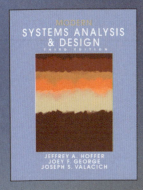
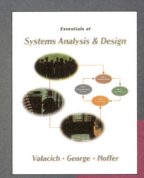
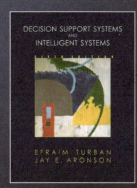

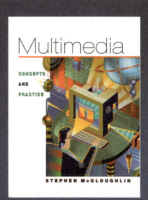

Essentials of
Management
Information
Systems

ESSENTIALS OF MANAGEMENT INFORMATION SYSTEMS

MANAGING THE DIGITAL FIRM

Fifth Edition

KENNETH C. LAUDON
New York University

JANE P. LAUDON
Azimuth Information Systems

Prentice Hall

Upper Saddle River, New Jersey 07458

Library of Congress Cataloging-in-Publication Data
Laudon, Kenneth C., 1944–
    Essentials of management information systems: managing the digital firm
/Kenneth C. Laudon, Jane P. Laudon.—
5th ed.
        p. cm.
    Includes bibliographical references and index.
    ISBN 0-13-008734-3
    1. Management information systems. I. Laudon, Jane Price. II. Title.

T58.6.L3753 2003
658'4'038'011—dc21

2002022031

Executive Editor: David Alexander
Publisher: Natalie E. Anderson
Editorial Project Manager: Kyle Hannon
Editorial Assistant: Maat Van Uitert
Media Project Manager: Joan Waxman
Senior Marketing Manager: Sharon K. Turkovich
Marketing Assistant: Scott Patterson
Project Manager: Audri Anna Bazlen
Managing Editor (Production): Gail Steier de Acevedo
Buyer: Natacha St. Hill Moore
Permissions Coordinator: Suzanne Grappi
Photo Permissions Coordinator: Shirley Webster
Associate Director, Manufacturing: Vincent Scelta
Interior Design: Jill Little
Cover Design: Pat Smythe
Cover Illustration: © Guy Crittenden/SIS
Manager, Print Production: Christy Mahon
Composition: Carlisle Communications
Full-Service Project Management: Carlisle Publishers Services
Printer/Binder: Quebecor World/Versailles

Credits and acknowledgments borrowed from other sources and reproduced, with permission,
in this textbook appear on appropriate page within text and on the last two pages of the book.

Microsoft and Windows are registered trademarks of the Microsoft Corporation in the U.S.A.
and other countries. Microsoft screen shots and icons reprinted with permission from the
Microsoft Corporation. This book is not sponsored or endorsed by or affiliated with the
Microsoft Corporation.

Prentice
Hall

10 9 8 7 6 5 4 3 2
ISBN 0-13-008734-3

FOR
ERICA AND ELISABETH

ABOUT THE AUTHORS

Kenneth C. Laudon is a Professor of Information Systems at New York University's Stern School of Business. He holds a B.A. in Economics from Stanford and a Ph.D. from Columbia University. He has authored twelve books dealing with electronic commerce, information systems, organizations, and society. Professor Laudon has also written over forty articles concerned with the social, organizational, and management impacts of information systems, privacy, ethics, and multimedia technology.

Professor Laudon's current research is on the planning and management of large-scale information systems and multimedia information technology. He has received grants from the National Science Foundation to study the evolution of national information systems at the Social Security Administration, the IRS, and the FBI. A part of this research is concerned with computer-related organizational and occupational changes in large organizations, changes in management ideology, changes in public policy, and understanding productivity change in the knowledge sector.

Ken Laudon has testified as an expert before the United States Congress. He has been a researcher and consultant to the Office of Technology Assessment (United States Congress) and to the Office of the President, several executive branch agencies, and Congressional Committees. Professor Laudon also acts as an in-house educator for several consulting firms and as a consultant on systems planning and strategy to several Fortune 500 firms. Ken has worked with the Concours Group to provide advice to firms developing enterprise systems.

At NYU's Stern School of Business, Professor Laudon teaches courses on Managing the Digital Firm, Information Technology and Corporate Strategy, and Electronic Commerce and Digital Markets. Ken Laudon's hobby is sailing and he is a veteran Newport to Bermuda Race captain.

Jane Price Laudon is a management consultant in the information systems area and the author of seven books. Her special interests include systems analysis, data management, MIS auditing, software evaluation, and teaching business professionals how to design and use information systems.

Jane received her Ph.D. from Columbia University, her M.A. from Harvard University, and her B.A. from Barnard College. She has taught at Columbia University and the New York University Graduate School of Business. She maintains a lifelong interest in Oriental languages and civilizations.

The Laudons have two daughters, Erica and Elisabeth.

Essentials of Management Information Systems: Managing the Digital Firm reflects a deep understanding of MIS research and teaching as well as practical experience designing and building real-world systems.

BRIEF CONTENTS

CONTENTS

PREFACE

WELCOME TO THE DIGITAL FIRM

Essentials of Management Information Systems: Managing the Digital Firm, Fifth Edition, is based on the premise that information systems knowledge is essential for creating competitive firms, managing global corporations, and providing useful products and services to customers. This book provides an introduction to management information systems (MIS) that undergraduate and MBA students will find vital to their professional success.

THE INFORMATION REVOLUTION IN BUSINESS AND MANAGEMENT: THE EMERGING DIGITAL FIRM

The growth of the Internet, the globalization of trade, and the rise of information economies have recast the role of information systems (IS) in business and management. Internet technology is supplying the foundation for new business models, new business processes, and new ways of distributing knowledge. The wave of dot.com failures has not deterred companies from using Internet technology to drive their businesses.

Companies are relying on Internet and networking technology to conduct more of their work electronically, seamlessly linking factories, offices, and sales forces around the globe. Leading-edge firms, such as Cisco Systems, Dell Computer, and Procter & Gamble, are extending their networks to suppliers, customers, and other groups outside the organization so they can react instantly to customer demands and market shifts. Cisco Systems corporate managers can use information systems to "virtually close" their books at any time, generating consolidated financial statements based on up-to-the-minute figures on orders, discounts, revenue, product margins, and staffing expenses. Executives can constantly analyze performance at all levels of the organization. This digital integration both within the firm and without, from the warehouse to the executive suite, from suppliers to customers, is changing how we organize and manage a business. Ultimately, these changes are leading to fully digital firms where all internal business processes and relationships with customers and suppliers are digitally enabled. In digital firms, information to support business decisions is available any time and anywhere in the organization. Accordingly, we have changed the subtitle of this text to *Managing the Digital Firm.*

NEW TO THE FIFTH EDITION

This edition more fully explores the digital integration of the firm and the use of the Internet to digitally enable business processes for electronic commerce and electronic business. It pays special attention to new technology applications that improve firms' relationships with customers and create additional value through closer collaboration with suppliers and other business partners. To meet the needs of instructors teaching MIS to general business majors, we have added features that make this text more relevant to the general manager without omitting any of the coverage necessary to the IS major.

The following features and content reflect this new direction:

NEW COVERAGE OF THE DIGITAL FIRM

Chapter 1 introduces and defines the emerging digital firm, using examples of leading-edge companies such as Cisco Systems and Procter & Gamble. Chapter 2 highlights the importance of integrating the flow of information across the enterprise and using digital technology to create close relationships with customers and suppliers. Chapter 3 explains how information systems and business strategy have changed as a result of digital firm technology, and Chapter 11 describes digital firm applications of decision-support systems and executive support systems. The entire text details the management, organization, and technology issues surrounding the digital integration of the firm and the formation of industry-wide networks and global supply chains.

DETAILED COVERAGE OF CUSTOMER RELATIONSHIP MANAGEMENT, SUPPLY CHAIN MANAGEMENT, COLLABORATIVE COMMERCE, AND ENTERPRISE SYSTEMS

Digital firm technology helps firms improve their relationships with customers and collaborate more closely with suppliers and other business partners. Chapter 2 provides detailed treatment of customer relationship management, supply chain management, collaborative commerce, enterprise systems, and the digital integration of business processes. Subsequent chapters include additional descriptions, discussions, and case studies of these topics, emphasizing the importance of integrating information across business processes and electronically linking firms to suppliers, customers, and other business partners. "Before and after" snapshots throughout the text illustrate how firms have changed their business processes using digital technology. (The "Before-After" diagram in Chapter 10 showing changes in the Toys R Us construction project management process using new Web-based tools is one example.)

MORE ATTENTION TO FUNCTIONAL BUSINESS APPLICATIONS

The Make IT Your Business icon helps students identify functional business applications of chapter concepts.

A new Make IT Your Business section concluding every chapter shows how the topics in each chapter specifically relate to the major functional areas of business: finance and accounting, human resources, manufacturing and production, and sales and marketing. This section also directs students to pages in the chapter on which functional business examples can be found. To further aid students in identifying these functional applications, icons are positioned adjacent to functional business examples in chapter opening vignettes, Window On boxes, chapter ending cases, and in the body of the chapter itself.

NEW MANAGER'S TOOLKIT WITH HOW-TO CHECKLISTS FOR MANAGERS

Each chapter contains a MIS in Action: Manager's Toolkit section with a checklist to help students use chapter concepts to deal with a specific business problem, such as how to integrate the Wireless Web into business strategy, how to benefit from customer relationship management, or how to develop a disaster recovery plan. Students will find these sections useful guides when they work on projects for the course and in their future jobs.

MORE APPLIED CHAPTER OBJECTIVES

We have redesigned the chapter learning Objectives to demonstrate the chapter's relevance to general business managers as well as information systems majors. The Objectives now list questions that each chapter answers in language that both general business managers and IS professionals can easily understand and the Chapter Summary shows how the chapter answers those questions. Examples of these new Objectives are, "How can Internet technology support e-business and supply chain management?" "What computer processing and storage capability does our organization need to handle its information and business transactions?" "What alternative network services are available to our organization?" "How should we manage our firm's hardware and software assets?" Students can see clearly how they can use this knowledge in their jobs.

EXPANDED COVERAGE OF ELECTRONIC COMMERCE, ELECTRONIC BUSINESS, AND THE INTERNET

The Internet, electronic commerce, and electronic business are introduced in Chapter 1 and integrated throughout the text and the entire learning package. The text features two full chapters on these topics. Chapter 4, "The Digital Firm: Electronic Commerce and Electronic Business" discusses electronic commerce, Internet business models, e-business, and the management and organizational transformations driving the move toward digital firms. Chapter 9, "The Internet and the New Information Technology Infrastructure" describes the underlying technology, capabilities, and benefits of the Internet, including new coverage of the Wireless Web, m-commerce, and digital firm infrastructure. Every chapter contains a Window On box or a case study devoted to electronic commerce, electronic business, or digital firm issues, as well as in-text descriptions of how Internet technology is changing a particular aspect of information systems.

MORE ACTIVE HANDS-ON LEARNING PROJECTS AND PROBLEM SOLVING

This edition is more problem-solving-oriented and project-oriented than earlier editions. It includes new active hands-on learning projects that help students make text concepts more meaningful.

New Comprehensive Projects

We have added four new, longer comprehensive projects, each concluding a major part of the text. These projects require students to apply text concepts to demanding problems that they might encounter as firms become more digitally integrated and Internet enabled. These projects include the following:

▌ Analyzing business processes for an enterprise system (Part I project)
▌ Creating a new Internet business (Part II project)
▌ Designing an enterprise information portal (Part III project)
▌ Redesigning business processes (Part IV project)

New Improved Hands-on Application Software Exercises

Each chapter features more challenging hands-on Application Software Exercises where students can solve problems using spreadsheet, database, Web page development tool, or electronic presentation software. Some of these exercises require students to use these application software tools in conjuction with Web activities. The exercises have been redesigned so that they require more critical thinking than the exercises in previous editions and so that they are more relevant to the topics in each chapter. The new Application Software Exercises include business problems such as the following:

▌ Improving supply chain management (Chapter 2)
▌ Analyzing a dot.com business (Chapter 4)
▌ Capital budgeting for information technology investments (Chapter 13)
▌ Using a database for strategic business development (Chapter 3)

The application exercises are included in each chapter and on the Laudon Web site along with the required data files and complete instructions.

New E-Business Projects

New e-business projects have been added to the Tools for Interactive Learning sections concluding each chapter. Students can engage in e-business projects (such as redesigning business processes for supply chain management) as well as e-commerce projects at the Laudon Web site.

NEW LEADING-EDGE TOPICS

In addition to the new digital firm coverage we have already described, this edition includes up-to-date treatment of topics such as

- Collaborative commerce (Chapter 2)
- Expanded coverage of B2B business models, including private exchanges and private industrial networks (Chapter 4)
- Web services (Chapter 12)
- Application development for e-commerce and e-business (Chapter 12)
- M-commerce and the Wireless Web (Chapter 9)
- Scalability and high-availability computing (Chapters 9 and 14)
- Application service providers and on-line storage service providers (Chapter 6)
- Peer-to-peer computing (Chapter 6)
- Bluetooth and Wi-Fi (Chapter 9)
- XML (Chapter 6)

INCREASED ATTENTION TO ETHICS AND PRIVACY

The chapter on ethics has been moved earlier in the text to reflect its new importance. Chapter 5 provides a fresh, new look at ethical and social issues in the digital firm. E-commerce has made privacy and intellectual property protection among the most pressing ethical and social issues today—issues that managers and business professionals cannot afford to ignore.

BOOK OVERVIEW

Part I is concerned with the organizational foundations of systems, their strategic role, and the organizational and management changes driving electronic commerce, electronic business, and the emerging digital firm. It provides an extensive introduction to real-world systems, focusing on their relationships to organizations, management, business processes, and important ethical and social issues.

Part II provides the technical foundation for understanding information systems. It describes the hardware, software, data storage, and telecommunications technologies that comprise the organization's information technology infrastructure. Part II concludes by describing how all of these information technologies work together with the Internet to create a new infrastructure for the digital integration of the enterprise.

Part III describes the role of information systems in capturing and distributing organizational knowledge and in enhancing management decision making across the enterprise. It shows how knowledge management, work group collaboration, and individual and group decision making are supported by knowledge work, group collaboration, artificial intelligence, decision support, and executive support systems.

Part IV focuses on the process of redesigning organizations using information systems, including the reengineering of critical business processes and the development of Web applications. Managers must understand the business value of systems; manage system-related change; and ensure that the right set of technologies, policies, and procedures are in place for quality, security, and control. Throughout the text emphasis is placed on using information technology to redesign the organization's products, services, procedures, jobs, and management structures; numerous examples are drawn from multinational systems and global business environments.

CHAPTER OUTLINE

Each chapter contains the following:

- A detailed outline to provide an overview
- An opening vignette describing a real-world organization to establish the theme and importance of the chapter

❚ A diagram analyzing the opening vignette in terms of the management, organization, and technology model used throughout the text

❚ A series of chapter Objectives in easy-to-understand language for business professionals

❚ Management Challenges related to the chapter theme

❚ A Manager's Toolkit with checklists to help students apply chapter concepts to specific business problems

❚ Marginal glosses of key terms in the text

❚ An Internet Connection icon directing students to related material on the Internet

❚ Make IT Your Business icons and discussions directing students to portions of the chapter dealing with functional business applications of chapter concepts

❚ A Management Wrap-Up tying together the key management, organization, and technology issues for the chapter, with questions for discussion

❚ A chapter Summary keyed to the learning Objectives

❚ A list of Key Terms that students can use to review concepts

❚ Review Questions for students to test their comprehension of chapter material

❚ An Application Software Exercise requiring students to use application software tools to develop solutions to real-world business problems based on chapter concepts

❚ A Group Project to develop teamwork and presentation skills

❚ A Tools for Interactive Learning section showing specifically how the chapter can be integrated with the Laudon Web site and CD-ROM edition of the text

❚ A chapter ending case study illustrating important themes

IMPROVED COMPANION WEB SITE (WWW.PRENHALL.COM/LAUDON)

The text is accompanied by a Companion Web site that brings students a rich Web experience.

Further enhancements have been made to the Laudon & Laudon Web site to provide a wide array of capabilities for interactive learning and management problem solving that have been carefully prepared for use with the text. They include the following:

Electronic Commerce and Electronic Business Projects for Every Chapter

On the Web site are Web-based electronic commerce and electronic business exercises for each chapter. Students can use interactive software at various company Web sites and other Web tools to solve specific business problems related to chapter concepts. These exercises encourage critical thinking skills as students explore business resources on the Internet and take learning MIS on the Internet to the next level.

Interactive Study Guide and Internet Connections for Each Chapter

Each chapter of the text features a Web site and an Interactive Study Guide and Internet Connection exercise.

❚ The on-line Interactive Study Guide helps students review skills and test

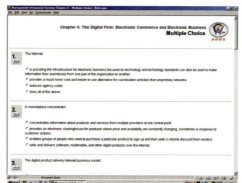

Students are presented with a problem to develop a budget for annual shipping costs. To obtain the information required for the solution, they can input data on-line and use the interactive software at this Web site to perform the required calculations or analysis.

Student responses to questions are automatically graded and can be e-mailed to the instructor.

their mastery of chapter concepts with a series of multiple-choice, true–false, and essay questions.

▌ Internet Connections noted by marginal icons in the chapter direct students to exercises and projects on the Laudon Web site that are related to organizations and concepts in the chapter.

Internet Connections direct students to Web-based exercises on the Laudon Web site. Students can e-mail their work to their professors.

Additional Case Studies

The Web site contains additional case studies with hyperlinks to the Web sites of the organizations discussed.

International Resources

Links to Web sites of non-U.S. companies are provided for users interested in international material.

UNIQUE FEATURES OF THIS TEXT FOR THE STUDENT

Essentials of Management Information Systems: Managing the Digital Firm, Fifth Edition, has many unique features designed to create an active, dynamic learning environment.

A special diagram accompanying each chapter opening vignette graphically illustrates how management, organization, and technology elements work together to create an information system solution to the business challenges discussed in the vignette.

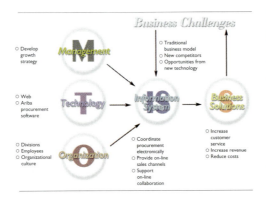

INTEGRATED FRAMEWORK FOR DESCRIBING AND ANALYZING INFORMATION SYSTEMS

An integrated framework portrays information systems as being composed of management, organization, and technology elements. This framework is used throughout the text to describe and analyze information systems and information system problems.

REAL-WORLD EXAMPLES

Real-world examples drawn from business and public organizations are used throughout the text to illustrate text concepts. More than 100 companies in the United States and nearly 100 organizations in Canada, Europe, Australia, Asia, and Africa are discussed.

Each chapter opens with a vignette illustrating the themes of the chapter and showing how a real-world organization meets a business challenge using information systems. Each chapter also contains two Window On boxes (Window on Management, Window on Organizations, or Window on Technology) that present real-world examples illustrating the management, organization, and technology issues in the chapter. Each Window On box concludes with a section called To Think About containing questions for students to consider in applying chapter concepts to management problem solving. The themes for each box are as follows:

Window on Management

Management problems raised by systems and their solution; management strategies and plans; careers and experiences of managers using systems.

Window on Technology

Hardware, software, telecommunications, data storage, standards, and systems-building methodologies.

Window on Organizations

Activities of private and public organizations using information systems; experiences of people working with systems.

MANAGEMENT WRAP-UP OVERVIEWS OF KEY ISSUES

Management Wrap-Up sections at the end of each chapter summarize key issues using the authors' management, organization, and technology framework for analyzing information systems.

The Management Wrap-Up provides a quick overview of the key issues in each chapter, reinforcing the authors' management, organization, and technology framework.

MANAGEMENT WRAP-UP

Managers need to carefully review their strategy and business models to determine how to maximize the benefits of Internet technology. Managers should anticipate making organizational changes to take advantage of this technology, including new business processes, new relationships with the firm's value partners and customers, and even new business designs. Determining how and where to digitally enable the enterprise with Internet technology is a key management decision.

The Internet can dramatically reduce transaction and agency costs and is fueling new business models. By using the Internet and other networks for electronic commerce, organizations can exchange purchase and sale transactions directly with customers and suppliers, eliminating inefficient intermediaries. Organizational processes can be streamlined by using the Internet and intranets to make communication and coordination more efficient. To take advantage of these opportunities, organizational processes must be redesigned.

Internet technology has created a universal computing platform that has become the primary infrastructure for electronic commerce, electronic business, and the emerging digital firm. Web-based applications integrating voice, data, video, and audio are providing new products, services, and tools for communicating with employees and customers. Intranets enable companies to make information flow between disparate systems, business processes, and parts of the organization.

For Discussion:
1. How does the Internet change consumer and supplier relationships?
2. The Internet may not make corporations obsolete, but they will have to change their business models. Do you agree? Why or why not?

A TRULY INTERNATIONAL PERSPECTIVE

Coverage of managing international information systems is integrated throughout the text, with special attention to this topic in Chapters 2 and 13. All chapters of the text are illustrated with real-world examples from nearly 100 corporations in Canada, Europe, Asia, Latin America, Africa, and Australia. Each chapter contains at least one Window On box, case study, or opening vignette drawn from a non-U.S. firm, and often more. The text concludes with four major international case studies contributed by leading MIS experts in Canada, Europe, and Hong Kong—Len Fertuck, University of Toronto (Canada); Gerhard Schwabe, University of Koblenz-Landau (Germany); Donald A. Marchand and Katarina Paddack, International Institute of Management Development (Switzerland); and Ali Farhoomand, Dennis Kira, Amir Hoosain, and Shamza Khan, The University of Hong Kong (Hong Kong).

ATTENTION TO SMALL BUSINESSES AND ENTREPRENEURS

A computer icon identifies in-text discussions and specially designated chapter opening vignettes, Window On boxes, and part ending case studies that highlight the experiences and challenges of small businesses and entrepreneurs using information systems.

PEDAGOGY TO PROMOTE ACTIVE LEARNING AND MANAGEMENT PROBLEM SOLVING

In addition to the new comprehensive projects and hands-on application exercises, Essentials of Management Information Systems: Managing the Digital Firm, Fifth Edition, contains many other features that encourage students to learn actively and to engage in management problem solving.

Management Challenges Section

Each chapter begins with several challenges relating to the chapter topic that managers are likely to encounter. These challenges are multifaceted and sometimes pose dilemmas. They make excellent springboards for class discussion. Some of the Management Challenges include finding the right Internet business model, overcoming the organizational obstacles to building a database environment, and agreeing on quality standards for information systems.

Case Studies

Each chapter concludes with a case study based on a real-world organization. These cases help students synthesize chapter concepts and apply this new knowledge to concrete problems and scenarios. Major international case studies and electronic case studies at the Laudon & Laudon Web site provide additional opportunities for management problem solving.

MIS in Action: Decisionmaking

MIS in Action: Decisionmaking problems appear in Chapters 1, 2, 5, 6, 7, 8, 13, and 14 to encourage students apply what they have learned to a real-world, management decision-making scenario. These problems can be used for practical group learning or individual learning both in and outside of the classroom. The problems require students to make decisions based on real-world MIS issues such as the following:

- Analyzing enterprise process integration (Chapter 2)
- Monitoring how much time employees spend on the Web (Chapter 5)
- Creating company-wide data standards (Chapter 7)

Group Projects

At the end of each chapter is a group project that encourages students to develop teamwork, and oral and written presentation skills. The group projects have been enhanced to make more use of the Internet. For instance, students might be asked to work in small groups to evaluate the Web sites of two competing businesses or to develop a corporate ethics code on privacy that considers e-mail privacy and the monitoring of employees using networks.

Students can reinforce and extend their knowledge of chapter concepts using the glossaries and other interactive resources in the CD-ROM edition.

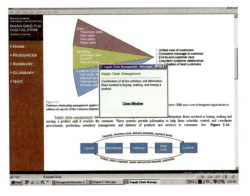

TOOLS FOR INTERACTIVE LEARNING: TECHNOLOGY INTEGRATED WITH CONTENT

An interactive CD-ROM multimedia version of the text can be packaged with the text. In addition to the full text and bullet text summaries by chapter, the CD-ROM features simulations, audio/video overviews explaining key concepts, on-line quizzes, hyperlinks to the exercises on the Laudon Web site, technology updates, and more. Students can use the CD-ROM edition as an interactive supplement or as an alternative to the traditional text.

The Tools for Interactive Learning section concluding each chapter shows students how they can extend their knowledge of each chapter with projects and exercises on the Laudon Web site and the CD-ROM multimedia edition.

TOOLS FOR INTERACTIVE LEARNING

■ INTERNET CONNECTION

The Internet Connection for this chapter will take you to the Rosenbluth Travel Web site where you can complete an exercise to analyze how Rosenbluth International uses the Web and communications technology in its daily operations. You can also use the Interactive Study Guide to test your knowledge of the topics in the chapter and get instant feedback where you need more practice.

■ ELECTRONIC BUSINESS PROJECT

At the Laudon Web site for Chapter 8, you can find an Electronic Business project to compare and evaluate the supply chain management services of Schneider National and J.B. Hunt.

■ CD-ROM

If you use the Multimedia Edition CD-ROM with this chapter, you can find a video demonstrating the capabilities of personal communication services, an audio overview of the major themes of this chapter, and bullet text summarizing the key points of the chapter.

> Students and instructors can see at a glance exactly how Internet connections and electronic commerce projects can be used to enhance student learning for each chapter. Students can also see immediately how the chapter can be used in conjunction with the optional CD-ROM edition.

INSTRUCTIONAL SUPPORT MATERIALS

INSTRUCTOR'S RESOURCE CD-ROM

Most of the support materials described in the following section are conveniently available for adopters on the Instructor's Resource CD-ROM. The CD includes the Instructor's Resource Manual, Test Item File, Windows PH Test Manager, PowerPoint slides, and the helpful lecture tool "Image Library."

IMAGE LIBRARY (ON INSTRUCTOR'S RESOURCE CD-ROM)

The Image Library is an impressive resource to help instructors create vibrant lecture presentations. Almost every figure and photo in the text is provided and organized by chapter for convenience. These images and lecture notes can be easily imported into Microsoft PowerPoint to create new presentations or to add to existing ones.

INSTRUCTOR'S MANUAL (ON WEB AND ON INSTRUCTOR'S RESOURCE CD-ROM)

The Instructor's Manual features not only answers to review, discussion, case study, and group project questions but also an in-depth lecture outline, teaching objectives, key terms, teaching suggestions, and Internet resources. This supplement can be downloaded from the secure faculty section of the Laudon & Laudon Web site and is also available on the Instructor's Resource CD-ROM.

TEST ITEM FILE (ON INSTRUCTOR'S RESOURCE CD-ROM)

The Test Item File, by Professor Betty Spaulding, is a comprehensive collection of true–false, multiple-choice, fill-in-the-blank, and essay questions. The questions are rated by difficulty level and the answers are referenced by section. An electronic version of the Test Item File is available as the Windows PH Test Manager on the Instructor's Resource CD-ROM.

POWERPOINT SLIDES (ON WEB AND INSTRUCTOR'S RESOURCE CD-ROM)

Electronic color slides were created by Azimuth Interactive, Inc., and are available in Microsoft PowerPoint, Version 2000. The slides illuminate and build on key concepts in the text. Both student and faculty can download the PowerPoint slides from the Web site, and they are also provided on the Instructor's Resource CD-ROM.

VIDEOS

Prentice Hall MIS Video, Volume 1

The first video in the Prentice Hall MIS Video Library includes custom clips created exclusively for Prentice Hall featuring real companies, such as Lands' End, Lotus Development Corporation, Oracle Corporation, and Pillsbury Company.

Prentice Hall MIS Video, Volume 2

Video clips are provided to adopters to enhance class discussion and projects. These clips highlight real-world corporations and organizations and illustrate key concepts found in the text.

WEB SITE

The Laudon/Laudon text is supported by an excellent Web site at http://www.prenhall.com/laudon that truly reinforces and enhances text material with Electronic Commerce and Electronic Business projects, hands-on Application Exercises, Internet Exercises, an Interactive Study Guide, International Resources, Additional Case Studies, and PowerPoint slides. The Web site also features a secure password-protected faculty area from which instructors can download the Instructor's Manual, and suggested answers to the Internet Connections and E-Commerce/E-Business Projects. The site has an improved on-line syllabus tool to help professors add their own personal syllabi to the site in minutes. Please see the complete description discussed earlier in the preface.

ON-LINE COURSES

WebCT www.prenhall.com/webct

Gold Level customer support, available exclusively to adopters of Prentice Hall courses, is provided free-of-charge on adoption and provides priority assistance, training discounts, and dedicated technical support.

Blackboard www.prenhall.com/blackboard

Prentice Hall's abundant on-line content, combined with Blackboard's popular tools and interface, result in robust Web-based courses that are easy to implement, manage, and use—taking your courses to new heights in student interaction and learning.

CourseCompass www.prenhall.com/coursecompass

CourseCompass is a dynamic, interactive, on-line course management tool powered exclusively for Pearson Education by Blackboard. This exciting product allows you to teach market-leading Pearson Education content in an easy-to-use customizable format.

TUTORIAL SOFTWARE

For instructors seeking Application Software support to use with this text, Prentice Hall is pleased to offer the PH Train IT CD-ROM and the Web-delivered PH Train & Assess IT for Office 2000 and XP. These exciting tutorial and assessment products are fully certified up to the expert level of the Microsoft Office User Specialist (MOUS) Certification Program. These items are not available as stand-alone items but can be packaged with the Laudon/Laudon text at an additional charge. Please go to www.prenhall.com/phit for an on-line demonstration of these products or contact your local Prentice Hall representative for more details.

SOFTWARE CASES

A series of optional management software cases, *Solve it! Management Problem Solving with PC Software,* has been developed to support the text. *Solve it!* consists of 10 spreadsheet cases, 10 database cases, and 6 Internet projects drawn from real-world businesses, plus a data disk with the files associated with the cases. The cases are graduated in difficulty. The case book contains complete tutorial documentation showing how to use spreadsheet, database, and Web browser software to solve the problems. A new version of *Solve it!* with all new cases is published every year. *Solve it!* must be adopted for an entire class. It can be purchased directly from the supplier, Azimuth Interactive Corporation, 23 North Division Street, Peekskill, New York, 10566 (telephone: 800-416-6786 extension 14; Web site www.mysolveit.com).

ACKNOWLEDGMENTS

The production of any book involves valued contributions from a number of persons. We would like to thank all of our editors for encouragement, insight, and strong support for many years. David Alexander is a truly outstanding editor who guided the development of this edition. We remain grateful to Natalie Anderson for her support of this project. We thank Sharon K. Turkovich, senior marketing manager, for her superb marketing work.

We praise Kyle Hannon for her role in managing this project and for her supervision of ancillary material preparation. Audri Anna Bazlen and Kathy Davis must be commended for production/manufacturing of this text under an extraordinarily ambitious schedule. We thank Shirley Webster for her energetic photo research work.

Our special thanks go to Professor Betty Spaulding for developing the testing systems that accompany our text and to all those who worked on supporting materials.

We remain deeply indebted to Marshall R. Kaplan for his invaluable assistance in the preparation of the text and to David Langley for his help with application software projects. Jiri Rodovsky and Todd Traver provided additional suggestions for improvements.

The Stern School of Business at New York University and the Information Systems Department provided a very special learning environment—one in which we and others could rethink the MIS field. Special thanks to Professors Vasant Dhar, Michael Davern, and Alex Tuzhilin for providing critical feedback and support where deserved. Professor William H. Starbuck of the Management Department at New York University provided valuable comments and insights in our joint graduate seminar on organization theory.

Professor Edward Stohr of Stevens Institute of Technology, Professor Gordon Everest of the University of Minnesota, Professors Al Croker and Michael Palley of Baruch College and New York University, and Professor Thomas J. Housel of the Naval Postgraduate School provided additional suggestions for improvement. We continue to remember the late Professor James Clifford of the Stern School as a wonderful friend and colleague who also made valuable recommendations for improving our discussion of files and databases.

One of our goals was to write a book that was authoritative, synthesized diverse views in the MIS literature, and helped define a common academic field. A large number of leading scholars in the field were contacted and assisted us in this effort. Reviewers and consultants for *Essentials of Management Information Systems: Managing the Digital Firm* are listed in the back endpapers of the book. We thank them for their contributions. Consultants for the Fifth Edition include Professor Arben Asllani of Fayetteville State University, Professor John DiRenzo of Cameron University, Professor Rick Hicks of Florida Atlantic University, Professor Virginia Kleist of West Virginia State University, Professor Brian Kovar of Kansas State University, Professor Treise Lynn of Wingate University, Professor Jennifer Thomas of Pace University, and Professor Kathie Wright of Purdue University.

It is our hope that this group endeavor contributes to a shared vision and understanding of the MIS field.

—K.C.L.
—J.P.L.

ORGANIZATIONS, MANAGEMENT, AND THE NETWORKED ENTERPRISE

1 Chapter

MANAGING THE DIGITAL FIRM

c h a p t e r
c h a p t e r

objectives

As a manager, you'll need to know how information systems can make businesses more competitive and efficient. After completing this chapter, you will be able to answer the following questions:

1. What is the role of information systems in today's competitive business environment?
2. What exactly is an information system? What do managers need to know about information systems?
3. How are information systems transforming organizations and management?
4. How has the Internet and Internet technology transformed business?
5. What are the major management challenges to building and using information systems?

Procter & Gamble Builds New Relationships as a Digital Firm

Procter & Gamble Co. (P&G), the 163-year-old consumer goods giant, has traditionally aimed at doubling its sales every decade and has usually succeeded—until recently. During the last five years, annual sales growth slowed from 5 to 2.6 percent. A.G. Lafley, P&G's new CEO, is trying to revitalize the company to make faster and better decisions, cut red tape, wring costs out of systems and procedures, and fuel innovation. Key components in P&G's ambitious change program include using Internet technology to drive inefficiencies out of its supplier relationships, forging new ties to consumers, and pulling in new revenue from one-to-one marketing and electronic commerce.

P&G has launched dozens of Web sites to promote old brands and build new ones, hoping to deepen its relationship with consumers in the process. PG.com, its main corporate Web site, links to numerous other subsites devoted to P&G products such as Tide, Pampers, or Mr. Clean. If consumers enter details at Tide.com about a coffee stain, the site offers on-line advice on how to remove it. Reflect.com targets upscale women by letting them design their own custom-blended cosmetics and place orders for these items via the Web. An icon of a stylized test tube and beaker on PG.com invites visitors to send new product suggestions to the company. By using the Internet to interact with customers and test their interest in new products, P&G has cut its marketing research costs between 50 to 75 percent.

P&G's management hopes its Internet and intranet initiatives will encourage employees to be more creative and to take more responsibility. An internal InnovationNet intranet allows users to post reports, charts, and videos to a common shared repository and to contact other people

2

working on similar problems and issues. Another intranet called MyIdea provides a forum for employees to publicize their ideas for improving the company.

To slash inventory and cycle time, P&G instituted a collaborative planning, forecasting, and replenishment (CPFR) system in which it shares sales forecasts

with its retailers such as Kmart, Target, and Wal-Mart in the United States and Dansk, Sainsbury, and Tesco in Europe. If actual sales are in line with forecasts, the system automatically orders items to replenish what has been sold in stores. If the results are sharply different from forecasts, the system automatically notifies companies about such "exceptions," allowing company planners to adjust orders to accommodate spikes or dips in demand. Early tests showed that the CPFR system helped P&G reduce inventory by 10 percent and cycle time (the time required to get a product from the assembly line to the retailer's shelf) by 10 percent. Sales increased by 2 percent as well because P&G was able to use the information in the system to take immediate actions to prevent out-of-stock items.

P&G recently developed an even more efficient system using point-of-sale data to keep retail store shelves stocked while meeting local customer demands. The system was first piloted in four U.S. food and drug retail chains, which collect data on customer purchases of P&G products from their checkout scanners and cash registers. These data are transmitted to a third-party company for analysis to detect changes in an item's selling patterns that might indicate a potential out-of-stock situation. The system then sends alerts over computers and wireless devices to appropriate store personnel to reorder. P&G's ultimate goal is a fully automated system that uses point-of-sale data to automatically trigger every event in the production and delivery of the product, from manufacturing and delivery to resupplying and restocking.

Sources: Kayte VanScoy, "Can the Internet Hot-Wire P&G?" *Smart Business Magazine*, January 2001; "Procter & Gamble Takes on the Supply Chain," *Intelligent Enterprise*, July 20, 2001; Michael Totty, "Information, Please," *Wall Street Journal E-Commerce section*, October 29, 2001; and Noah Schachtman, "Trading Partners Collaborate to Increase Sales," *Information Week*, October 9, 2000.

The changes taking place at Procter & Gamble exemplify the transformation of business firms throughout the world as they rebuild themselves as fully digital firms. Such digital firms use the Internet and networking technology to make data flow seamlessly among different parts of the organization; streamline the flow of work; and create electronic links with customers, suppliers, and other organizations.

All types of businesses, both large and small are using information systems, networks, and Internet technology to conduct more of their business electronically, achieving new levels of efficiency and competitiveness. This chapter starts our investigation of information systems and organizations by describing information systems from both technical and behavioral perspectives and by surveying the changes they are bringing to organizations and management.

1.1   WHY INFORMATION SYSTEMS?

Today it is widely recognized that information systems knowledge is essential for managers because most organizations need information systems to survive and prosper. Information systems can help companies extend their reach to faraway locations, offer new products and services, reshape jobs and work flows, and perhaps profoundly change the way they conduct business.

THE COMPETITIVE BUSINESS ENVIRONMENT AND THE EMERGING DIGITAL FIRM

Four powerful worldwide changes have altered the business environment. The first change is the emergence and strengthening of the global economy. The second change is the transformation of industrial economies and societies into knowledge- and information-based service economies. The third is the transformation of the business enterprise. The fourth is the emergence of the digital firm. These changes in the business environment and climate, summarized in Table 1-1, pose a number of new challenges to business firms and their management.

Emergence of the Global Economy

A growing percentage of the American economy—and other advanced industrial economies in Europe and Asia—depends on imports and exports. Foreign trade, both exports and imports, accounts for more than 25 percent of the goods and services produced in the United States, and even more in countries such as Japan and Germany. Companies are also distrib-

TABLE 1-1   THE CHANGING CONTEMPORARY BUSINESS ENVIRONMENT

Globalization

Management and control in a global marketplace

Competition in world markets

Global work groups

Global delivery systems

Transformation of Industrial Economies

Knowledge- and information-based economies

New products and services

Knowledge: a central productive and strategic asset

Time-based competition

Shorter product life

Turbulent environment

Limited employee knowledge base

Transformation of the Enterprise

Flattening

Decentralization

Flexibility

Location independence

Low transaction and coordination costs

Empowerment

Collaborative work and teamwork

Emergence of the Digital Firm

Digitally enabled relationships with customers, suppliers, and employees

Core business processes accomplished via digital networks

Digital management of key corporate assets

Rapid sensing and responding to environmental changes

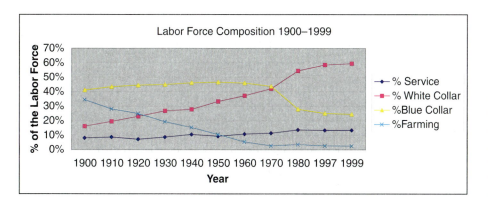

Figure 1-1 The growth of the information economy. Since the beginning of the twentieth century, the United States has experienced a steady decline in the number of farm workers and blue-collar workers who are employed in factories. At the same time, the country is experiencing a rise in the number of white-collar workers who produce economic value using knowledge and information.
Sources: U.S. Department of Commerce, *Bureau of the Census, Statistical Abstract of the United States, 2000,* Table 669 and *Historical Statistics of the United States, Colonial Times to 1970,* Vol. 1, Series D 182–232.

uting core business functions in product design, manufacturing, finance, and customer support to locations in other countries where the work can be performed more cost effectively. The success of firms today and in the future depends on their ability to operate globally.

Today, information systems provide the communication and analytic power that firms need for conducting trade and managing businesses on a global scale. Controlling the far-flung global corporation—communicating with distributors and suppliers, operating 24 hours a day in different national environments, coordinating global work teams, and servicing local and international reporting needs—is a major business challenge that requires powerful information system responses.

Globalization and information technology also bring new threats to domestic business firms: Because of global communication and management systems, customers now can shop in a worldwide marketplace, obtaining price and quality information reliably 24 hours a day. To become competitive participants in international markets, firms need powerful information and communication systems.

Transformation of Industrial Economies

The United States, Japan, Germany, and other major industrial powers are being transformed from industrial economies to knowledge- and information-based service economies, whereas manufacturing has been moving to low-wage countries. In a knowledge- and information-based economy, knowledge and information are key ingredients in creating wealth.

The knowledge and information revolution began at the turn of the twentieth century and has gradually accelerated. By 1976 the number of white-collar workers employed in offices surpassed the number of farm workers, service workers, and blue-collar workers employed in manufacturing (see Figure 1-1). Today, most people no longer work on farms or in factories but instead are found in sales, education, healthcare, banks, insurance firms, and law firms; they also provide business services like copying, computer programming, or making deliveries. These jobs primarily involve working with, distributing, or creating new knowledge and information. In fact, knowledge and information work now account for a significant 60 percent of the American gross national product and nearly 55 percent of the labor force.

Knowledge and information are becoming the foundation for many new services and products. **Knowledge- and information-intense products** such as computer games require a great deal of knowledge to produce. Entire new information-based services have sprung up, such as Lexis, Dow Jones News Service, and America Online. These fields are employing millions of people. Knowledge is used more intensively in the production of traditional products as well. In the automobile industry, for instance, both design and production now rely heavily on knowledge and information technology.

In a knowledge- and information-based economy, information technology and systems take on great importance. Knowledge-based products and services of great economic value, such as credit cards, overnight package delivery, and worldwide reservation systems, are based on new information technologies. Information technology constitutes more than 70 percent of the invested capital in service industries such as finance, insurance, and real estate.

Across all industries, information and the technology that delivers it have become critical, strategic assets for business firms and their managers (Leonard-Barton, 1995). Information systems are needed to optimize the flow of information and knowledge within

knowledge- and information-intense products
Products that require a great deal of learning and knowledge to produce.

the organization and to help management maximize the firm's knowledge resources. Because employees' productivity depends on the quality of the systems serving them, management decisions about information technology are critically important to the firm's prosperity and survival.

Transformation of the Business Enterprise

There has been a transformation in the possibilities for organizing and managing the business enterprise. Some firms have begun to take advantage of these new possibilities.

The traditional business firm was—and still is—a hierarchical, centralized, structured arrangement of specialists that typically relied on a fixed set of standard operating procedures to deliver a mass-produced product (or service). The new style of business firm is a flattened (less hierarchical), decentralized, flexible arrangement of generalists who rely on nearly instant information to deliver mass-customized products and services uniquely suited to specific markets or customers.

The traditional management group relied—and still relies—on formal plans, a rigid division of labor, and formal rules. The new manager relies on informal commitments and networks to establish goals (rather than formal planning), a flexible arrangement of teams and individuals working in task forces, and a customer orientation to achieve coordination among employees. The new manager appeals to the knowledge, learning, and decision making of individual employees to ensure proper operation of the firm. Once again, information technology makes this style of management possible.

The Emerging Digital Firm

The intensive use of information technology in business firms since the mid-1990s, coupled with equally significant organizational redesign, has created the conditions for a new phenomenon in industrial society—the fully digital firm. The **digital firm** can be defined along several dimensions. A digital firm is one where nearly all of the organization's *significant business relationships* with customers, suppliers, and employees are digitally enabled and mediated. *Core business processes* are accomplished through digital networks spanning the entire organization or linking multiple organizations. **Business processes** refer to the unique manner in which work is organized, coordinated, and focused to produce a valuable product or service. Developing a new product, generating and fulfilling an order, or hiring an employee are examples of business processes, and the way organizations accomplish their business processes can be a source of competitive strength. (A detailed discussion of business processes can be found in Chapter 2.) *Key corporate assets*—intellectual property, core competencies, financial, and human assets—are managed through digital means. In a digital firm, any piece of information required to support key business decisions is available at any time and anywhere in the firm. Digital firms *sense and respond* to their environments far more rapidly than traditional firms, giving them more flexibility to survive in turbulent times. Digital firms offer extraordinary opportunities for more global organization and management. By digitally enabling and streamlining their work, digital firms have the potential to achieve unprecedented levels of profitability and competitiveness.

Digital firms are distinguished from traditional firms by their near total reliance on a set of information technologies to organize and manage. For managers of digital firms, information technology is not simply a useful handmaiden, an enabler, but rather it is the core of the business and the primary management tool.

There are very few fully digital firms today. Yet nearly all firms—especially larger traditional firms—are being driven in this direction by a number of business forces and opportunities. Despite the recent decline in technology investments and Internet-only dot.com businesses, firms are continuing to invest heavily in information systems that integrate internal business processes and build closer links with suppliers and customers. Cisco Systems, described in the chapter ending case study, is close to becoming a fully digital firm, using Internet technology to drive every aspect of its business. Procter & Gamble, described in the chapter opening vignette is another digital firm in the making.

Moving from a traditional firm foundation toward a digital firm requires insight, skill, and patience (see the chapter ending case study). Managers need to identify the challenges facing their firms; discover the technologies that will help them meet these challenges; or-

digital firm
Organization where nearly all significant business processes and relationships with customers, suppliers, and employees are digitally enabled, and key corporate assets are managed through digital means.

business processes
The unique ways in which organizations coordinate and organize work activities, information, and knowledge to produce a product or service.

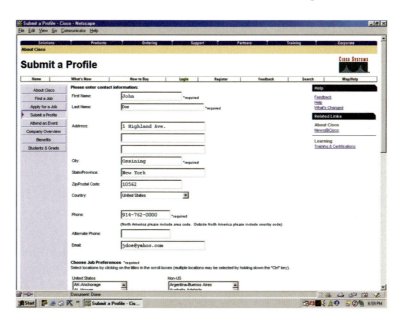

Cisco Systems uses the Web to recruit almost all of its employees. With many of its business processes enabled by the Internet, Cisco is becoming a digital firm.

ganize their firms and business processes to take advantage of the technology; and create management procedures and policies to implement the required changes. This book is dedicated to helping managers prepare for these tasks.

WHAT IS AN INFORMATION SYSTEM?

An **information system** can be defined technically as a set of interrelated components that collect (or retrieve), process, store, and distribute information to support decision making, coordination, and control in an organization. In addition to supporting decision making, coordination, and control, information systems may also help managers and workers analyze problems, visualize complex subjects, and create new products.

Information systems contain information about significant people, places, and things within the organization or in the environment surrounding it. By **information** we mean data that have been shaped into a form that is meaningful and useful to human beings. **Data**, in contrast, are streams of raw facts representing events occurring in organizations or the physical environment before they have been organized and arranged into a form that people can understand and use.

A brief example contrasting information to data may prove useful. Supermarket check-out counters ring up millions of pieces of data, such as product identification numbers or the cost of each item sold. Such pieces of data can be totaled and analyzed to provide meaningful information such as the total number of bottles of dish detergent sold at a particular store, which brands of dish detergent were selling the most rapidly at that store or sales territory, or the total amount spent on that brand of dish detergent at that store or sales region (see Figure 1-2).

Three activities in an information system produce the information that organizations need to make decisions, control operations, analyze problems, and create new products or services. These activities are input, processing, and output (see Figure 1-3). **Input** captures or collects raw data from within the organization or from its external environment. **Processing** converts this raw input into a more meaningful form. **Output** transfers the processed information to the people who will use it or to the activities for which it will be used. Information systems also require **feedback**, which is output that is returned to appropriate members of the organization to help them evaluate or correct the input stage.

In Procter & Gamble's point-of-sale system, the raw input consists of the item identification number, item description, and amount of each item sold along with the retailer's name and identification number. A computer processes these data by comparing the amount of each item sold to the historical sales pattern for that item to determine if the item might soon be out of stock. The system then sends alerts over computers and wireless devices to appropriate store personnel to reorder the item, which become the system outputs. The

information system
Interrelated components working together to collect, process, store, and disseminate information to support decision making, coordination, control, analysis, and visualization in an organization.

information
Data that have been shaped into a form that is meaningful and useful to human beings.

data
Streams of raw facts representing events occurring in organizations or the physical environment before they have been organized and arranged into a form that people can understand and use.

input
The capture or collection of raw data from within the organization or from its external environment for processing in an information system.

processing
The conversion, manipulation, and analysis of raw input into a form that is more meaningful to humans.

output
The distribution of processed information to the people who will use it or to the activities for which it will be used.

feedback
Output that is returned to the appropriate members of the organization to help them evaluate or correct input.

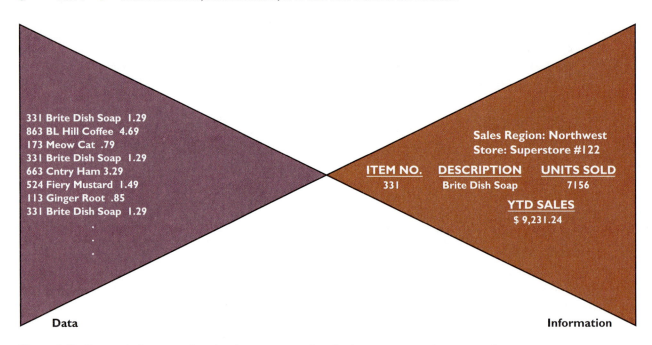

331 Brite Dish Soap 1.29
863 BL Hill Coffee 4.69
173 Meow Cat .79
331 Brite Dish Soap 1.29
663 Cntry Ham 3.29
524 Fiery Mustard 1.49
113 Ginger Root .85
331 Brite Dish Soap 1.29
.
.
.

Sales Region: Northwest
Store: Superstore #122

ITEM NO.	DESCRIPTION	UNITS SOLD
331	Brite Dish Soap	7156

YTD SALES
$ 9,231.24

Data

Information

Figure 1-2 Data and information. Raw data from a supermarket checkout counter can be processed and organized in order to produce meaningful information such as the total unit sales of dish detergent or the total sales revenue from dish detergent for a specific store or sales territory.

computer-based information systems (CBIS)
Information systems that rely on computer hardware and software for processing and disseminating information.

formal system
System resting on accepted and fixed definitions of data and procedures, operating with predefined rules.

Figure 1-3 Functions of an information system. An information system contains information about an organization and its surrounding environment. Three basic activities—input, processing, and output—produce the information organizations need. Feedback is output returned to appropriate people or activities in the organization to evaluate and refine the input. Environmental factors such as customers, suppliers, competitors, stockholders, and regulatory agencies interact with the organization and its information systems.

system thus provides meaningful information, such as lists of what retailer ordered what items, the total number of each item ordered daily, the total number of each item ordered by each retailer, and items that need to be restocked.

Our interest in this book is in formal, organizational **computer-based information systems (CBIS)** like those designed and used by Procter & Gamble and its customers, suppliers, and employees. **Formal systems** rest on accepted and fixed definitions of data and procedures for collecting, storing, processing, disseminating, and using these data. The formal systems we describe in this text are structured; that is, they operate in conformity with

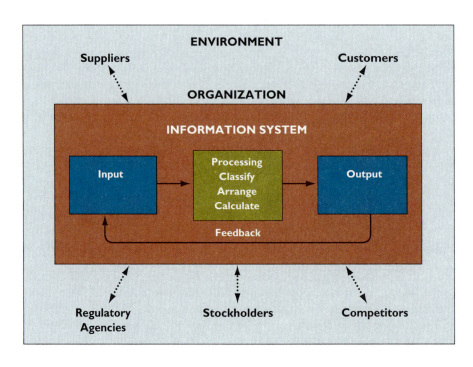

predefined rules that are relatively fixed and not easily changed. For instance, Procter & Gamble's point-of-sale system requires that all orders include the retailer's name and identification number and a unique number for identifying each item.

Informal information systems (such as office gossip networks) rely, by contrast, on unstated rules of behavior. There is no agreement on what is information, or on how it will be stored and processed. Such systems are essential for the life of an organization, but an analysis of their qualities is beyond the scope of this text.

Formal information systems can be either computer-based or manual. Manual systems use paper-and-pencil technology. These manual systems serve important needs, but they too are not the subject of this text. Computer-based information systems, in contrast, rely on computer hardware and software technology to process and disseminate information. From this point on, when we use the term *information systems,* we are referring to computer-based information systems—formal organizational systems that rely on computer technology. The Window on Technology describes some of the typical technologies used in computer-based information systems today.

Although computer-based information systems use computer technology to process raw data into meaningful information, there is a sharp distinction between a computer and a computer program on the one hand, and an information system on the other. Electronic computers and related software programs are the technical foundation, the tools and materials, of modern information systems. Computers provide the equipment for storing and processing information. Computer programs, or software, are sets of operating instructions that direct and control computer processing. Knowing how computers and computer programs work is important in designing solutions to organizational problems, but computers are only part of an information system. A house is an appropriate analogy. Houses are built with hammers, nails, and wood, but these do not make a house. The architecture, design, setting, landscaping, and all of the decisions that lead to the creation of these features are part of the house and are crucial for solving the problem of putting a roof over one's head. Computers and programs are the hammer, nails, and lumber of CBIS, but alone they cannot produce the information a particular organization needs. To understand information systems, one must understand the problems they are designed to solve, their architectural and design elements, and the organizational processes that lead to these solutions.

A BUSINESS PERSPECTIVE ON INFORMATION SYSTEMS

From a business perspective, an information system is an organizational and management solution, based on information technology, to a challenge posed by the environment. Examine this definition closely because it emphasizes the organizational and managerial nature of information systems: To fully understand information systems, a manager must understand the broader organization, management, and information technology dimensions

Using a handheld computer called a Delivery Information Acquisition Device (DIAD), UPS drivers automatically capture customers' signatures along with pickup, delivery, and time-card information.

UPS COMPETES GLOBALLY WITH INFORMATION TECHNOLOGY

United Parcel Service, the world's largest air and ground package-distribution company, started out in 1907 in a closet-size basement office. Jim Casey and Claude Ryan—two teenagers from Seattle with two bicycles and one phone—promised the "best service and lowest rates." UPS has used this formula successfully for more than 90 years.

Today UPS delivers more than 3 billion parcels and documents annually to the United States and to more than 200 other countries and territories. The firm has been able to maintain its leadership in small-package delivery services in the face of stiff competition from Federal Express and Airborne Express by investing heavily in advanced information technology. During the past decade, UPS has poured more than $1 billion a year into technology and systems to boost customer service while keeping costs low and streamlining its overall operations.

Using a handheld computer called a Delivery Information Acquisition Device (DIAD), UPS drivers automatically capture customers' signatures along with pickup, delivery, and time-card information. The drivers then place the DIAD into their truck's vehicle adapter, an information-transmitting device that is connected to the cellular telephone network. (Drivers may also transmit and receive information using an internal radio in the DIAD.) Package tracking information is then transmitted to UPS's computer network for storage and processing in UPS's main computers in Mahwah, New Jersey, and Alpharetta, Georgia. From there, the information can be accessed worldwide to provide proof of delivery to the customer or respond to customer queries.

Through its automated package tracking system, UPS can monitor packages throughout the delivery process. At various points along the route from sender to receiver, a barcode device scans shipping information on the package label; the information is then fed into the central computer. Customer service representatives can check the status of any package from desktop computers linked to the central computers and are able to respond immediately to inquiries from customers. UPS customers can also access this information from the company's Web site using their own computers or wireless devices such as pagers and cell phones.

Anyone with a package to ship can access the UPS Web site to track packages, check delivery routes, calculate shipping rates, determine time in transit, and schedule a pickup. Businesses anywhere can use the Web site to arrange UPS shipments and bill the shipments to the company's UPS account number or to a credit card. The data collected at the UPS Web site are transmitted to the UPS central computer and then back to the customer after processing. UPS also provides tools that enable its customers, such as Cisco Systems, described in the chapter ending case study, to embed UPS functions such as tracking and cost calculations into their own Web sites so that they can track shipments without visiting the UPS site. UPS started a new service called UPS Document Exchange to deliver business documents electronically using the Internet. The service provides a high level of security for these important documents as well as document tracking.

UPS recently set up a subsidiary called UPS e-Logistics to provide a complete bundle of standardized services to Internet businesses at a fraction of what it would cost to build their own systems and infrastructure. UPS e-Logistics provides subscribing companies with a network of distribution centers, warehousing, order fulfillment, inventory management, inbound and outbound transportation services, returns management, and customer call centers so that they can concentrate on taking orders on their Web sites.

To Think About: What are the inputs, processing, and outputs of UPS's package tracking system? What technologies are used? How are these technologies related to UPS's business strategy? What would happen if these technologies were not available?

Sources: Samuel Greengard, "United Parcel Service: Ahead of Time," *IQ Magazine*, May/June 2001; Matthew G. Nelson, "Wireless Delivers for UPS Overhaul," *Information Week*, June 11, 2001; Rick Brooks, "Got Mail?" *Wall Street Journal*, June 22, 2001; "Outside the Box," *Wall Street Journal E-Commerce section*, February 12, 2001; United Parcel Service, "Round UPS," Winter, 2001; and Kelly Barron, "Logistics in Brown," *Forbes*, January 10, 2000.

---

of systems (see Figure 1-4) and their power to provide solutions to challenges and problems in the business environment. We refer to this broader understanding of information systems, which encompasses an understanding of the management and organizational dimensions of systems as well as the technical dimensions of systems as **information systems literacy**. Information systems literacy includes a behavioral as well as a technical approach to studying information systems. **Computer literacy**, in contrast, focuses primarily on knowledge of information technology.

Review the diagram at the beginning of the chapter, which reflects this expanded definition of an information system. The diagram shows how Procter & Gamble's Web site, intranet, and sales and replenishment systems solve the business challenge of being a mature

information systems literacy
Broad-based understanding of information systems that includes behavioral knowledge about organizations and individuals using information systems as well as technical knowledge about computers.

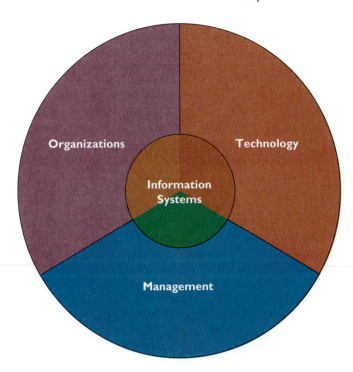

Figure 1-4 Information systems are more than computers. Using information systems effectively requires an understanding of the organization, management, and information technology shaping the systems. All information systems can be described as organizational and management solutions to challenges posed by the environment.

business with inefficient business processes. The diagram also illustrates how management, technology, and organization elements work together to create the systems. Each chapter of this text begins with a diagram similar to this one to help you analyze the chapter opening case. You can use this diagram as a starting point for analyzing any information system or information system problem you encounter. The Manager's Toolkit provides guidelines on how to use this framework for problem solving.

computer literacy
Knowledge about information technology, focusing on understanding how computer-based technologies work.

Organizations

Information systems are an integral part of organizations. Indeed, for some companies, such as credit reporting firms, without the information system there would be no business. The key elements of an organization are its people, structure, operating procedures, politics, and culture. We introduce these components of organizations here and describe them in greater detail in Chapter 3. Organizations are composed of different levels and specialties. Their structures reveal a clear-cut division of labor. Experts are employed and trained for different functions. The major **business functions**, or specialized tasks performed by business organizations, consist of sales and marketing, manufacturing and production, finance, accounting, and human resources (see Table 1-2).

Chapter 2 provides more detail on these business functions and the ways in which they are supported by information systems. Each chapter of this text now concludes with a Make

business functions
Specialized tasks performed in a business organization, including manufacturing and production, sales and marketing, finance, accounting, and human resources.

MIS IN ACTION   MANAGER'S TOOLKIT

HOW TO ANALYZE A BUSINESS INFORMATION SYSTEM PROBLEM

Information system problems in the business world represent a combination of management, organization, and technology issues. Here is a five-step process for analyzing a business problem involving information systems.

1. Identify the problem. What kind of problem is it? Is it a management problem, an organizational problem, a technology problem, or a combination of these? What are the management, organization, and technology issues that contributed to the problem?

2. What is the solution to the problem? What are the objectives of this solution? Are several alternative solutions possible? Which is the best alternative and why?

3. What technologies could be used to generate a solution?

4. What changes to organizational processes will be required by the solution?

5. What management policy will be required to implement the solution?

TABLE 1-2   **MAJOR BUSINESS FUNCTIONS**

Function	Purpose
Sales and marketing	Selling the organization's products and services
Manufacturing and production	Producing products and services
Finance	Managing the organization's financial assets (cash, stocks, bonds, etc.)
Accounting	Maintaining the organization's financial records (receipts, disbursements, paychecks, etc.); accounting for the flow of funds
Human resources	Attracting, developing, and maintaining the organization's labor force; maintaining employee records

IT Your Business section showing how chapter topics relate to each of these functional areas. The section also provides page numbers in each chapter where these functional examples can be found. Icons placed next to these functional business examples in the chapter-opening vignettes, Window On boxes, chapter ending case studies, and in the body of the chapters will help you identify them.

An organization coordinates work through a structured hierarchy and formal, standard operating procedures. The hierarchy arranges people in a pyramid structure of rising authority and responsibility. The upper levels of the hierarchy consist of managerial, professional, and technical employees, whereas the lower levels consist of operational personnel.

standard operating procedures (SOPs)
Formal rules for accomplishing tasks that have been developed to cope with expected situations.

Standard operating procedures (SOPs) are formal rules that have been developed over a long time for accomplishing tasks. These rules guide employees in a variety of procedures, from writing an invoice to responding to customer complaints. Most procedures are formalized and written down, but others are informal work practices, such as a requirement to return telephone calls from co-workers or customers, that are not formally documented. The firm's business processes, which we defined earlier, are based on its standard operating procedures. Many business processes and SOPs are incorporated into information systems, such as how to pay a supplier or how to correct an erroneous bill.

knowledge workers
People such as engineers or architects who design products or services and create knowledge for the organization.

Organizations require many different kinds of skills and people. In addition to managers, **knowledge workers** (such as engineers, architects, or scientists) design products or services and create new knowledge and **data workers** (such as secretaries, bookkeepers, or clerks) process the organization's paperwork. **Production or service workers** (such as machinists, assemblers, or packers) actually produce the organization's products or services.

data workers
People such as secretaries or bookkeepers who process the organization's paperwork.

Each organization has a unique culture, or fundamental set of assumptions, values, and ways of doing things, that has been accepted by most of its members. Parts of an organization's culture can always be found embedded in its information systems. For instance, the United Parcel Service's concern with placing service to the customer first is an aspect of its organizational culture that can be found in the company's package tracking systems.

production or service workers
People who actually produce the products or services of the organization.

Different levels and specialties in an organization create different interests and points of view. These views often conflict. Conflict is the basis for organizational politics. Information systems come out of this cauldron of differing perspectives, conflicts, compromises, and agreements that are a natural part of all organizations. In Chapter 3 we examine these features of organizations in greater detail.

Management

Managers perceive business challenges in the environment, they set the organizational strategy for responding and allocate the human and financial resources to achieve the strategy and coordinate the work. Throughout, they must exercise responsible leadership. Management's job is to "make sense" out of the many situations faced by organizations and formulate action plans to solve organizational problems. The business information systems described in this book reflect the hopes, dreams, and realities of real-world managers.

But managers must do more than manage what already exists. They must also create new products and services and even re-create the organization from time to time. A substantial part of management responsibility is creative work driven by new knowledge and information. Information technology can play a powerful role in redirecting and redesigning the organization. Chapter 3 describes managers' activities and management decision making in detail.

It is important to note that managerial roles and decisions vary at different levels of the organization. **Senior managers** make long-range strategic decisions about what products and services to produce. **Middle managers** carry out the programs and plans of senior management. **Operational managers** are responsible for monitoring the firm's daily activities. All levels of management are expected to be creative, to develop novel solutions to a broad range of problems. Each level of management has different information needs and information system requirements.

Technology

Information technology is one of many tools managers use to cope with change. **Computer hardware** is the physical equipment used for input, processing, and output activities in an information system. It consists of the following: the computer processing unit; various input, output, and storage devices; and physical media to link these devices together. Chapter 6 describes computer hardware in greater detail.

Computer software consists of the detailed preprogrammed instructions that control and coordinate the computer hardware components in an information system. Chapter 6 explains the importance of computer software in information systems.

Storage technology includes both the physical media for storing data, such as magnetic or optical disk or tape, and the software governing the organization of data on these physical media. More detail on physical storage media can be found in Chapter 6, whereas Chapter 7 covers data organization and access methods.

Communications technology, consisting of both physical devices and software, links the various pieces of hardware and transfers data from one physical location to another. Computers and communications equipment can be connected in networks for sharing voice, data, images, sound, or even video. A **network** links two or more computers to share data or resources such as a printer. Chapters 8 and 9 provide more details on communications and networking technology and issues.

All of these technologies represent resources that can be shared throughout the organization and constitute the firm's **information technology (IT) infrastructure**. The IT infrastructure provides the foundation or platform on which the firm can build its specific information systems. Each organization must carefully design and manage its information technology infrastructure so that it has the set of technology services it needs for the work it wants to accomplish with information systems. Chapters 6 through 9 of this text examine each major technology component of information technology infrastructure and show how they all work together to create the technology platform for the organization.

Let us return to UPS's package tracking system in the Window on Technology and identify the organization, management, and technology elements. The organization element anchors the package tracking system in UPS's sales and production functions (the main product of UPS is a service—package delivery). It specifies the required procedures for identifying packages with both sender and recipient information, taking inventory, tracking the packages en route, and providing package status reports for UPS customers and customer service representatives. The system must also provide information to satisfy the needs of managers and workers. UPS drivers need to be trained in both package pickup and delivery procedures and in how to use the package tracking system so that they can work efficiently and effectively. UPS customers may need some training to use UPS in-house package tracking software or the UPS World Wide Web site. UPS's management is responsible for monitoring service levels and costs and for promoting the company's strategy of combining low cost and superior service. Management decided to use automation to increase the ease of sending a package via UPS and of checking its delivery status, thereby reducing delivery costs and increasing sales revenues. The technology supporting this system consists of handheld computers, barcode scanners, wired and wireless communications networks, desktop computers, UPS's central computer, storage technology for the package delivery data, UPS in-house package tracking software, and software to access the World Wide Web. The result is an information system solution to the business challenge of providing a high level of service with low prices in the face of mounting competition.

---

senior managers
People occupying the topmost hierarchy in an organization who are responsible for making long-range decisions.

middle managers
People in the middle of the organizational hierarchy who are responsible for carrying out the plans and goals of senior management.

operational managers
People who monitor the day-to-day activities of the organization.

computer hardware
Physical equipment used for input, processing, and output activities in an information system.

computer software
Detailed, preprogrammed instructions that control and coordinate the work of computer hardware components in an information system.

storage technology
Physical media and software governing the storage and organization of data for use in an information system.

communications technology
Physical devices and software that link various computer hardware components and transfer data from one physical location to another.

network
The linking of two or more computers to share data or resources, such as a printer.

information technology (IT) infrastructure
Computer hardware, software, data and storage technology, and networks providing a portfolio of shared information technology resources for the organization.

1.2 CONTEMPORARY APPROACHES TO INFORMATION SYSTEMS

Multiple perspectives on information systems show that the study of information systems is a multidisciplinary field. No single theory or perspective dominates. Figure 1-5 illustrates the major disciplines that contribute problems, issues, and solutions in the study of information systems. In general, the field can be divided into technical and behavioral approaches. Information systems are sociotechnical systems. Though they are composed of machines, devices, and "hard" physical technology, they require substantial social, organizational, and intellectual investments to make them work properly.

TECHNICAL APPROACH

The technical approach to information systems emphasizes mathematically based models to study information systems, as well as the physical technology and formal capabilities of these systems. The disciplines that contribute to the technical approach are computer science, management science, and operations research. Computer science is concerned with establishing theories of computability, methods of computation, and methods of efficient data storage and access. Management science emphasizes the development of models for decision-making and management practices. Operations research focuses on mathematical techniques for optimizing selected parameters of organizations, such as transportation, inventory control, and transaction costs.

BEHAVIORAL APPROACH

An important part of the information systems field is concerned with behavioral issues that arise in the development and long-term maintenance of information systems. Issues such as strategic business integration, design, implementation, utilization, and management cannot be explored usefully with the models used in the technical approach. Other behavioral disciplines contribute important concepts and methods. For instance, sociologists study information systems with an eye toward how groups and organizations shape the development of systems and also how systems affect individuals, groups, and organizations. Psychologists study information systems with an interest in how human decision makers perceive and use formal information. Economists study information systems with an interest in what impact systems have on control and cost structures within the firm and within markets.

The behavioral approach does not ignore technology. Indeed, information systems technology is often the stimulus for a behavioral problem or issue. But the focus of this approach is generally not on technical solutions. Instead it concentrates on changes in attitudes, management and organizational policy, and behavior (Kling and Dutton, 1982).

APPROACH OF THIS TEXT: SOCIOTECHNICAL SYSTEMS

The study of **management information systems (MIS)** arose in the 1970s to focus on computer-based information systems aimed at managers (Davis and Olson, 1985). MIS

management information systems (MIS)
The study of information systems focusing on their use in business and management.

Figure 1-5 Contemporary approaches to information systems. The study of information systems deals with issues and insights contributed from technical and behavioral disciplines.

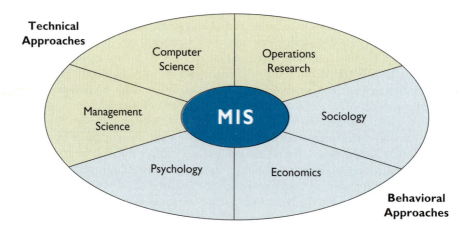

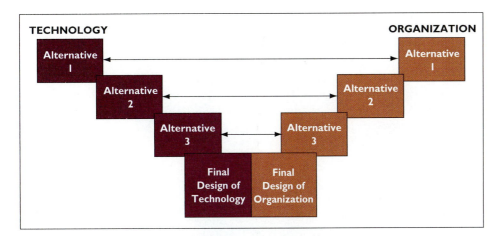

Figure 1-6 A sociotechnical perspective on information systems. In a sociotechnical perspective, the performance of a system is optimized when both the technology and the organization mutually adjust to one another until a satisfactory fit is obtained.

combines the theoretical work of computer science, management science, and operations research with a practical orientation toward developing system solutions to real-world problems and managing information technology resources. It also pays attention to behavioral issues surrounding the development, use, and impact of information systems raised by sociology, economics, and psychology.

Our experience as academics and practitioners leads us to believe that no single perspective effectively captures the reality of information systems. Problems with systems—and their solutions—are rarely all technical or all behavioral. Our best advice to students is to understand the perspectives of all disciplines. Indeed, the challenge and excitement of the information systems field is that it requires an appreciation and tolerance of many different approaches.

Adopting a sociotechnical systems perspective helps to avoid a purely technological approach to information systems. For instance, the fact that information technology is rapidly declining in cost and growing in power does not necessarily or easily translate into productivity enhancement or bottom-line profits.

In this book, we stress the need to optimize the system's performance as a whole. Both the technical and behavioral components need attention. This means that technology must be changed and designed in such a way as to fit organizational and individual needs. At times, the technology may have to be "de-optimized" to accomplish this fit. Organizations and individuals must also be changed through training, learning, and planned organizational change in order to allow the technology to operate and prosper (see, for example, Liker et al., 1987). People and organizations change to take advantage of new information technology. Figure 1-6 illustrates this process of mutual adjustment in a sociotechnical system.

1.3 TOWARD THE DIGITAL FIRM: THE NEW ROLE OF INFORMATION SYSTEMS IN ORGANIZATIONS

Managers cannot ignore information systems because they play such a critical role in contemporary organizations. Today's systems directly affect how managers decide, plan, and manage their employees, and, increasingly, they shape what products are produced, and where, when, and how. Therefore, responsibility for systems cannot be delegated to technical decision makers.

THE WIDENING SCOPE OF INFORMATION SYSTEMS

Figure 1-7 illustrates the new relationship between organizations and information systems. There is a growing interdependence between business strategy, rules, and procedures on the one hand, and information systems software, hardware, databases, and telecommunications on the other. A change in any of these components often requires changes in other components. This relationship becomes critical when management plans for the future. What a business would like to do in five years often depends on what its systems will be able to do.

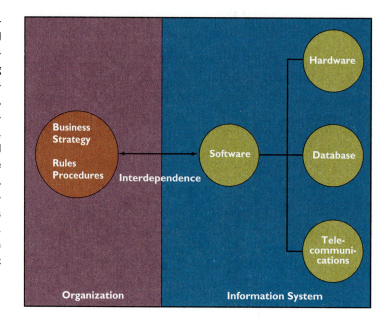

Figure 1-7 The interdependence between organizations and information systems. In contemporary systems there is a growing interdependence between organizational business strategy, rules, and procedures and the organization's information systems. Changes in strategy, rules, and procedures increasingly require changes in hardware, software, databases, and telecommunications. Existing systems can act as a constraint on organizations. Often, what the organization would like to do depends on what its systems will permit it to do.

Increasing market share, becoming the high-quality or low-cost producer, developing new products, and increasing employee productivity depend more and more on the kinds and quality of information systems in the organization.

A second change in the relationship between information systems and organizations results from the growing reach and scope of system projects and applications. Building and managing systems today involves a much larger part of the organization than it did in the past. As firms become more like "digital firms," the system enterprise extends to customers, vendors, and even industry competitors (see Figure 1-8). Where early systems produced largely technical changes that affected only a few people in the firm, contemporary systems have been bringing about managerial changes (who has what information about whom, when, and how often) and institutional "core" changes (what products and services are produced, under what conditions, and by whom). As companies move toward digital firm organizations, nearly all the firm's managers and employees—as well as customers and vendors—participate in a variety of firm systems, tied together by a digital information web. For instance, what a customer does on a firm's Web site can trigger an employee to make an on-the-spot pricing decision or alert a firm's suppliers of potential "stockout" situations.

THE NETWORK REVOLUTION AND THE INTERNET

One reason information systems play such a large role in organizations and affect so many people is the soaring power and declining cost of computer technology. Computing power, which has been doubling every 18 months, has improved the performance of microprocessors over 25,000 times since their invention 30 years ago. With powerful, easy-to-use soft-

Figure 1-8 The widening scope of information systems. Over time, information systems have come to play a larger role in the life of organizations. Early systems brought about largely technical changes that were relatively easy to accomplish. Later systems affected managerial control and behavior and subsequently "core" institutional activities. In the digital firm era, information systems extend far beyond the boundaries of the firm to encompass vendors, customers, and even competitors.

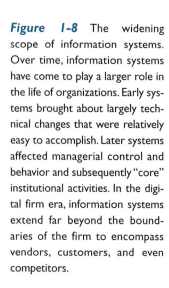

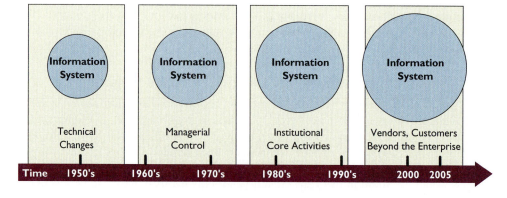

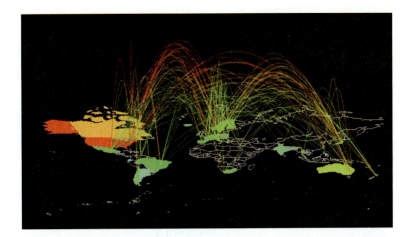

The Internet. This global network of networks provides a highly flexible platform for information sharing. Digital information can be distributed at almost no cost to millions of people throughout the world.

ware, the computer can crunch numbers, analyze vast pools of data, or simulate complex physical and logical processes with animated drawings, sounds, and even tactile feedback.

The soaring power of computer technology has spawned powerful communication networks that organizations can use to access vast storehouses of information from around the world and to coordinate activities across space and time. These networks are transforming the shape and form of business enterprises, creating the foundation for the digital firm.

The world's largest and most widely used network is the **Internet**. The Internet is an international network of networks that are both commercial and publicly owned. The Internet connects hundreds of thousands of different networks from more than 200 countries around the world. More than 500 million people working in science, education, government, and business use the Internet to exchange information or perform business transactions with other organizations around the globe.

The Internet is extremely elastic. If networks are added or removed or failures occur in parts of the system, the rest of the Internet continues to operate. Through special communication and technology standards, any computer can communicate with virtually any other computer linked to the Internet using ordinary telephone lines. Companies and private individuals can use the Internet to exchange business transactions, text messages, graphic images, and even video and sound, whether they are located next door or on the other side of the globe. Table 1-3 describes some of the Internet's capabilities.

The Internet is creating a new "universal" technology platform on which to build all sorts of new products, services, strategies, and organizations. It is reshaping the way information systems are being used in business and daily life. By eliminating many technical, geographic, and cost barriers obstructing the global flow of information, the Internet is inspiring new uses of information systems and new business models. The Internet provides the primary technology platform for the digital firm.

Because it offers so many new possibilities for doing business, the Internet capability known as the **World Wide Web** is of special interest to organizations and managers. The World Wide Web is a system with universally accepted standards for storing, retrieving, formatting, and displaying information in a networked environment. Information is stored and displayed as electronic "pages" that can contain text, graphics, animations, sound, and video. These Web pages can be linked electronically to other Web pages, regardless of where they are located, and viewed by any type of computer. By clicking on highlighted words or buttons on a Web page, you can link to related pages to find additional information, software programs, or still more links to other points on the Web. The Web can serve as the foundation for new kinds of information systems such as those based on Procter & Gamble's Web site described in the chapter opening vignette.

All of the Web pages maintained by an organization or individual are called a **Web site**. Businesses are creating Web sites with stylish typography, colorful graphics, push-button interactivity, and often sound and video to disseminate product information widely, to "broadcast" advertising and messages to customers, to collect electronic orders and customer data, and, increasingly, to coordinate far-flung sales forces and organizations on a global scale.

Internet

International network of networks that is a collection of hundreds of thousands of private and public networks.

World Wide Web

A system with universally accepted standards for storing, retrieving, formatting, and displaying information in a networked environment.

Web site

All of the World Wide Web pages maintained by an organization or an individual.

TABLE 1-3

WHAT YOU CAN DO ON THE INTERNET

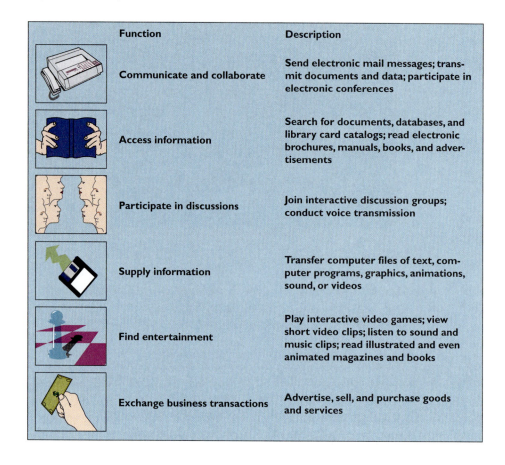

	Function	Description
	Communicate and collaborate	Send electronic mail messages; transmit documents and data; participate in electronic conferences
	Access information	Search for documents, databases, and library card catalogs; read electronic brochures, manuals, books, and advertisements
	Participate in discussions	Join interactive discussion groups; conduct voice transmission
	Supply information	Transfer computer files of text, computer programs, graphics, animations, sound, or videos
	Find entertainment	Play interactive video games; view short video clips; listen to sound and music clips; read illustrated and even animated magazines and books
	Exchange business transactions	Advertise, sell, and purchase goods and services

In Chapters 4 and 9 we describe the Web and other Internet capabilities in greater detail. We also discuss relevant features of the Internet throughout the text because the Internet affects so many aspects of information systems in organizations.

NEW OPTIONS FOR ORGANIZATIONAL DESIGN: THE DIGITAL FIRM AND THE COLLABORATIVE ENTERPRISE

The explosive growth in computing power and networks, including the Internet, is turning organizations into networked enterprises, allowing information to be instantly distributed within and beyond the organization. Companies can use this information to improve their internal business processes and to coordinate these business processes with those of other organizations. These new technologies for connectivity and collaboration can be used to redesign and reshape organizations, transforming their structure, scope of operations, reporting and control mechanisms, work practices, work flows, products, and services. The ultimate end product of these new ways of conducting business electronically is the digital firm.

Flattening Organizations and the Changing Management Process

Large, bureaucratic organizations, which primarily developed before the computer age, are often inefficient, slow to change, and less competitive than newly created organizations. Some of these large organizations have downsized, reducing the number of employees and the number of levels in their organizational hierarchies. For example, when Eastman Chemical Co. split off from Kodak in 1994 it had $3.3 billion in revenue and 24,000 full-time employees. By 2000 it generated $5 billion in revenue with only 17,000 employees (*Information Week*, 2000).

In digital firms, hierarchy and organizational levels do not disappear. But digital firms develop "optimal hierarchies" that balance the decision-making load across an organization, resulting in flatter organizations. Flatter organizations have fewer levels of management, with lower-level employees being given greater decision-making authority (see Figure 1-9). Those

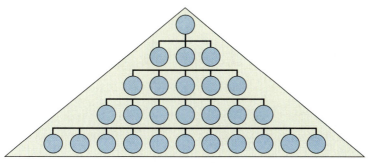

A traditional hierarchical organization with many levels of management

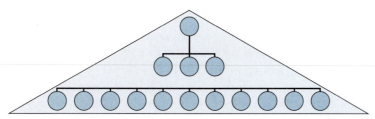

An organization that has been "flattened" by removing layers of management

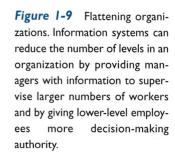

Figure 1-9 Flattening organizations. Information systems can reduce the number of levels in an organization by providing managers with information to supervise larger numbers of workers and by giving lower-level employees more decision-making authority.

employees are empowered to make more decisions than in the past, they no longer work standard nine-to-five hours, and they no longer necessarily work in an office. Moreover, such employees may be scattered geographically, sometimes working half a world away from the manager.

These changes mean that the management span of control has also been broadened, allowing high-level managers to manage and control more workers spread over greater distances. Many companies have eliminated thousands of middle managers as a result of these changes. AT&T, IBM, and General Motors are only a few of the organizations that have eliminated more than 30,000 middle managers in one fell swoop.

Information technology is also recasting the management process by providing powerful new tools for more precise planning, forecasting, and monitoring. For instance, it is now possible for managers to obtain information on organizational performance down to the level of specific transactions from just about anywhere in the organization at any time. Product managers at Frito-Lay Corporation, the world's largest manufacturer of salty snack foods, can know within hours precisely how many bags of Fritos have sold on any street in America at its customers' stores, how much they sold for, and what the competition's sales volumes and prices are. (The Chapter 10 case study provides more detail about this company.)

Separating Work from Location

Communications technology has eliminated distance as a factor for many types of work in many situations. Salespersons can spend more time in the field with customers and have more up-to-date information with them while carrying much less paper. Many employees can work remotely from their homes or cars, and companies can reserve space at smaller central offices for meeting clients or other employees. Collaborative teamwork across thousands of miles has become a reality as designers work on a new product together even if they are located on different continents. Lockheed Martin Aeronautics developed a real-time system for collaborative product design and engineering based on the Internet, which it uses to coordinate tasks with its partners such as BAE and Northrup Grumman. Engineers from all three companies work jointly on designs over the Internet. Previously, the company and its partners worked separately on designs, hammering out design differences in lengthy face-to-face meetings. A drawing that once took 400 hours now takes 125 and the design phase of projects has been cut in half (Konicki, 2001).

Reorganizing Work Flows

Information systems have been progressively replacing manual work procedures with automated work procedures, work flows, and work processes. Electronic work flows have reduced

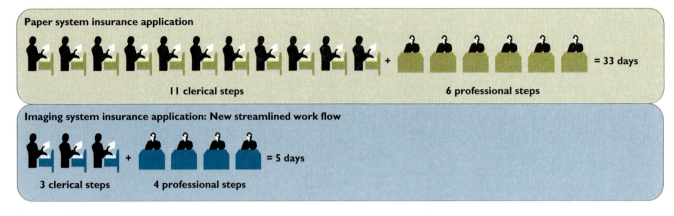

Figure 1-10 Redesigned work flow for insurance underwriting. An application requiring 33 days in a paper system would only take five days using computers, networks, and a streamlined work flow.

the cost of operations in many companies by displacing paper and the manual routines that accompany it. Improved work flow management has enabled many corporations not only to cut costs significantly but also to improve customer service at the same time. For instance, insurance companies can reduce processing of applications for new insurance from weeks to days (see Figure 1-10).

Redesigned work flows can have a profound impact on organizational efficiency and can even lead to new organizational structures, products, and services. We discuss the impact of restructured work flows on organizational design in greater detail in Chapters 3 and 12.

Increasing Flexibility of Organizations

Companies can use communications technology to organize in more flexible ways, increasing their ability to sense and respond to changes in the marketplace and to take advantage of new opportunities. Information systems can give both large and small organizations additional flexibility to overcome some of the limitations posed by their size. Table 1-4 describes some of the ways in which information technology can help small companies act "big" and help big companies act "small." Small organizations can use information systems to acquire some of the muscle and reach of larger organizations. They can perform coordinating activities, such as processing bids or keeping track of inventory, and many manufacturing tasks with very few managers, clerks, or production workers.

mass customization
The capacity to offer individually tailored products or services on a large scale.

Large organizations can use information technology to achieve some of the agility and responsiveness of small organizations. One aspect of this phenomenon is **mass customization**, the ability to offer individually tailored products or services on a large scale. Information systems can make the production process more flexible so that products can be

HOW INFORMATION TECHNOLOGY INCREASES ORGANIZATIONAL FLEXIBILITY

Small Companies

Desktop machines, inexpensive computer-aided design (CAD) software, and computer-controlled machine tools provide the precision, speed, and quality of giant manufacturers.

Information immediately accessed by telephone and communications links eliminates the need for research staff and business libraries.

Managers can easily obtain the information they need to manage large numbers of employees in widely scattered locations.

Large Companies

Custom manufacturing systems allow large factories to offer customized products in small quantities.

Massive databases of customer purchasing records can be analyzed so that large companies can know their customers' needs and preferences as easily as local merchants.

Information can be easily distributed down the ranks of the organization to empower lower-level employees and work groups to solve problems.

tailored to each customer's unique set of requirements (Zipkin, 2001). Software and computer networks can be used to link the plant floor tightly with orders, design, and purchasing and to finely control production machines so that products can be turned out in greater variety and easily customized with no added cost for small production runs. For example, Levi Strauss has equipped its stores with an option called Original Spin, which allows customers to design jeans to their own specifications, rather than picking the jeans off the rack. Customers enter their measurements into a personal computer, which then transmits the customer's specifications over a network to Levi's plants. The company is able to produce the custom jeans on the same lines that manufacture its standard items. There are almost no extra production costs because the process does not require additional warehousing, production overruns, and inventories. Lands' End has implemented a similar system for customizing chino slacks that allows customers to enter their measurements over its Web site.

A related trend is micromarketing, in which information systems can help companies pinpoint tiny target markets for these finely customized products and services—as small as individualized "markets of one." We discuss micromarketing in more detail in Chapters 2, 3, and 11.

Redefining Organizational Boundaries: New Avenues for Collaboration

A key feature of the emerging digital firm is the ability to conduct business across firm boundaries almost as efficiently and effectively as it can conduct business within the firm. Networked information systems allow companies to coordinate with other organizations across great distances. Transactions such as payments and purchase orders can be exchanged electronically among different companies, thereby reducing the cost of obtaining products and services from outside the firm. Organizations can also share business data, catalogs, or mail messages through networks. These networked information systems can create new efficiencies and new relationships between an organization, its customers, and suppliers, redefining organizational boundaries.

For example, the Toyota Motor Corporation is networked to suppliers, such as the Dana Corporation of Toledo, Ohio, a tier-one supplier of chassis, engines, and other major automotive components. Through this electronic link, the Dana Corporation monitors Toyota production and ships components exactly when needed (McDougall, 2001). Toyota and Dana have thus become linked business partners with mutually shared responsibilities.

The information system linking Toyota to its supplier is called an interorganizational information system. Systems linking a company to its customers, distributors, or suppliers are termed **interorganizational systems** because they automate the flow of information across organizational boundaries. Digital firms use interorganizational systems to link with suppliers, customers, and sometimes even competitors, to create and distribute new products and services without being limited by traditional organizational boundaries or physical locations. For example, Cisco Systems, described in the chapter ending case study, does not manufacture the networking products it sells; it uses other companies, such as Flextronics, for this purpose. Cisco uses the Internet to transmit orders to Flextronics and to monitor the status of orders as they are being shipped. (More detail on Flextronics can be found in the Chapter 2 opening vignette.)

Many of these interorganizational systems are becoming increasingly based on Web technology and providing more intense sharing of knowledge, resources, and business processes than in the past. Firms are using these systems to work jointly with suppliers and other business partners on product design and development and on the scheduling and flow of work in manufacturing, procurement, and distribution. These new levels of interfirm collaboration and coordination can lead to higher levels of efficiency, value to customers, and ultimately significant competitive advantage (see the Window on Organizations).

interorganizational systems
Information systems that automate the flow of information across organizational boundaries and link a company to its customers, distributors, or suppliers.

THE DIGITAL FIRM: ELECTRONIC COMMERCE, ELECTRONIC BUSINESS, AND NEW DIGITAL RELATIONSHIPS

The changes we have just described represent new ways of conducting business electronically both inside and outside the firm that can ultimately result in the creation of digital firms. Increasingly, the Internet is providing the underlying technology for these changes. The

FAST-PACED FASHIONS AT LI & FUNG

A clerk at a Fifth Avenue store of the nationwide Express chain said of the clothing retailer, "We rotate the front of the store every Thursday." She noted that "The changes are getting faster and faster." Instead of the traditional four clothing fashion seasons (spring, summer, autumn, and winter), styles now change once a month or even faster. According to Jane Werner, an associate professor of fashion merchandising management at New York's Fashion Institute of Technology, stores now "get a new delivery every two weeks." In the face of the speedup, some retailers, such as The Gap and the Spanish chain Zara, manage their own production. Many others, including Levi Strauss, Ann Taylor, Disney, and the Limited, turn to Li & Fung of Hong Kong.

Founded in 1906 as a trading house exporting ceramics and fireworks, Li & Fung now manages the production and shipping of garments for retailers. It provides a one-stop shop for product development, raw material sourcing, production planning management, quality assurance, and shipping. Li & Fung owns neither fabric nor factories nor machines, outsourcing all of its work to other companies. Its clients include such giants as Ann Taylor, Guess, Laura Ashley, Levi Strauss, and Reebok. Its 2000 revenue was $3.2 billion and it is growing by 32 percent annually.

One key to Li & Fung's business success is its ability to have the products ordered by its clients manufactured very rapidly. Whereas companies such as The Gap used to need a nine-month lead to go from design to a retail store, Li & Fung can have the product in the store only five weeks after it receives an order. The company's management believes that not owning any production facilities keeps it flexible and adaptable for quick-response manufacturing, and encourages a constant search for quality-conscious, cost-effective producers that can meet their

clients' deadlines. Li & Fung's widespread network includes more than 7,500 suppliers in 37 countries around the world. Li & Fung maintains 64 offices in 37 countries and uses Internet and Web technology extensively to coordinate this network.

Customers can place their orders to Li & Fung over its private Web site. When Li & Fung receives an order, it first communicates with the customer using e-mail to fine tune the specifications. Next it sends those instructions to the appropriate raw materials suppliers. The fabrics and instructions are then forwarded to a carefully selected factory where the clothing is produced. Ada Liu, a division manager at Li & Fung, described one transaction. She received a pants order from a major American company. She had the fabric woven in China where it would be dyed to the exact color she required. She ordered fastenings from factories in both Hong Kong and Korea. Next the materials were sent to Guatemala because, she said, "For simple things like pants with four seams, Guatemala is great." She also noted, "They can do things quickly, and it's close to the U.S."

The Li & Fung Web site tracks the entire production process for each order. At each stage customers are able to use the Web site to modify specifications before the next step takes place. For example, they can change the color before the fabric has been dyed and can even cancel their orders if material has not yet been purchased.

To Think About: How has the Internet affected the strategy and operation of fashion industry businesses? How has it affected Li & Fung's relationships with its suppliers and customers? What benefits does it provide organizations such as Li & Fung and its clients?

Sources: Joanne Lee-Young, "Furiously Fast Fashions," *The Industry Standard,* June 11, 2001; and www.lifung.com.

---

electronic market
A marketplace that is created by computer and communication technologies that link many buyers and sellers.

Internet can link thousands of organizations into a single network, creating the foundation for a vast electronic marketplace. An **electronic market** is an information system that links together many buyers and sellers to exchange information, products, services, and payments. Through computers and networks, these systems function like electronic intermediaries, with lowered costs for typical marketplace transactions, such as matching buyers and sellers, establishing prices, ordering goods, and paying bills (Bakos, 1998). Buyers and sellers can complete purchase and sale transactions digitally, regardless of their location.

A vast array of goods and services are being advertised, bought, and exchanged worldwide using the Internet as a global marketplace. Companies are furiously creating eye-catching electronic brochures, advertisements, product manuals, and order forms on the World Wide Web. All kinds of products and services are available on the Web, including fresh flowers, books, real estate, musical recordings, electronics, and steaks. Even electronic financial trading has arrived on the Web for stocks, bonds, mutual funds, and other financial instruments.

Increasingly the Web is being used for business-to-business transactions as well. For example, airlines can use the Boeing Corporation's Web site to order parts electronically and check the status of their orders. Altranet Energy Technologies of Houston operates an on-line marketplace called altranet.com where many different energy industry suppliers and buyers

Li & Fung uses the Internet to communicate with clients and its global sourcing network of more than 7500 suppliers in 37 countries. Interorganizational systems based on the Web are making it possible for multiple firms to coordinate their activities even though they are many miles apart.

can meet any time of day or night to trade natural gas, liquids, electricity, and crude oil in a spot market for immediate delivery. Participants can select their trading partners, confirm transactions, and obtain credit and insurance.

The global availability of the Internet for the exchange of transactions between buyers and sellers has fueled the growth of electronic commerce. **Electronic commerce** is the process of buying and selling goods and services electronically with computerized business transactions using the Internet, networks, and other digital technologies. It also encompasses activities supporting those market transactions, such as advertising, marketing, customer support, delivery, and payment. By replacing manual and paper-based procedures with electronic alternatives, and by using information flows in new and dynamic ways, electronic commerce can accelerate ordering, delivery, and payment for goods and services while reducing companies' operating and inventory costs.

The Internet has emerged as the primary technology platform for electronic commerce. Equally important, Internet technology is facilitating management of the rest of the business—publishing employee personnel policies, reviewing account balances and production plans, scheduling plant repairs and maintenance, and revising design documents. Companies are taking advantage of the connectivity and ease of use of Internet technology to create internal corporate networks called **intranets** that are based on Internet technology. The chapter opening vignette described how Procter & Gamble set up a private intranet for employees to publish reports, charts, and their ideas for improving the company. The number of these private intranets for organizational communication, collaboration, and coordination is soaring. In this text, we use the term **electronic business** to distinguish these uses of Internet and digital technology for the management and coordination of other business processes from electronic commerce.

The Window on Organizations showed how Li & Fung allowed its suppliers and business partners to access portions of its private intranet. Private intranets extended to authorized users outside the organization are called **extranets**, and firms use such networks to coordinate their activities with other firms for electronic commerce and electronic business. Table 1-5 lists some examples of electronic commerce and electronic business.

Figure 1-11 illustrates a digital firm making intensive use of Internet and digital technology for electronic commerce and electronic business. Information can flow seamlessly among different parts of the company and between the company and external entities—its customers, suppliers, and business partners. Organizations will move toward this digital firm vision as they use the Internet, intranets, and extranets to manage their internal processes and their relationships with customers, suppliers, and other external entities.

Both electronic commerce and electronic business can fundamentally change the way business is conducted. To use the Internet and other digital technologies successfully for

electronic commerce
The process of buying and selling goods and services electronically involving transactions using the Internet, networks, and other digital technologies.

intranet
An internal network based on Internet and World Wide Web technology and standards.

electronic business
The use of Internet and other digital technology for organizational communication and coordination and the management of the firm.

extranet
Private intranet that is accessible to authorized outsiders.

TABLE 1-5

EXAMPLES OF ELECTRONIC COMMERCE AND ELECTRONIC BUSINESS

Electronic Commerce

Drugstore.com operates a virtual pharmacy on the Internet selling prescription medicine and over-the-counter health, beauty, and wellness products. Customers can input their orders via the drugstore.com™ web site and have their purchases shipped to them.

Travelocity provides a Web site that can be used by consumers for travel and vacation planning. Visitors can find out information on airlines, hotels, vacation packages, and other travel and leisure topics, and they can make airline and hotel reservations on-line through the Web site.

Milwaukee Electric Tool, a subsidiary of the **Atlas Copco AB** global industrial machine tools conglomerate based in Stockholm, created a secure sales extranet that allows its distributors to search the company's product catalog and order equipment.

Electronic Business

Roche Bioscience scientists worldwide use an intranet to share research results and discuss findings. The intranet also provides a company telephone directory and newsletter.

Texas Instruments uses an intranet to provide employees with a consolidated report of all of their compensation and benefits, including pension plans, 401K employee savings plans, and stock purchase plans. Employees can use charts and modeling tools to see the value of their portfolios and benefits now and in the future.

Dream Works SKG uses an intranet to check the daily status of projects, including animation objects, and to coordinate movie scenes.

---

electronic commerce, electronic business, and the creation of digital firms, organizations may have to redefine their business models, reinvent business processes, change corporate cultures, and create much closer relationships with customers and suppliers. We discuss these issues in greater detail in following chapters.

1.4 LEARNING TO USE INFORMATION SYSTEMS: NEW OPPORTUNITIES WITH TECHNOLOGY

Although information systems are creating many exciting opportunities for both businesses and individuals, they are also a source of new problems, issues, and challenges for managers. In this course, you will learn about both the challenges and opportunities information systems present, and you will be able to use information technology to enrich your learning experience.

At the drugstore.com™ Web site, customers can make on-line purchases of prescription medicine and over-the-counter health, beauty, and wellness products. The Internet is fueling the growth of electronic commerce.

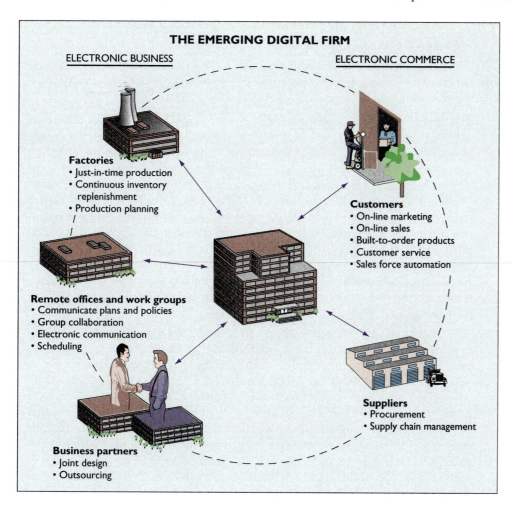

THE EMERGING DIGITAL FIRM

ELECTRONIC BUSINESS **ELECTRONIC COMMERCE**

Factories
• Just-in-time production
• Continuous inventory replenishment
• Production planning

Remote offices and work groups
• Communicate plans and policies
• Group collaboration
• Electronic communication
• Scheduling

Business partners
• Joint design
• Outsourcing

Customers
• On-line marketing
• On-line sales
• Built-to-order products
• Customer service
• Sales force automation

Suppliers
• Procurement
• Supply chain management

Figure 1-11 Electronic commerce and electronic business in the emerging digital firm. Electronic commerce uses Internet and digital technology to conduct transactions with customers and suppliers, whereas electronic business uses these technologies for the management of the rest of the business.

MIS IN ACTION DECISIONMAKING

PLANNING A NEW INTERNET BUSINESS

You would like to create a new business on the Web that provides cat and dog owners with advice on animal health, behavior, and nutrition and sells products such as pet beds, carriers, dishes, toys, flea treatments, and grooming aids. Your Web site would also have capabilities for pet owners to exchange electronic messages about their pets and pet care with other pet owners. In researching the U.S. market for your business, you have found the following statistics from the U.S. Commerce Department's *Statistical Abstract of the United States*.

Household Pet Ownership by Income Level

Annual Income	Dog Owners	Cat Owners
Less than $12,500	14%	15%
$12,500–$24,999	20	20
$25,000–$39,999	24	23
$40,000–$59,999	22	22
$60,000 and over	20	20
Total	**100**	**100**

Internet Use by Income Level

Annual Income	Percentage Using the Internet
Less than $20,000	5%
$20,000–$49,999	26
$50,000–$74,999	28
$75,000 and over	41
Total	**100**

1. What are the implications of this information for starting this business on the Internet?
2. What additional information might be useful to help you decide whether such a business could be profitable and what type and price range of products to sell?

The Challenge of Information Systems: Key Management Issues

Although information technology is advancing at a blinding pace, there is nothing easy or mechanical about building and using information systems. There are five key challenges confronting managers:

1. **The Strategic Business Challenge: Realizing the Digital Firm: How can businesses use information technology to become competitive, effective, and digitally enabled?** Creating a digital firm and obtaining benefits is a long and difficult journey for most organizations. Despite heavy information technology investments, many organizations are not obtaining significant business benefits, nor are they becoming digitally enabled. The power of computer hardware and software has grown much more rapidly than the ability of organizations to apply and use this technology. To fully benefit from information technology, realize genuine productivity, and take advantage of digital firm capabilities, many organizations actually need to be redesigned. They will have to make fundamental changes in organizational behavior, develop new business models, and eliminate the inefficiencies of outmoded organizational structures. If organizations merely automate what they are doing today, they are largely missing the potential of information technology.

2. **The Globalization Challenge: How can firms understand the business and system requirements of a global economic environment?** The rapid growth in international trade and the emergence of a global economy call for information systems that can support both producing and selling goods in many different countries. In the past, each regional office of a multinational corporation focused on solving its own unique information problems. Given language, cultural, and political differences among countries, this focus frequently resulted in chaos and the failure of central management controls. To develop integrated, multinational, information systems, businesses must develop global hardware, software, and communications standards; create cross-cultural accounting and reporting structures (Roche, 1992); and design transnational business processes.

3. **The Information Architecture and Infrastructure Challenge: How can organizations develop an information architecture and information technology infrastructure that can support their goals when business conditions and technologies are changing so rapidly?** Meeting the business and technology challenges of today's digital economy requires redesigning the organization and building a new information architecture and information technology (IT) infrastructure.

   Information architecture is the particular form that information technology takes in an organization to achieve selected goals or functions. It is a design for the business application systems that serve each functional specialty and level of the organization and the specific ways that they are used by each organization. As firms move toward digital firm organizations and technologies, information architectures are increasingly being designed around business processes and clusters of system applications spanning multiple functions and organizational levels (Kalakota and Robinson, 2001). Because managers and employees directly interact with these systems, it is critical for organizational success that the information architecture meet business requirements now and in the future.

   Figure 1-12 illustrates the major elements of information architecture that managers will need to develop now and in the future. The architecture shows the firm's business application systems for each of the major functional areas of the organization, including sales and marketing, manufacturing, finance, accounting, and human resources. It also shows application systems supporting business processes spanning multiple organizational levels and functions within the enterprise and extending outside the enterprise to systems of suppliers, distributors, business partners, and customers. The firm's IT infrastructure provides the technology platform for this architecture. Computer hardware, software, data and storage technology, networks, and human resources required to operate the equipment constitute the shared IT resources of the firm and are available to all of its applications. Contemporary IT infrastructures are

information architecture
The particular design that information technology takes in a specific organization to achieve selected goals or functions.

INFORMATION
ARCHITECTURE
OF THE
ORGANIZATION

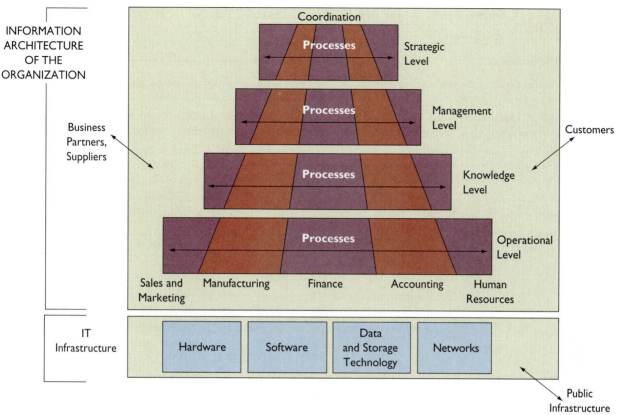

Figure 1-12 Information architecture and information technology infrastructure. Today's managers must know how to arrange and coordinate the various computer technologies and business system applications to meet the information needs of each level of the organization, and the needs of the organization as a whole.

linked to public infrastructures such as the Internet. Although this technology platform is typically operated by technical personnel, general management must decide how to allocate the resources it has assigned to hardware, software, data storage, and telecommunications networks to make sound information technology investments (Weill and Broadbent, 1997 and 1998).

Typical questions regarding information architecture and IT infrastructure facing today's managers include the following: Should the corporate sales data and function be distributed to each corporate remote site, or should they be centralized at headquarters? Should the organization build systems to connect the entire enterprise or separate islands of applications? Should the organization extend its infrastructure outside its boundaries to link to customers or suppliers? There is no one right answer to each of these questions (see Allen and Boynton, 1991). Moreover, business needs are constantly changing, which requires the IT architecture to be reassessed continually (Feeny and Willcocks, 1998).

Creating the information architecture and IT infrastructure for a digital firm is an especially formidable task. Most companies are crippled by fragmented and incompatible computer hardware, software, telecommunications networks, and information systems that prevent information from flowing freely between different parts of the organization. Although Internet standards are solving some of these connectivity problems, creating data and computing platforms that span the enterprise—and, increasingly, link the enterprise to external business partners—is rarely as seamless as promised. Many organizations are still struggling to integrate their islands of information and technology into a coherent architecture. Chapters 6 through 9 provide more detail on information architecture and IT infrastructure issues.

4. The Information Systems Investment Challenge: How can organizations determine the business value of information systems? A major problem raised by the

| TABLE 1-6 | POSITIVE AND NEGATIVE IMPACTS OF INFORMATION SYSTEMS |

Benefit of Information System	Negative Impact
Information systems can perform calculations or process paperwork much faster than people.	By automating activities that were previously performed by people, information systems may eliminate jobs.
Information systems can help companies learn more about the purchase patterns and preferences of their customers.	Information systems may allow organizations to collect personal details about people that violate their privacy.
Information systems provide new efficiencies through services such as automated teller machines (ATMs), telephone systems, or computer-controlled airplanes and air terminals.	Information systems are used in so many aspects of everyday life that system outages can cause shutdowns of businesses or transportation services, paralyzing communities.
Information systems have made possible new medical advances in surgery, radiology, and patient monitoring.	Heavy users of information systems may suffer repetitive stress injury, technostress, and other health problems.
The Internet distributes information instantly to millions of people across the world.	The Internet can be used to distribute illegal copies of software, books, articles, and other intellectual property.

development of powerful, inexpensive computers involves not technology but management and organizations. It's one thing to use information technology to design, produce, deliver, and maintain new products. It's another thing to make money doing it. How can organizations obtain a sizable payoff from their investment in information systems?

Engineering massive organizational and system changes in the hope of positioning a firm strategically is complicated and expensive. Senior management can be expected to ask these questions: Are we receiving the kind of return on investment from our systems that we should be? Do our competitors get more? Understanding the costs and benefits of building a single system is difficult enough; it is daunting to consider whether the entire systems effort is "worth it." Imagine, then, how a senior executive must think when presented with a major transformation in information architecture and IT infrastructure —a bold venture in organizational change costing tens of millions of dollars and taking many years.

5. **The Responsibility and Control Challenge: How can organizations ensure that their information systems are used in an ethically and socially responsible manner?** How can we design information systems that people can control and understand? Although information systems have provided enormous benefits and efficiencies, they have also created new problems and challenges of which managers should be aware. Table 1-6 describes some of these problems and challenges.

Many chapters of this text describe scenarios that raise these ethical issues, and Chapter 5 is devoted entirely to this topic. A major management challenge is making informed decisions that are sensitive to the negative consequences of information systems as well to the positive ones.

Managers will also be faced with ongoing problems of security and control. Information systems are so essential to business, government, and daily life that organizations must take special steps to ensure that they are accurate, reliable, and secure. A firm invites disaster if it uses systems that don't work as intended, that don't deliver information in a form that people can interpret correctly and use, or that have control rooms where controls don't work or where instruments give false signals. Information systems must be designed so that they function as intended and so that humans can control the process.

Managers will need to ask: Can we apply high quality assurance standards to our information systems, as well as to our products and services? Can we build information systems that respect people's rights of privacy while still pursuing our organization's goals? Should information systems monitor employees? What do we do when an information system designed to increase efficiency and productivity eliminates people's jobs?

This text is designed to provide future managers with the knowledge and understanding required to deal with these challenges. To further this objective, each succeeding chapter

MAKE IT YOUR BUSINESS

FINANCE AND ACCOUNTING

The Internet has created vast electronic marketplaces for the purchase and sale of stocks, bonds, and other financial products. On-line management of investment accounts is also available. Corporate financial systems, some of the first to computerize, are based today on high-speed computers and networks. Financial and accounting information can be obtained instantly from internal computer systems and can flow smoothly across entire organizations. Financial information from sources outside the firm can also be obtained instantly on the Internet. You can find examples of finance and accounting applications on pages 33–35.

MANUFACTURING AND PRODUCTION

Internet and network technology have enhanced the precision and flexibility of the manufacturing and production function in both large and small companies. Large manufacturers can use software and networks for mass customization, whereas small manufacturers can use desktop computers with computer-aided design software and computer-controlled machines to output products with the precision and speed of larger firms. Companies can also use these technologies to work collaboratively with other companies and coordinate their production processes more tightly with those of suppliers and distributors. You can find examples of manufacturing and production applications on pages 3, 10, 21, 22, and 33–35.

HUMAN RESOURCES

Human resources record keeping is now largely computer based, allowing companies to instantly track their employee resources. Networked communication systems and the Internet make it much easier for managers to communicate with many employees simultaneously, and manage distant task forces and worker teams. Work can be separated from location and managed from afar. You can find examples of human resources applications on pages 2 and 33–35.

SALES AND MARKETING

The Internet and the Web have opened up a powerful new sales and marketing channel to retail consumers and to other businesses. Companies can use the Internet for advertising, customer support, and even some forms of product testing, with customers ordering products and services over the Web from their desktop computers. The ubiquity of the Internet makes it possible for small businesses to sell their wares in many areas of the globe without a physical sales force or front offices. You can find examples of sales and marketing applications on pages 2, 3, and 33–35.

begins with a Management Challenges box that outlines the key issues of which managers should be aware.

INTEGRATING TEXT WITH TECHNOLOGY: NEW OPPORTUNITIES FOR LEARNING

In addition to the changes in business and management that we have just described, we believe that information technology creates new opportunities for learning that can make the MIS course more meaningful and exciting. We have provided a Web site and an interactive multimedia CD-ROM for integrating the text with leading-edge technology.

As you read each chapter of the text, you can visit the Prentice Hall Laudon Web site (www.prenhall.com/laudon) and use the Internet for interactive learning and management problem solving. The Internet Connection icon in the chapter directs you to Web sites for which we have provided additional exercises and projects related to the concepts and organizations described in that particular chapter. For each chapter, you will also find an Electronic Commerce or Electronic Business project where you can use Web research and interactive software at various company Web sites to solve specific problems. A graded on-line interactive Study Guide contains questions to help you review what you have learned and test your mastery of chapter concepts. You can also use the Laudon Web site to find links to additional on-line case studies, international resources, and technology updates.

An interactive CD-ROM multimedia version of the text features bullet text summaries of key points in each chapter, full-color graphics and photos, Web links to the companion Web site, videos, interactive quizzes, Dynamic Blackboard, and a hyperlinked digital glossary. You can use the CD-ROM as an interactive study guide or as an alternative to the traditional text.

Application software exercises require students to use spreadsheet, database, Web browser, and other application software in hands-on projects related to chapter concepts. They have been redesigned for this edition to make them more challenging and relevant to chapter topics. Students can apply the application software skills they have learned in other courses to real-world business problems. You can find these exercises following the Review Questions at the end of each chapter and both the exercises and their data files on the Laudon Web site.

New to this edition are longer, comprehensive projects concluding each major section of the text. These projects require students to apply what they have learned to more demanding problems, such as analyzing enterprise system requirements, developing an Internet business model, redesigning business processes, and designing a corporate knowledge intranet. Some of these projects require use of the Web.

You will find a Tools for Interactive Learning section with this icon toward the end of every chapter to show how you can use the Web and interactive multimedia to enrich your learning experience.

MANAGEMENT WRAP-UP

Managers are problem solvers who are responsible for analyzing the many challenges confronting organizations and for developing strategies and action plans. Information systems are one of their tools, delivering the information required for solutions. Information systems both reflect management decisions and serve as instruments for changing the management process.

Information systems are rooted in organizations, an outcome of organizational structure, culture, politics, work flows, and standard operating procedures. They are instruments for organizational change, making it possible to recast these organizational elements into new business models and redraw organizational boundaries. Advances in information systems are accelerating the trend toward globalized, knowledge-driven economies and flattened, flexible, decentralized organizations that can coordinate with other organizations across great distances.

A network revolution is under way. Information systems technology is no longer limited to computers but consists of an array of technologies that enable computers to be networked together to exchange information across great distances and organizational boundaries. The Internet provides global connectivity and a flexible platform for the seamless flow of information across the enterprise and between the firm and its customers and suppliers.

For Discussion

1. Information systems are too important to be left to computer specialists. Do you agree? Why or why not?

2. As computers become faster and cheaper and the Internet becomes more widely used, most of the problems we have with information systems will disappear. Do you agree? Why or why not?

SUMMARY

1. *What is the role of information systems in today's competitive business environment?* Information systems have become essential for helping organizations deal with changes in global economies and the business enterprise. Information systems provide firms with communication and analytic tools for conducting trade and managing businesses on a global scale. Information systems are the foundation of new knowledge-based products and services in knowledge economies and help firms manage their knowledge assets. Information systems make it possible for businesses to adopt flatter, more decentralized structures and more flexible arrangements of employees and management. Organizations are trying to become more competitive and efficient by transforming themselves into digital firms where nearly all core business processes and relationships with customers, suppliers, and employees are digitally enabled.

2. *What exactly is an information system? What do managers need to know about information systems?* The purpose of an information system is to collect, store, and disseminate information from an organization's environment and internal operations to support organizational functions and decision making, communication, coordination, control, analysis, and visualization. Information systems transform raw data into useful information through three basic activities: input, processing, and output. From a business perspective, an information system represents an organizational and management solution based on information technology to a challenge posed by the environment.

Information systems literacy requires an understanding of the organizational and management dimensions of information systems as well as the technical dimensions addressed by computer literacy. Information systems literacy draws on both technical and behavioral approaches to studying information systems. Both perspectives can be combined into a sociotechnical approach to systems.

3. *How are information systems transforming organizations and management?* The kinds of systems built today are very important for the organization's overall performance, especially in today's highly globalized and information-based economy. Information systems are driving both daily operations and organizational strategy. Powerful computers, software, and networks, including the Internet, have helped organizations become more flexible, eliminate layers of management, separate work from location, coordinate with suppliers and customers, and restructure work flows, giving new powers to both line workers and management. Information technology provides managers with tools for more precise planning, forecasting, and monitoring of the business. To maximize the advantages of information technology, there is a much greater need to plan the organization's information architecture and information technology (IT) infrastructure.

4. *How has the Internet and Internet technology transformed business?* The Internet provides the primary technology infrastructure for electronic commerce, electronic business, and the emerging digital firm. The Internet and other networks have made it possible for businesses to replace manual and paper-based processes with electronic flows of information. In electronic commerce, businesses can exchange electronic purchase and sale transactions with each other and with individual customers. Electronic business uses the Internet and digital technology to expedite the exchange of information that can facilitate communication and coordination both inside the organization and between the organization and its business partners. Digital firms use Internet technology intensively for electronic commerce and electronic business to manage their internal processes and relationships with customers, suppliers, and other external entities.

5. *What are the major management challenges to building and using information systems?* There are five key management challenges in building and using information systems: (1) designing systems that are competitive and efficient; (2) understanding the system requirements of a global business environment; (3) creating an information architecture that supports the organization's goals; (4) determining the business value of information systems; and (5) designing systems that people can control, understand, and use in a socially and ethically responsible manner.

KEY TERMS

Business functions, 11

Business processes, 6

Communications technology, 13

Computer-based information systems (CBIS), 8

Computer hardware, 13

Computer literacy, 11

Computer software, 13

Data, 7

Data workers, 12

Digital firm, 6

Electronic business, 23

Electronic commerce, 23

Electronic market, 22

Extranet, 23

Feedback, 7

Formal system, 8

Information, 7

Information architecture, 26

Information system, 7

Information systems literacy, 10

Information technology (IT) infrastructure, 13

Input, 7

Internet, 17

Interorganizational systems, 21

Intranet, 23

Knowledge- and information-intense products, 5

Knowledge workers, 12

Management information systems (MIS), 14

Mass customization, 20

Middle managers, 13

Network, 13

Operational managers, 13

Output, 7

Processing, 7

Production or service workers, 12

Senior managers, 13

Standard operating procedures (SOPs), 12

Storage technology, 13

Web site, 17

World Wide Web, 17

REVIEW QUESTIONS

1. Why are information systems essential in business today? Describe four trends in the global business environment that have made information systems so important.

2. Describe the capabilities of a digital firm. Why are digital firms so powerful?

3. What is an information system? Distinguish between a computer, a computer program, and an information system. What is the difference between data and information?

4. What activities convert raw data to usable information in information systems? What is their relationship to feedback?

5. What is information systems literacy? How does it differ from computer literacy?

6. What are the organization, management, and technology dimensions of information systems?

7. Distinguish between a behavioral and a technical approach to information systems in terms of the questions asked and the answers provided. What major disciplines contribute to an understanding of information systems?

8. What is the relationship between an organization and its information systems? How has this relationship changed over time?

9. What are the Internet and the World Wide Web? How have they changed the role played by information systems in organizations?

10. Describe some of the major changes that information systems are bringing to organizations.

11. How are information systems changing the management process?

12. What is the relationship between the network revolution, the digital firm, electronic commerce, and electronic business?

13. What are interorganizational systems? Why are they becoming more important? How has Internet and Web technology affected these systems?

14. What do we mean by information architecture and information technology infrastructure? Why are they important concerns for managers?

15. What are the key management challenges involved in building, operating, and maintaining information systems today?

APPLICATION SOFTWARE EXERCISE

DATABASE EXERCISE: CONVERTING DATA TO USEFUL INFORMATION FOR MANAGEMENT ANALYSIS

Effective managers not only gather business data for their company, but also analyze and interpret the data to create meaningful information for improving the company's opportunities for success. At the Laudon Web site for Chapter 1 you can find a Store and Regional Sales Database with raw data on weekly store sales of computer equipment in various sales regions. The database includes fields for store identification number, sales region number, item number, item description, unit price, units sold, and the weekly sales period when the sales were made. Develop

some reports and queries to make this information more useful for management. Modify the database table, if necessary, to provide all of the information you require. Here are some questions you might consider:

a) Which are the best performing stores and sales regions?
b) What are the best selling products?
c) Which stores and sales regions are strongest in which products?
d) What are the strongest and weakest selling periods? For which stores? Which sales regions? Which products?
e) How can your company improve sales in the weakest store and sales region? (Answers will vary.)

GROUP PROJECT

In a group with three or four classmates, find a description in a computer or business magazine of an information system used by an organization. Look for information about the company on the Web to gain further insight into the company and prepare a brief description of the business. Describe the system you have

selected in terms of its inputs, processes, and outputs, and in terms of its organization, management, and technology features and the importance of the system to the company. If possible, use electronic presentation software to present your analysis to the class.

TOOLS FOR INTERACTIVE LEARNING

■ INTERNET CONNECTION

The Internet Connection for this chapter will take you to the United Parcel Service Web site, where you can complete an exercise to evaluate how UPS uses the Web and other information technology in its daily operations. You can also use the Interactive Study Guide to test your knowledge of the topics in this chapter, and get instant feedback where you need more practice.

■ ELECTRONIC COMMERCE PROJECT

At the Laudon Web site for Chapter 1, you will find an Electronic Commerce project that will use the interactive soft-

ware at the UPS Web site to help a company calculate and budget for its shipping costs.

■ CD-ROM

If you use the Multimedia Edition CD-ROM with this chapter, you will find a video clip illustrating UPS's package tracking system, an audio overview of the major themes of this chapter, and bullet text summarizing the key points of the chapter.

CASE STUDY—*Cisco Systems: Poster Child for the Digital Firm?*

Cisco Systems advertises itself as the company on which the Internet runs, and this San Jose, California, company does dominate the sale of network routers and switching equipment used for Internet infrastructure. Under the leadership of CEO John Chambers, it has been so successful that it even briefly became the most valuable company on earth in early 2000, reaching a valuation of $555 billion and a stock price of more than $80 per share. One key to its success is that Cisco uses information systems and the Internet in every way it can. However, by April 2001 the stock closed below $14, a decline of more than 80 percent, while the company value fell to around $100 billion. What was to blame for this precipitous plunge? What role did Cisco's information systems play?

Cisco was founded in 1984 by Stanford University computer scientists looking for an easier and better way to connect different types of computer systems. By 1990 the company was growing at a double-digit rate, which it maintained for 10 years, even surpassing 50 percent in growth during some years. The company claims it now has 85 percent of the Internet switching equipment market.

Cisco's growth was based on two main strategies. First, the company outsources much of its production, and second, a significant portion of its growth has been through strategic acquisitions of and investments in other companies, amounting to $20 billion to $30 billion between 1993 and 2000. Cisco's investments were carefully selected as a means of building internal competencies in areas where the market was evolving. In September 2000, six months after the stock market decline began, Cisco announced its sales were growing at an annual rate of 66 percent.

Cisco was very proud of its use of the Internet to drive its business and has actively promoted itself as a model for other companies. It is generally believed that "Cisco uses the Web more effectively than any other big company in the world. Period," according to *Fortune Magazine*. If any company epitomized the digital firm, it was—and still is—Cisco.

Cisco began selling its products over the Internet in 1995. In 2000 Cisco was selling about $50 million in products daily via the Web. Customers can use Cisco's Web site, called the Cisco Connection Online, or CCO, to configure, price, route, and submit orders electronically to Cisco. More than half of the orders entered on CCO are sent directly to the supplier, and once the product has been manufactured, it is shipped directly to the customer. Those orders are never touched by Cisco. The result is that the company has reduced its order-to-delivery cycle from six to eight weeks to less than three weeks. Moreover, this has enabled Cisco and its suppliers to manufacture based on actual orders, not on projections, lowering inventory costs for both Cisco and its suppliers, while leaving customers pleased with the speed of fulfillment. In addition, 85 percent of customer support queries are handled through Cisco's Web site, saving the company $600 million in 2000 alone, according to Chambers. Cisco claims it has seen a 25 percent increase in customer satisfaction since it established these portals in 1995.

Cisco uses the Internet in many other ways. It has established a business-to-business supply chain extranet called Cisco Manufacturing Connection Online (MCO) for its manufacturers and suppliers, which is used to purchase supplies, make reports, and submit forecasts and inventory information. This Web site has helped Cisco and its manufacturing partners reduce their inventories by 45 percent.

Cisco shares a great deal of its own knowledge on its intranet, whereas many corporations believe that most of their knowledge must be guarded. The company's stated goal for admitting many customers, suppliers, and distributors to selected portions of its intranet, according to Peter Solvik, Cisco's CIO and senior vice president, is "to create a relationship where customers can get access to every aspect of their relationship with our company over the intranet or Internet."

Although the employee turnover rate is very high in most technology companies, at Cisco it is very low. One reason may be Cisco's use of its employee intranet, called the Cisco Employee Connection. Employees use it to enroll in company benefits and file expense reports, and they are usually reimbursed within 48 hours. Four-fifths of employee technical training take place online, saving the company employee time and travel money while enabling employees to receive more training. Managers review their employees, collect information on competitors, and monitor sales or other functions the manager is responsible for, all on-line.

The company's sales database is updated three times daily, enabling managers to determine which salespeople and regions are not meeting quotas. Engineering managers receive e-mail alerts if a big problem occurs that is not solved within one hour. The manager will then call the appropriate customer and offer help. When customers call Cisco with problems, Cisco employees use its Web site to help solve the problems. About 85 percent of 25,000 monthly job applications to Cisco come over the Internet. If most came on paper, the firm simply could not sort or read them all, much less select out and consider the most promising of them.

Cisco even developed what it calls its "virtual close." Larry Carter, Cisco's chief financial officer, said that it used to take Cisco 14 days to close its books, "a real hindrance." Now the finance group achieves its close in only a few hours, giving employees "real-time access to detailed operating data." Today, "we update our bookings, revenues, and product margins by the minute," said Carter. "These tools and data have been invaluable in helping Cisco manage its rapid growth. Executives can constantly analyze performance at all levels of the organization," he claims. Cisco's systems also are used to forecast sales. The forecasts primarily are based on past sales and current orders. "Daily information about our product backlog, product margins, and lead times," are included, according to Carter, and that triggers decisions throughout Cisco's chain of suppliers. These forecasts also include information about bookings, shortfalls in supplies, and delayed product deliveries.

Although the stock market reached its all time high in March 2000 and then started to correct, Cisco continued to thrive a while longer and its management remained absolutely optimistic. During market declines in past years when sales of networking devices slowed (1994 and 1997–98), Cisco had continued to aggressively expand even though its competitors slowed their activities or merged with other companies. Each time Cisco had increased its market share.

However, this time proved to be different. Cisco faced a decline of two-thirds in the technology-laden Nasdaq stock market which included a major pull back in telecommunications, a pivotal field for Cisco. Cisco had previously projected telecommunications sales to double in 2000–2001, but the opposite happened, resulting in the sharp decline in Cisco's stock. In the summer of 2000 Cisco still believed its situation was very positive. It received an outpouring of orders, so many in fact that it lacked many parts, causing massive delays in fulfilling orders. Many customers waited as long as 15 weeks for delivery. Cisco launched a two-fold strategy to resume filling orders quickly. It started purchasing key components months before they were ordered, so they would be available when needed. Also the company lent $600 million interest-free to its contract producers so they could purchase the missing parts. Although some of these manufacturers were concerned that Cisco was being too expansive, Cisco's July 29 year end showed a revenue jump of 60 percent from the previous year. By September the company backlog was more than seven weeks with a value of $3.8 billion. Although the stock for Nortel Networks Corp., a Cisco rival, did fall 33 percent in two days because Nortel announced slower-than-expected sales, Michelangelo Volpi, Cisco's chief strategy officer, said Nortel had fallen prey to management "exuberance." This was not true of Cisco, he said, because, "We try to very precisely set expectations [using our virtual close]." Chambers emphasized that Cisco could meet Wall Street projections. Meanwhile, two Cisco manufacturers informed the company that their shipments were slowing.

In November 2000 Cisco's orders for its telecom division reported a sales decline of 10 percent from the previous quarter. Moreover, Cisco's sales to newer companies didn't grow at all. Some of these companies, including several that had borrowed funds from Cisco, declared bankruptcy. Yet according to Chambers, orders were "comfortably" up by more than 70 percent from the previous year, and Carter said Cisco expected sales to grow by nearly 60 percent in the current quarter. The company aggressively hired new staff. On December 4 Chambers again described the perceived slowdown as a Cisco opportunity, following its earlier slowdown strategy. "Cisco is actually better off if the stock market stays tough for the next 12 to 18 months," he said. However, just before December 15, after Chambers's vaunted virtual close system told him that daily sales were 10 percent below expectation for two weeks, he called his top sales executives, who verified the unexpected numbers. He then met with his senior executives to let them know about his concern over the sudden drop in quarterly sales. The group agreed to delay both hiring and inventory building for the next 45 to 60 days.

Earlier, in late spring 2000 as Cisco was planning its 2000–2001 fiscal year to begin in October, Chambers had said the dot.coms "had money" and "they were buying." His view

was, "To not plan to meet that growth is the quickest way to lose customers." However, at the end of January 2001, Cisco's second quarter ended with sales to young telecom companies down by 40 percent. Sales to dot.coms were down by half rather than rising by half as the Cisco's vaunted computer systems had predicted. Between November 2000 and March 2001, the company had hired about 5,000 new staff, but on March 9 Cisco announced it would lay off 5,000 (soon increased to 6,000) employees and up to 3,000 temporary workers while restructuring its business. By April Cisco was selling to only about 150 young telecom companies, down from 3,000 companies only one year earlier. On April 16, 2001, Cisco announced it would write off $2.5 billion of its swollen inventory, although it was still left with an inventory of $1.6 billion, one-third higher than the previous summer. In addition, with so many bankruptcies, barely used network equipment had come on the market at steep discounts of around 15 cents on the dollar.

What went wrong? It was crystal clear the company was suffering from overordering. Cisco was focused on what their customers were ordering. No one looked at the macroeconomic factors overshadowing the entire communications industry. Someone should have said, "These orders can't be sustained." One explanation was that, facing delays in shipments after ordering, many customers began ordering from Cisco and also ordering from two or three other suppliers, causing the backlog to look greatly larger than it actually was. When an order did arrive, those companies cancelled the other orders, resulting in a sudden, rapid backlog decline. Cisco's information systems could not account for that situation, and so the company was misled by the very systems in which it had so much pride. "We knew there were multiple orders," said Volpi. "We just didn't know the magnitude." Cisco's forecasting software focused on growth data and ignored such macroeconomic data as debt levels, economic spending, interest rates, the bank market, and the stock market. The software was not designed to deal well with declining demand. Misleading, though accurate, information had resulted in bad decisions.

Some observers expressed their belief that Cisco sales forecasts were way too high because the company suffered from overconfidence after years of remarkable sales growth. It had relied on past rosy sales and never considered the possibility that sales might actually decline. Management was more concerned about turning away orders than about whether the orders were real. Moreover, "People see a shortage and intuitively they forecast higher," commented Ajay Shah, the CEO of Solectron Technology Solutions Business Unit, a company that produced networking parts for Cisco. He went on, "Salespeople don't want to be caught without supply, so they make sure they have supply by forecasting more sales than they expect." Shah also noted that his company (and some others) saw a decline and began to cut back. He did not urge Cisco to do the same, because, he said, "Can you really sit there and confront a customer and tell him he doesn't know what he's doing with his business? The numbers might suggest you should." M. Eric Johnson, an associate professor of business administration at the Tuck School of Business and an expert in supply chains, said Cisco's outsourcing business model ultimately worked against the company. He said the outsourcing model has "done some wonderful things. But Solectron has to watch its own business. It matters less to them if Cisco's numbers look off."

In sum, Cisco may have overrelied on forecasting technology, leading people to undervalue or ignore human judgment and intuition. In November 2000, when the economic troubles were clear to many, Volpi said, "We haven't seen any sign of a slow-down," and Chambers announced, "I have never been more optimistic about the future of our industry as a whole or of Cisco." Only when the virtual close showed the actual sales line crossing under the sales forecast line in mid-December did the company see a problem for the first time, according to Peter Solvik, who was in charge of Cisco's information systems function.

Chambers has expressed a very different view. According to him, Cisco is suffering because of the sudden and unexpected economic deterioration. He denies that the company relies exclusively on its software. "Do our systems do a great job of telling us where we are today? Yes, but they don't tell the future." He admitted that if they had instituted a hiring freeze in the autumn of 2000, there would be no layoffs now. But, he added, that would have cost sales and market share. "We will always err on the side of meeting customer expectations," he said, also noting that pausing when sales hit a small decline would have prevented the company from reaching its $19 billion sales mark last year.

In late August 2001, Cisco underwent a major reorganization, abandoning its "line of business" organization that had been in place since 1997. The old lines of business, including commercial, consumer, enterprise, and service provider, were less useful as Cisco customer interest increasingly cut across multiple product lines. Cisco replaced this structure with a centralized engineering and marketing organization with 11 technology groups, focusing on access; core routing; Internet switching and services; network management services; and optical, voice, and wireless technologies. The reorganization enables Cisco to more closely track which products and technologies are the most and least profitable so that it can focus on them. Cisco found through this reorganization, that its service provider business was its poorest performer and that wireless networking technology promises rapid sales growth. The question is, how quickly and effectively can Cisco rebound? Can it maintain its leadership role in networking technology? And is its digital firm strategy a recipe for future successes or pitfalls?

Sources: Scott Berinato, "What Went Wrong at Cisco," *CIO Magazine*, August 1, 2001; Larry Carter, "Cisco's Virtual Close," *Harvard Business Review*, April 2001; Dan Goodin, "Cisco Expects Tornadoes to Power Growth," *Wall Street Journal*, July 20, 2001; Lee Sherman, "A Matter of Connections," *Knowledge Management*, July 2000; Bret Swanson, "For Cisco, It's Change or Perish," *Wall Street Journal*, April 18, 2001; Scott Thurm, "Even as Rivals Began to Stumble, Cisco Believed Itself to be Immune," *Wall Street Journal*, April 18, 2001; John Pallatto, "Inside Cisco," *Internet World*, October, 2001; and Scott Thurm, "Eating Their Own Dog Food," *Wall Street Journal*, April 19, 2000.

CASE STUDY QUESTIONS

1. Analyze the relationship between information systems, Internet technology and Cisco's business strategy.

2. To what extent is Cisco a digital firm?

3. How successful was Cisco's reliance on information systems and the Internet?

4. Why did Cisco react so slowly to deteriorating economic conditions and declining sales in 2000? What management, organization, and technology factors influenced the way Cisco responded? Include evidence to support your analysis.

5. What do you think Chambers and Cisco could and should have done differently in 2000 and early 2001? Do you agree or disagree with Chambers's conclusion that the company had to take the steps it did? Why or why not?

chapter 2

INFORMATION SYSTEMS IN THE ENTERPRISE

As a manager, you will need to understand the role of the various types of information systems in organizations. After completing this chapter, you will be able to answer the following questions:

1. *What are the key system applications in a business? What role do they play?*
2. *How do information systems support the major business functions: sales and marketing, manufacturing and production, finance and accounting, and human resources?*
3. *Why should managers pay attention to business processes? What are the benefits of using information systems to support business processes, including those for customer relationship management and supply chain management?*
4. *What are the business benefits of using collaborative commerce, private industrial networks, and enterprise systems?*
5. *What types of information systems are used by companies that operate internationally?*

Flextronics Orchestrates Its Supply Chain

You may not have heard of Flextronics, but you probably use something they've made every day. Flextronics is a contract manufacturer that makes the innards of technology products such as cell phones; PCs; and Internet hardware for household names such as Cisco Systems, Dell Computers, and Ericsson mobile phones. In the fast-paced, hyper-competitive technology industry, profit margins for electronic manufacturing services, such as Flextronics, are razor-thin, amounting to no more than 3 to 5 percent. Yet during the past seven years Flextronics has been able to skyrocket from a tiny company into a multibillion dollar global operation. How did Flextronics do it?

The answer lies in skillful supply chain management. Flextronics continually collects and analyzes its supply chain information to standardize and coordinate the work of its factories around the globe. The company built a low-cost manufacturing network in China, Singapore, Mexico, and other locations around the world. Flextronics facilities are built like campuses with water, sewers, computer lines, and buildings for suppliers so that they can be close to its factories.

The campuses are standardized so that they look and perform the same way, regardless of their location. Flextronics thus can offer inexpensive manufacturing facilities that are not too far away from its European and U.S clients.

Flextronics uses the same enterprise resource planning software in the same configuration in all of its factories so that it can standardize and coordinate their

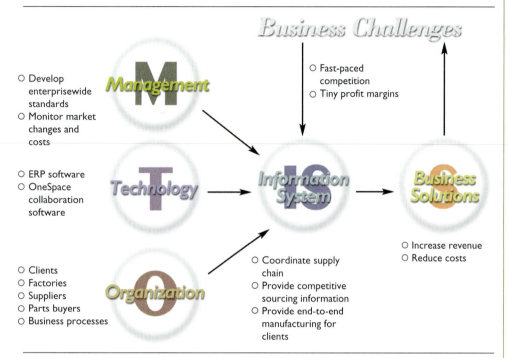

work more precisely. The same business processes for doing manufacturing work are thus replicated worldwide. Employees accessing Flextronics's global information system can see data from every Flextronics factory. A parts buyer in Mexico can see what prices a Singapore parts buyer is obtaining for a specific component and use that information to get a price break from suppliers. When someone uses the system to place an order, the system displays a pop-up window that might show where he or she could get a better price on that same item and whether the component could be obtained from a Flextronics factory that overstocked on that item. Flextronics's 2000 design engineers can work jointly on design specifications from many different locations using OneSpace Web-based collaboration software.

Armed with such powerful software and well-designed business processes, Flextronics is now assuming responsibility for even larger portions of its clients' supply chains. About 85 to 90 percent of Flextronics's revenue comes from its traditional outsourced manufacturing work, where the company makes a part of a product for a client and then ships it to the client for assembly into the finished product. What Flextronics's new strategy will do is enable customers, such as Cisco Systems, to entrust the manufacturing process for entire products to Flextronics. Cisco will focus on product design and marketing and Flextronics will do the rest. Flextronics can also use its new end-to-end manufacturing capabilities for other clients. Ericsson, the Swedish cell phone manufacturer recently contracted to hand over its entire manufacturing process to Flextronics.

Flextronics would like to take over design work for customers as well. In the works is a Web-based product design system that extracts individual component information from a repository of product data and delivers it to designers so they can see each potential component's quality, availability, and supplier history. Flextronics will then be able to use that information for bulk purchases of materials so they can charge less for manufacturing and, hopefully, win more clients.

Sources: Christopher Koch, "Yank Your Chain," *Darwin Magazine*, October 2001; John Markoff, "Ignore the Label: It's Flextronics Inside," *New York Times*, February 15, 2001; and Jeff Sweat, "Customer Collaboration Counts," *Information Week*, December 10, 2001.

MANAGEMENT CHALLENGES

Businesses need different types of information systems to support decision making and work activities for various organizational levels and functions. Many may need systems that integrate information and business processes from different functional areas. Flextronics, for instance, needed information systems that would allow it to precisely coordinate its supply chain. It found a solution in using the same enterprise system in all of its locations for important business processes for sales, production, and logistics. The opening vignette presents the potential rewards to firms with well-conceived systems linking the entire enterprise. Such systems typically require a significant amount of organizational and management change and raise the following management challenges:

1. **Integration.** Although it is necessary to design different systems serving different levels and functions in the firm, more and more firms are finding advantages in integrating systems. However, integrating systems for different organizational levels and functions to freely exchange information can be technologically difficult and costly. Managers need to determine what level of system integration is required and how much it is worth in dollars.

2. **Enlarging the scope of management thinking.** Most managers are trained to manage a product line, a division, or an office. They are rarely trained to optimize the performance of the organization as a whole and often are not given the means to do so. But enterprise systems and industrial networks require managers to take a much larger view of their own behavior, including other products, divisions, departments, and even outside business firms. Investments in enterprise systems are huge, they must be developed over long periods of time, and they must be guided by a shared vision of the objectives.

In this chapter we examine the role of the various types of information systems in organizations. First, we look at ways of classifying information systems based on the organizational level they support. Next, we look at systems in terms of the organizational function they serve. We show how systems can support business processes for the major business functions and processes that span more than one function, such as supply chain management. We then examine enterprise systems and industrial networks, which enable organizations to integrate information and business processes across entire firms and even entire industries. Finally, we discuss different ways that information systems can be configured when businesses operate internationally.

2.1   KEY SYSTEM APPLICATIONS IN THE ORGANIZATION

Because there are different interests, specialties, and levels in an organization, there are different kinds of systems. No single system can provide all the information an organization needs. Figure 2-1 illustrates one way to depict the kinds of systems found in an organization. In the illustration, the organization is divided into strategic, management, knowledge, and operational levels and then is further divided into functional areas such as sales and market-

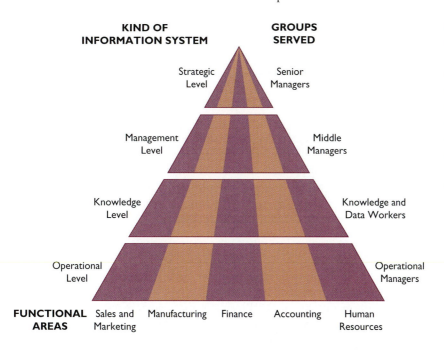

KIND OF INFORMATION SYSTEM | **GROUPS SERVED**

Strategic Level — Senior Managers
Management Level — Middle Managers
Knowledge Level — Knowledge and Data Workers
Operational Level — Operational Managers

FUNCTIONAL AREAS Sales and Marketing Manufacturing Finance Accounting Human Resources

Figure 2-1 Types of information systems. Organizations can be divided into strategic, management, knowledge, and operational levels and into five major functional areas: sales and marketing, manufacturing, finance, accounting, and human resources. Information systems serve each of these levels and functions.

ing, manufacturing, finance, accounting, and human resources. Systems are built to serve these different organizational interests (Anthony, 1965).

DIFFERENT KINDS OF SYSTEMS

Four main types of information systems serve different organizational levels: operational-level systems, knowledge-level systems, management-level systems, and strategic-level systems. **Operational-level systems** support operational managers by keeping track of the elementary activities and transactions of the organization, such as sales, receipts, cash deposits, payroll, credit decisions, and the flow of materials in a factory. The principal purpose of systems at this level is to answer routine questions and to track the flow of transactions through the organization. How many parts are in inventory? What happened to Mr. Williams's payment? To answer these kinds of questions, information generally must be easily available, current, and accurate. Examples of operational-level systems include a system to record bank deposits from automatic teller machines or one that tracks the number of hours worked each day by employees on a factory floor.

Knowledge-level systems support the organization's knowledge and data workers. The purpose of knowledge-level systems is to help the business firm integrate new knowledge into the business and to help the organization control the flow of paperwork. Knowledge-level systems, especially in the form of workstations and office systems, are among the fastest-growing applications in business today.

Management-level systems serve the monitoring, controlling, decision-making, and administrative activities of middle managers. The principal question addressed by such systems is, Are things working well? Management-level systems typically provide periodic reports rather than instant information on operations. An example is a relocation control system that reports on the total moving, house-hunting, and home financing costs for employees in all company divisions, noting wherever actual costs exceed budgets.

Some management-level systems support nonroutine decision making (Keen and Morton, 1978). They tend to focus on less-structured decisions for which information requirements are not always clear. These systems often answer "what-if" questions: What would be the impact on production schedules if we were to double sales in the month of December? What would happen to our return on investment if a factory schedule were delayed for six months? Answers to these questions frequently require new data from outside the organization, as well as data from inside that cannot be easily drawn from existing operational-level systems.

Strategic-level systems help senior management tackle and address strategic issues and long-term trends, both in the firm and in the external environment. Their principal concern

operational-level systems
Information systems that monitor the elementary activities and transactions of the organization.

knowledge-level systems
Information systems that support knowledge and data workers in an organization.

management-level systems
Information systems that support the monitoring, controlling, decision-making, and administrative activities of middle managers.

strategic-level systems
Information systems that support the long-range planning activities of senior management.

is matching changes in the external environment with existing organizational capability. What will employment levels be in five years? What are the long-term industry cost trends, and where does our firm fit in? What products should we be making in five years?

Information systems also serve the major business functions, such as sales and marketing, manufacturing, finance, accounting, and human resources. A typical organization has operational-, management-, knowledge-, and strategic-level systems for each functional area. For example, the sales function generally has a sales system on the operational level to record daily sales figures and to process orders. A knowledge-level system designs promotional displays for the firm's products. A management-level system tracks monthly sales figures by sales territory and reports on territories where sales exceed or fall below anticipated levels. A system to forecast sales trends over a five-year period serves the strategic level. We first describe the specific categories of systems serving each organizational level and their value to the organization. Then we show how organizations use these systems for each major business function.

SIX MAJOR TYPES OF SYSTEMS

Figure 2-2 shows the specific types of information systems that correspond to each organizational level. The organization has executive support systems (ESS) at the strategic level; management information systems (MIS) and decision-support systems (DSS) at the management level; knowledge work systems (KWS) and office systems at the knowledge level; and transaction processing systems (TPS) at the operational level. Systems at each level in turn are specialized to serve each of the major functional areas. Thus, the typical systems found in organizations are designed to assist workers or managers at each level and in the functions of sales and marketing, manufacturing, finance, accounting, and human resources.

Table 2-1 summarizes the features of the six types of information systems. It should be noted that each of the different systems may have components that are used by organizational levels and groups other than their main constituencies. A secretary may find information on an MIS, or a middle manager may need to extract data from a TPS.

Figure 2-2 The six major types of information systems. This figure provides examples of TPS, office systems, KWS, DSS, MIS, and ESS, showing the level of the organization and business function that each supports.

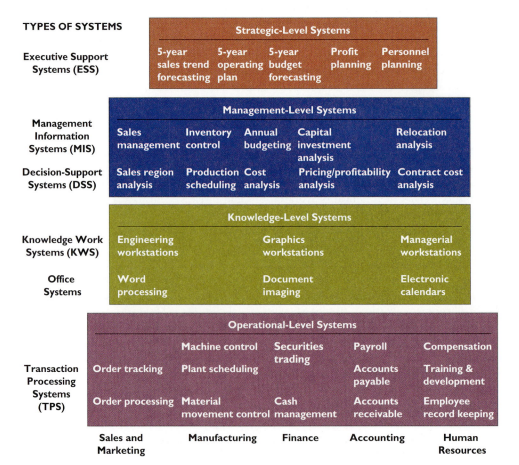

TABLE 2-1 ## CHARACTERISTICS OF INFORMATION PROCESSING SYSTEMS

Type of System	Information Inputs	Processing	Information Outputs	Users
ESS	Aggregate data; external, internal	Graphics; simulations; interactive	Projections; responses to queries	Senior managers
DSS	Low-volume data or massive databases optimized for data analysis; analytic models and data analysis tools	Interactive; simulations; analysis	Special reports; decision analyses; responses to queries	Professionals; staff managers
MIS	Summary transaction data; high-volume data; simple models	Routine reports; simple models; low-level analysis	Summary and exception reports	Middle managers
KWS	Design specifications; knowledge base	Modeling; simulations	Models; graphics	Professionals; technical staff
Office systems	Documents; schedules	Document management; scheduling; communication	Documents; schedules; mail	Clerical workers
TPS	Transactions; events	Sorting; listing; merging; updating	Detailed reports; lists; summaries	Operations personnel; supervisors

Transaction Processing Systems

Transaction processing systems (TPS) are the basic business systems that serve the operational level of the organization. A transaction processing system is a computerized system that performs and records the daily routine transactions necessary to the conduct of the business. Examples are sales order entry, hotel reservation systems, payroll, employee record keeping, and shipping.

At the operational level, tasks, resources, and goals are predefined and highly structured. The decision to grant credit to a customer, for instance, is made by a lower-level supervisor according to predefined criteria. All that must be determined is whether the customer meets the criteria.

Figure 2-3 depicts a payroll TPS, which is a typical accounting transaction processing system found in most firms. A payroll system keeps track of the money paid to employees. The master file is composed of discrete pieces of information (such as a name, address, or employee number) called data elements. Data are keyed into the system, updating the data elements. The elements on the master file are combined in different ways to make up reports of interest to management and government agencies and to send paychecks to employees. These TPS can generate other report combinations of existing data elements.

Other typical TPS applications are identified in Figure 2-4. The figure shows that there are five functional categories of TPS: sales/marketing, manufacturing/production, finance/accounting, human resources, and other types of TPS that are unique to a particular industry. The UPS package tracking system described in Chapter 1 is an example of a manufacturing TPS. UPS sells package delivery services; the system keeps track of all of its package shipment transactions.

Transaction processing systems are often so central to a business that TPS failure for a few hours can spell a firm's demise and perhaps harm other firms linked to it. Imagine what would happen to UPS if its package tracking system were not working! What would the airlines do without their computerized reservation systems?

Managers need TPS to monitor the status of internal operations and the firm's relations with the external environment. TPS are also major producers of information for the other types of systems. (For example, the payroll system illustrated here, along with other accounting TPS, supplies data to the company's general ledger system, which is responsible for maintaining records of the firm's income and expenses and for producing reports such as income statements and balance sheets.)

transaction processing systems (TPS)
Computerized systems that perform and record the daily routine transactions necessary to conduct the business; they serve the organization's operational level.

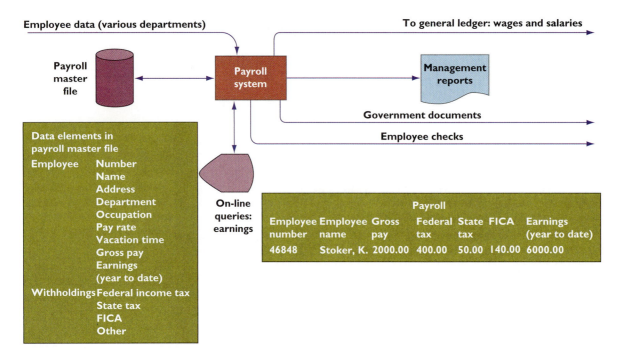

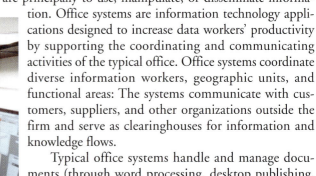

Figure 2-3   A symbolic representation for a payroll TPS.

Knowledge Work and Office Systems

Knowledge work systems (KWS) and **office systems** serve the information needs at the knowledge level of the organization. Knowledge work systems aid knowledge workers, whereas office systems primarily aid data workers (although they are also used extensively by knowledge workers).

In general, *knowledge workers* are people who hold formal university degrees and who are often members of recognized professions, such as engineers, doctors, lawyers, and scientists. Their jobs consist primarily of creating new information and knowledge. KWS, such as scientific or engineering design workstations, promote the creation of new knowledge and ensure that new knowledge and technical expertise are properly integrated into the business. *Data workers* typically have less formal, advanced educational degrees and tend to process rather than create information. They consist primarily of secretaries, bookkeepers, filing clerks, or managers whose jobs are principally to use, manipulate, or disseminate information. Office systems are information technology applications designed to increase data workers' productivity by supporting the coordinating and communicating activities of the typical office. Office systems coordinate diverse information workers, geographic units, and functional areas: The systems communicate with customers, suppliers, and other organizations outside the firm and serve as clearinghouses for information and knowledge flows.

Typical office systems handle and manage documents (through word processing, desktop publishing, document imaging, and digital filing), scheduling (through electronic calendars), and communication (through electronic mail, voice mail, or videoconferencing). **Word processing** refers to the software and hardware that creates, edits, formats, stores, and prints documents (see Chapter 6). Word processing systems represent the single most common application of information technology to office work, in part because pro-

Graphics designers use desktop publishing software to design a page for "La Opinion." Desktop publishing software enables users to control all aspects of the design and layout process for professional-looking publications.

TYPE OF TPS SYSTEM				
Sales/ marketing systems	**Manufacturing/ production systems**	**Finance/ accounting systems**	**Human resources systems**	**Other types (e.g., university)**
Major functions of system				
Sales management	Scheduling	Budgeting	Personnel records	Admissions
Market research	Purchasing	General ledger	Benefits	Grade records
Promotion	Shipping/receiving	Billing	Compensation	Course records
Pricing	Engineering	Cost accounting	Labor relations	Alumni
New products	Operations		Training	
Major application systems				
Sales order information system	Machine control systems	General ledger	Payroll	Registration system
Market research system	Purchase order systems	Accounts receivable/payable	Employee records	Student transcript system
Sales commission system	Quality control systems	Funds management systems	Benefit systems	Curriculum class control systems
			Career path systems	Alumni benefactor system

Figure 2-4   Typical applications of TPS. There are five functional categories of TPS: sales/marketing, manufacturing/production, finance/accounting, human resources, and other types of systems specific to a particular industry. Within each of these major functions are subfunctions. For each of these subfunctions (e.g., sales management) there is a major application system.

ducing documents is what offices are all about. **Desktop publishing** produces professional publishing-quality documents by combining output from word processing software with design elements, graphics, and special layout features. Companies are now starting to publish documents in the form of Web pages for easier access and distribution. We describe Web publishing in more detail in Chapter 10.

Document imaging systems are another widely used knowledge application. Document imaging systems convert documents and images into digital form so that they can be stored and accessed by the computer.

Management Information Systems

In Chapter 1, we defined management information systems as the study of information systems in business and management. The term *management information systems (MIS)* also designates a specific category of information systems serving management-level functions. **Management information systems (MIS)** serve the management level of the organization, providing managers with reports or with on-line access to the organization's current performance and historical records. Typically, they are oriented almost exclusively to internal, not environmental or external, events. MIS primarily serve the functions of planning, controlling, and decision making at the management level. Generally, they depend on underlying transaction processing systems for their data.

MIS summarize and report on the company's basic operations. The basic transaction data from TPS are compressed and are usually presented in long reports that are produced on a regular schedule. Figure 2-5 shows how a typical MIS transforms transaction level data from inventory, production, and accounting into MIS files that are used to provide managers with reports. Figure 2-6 shows a sample report from this system.

MIS usually serve managers interested in weekly, monthly, and yearly results—not day-to-day activities. MIS generally provide answers to routine questions that have been specified in advance and have a predefined procedure for answering them. For instance, MIS reports might list the total pounds of lettuce used this quarter by a fast-food chain or, as illustrated in Figure 2-6, compare total annual sales figures for specific products to planned targets. These systems are generally not flexible and have little analytical capability. Most MIS use simple routines such as summaries and comparisons, as opposed to sophisticated mathematical models or statistical techniques.

desktop publishing
Technology that produces professional-quality documents combining output from word processors with design, graphics, and special layout features.

document imaging systems
Systems that convert documents and images into digital form so that they can be stored and accessed by the computer.

management information systems (MIS)
Information systems at the management level of an organization that serve the functions of planning, controlling, and decision making by providing routine summary and exception reports.

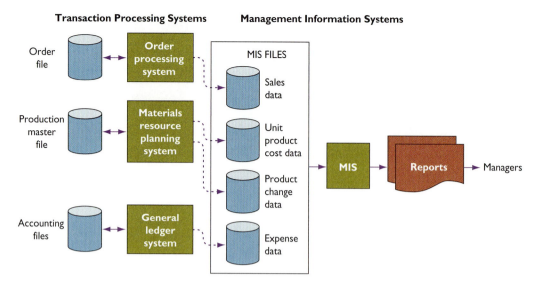

Figure 2-5 How management information systems obtain their data from the organization's TPS. In the system illustrated by this diagram, three TPS supply summarized transaction data at the end of the time period to the MIS reporting system. Managers gain access to the organizational data through the MIS, which provides them with the appropriate reports.

Decision-Support Systems

decision-support systems (DSS)
Information systems at the organization's management level that combine data and sophisticated analytical models or data analysis tools to support non-routine decision making.

Decision-support systems (DSS) also serve the management level of the organization. DSS help managers make decisions that are unique, rapidly changing, and not easily specified in advance. They address problems where the procedure for arriving at a solution may not be fully predefined in advance. Although DSS use internal information from TPS and MIS, they often bring in information from external sources, such as current stock prices or product prices of competitors.

Clearly, by design, DSS have more analytical power than other systems. They are built explicitly with a variety of models to analyze data, or they condense large amounts of data into a form in which they can be analyzed by decision makers. DSS are designed so that users can work with them directly; these systems explicitly include user-friendly software. DSS are interactive; the user can change assumptions, ask new questions, and include new data.

An interesting, small, but powerful DSS is the voyage-estimating system of a subsidiary of a large American metals company that exists primarily to carry bulk cargoes of coal, oil, ores, and finished products for its parent company. The firm owns some vessels, charters others, and bids for shipping contracts in the open market to carry general cargo. A voyage-

Figure 2-6 A sample report that might be produced by the MIS in Figure 2-5.

Consolidated Consumer Products Corporation
Sales by Product and Sales Region: 2002

PRODUCT CODE	PRODUCT DESCRIPTION	SALES REGION	ACTUAL SALES	PLANNED	ACTUAL VS. PLANNED
4469	Carpet Cleaner	Northeast	4,066,700	4,800,000	0.85
		South	3,778,112	3,750,000	1.01
		Midwest	4,867,001	4,600,000	1.06
		West	4,003,440	4,400,000	0.91
	TOTAL		16,715,253	17,550,000	0.95
5674	Room Freshener	Northeast	3,676,700	3,900,000	0.94
		South	5,608,112	4,700,000	1.19
		Midwest	4,711,001	4,200,000	1.12
		West	4,563,440	4,900,000	0.93
	TOTAL		18,559,253	17,700,000	1.05

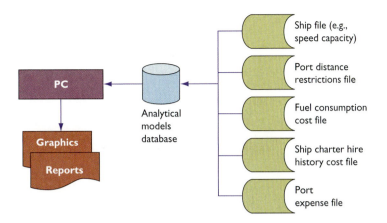

Figure 2-7 Voyage-estimating decision-support system. This DSS operates on a powerful PC. It is used daily by managers who must develop bids on shipping contracts.

estimating system calculates financial and technical voyage details. Financial calculations include ship/time costs (fuel, labor, capital), freight rates for various types of cargo, and port expenses. Technical details include a myriad of factors such as ship cargo capacity, speed, port distances, fuel and water consumption, and loading patterns (location of cargo for different ports). The system can answer questions such as the following: Given a customer delivery schedule and an offered freight rate, which vessel should be assigned at what rate to maximize profits? What is the optimum speed at which a particular vessel can optimize its profit and still meet its delivery schedule? What is the optimal loading pattern for a ship bound for the U.S. west coast from Malaysia? Figure 2-7 illustrates the DSS built for this company. The system operates on a powerful desktop personal computer, providing a system of menus that makes it easy for users to enter data or obtain information. We describe other types of DSS in Chapter 11.

Executive Support Systems

Senior managers use **executive support systems (ESS)** to make decisions. ESS serve the strategic level of the organization. They address nonroutine decisions requiring judgment, evaluation, and insight because there is no agreed-on procedure for arriving at a solution. ESS create a generalized computing and communications environment rather than providing any fixed application or specific capability. ESS are designed to incorporate data about external events such as new tax laws or competitors, but they also draw summarized information from internal MIS and DSS. They filter, compress, and track critical data, emphasizing the reduction of time and effort required to obtain information useful to executives. ESS employ the most advanced graphics software and can deliver graphs and data from many sources immediately to a senior executive's office or to a boardroom.

   Unlike the other types of information systems, ESS are not designed primarily to solve specific problems. Instead, ESS provide a generalized computing and communications capacity that can be applied to a changing array of problems. Although many DSS are designed to be highly analytical, ESS tend to make less use of analytical models.

   Questions ESS assist in answering include the following: What business should we be in? What are the competitors doing? What new acquisitions would protect us from cyclical business swings? Which units should we sell to raise cash for acquisitions (Rockart and Treacy, 1982)? Figure 2-8 illustrates a model of an ESS. It consists of workstations with menus, interactive graphics, and communications capabilities that can access historical and competitive data from internal corporate systems and external databases such as Dow Jones News/Retrieval or the Gallup Poll. Because ESS are designed to be used by senior managers who often have little, if any, direct contact or experience with computer-based information systems, they incorporate easy-to-use graphic interfaces. More details on leading-edge applications of DSS and ESS can be found in Chapter 11.

executive support systems (ESS)
Information systems at the organization's strategic level designed to address unstructured decision making through advanced graphics and communications.

RELATIONSHIP OF SYSTEMS TO ONE ANOTHER

Figure 2-9 illustrates how the systems serving different levels in the organization are related to one another. TPS are typically a major source of data for other systems, whereas ESS are

Figure 2-8 Model of a typical executive support system. This system pools data from diverse internal and external sources and makes them available to executives in an easy-to-use form.

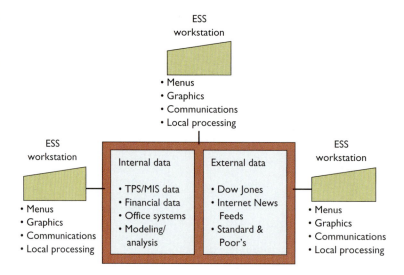

primarily a recipient of data from lower-level systems. The other types of systems may exchange data with each other as well. Data may also be exchanged among systems serving different functional areas. For example, an order captured by a sales system may be transmitted to a manufacturing system as a transaction for producing or delivering the product specified in the order.

It is definitely advantageous to have some measure of integration among these systems so that information can flow easily between different parts of the organization. But integration costs money, and integrating many different systems is extremely time consuming and complex. Each organization must weigh its needs for integrating systems against the difficulties of mounting a large-scale systems integration effort. The discussion of enterprise systems in Section 2.3 treats this issue in greater detail.

2.2 SYSTEMS FROM A FUNCTIONAL PERSPECTIVE

Information systems can be classified by the specific organizational function they serve as well as by organizational level. We now describe typical information systems that support each of the major business functions and provide examples of functional applications for each organizational level.

Figure 2-9 Interrelationships among systems. The various types of systems in the organization have interdependencies. TPS are major producers of information that is required by the other systems, which, in turn, produce information for other systems. These different types of systems are only loosely coupled in most organizations.

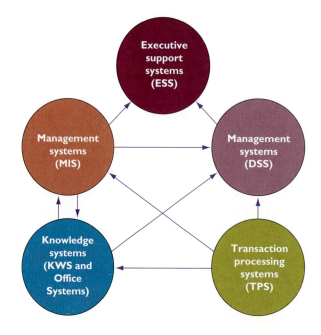

TABLE 2-2	EXAMPLES OF SALES AND MARKETING INFORMATION SYSTEMS	
System	**Description**	**Organizational Level**
Order processing	Enter, process, and track orders	Operational
Market analysis	Identify customers and markets using data on demographics, markets, consumer behavior, and trends	Knowledge
Pricing analysis	Determine prices for products and services	Management
Sales trend forecasting	Prepare 5-year sales forecasts	Strategic

SALES AND MARKETING SYSTEMS

The sales and marketing function is responsible for selling the organization's product or service. Marketing is concerned with identifying the customers for the firm's products or services, determining what they need or want, planning and developing products and services to meet their needs, and advertising and promoting these products and services. Sales is concerned with contacting customers, selling the products and services, taking orders, and following up on sales. **Sales and marketing information systems** support these activities.

Table 2-2 shows that information systems are used in sales and marketing in a number of ways. At the strategic level, sales and marketing systems monitor trends affecting new products and sales opportunities, support planning for new products and services, and monitor the performance of competitors. At the management level, sales and marketing systems support market research, advertising and promotional campaigns, and pricing decisions. They analyze sales performance and the performance of the sales staff. Knowledge-level sales and marketing systems support marketing analysis workstations. At the operational level, sales and marketing systems assist in locating and contacting prospective customers, tracking sales, processing orders, and providing customer service support.

Review Figure 2-6. It shows the output of a typical sales information system at the management level. The system consolidates data about each item sold (such as the product code, product description, and sales amount) for further management analysis. Company managers examine these sales data to monitor sales activity and buying trends. The Window on Management describes the business benefits of another sales and marketing system.

sales and marketing information systems Systems that help the firm identify customers for the firm's products or services, develop products and services to meet customers' needs, promote these products and services, sell the products and services, and provide ongoing customer support.

MANUFACTURING AND PRODUCTION SYSTEMS

The manufacturing and production function is responsible for actually producing the firm's goods and services. Manufacturing and production systems deal with the planning, development, and maintenance of production facilities; the establishment of production goals; the acquisition, storage, and availability of production materials; and the scheduling of equipment, facilities, materials, and labor required to fashion finished products. **Manufacturing and production information systems** support these activities.

Table 2-3 shows some typical manufacturing and production information systems arranged by organizational level. Strategic-level manufacturing systems deal with the firm's long-term manufacturing goals, such as where to locate new plants or whether to invest in

manufacturing and production information systems Systems that deal with the planning, development, and production of products and services, and with controlling the flow of production.

TABLE 2-3	EXAMPLES OF MANUFACTURING AND PRODUCTION INFORMATION SYSTEMS	
System	**Description**	**Organizational Level**
Machine control	Control the actions of machines and equipment	Operational
Computer-aided design (CAD)	Design new products using the computer	Knowledge
Production planning	Decide when and how many products should be produced	Management
Facilities location	Decide where to locate new production facilities	Strategic

SAFILO SEES ITS WAY TO BETTER SALES

Selling eyeglasses and sunglasses presents the same challenge to the sales staff as do sales of most other products. The sales persons need to know the brands the customer purchases, recent orders, delivery status, payment information, the customer's ordering history, which sales reps were calling on the particular customer, and other key sales information. Safilo, an Italian eyewear company with annual sales of $625 million worldwide, carries many brands of frames, including such famous ones as Burberry, Polo Ralph Lauren, Diesel, Pierre Cardin, and Carrera. The company has a sales team of 30 in Canada, each of whom represents one or more of the brands Safilo carries when the person calls on any of its 2,500 Canadian customers. Each salesperson handles a different line of frames or sometimes several different brands.

To sell all of its products, Safilo has to dispatch three or four salespeople to each of its customers three or four times per year. In the past the company distributed to its sales staff valuable information on all customers by printing reports the size of a Manhattan telephone book that covered all Safilo customers. Paper companies loved them: They used reams and reams of paper. There was so much detail in these reports that the sales representatives would flip right to the back to get a summary. They did not really make use of valuable data that were available. The sales staff had no choice but to haul this weighty tome to each customer because they might need to comb the giant report for a tiny amount of data that relates to that specific customer. It was a difficult and time consuming task. Even the report itself required three days to produce.

Claude Groppi, Safilo's information technology manager, looked for another way to handle the problem and turned to Syntax.net, a Montreal-based firm specializing in business intelligence and enterprise system solutions. Early in 1999 Syntax.net

proposed that Safilo install PowerPlay business intelligence software from Cognos in combination with Syntax.net's Distribution Management (SDM) software. Working together, the two pieces of software produced the necessary data on-line where they can be easily searched and organized the way the individual salesperson wants them. The new system makes it much easier to find out what individual customers have been buying, what brands they were purchasing, and which sales reps were selling to each account. A sales rep can use the system to view high-level summary data or drill down into more detailed information on a case-by-case basis. Members of the sales staff were issued laptop computers so they could easily carry the data with them and bring up what was needed in the quest for more sales. Safilo was able to jettison the giant paper reports. Some of the sales staff used the computer to print off a report, but it would be on one particular customer only. Most carried the computer to the customer's business site. But in any case, "Our salesmen are really happy with the solution," said Groppi. "It is fast to find the information." The whole project cost the company $170,000 Canadian (about $108,000 U.S.) and only took three months to install. Key to its success was the training the entire sales staff received on both the computer and the software when they came together for a weekend. "The information helps them sell the products," exclaimed Groppi. "The information is good and accurate, and I think sales are better."

To Think About: Describe the sales and marketing system Safilo adopted. How does this system support the sales and marketing function? What level or levels of the organization are supported by the system? What management benefits does it provide?

Sources: David Aponovich, "Case Study: Data Software Has Eyewear Seller Seeing Clearly," *Datamation*, September 14, 2001; www.safilo.com; and www.scancode.com.

---

new manufacturing technology. At the management level, manufacturing and production systems analyze and monitor manufacturing and production costs and resources. Knowledge manufacturing and production systems create and distribute design knowledge or expertise to drive the production process, and operational manufacturing and production systems deal with the status of production tasks.

Most manufacturing and production systems use some sort of inventory system, as illustrated in Figure 2-10. Data about each item in inventory, such as the number of units depleted because of a shipment or purchase or the number of units replenished by reordering or returns, are either scanned or keyed into the system. The inventory master file contains basic data about each item, including the unique identification code for each item, the description of the item, the number of units on hand, the number of units on order, and the reorder point (the number of units in inventory that triggers a decision to reorder to prevent a stockout). Companies can estimate the number of items to reorder or they can use a for-

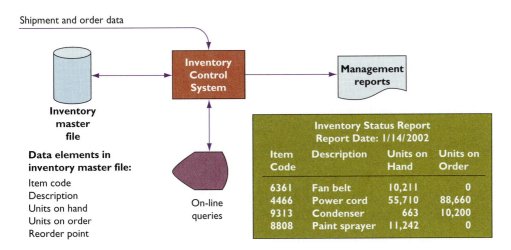

mula for calculating the least expensive quantity to reorder called the *economic order quantity*. The system produces reports such as the number of each item available in inventory, the number of units of each item to reorder, or items in inventory that must be replenished.

FINANCE AND ACCOUNTING SYSTEMS

The finance function is responsible for managing the firm's financial assets, such as cash, stocks, bonds, and other investments in order to maximize the return on these financial assets. The finance function is also in charge of managing the capitalization of the firm (finding new financial assets in stocks, bonds, or other forms of debt). In order to determine whether the firm is getting the best return on its investments, the finance function must obtain a considerable amount of information from sources external to the firm.

The accounting function is responsible for maintaining and managing the firm's financial records—receipts, disbursements, depreciation, payroll—to account for the flow of funds in a firm. Finance and accounting share related problems—how to keep track of a firm's financial assets and fund flows. They provide answers to questions such as these: What is the current inventory of financial assets? What records exist for disbursements, receipts, payroll, and other fund flows?

Table 2-4 shows some of the typical **finance and accounting information systems** found in large organizations. Strategic-level systems for the finance and accounting function establish long-term investment goals for the firm and provide long-range forecasts of the firm's financial performance. At the management level, information systems help managers oversee and control the firm's financial resources. Knowledge systems support finance and accounting by providing analytical tools and workstations for designing the right mix of investments to maximize returns for the firm. Operational systems in finance and accounting track the flow of funds in the firm through transactions such as paychecks, payments to vendors, securities reports, and receipts.

Review Figure 2-3, which illustrates a payroll system, a typical accounting TPS found in all businesses with employees.

finance and accounting information systems
Systems that keep track of the firm's financial assets and fund flows.

TABLE 2-4	EXAMPLES OF FINANCE AND ACCOUNTING INFORMATION SYSTEMS	
System	**Description**	**Organizational Level**
Accounts receivable	Track money owed the firm	Operational
Portfolio analysis	Design the firm's portfolio of investments	Knowledge
Budgeting	Prepare short-term budgets	Management
Profit planning	Plan long-term profits	Strategic

TABLE 2-5

EXAMPLES OF HUMAN RESOURCES INFORMATION SYSTEMS

System	Description	Organizational Level
Training and development	Track employee training, skills, and performance appraisals	Operational
Career pathing	Design career paths for employees	Knowledge
Compensation analysis	Monitor the range and distribution of employee wages, salaries, and benefits	Management
Human resources planning	Plan the long-term labor force needs of the organization	Strategic

HUMAN RESOURCES SYSTEMS

human resources information systems

Systems that maintain employee records; track employee skills, job performance, and training; and support planning for employee compensation and career development.

The human resources function is responsible for attracting, developing, and maintaining the firm's work force. **Human resources information systems** support activities such as identifying potential employees, maintaining complete records on existing employees, and creating programs to develop employees' talents and skills.

Strategic-level human resources systems identify the manpower requirements (skills, educational level, types of positions, number of positions, and cost) for meeting the firm's long-term business plans. At the management level, human resources systems help managers monitor and analyze the recruitment, allocation, and compensation of employees. Knowledge systems for human resources support analysis activities related to job design, training, and the modeling of employee career paths and reporting relationships. Human resources operational systems track the recruitment and placement of the firm's employees (see Table 2-5).

Figure 2-11 illustrates a typical human resources TPS for employee record keeping. It maintains basic employee data, such as the employee's name, age, sex, marital status, address, educational background, salary, job title, date of hire, and date of termination. The system can produce a variety of reports, such as lists of newly hired employees, employees who are terminated or on leaves of absence, employees classified by job type or educational level, or employee job performance evaluations. Such systems are typically designed to provide data that can satisfy federal and state record keeping requirements for Equal Employment Opportunity (EEO) and other purposes.

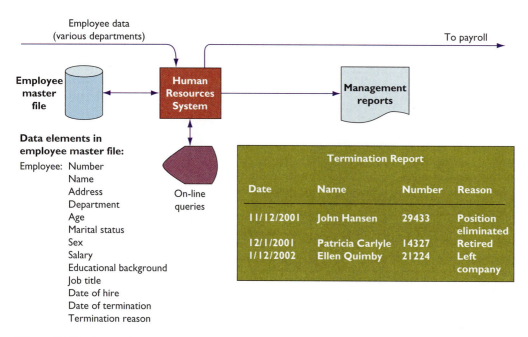

Figure 2-11 An employee record keeping system. This system maintains data on the firm's employees to support the human resources function.

2.3 INTEGRATING FUNCTIONS AND BUSINESS PROCESSES: CUSTOMER RELATIONSHIP MANAGEMENT, SUPPLY CHAIN MANAGEMENT, COLLABORATIVE COMMERCE, AND ENTERPRISE SYSTEMS

Organizations are using information systems to coordinate activities and decisions across entire firms and even entire industries. Information systems for customer relationship management (CRM) and supply chain management (SCM) can help coordinate processes that span multiple business functions, including those shared with customers and other supply chain partners. Enterprise systems can automate the flow of information across business processes throughout the entire organization.

BUSINESS PROCESSES AND INFORMATION SYSTEMS

The systems we have just described support flows of work and activities called *business processes,* which we introduced in Chapter 1. Business processes refer to the manner in which work is organized, coordinated, and focused to produce a valuable product or service. On the one hand, business processes are concrete work flows of material, information, and knowledge—sets of activities. Business processes also refer to the unique ways in which organizations coordinate work, information, and knowledge, and the ways in which management chooses to coordinate work. Table 2-6 describes typical business processes for each of the functional areas.

Although each of the major business functions has its own set of business processes, many other business processes are cross-functional, transcending the boundaries between sales, marketing, manufacturing, and research and development. These cross-functional processes cut across the traditional organizational structure, grouping employees from different functional specialties to complete a piece of work. For example, the order fulfillment process at many companies requires cooperation among the sales function (receiving the order, entering the order), the accounting function (credit checking and billing for the order), and the manufacturing function (assembling and shipping the order). Figure 2-12 illustrates how this cross-functional process might work. Information systems support these cross-functional processes as well as processes for the separate business functions.

Information systems can help organizations achieve great efficiencies by automating parts of these processes or by helping organizations rethink and streamline these processes. However, redesigning business processes requires careful analysis and planning. When systems are used to strengthen the wrong business model or business processes, the business can

TABLE 2-6 EXAMPLES OF BUSINESS PROCESSES

Functional Area	Business Process
Manufacturing and production	Assembling the product
	Checking for quality
	Producing bills of materials
Sales and marketing	Identifying customers
	Making customers aware of the product
	Selling the product
Finance and accounting	Paying creditors
	Creating financial statements
	Managing cash accounts
Human resources	Hiring employees
	Evaluating employees' job performance
	Enrolling employees in benefits plans

Figure 2-12 The order fulfillment process. Generating and fulfilling an order is a multi-step process involving activities performed by the sales, manufacturing and production, and accounting functions.

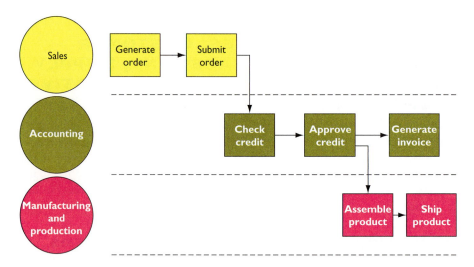

become more efficient at doing what it should not do. As a result, the firm becomes vulnerable to competitors who may have discovered the right business model. Therefore, one of the most important strategic decisions that a firm can make is not deciding how to use computers to improve business processes, but instead to first understand what business processes need improvement (Keen, 1997). Chapter 12 treats this subject in greater detail, because it is fundamental to systems analysis and design.

CUSTOMER RELATIONSHIP MANAGEMENT AND SUPPLY CHAIN MANAGEMENT

Electronic commerce, global competition, and the rise of digital firms have made companies think strategically about their business processes for managing their relationships with customers and suppliers. Consumers can now use the Web to comparison shop and switch companies on a moment's notice. To survive, businesses need to find ways of providing more value and service to customers at lower cost. Many believe the solution lies in improving business processes for interacting with customers and for producing and delivering products or services.

Customer Relationship Management (CRM)

customer relationship management (CRM)
Business and technology discipline to coordinate all of the business processes for dealing with customers.

Instead of treating customers as exploitable sources of income, businesses are now viewing them as long-term assets to be nurtured through customer relationship management. **Customer relationship management (CRM)** focuses on managing all of the ways that a firm deals with its existing and potential new customers. CRM is both a business and technology discipline that uses information systems to coordinate all of the business processes surrounding the firm's interactions with its customers in sales, marketing, and service. The ideal CRM system provides end-to-end customer care from receipt of an order through product delivery and service.

In the past, a firm's processes for sales, service, and marketing were highly compartmentalized and did not share much essential customer information. Some information on a specific customer might be stored and organized in terms of that person's account with the company. Other pieces of information about the same customer might be organized by products that were purchased. There was no way to consolidate all of this information to provide a unified view of a customer across the company. CRM tools try to solve this problem by integrating the firm's customer-related processes and consolidating customer information from multiple communication channels—telephone, e-mail, wireless devices, or the Web—so that the firm can present one coherent face to the customer (see Figure 2-13).

Good CRM systems consolidate customer data from multiple sources and provide analytical tools for answering questions such as, What is the value of a particular customer to the firm over his or her lifetime? Who are our most loyal customers? (It costs six times more to sell to a new customer than to an existing customer [Kalakota and Robinson, 2001].) Who

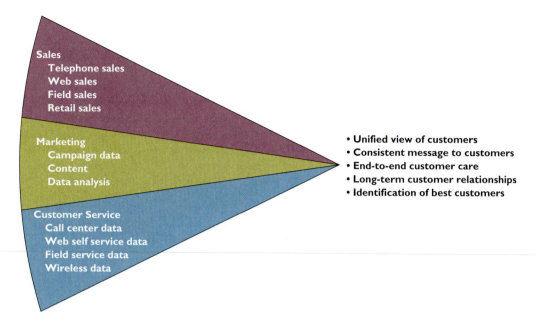

- Unified view of customers
- Consistent message to customers
- End-to-end customer care
- Long-term customer relationships
- Identification of best customers

Sales
Telephone sales
Web sales
Field sales
Retail sales

Marketing
Campaign data
Content
Data analysis

Customer Service
Call center data
Web self service data
Field service data
Wireless data

Figure 2-13 Customer relationship management (CRM). Customer relationship management applies technology to look at customers from a multifaceted perspective. CRM uses a set of integrated applications to address all aspects of the customer relationship, including customer service, sales, and marketing.

are our most profitable customers? (Typically 80 to 90 percent of a firm's profits are generated by 10 to 20 percent of its customers.) What do these profitable customers want to buy? Firms can then use the answers to acquire new customers, provide better service and support, customize their offerings more precisely to customer preferences, and provide ongoing value to retain profitable customers. Chapters 3, 4, 9, and 11 provide additional details on customer relationship management applications and technologies. The Window on Organizations shows how some European companies have benefited from customer relationship management.

Investing in CRM software alone won't automatically produce better information about customers, and many customer relationship management systems fall short of their objectives. These systems require changes in sales, marketing, and customer service processes to encourage sharing of customer information; support from top management; and a very clear idea of the benefits that could be obtained from consolidating customer data (see

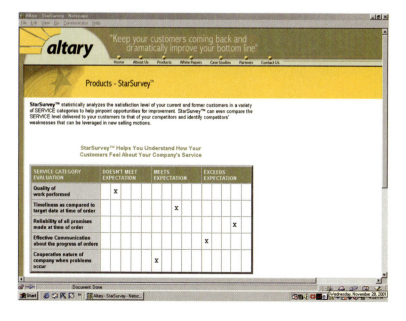

Altary's StarSurvey and StarService software monitor processes that span multiple departments to ensure customer expectations are always met or exceeded. Identifying and cultivating repeat customers is an important goal of customer relationship management.

CUSTOMER RELATIONSHIP MANAGEMENT SWEEPS EUROPE

European firms looking for better ways to understand and serve their customers are turning to customer relationship management systems. Heineken Ireland, a subsidiary of the Netherlands beverage company, Heineken N.V., has traditionally sold directly to pubs. Even sales to such customers as hotels usual went through the pub owners. Thus Heineken Ireland didn't have basic customer information, such as the amount of purchases or the customer's normal restocking time. One result was that its best customers were not given special treatment. "At the time, we treated all customers exactly the same," explained Denise Burke, Heineken's customer-services manager. "[Top customers] told us they weren't happy with the way we did business with them." And so the company implemented a customer relationship management (CRM) system from Siebel.

The software emphasizes collecting customer data through call center and sales force automation applications. Using CRM Heineken Ireland monitors customers' purchasing patterns, recording how much sales and marketing resources were devoted to each customer and classifying customers according to their value to the company. The sales and marketing staffs are given full access to these data. According to Burke, "We're more able to predict reactions of customers and respond quickly to change." Heineken's most valuable customers now get a weekly call or visit from the sales staff. When the Heineken staff contacts customers, the information the staff receives is stored in the system for use when other staff members follow up later. "It's much easier to maintain the relationship if the information's all there," explained Burke. She added, "Irish culture is all about relationships. It's about building trust and credibility over time."

Winterthur International, a Swiss insurance group and subsidiary of Credit Suisse, sells tailor-made insurance solutions for property, casualty, employee benefits, and alternative risk transfer to large national and multinational companies. It keeps records on at least 70 to 80 employees per customer, and it must be able work with information from different countries. Winterthur was facing mounting pressures from new competitors and a need to provide customers with greater service and value. Siebel's CRM system provided a solution that would work internationally and could monitor any sales interaction Winterthur had with a customer. If, for example, a pension fund manager made a deal with Winterthur, the Winterthur sales representative would have access to that information before pitching a health insurance product to another contact within the company. By seamlessly sharing customer information across its teams worldwide, Winterthur can create profiles of important global customers and develop products and services to meet their specific needs.

Because Europeans demand their governments meet more of their needs than Americans do, governments take a more active role in business practices. Kingston-on-Hull, a city of 250,000 people on England's Yorkshire coast, turned to CRM because its city council provides many services, including education, public housing, building and repair, community development, and telecommunications services. Prior to CRM, residents had no single way to contact the city. They had to choose from a bewildering 250 face-to-face access points or 200 telephone numbers. There was a good chance a resident would not know the right number to call. Kingston also had 37 independent, isolated computer systems, so actions by one department were unknown to others. Kingston-on-Hull turned to the Oracle 11i CRM package, with a goal of bringing all its customer contact points and relevant information together in one system. Using the software, the city established one call center for all services and one computer system with all the information. It is the contact for all departments, providing a single view for the customers. If a resident calls, a government employee can look up his or her information and discuss other services that might be useful.

To Think About   How have customer relationship management systems changed how organizations are able to service their customers? How have the organizations described here benefited from using CRM systems?

Source: Jeff Sweat, "CRM Migration," *Information Week,* May 21, 2001 and "Winterthur Reaps the Benefits of Intimate Customer Relationship Management," www.siebel.com.

Chapter 13). The Manager's Toolkit describes some of the customer data issues that managers must address.

Supply Chain Management

To deliver the product more rapidly to the customer and lower costs, companies are also trying to streamline their business processes for supply chain management. **Supply chain management** is the close linkage and coordination of activities involved in buying, making, and moving a product. It integrates supplier, manufacturer, distributor, and customer logistics processes to reduce time, redundant effort, and inventory costs. The **supply chain** is a net-

supply chain management
Close linkage and coordination of activities involved in buying, making, and moving a product.

MIS IN ACTION   MANAGER'S TOOLKIT

HOW TO BENEFIT FROM CUSTOMER RELATIONSHIP MANAGEMENT

When setting up CRM systems, managers need to have a clear understanding of the business questions concerning customers that the system should answer. Here are some key questions to ask when gathering customer information:

Customer status: Is the firm interested in information about existing customers, new customers, or both?

Customer value: What is the customer's value to the business? Why is this customer important?

Channels: What channel or channels did the customer use to interact with the company? Were these interactions over the tele-

phone, via e-mail, through the corporate Web site, or through company sales representatives? Which channel or channels are the most important?

Nature of interaction: Why did the customer interact with the company? Was it to purchase an item, to secure customer service, or to return merchandise? What is the intended outcome for this interaction?

Metrics: How can the company measure the value of its interaction with the customer? Can it be measured in terms of cost savings, increased revenue, or higher levels of customer satisfaction?

---

work of organizations and business processes for procuring materials, transforming raw materials into intermediate and finished products, and distributing the finished products to customers. It links suppliers, manufacturing plants, distribution centers, conveyances, retail outlets, people, and information through processes such as procurement, inventory control, distribution, and delivery to supply goods and services from source through consumption. Materials, information, and payments flow through the supply chain in both directions. Goods start out as raw materials and move through logistics and production systems until they reach customers. The supply chain includes **reverse logistics** in which returned items flow in the reverse direction from the buyer back to the seller .

The supply chain illustrated in Figure 2-14 has been simplified. Most supply chains, especially those for large manufacturers such as automakers, are multitiered, with thousands of primary, secondary, and tertiary suppliers. To manage the supply chain, a company tries to eliminate redundant steps, delays, and the amount of resources tied up along the way.

Companies that skillfully manage their supply chains get the right amount of their products from their source to their point of consumption with the least amount of time and the lowest cost. Information systems make supply chain management more efficient by helping

supply chain

Network of organizations and business processes for procuring materials, transforming raw materials into intermediate and finished products, and distributing the finished products to customers.

reverse logistics

The return of items from buyers to sellers in a supply chain.

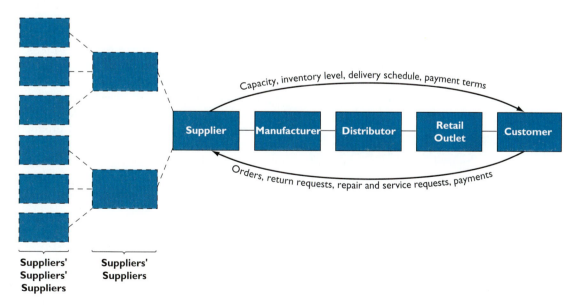

Figure 2-14 Supply chain management. This figure illustrates the major entities in the supply chain and the flow of information upstream and downstream to coordinate the activities involved in buying, making, and moving a product. Suppliers transform raw materials into intermediate products or components, and then manufacturers turn them into finished products. The products are shipped to distribution centers and from there to retailers and customers.

TABLE 2-7	HOW INFORMATION SYSTEMS CAN FACILITATE SUPPLY CHAIN MANAGEMENT

Information Systems Can Help Participants in the Supply Chain

Decide when and what to produce, store, and move

Rapidly communicate orders

Track the status of orders

Check inventory availability and monitor inventory levels

Reduce inventory, transportation, and warehousing costs

Track shipments

Plan production based on actual customer demand

Rapidly communicate changes in product design

companies coordinate, schedule, and control procurement, production, inventory management, and delivery of products and services. Supply chain management systems can be built using intranets, extranets, or special supply chain management software. Table 2-7 describes how companies can benefit from using information systems for supply chain management.

Inefficiencies in the supply chain, such as parts shortages, underutilized plant capacity, excessive finished goods inventory, or runaway transportation costs, are caused by inaccurate or untimely information. For example, manufacturers may keep too many parts in inventory because they don't know exactly when they will receive their next shipment from their suppliers. Suppliers may order too few raw materials because they don't have precise information on demand. These supply chain inefficiencies can waste as much as 25 percent of a company's operating costs.

bullwhip effect
Large fluctuations in inventories along the supply chain resulting from small unanticipated fluctuations in demand.

One recurring problem in supply chain management is the **bullwhip effect**, in which information about the demand for a product gets distorted as it passes from one entity to the next across the supply chain (Lee, Padmanabhan and Wang, 1997). A slight rise in demand for an item might cause different members in the supply chain—distributors, manufacturers, suppliers, suppliers' suppliers, and suppliers' suppliers' suppliers—to stockpile inventory so each has enough "just in case." These changes will ripple throughout the supply chain, magnifying what started out as a small change from planned orders, creating excess inventory, production, warehousing, and shipping costs. If all members of the supply chain could share dynamic information about inventory levels, schedules, forecasts, and shipments they would have a more precise idea of how to adjust their sourcing, manufacturing, and distribution plans.

Supply chain management uses systems for supply chain planning (SCP) and supply chain execution (SCE). *Supply chain planning systems* enable the firm to generate demand forecasts for a product and to develop sourcing and manufacturing plans for that product. *Supply chain execution systems* manage the flow of products through distribution centers and warehouses to ensure that products are delivered to the right locations in the most efficient manner. Table 2-8 provides more details on supply chain planning and execution systems.

Hewlett-Packard and other computer manufacturers use supply chain management software to help them produce PCs to order, while minimizing the parts, goods in process, and completed products in inventory.

COLLABORATIVE COMMERCE AND INDUSTRIAL NETWORKS

Successful supply chain management requires an atmosphere of trust where all the members of the supply chain agree to cooperate and to honor the commitments they have made to each other (Welty and Becerra-Fernandez, 2001). They must be able to work together on the same goal and to redesign some of their business processes so that they can coordinate their activities more easily. In some industries, companies

TABLE 2-8	**SUPPLY CHAIN PLANNING AND EXECUTION SYSTEMS**

Capabilities of Supply Chain Planning Systems

Order planning: Select an order fulfillment plan that best meets the desired level of service to the customer given existing transportation and manufacturing constraints.

Advanced scheduling and manufacturing planning: Provide detailed coordination of scheduling based on analysis of changing factors such as customer orders, equipment outages, or supply interruptions. Scheduling modules create job schedules for the manufacturing process and supplier logistics.

Demand planning: Generate demand forecasts from all business units using statistical tools and business forecasting techniques.

Distribution planning: Create operating plans for logistics managers for order fulfillment, based on input from demand and manufacturing planning modules.

Transportation planning: Track and analyze inbound and outbound movement of materials and products to ensure that materials and finished goods are delivered at the right time and place at the minimum cost.

Capabilities of Supply Chain Execution Systems

Order commitments: Allow vendors to quote accurate delivery dates to customers by providing more real-time detailed information on the status of orders from availability of raw materials and inventory to production and shipment status.

Final Production: Organize and schedule final subassemblies required to make each final product.

Replenishment: Coordinate component replenishment work so that warehouses remain stocked with the minimum amount of inventory in the pipeline.

Distribution management: Coordinate the process of transporting goods from the manufacturer to distribution centers to the final customer. Provide on-line customer access to shipment and delivery data.

Reverse distribution: Track the shipment and accounting for returned goods or remanufactured products.

have extended their supply chain management systems to work more collaboratively with customers, suppliers, and other firms in their industry. This is a much broader mission than traditional supply chain management systems, which focused primarily on managing the flow of transactions among organizations. It focuses on using shared systems and business processes to optimize the value of relationships.

Companies are relying on these new collaborative relationships to further improve their planning, production, and distribution of goods and services. The use of digital technologies to enable multiple organizations to collaboratively design, develop, build, move, and manage products through their lifecycles is called **collaborative commerce**. Firms can integrate their systems with those of their supply chain partners to coordinate demand forecasting, resource planning, production planning, replenishment, shipping, and warehousing. They can work jointly with suppliers on product design and marketing. Customers can provide feedback for marketers to use to improve product design, support, and service. A firm engaged in collaborative commerce with its suppliers and customers can achieve new levels of efficiency in

collaborative commerce
The use of digital technologies to enable multiple organizations to collaboratively design, develop, build, and manage products through their lifecycles.

LOG-Net Inc. provides software for tracking purchase orders and shipments from any location via the Web. Companies can use such tools to improve their supply chain management.

Figure 2-15 Collaborative commerce. Collaborative commerce is a set of digitally enabled collaborative interactions between an enterprise and its business partners and customers. Data and processes that were once considered internal can be shared by the collaborative community.

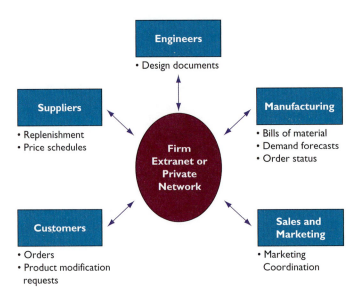

reducing product design cycles, minimizing excess inventory, forecasting demand, and keeping partners and customers informed (see Figure 2-15).

For example, Briggs & Stratton, based in Wauwatosa, Wisconsin, built a collaborative extranet called BriggsNetwork.com, linking it to its customers and suppliers, that is available in eight different languages. The company produces air-cooled gasoline engines for outdoor power equipment and uses more than 35,000 distributors worldwide. Suppliers and manufacturing customers can log onto the extranet to check manufacturing specifications, view upcoming sales promotions, and obtain parts and warranty information. Distributors can link their own Web sites to portions of the Briggs & Stratton extranet of special interest to their customers so that these customers see information that is immediately available and up to date.

Users of the extranet see different data, depending on whether they are manufacturing customers, distributors, or dealers. The information available includes searchable libraries of product brochures, marketing material, and two- and three-dimensional engine drawings, as well as an on-line calendar to help dealers schedule training classes with their distributors. The company's regional managers can publish information unique to the regions they oversee. Briggs & Stratton provides its end customers with some of this company information through BriggsandStratton.com. Through this consumer Web site, users can access sales catalogs of equipment powered by Briggs & Stratton; obtain on-line advice to locate products that meet their needs; and locate retail outlets, such as Home Depot, Sears or Lowe's, that carry the company's products. Briggs & Stratton also uses Digex to host Web sites for smaller retailers who lack the resources to maintain their own Web presence (McDougall, 2001). Table 2-9 provides other examples of collaborative commerce.

Internet technology is making this level of collaboration possible by providing a platform where systems from different companies can seamlessly exchange information. Web enabled networks for the coordination of transorganizational business processes provide an infrastructure for collaborative commerce activities. Such networks can be termed **private industrial networks**, and they permit firms and their business partners to share information about product design and development, marketing, inventory, and production scheduling, including transmission of graphics, e-mail, and CAD drawings. Many of these networks are "owned" and managed by large companies who use them to coordinate purchases, orders, and other activities with their suppliers, distributors, and selected business partners.

For instance, Procter & Gamble (P&G), the world's largest consumer goods company, developed an integrated industry-wide system to coordinate grocery store point-of-sale systems with grocery store warehouses, shippers, its own manufacturing facilities, and its suppliers of raw materials. This single industry-spanning system effectively allows P&G to monitor the movement of all its products from raw materials to customer purchase. P&G uses data collected from point-of-sale terminals to trigger shipments to retailers of items that cus-

private industrial networks
Web-enabled networks linking systems of multiple firms in an industry for the coordination of transorganizational business processes.

TABLE 2-9	HOW BUSINESSES ARE ENGAGING IN COLLABORATIVE COMMERCE	
Business	**Collaborative Commerce Activities**
Cummins Inc.	Extranet enables customers to access updates on their engine orders. Truck manufacturers can view early prototypes for Cummins line of engines and ask for modifications. Real-time design collaboration tools let Cummins engineers work with customers' engineers via the Web. A customer council reviews all significant updates to the Cummins site.
Group Dekko	Group of 12 independently operated manufacturing companies that produce components such as wire harnesses, molded plastic parts, metal stamping for automobiles, and office furniture uses a common shared data repository to coordinate partner firms to make sure they satisfy ISO 9000 international quality control standards. Partner firms share quality standards, documents, graphics, engineering drawings, bills of material, pricing, and routing information. Partner firms, suppliers, and customers can be involved in the complete flow of design and product information.
Menasha	Packaging company lets customers use the Web to proof products, change colors and specifications, and check scheduling directly in its enterprise resource planning (ERP) system.
American Axle and Manufacturing	Manufacturer of automobile driveline systems, chassis components, and forged products uses the Web to share with suppliers photos of defective parts that stall its assembly line, discuss the problem, and solve it on the spot.

tomers have purchased and that need restocking. Electronic links to suppliers enable P&G to order materials from its own suppliers when its inventories are low. The system helps P&G reduce its inventory by allowing the company to produce products as they are demanded by retailers. P&G is implementing an Ultimate Supply System that uses Internet technology to link retailers and suppliers to its private corporate intranet. By having retailers and suppliers integrate their systems with P&G's systems, P&G hopes to reduce product cycle time by half, inventory costs by $4.5 billion, and systems costs by $5 billion.

Similarly, Safeway U.K. has electronic links to suppliers where it can share information about forecasts, shelf space, and inventory in its supermarkets so suppliers can track demand for their products, adjust production, and adjust the timing and size of deliveries. The suppliers can download Safeway's information into their enterprise systems or production planning systems. Suppliers send Safeway information about product availability, production capacity, and inventory levels.

Although private industrial networks are primarily used today to coordinate the activities of a single firm and its business partners, some can encompass an entire industry, coordinating the business processes for the key players in that industry, including suppliers, transporters, production firms, distributors, and retailers. For example, the OASIS system Web sites link U.S. electrical utility companies in regional power pool groups to sell their surplus power to wholesalers and to locate the transmission facilities for moving the power between its source and the customers.

A few industrial networks have been built to support collaboration among firms in multiple industries. General Mills, Kellogg, Land O'Lakes, and Monsanto now use a common system based on Internet technology to share their excess shipping capacity. The system uses a private network to coordinate underutilized shipping capacity of container trucks and railroad cars to reduce participating members' logistics costs.

ENTERPRISE SYSTEMS

Organizations have internal business processes and flows of information that can also benefit from tighter integration. A large organization typically has many different kinds of information systems that support different functions, organizational levels, and business processes. Most of these systems are built around different functions, business units and business processes that do not "talk" to each other, and managers might have a hard time assembling the data they need for a comprehensive, overall picture of the organization's operations. For instance, sales personnel might not be able to tell at the time they place an order whether the items that were ordered were in inventory; customers could not track their orders; and manufacturing could not communicate easily with finance to plan for new production. This fragmentation of data in hundreds of separate systems could thus have a negative impact on

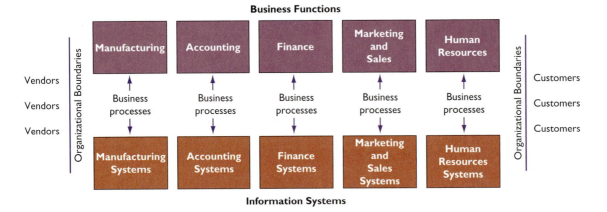

Figure 2-16   Traditional view of systems. In most organizations today, separate systems built over a long period of time support discrete business processes and discrete business functions. The organization's systems rarely include vendors and customers.

organizational efficiency and business performance. Figure 2-16 illustrates the traditional arrangement of information systems.

enterprise systems

Firmwide information systems that integrate key business processes so that information can flow freely between different parts of the firm.

Many organizations are now building **enterprise systems**, also known as enterprise resource planning (ERP) systems, to solve this problem. Enterprise software models and automates many business processes, such as filling an order or scheduling a shipment, with the goal of integrating information across the company and eliminating complex, expensive links between computer systems in different areas of the business. Information that was previously fragmented in different systems can seamlessly flow throughout the firm so that it can be shared by business processes in manufacturing, accounting, human resources, and other areas of the firm. Discrete business processes from sales, production, finance, and logistics can be integrated into company-wide business processes that flow across organizational levels and functions. An enterprise-wide technical platform serves all processes and levels. Figure 2-17 illustrates how enterprise systems work.

The enterprise system collects data from various key business processes (see Table 2-10) and stores the data in a single comprehensive data repository where they can be used by other parts of the business. Managers emerge with more precise and timely information for coordinating the daily operations of the business and a firmwide view of business processes and information flows.

For instance, when a sales representative in Brussels enters a customer order, the data flow automatically to others in the company who need to see them. The factory in Hong Kong receives the order and begins production. The warehouse checks its progress on-line and schedules the shipment date. The warehouse can check its stock of parts and replenish whatever the factory has depleted. The enterprise system stores production information,

Figure 2-17   Enterprise systems. Enterprise systems can integrate the key business processes of an entire firm into a single software system that allows information to flow seamlessly throughout the organization. These systems may include transactions with customers and vendors.

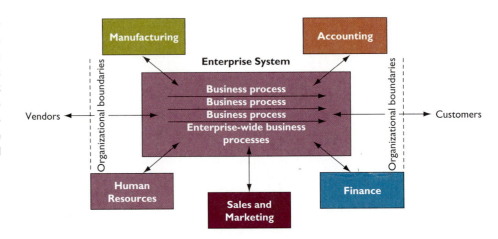

TABLE 2-10	**BUSINESS PROCESSES SUPPORTED BY ENTERPRISE SYSTEMS**

Manufacturing processes, including inventory management, purchasing, shipping, production planning, material requirements planning, and plant and equipment maintenance

Financial and accounting processes, including accounts payable, accounts receivable, cash management and forecasting, product-cost accounting, cost-center accounting, asset accounting, general ledger, and financial reporting

Sales and marketing processes, including order processing, pricing, shipping, billing, sales management, and sales planning

Human resource processes, including personnel administration, time accounting, payroll, personnel planning and development, benefits accounting, applicant tracking, and travel expense reporting

where it can be accessed by customer service representatives to track the progress of the order through every step of the manufacturing process. Updated sales and production data automatically flow to the accounting department. The system transmits information for calculating the salesperson's commission to the payroll department. The system also automatically recalculates the company's balance sheets, accounts receivable and payable ledgers, cost-center accounts, and available cash. Corporate headquarters in London can view up-to-the-minute data on sales, inventory, and production at every step of the process, as well as updated sales and production forecasts and calculations of product cost and availability.

Benefits and Challenges of Enterprise Systems

Enterprise systems promise to integrate the diverse business processes of a firm into a single, integrated information architecture, but they also present major challenges.

Benefits of Enterprise Systems Enterprise systems promise to greatly change four dimensions of business: firm structure, management process, technology platform, and business capability. Companies can use enterprise systems to support organizational structures that were not previously possible or to create a more disciplined organizational culture. For example, they might use enterprise systems to integrate the corporation across geographic or business unit boundaries or to create a more uniform organizational culture in which everyone uses similar processes and information. An enterprise-enabled organization does business the same way worldwide, with cross-functional coordination and information flowing freely across business functions. Information supplied by an enterprise system is

MIS IN ACTION   DECISIONMAKING

ANALYZING ENTERPRISE PROCESS INTEGRATION
Management at your agricultural chemicals corporation has been dissatisfied with production planning. Production plans are created using best guesses of demand for each product, which are based on how much of each product has been ordered in the past. If a customer places an unexpected order or requests a change to an existing order after it has been placed, there is no way to adjust production plans. The company may have to tell customers it can't fill their orders, or it may run up extra costs maintaining additional inventory to prevent stockouts.

At the end of each month, orders are totaled and manually keyed into the company's production planning system. Data from the past month's production and inventory systems are manually entered into the firm's order management system. Analysts from the sales department and from the production department analyze the data from their respective systems to determine what the sales targets and production

targets should be for the next month. These estimates are usually different. The analysts then get together at a high-level planning meeting to revise the production and sales targets to take into account senior management's goals for market share, revenues, and profits. The outcome of the meeting is a finalized production master schedule.

The entire production planning process takes 17 business days to complete. Nine of these days are required to enter and validate the data. The remaining days are spent developing and reconciling the production and sales targets and finalizing the production master schedule.

1. Draw a diagram of the production planning process.
2. Analyze the problems this process creates for the company.
3. How could an enterprise system solve these problems? In what ways could it lower costs? Diagram what the production planning process might look like if the company implemented enterprise software.

structured around cross-functional business processes, and it can improve management reporting and decision making. For example, an enterprise system might help management more easily determine which products are most or least profitable. An enterprise system could potentially supply management with better data about business processes and overall organizational performance.

Enterprise systems promise to provide firms with a single, unified, and all-encompassing information system technology platform that houses data on all the key business processes. The data have common, standardized definitions and formats that are accepted by the entire organization. You will learn more about the importance of standardizing organizational data in Chapter 7.

Enterprise systems can also help create the foundation for a customer or demand-driven organization. By integrating discrete business processes, such as sales, production, finance, and logistics, the entire organization can respond more efficiently to customer requests for products or information, forecast new products, and build and deliver them as demand requires. Manufacturing has better information to produce only what customers have ordered, procure exactly the right amount of components or raw materials to fill actual orders, stage production, and minimize the time that components or finished products are in inventory.

Enterprise systems have primarily focused on helping companies manage their internal manufacturing, financial, and human resource processes and were not originally designed to support supply chain management processes involving entities outside the firm. However, enterprise software vendors are starting to enhance their products so that firms can link their enterprise systems with vendors, suppliers, manufacturers, distributors, and retailers.

Enterprise systems can produce the integration among internal supply chain processes, such as sales, inventory, and production, that makes it easier for the firm to coordinate its activities with manufacturing partners and customers. If participants in the supply chain use the same enterprise software systems, their systems can exchange data without manual intervention.

Challenges of Enterprise Systems   Although enterprise systems can improve organizational coordination, efficiency, and decision making, they have proven very difficult to build. They require not only large technology investments but also fundamental changes in the way the business operates. Companies will need to rework their business processes to make information flow smoothly between them. Employees will have to take on new job functions and responsibilities. Organizations that don't understand that such changes will be required or are unable to make them will have problems implementing enterprise systems or they may not be able to achieve a higher level of functional and business process integration.

Enterprise systems require complex pieces of software and large investments of time, money, and expertise. This software is deeply intertwined with corporate business processes. It might take a large company three to five years to fully implement all of the organizational and technological changes required by an enterprise system. Because enterprise systems are integrated, it is difficult to make a change in only one part of the business without affecting other parts as well. There is the prospect that the new enterprise systems could eventually prove as brittle and hard to change as the old systems they replaced, binding firms to outdated business processes and systems.

Companies may also fail to achieve strategic benefits from enterprise systems if integrating business processes using the generic models provided by standard ERP software prevents the firm from using unique business processes that had been sources of advantage over competitors. Enterprise systems promote centralized organizational coordination and decision making, which may not be the best way for some firms to operate. There are companies that clearly do not need the level of integration provided by enterprise systems (Davenport, 2000 and 1998). Chapter 13 provides more detail on the organizational and technical challenges to enterprise system implementation.

2.4   INTERNATIONAL INFORMATION SYSTEMS

There are different ways of configuring information systems when businesses operate internationally, based on the firm's organizational structure.

FORMS OF GLOBAL BUSINESS ORGANIZATION

There are four main forms of international business organization: domestic exporter, multinational, franchiser, and transnational, each with different patterns of organizational structure or governance. In each type of global business organization, business functions may be centralized (in the home country), decentralized (to local foreign units), and coordinated (all units participate as equals).

The **domestic exporter** is characterized by heavy centralization of corporate activities in the home country of origin. Production, finance/accounting, sales/marketing, human resources, and strategic management are set up to optimize resources in the home country. International sales are sometimes dispersed using agency agreements or subsidiaries, but even here foreign marketing is totally reliant on the domestic home base for marketing themes and strategies. Caterpillar Corporation and other heavy capital-equipment manufacturers fall into this category of firm.

The **multinational** firm concentrates financial management and control out of a central home base while decentralizing production, sales, and marketing operations to units in other countries. The products and services on sale in different countries are adapted to suit local market conditions. The organization becomes a far-flung confederation of production and marketing facilities in different countries. Many financial service firms, along with a host of manufacturers such as General Motors, Chrysler, and Intel, fit this pattern.

Franchisers have the product created, designed, financed, and initially produced in the home country, but rely heavily on foreign personnel for further production, marketing, and human resources. Food franchisers such as McDonald's, Mrs. Fields Cookies, and Kentucky Fried Chicken fit this pattern. McDonald's created a new form of fast-food chain in the United States and continues to rely largely on the United States for inspiration of new products, strategic management, and financing. Nevertheless, because the product must be produced locally—it is perishable—extensive coordination and dispersal of production, local marketing, and local recruitment of personnel are required.

Transnational firms have no single national headquarters but instead have many regional headquarters and perhaps a world headquarters. In a **transnational** strategy, nearly all the value-adding activities are managed from a global perspective without reference to national borders, optimizing sources of supply and demand wherever they appear, and taking advantage of any local competitive advantages. The governance of these firms has been likened to a federal structure in which there is a strong central management core of decision making, but considerable dispersal of power and financial muscle throughout the global divisions. Few companies have actually attained transnational status, but Citicorp, Sony, Ford, and others are attempting this transition.

GLOBAL SYSTEM CONFIGURATION

Information technology and improvements in global telecommunications are giving international firms more flexibility in their global business design. Figure 2-18 depicts four types of systems configuration for global business organizations. *Centralized systems* are those in which systems development and operation occur totally at the domestic home base. *Duplicated systems* are those in which development occurs at the home base but operations are handed over to autonomous units in foreign locations. *Decentralized systems* are those in which each foreign unit designs its own unique solutions and systems. *Networked systems* are those in which systems development and operations occur in an integrated and coordinated fashion across all units.

domestic exporter
Form of business organization characterized by heavy centralization of corporate activities in the home country of origin.

multinational
Form of business organization that concentrates financial management and control out of a central home base while decentralizing production, sales, and marketing operations to units in other countries.

franchiser
Form of business organization in which a product is created, designed, financed, and initially produced in the home country, but for product-specific reasons relies heavily on foreign personnel for further production, marketing, and human resources.

transnational
Truly global form of business organization with no national headquarters; value-added activities are managed from a global perspective without reference to national borders, optimizing sources of supply and demand and local competitive advantage.

SYSTEM CONFIGURATION	BUSINESS ORGANIZATION			
	Domestic Exporter	Multinational	Franchiser	Transnational
Centralized	X			
Duplicated			X	
Decentralized	x	X	x	
Networked		x		X

Figure 2-18 Global business organization and systems configurations. The large Xs show the dominant patterns, and the small Xs show the emerging patterns. For instance, domestic exporters rely predominantly on centralized systems, but there is continual pressure and some development of decentralized systems in local marketing regions.

MAKE **IT** YOUR BUSINESS

FINANCE AND ACCOUNTING

Finance and accounting systems help firms keep track of their assets and fund flows. They can help firms maximize returns on their financial assets and investments, and maintain financial records. Enterprise systems can integrate financial information with production and sales information so that the impact of sales and manufacturing transactions can be immediately reflected on the firm's balance sheets, accounts receivable and payable ledgers, and reports of cash flows. Management can use enterprise systems to obtain up-to-the-minute reports of the firm's overall financial performance.

HUMAN RESOURCES

Human resources systems help businesses develop staffing requirements; identify potential new employees; maintain employee records; and track employee training, skills, and job performance. They help managers develop appropriate plans for employee compensation and career development. Enterprise systems can help businesses coordinate their staffing levels with sales and production activities and financial resources.

MANUFACTURING AND PRODUCTION

Manufacturing and production systems solve problems related to the planning, development, and delivery of products and services, and control the flow of production. Supply chain management (SCM) systems provide information to coordinate sourcing and procurement, production scheduling, order fulfillment, inventory management, product development, warehousing, and customer service. When these processes are coordinated among supply chain members, goods can move smoothly and on time from suppliers to manufacturers to customers. Collaborative commerce can promote further supply chain and product development efficiencies by facilitating collaborative interactions between the firm and its suppliers, customers, and other business partners. You can find examples of manufacturing and production applications on pages 36, 44, 58, and 67–69.

SALES AND MARKETING

Information systems help businesses promote products, contact customers, track sales, and provide ongoing service and support, and they can also be used to analyze the performance of the firm's sales staff. Systems for customer relationship management (CRM) are especially useful for consolidating customer data from different sources so that the firm can coordinate its interactions with customers and provide better long-term customer relationships. You can find examples of sales and marketing applications on pages 48, 54, 58, and 67–69.

As can be seen in Figure 2-18, domestic exporters tend to have highly centralized systems in which a single domestic systems development staff develops worldwide applications. Multinationals allow foreign units to devise their own systems solutions based on local needs with few if any applications in common with headquarters (the exceptions being financial reporting and some telecommunications applications). Franchisers typically develop a single system, usually at the home base, and then replicate it around the world. Each unit, no matter where it is located, has identical applications. Firms organized along transnational lines use networked systems that span multiple countries using a powerful telecommunications backbone and a shared management culture that crosses cultural barriers. One can see the networked systems structure in financial services where the homogeneity of the product—money and money instruments—seems to overcome national and cultural barriers.

MANAGEMENT WRAP-UP

Enterprise systems require management to take a firmwide view of business processes and information flows. Managers need to determine which business processes should be integrated, the short- and long-term benefits of this integration, and the appropriate level of financial and organizational resources to support this integration.

There are many types of information systems in an organization that support different organizational levels, functions, and business processes. Some of these systems, including those for supply chain management and customer relationship management, span more than one function or business process and may be tied to the business processes of other organizations. Systems integrating information from different business functions, business processes and organizations often require extensive organizational change.

Information systems that create firmwide or industry-wide information flows and business processes require major technology investments and planning. Firms must have an information technology (IT) infrastructure that can support organization-wide or industry-wide computing.

For Discussion

1. Review the payroll TPS illustrated in Figure 2-3. How could it provide information for other types of systems in the firm?

2. Adopting an enterprise system is a key business decision as well as a technology decision. Do you agree? Why or why not? Who should make this decision?

SUMMARY

1. *What are the key system applications in a business? What role do they play?* There are six major types of information systems in contemporary organizations. Operational-level systems are transaction processing systems (TPS), such as payroll or order processing, that track the flow of the daily routine transactions that are necessary to conduct business. Knowledge-level systems support clerical, managerial, and professional workers. They consist of office systems for increasing data workers' productivity and knowledge work systems for enhancing knowledge workers' productivity. Management-level systems (MIS and DSS) provide the management control level with information for monitoring, controlling, and decision-making. Most MIS reports condense information from TPS and are not highly analytical. Decision-support systems (DSS) support management decisions when these decisions are unique, rapidly changing, and not specified easily in advance. They have more advanced analytical models and data analysis capabilities than MIS and often draw on information from external as well as internal sources. Executive support systems (ESS) support the strategic level by providing a generalized computing and communications environment to assist senior management's decision making. They have limited analytical capabilities but can draw on sophisticated graphics software and many sources of internal and external information.

   The various types of systems in the organization exchange data with one another. TPS are a major source of data for other systems, especially MIS and DSS. ESS primarily receive data from lower-level systems. The different systems in an organization have traditionally been loosely integrated.

2. *How do information systems support the major business functions: sales and marketing, manufacturing and production, finance and accounting, and human resources?* At each level of the organization there are information systems supporting the major functional areas of the business. Sales and marketing systems help the firm identify customers for the firm's products or services, develop products and services to meet customers' needs, promote the products and services, sell the products and services, and provide ongoing customer support. Manufacturing and production systems deal with the planning, development, and production of products and services, and controlling the flow of production. Finance and accounting systems keep track of the firm's financial assets and fund flows. Human resources systems maintain employee records; track employee skills, job performance,

and training; and support planning for employee compensation and career development.

3. *Why should managers pay attention to business processes? What are the benefits of using information systems to support business processes, including those for customer relationship management and supply chain management?* Business processes refer to the manner in which work is organized, coordinated, and focused to produce a valuable product or service. Business processes are concrete work flows of material, information, and knowledge. They also represent unique ways in which organizations coordinate work, information, and knowledge and the ways in which management chooses to coordinate work. Managers need to pay attention to business processes because they determine how well the organization can execute, and thus are a potential source of strategic success or failure. Although each of the major business functions has its own set of business processes, many other business processes are cross-functional, such as fulfilling an order. Information systems can help organizations achieve great efficiencies by automating parts of these processes or by helping organizations rethink and streamline these processes, especially those for customer relationship management and supply chain management. Customer relationship management uses information systems to coordinate all of the business processes surrounding the firm's interactions with its customers. Supply chain management is the close linkage of activities involved in buying, making, and moving products. Information systems make supply chain management more efficient by helping companies coordinate, schedule, and control procurement, production, inventory management, and delivery of products and services to customers.

4. *What are the business benefits of using collaborative commerce, private industrial networks and enterprise systems?* Collaborative commerce relies on digital technologies to enable multiple organizations to collaboratively design, develop, build, move, and manage products through their lifecycles. A firm engaged in collaborative commerce with its suppliers and customers can achieve new efficiencies by reducing product design cycles, minimizing excess inventory, forecasting demand, and keeping partners and customers informed. Private industrial networks are Web-enabled networks that support collaborative commerce activities by providing an infrastructure for transorganizational business processes and information flows.

Enterprise systems integrate the key business processes of a firm into a single software system so that information can flow throughout the organization, improving coordination, efficiency, and decision making. Enterprise systems promise efficiencies from better coordination of both internal and external business processes. Enterprise systems can help create a more uniform organization in which everyone uses similar processes and information, and measures their work in terms of organization-wide performance standards. The coordination of sales, production, finance, and logistics processes provided by enterprise systems helps organizations respond more rapidly to customer demands.

Enterprise systems are very difficult to implement successfully. They require extensive organizational change, use complicated technologies, and require large up-front costs for long-term benefits that are difficult to quantify. Once implemented, enterprise systems are very difficult to change.

Management vision and foresight are required to take a firmwide and industry-wide view of problems and to find solutions that realize strategic value from the investment.

5. *What types of information systems are used by companies that operate internationally?* There are four basic global forms of business organization: domestic exporter, multinational, franchiser, and transnational. Each works best with a different systems configuration. Transnational firms must develop networked system configurations and permit considerable decentralization of development and operations. Franchisers tend to duplicate systems across many countries and use centralized financial controls. Multinationals typically rely on decentralized independence among foreign units with some movement toward development of networks. Domestic exporters typically are centralized in domestic headquarters with some decentralized operations permitted.

KEY TERMS

Bullwhip effect, 56

Collaborative commerce, 57

Customer relationship management (CRM), 52

Decision-support systems (DSS), 44

Desktop publishing, 43

Document imaging systems, 43

Domestic exporter, 63

Enterprise systems, 60

Executive support systems (ESS), 45

Finance and accounting information systems, 49

Franchiser, 63

Human resources information systems, 50

Knowledge-level systems, 39

Knowledge work systems (KWS), 42

Management information systems (MIS), 43

Management-level systems, 39

Manufacturing and production information systems, 47

Multinational, 63

Office systems, 42

Operational-level systems, 39

Private industrial networks, 58

Reverse logistics, 55

Sales and marketing information systems, 47

Strategic-level systems, 39

Supply chain, 54

Supply chain management, 54

Transnational, 63

Transaction processing systems (TPS), 41

Word processing, 42

REVIEW QUESTIONS

1. Identify and describe the four levels of the organizational hierarchy. What types of information systems serve each level?

2. List and briefly describe the major types of systems in organizations.

3. What are the five types of TPS in business organizations? What functions do they perform? Give examples of each.

4. Describe the functions performed by knowledge work and office systems and some typical applications of each.

5. What are the characteristics of MIS? How do MIS differ from TPS? From DSS?

6. What are the characteristics of DSS? How do they differ from those of ESS?

7. Describe the relationship between TPS, office systems, KWS, MIS, DSS, and ESS.

8. List and describe the information systems serving each of the major functional areas of a business.

9. What is a business process? Give two examples of processes for functional areas of the business and one example of a cross-functional process.

10. What is customer relationship management? Why is it so important to businesses? How do information systems facilitate customer relationship management?

11. What is supply chain management? What activities does it comprise? Why is it so important to businesses?

12. How do information systems facilitate supply chain management?

13. What is collaborative commerce? How can organizations benefit from it?

14. How can organizations benefit from participating in private industrial networks?

15. What are enterprise systems? How do they change the way an organization works?

16. What are the benefits and challenges of implementing enterprise systems?

17. Describe the four major types of global business organization and the system configuration that is most appropriate for supporting each type.

APPLICATION SOFTWARE EXERCISE

SPREADSHEET EXERCISE: IMPROVING SUPPLY CHAIN MANAGEMENT

You run a company that manufactures aircraft components. You have many competitors who are trying to offer lower prices and better service to customers and you are trying to determine if you can benefit from better supply chain management. At the Laudon Web site for Chapter 2 you can find a spreadsheet file that contains a list of all of the items that your firm has ordered from its suppliers over the past three months. The fields on the spreadsheet file include vendor name, vendor identification number, the purchaser's order number, item identification number and item description (for each item ordered from the vendor), the cost per item, number of units of the item ordered, the

total cost of each order, the vendor's accounts payable terms, promised shipping date, promised transit time, and actual arrival date for each order.

Prepare a recommendation of how you can use the data in this spreadsheet database to improve your supply chain management. You may wish to look at ways to identify preferred suppliers or other ways of improving the movement and production of your products. Some criteria you might consider include: the supplier's track record for on-time deliveries, suppliers offering the best accounts payable terms, and suppliers offering lower pricing when the same item can be provided by multiple suppliers. Use your spreadsheet software to prepare reports and, if appropriate, graphs to support your recommendations.

GROUP PROJECT

With a group of three or four other students, select a business using an industrial network for supply chain management. Use the Web, newspapers, journals, and computer or business magazines to find out more about that organization and its use of

information technology, and to provide links to other organizations. If possible, use presentation software to present your findings to the class.

TOOLS FOR INTERACTIVE LEARNING

■ INTERNET CONNECTION

The Internet Connection for this chapter will take you to a series of Web sites where you can complete an exercise to evaluate the use of supply chain management software. You can also use the Interactive Study Guide to test your knowledge of the topics in this chapter and get instant feedback when you need more practice.

■ ELECTRONIC BUSINESS PROJECT

At the Laudon Web site for Chapter 2 you will find an electronic business project for logistics planning.

■ CD-ROM

If you use the Multimedia Edition CD-ROM with this chapter, you can find an audio overview of the major themes of this chapter and bullet text summarizing the key points of the chapter.

CASE STUDY—*Can A&P Renew Itself with New Information Systems?*

Is A&P, the most famous supermarket chain in the United States, about to disappear? Maybe, but if it happens, it won't be immediately because management is fighting hard to survive. The Great Atlantic & Pacific Tea Co. (A&P's official name), headquartered in Montvale, New Jersey, had about 750 stores in 16 states, Washington D.C., and Ontario, Canada. These stores include the A&P chain but also the Food Emporium, SuperFresh, and Waldbaum's chains. They have about 24,400 full-time employees plus 56,600 part timers.

This "granddaddy" of grocery store chains was founded in 1859 and has been a leader right from the start. In the 1920s A&P was one of the first chains to offer store brands, such as A&P's Bokar Coffee. In 1937 it launched its own magazine, *Women's Day*. A&P became so large that in 1950 its annual revenue was second only to General Motors in the United States. However, by 1990 its sales were no longer growing, and it was facing stiff competition from such giant chains as Safeway and Kroger.

In 1993, 34-year old Christian Haub became the CEO of A&P. Haub is a member of the family that owns Germany's Tengelmann Group, which in turn holds 53 percent of A&P. Tengelmann is one of the 10 largest retailers in the world, with annual sales of about $25 billion. Haub immediately began to address A&P's problems. He launched a program he named the "Great Renewal" and rapidly closed more than 100 "underperforming" stores, while establishing a number of "superstores." Next he reorganized management into regional divisions, and in mid-1999 he hired Nicholas L. Ioli as A&P's senior vice president and CIO. Ioli, with strong and active support from Haub, immediately embarked on a project to reconstruct and modernize the company, including its whole supply chain.

A&P was facing a number of serious problems in addition to its stagnant sales. Its obsolete information technology infrastructure was composed of a complex web of stitched-together old legacy systems. The company was primarily using 12- to 20-year-old software running on two large mainframe computers. "We had extremely antiquated systems, from finance to merchandising to store and warehousing systems," explained Ioli. The company had fragmented distribution systems, resulting in little knowledge of what sells in which stores. Moreover, A&P's supply chain was not using the Web to work better and more inexpensively. The company also had outdated, ineffective business processes, such as not having systems to analyze data from either customers or suppliers.

The grocery business operates on high volumes of transactions and tiny profit margins of 1 to 2 percent of sales. In addition to traditional competitors, A&P was losing market share to new types of stores, such as Wal-Mart, that had entered the grocery business as part of their attempt to meet most home needs. Also the company was facing a challenge from discount club stores, such as Sam's Choice, and from convenience stores such as Seven-Eleven.

Haub's plan to revive A&P called for using new information systems to refocus the company on serving customers better and managing inventory more efficiently. Management expected the new systems to save about $325 million over four years by decreasing operating costs while making desirable products more easily available to customers. It also hoped the systems would eliminate inefficiencies in its supply chain. After that, Haub expected the project to result in an increase of $100 million annual pretax operating profits.

In March 2000, the company launched a $250 million project for a four-year redesign of its information systems. In describing the planned project, A&P estimated that, of the $250 million, 35 percent would be technology costs, whereas the remaining 65 percent would be for training, communications, and managing and measuring performance. One objective was to enable customers to use self-checkout lines to save time. Customers would even be able to order on the Web so, for example, they could order at work and pick up merchandise on the way home. Ioli expects the company to have store-specific data so that it can serve local customers. The project would also address A&P's technical staffing problems. Management plans to double A&P's IT department, from 150 people to 300. In addition, they will outsource noncore IT functions, which depend on the old legacy systems, so that A&P staff time is not wasted on such tasks. The project is planning for a Web-enabled, e-commerce supply chain and the modernization of other systems as well, replacing up to 95 percent of current applications. Ioli also expects to supervise training and other large-scale, change-management programs. Haub named the project "Great Renewal II" and set it up as a shared-risk partnership.

Wall Street's reaction was sharply negative. "The Great Renewal projects are absolutely needed, but they are significantly late," stated Mark Husson, a Merrill Lynch equity analyst. Analysts have criticized the project as being too expensive, thereby reducing company earnings and reducing shareholder value. Many analysts recommended that their clients sell the stock.

Ioli quickly turned to IBM as a consultant and partner for the Great Renewal project. Developing software was a major challenge, partly because there is very little prewritten software available for the grocery business. Most grocery retailers have to write their own software, which would be extremely time consuming and expensive for A&P. If the company did try to use the best prewritten software commercially available, it would have to create additional software to link different portions of the system together so they could communicate with each other. Creating this interface software would consume a great deal of time in a project that needed to be completed rapidly. Another possible solution was an enterprise system to integrate data and business processes for different functions. However, no ERP system had ever been designed specifically for the grocery business with its special problems, such as its need to move perishable items (fruits, vegetables, milk, ice cream, and meats) rapidly through the supply chain. Many products have to be purchased regionally. As a result, this would be "the first attempt to strategically reengineer a company and get as close to an ERP as we can" in the grocery industry, said Ioli. However, he added, "We believe the technology and functionality will allow us to move ahead of the competition."

A&P wanted a core system where all of its item and merchandising information would reside; it also wanted functionality for category management, merchandising, procurement, promotion, pricing, and forecasting, including the perishable side of the grocery industry. Management selected Retek, a small Minneapolis-based software company that had developed systems for European and Asian grocery chains and for other major retailers, such as Ann Taylor and Eckard.

Retek provided a merchandising system that A&P could use to execute core merchandising activities; a demand forecasting system to produce accurate forecasts for supply chain planning, allocation, and replenishment; a merchandising planning application; a retail intelligence tool that identifies opportunities; and a data warehouse for analyzing vast pools of transaction data to discern patterns of customer behavior and sales trends.

Many observers considered the project risky; A&P was betting the future of the company on new technology. The whole grocery business is watching A&P's project very closely. A&P had invested comparatively less in information technology than its rivals. "If A&P does succeed, it will reinforce the inclination of grocery chains and their senior management boards to bet their thin margin businesses on IT investments," explained Greg Girard, an analyst at Boston's AMR Research. Observers feared that the project and its budget would grow beyond what was originally targeted. Yet another fear concerns training and support once the software portion has been completed. With 750 stores, a lot of part-time help and high turnover, A&P has a great deal to absorb.

Numerous other companies have experienced enterprise system failures. Fox Meyer, a large drug distributor, was liquidated after its project failed, whereas profits for Hershey Foods were badly slashed when serious project problems forced it to miss the highly profitable Halloween and Christmas/New Year's rushes. In the grocery business, Nash Finch Co., a supermarket operator, lost more than $70 million when it abandoned its enterprise project, and A&P's project is much larger. To address these risks, the A&P project team has developed and uses an elaborate business plan that includes holding weekly meetings with top management, team leaders, and representatives from Retek and IBM.

The core portion of the project, retail application development, was divided into three stages: purchasing, merchandising, and inventory management. The new applications must communicate with several other major pieces of software: OMI International's warehouse management system, Manugistics's transportation system, and both Tomax's and SofTechnics's store systems. Oracle systems were selected for the financial and human resources functions. The first of the three development stages was scheduled to be completed by December 2000, and the transportation system was actually operating in Canada by February 2001. The project's primary teams include technical and development teams; a change management team; a business processes team; a team to oversee information technology; and a team of eight A&P employees who monitor the project, including its schedule and costs.

Sources: Susannah Patton, "Can I.T. Save A&P?" and "A More Perfect Union," *CIO Magazine*, February 15, 2001; Sami Lais, "A&P's $250M IT Plan Shunned by Wall Street," *Computerworld*, March 20, 2000; Retek Corp., "A&P's Project Great Renewal Powered by Retek and IBM," www.retek.com; and www.aptea.com.

CASE STUDY QUESTIONS

1. What problems did A&P have with its business? What management, organization, and technology factors contributed to those problems?

2. To what extent was the Great Renewal project a solution to those problems? What problems could system modernization solve? What A&P problems could it not solve?

3. How would implementing new systems change the way A&P ran its business?

4. Evaluate the chances of success for the Great Renewal project. What else do you think A&P needs to do if it is to be successful in redesigning its company? Explain your answers.

c h a p t e r
3

INFORMATION SYSTEMS, ORGANIZATIONS, MANAGEMENT, AND STRATEGY

objectives

As a manager, you'll need to know how to use information systems strategically and how systems can help you make better decisions. After completing this chapter, you will be able to answer the following questions:

1. *What do managers need to know about organizations in order to build and use information systems successfully?*
2. *What impact do information systems have on organizations?*
3. *How do information systems support the activities of managers in organizations?*
4. *How can businesses use information systems for competitive advantage?*
5. *Why is it so difficult to build successful information systems, including systems that promote competitive advantage?*

Can Textron Transform Itself with the Internet?

Textron is an old-line business that makes everything from corporate airplanes and power transmissions to turf mowers and sod cutters. Its aircraft division includes Bell Helicopter and Cessna Aircraft, and its automotive division supplies major automobile manufacturers with everything from airbag doors to modular fluid systems. Textron's industrial division is a world market leader in fasteners, which are used to bind two manufactured elements together. Textron Financial provides financial services and financing for company products. The company's track record is hard to match, with more than 44 consecutive quarters of earnings growth and earnings per share growing an average of 19 percent each year. Textron is among *Fortune* magazine's "Global Most Admired Companies" and *Industry Week* magazine's "Best Managed Companies."

So what's the problem? Textron's managers think that Textron is too much of a traditional conglomerate to keep on growing this way. The Internet has changed

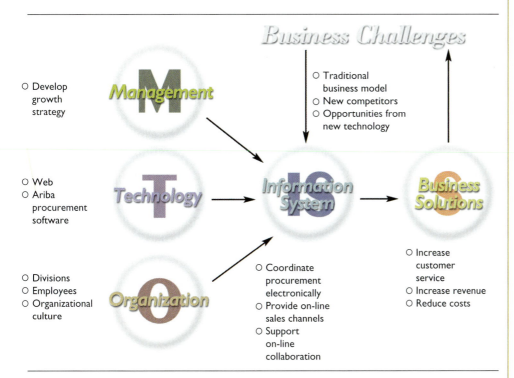

Business Challenges

○ Develop growth strategy

Management

○ Traditional business model
○ New competitors
○ Opportunities from new technology

○ Web
○ Ariba procurement software

Technology

Information System

Business Solutions

○ Divisions
○ Employees
○ Organizational culture

Organization

○ Coordinate procurement electronically
○ Provide on-line sales channels
○ Support on-line collaboration

○ Increase customer service
○ Increase revenue
○ Reduce costs

the rules of the game, and smaller competitors are starting to move more quickly and provide better customer service. Textron needs to become more nimble and responsive. Management would like employees to take advantage of the Internet to find more efficient ways to perform their jobs and to freely exchange information and ideas. Employees have been encouraged to "be curious, think differently, innovate."

Given Textron's structure and organizational culture, it's a tall order. Textron's four divisions have operated independently for many years, each with its own finance, human resources, and information technology departments. The company was unable to take maximum advantage of discounts for bulk orders because different Textron factories and facilities did their purchasing independently. Even products that were used by all Textron groups, such as copy paper, argon gas, or shop towels, were purchased by each division using different procedures for ordering.

Now Textron's leaders want to link the divisions together to reduce costs by standardizing procurement and streamlining other business processes. Using Ariba e-procurement software, Textron created an e-procurement system to be used by all of its divisions. All of Textron's purchasing catalogs are available on-line, and all purchases are executed electronically and uniformly. Prices for most products are prenegotiated. Textron expects to save $150 million by 2002 through e-procurement alone. Textron is also trying to standardize Internet services and to consolidate all the different computer networks run by its divisions into a single company-wide network.

Textron now has 50 Web sites up and running. Although a few merely provide on-line brochures for electronic and cable-testing equipment, others have more extensive e-commerce capabilities. Textron's Assetcontrol.com Web site provides an on-line marketplace for millions of dollars worth of assets the company no longer needs. In 2000 it sold $12 million worth of inventory, a 388 percent increase over the previous year. Textron Financial can now take on-line applications for 50 percent of its business.

Textron has other plans for Internet technology as well. It would like to consolidate human resources activities across divisions. Benefits information could be placed on-line and job applicant resumes could be shared across all divisions. The Internet could help Textron improve supply chain management and customer service by making it easier to produce only the products customers have ordered.

Will these efforts result in success for Textron? Management thinks that much more innovation and change are required. According to Ken Bohlen, Textron's chief innovation officer, "The Internet part is easy. A lot of what we are talking about is cultural." Textron's traditional corporate culture did not promote sharing ideas across divisions, and the company's future depends on finding more ways to unlock innovation.

Sources: John Galvin, "Manufacturing the Future," *Smart Business Magazine,* March 2001; and "Textron Honors Breakthrough Innovations," Textron Public Relations, www.Textron.com, accessed July 31, 2001.

MANAGEMENT CHALLENGES

Textron's story illustrates the interdependence of business environments, organizational culture, management strategy, and the development of information systems. Textron is attempting to create a series of Internet-based information systems in response to changes in competitive pressures from its surrounding environment, but this systems effort cannot succeed without a significant amount of organizational and management change. The new information system is changing the way Textron runs its business and makes management decisions. Textron's experience raises the following management challenges:

1. **Sustainability of competitive advantage.** The competitive advantages strategic systems confer do not necessarily last long enough to ensure long-term profitability. Because competitors can retaliate and copy strategic systems, competitive advantage isn't always sustainable. Markets, customer expectations, and technology change. The Internet can make competitive advantage disappear very quickly as virtually all companies can use this technology (Porter, 2001). Classic strategic systems, such as American Airlines's SABRE computerized reservation system, Citibank's ATM system, and Federal Express's package tracking system, benefited by being the first in their industries. Then rival systems emerged. Information systems alone cannot provide an enduring business advantage. Systems originally intended to be strategic frequently become tools for survival, required by every firm to stay in business, or they may inhibit organizations from making the strategic changes essentials for future success (Eardley, Avison, and Powell, 1997).

2. **Fitting technology to the organization (or vice-versa).** On the one hand, it is important to align information technology to the business plan, to the firm's business processes, and to senior management's strategic business plans. Information technology is, after all, supposed to serve the organization. On the other hand, these business plans, processes, and management strategy all may be very outdated or incompatible with the envisioned technology. In such instances, managers will need to change the organization to fit the technology or to adjust both the organization and the technology to achieve an optimal "fit."

This chapter explores the relationships between organizations, management, information systems, and business strategy. We introduce the features of organizations that you will need to understand when you design, build, and operate information systems. We also scrutinize the role of a manager and the management decision-making process, identifying areas where information systems can enhance managerial effectiveness. We conclude by examining the problems firms face from competition and the ways in which information systems can provide competitive advantage.

3.1   ORGANIZATIONS AND INFORMATION SYSTEMS

Information systems and organizations influence one another. Information systems must be aligned with the organization to provide information that important groups within the organization need. At the same time, the organization must be aware of and be open to the influences of information systems in order to benefit from new technologies.

The interaction between information technology and organizations is very complex and is influenced by a great many mediating factors, including the organization's structure, standard operating procedures, politics, culture, surrounding environment, and management decisions (see Figure 3-1). Managers must be aware that information systems can markedly alter life in the organization. They cannot successfully design new systems or understand existing systems without understanding organizations. Managers do decide what systems will be built, what they will do, how they will be implemented, and so forth. Sometimes, however, the outcomes are the result of pure chance and of both good and bad luck.

WHAT IS AN ORGANIZATION?

An **organization** is a stable, formal, social structure that takes resources from the environment and processes them to produce outputs. This technical definition focuses on three elements of an organization. Capital and labor are primary production factors provided by the environment. The organization (the firm) transforms these inputs into products and services in a production function. The products and services are consumed by environments in return for supply inputs (see Figure 3-2). An organization is more stable than an informal group (such as a group of friends that meets every Friday for lunch) in terms of longevity and routineness. Organizations are formal legal entities, with internal rules and procedures, that must abide by laws. Organizations are also social structures because they are a collection of social elements, much as a machine has a structure—a particular arrangement of valves, cams, shafts, and other parts.

This definition of organizations is powerful and simple, but it is not very descriptive or even predictive of real-world organizations. A more realistic behavioral definition of an **organization** is that it is a collection of rights, privileges, obligations, and responsibilities that are delicately balanced over a period of time through conflict and conflict resolution (see Figure 3-3). In this behavioral view of the firm, people who work in organizations develop customary ways of working; they gain attachments to existing relationships; and they make

organization (technical definition)
A stable, formal, social structure that takes resources from the environment and processes them to produce outputs.

organization (behavioral definition)
A collection of rights, privileges, obligations, and responsibilities that are delicately balanced over a period of time through conflict and conflict resolution.

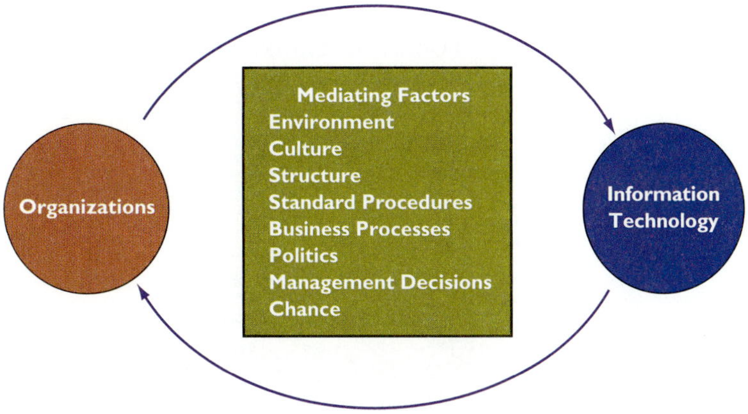

Figure 3-1 The two-way relationship between organizations and information technology. This complex two-way relationship is mediated by many factors, not the least of which are the decisions made—or not made—by managers. Other factors mediating the relationship include the organizational culture, bureaucracy, politics, business processes, and pure chance.

Organizations ⟷ Mediating Factors: Environment, Culture, Structure, Standard Procedures, Business Processes, Politics, Management Decisions, Chance ⟷ Information Technology

Figure 3-2 The technical microeconomic definition of the organization. In the microeconomic definition of organizations, capital and labor (the primary production factors provided by the environment) are transformed by the firm through the production process into products and services (outputs to the environment). The products and services are consumed by the environment, which supplies additional capital and labor as inputs in the feedback loop.

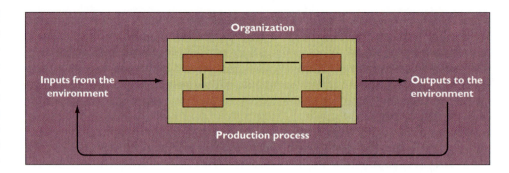

arrangements with subordinates and superiors about how work will be done, how much work will be done, and under what conditions. Most of these arrangements and feelings are not discussed in any formal rule book.

How do these definitions of organizations relate to information system technology? A technical view of organizations encourages us to focus on the way inputs are combined into outputs when technology changes are introduced into the company. The firm is seen as infinitely malleable, with capital and labor substituting for each other quite easily. But the more realistic behavioral definition of an organization suggests that building new information systems or rebuilding old ones involves much more than a technical rearrangement of machines or workers—that some information systems change the organizational balance of rights, privileges, obligations, responsibilities, and feelings that have been established over a long period of time.

Technological change requires changes in who owns and controls information, who has the right to access and update that information, and who makes decisions about whom, when, and how. For instance, Textron is hoping to use Internet technology to provide employees with more information so that they can innovate and make more decisions on their own. This more complex view forces us to look at the way work is designed and the procedures used to achieve outputs.

The technical and behavioral definitions of organizations are not contradictory. Indeed, they complement each other: The technical definition tells us how thousands of firms in competitive markets combine capital, labor, and information technology, whereas the behavioral model takes us inside the individual firm to see how that technology affects the organization's inner workings. Section 3.2 describes how each of these definitions of organizations can help explain the relationships between information systems and organizations.

Some features of organizations are common to all organizations; others distinguish one organization from another. Let us look first at the features common to all organizations.

COMMON FEATURES OF ORGANIZATIONS

You might not think that Apple Computer, United Airlines, and the Aspen, Colorado, Police Department have much in common, but they do. In some respects, all modern organizations are alike because they share the characteristics that are listed in Table 3-1. A German sociol-

Figure 3-3 The behavioral view of organizations. The behavioral view of organizations emphasizes group relationships, values, and structures.

TABLE 3-1	**STRUCTURAL CHARACTERISTICS OF ALL ORGANIZATIONS**

Clear division of labor

Hierarchy

Explicit rules and procedures

Impartial judgments

Technical qualifications for positions

Maximum organizational efficiency

ogist, Max Weber, was the first to describe these "ideal-typical" characteristics of organizations in 1911. He called organizations **bureaucracies** that have certain "structural" features.

According to Weber, all modern bureaucracies have a clear-cut division of labor and specialization. Organizations arrange specialists in a hierarchy of authority in which everyone is accountable to someone and authority is limited to specific actions. Authority and action are further limited by abstract rules or procedures (standard operating procedures, or SOPs) that are interpreted and applied to specific cases. These rules create a system of impartial and universal decision making; everyone is treated equally. Organizations try to hire and promote employees on the basis of technical qualifications and professionalism (not personal connections). The organization is devoted to the principle of efficiency: maximizing output using limited inputs.

According to Weber, bureaucracies are prevalent because they are the most efficient form of organization. Other scholars have supplemented Weber, identifying additional features of organizations. All organizations develop standard operating procedures, politics, and cultures.

bureaucracy
Formal organization with a clear-cut division of labor, abstract rules and procedures, and impartial decision making that uses technical qualifications and professionalism as a basis for promoting employees.

Standard Operating Procedures

Organizations that survive over time become very efficient, producing a limited number of products and services by following standard routines. These standard routines become codified into reasonably precise rules, procedures, and practices called **standard operating procedures (SOPs)** that are developed to cope with virtually all expected situations. Some of these rules and procedures are written, formal procedures. Most are "rules of thumb" to be followed in select situations. Business processes are based on standard operating procedures.

These standard operating procedures have a great deal to do with the efficiency that modern organizations attain. For instance, in the assembly of a car, managers and workers develop complex standard procedures to handle thousands of motions in a precise fashion, permitting the finished product to roll off the assembly line. Any change in SOPs requires an enormous organizational effort. Indeed, the organization may need to halt the entire production process before the old SOPs can be retired.

Difficulty in changing standard operating procedures is one reason Detroit automakers have been slow to adopt Japanese mass-production methods. For many years, U.S. automakers followed Henry Ford's mass-production principles. Ford believed that the cheapest way to build a car was to churn out the largest number of autos by having workers repeatedly perform a simple task. By contrast, Japanese automakers have emphasized "lean production" methods whereby a smaller number of workers, each performing several tasks, can produce cars with less inventory, less investment, and fewer mistakes. Workers have multiple job responsibilities and are encouraged to stop production in order to correct a problem.

standard operating procedures (SOPs)
Precise rules, procedures, and practices developed by organizations to cope with virtually all expected situations.

Organizational Politics

People in organizations occupy different positions with different specialties, concerns, and perspectives. As a result, they naturally have divergent viewpoints about how resources, rewards, and punishments should be distributed. These differences matter to both managers and employees, and they result in political struggle, competition, and conflict within every organization. Political resistance is one of the great difficulties of bringing about organizational change—especially the development of new information systems. Virtually all information systems that bring about significant changes in goals, procedures, productivity, and personnel are politically charged and will elicit serious political opposition.

Organizational Culture

All organizations have bedrock, unassailable, unquestioned (by the members) assumptions that define their goals and products. **Organizational culture** is this set of fundamental assumptions about what products the organization should produce, how it should produce them, where, and for whom. Generally, these cultural assumptions are taken totally for granted and are rarely publicly announced or spoken about (Schein, 1985).

You can see organizational culture at work by looking around your university or college. Some bedrock assumptions of university life are that professors know more than students, the reason students attend college is to learn, and classes follow a regular schedule. Organizational culture is a powerful unifying force that restrains political conflict and promotes common understanding, agreement on procedures, and common practices. If we all share the same basic cultural assumptions, then agreement on other matters is more likely.

At the same time, organizational culture is a powerful restraint on change, especially technological change. Most organizations will do almost anything to avoid making changes in basic assumptions. Any technological change that threatens commonly held cultural assumptions usually meets a great deal of resistance. However, there are times when the only sensible way for a firm to move forward is to employ a new technology that directly opposes an existing organizational culture. When this occurs, the technology is often stalled while the culture slowly adjusts.

UNIQUE FEATURES OF ORGANIZATIONS

Although all organizations do have common characteristics, no two organizations are identical. Organizations have different structures, goals, constituencies, leadership styles, tasks, and surrounding environments.

Different Organizational Types

One important way in which organizations differ is in their structure or shape. The differences among organizational structures are characterized in many ways. Mintzberg's classification, described in Table 3-2, identifies five basic kinds of organizations (Mintzberg, 1979).

Organizations and Environments

Organizations reside in environments from which they draw resources and to which they supply goods and services. Organizations and environments have a reciprocal relationship. On

---

TABLE 3-2   ORGANIZATIONAL STRUCTURES

Organizational Type	Description	Example
Entrepreneurial structure	Young, small firm in a fast-changing environment. It has a simple structure and is managed by an entrepreneur serving as its single chief executive officer.	Small start-up business
Machine bureaucracy	Large bureaucracy existing in a slowly changing environment, producing standard products. It is dominated by a centralized management team and centralized decision making.	Midsize manufacturing firm
Divisionalized bureaucracy	Combination of multiple machine bureaucracies, each producing a different product or service, all topped by one central headquarters.	Fortune 500 firms such as General Motors
Professional bureaucracy	Knowledge-based organization where goods and services depend on the expertise and knowledge of professionals. Dominated by department heads with weak centralized authority.	Law firms, school systems, hospitals
Adhocracy	"Task force" organization that must respond to rapidly changing environments. Consists of large groups of specialists organized into short-lived multidisciplinary teams and has weak central management.	Consulting firms such as the Rand Corporation

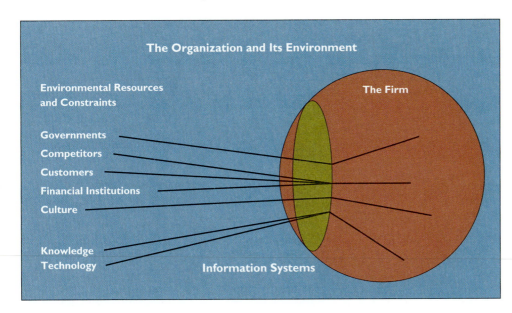

Figure 3-4 Environments and organizations have a reciprocal relationship. Environments shape what organizations can do, but organizations can influence their environments and decide to change environments altogether. Information technology plays a critical role in helping organizations perceive environmental change, and in helping organizations act on their environment. Information systems act as a filter between organizations and their environments.

the one hand, organizations are open to, and dependent on, the social and physical environment that surrounds them. Without financial and human resources—people willing to work reliably and consistently for a set wage or revenue from customers—organizations could not exist. Organizations must respond to legislative and other requirements imposed by government, as well as the actions of customers and competitors. On the other hand, organizations can influence their environments. Organizations form alliances with others to influence the political process; they advertise to influence customer acceptance of their products.

Figure 3-4 shows that information systems play an important role in helping organizations perceive changes in their environments and also in helping organizations act on their environments. Information systems are key instruments for *environmental scanning*, helping managers identify external changes that might require an organizational response.

Environments generally change much faster than organizations. The main reasons for organizational failure are an inability to adapt to a rapidly changing environment and a lack of resources—particularly among young firms—to sustain even short periods of troubled times (Freeman et al., 1983). New technologies, new products, and changing public tastes and values (many of which result in new government regulations) put strains on any organization's culture, politics, and people. Most organizations do not cope well with large environmental shifts. The inertia built into an organization's standard operating procedures, the political conflict raised by changes to the existing order, and the threat to closely held cultural values typically inhibit organizations from making significant changes. It is not surprising that only 10 percent of the Fortune 500 companies in 1919 still exist today.

Other Differences Among Organizations

Organizations have different shapes or structures for many other reasons also. They differ in their ultimate goals and the types of power used to achieve them. Some organizations have coercive goals (e.g., prisons); others have utilitarian goals (e.g., businesses). Still others have normative goals (universities, religious groups). Organizations also serve different groups or have different constituencies, some primarily benefiting their members, others benefiting clients, stockholders, or the public. The nature of leadership differs greatly from one organization to another—some organizations may be more democratic or authoritarian than others. Another way organizations differ is by the tasks they perform and the technology they use. Some organizations perform primarily routine tasks that could be reduced to formal rules that require little judgment (such as manufacturing auto parts), whereas others (such as consulting firms) work primarily with nonroutine tasks.

As you can see in Table 3-3, the list of unique features of organizations is longer than the common features list. It stands to reason that information systems will have different impacts on different types of organizations. Different organizations in different circumstances will

TABLE 3-3	A SUMMARY OF SALIENT FEATURES OF ORGANIZATIONS

Common Features	Unique Features
Formal structure	Organizational type
Standard operating procedures (SOPs)	Environments
Politics	Goals
Culture	Power
	Constituencies
	Function
	Leadership
	Tasks
	Technology
	Business processes

Window on Organizations

MIS In Action

E-COMMERCE, CHINESE STYLE

China is surely one of the most exciting countries to think about when contemplating the future use of Internet-based electronic commerce. It is the largest country in the world with well over 1.3 billion people, and for a decade or more it has had one of the fastest growing economies on the planet. One forward-looking company is Sata, a Chinese-brand hand-tool manufacturer and division of Danaher Tool (Shanghai) Limited, which in turn is a subsidiary of Fortune 500 Danaher Corporation. Sata has established a Web site, Satatools.com, with a goal of having all orders in China coming through the Web by the end of 2001. However, Sata, along with any Chinese e-commerce enterprise, faces many impediments.

As fast as China's economy is growing, it is still a poor country. Moreover, business cannot consider China as a free enterprise country because of its strong economic, political, and speech controls, including controls over the Internet. Perhaps the biggest problem, however, is that China is still in the early stages of using the Internet. In 2001 it had about 36 million users, less than 3 percent of China's population. Much has to happen before e-commerce can play a major role in China.

One underlying problem is that most Chinese companies as well as large multinationals in China spend less than 1 percent of their income per year on information technology. Many companies do not have Internet connections and often do not have the technical ability to move ahead. Many companies do not even have computers. Sata has to train its customers to use the Internet. Another problem that is almost as basic is that both good software written in Chinese and domestic computer support are not available. Derek Palaschuk, the vice president of finance of Sohu.com, a popular Chinese information portal and

seller of such products as books and CDs, says, "There isn't a local company that we can call on to provide us with [the] world-class service you would have in the U.S." Even if a company could develop its own B2B software, as has Sata, the back-end systems of most companies are not adequately developed to support such trade. In many cases, one would have to reorganize a Chinese company in order to use software that's been developed overseas.

Another major problem is that China does not have the legal guarantees to protect businesses, particularly if their security is compromised. Related to that and critical to the expansion of e-commerce, are the legal and cultural roadblocks to paying for products over the Internet. Without adequate legal protection, purchasers are afraid of losses caused by Internet transactions. Neither credit cards nor debit cards are widely used in China. People are unaccustomed to buying goods without looking them over first. "The majority still prefer to buy anything with cash," said Vivian Zhao, the e-business director at GE (China) Co. in Beijing. Sixty percent of sales are cash-on-delivery (COD) using bicycle couriers for delivery, whereas 35 percent of purchases are paid for at the post office. Even delivery is a major problem, although the road and railroad infrastructures are improving. The encouraging sign is that companies like Sata are starting to risk using e-commerce as a primary tool in China.

To Think About: What organizational factors describe why China is so slow in adopting e-commerce? How would a company's management, organization, and technology have to change to either purchase or sell goods in China?

Sources: Steven Schwankert, "Global Value Chain Comes to China," *Internet World,* August 1, 2001; and Carol Sliwa, "China: The Web's Next Frontier?" *Computerworld,* May 28, 2001.

experience different effects from the same technology. The Window on Organizations shows, for example, how China's unique environment, culture, and organizational characteristics have affected Internet use and electronic commerce. Only by close analysis of a specific organization can a manager effectively design and manage information systems.

3.2 THE CHANGING ROLE OF INFORMATION SYSTEMS IN ORGANIZATIONS

Information systems have become integral, on-line, interactive tools deeply involved in the minute-to-minute operations and decision making of large organizations. We now describe the changing role of systems in organizations and how it has been shaped by the interaction of organizations and information technology.

INFORMATION TECHNOLOGY INFRASTRUCTURE AND INFORMATION TECHNOLOGY SERVICES

One way that organizations can influence how information technology will be used is through decisions about the technical and organizational configuration of systems. Previous chapters described the ever-widening role of information systems in organizations. Supporting this widening role have been changes in information technology (IT) infrastructure, which we defined in Chapter 1. Each organization determines exactly how its infrastructure will be configured. Chapters 6 through 9 detail the various technology alternatives that organizations can use to design their infrastructures.

Another way that organizations have affected information technology is through decisions about who will design, build and maintain the organization's IT infrastructure. These decisions determine how information technology services will be delivered.

The formal organizational unit or function responsible for technology services is called the **information systems department.** The information systems department is responsible for maintaining the hardware, software, data storage, and networks that comprise the firm's IT infrastructure.

The information systems department consists of specialists, such as programmers, systems analysts, project leaders, and information systems managers (see Figure 3-5). **Programmers** are highly trained technical specialists who write the software instructions for the computer. **Systems analysts** constitute the principal liaisons between the information systems groups and the rest of the organization. It is the systems analyst's job to translate business problems and requirements into information requirements and systems. **Information systems managers** are leaders of teams of programmers and analysts, project managers, physical facility managers, telecommunications managers, and heads of office system groups. They are also managers of computer operations and data entry staff. Also external specialists, such as hardware vendors and manufacturers, software firms, and consultants

information systems department
The formal organizational unit that is responsible for the information systems function in the organization.

programmers
Highly trained technical specialists who write computer software instructions.

systems analysts
Specialists who translate business problems and requirements into information requirements and systems, acting as liaisons between the information systems department and the rest of the organization.

information systems managers
Leaders of the various specialists in the information systems department.

THE ORGANIZATION
Senior management
Major end users (divisions)

Information Systems Department

IT Infrastructure
Hardware
Software
Data storage
Networks

Information Systems Specialists
CIO
Managers
Systems analysts
Systems designers
Programmers
Network specialists
Database administrator
Clerical

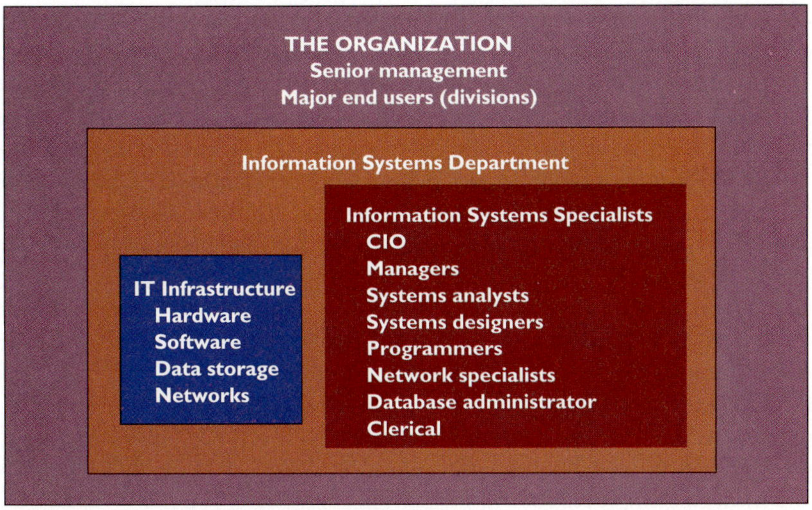

Figure 3-5 Information technology services. Many types of specialists and groups are responsible for the design and management of the organization's information technology (IT) infrastructure.

frequently participate in the day-to-day operations and long-term planning of information systems.

In many companies, the information systems department is headed by a **chief information officer (CIO)**. The CIO is a senior management position that oversees the use of information technology in the firm.

End users are representatives of departments outside of the information systems group for whom applications are developed. These users are playing an increasingly large role in the design and development of information systems.

In the early years, the information systems group was composed mostly of programmers, who performed very highly specialized but limited technical functions. Today a growing proportion of staff members are systems analysts and network specialists, with the information systems department acting as a powerful change agent in the organization. The information systems department suggests new business strategies and new information-based products and services, and coordinates both the development of the technology and the planned changes in the organization.

In the past, firms generally built their own software and managed their own computing facilities. Today, many firms are turning to external vendors to provide these services (see Chapters 6, 9, and 12) and using their information systems departments to manage these service providers.

How Information Systems Affect Organizations

How have changes in information technology affected organizations? To find answers, we draw on research and theory based on both economic and behavioral approaches.

Economic Theories

From an economic standpoint, information system technology can be viewed as a factor of production that can be freely substituted for capital and labor. As the cost of information system technology falls, it is substituted for labor, which historically has been a rising cost. Hence, information technology should result in a decline in the number of middle managers and clerical workers as information technology substitutes for their labor.

Information technology also helps firms contract in size because it can reduce transaction costs—the costs incurred when a firm buys on the marketplace what it cannot make itself. According to **transaction cost theory**, firms and individuals seek to economize on transaction costs, much as they do on production costs. Using markets is expensive (Williamson, 1985; Coase, 1937) because of costs such as locating and communicating with distant suppliers, monitoring contract compliance, buying insurance, obtaining information on products, and so forth. Traditionally, firms have tried to reduce transaction costs by getting bigger, hiring more employees or buying their own suppliers and distributors, as General Motors used to do.

Information technology, especially the use of networks, can help firms lower the cost of market participation (transaction costs), making it worthwhile for firms to contract with external suppliers instead of using internal sources. For example, by using computer links to external suppliers, the Chrysler Corporation can achieve economies by obtaining more than 70 percent of its parts from the outside. Figure 3-6 shows that as transaction costs decrease, firm size (the number of employees) should shrink because it becomes easier and cheaper for the firm to contract for the purchase of goods and services in the marketplace rather than to make the product or service itself. Firm size can stay constant or contract even if the company increases its revenues. (For example, General Electric reduced its workforce from about 400,000 people in the early 1980s to about 230,000 while increasing revenues 150 percent.)

Information technology also can reduce internal management costs. According to **agency theory**, the firm is viewed as a "nexus of contracts" among self-interested individuals rather than as a unified, profit-maximizing entity (Jensen and Meckling, 1976). A principal (owner) employs "agents" (employees) to perform work on his or her behalf. However, agents need constant supervision and management because otherwise they will tend to pursue their own interests rather than those of the owners. As firms grow in size and scope, agency costs or coordination costs rise, because owners must expend more and more effort supervising and managing employees.

chief information officer (CIO)
Senior manager in charge of the information systems function in the firm.

end users
Representatives of departments outside the information systems group for whom applications are developed.

transaction cost theory
Economic theory stating that firms grow larger because they can conduct marketplace transactions internally more cheaply than they can with external firms in the marketplace.

agency theory
Economic theory that views the firm as a nexus of contracts among self-interested individuals who must be supervised and managed.

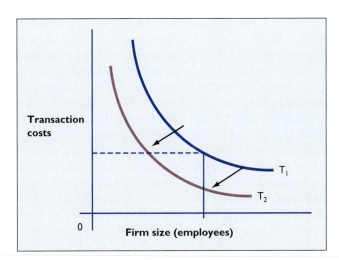

Figure 3-6 The transaction cost theory of the impact of information technology on the organization. Firms traditionally grew in size in order to reduce transaction costs. IT potentially reduces the costs for a given size, shifting the transaction cost curve inward, opening up the possibility of revenue growth without increasing size, or even revenue growth accompanied by shrinking size.

Information technology, by reducing the costs of acquiring and analyzing information, permits organizations to reduce agency costs because it becomes easier for managers to oversee a greater number of employees. Figure 3-7 shows that by reducing overall management costs, information technology allows firms to increase revenues while shrinking the number of middle management and clerical workers. We have seen examples in earlier chapters where information technology expanded the power and scope of small organizations by allowing them to perform coordinating activities such as processing orders or keeping track of inventory with very few clerks and managers.

Behavioral Theories

Although economic theories try to explain how large numbers of firms act in the marketplace, behavioral theories from sociology, psychology, and political science are more useful for describing the behavior of individual firms. Behavioral research has found little evidence that information systems automatically transform organizations, although the systems may be instrumental in accomplishing this goal once senior management decides to pursue this end.

Behavioral researchers have theorized that information technology could change the hierarchy of decision making in organizations by lowering the costs of information acquisition and broadening the distribution of information (Malone, 1997). Information technology could bring information directly from operating units to senior managers, thereby eliminating middle managers and their clerical support workers. Information technology could permit senior managers to contact lower-level operating units directly by using networked telecommunications and computers, eliminating middle management intermediaries. Information technology could also distribute information directly to lower-level workers, who could then make their own decisions based on their own knowledge and information without any management

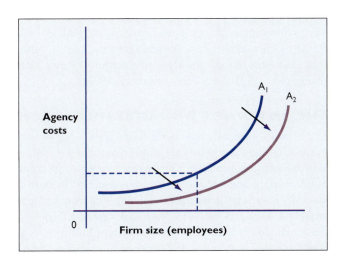

Figure 3-7 The agency cost theory of the impact of information technology on the organization. As firms grow in size and complexity, traditionally they experience rising agency costs. IT shifts the agency cost curve down and to the right, allowing firms to increase size while lowering agency costs.

intervention. However, some research suggests that computerization increases the information given to middle managers, empowering them to make more important decisions than in the past, thus reducing the need for large numbers of lower-level workers (Shore, 1983).

In postindustrial societies, authority increasingly relies on knowledge and competence, and not merely on formal positions. Hence, the shape of organizations should "flatten," because professional workers tend to be self-managing; and decision making should become more decentralized as knowledge and information become more widespread throughout (Drucker, 1988). Information technology may encourage "task force" networked organizations in which groups of professionals come together—face-to-face or electronically—for short periods of time to accomplish a specific task (e.g., designing a new automobile); once the task is accomplished, the individuals join other task forces. More firms may operate as **virtual organizations**, where work no longer is tied to geographic location. Virtual organizations use networks to link people, assets, and ideas. They can ally with suppliers, customers, and sometimes even competitors to create and distribute new products and services without being limited by traditional organizational boundaries or physical locations. For example, Calyx and Corolla is a networked virtual organization selling fresh flowers directly to customers, bypassing traditional florists. The firm takes orders via telephone or from its Web site and transmits them to grower farms, which ship them in Federal Express vans directly to customers.

Who makes sure that self-managed teams do not head off in the wrong direction? Who decides which person works on what team and for how long? How can managers evaluate the performance of someone who is constantly rotating from team to team? How do people know where their careers are headed? New approaches for evaluating, organizing, and informing workers are required; and not all companies can make virtual work effective (Davenport and Pearlson, 1998).

No one knows the answers to these questions, and it is not clear that all modern organizations will undergo this transformation. General Motors, for example, may have many self-managed knowledge workers in certain divisions, but it still will have a manufacturing division structured as a large, traditional bureaucracy. In general, the shape of organizations historically changes with the business cycle and with the latest management fashions. When times are good and profits are high, firms hire large numbers of supervisory personnel; when times are tough, they let go many of these same people (Mintzberg, 1979).

Another behavioral approach views information systems as the outcome of political competition between organizational subgroups for influence over the organization's policies, procedures, and resources (Laudon, 1974; Keen, 1981; Kling, 1980; Laudon, 1986). Information systems inevitably become bound up in organizational politics because they influence access to a key resource—namely, information. Information systems can affect who does what to whom, when, where, and how in an organization. Because information systems potentially change an organization's structure, culture, politics, and work, there is often considerable resistance to them when they are introduced.

There are several ways to visualize organizational resistance. Leavitt (1965) used a diamond shape to illustrate the interrelated and mutually adjusting character of technology and organization (see Figure 3-8). Here, changes in technology are absorbed, deflected, and defeated by organizational task arrangements, structures, and people. In this model, the only way to bring about change is to change the technology, tasks, structure, and people simultaneously. Other authors have spoken about the need to "unfreeze" organizations before introducing an innovation, quickly implementing it, and "refreezing" or institutionalizing the change (Kolb, 1970; Alter and Ginzberg, 1978).

THE INTERNET AND ORGANIZATIONS

The Internet, especially the World Wide Web, is beginning to have an important impact on the relationships between firms and external entities, and even on the organization of business processes inside a firm. The Internet increases the accessibility, storage, and distribution of information and knowledge for organizations. In essence, the Internet is capable of dramatically lowering the transaction and agency costs facing most organizations. For instance, brokerage firms and banks in New York can now "deliver" their internal-operations procedures manuals to their employees at distant locations by posting them on their corporate Web sites, saving millions of dollars in distribution costs. A global sales force can receive

---

virtual organization

Organization using networks to link people, assets, and ideas to create and distribute products and services without being limited to traditional organizational boundaries or physical locations.

nearly instant price product information updates via the Web or instructions from management via e-mail. Vendors of some large retailers can access retailers' internal Web sites directly for up-to-the-minute sales information and initiate replenishment orders instantly.

Businesses are rapidly rebuilding some of their key business processes based on Internet technology and making this technology a key component of their information technology (IT) infrastructures. If prior networking is any guide, one result will be simpler business processes, fewer employees, and much flatter organizations than in the past.

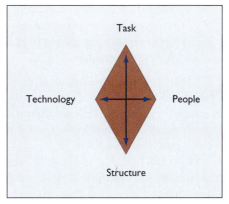

Figure 3-8 Organizational resistance and the mutually adjusting relationship between technology and the organization. Implementing information systems has consequences for task arrangements, structures, and people. According to this model, in order to implement change, all four components must be changed simultaneously.
Source: Leavitt, 1965.

3.3 MANAGERS, DECISION MAKING, AND INFORMATION SYSTEMS

To determine how information systems can benefit managers, we must first examine what managers do and what information they need for decision making and other functions. We must also understand how decisions are made and what kinds of decisions can be supported by formal information systems.

THE ROLE OF MANAGERS IN ORGANIZATIONS

Managers play a key role in organizations. Their responsibilities range from making decisions, to writing reports, to attending meetings, to arranging birthday parties. We can better understand managerial functions and roles by examining classical and contemporary models of managerial behavior.

Classical Descriptions of Management

The **classical model of management,** which describes what managers do, was largely unquestioned for more than 70 years since the 1920s. Henri Fayol and other early writers first described the five classical functions of managers as planning, organizing, coordinating, deciding, and controlling. This description of management activities dominated management thought for a long time, and it is still popular today.

But these terms describe formal managerial functions and are unsatisfactory as a description of what managers actually do. The terms do not address what managers do when they plan, decide things, and control the work of others. We need a more fine-grained understanding of how managers actually behave.

classical model of management
Traditional description of management that focused on its formal functions of planning, organizing, coordinating, deciding, and controlling.

Behavioral Models

Contemporary behavioral scientists have observed that managers do not behave as the classical model of management led us to believe. Kotter (1982), for example, describes the morning activities of the president of an investment management firm.

7:35 A.M. Richardson arrives at work, unpacks her briefcase, gets some coffee, and begins making a list of activities for the day.

7:45 A.M. Bradshaw (a subordinate) and Richardson converse about a number of topics and exchange pictures recently taken on summer vacations.

8:00 A.M. They talk about a schedule of priorities for the day.

8:20 A.M. Wilson (a subordinate) and Richardson talk about some personnel problems, cracking jokes in the process.

8:45 A.M. Richardson's secretary arrives, and they discuss her new apartment and arrangements for a meeting later in the morning.

8:55 A.M. Richardson goes to a morning meeting run by one of her subordinates. Thirty people are there, and Richardson reads during the meeting.

11:05 A.M. Richardson and her subordinates return to the office and discuss a difficult problem. They try to define the problem and outline possible alternatives. She lets the discussion roam away from and back to the topic again and again. Finally, they agree on a next step.

In this example, it is difficult to determine which activities constitute Richardson's planning, coordinating, and decision making. **Behavioral models** state that the actual behavior of managers appears to be less systematic, more informal, less reflective, more reactive, less well-organized, and much more frivolous than students of information systems and decision making generally expect it to be.

Observers find that managerial behavior actually has five attributes that differ greatly from the classical description: First, managers perform a great deal of work at an unrelenting pace—studies have found that managers engage in more than 600 different activities each day, with no break in their pace. Second, managerial activities are fragmented; most activities last for less than nine minutes; only 10 percent of the activities exceed one hour in duration. Third, managers prefer speculation, hearsay, gossip—they want current, specific, and ad hoc information (printed information often will be too old). Fourth, they prefer oral forms of communication to written forms because oral media provide greater flexibility, require less effort, and bring a faster response. Fifth, managers give high priority to maintaining a diverse and complex web of contacts that acts as an informal information system and helps them execute their personal agendas and short- and long-term goals.

Analyzing managers' day-to-day behavior, Mintzberg found that it could be classified into 10 **managerial roles**. Managerial roles are expectations of the activities that managers should perform in an organization. Mintzberg found that these managerial roles fell into three categories: interpersonal, informational, and decisional.

Interpersonal Roles   Managers act as figureheads for the organization when they represent their companies to the outside world and perform symbolic duties such as giving out employee awards. Managers act as leaders, attempting to motivate, counsel, and support subordinates. Managers also act as liaisons between various organizational levels; within each of these levels, they serve as liaisons among the members of the management team. Managers provide time and favors, which they expect to be returned.

Informational Roles   Managers act as the nerve centers of their organization, receiving the most concrete, up-to-date information and redistributing it to those who need to be aware of it. Managers are therefore information disseminators and spokespersons for their organizations.

Decisional Roles   Managers make decisions. They act as entrepreneurs by initiating new kinds of activities; they handle disturbances arising in the organization; they allocate resources to staff members who need them; and they negotiate conflicts and mediate between conflicting groups in the organization.

Table 3-4, based on Mintzberg's role classifications, is one look at where systems can and cannot help managers. The table shows that information systems do not yet contribute a great deal to important areas of management life. These areas will provide great opportunities for future systems efforts.

MANAGERS AND DECISION MAKING

Decision making is often a manager's most challenging role. Information systems have helped managers communicate and distribute information; however, they have provided only limited assistance for management decision making. Because decision making is an area that system designers have sought most of all to affect (with mixed success), we now turn our attention to this issue.

The Process of Decision Making

Decision making can be classified by organizational level, corresponding to the strategic, management, knowledge, and operational levels of the organization introduced in Chapter 2. **Strategic decision making** determines the objectives, resources, and policies of the organization. Decision making for **management control** is principally concerned with how effi-

---

behavioral models

Descriptions of management based on behavioral scientists' observations of what managers actually do in their jobs.

managerial roles

Expectations of the activities that managers should perform in an organization.

interpersonal roles

Mintzberg's classification for managerial roles where managers act as figureheads and leaders for the organization.

informational roles

Mintzberg's classification for managerial roles where managers act as the nerve centers of their organizations, receiving and disseminating critical information.

decisional roles

Mintzberg's classification for managerial roles where managers initiate activities, handle disturbances, allocate resources, and negotiate conflicts.

strategic decision making

Determining the long-term objectives, resources, and policies of an organization.

management control

Monitoring how efficiently or effectively resources are used and how well operational units are performing.

TABLE 3-4	MANAGERIAL ROLES AND SUPPORTING INFORMATION SYSTEMS	
Role	**Behavior**	**Support Systems**
Interpersonal Roles		
Figurehead - →		None exist
Leader - - - - - - - - - - - - -Interpersonal- - →		None exist
Liaison - →		Electronic communication systems
Informational Roles		
Nerve center - - - - - - - - - - - - - - - - - - →		Management information systems, ESS
Disseminator - - - - - - - - - -Information- - →		Mail, office systems
Spokesperson - - - - - - - - - - processing - - →		Office and professional systems, workstations
Decisional Roles		
Entrepreneur - - - - - - - - - - - - - - - - - - →		None exist
Disturbance handler - - - - - -Decision - - - →		None exist
Resource allocator- - - - - - - - making - - - →		DSS systems
Negotiator- →		None exist

Source: Kenneth C. Laudon and Jane P. Laudon; and Mintzberg, 1971.

ciently and effectively resources are used and how well operational units are performing. **Operational control** decision making determines how to carry out the specific tasks set forth by strategic and middle-management decision makers. **Knowledge-level decision making** deals with evaluating new ideas for products and services, ways to communicate new knowledge, and ways to distribute information throughout the organization.

Within each of these levels of decision making, researchers classify decisions as structured and unstructured. **Unstructured decisions** are those in which the decision maker must provide judgment, evaluation, and insights into the problem definition. Each of these decisions is novel, important, and nonroutine, and there is no well-understood or agreed-on procedure for making them (Gorry and Scott-Morton, 1971). **Structured decisions**, by contrast, are repetitive and routine, and they involve a definite procedure for handling them so that they do not have to be treated each time as if they were new. Some decisions are semistructured; in such cases, only part of the problem has a clear-cut answer provided by an accepted procedure.

Combining these two views of decision making produces the grid shown in Figure 3-9. In general, operational control personnel face fairly well structured problems. In contrast, strategic planners tackle highly unstructured problems. Many of the problems knowledge workers encounter are fairly unstructured as well. Nevertheless, each level of the organization contains both structured and unstructured problems.

operational control

Deciding how to carry out specific tasks specified by upper and middle management, and establishing criteria for completion and resource allocation.

knowledge-level decision making

Evaluating new ideas for products, services, ways to communicate new knowledge, and ways to distribute information throughout the organization.

unstructured decisions

Nonroutine decisions in which the decision maker must provide judgment, evaluation, and insights into the problem definition; there is no agreed-on procedure for making such decisions.

structured decisions

Decisions that are repetitive, routine, and have a definite procedure for handling them.

A corporate chief executive learns how to use a computer. Many senior managers lack computer knowledge or experience and require systems that are extremely easy to use.

Figure 3-9 Different kinds of information systems at the various organization levels support different types of decisions.

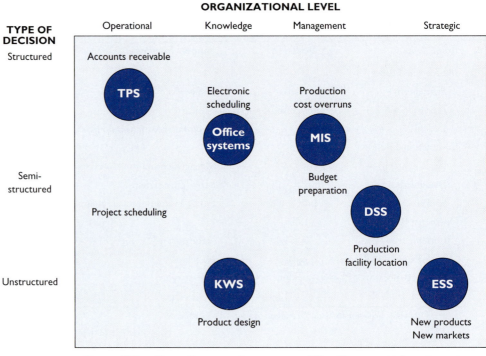

Key: TPS = Transaction processing system   MIS = Management information system
       KWS = Knowledge work system   DSS = Decision-support system
                                               ESS = Executive support system

Stages of Decision Making

Making decisions consists of several different activities. Simon (1960) described four different stages in decision making: intelligence, design, choice, and implementation.

Intelligence consists of identifying and understanding the problems occurring in the organization—why the problem, where, and with what effects. Traditional MIS systems that deliver a wide variety of detailed information can help identify problems, especially if the systems report exceptions.

During solution **design**, the individual designs possible solutions to the problems. Smaller DSS systems are ideal in this stage of decision making because they operate on simple models, can be developed quickly, and can be operated with limited data.

Choice consists of choosing among solution alternatives. Here the decision maker might need a larger DSS system to develop more extensive data on a variety of alternatives and complex models, or data analysis tools to account for all of the costs, consequences, and opportunities.

During solution **implementation**, when the decision is put into effect, managers can use a reporting system that delivers routine reports on the progress of a specific solution. Support systems can range from full-blown MIS systems to much smaller systems, as well as project-planning software operating on personal computers.

In general, the stages of decision making do not necessarily follow a linear path. Think again about the decision you made to attend a specific college. At any point in the decision-making process, you may have to loop back to a previous stage (see Figure 3-10). For instance, one can often come up with several designs but may not be certain about whether a specific design meets the requirements for the particular problem. This situation requires additional intelligence work. Alternatively, one can be in the process of implementing a decision, only to discover that it is not working. In such a case, one is forced to repeat the design or choice stage.

Models of Decision Making

A number of models attempt to describe how people make decisions. Some of these models focus on individual decision making, whereas others focus on decision making in groups.

intelligence
The first of Simon's four stages of decision making, when the individual collects information to identify problems occurring in the organization.

design
Simon's second stage of decision making, when the individual conceives of possible alternative solutions to a problem.

choice
Simon's third stage of decision making, when the individual selects among the various solution alternatives.

implementation
Simon's final stage of decision making, when the individual puts the decision into effect and reports on the progress of the solution.

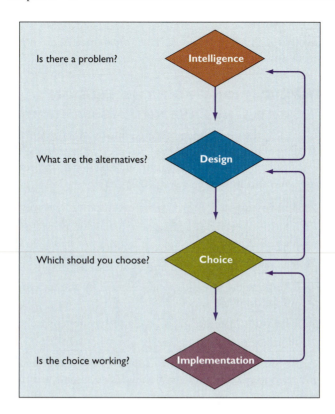

Figure 3-10 The decision-making process. Decisions are often arrived at after a series of iterations and evaluations at each stage in the process. The decision maker often must loop back through one or more of the stages before completing the process.

Individual models of decision making assume that human beings are in some sense rational. The **rational model** of human behavior is built on the idea that people engage in basically consistent, rational, value-maximizing calculations. According to this model, an individual identifies goals, ranks all possible alternative actions by their contributions to those goals, and chooses the alternative that contributes most to those goals.

Critics of this model show that in fact people cannot specify all of the alternatives, and that most individuals do not have singular goals and so are unable to rank all alternatives and consequences. Many decisions are so complex that calculating the choice (even if done by computer) is virtually impossible. Instead of searching through all alternatives, people tend to choose the first available alternative that moves them toward their ultimate goal. In making policy decisions, people choose policies most like the previous policy (Lindblom, 1959). Finally, some scholars point out that decision making is a continuous process in which final decisions are always being modified.

Other research has found that humans differ in how they maximize their values and in the frames of reference they use to interpret information and make choices. Tversky and Kahneman showed that humans have built-in biases that can distort decision making. People can be manipulated into choosing alternatives that they might otherwise reject simply by changing the frame of reference (Tversky and Kahneman, 1981).

Cognitive style describes underlying personality dispositions toward the treatment of information, the selection of alternatives, and the evaluation of consequences. **Systematic decision makers** approach a problem by structuring it in terms of some formal method. They evaluate and gather information in terms of their structured method. **Intuitive decision makers** approach a problem with multiple methods, using trial and error to find a solution. They tend not to structure information gathering or evaluation (McKenney and Keen, 1974) . Neither style is considered superior to the other and each may be advantageous in certain decision situations. While structured problems with clearcut issues can be best handled by "thinking first" in logical steps, others requiring novel, creative solutions may be best solved through a flash of intuition or by trying out several courses of action and seeing what works (Mintzberg and Westley, 2001).

Decision making often is not performed by a single individual but by entire groups or organizations. **Organizational models of decision making** take into account the bureaucratic and political characteristics of an organization. Some actions taken by organizations

rational model
Model of human behavior based on the belief that people, organizations, and nations engage in basically consistent, value-maximizing calculations.

cognitive style
Underlying personality dispositions toward the treatment of information, selection of alternatives, and evaluation of consequences.

systematic decision makers
Cognitive style that describes people who approach a problem by structuring it in terms of some formal method.

intuitive decision makers
Cognitive style that describes people who approach a problem with multiple methods in an unstructured manner, using trial and error to find a solution.

organizational models of decision making
Models of decision making that take into account the structural and political characteristics of an organization.

may be based on their standard operating procedures because radical policy departures involve too much uncertainty. What organizations do may also result from political bargains struck among key leaders and interest groups.

IMPLICATIONS FOR THE DESIGN AND UNDERSTANDING OF INFORMATION SYSTEMS

In order to deliver genuine benefits, information systems must be built with a clear understanding of the organization in which they will reside and of exactly how they can contribute to managerial decision making. In our experience, the central organizational factors to consider when planning a new system are

- ▮ The environment in which the organization must function.
- ▮ The structure of the organization: hierarchy, specialization, standard operating procedures.
- ▮ The organization's culture and politics.
- ▮ The type of organization and its style of leadership.
- ▮ The principal interest groups affected by the system and the attitudes of workers who will be using the system.
- ▮ The kinds of tasks, decisions, and business processes that the information system is designed to assist.

Systems should be built to support both group and organizational decision making. Information systems builders should design systems that have the following characteristics:

- ▮ They are flexible and provide many options for handling data and evaluating information.
- ▮ They are capable of supporting a variety of styles, skills, and knowledge as well as keeping track of many alternatives and consequences.
- ▮ They are sensitive to the organization's bureaucratic and political requirements.

3.4 INFORMATION SYSTEMS AND BUSINESS STRATEGY

Certain types of information systems have become especially critical to firms' long-term prosperity and survival. Such systems, which are powerful tools for staying ahead of the competition, are called *strategic information systems*.

WHAT IS A STRATEGIC INFORMATION SYSTEM?

strategic information systems
Computer systems at any level of the organization that change goals, operations, products, services, or environmental relationships to help the organization gain a competitive advantage.

Strategic information systems change the goals, operations, products, services, or environmental relationships of organizations to help them gain an edge over competitors. Systems that have these effects may even change the business of organizations. For instance, State Street Bank and Trust Co. of Boston transformed its core business from traditional banking services, such as customer checking and savings accounts and loans, to electronic record keeping and financial information services, providing data processing services for securities and mutual funds, and services for pension funds to monitor their money managers.

Strategic information systems should be distinguished from strategic-level systems for senior managers that focus on long-term, decision-making problems. Strategic information systems can be used at all organizational levels and are more far reaching and deep rooted than the other kinds of systems we have described. Strategic information systems profoundly alter the way a firm conducts its business or the very business of the firm itself. As we will see, organizations may need to change their internal operations and relationships with customers and suppliers in order to take advantage of new information systems technology.

Traditional models of strategy are being modified to accommodate the impact of digital firms and new information flows. Before the emergence of the digital firm, business strategy emphasized competing head-to-head against other firms in the same marketplace. Today, the emphasis is increasingly on exploring, identifying, and occupying new market niches before competitors; understanding the customer value chain better; and learning faster and more deeply than competitors.

There is generally no single all-encompassing strategic system, but instead there are a number of systems operating at different levels of strategy—the business, the firm, and the industry level. For each level of business strategy, there are strategic uses of systems. And for each level of business strategy, there is an appropriate model used for analysis.

BUSINESS-LEVEL STRATEGY AND THE VALUE CHAIN MODEL

At the business level of strategy, the key question is, "How can we compete effectively in this particular market?" The market might be light bulbs, utility vehicles, or cable television. The most common generic strategies at this level are (1) to become the low-cost producer, (2) to differentiate your product or service, and/or (3) to change the scope of competition by either enlarging the market to include global markets or narrowing the market by focusing on small niches not well served by your competitors. Digital firms provide new capabilities for supporting business-level strategy by managing the supply chain, building efficient customer "sense and response" systems, and participating in "value webs" to deliver new products and services to market.

Leveraging Technology in the Value Chain

At the business level the most common analytical tool is value chain analysis. The **value chain model** highlights specific activities in the business where competitive strategies can be best applied (Porter, 1985) and where information systems are most likely to have a strategic impact. The value chain model identifies specific, critical leverage points where a firm can use information technology most effectively to enhance its competitive position. Exactly where can it obtain the greatest benefit from strategic information systems—what specific activities can be used to create new products and services, enhance market penetration, lock in customers and suppliers, and lower operational costs? This model views the firm as a series or "chain" of basic activities that add a margin of value to a firm's products or services. These activities can be categorized as either primary activities or support activities.

Primary activities are most directly related to the production and distribution of the firm's products and services that create value for the customer. Primary activities include inbound logistics, operations, outbound logistics, sales and marketing, and service. Inbound logistics include receiving and storing materials for distribution to production. Operations transforms inputs into finished products. Outbound logistics entail storing and distributing finished products. Sales and marketing includes promoting and selling the firm's products. The service activity includes maintenance and repair of the firm's goods and services. **Support activities** make the delivery of the primary activities possible and consist of organization infrastructure (administration and management), human resources (employee recruiting, hiring, and training), technology (improving products and the production process), and procurement (purchasing input).

Organizations have competitive advantage when they provide more value to their customers or when they provide the same value to customers at a lower price. An information system could have a strategic impact if it helped the firm provide products or services at a lower cost than competitors or if it provided products and services at the same cost as competitors but with greater value. The value activities that add the most value to products and services depend on the features of each particular firm.

The firm's value chain can be linked to the value chains of its other partners, including suppliers, distributors, and customers. Figure 3-11 illustrates the activities of the firm value chain and the industry value chain, showing examples of strategic information systems that could be developed to make each of the value activities more cost effective. A firm can achieve a strategic advantage by providing value, not only through its internal value chain processes but also through powerful, efficient ties to industry value partners.

Digitally enabled networks can be used not only to purchase supplies but also to closely coordinate production of many independent firms. For instance, Italian casual wear company Bennetton uses subcontractors and independent firms for labor-intensive production processes such as tailoring, finishing, and ironing while maintaining control of design, procurement, marketing, and distribution. Bennetton uses computer networks to provide independent businesses

value chain model
Model that highlights the primary or support activities that add a margin of value to a firm's products or services where information systems can best be applied to achieve a competitive advantage.

primary activities
Activities most directly related to the production and distribution of a firm's products or services.

support activities
Activities that make the delivery of a firm's primary activities possible. Consist of the organization's infrastructure, human resources, technology, and procurement.

Figure 3-11 The firm value chain and the industry value chain. Illustrated are various examples of strategic information systems for the primary and support activities of a firm and of its value partners that would add a margin of value to a firm's products or services.

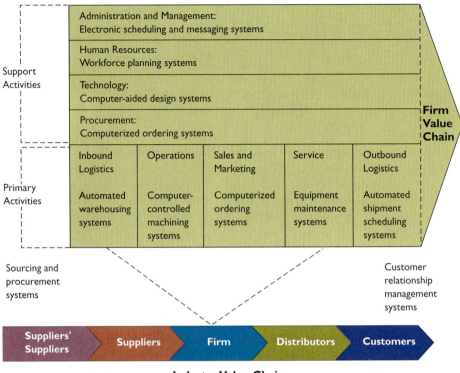

Industry Value Chain

value web

Customer-driven network of independent firms who use information technology to coordinate their value chains to collectively produce a product or service for a market.

and foreign production centers with production specifications so that they can efficiently produce the items needed by Benetton retail outlets (Camuffo, Romano and Vinelli, 2001).

Internet technology has made it possible to extend the value chain so that it ties together all the firm's suppliers, business partners, and customers into a value web. A **value web** is a collection of independent firms who use information technology to coordinate their value chains to collectively produce a product or service for a market. It is more customer-driven and operates in less linear fashion than the traditional value chain. Figure 3-12 shows that this value web functions like a dynamic business ecosystem, synchronizing the business

Figure 3-12 The value web. The value web is a networked business ecosystem that can synchronize the value chains of business partners within an industry to rapidly respond to changes in supply and demand.

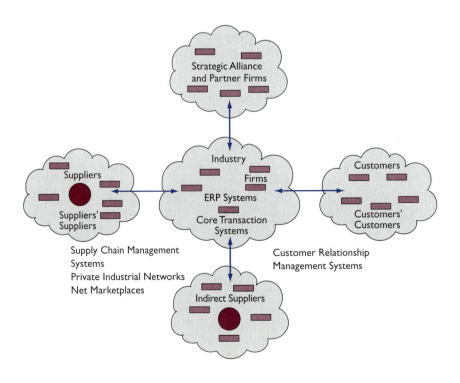

NEXTCARD DIRECT MARKETS WITH THE INTERNET

Window on Technology

MIS In Action

Most people in the United States already have too many credit cards. If they already have three or four credit cards, why would they want another one? This has been the challenge of NextCard, an Internet-only credit card issuer, and so far it has succeeded, thanks to new direct marketing efficiencies provided by Internet technology.

The credit card industry has had many years of success soliciting customers via direct mail. (About 3 billion credit card solicitations are mailed yearly in the United States.) Credit card firms constantly tinker with the mailings, tweaking their design, wording, and even the positioning of MasterCard or Visa logos to see what triggers the greatest response rate. NextCard has transferred some of these direct mailing techniques to the Internet while taking advantage of capabilities that are way beyond the reach of conventional direct marketing.

NextCard runs about 100 different banner ads on the Web, based on its stock of 2,000 different designs. In any given month, NextCard ads appear about 3 billion different times on 200 different Web sites of other companies. Within a two-week period NextCard has 200,000 different opportunities to test what combination of design and Web site positioning is most likely to elicit a credit card application, and the exact cost to the company of such advertisements. NextCard even has tools to monitor what Web banner ads generate the most profitable customers, the amount of balances from a customer's other credit card accounts transferred to NextCard, and whether customers stay after their low introductory rates expire.

Signing up for a credit card is often an impulse move. By placing its ads on other Web sites of interest to potential credit card users, NextCard creates opportunities for individuals to transact at the precise moment when they are most likely to be interested in a credit card. Once a visitor to an affiliated Web site clicks on a NextCard banner ad, that person is transported to NextCard's Web site where he or she can immediately apply for a NextCard. In the non-Internet world, a credit card applicant would have to fill out a paper application form, mail it in (or perhaps phone in the information) and wait for days or weeks to obtain credit approval and the physical card itself. Thanks to Internet technology, all of these events can now take place simultaneously.

NextCard's Web site has software that can approve (or decline) a potential credit card customer, issue a NextCard number within 30 seconds, and immediately transfer the applicant's balances from other credit card accounts to NextCard on-line. The system also presents approved cardholders with at least two options on terms, such as interest rates, airline tickets, or other rewards. Although other dot.com businesses are falling by the wayside, NextCard is starting to become profitable.

To Think About: What is the relationship of Internet technology to NextCard's business model and business strategy? How is NextCard using value chain strategy?

Sources: Paul Beckett, "NextCard Is a Dot-Com Rarity: Its Online Ads Prove Effective," *Wall Street Journal*, January 29, 2001; and Jason Black, "Sales by Association," *Internet World*, February 1, 2001.

---

processes of customers, suppliers, and trading partners among different companies in an industry or related industries. These value webs are flexible and adaptive to changes in supply and demand. Relationships can be bundled or unbundled in response to changing market conditions. A company can use this value web to maintain long-standing relationships with many customers over long periods or to respond immediately to individual customer transactions. Firms can accelerate time to market and to customers by optimizing their value web relationships to make quick decisions on who can deliver the required products or services at the right price and location. The industrial networks we introduced in Chapter 2 form the infrastructure for such value webs.

Businesses should try to develop strategic information systems for both the internal value chain activities and the external value activities that add the most value. A strategic analysis might, for example, identify sales and marketing activities where information systems could provide the greatest boost. The analysis might recommend a system to reduce marketing costs by targeting marketing campaigns more efficiently or by providing information for developing products more finely attuned to a firm's target market. A series of systems, including some linked to systems of other value partners, might be required to create a strategic advantage. The Window on Technology describes how NextCard developed systems for such purposes.

We now show how information technology at the business level helps the firm reduce costs, differentiate products, and serve new markets.

Information System Products and Services

Firms can use information systems to create unique new products and services that can be easily distinguished from those of competitors. Strategic information systems for **product differentiation** can prevent the competition from responding in kind so that firms with these differentiated products and services no longer have to compete on the basis of cost.

Many of these information technology-based products and services have been created by financial institutions. Citibank developed automatic teller machines (ATMs) and bank debit cards in 1977. Citibank became at one time the largest bank in the United States. Citibank ATMs were so successful that Citibank's competitors were forced to counterstrike with their own ATM systems. Citibank, Wells Fargo Bank, and others have continued to innovate by providing on-line electronic banking services so that customers can do most of their banking transactions with home computers linked to proprietary networks or the Internet. These banks have recently launched new account aggregation services that let customers view all of their accounts, including their credit cards, investments, on-line travel rewards, and even accounts from competing banks, from a single on-line source. Some companies such as E*Trade Bank have used the Web to set up "virtual banks" offering a full array of banking services without any physical branches. (Customers mail in their deposits.) NextCard, described in the Window on Technology, is another example of a new Internet-based financial product.

Manufacturers and retailers are starting to use information systems to create products and services that are custom-tailored to fit the precise specifications of individual customers. Dell Computer Corporation sells directly to customers using assemble-to-order manufacturing. Individuals, businesses, and government agencies can buy computers directly from Dell, customized with exactly the features and components they need. They can place their orders directly using a toll-free telephone number or Dell's Web site. Once Dell's production control receives an order, it directs an assembly plant to assemble the computer based on the configuration specified by the customer using components from an on-site warehouse. Chapter 1 describes other instances in which information technology is creating customized products and services while retaining the cost efficiencies of mass-production techniques. These build-to-order strategies require careful coordination of customer requirements with production and flexible processes throughout the firm's value chain (Holweg and Pil, 2001).

Systems to Focus on Market Niche

Businesses can create new market niches by identifying a specific target for a product or service that it can serve in a superior manner. Through **focused differentiation**, the firm can provide a specialized product or service for this narrow target market better than competitors.

---

product differentiation
Competitive strategy for creating brand loyalty by developing new and unique products and services that are not easily duplicated by competitors.

focused differentiation
Competitive strategy for developing new market niches for specialized products or services where a business can compete in the target area better than its competitors.

At Dell Computer Corporation's Web site, customers can select the options they want and order their computer custom-built to these specifications. Dell's assemble-to-order system is a major source of competitive advantage.

An information system can give companies a competitive advantage by producing data for finely tuned sales and marketing techniques. Such systems treat existing information as a resource that the organization can "mine" to increase profitability and market penetration. Information systems enable companies to finely analyze customer buying patterns, tastes, and preferences so that they efficiently pitch advertising and marketing campaigns to smaller and smaller target markets.

The data come from a range of sources—credit card transactions, demographic data, purchase data from checkout counter scanners at supermarkets and retail stores, and data collected when people access and interact with Web sites. Sophisticated software tools can find patterns in these large pools of data and infer rules from them that can be used to guide decision making. Analysis of such data can drive one-to-one marketing where personal messages can be created based on individualized preferences.

For example, Sears Roebuck continually analyzes purchase data from its 60 million past and present credit card users to target appliance buyers, gardening enthusiasts, and mothers-to-be with special promotions. The company might mail customers who purchase a washer and dryer a maintenance contract and annual contract renewal forms. Stein Roe Investors, a mutual fund company, captures and analyzes data generated when people visit its Web site. It uses this information to target existing and potential customers with personalized content and advertising geared to their interests, such as retirement planning. The Canadian Imperial Bank of Commerce (CIBC) analyzes its customer account data to identify its most profitable customers so that it can offer them special services. The level of fine-grained customization provided by these data analysis systems parallels that for mass customization described in Chapter 1. More examples of customer data analysis can be found in Chapters 7 and 11.

The cost of acquiring a new customer has been estimated to be five times that of retaining an existing customer. By carefully examining transactions of customer purchases and activities, firms can identify profitable customers and win more of their business. Likewise, companies can use these data to identify nonprofitable customers. Companies that skillfully use customer data will focus on identifying their most valued customers and use data from a variety of sources to understand their needs (Davenport, Harris, and Kohli, 2001; Clemons and Weber, 1994.)

Supply Chain Management and Efficient Customer Response Systems

Digital firms have the capabilities to go far beyond traditional strategic systems for taking advantage of digital links with other organizations. A powerful business-level strategy available to digital firms involves linking the value chains of vendors and suppliers to the firm's value chain. Integration of value chains can be carried further by digital firms by linking the customer's value chain to the firm's value chain in an "efficient customer response system." Firms using systems to link with customers and suppliers can reduce their inventory costs while responding rapidly to customer demands.

By keeping prices low and shelves well stocked using a legendary inventory replenishment system, Wal-Mart has become the leading retail business in the United States. Wal-Mart's "continuous replenishment system" sends orders for new merchandise directly to suppliers as soon as consumers pay for their purchases at the cash register. Point-of-sale terminals record the bar code of each item passing the checkout counter and send a purchase transaction directly to a central computer at Wal-Mart headquarters. The computer collects the orders from all Wal-Mart stores and transmits them to suppliers. Suppliers can also access Wal-Mart's sales and inventory data using Web technology. Because the system can replenish inventory with lightning speed, Wal-Mart does not need to spend much money on maintaining large inventories of goods in its own warehouses. The system also allows Wal-Mart to adjust purchases of store items to meet customer demands. Competitors such as Kmart were spending 21 percent of sales on overhead. But by using systems to keep operating costs low, Wal-Mart pays only 15 percent of sales revenue for overhead.

Wal-Mart's continuous replenishment system is an example of efficient supply chain management, which we introduced in Chapter 2. Supply chain management systems can not only lower inventory costs but they can also deliver the product or service more rapidly to the customer. Supply chain management can thus be used to create **efficient customer response systems** that respond to customer demands more efficiently. An efficient customer response

efficient customer response system

System that directly links consumer behavior back to distribution, production, and supply chains.

Wal-Mart's continuous inventory replenishment system uses sales data captured at the checkout counter to transmit orders to restock merchandise directly to its suppliers. The system enables Wal-Mart to keep costs low while fine-tuning its merchandise to meet customer demands.

switching costs

The expense a customer or company incurs in lost time and resources when changing from one supplier or system to a competing supplier or system.

system directly links consumer behavior back to distribution, and production and supply chains. Wal-Mart's continuous replenishment system provides such efficient customer response. Dell Computer Corporation's assemble-to-order system, described earlier, is another example of an efficient customer response system.

The convenience and ease of using these information systems raise **switching costs** (the cost of switching from one product to a competing product), which discourages customers from going to competitors. For example, Baxter Healthcare International's "stockless inventory" and ordering system uses supply chain management to create an efficient customer response system. Participating hospitals become unwilling to switch to another supplier because of the system's convenience and low cost. Baxter supplies nearly two-thirds of all products used by U.S. hospitals. Terminals tied to Baxter's own computers are installed in hospitals. When hospitals want to place an order, they do not need to call a salesperson or send a purchase order—they simply use a Baxter computer terminal on-site to order from the full Baxter supply catalog. The system generates shipping, billing, invoicing, and inventory information, and the hospital terminals provide customers with an estimated delivery date. With more than 80 distribution centers in the United States, Baxter can make daily deliveries of its products, often within hours of receiving an order.

Baxter delivery personnel no longer drop off their cartons at loading docks to be placed in hospital storerooms. Instead, they deliver orders directly to the hospital corridors, dropping them at nursing stations, operating rooms, and supply closets. This has created in effect a "stockless inventory," with Baxter serving as the hospitals' warehouse.

Figure 3-13 compares stockless inventory with the just-in-time supply method and traditional inventory practices. Whereas just-in-time inventory allows customers to reduce their inventories by ordering only enough material for a few days' inventory, stockless inventory allows them to eliminate their inventories entirely. All inventory responsibilities shift to the

Figure 3-13 Stockless inventory compared to traditional and just-in-time supply methods. The just-in-time supply method reduces inventory requirements of the customer, whereas stockless inventory allows the customer to eliminate inventories entirely. Deliveries are made daily, sometimes directly to the departments that need the supplies.

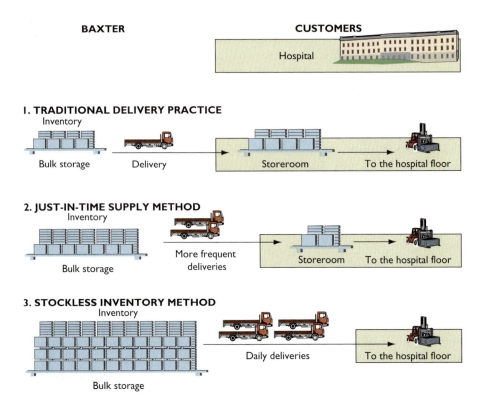

distributor, who manages the supply flow. The stockless inventory is a powerful instrument for "locking in" customers, thus giving the supplier a decided competitive advantage.

Supply chain management and efficient customer response systems are two examples of how emerging digital firms can engage in business strategies not available to traditional firms. Both types of systems require network-based information technology infrastructure investment and software competence to make customer and supply chain data flow seamlessly among different organizations. Both types of strategies have greatly enhanced the efficiency of individual firms and the U.S. economy as a whole by moving toward a *demand-pull production system,* and away from the *traditional supply-push economic system* in which factories were managed on the basis of 12-month official plans rather than on near-instantaneous customer purchase information. Figure 3-14 illustrates the relationships between supply chain management, efficient customer response, and the various business-level strategies.

FIRM-LEVEL STRATEGY AND INFORMATION TECHNOLOGY

A business firm is typically a collection of businesses. Often, the firm is organized financially as a collection of strategic business units, and the returns to the firm are directly tied to strategic business unit performance. Information systems can improve the overall performance of these business units by promoting synergies and core competencies. The idea driving synergies is that when some units can be used as inputs to other units, or two organizations can pool markets and expertise, these relationships can lower costs and generate profits. Recent bank and financial firm mergers, such as the merger of Chemical Bank and Chase Manhattan Corp., Wells Fargo and Norwest Corp., Deutsche Bank and Bankers Trust, and Citicorp and Travelers Insurance occurred precisely for this purpose. One use of information technology in these synergy situations is to tie together the operations of disparate business units so that they can act as a whole. For example, Citigroup can cross-market both Citicorp and Travelers financial products to customers. Such systems would lower retailing costs, increase customer access to new financial products, and speed up the process of marketing new instruments.

Enhancing Core Competencies

A second concept for firm-level strategy involves the notion of "core competency." The argument is that the performance of all business units can increase insofar as these business units

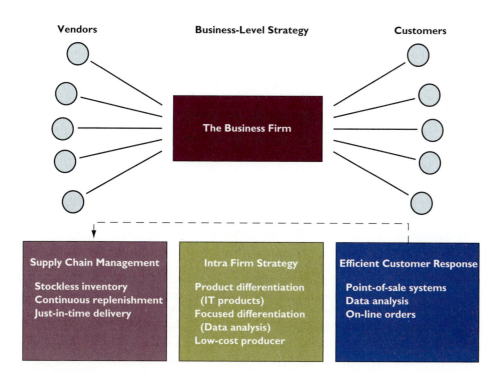

Figure 3-14 Business-level strategy. Efficient customer response and supply chain management systems are often interrelated, helping firms "lock in" customers and suppliers while lowering operating costs. Other types of systems can be used to support product differentiation, focused differentiation, and low-cost producer strategies.

core competency
Activity at which a firm excels as a world-class leader.

develop, or create, a central core of competencies. A **core competency** is an activity at which a firm is a world-class leader. Core competencies may involve being the world's best miniature parts designer, the best package delivery service, or the best thin-film manufacturer. In general, a core competency relies on knowledge that is gained over many years of experience and a first-class research organization or simply key people who follow the literature and stay abreast of new external knowledge.

Any information system that encourages the sharing of knowledge across business units enhances competency. Such systems might encourage or enhance existing competencies and help employees become aware of new external knowledge; such systems might also help a business leverage existing competencies to related markets.

INDUSTRY-LEVEL STRATEGY AND INFORMATION SYSTEMS: COMPETITIVE FORCES AND NETWORK ECONOMICS

Firms together comprise an industry, such as the automotive industry, telephone, television broadcasting, and forest products industries, to name a few. The key strategic question at this level of analysis is, "How and when should we compete with as opposed to cooperate with others in the industry?" Whereas most strategic analyses emphasize competition, a great deal of money can be made by cooperating with other firms in the same industry or firms in related industries. For instance, firms can cooperate to develop industry standards in a number of areas; they can cooperate by working together to build customer awareness, and by working collectively with suppliers to lower costs (Shapiro and Varian, 1999). The three principal concepts for analyzing strategy at the industry level are information partnerships, the competitive forces model, and network economics.

Information Partnerships

information partnership
Cooperative alliance formed between two or more corporations for the purpose of sharing information to gain strategic advantage.

Firms can form information partnerships and even link their information systems to achieve unique synergies. In an **information partnership**, both companies can join forces without actually merging by sharing information (Konsynski and McFarlan, 1990). American Airlines has an arrangement with Citibank to award one mile in its frequent flier program for every dollar spent using Citibank credit cards. American benefits from increased customer loyalty, and Citibank gains new credit card subscribers and a highly creditworthy customer base for cross-marketing. Northwest Airlines has a similar arrangement with U.S. Bank. American and Northwest have also allied with MCI, awarding frequent flier miles for each dollar of long-distance billing.

Such partnerships help firms gain access to new customers, creating new opportunities for cross-selling and targeting products. Companies that have been traditional competitors may find such alliances to be mutually advantageous. Baxter Healthcare International offers its customers medical supplies from competitors and office supplies through its electronic ordering channel.

The Competitive Forces Model

competitive forces model
Model used to describe the interaction of external influences, specifically threats and opportunities, that affect an organization's strategy and ability to compete.

In Porter's **competitive forces model**, which is illustrated in Figure 3-15, a firm faces a number of external threats and opportunities: the threat of new entrants into its market, the pressure from substitute products or services, the bargaining power of customers, the bargaining power of suppliers, and the positioning of traditional industry competitors (Porter, 1985).

Competitive advantage can be achieved by enhancing the firm's ability to deal with customers, suppliers, substitute products and services, and new entrants to its market, which in turn may change the balance of power between a firm and other competitors in the industry in the firm's favor.

How can information systems be used to achieve strategic advantage at the industry level? By working with other firms, industry participants can use information technology to develop industry-wide standards for exchanging information or business transactions electronically (see Chapters 6 and 9), which force all market participants to subscribe to similar standards. Earlier we described how firms can benefit from value webs with complementary firms in the industry. Such efforts increase efficiency at the industry level as well as the busi-

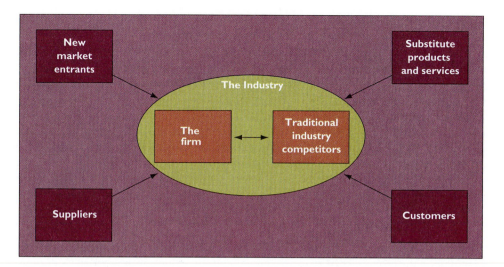

Figure 3-15 Porter's competitive forces model. There are various forces that affect an organization's ability to compete and therefore greatly influence a firm's business strategy. There are threats from new market entrants and from substitute products and services. Customers and suppliers wield bargaining power. Traditional competitors constantly adapt their strategies to maintain their market positioning.

ness level—making product substitution less likely and perhaps raising entry costs—thus discouraging new entrants. Also, industry members can build industry-wide, IT-supported consortia, symposia, and communications networks to coordinate activities concerning government agencies, foreign competition, and competing industries.

An example of such industry-level cooperation can be found in the Chapter 4 Window on Organizations describing Covisint, an electronic marketplace shared by the major automobile manufacturers for procurement of auto parts. Although the Big 3 U.S. auto manufacturers aggressively compete on such factors as design, service, quality, and price, they can raise the industry's productivity by working together to create an integrated supply chain. Covisint enables all manufacturers and suppliers to trade on a single Internet site, sparing manufacturers the cost of setting up their own Web-based marketplaces.

In the digital firm era, the competitive forces model needs modification. The traditional Porter model assumes a relatively static industry environment; relatively clear-cut industry boundaries; and a relatively stable set of suppliers, substitutes, and customers. Instead of participating in a single industry, today's firms are much more aware that they participate in "industry sets"— multiple related industries that consumers can choose from to obtain a product or service (see Figure 3-16). For instance, automobile companies compete against other automobile companies in the "auto industry," but they also compete against many other industries in the transportation industry "set" such as train, plane, and bus transportation companies. Success or failure for a single auto company may depend on the success or failure of various other industries. Colleges may think they are in competition with other traditional colleges, but in fact they are in competition with electronic distance learning universities, publishing companies who have created on-line college courses, and private training firms who offer technical certificates—all of whom are members of a much larger "education

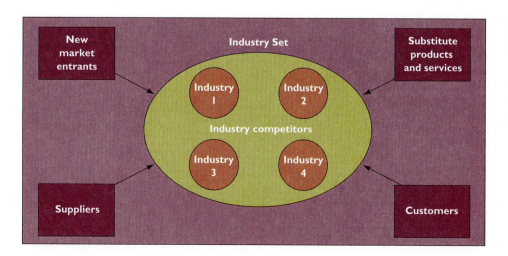

Figure 3-16 The new competitive forces model. The digital firm era requires a more dynamic view of the boundaries between firms, customers, and suppliers, with competition occurring among industry sets.

industry set." In the digital firm era we can expect greater emphasis on building strategies to compete—and cooperate—with members of the firm's industry set.

Nevertheless, the competitive forces model remains a valid model for analyzing strategy, even considering the impact of the Internet. Internet technology has affected industry structure by providing technologies that make it easier for rivals to compete on price alone and for new competitors to enter the market. Profits have also been dampened because the Internet dramatically increases the information available to customers for comparison shopping, thus raising their bargaining power. Although the Internet can provide benefits, such as new channels to customers and new operating efficiencies, firms cannot achieve competitive advantage unless they have carefully integrated Internet initiatives into their overall strategy and operations. In the age of the Internet, the traditional competitive forces are still at work, but competitive rivalry has become much more intense (Porter, 2001).

Network Economics

network economics

Model of strategic systems at the industry level based on the concept of a network where adding another participant entails zero marginal costs but can create much larger marginal gain.

A third strategic concept useful at the industry level is **network economics**. In traditional economics—the economics of factories and agriculture—production experiences diminishing returns. The more any given resource is applied to production, the lower the marginal gain in output, until a point is reached where the additional inputs produce no additional outputs. This is the law of diminishing returns, and it is the foundation for most of modern economics.

In some situations the law of diminishing returns does not work. For instance, in a network, the marginal costs of adding another participant are about zero, whereas the marginal gain is much larger. The larger the number of subscribers in a telephone system, or the Internet, the greater the value to all participants. It's no more expensive to operate a television station with 1,000 subscribers than with 10 million subscribers. And the value of a community of people grows with size, whereas the cost of adding new members is inconsequential.

From this network economics perspective, information technology can be strategically useful. Internet sites can be used by firms to build "communities of users"—like-minded customers who want to share their experiences. This can build customer loyalty and enjoyment, and build unique ties to customers. Microsoft Corporation—the world's dominant PC software manufacturer—uses information technology to build communities of software developers around the world. Using the Microsoft Developer's Network, these small software development firms work closely with Microsoft to debug its operating system software, pro-

MIS IN ACTION   MANAGER'S TOOLKIT

IDENTIFYING OPPORTUNITIES FOR STRATEGIC INFORMATION SYSTEMS

Managers are expected to identify the types of systems that would provide a strategic advantage to their firms. Here are some key questions to ask:

1. Examine the structure of the industry where the firm is located.
   ❚ What are some of the competitive forces at work in the industry? Are there new entrants to the industry? What is the relative power of suppliers, customers, and substitute products and services over prices?
   ❚ Is the basis of competition quality, price or brand?
   ❚ What are the direction and nature of change within the industry? From where are the momentum and change coming?
   ❚ How is the industry currently using information technology? Is the organization behind or ahead of the industry in its application of information systems?

2. Examine business, firm, and industry value chains.
   ❚ How is the company creating value for the customer? Through lower prices and transaction costs or higher quality?
   ❚ Does the firm understand and manage its business processes using the best practices available? Is it taking maximum advantage of supply chain management, customer relationship management, and enterprise systems?
   ❚ Does the firm leverage its core competencies?
   ❚ Is the industry supply chain and customer base changing in ways that benefit or harm the firm?
   ❚ Could the firm benefit from strategic partnerships and value webs?
   ❚ Where in the value chain would information systems provide the greatest value to the firm?

MAKE IT YOUR BUSINESS

FINANCE AND ACCOUNTING

Information systems promote better management of the firm's assets and cash flows that can increase revenues and reduce operating costs, thereby enhancing its competitive position. On-line systems provide more immediate tracking and identification of the firm's assets and the return on the firm's investments. The accounting function can monitor transaction flows and keep track of costs and revenues more precisely in real-time. Tracking and identifying changes in assets and fund flows that used to take weeks can now be accomplished in hours or days.

HUMAN RESOURCES

Information systems lower agency costs, enabling the firm to manage more employees with fewer resources. Networked systems also make it possible to create work groups outside traditional places of work. Employees from many different locations can use information systems to work together on virtual teams. Understanding human resource issues is essential for successful system implementation because people need to adjust to the organizational change created by introducing a new information system. You can find examples of human resources applications on page 72.

MANUFACTURING AND PRODUCTION

Information systems can be used to streamline manufacturing and production processes so that they require fewer steps and less human intervention. By taking advantage of more precise flows of information, firms can tighten coordination of production and distribution, lowering transaction and agency costs. You can find examples of manufacturing and production applications on pages 71–72, 92–95, and 103–105.

SALES AND MARKETING

Information systems provide a rich new set of capabilities for fine tuning sales and marketing that are often a source of competitive advantage. Systems can be used to analyze vast pools of data for highly targeted marketing campaigns, and they can also generate unique new products and services that the organization can sell. Efficient customer response systems can improve sales by tightly coordinating production and distribution with customer orders. You can find examples of sales and marketing applications on pages 71–72, 78, 91–93, and 103–105.

---

vide new software ideas and extensions, supply customers with tips and new software applications, and in general participate in a powerful and useful network.

USING SYSTEMS FOR COMPETITIVE ADVANTAGE: MANAGEMENT ISSUES

Strategic information systems often change the organization as well as its products, services, and operating procedures, driving the organization into new behavior patterns. Using technology for strategic benefit requires careful planning and management. Managers interested in using information systems for competitive advantage will need to perform a strategic systems analysis. The Manager's Toolkit describes some of the issues this analysis will have to address.

Managing Strategic Transitions

Adopting the kinds of strategic systems described in this chapter generally requires changes in business goals, relationships with customers and suppliers, internal operations, and information architecture. These sociotechnical changes, affecting both social and technical elements of the organization, can be considered **strategic transitions**—a movement between levels of sociotechnical systems.

Such changes often entail blurring of organizational boundaries, both external and internal. Suppliers and customers must become intimately linked and may share each other's responsibilities. For instance, in Baxter International's stockless inventory system, Baxter has assumed responsibility for managing its customers' inventories (Johnston and Vitale, 1988). Managers will need to devise new business processes for coordinating their firms' activities with those of customers, suppliers, and other organizations. The organizational change requirements surrounding new information systems are so important that they merit attention throughout this text. Chapters 12 and 13 examine organizational change issues in great detail.

strategic transitions
A movement from one level of sociotechnical system to another. Often required when adopting strategic systems that demand changes in the social and technical elements of an organization.

MANAGEMENT WRAP-UP

Management

Information technology provides tools for managers to carry out both their traditional and newer roles, allowing them to monitor, plan, and forecast with more precision and speed than ever before and to respond more rapidly to the changing business environment. Finding ways to use information technology to achieve competitive advantage at the business, firm, and industry level is a key management responsibility. In addition to identifying the business processes, core competencies, and the relationships with others in the industry that can be enhanced with information technology, managers need to oversee the sociotechnical changes required to implement strategic systems.

Organization

Each organization has a unique constellation of information systems that result from its interaction with information technology. Contemporary information technology can lead to major organizational changes—and efficiencies—by reducing transaction and agency costs and can also be a source of competitive advantage. Developing meaningful strategic systems generally requires extensive changes in organizational structure, culture, and business processes that often encounter resistance.

Technology

Information technology offers new ways of organizing work and using information that can promote organizational survival and prosperity. Technology can be used to differentiate existing products, create new products and services, nurture core competencies, and reduce operational costs. Selecting an appropriate technology for the firm's competitive strategy is a key decision.

For Discussion

1. A number of information system experts have claimed that there is no such thing as a sustainable strategic advantage. Do you agree? Why or why not?

2. How has the Internet changed the management process?

SUMMARY

1. *What do managers need to know about organizations in order to build and use information systems successfully?* Managers need to understand certain essential features of organizations in order to build and use information systems successfully. All modern organizations are hierarchical, specialized, and impartial. They use explicit standard operating procedures to maximize efficiency. All organizations have their own cultures and politics arising from differences in interest groups. Organizations differ in goals, groups served, social roles, leadership styles, incentives, surrounding environments, and types of tasks performed. These differences create varying types of organizational structures and they also help explain differences in organizations' use of information systems.

2. *What impact do information systems have on organizations?* Information systems and the organizations in which they are used interact with and influence each other. The introduction of a new information system will affect organizational structure, goals, work design, values, competition between interest groups, decision making, and day-to-day behavior. At the same time, information systems must be designed to serve the needs of important organizational groups and will

be shaped by the organization's structure, tasks, goals, culture, politics, and management. Information technology can reduce transaction and agency costs, and such changes have been accentuated in organizations using the Internet. The information systems department is the formal organizational unit that is responsible for the organization's information systems function. Organizational characteristics and managerial decisions determine the role this group will actually play.

3. *How do information systems support the activities of managers in organizations?* There are several different models of what managers actually do in organizations that show how information systems can be used for managerial support. Early classical models of managerial activities stressed the functions of planning, organizing, coordinating, deciding, and controlling. Contemporary research looking at the actual behavior of managers has found that managers' real activities are highly fragmented, variegated, and brief in duration, with managers moving rapidly and intensely from one issue to another. Managers spend considerable time pursuing personal agendas and goals, and contemporary managers shy away from making grand, sweeping policy decisions.

The nature and level of decision making are important factors in building information systems for managers. Decisions can be structured, semistructured, or unstructured, with structured decisions clustering at the operational level of the organization and unstructured decisions at the strategic planning level. Decision making can also take place at the individual or group level. Individual models of decision making assume that human beings can rationally choose alternatives and consequences based on the priority of their objectives and goals. Organizational models of decision making illustrate that real decision making in organizations takes place in arenas where many psychological, political, and bureaucratic forces are at work.

Information systems have been most helpful to managers by providing support for their roles in disseminating information, providing liaison between organizational levels, and allocating resources. However, some managerial roles cannot be supported by information systems, and information systems are less successful at supporting unstructured decisions.

4. *How can businesses use information systems for competitive advantage?* Businesses can use strategic information systems to gain an edge over competitors. Such systems change organizations' goals, business processes, products, services, or environmental relationships, driving them into new forms of behavior.

Information systems can be used to support strategy at the business, firm, and industry level. At the business level of strategy, information systems can be used to help firms become the low-cost producers, differentiate products and services, or serve new markets. Information systems can also be used to "lock in" customers and suppliers using efficient customer response and supply chain management applications. Value chain analysis is useful at the business level to highlight specific activities in the business where information systems are most likely to have a strategic impact.

At the firm level, information systems can be used to achieve new efficiencies or to enhance services by tying together the operations of disparate business units so that they can function as a whole or promote the sharing of knowledge across business units. At the industry level, systems can promote competitive advantage by facilitating cooperation with other firms in the industry, creating consortiums or communities for sharing information, exchanging transactions, or coordinating activities. The competitive forces model, information partnerships and network economics are useful concepts for identifying strategic opportunities for systems at the industry level.

5. *Why is it so difficult to build successful information systems, including systems that promote competitive advantage?* Information systems are closely intertwined with an organization's structure, culture, and business processes. New systems disrupt established patterns of work and power relationships, so there is often considerable resistance to them when they are introduced.

Implementing strategic systems often requires extensive organizational change and a transition from one sociotechnical level to another. Such changes are called *strategic transitions* and are often difficult and painful to achieve. Moreover, not all strategic systems are profitable, and they can be expensive to build. Many strategic information systems are easily copied by other firms, so that strategic advantage is not always sustainable.

KEY TERMS

Agency theory, 80

Behavioral models, 84

Bureaucracy, 75

Chief information officer (CIO), 80

Choice, 86

Classical model of management, 83

Cognitive style, 87

Competitive forces model, 96

Core competency, 96

Decisional roles, 84

Design, 86

Efficient customer response system, 93

End users, 80

Focused differentiation, 92

Implementation, 86

Information partnership, 96

Information systems department, 79

Information systems managers, 79

Informational roles, 84

Intelligence, 86

Interpersonal roles, 84

Intuitive decision makers, 87

Knowledge-level decision making, 85

Management control, 84

Managerial roles, 84

Network economics, 98

Operational control, 85

Organization, 73

Organizational culture, 76

Organizational models of decision making, 87

Primary activities, 89

Product differentiation, 92

Programmers, 79

Rational model, 87

Standard operating procedures (SOPs), 75

Strategic decision making, 84

Strategic information system, 88

Strategic transitions, 99

Structured decisions, 85

Support activities, 89

Switching costs, 94

Systematic decision makers, 87

Systems analysts, 79

Transaction cost theory, 80

Unstructured decisions, 85

Value chain model, 89

Value web, 90

Virtual organization, 82

REVIEW QUESTIONS

1. What is an organization? Compare the technical definition of organizations with the behavioral definition.

2. What features do all organizations have in common? In what ways can organizations differ?

3. How are information technology services delivered in organizations? Describe the role played by programmers, systems analysts, information systems managers, and the chief information officer (CIO).

4. Describe the major economic theories that help explain how information systems affect organizations.

5. Describe the major behavioral theories that help explain how information systems affect organizations.

6. Why is there considerable organizational resistance to the introduction of information systems?

7. Compare the descriptions of managerial behavior in the classical and behavioral models.

8. What specific managerial roles can information systems support? Where are information systems particularly strong in supporting managers, and where are they weak?

9. What are the four stages of decision making described by Simon?

10. Compare individual and organizational models of decision making.

11. What is the impact of the Internet on organizations and the process of management?

12. What is a strategic information system? What is the difference between a strategic information system and a strategic-level system?

13. Describe appropriate models for analyzing strategy at the business level, and the types of strategies and information systems that can be used to compete at this level.

14. Describe appropriate strategies for the firm level and how information systems can help companies compete at this level.

15. How can the competitive forces model, information partnerships, and network economics be used to identify strategies and system opportunities at the industry level?

16. How have the value chain and competitive forces models changed as a result of the Internet and the emergence of digital firms?

17. Why are strategic information systems difficult to build?

APPLICATION SOFTWARE EXERCISE

DATABASE EXERCISE: USING A DATABASE FOR STRATEGIC BUSINESS DEVELOPMENT

The Presidents' Inn is a small three-story hotel on the Atlantic Ocean in Cape May, NJ, a popular Northeastern U.S. resort. Ten rooms overlook side streets, ten rooms have bay windows that offer limited views of the ocean, and the remaining ten rooms in the front of the hotel face the ocean. Room rates are based on room choice, length of stay, and number of guests per room. Room rates are the same for one to four guests per room. Fifth and sixth guests must pay an additional $20 charge each per day. Guests staying for seven days or more receive a ten-percent discount on their daily room rates.

Business has grown steadily over the past ten years. Now totally renovated, the hotel uses a romantic weekend package to attract couples, a vacation package to attract young families, and a weekday discount package to attract business travelers. The owners currently use a manual reservation and bookkeeping system, which has caused many problems. Sometimes two families

have been booked in the same room at the same time. Management does not have immediate data about the hotel's daily operations and income.

Use the information provided in this description and in the database tables on the Laudon Web site for Chapter 3 to develop reports that would provide information to help management make the business more competitive and profitable. The database and related queries should be designed to make it easy to identify information such as the average length of stay per room type, the average number of visitors per room type, and the base income per room (i.e., length of visit multiplied times the daily rate) during a specified period of time.

After identifying the above information, write a brief report describing what your database information tells you about your current business situation. For example, what is your strongest customer base? What specific business strategies might you pursue to increase room occupancy and revenue? For example, would you add, modify, or delete discount packages? Why or why not?

GROUP PROJECT

With a group of three or four students, select a company described in the *Wall Street Journal, Fortune, Forbes,* or another business publication. Visit the company's Web site to find out additional information about that company and to see how the firm is using the Web. On the basis of this information, analyze the business. Include a description of the organization's features,

such as important business processes, culture, structure, and environment, as well as its business strategy. Suggest strategic information systems appropriate for that particular business, including those based on Internet technology, if appropriate. If possible, use electronic presentation software to present your findings to the class.

TOOLS FOR INTERACTIVE LEARNING

■ INTERNET CONNECTION

The Internet Connection for this chapter will take you to the E*Trade Web site where you can see how one company used the Internet to create an entirely new type of business. You can complete an exercise for analyzing this Web site's capabilities and its strategic benefits. You can also use the Interactive Study Guide to test your knowledge of this chapter and get instant feedback where you need more practice.

■ ELECTRONIC COMMERCE PROJECT

At the Laudon Web site for Chapter 3, you will find an Electronic Commerce project on competitive auto pricing and sales on the Web.

■ CD-ROM

If you use the Multimedia Edition CD-ROM with this chapter, you will find a video clip illustrating the role of information systems in Schneider National's organization, an audio overview of the major themes of this chapter, and bullet text summarizing the key points of the chapter.

CASE STUDY—*Can GE Prosper with a Digital Firm Strategy?*

General Electric (GE) is the world's largest diversified manufacturer. Headquartered in Fairfield, Connecticut, the company consists of 20 major units, including Appliances, Broadcasting (NBC), Capital, Medical Systems, and Transportation Systems.

Jack Welch, GE's CEO and chairman from 1981 until September 2001, has been often cited as the most admired CEO in the United States. Under Welch's leadership GE became a company of $130 billion in revenue, earnings of $12.7 billion, capitalization of $400 billion and 314,000 employees in 100 countries. Welch achieved spectacular results by pressuring GE workers to stretch themselves to meet ever-more demanding quality and efficiency standards. Welch demanded that his managers find ways of making each of the company's major businesses rank first or second in the world. Welch tried to overhaul the company over and over again—through globalization of the company in the late 1980s; "products plus service" programs in 1995, which placed emphasis on customer service; and Six Sigma in 1996, a quality program that mandated GE units to use feedback from customers as the center of the program.

Fortune named GE "America's Most Admired Company" in 1998, 1999, and 2000. Welch retired in September 2001 and was succeeded by Jeffrey Immelt. Well before Welch retired, GE had already become one of the biggest corporations in the world and an old economy business. How could it continue to throw off profits at the same furious pace it had in the past? Welch and his management team decided to explore using Internet technology for this purpose.

At a January 1999 meeting of 500 top GE executives in Boca Raton, Florida, Welch announced a new initiative to turn GE into an Internet company. Welch proclaimed that the Internet "will forever change the way business is done. It will change every relationship, between our businesses, between our customers, between our suppliers." By Internet-enabling its business processes, GE could reduce overhead costs by half, saving as much as $10 billion in the first two years. Gary Reiner, GE's corporate CIO, later explained, "We are Web-enabling nearly all of the [purchasing] negotiations process, and we are targeting 100 percent of our transactions on the buy side being done electronically." On the sell side Reiner also wanted to automate as much as possible, including providing customer service and order taking.

GE had quietly been involved with the Internet years before the 1999 meeting, conducting more purchasing and selling on the Internet than any other noncomputer manufacturer. For example within six months after beginning to use the Internet for purchasing in mid-1996, GE Lighting had reduced its purchasing cycle from 14 to 7 days. It also reduced supply prices by 10 to 15 percent as a result of open bidding on the Internet. In 1997, seven other GE units began purchasing via the Net. The company even sold the concept to others, including Boeing and 3M.

Polymerland, GE Plastic's distribution arm, began distributing technical documentation over the Web in 1994. It put its product catalog on the Net in 1995, and in 1997 it established a site for sales transactions. Its on-line system enables customers to search for product by name, number, or product characteristics; download product information; verify that the product meets their specifications; apply for credit; order; track shipments; and even return merchandise. Polymerland's weekly on-line sales climbed from $10,000 in 1997 to $6 million in 2000.

Welch ordered all GE units to determine how dot.com companies could destroy their businesses, dubbing this project DYB (destroy your business). He explained that if these units didn't identify their weaknesses, others would. Once armed with these answers, managers were to change their units to prevent this from happening. Each of GE's 20 units created small cross-functional teams to execute the initiative. Welch also wanted them to move current operations to the Web and to uncover new Net-related business opportunities. The final product was to be an Internet-based business plan that a competitor could have used to take away each GE unit's customers, and a plan for changes to their unit to combat this threat. Reiner ordered GE units to "come back with alternative approaches that enhance value to the customer and reduce total costs."

The Internet initiative started by changing GE's culture at the very top. GE's internal newsletters and many of Welch's memos became available only on-line. To give blue-collar workers access to the Net, GE installed computer kiosks on factory floors. One thousand top managers and executives, including Welch (who also had to take typing lessons), were assigned young, skilled mentors to work with them three to four hours per week to help them become comfortable with the Web. They had to be able to evaluate their competitors' Web sites and to use the Web in other beneficial ways. Every GE employee was given Internet training. Welch announced in 2000, that GE would reduce administrative expenses by 30 to 50 percent (about $10 billion) within 18 months by using the Internet. Employees can handle all of their business travel arrangements via the Internet and access employee information on-line through a corporate intranet.

Many projects came out of the initiative. For example GE Medical Systems, which manufactures diagnostic imaging systems such as CAT scanners and mammography equipment, identified its DYB threat as aggregators, such as WebMD, which offered unbiased information on competing products as well as selling them. GE products on these sites looked like any other commodity. The unit's major response was iCenter, a Web connection to customers' GE equipment to monitor the equipment operation at the customer site. iCenter collects data and feeds it back to each customer who can then ask questions about the operation of the equipment through the same site. GE compares a customer's operating data with the same equipment operating elsewhere to aid that customer in improving performance. "We can say, 'Do you know you're only 60 percent as productive as another customer using the same equipment in another part of the world,'" explained Joe Hogan, Medical Systems' CEO, "'and by doing x, y and z, you can increase productivity?'" In addition customers are now able to download and test upgraded software for 30 days prior to having to purchase it. The unit also began offering its equipment training classes on-line, enabling clients to take them at any time. The aggregators were also auctioning off used equipment, which was in demand in poorer countries. Medical Systems established its own site to auction its own used equipment, thus opening new markets (outside the United States). GE Aircraft adapted iCenter and now monitors its customers' engines while they are in flight.

GE Power Systems then developed its Turbine Optimizer, which uses the Web to monitor any GE turbine, comparing its performance (such as fuel burn rate) with other turbines of the same model anywhere in the world. Their site advises operators how to improve their turbines' performance and how much money the improvements would be worth. The operator can even schedule a service call in order to make further performance improvements.

Late in 1999 GE Transportation went live with an e-auction system for purchasing supplies. Soon other units, including Power and Medical, adopted the system. GE later estimated the system would handle $5 billion in GE purchasing in 2000, and the company would do at least 50 percent of its purchasing on-line in 2001. The system lowers prices for GE because approved suppliers bid against each other to obtain GE contracts. It also results in fewer specification errors and speeds up the purchasing process.

GE Appliances realized that appliances are traditionally sold through large and small retailers and that the Internet might destroy that model, turning appliances into commodities sold on big retail and auction sites. GE wanted to maintain the current system, keeping consumer loyalty for their GE brand (versus Maytag, Whirlpool, or Frigidaire). Appliances developed a point-of-sale system to be placed in retail stores, such as Home Depot, where customers could enter their own orders. The retailer is paid a percentage of the sale. The product is shipped from GE directly to the customer. GE Appliances claims it can now ship products from its factories anywhere in the United States virtually overnight on a cost-effective basis. Today, nearly 100 percent of its sales take place over the Web. Instead of $5 per telephone call, each order taken over the Web only costs 20 cents.

The corporation and its units issued a blizzard of press releases touting the successes of each of GE's Internet initiatives and the subsequent positive effect on financial results. CIO Reiner said, "We are not talking about incremental change. We're talking total transformation."

A January 2001 article by Mark Roberti of *The Industry Standard* was skeptical. Roberti commended GE for embracing the Internet so quickly. He also noted that, "these endeavors are unlikely to make GE vastly more profitable . . . because the company isn't using the Internet to reach new markets or create major new sources of revenue." Roberti questioned the great savings through Internet-based cost cutting that GE claimed. To cut costs by moving business processes on-line, a firm "must eliminate—or re-deploy—a significant number of employees" and eliminate redundant systems. "GE hasn't." For example, Roberti said, 60 percent of orders to GE Capital Fleet Services were being placed on-line, but GE had not reduced its call center staff (nor has GE reduced the call center staff of GE Appliances). GE reported that its selling and general and administrative expenses as a percentage of sales fell for the first nine months of 2000 from 24.3 percent in 1999 to 23.6 percent, a minor drop at best. Reducing costs by having customers and employees serve themselves via the Web has proved elusive at other companies as well, such as IBM and UPS. Overall, Roberti pointed out, GE has achieved genuine progress and even leadership, but the company could not be generating the savings management had been predicting.

Since the publication of Roberti's article, GE has agreed with some of his points. In May 2001, GE acknowledged that its expected $10 billion savings would only reach $1.6 billion, a giant savings but severely short of the company's predictions. Moreover, much of that saving resulted from internal Web use. Analysts say that perhaps $1 billion of the savings came from Web-based production efficiencies within GE's 20 major business units—sharing design plans and best practices, monitoring performance data, and automating and consolidating procurement. These gains will start leveling off within the next few years.

Although e-commerce sales amounted to 10 percent of GE's $130 billion in total revenue, connecting GE's suppliers and customers to its Web trading systems has been a major problem. For example observers claim GE has only been able to connect about 25 percent of its suppliers, with another 25 percent still using traditional private networks. That leaves about 15,000 of the 30,000 suppliers using nonelectronic methods of selling to GE. Suppliers appear to have two main reasons for not using the Web. First, using the Web presents complex changes to link the GE Web purchases to the suppliers' own back-end systems. Second, and perhaps more important, GE relies on electronic auctions, and the increased competition by using the Web is reducing GE's purchase prices, making electronic methods more unattractive to the suppliers. Analysts believe that only 60 percent of GE suppliers will switch to electronic methods and that the Web will not enable GE to expand into new markets.

GE continues to have faith in e-commerce and e-business. It has budgeted about $3 billion for computer spending in 2001, an increase of about 12 percent over the previous year. It also has indicated it will design and offer to its customers Web-based systems, such as monitoring airline, hospital, and auto production equipment purchased from GE. Customers will be supplied with software that they can use to constantly keep tabs on their businesses while linking with GE systems. GE is also developing a new system that supposedly will enable its suppliers to be paid in 15 days instead of the usual 60 days. The effect will be that the supplier will no longer have to sell its debts to a factoring company that charges a fee to collect these debts. GE and its suppliers would split the savings from not selling debts, and GE projects an annual accounts payable savings of 12 percent.

Some of GE's remaining hurdles are cultural. In the past, GE achieved major breakthroughs under Jack Welch. Will GE's bet on Internet technology pay off? Only the future will tell whether his successors can provide the same kind of exceptional leadership.

Sources: Tom Kaneshige, "New Man, Same Plan," *Line56*, September 15, 2001; Matt Murray and Jathon Sapsford, "GE Reshuffles Its Dot-Com Strategy to Focus on Internal 'Digitizing,'" *Wall Street Journal*, May 4, 2001; Matt Murray, "Why Jack Welch's Leadership Matters to Business World-Wide," *Wall Street Journal*, September 5, 2001; Chuck Moozakis, "GE Scales Back," *Internet Week*, May 10, 2001; Bob Tedeschi, "GE Has Bright Ideas," *Smart Business*, June 2001; Mark Roberti, "General Electric's Spin Machine," *The Industry Standard*, January 15, 2001; Ramona Dzinkowski, "Removing Boundaries to Learning," *Knowledge Management*, May 2001; Meridith Levinson, "Destructive Behavior," *CIO Magazine*, July 15, 2000; Jon Burke, "Is GE the Last Internet Company?" *Red Herring*, December 19, 2000; Geoffrey Colvin, "How Leading Edge Are They?" *Fortune*, February 21, 2000; Cheryl Dahle, "Adventures in Polymerland," *Fast Company*, May 2000; David Bicknell, "Let There Be Light," *ComputerWeekly.com*, September 7, 2000; David Drucker, "Virtual Teams Light Up GE," *Internet Week*, April 6, 2000; David Joachim, "GE's E-Biz Turnaround Proves That Big Is Back," *Internet Week*, April 3, 2000; Mark Baard, "GE's WebCity," *Publish*, September 2000; Faith Keenan, "Giants Can Be Nimble," *Business Week*, September 18, 2000; Marianne Kolbasuk McGee, "E-Business Makes General Electric a Different Company," *Information Week*, January 31, 2000; Marianne Kolbasuk McGee, "Wake-Up Call," *Information Week*, September 18, 2000; Pamela L. Moore, "GE's Cyber Payoff," *Business Week*, April 13, 2000; Srikumar S. Rao, "General Electric, Software Vendor," *Forbes*, January 24, 2000; and Jim Rohwer, Jack Welch, Scott McNealy, John Huey, and Brent Schlender, "The Odd Couple," *Fortune*, May 1, 2000.

CASE STUDY QUESTIONS

1. Use the value chain and competitive forces models to analyze GE and its business strategy. Summarize the business and technology conditions causing GE to launch its Internet initiative.

2. How is GE using Internet technology in its internal and external business processes? How is the Internet related to its business strategy? How is it changing the way the company conducts its business?

3. What management, organization, and technology issues did GE have to address in its Internet initiative?

4. Evaluate GE's Internet initiative. Has it been successful? Is the company transforming itself into a digital firm? Why or why not?

chapter

4

THE DIGITAL FIRM: ELECTRONIC COMMERCE AND ELECTRONIC BUSINESS

As a manager, you'll want to know how your firm can benefit from electronic commerce and electronic business. After completing this chapter, you will be able to answer the following questions:

1. *How has Internet technology changed value propositions and business models?*

2. *What is electronic commerce? How has electronic commerce changed consumer retailing and business-to-business transactions?*

3. *What are the principal payment systems for electronic commerce?*

4. *How can Internet technology support electronic business and supply chain management?*

5. *What are the major managerial and organizational challenges posed by electronic commerce and electronic business?*

GUESS Goes Digital

During the 1980s and early 1990s, GUESS dominated the designer jeans and casual clothing market. But by 1997 the company was gasping for air. It had started out as a family business but had mushroomed into a corporate empire that had become difficult to manage. Competitors such as Levi's and the Gap sharpened their designs to grab GUESS's market.

At that point, Paul Marciano, the company's cochairman and co-chief executive officer called for overhauling GUESS from head to toe. Marciano cut the workforce by 6 percent, shifting three-fourths of production from domestic to overseas plants. He set an ambitious sales target to triple sales to $2 billion by 2003. He also turned to the Internet to help him keep costs low while increasing sales.

GUESS launched a major initiative to shift its internal and external business processes to the Internet. Working with Cisco Systems, GUESS replaced a tangle of

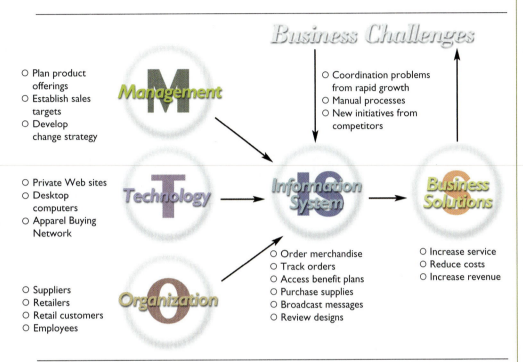

Business Challenges

Management
○ Plan product offerings
○ Establish sales targets
○ Develop change strategy

Technology
○ Private Web sites
○ Desktop computers
○ Apparel Buying Network

Organization
○ Suppliers
○ Retailers
○ Retail customers
○ Employees

○ Coordination problems from rapid growth
○ Manual processes
○ New initiatives from competitors

Information System
○ Order merchandise
○ Track orders
○ Access benefit plans
○ Purchase supplies
○ Broadcast messages
○ Review designs

Business Solutions
○ Increase service
○ Reduce costs
○ Increase revenue

outdated networking equipment with up-to-date standardized technology. With the help of software vendors PeopleSoft and CommerceOne, GUESS created an Apparel Buying Network for its suppliers and independent retailers in the United States and 230 other countries. The company can use the Apparel Buying Network to purchase direct items such as trim, fabric, and finished goods and indirect items such as office and maintenance supplies. Store buyers can order merchandise directly from GUESS by entering their purchases on a private Web site called ApparelBuy.com, which is integrated with the firm's core order processing systems. Users can then track their orders through fulfillment or delivery any time of the day or night. The ApparelBuy.com system features software to maintain an on-line catalog and to integrate information from sales, inventory, and other business functions. ApparelBuy.com can detect order errors by checking catalog product numbers, correct the orders, and avoid shipping the wrong products, thereby reducing the amount of returns. GUESS used to take one to two weeks to place and receive orders using manual, paper-based processes. With its new system, it has reduced its ordering process to one or two days and cut warehouse operations staff from 350 to 110 people. ApparelBuy.com is open to other companies in the fashion industry, including GUESS's competitors.

GUESS maintains a public Web site for retail customers called GUESS.com, which offers product catalogs and merchandise ordering on-line. This e-commerce site generates as many sales as one of the GUESS flagship stores, and GUESS expects sales to grow even more as it offers more merchandise on this site. GUESS established www.babyguess.com and www.guesskids.com as e-commerce sites for retailing infants' and children's clothing and accessories.

GUESS is also using Internet technology to streamline its internal business processes. GUESSExpress is an internal private network based on Internet technology that is used for purchasing supplies, reviewing architectural plans for new stores, making travel arrangements, and broadcasting messages to managers about operating instructions and company and industry trends. Employees can use GUESSExpress to access their benefits records on-line and make changes to their benefits plans.

All of these systems will eventually replace most of GUESS's telephone and fax-based processes. Management believes these systems will increase revenue and decrease costs by providing more efficient supply chain management and customer service while reducing internal administrative expenses. GUESS management is counting on the Internet to change the whole backbone of how the company does business in the twenty-first century.

Sources: Thomas York, "Perfect Fit," *Cisco IQ Magazine*, January/February 2001; GUESS Annual Report, March 30, 2000; and www.apparelbuy.com.

MANAGEMENT CHALLENGES

Like GUESS, many companies are starting to use the Internet to communicate with both their customers and suppliers, creating new digital electronic commerce networks that bypass traditional distribution channels. They are using Internet technology to streamline their internal business processes as well. Digitally enabling business processes and relationships with other organizations can help companies achieve new levels of competitiveness and efficiency, but they raise the following management challenges:

1. **Electronic commerce and electronic business require a complete change of mindset.** Digital firms require new organizational designs and management processes. To implement electronic commerce and electronic business successfully, companies must examine and perhaps redesign entire business processes rather than trying to graft new technology on existing business practices. Companies must consider a different organizational structure, changes in organizational culture, a different support structure for information systems, different procedures for managing employees and networked processing functions, and perhaps a different business strategy. Electronic commerce requires different strategies for ordering, advertising, and customer support than traditional business strategies (Chaudhury, Mallick, and Rao, 2001).

2. **Finding a successful Internet business model.** Companies have raced to put up Web sites in the hope of increasing earnings through electronic commerce. However, many electronic commerce sites have yet to turn a profit or to make a tangible difference in firms' sales and marketing efforts. Cost savings or access to new markets promised by the Web may not materialize. Companies need to think carefully about whether they can create a genuinely workable business model on the Internet and how the Internet relates to their overall business strategy. Internet technology alone is not a substitute for an effective business strategy (Rangan and Adner, 2001; Willcocks and Plant, 2001).

I nternet technology is creating a universal technology platform for buying and selling goods and for driving important business processes inside the firm. It has inspired new ways of organizing and managing that are transforming businesses and the use of information systems in everyday life. In addition to bringing many new benefits and opportunities, electronic commerce and electronic business are creating new sets of management challenges. We describe these challenges so that organizations can understand the management, organization, and technology issues that must be addressed to benefit from electronic commerce, electronic business, and the emerging digital firm.

4.1   ELECTRONIC COMMERCE, ELECTRONIC BUSINESS, AND THE EMERGING DIGITAL FIRM

Throughout this edition, we emphasize the benefits of integrating information across the enterprise, creating an information technology infrastructure in which information can flow seamlessly from one part of the organization to another and from the organization to its customers, suppliers, and business partners. The emerging digital firm requires this level of information integration, and companies increasingly depend on such an infrastructure today to remain efficient and competitive. Internet technology has emerged as the key enabling technology for this digital integration.

INTERNET TECHNOLOGY AND THE DIGITAL FIRM

For a number of years, companies used proprietary systems to integrate information from their internal systems and to link to their customers and trading partners. Such systems were expensive and based on technology standards that only a few could follow. The Internet is rapidly becoming the infrastructure of choice for electronic commerce because it offers businesses an even easier way to link with other businesses and individuals at a very low cost. It provides a universal and easy-to-use set of technologies and technology standards that can be adopted by all organizations, no matter what computer system or information technology platform the organizations are using.

Trading partners can directly communicate with each other, bypassing intermediaries and inefficient multilayered procedures. Web sites are available to consumers 24 hours a day. Some information-based products, such as software, music, and videos, can actually be physically distributed via the Internet. Vendors of other types of products and services can use the Internet to distribute the information surrounding their wares, such as product pricing, options, availability, and delivery time. The Internet can replace existing distribution channels or extend them, creating outlets for attracting and serving customers who otherwise would not patronize the company. For example, Web-based discount brokerages have attracted new customers who could not afford paying the high commissions and fees charged by conventional brokerage and financial services firms.

Companies can use Internet technology to radically reduce their transaction costs. Chapter 3 introduced the concept of transaction costs, which include the costs of searching for buyers and sellers, collecting information on products, negotiating terms, writing and enforcing contracts, and transporting merchandise. Information on buyers, sellers, and prices for many products is immediately available on the Web. For example, manually processing a purchase order can cost $100 to $125, whereas purchasing goods via an Internet marketplace can reduce those costs by nearly 80 percent. Table 4-1 provides other examples

TABLE 4-1	HOW THE INTERNET REDUCES TRANSACTION COSTS	
Transaction	**Traditional**	**Internet**
Checking bank account balance	$1.08	$.13
Answering a customer question	$10 to $20	$.10 to $.20
Trading 100 shares of stock	$100	$9.95
Correcting an employee record	$128	$2.32
Processing a customer order	$15	$.80
Sending an advertising brochure	$.75–$10.00	$0–$.25
Paying a bill	$2.22–$3.32	$.65–$1.10

of transaction cost reductions from the Internet or Internet technology. Handling transactions electronically can reduce transaction costs and delivery time for some goods, especially those that are purely digital (such as software, text products, images, or videos) because these products can be distributed over the Internet as electronic versions.

Equally important, Internet technology is providing the infrastructure for electronic business because its technology and technology standards can also be used to make information flow seamlessly from one part of the organization to another. Internet technology provides a much lower cost and easier to use alternative for coordination activities than proprietary networks. Managers can use e-mail and other Internet communication capabilities to oversee larger numbers of employees, to manage many tasks and subtasks in projects, and to coordinate the work of multiple teams working in different parts of the world. Internet standards can be used to link disparate systems, such as ordering and logistics tracking, which previously could not communicate with each other. The Internet also reduces other agency costs, such as the cost to coordinate activities of the firm with suppliers and other external business partners. The low-cost connectivity and universal standards provided by Internet technology are the driving force behind the explosion of electronic business and the emergence of the digital firm.

New Business Models and Value Propositions

The Internet has introduced major changes in the way companies conduct business. It has created a dramatic drop in the cost of developing, sending, and storing information while making that information more widely available. Millions of people can exchange massive amounts of information directly, instantly, and for free.

In the past, information about products and services was usually tightly bundled with the physical value chain for those products and services. If a consumer wanted to find out about the features, price, and availability of a refrigerator or an automobile, for instance, that person had to visit a retail store that sold those products. The cost of comparison shopping was very high because people had to physically travel from store to store.

The Internet has changed that relationship. Once everyone is connected electronically, information about products and services can flow on its own directly and instantly to consumers. The traditional link between the flow of the product and the flow of product-related information can be broken. Information is not limited to traditional physical methods of delivery. Customers can find out about products on their own on the Web and buy directly from product suppliers instead of using intermediaries such as retail stores.

business model

An abstraction of what an enterprise is and how the enterprise delivers a product or service, showing how the enterprise creates wealth.

This unbundling of information from traditional value chain channels is having a disruptive effect on old business models and is creating new business models as well. A **business model** describes how the enterprise delivers a product or service, showing how the enterprise creates wealth. Some of the traditional channels for exchanging product information have become unnecessary or uneconomical, and business models based on the coupling of information with products and services may no longer be necessary.

For example, in pre-Internet retailing days, people who wanted to purchase books had to go to a physical bookstore in order to learn what titles were available, the books' contents, and prices. The bookstore had a monopoly on this information. When Amazon.com opened as an on-line bookstore, it provided visitors a Web site with a vast electronic catalog containing close to 3 million titles, along with tables of contents, reviews, and other information about those titles. People could order books directly from their desktop computers. Amazon.com was able to sell books at lower cost because it did not have to pay rent, employee salaries, warehousing, and other overhead to maintain physical retail bookstores. (Amazon had almost no inventory costs because it relied on book distributors to stock most of its books.) Traditional booksellers who maintained physical storefronts were threatened. Selling books and other goods directly to consumers on-line without using physical storefronts represents a new business model. Publishers are now challenging this business model by selling digital electronic books directly to consumers without any intermediaries at all.

Financial service business models underwent a similar revolution. In the past, people wishing to purchase stocks or bonds had to pay high commissions to full-service brokers such as Merrill Lynch. Individual investors relied on these firms both to execute their trading transactions and to provide them with investment information. It was difficult for individual

Internet brokerage firms such as E*Trade deliver real-time market quotes and other investment information directly to users' desktops. Customers can place their own trades for a fraction of the cost of using a traditional full-service broker.

investors to obtain stock quotes, charts, investment news, historical data, investment advice, and other financial information on their own. Such information can be found now in abundance on the Web, and investors can use financial Web sites to place their own trades directly for very small transaction fees. The unbundling of financial information from trading has sharply reduced the need for full-service retail brokers.

The Changing Economics of Information

The Internet shrinks information asymmetry. An **information asymmetry** exists when one party in a transaction has more information that is important for the transaction than the other party. That information can determine their relative bargaining power. For example, until auto retailing sites appeared on the Web, there was a pronounced information asymmetry between auto dealers and customers. Only the auto dealers knew the manufacturers' prices, and it was difficult for consumers to shop around for the best price. Auto dealers' profit margins depended on this asymmetry of information. Now consumers have access to a legion of Web sites providing competitive pricing information, and the majority of auto buyers use the Internet to shop around for the best deal. Thus, the Web has reduced the information asymmetry surrounding an auto purchase. The Internet has also helped businesses seeking to purchase from other businesses reduce information asymmetries and locate better prices and terms.

Before the Internet, businesses had to make tradeoffs between the richness and reach of their information. **Richness** refers to the depth and detail of information—the amount of information the business can supply to the customer as well as information the business collects about the customer. **Reach** refers to how many people a business can connect with and how many products it can offer those people. Rich communication occurs, for example, when a sales representative meets with a customer, sharing information that is very specific to that interaction. Such an interaction is very expensive for a business because it can only take place with a small audience. Newspaper and television ads could reach millions of people quite inexpensively, but the information they provide is much more limited. It used to be prohibitively expensive for traditional businesses to have both richness and reach. Few, if any, companies could afford to provide highly detailed, customized information to a large mass audience. The Internet has transformed the richness and reach relationships (see Figure 4-1). Using the Internet and Web multimedia capabilities, companies can quickly and inexpensively provide detailed product information and detailed information specific to each customer to very large numbers of people simultaneously (Evans and Wurster, 2000).

Internet-enabled relationships between richness and rich are changing internal operations as well. Organizations can now exchange rich, detailed information among large numbers of people, making it easier for management to coordinate more jobs and tasks. In the

information asymmetry
Situation where the relative bargaining power of two parties in a transaction is determined by one party in the transaction possessing more information essential to the transaction than the other party.

richness
Measurement of the depth and detail of information that a business can supply to the customer as well as information the business collects about the customer.

reach
Measurement of how many people a business can connect with and how many products it can offer those people.

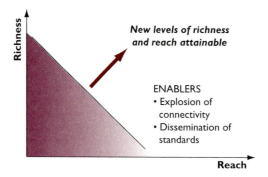

Figure 4-1 The changing economics of information. In the past, companies have had to trade off between the richness and reach of their information. Internet connectivity and universal standards for information-sharing radically lower the cost of providing rich, detailed information to large numbers of people, reducing the tradeoff.

past, management's span of control had to be much narrower because rich communication could only be channeled among a few people at a time using cumbersome manual paper-based processes. Digitally enabled business processes have become new sources of organizational efficiency, reducing operating costs while improving the accuracy and timeliness of customer service.

Internet Business Models

The Internet can help companies create and capture profit in new ways by adding extra value to existing products and services or by providing the foundation for new products and services. Table 4-2 describes some of the most important Internet business models that have emerged. All in one way or another add value: They provide the customer with a new product or service; they provide additional information or service along with a traditional product or service; or they provide a product or service at much lower cost than traditional means.

Some of these new business models take advantage of the Internet's rich communication capabilities. EBay is an on-line auction forum, using e-mail and other interactive features of the Web. People can make on-line bids for items, such as computer equipment, antiques and collectibles, wine, jewelry, rock-concert tickets, and electronics, that are posted by sellers from around the world. The system accepts bids for items entered on the Internet, evaluates the bids, and notifies the highest bidder. EBay collects a small commission on each listing and sale.

Business-to-business auctions are proliferating as well. AssetTrade, for instance, features Web-based auction services for business-to-business sales of used heavy industrial equipment and machinery. On-line bidding, also known as **dynamic pricing**, is expected to grow rapidly because buyers and sellers can interact so easily through the Internet to determine what an item is worth at any particular moment.

The Internet has created on-line communities, where people with similar interests can exchange ideas from many different locations. Some of these virtual communities are providing the foundation for new businesses. Tripod, Geocities, and FortuneCity (which started out in Great Britain) provide communities for people wishing to communicate with others about art, careers, health and fitness, sports, business, travel, and many other interests. Members can post their own personal Web pages, participate in on-line discussion groups, and join on-line "clubs" with other like-minded people. A major source of revenue for these communities is providing ways for corporate clients to target customers, including the placement of banner ads on their Web sites. A **banner ad** is a graphic display on a Web page used for advertising. The banner is linked to the advertiser's Web site so that a person clicking on the banner will be transported to a Web page with more information about the advertiser.

Even traditional retailing businesses are enhancing their Web sites with chat, message boards, and community-building features as a means of encouraging customers to spend more time, return more frequently, and hopefully make more purchases on-line. For example, iGo.com, a Web site selling mobile computing technology, found that its average sale shot up more than 50 percent after it added the ability to communicate interactively on-line with customer service representatives (Bannan, 2000).

The Web's information resources are so vast and rich that special business models called **portals** have emerged to help individuals and organizations locate information more efficiently. A portal is a Web site or other service that provides an initial point of entry to the Web or to internal company data. Yahoo! is an example. It provides a directory of informa-

dynamic pricing
Pricing of items based on real-time interactions between buyers and sellers that determine what a item is worth at any particular moment.

banner ad
A graphic display on a Web page used for advertising. The banner is linked to the advertiser's Web site so that a person clicking on it will be transported to the advertiser's Web site.

portal
Web site or other service that provides an initial point of entry to the Web or to internal company data.

TABLE 4-2 INTERNET BUSINESS MODELS

Category	Description	Examples
Virtual storefront	Sells physical products directly to consumers or to individual businesses.	Amazon.com EPM.com
Information broker	Provides product, pricing, and availability information to individuals and businesses. Generates revenue from advertising or from directing buyers to sellers.	Edmunds.com Kbb.com Insweb.com ehealthinsurance.com IndustrialMall.com
Transaction broker	Saves users money and time by processing on-line sales transactions, generating a fee each time a transaction occurs. Also provides information on rates and terms.	E*Trade.com Expedia.com
Online Marketplace	Provides a digital environment where buyers and sellers can meet, search for products, display products, and establish prices for those products. Can provide on-line auctions or reverse auctions where buyers submit bids to multiple sellers to purchase at a buyer-specified price as well as negotiated or fixed pricing. Can serve consumers or B2B e-commerce, generating revenue from transaction fees.	eBay.com Priceline.com ChemConnect.com Pantellos.com
Content provider	Creates revenue by providing digital content, such as digital news, music, photos, or video, over the Web. The customer may pay to access the content, or revenue may be generated by selling advertising space.	WSJ.com CNN.com TheStreet.com PhotoDisc.com MP3.com
On-line service provider	Provides on-line service for individuals and businesses. Generates revenue from subscription or transaction fees, from advertising or from collecting marketing information from users.	@Backup.com Xdrive.com Employease.com Salesforce.com
Virtual community	Provides on-line meeting place where people with similar interests can communicate and find useful information.	Geocities.com FortuneCity.com Tripod.com iVillage.com
Portal	Provides initial point of entry to the Web along with specialized content and other services.	Yahoo.com MSN.com StarMedia.com

tion on the Internet along with news, sports, weather, telephone directories, maps, games, shopping, e-mail, and other services. There are also specialized portals to help users with specific interests. For example, StarMedia is a portal customized for Latin American Internet users. (Companies are also building their own internal portals to provide employees with streamlined access to corporate information resources—see Chapter 10.)

Yahoo and other portals and Web content sites often combine content and applications from many different sources and service providers. Other Internet business models use syndication as well to provide additional value. For example, E*Trade, the discount Web trading site, purchases most of its content from outside sources such as Reuters (news), Bridge Information Systems (quotes), and BidCharts.com (charts). On-line **syndicators** who aggregate content or applications from multiple sources, package them for distribution, and resell them to third-party Web sites have emerged as another variant of the on-line content provider business model (Werbach, 2000). The Web makes it much easier for companies to aggregate, repackage, and distribute information and information-based services.

Chapter 6 describes application service providers such as Employease.com or Salesforce.com that feature software that runs over the Web. They provide on-line services to businesses. Other on-line service providers offer services to individual consumers, such as remote storage of data at Xdrive.com. Service providers generate revenue through subscription fees or from advertising.

Most of the business models described in Table 4-2 are called **pure-play** business models because they are based purely on the Internet. These firms did not have an existing

syndicator

Business aggregating content or applications from multiple sources, packaging them for distribution, and reselling them to third-party Web sites.

pure-play

Business models based purely on the Internet.

iVillage is an Internet business based on an on-line community for women sharing similar interests, such as diet and fitness, parenting, pregnancy, home and garden, and food. The company generates revenue from advertising banners on its Web pages.

bricks-and-mortar business when they designed their Internet business. However, many existing retail firms such as L. L. Bean, Office Depot, R.E.I., or the Wall Street Journal have developed Web sites as extensions of their traditional bricks-and-mortar businesses. Such businesses represent a hybrid **clicks-and-mortar** business model.

clicks-and-mortar
Business model where the Web site is an extension of a traditional bricks-and-mortar business.

4.2   Electronic Commerce

Although most commercial transactions still take place through conventional channels, rising numbers of consumers and businesses are using the Internet for electronic commerce. Projections show that by 2006, total e-commerce spending by consumers and businesses could surpass $5 trillion.

Categories of Electronic Commerce

There are many ways in which electronic commerce transactions can be classified. One is by looking at the nature of the participants in the electronic commerce transaction. The three major electronic commerce categories are business-to-consumer (B2C) e-commerce, business-to-business (B2B) e-commerce, and consumer-to-consumer (C2C) e-commerce.

business-to-consumer (B2C) electronic commerce
Electronic retailing of products and services directly to individual consumers.

❚ **Business-to-consumer (B2C) electronic commerce** involves retailing products and services to individual shoppers. Barnes&Noble.com, which sells books, software, and music to individual consumers, is an example of B2C e-commerce.

business-to-business (B2B) electronic commerce
Electronic sales of goods and services among businesses.

❚ **Business-to-business (B2B) electronic commerce** involves sales of goods and services among businesses. Milpro.com, Milacron Inc.'s Web site for selling cutting tools, grinding wheels, and metal working fluids to more than 100,000 small machining businesses, is an example of B2B e-commerce.

❚ **Consumer-to-consumer (C2C) electronic commerce** involves consumers selling directly to consumers. For example, eBay, the giant Web auction site, allows people to sell their goods to other consumers by auctioning the merchandise off to the highest bidder.

consumer-to-consumer (C2C) electronic commerce
Consumers selling goods and services electronically to other consumers.

Another way of classifying electronic commerce transactions is in terms of the participants' physical connection to the Web. Until recently, almost all e-commerce transactions took place over wired networks. Now cell phones and other wireless handheld digital appliances are Internet enabled so that they can be used to send e-mail or access Web sites. Companies are rushing to offer new sets of Web-based products and services that can be accessed by these wireless devices. For example, in Britain, customers of Virgin Mobile can use their cell phones to browse Virgin's Web site and purchase compact disks, wine, TV sets, and washing machines. Subscribers to Japan's NTT DoCoMo Internet cell phone service can send and receive e-mail, tap into on-line news, purchase airplane tickets, trade stocks, and browse through restaurant guides, linking to Web sites that have been redesigned to fit on tiny screens. The use of handheld wireless devices for purchasing goods and services has been termed **mobile commerce** or **m-commerce**. Both business-to-business and business-to-consumer e-commerce transactions can take place using m-commerce technology. Chapter 9 discusses m-commerce and wireless Web technology in detail.

CUSTOMER-CENTERED RETAILING

Despite the many failures of dot.com retail companies since mid-2000, on-line retailing continues to grow at a rapid pace. The Internet provides companies with new channels of communication and interaction that can create closer yet more cost-effective relationships with customers in sales, marketing, and customer support. Companies can use the Web to provide ongoing information, service, and support, creating positive interactions with customers that can serve as the foundations for long-term relationships and repeat purchases.

Direct Sales over the Web

Manufacturers can sell their products and services directly to retail customers, bypassing intermediaries such as distributors or retail outlets. Eliminating intermediaries in the distribution channel can significantly lower purchase transaction costs. Operators of virtual storefronts, such as Amazon.com or EPM.com, do not have large expenditures for rent, sales staff, and the other operations associated with a traditional retail store. Airlines can sell tickets directly to passengers through their own Web sites or through travel sites such as Travelocity without paying commissions to travel agents.

To pay for all the steps in a traditional distribution channel, a product may have to be priced as high as 135 percent of its original cost to manufacture (Mougayar, 1998). Figure 4-2 illustrates how much savings can result from eliminating each of these layers in the distribution process. By selling directly to consumers or reducing the number of intermediaries, companies can achieve higher profits while charging lower prices. The removal of organizations or business process layers responsible for intermediary steps in a value chain is called **disintermediation**.

The Internet is accelerating disintermediation in some industries and creating opportunities for new types of intermediaries in others. In certain industries, distributors with warehouses of goods, or intermediaries such as real estate agents may be replaced by new intermediaries or "infomediaries" specializing in helping Internet users efficiently obtain product and price information, locate on-line sources of goods and services, or manage or maximize the value of the information captured about them in electronic commerce transactions (Hagel, III, and Singer, 1999). The information brokers listed in Table 4-2 are examples. The

mobile commerce (m-commerce)
The use of wireless devices, such as cell phones or handheld digital information appliances, to conduct both business-to-consumer and business-to-business e-commerce transactions over the Internet.

disintermediation
The removal of organizations or business process layers responsible for certain intermediary steps in a value chain.

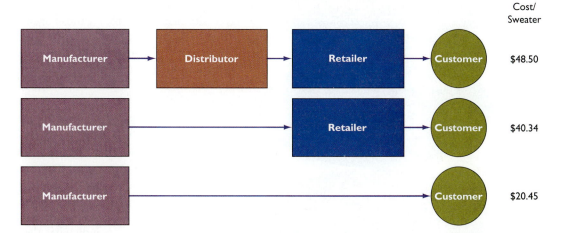

Figure 4-2 The benefits of disintermediation to the consumer. The typical distribution channel has several intermediary layers, each of which adds to the final cost of a product, such as a sweater. Removing layers lowers the final cost to the consumer.

reintermediation

The shifting of the intermediary role in a value chain to a new source.

process of shifting the intermediary function in a value chain to a new source is called **reintermediation**.

Interactive Marketing and Personalization

Marketers can use the interactive features of Web pages to hold consumers' attention or to capture detailed information about their tastes and interests for one-to-one marketing (see Chapter 3). Web sites have become a bountiful source of detailed information about customer behavior, preferences, needs, and buying patterns that companies can use to tailor promotions, products, services, and pricing. Some customer information may be obtained by asking visitors to "register" on-line and provide information about themselves, but many companies are also collecting customer information by using software tools that track the activities of Web site visitors. Companies can use special Web site auditing software capable of tracking the number of times visitors request Web pages, the Web pages of greatest interest to visitors after they have entered the sites, and the path visitors followed as they clicked from Web page to Web page. They can analyze this information about customer interests and behavior to develop more precise profiles of existing and potential customers.

For instance, TravelWeb, a Web site offering electronic information on more than 16,000 hotels in 138 countries and an on-line reservation capability, tracks the origin of each user and the screens and Web page links he or she uses to learn about customer preferences. The Hyatt hotel chain found that Japanese users are most interested in the resort's golf facilities, valuable information in shaping market strategies and for developing hospitality-related products.

Communications and product offerings can be tailored precisely to individual customers (Bakos, 1998). Generic Web sites that force users to wade through options and content that are irrelevant to them are considered frustrating, but firms can create unique personalized Web pages that display content or ads for products or services of special interest to each user, improving the customer's experience and creating additional value (see Figure 4-3). By using **Web personalization** technology to modify the Web pages presented to each customer, marketers can achieve the benefits of using individual salespeople at dramatically lower costs. Personalization can also help firms form lasting relationships with customers by providing individualized content, information, and services. Here are some examples:

Web personalization

The tailoring of Web content directly to a specific user.

❚ Amazon.com retains information on each customer's purchases. When a customer returns to the Amazon.com Web site, that person will be greeted with a Web page recommending books based on that person's purchase history or past purchases of other buyers with similar histories.

Figure 4-3 Web site personalization. Firms can create unique personalized Web pages that display content or ads for products or services of special interest to individual users, improving the customer experience and creating additional value.

❚ American Airlines is using personalization to reduce its cost structure by encouraging customers to manage their frequent flyer accounts and purchase tickets through its Web site instead of from a travel agent. American Airlines can create individual "travel agencies" for its customers on the Web, informing them that if they take one more domestic flight this year, they can achieve platinum frequent flyer status next year. American expects to sell $500 million worth of tickets from its Web site.

❚ Dell Computer allows users to create their own personal "Dell sites," where Dell can offer them special prices and deals based on the information they provide about their interests and computing requirements. Users can buy exactly what they want without having to call a representative, hunt down the products available, and try to work out deals.

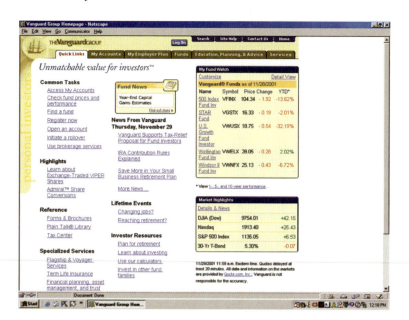

Web sites can tailor their content to the specific interests of individual visitors. The Vanguard Group home page can be personalized to display mutual fund information of special interest to the user.

Many other Web sites are using personalization technologies to deliver Web pages with content and banner ads geared to the specific interests of the visitor. Chapters 5, 9, and 11 describe additional technologies that gather the information on Web site visitors to make such personalized advertising and customer interaction possible. They also describe how companies are trying to combine Web visitor data with customer data from other sources such as off-line purchases, customer service records, or product registrations to create detailed profiles of individuals. Critics worry that companies gathering so much personal information on Web site visitors pose a threat to individual privacy, especially when much of this information is gathered without the customer's knowledge. Chapter 5 provides a detailed discussion of Web site privacy issues raised by these practices.

The cost of customer surveys and focus groups is very high. Learning how customers feel or what they think about one's products or services through electronic visits to Web sites is much cheaper. Web sites providing product information also lower costs by shortening the sales cycle and reducing the amount of time sales staff must spend in customer education. The Web shifts more marketing and selling activities to the customer, because customers fill out their own on-line order forms. By using the Web to provide vendors with more precise information about their preferences and suggestions for improving products and services, customers are being transformed from passive buyers to active participants in creating value (Prahalad and Ramaswamy, 2000).

M-Commerce and Next Generation Marketing

Within the next few years, the Web will be accessible from almost anywhere, as consumers turn to wireless telephones, handheld digital appliances, interactive television, or other information appliances to link to the Internet. Chapter 9 discusses m-commerce and new wireless Internet devices in greater detail. Travelers will be able to access the Internet in automobiles, airports, hotels, and train stations. Mobile commerce will provide businesses with additional channels for reaching customers and with new opportunities for personalization. Location tracking software in some of these devices will enable businesses to track users' movements and supply information, advertisements, and other services, such as local weather reports or directions to the nearest restaurant, while they are on the go. Instead of focusing on how to bring a customer to a Web site, marketing strategies will shift to finding ways of bringing the message directly to the customer at the point of need (Kenny and Marshall, 2000). Figure 4-4 illustrates how personalization can be extended via the ubiquitous Internet and m-commerce.

Customer Self-Service

The Web and other network technologies are inspiring new approaches to customer service and support. Many companies are using their Web sites and e-mail to answer customer questions or

Figure 4-4 Customer personalization with the ubiquitous Internet. Companies can use mobile wireless devices to deliver new value-added services directly to customers at any time and place, extending personalization and deepening their relationships.

Target	Platform	When	Content and Service
Traveler	Computer-equipped car	Whenever car is moving	Provide maps, driving directions, weather reports, ads for nearby restaurants and hotels.
Parent	Cell phone	During school days	Notify about school-related closings: Hello, Caroline. Your children's school is closing early. Press 1 for closure reason Press 2 for weather reports Press 3 for traffic reports
Stock Broker	Pager	During trading days. Notify if unusually high trading volume.	Summary portfolio analysis showing changes in positions for each holding.

to provide customers with helpful information. The Web provides a medium through which customers can interact with the company, at the customers' convenience, and find information that previously required a human customer-support expert. Automated self-service or other Web-based responses to customer questions cost a tiny fraction of the price of using a live customer service representative on the telephone.

Companies are realizing substantial cost savings from Web-based customer self-service applications. American, Northwest, and other major airlines have created Web sites where customers can review flight departure and arrival times, seating charts, and airport logistics; check frequent-flyer miles; and purchase tickets on-line. Yamaha Corporation of America has reduced customer calls concerning questions or problems by allowing customers to access technical solutions information from the service and support area of its Web site. If they can't find answers on their own, customers can send e-mail to a live technician. Chapter 1 described how customers of UPS can use its Web site to track shipments, calculate shipping costs, determine time in transit, and arrange for a package pickup. FedEx and other package delivery firms provide similar Web-based services.

New software products are even integrating the Web with customer call centers, where customer service problems have been traditionally handled over the telephone. A **call center** is an organizational department responsible for handling customer service issues by telephone and other channels. For example, visitors can click on a "push to talk" link on the Lands' End Web site that lets a user request a phone call. The user enters his or her telephone number and a call-center system directs a customer service representative to place a voice telephone call to the user's phone. Some systems also let the customer interact with a service representative on the Web while talking on the phone at the same time. The Lands' End site even offers a "shop with a friend" feature that lets site visitors contact friends by phone to help them with their purchasing decisions.

call center

An organizational department responsible for handling customer service issues by telephone and other channels.

BUSINESS-TO-BUSINESS ELECTRONIC COMMERCE: NEW EFFICIENCIES AND RELATIONSHIPS

For a number of years, companies have used proprietary systems for business-to-business (B2B) e-commerce. Now they are turning to the Web and Internet technology. By eliminating inefficient paper-based processes for locating suppliers, ordering supplies, or delivering

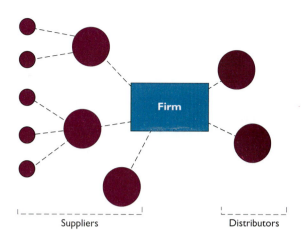

Figure 4-5 A private industrial network. A private industrial network links a firm to its suppliers, distributors, and other key business partners for efficient supply chain management and other collaborative commerce activities.

Suppliers   Distributors

goods, and by providing more opportunities for finding the lowest-priced products and services, business-to-business Web sites can save participants anywhere from 5 to 45 percent.

For business-to-business electronic commerce, companies can sell to other businesses using their own Web sites as electronic storefronts or they can execute purchase and sale transactions through private industrial networks or net marketplaces. We introduced *private industrial networks* in Chapter 2. Private industrial networks focus on continuous business process coordination between companies for collaborative commerce and supply chain management. A private industrial network typically consists of a large firm using an extranet to link to its suppliers and other key business partners (see Figure 4-5). The network is owned by the buyer and it permits the firm and designated suppliers, distributors, and other business partners to share product design and development, marketing, production scheduling, inventory management, and unstructured communication, including graphics and e-mail. Another term for a private industrial network is a **private exchange**. The Window on Management describes how Mitsubish's truck and motor sales divisions benefited from setting up such networks with dealers. Private industrial networks are currently the fastest-growing type of B2B commerce.

Net marketplaces, which are sometimes called *e-hubs*, provide a single digital marketplace based on Internet technology for many different buyers and sellers (see Figure 4-6). They are industry-owned or operate as independent intermediaries between buyers and sellers. Net marketplaces are more transaction-oriented (and less relationship-oriented) than private industrial networks, generating revenue from purchase and sale transactions and other services provided to clients. Participants in net marketplaces can establish prices through on-line negotiations, auctions, or requests for quotations, or they can use fixed prices.

There are many different types of net marketplaces and ways of classifying them. Some net marketplaces sell direct goods and some sell indirect goods. *Direct goods* are goods used in a production process, such as sheet steel for auto body production. *Indirect goods* are all other goods not directly involved in the production process, such as office supplies or products for maintenance and repair. Some net marketplaces support contractual purchasing based on long-term relationships with designated suppliers and others support short-term

private exchange
Another term for a private industrial network.

net marketplace
A single digital marketplace based on Internet technology linking many buyers to many sellers.

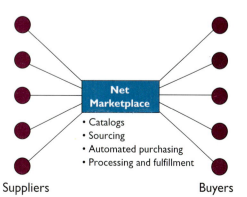

Figure 4-6 A net marketplace. Net marketplaces are on-line marketplaces where multiple buyers can purchase from multiple sellers.

Net Marketplace
- Catalogs
- Sourcing
- Automated purchasing
- Processing and fulfillment

Suppliers   Buyers

MITSUBISHI REVS UP ITS DEALER NETWORKS

For any manufacturer that relies on dealers and distributors, strong communication is essential to remain competitive. This is especially true for Mitsubishi, which suffered from a steep drop in automotive sales in 2001. The company has launched multiple Web-based initiatives to provide better information to dealers so that the dealers can work more efficiently and improve their customer service.

Mitsubishi Fuso Truck of North America used to share information with its network of 150 dealers in the United States primarily through the mail. Dealers received a pile of printed brochures, telephone-book size manuals, and bulletins, and they complained that they could not wade through the piles of paper to find the specific information they needed. Mitsubishi spent hundred of thousands of dollars on publishing.

Dealers had to use an outdated, homegrown system to enter orders for trucks and parts, submit warranty claims, and transmit inquiries to corporate headquarters in Bridgeport, New Jersey. The system was slow and cumbersome. Mitsubishi was afraid that dealers would find it so difficult to obtain up-to-date information that they would stop carrying Mitsubishi trucks. (About 75 percent of Mitsubishi dealers sell trucks from other manufacturers.)

In July 2000 Mitsubishi launched FusoNet, a private network based on Internet technology that could provide sales and support services to dealers via a Web interface. The system was designed to facilitate communication between dealers and company headquarters, to allow dealers to perform some transactions themselves, and to facilitate training and information gathering. Mitsubishi management instructed all dealers to start using FusoNet by January 2001. The network would be deemed successful if it increased dealership productivity by 25 percent.

The team that built FusoNet interviewed dealers to determine their information needs. Each dealer would have to be able to personalize the application to find exactly what she or he needed. Collaborative tools, such as e-mail, on-line instant messaging, electronic bulletin boards, and discussion areas, were added to the system. FusoNet also included aggregated news feeds from industry sources, on-line training, and on-line access to company publications.

The system was designed for ease of use. To access the system, the user only needs to log in once. InfoImage Inc., an enterprise portal software developer in Phoenix, provided tools to combine data from the company's existing systems and distribute it through a single user-friendly interface. The system provides dealers with an organized environment that assembles sales, customer service, and competitive information in a single location that can be accessed by all parties involved in selling trucks. Dealers can search electronically for any information they need, including information from third parties, such as industry news sources, finance companies, and suppliers. They can also electronically access diagrams, repair manuals, and time guides that used to be stored in telephone-book sized manuals. The new system processes warranty claims and parts orders from dealers almost immediately.

FusoNet is expected to save Mitsubishi hundreds of thousands of dollars annually in publishing costs alone. What's more, the system has improved the company's relationship with its dealers, who can use e-mail to fire off suggestions and criticisms. Mitsubishi management says it is hearing from dealers in ways it never did before. For example, Michele Royals, a sales manager for a Mitsubishi truck dealership outside of Chicago, uses FusoNet to gather data on inventory, sales, parts, competitor products, and advertising. She believes that FusoNet provides timely information whenever she needs it, which is critical in an industry that is constantly changing.

Mitsubishi Motor Sales of America took similar action to replace outdated systems with a Web-based private network for its 500 U.S. dealerships. Mitsubishi auto dealers can use the system to access reports on warranty repairs, billing, and the status of car and parts orders, and to search for invoices. The system lets dealers see whether they have met their sales targets and submit required financial statements about their operations. With more data in dealers' hands, they can react more quickly to the marketplace and be more responsive to customers.

To Think About: What are the management benefits of using these private industrial networks? How did they change the way Mitsubishi's auto and truck divisions conducted their business?

Sources: Phat X. Chiem, "Tools for Trucking," *Knowledge Management*, July 2001; and Antone Gonsalves, "Dealers Try Online CRM," *Information Week*, July 23, 2001.

---

spot purchasing, where goods are purchased based on immediate needs, often from many different suppliers. Some net marketplaces serve vertical markets for specific industries, such as automobiles, telecommunications, or machine tools, while others serve horizontal markets for goods and services that can be found in many different industries, such as office equipment or transportation.

W. W. Grainger serves the horizontal market for sourcing MRO (maintenance, repair, and operations) products used in many different industries. Its Web site provides a single source from which customers can make spot purchases of indirect goods from many different

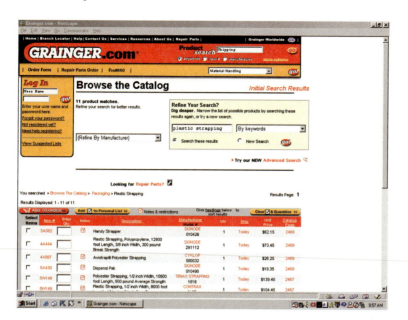

Grainger.com provides a single on-line source from which customers can make spot purchases of maintenance, repair, and operations products from many different companies.

suppliers. Grainger.com features on-line versions of Grainger's seven-pound paper catalog plus access to parts and supplies from other sources and capabilities for electronic ordering and payment. Most of this site is open to the public. Customers benefit from lower search costs, lower transaction costs, wide selection, and lower prices, while Grainger earns revenue by charging a markup on the products it distributes.

Ariba and CommerceOne are independently owned, third-party intermediaries that bundle extensive e-commerce services with net marketplaces for long-term contractual purchasing of both indirect and direct goods. They provide both buyers and sellers with software systems and services to run net marketplaces, aggregating hundreds of catalogs into a single marketplace and customizing procurement and sales processes to work with their systems. For buyers, Ariba and CommerceOne automate sourcing, contract management, purchase orders, requisitions, business rules enforcement, and payment. For sellers, these net marketplaces provide services for catalog creation and content management, order management, invoicing, and settlement. For example, Federal Express uses Ariba's e-procurement system for $8 million in purchases. Employees use Ariba to order from more than 32 MRO suppliers and catalogs. The system automatically invokes FedEx's business rules for purchasing to route, review, and approve requisitions electronically. By using this net marketplace, FedEx has reduced the cost of processing purchases by 75 percent and the prices paid for MRO supplies by 12 percent, and it has cut parts delivery time from an average of seven days to two days.

Covisint is an example of an industry-owned net marketplace serving the vertical market for automobile manufacturing. It brings a small number of prechosen buyers in contact with thousands of preselected suppliers and provides value-added software services for procurement, transaction management, and payment. Industry-owned net marketplaces focus on long-term contract purchasing relationships and on providing common networks and computing platforms for reducing supply chain inefficiencies. Buyer firms can benefit from competitive pricing among alternative suppliers, and suppliers can benefit by having stable long-term selling relationships with large firms. The ultimate goal of some industry-owned net marketplaces is the unification of an entire industry supply chain. The Window on Organizations provides more detail on the challenges facing Covisint as it struggles to become a viable business model.

Exchanges are third-party net marketplaces that can connect thousands of suppliers and buyers for spot purchasing. Many exchanges provide vertical markets for a single industry, such as food, electronics, or industrial equipment, and they primarily deal with direct inputs. For example, Altra Energy Technologies operates an on-line exchange for spot purchases in the energy industry. Suppliers use the exchange to sell natural gas, liquids, power, and crude oil to small utilities and energy distributors.

exchange

Third-party net marketplace that is primarily transaction oriented and that connects many buyers and suppliers for spot purchasing.

CAN COVISINT SUCCEED AS AN AUTO INDUSTRY NET MARKETPLACE?

On February 25, 2000, General Motors, Ford, and Daimler-Chrysler announced the formation of a new automotive industry business-to-business net marketplace called Covisint to squeeze excess costs out of the process of purchasing auto parts and equipment. The Big 3 spend about $240 billion each year on direct and indirect supplies. Lower prices would be achieved by requiring suppliers to bid for orders together over the Covisint Web site and by reducing the cost of each purchase order transaction. Covisint is expected to reduce the transaction cost of each purchase order from $100 to $10 or $20. Covisint includes an analysis tool to help the manufacturers weigh competing bids from suppliers using attributes such as quality, price, and delivery date. The automobile producers believe they will save billions every year, trimming costs by $1,200 to $3,000 per car. The rival automakers believe they could realize additional savings by sharing one common industry exchange rather than bearing the costs of setting up their own exchanges. Covisint could also provide savings to suppliers by providing a low-cost point of entry for trading with manufacturers. Covisint is controlled by the Big 3 automobile manufacturers (who were later joined by Renault and Nissan Motors) and two companies supplying the software: Oracle and CommerceOne.

Covisint has already enrolled close to 2,000 Tier 1 suppliers—the largest suppliers in the industry—such as Dana and Johnson Controls, which sell completed components, such as axles, brake systems, instrument panels, and seats. It is soliciting participation from Tier 2 and Tier 3 suppliers—the smaller suppliers who sell parts to Tier 1 suppliers. Once Covisint can link automakers to the entire supply chain, it hopes to provide on-line global communication for demand forecasting, capacity planning, and logistics that would make it possible build automobiles to order. The automakers also hope Covisint will reduce the time it takes to develop a new automobile from 42 months to 12 to 18 months by providing collaborative software tools for car designers, engineers, parts manufacturers, and materials suppliers to share design documents and schedules.

Covisint has faced challenges from its inception. The U.S. Federal Trade Commission (FTC) investigated whether the giant automobile manufacturers were using Covisint to control parts prices. The supply chain for the automotive industry is large and complex, with a car or light truck requiring 5,000 different components sourced from 90,000 suppliers. Many auto industry suppliers have been reluctant to participate in the exchange. Many of the auto industry's 8,000 first-tier suppliers have already built their own private networks to be used with their lower-tier suppliers. Covisint has now assured these suppliers that Covisint is being designed to enable the suppliers to use their own private networks in conjunction with Covisint. The Tier 1 suppliers fear they could lose money and control over their own supply chains if Covisint becomes a single point of entry for transactions among all suppliers in the entire auto industry. Suppliers also worry that bidding for orders with competitors in an industry-wide net marketplace will turn their products into commodities, that they will lose the benefit of loyalty to their brands. But one advantage seen by the smaller suppliers is that Covisint will enable them to participate in e-commerce; previously more than 60 percent of them could not afford their own electronic networks.

The entire business world is watching Covisint very closely, because Covisint is the largest and most visible B2B exchange in operation. By mid-2001 Covisint had generated nearly $38 billion in auction revenue and hosted 26,000 transactions from more than 200 on-line supplier catalogs. Ford Motor Company claimed it would save $350 million in indirect procurement costs in 2001. Can Covisint sustain profits and deliver on its promises?

To Think About: Do you think Covisint can succeed. If so, how and why? If not, why not? What are the strengths and weaknesses of its business model?

Sources: Christopher Koch, "Motorcity Shakeup," *Darwin Magazine,* January 2002; Ruhan Memishi, "Covisint's Starts and Stops," *Internet World,* January 1, 2001; Bill Robinson," Covisint; Driving the Automotive Industry," *IQ Magazine,* January/February 2001; Richard Brown, "GM Spends $98 Billion Via Covisint," *Line 56,* August 21, 2001; and Chuck Moozakis, "Big Auto Suppliers to Wield Tech Clout," *Internet Week,* August 13, 2001.

Exchanges proliferated during the early years of e-commerce, but many have failed. Suppliers were reluctant to participate because the exchanges encouraged competitive bidding that drove prices down and did not offer any long-term relationships with buyers or services to make lowering prices worthwhile. Many essential direct purchases are not conducted on a spot basis, requiring contracts and consideration of issues such as delivery timing, customization, and quality of products (Laudon, 2002; Wise and Morrison, 2000). The early exchanges primarily performed relatively simple transactions and could not handle these complexities as well as the more sophisticated B2B net marketplaces we previously described (Andrew, Blackburn and Sirkin, 2000).

ELECTRONIC COMMERCE PAYMENT SYSTEMS

Special **electronic payment systems** have been developed to handle ways of paying for goods electronically on the Internet. Electronic payment systems for the Internet include systems for credit card payments, digital cash, digital wallets, accumulated balance digital payment systems, stored value payment systems, peer-to-peer payment systems, electronic checks, and electronic billing presentment and payment systems.

Credit cards account for 95 percent of on-line payments in the United States and about 50 percent of all on-line transactions outside the United States. The more sophisticated electronic commerce software (see Chapter 9) has capabilities for processing credit card purchases on the Web. Businesses can also contract with services that extend the functionality of existing credit card payment systems. **Digital credit card payment systems** extend the functionality of credit cards so they can be used for on-line shopping payments. They make credit cards safer and more convenient for merchants and consumers by providing mechanisms for authenticating the purchaser's credit card to make sure it is valid and arranging for the bank that issued the credit card to deposit money for the amount of the purchase in the seller's bank account. Chapter 14 describes the technologies for secure credit card processing in more detail.

Digital wallets make paying for purchases over the Web more efficient by eliminating the need for shoppers to repeatedly enter their address and credit card information each time they buy something. A **digital wallet** securely stores credit card and owner identification information and provides that information at an electronic commerce site's "checkout counter." The electronic wallet enters the shopper's name, credit card number, and shipping information automatically when invoked to complete the purchase. Amazon.com's 1-Click shopping, which enables a consumer to automatically fill in shipping and credit card information by clicking one button, uses electronic wallet technology. Gator and America Online's Quick Checkout are other digital wallet systems.

Micropayment systems have been developed for purchases of less than $10, such as downloads of individual articles or music clips, that would be too small for conventional credit card payments. Accumulated balance payment systems or stored value payment systems are useful for such purposes. **Accumulated balance digital payment systems** allow users to make micropayments and purchases on the Web, accumulating a debit balance that they must pay periodically on their credit card or telephone bills. Qpass, for instance, collects all of a consumer's tiny purchases for monthly billing on a credit card. The New York Times uses Qpass to bill consumers wishing to access articles from its Web site. Trivnet lets consumers charge small purchases to their monthly telephone bill.

Stored value payment systems enable consumers to make instant on-line payments to merchants and other individuals based on value stored in a digital account. On-line value

---

electronic payment system
The use of digital technologies, such as credit cards, smart cards, and Internet-based payment systems, to pay for products and services electronically.

digital credit card payment system
Secure services for credit card payments on the Internet that protect information transmitted among users, merchant sites, and processing banks.

digital wallet
Software that stores credit card and owner identification information and provides these data automatically during electronic commerce purchase transactions.

micropayment
Payment for a very small sum of money, often less than $10.

accumulated balance digital payment systems
Systems enabling users to make micropayments and purchases on the Web, accumulating a debit balance on their credit card or telephone bills.

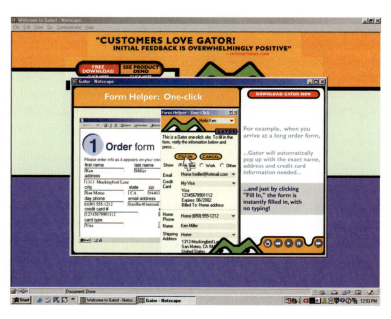

Gator (www.gator.com) is a digital wallet system which stores personal information securely on the user's computer. When the user encounters a registration or order form on the Web, Gator Form Helper pops up and fills in the form with one or just a few clicks.

TABLE 4-3

EXAMPLES OF ELECTRONIC PAYMENT SYSTEMS FOR E-COMMERCE

Payment System	Description	Commercial Example
Digital credit card payment systems	Secure services for credit card payments on the Internet protect information transmitted among users, merchant sites, and processing banks	CyberSource eCharge IC Verify
Digital wallet	Software that stores credit card and other information to facilitate payment for goods on the Web	Gator AOL Quick Checkout
Accumulated balance payment systems	Accumulates micropayment purchases as a debit balance that must be paid periodically on credit card or telephone bills	Qpass Trivnet
Stored value payment systems	Enables consumers to make instant payments to merchants based on value stored in a digital account	Mondex smart card American Express Blue smart card
Digital cash	Digital currency that can be used for micropayments or larger purchases	eCoin InternetCash
Peer-to-peer payment systems	Sends money using the Web to individuals or vendors who are not set up to accept credit card payments	PayPal
Digital checking	Electronic check with a secure digital signature	Achex CHEXpedite
Electronic billing presentment and payment	Supports electronic payment for on-line and physical store purchases of goods or services after the purchase has taken place	CheckFree

stored value payment systems

Systems enabling consumers to make instant on-line payments to merchants and other individuals based on value stored in a digital account.

smart card

A credit-card-size plastic card that stores digital information and that can be used for electronic payments in place of cash.

digital cash

Currency represented in electronic form that moves outside the normal network of money.

peer-to-peer payment system

Electronic payment system for people who want to send money to vendors or individuals who are not set up to accept credit card payments.

Digital checking

Systems that extend the functionality of existing checking accounts so they can be used for on-line shopping payments.

systems rely on the value stored in a consumer's bank, checking, or credit card account and some of these systems require the use of a digital wallet. Smart cards are another type of stored value system used for micropayments. A **smart card** is a plastic card the size of a credit card that stores digital information. The smart card can store health records, identification data, or telephone numbers, or it can serve as an "electronic purse" in place of cash. The Mondex and American Express Blue smart cards contain electronic cash and can be used to transfer funds to merchants in physical storefronts and to merchants on the Internet. Both are contact smart cards that require use of special card reading devices whenever the cards need to transfer cash to either an on-line or off-line merchant. (Internet users must attach a smart card reader to their PCs to use the card. To pay for a Web purchase, the user would swipe the smart card through the card reader.)

Digital cash (also known as electronic cash or e-cash) can also be used for micropayments or larger purchases. **Digital cash** is currency represented in electronic form that moves outside the normal network of money (paper currency, coins, checks, credit cards). Users are supplied with client software and can exchange money with another e-cash user over the Internet or with a retailer accepting e-cash. ECoin and InternetCash.com are examples of digital cash services. In addition to facilitating micropayments, digital cash can be useful for people who don't have credit cards and wish to make Web purchases.

New Web-based **peer-to-peer payment systems** have sprung up to serve people who want to send money to vendors or individuals who are not set up to accept credit card payments. The party sending money uses his or her credit card to create an account with the designated payment at a Web site dedicated to peer-to-peer payments. The recipient "picks up" the payment by visiting the Web site and supplying information about where to send the payment (a bank account or a physical address.) PayPal has become a popular person-to-person payment system.

Digital checking payment systems, such as CHEXpedite and Achex, extend the functionality of existing checking accounts so they can be used for on-line shopping payments. Digital checks are less expensive than credit cards and much faster than traditional paper-based checking. These checks are encrypted with a digital signature that can be verified and used for payments in electronic commerce. Electronic check systems are useful in business-to-business electronic commerce.

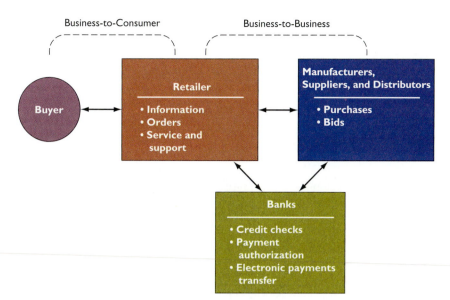

Figure 4-7 Electronic commerce information flows. Individuals can purchase goods and services electronically from on-line retailers, who in turn can use electronic commerce technologies to link directly to their suppliers or distributors. Electronic payment systems are used in both business-to-consumer and business-to-business electronic commerce.

Electronic billing presentment and payment systems are used for paying routine monthly bills. They allow users to view their bills electronically and pay them through electronic fund transfers from bank or credit card accounts. These services support payment for on-line and physical store purchases of goods or services after the purchase has taken place. They notify purchasers about bills that are due, present the bills, and process the payments. Some of these services, such as CheckFree, consolidate subscribers' bills from various sources so that they can all be paid at one time. Table 4-3 summarizes the features of these payment systems.

The process of paying for products and services purchased on the Internet is complex and merits additional discussion. We discuss electronic commerce security in detail in Chapter 14. Figure 4-7 provides an overview of the key information flows in electronic commerce.

electronic billing presentment and payment systems Systems used for paying routine monthly bills that allow users to view their bills electronically and pay them through electronic funds transfers from bank or credit card accounts.

4.3 ELECTRONIC BUSINESS AND THE DIGITAL FIRM

Businesses are finding that some of the greatest benefits of Internet technology come from applications that lower agency and coordination costs. Although companies have used internal networks for many years to manage and coordinate internal business processes, intranets quickly are becoming the technology of choice for electronic business.

HOW INTRANETS SUPPORT ELECTRONIC BUSINESS

Intranets are inexpensive, scalable to expand or contract as needs change, and accessible from most computing platforms. Whereas most companies, particularly the larger ones, must support a multiplicity of computer platforms that cannot communicate with each other, intranets provide instant connectivity, uniting all computers into a single, virtually seamless, network system. Web software presents a uniform interface, which can be used to integrate many different processes and systems throughout the company. Companies can connect their intranets to internal company transaction systems, enabling employees to take actions central to a company's operations. For instance, customer service representatives for Qwest Communications can access the firm's main customer system through the corporate intranet to turn on services, such as call waiting, or to check installation dates for new phone lines, all while the customer is on the telephone.

Intranets can help organizations create a richer, more responsive information environment. Internal corporate applications based on the Web page model can be made interactive using a variety of media, text, audio, and video. A principal use of intranets has been to create on-line repositories of information that can be updated as often as required. Product catalogs, employee handbooks, telephone directories, or benefits information can be revised

TABLE 4-4	ORGANIZATIONAL BENEFITS OF INTRANETS

Connectivity: accessible from most computing platforms

Can be tied to internal corporate systems and core transaction databases

Can create interactive applications with text, audio, and video

Scalable to larger or smaller computing platforms as requirements change

Easy to use, universal Web interface

Low start-up costs

Richer, more responsive information environment

Reduced information distribution costs

immediately as changes occur. This "event-driven" publishing allows organizations to respond more rapidly to changing conditions than traditional paper-based publishing, which requires a rigid production schedule. Made available via intranets, documents always can be up-to-date, eliminating paper, printing, and distribution costs. For instance, Sun Healthcare, a chain of nursing and long-term care facilities headquartered in Albuquerque, New Mexico, saved $400,000 in printing and mailing costs when it put its corporate newsletter on an intranet. The newsletter is distributed to 69,000 employees in 49 states.

Conservative studies of returns on investment (ROIs) from intranets show ROIs of 23 to 85 percent, and some companies have reported ROIs of more than 1,000 percent. For example, the Mitre Corporation reported that its $7.9 million invested in the intranet collaboration environment described in the following section produced $62.1 million in reduced costs and increased productivity. Mitre also realized nonquantifiable benefits, such as higher quality and more innovative solutions for clients (Young, 2000). More information on the business value of intranets can be found in Chapter 13. Table 4-4 summarizes the organizational benefits of intranets.

INTRANETS AND GROUP COLLABORATION

Intranets provide a rich set of tools for creating collaborative environments in which members of an organization can exchange ideas, share information, and work together on common projects and assignments regardless of their physical location. For example, Noranda Inc., a large Canadian mining company, uses an intranet to keep track of its mineral exploration research in a dozen offices in North and South America, Australia, and Europe.

Some companies are using intranets to create enterprise collaboration environments linking diverse groups, projects, and activities throughout the organization. For example, the Mitre Corporation, which conducts research and development work for the U.S. federal government, set up a collaborative environment called Mitre Information Infrastructure for sharing personnel, planning, and project information. This intranet includes a corporate directory with names, telephone numbers, and resumes of Mitre employees; a Lessons Learned Library with best practices and lessons learned from 10 years of Mitre projects; and capabilities for filing human resources reports, such as time sheets, service requests, and property inventory and tracking forms. Chapter 10 provides a detailed discussion of intranets in collaborative work.

INTRANET APPLICATIONS FOR ELECTRONIC BUSINESS

Intranets are springing up in all the major functional areas of businesses, allowing organizations to manage more business processes electronically. Figure 4-8 illustrates some of the intranet applications that have been developed for finance and accounting, human resources, sales and marketing, and manufacturing and production.

Finance and Accounting

Many organizations have extensive TPS that collect operational data on financial and accounting activities, but their traditional management reporting systems, such as general

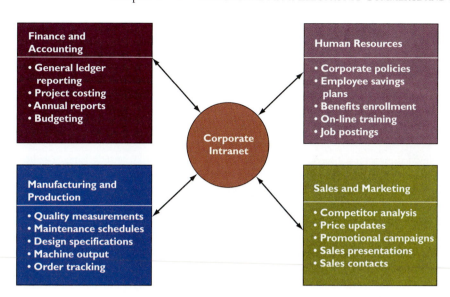

Figure 4-8 Functional applications of intranets. Intranet applications have been developed for each of the major functional areas of the business.

ledger systems and spreadsheets, often cannot bring this detailed information together for decision making and performance measurement. Intranets can be very valuable for finance and accounting because they can provide an integrated view of financial and accounting information on-line in an easy-to-use format. Table 4-5 provides some examples.

Human Resources

Principal responsibilities of human resources departments include keeping employees informed of company issues and providing information about employees' personnel records and benefits. Human resources can use intranets for on-line publishing of corporate policy manuals, job postings and internal job transfers, company telephone directories, and training classes. Employees can use an intranet to enroll in healthcare, employee savings, and other benefit plans if it is linked to the firm's human resources or benefits database, or to take on-line competency tests. Human resources departments can rapidly deliver information about upcoming events or company developments to employees using newsgroups or e-mail broadcasts. Table 4-6 lists examples of how intranets are used in the area of human resources.

TABLE 4-5 **INTRANETS IN FINANCE AND ACCOUNTING**

Organization	Intranet Application
J.P. Morgan Chase	Web-based system based on software from Hyperion Solutions manages how corporate units charge each other for services provided inside the corporation. Software consolidates information from a series of business and accounting systems and presents users with customizable pages that show the amounts their departments are being billed for services, such as information processing or use of conference rooms. Users can compare actual bills with the amounts they budgeted and drill down to obtain additional information.
Charles Schwab	SMART reporting and analysis application provides managers with a comprehensive view of Schwab's financial activities, including a risk-evaluation template that helps managers assess nine categories of risk. Schwab's intranet also delivers the FinWeb General Ledger reporting system on-line in an easy-to-digest format.
U.S. Department of Agriculture Rural Development	Intranet makes information about its loan and grant programs for rural and small communities available to its 7,200 employees. Employees can use standard Web browsing software to find out which projects have been funded in specific local areas.
Pacific Northwest National Laboratory	Intranet Web Reporting System provides financial statistics for laboratory activities, including current costs charged to each project, number of hours spent on each project by individual employees, and how actual costs compare to projected costs. Lab employees can use the intranet to perform ad hoc queries on financial data.

TABLE 4-6 INTRANETS IN HUMAN RESOURCES

Organization	Intranet Application
Sandia National Laboratories	Tech Web intranet posts weekly newsletter and employee directory on-line. Employees can use the intranet for time and expense calculations and for project management.
TransCanada Pipelines	Employees process their timesheets and expense reports, and manage their own health and pension benefits accounts using an intranet.
Medtronics	Employees use myMedtronic for self-service human resources administration tasks, such as changing addresses or employee payroll information or enrolling in benefit plans. Managers use myMedtronic to enter pay changes and promotions. A Life Event section provides information to guide employees through employee data and benefit changes that would have to be made if employees changed marital status or had a child.
E*Trade	Uses Icarian Workforce software on the corporate intranet to automate the entire job applicant tracking process. The software automatically takes in applicant information from sources such as on-line headhunters and on-line job posting sites, tracking all applicants from requisition through interviewing. The data are integrated with the corporate human resources system.

Sales and Marketing

Earlier we described how the Internet and the Web can be used for selling to individual customers and to other businesses. Internet technology also can be applied to the internal management of the sales and marketing function. One of the most popular applications for corporate intranets is to oversee and coordinate the activities of the sales force. Sales staff can dial in for updates on pricing, promotions, rebates, or customers, or to obtain information about competitors. They can access presentations and sales documents and customize them for customers. Table 4-7 describes examples of these applications.

Manufacturing and Production

In manufacturing, information-management issues are highly complex, involving massive inventories, capturing and integrating real-time production data flows, changing relationships with suppliers, and volatile costs. The manufacturing function typically uses multiple types of data, including graphics as well as text, which are scattered in many disparate systems. Manufacturing information is often very time sensitive and difficult to retrieve because files must be continuously updated. Developing intranets that integrate manufacturing data under a uniform user interface is more complicated than in other functional areas.

Despite these difficulties, companies are launching intranet applications for manufacturing. Intranets coordinating the flow of information between lathes, controllers, inventory systems, and other components of a production system can make manufacturing informa-

TABLE 4-7 INTRANETS IN SALES AND MARKETING

Organization	Intranet Application
American Express	Uses a Web-based sales management system by Salesnet to help its North American sales team (which sells gift checks and incentive cards to corporate clients) distribute and track qualified sales leads. More than 50 members of the sales team can access the system using wireless devices.
Yesmail.com	E-mail marketing company set up a sales intranet for sharing tools and documents about contacts, sales leads, and prospects, and used Web conferencing technologies to train remote sales staff. The application includes a methodology to measure the company's progress in different stages of the sales process.
Haworth Inc.	Customized eRoom teamware for sales force support, creating "virtual workspaces" dedicated to sales reporting, sales strategy development, sales forecasting, field sales processes, and education and training. The system helps salespeople in many different countries work together on multinational accounts.
Case Corp.	Supports sales and marketing teams with intranet collaboration tools for contact management, discussion forums, document management, and calendars. The intranet applications facilitate sharing of information on competitors, potential product-development, and research tasks, and include time-sensitive accountability to measure results.

TABLE 4-8	INTRANETS IN MANUFACTURING AND PRODUCTION
Organization	**Intranet Application**
Noranda Inc.	Intranet for its Magnola magnesium production facility in Quebec monitors plant operations remotely using a virtual control panel and video cameras.
Sony Corporation	Intranet delivers financial information to manufacturing personnel so that workers can monitor the production line's profit-and-loss performance and adapt performance accordingly. The intranet also provides data on quality measurements, such as defects and rejects, as well as maintenance and training schedules.
TransCanada Pipelines	Managers can schedule plant maintenance using an on-line system linked to procurement software that automatically secures needed parts from inventory or generates purchase orders.
Duke Power	Intranet provides on-line access to a computer-aided engineering tool for retrieving equipment designs and operating specifications that allows employees to view every important system in the plant at various levels of detail. Different subsets of systems can be formatted together to create a view of all the equipment in a particular room. Maintenance technicians, plant engineers, and operations personnel can use this tool with minimal training.
Rockwell International	Intranet improves process and quality of manufactured circuit boards and controllers by establishing home pages for its Milwaukee plant's computer-controlled machine tools that are updated every 60 seconds. Quality control managers can check the status of a machine by calling up its home page to learn how many pieces the machine output that day, what percentage of an order that output represents, and to what tolerances the machine is adhering.

tion more accessible to different parts of the organization, increasing precision and lowering costs. Table 4-8 describes some of these uses.

SUPPLY CHAIN MANAGEMENT AND COLLABORATIVE COMMERCE

Intranets can also be used to simplify and integrate business processes spanning more than one functional area. These cross-functional processes can be coordinated electronically, increasing organizational efficiency and responsiveness, and they can also be coordinated with the business processes of other companies. Internet technology has proved especially useful for supply chain management and collaborative commerce.

Chapter 2 introduced the concept of supply chain management, which integrates procurement, production, and logistics processes to supply goods and services from their source to final delivery to the customer. In the pre-Internet environment, supply chain coordination was hampered by the difficulties of making information flow smoothly among many different kinds of systems servicing different parts of the supply chain, such as purchasing, materials management, manufacturing, and distribution. Enterprise systems could supply some of this integration for internal business processes, but such systems are difficult and costly to build.

Some of this integration can be supplied more inexpensively using Internet technology. Firms can use intranets to improve coordination among their internal supply chain processes, and they can use extranets to coordinate supply chain processes shared with their business partners. *Extranets*, which we introduced in Chapter 1, are private intranets extended to authorized users outside the company. Many of the private industrial networks discussed in this chapter and in Chapter 2, are based on extranets for streamlining supply chain management.

Using Internet technology, all members of the supply chain can instantly communicate with each other, using up-to-date information to adjust purchasing, logistics, manufacturing, packaging, and schedules. A manager can use a Web interface to tap into suppliers' systems to see if inventory and production capabilities match demand for the manufacturer's products. Business partners can use Web-based supply chain management tools to collaborate on-line on forecasts. Sales representatives can tap into suppliers' production schedules and logistics information to monitor customers' order status. As extended supply chains start sharing production, scheduling, inventory, forecasting, and logistics information on-line instead of by phone or fax, companies can respond more accurately to changing customer demand. Manufacturers can communicate up-to-the-minute information to suppliers so they can

TABLE 4-9	EXAMPLES OF WEB-BASED SUPPLY CHAIN MANAGEMENT APPLICATIONS
Organization	**Supply Chain Management Application**
Celestica	Toronto-based electronics manufacturing services provider has an extranet for its 1,000 suppliers, which use it to pull production planning information from Celestica's supply chain systems. When Celestica gets demand forecast data from one of its large customers, suppliers can view the data through Celestica's corporate portal and let Celestica know how quickly they can deliver the required materials.
Acma Computers	Uses Datasweep Advantage Web-based supply chain management tool to track work orders for specific customers on-line, flag and manage product shortages, manage change orders, and monitor production and quality information throughout the product lifecycle. Increased on-time delivery of customer units from 78 to 96%.
SMTC Manufacturing	Uses Web-based OrderIT software to enable customers for its circuit boards and computer components to check the status of orders. Customers can also check SMTC's master production schedule to help them respond to dynamic customer demand.
Nabisco and Wegman's Food Markets	Created a joint Web-based forecast to maximize the profitability of shelf space for Nabisco Planter's products. The forecast initiated replenishment orders, refined the established forecasting–replenishment plan to drive sourcing, production, and transportation plans, and monitored execution against these plans. After this system was implemented Planters' sales increased by 54% while stock availability rose from 92.8 to 96.6%.
Chrysler Corporation	Supplier Partner Information Network (SPIN) allows 3,500 of Chrysler's 12,000 suppliers to access portions of its intranet, where they can get the most current data on design changes, parts shortages, packaging information, and invoice tracking. Chrysler can use the information from SPIN to reassign workers so that shortages do not hold up assembly lines. Chrysler believes SPIN has reduced the time to complete various business processes by 25 to 50%.

postpone their products' final configuration and delivery until the last moment. The low cost of providing this information with Web-based tools instead of costly proprietary systems encourages companies to share critical business information with a greater number of suppliers. Table 4-9 provides examples of Web-based supply chain management applications.

The Web-based B2B marketplaces and exchanges we described earlier also provide supply chain management functions. When it is completed, Covisint, the giant automotive industry net marketplace described in the Window on Organizations, will help the participating automotive manufacturers view their supply chains as components move through the system. Purchase orders, supplier ship dates, and production schedules are all available on the Covisint Web site. The auto manufacturers and their suppliers can use this real-time information to reduce their inventories and respond more quickly to customers.

Logistics and fulfillment are receiving new attention in the quest for optimal supply chain management and successful e-commerce execution. As more and more companies embrace the Internet and e-commerce, they are reexamining how they move products to customers. Order fulfillment can be the most expensive—and sometimes the most critical—operation in electronic commerce. The Internet has introduced new ways of managing warehousing, shipping, and packaging based on access to supply chain information that can give companies an edge in delivering goods and services at a reasonable cost. Companies can use information flows from the supply chain to postpone delivery decisions until they have the most up-to-date and complete information on what the customer wants so that products can be delivered in the most direct and cost-effective way (Lee and Whang, 2001).

Internet-based supply chain management applications are clearly changing the way businesses work internally and with each other. In addition to reducing costs, these supply chain management systems provide more responsive customer service, allowing the workings of the business to be driven more by customer demand. Earlier supply chain management systems were driven by production master schedules based on forecasts or best guesses of demand for products. With new flows of information made possible by Web-based tools, supply chain management can follow a demand-driven model.

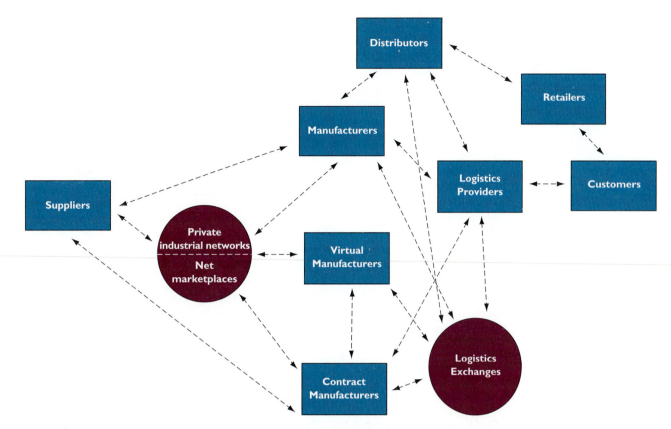

Figure 4-9 The future Internet-driven supply chain. The future Internet-driven supply chain operates like a digital logistics nervous system. It provides multidirectional communication among firms, networks of firms, and e-marketplaces so that entire networks of supply chain partners can immediately adjust inventories, orders, and capacities.

Internet technology has given a great boost to collaborative product development that is more customer-driven as well. The development of a new product usually involves collaboration among different departments in a single firm and, increasingly, among several different organizations. Internet technology provides communication and collaboration tools to connect designers, engineers, marketing, and manufacturing employees. Companies can work internally or with their business partners more efficiently to bring products more rapidly to market, from their initial design and engineering to marketing and sales. Internet-based tools also help companies work with contract manufacturers to build these new products. Customer feedback from Web sites or on-line communities can be fed into product design.

Ultimately, the Internet could create a "digital logistics nervous system" throughout the supply chain. This system permits simultaneous, multidirectional communication of information about participants' inventories, orders, and capacities, and works to optimize the activities of individual firms and groups of firms interacting in e-commerce marketplaces (see Figure 4-9). As more digital firms evolve, this future "digital logistics nervous system" will come closer to being realized.

4.4 MANAGEMENT CHALLENGES AND OPPORTUNITIES

Although electronic commerce and electronic business offer organizations a wealth of new opportunities, they also present managers with a series of challenges. Many new Internet business models have yet to prove enduring sources of profit. Web-enabling business processes for electronic commerce and electronic business requires far-reaching organizational change. The legal environment for electronic commerce has not yet solidified, and companies pursuing electronic commerce must be vigilant about security and consumer privacy.

UNPROVEN BUSINESS MODELS

Not all companies make money on the Web. Hundreds of retail dot.com firms, including Garden.com, Chinese Books Cyberstore, Productopia.com, and Pets.com, have closed their doors. Fleetscape.com, M-Xchange.com, IndustrialVortex.com, and other exchanges have shut down. Dot.com stock prices collapsed after many of these companies failed to generate enough revenue to sustain their costly marketing campaigns, infrastructures, and staff salaries, losing money on every sale they made. Business models built around the Internet are new and largely unproven. The chapter ending case study on the failure of Webvan is devoted to this topic.

Doing business over the Internet is not necessarily more efficient or cost effective than traditional business methods. Virtual retailers may not need to pay for costly storefronts and retail workers, but they require heavy outlays for warehousing, customer service call centers, and customer acquisition. Challenges also confront businesses that are trying to use the Web to supplement or enhance a traditional business model. Businesses that are unclear about their on-line strategy—and its relationship to their overall business strategy—can waste thousands and even millions of dollars building and maintaining a Web site that fails to deliver the desired results. Even successful Web sites can incur very high costs. For example, Recreational Equipment Inc. (REI), the famous seller of outdoor gear, headquartered in Kent, Washington, has bricks-and-mortar retail stores, hefty catalog sales, and a profitable Web site that dominates its market. It has high payroll expenditures to pay for the skilled technical staff supporting the Web site and additional shipping expenses to make sure Web orders are delivered to customers in a timely fashion. REI has spent many millions of dollars upgrading and remodeling the Web site.

BUSINESS PROCESS CHANGE REQUIREMENTS

Electronic commerce and electronic business require careful orchestration of the firm's divisions, production sites, and sales offices, as well as closer relationships with customers, suppliers, and other business partners in its network of value creation. Essential business processes must be redesigned and more closely integrated, especially those for supply chain management. In addition to integrating processes inside the firm, supply chain management requires aligning the business practices and behaviors of a number of different companies participating in the supply chain. Companies will need well-defined policies and procedures for sharing data with other organizations, including specifications for the type, format, level of precision, and security of the data to be exchanged (Barua, Konana, Whinston, and Yin, 2001). Traditional boundaries between departments and divisions, companies and suppliers can be an impediment to collaboration and relationship building. The digitally enabled enterprise must transform the way it conducts business on many levels to act rapidly and with precision.

Channel Conflicts

channel conflict

Competition between two or more different distribution chains used to sell the products or services of the same company.

Using the Web for on-line sales and marketing may create **channel conflict** with the firm's traditional channels, especially for less information-intensive products that require physical intermediaries to reach buyers. A company's sales force and distributors may fear that their revenues will drop as customers make purchases directly from the Web or that they will be displaced by this new channel.

Channel conflict is an especially troublesome issue in business-to-business electronic commerce, where customers buy directly from manufacturers via the Web instead of through distributors or sales representatives. Milacron Inc. operates one of heavy industry's most extensive Web sites for selling machine tools to contract manufacturers. To minimize negative repercussions from channel conflict, Milacron is paying full commissions to its reps for on-line sales made in their territory, even if they do not do any work on the sale or meet the buyer. Other companies are devising other solutions, such as offering only a portion of their full product line on the Web. Using alternative channels created by the Internet requires very careful planning and management.

LEGAL ISSUES

Laws governing electronic commerce are still being written. Legislatures, courts, and international agreements are just starting to settle such questions as the legality and force of e-mail contracts, the role of electronic signatures, and the application of copyright laws to electronically copied documents. Moreover, the Internet is global, and it is used by individuals and organizations in hundreds of different countries. If a product were offered for sale in Thailand via a server in Singapore and the purchaser lived in Hungary, whose law would apply? The legal and regulatory environment for electronic commerce has not been fully established.

SECURITY AND PRIVACY

Internet-based systems are even more vulnerable to penetration by outsiders than private networks, because the Internet was designed to be open to everyone. Any information, including e-mail, passes through many computer systems on the Net before it reaches its destination. It can be monitored, captured, and stored at any of these points along the route. Valuable data that might be intercepted include credit card numbers and names, private personnel data, marketing plans, sales contracts, product development and pricing data, negotiations between companies, and other data that might be of value to the competition. Hackers, vandals, and computer criminals have exploited Internet weaknesses to break into computer systems, causing harm by stealing passwords, obtaining sensitive information, electronic eavesdropping, or "jamming" corporate Web servers to make them inaccessible. We explore Internet security, computer crime, and technology for secure electronic payments in greater detail in Chapters 5 and 14.

The Web provides an unprecedented ability to learn about and target customers. But the same capability can also undermine individual privacy. Using Web site monitoring software and other technology for tracking Web visitors, companies can gather detailed information about individuals without their knowledge. In other instances, Web site visitors knowingly supply personal information, such as their names, addresses, e-mail addresses, and special interests, in exchange for access to the site without realizing how the organization owning the Web site may be using the information. Companies collecting detailed customer information over the Web will need to balance their desire to profit from such information with the need to safeguard individual privacy.

Digitally enabling the enterprise with Internet technology requires careful management planning. The Manager's Toolkit lists some important questions managers should ask when exploring the use of the Internet for electronic commerce and electronic business.

MIS IN ACTION   MANAGER'S TOOLKIT

DIGITALLY ENABLING THE ENTERPRISE: TOP QUESTIONS TO ASK

Managers need to understand precisely how Internet technology will benefit their company and the challenges they face when implementing electronic commerce and electronic business applications. Here are some key questions to ask:

1. How much digital integration does our business need to remain competitive? How can the digital integration provided by Internet technology change our business model? Should we change our business model?

2. How can we measure the success of digitally enabling the enterprise? Will the benefits outweigh the costs?

3. How will business processes have to be changed to use Internet technology seriously for electronic commerce or electronic business? How much process integration is required?

4. How will we have to recast our relationships with customers, suppliers, and other business partners to take advantage of digitally enabled business processes?

5. Do we have the appropriate information technology infrastructure for digitally enabling our business? What technical skills and employee training will be required to use Internet technology? How can we integrate Internet applications with existing applications and data?

6. How can we make sure our intranet is secure from entry by outsiders? How secure is the electronic payment system we are using for electronic commerce?

7. Are we doing enough to protect the privacy of customers we reach electronically?

MAKE IT YOUR BUSINESS

FINANCE AND ACCOUNTING

Internet technology facilitates access to and integration of financial data from sources inside and outside the firm. Companies can use the Internet to obtain data on interest rates, market conditions, and other factors to help them monitor and plan their investments. Firms that have embarked on ambitious programs to integrate their systems can use corporate intranets to obtain company-wide views of their firm's financial performance. The Internet has also opened up new avenues for businesses to make and receive payments electronically and has provided the financial industry with new products and channels to customers. Collaborative commerce requires new types of accounting systems that can handle coordination among business partners and their supply chains. You can find examples of finance and accounting applications on page 127.

HUMAN RESOURCES

Internet technology has led to efficiencies and cost savings in employee communication and training as well as the processing of basic human resources transactions. Many companies are installing self-service human resources (HR) systems on intranets to deliver HR-related services, such as enrolling in insurance and medical plans, maintaining employee savings plans, and applying for company jobs. Companies can realize productivity and savings by using Web technology to deliver interactive employee training and human resources policy manuals and company directories. Human resources staff members can use intranets to access employee records from the firm's basic human resources transaction systems. You can find examples of human resources applications on pages 108 and 128.

MANUFACTURING AND PRODUCTION

Internet technology creates a common platform for communication and data exchange that can be used to integrate manufacturing and production data from disparate systems inside the firm and to coordinate manufacturing and production processes with those of suppliers and distributors. Internet technology can help companies bring products to market more quickly, optimize inventory management, and, in

some cases, outsource most and even all of their production or order fulfillment. Public B2B commerce systems and private industrial networks can help reduce procurement costs and make other supply chain processes more efficient. The Internet can play a role in every step of the manufacturing and production process, from gauging demand and taking orders to scheduling production jobs, managing inventory, and handling shipping and logistics. You can find examples of manufacturing and production applications on pages 106–108, 122, 129–130, and 137–139.

SALES AND MARKETING

Although the Internet may not have overwhelmed traditional retailing, it has spawned powerful new channels for reaching consumers and new digital products and services. A significant percentage of financial products and services, books, computers, music, video, and travel services are now purchased on the Web. Some of these products were actually created with Internet technology, such as on-line Web investing services and digital music.

The Internet has reduced consumer search costs and transaction costs, making it much easier to comparison shop and find the right combination of trust, fulfillment, customer service, and price to meet consumers' needs. Internet technologies can help differentiate products by using personalization, customization techniques, and community marketing techniques.

The Internet has broadened the scope of marketing communications by making it much easier for firms to reach large numbers of people. The Internet has also increased the richness of marketing communications by combining text, video, and audio content into rich messages and providing capabilities for users to interactively control the experience. Personalized messages can be delivered at very low cost to individuals and groups. Finally, the Internet provides marketers with unparalleled, fine-grained, detailed real-time information about consumers as they transact on the Web. You can find examples of sales and marketing applications on pages 106–108, 116–118, 120, 122, 128, and 137–139.

MANAGEMENT WRAP-UP

Managers need to carefully review their strategy and business models to determine how to maximize the benefits of Internet technology. Managers should anticipate making organizational changes to take advantage of this technology, including new business processes, new relationships with the firm's value partners and customers, and even new business designs. Determining how and where to digitally enable the enterprise with Internet technology is a key management decision.

The Internet can dramatically reduce transaction and agency costs and is fueling new business models. By using the Internet and other networks for electronic commerce, organizations can exchange purchase and sale transactions directly with customers and suppliers, eliminating inefficient intermediaries. Organizational processes can be streamlined by using the Internet and intranets to make communication and coordination more efficient. To take advantage of these opportunities, organizational processes must be redesigned.

Internet technology has created a universal computing platform that has become the primary infrastructure for electronic commerce, electronic business, and the emerging digital firm. Web-based applications integrating voice, data, video, and audio are providing new products, services, and tools for communicating with employees and customers. Intranets enable companies to make information flow between disparate systems, business processes, and parts of the organization.

For Discussion:

1. How does the Internet change consumer and supplier relationships?

2. The Internet may not make corporations obsolete, but they will have to change their business models. Do you agree? Why or why not?

SUMMARY

1. *How has Internet technology changed value propositions and business models?* The Internet is rapidly becoming the infrastructure of choice for electronic commerce and electronic business because it provides a universal and easy-to-use set of technologies and technology standards that can be adopted by all organizations, no matter what computer system or information technology platform they are using. Internet technology provides a much lower cost and easier to use alternative for coordination activities than proprietary networks. Companies can use Internet technology to radically reduce their transaction costs.

The Internet radically reduces the cost of creating, sending, and storing information while making that information more widely available. Information is not limited to traditional physical methods of delivery. Customers can find out about products on their own on the Web and buy directly from product suppliers instead of using intermediaries such as retail stores. This unbundling of information from traditional value chain channels is having a disruptive effect on old business models, and it is creating new business models as well. Some of the traditional channels for exchanging product information have become unnecessary or uneconomical, and business models based on the coupling of information with products and services may no longer be necessary.

The Internet shrinks information asymmetry and has transformed the relationship between information richness and reach. Using the Internet and Web multimedia capabilities, companies can quickly and inexpensively provide detailed product information and detailed information specific to each customer to very large numbers of people simultaneously. The Internet can help companies create and capture profit in new ways by adding extra value to existing products and services or by providing the foundation for new products and services. Many different business models for electronic commerce on the Internet have emerged, including virtual storefronts, information brokers, transaction brokers, online marketplaces, content providers, on-line service providers, virtual communities, and portals.

2. *What is electronic commerce? How has electronic commerce changed consumer retailing and business-to-business transactions?* Electronic commerce is the process of buying and selling goods electronically with computerized business transactions using the Internet or other digital network technology. It includes marketing, customer support, delivery, and payment. The three major type of electronic commerce are business-to-consumer (B2C), business-to-business (B2B), and consumer-to-consumer (C2C). Another way of classifying electronic commerce transactions is in terms of the participants' physical connection to the Web. Conventional e-commerce transactions, which take place over wired networks, can be distinguished from mobile commerce or m-commerce, the purchase of goods and services using handheld wireless devices.

The Internet provides a universally available set of technologies for electronic commerce that can be used to create new channels for marketing, sales, and customer support, and to eliminate intermediaries in buy and sell transactions. Interactive capabilities on the Web can be used to build closer relationships with customers in marketing and customer support. Firms can use various Web personalization technologies to deliver Web pages with content geared to the specific interests of each user, including technologies to deliver personalized information and ads through m-commerce channels. Companies can also reduce costs and improve customer service by using Web sites to provide helpful information as well as e-mail and even telephone access to customer service representatives.

B2B e-commerce generates efficiencies by enabling companies to electronically locate suppliers, solicit bids, place orders, and track shipments in transit. Businesses can use their own Web sites to sell to other businesses or use net marketplaces or private industrial networks. Net marketplaces provide a single digital marketplace based on Internet technology for many buyers and sellers. Net marketplaces can be differentiated by whether they sell direct or indirect goods, support spot or long-term purchasing, or serve vertical or horizontal markets. Private industrial networks link a firm with its suppliers and other strategic business partners to develop highly efficient supply chains and to respond quickly to customer demands.

3. *What are the principal payment systems for electronic commerce?* The principal electronic payment systems for electronic commerce are credit card systems, digital wallets, accumulated balance digital payment systems, stored value systems, digital cash, peer-to-peer payment systems, electronic checks, and electronic billing presentment and payment systems. Accumulated balance systems, stored value systems (including smart cards), and digital cash are useful for small micropayments.

4. *How can Internet technology support electronic business and supply chain management?* Private, internal corporate networks called intranets can be created using Internet connectivity standards. Extranets are private intranets that are extended to selected organizations or individuals outside the firm. Intranets and extranets are forming the underpinnings of electronic business by providing a low-cost technology that can run on almost any computing platform. Organizations can use intranets to create collaboration environments for coordinating work and information sharing, and they can use intranets to make information flow between different functional areas of the firm. Intranets also provide a low-cost alternative for improving coordination among organizations' internal supply chain processes. Extranets can be used to coordinate supply chain processes shared with external organizations.

5. *What are the major managerial and organizational challenges posed by electronic commerce and electronic business?* Many new business models based on the Internet have not yet found proven ways to generate profits or reduce costs. Digitally enabling a firm for electronic commerce and electronic business requires far-reaching organizational change, including redesign of business processes; recasting relationships with customers, suppliers, and other business partners; and new roles for employees. Channel conflicts may erupt as the firm turns to the Internet as an alternative outlet for sales. Security, privacy and legal issues pose additional electronic commerce challenges.

KEY TERMS

Accumulated balance digital payment systems, 123
Banner ad, 112
Business model, 110
Business-to-business (B2B) electronic commerce, 114
Business-to-consumer (B2C) electronic commerce, 114
Call center, 118
Channel conflict, 132
Clicks-and-mortar, 114

Consumer-to-consumer (C2C) electronic commerce, 114
Digital cash, 124
Digital checking, 124
Digital credit card payment system, 123
Digital wallet, 123
Disintermediation, 115
Dynamic pricing, 112
Electronic billing presentment and payment systems, 125

Electronic payment system, 123
Exchange, 121
Information asymmetry, 111
Micropayment, 123
Mobile commerce (m-commerce), 115
Net marketplace, 119
Peer-to-peer payment system, 124
Portal, 112
Private exchange, 119

Pure-play, 113
Reach, 111
Reintermediation, 116
Richness, 111
Smart card, 124
Stored value payment systems, 124
Syndicator, 113
Web personalization, 116

REVIEW QUESTIONS

1. What are the advantages of using the Internet as the infrastructure for electronic commerce and electronic business?

2. How is the Internet changing the economics of information and business models?

3. Name and describe six Internet business models for electronic commerce. Distinguish between a pure-play Internet business model and a clicks-and-mortar business model.

4. Name and describe the various categories of electronic commerce.

5. How can the Internet facilitate sales and marketing to individual customers? Describe the role played by Web personalization.

6. How can the Internet help provide customer service?

7. How can Internet technology support business-to-business electronic commerce?

8. What are net marketplaces? Why do they represent an important business model for B2B e-commerce? How do they differ from private industrial networks?

9. Name and describe the principal electronic payment systems used on the Internet.

10. Why are intranets so useful for electronic business?

11. How can intranets support organizational collaboration?

12. Describe the uses of intranets for electronic business in sales and marketing, human resources, finance and accounting, and manufacturing.

13. How can companies use Internet technology for supply chain management?

14. Describe the management challenges posed by electronic commerce and electronic business on the Internet.

15. What is channel conflict? Why is it becoming a growing problem in electronic commerce?

APPLICATION SOFTWARE EXERCISE

SPREADSHEET EXERCISE: ANALYZING A DOT.COM BUSINESS

Pick one e-commerce company on the Internet such as Ashford.com, Buy.com, Yahoo.com or Priceline.com. Study the Web pages that describe the company and explain its purpose and structure. Look for articles at Web sites such as Bigcharts.com that comment upon the company. Then visit the Securities and Exchange Commission's Web site at www.sec.gov and access the company's 10-K forms showing income statements and balance sheets. Select only the sections of the 10-K form containing the desired portions of financial statements that you need to examine and download them into your spreadsheet. (Hint: When you find the page that lists specific forms, select the text version. Do not select the HTML version. The Laudon Web site for Chapter 4 provides more detailed instructions on how to download this 10-K data into a spreadsheet.) Create sim-plified spreadsheets of the company's balance sheets and income statements for the past three years.

Is the company a dot.com success, borderline business, or failure? What information is the basis of your decision? Why? When answering these questions, pay special attention to the company's three-year trends in revenues, costs of sales, gross margins, operating expenses, and net margins. The Laudon Web site provides definitions of these terms and how they are calculated. Prepare an overhead presentation (minimum of five slides), including appropriate spreadsheets or charts, and present your work to your professor and/or classmates. If the company is successful, what additional business strategies could it pursue to become even more successful? If the company is a borderline or failing business, what specific business strategies (if any) could make it more successful?

GROUP PROJECT

Form a group with three or four of your classmates. Select two businesses that are competitors in the same industry and using their Web sites for electronic commerce. Visit their Web sites. You might compare, for example, the Web sites for virtual banking created by Citibank and Wells Fargo Bank, or the Internet trading Web sites of E*Trade and Ameritrade. Prepare an evaluation of each business's Web site in terms of its functions, user friendliness, and how well it supports the company's business strategy. Which Web site does a better job? Why? Can you make some recommendations to improve these Web sites?

TOOLS FOR INTERACTIVE LEARNING

■ INTERNET CONNECTION

The Internet Connection for this chapter will take you to several Web sites where you can complete an exercise to evaluate several virtual storefront businesses. You can also use the Interactive Study Guide to test your knowledge of the topics in this chapter and get instant feedback where you need more practice.

■ ELECTRONIC COMMERCE PROJECT

At the Laudon Web site for Chapter 4, you will find an electronic commerce project where you can build an electronic commerce storefront.

■ CD-ROM

If you use the Multimedia Edition CD-ROM with this chapter, you can find an audio overview of the major themes of this chapter and bullet text summarizing the key points of the chapter.

CASE STUDY—*The Collapse of Webvan*

The grocery business is gigantic, with annual retail store sales that are estimated at $650 billion. However, it is a very tough business because the profit margins are tiny, only 1 to 2 percent of sales. Moreover, the industry is very price competitive. Yet Webvan, which was founded in late 1996, chose groceries as the way to establish itself as a Web-based powerhouse.

Aside from the tiny profit margin, on-line grocery sales face other problems. Most successful Web retail sales involve delivery several days after ordering via parcel delivery services such as UPS or FedEx. Yet people usually need grocery delivery right away, and the groceries usually include such spoilables as milk, ice cream, fresh vegetables, and meats.

A number of companies, including Peapod, HomeGrocer.com, Kozmo.com, and Safeway have struggled to establish on-line grocery businesses. Webvan Group Inc. of Foster City, California (in the Silicon Valley), was the brainchild of Louis Borders, the cofounder of the very successful Borders bookstore chain. Webvan's founders and management believed they could succeed where others were faltering by using a different business model. The company carried about 20,000 high-quality grocery items, including fresh fruits and vegetables, meats, and frozen foods, and delivered the orders to customers throughout a large metropolitan region. Webvan had no retail outlets, but instead it operated out of massive regional distribution centers of about 350,000 square feet each.

Management claimed one distribution center could sell as many products in one day as 18 metropolitan-area supermarkets. Orders could be entered on the Internet 24 hours per day, every day, and the goods would be delivered from the distribution centers. The company expected to have only about 900 to 1,000 employees per center, compared with about 2,200 to 2,700 for the supermarkets. The company kept real estate costs low by having only one large site per metropolitan region, and the sites were located in low-cost industrial areas rather than in high-priced residential neighborhoods. Thus Webvan would achieve a much higher operating margin than supermarkets, more than enough to pay for such added expenses as software and delivery.

The grocery business is difficult to break into. Customers expect high quality and yet prefer not to pay extra for convenience. Polls show the majority wants to smell the strawberries and squeeze the tomatoes before purchasing them. The most difficult challenge is breaking consumers' habits of actually going to the store.

Webvan's top management believed that the leverage in groceries was distribution. The company decided on a hub-and-spoke model in which orders would be filled in the massive warehouses and then taken to tiny transfer stations that served specific neighborhoods where they would be transferred to a leased fleet of Webvan trucks for delivery. Thus, Webvan could efficiently serve a 60-mile, heavily populated radius. Time-starved shoppers would be lured by the convenience of being able to order products 24 hours a day and having the goods home delivered exactly at the time of their choosing.

The original plan was for a rapid rollout in 26 U.S. metropolitan areas by the end of 2001. Customers included not only people who are at home but also office workers who would use their work computers to order groceries for home and even order lunches and snacks for the office. The long-range plan was to expand into other businesses. If Webvan could deliver groceries to a number of places in a neighborhood, it was set up to deliver other products as well.

The model relied on extremely sophisticated, highly automated information systems centered in the warehouses. An in-house engineering team worked with Optimum Inc. of White Plains, New York, to design and build systems for warehouse management, routing and scheduling, and for communication with suppliers. The systems were designed to handle as many as 50,000 items, leaving plenty of room for expansion into non-grocery products. A data repository in San Jose, California, served as the information center for all the warehouses.

The warehouses had three temperature zones for shelf items, fresh items (such as vegetables and meats), and frozen foods. Every warehouse had 12 huge carousels, each of which held up to 7,500 items. An employee stationed at each carousel could stand still rather than having to move around to pick the items. When they were picked, the items were placed in totes and moved around using the warehouse's 4½ miles of conveyer belts.

The ordering process began when customers placed their orders on Webvan's Web site. When the order was completed, customers selected an open 30-minute delivery time slot in any of the next seven days. The delivery optimizer marked slots as taken if they had already been reserved or if they were too far away from the delivery location of the new order for on-time delivery.

The order was electronically transmitted to the relevant warehouse where it would be filled. The software system devised an optimal picking plan, and the totes were automatically marked with a barcode, tying them to a specific order. The totes were color-coded to identify the type of products that were in them. The software determined how many totes were needed. Webvan stored data on many characteristics of each item. For example, it needed item size to determine if that item would fit into the tote, whereas weight was needed to be certain the tote would not become too heavy for the staff to lift. Some items could not be split, such as watermelons. "Crushability" was necessary to track that fragile items, such as eggs, would be on top of the totes, and heavy items, such as big cans would be on the bottom. Totes for frozen items were styrofoam-lined and contained dry-ice packs. Shelf items were collected in sequence according to the picking plan, and then the tote was conveyed to the carousel station where the picker checked the products from a list and loaded the remaining items (often working on more than one order at a time). When a tote was completed, the picker closed it and placed it on a conveyor that moved it to shipping. The system even calculated the amount of picking time required for each part of the order. Based on the scheduled delivery time and workload, it determined when to start loading each tote to arrive at shipping at the proper time. The totes were then rolled onto a truck designated for the specific transfer station where they were placed on delivery trucks and delivered according to a route prepared by route optimization software. This complex system was unprecedented.

Delivery was technically complex as well. Webvan's software optimized delivery schedules so that deliveries could be made every 10 to 30 minutes. Webvan used sophisticated route-planning software to map out the most efficient delivery route for each order. The driver's location was monitored by dispatch using the Global Positioning System (GPS) in each van. When an unplanned delay occurred, dispatchers called to inform customers who could choose either to accept a late delivery or to reschedule it. The drivers also used the GPS to plot alternate routes to circumvent traffic problems, thereby more easily meeting their schedules. At the home, the driver carried the totes inside and unpacked them. Alternatively, the customer could have the totes left unpacked for a small deposit per tote. The driver then used a handheld wireless device to print out a receipt and an itemized order list. The device also notified dispatch that the delivery was completed.

Webvan also developed a system of ordering products from its suppliers. Webvan determined what to order based on both actual and expected demand. If an item was not in the warehouse at the time a customer ordered it, Webvan used a rapid and reliable communication Web site (harbinger.net) to automatically inform suppliers. Harbinger software formatted orders for all suppliers and forwarded the orders to them. When goods arrived at a warehouse, receiving opened the cartons and scanned the products. Shelf items were put into trays, and the system used a very complex "round-robin" algorithm to assign each tray to a specific carousel. However, like many of its supermarket rivals, Webvan did little else to automate its supply chain because it was too small to force its suppliers to invest in supply chain technology.

Webvan took its first orders on June 2, 1999, in the San Francisco Bay area, and by the end of June it had nearly $400,000 is sales. On July 8, the company signed a blockbuster $1 billion deal with Bechtel to design and construct 26 distribution centers within the next two years, reflecting both the large amount of capital Webvan had raised and its plan for rapid expansion. In October, George Shaheen, the former CEO of Andersen Consulting (now Accenture), became the CEO of Webvan. The company was flying high, even though it had no profit and was spending investor capital rapidly, much of it devoted to building warehouses.

In February 2000, Webvan announced its average order size had risen from $72 to $80. By June Webvan had spread to Atlanta, Georgia, and Sacramento, California. At the same time it purchased a rival, HomeGrocer.com, allowing Webvan to move into Dallas, Los Angeles, San Diego, Seattle, Portland, and Orange County, California, at a very low cost while eliminating the need to compete with HomeGrocer for customers.

However, Webvan's situation was worsening. On February 21, Webvan shut down the Dallas operation. Atlanta was receiving only half the number of orders it needed to break even, and no site had yet become profitable. Unintimidated and confident of its future success, in August Webvan opened in Chicago. The San Francisco area facility had failed to break even as had been predicted, and the company curtailed its growth plans in order to preserve cash, delaying expansion into Washington, D.C., Baltimore, and New Jersey (even though each had $35-million warehouses). In November Webvan announced that its average order had risen only to $91. In addition to groceries, the company was selling drugstore and pet items, books and CDs, electronics, games, and toys. Webvan stock kept plummeting.

Webvan was forced into brutal cost cutting. More Webvan centers closed—Dallas on February 21, 2001, and Sacramento and Atlanta in April of that year. The company slashed marketing expenses and started charging for deliveries. Borders had been replaced by Shaheen as CEO, and Shaheen resigned on April 16, replaced by COO Robert Swann. The company noted that only 6.5 percent of San Francisco households had ordered from Webvan, and less than half of them had placed a second order.

On July 9, 2001, Webvan ceased all operations, laying off 2,000 employees and announcing plans to file for Chapter 11 bankruptcy protection. During its short life it had burned through $1.2 billion in investor capital, making it one of the most spectacular dot.com failures on record. Since then, the company has been liquidating its assets.

Does Webvan's demise mean that on-line grocery retailing is a dead end? Or was the problem Webvan's ambitious business model? One of the few on-line grocers to turn a profit is Tesco.com, the on-line arm of the British supermarket chain. Tesco.com serves nearly 1 million registered customers in the United Kingdom and handles 70,000 orders per week. It is ringing up annual sales of $420 million. Tesco.com moved slowly into on-line retailing. It experimented with having customers order groceries on-line and having their groceries prepackaged and waiting for them at an existing Tesco store. Customers saved time by not having to cruise around supermarket aisles to pick out products, and Tesco was able to use its existing infrastructure

to provide the groceries. Tesco recently started to deliver groceries to customer homes near their stores but charges delivery fees. Shopper order sizes actually grew because households wanted to get maximum mileage for the delivery charge. Tesco's on-line customers have increased purchases from the stores, and people who used to shop in the stores have increased their shopping on the Web. Tesco used technology to make the existing shopping process more efficient rather than trying to create an entirely new shopping process unfamiliar to people. But Tesco also benefits from higher profit margins in grocery retailing in the United Kingdom, which run around 8 percent. This means that Tesco could lose close to 6 percent on its on-line operations and still reap the same percentage of profit as U.S. grocery retailers.

Sources: Christopher T. Heun, "Delivery, Anyone?" *Information Week*, July 16, 2001; "What Webvan Could Have Learned from Tesco," *Knowledge@Wharton,* October 10–23, 2001; "Why Webvan Crashed," *FTDynamo*, July 25, 2001; Miguel Helft, "The End of the Road," *The Industry Standard*, July 23, 2001; Ronna Abramson, "Webvan Checks Out of Dallas Market," *The Industry Standard*, February 20, 2001; Saul Hansell, "Some Hard Lessons for Online Grocer," *New York Times*, February 19, 2001; Miguel Helft, "Amazon.com Sues Webvan over Marketing Deal," *Computerworld*, April 3, 2001; Andrew Edgecliffe-Johnson, "Webvan Job Cuts Dent Online Grocery Dreams," *Financial Times*, April 27, 2001; Jen Muehlbauer, "Webvan Delivers Corporate Welfare," *The Industry Standard*, May 17, 2001; "Disaster of the Day: Webvan," Forbes.com, January 10, 2001; Nick Wingfield, "Grocer Webvan Reveals Initiatives for Recovery, Including Job Cuts," *Wall Street Journal,* April 26, 2001; Jean V. Murphy, "Webvan: Rewriting the Rules on 'Last Mile' Delivery," *Global Logistics & Supply Chain Strategies*, August 2000; "Unlike Many, Grocers Haven't Given Up on the Net," Forbes.com, April 23, 2001; Miguel Helft, "Webvan's CEO Resigns," *The Industry Standard*, April 13, 2001; Jim Carlton, "Stalled, Webvan Hits New Roads," *Wall Street Journal*, July 31, 2000; Miguel Helft, "Going the Last Mile," *The Industry Standard*, November 10, 2000; "Webvan Fails to Deliver," *The Industry Standard*, October 18, 2000; "Webvan Goes Shopping," *The Industry Standard*, July 10, 2000; Christine McGeever, "Online Grocer Inks Deals with Consumer Goods Makers," *Computerworld*, January 25, 2000; Jen Muehlbauer, "Webvan's Knockin', But Is It Rockin'?" *The Industry Standard*, June 27, 2000; Don Tapscott and David Ticoll, "Retail Revolution," *The Industry Standard*, July 24, 2000; and Rusty Weston, "Return of the Milkman," *Upside Today*, February 18, 2000.

CASE STUDY QUESTIONS

1. Describe the Webvan business model and then analyze it using the value chain and competitive forces models. What were the assumptions that drove this business model?

2. Describe the role of technology in the Webvan model. What Webvan problems could computer technology solve, and what could it not solve? Explain your answer.

3. Critique the Webvan strategy and give your views as to whether this strategy is or can ever be viable. Explain your answer.

4. What management, organization, and technology factors were responsible for Webvan's failure? Explain.

chapter

5

ETHICAL AND SOCIAL ISSUES IN THE DIGITAL FIRM

objectives

One of your managerial responsibilities is to make informed decisions that reflect an understanding of the ethical and social issues as well as the business issues surrounding the use of information systems. After completing this chapter, you will be able to answer the following questions:

1. *What ethical, social, and political issues are raised by information systems?*

2. *Are there specific principles for conduct that can be used to guide decisions about ethical dilemmas?*

3. *Why does contemporary information systems technology pose challenges to the protection of individual privacy and intellectual property?*

4. *How have information systems affected everyday life?*

5. *How can organizations develop corporate policies for ethical conduct?*

M-Commerce: No Place to Hide?

As the Web goes wireless, the old real estate adage "location, location, location" is taking on new importance. Location can matter in electronic commerce as people tap into the Internet while they are on the go. Web-enabled cell phones, PDA devices, or automobiles with location-tracking systems have the potential to figure out exactly where people are and put that information to use. For example, one could use location information to find the nearest restaurant or hotel, with the answer delivered on a tiny Web screen. Users could obtain this information on request or even have the information automatically delivered to them when they were in the vicinity of hotels and restaurants. Businesses might even use these systems to send electronic coupons directly to a consumer's cell phone or car as the person nears a particular store or restaurant.

But privacy groups have raised concerns about the potential threat to individual privacy posed by location-tracking technology. Many people may not like having their physical move-

140

ments tracked so closely. Location information might help direct a tow truck to your broken down car, but it could also be used to find out where you went on your lunch hour.

Privacy concerns are also erupting over mushrooming m-commerce spam. Spammers are using short messaging capabilities of mobile phones to broadcast

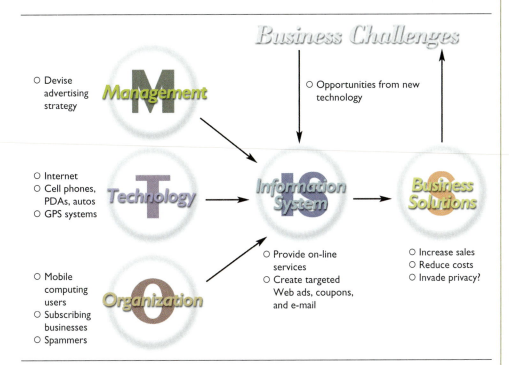

Business Challenges

- O Devise advertising strategy **Management**
- O Opportunities from new technology

- O Internet
- O Cell phones, PDAs, autos
- O GPS systems **Technology**

Information System

Business Solutions

- O Mobile computing users
- O Subscribing businesses
- O Spammers **Organization**

- O Provide on-line services
- O Create targeted Web ads, coupons, and e-mail

- O Increase sales
- O Reduce costs
- O Invade privacy?

indiscriminate pitches for Web sites. In the Netherlands, one man sent a short text message to thousands of Dutch mobile phone users asking them to call him back. His number turned out to be a phone pornography service. Although many Dutch consumers found this spam intrusive and offensive, it was not illegal.

The cost and "nuisance factor" for unsolicited mobile phone messages is much greater than for unsolicited postal mail. Unlike postal junk mail, the cost of electronic spam is generally borne by its recipients, who are charged for both sending and receiving short text messages. Some of these unsolicited messages are from wireless service providers, who send "welcome messages" when users cross a national border or move from one network to another. Travelers to Luxembourg, for instance, receive two welcome messages from Omnitel in French and in German, as well as a plug for local cultural events.

But one person's spam is another person's business model and some electronic pitches provide benefits. London-based Boltblue Ltd. offers a service that lets people send short messages of up to 160 characters to any mobile phone user in the world free of charge. Boltblue pays for this service by appending short advertisements at the end of each message and subscribers are informed of this practice in advance. Alastair Tempest, director-general of the European Direct Marketing Association, points out that direct marketing is much more targeted than unsolicited spam and that a ban on spam would hamper "legitimate" marketing.

Sources: Brandon Mitchener, "All Spam, All the Time, " *Wall Street Journal*, October 29, 2001; and Thomas E. Weber, "With Wireless Gadgets, Web Companies Plan to Map Your Moves," *Wall Street Journal*, May 8, 2000.

Technology can be a double-edged sword. It can be the source of many benefits. One great achievement of contemporary computer systems is the ease with which digital information can be analyzed, transmitted, and shared among many people. But at the same time, this powerful capability creates new opportunities for breaking the law or taking benefits away from others. Balancing the convenience and privacy implications of using m-commerce technology to track consumer locations and send unsolicited e-mail is one of the compelling ethical issues raised by contemporary information systems. As you read this chapter, you should be aware of the following management challenges:

MANAGEMENT CHALLENGES

1. **Understanding the moral risks of new technology.** Rapid technological change means that the choices facing individuals also rapidly change, and the balance of risk and reward and the probabilities of apprehension for wrongful acts change as well. Protecting individual privacy has become a serious ethical issue precisely for this reason, in addition to other issues described in this chapter. In this environment it will be important for management to conduct an ethical and social impact analysis of new technologies. One might take each of the moral dimensions described in this chapter and briefly speculate on how a new technology will impact each dimension. There may not always be right answers for how to behave but there should be management awareness on the moral risks of new technology.

2. **Establishing corporate ethics policies that include information systems issues.** As managers you will be responsible for developing, enforcing, and explaining corporate ethics policies. Historically, corporate management has paid much more attention to financial integrity and personnel policies than to the information systems area. But from what you will know after reading this chapter, it is clear your corporation should have an ethics policy in the information systems area covering such issues as privacy, property, accountability, system quality, and quality of life. The challenge will be in educating non-IS managers to the need for these policies, as well as educating your workforce.

The Internet and electronic commerce have awakened new interest in the ethical and social impact of information systems. Internet and digital firm technologies that make it easier than ever to assemble, integrate, and distribute information have unleashed new concerns about appropriate use of customer information, the protection of personal privacy, and the protection of intellectual property. These issues have moved to the forefront of social and political debate in the United States and many other countries.

Although protecting personal privacy and intellectual property on the Internet are now in the spotlight, there are other pressing ethical issues raised by the widespread use of information systems. They include establishing accountability for the consequences of information systems; setting standards to safeguard system quality that protect the safety of the individual and society; and preserving values and institutions considered essential to the quality of life in an information society. This chapter describes these issues and suggests guidelines for dealing with these questions, with special attention to the ethical challenges posed by the Internet.

5.1   UNDERSTANDING ETHICAL AND SOCIAL ISSUES RELATED TO SYSTEMS

ethics

Principles of right and wrong that can be used by individuals acting as free moral agents to make choices to guide their behavior.

Ethics refers to the principles of right and wrong that individuals, acting as free moral agents, use to make choices to guide their behavior. Information technology and information systems raise new ethical questions for both individuals and societies because they create opportunities for intense social change, and thus threaten existing distributions of power, money, rights, and obligations. Like other technologies, such as steam engines, electricity, telephone, and radio, information technology can be used to achieve social progress, but it can also be used to commit crimes and threaten cherished social values. The development of information technology will produce benefits for many, and costs for others. When using information systems, it is essential to ask, what is the ethical and socially responsible course of action?

A MODEL FOR THINKING ABOUT ETHICAL, SOCIAL, AND POLITICAL ISSUES

Ethical, social, and political issues are closely linked. The ethical dilemma you may face as a manager of information systems typically is reflected in social and political debate. One way to think about these relationships is given in Figure 5-1. Imagine society as a more or less calm pond on a summer day, a delicate ecosystem in partial equilibrium with individuals and with social and political institutions. Individuals know how to act in this pond because social institutions (family, education, organizations) have developed well-honed rules of behavior, and these are backed by laws developed in the political sector that prescribe behavior and promise sanctions for violations. Now toss a rock into the center of the pond. But imagine instead of a rock that the disturbing force is a powerful shock of new information technology and systems hitting a society more or less at rest. What happens? Ripples, of course.

Suddenly individual actors are confronted with new situations often not covered by the old rules. Social institutions cannot respond overnight to these ripples—it may take years to develop etiquette, expectations, social responsibility, "politically correct" attitudes, or approved rules. Political institutions also require time before developing new laws and often require the demonstration of real harm before they act. In the meantime, you may have to act. You may be forced to act in a legal "gray area."

We can use this model to illustrate the dynamics that connect ethical, social, and political issues. This model is also useful for identifying the main moral dimensions of the "information society," which cut across various levels of action—individual, social, and political.

MORAL DIMENSIONS OF THE INFORMATION AGE

The major ethical, social, and political issues raised by information systems include the following moral dimensions:

▌ Information rights and obligations: What **information rights** do individuals and organizations possess with respect to information about themselves? What can they protect? What obligations do individuals and organizations have concerning this information?

information rights
The rights that individuals and organizations have with respect to information that pertains to themselves.

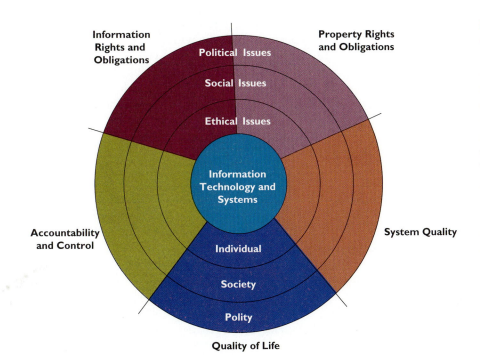

Quality of Life

Figure 5-1 The relationship between ethical, social, and political issues in an information society. The introduction of new information technology has a ripple effect, raising new ethical, social, and political issues that must be dealt with on the individual, social, and political levels. These issues have five moral dimensions: information rights and obligations, property rights and obligations, system quality, quality of life, and accountability and control.

▌ Property rights: How will traditional intellectual property rights be protected in a digital society in which tracing and accounting for ownership is difficult, and ignoring such property rights is so easy?

▌ Accountability and control: Who can and will be held accountable and liable for the harm done to individual and collective information and property rights?

▌ System quality: What standards of data and system quality should we demand to protect individual rights and the safety of society?

▌ Quality of life: What values should be preserved in an information- and knowledge-based society? What institutions should we protect from violation? What cultural values and practices are supported by the new information technology?

We explore these moral dimensions in detail in Section 5.3.

KEY TECHNOLOGY TRENDS THAT RAISE ETHICAL ISSUES

Ethical issues long preceded information technology—they are the abiding concerns of free societies everywhere. Nevertheless, information technology has heightened ethical concerns, put stress on existing social arrangements, and made existing laws obsolete or severely crippled. There are four key technological trends responsible for these ethical stresses and they are summarized in Table 5-1.

The doubling of computing power every 18 months has made it possible for most organizations to use information systems for their core production processes. As a result, our dependence on systems and our vulnerability to system errors and poor data quality have increased. Social rules and laws have not yet adjusted to this dependence. Standards for ensuring the accuracy and reliability of information systems (see Chapter 14) are not universally accepted or enforced.

Advances in data storage techniques and rapidly declining storage costs have been responsible for the multiplying databases on individuals—employees, customers, and potential customers—maintained by private and public organizations. These advances in data storage have made the routine violation of individual privacy both cheap and effective. For example, IBM has developed a wafer-sized disk that can hold the equivalent of more than 500 large novels. Already massive data storage systems are cheap enough for regional and even local retailing firms to use in identifying customers.

Advances in data analysis techniques for large pools of data are a third technological trend that heightens ethical concerns, because they enable companies to find out much detailed personal information about individuals. With contemporary information systems technology, companies can assemble and combine the myriad pieces of information stored on you by computers much more easily than in the past. Think of all the ways you generate computer information about yourself—credit card purchases, telephone calls, magazine subscriptions, video rentals, mail-order purchases, banking records, and local, state, and federal

TABLE 5-1   TECHNOLOGY TRENDS THAT RAISE ETHICAL ISSUES

Trend	Impact
Computing power doubles every 18 months	More organizations depend on computer systems for critical operations
Rapidly declining data storage costs	Organizations can easily maintain detailed databases on individuals
Data analysis advances	Companies can analyze vast quantities of data gathered on individuals to develop detailed profiles of individual behavior
Networking advances and the Internet	Copying data from one location to another and accessing personal data from remote locations are much easier

Credit card purchases can make personal information available to market researchers, telephone marketers, and direct mail companies. Advances in information technology facilitate the invasion of privacy.

government records (including court and police records). Put together and mined properly, this information could reveal not only your credit information but also your driving habits, your tastes, your associations, and your political interests.

Companies with products to sell purchase relevant information from these sources to help them more finely target their marketing campaigns. Chapters 3 and 7 describe how companies can analyze very large pools of data from multiple sources to rapidly identify buying patterns of customers and suggest individual responses. The use of computers to combine data from multiple sources and create electronic dossiers of detailed information on individuals is called **profiling**. For example, hundreds of Web sites allow DoubleClick (www.doubleclick.net), an Internet advertising broker, to track the activities of their visitors in exchange for revenue from advertisements based on visitor information DoubleClick gathers. DoubleClick uses this information to create a profile of each on-line visitor, adding more detail to the profile as the visitor accesses an associated DoubleClick site. Over time DoubleClick can create a detailed dossier of a person's spending and computing habits on the Web that can be sold to companies to help them target their Web ads more precisely.

Last, advances in networking, including the Internet, promise to reduce greatly the costs of moving and accessing large quantities of data, and open the possibility of mining large pools of data remotely using small desktop machines, permitting an invasion of privacy on a scale and precision heretofore unimaginable.

The development of global digital-superhighway communication networks widely available to individuals and businesses poses many ethical and social concerns. Who will account for the flow of information over these networks? Will you be able to trace information collected about you? What will these networks do to the traditional relationships between family, work, and leisure? How will traditional job designs be altered when millions of "employees" become subcontractors using mobile offices for which they themselves must pay?

In the next section we consider some ethical principles and analytical techniques for dealing with these kinds of ethical and social concerns.

profiling
The use of computers to combine data from multiple sources and create electronic dossiers of detailed information on individuals.

5.2 ETHICS IN AN INFORMATION SOCIETY

Ethics is a concern of humans who have freedom of choice. Ethics is about individual choice: When faced with alternative courses of action, what is the correct moral choice? What are the main features of "ethical choice"?

BASIC CONCEPTS: RESPONSIBILITY, ACCOUNTABILITY, AND LIABILITY

Ethical choices are decisions made by individuals who are responsible for the consequences of their actions. **Responsibility** is a key element of ethical action. Responsibility means that

responsibility
Accepting the potential costs, duties, and obligations for the decisions one makes.

MIS IN ACTION   MANAGER'S TOOLKIT

HOW TO CONDUCT AN ETHICAL ANALYSIS

When confronted with a situation that presents ethical issues, how should you analyze and reason about the situation? Here is a five-step process to guide your decision making:

1. *Identify and describe clearly the facts.* Find out who did what to whom, and where, when, and how. In many instances, you will be surprised at the errors in the initially reported facts, and often you will find that simply getting the facts straight helps define the solution. It also helps to get the opposing parties involved in an ethical dilemma to agree on the facts.

2. *Define the conflict or dilemma and identify the higher-order values involved.* Ethical, social, and political issues always reference higher values. The parties to a dispute all claim to be pursuing higher values (e.g., freedom, privacy, protection of property, and the free enterprise system). Typically, an ethical issue involves a dilemma: two diametrically opposed courses of action that support worthwhile values. For example, the chapter opening vignette and Window on Organizations illustrate two competing values: the need for companies to use marketing to become more efficient and the need to protect individual privacy.

3. *Identify the stakeholders.* Every ethical, social, and political issue has stakeholders: players in the game who have an interest in the outcome, who have invested in the situation, and usually who have vocal opinions. Find out the identity of these groups and what they want. This will be useful later when designing a solution.

4. *Identify the options that you can reasonably take.* You may find that none of the options satisfy all the interests involved, but that some options do a better job than others. Sometimes arriving at a "good" or ethical solution may not always be a "balancing" of consequences to stakeholders.

5. *Identify the potential consequences of your options.* Some options may be ethically correct, but disastrous from other points of view. Other options may work in this one instance, but not in other similar instances. Always ask yourself, "What if I choose this option consistently over time?"

---

accountability

The mechanisms for assessing responsibility for decisions made and actions taken.

liability

The existence of laws that permit individuals to recover the damages done to them by other actors, systems, or organizations.

due process

A process in which laws are well-known and understood and there is an ability to appeal to higher authorities to ensure that laws are applied correctly.

you accept the potential costs, duties, and obligations for the decisions you make. **Accountability** is a feature of systems and social institutions: It means that mechanisms are in place to determine who took responsible action, who is responsible. Systems and institutions in which it is impossible to find out who took what action are inherently incapable of ethical analysis or ethical action. Liability extends the concept of responsibility further to the area of laws. **Liability** is a feature of political systems in which a body of law is in place that permits individuals to recover the damages done to them by other actors, systems, or organizations. **Due process** is a related feature of law-governed societies and is a process in which laws are known and understood and there is an ability to appeal to higher authorities to ensure that the laws are applied correctly.

These basic concepts form the underpinning of an ethical analysis of information systems and those who manage them. First, as discussed in Chapter 3, information technologies are filtered through social institutions, organizations, and individuals. Systems do not have "impacts" by themselves. Whatever information system impacts exist are products of institutional, organizational, and individual actions and behaviors. Second, responsibility for the consequences of technology falls clearly on the institutions, organizations, and individual managers who choose to use the technology. Using information technology in a "socially responsible" manner means that you can and will be held accountable for the consequences of your actions. Third, in an ethical political society, individuals and others can recover damages done them through a set of laws characterized by due process. The Manager's Toolkit provides some guidelines for performing an ethical analysis.

CANDIDATE ETHICAL PRINCIPLES

Once your analysis is complete, what ethical principles or rules should you use to make a decision? What higher-order values should inform your judgment? Although you are the only one who can decide which among many ethical principles you will follow, and how you will prioritize them, it is helpful to consider some ethical principles with deep roots in many cultures that have survived throughout recorded history.

1. Do unto others as you would have them do unto you (the Golden Rule). Putting yourself into the place of others, and thinking of yourself as the object of the decision, can help you think about "fairness" in decision making.

2. If an action is not right for everyone to take, then it is not right for anyone (**Immanuel Kant's Categorical Imperative**). Ask yourself, "If everyone did this, could the organization, or society, survive?"

Immanuel Kant's Categorical Imperative

A principle that states that if an action is not right for everyone to take it is not right for anyone.

3. If an action cannot be taken repeatedly, then it is not right to take at all (**Descartes' rule of change**). This is the slippery-slope rule: An action may bring about a small change now that is acceptable, but if repeated would bring unacceptable changes in the long run. In the vernacular, it might be stated as "once started down a slippery path you may not be able to stop."

4. Take the action that achieves the higher or greater value (**the Utilitarian Principle**). This rule assumes you can prioritize values in a rank order and understand the consequences of various courses of action.

5. Take the action that produces the least harm, or the least potential cost (**Risk Aversion Principle**). Some actions have extremely high failure costs of very low probability (e.g., building a nuclear generating facility in an urban area) or extremely high failure costs of moderate probability (speeding and automobile accidents). Avoid these high failure cost actions, paying greater attention obviously to high failure cost potential of moderate to high probability.

6. Assume that virtually all tangible and intangible objects are owned by someone else unless there is a specific declaration otherwise. (This is the **ethical "no free lunch" rule**.) If something someone else has created is useful to you, it has value, and you should assume the creator wants compensation for this work.

Although these ethical rules cannot be guides to action, actions that do not easily pass these rules deserve some very close attention and a great deal of caution. The appearance of unethical behavior may do as much harm to you and your company as actual unethical behavior.

PROFESSIONAL CODES OF CONDUCT

When groups of people claim to be professionals, they take on special rights and obligations because of their special claims to knowledge, wisdom, and respect. Professional codes of conduct are promulgated by associations of professionals such as the American Medical Association (AMA), the American Bar Association (ABA), the Association of Information Technology Professionals (AITP), and the Association of Computing Machinery (ACM). These professional groups take responsibility for the partial regulation of their professions by determining entrance qualifications and competence. Codes of ethics are promises by professions to regulate themselves in the general interest of society. For example, avoiding harm to others, honoring property rights (including intellectual property), and respecting privacy are among the General Moral Imperatives of the ACM's Code of Ethics and Professional Conduct (ACM, 1993).

SOME REAL-WORLD ETHICAL DILEMMAS

Information systems have created new ethical dilemmas in which one set of interests is pitted against another. For example, many of the large telephone companies in the United States are using information technology to reduce the sizes of their workforces. AT&T has been using voice recognition software to reduce the need for human operators by allowing computers to recognize a customer's responses to a series of computerized questions. AT&T planned for the new technology to eliminate 3,000 to 6,000 operator jobs nationwide, 200 to 400 management positions, and 31 offices in 21 states.

Many companies monitor what their employees are doing on the Internet to prevent them from wasting company resources on nonbusiness activities. Computer Associates International fired at least 10 employees at its Herndon office in December 2000 for sending sexually explicit e-mail; Xerox Corporation fired 40 workers in 1999 for spending too much of their work time surfing the Web. Firms believe they have the right to monitor employee e-mail and Web use because they own the facilities, intend their use to be for business purposes only, and create the facility for a business purpose (see the Chapter 8 Window on Management).

In each instance, you can find competing values at work, with groups lined on either side of a debate. A company may argue, for example, that it has a right to use information systems to increase productivity and reduce the size of its workforce to lower costs and stay in

Descartes' rule of change
A principle that states that if an action cannot be taken repeatedly, then it is not right to be taken at any time.

Utilitarian Principle
Principle that assumes one can put values in rank order and understand the consequences of various courses of action.

Risk Aversion Principle
Principle that one should take the action that produces the least harm or incurs the least cost.

ethical "no free lunch" rule
Assumption that all tangible and intangible objects are owned by someone else, unless there is a specific declaration otherwise, and that the creator wants compensation for this work.

MIS IN ACTION   DECISIONMAKING

WHAT TO DO ABOUT EMPLOYEE WEB USAGE

As the head of a small insurance company with six employees, you are concerned about how effectively your company is using its networking and human resources. Budgets are tight, and you are struggling to meet payrolls because employees are reporting many overtime hours. You do not believe that the employees have a sufficiently heavy workload to warrant working longer hours and are looking into the amount of time they spend on the Internet. Each employee uses a computer with Internet access on the job. You requested the following weekly report of employee Web usage from your information systems department.

Web Usage Report for the Week Ending January 12, 2002

User Name	Minutes On-line	Web Site Visited
Kelleher, Claire	45	www.doubleclick.net
Kelleher, Claire	57	www.yahoo.com
Kelleher, Claire	96	www.insuremarket.com
McMahon, Patricia	83	www.e-music.com
Milligan, Robert	112	www.shopping.com
Milligan, Robert	43	www.travelocity.com
Olivera, Ernesto	40	www.internetnews.com
Talbot, Helen	125	www.etrade.com
Talbot, Helen	27	www.nordstrom.com
Talbot, Helen	35	www.yahoo.com
Talbot, Helen	73	www.ebay.com
Wright, Steven	23	www.geocities.com
Wright, Steven	15	www.autobytel.com

1. Calculate the total amount of time each employee spent on the Web for the week and the total amount of time that company computers were used for this purpose. Rank the employees in the order of the amount of time each spent on-line.
2. Do your findings and the contents of the report indicate any ethical problems employees are creating? Is the company creating an ethical problem by monitoring its employees' use of the Internet?
3. Use the guidelines for ethical analysis presented in this chapter to develop a solution to the problems you have identified.

---

business. Employees displaced by information systems may argue that employers have some responsibility for their welfare. Business owners might feel obligated to monitor employee e-mail and Internet use to minimize drains on productivity (Urbaczewski and Jessup, 2002). Employees might believe they should be able to use the Internet for short personal tasks in place of the telephone. A close analysis of the facts can sometimes produce compromised solutions that give each side "half a loaf." Try to apply some of the principles of ethical analysis described to each of these cases. What is the right thing to do?

5.3 THE MORAL DIMENSIONS OF INFORMATION SYSTEMS

In this section, we take a closer look at the five moral dimensions of information systems first described in Figure 5-1. In each dimension we identify the ethical, social, and political levels of analysis and use real-world examples to illustrate the values involved, the stakeholders, and the options chosen.

INFORMATION RIGHTS: PRIVACY AND FREEDOM IN THE INTERNET AGE

privacy
The claim of individuals to be left alone, free from surveillance or interference from other individuals, organizations, or the state.

Privacy is the claim of individuals to be left alone, free from surveillance or interference from other individuals or organizations, including the state. Claims to privacy are also involved at the workplace: Millions of employees are subject to electronic and other forms of high-tech surveillance (Ball, 2001). Information technology and systems threaten individual claims to privacy by making the invasion of privacy cheap, profitable, and effective.

The claim to privacy is protected in the U.S., Canadian, and German constitutions in a variety of different ways, and in other countries through various statutes. In the United States, the claim to privacy is protected primarily by the First Amendment guarantees of freedom of speech and association, the Fourth Amendment protections against unreasonable search and seizure of one's personal documents or home, and the guarantee of due process.

Due process has become a key concept in defining privacy. Due process requires that a set of rules or laws exist that clearly define how information about individuals will be treated, and what appeal mechanisms are available. Perhaps the best statement of due process in record keeping is given by the Fair Information Practices Doctrine developed in the early 1970s.

TABLE 5-2   FAIR INFORMATION PRACTICES PRINCIPLES

1. There should be no personal record systems whose existence is secret.

2. Individuals have rights of access, inspection, review, and amendment to systems that contain information about them.

3. There must be no use of personal information for purposes other than those for which it was gathered without prior consent.

4. Managers of systems are responsible and can be held accountable and liable for the damage done by systems.

5. Governments have the right to intervene in the information relationships among private parties.

Most American and European privacy law is based on a regime called Fair Information Practices (FIP) first set forth in a report written in 1973 by a federal government advisory committee (U.S. Department of Health, Education, and Welfare, 1973). **Fair Information Practices (FIP)** is a set of principles governing the collection and use of information about individuals. The five Fair Information Practices principles are shown in Table 5-2.

FIP principles are based on the notion of a "mutuality of interest" between the record-holder and the individual. The individual has an interest in engaging in a transaction, and the record keeper—usually a business or government agency—requires information about the individual to support the transaction. Once gathered, the individual maintains an interest in the record, and the record may not be used to support other activities without the individual's consent.

Fair Information Practices form the basis of the federal statutes listed in Table 5-3 that set forth the conditions for handling information about individuals in such areas as credit reporting, education, financial records, newspaper records, and electronic communications. The Privacy Act of 1974 has been the most important of these laws, regulating the federal government's collection, use, and disclosure of information. At present, most U.S. federal privacy laws apply only to the federal government and regulate very few areas of the private sector.

Efforts are under way to develop appropriate legislation to protect the privacy of Internet users. The Federal Trade Commission (FTC) has made a series of recommendations to the U.S. Congress for on-line privacy protection, issuing its own set of Fair Information Practice

Fair Information Practices (FIP)

A set of principles originally set forth in 1973 that governs the collection and use of information about individuals and forms the basis of most U.S. and European privacy laws.

TABLE 5-3   FEDERAL PRIVACY LAWS IN THE UNITED STATES

General Federal Privacy Laws

Freedom of Information Act, 1968 as Amended (5 USC 552)

Privacy Act of 1974 as Amended (5 USC 552a)

Electronic Communications Privacy Act of 1986

Computer Matching and Privacy Protection Act of 1988

Computer Security Act of 1987

Federal Managers Financial Integrity Act of 1982

Privacy Laws Affecting Private Institutions

Fair Credit Reporting Act of 1970

Family Educational Rights and Privacy Act of 1978

Right to Financial Privacy Act of 1978

Privacy Protection Act of 1980

Cable Communications Policy Act of 1984

Electronic Communications Privacy Act of 1986

Video Privacy Protection Act of 1988

Children's Online Privacy Protection Act of 1998

Principles (FIP) in 1998. The FTC's FIP restate and extend the original FIP to provide guidelines more appropriate for privacy protection in the age of the Internet. Core principles specify that Web sites must disclose their information practices before collecting data and that consumers must be allowed to choose how information about them will be used for secondary purposes (purposes other than those supporting the immediate transaction).

In the United States, privacy law is enforced by individuals who must sue agencies or companies in court to recover damages. European countries and Canada define privacy in a similar manner to that in the United States, but they have chosen to enforce their privacy laws by creating privacy commissions or data protection agencies to pursue complaints brought by citizens.

The European Directive on Data Protection

In Europe, privacy protection is much more stringent than in the United States. Unlike the United States, European countries do not allow businesses to use personally identifiable information without consumers' prior consent. On October 25, 1998, the European Commission's Directive on Data Protection came into effect, broadening privacy protection in the European Union (EU) nations. The directive requires companies to inform people when they collect information about them and disclose how it will be stored and used. Customers must provide their informed consent before any company can legally use data about them, and they have the right to access that information, correct it, and request that no further data be collected. **Informed consent** can be defined as consent given with knowledge of all the facts needed to make a rational decision. EU member nations must translate these principles into their own laws and cannot transfer personal data to countries such as the United States that don't have similar privacy protection regulations.

informed consent
Consent given with knowledge of all the facts needed to make a rational decision.

Working with the European Commission, the U.S. Department of Commerce developed a safe harbor framework for U.S. firms. U.S. businesses would be allowed to use personal data from EU countries if they develop privacy protection policies that meet EU standards. Enforcement would occur in the United States, using self-policing, regulation, and government enforcement of fair trade statutes.

Internet Challenges to Privacy

The Internet introduces technology that poses new challenges to the protection of individual privacy that the original Fair Information Practices principles have been inadequate in addressing. Information sent over this vast network of networks may pass through many different computer systems before it reaches its final destination. Each of these systems is capable of monitoring, capturing, and storing communications that pass through it.

It is possible to record many on-line activities, including which on-line newsgroups or files a person has accessed, which Web sites and Web pages he or she has visited, and what items that person has inspected or purchased over the Web. Much of this monitoring and tracking of Web site visitors occurs in the background without the visitor's knowledge. Tools to monitor visits to the World Wide Web have become popular because they help organizations determine who is visiting their Web sites and how to better target their offerings. (Some firms also monitor the Internet usage of their employees to see how they are using company network resources.) Web retailers now have access to software that lets them watch the on-line shopping behavior of individuals and groups while they are visiting a Web site and making purchases. The commercial demand for this personal information is virtually insatiable.

Web sites can learn the identity of their visitors if the visitors voluntarily register at the site to purchase a product or service or to obtain a free service, such as information. Web sites can also capture information about visitors without their knowledge using "cookie" technology. **Cookies** are tiny files deposited on a computer hard drive when a user visits certain Web sites. Cookies identify the visitor's Web browser software and track visits to the Web site. When the visitor returns to a site that has stored a cookie, the Web site software will search the visitor's computer, find the cookie, and "know" what that person has done in the past. It may also update the cookie, depending on the activity during the visit. In this way, the site can customize its contents for each visitor's interests. For example, if you purchase a book on the Amazon.com Web site and return later from the same browser, the site will welcome you

cookie
Tiny file deposited on a computer hard drive when an individual visits certain Web sites. Used to identify the visitor and track visits to the Web site.

by name and recommend other books of interest based on your past purchases. DoubleClick, introduced earlier in this chapter, uses cookies to build its dossiers with details of on-line purchases and the behavior of Web site visitors. Figure 5-2 illustrates how cookies work.

Web sites using "cookie" technology cannot directly obtain visitors' names and addresses. However, if a person has registered at a site, that information can be combined with cookie data to identify the visitor. Web sites owners can also combine the data they have gathered from "cookies" and other Web site monitoring tools with personal data from other sources such as off-line data collected from surveys or paper catalog purchases to develop very detailed profiles of their visitors.

The Internet is inspiring even more subtle and surreptitious tools for surveillance (Bennett, 2001). **Web bugs** (sometimes called *invisible.GIFs* or *clear.GIFS*) are tiny graphic files embedded in e-mail messages and Web pages that are designed to monitor who is reading the e-mail message or Web page. They transmit information about the user and the page being viewed to a monitoring computer. Because Web bugs are very tiny, colorless, and virtually invisible, they can be difficult for unsophisticated Internet users to detect. Marketers use these Web bugs as another tool to monitor on-line behavior and can develop detailed consumer profiles by combining Web bug data with data from other sources.

The United States has allowed businesses to gather transaction information generated in the marketplace and then use that information for other marketing purposes without obtaining the informed consent of the individual whose information is being used. U.S. e-commerce sites are largely content to publish statements on their Web sites informing visitors about how their information will be used. Some have added *opt-out* selection boxes to these information policy statements. An **opt-out** model of informed consent permits the collection of personal information until the consumer specifically requests that the data not be collected. Privacy advocates would like to see wider use of an **opt-in** model of informed consent in which a business is prohibited from collecting any personal information unless the consumer specifically takes action to approve information collection and use.

Cookies? I Didn't Order Any Cookies

Here is how a cookie works:

1. A user opens a Web browser and selects a Web site to visit.

2. The user's computer sends a request for information to the computer running the Web site.

3. The Web site computer, called a server, sends the information that allows the user's computer to display the Web site. It also sends a cookie —a data file that contains information like an encrypted user ID and information about when the user visited and what he did on the site.

www

4. The user's computer receives the cookie and places it in a file on the hard drive.

5. Whenever the user goes back to the Web site, the server running the site retrieves the cookie to help it identify the user.

www

Figure 5-2 How cookies can identify Web visitors. Cookies are written by a Web site on a visitor's hard drive. When the visitor returns to that Web site, the Web server requests the ID number from the cookie and uses it to access the data stored by that server on that visitor. The Web site can then use these data to display personalized information. *Source:* Cookies? I Didn't Order Any Cookies. From "Giving Web a Memory Costs Its Users Privacy" by John Swartz, *New York Times*, September 4, 2001.

Web bugs

Tiny graphic files embedded in e-mail messages and Web pages that are designed to monitor on-line Internet user behavior.

opt-out

Model of informed consent permitting the collection of personal information until the consumer specifically requests that the data not be collected.

opt-in

Model of informed consent prohibiting an organization from collecting any personal information unless the individual specifically takes action to approve information collection and use.

Governments around the world are trying to address the issue of on-line privacy. In the United States, the Federal Trade Commission (FTC) has played a leading role in recommending on-line privacy legislation to the U.S. Congress. The FTC is responsible for protecting consumers from unfair or deceptive practices and for promoting competition to increase consumer choice. In 1998 the FTC issued a set of Fair Information Practice Principles that restated the 1973 FIP to make them more applicable to on-line privacy in e-commerce.

The new FIP, which we described earlier, are being used as guidelines to drive changes in privacy legislation. In July 1998 the U.S. Congress passed the Children's Online Privacy Protection Act (COPPA), requiring Web sites to obtain parental permission before collecting information on children under the age of 13. In July 2000 the FTC recommended additional legislation to protect on-line consumer privacy in advertising networks such as DoubleClick, which collect records of consumer Web activity to develop detailed profiles that are then used by other companies to target on-line ads. Other proposed e-commerce

"Cookies" are tiny files deposited on a computer hard drive when users visit certain Web sites. Although cookies can provide valuable marketing information, the practice of collecting Web site visitor data raises worries about protecting individual privacy.

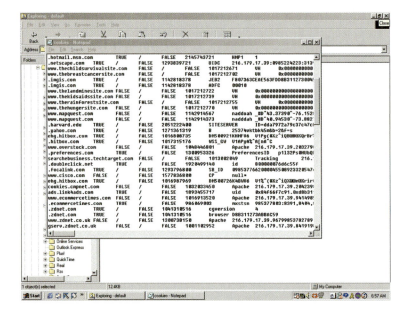

privacy legislation is focusing on protecting the on-line use of personal identification numbers such as social security numbers and prohibiting the use of "spyware" programs that trace on-line user activities without the users' permission or knowledge.

The on-line industry has preferred self-regulation to privacy legislation for protecting consumers. In 1998 the on-line industry formed the Online Privacy Alliance to encourage self-regulation to develop a set of privacy guidelines for its members. The group is promoting the use of on-line "seals" such as that of TRUSTe, certifying Web sites adhering to certain privacy principles. Members of the advertising network industry, including DoubleClick, Adforce, Avenue A, and 24/7 Media, have created an additional industry association called the Network Advertising Initiative (NAI) to develop its own privacy policies to help consumers opt-out of advertising network programs and provide consumer redress from abuses.

Technical Solutions

In addition to legislation, new technologies are being developed to protect user privacy during interactions with Web sites (Vijayan, 2000). Many of these tools are used for encrypting

Web sites are starting to post their privacy policies for visitors to review. The TRUSTe seal designates Web sites that have agreed to adhere to TRUSTe's established privacy principles of disclosure, choice, access, and security.

TABLE 5-4   PRIVACY PROTECTION TOOLS

Privacy Protection Function	Description	Example
Managing cookies	Block or limit cookies from being placed on the user's computer	Microsoft Internet Explorer 5 and 6 CookieCrusher
Blocking ads	Control ads that pop up based on user profiles and prevent them from collecting or sending information	AdSubtract
Encrypting e-mail or data	Scramble e-mail or data so that it can't be read	Pretty Good Privacy (PGP) SafeMessage.com
Anonymizers	Allow users to surf the Web without being identified or to send anonymous e-mail	Anonymizer.com

e-mail, for making e-mail or surfing activities appear anonymous, or for preventing client computers from accepting "cookies." Table 5-4 describes some of these tools.

Interest is now growing in tools to help users determine the kind of personal data that can be extracted by Web sites. The Platform for Privacy Preferences, known as P3P enables automatic communication of privacy policies between an e-commerce site and its visitors. **P3P** provides a standard for communicating a Web site's privacy policy to Internet users and for comparing that policy to the user's preferences or to other standards such as the FTC's new FIP guidelines or the European Directive on Data Protection. Users can use P3P to select the level of privacy they wish to maintain when interacting with the Web site. The Window on Organizations describes how P3P works and its potential impact on organizations and individuals.

P3P
Industry standard designed to give users more control over personal information gathered on Web sites they visit. Stands for Platform for Privacy Preferences.

Ethical Issues

The ethical privacy issue in this information age is as follows: Under what conditions should I (you) invade the privacy of others? What legitimates intruding into others' lives through unobtrusive surveillance, through market research, or by whatever means? Do we have to inform people that we are eavesdropping? Do we have to inform people that we are using credit history information for employment screening purposes?

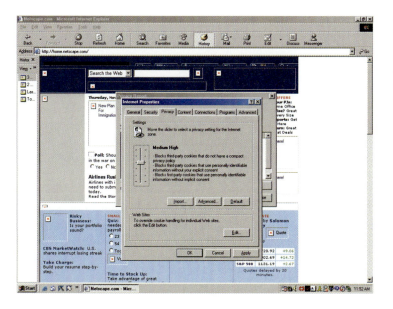

New versions of Microsoft's Internet Explorer Web browsing software support the P3P system for establishing Web site visitor privacy preferences. Users can adjust P3P settings to the level of privacy protection they desire when accessing a Web site.

Can P3P Give Users Back Their Privacy?

Internet users are never alone. They are always surrounded by cookies deposited on their hard drives by nearly every Web site they visit and users can't easily tell what these cookies are doing. The Platform for Privacy Preferences (P3P) has been touted as a tool to give users a closer look at cookies and much more control over what they do.

The P3P system is a product of years of work by the World Wide Web Consortium, an industry group with 513 members. P3P is a standard that allows Web sites to publish privacy policies in a form that computers can understand. Once codified according to P3P rules, the privacy policy becomes part of the software for individual Web pages. P3P is built into Microsoft Internet Explorer 6 Web browsing software so that Internet Explorer 6 users can access and read the P3P site's privacy policy. This feature allows users to see what Web sites are sending a cookie, what kind of information they're after, and who will get to use it. If you visit the Web site of any consortium member that has adopted P3P, you can double-click on a small eye icon at the bottom of Internet Explorer 6.0 to see the site's privacy policy and an updated list of all the cookies coming from the site. Double click on each cookie and you'll see the name of the sender and its privacy statement describing what information the cookie is collecting. If you hit another button, Internet Explorer lets you screen out cookies you don't want. You can adjust your computer to screen out all cookies or let in selected cookies based on specific levels of privacy. For example, the "medium" level accepts cookies from "first-party" host sites that have opt-in or opt-out policies but rejects third-party cookies that use personally identifiable information without an opt-in policy.

P3P sounds like a pair of magic glasses, but experts aren't so sure. P3P only works with Web sites of members of the World Wide Web Consortium who have translated their Web site privacy policies into P3P format. The technology will display cookies from Web sites that are not part of the consortium, but users won't be able to obtain sender information or privacy statements. It is difficult for businesses to rewrite their privacy statements to fit the P3P format. According to Jules Polonetsky, chief privacy officer at the e-mail marketing company DoubleClick, "most privacy policies don't go into as much detail as P3P does." Additionally, users may not fully grasp the meaning of P3P terms such as a "third party." (This term refers to networks such as DoubleClick that use cookies and other data to develop user profiles to beam targeted ads onto Web sites.) Users also need to understand the difference between blocking a cookie and restricting it (which essentially means accepting the cookie but deleting it once one leaves the browser) and the difference between explicit and implicit consent, which are equivalent to "opt-in" and "opt-out." Most users would need to read help files and visit other Web sites for more data in order to understand all of this language. Microsoft says privacy issues are complex and can only be boiled down so far. The company believes the main challenge is to get consumers to use its P3P tools so that more Web sites will publish their privacy policies in P3P format. Critics would also like to see P3P make e-businesses more accountable for the promises they make.

To Think About   What are the benefits of P3P for businesses? For consumers? How effective is P3P as a privacy protection tool?

Sources: Deborah Radcliff, "Giving Users Back Their Privacy," *Computerworld*, July 9, 2001; Thomas W. Weber, "A New Privacy Tool Is at Your Disposal Now-Warts and All," *Wall Street Journal*, September 10, 2001; Glenn R. Simpson, "As Congress Mulls New Web-Privacy Laws, Microsoft Pushes System Tied to Its Browser," *Wall Street Journal*, October 29, 2001; and Bill Richards, "Following the Crumbs," *Wall Street Journal*, October 29, 2001.

Social Issues

The social issue of privacy concerns the development of "expectations of privacy" or privacy norms, as well as public attitudes. In what areas of life should we as a society encourage people to think they are in "private territory" as opposed to public view? For instance, should we as a society encourage people to develop expectations of privacy when using electronic mail, cellular telephones, bulletin boards, the postal system, the workplace, the street? Should expectations of privacy be extended to criminal conspirators?

Political Issues

The political issue of privacy concerns the development of statutes that govern the relations between record keepers and individuals. Should we permit the FBI to monitor e-mail at will in order to apprehend suspected criminals and terrorists (see the chapter ending case study). To what extent should e-commerce sites and other businesses be allowed to maintain personal data about individuals?

PROPERTY RIGHTS: INTELLECTUAL PROPERTY

Contemporary information systems have severely challenged existing law and social practices that protect private intellectual property. **Intellectual property** is considered to be intangible property created by individuals or corporations. Information technology has made it difficult to protect intellectual property because computerized information can be so easily copied or distributed on networks. Intellectual property is subject to a variety of protections under three different legal traditions: trade secret, copyright, and patent law.

Trade Secrets

Any intellectual work product—a formula, device, pattern, or compilation of data—used for a business purpose can be classified as a **trade secret**, provided it is not based on information in the public domain. Protections for trade secrets vary from state to state. In general, trade secret laws grant a monopoly on the ideas behind a work product, but it can be a very tenuous monopoly.

Software that contains novel or unique elements, procedures, or compilations can be included as a trade secret. Trade secret law protects the actual ideas in a work product, not only their manifestation. To make this claim, the creator or owner must take care to bind employees and customers with nondisclosure agreements and to prevent the secret from falling into the public domain.

The limitation of trade secret protection is that although virtually all software programs of any complexity contain unique elements of some sort, it is difficult to prevent the ideas in the work from falling into the public domain when the software is widely distributed.

Copyright

Copyright is a statutory grant that protects creators of intellectual property from having their work copied by others for any purpose for a period of 28 years. Since the first Federal Copyright Act of 1790, and the creation of the Copyright Office to register copyrights and enforce copyright law, Congress has extended copyright protection to books, periodicals, lectures, dramas, musical compositions, maps, drawings, artwork of any kind, and motion pictures. The congressional intent behind copyright laws has been to encourage creativity and authorship by ensuring that creative people receive the financial and other benefits of their work. Most industrial nations have their own copyright laws, and there are several international conventions and bilateral agreements through which nations coordinate and enforce their laws.

In the mid-1960s the Copyright Office began registering software programs, and in 1980 Congress passed the Computer Software Copyright Act, which clearly provides protection for software program code and for copies of the original sold in commerce, and sets forth the rights of the purchaser to use the software while the creator retains legal title.

Copyright protection is clear-cut: It protects against copying of entire programs or their parts. Damages and relief are readily obtained for infringement. The drawback to copyright protection is that the underlying ideas behind a work are not protected, only their manifestation in a work. A competitor can use your software, understand how it works, and build new software that follows the same concepts without infringing on a copyright.

"Look and feel" copyright infringement lawsuits are precisely about the distinction between an idea and its expression. For instance, in the early 1990s Apple Computer sued Microsoft Corporation and Hewlett-Packard Inc. for infringement of the expression of Apple's Macintosh interface. Among other claims, Apple claimed that the defendants copied the expression of overlapping windows. The defendants counterclaimed that the idea of overlapping windows can only be expressed in a single way and, therefore, was not protectable under the "merger" doctrine of copyright law. When ideas and their expression merge, the expression cannot be copyrighted. In general, courts appear to be following the reasoning of a 1989 case—*Brown Bag Software* vs. *Symantec Corp.*—in which the court dissected the elements of software alleged to be infringing. The court found that similar concept, function, general functional features (e.g., drop-down menus), and colors are not protectable by copyright law (*Brown Bag* vs. *Symantec Corp.*, 1992).

intellectual property

Intangible property created by individuals or corporations that is subject to protections under trade secret, copyright, and patent law.

trade secret

Any intellectual work or product used for a business purpose that can be classified as belonging to that business, provided it is not based on information in the public domain.

copyright

A statutory grant that protects creators of intellectual property against copying by others for any purpose for a period of 28 years.

Patents

patent

A legal document that grants the owner an exclusive monopoly on the ideas behind an invention for 20 years; designed to ensure that inventors of new machines or methods are rewarded for their labor while making widespread use of their inventions.

A **patent** grants the owner an exclusive monopoly on the ideas behind an invention for 20 years. The congressional intent behind patent law was to ensure that inventors of new machines, devices, or methods receive the full financial and other rewards of their labor and yet still make widespread use of the invention possible by providing detailed diagrams for those wishing to use the idea under license from the patent's owner. The granting of a patent is determined by the Patent Office and relies on court rulings.

The key concepts in patent law are originality, novelty, and invention. The Patent Office did not accept applications for software patents routinely until a 1981 Supreme Court decision that held that computer programs could be a part of a patentable process. Since that time hundreds of patents have been granted and thousands await consideration.

The strength of patent protection is that it grants a monopoly on the underlying concepts and ideas of software. The difficulty is passing stringent criteria of nonobviousness (e.g., the work must reflect some special understanding and contribution), originality, and novelty, as well as years of waiting to receive protection.

Challenges to Intellectual Property Rights

Contemporary information technologies, especially software, pose a severe challenge to existing intellectual property regimes and, therefore, create significant ethical, social, and political issues. Digital media differ from books, periodicals, and other media in terms of ease of replication; ease of transmission; ease of alteration; difficulty classifying a software work as a program, book, or even music; compactness—making theft easy; and difficulties in establishing uniqueness.

The proliferation of electronic networks, including the Internet, has made it even more difficult to protect intellectual property. Before widespread use of networks, copies of software, books, magazine articles, or films had to be stored on physical media, such as paper, computer disks, or videotape, creating some hurdles to distribution. Using networks, information can be more widely reproduced and distributed.

With the World Wide Web in particular, one can easily copy and distribute virtually anything to thousands and even millions of people around the world, even if they are using different types of computer systems. Information can be illicitly copied from one place and distributed through other systems and networks even though these parties do not willingly participate in the infringement. For example, the music industry is worried because individuals can illegally copy digitized MP3 music files to Web sites where they can be downloaded by others who do not know that the MP3 files are not licensed for copying or distribution (see the Window on Technology). The Internet was designed to transmit information freely around the world, including copyrighted information. Intellectual property that can be easily copied is likely to be copied (Cavazos, 1996; Chabrow, 1996).

The manner in which information is obtained and presented on the Web further challenges intellectual property protections (Okerson, 1996). Web pages can be constructed from bits of text, graphics, sound, or video that may come from many different sources. Each item may belong to a different entity, creating complicated issues of ownership and compensation (see Figure 5-3). Web sites can also use a capability called **framing** to let one site construct an on-screen border around content obtained by linking to another Web site. The first site's border and logo stay on screen, making the content of the new Web site appear to be "offered" by the previous Web site.

framing

Displaying the content of another Web site inside one's own Web site within a frame or a window.

Mechanisms are being developed to sell and distribute books, articles, and other intellectual property on the Internet, and some copyright protection is being provided by the Digital Millennium Copyright Act (DMCA) of 1998. The DMCA implements a World Intellectual Property Organization treaty that makes it illegal to circumvent technology-based protections of copyrighted materials. Internet Service Providers (ISPs) are required to "take down" sites of copyright infringers that they are hosting once they are notified of the problem.

Ethical Issues

The central ethical issue concerns the protection of intellectual property such as software, digital books, digital music, or digitized video. Should I (you) copy for my own use a piece of

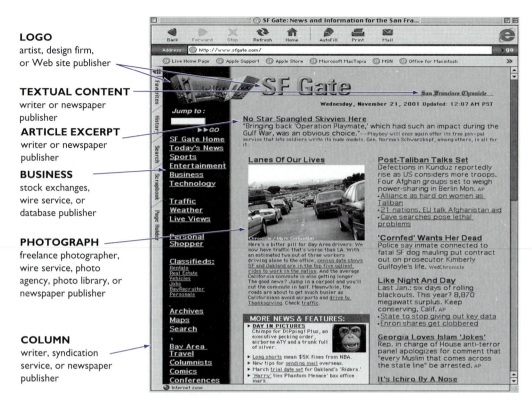

LOGO
artist, design firm,
or Web site publisher

TEXTUAL CONTENT
writer or newspaper
publisher

ARTICLE EXCERPT
writer or newspaper
publisher

BUSINESS
stock exchanges,
wire service, or
database publisher

PHOTOGRAPH
freelance photographer,
wire service, photo
agency, photo library, or
newspaper publisher

COLUMN
writer, syndication
service, or newspaper
publisher

Figure 5-3   Who Owns the Pieces? Anatomy of a Web page. Web pages are often constructed with elements from many different sources, clouding issues of ownership and intellectual property protection.

software or other digital content material protected by trade secret, copyright, and/or patent law? Is there continued value in protecting intellectual property when it can be so easily copied and distributed over the Internet?

Social Issues

There are several property-related social issues raised by new information technology. Most experts agree that the current intellectual property laws are breaking down in the information age. The vast majority of Americans report in surveys that they routinely violate some minor laws—everything from speeding to taking paper clips from work to copying books and software. The ease with which software and digital content can be copied contributes to making us a society of lawbreakers. These routine thefts threaten significantly to reduce the speed with which new information technologies can and will be introduced and, therefore, threaten further advances in productivity and social well-being.

Political Issues

The main property-related political issue concerns the creation of new property protection measures to protect investments made by creators of new software, digital books, and digital entertainment. Microsoft and 1,400 other software and information content firms are represented by the Software and Information Industry Association (SIIA), which lobbies for new laws and enforcement of existing laws to protect intellectual property around the world. (SIIA was formed on January 1, 1999, from the merger of the Software Publishers Association [SPA] and the Information Industry Association [IIA]). The SIIA runs an antipiracy hotline for individuals to report piracy activities and educational programs to help organizations combat software piracy. The SIIA has developed model Employee Usage Guidelines for software, described in Table 5-5.

Allied against SIIA are a host of groups and millions of individuals who believe that antipiracy laws cannot be enforced in the digital age and that software should be free or be paid for on a voluntary basis (shareware software). According to these groups, the greater social benefit results from the free distribution of software.

Napster and Gnutella Rock the Entertainment Industry

Would you pay $5.99 for a CD of your favorite recording artist when you could get it for free on the Web? That's what the music industry has been worrying about since the advent of Napster. Napster is a Web site that provides software and services that enable users to find and share MP3 music files. To use the company's service, users must download software that allows their computer to search the hard drives of other Napster subscribers for MP3 files. The MP3 files can then be downloaded directly from the user's computer.

Napster computers do not store any music files. They act as matchmakers. After you type in the name of the song you want, Napster shows all the users who are connected and who have that song on their computer available for downloading. Napster software then sets up a connection between your computer and the computer with the MP3 file, so the download can proceed. The song can then be played through computer speakers, transferred to an audio CD with a CD-R drive, or left in the shared music folder on your hard drive so other Napster users can copy it from you. Napster attracted about 38 million users in its first 18 months of existence.

Napster software can be used in a perfectly legal fashion to trade uncopyrighted music files, but many Napster users are sharing digital MP3 music files that have been copied from commercial audio CDs. In December 1999 the Recording Industry of America, representing the five major music recording companies, sued Napster for violating copyright laws. This suit is one of a series of legal actions the recording industry has taken against on-line music companies that are violating copyrights. In February 2001, a federal appeals court upheld an earlier ruling ordering Napster to stop allowing users to share and download copyrighted music files. On October 31, 2000, Napster announced it would join Bertelsmann, one of the world's five major music companies to create a fee-based Internet music service. Napster announced an additional distribution deal in June 2001 with MusicNet, another music subscription service, to sell music offered by major record labels for a fee.

But reforming Napster won't solve the problem. Other software and Web sites allow people to do the same thing. Gnutella, for example, allows individuals to send and receive all kinds of files without going through a central computer. In addition to MP3 music files, digital files of any type, size, or origin, including files of films, books, TV shows, or software—anything that can be digitized—can be shared with other computers without going through a central service. Each Gnutella.Net client can share files, search for files, and download files from any other user. Gnutella users have been actively trading movies as well as CDs over the Internet.

Gnutella was developed by Nullsoft, the maker of the Winamp MP3 player. Nullsoft's owner, America Online, shut down the Gnutella site immediately after it became active, but the Gnutella source code was openly distributed to developers outside the company and versions are available on the Internet. It is nearly impossible for ISPs, governments, or other groups to disable the network. According to Thomas Hale, CEO of Wired Planet, "The only way to stop [Gnutella] is to turn off the Internet."

Viewed in a positive light, Gnutella provides technology that can help break through censorship in other countries. Viewed more negatively, the same technology can be used to systematically violate copyright laws. The publishing and computer software industries are especially worried about potential losses from Gnutella and other similar programs such as Hotline, JungleMonkey, and Freenet because there is no central service, as in the case of Napster, that can be shut down to stop the flow of files.

To Think About Should you use programs like Gnutella to obtain software, movies, or other digital files for free? Explain your answer.

Sources: "Napster Strikes Deal with Labels," *Associated Press,* June 6, 2001; Dan Goodis, "Napster Blocks over 115,000 Songs," *The Industry Standard,* March 12, 2001, and "Can Napster Change Its Tune?" *The Industry Standard,* February 18, 2001; Amy Harmon, "Napster Users Mourn End of Free Music," *New York Times,* November 1, 2000; Amy Harmon with John Sullivan, "Music Industry Wins Ruling in U.S. Court," *New York Times,* April 29, 2000; Peter H. Lewis, "Napster Rocks the Web," *New York Times,* June 2000; Lee Gomes, "Software 'Free Spirits' Release Version of Program Mimicking Napster Product," *Wall Street Journal,* March 5, 2000; and Don Clark and Martin Peers, "Can the Record Industry Beat Free Web Music?" *Wall Street Journal,* June 20, 2000.

Accountability, Liability, and Control

Along with privacy and property laws, new information technologies are challenging existing liability law and social practices for holding individuals and institutions accountable. If a person is injured by a machine controlled, in part, by software, who should be held accountable and, therefore, held liable? Should a public bulletin board or an electronic service such as America Online permit the transmission of pornographic or offensive material (as broadcasters), or should they be held harmless against any liability for what users transmit (as is true of common carriers such as the telephone system)? What about the Internet? If you out-

TABLE 5-5   EMPLOYEE USAGE GUIDELINES FOR [ORGANIZATION]

Purpose

Software will be used only in accordance with its license agreement. Unless otherwise provided in the license, any duplication of copyrighted software, except for backup and archival purposes by software manager or designated department, is a violation of copyright law. In addition to violating copyright law, unauthorized duplication of software is contrary to [organization's] standards of conduct. The following points are to be followed to comply with software license agreements:

1. All users must use all software in accordance with its license agreements and the [organization's] software policy. All users acknowledge that they do not own this software or its related documentation, and unless expressly authorized by the software publisher, may not make additional copies except for archival purposes.

2. [Organization] will not tolerate the use of any unauthorized copies of software or fonts in our organization. Any person illegally reproducing software can be subject to civil and criminal penalties including fines and imprisonment. All users must not condone illegal copying of software under any circumstances and anyone who makes, uses, or otherwise acquires unauthorized software will be appropriately disciplined.

3. No user will give software or fonts to any outsiders including clients, customers, and others. Under no circumstances will software be used within [organization] that has been brought in from any unauthorized location under [organization's] policy, including, but not limited to, the Internet, the home, friends, and colleagues.

4. Any user who determines that there may be a misuse of software within the organization will notify the Certified Software Manager, department manager, or legal counsel.

5. All software used by the organization on organization-owned computers will be purchased through appropriate procedures.

I have read [organization's] software code of ethics. I am fully aware of our software compliance policies and agree to abide by them. I understand that violation of any above policies may result in my termination.

_____

EMPLOYEE SIGNATURE

_____

DATE

Published by the SPA Anti-Piracy. You are given permission to duplicate and modify this policy statement so long as attribution to the original document comes from SPA Anti-Piracy.

source your information processing, can you hold the external vendor liable for injuries done to your customers? Some real-world examples may shed light on these questions.

Some Liability Problems

On March 13, 1993, a blizzard hit the East Coast of the United States, knocking out an Electronic Data Systems Inc. (EDS) computer center in Clifton, New Jersey. The center operated 5,200 ATM machines in 12 different networks across the country involving more than 1 million cardholders. In the two weeks required to recover operations, EDS informed its customers to use alternative ATM networks operated by other banks or computer centers, and offered to cover more than $50 million in cash withdrawals. Because the alternative networks did not have access to the actual customer account balances, EDS was at substantial risk of fraud. Cash withdrawals were limited to $100 per day per customer to reduce the exposure. Most service was restored by March 26. Although EDS had a disaster-recovery plan, it did not have a dedicated backup facility. Who is liable for any economic harm caused to individuals or businesses that could not access their full account balances in this period (Joes, 1993)?

In April 1990, a computer system at Shell Pipeline Corporation failed to detect a human operator error. As a result, 93,000 barrels of crude oil were shipped to the wrong trader. The error cost $2 million because the trader sold oil that should not have been delivered to him. A court ruled later that Shell Pipeline was liable for the loss of the oil because the error was caused by a human operator who entered erroneous information into the system. Shell was held liable for not developing a system that would prevent the possibility of misdeliveries (King, 1992). Who would you have held liable—Shell Pipeline? The trader for not being more careful about deliveries? The human operator who made the error?

These cases point out the difficulties faced by information systems executives who ultimately are responsible for the harm done by systems developed by their staffs. In general, insofar as computer software is part of a machine, and the machine injures someone physically or economically, the producer of the software and the operator can be held liable for damages. Insofar as the software acts more like a book, storing and displaying information, courts have been reluctant to hold authors, publishers, and booksellers liable for contents (the exception being instances of fraud or defamation), and hence courts have been wary of holding software authors liable for "booklike" software.

In general, it is very difficult (if not impossible) to hold software producers liable for their software products when those products are considered like books, regardless of the physical or economic harm that results. Historically, print publishers, books, and periodicals have not been held liable because of fears that liability claims would interfere with First Amendment rights guaranteeing freedom of expression.

What about "software as service"? ATM machines are a service provided to bank customers. Should this service fail, customers will be inconvenienced and perhaps harmed economically if they cannot access their funds in a timely manner. Should liability protections be extended to software publishers and operators of defective financial, accounting, simulation, or marketing systems?

Software is very different from books. Software users may develop expectations of infallibility about software; software is less easily inspected than a book, and more difficult to compare with other software products for quality; software claims actually to perform a task rather than describe a task like a book; and people come to depend on services essentially based on software. Given the centrality of software to everyday life, the chances are excellent that liability law will extend its reach to include software even when it merely provides an information service.

Telephone systems have not been held liable for the messages transmitted because they are regulated "common carriers." In return for their right to provide telephone service, they must provide access to all, at reasonable rates, and achieve acceptable reliability. But broadcasters and cable television systems are subject to a wide variety of federal and local constraints on content and facilities. Organizations can be held liable for offensive content on their Web sites; and on-line services such as America Online might be held liable for postings by their users.

Ethical Issues

The central liability-related ethical issue raised by new information technologies is whether individuals and organizations that create, produce, and sell systems (both hardware and software) are morally responsible for the consequences of their use (see Johnson and Mulvey, 1995). If so, under what conditions? What liabilities (and responsibilities) should the user assume, and what should the provider assume?

Social Issues

The central liability-related social issue concerns the expectations that society should allow to develop around service-providing information systems. Should individuals (and organizations) be encouraged to develop their own backup devices to cover likely or easily anticipated system failures, or should organizations be held strictly liable for system services they provide? If organizations are held strictly liable, what impact will this have on the development of new system services? Can society permit networks and bulletin boards to post libelous, inaccurate, and misleading information that will harm many persons? Or should information service companies become self-regulating, and self-censoring?

Political Issues

The leading liability-related political issue is the debate between information providers of all kinds (from software developers to network service providers), who want to be relieved of liability as much as possible (thereby maximizing their profits), and service users—individuals, organizations, and communities—who want organizations to be held responsible for providing high-quality system services (thereby maximizing the quality of service). Service providers argue they will withdraw from the marketplace if they are held liable, whereas service users argue that only by holding providers liable can they guarantee a high level of service and compensate injured parties. Should legislation impose liability or restrict liability on service providers? This fundamental cleavage is at the heart of numerous political and judicial conflicts.

SYSTEM QUALITY: DATA QUALITY AND SYSTEM ERRORS

The debate over liability and accountability for unintentional consequences of system use raises a related but independent moral dimension: What is an acceptable, technologically feasible level of system quality (see Chapter 14)? At what point should system managers say, "Stop testing, we've done all we can to perfect this software. Ship it!" Individuals and organizations may be held responsible for avoidable and foreseeable consequences, which they have a duty to perceive and correct. And the gray area is that some system errors are foreseeable and correctable only at very great expense, an expense so great that pursuing this level of perfection is not feasible economically—no one could afford the product. For example, although software companies try to debug their products before releasing them to the marketplace, they knowingly ship buggy products because the time and cost of fixing all minor errors would prevent these products from ever being released (Rigdon, 1995). What if the product was not offered on the marketplace, would social welfare as a whole not advance and perhaps even decline? Carrying this further, just what is the responsibility of a producer of computer services—should they withdraw the product that can never be perfect, warn the user, or forget about the risk (let the buyer beware)?

Three principal sources of poor system performance are software bugs and errors, hardware or facility failures caused by natural or other causes, and poor input data quality. Chapter 14 discusses why zero defects in software code of any complexity cannot be achieved and why the seriousness of remaining bugs cannot be estimated. Hence, there is a technological barrier to perfect software, and users must be aware of the potential for catastrophic failure. The software industry has not yet arrived at testing standards for producing software of acceptable but not perfect performance (Collins et al., 1994).

Although software bugs and facility catastrophe are likely to be widely reported in the press, by far the most common source of business system failure is data quality. Few companies routinely measure the quality of their data, but studies of individual organizations report data error rates ranging from 0.5 to 30 percent (Redman, 1998).

Ethical Issues

The central quality-related ethical issue that information systems raise is at what point should I (or you) release software or services for consumption by others? At what point can you conclude that your software or service achieves an economically and technologically adequate level of quality? What are you obliged to know about the quality of your software, its procedures for testing, and its operational characteristics?

Social Issues

The leading quality-related social issue once again deals with expectations: As a society, do we want to encourage people to believe that systems are infallible, that data errors are impossible? Do we instead want a society where people are openly skeptical and questioning of the output of machines, where people are at least informed of the risk? By heightening awareness of system failure, do we inhibit the development of all systems, which in the end contribute to social well-being?

Political Issues

The leading quality-related political issue concerns the laws of responsibility and accountability. Should Congress establish or direct the National Institute of Science and Technology

(NIST) to develop quality standards (software, hardware, and data quality) and impose those standards on industry? Or should industry associations be encouraged to develop industry-wide standards of quality? Or should Congress wait for the marketplace to punish poor system quality, recognizing that in some instances this will not work (e.g., if all retail grocers maintain poor quality systems, then customers have no alternatives)?

QUALITY OF LIFE: EQUITY, ACCESS, AND BOUNDARIES

The negative social costs of introducing information technologies and systems are beginning to mount along with the power of the technology. Many of these negative social consequences are not violations of individual rights, nor are they property crimes. Nevertheless, these negative consequences can be extremely harmful to individuals, societies, and political institutions. Computers and information technologies potentially can destroy valuable elements of our culture and society even while they bring us benefits. If there is a balance of good and bad consequences of using information systems, whom do we hold responsible for the bad consequences? Next, we briefly examine some of the negative social consequences of systems, considering individual, social, and political responses.

Balancing Power: Center Versus Periphery

An early fear of the computer age was that huge, centralized mainframe computers would centralize power at corporate headquarters and in the nation's capital, resulting in a Big Brother society, as was suggested in George Orwell's novel, *1984*. The shift toward highly decentralized computing, coupled with an ideology of "empowerment" of thousands of workers, and the decentralization of decision making to lower organizational levels, have reduced fears of power centralization in institutions. Yet much of the "empowerment" described in popular business magazines is trivial. Lower-level employees may be empowered to make minor decisions, but the key policy decisions may be as centralized as in the past.

Rapidity of Change: Reduced Response Time to Competition

Information systems have helped to create much more efficient national and international markets. The now-more-efficient global marketplace has reduced the normal social buffers that permitted businesses many years to adjust to competition. "Time-based competition" has an ugly side: The business you work for may not have enough time to respond to global competitors and may be wiped out in a year, along with your job. We stand the risk of developing a "just-in-time society" with "just-in-time jobs" and "just-in-time" workplaces, families, and vacations.

Although some people may enjoy the convenience of working at home, the "do anything anywhere" computing environment can blur the traditional boundaries between work and family time.

Maintaining Boundaries: Family, Work, and Leisure

Parts of this book were produced on trains, planes, as well as on family "vacations" and what otherwise might have been "family" time. The danger to ubiquitous computing, telecommuting, nomad computing, and the "do anything anywhere" computing environment is that it might actually come true. If so, the traditional boundaries that separate work from family and just plain leisure will be weakened. Although authors have traditionally worked just about anywhere (typewriters have been portable for nearly a century), the advent of information systems, coupled with the growth of knowledge-work occupations, means that more and more people will be working when traditionally they would have been playing or communicating with family and friends. The "work umbrella" now extends far beyond the eight-hour day.

Weakening these institutions poses clear-cut risks. Family and friends historically have provided powerful support mechanisms for individuals, and they act as balance points in a society by preserving "private life," providing a place for one to collect one's thoughts, think in ways contrary to one's employer, and dream.

Dependence and Vulnerability

Today, our businesses, governments, schools, and private associations, such as churches, are incredibly dependent on information systems and are, therefore, highly vulnerable if these systems should fail. With systems now as ubiquitous as the telephone system, it is startling to remember that there are no regulatory or standard-setting forces in place similar to telephone, electrical, radio, television, or other public-utility technologies. The absence of standards and the criticality of some system applications will probably call forth demands for national standards and perhaps regulatory oversight.

Computer Crime and Abuse

Many new technologies in the industrial era have created new opportunities for committing crime. Technologies, including computers, create new valuable items to steal, new ways to steal them, and new ways to harm others. **Computer crime** is the commission of illegal acts through the use of a computer or against a computer system. Computers or computer systems can be the object of the crime (destroying a company's computer center or a company's computer files), as well as the instrument of a crime (stealing computer lists by illegally gaining access to a computer system using a home computer). Simply accessing a computer system without authorization, or intent to do harm, even by accident, is now a federal crime. **Computer abuse** is the commission of acts involving a computer that may not be illegal but are considered unethical.

No one knows the magnitude of the computer crime problem—how many systems are invaded, how many people engage in the practice, or what is the total economic damage, but it is estimated to cost more than $1 billion in the United States alone. Many companies are reluctant to report computer crimes because they may involve employees. The most economically damaging kinds of computer crime are introducing viruses, theft of services, disruption of computer systems, and theft of telecommunications services. "Hackers" is the pejorative term for persons who use computers in illegal ways. Hacker attacks are on the rise, posing new threats to organizations linked to the Internet (see Chapter 14).

Computer viruses (see Chapter 14) have grown exponentially during the past decade. More than 20,000 viruses have been documented, many causing huge losses because of lost data or crippled computers. Although many firms now use antivirus software, the proliferation of computer networks will increase the probability of infections.

Following are some illustrative computer crimes:

▮ Michael Whitt Ventimiglia, a former information technology worker at GTE Corporation, pled guilty to the charge of unintentionally damaging protected computers on May 15, 2000, at a Verizon Communications network support center in Tampa. Ventimiglia used his ability to gain access to GTE's secure computers and began to erase data on the computers, entering a command that prevented anyone from stopping the destruction. Ventimiglia's actions created more than $200,000 in damage (Sullivan, 2001).

computer crime
The commission of illegal acts through the use of a computer or against a computer system.

computer abuse
The commission of acts involving a computer that may not be illegal but are considered unethical.

The Black ICE Defender Firewall protects home and small office systems from hacker attacks and provides reports documenting attempted attacks. Hackers illegally accessing systems can cause widespread disruption and harm.

▍ An 11-member group of hackers, dubbed "The Phonemasters" by the FBI, gained access to telephone networks of companies including British Telecommunications, AT&T Corporation, MCI, Southwestern Bell, and Sprint. They were able to access credit-reporting databases belonging to Equifax and TRW Inc., as well as databases owned by Nexis/Lexis and Dunn & Bradstreet information services. Members of the ring sold credit reports, criminal records, and other data they pilfered from the databases, causing $1.85 million in losses. The FBI apprehended group members Calvin Cantrell, Corey Lindsley, and John Bosanac, and they were sentenced to jail terms of two to four years in federal prison. Other members remain at large (Simons, 1999).

▍ Santo Polanco, an 18-year-old student at the New York Institute of Technology and 26-year-old Eric Bilejhy were charged with a scheme to defraud in First District Court in New York. Both men allegedly raised at least $16,000 through fraudulent sales at eBay, Yahoo, and other Web sites, offering computers for auction that were never delivered after purchasers paid them thousands of dollars (Angwin, 00).

In general, it is employees—insiders—who have inflicted the most injurious computer crimes because they have the knowledge, access, and frequently a job-related motive to commit such crimes.

Congress responded to the threat of computer crime in 1986 with the Computer Fraud and Abuse Act. This act makes it illegal to access a computer system without authorization. Most states have similar laws, and nations in Europe have similar legislation. Other existing legislation covering wiretapping, fraud, and conspiracy by any means, regardless of technology employed, is adequate to cover computer crimes committed thus far.

The Internet's ease of use and accessibility have created new opportunities for computer crime and abuse. One widespread form of abuse is **spamming**, in which organizations or individuals send out thousands and even hundreds of thousands of unsolicited e-mail and electronic messages. This practice has been growing because it only costs a few cents to send thousands of messages advertising one's wares to Internet users. Some states' laws prohibit spamming, but it remains largely unregulated. Table 5-6 describes other practices where the Internet has been used for illegal or malicious purposes.

spamming
The practice of sending unsolicited e-mail and other electronic communication.

Employment: Trickle-Down Technology and Reengineering Job Loss

Reengineering work (see Chapter 12) is typically hailed in the information systems community as a major benefit of new information technology. It is much less frequently noted that redesigning business processes could potentially cause millions of middle-level managers and clerical workers to lose their jobs. One economist has raised the possibility that we will create

TABLE 5-6   INTERNET CRIME AND ABUSE

Problem	Description
Spamming	Marketers send out unsolicited mass e-mail to recipients who have not requested this information.
Hacking	Hackers exploit weaknesses in Web site security to obtain access to proprietary data, such as customer information and passwords. They may use "Trojan horses" posing as legitimate software to obtain information from the host computer.
Jamming	Jammers use software routines to tie up the computer hosting a Web site so that legitimate visitors can't access the site.
Malicious software	Cyber vandals use data flowing through the Internet to transmit computer viruses, which can disable computers that they "infect" (see Chapter 14).
Sniffing	Sniffing, a form of electronic eavesdropping, involves placing a piece of software to intercept information passing from a user to the computer hosting a Web site. This information can include credit card numbers and other confidential data.
Spoofing	Spoofers fraudulently misrepresent themselves as other organizations, setting up false Web sites where they can collect confidential information from unsuspecting visitors to the site.

a society run by a small "high tech elite of corporate professionals . . . in a nation of the permanently unemployed" (Rifkin, 1993).

Other economists are much more sanguine about the potential job losses. They believe relieving bright, educated workers from reengineered jobs will result in these workers moving to better jobs in fast-growth industries. Left out of this equation are blue-collar workers, and older, less well educated middle managers. It is not clear that these groups can be retrained easily for high-quality (high-paying) jobs. Careful planning and sensitivity to employee needs can help companies redesign work to minimize job losses.

Equity and Access: Increasing Racial and Social Class Cleavages

Does everyone have an equal opportunity to participate in the digital age? Will the social, economic, and cultural gaps that exist in America and other societies be reduced by information systems technology? Or will the cleavages be increased, permitting the "better off" to become even better off relative to others?

These questions have not yet been fully answered because the impact of systems technology on various groups in society has not been thoroughly studied. What is known is that information, knowledge, computers, and access to these resources through educational institutions and public libraries are inequitably distributed along racial and social class lines, as are many other information resources. Several studies have found that certain ethnic and income groups in the United States are much less likely to have computers or on-line Internet access even though computer ownership and Internet access have soared in the past five years. The gap between white and African American and Hispanic American household Internet use actually grew larger in 2000. Higher-income families in each ethnic group were much more likely to have home computers and Internet access than lower-income families in the same group (U.S. Department of Commerce, 1998; Rainie and Packel, 2001). A similar digital divide exists in U.S. schools, with schools in high-poverty areas much less likely to have computers, high-quality educational technology programs, or Internet access available for their students. Left uncorrected, the "digital divide" could lead to a society of information haves, computer literate and skilled, versus a large group of information have-nots, computer illiterate and unskilled.

Public interest groups want to narrow this "digital divide" by making digital information services—including the Internet—available to "virtually everyone" just as basic telephone service is now. The U.S. Department of Education and the National Science Foundation

Advanced Networking Project have undertaken programs to promote the use of computers and the Internet in rural and poor urban schools, but this is only a partial solution to the problem.

Health Risks: RSI, CVS, and Technostress

repetitive stress injury (RSI)
Occupational disease that occurs when muscle groups are forced through repetitive actions with high-impact loads or thousands of repetitions with low-impact loads.

carpal tunnel syndrome (CTS)
Type of RSI in which pressure on the median nerve through the wrist's bony carpal tunnel structure produces pain.

computer vision syndrome (CVS)
Eyestrain condition related to computer display screen use; symptoms include headaches, blurred vision, and dry and irritated eyes.

technostress
Stress induced by computer use; symptoms include aggravation, hostility toward humans, impatience, and enervation.

The most important occupational disease today is **repetitive stress injury (RSI)**. RSI occurs when muscle groups are forced through repetitive actions often with high-impact loads (such as tennis) or tens of thousands of repetitions under low-impact loads (such as working at a computer keyboard).

The single largest source of RSI is computer keyboards. About 50 million Americans use computers at work. The most common kind of computer-related RSI is **carpal tunnel syndrome (CTS),** in which pressure on the median nerve through the wrist's bony structure, called a "carpal tunnel," produces pain. The pressure is caused by constant repetition of keystrokes: In a single shift, a word processor may perform 23,000 keystrokes. Symptoms of carpal tunnel syndrome include numbness, shooting pain, inability to grasp objects, and tingling. Millions of workers have been diagnosed with carpal tunnel syndrome.

RSI is avoidable. Designing workstations for a neutral wrist position (using a wrist rest to support the wrist), proper monitor stands, and footrests all contribute to proper posture and reduced RSI. New, ergonomically correct keyboards are also an option, although their effectiveness has yet to be clearly established. These measures should be backed by frequent rest breaks, rotation of employees to different jobs, and moving toward voice or scanner data entry.

RSI is not the only occupational illness computers cause. Back and neck pain, leg stress, and foot pain also result from poor ergonomic designs of workstations. **Computer vision syndrome (CVS)** refers to any eyestrain condition related to computer display screen use. Its symptoms, usually temporary, include headaches, blurred vision, and dry and irritated eyes.

The newest computer-related malady is **technostress**, which is stress induced by computer use. Its symptoms include aggravation, hostility toward humans, impatience, and fatigue. The problem according to experts is that humans working continuously with computers come to expect other humans and human institutions to behave like computers, providing instant response, attentiveness, and an absence of emotion. Computer-intense workers are aggravated when put on hold during phone calls, becoming incensed or alarmed when their PCs take a few seconds longer to perform a task. Technostress is thought to be related to high levels of job turnover in the computer industry, high levels of early retirement from computer-intense occupations, and elevated levels of drug and alcohol abuse.

The incidence of technostress is not known but is thought to be in the millions in the United States and growing rapidly. Computer-related jobs now top the list of stressful occupations based on health statistics in several industrialized countries.

Repetitive stress injury (RSI) is the leading occupational disease today. The single largest cause of RSI is computer keyboard work.

To date the role of radiation from computer display screens in occupational disease has not been proved. Video display terminals (VDTs) emit nonionizing electric and magnetic fields at low frequencies. These rays enter the body and have unknown effects on enzymes, molecules, chromosomes, and cell membranes. Long-term studies are investigating low-level electromagnetic fields and birth defects, stress, low birth weight, and other diseases. All manufacturers have reduced display screen emissions since the early 1980s, and European countries such as Sweden have adopted stiff radiation emission standards.

The computer has become a part of our lives—personally as well as socially, culturally, and politically. It is unlikely that the issues and our choices will become easier as information technology continues to transform our world. The growth of the Internet and the information economy suggests that all the ethical and social issues we have described will be heightened further as we move into the first digital century.

MANAGEMENT ACTIONS: A CORPORATE CODE OF ETHICS

Some corporations have developed far-reaching corporate IS codes of ethics, including Federal Express, IBM, American Express, and Merck and Co. Most firms, however, have not developed these codes of ethics, leaving their employees in the dark about expected correct behavior. There is some dispute concerning a general code of ethics versus a specific information systems code of ethics. As managers, you should strive to develop an IS-specific set of ethical standards for each of the five moral dimensions:

▌ Information rights and obligations. A code should cover topics such as employee e-mail and Internet privacy, workplace monitoring, treatment of corporate information, and policies on customer information.

▌ Property rights and obligations. A code should cover topics such as software licenses, ownership of firm data and facilities, ownership of software created by employees on company hardware, and software copyrights. Specific guidelines for contractual relationships with third parties should be covered as well.

MAKE **IT** YOUR BUSINESS

FINANCE AND ACCOUNTING
Poor data quality and software errors can have a devastating impact on the firm's financial and accounting systems because errors in these systems can easily lead to huge losses. Financial and accounting systems are prime targets for computer crime, as are the specialized financial systems of financial and banking institutions. One growing area of computer crime is securities fraud over the Internet. You can find examples of finance and accounting applications on pages 159 and 163–164.

HUMAN RESOURCES
Developing and enforcing a corporate ethics policy and procedures that balance the need to run the business responsibly and efficiently with the need to safeguard employee privacy, health, and well-being has become an important responsibility of the human resources function. Employees and their managers may need special training to sensitize them to the new ethical issues surrounding information systems, such as personal use of the Internet or corporate systems or copying digital material and software.

MANUFACTURING AND PRODUCTION
Economic prosperity and the quality of daily life are highly dependent on the smooth and accurate flow of information among disparate manufacturing and production systems. Data quality problems and software errors in one system can affect the performance of other systems inside the firm and the performance of suppliers, distributors, and logistics services that depend on information from these systems.

SALES AND MARKETING
The Internet has provided powerful new ways of reaching customers and gathering information about them in order to provide more targeted marketing and products. Information about consumers' activities is marketing gold—and often a critical success factor—for companies doing business on-line. However, the customer information that's required to create a personalized Web experience raises serious privacy concerns, because contemporary information technology makes it so easy for businesses to monitor on-line behavior and assemble highly detailed profiles of individual consumers. You can find examples of sales and marketing applications on pages 140–141, 154, 158, and 171–173.

▍ Accountability and control. The code should specify a single individual responsible for all information systems, and reporting to this individual should be others who are responsible for individual rights, the protection of property rights, system quality, and quality of life (e.g., job design, ergonomics, employee satisfaction). Responsibilities for control of systems, audits, and management should be clearly defined. The potential liabilities of systems officers and the corporation should be detailed in a separate document.

▍ System quality. The code should describe the general levels of data quality and system error that can be tolerated with detailed specifications left to specific projects. The code should require that all systems attempt to estimate data quality and system error probabilities.

▍ Quality of life. The code should state that the purpose of systems is to improve the quality of life for customers and for employees by achieving high levels of product quality, customer service, and employee satisfaction and human dignity through proper ergonomics, job and work flow design, and human resource development.

MANAGEMENT WRAP-UP

Managers are ethical rule makers for their organizations. They are charged with creating the policies and procedures to establish ethical conduct, including the ethical use of information systems. Managers are also responsible for identifying, analyzing, and resolving the ethical dilemmas that invariably crop up as they balance conflicting needs and interests.

Rapid changes fueled by information technology are creating new situations where existing laws or rules of conduct may not be relevant. New "gray areas" are emerging in which ethical standards have not yet been codified into law. A new system of ethics for the information age is required to guide individual and organizational choices and actions.

Information technology is introducing changes that create new ethical issues for societies to debate and resolve. Increasing computing power, storage, and networking capabilities—including the Internet—can expand the reach of individual and organizational actions and magnify their impact. The ease and anonymity with which information can be communicated, copied, and manipulated in on-line environments are challenging traditional rules of right and wrong behavior.

For Discussion

1. Should producers of software-based services such as ATMs be held liable for economic injuries suffered when their systems fail?

2. Should companies be responsible for unemployment caused by their information systems? Why or why not?

SUMMARY

1. *What ethical, social, and political issues are raised by information systems?* Information technology has raised new possibilities for behavior for which laws and rules of acceptable conduct have not yet been developed. The main ethical, social, and political issues raised by information systems center around information rights and obligations, property rights, accountability and control, system quality, and quality of life. Ethical, social, and political issues are closely related. Ethical issues confront individuals who must choose a course of action, often in a situation in which two or more ethical principles are in conflict (a dilemma). Social issues spring from ethical issues as societies develop expectations in individuals about the correct course of action. Political issues spring from social conflict and have to do largely with laws that prescribe behavior and seek to use the law to create situations in which individuals behave correctly.

2. *Are there specific principles for conduct that can be used to guide decisions about ethical dilemmas?* Six ethical principles are available to judge conduct. These principles are derived independently from several cultural, religious, and intellectual

traditions and include the Golden Rule, Immanuel Kant's Categorical Imperative, Descartes' rule of change, the Utilitarian Principle, the Risk Aversion Principle, and the ethical "no free lunch" rule. These principles should be used in conjunction with an ethical analysis to guide decision making. The ethical analysis involves identifying the facts, values, stakeholders, options, and consequences of actions. Once completed, one can consider what ethical principle to apply to a situation to arrive at a judgment.

3. *Why does contemporary information systems technology pose challenges to the protection of individual privacy and intellectual property?* Contemporary information systems technology, including the Internet technology, challenges traditional regimens for protecting individual privacy and intellectual property. Database and data analysis technology allows companies to easily gather personal data about individuals from many different sources and analyze these data to create detailed electronic profiles about individuals and their behavior. Data flowing over the Internet can be monitored at many points. The activities of Web site visitors can be closely tracked using "cookies" and other Web monitoring tools. Not all Web sites have strong privacy protection policies, and they do not always allow for informed consent regarding the use of personal information. The on-line industry prefers self-regulation to the U.S. government tightening privacy protection legislation.

Traditional copyright laws are insufficient to protect software piracy because digital material can be so easily copied. Internet technology also makes intellectual property even more difficult to protect because digital material can be copied and transmitted to many different locations simultaneously over the Net. Web pages can be easily con-structed by using pieces of content from other Web sites without permission.

4. *How have information systems affected everyday life?* Although computer systems have been sources of efficiency and wealth, they have some negative impacts. Errors in large computer systems are impossible to totally eradicate. Computer errors can cause serious harm to individuals and organizations, and existing laws and social practices are often unable to establish liability and accountability for these problems. Less serious errors are often attributable to poor data quality, which can cause disruptions and losses for businesses. Jobs can be lost when workers are replaced by computers or tasks become unnecessary in reengineered business processes. The ability to own and use a computer may be exacerbating socioeconomic disparities among different racial groups and social classes. Widespread use of computers increases opportunities for computer crime and computer abuse. Computers can also create health problems such as repetitive stress injury, computer vision syndrome, and technostress.

5. *How can organizations develop corporate polices for ethical conduct?* For each of the five moral dimensions of information systems, corporations should develop an ethics policy statement to assist individuals and to encourage the correct decisions. The policy areas are as follows. Individual information rights: Spell out corporate privacy and due process policies. Property rights: Clarify how the corporation will treat property rights of software owners. Accountability and control: Clarify who is responsible and accountable for corporate information. System quality: Identify methodologies and quality standards to be achieved. Quality of life: Identify corporate policies on family, computer crime, decision making, vulnerability, job loss, and health risks.

KEY TERMS

Accountability, 146
Carpal tunnel syndrome (CTS), 166
Computer abuse, 163
Computer crime, 163
Computer vision syndrome (CVS), 166
Cookie, 150
Copyright, 155
Descartes' rule of change, 147

Due process, 146
Ethical "no free lunch" rule, 147
Ethics, 142
Fair Information Practices (FIP), 149
Framing, 156
Immanuel Kant's Categorical Imperative, 146
Information rights, 143

Informed consent, 150
Intellectual property, 155
Liability, 146
Opt-in, 151
Opt-out, 151
P3P, 153
Patent, 156
Privacy, 148
Profiling, 145

Repetitive stress injury (RSI), 166
Responsibility, 145
Risk Aversion Principle, 147
Spamming, 164
Technostress, 166
Trade secret, 155
Utilitarian Principle, 147
Web bugs, 151

REVIEW QUESTIONS

1. In what ways are ethical, social, and political issues connected? Give some examples.
2. What are the key technological trends that heighten ethical concerns?
3. What are the differences between responsibility, accountability, and liability?
4. What are the five steps in an ethical analysis?

5. Identify and describe six ethical principles.
6. What is a professional code of conduct?
7. What are meant by "privacy" and "fair information practices"?
8. How is the Internet challenging the protection of individual privacy?

9. What role can informed consent, legislation, industry self-regulation, and technology tools play in protecting individual privacy of Internet users?

10. What are the three different regimes that protect intellectual property rights? What challenges to intellectual property rights are posed by the Internet?

11. Why is it so difficult to hold software services liable for failure or injury?

12. What is the most common cause of system quality problems?

13. Name and describe four "quality of life" impacts of computers and information systems.

14. What is technostress, and how would you identify it?

15. Name three management actions that could reduce RSI injuries.

APPLICATION SOFTWARE EXERCISE

WORD PROCESSING AND WEB PAGE DEVELOPMENT TOOL EXERCISE: CREATING A SIMPLE WEB SITE

Build a simple Web site of your own design for a business using the Web page creation function of Microsoft Word 97, 2000, or XP or a Web page development tool of your choice. Your Web site should include a Home page with a description of your business and at least one picture or graphic. From the Home page you must be able to link to a second Web page and, from there, link to a third Web page. Make the Home page long enough so that when you arrive at the bottom of the page, you can no longer see the top. There you must include a link back to the top. Also include a link to one of the secondary Web pages. On that secondary page, include a link to the top of that page, and a link back to the top of the *Home* page. Also include a link to the third page, which should contain a link to its own top and a link back to the top of the *Home* page. Finally, on one of the secondary pages, include another picture or graphic, and on the other page include an object that you create using Microsoft Excel or other spreadsheet software. The Laudon Web site for Chapter 5 includes sample pages that you can use as a model and instructions for completing this project. If you have tested every function and all are now working to your satisfaction, save the pages you have created for submission to your instructor.

GROUP PROJECT

With three or four of your classmates, develop a corporate ethics code on privacy that addresses both employee privacy and the privacy of customers and users of the corporate Web site. Be sure to consider e-mail privacy and employer monitoring of worksites, as well as corporate use of information about employees concerning their off-job behavior (e.g., lifestyle, marital arrangements, and so forth). If possible, use electronic presentation software to present your ethics code to the class.

TOOLS FOR INTERACTIVE LEARNING

▮ INTERNET CONNECTION

The Internet Connection for this chapter will direct you to a series of Web sites where you can learn more about the privacy issues raised by the use of the Internet and the Web. You can complete an exercise to analyze the privacy implications of existing technologies for tracking Web site visitors. You can also use the Interactive Study Guide to test your knowledge of the topics in this chapter, and get instant feedback where you need more practice.

▮ ELECTRONIC COMMERCE PROJECT

At the Laudon Web site for Chapter 5, you will find an Electronic Commerce project that uses the interactive software at the Google Groups Web site to explore the use of Internet discussion groups for targeted marketing.

▮ CD-ROM

If you use the Multimedia Edition CD-ROM with this chapter, you can find a video clip on software piracy and the activities of the Software and Information Industry Association (SIIA), an audio overview of the major themes of this chapter, and bullet text summarizing the key points of the chapter.

CASE STUDY—*Will FBI's Carnivore Eat Our Privacy?*

In the 1960s the U.S. Federal Bureau of Investigation (FBI) began compiling files on citizens considered a threat to U.S. security. Its secret files included thousands of Vietnam War protestors, civil rights activists, and such celebrities as Albert Einstein, Rock Hudson, and even Henry Ford. The Privacy Act of 1974 later became law in order to forbid the collection of such information unless the Justice Department could show reason to suspect that the person had committed a crime.

Starting in the 1960s many people feared the FBI because it had gained a reputation of being antiprivacy, mismanaged, and even inept. Strong opposition to the FBI's ability to secretly collect data on ordinary citizens surfaced in 1999 when the FBI admitted that it had developed and was using a computer product it named Carnivore (also known as DCS1000) to secretly collect e-mail information. However, the growing fear of the FBI may have been reversed when terrorists attacked the World Trade Center and the Pentagon on September 11, 2001. Many appear to be reevaluating how much privacy they are willing to surrender in order to gain more security.

Carnivore, which is used to eavesdrop on communication flowing through the Internet, is a computer-age version of wire-tapping. Wiretaps gather analog information (voices) from telephones, whereas Carnivore gathers digital information from e-mail and other network traffic flowing to or from a specific user or Internet address. The FBI named it Carnivore because, they say, Carnivore finds the "meat" in "suspicious" or "interesting" communications. However, the two have two major differences. First, wiretaps require high-level court orders because they give the FBI the right to listen to all telephone call conversations on the tapped line of the person being investigated. Carnivore court orders are easier to obtain because they only grant permission to gather certain data from e-mail headers and not from the content of the message itself.

Second, the two differ in their methods of collection. Wiretaps are placed on the telephone line(s) of individuals under investigation. The FBI taps Internet communication by installing Carnivore on a special computer at the site of the target's Internet Service Provider (ISP). There it must review the headers of all messages that pass through the ISP's computer (multiple millions of messages daily for larger ISPs) in order to identify those that fall within the court order. When identified, Carnivore will select those messages and their contents.

Why would the FBI seek only the header information? First, because the legal standard for court orders on collecting header information is much lower than that for the message itself. To meet the higher standard needed to read e-mail and other messages, the FBI would have to prove "probable cause" (strong evidence of possible criminal activity). Second, according to the FBI, header information has proven valuable in its pursuits. Opponents do point out, however, that although Carnivore has been used about 30 times, the evidence it collected has never been cited in a single court trial.

Many believed the use of Carnivore was an invasion of personal privacy partly because Carnivore is controlled by FBI agents, and much of the data Carnivore collects may not even be within the scope of the court order. Headers often contain more data than that allowed in the court order, illegally giving the FBI access to data it has no right to see. Also, because Carnivore must access every header for all e-mails to locate the ones authorized by the court order, the agents could illegally use it to select data from any of the headers they desire, and only the FBI would know. Donald Kerr, the director of the FBI lab division, agreed that Carnivore enables FBI agents to use the system illegally to check up on someone's ex-spouse or political enemy. Nonetheless, he claimed, it was very unlikely to happen because agents who acted illegally would face heavy fines and up to five years in prison.

Carnivore does not produce audit trails. Many have viewed the system as "the electronic equivalent of listening to everybody's phone calls to see if it's the phone call you should be monitoring," according to Mark Rasch, a former federal prosecutor. Opponents also feared that local law enforcement agencies could begin to use Carnivore, noting that the Fourth Amendment, used to protect privacy, only applies to the federal government and not to state or local governments. According to Paul Bresson, an FBI spokesperson, the FBI position was that it was seeking ways to modify Carnivore so that it would only collect information on targeted people. He said, "We never denied that it had the capability to capture more [data than an investigation requires]. What we maintained was that it had the filtering devices to capture only the data pertaining to the court order." The view of David Sobel, the general counsel of the Electronic Privacy Information Center (EPIC), a Washington D.C.–based electronic privacy group, was, "If it's that easy for the FBI to accidentally collect too much data, imagine how simple it would be for agents to do so intentionally."

Before the September 11 terrorist attack, congressional fears were strong, as expressed at a July 2000 House of Representative hearing on Carnivore. "There's new legal ground that you all are trying to break here where you are saying you have the authority to harvest large quantities of information, then you filter out what you want," explained Bob Barr, a Republican Representative from Georgia. "Those are two very, very large steps we are taking here. I don't think this has been well thought out." At a September 2000 Senate hearing, Orin Hatch, Republican Senator from Utah and chair of the Senate Judiciary Committee, said, "I don't want to have 1984 in 2004. We're already there with technology." However, on October 26, 2001, President George W. Bush signed a new bill to combat terrorism, a bill that had passed the Senate 98 to 1 and the House 356 to 66. The bill, which was passed in reaction to the terrorist attacks, expands the government's ability not only to detain immigrants and penetrate money-laundering banks but also to conduct more electronic surveillance. For example, it authorizes the government to approve wiretaps even if intelligence gathering is only a minor purpose. The new law does include a sunset provision, however. The increased power to keep more computers and telephones under surveillance will expire in 2005.

The FBI's position is simple: ISPs must allow the FBI to install and control Carnivore. Even at the 2000 hearings, the FBI refused to give any information on Carnivore technology or on its uses. It simply claimed Carnivore was necessary to catch drug dealers, pornographers, and terrorists. Most ISPs have been in opposition.

Even prior to the September 11 terrorist attacks, some organizations had agreed to use Carnivore because they believed they had no alternative even though they still did not like it. "There's no way to stop Carnivore. It's become a fact of life," said Steve Lopez, the vice president of technology services for the National Board of Medical Examiners in Philadelphia. "It's being forced down our throats." That view seems to have been strengthened for many people since the terrorist attacks. But strong opposition does remain. Patrick Leahy, the chair of the Senate Judiciary Committee, said, "We must not let the terrorists win." He explained, "If we abandon our democracy to battle them, they win." David Boaz, a vice president of the conservative Cato Institute still said after the attacks, "We need strong protections against government access to information about individuals."

Clearly, the FBI already does gather a lot of other information. For example, they use the immense Lexis-Nexis database that contains legal briefs, newspaper articles, and other public records. They also gather such data as taxpayer assets, credit card charges (including activity locations), telephone numbers, and even driving histories. Because it is illegal for government organizations (including the FBI) to collect much of this type of information themselves, they outsource the collection, purchasing such data from commercial organizations that legally collect them for their own use or for sale to their customers, of which the government is one. However, many people have opposed this method.

One publicly held company that sells such data to the FBI is ChoicePoint Inc. of Alpharetta, Georgia. It supplies its commercial customers with information primarily to enable them to check out prospective clients and partners, and it claims its dealings with government organizations are "a natural extension" of its business. Derek Smith, ChoicePoint's CEO, maintains it helps the government to unearth fraud and to convict criminals. The FBI contends it has "located nearly 1,300 subjects of criminal cases using these kinds of searches." John Collingwood, another FBI spokesperson, adds that this method "saves countless hours of manual record checks, a process the FBI has relied on for decades." The federal Health Care Financing Administration also relies on information from ChoicePoint. It compares its data with ChoicePoint's 2 million "high-risk and fraudulent business addresses" to help locate fraud.

One problem is the potential for inaccurate ChoicePoint data. In 2001 the NAACP sued both ChoicePoint and the state of Florida, charging the data supplied to Florida in 2000 contained faulty information on criminal records causing thousands of voters to be illegally purged from Florida voter rolls. ChoicePoint admitted supplying some faulty data, and that data may have helped swing the presidential election from Albert Gore (Democrat) to George W. Bush (Republican).

Many ways currently exist for criminals and terrorists to circumvent the use of Carnivore so that the FBI would not be able to collect header information. First, Carnivore cannot even read many Web-based e-mails, such as those sent from Hotmail and Yahoo! This may be overcome as technology increases in sophistication. Second, effective software to encrypt messages, such as PGP, is easily obtainable. Individuals can even download PGP for free. Programs even exist that can collect and deliver the information the FBI requires without using Carnivore and without each ISP developing its own system. One such program is Altivore from Network Ice, which is a leading developer of security-related software.

One issue that has only emerged since the terrorist attacks is the great power of steganography, the embedding of secret messages within other more public messages. Computer technology now enables users to hide messages within digitized, written, graphics, and even music documents, and they are virtually undetectable, making it even more difficult to find the message than to decode it. In 1998, referring not only to encryption but also to steganography, the then FBI director Louis Freeh told the U.S. Senate Judiciary committee, "Not just Bin Laden, but many other people who work against us in the area of terrorism, are becoming sophisticated enough to equip themselves with encryption devices."

Sources: David Armstrong and Joseph Pereira, "FBI Gives Carriers Access to Watchlists; Database Plays New Role After Attacks," *Wall Street Journal*, October 23, 2001; Ariana Eunjung Cha and Jonathan Krim, "Privacy Trade-Offs Reassessed," *The Washington Post*, September 13, 2001, and "Terrorists' Online Methods Elusive," *The Washington Post*, September 19, 2001; Nick Wingfield, "Some Fear Fight Against Terror Will Imperil Privacy," *Wall Street Journal*, September 13, 2001; Adam Clymer, "Antiterrorism Bill Passes; U.S. Gets Expanded Powers," *New York Times*, October 26, 2001; Adam Clymer, "Bush Signs Bipartisan Bill to Combat Terrorism," *New York Times*, October 26, 2001; Larry Kahaner, "Hungry for Your E-Mail," *Informationweek.com*, April 23, 2001, and "Taking a Bite Out of Carnivore," *Informationweek.com*, April 23, 2001; Glenn R. Simpson, "FBI's Reliance on the Private Sector Has Raised Some Privacy Concerns," *Wall Street Journal*, April 13, 2001; Jennifer DiSabatino, "Carnivore Probe Mollifies Some," *The Industry Standard*," November 23, 2000; Bill Frezza, "Carnivore Takes a Bite Out of the Fourth Amendment," *TechWeb*, August 7, 2000; David Johnston, "Citing FBI Lapse, Ashcroft Delays McVeigh Execution," *New York Times*, May 13, 2001; Margret Johnston, "Lawmakers Find Carnivore Unappetizing," *The Industry Standard*, July 25, 2000; Larry Kahaner, "Carnivore's Legal Teeth," *Informationweek.com*, April 23, 2001; Declan McCullagh, "Ashcroft to Chew on Carnivore" *Wired News*, January 27, 2001; Declan McCullagh, "Bin Laden: Steganography Master?" *Wired News*, February 7, 2001, and "Regulating Privacy: At What Cost?" *Wired News*, September 19, 2000; Mary Mosquera, "Lawmakers Want Privacy Protections with Carnivore," *TechWeb*, September 6, 2000; and Peter Rojas, "Is It Spam or Spammimic?" *Red Herring*, February 15, 2001.

CASE STUDY QUESTIONS

1. Does Carnivore present an ethical dilemma? Explain your answer.

2. Apply an ethical analysis to the issue of the FBI's use of information technology and U.S. citizens' privacy rights.

3. What are the ethical, social, and political issues raised by the FBI tapping the e-mails of individuals and collecting personal data on them?

4. How effective is Carnivore as a terrorism and crime-prevention tool?

5. State your views on ways to solve the problems of collecting the key data the FBI can gain through Carnivore without interfering with the privacy of people not related to the crime involved.

Part 1 Project

ANALYZING BUSINESS PROCESSES FOR AN ENTERPRISE SYSTEM

Your firm manufactures specialty chemicals and dyestuffs used in plastics, fibers, and coatings. It operates five different production facilities in the southeastern United States, with corporate headquarters in Memphis, Tennessee.

Rapid time-to-market of new products, strong customer service, and low costs are essential for remaining competitive in the chemical industry. Management is looking for ways to make the company operate more efficiently and would like to start by examining order processing.

This is how the firm's order processing works. A customer can call, fax, or mail in an order. A customer service representative writes down order information on an order pad. This information includes the customer name, shipping address, billing address, product number, product description, quantity, and shipping instructions (such as to call the receiving manager to make an appointment for delivery). After gathering all the relevant information, the representative confirms the entire order with the customer.

While taking down the order information, the customer service representative accesses the company's order entry system and checks the inventory for each product ordered. The customer service representative first checks the warehouse closest to the customer's shipping address. If the product is not available there, the representative checks another warehouse. If the order is placed on the telephone, the customer service representative suggests a delivery date, which is four to five business days away. If the customer needs the order sooner, the customer service representative queries the existing order entry information system to see which warehouse might have the inventory to fulfill the order. Generally, the order will be filled by the warehouse closest to the customer's shipping address.

All current orders are collected manually and entered into the firm's order entry system. The order will not be accepted by the system unless it includes the customer's identification number, shipping address, and billing address. (If the order is from a new customer, the system can assign a new customer number.) If the order has a delivery date of 8 to 10 business days in the future, the order form will be held manually for several days and then input into the system. If an order is for more than 10 days in the future, it will be treated as a back order when it is input into the system. The system generates a back order report daily to remind customer service representatives of orders that they have on back order.

When each order has been entered, the system performs a credit check on the customer. Some customers are assigned "credit hold" status and are not shipped their orders until payment has been received for the purchase. Other customer orders are processed immediately, and the customer pays for the purchase after receiving the shipment and an invoice. A report on credit holds is forwarded to the credit department, and the customer service representatives receive a daily report on orders placed on credit hold.

Different business units at your company use different identification systems for the same products. In other words, corporate headquarters might use a different product number for a product such as purple dye 211, than the product identification number used at the plant at which it was manufactured.

1. Diagram the order process. What are the outputs of this process?

2. What other major business processes outside of the order process are likely to be impacted by the order process? Explain.

3. How could this process be made more efficient? Draw a diagram of your proposed process and information changes.

4. Prepare descriptions of two reports from the order entry system: one that would be important to the order entry staff and one that would be important to corporate management.

5. Your company is thinking about installing enterprise software. You would like to learn more about enterprise software and how it could handle your order entry process. Explore the Industry Solutions and Business Map for the chemical industry on the SAP Web site (www.sap.com). Which SAP processes are likely to address the activities in order processing that we have described? What questions would you ask to determine whether SAP's software could handle your order process?

You have heard that enterprise software might not be able to handle the following situations:

- When the system checks for available inventory, it treats batches of chemicals that are still undergoing quality control inspection as available inventory as well as material in inventory that has already passed quality control inspection.

- There is no way to automatically check customer records to determine which qualify for sales tax exemptions.

- The system assigns a date for back orders of items that are currently out of stock rather than the original requested date on the customer order.

What impact might this lack of functionality have on order processing in other parts of the company? How could you determine how serious a problem this creates? What questions would you ask?

PART II

INFORMATION TECHNOLOGY INFRASTRUCTURE

Part II Project
Creating a New Internet Business

6

MANAGING HARDWARE AND SOFTWARE ASSETS

objectives

As a manager, you'll face many decisions about using hardware and software to improve the performance of your firm. After completing this chapter, you will be able to answer the following questions:

1. *What computer processing and storage capability does our organization need to handle its information and business transactions?*

2. *What arrangement of computers and computer processing would best benefit our organization?*

3. *What kinds of software and software tools do we need to run our business? What criteria should we use to select our software technology?*

4. *Of what new software technologies should we be aware? How would they benefit our organization?*

5. *How should we acquire and manage the firm's hardware and software assets?*

Rogers Communications Selects New Workforce Technology

Rogers Communications consists of three Canadian communications companies with combined revenues of more than $3 billion per year from wireless telephone and cable services. These three companies—Rogers AT&T Wireless, Rogers Cable, and Rogers Media—together have more than 14,000 employees in 100 locations across Canada. It is not surprising that Rogers's human resources department has a great deal to manage.

Until recently, human resources was mired in paperwork. More than 7,000 employee time sheets were submitted via courier, fax, and interoffice mail to a central payroll office every other week. Payroll clerks would take two to three days to key the data into the payroll system so that employees could be paid. Management could not make sure that all the paperwork for processing the payroll was submitted on time. The manual data input process increased the incidence of

MAKE **IT** YOUR BUSINESS

errors and lost paperwork. Rogers's payroll office often had to write out many corrected checks by hand. Because there was no central location where all the employee data were stored, management had no way to analyze overall staffing and payroll issues or to ensure that employees in the same business unit were being treated equally.

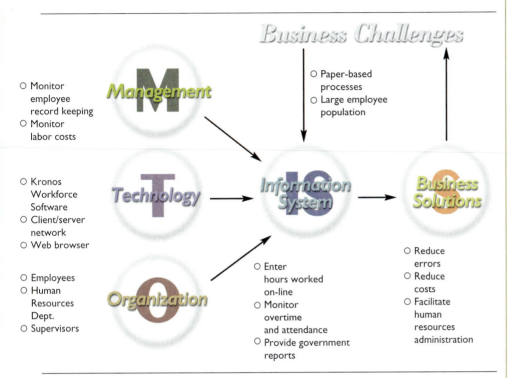

Business Challenges

- Monitor employee record keeping
- Monitor labor costs

Management

- Paper-based processes
- Large employee population

- Kronos Workforce Software
- Client/server network
- Web browser

Technology

Information System

Business Solutions

- Reduce errors
- Reduce costs
- Facilitate human resources administration

- Employees
- Human Resources Dept.
- Supervisors

Organization

- Enter hours worked on-line
- Monitor overtime and attendance
- Provide government reports

Rogers Communications management believed the company could increase the timeliness and accuracy of employee attendance reporting by replacing these old systems and processes with more up-to-date technology. After reviewing many different application software packages, Rogers selected several workforce management software tools from Kronos Inc. of Chelmsford, Massachusetts. Rogers employees can use the software to enter their timesheets on-line, while supervisors can use the software to monitor overtime and attendance. The software helps corporate management as well to meet government reporting requirements and to find the data they need to make policies consistent among Rogers's different divisions. Kronos software features both English and French language versions for Canadian users.

In March 1999 Rogers installed Kronos Workforce Manager Client/Server, which runs on a client/server computing network and provides up to 1,000 supervisors with decentralized administrative and managerial functions. A year later, the firm installed Kronos Workforce Web, which enables 5,000 salaried and hourly employees across the company to report their hours and attendance on a corporate network using Web browser software. Employees can also use this software to access information such as their overtime or the number of vacation days they have available. Previously, such tasks were impossible.

Middle managers and administrators can use the software to review employee time listings, process approvals, and monitor attendance and overall labor costs. Managers can also use the system to set tolerances or create "trigger events" to alert them to problems requiring their attention. For example, they could produce reports showing which employees have used up more sick days than are standard for their industry so that the employees' managers and the human resources department can manage these employees before they become a serious problem. Such reporting can now be performed consistently throughout the company.

Sources: Dennis Fowler, "All on the Same Page," *Knowledge Management,* April 2001; Jim Kizielewicz, "Web-Based Labor-Related Functions Increase Organizational Efficiency," *Paytech,* July/August 2001; and www.rogers.ca.

Although Rogers Communications provides leading-edge technology services, its own internal operations and business processes were hampered by outdated technology. The company found it could improve the performance of its human resources function by using the right hardware and software. In order to select the technology it needed, Rogers had to understand the capabilities of computer hardware and software technology, how to select hardware and software to meet its specific business requirements, and the financial and business rationale for its hardware and software investments. The workforce management software Rogers selected transformed a jumble of tangled paperwork into manageable information and became an important technology asset. Computer hardware and software technology can improve organizational performance, but they raise the following management challenges:

MANAGEMENT CHALLENGES

1. **The centralization versus decentralization debate.** A long-standing issue among information system managers and CEOs has been the question of how much to centralize or distribute computing resources. Should processing power and data be distributed to departments and divisions, or should they be concentrated at a single location using a large central computer? Should organizations deliver application software to users over networks from a central location or allow users to maintain software and data on their own desktop computers? Client/server computing facilitates decentralization, but network computers and mainframes support a centralized model. Which is the best for the organization? Each organization will have a different answer based on its own needs. Managers need to make sure that the computing model they select is compatible with organizational goals (Schuff and St. Louis, 2001).

2. **The application backlog.** Advances in computer software have not kept pace with the breathtaking productivity gains in computer hardware. Developing software has become a major preoccupation for organizations. A great deal of software must be intricately crafted. Moreover, the software itself is only one component of a complete information system that must be carefully designed and coordinated with organizational and hardware components. The "software crisis" is actually part of a larger systems analysis, design, and implementation issue, which will be treated in detail later. Despite the gains from fourth-generation languages, personal desktop software tools, object-oriented programming, and software tools for the World Wide Web, many businesses continue to face a backlog of two to three years in developing the information systems they need, or they will not be able to develop them at all.

Although managers and business professionals do not need to be computer technology experts, they should have a basic understanding of the role of hardware and software in the organization's information technology (IT) infrastructure so that they can make technology decisions that promote organizational performance and productivity. This chapter surveys the capabilities of computer hardware and computer software and highlights the major issues in the management of the firm's hardware and software assets.

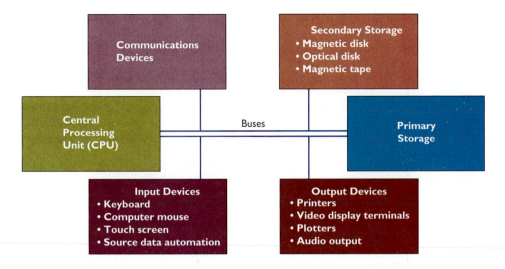

Figure 6-1 Hardware components of a computer system. A contemporary computer system can be categorized into six major components. The central processing unit manipulates data and controls the other parts of the computer system; primary storage temporarily stores data and program instructions during processing; secondary storage stores data and instructions when they are not used in processing; input devices convert data and instructions for processing in the computer; output devices present data in a form that people can understand; and communications devices control the passing of information to and from communications networks.

6.1 COMPUTER HARDWARE AND INFORMATION TECHNOLOGY INFRASTRUCTURE

Computer hardware, which we defined in Chapter 1, provides the underlying physical foundation for the firm's IT infrastructure. Other infrastructure components—software, data, and networks—require computer hardware for their storage or operation.

THE COMPUTER SYSTEM

A contemporary computer system consists of a central processing unit, primary storage, secondary storage, input devices, output devices, and communications devices (see Figure 6-1). The central processing unit manipulates raw data into a more useful form and controls the other parts of the computer system. Primary storage temporarily stores data and program instructions during processing, whereas secondary storage devices (magnetic and optical disks, magnetic tape) store data and programs when they are not being used in processing. Input devices, such as a keyboard or mouse, convert data and instructions into electronic form for input into the computer. Output devices, such as printers and video display terminals, convert electronic data produced by the computer system and display them in a form that people can understand. Communications devices provide connections between the computer and communications networks. Buses are circuitry paths for transmitting data and signals among the parts of the computer system.

In order for information to flow through a computer system and be in a form suitable for processing, all symbols, pictures, or words must be reduced to a string of binary digits. A binary digit is called a **bit** and represents either a 0 or a 1. In the computer, the presence of an electronic or magnetic signal means one, and its absence signifies zero. Digital computers operate directly with binary digits, either singly or strung together to form bytes. A string of eight bits that the computer stores as a unit is called a **byte**. Each byte can be used to store a decimal number, a symbol, a character, or part of a picture (see Figure 6-2).

Computers can represent pictures by creating a grid overlay of the picture. Each single point in this grid or matrix is called a *pixel* (picture element) and consists of a number of bits. The computer then stores this information on each pixel.

THE CPU AND PRIMARY STORAGE

The **central processing unit (CPU)** is the part of the computer system where the manipulation of symbols, numbers, and letters occurs, and it controls the other parts of the computer system (see Figure 6-3). Located near the CPU is **primary storage** (sometimes called primary memory or main memory), where data and program instructions are stored temporarily during processing. Buses provide pathways for transmitting data and signals between the

bit
A binary digit representing the smallest unit of data in a computer system. It can only have one of two states, representing 0 or 1.

byte
A string of bits, usually eight, used to store one number or character in a computer system.

central processing unit (CPU)
Area of the computer system that manipulates symbols, numbers, and letters, and controls the other parts of the computer system.

primary storage
Part of the computer that temporarily stores program instructions and data being used by the instructions.

arithmetic-logic unit (ALU)
Component of the CPU that performs the computer's principal logic and arithmetic operations.

control unit
Component of the CPU that controls and coordinates the other parts of the computer system.

machine cycle
Series of operations required to process a single machine instruction.

nanosecond
One-billionth of a second.

RAM (random access memory)
Primary storage of data or program instructions that can directly access any randomly chosen location in the same amount of time.

CPU, primary storage, and the other devices in the computer system. The characteristics of the CPU and primary storage are very important in determining a computer's speed and capabilities.

The Arithmetic-Logic Unit and Control Unit

Figure 6-3 also shows that the CPU consists of an arithmetic-logic unit and a control unit. The **arithmetic-logic unit (ALU)** performs the computer's principal logical and arithmetic operations. It adds, subtracts, multiplies, and divides, determining whether a number is positive, negative, or zero. In addition to performing arithmetic functions, an ALU must be able to determine when one quantity is greater than or less than another and when two quantities are equal. The ALU can perform logic operations on letters as well as numbers.

The **control unit** coordinates and controls the other parts of the computer system. It reads a stored program, one instruction at a time, and directs other components of the computer system to perform the program's required tasks. The series of operations required to process a single machine instruction is called the **machine cycle**. Older computers and PCs have machine cycle times measured in *microseconds* (millionths of a second). More powerful machines have machine cycle times measured in **nanoseconds** (billionths of a second) or picoseconds (trillionths of a second). Another measure of machine cycle time is by *MIPS*, or millions of instructions per second.

Primary Storage

Primary storage has three functions. It stores all or part of the software program that is being executed. Primary storage also stores the operating system programs that manage the operation of the computer (see Section 6.4). Finally, the primary storage area holds data that the program is using. Internal primary storage is often called **RAM, or random access memory**. It is called RAM because it can directly access any randomly chosen location in the same amount of time.

Figure 6-3 The CPU and primary storage. The CPU contains an arithmetic-logic unit and a control unit. Data and instructions are stored in unique addresses in primary storage that the CPU can access during processing. The data bus, address bus, and control bus transmit signals between the central processing unit, primary storage, and other devices in the computer system.

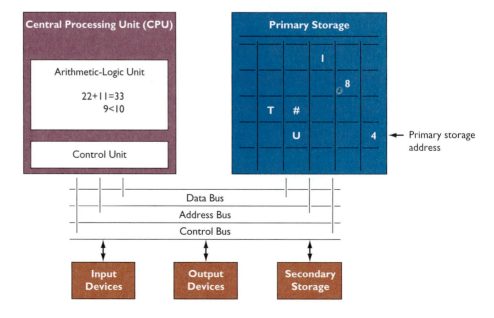

TABLE 6-1   COMPUTER STORAGE CAPACITY

Byte	String of eight bits
Kilobyte	1,000 bytes*
Megabyte	1,000,000 bytes
Gigabyte	1,000,000,000 bytes
Terabyte	1,000,000,000,000 bytes

*Actually 1,024 storage positions

Primary memory is divided into storage locations called bytes. Each location contains a set of eight binary switches or devices, each of which can store one bit of information. The set of eight bits found in each storage location is sufficient to store one letter, one digit, or one special symbol (such as $). Each byte has a unique address, similar to a mailbox, indicating where it is located in RAM. The computer can remember where the data in all of the bytes are located simply by keeping track of these addresses.

Computer storage capacity is measured in bytes. Table 6-1 lists computer storage capacity measurements. One thousand bytes (actually 1,024 storage positions) is called a **kilobyte**. One million bytes is called a **megabyte,** one billion bytes is called a **gigabyte,** and one trillion bytes is called a **terabyte**.

Primary storage is composed of *semiconductors,* which are integrated circuits made by printing thousands and even millions of tiny transistors on small silicon chips. There are several different kinds of semiconductor memory used in primary storage. RAM is used for short-term storage of data or program instructions. RAM is volatile: Its contents will be lost when the computer's electric supply is disrupted by a power outage or when the computer is turned off. **ROM, or read-only memory,** can only be read from; it cannot be written to. ROM chips come from the manufacturer with programs already burned in, or stored. ROM is used in general-purpose computers to store important or frequently used programs.

COMPUTER PROCESSING

The processing capability of the CPU plays a large role in determining the amount of work that a computer system can accomplish.

Microprocessors and Processing Power

Contemporary CPUs use semiconductor chips called **microprocessors,** which integrate all of the memory, logic, and control circuits for an entire CPU onto a single chip. The speed and performance of a computer's microprocessors help determine a computer's processing power and are based on the microprocessor's word length, cycle speed, and data bus width. *Word length* refers to the number of bits that the computer can process at one time. A 32-bit chip can process 32 bits, or 4 bytes, of data in a single machine cycle. A 64-bit chip can process 64 bits or 8 bytes in a single cycle. The larger the word length, the greater the computer's speed.

A second factor affecting chip speed is cycle speed. Every event in a computer must be sequenced so that one step logically follows another. The control unit sets a beat to the chip. This beat is established by an internal clock and is measured in **megahertz** (abbreviated MHz, which stands for millions of cycles per second). The Intel 8088 chip, for instance, originally had a clock speed of 4.47 megahertz, whereas the Intel Pentium III chip has a clock speed that ranges from 450 to more than 900 megahertz and the Pentium 4 chip clock speed can reach up to 2 gigahertz.

A third factor affecting speed is the *data bus width.* The data bus acts as a highway between the CPU, primary storage, and other devices, determining how much data can be moved at one time. The 8088 chip used in the original IBM personal computer, for example, had a 16-bit word length but only an 8-bit data bus width. This meant that data were processed within the CPU chip itself in 16-bit chunks but could only be moved 8 bits at a time between the CPU, primary storage, and external devices. On the other hand, Intel's

kilobyte
One thousand bytes (actually 1,024 storage positions). Unit of computer storage capacity.

megabyte
Approximately one million bytes. Unit of computer storage capacity.

gigabyte
Approximately one billion bytes. Unit of computer storage capacity.

terabyte
Approximately one trillion bytes. Unit of computer storage capacity.

ROM (read-only memory)
Semiconductor memory chips that contain program instructions. These chips can only be read from; they cannot be written to.

microprocessor
Very large scale integrated circuit technology that integrates the computer's memory, logic, and control on a single chip.

megahertz
A measure of cycle speed, or the pacing of events in a computer; one megahertz equals one million cycles per second.

Figure 6-4 Sequential and parallel processing. During sequential processing, each task is assigned to one CPU that processes one instruction at a time. In parallel processing, multiple tasks are assigned to multiple processing units to expedite the result.

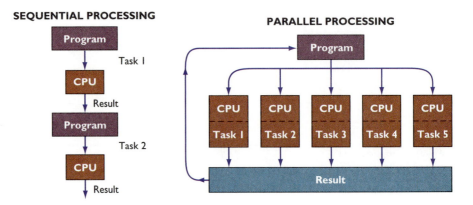

Itanium chip has both a 64-bit word length and a 64-bit data bus width. To have a computer execute more instructions per second and work through programs or handle users expeditiously, it is necessary to increase the processor's word length, the data bus width, or the cycle speed—or all three.

Microprocessors can be made faster by using **reduced instruction set computing (RISC)** in their design. Conventional chips, based on complex instruction set computing, have several hundred or more instructions hard-wired into their circuitry, and they may take several clock cycles to execute a single instruction. If the little-used instructions are eliminated, the remaining instructions can execute much faster. RISC processors have only the most frequently used instructions embedded in them. A RISC CPU can execute most instructions in a single machine cycle and sometimes multiple instructions at the same time. RISC is often used in scientific and workstation computing.

reduced instruction set computing (RISC)
Technology used to enhance the speed of microprocessors by embedding only the most frequently used instructions on a chip.

Parallel Processing

Processing can also be sped up by linking several processors to work simultaneously on the same task. Figure 6-4 compares parallel processing to serial processing used in conventional computers. In **parallel processing,** multiple processing units (CPUs) break down a problem into smaller parts and work on it simultaneously. Getting a group of processors to attack the same problem at once requires both rethinking the problems and special software that can divide problems among different processors in the most efficient way possible, providing the needed data, and reassembling the many subtasks to reach an appropriate solution.

Massively parallel computers have huge networks of hundreds or even thousands of processor chips interwoven in complex and flexible ways to attack large computing problems. As opposed to parallel processing, where small numbers of powerful but expensive specialized chips are linked together, massively parallel machines link hundreds or even thousands of inexpensive, commonly used chips to break problems into many small pieces and solve them.

parallel processing
Type of processing in which more than one instruction can be processed at a time by breaking down a problem into smaller parts and processing them simultaneously with multiple processors.

massively parallel computers
Computers that use hundreds or thousands of processing chips to attack large computing problems simultaneously.

6.2   Storage, Input and Output Technology

The capabilities of computer systems depend not only on the speed and capacity of the CPU but also on the speed, capacity, and design of storage, input and output technology. Storage, input and output devices are called *peripheral devices* because they are outside the main computer system unit.

Secondary Storage Technology

The rise of digital firms has made storage a strategic technology. Although electronic commerce and electronic business are reducing manual processes, data of all types must be stored electronically and available whenever needed. Most of the information used by a computer application is stored on secondary storage devices located outside of the primary storage area. **Secondary storage** is used for relatively long term storage of data outside the CPU.

secondary storage
Relatively long term, nonvolatile storage of data outside the CPU and primary storage.

Secondary storage devices such as floppy disks, optical disks, and hard disks are used to store large quantities of data outside the CPU and primary storage. They provide direct access to data for easy retrieval.

Secondary storage is nonvolatile and retains data even when the computer is turned off. The most important secondary storage technologies are magnetic disk, optical disk, and magnetic tape.

Magnetic Disk

The most widely used secondary storage medium today is **magnetic disk**. There are two kinds of magnetic disks: floppy disks (used in PCs) and **hard disks** (used on large commercial disk drives and PCs). Large mainframe or midrange computer systems have multiple hard disk drives because they require immense disk storage capacity in the gigabyte and terabyte range. PCs also use **floppy disks,** which are removable and portable, with storage of up to 2.8 megabytes and a much slower access rate than hard disks. Removable disk drives are popular backup storage alternatives for PC systems. Magnetic disks on both large and small computers permit direct access to individual records so that data stored on the disk can be directly accessed regardless of the order in which the data were originally recorded. Disk technology is useful for systems requiring rapid and direct access to data.

Disk drive performance can be further enhanced by using a disk technology called **RAID (Redundant Array of Inexpensive Disks)**. RAID devices package more than a hundred disk drives, a controller chip, and specialized software into a single large unit. Traditional disk drives deliver data from the disk drive along a single path, but RAID delivers data over multiple paths simultaneously, improving disk access time and reliability. For most RAID systems, data on a failed disk can be restored automatically without the computer system having to be shut down.

Optical Disks

Optical disks, also called compact disks or laser optical disks, user laser technology to store massive quantities of data in a highly compact form. They are available for both PCs and large computers. The most common optical disk system used with PCs is called **CD-ROM (compact disk read-only memory)**. A 4.75-inch compact disk for PCs can store up to 660 megabytes, nearly 300 times more than a high-density floppy disk. Optical disks are most appropriate for applications where enormous quantities of unchanging data must be stored compactly for easy retrieval or for applications combining text, sound, and images.

CD-ROM is read-only storage. No new data can be written to it; it can only be read. *WORM (write once/read many)* and *CD-R (compact disk-recordable)* optical disk systems allow users to record data only once on an optical disk. Once written, the data cannot be erased but can be read indefinitely. *CD-RW (CD-ReWritable)* technology has been developed to allow users to create rewritable optical disks for applications requiring large volumes of storage where the information is only occasionally updated.

Digital video disks (DVDs), also called digital versatile disks, are optical disks the same size as CD-ROMs but of even higher capacity. They can hold a minimum of 4.7 gigabytes of data, enough to store a full-length, high-quality motion picture. DVDs are initially being used to store movies and multimedia applications using large amounts of video and graphics, but they may replace CD-ROMs because they can store large amounts of digitized text, graphics, audio, and video data. Once read-only, writable and re-writable DVD drives and media are now available.

magnetic disk
A secondary storage medium in which data are stored by means of magnetized spots on a hard or floppy disk.

hard disk
Magnetic disk resembling a thin magnetic platter used in large computer systems and in most PCs.

floppy disk
Removable magnetic disk storage primarily used with PCs.

RAID (Redundant Array of Inexpensive Disks)
Disk storage technology to boost disk performance by packaging more than 100 smaller disk drives with a controller chip and specialized software in a single large unit to deliver data over multiple paths simultaneously.

CD-ROM (compact disk read-only memory)
Read-only optical disk storage used for imaging, reference, and other applications with massive amounts of unchanging data and for multimedia.

digital video disk (DVD)
High-capacity optical storage medium that can store full-length videos and large amounts of data.

Magnetic Tape

Magnetic tape is an older storage technology that still is employed for secondary storage of large quantities of data that are needed rapidly but not instantly. Magnetic tape is very inexpensive and relatively stable. However, it stores data sequentially and is relatively slow compared to the speed of other secondary storage media. In order to find an individual record stored on magnetic tape, such as an employment record, the tape must be read from the beginning up to the location of the desired record.

New Storage Alternatives: Storage Area Networks (SANs)

To meet the escalating demand for data-intensive multimedia, Web, and other services, the amount of data that companies need to store is increasing from 75 to 150 percent every year. Companies are turning to new kinds of storage infrastructures to deal with their mushrooming storage requirements and their difficulties managing large volumes of data.

Storage area networks (SANs) can provide a solution for companies with the need to share information across applications and computing platforms. A **storage area network (SAN)** is a high-speed network dedicated to storage that connects different kinds of storage devices, such as tape libraries and disk arrays. The network moves data among pools of servers and storage devices, creating an enterprise-wide infrastructure for data storage. The SAN creates a large central pool of storage that can be shared by multiple servers so that users can rapidly share data across the SAN. Every user in a company can access data from any server in the organization. Figure 6-5 illustrates how a SAN works. The SAN storage devices are located on their own network and connected using a high-transmission technology such as Fibre Channel. SANs can be expensive and difficult to manage, but they are very useful for companies that can benefit from consolidating their storage resources and providing rapid data access to widely distributed users.

INPUT AND OUTPUT DEVICES

Human beings interact with computer systems largely through input and output devices. Input devices gather data and convert them into electronic form for use by the computer, whereas output devices display data after they have been processed. Table 6-2 describes the principal input devices, and Table 6-3 describes the major output devices.

Figure 6-5 A storage area network (SAN). The SAN stores data on many different types of storage devices, providing data to the enterprise. The SAN supports communication between any server and the storage unit as well as between different storage devices in the network.

TABLE 6-2   PRINCIPAL INPUT DEVICES

Input Device	Description
Keyboard	Principal method of data entry for text and numerical data.
Computer mouse	Handheld device with point-and-click capabilities that is usually connected to the computer by a cable. The computer user can move the mouse around on a desktop to control the cursor's position on a computer display screen, pushing a button to select a command. Trackballs and touch pads often are used in place of the mouse as pointing devices on laptop PCs.
Touch screen	Allows users to enter limited amounts of data by touching the surface of a sensitized video display monitor with a finger or a pointer. Often found in information kiosks in retail stores, restaurants, and shopping malls.
Optical character recognition	Devices that can translate specially designed marks, characters, and codes into digital form. The most widely used optical code is the *bar code*, which is used in point-of-sale systems in supermarkets and retail stores. The codes can include time, date, and location data in addition to identification data.
Magnetic ink character recognition (MICR)	Used primarily in check processing for the banking industry. Characters on the bottom of a check identify the bank, checking account, and check number and are preprinted using a special magnetic ink. A MICR reader translates these characters into digital form for the computer.
Pen-based input	Handwriting-recognition devices such as pen-based tablets, notebooks, and notepads convert the motion made by an electronic stylus pressing on a touch-sensitive tablet screen into digital form.
Digital scanner	Translates images such as pictures or documents into digital form and is an essential component of image-processing systems.
Audio input	Voice input devices that convert spoken words into digital form for processing by the computer. Microphones and tape cassette players can serve as input devices for music and other sounds.
Sensors	Devices that collect data directly from the environment for input into a computer system. For instance, today's farmers can use sensors to monitor the moisture of the soil in their fields to help them with irrigation.

The principal input devices consist of keyboards, pointing devices (such as the computer mouse and touch screens), and source data automation technologies (optical and magnetic ink character recognition, pen-based input, digital scanners, audio input, and sensors), which capture data in computer-readable form at the time and place they are created.

The principal output devices are cathode ray tube terminals (CRTs), sometimes called video display terminals or VDTs, and printers.

BATCH AND ON-LINE INPUT AND PROCESSING

The manner in which data are input into the computer affects how the data can be processed. Information systems collect and process information in one of two ways: through batch or through on-line processing. In **batch processing,** transactions, such as orders or

batch processing
A method of collecting and processing data in which transactions are accumulated and stored until a specified time when it is convenient or necessary to process them as a group.

TABLE 6-3   PRINCIPAL OUTPUT DEVICES

Output Device	Description
Cathode ray tube (CRT)	Electronic gun that shoots a beam of electrons illuminating pixels on a display screen. Laptop computers use flat panel displays, which are less bulky than CRT monitors.
Printers	Produce a printed hard copy of information output. They include impact printers (such as dot matrix printers) and nonimpact printers (laser, inkjet, and thermal transfer printers).
Audio output	Voice output devices convert digital output data back into intelligible speech. Other audio output, such as music, can be delivered by speakers connected to the computer.
Microfilm and microfiche	Used to store large quantities of output as microscopic filmed documents; being replaced by optical disk technology.

payroll time cards, are accumulated and stored in a group or batch until the time when, because of some reporting cycle, it is efficient or necessary to process them. Batch processing is found primarily in older systems where users need only occasional reports. In **on-line processing,** the user enters transactions into a device (such as a data entry keyboard or bar code reader) that is directly connected to the computer system. The transactions usually are processed immediately. Most processing today is on-line processing.

Figure 6-6 compares batch and on-line processing. Batch systems often use tape as a storage medium, whereas on-line processing systems use disk storage, which permits immediate access to specific items. In batch systems, transactions are accumulated in a **transaction file**, which contains all the transactions for a particular time period. Periodically, this file is used to update a **master file,** which contains permanent information on entities. (An example is a payroll master file with employee earnings and deduction data. It is updated with weekly time-card transactions.) Adding the transaction data to the existing master file creates a new master file. In on-line processing, transactions are entered into the system immediately using a keyboard, pointing device, or source data automation, and the system usually responds immediately. The master file is updated continually.

INTERACTIVE MULTIMEDIA

The processing, input, output, and storage technologies we have just described can be used to create **multimedia** applications that integrate sound and full-motion video, or animation with graphics and text into a computer-based application. Multimedia is becoming the foundation of new consumer products and services, such as electronic books and newspapers, electronic classroom-presentation technologies, full-motion videoconferencing, imaging, graphics design tools, and video and voice mail. PCs today come with built-in multimedia capabilities, including high-resolution color monitors, CD-ROM drives or DVD drives to store video, audio, and graphic data, and stereo speakers for amplifying audio output.

Interactive Web pages replete with graphics, sound, animations, and full-motion video have made multimedia popular on the Internet. For example, visitors to the CNN Interactive Web site can access news stories from CNN, photos, on-air transcripts, video clips, and audio clips. The video and audio clips are made available using **streaming tech-**

Figure 6-6 A comparison of batch and on-line processing. In batch processing, transactions are accumulated and stored in a group. Because batches are processed at regular intervals, such as daily, weekly, or monthly, information in the system will not always be up to date. In on-line processing, transactions are input immediately and usually processed immediately. Information in the system is generally up to date. A typical on-line application is an airline reservation system.

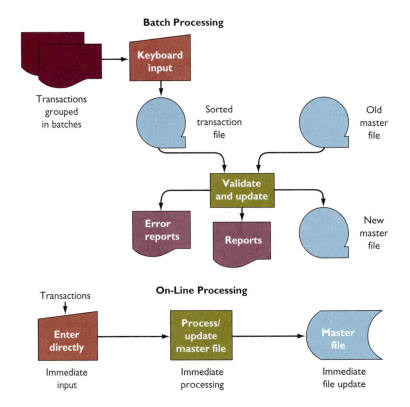

Multimedia combines text, graphics, sound, and video into a computer-based experience that permits two-way communication. Many organizations use this technology for interactive training.

nology, which allows audio and video data to be processed as a steady and continuous stream as they are downloaded from the Web.

Multimedia Web sites are also being used to sell digital products, such as digitized music clips. A compression standard known as **MP3,** also called **MPEG3,** which stands for Motion Picture Experts Group, audio layer 3, can compress audio files down to one-tenth or one-twelfth of their original size with virtually no loss in quality. Visitors to Web sites such as MP3.com can download MP3 music clips over the Internet and play them on their own computers.

MP3 (MPEG3)
Compression standard that can compress audio files for transfer over the Internet with virtually no loss in quality.

6.3 CATEGORIES OF COMPUTERS AND COMPUTER SYSTEMS

Contemporary computers can be categorized as mainframes, midrange computers, PCs, workstations, and supercomputers. Managers need to understand the capabilities of each of these types of computers, and why some types are more appropriate for certain processing work than others.

CLASSIFYING COMPUTERS

A **mainframe** is the largest computer, a powerhouse with massive memory and extremely rapid processing power. It is used for very large business, scientific, or military applications where a computer must handle massive amounts of data or many complicated processes. A **midrange computer** is less powerful, less expensive and smaller than a mainframe but capable of supporting the computing needs of smaller organizations or of managing networks of other computers. Midrange computers can be **minicomputers,** which are used in systems for universities, factories, or research laboratories, or they can be **servers,** which are used for managing internal company networks or Web sites. Server computers are specifically optimized to support a computer network, enabling users to share files, software, peripheral devices (such as printers), or other network resources. Servers have large memory and disk-storage capacity, high-speed communications capabilities, and powerful CPUs.

Servers have become important components of firms' IT infrastructures, because they provide the hardware platform for electronic commerce. By adding special software, they can be customized to deliver Web pages, process purchase and sale transactions, or exchange data with systems inside the company. Organizations with heavy electronic commerce requirements and massive Web sites are running their Web and electronic commerce applications

mainframe
Largest category of computer, used for major business processing.

midrange computer
Middle-size computer that is capable of supporting the computing needs of smaller organizations or of managing networks of other computers.

minicomputer
Middle-range computer used in systems for universities, factories, or research laboratories.

server
Computer specifically optimized to provide software and other resources to other computers over a network.

server farm
Large group of servers maintained by a commercial vendor and made available to subscribers for electronic commerce and other activities requiring heavy use of servers.

personal computer (PC)
Small desktop or portable computer.

workstation
Desktop computer with powerful graphics and mathematical capabilities and the ability to perform several complicated tasks at once.

supercomputer
Highly sophisticated and powerful computer that can perform very complex computations extremely rapidly.

distributed processing
The distribution of computer processing work among multiple computers linked by a communications network.

centralized processing
Processing that is accomplished by one large central computer.

client/server computing
A model for computing that splits processing between "clients" and "servers" on a network, assigning functions to the machine most able to perform the function.

on multiple servers in **server farms** in computing centers run by commercial vendors such as IBM.

A **personal computer (PC),** which is sometimes referred to as a microcomputer, is one that can be placed on a desktop or carried from room to room. Smaller laptop PCs are often used as portable desktops on the road. PCs are used as personal machines as well as in business. A **workstation** also fits on a desktop but has more powerful mathematical and graphics-processing capabilities than a PC and can perform more complicated tasks than a PC in the same amount of time. Workstations are used for scientific, engineering, investment, and design work that requires powerful graphics or computational capabilities.

A **supercomputer** is a highly sophisticated and powerful computer that is used for tasks requiring extremely rapid and complex calculations with hundreds of thousands of variable factors. Supercomputers use parallel processors and traditionally have been used in scientific and military work, such as classified weapons research and weather forecasting, which use complex mathematical models. They are now starting to be used in business for the manipulation of vast quantities of data.

COMPUTER NETWORKS AND CLIENT/SERVER COMPUTING

Today, stand-alone computers have been replaced by computers in networks for most processing tasks. The use of multiple computers linked by a communications network for processing is called **distributed processing.** In contrast to **centralized processing,** in which all processing is accomplished by one large central computer, distributed processing distributes the processing work among PCs, midrange computers, and mainframes linked together.

One widely used form of distributed processing is **client/server computing.** Client/server computing splits processing between "clients" and "servers." Both are on the network, but each machine is assigned functions it is best suited to perform. The **client** is the user point-of-entry for the required function and is normally a desktop computer, workstation, or laptop computer. The user generally interacts directly only with the client portion of the application, often to input data or retrieve data for further analysis. The *server* provides the client with services. The server could be a mainframe to another desktop computer, but specialized server computers are often used in this role. Servers store and process shared data and also perform back-end functions not visible to users, such as managing network activities. Figure 6-7 illustrates the client/server computing concept. Computing on the Internet uses the client/server model (see Chapter 9).

Figure 6-8 illustrates five different ways that the components of an application could be partitioned between the client and the server. The interface component is essentially the application interface—how the application appears visually to the user. The application logic component consists of the processing logic, which is shaped by the organization's business rules. (An example might be that a salaried employee is only to be paid monthly.) The data management component consists of the storage and management of the data used by the application. The exact division of tasks depends on the requirements of each application, including its processing needs, the number of users, and the available resources.

In some firms client/server networks with PCs have actually replaced mainframes and minicomputers. The process of transferring applications from large computers to smaller ones is called **downsizing**. Downsizing can potentially reduce computing costs, because

Figure 6-7 Client/server computing. In client/server computing, computer processing is split between client machines and server machines linked by a network. Users interface with the client machines.

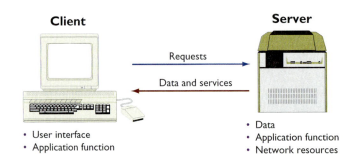

Client

Server

Requests →

← Data and services

• User interface
• Application function

• Data
• Application function
• Network resources

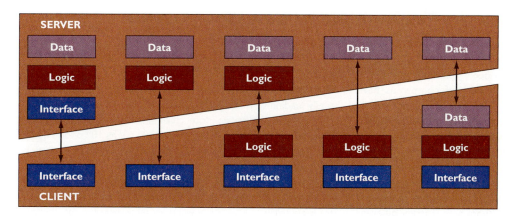

Figure 6-8 Types of client/ server computing. There are various ways in which an application's interface, logic, and data management components can be divided among the clients and servers in a network.

memory and processing power on a PC cost a fraction of their equivalent on a mainframe. The decision to downsize involves many factors in addition to the cost of computer hardware, including the need for new software, training, and perhaps new organizational procedures (see the discussion of total cost of ownership in Section 6.6).

NETWORK COMPUTERS AND PEER-TO-PEER COMPUTING

In one form of client/server computing, client processing and storage capabilities are so minimal that the bulk of computer processing occurs on the server. The term *thin client* is sometimes used to refer to the client in this arrangement. Thin clients with minimal memory, storage and processor power and which are designed to work on networks are called **network computers (NCs)**. NC users download whatever software or data they need from a central computer over the Internet or an organization's internal network. The central computer also saves information for the user and makes it available for later retrieval, effectively eliminating the need for secondary storage devices such as hard disks, floppy disks, CD-ROMs, and their drives.

NCs are less expensive to purchase than PCs with local processing and storage, and can be administered and updated from a central network server. Software programs and applications would not have to be purchased, installed, and upgraded for each user because software would be delivered and maintained from one central point. Network computers and centralized software distribution thus could increase management control over the organization's computing function.

However, PC prices have fallen so that units can be purchased for almost the same cost as NCs. If a network failure occurs, hundreds or thousands of employees would not be able to use their computers, whereas people could keep working if they had full-function PCs. Companies should closely examine how network computers might fit into their information technology infrastructure.

Peer-to-Peer Computing

Another form of distributed processing, called **peer-to-peer computing,** puts processing power back on users' desktops, linking these computers so that they can share processing tasks. Individual PCs, workstations, or other computers can share data, disk space, and even processing power for a variety of tasks when they are linked in a network, including the Internet. The peer-to-peer computing model stands in contrast to the network computing model, because processing power resides only on individual desktops and these computers work together without a server or any central controlling authority. It has been estimated that most companies—and individuals—use less than 25 percent of their processing and storage capacity. Peer-to-peer computing taps the unused disk space or processing power on PC or workstation networks for large computing tasks that can now only be performed by large expensive server computers or even supercomputers.

Each form of computer processing can provide benefits, depending on the business needs of the organization. The Window on Organizations explores this topic.

client
The user point-of-entry for the required function in client/server computing. Normally a desktop computer, workstation, or laptop computer.

downsizing
The process of transferring applications from large computers to smaller ones.

network computer (NC)
Simplified desktop computer that does not store software programs or data permanently. Users download whatever software or data they need from a central computer over the Internet or an organization's own internal network.

peer-to-peer computing
Form of distributed processing that links computers via the Internet or private networks so that they can share processing tasks.

PEER-TO-PEER OR NETWORK COMPUTING: WHICH IS BEST FOR YOUR FIRM?

Peer-to-peer computing is catching on. A variety of companies have discovered that this technology helps them do business faster, cheaper, and better. Unlike client/server computing, peer-to-peer computing lets different groups of users collaborate without having to go through the bottleneck of a central corporate server. The technology can also break down large tasks into smaller assignments and distribute them across many different interconnected desktops so that many different computers can be directed toward the solution simultaneously.

Peer-to-peer computing is especially useful for research and design collaboration work. Intel is using peer-to-peer technology to shave weeks off its schedule for chip design. An Intel chip designer in Oregon can, for example, run a computer processing job on company desktops in Israel when the workday there has ended. GlaxoSmithKline, the global pharmaceutical firm, started using peer-to-peer software from Groove Networks Inc. to help its researchers create a worldwide collaborative network with scientists from universities and biotechnology companies. GlaxoSmithKline works closely with these organizations in clinical studies and drug trials, and must exchange many confidential documents and images with them. The company's first peer-to-peer task was to expedite a patent filing by linking a company lawyer in the United States with a company scientist in Britain and an outside intellectual property lawyer in London.

First Union Bank is another peer-to-peer convert. The bank's fixed-income derivatives trading group is using DataSynapse software to increase trading volume and conduct portfolio risk analysis continuously instead of waiting for its central computers to be freed up at the end of a trading day. Peer-to-peer computing with the DataSynapse software has reduced computing times for most assets from hours to minutes. Faster response times help First Union edge out its competitors, eventually leading to more profits.

Radisson's Edwardian Hotel chain in London took the opposite tack: It decided to scrap its servers and PCs at its 10 London hotels in favor of a single computer center and storage facility at Heathrow linked to thin clients in each of the hotels. The hotel chain will use a portal to give users a single point of entry to all applications, including human resources, financial systems, office tools, and training. The portal will tailor information to the needs of individual users so that they can use their time on the system more efficiently. Management plans to roll out the same infrastructure to new hotels planned for Manchester, Birmingham, and London.

To set up a new hotel, the company needs to buy the computer, hook into Radisson's private network, and add PCs with Web browser software. Because all hotels will use the same applications, there will be no need to install special hardware or software for each hotel. Radisson's management believes this ease of administration will save money, because it can deliver all software tools and upgrades to 400 desktops centrally from the head office. Individual hotels will no longer need their own information systems staff.

To Think About: Compare the business benefits of peer-to-peer and network computing. What management, organization, and technology factors should be used to determine whether to use peer-to-peer or network computing?

Sources: Sarah Arnott, "Radisson Books into a Single Datacentre," *Computing,* July 7, 2001; Jonathan Burton, "Peer-to-Peer Grows Up and Gets a Real Job," *New York Times,* June 13, 2001; and Paul McDougall, "Napster-Like Networks May Be Peerless for Collaboration," *Information Week,* May 7, 2001.

6.4 TYPES OF SOFTWARE

To play a useful role in the firm's information technology infrastructure, computer hardware requires computer software. Chapter 1 defined computer *software* as the detailed instructions that control the operation of a computer system. Selecting appropriate software for the organization is a key management decision.

A software **program** is a series of statements or instructions to the computer. The process of writing or coding programs is termed *programming,* and individuals who specialize in this task are called *programmers.*

There are two major types of software: system software and application software. Each kind performs a different function. **System software** is a set of generalized programs that manage the computer's resources, such as the central processor, communications links, and peripheral devices. Programmers who write system software are called *system programmers.*

Application software describes the programs that are written for or by users to apply the computer to a specific task. Software for processing an order or generating a mailing list is application software. Programmers who write application software are called *application programmers.*

program
A series of statements or instructions to the computer.

system software
Generalized programs that manage the computer's resources, such as the central processor, communications links, and peripheral devices.

application software
Programs written for a specific application to perform functions specified by end users.

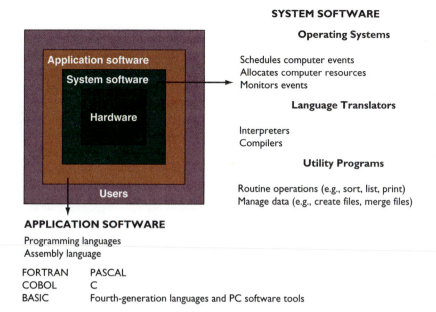

SYSTEM SOFTWARE

Operating Systems

Schedules computer events
Allocates computer resources
Monitors events

Language Translators

Interpreters
Compilers

Utility Programs

Routine operations (e.g., sort, list, print)
Manage data (e.g., create files, merge files)

APPLICATION SOFTWARE
Programming languages
Assembly language

FORTRAN	PASCAL
COBOL	C
BASIC	Fourth-generation languages and PC software tools

Figure 6-9 The major types of software. The relationship between system software, application software, and users can be illustrated by a series of nested boxes. System software—consisting of operating systems, language translators, and utility programs—controls access to the hardware. Application software, such as programming languages and "fourth-generation" languages, must work through the system software to operate. The user interacts primarily with the application software.

The types of software are interrelated and can be thought of as a set of nested boxes, each of which must interact closely with the other boxes surrounding it. Figure 6-9 illustrates this relationship. The system software surrounds and controls access to the hardware. Application software must work through the system software in order to operate. End users work primarily with application software. Each type of software must be specially designed for a specific machine to ensure its compatibility.

SYSTEM SOFTWARE AND PC OPERATING SYSTEMS

System software coordinates the various parts of the computer system and mediates between application software and computer hardware. The system software that manages and controls the computer's activities is called the **operating system**. Other system software consists of computer language translation programs that convert programming languages into machine language that can be understood by the computer and utility programs that perform common processing tasks.

operating system
The system software that manages and controls the activities of the computer.

Functions of the Operating System

The operating system is the computer system's chief manager. The operating system allocates and assigns system resources, schedules the use of computer resources and computer jobs, and monitors computer system activities. The operating system provides locations in primary memory for data and programs, and controls the input and output devices, such as printers, terminals, and telecommunication links. The operating system also coordinates the scheduling of work in various areas of the computer so that different parts of different jobs can be worked on at the same time. Finally, the operating system keeps track of each computer job and may also keep track of who is using the system, of what programs have been run, and of any unauthorized attempts to access the system.

Multiprogramming

A series of specialized operating system capabilities enables the computer to handle many different tasks and users at the same time. **Multiprogramming** permits multiple programs to share a computer system's resources at any one time through concurrent use of a CPU. Only one program is actually using the CPU at any given moment, but the input/output needs of other programs can be serviced at the same time. Two or more programs are active at the same time, but they do not use the same computer resources simultaneously. With multiprogramming, a group of programs takes turns using the processor. Figure 6-10 shows how three programs in a multiprogramming environment can be stored in primary storage.

multiprogramming
A method of executing two or more programs concurrently using the same computer. The CPU executes only one program but can service the input/output needs of others at the same time.

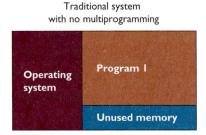

Traditional system with no multiprogramming

Multiprogramming environment

Figure 6-10 Single-program execution versus multiprogramming. In multiprogramming, the computer can be used much more efficiently because a number of programs can be executing concurrently. Several complete programs are loaded into memory. The first program executes until an input/output event is read in the program. The CPU then moves to the second program until an input/output statement occurs. At this point, the CPU switches to the execution of the third program, and so forth, until eventually all three programs have been executed.

Multiprogramming on single-user operating systems such as those in older personal computers is called **multitasking.**

Virtual Storage

Virtual storage handles programs more efficiently because the computer divides the programs into small fixed- or variable-length portions, storing only a small portion of the program in primary memory at one time. Only a few statements of a program actually execute at any given moment. This permits a very large number of programs to reside in primary memory, because only a tiny portion of each program is actually located there (see Figure 6-11), using this resource more efficiently. All other program pages are stored on a peripheral disk unit until they are ready for execution.

Time Sharing

Time sharing is an operating system capability that allows many users to share computer processing resources simultaneously. It differs from multiprogramming in that the CPU spends a fixed amount of time on one program before moving on to another. Thousands of users are each allocated a tiny slice of computer time, when each is free to perform any required operations; at the end of this period, another user is given another tiny time slice of the CPU. This arrangement permits many users to be connected to a CPU simultaneously, with each receiving only a tiny amount of CPU time.

Multiprocessing

Multiprocessing is an operating system capability that links together two or more CPUs to work in parallel in a single computer system. The operating system can assign multiple CPUs to execute different instructions from the same program or from different programs simulta-

---

multitasking
The multiprogramming capability of primarily single-user operating systems, such as those for older PCs.

virtual storage
Handling programs more efficiently by dividing the programs into small fixed- or variable-length portions with only a small portion stored in primary memory at one time.

time sharing
The sharing of computer resources by many users simultaneously by having the CPU spend a fixed amount of time on each user's program before proceeding to the next.

multiprocessing
An operating system feature for executing two or more instructions simultaneously in a single computer system by using multiple central processing units.

Figure 6-11 Virtual storage. In virtual storage, programs are broken down into small sections that are read into memory only when needed. The rest of the program is stored on disk until it is required. In this way, very large programs can be executed by small machines, or a large number of programs can be executed concurrently by a single machine.

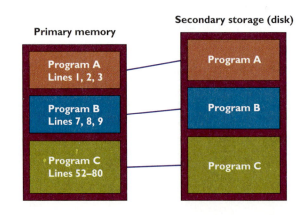

neously, dividing the work between the CPUs. Whereas multiprogramming uses concurrent processing with one CPU, multiprocessing uses simultaneous processing with multiple CPUs.

Language Translation and Utility Software

System software includes special language translator programs that translate high-level language programs written in programming languages such as COBOL, FORTRAN, or C into machine language that the computer can execute. The program in the high-level language before translation into machine language is called **source code.** A **compiler** translates source code into machine code called *object code,* which is linked to other object code modules and then executed by the computer. Some programming languages, such as BASIC, do not use a compiler but an *interpreter,* which translates each source code statement one at a time into machine code and executes it.

System software includes *utility programs* for routine, repetitive tasks, such as copying, clearing primary storage, computing a square root, or sorting. Utility programs can be shared by all users of a computer system and can be used in many different information system applications when requested.

PC Operating Systems and Graphical User Interfaces

Like any other software, PC software is based on specific operating systems and computer hardware. Software written for one PC operating system generally cannot run on another. Table 6-4 compares the leading PC operating systems: Windows XP, Windows 98 and Windows Me, Windows 2000, Windows CE, UNIX, Linux, OS/2, the Macintosh operating system, and DOS.

When a user interacts with a computer, including a PC, the interaction is controlled by an operating system. A user communicates with an operating system through the user interface of that operating system. Contemporary PC operating systems use a **graphical user interface**, often called a **GUI,** which makes extensive use of icons, buttons, bars, and boxes to perform tasks. It has become the dominant model for the user interface of PC operating systems and for many types of application software.

source code
Program instructions written in a high-level language that must be translated into machine language to be executed by the computer.

compiler
Special system software that translates a high-level language into machine language for execution by the computer.

graphical user interface (GUI)
The part of an operating system users interact with that uses graphic icons and the computer mouse to issue commands and make selections.

TABLE 6-4   LEADING PC OPERATING SYSTEMS

Operating System	Features
Windows XP	Reliable, robust operating system for powerful PCs with versions for both home and corporate users. Features support of Internet and multimedia and improved networking, security, and corporate management capabilities.
Windows 98/Me	32-bit operating system for personal computing with a streamlined graphical user interface and powerful multitasking and networking capabilities. Can be integrated with the information resources of the Web.
Windows 2000	32-bit operating system for PCs, workstations, and network servers. Supports multitasking, multiprocessing, intensive networking, and Internet services for corporate computing.
Windows CE	Pared-down version of the Windows operating system, including its graphical user interface, for handheld computers and wireless communication devices. Designed to run on small, handheld computers, personal digital assistants, wireless communication devices, and other information appliances.
UNIX	Used for powerful PCs, workstations, and network servers. Supports multitasking, multiuser processing, and networking. Is portable to different models of computer hardware.
Linux	Free, reliable alternative to UNIX and Windows 2000 that runs on many different types of computer hardware and can be modified by software developers.
OS/2	Robust 32-bit operating system for powerful IBM or IBM-compatible PCs with Intel microprocessors. Used for complex, memory-intensive applications or those that require networking, multitasking, or large programs. Has its own graphical user interface and desktop and server versions.
Mac OS	Operating system for the Macintosh computer, featuring multitasking, powerful multimedia and networking capabilities, and a mouse-driven graphical user interface. Supports connecting to and publishing on the Internet.
DOS	16-bit operating system for older PCs based on the IBM PC standard. Does not support multitasking and limits the size of a program in memory to 640 kilobytes.

Windows 98

Version of the Windows operating system that is closely integrated with the Internet and that supports multitasking, networking and hardware technologies such as digital video disk, videoconferencing cameras, scanners, TV tuner-adapter cards, and joysticks.

Windows Millennium Edition (Windows Me)

Enhanced Windows operating system for consumer users featuring tools for working with video, photos, music, and home networking.

Windows 2000

Powerful operating system developed by Microsoft for use with 32-bit PCs, workstations, and network servers. Supports networking, multitasking, multiprocessing, and Internet services.

Windows XP

Powerful Windows operating system that provides reliability, robustness, and ease of use for both corporate and home PC users.

UNIX

Operating system for all types of computers, which is machine independent and supports multiuser processing, multitasking, and networking. Used in high-end workstations and servers.

Linux

Reliable and compactly designed operating system that is an offshoot of UNIX, that can run on many different hardware platforms and is available free or at very low cost.

open-source software

Software that provides free access to its program code, allowing users to modify the program code to make improvements or fix errors.

Microsoft's **Windows 98** is a genuine 32-bit operating system that provides a streamlined graphical user interface that arranges icons to provide instant access to common tasks. Windows 98 features multitasking and powerful networking capabilities, including the capability to integrate fax, e-mail, and scheduling programs. (*Windows 95* was an earlier version of this operating system.) It can support additional hardware technologies, such as digital video disk (DVD), videoconferencing cameras, scanners, TV tuner-adapter cards, and joysticks. Users can work with the traditional Windows interface or use the Web browser interface to display information. Windows 98 also includes a group collaboration tool called NetMeeting and Front Page Express, a tool for creating and storing Web pages.

Windows Millennium Edition (Windows Me) is an enhanced version of this operating system for consumer users. It has tools for working with photos and video recordings and tools to simplify home networking of two or more PCs. A media player bundled with Windows Me can record, store, and play CDs, digital music downloaded from the Internet, and videos.

Windows 2000 is another 32-bit operating system developed by Microsoft with features that make it appropriate for applications in large networked organizations. Earlier versions of this operating system were known as *Windows NT* (for New Technology). Windows 2000 is used as an operating system for high-performance desktop and laptop computers and network servers. Windows 2000 shares the same graphical user interface as the other Windows operating systems, but it has more powerful networking, multitasking, and memory-management capabilities. Windows 2000 can support software written for Windows and it can provide mainframelike computing power for new applications with massive memory and file requirements. It can even support multiprocessing with multiple CPUs.

There are two basic versions of Windows 2000—a Professional version for users of stand-alone or client desktop and laptop computers, and several server versions designed to run on network servers and provide network management functions, including tools for creating and operating Web sites and other Internet services.

Windows XP (for eXPerience) combines the reliability and robustness of Windows 2000 with the ease of use and consumer features of Windows 98/Me, and an improved graphical user interface. The Windows XP Home Edition is for home users and the Windows XP Professional Edition targets mobile and business users. This operating system is meant for powerful new PCs with at least 400 megahertz of processing power and 128 megabytes of RAM.

UNIX is an interactive, multiuser, multitasking operating system developed by Bell Laboratories in 1969 to help scientific researchers share data. UNIX was designed to connect various machines together and is highly supportive of communications and networking. UNIX is often used on workstations and servers and provides the reliability and scalability for running large systems on high-end servers. UNIX can run on many different kinds of computers and can be easily customized. Application programs that run under UNIX can be ported from one computer to run on a different computer with little modification.

UNIX is considered powerful but very complex, with a legion of commands. Graphical user interfaces have been developed for UNIX. UNIX also poses some security problems, because multiple jobs and users can access the same file simultaneously. Vendors have developed different versions of UNIX that are incompatible, thereby limiting software portability.

Linux is a UNIX-like operating system that can be downloaded from the Internet free of charge or purchased for a small fee from companies that provide additional tools for the software. It is free, reliable, compactly designed, and capable of running on many different hardware platforms, including servers, handheld computers, and consumer electronics. Linux has become popular during the past few years among sophisticated computer users and businesses as a robust low-cost alternative to UNIX and Windows 2000. Major hardware and software vendors are starting to provide versions of their products that can run on Linux. The software instructions for Linux are available along with the operating system software, so the software can be modified by software developers to fit their particular needs.

Linux is an example of **open-source software,** which provides all computer users with free access to its program code, so they can modify the code to fix errors or to make improvements. Open-source software such as Linux is not owned by any company or individual. A

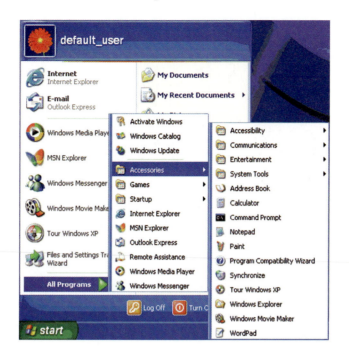

Microsoft's Windows XP is a robust and easy-to-use operating system for corporate and home applications.

global network of programmers and users manages and modifies the software, usually without being paid to do so.

APPLICATION SOFTWARE AND PROGRAMMING LANGUAGES

Application software is primarily concerned with accomplishing the tasks of end users. Many different languages and software tools can be used to develop application software. Managers should understand which software tools and programming languages are appropriate for their organization's objectives.

Programming Languages

The first generation of computer languages consisted of **machine language,** which required the programmer to write all program instructions in the 0s and 1s of binary code and to specify storage locations for every instruction and item of data used. Programming in machine language was a very slow, labor-intensive process. As computer hardware improved and processing speed and memory size increased, programming languages became progressively easier for humans to understand and use. From the mid-1950s to the mid-1970s, high-level programming languages emerged, allowing programs to be written with regular words using sentence-like statements. We now briefly describe the most important high-level languages.

Assembly Language

Assembly language is the next level of programming language up from machine language and is considered a "second-generation" language. Like machine language, **assembly language** (Figure 6-12) is designed for a specific machine and specific microprocessors.

> **machine language**
> A programming language consisting of the 1s and 0s of binary code.

> **assembly language**
> A programming language developed in the 1950s that resembles machine language but substitutes mnemonics for numeric codes.

> **Figure 6-12** Assembly language. This sample assembly language command adds the contents of register 3 to register 5 and stores the result in register 5. (A register is a temporary storage location in the CPU for small amounts of data or instructions).

```
AR 5, 3
```

Figure 6-13 FORTRAN. This sample FORTRAN program code is part of a program to compute sales figures for a particular item.

```
READ (5,100) ID, QUANT, PRICE
TOTAL = QUANT * PRICE
```

Figure 6-14 COBOL. This sample COBOL program code is part of a routine to compute total sales figures for a particular item.

```
MULTIPLY QUANT-SOLD BY UNIT-PRICE GIVING SALES-TOTAL.
```

Assembly language makes use of certain mnemonics (e.g., load, sum) to represent machine language instructions and storage locations. Although assembly language gives programmers great control, it is difficult and costly to write and learn. Assembly language is used primarily today in system software.

Third-Generation Languages: FORTRAN, COBOL, BASIC, Pascal, and C

Third-generation languages specify instructions as brief statements that are more like natural languages than assembly language. All are less efficient in the use of computer resources than earlier languages, they are easier to write and understand and have made it possible to create software for business and scientific problems. Important third-generation languages include FORTRAN, COBOL, BASIC, and C.

FORTRAN (FORmula TRANslator)
A programming language developed in 1956 for scientific and mathematical applications.

FORTRAN FORTRAN (FORmula TRANslator) (Figure 6-13) was developed in 1956 to provide an easy way of writing scientific and engineering applications. FORTRAN is especially useful in processing numeric data. Some business applications can be written in FORTRAN, and contemporary versions provide sophisticated structures for controlling program logic.

COBOL (COmmon Business Oriented Language)
Major programming language for business applications because it can process large data files with alphanumeric characters.

COBOL COBOL (COmmon Business Oriented Language) (Figure 6-14) was developed in the early 1960s by a committee representing both government and industry. Rear Admiral Grace M. Hopper was a key committee member who played a major role in COBOL development. COBOL was designed with business administration in mind, for processing large data files with alphanumeric characters (mixed alphabetic and numeric data) and for performing repetitive tasks such as payroll. It is poor at complex, mathematical calculations. Also, there are many versions of COBOL, and not all are compatible with each other.

BASIC and Pascal BASIC and Pascal are used primarily in education to teach programming. *BASIC (Beginners All-purpose Symbolic Instruction Code)* was developed in 1964 by John Kemeny and Thomas Kurtz to teach students at Dartmouth College how to use computers. BASIC is easy to use but does few computer processing tasks well, even though it does them all. Different versions of BASIC exist.

Named after Blaise Pascal, the seventeenth-century mathematician and philosopher, *Pascal* was developed by the Swiss computer science professor Niklaus Wirth of Zurich in the late 1960s. Pascal is used primarily in computer science courses to teach sound programming practices.

C
A powerful programming language with tight control and efficiency of execution; is portable across different microprocessors and is used primarily with PCs.

C and C++ C is a powerful and efficient language developed at AT&T's Bell Labs in the early 1970s. It combines machine portability with tight control and efficient use of computer resources, and it can work on a variety of different computers. It is used primarily by professional programmers to create operating systems and application software, especially for PCs.

C++
Object-oriented version of the C programming language.

C++ is a newer version of C that is object-oriented (see Section 6.5). It has all the capabilities of C plus additional features for working with software objects. C++ is used for developing application software.

FOURTH-GENERATION LANGUAGES AND PC SOFTWARE TOOLS

Fourth-generation languages consist of a variety of software tools that enable end users to develop software applications with minimal or no technical assistance or that enhance professional programmers' productivity. Fourth-generation languages tend to be nonprocedural, or less procedural, than conventional programming languages. Procedural languages require specification of the sequence of steps, or procedures, that tell the computer what to do and how to do it. Nonprocedural languages need only specify what has to be accomplished rather than provide details about how to carry out the task. Some of these nonprocedural languages are **natural languages** that enable users to communicate with the computer using conversational commands resembling human speech.

Table 6-5 shows that there are seven categories of fourth-generation languages: PC software tools, query languages, report generators, graphics languages, application generators, application software packages, and very high-level programming languages. The table shows the tools ordered in terms of ease of use by nonprogramming end users. End users are most likely to work with PC software tools and query languages. **Query languages** are software tools that provide immediate on-line answers to requests for information that are not predefined, such as "Who are the highest-performing sales representatives?" Query languages are often tied to data management software and to database management systems (see Chapter 7).

Application Software Packages and PC Software Tools

A **software package** is a prewritten, precoded, commercially available set of programs that eliminates the need for individuals or organizations to write their own software programs for certain functions. There are software packages for system software, but most package software is application software.

Software packages that run on mainframes and larger computers usually require professional programmers for their installation and support. However, there are also application

---

fourth-generation language
A programming language that can be employed directly by end users or less-skilled programmers to develop computer applications more rapidly than conventional programming languages.

natural languages
Programming language that is very close to human language.

query language
Software tool that provides immediate on-line answers to requests for information that are not predefined.

software package
A prewritten, precoded, commercially available set of programs that eliminates the need to write software programs for certain functions.

TABLE 6-5   CATEGORIES OF FOURTH-GENERATION LANGUAGES

Fourth-Generation Tool	Description	Example	Oriented toward end users
PC software tools	General-purpose application software packages for PCs.	WordPerfect Internet Explorer Access	
Query language	Languages for retrieving data stored in databases or files. Capable of supporting requests for information that are not predefined.	SQL	
Report generator	Extract data from files or databases to create customized reports in a wide range of formats not routinely produced by an information system. Generally provide more control over the way data are formatted, organized, and displayed than query languages.	RPG III	
Graphics language	Retrieve data from files or databases and display them in graphic format. Some graphics software can perform arithmetic or logical operations on data as well.	SAS Graph Systat	
Application generator	Contain preprogrammed modules that can generate entire applications, including Web sites, greatly speeding development. A user can specify what needs to be done, and the application generator will create the appropriate program code for input, validation, update, processing, and reporting.	FOCUS PowerBuilder Microsoft FrontPage	
Application software package	Software programs sold or leased by commercial vendors that eliminate the need for custom-written, in-house software.	PeopleSoft HRMS SAP R/3	
Very high-level programming language	Generate program code with fewer instructions than conventional languages, such as COBOL or FORTRAN. Designed primarily as productivity tools for professional programmers.	APL Nomad2	Oriented toward IS professionals

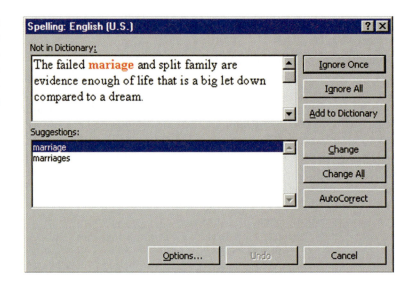

Figure 6-15 Text and the spelling checking option in Microsoft Word. Word processing software provides many easy-to-use options to create and output a text document to meet a user's specifications.
Source: Courtesy of Microsoft.

software packages developed explicitly for end users. These PC application packages for word processing, spreadsheet, data management, presentation graphics, integrated software packages, e-mail, Web browsers, and groupware are the most widely used software tools among business and consumer users.

Word Processing Software.   *Word processing software,* which we introduced in Chapter 2, stores text data electronically as a computer file rather than on paper. The word processing software allows the user to make changes in the document electronically in memory. This eliminates the need to retype an entire page to incorporate corrections. The software has formatting options to make changes in line spacing, margins, character size, and column width. Microsoft Word and WordPerfect are popular word processing packages. Figure 6-15 illustrates a Microsoft Word screen displaying text, spelling checking, and menu options.

Most word processing software has advanced features that automate other writing tasks: spelling checkers, style checkers (to analyze grammar and punctuation), thesaurus programs, and mail merge programs, which link letters or other text documents with names and addresses in a mailing list. The newest versions of this software can create and access Web pages.

Businesses that need to create highly professional looking brochures, manuals, or books will likely use desktop publishing software for this purpose. *Desktop publishing* software provides more control over the placement of text, graphics, and photos in the layout of a page than does word processing software. Adobe PageMaker and QuarkXpress are two popular desktop publishing packages.

spreadsheet

Software displaying data in a grid of columns and rows, with the capability of easily recalculating numerical data.

Spreadsheets.   Electronic **spreadsheet** software provides computerized versions of traditional financial modeling tools, such as the accountant's columnar pad, pencil, and calculator. An electronic spreadsheet is organized into a grid of columns and rows. The power of the electronic spreadsheet is evident when one changes a value or series of values because all other related values on the spreadsheet will be automatically recomputed.

Spreadsheets are valuable for applications in which numerous calculations with pieces of data must be related to each other. Spreadsheets also are useful for applications that require modeling and what-if analysis. After the user has constructed a set of mathematical relationships, the spreadsheet can be recalculated instantaneously using a different set of assumptions. A number of alternatives can easily be evaluated by changing one or two pieces of data without having to rekey in the rest of the worksheet. Many spreadsheet packages include graphics functions that can present data in the form of line graphs, bar graphs, or pie charts. The most popular spreadsheet packages are Microsoft Excel and Lotus 1-2-3. The newest versions of this software can read and write Web files. Figure 6-16 illustrates the output from a spreadsheet for a breakeven analysis and its accompanying graph.

		Custom Neckties Pro Forma Income Statement			
Total fixed cost	19,000.00				
Variable cost per unit	3.00				
Average sales price	17.00				
Contribution margin	14.00				
Breakeven point	1,357				
Units sold	0.00	679	1,357	2,036	2,714
Revenue	0	11,536	23,071	34,607	46,143
Fixed cost	19,000	19,000	19,000	19,000	19,000
Variable cost	0	2,036	4,071	6,107	8,143
Total cost	19,000	21,036	23,071	25,107	27,143
Profit/Loss	(19,000)	(9,500)	0	9,500	19,000

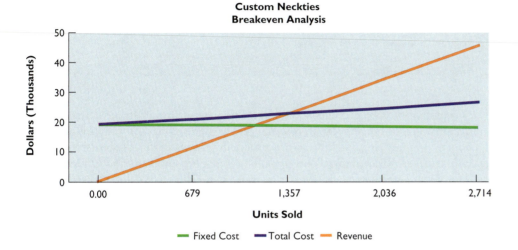

Custom Neckties Breakeven Analysis

Fixed Cost — Total Cost — Revenue

Figure 6-16 Spreadsheet software. Spreadsheet software organizes data into columns and rows for analysis and manipulation. Contemporary spreadsheet software provides graphing abilities for clear visual representation of the data in the spreadsheets. This sample breakeven analysis is represented as numbers in a spreadsheet as well as a line graph for easy interpretation.

Data Management Software. Although spreadsheet programs are powerful tools for manipulating quantitative data, **data management software** is more suitable for creating and manipulating lists and for combining information from different files. PC database management packages have programming features and easy-to-learn menus that enable non-specialists to build small information systems.

Data management software typically has facilities for creating files and databases and for storing, modifying, and manipulating data for reports and queries. A detailed treatment of data management software and database management systems can be found in Chapter 7. Popular database management software for the personal computer includes Microsoft Access, which has been enhanced to publish data on the Web. Figure 6-17 shows a screen from Microsoft Access illustrating some of its capabilities.

data management software
Software used for creating and manipulating lists, creating files and databases to store data, and combining information for reports.

Presentation Graphics. **Presentation graphics** software allows users to create professional-quality graphics presentations. This software can convert numeric data into charts and other types of graphics and can include multimedia displays of sound, animation, photos, and video clips. The leading presentation graphics packages include capabilities for computer-generated slide shows and translating content for the Web. Microsoft PowerPoint and Lotus Freelance Graphics are popular presentation graphics packages.

presentation graphics
Software to create professional-quality graphics presentations that can incorporate charts, sound, animation, photos, and video clips.

Integrated Software Packages and Software Suites. **Integrated software packages** combine the functions of the most important PC software packages, such as word processing, spreadsheets, presentation graphics, and data management. This integration provides a more general-purpose software tool and eliminates redundant data entry and data maintenance. For example, the breakeven analysis spreadsheet illustrated in Figure 6-16 could be reformatted into a polished report with word processing software without separately keying the data into both programs. Although integrated packages can do many things well, they generally do not have the same power and depth as single-purpose packages.

integrated software package
A software package that provides two or more applications, such as word processing and spreadsheets, providing for easy transfer of data between them.

Figure 6-17 Data management software. This screen from Microsoft Access illustrates some of its powerful capabilities for managing and organizing information.

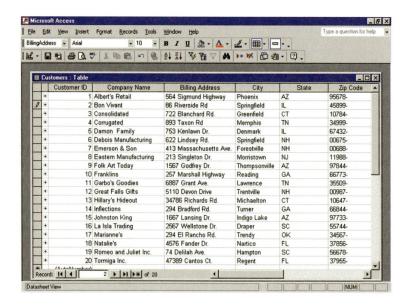

Integrated software packages should be distinguished from software suites, which are full-featured versions of application software sold as a unit. Microsoft Office is an example. This software suite contains Word word processing software, Excel spreadsheet software, Access database software, PowerPoint presentation graphics software, and Outlook, a set of tools for e-mail, scheduling, and contact management. **Office 2000** and **Office XP** contain additional capabilities to support collaborative work on the Web, including the ability to manage multiple comments and revisions from several reviewers in a single document and the ability to automatically notify others about changes to documents. Documents created with Office tools can be viewed with a Web browser and published on the Web. Office XP users can automatically refresh their documents with information from the Web, such as stock quotes and news flashes, and manage their e-mail accounts from a single view.

Office 2000 and Office XP
Integrated software suites with capabilities for supporting collaborative work on the Web or incorporating information from the Web into documents.

electronic mail (e-mail)
The computer-to-computer exchange of messages.

E-mail Software. **Electronic mail (e-mail)** is used for the computer-to-computer exchange of messages and is an important tool for communication and collaborative work. A person can use a networked computer to send notes or lengthier documents to a recipient on the same network or a different network. Many organizations operate their own electronic-mail systems, but communications companies, such as MCI and AT&T, offer these services,

Users can create professional-looking electronic presentations incorporating text, diagrams, and other multimedia elements using presentation graphics software. This slide was created with Microsoft PowerPoint.

along with commercial on-line information services, such as America Online and public networks on the Internet.

Web browsers and the PC software suites have e-mail capabilities, but specialized e-mail software packages are also available for use on the Internet. In addition to providing electronic messaging, e-mail software has capabilities for routing messages to multiple recipients, message forwarding, and attaching text documents or multimedia to messages.

Web Browsers. **Web browsers** are easy-to-use software tools for displaying Web pages and for accessing the Web and other Internet resources. Web browser software features a point-and-click graphical user interface that can be employed throughout the Internet to access and display information stored on computers at other Internet sites. Browsers can display or present graphics, audio, and video information as well as traditional text, and they allow you to click on-screen buttons or highlighted words to link to related Web sites. Web browsers have become the primary interface for accessing the Internet or for using networked systems based on Internet technology. You can see examples of Web browser software by looking at the illustrations of Web pages in each chapter of this text.

The two leading commercial Web browsers are Microsoft's Internet Explorer and Netscape Navigator, which is also available as part of the Netscape Communicator software suite. They include capabilities for using e-mail, file transfer, on-line discussion groups and bulletin boards, along with other Internet services. Newer versions of these browsers contain support for Web publishing and workgroup computing. (See the following discussion of groupware.)

Groupware. **Groupware** provides functions and services to support the collaborative activities of work groups. Groupware includes software for group writing and commenting, information-sharing, electronic meetings, scheduling, and e-mail and a network to connect the members of the group as they work on their own desktop computers, often in widely scattered locations. Any group member can review the ideas of others at any time and add to them, or individuals can post a document for others to comment on or edit. Leading commercial groupware products include Lotus Notes and Opentext's Livelink. Groove is a new groupware tool based on peer-to-peer technology, which enables people to work directly with other people over the Internet without going through a central server. Microsoft Internet Explorer and Netscape Communicator Web browser software includes groupware functions, such as e-mail, electronic scheduling and calendaring, audio and data conferencing, and electronic discussion groups and databases (see Chapter 10). Microsoft's Office 2000 and Office XP software suites include groupware features using Web technology.

Web browser
An easy-to-use software tool for accessing the World Wide Web and the Internet.

groupware
Software that provides functions and services that support the collaborative activities of work groups.

Groupware facilitates collaboration by enabling members of a group to share documents, schedule meetings, and discuss activities, events, and issues. Illustrated are capabilities for following a threaded discussion, where a series of messages have been posted as replies to each other.

Software for Enterprise Integration

Chapters 2 and 3 discussed the growing organizational need to integrate functions and business processes to improve organizational control, coordination, and responsiveness by allowing data and information to flow freely between different parts of the organization. Poorly integrated applications can create costly inefficiencies or slowed down customer service that become competitive liabilities. Alternative software solutions are available to promote enterprise integration.

enterprise software

Set of integrated modules for applications such as sales and distribution, financial accounting, investment management, materials management, production planning, plant maintenance, and human resources that allow data to be used by multiple functions and business processes.

One alternative, which we introduced in Chapter 2, is to replace isolated systems that cannot communicate with each other with an enterprise system. **Enterprise software** consists of a set of interdependent modules for applications such as sales and distribution, financial accounting, investment management, materials management, production planning, plant maintenance, and human resources that allow data to be used by multiple functions and business processes for more precise organizational coordination and control. The modules can communicate with each other directly or by sharing a common repository of data. Contemporary enterprise systems use a client/server computing architecture. Major enterprise software vendors include SAP, Oracle, PeopleSoft, and Baan. These vendors are now enhancing their products to provide more capabilities for supply chain management and exchange of data with other enterprises.

Individual companies can implement all of the enterprise software modules offered by a vendor or select only the modules of interest to them. They can also configure the software they select to support the way they do business. For example, they could configure the software to track revenue by product line, geographical unit, or distribution channel. However, the enterprise software may not be able to support some companies' unique business processes and often requires firms to change the way they work. Chapter 13 describes the challenges of implementing enterprise software in greater detail.

Most firms cannot jettison all of their existing systems and create enterprise-wide integration from scratch. Many existing legacy mainframe applications are essential to daily operations and very risky to change, but they can be made more useful if their information and business logic can be integrated with other applications (Noffsinger, Niedbalski, Blanks, and Emmart, 1998). One way to integrate various legacy applications is to use special software called **middleware** to create an interface or bridge between two different systems. Middleware is software that connects two otherwise separate applications, allowing them to communicate with each other and to pass data between them (see Figure 6-18). Middleware may consist of custom software written in-house or a software package.

middleware

Software that connects two disparate applications, allowing them to communicate with each other and to exchange data.

There are many different types of middleware. One important use of middleware is to link client and server machines in client/server computing and increasingly to link a Web server to data stored on another computer. A **Web server** is the software for locating and managing stored Web pages. It locates the Web pages requested by a user on the computer where they are stored and delivers the Web pages to the user's computer. Middleware allows users to request data (such as an order) from the actual transaction system (such as an order processing system) housing the data by entering the request on forms displayed on a Web browser, and it enables the Web server to return dynamic Web pages based on information users request.

Web server

Software that manages requests for Web pages on the computer where they are stored and that delivers the page to the user's computer.

Instead of custom-writing software to connect one application to another, companies can now purchase **enterprise application integration software** to connect disparate applications or application clusters. Enterprise application integration is the process of tying together multiple applications to support the flow of information across multiple business units and systems. Enterprise application integration software can consist of middleware for passing data between two different systems or business process integration tools that link applications together through business process modeling. The software allows system builders to model their business processes graphically and define the rules that applications should follow to make these processes work. The software then generates the underlying pro-

enterprise application integration software

Software that ties together multiple applications to support enterprise integration.

gram instructions to link existing applications to each other to support those processes. Because the enterprise application integration software is largely independent of the individual applications it connects, the organization can change its business processes and grow without requiring changes to the applications. A few enterprise application integration tools allow multiple businesses to integrate their systems into an extended supply chain.

6.5   CONTEMPORARY TOOLS FOR SOFTWARE DEVELOPMENT

A growing backlog of software projects and the need for businesses to fashion systems that are flexible or that can run over the Internet have stimulated approaches to software development based on object-oriented programming tools and new programming languages such as Java, hypertext markup language (HTML), and eXtensible Markup Language (XML).

OBJECT-ORIENTED PROGRAMMING

Traditional software development methods have treated data and procedures as independent components. A separate programming procedure must be written every time someone wants to take an action on a particular piece of data. The procedures act on data that the program passes to them.

Object-oriented programming combines data and the specific procedures that operate on those data into one object. The object combines data and program code. Instead of passing data to procedures, programs send a message for an object to perform a procedure that is already embedded in it. (Procedures are termed *methods* in object-oriented languages.) The same message may be sent to many different objects, but each will implement that message differently.

For example, an object-oriented financial application might have Customer objects sending debit and credit messages to Account objects. The Account objects in turn might maintain Cash-on-Hand, Accounts-Payable, and Accounts-Receivable objects.

An object's data are encapsulated from other parts of the system, so each object is an independent software building block that can be used in many different systems without changing the program code. Thus, object-oriented programming is expected to reduce the time and cost of writing software by producing reusable program code or software chips that can be reused in other related systems. Productivity gains from object-oriented technology could be magnified if objects were stored in reusable software libraries and explicitly designed for reuse (Fayad and Cline, 1996). However, such benefits are unlikely to be realized unless organizations develop appropriate standards and procedures for reuse (Kim and Stohr, 1998).

Object-oriented programming has spawned a new programming technology known as **visual programming**. With visual programming, programmers do not write code. Rather, they use a mouse to select and move around programming objects, copying an object from a library into a specific location in a program, or drawing a line to connect two or more objects. Visual Basic is a widely used visual programming tool for creating applications that run on Microsoft Windows.

object-oriented programming
An approach to software development that combines data and procedures into a single object.

visual programming
The construction of software programs by selecting and arranging programming objects rather than by writing program code.

Object-Oriented Programming Concepts

Object-oriented programming is based on the concepts of class and inheritance. Program code is not written separately for every object but for classes, or general categories, of similar objects. Objects belonging to a certain class have the features of that class. Classes of objects in turn can inherit all the structure and behaviors of a more general class and then add variables and behaviors unique to each object. New classes of objects are created by choosing an existing class and specifying how the new class differs from the existing class, instead of starting from scratch each time.

We can see how class and inheritance work in Figure 6-19, which illustrates a tree of classes concerning employees and how they are paid. Employee is the common ancestor of the other four classes. Nonsalaried and Salaried are subclasses of Employee, whereas Temporary and Permanent are subclasses of Nonsalaried. The variables for the class are in the

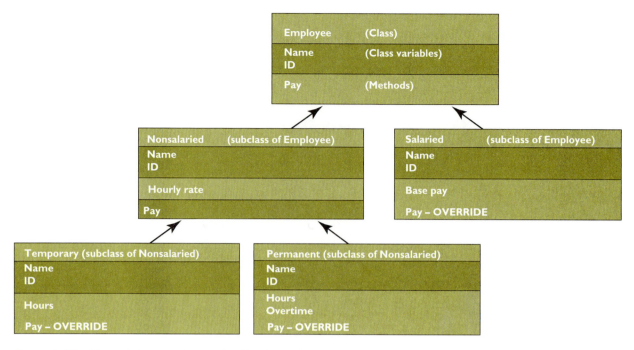

Figure 6-19 Class, subclasses, and overriding. This figure illustrates how a message's method can come from the class itself or from an ancestor class. Class variables and methods are shaded when they are inherited from above.

top half of the box, and the methods are in the bottom half. Darker items in each box are inherited from some ancestor class. (For example, by following the tree upward, we can see that Name and ID in the Nonsalaried, Salaried, Temporary, and Permanent subclasses are inherited from the Employee superclass [ancestor class].) Lighter methods, or class variables, are unique to a specific class and they override, or redefine, existing methods. When a subclass overrides an inherited method, its object still responds to the same message, but it executes its definition of the method rather than its ancestor's. Whereas Pay is a method inherited from some superclass, the method Pay-OVERRIDE is specific to the Temporary, Permanent, and Salaried classes.

JAVA

Java is a platform-independent, object-oriented programming language developed by Sun Microsystems. Java software is designed to run on any computer or computing device,

Java
Programming language that can deliver only the software functionality needed for a particular task, such as a small applet downloaded from a network; can run on any computer and operating system.

With visual programming tools, such as IBM's Visual Age Generator, working software programs can be created by drawing, pointing, and clicking instead of writing program code.

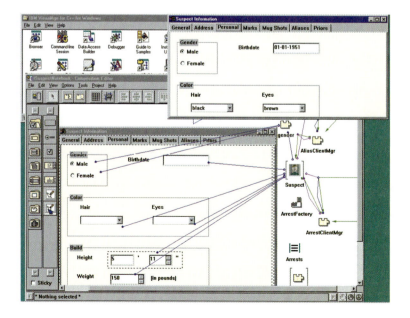

regardless of the specific microprocessor or operating system it uses. A Macintosh PC, an IBM PC running Windows, a Sun server running UNIX, and even a smart cellular phone or personal digital assistant can share the same Java application.

Java can be used to create miniature programs called "applets" designed to reside on centralized network servers. The network delivers only the applets required for a specific function. With Java applets residing on a network, a user can download only the software functions and data that he or she needs to perform a particular task, such as analyzing the revenue from one sales territory. The user does not need to maintain large software programs or data files on his or her desktop machine. When the user is finished with processing, the data can be saved through the network.

Java is also a very robust language that can handle text, data, graphics, sound, and video, all within one program if needed. Java applets often are used to provide interactive capabilities for Web pages. For example, Java applets can be used to create animated cartoons or real-time news tickers for a Web site, or to add a capability to a Web page to calculate a loan payment schedule on-line in response to financial data input by the user.

Companies are starting to develop more extensive Java applications running over the Internet or over their private networks because such applications can potentially run in Windows, UNIX, IBM mainframe, Macintosh, and other environments without having to be rewritten for each computing platform. Java can let PC users manipulate data on networked systems using Web browsers, reducing the need to write specialized software.

Despite these benefits, Java has not yet fulfilled its early promise to revolutionize software development and use. Programs written in current versions of Java tend to run slower than "native" programs, although high-performance versions of Java are under development (Pancake and Lengauer, 2001). Vendors such as Microsoft are supporting alternative versions of Java that include subtle differences that affect Java's performance in different pieces of hardware and operating systems.

HYPERTEXT MARKUP LANGUAGE (HTML) AND XML

Hypertext markup language (HTML) is a page description language for creating hypertext or hypermedia documents such as Web pages. (See the discussions of hypermedia in Chapter 7 and of Web pages in Chapter 9.) HTML uses instructions called *tags* to specify how text, graphics, video, and sound are placed on a document and to create dynamic links to other documents and objects stored in the same or remote computers. Using these links, a user need only point at a highlighted key word or graphic, click on it, and immediately be transported to another document.

HTML programs can be custom written, but they also can be created using the HTML authoring capabilities of Web browsers or of popular word processing, spreadsheet, data management, and presentation graphics software packages. HTML editors, such as Claris Home Page and Adobe PageMill, are more powerful HTML authoring tool programs for creating Web pages.

hypertext markup language (HTML)
Page description language for creating Web pages and other hypermedia documents.

XML

XML, which stands for **eXtensible Markup Language,** is a new specification originally designed to improve usefulness of Web documents. Whereas HTML only determines how text and images should be displayed on a Web document, XML describes what the data in these documents mean so the data can be used in computer programs. In XML, a number is not simply a number; the XML tag specifies whether the number represents a price, a date, or a ZIP code. Table 6-6 illustrates the differences between HTML and XML.

XML (eXtensible Markup Language)
General-purpose language that describes the structure of a document and supports links to multiple documents, allowing data to be manipulated by the computer. Used for both Web and non-Web applications.

TABLE 6-6	COMPARISON OF HTML AND XML	
Plain English	**HTML**	**XML**
Subcompact	<TITLE>Automobile</TITLE>	<AUTOMOBILETYPE="Subcompact">
4 passenger	<LI>4 passenger	<PASSENGER UNIT="PASS">4</PASSENGER>
$16,800	<LI>$16,800	<PRICE CURRENCY="USD">$16,800</PRICE>

HOW CAN XML HELP BUSINESSES?

In the fast-paced world of electronic commerce and electronic business, companies should benefit by being able to respond quickly to customers, partners, and suppliers. XML provides a new tool to accomplish this because it helps disparate applications identify and use a variety of information from otherwise incompatible sources.

Does XML really help a company? Clearly Fidelity Investments believes it does. Although many corporations are converting to XML one application at a time, Fidelity is taking a more confident and comprehensive approach, converting many programs and systems all at once. Fidelity believes that making a large investment in this technology will keep it ahead of competitors by simplifying communication between consumer Web applications and back-end systems.

XML is a common language for the translation of all corporate data, eliminating the need and time to translate data from one program or system to another. Such translations have particularly been a problem in linking data from legacy systems to Web systems. When a Fidelity customer requested a specific piece of data, that data had to go through up to six translations using some type of middleware. With the use of XML, Fidelity has been able to eliminate half of those translations so that customers can now obtain their data a little faster (only a matter of seconds, but nevertheless important seconds to persons waiting for a Web query response). Now, using XML, a single query is able to collect and manipulate data from multiple systems and sources of data. XML is not only making Fidelity customers happier, but it also is saving Fidelity money. Fidelity hopes to eliminate 75 percent of the hardware and software devoted to translating between systems and to develop applications more

rapidly by using XML technology. Programming staff that had been preoccupied with writing business interfaces can now focus on important business functions.

XML also is making it easier and cheaper for Fidelity to develop many of its new programs because, in many cases, new translation programs no longer need to be developed. Steve Elterich, who is Fidelity's e-business president, predicts that standardizing data on XML will reduce development time for a typical application by 25 percent. In one recent case, Fidelity developed a system that enabled 401K customers to access their accounts from handheld devices running the Palm operating system, and using XML saved the company 50 percent of its development time and cost.

Other companies are embracing XML as well, including companies in the computer industry and firms with complicated and distributed supply chains. XML offers a neutral method for exchanging data between two systems. For example, CrossMark Performance Group adopted XML to link 1,100 product manufacturers and more than 300 retail outlets. All incoming transactions are converted to XML, processed, and then sent back in the format used by the recipient. The company handles 1.5 million transactions each year, all in XML.

To Think About: How does XML support electronic commerce and electronic business? What technology, management, and organizational issues need to be addressed when adopting XML? How will Fidelity's commitment to XML likely affect its competitive situation, and why?

Sources: Jeffrey Schwartz, "Fidelity Pours Resources into XML," *InternetWeek.com,* August 6, 2001; Lucas Mearian, "Fidelity Makes Big XML Conversion," *Computerworld,* October 2001; and Andy Patrizio, "XML Passes from Development to Implementation," *InformationWeek.com,* March 26, 2001.

By tagging selected elements of the content of documents for their meanings, XML makes it possible for computers to automatically manipulate and interpret their data and perform operations on the data without human intervention. Web browsers and computer programs, such as order processing or ERP software, can follow programmed rules for applying and displaying the data. XML provides a standard format for data exchange.

XML is already becoming a serious technology for Web-based applications. The key to XML is the setting of standards (or vocabulary) that enable both sending and receiving parties to describe data the same way. Each standard is contained in an XML Document Type Definition (DTD), usually simply called a dictionary. For example, RosettaNet is an XML dictionary developed by 34 leading companies within the PC industry. It defines all properties of a personal computer, such as modems, monitors, and cache memory. As a result the entire PC industry is now able to speak the same language. The entire supply chain of the industry can now easily be linked without requiring business partners or customers to use a particular programming language, application, or operating system to exchange data. Companies can also use XML to help them and their suppliers access and manipulate their own internal data without high software development costs. The Window on Technology describes how some companies are benefiting from using XML.

6.6 MANAGING HARDWARE AND SOFTWARE ASSETS

Selection and use of computer hardware and software technology can have a profound impact on business performance. Computer hardware and software thus represent important organizational assets that must be properly managed. We now describe the most important issues in managing hardware and software technology assets: understanding the new technology requirements for electronic commerce and the digital firm; determining the total cost of ownership (TCO) of technology assets; and determining whether to own and maintain technology assets or use external technology service providers for the firm's IT infrastructure.

HARDWARE REQUIREMENTS FOR ELECTRONIC COMMERCE AND THE DIGITAL FIRM

Electronic commerce and electronic business are placing heavy new demands on hardware technology because organizations are replacing so many manual and paper-based processes with electronic ones. Much larger processing and storage resources are required to process and store the surging digital transactions flowing between different parts of the firm and between the firm and its customers and suppliers. Many people using a Web site simultaneously place great strains on a computer system, as does hosting large numbers of interactive Web pages with data-intensive graphics or video.

Capacity Planning and Scalability

Managers and information systems specialists now need to pay more attention to hardware capacity planning and scalability than they did in the past. **Capacity planning** is the process of predicting when a computer hardware system becomes saturated. It considers factors such as the maximum number of users that the system can accommodate at one time, the impact of existing and future software applications, and performance measures such as minimum response time for processing business transactions. Capacity planning ensures that the firm has enough computing power for its current and future needs. For example, the Nasdaq Stock Market performs ongoing capacity planning to identify peaks in the volume of stock trading transactions and to ensure it has enough computing capacity to handle large surges in volume when trading is very heavy.

> **capacity planning**
> The process of predicting when a computer hardware system becomes saturated to ensure that adequate computing resources are available for work of different priorities and that the firm has enough computing power for its current and future needs.

Although capacity planning is performed by information system specialists, input from business managers is essential. Business managers need to determine acceptable levels of computer response time and availability for the firm's mission-critical systems to maintain the level of business performance they expect. New applications, mergers and acquisitions, and changes in business volume will all impact computer workload and must be taken into account when planning hardware capacity.

Scalability refers to the ability of a computer, product, or system to expand to serve a large number of users without breaking down. Electronic commerce and electronic business both call for scalable IT infrastructures that have the capacity to grow with the business as the size of a Web site and number of visitors increase. Organizations must make sure they have sufficient computer processing, storage, and network resources to handle surging volumes of digital transactions and to make such data immediately available on-line.

> **scalability**
> The ability of a computer, product, or system to expand to serve a larger number of users without breaking down.

TOTAL COST OF OWNERSHIP (TCO) OF TECHNOLOGY ASSETS

The purchase and maintenance of computer hardware and software is but one of a series of cost components that managers must consider when selecting and managing hardware technology assets. The actual cost of owning technology resources includes the original cost of computers and software, hardware and software upgrades, maintenance, technical support, and training. The **total cost of ownership (TCO)** model can be used to analyze these direct and indirect costs to help firms determine the actual cost of specific technology implementations. The Manager's Toolkit describes the most important TCO components to help you perform a TCO analysis.

> **total cost of ownership (TCO)**
> Designates the total cost of owning technology resources, including initial purchase costs, the cost of hardware and software upgrades, maintenance, technical support, and training.

MIS IN ACTION DECISIONMAKING

CAPACITY PLANNING FOR ELECTRONIC COMMERCE
Your company implemented its own electronic commerce site using its own hardware and software, and business is growing rapidly. The company Web site has not experienced any outages, and customers are always able to have requests for information or purchase transactions processed very rapidly. Your information systems department has instituted a formal operations review program that continuously monitors key indicators of system usage that affect processing capacity and response time. The following report for management illustrates two of those indicators, daily CPU usage and daily I/O usage for the system. I/O usage measures the number of times a disk has been read.

Your server supports primarily U.S. customers who access the Web site during the day and early evening. I/O usage should be kept below 70 percent if the CPU is very busy so that the CPU does not waste machine cycles looking for data. I/O usage is high between 1 A.M. and 6 A.M. because the firm backs up its data stored on disk when the CPU is not busy.

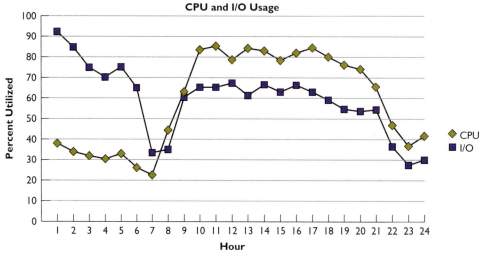

Daily CPU and I/O usage (hours are for U.S. Eastern Standard Time).

1. Anticipated e-commerce business over the next year is expected to increase CPU usage and I/O usage by 20 percent between 1:00 P.M. and 9:00 P.M. and by 10 percent during the rest of the day. Does your company have enough processing capacity to handle this increased load?

2. What would happen if your organization did not attend to capacity issues?

When all these cost components are considered, the TCO for a PC might run up to three times the original purchase price of the equipment. "Hidden costs" for support staff and additional network management can make distributed client/server architectures more expensive than centralized mainframe architectures.

RENT OR BUILD DECISIONS: USING TECHNOLOGY SERVICE PROVIDERS

Some of the most important questions facing managers are, "How should we acquire and maintain our technology assets? Should we build and run them ourselves or acquire them from outside sources?" In the past, most companies built and ran their own computer facilities and developed their own software. Today, more and more companies are obtaining their hardware and software technology from external service vendors. On-line services for storage and for running application software have become especially attractive options for many firms.

On-Line Storage Service Providers

storage service provider (SSP)
Third-party provider that rents out storage space to subscribers over the Web, allowing customers to store and access their data without having to purchase and maintain their own storage technology.

Some companies are using storage service providers (SSPs) to replace or supplement their own in-house storage infrastructure. A **storage service provider (SSP)** is a third-party provider that rents out storage space to subscribers over the Web. Storage service providers sell storage as a pay-per-use utility, allowing customers to store and access their data without

MIS IN ACTION   MANAGER'S TOOLKIT

HOW TO CALCULATE THE TOTAL COST OF OWNERSHIP (TCO) OF TECHNOLOGY ASSETS

In order to determine the total cost of ownership (TCO) of an organization's technology assets, you will need to calculate the cost of the following components:

Hardware acquisition: Purchase price of computer hardware equipment, including computers, terminals, storage, printers

Software acquisition: Purchase or license of software for each user

Installation: Costs to install computers and software

Training: Costs to provide training to information system specialists and end users

Support: Costs to provide ongoing technical support, help desks, and so forth

Maintenance: Costs to upgrade the hardware and software

Infrastructure: Costs to acquire, maintain, and support related infrastructure such as networks and specialized equipment (including storage backup units)

---

having to purchase and maintain their own storage infrastructure and storage support staff. To be successful SSPs must offer very high availability and reliability and also must keep up with the latest technology. SSPs are responsible for monitoring the stored data and for managing their own capacity, response time, and reliability.

Application Service Providers (ASPs)

Section 6.3 described hardware capabilities for providing data and software programs to desktop computers over networks. It is clear that software will be increasingly delivered and used over networks. On-line application service providers (ASPs) are springing up to provide these software services over the Web and over private networks. An **application service provider (ASP)** is a business that delivers and manages applications and computer services from remote computer centers to multiple users via the Internet or a private network. Instead of buying and installing software programs, subscribing companies can rent the same functions from these services. Users pay for the use of this software either on a subscription or per transaction basis. The ASP's solution combines package software applications and all of the related hardware, system software, network, and other infrastructure services that the customer would have to purchase, integrate, and manage on his or her own. The ASP customer interacts with a single entity instead of an array of technologies and service vendors.

The "timesharing" services of the 1970s, which ran applications such as payroll on their computers for other companies, were an earlier version of this application hosting. But today's ASPs run a wider array of applications than these earlier services and deliver many of these software services over the Web. At Web-based services, servers perform the bulk of the processing and the only essential program needed by users is their Web browser. Large and medium-size businesses are using ASPs for enterprise systems, sales force automation, or financial management, and small businesses are using them for functions such as invoicing, tax calculations, electronic calendars, and accounting.

Companies are turning to this "software utility" model as an alternative to developing their own software. Some companies will find it much easier to "rent" software from another firm and avoid the expense and difficulty of installing, operating, and maintaining complex systems, such as enterprise resource planning (ERP). The ASP contracts guarantee a level of service and support to make sure that the software is available and working at all times. Today's Internet-driven business environment is changing so rapidly that getting a system up and running in three months instead of six could mean the difference between success and failure. Application service providers also enable small and medium-size companies to use applications that they otherwise could not afford.

Companies considering the software utility model need to carefully assess application service provider costs and benefits, weighing all management, organizational, and technology issues. In some cases, the cost of renting software can add up to more than purchasing and maintaining the application in-house. Yet there may be benefits to paying more for software through an ASP if this decision allows the company to focus on core business issues instead of technology challenges. More detail on application service providers can be found in the chapter ending case study and in Chapter 12.

application service provider (ASP)
Company providing software that can be rented by other companies over the Web or a private network.

MAKE IT YOUR BUSINESS

FINANCE AND ACCOUNTING

One of the earliest tasks assigned computers was to automate calculations for finance and accounting, and these functions have remained high-priority targets for computerization. Many application software packages for individuals as well as for large businesses support financial processes such as corporate accounting, tax calculations, payroll processing, or investment planning. Calculating the Total Cost of Ownership (TCO) of technology assets requires models and expertise supplied by finance and accounting. You can find examples of finance and accounting applications on pages 190, 206, and 215–216.

HUMAN RESOURCES

Hardware and software technologies are changing very rapidly, providing many new productivity tools to employees and powerful software package and services for the Human Resources department. Employees will need frequent retraining in order to use these tools effectively. You can find examples of human resources applications on pages 176–178.

MANUFACTURING AND PRODUCTION

Many manufacturing applications are based on client/server networks, which use networked computers to control the flow of work on the factory floor. Handheld computers and bar code scanners are widely used to track items in inventory and to track package shipments. XML provides a set of standards through which all systems of participants in an industry supply chain can exchange data with each other without high expenditures for specialized translation programs and middleware. You can find examples of manufacturing and production applications on pages 190, 206, and 215–216.

SALES AND MARKETING

Sales and marketing has benefited from hardware and software technologies that provide customers and sales staff with rapid access to information, responses to customer questions, and order-taking. Web browser software provides an easy-to-use interface for accessing product information or placing orders over the Web, while e-mail software is a quick and inexpensive tool for answering customer queries. Web sites can be enhanced with Java applets that allow users to perform calculations or view interactive product demonstrations using standard Web browser software.

Other Types of Service Providers

Other types of specialized service providers provide additional resources for helping organizations manage their technology assets. *Management service providers* can be enlisted to manage combinations of applications, networks, storage, and security as well as to provide Web site and systems performance monitoring. *Business continuity service providers* offer disaster recovery and continuous Web availability services to help firms continue essential operations when their systems malfunction (see Chapter 14). Table 6-7 provides examples of the major types of technology service providers.

TABLE 6-7   EXAMPLES OF TECHNOLOGY SERVICE PROVIDERS

Type of Service Provider	Description	Example
Storage service provider	Provides on-line access over networks to storage devices and storage area network technology.	IBM On-Demand storage services range from $25 to $75 per gigabyte per month.
Application service provider	Uses centrally managed facilities to host and manage access to package applications delivered over networks on a subscription basis.	Corio Inc., which offers a suite of hosted enterprise application software, charges $70 to $100 per user per month to host the ChangePoint professional services application.
Management service provider	Manages combinations of applications, networks, systems, storage, and security as well as providing Web site and systems performance monitoring to subscribers over the Internet.	Vendors include Nuclio, Silverback, Totality, Tractive, and SiteRock. Monthly charges range from several thousand dollars to more than $100,000.
Business continuity service provider	Defines and documents procedures for planning and recovering from system malfunctions that threaten vital business operations.	Comdisco disaster recovery, rapid recovery, and continuous Web availability services range from $10,000 to $100,000 per month.

MANAGEMENT WRAP-UP

Managers should know how to select and manage the organization's hardware and software assets in the firm's information technology (IT) infrastructure. General managers should understand the costs and capabilities of various hardware and software technologies and should understand the advantages and disadvantages of building and owning these assets or of renting them from outside services.

Computer hardware and software technology can either enhance or impede organizational performance. Computer hardware and software selection should be based on organizational and business needs, considering how well the technology meshes with the organization's culture and structure as well as information-processing requirements. Hardware and software services provided by outside vendors should fit into organizational computing plans.

A range of hardware and software technologies is available to organizations. Organizations have many computer processing options to choose from, including mainframes, workstations, PCs, and network computers, and many different ways of configuring hardware components to create systems. Firms can also select among alternative operating systems and application software tools. Key technology decisions include the appropriateness of the hardware or software for the problem to be addressed and compatibility with other components of the firm's IT infrastructure.

For Discussion

1. Why is selecting computer hardware and software for the organization an important management decision? What management, organization, and technology issues should be considered when selecting computer hardware?

2. Should organizations use application service providers (ASPs) and storage service providers (SSPs) for all their software and storage needs? Why or why not? What management, organization, and technology factors should be considered when making this decision?

SUMMARY

1. *What computer processing and storage capability does our organization need to handle its information and business transactions?* Managers should understand the alternative computer hardware technologies available for processing and storing information so that they can select the right technologies for their business. Modern computer systems have six major components: a central processing unit (CPU), primary storage, input devices, output devices, secondary storage, and communications devices. All of these components need to work together to process information for the organization. The CPU is the part of the computer where the manipulation of symbols, numbers, and letters occurs. The CPU has two components: an arithmetic-logic unit and a control unit.

The CPU is closely tied to primary memory, or primary storage, which stores data and program instructions temporarily before and after processing. Several different kinds of semiconductor memory chips are used with primary storage: RAM (random access memory) is used for short-term storage of data and program instructions; and ROM (read-only memory) permanently stores important program instructions.

Computer processing power depends in part on the speed of microprocessors, which integrate the computer's logic and control on a single chip. Microprocessor capabilities can be gauged by their word length, data bus width, and cycle speed. Most conventional computers process one instruction at a time, but computers with parallel processing can process multiple instructions simultaneously.

The principal secondary storage technologies are magnetic disk, optical disk, and magnetic tape. Disk permits direct access to specific records and is much faster than tape. Disk technology is used in on-line processing. Optical disks can store vast amounts of data compactly. CD-ROM disk systems can only be read from, but rewritable optical disk systems are becoming available. Magnetic tape stores records in sequence and only can be used in batch processing.

The principal input devices are keyboards, computer mice, touch screens, magnetic ink and optical character recognition, pen-based instruments, digital scanners, sensors, and voice input. The principal output devices are video display terminals, printers, plotters, voice output devices, and microfilm and microfiche. In batch processing, transactions are accumulated and stored in a group until the time when it is efficient or necessary to process them. In on-line processing, the user enters transactions into a device that is directly connected to the computer system. The transactions are usually processed immediately. Multimedia integrates two or more types of media, such as text, graphics, sound, voice, full-motion video, still video, and/or animation into a computer-based application.

2. *What arrangement of computers and computer processing would best benefit our organization?* Managers should understand the capabilities of various categories of computers and arrangements of computer processing. The type of computer and arrangement of processing power that should be used by the business depends on the nature of the organization and its problems.

Computers are categorized as mainframes, midrange computers, PCs, workstations, or supercomputers. Mainframes are the largest computers; midrange computers can be minicomputers used in factory, university, or research lab systems or servers providing software and other resources to computers on a network. PCs are desktop or laptop machines; workstations are desktop machines with powerful mathematical and graphic capabilities; and supercomputers are sophisticated, powerful computers that can perform massive and complex computations rapidly. Because of continuing advances in microprocessor technology, the distinctions between these types of computers are constantly changing.

Computers can be networked together to distribute processing among different machines. In the client/server model of computing, computer processing is split between "clients" and "servers" connected via a network. The exact division of tasks between client and server depends on the application. Network computers are pared-down desktop machines with minimal or no local storage and processing capacity. They obtain most or all of their software and data from a central network server. Whereas network computers help organizations maintain central control over computing, peer-to-peer computing puts processing power back on users' desktops, linking individual PCs, workstations, or other computers through the Internet or private networks to share data, disk space, and processing power for a variety of tasks.

3. *What kinds of software and software tools do we need to run our business? What criteria should we use to select our software technology?* Managers should understand the capabilities of various types of software so they can select software technologies that provide the greatest benefit for their firms. There are two major types of software: system software and application software. System software coordinates the various parts of the computer system and mediates between application software and computer hardware. Application software is used by application programmers and some end users to develop specific business applications.

The system software that manages and controls the activities of the computer is called the operating system. The operating system acts as the chief manager of the information system, allocating, assigning, and scheduling system resources and monitoring the use of the computer. Multiprogramming, multitasking, virtual storage, time sharing, and multiprocessing are operating system capabilities that enable system resources to be used more efficiently so that the computer can attack many problems at the same time. Other system software includes computer-language translation programs that convert programming languages into machine language and utility programs that perform common processing tasks.

PC operating systems have developed sophisticated capabilities such as multitasking and support for multiple users on networks. Leading PC operating systems include Windows XP, Windows 98 and Windows Me; Windows 2000, Windows CE, UNIX, Linux, OS/2, Mac OS, and DOS. PC operating systems and many kinds of application software now use graphical user interfaces.

The general trend in software is toward user-friendly, high-level languages that both increase professional programmer productivity and make it possible for end users to work directly with information systems. Conventional programming languages include assembly language, FORTRAN, COBOL, BASIC and Pascal, and C, and each is designed to solve specific types of problems. Fourth-generation languages are less procedural than conventional programming languages and enable end users to perform many software tasks that previously required technical specialists. They include popular PC software tools such as word processing, spreadsheet, data management, presentation graphics, and e-mail software along with Web browsers and groupware. Enterprise software, middleware, and enterprise application integration software are all software tools for promoting enterprise-wide integration of business processes and information system applications.

Software selection should be based on criteria such as efficiency, compatibility with the organization's technology platform, vendor support, and whether the software tool is appropriate for the problems and tasks of the organization.

4. *Of what new software technologies should we be aware? How would they benefit our organization?* Object-oriented programming tools and new programming languages such as Java, hypertext markup language (HTML), and eXtensible Markup Language (XML) can help firms create software more rapidly and efficiently and produce applications based on the Internet or data in Web sites. Object-oriented programming combines data and procedures into one object, which can act as an independent software building block. Each object can be used in many different systems without changing program code.

Java is an object-oriented programming language designed to operate on the Internet. It can deliver precisely the software functionality needed for a particular task as a small applet that is downloaded from a network. Java can run on any computer and operating system. HTML is a page description language for creating Web pages. XML is a language for creating structured documents in which data are tagged for meanings. The tagged data in XML documents and Web pages can be manipulated and used by other computer systems. XML can thus be used to exchange data between Web sites and different legacy systems within a firm and between the systems of different partners in a supply chain.

5. *How should we acquire and manage the firm's hardware and software assets?* Both hardware and software are major organizational assets that must be carefully managed. Electronic commerce and electronic business have put new strategic emphasis on technologies that can store vast quantities of transaction data and make them immediately available on-line. Managers and information systems specialists need to pay special attention to hardware capacity planning and scalability to ensure that the firm has enough computing power for its current and future needs.

They also need to balance the costs and benefits of owning and maintaining their own hardware and software or renting these assets from external service providers. On-line storage service providers (SSPs) rent out storage space to subscribers over the Web, selling computer storage as a pay-per-use utility. Application service providers (ASPs) rent out software applications and computer services from remote computer centers to subscribers over the Internet or private networks.

Calculating the total cost of ownership (TCO) of the organization's technology assets can help provide managers with the information they need to manage these assets and decide whether to rent or own these assets. The total cost of owning technology resources includes not only the original cost of computer hardware and software but also costs for hardware and software upgrades, maintenance, technical support, and training.

KEY TERMS

Application service provider (ASP), 209

Application software, 190

Arithmetic-logic unit (ALU), 180

Assembly language, 195

Batch processing, 185

Bit, 179

Byte, 179

C, 196

C++, 196

Capacity planning, 207

CD-ROM (compact disk read-only memory), 183

Central processing unit (CPU), 179

Centralized processing, 188

Client, 189

Client/server computing, 188

COBOL (COmmon Business Oriented Language), 196

Compiler, 193

Control unit, 180

Data management software, 199

Digital video disk (DVD), 183

Distributed processing, 188

Downsizing, 189

Electronic mail (e-mail), 200

Enterprise application integration software, 202

Enterprise software, 202

Floppy disk, 183

FORTRAN (FORmula TRANslator), 196

Fourth-generation language, 197

Gigabyte, 181

Graphical user interface (GUI), 193

Groupware, 201

Hard disk, 183

Hypertext markup language (HTML), 205

Integrated software package, 199

Java, 204

Kilobyte, 181

Linux, 194

Machine cycle, 180

Machine language, 195

Magnetic disk, 183

Magnetic tape, 184

Mainframe, 187

Massively parallel computers, 182

Master file, 186

Megabyte, 181

Megahertz, 181

Microprocessor, 181

Middleware, 202

Midrange computer, 187

Minicomputer, 187

MP3 (MPEG3), 187

Multimedia, 186

Multiprocessing, 192

Multiprogramming, 191

Multitasking, 192

Nanosecond, 180

Natural language, 197

Network computer (NC), 189

Object-oriented programming, 203

Office 2000 and Office XP, 200

On-line processing, 186

Open-source software, 194

Operating system, 191

Parallel processing, 182

Peer-to-peer computing, 189

Personal computer (PC), 188

Presentation graphics, 199

Primary storage, 179

Program, 190

Query language, 197

RAID (Redundant Array of Inexpensive Disks), 183

RAM (random access memory), 180

Reduced instruction set computing (RISC), 182

ROM (read-only memory), 181

Scalability, 207

Secondary storage, 182

Server, 187

Server farm, 188

Software package, 197

Source code, 193

Spreadsheet, 198

Storage area network (SAN), 184

Storage service provider (SSP), 208

Streaming technology, 186

Supercomputer, 188

System software, 190

Terabyte, 181

Time sharing, 192

Total cost of ownership (TCO), 207

Transaction file, 186

UNIX, 194

Virtual storage, 192

Visual programming, 203

Web browser, 201

Web server, 202

Windows 2000, 194

Windows 98, 194

Windows Millennium Edition (Windows Me), 194

Windows XP, 194

Workstation, 188

XML (eXtensible Markup Language), 205

Review Questions

1. What are the components of a contemporary computer system?

2. Distinguish between a bit and a byte, and describe how information is stored in primary memory.

3. Name the major components of the CPU and the function of each.

4. Name and describe the factors affecting a microprocessor's speed and performance

5. Distinguish between serial, parallel, and massively parallel processing.

6. List the most important secondary storage media. What are the strengths and limitations of each?

7. List and describe the major computer input and output devices.

8. What is the difference between batch and on-line processing? Diagram the difference.

9. What is multimedia? What technologies are involved?

10. What is the difference between a mainframe, a midrange computer, a server, and a PC? Between a PC and a workstation?

11. Compare the client/server, network computer, and peer-to-peer models of computing.

12. What are the major types of software? How do they differ in terms of users and uses?

13. What is the operating system of a computer? What does it do? What role do multiprogramming, virtual storage, time sharing, and multiprocessing play in the operation of an information system?

14. List and describe the major PC operating systems.

15. List and describe the major application programming languages. How do they differ from fourth-generation languages?

16. Name and describe the most important PC software tools.

17. Name and describe the kinds of software that can be used for enterprise integration.

18. What is object-oriented programming? How does it differ from conventional software development?

19. What are Java, HTML, and XML? Compare their capabilities. Why are they becoming important?

20. List and describe the principal issues in managing hardware and software assets.

Application Software Exercise

SPREADSHEET EXERCISE: EVALUATING COMPUTER HARDWARE AND SOFTWARE OPTIONS

You have been asked to obtain pricing information on hardware and software for an office of 30 people. Using the Internet, get pricing for 30 PC desktop systems (monitor, computer, and keyboard) manufactured by IBM, Dell, and Compaq as listed at their respective corporate Web sites. (For the purposes of this exercise, ignore the fact that desktop systems usually come with pre-loaded software packages). Also get pricing on 15 monochrome desktop printers manufactured by Hewlett Packard and by Xerox. Each desktop system must satisfy the minimum specifications shown in Table 1 below:

TABLE 1

MINIMUM DESKTOP SPECIFICATIONS

Processor speed (in gigahertz)	1.5 GHz
Hard Drive (in gigabytes)	20 GB
RAM (in megabytes)	128 MB
CD-ROM speed	48 speed
Monitor (diagonal measurement)	17 inches

Each desktop printer must satisfy the minimum specifications shown in the following table.

TABLE 2

MINIMUM MONOCHROME PRINTER SPECIFICATIONS

Print speed (pages per minute)	12
Print quality	600 × 600
Network ready?	Yes
Maximum price/unit	$1000

After getting pricing on the desktop systems and printers, obtain pricing on 30 copies of Microsoft's Office XP, Corel's WordPerfect Office 2002, and IBM's Lotus SmartSuite application packages and on 30 copies of Microsoft Windows XP Professional edition. The application software suite packages come in various versions, so be sure that each package contains programs for word processing, spreadsheet analysis, database analysis, graphics preparation, and e-mail.

Prepare a spreadsheet showing your research results for the desktop systems, for the printers, and for the software. Use your spreadsheet software to determine the desktop system, printer, and software combination that will offer both the best performance and pricing per worker. Since every two workers will share one printer (15 printers/30 systems), assume only half a printer cost per worker. Assume also that your company will take the standard warranty and servicing contract offered by each product's manufacturer.

GROUP PROJECT

Which is the better Internet software tool, Internet Explorer or Netscape Communicator? Your instructor will divide the class into two groups to research this question. Each group will present their findings to the class. To prepare your analysis, use articles from computer magazines and the Web, and examine the software's features and capabilities.

TOOLS FOR INTERACTIVE LEARNING

■ INTERNET CONNECTION

The Internet Connection for this chapter will direct you to a series of Web sites where you can complete an exercise to survey the products and services of major computer hardware vendors and the use of Web sites in the computer hardware industry. You can also use the Interactive Study Guide to test your knowledge of the topics in this chapter and get instant feedback where you need more practice.

■ ELECTRONIC BUSINESS PROJECT

At the Laudon Web site for Chapter 6, you will find an Electronic Business Project for salesforce budgeting.

■ CD-ROM

If you use the Multimedia Edition CD-ROM with this chapter, you can find a video clip by Intel showing the evolution of computer hardware, an audio overview of the key themes of this chapter, and bullet text summarizing the key points of the chapter.

CASE STUDY—*Enerline Turns to an ASP*

The oil and gas industries have always had to face an expensive and time-wasting problem—failure of the pipes used in the drilling and pumping of oil as well as in the pipelines used to transport the oil from the well to another place. The cost of replacing them is extremely high, entailing the cost of new pipes, excavation, labor, and most important of all, downtime. Other industries, such as water utilities and companies that produce industrial waste, also face the problem. In 1995 Enerline Restorations, Inc., of Calgary, Canada, was founded specifically to meet this market need.

The company currently produces three products: EnerCore for lining downhole tubes, EnerLiner for lining pipelines, and EnerBore, for lining casings. At first Enerline products were manufactured in Calgary, but in 2000 the firm opened a newly constructed manufacturing plant in Stettler, Alberta. Enerline started by selling its products in the major oil-producing areas of Alberta, where Calgary is located, and nearby Saskatchewan. It reached an agreement with C. E. Franklin to distribute its products through Franklin's 40 Western Canada locations. Because of the quality and cost effectiveness of its products, Enerline's sales took off and its products now sell in the United States, South America, Europe, and even Africa. However, start-up is normally slow and difficult, and Enerline is actually still a very small company.

In May 1996, when Enerline began to sell its products, it had only three employees, and its sales were only about $2 million (Canadian). Sales topped $7 million in the year 2000, a triple-digit growth rate. In 1998, when Enerline had expanded to 30 employees, Ron Hozjan joined the company as chief financial officer. Hozjan reported to Graham Illingworth, the president of Enerline, and to the five-member board of directors; all other employees reported to Hozjan. Hozjan was explicitly assigned to making the company more efficient and competitive, and the overall business of the company became his responsibility.

Given its rapid growth and the increased number of employees, Enerline needed more computerization. It had only one office that housed all of its employees and a single stand-alone desktop computer running the Microsoft Office PC productivity tools, a small accounting package, and on-line banking software. Inventory reports, reports informing customers of delivery schedules, timely production reports, and other essential tasks were both difficult to accomplish and very time consuming. For example, 40- to 80-page weekly production reports had to be faxed to Calgary where they were then keyed into a spreadsheet, a time-consuming and error-prone process. "If you hold up a customer for a few hours, you'll lose them forever," explained Hozjan. "An idle service rig or a well that's not fully productive can cost an oil and gas producer thousands or millions of dollars every day. We can't afford to keep them waiting." As demand for its money-saving products grew, it became more and more difficult for Enerline to satisfy its customers. To continue its growth, it became obvious that Enerline had no choice but to upgrade its information systems and information technology infrastructure.

Computerization can be very expensive, and a company as new and as small as Enerline needed to concentrate its assets on growing the business—marketing, sales, production, and research. Building the necessary IT infrastructure meant not only purchasing six or more desktop computers and server hardware and software, it also meant purchasing business and communications software and hardware, obtaining access to the Internet and a Web site, and installing computer backup facilities and security software. In addition Enerline would require hiring new staff to support the system and time to train them. Hozjan determined that the cost during the first year would be $80,000, an amount that should increase every year as the company grew. Hozjan did not want to commit so much of his company's limited resources to support when growth was the critical issue. He began to look around for an alternative, one that met most if not all of his requirements. He wanted to find a company that would supply his hardware, software, and communications needs, as well as give his company maintenance, backup, and full-time support. He also wanted consulting services whenever Enerline needed them. Finally, because his company was gaining customers on four continents, he wanted his services to be accessed over the Internet. He believed he found the solution in an application service provider (ASP).

An ASP manages applications and computer services for clients from its own site, delivering these services over the Web or over private networks. ASPs normally not only own the software and hardware but also manage the systems. They either charge the client a per-transaction fee or a set monthly fee. Hozjan later pointed out that the ASP computing model helped his firm quickly improve its market position and prepared it to serve new, larger and more geographically dispersed customers. Enerline was given a state-of-the-art infrastructure that it did not have to worry about so it could focus exclusively on serving customers. The ASP field only began about the same time as Enerline was founded, and so very few such companies were yet established. Hozjan's choice was further limited because he much preferred a Canadian-based firm, which would have made it easier for the two companies to work together. He really only had one Canadian company to look at, and that company was FutureLink.

Happily for Hozjan, FutureLink met most of Enerline's requirements. It was already supporting mission-critical systems for several other companies, it enabled its customers to work over the Internet, it gave what it called 24/7 free support, and it even guaranteed 99.8 percent uptime in its contract. In addition it had six offices already operating around Canada. Hozjan found that FutureLink was flexible and easy to work with. The biggest problem Enerline had was finding an appropriate accounting system. Hozjan wanted one that had a good reputation and was designed for the oil and gas industries. He finally selected PriceWaterhouseCooper's Qbyte system, and FutureLink had no problem installing it and then supporting it.

Enerline was up and running on the FutureLink system within 30 days. The software it had selected included Qbyte as well as Microsoft Office, Outlook, and Internet services. The company had no start-up costs (except for some time from its own staff)—Enerline did not have to pay FutureLink any start-up costs. However, it did have to sign a three-year contract for the services. Its cost was $1,800 a month for the first year, for a total of $21,000, and $1,600 per month for the remaining two years, totaling $38,400 for those two years, amounting to a three-year total of $60,000. The costs were to be paid out on a monthly basis, instead of paying $80,000 in the first year alone if Enerline had built its own systems.

FutureLink also helped Enerline set up a Web site where customers could find out where their tubulars were in the production cycle and visualize the progress of their pipelining projects. Customers could also submit questions about their projects through this Web site and receive rapid project quotes from Enerline.

Hozjan was pleased that Enerline scaled up from one to six computers overnight without any capital expenditures and has access to better technology than some companies five to ten times its size in Alberta. Hozjan also said "We have phenomenal access to technology for a company our size with our budget." Enerline was recently awarded a project in Africa that probably wouldn't have been available without the ASP approach. Employees are able to work much more efficiently. Production reporting and quotes are now done on-line and so are never faxed or re-keyed. Production decisions are made much more easily, quickly, and accurately because of the information that is readily available. And customers can simply go on-line and obtain the information they need immediately and with little effort.

A major problem in relying on FutureLink emerged in September 1999, only seven months after Enerline had begun operating its computer systems through FutureLink. Cameron Shell, FutureLink's founder and at that time its president, informed Hozjan that FutureLink was facing major financial adversity, although Shell assured Hozjan it would not affect FutureLink's service to Enerline. FutureLink was experiencing serious losses, and these losses were actually increasing as competition in the ASP business also grew. FutureLink's financial difficulty was a complete surprise to Hozjan. Two months later FutureLink merged with Citrix iBusiness, an ASP company headquartered in Irvine, California. Most of the FutureLink employees were replaced by Citrix employees, and even Shell left. In the year 2000 FutureLink's losses continued to grow. Hozjan noted that although 1999 had been a bad year for FutureLink, Enerline was still receiving reliable service, and the new management was still agreeable to changes that were requested in Enerline's business agreement. In the spring of 2001 FutureLink underwent a major restructuring and moved out of the ASP market in the United States. Hozjan expressed concern about their ability to continue serving Enerline. "They're basically our IT department," he said.

Sources: Evan Koblentz, "ASP Shakeout Could Benefit Buyers," *eWEEK*, April 8, 2001; www.citrix.com/ibusiness/profiles/enerline. htm; www.enerline.com; www.futurelink.ca/case_studies/case_ studies1/enerline.asp; tietovayla.fi/citrix/Citrix/section6/Enerline_ CustomerStory.pdf; http://www.charon.com/case_studies/downloads/ Enerline.pdf; and Jane Movold and Scott Sschneberger, "Enerline Restorations Inc: Stay with an ASP?" Richard Ivey School of Business, University of Western Ontario, 2000.

CASE STUDY QUESTIONS

1. Analyze Enerline and its business strategy using the competitive forces and value chain models. How well did Enerline's information systems support its business model and strategy?

2. Why was Hozjan concerned with computer system issues when the company had no real competition?

3. Why did Hozjan turn to working with an ASP? Was this a good decision? Identify the issues that were involved in this decision. What were the potential benefits of working with an ASP? The potential problems?

4. Was FutureLink a good choice of ASP for Enerline? Should Enerline continue working with FutureLink? Describe the implications of the changes in FutureLink's business plans for Enerline.

5. If Enerline decides to sever ties with FutureLink, should it switch to another ASP or build its own IT infrastructure? What management, organization, and technology issues should be addressed in answering this question?

7 MANAGING DATA RESOURCES

As a manager, you'll want to know how to organize your company's data so that they can be easily accessed and utilized. After completing this chapter, you will be able to answer the following questions:

1. *Why do businesses have trouble finding the information they need in their information systems?*

2. *How does a database management system help businesses improve the organization of their information?*

3. *How do the principal types of database models affect the way businesses can access and use information?*

4. *What are the managerial and organizational requirements of a database environment?*

5. *What new tools and technologies can make databases more accessible and useful?*

Chico's Revitalizes with Better Customer Data

Chico's FAS Inc. has come up with a successful retailing formula: provide loose, comfortable fashions for women between the ages of 40 and 60, a population group that is swelling with baby boomers. Over the past two decades Chico's has mushroomed into a 250-store chain with a loyal customer following. Loyal, that is, until Chico's stores started stocking trendy new fashions. Lacking any detailed information about customer preferences or behavior, Chico's managers and designers began experimenting with items that could only be worn by younger more slightly built women. Sales took a nosedive.

To find better information on what its customers wanted, Chico's launched a customer relationship management (CRM) program and revitalized a frequent-shopper loyalty program to boost the buying frequency of its best customers.

Chico's had tried earlier to find out more about its core customers and their buying preferences. In the early 1990s, it launched its Passport loyalty program, which offered a 5 percent discount to women who spent more than $500 each year. But the information provided by this system was of little use. Chico's had been managing its customer data using an older "flat" file management system running on an IBM AS/400 midrange computer. The way the data were arranged did not allow Chico's to analyze its sales transaction data to find out how many or what kinds of items were sold to which customers in which locations. Chico's obtained so few benefits from this customer loyalty program that it dropped it during the mid-1990s.

The company decided to revive Passport when it started a major growth campaign in 1998, with plans to open 60 new stores each year. Resurrecting Passport was part of a larger CRM initiative to find out more about Chico's better cus-

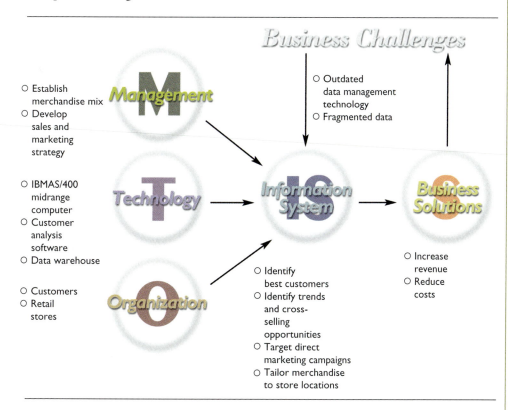

tomers. Chico's created a giant customer database in a data warehouse, where it can analyze its customer database to find its best clients, identify buying trends and cross-selling opportunities, and launch direct mail marketing campaigns. STS Systems of Montreal supplied the CRM software for this purpose. The data warehouse now includes data on 1.7 million customers, collected from in-store sales and other channels such as Chico's Web site and call center.

Since the data warehouse went live, Chico's has increased the number of customers eligible for the Passport loyalty program from 30,000 to 260,000. This group accounts for more than 58 percent of Chico's total sales. By learning how to tailor its merchandise and customer loyalty programs to its most profitable customers, Chico's has successfully run 22 targeted promotional campaigns to increase the purchasing frequency of its best customers. Each month it mails these good customers and promising sales prospects glossy catalogs that showcase Chico's new fashions and provide coupons offering 50 percent discounts when a customer spends a minimum of $100. Chico's also uses the customer database to help determine where to locate new stores and to decide which merchandise to stock in which locations based on purchasing patterns in each geographic area. According to Bari Horton, Chico's director of direct marketing, "Our numbers show that we're talking to the right customer at the right time. Chico's revenue climbed by 45 percent to $155 million in fiscal 2000 and to $186 million in the first nine months of fiscal 2001.

Sources: Beth Stackpole, "Chico's Fashions a New Plan," *eWEEK*, May 27, 2001 and Carol Sliwa, "Chico's IT Goes Up in Size," *Computerworld*, March 12, 2001.

MANAGEMENT CHALLENGES

Chico's experience illustrates how much the effective use of information depends on how data are stored, organized, and accessed. Proper delivery of information not only depends on the capabilities of computer hardware and software but also on the organization's ability to manage data as an important resource. Chico's inability to assemble the customer data required for identifying the buying patterns and interests of profitable customers led to inaccurate and inefficient sales, and marketing processes that impaired organizational performance. It has been very difficult for organizations to manage their data effectively. Two challenges stand out.

1. **Organizational obstacles to a database environment.** Implementing a database requires widespread organizational change in the role of information (and information managers), the allocation of power at senior levels, the ownership and sharing of information, and patterns of organizational agreement. A database management system (DBMS) challenges the existing power arrangements in an organization and for that reason often generates political resistance. In a traditional file environment, each department constructed files and programs to fulfill its specific needs. Now, with a database, files and programs must be built that take into account the full organization's interest in data. Although the organization has spent the money on hardware and software for a database environment, it may not reap the benefits it should if it is unwilling to make the requisite organizational changes.

2. **Cost/benefit considerations.** The costs of moving to a database environment are tangible, up front, and large in the short term (three years). Most firms buy a commercial DBMS package and related hardware. The software alone can cost $0.5 million for a full-function package with all options. New hardware may cost an additional $1 million to $2 million. Designing an enterprise-wide database that integrates all the organization's data can be a lengthy and costly process. It soon becomes apparent to senior management that a database system is a huge investment.

Unfortunately, the benefits of the DBMS are often intangible, back loaded, and long term (five years). Many millions of dollars have been spent over the years designing and maintaining existing systems. People in the organization understand the existing system after long periods of training and socialization. For these reasons, and despite the clear advantages of the DBMS, the short-term costs of developing a DBMS often appear to be as great as the benefits. Managers, especially those unfamiliar with (and perhaps unfriendly to) systems, tend to severely discount the obvious long-term benefits of the DBMS.

This chapter examines the managerial and organizational requirements as well as the technologies for managing data as a resource. Organizations need to manage their data assets very carefully to make sure that the data can be easily accessed and used by managers and employees across the organization. First we describe the typical challenges facing businesses trying to access information using traditional file management technologies. Then we describe the technology of database management systems, which can overcome many of the drawbacks of traditional file management and provide the firmwide integration of information required for digital firm applications. We include a discussion of the managerial and organizational requirements for successfully implementing a database environment.

7.1   ORGANIZING DATA IN A TRADITIONAL FILE ENVIRONMENT

An effective information system provides users with timely, accurate, and relevant information. This information is stored in computer files. When the files are properly arranged and maintained, users can easily access and retrieve the information they need. Well-managed, carefully arranged files make it easy to obtain data for business decisions, whereas poorly managed files lead to chaos in information processing, high costs, poor performance, and little, if any, flexibility. Despite the use of excellent hardware and software, many organizations have inefficient information systems because of poor file management. In this section we describe the traditional methods that organizations have used to arrange data in computer files. We also discuss the problems with these methods.

FILE ORGANIZATION TERMS AND CONCEPTS

A computer system organizes data in a hierarchy that starts with bits and bytes and progresses to fields, records, files, and databases (see Figure 7-1). A bit represents the smallest unit of data a computer can handle. A group of bits, called a byte, represents a single character, which can be a letter, a number, or another symbol. A grouping of characters into a word, a group of words, or a complete number (such as a person's name or age) is called a **field**. A group of related fields, such as the student's name, the course taken, the date, and the grade, comprises a **record**; a group of records of the same type is called a **file**. For instance, the student records in Figure 7-1 could constitute a course file. A group of related files makes up a **database**. The student course file illustrated in Figure 7-1 could be grouped with files on students' personal histories and financial backgrounds to create a student database.

A record describes an entity. An **entity** is a person, place, thing, or event on which we maintain information. An order is a typical entity in a sales order file, which maintains information on a firm's sales orders. Each characteristic or quality describing a particular entity is called an **attribute**. For example, order number, order date, order amount, item number, and item quantity would each be an attribute of the entity order. The specific values that these attributes can have can be found in the fields of the record describing the entity order (see Figure 7-2).

Every record in a file should contain at least one field that uniquely identifies that record so that the record can be retrieved, updated, or sorted. This identifier field is called a **key field**. An example of a key field is the order number for the order record illustrated in Figure 7-2 or an employee number or social security number for a personnel record (containing employee data such as the employee's name, age, address, job title, and so forth).

PROBLEMS WITH THE TRADITIONAL FILE ENVIRONMENT

In most organizations, systems tended to grow independently, and not according to some grand plan. Each functional area tended to develop systems in isolation from other functional areas. Accounting, finance, manufacturing, human resources, sales, and marketing all developed their own systems and data files. Figure 7-3 illustrates the traditional approach to information processing.

---

field
A grouping of characters into a word, a group of words, or a complete number, such as a person's name or age.

record
A group of related fields.

file
A group of records of the same type.

database
A group of related files.

entity
A person, place, thing, or event about which information must be kept.

attribute
A piece of information describing a particular entity.

key field
A field in a record that uniquely identifies instances of that record so that it can be retrieved, updated, or sorted.

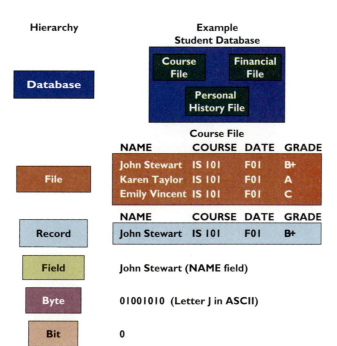

Figure 7-1 The data hierarchy. A computer system organizes data in a hierarchy that starts with the bit, which represents either a 0 or a 1. Bits can be grouped to form a byte to represent one character, number, or symbol. Bytes can be grouped to form a field, and related fields can be grouped to form a record. Related records can be collected to form a file, and related files can be organized into a database.

Figure 7-2 Entities and attributes. This record describes the entity called ORDER and its attributes. The specific values for order number, order date, item number, quantity, and amount for this particular order are the fields for this record. Order number is the key field because each order is assigned a unique identification number.

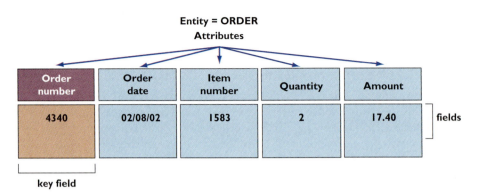

Each application, of course, required its own files and its own computer program to operate. For example, the human resources functional area might have a personnel master file, a payroll file, a medical insurance file, a pension file, a mailing list file, and so forth until tens, perhaps hundreds, of files and programs existed. In the company as a whole, this process led to multiple master files created, maintained, and operated by separate divisions or departments. As this process goes on for five or ten years, the organization is saddled with hundreds of programs and applications, with no one who knows what they do, what data they use, and who is using the data. The resulting problems are data redundancy, program-data dependence, inflexibility, poor data security, and inability to share data among applications.

Data Redundancy and Confusion

data redundancy

The presence of duplicate data in multiple data files.

Data redundancy is the presence of duplicate data in multiple data files. Data redundancy occurs when different divisions, functional areas, and groups in an organization independently collect the same piece of information. For instance, within the commercial loans division of a bank, the marketing and credit information functions might collect the same customer information. Because it is collected and maintained in so many different places, the same data item may have different meanings in different parts of the organization. Simple data items, such as the fiscal year, employee identification, and product code, can take on different meanings as programmers and analysts work in isolation on different applications.

Figure 7-3 Traditional file processing. The use of a traditional approach to file processing encourages each functional area in a corporation to develop specialized applications. Each application requires a unique data file that is likely to be a subset of the master file. These subsets of the master file lead to data redundancy, processing inflexibility, and wasted storage resources.

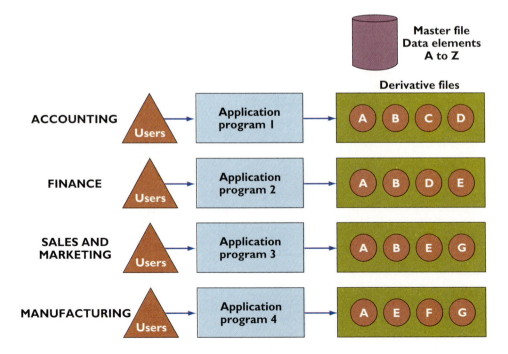

Program-Data Dependence

Program-data dependence is the tight relationship between data stored in files and the specific programs required to update and maintain those files. Every computer program has to describe the location and nature of the data with which it works. In a traditional file environment, any change in data requires a change in all programs that access the data. Changes, for instance, in tax rates or ZIP code length require changes in programs. Such programming changes may cost millions of dollars to implement in programs that require the revised data.

Lack of Flexibility

A traditional file system can deliver routine scheduled reports after extensive programming efforts, but it cannot deliver ad hoc reports or respond to unanticipated information requirements in a timely fashion. The information required by ad hoc requests is somewhere in the system but too expensive to retrieve. Several programmers would have to work for weeks to put together the required data items in a new file.

Poor Security

Because there is little control or management of data, access to and dissemination of information may be out of control. Management may have no way of knowing who is accessing or even making changes to the organization's data.

Lack of Data-Sharing and Availability

The lack of control over access to data in this confused environment does not make it easy for people to obtain information. Because pieces of information in different files and different parts of the organization cannot be related to one another, it is virtually impossible for information to be shared or accessed in a timely manner. Information cannot flow freely across different functional areas or different parts of the organization.

7.2   THE DATABASE APPROACH TO DATA MANAGEMENT

Database technology can cut through many of the problems a traditional file organization creates. A more rigorous definition of a **database** is a collection of data organized to serve many applications efficiently by centralizing the data and minimizing redundant data. Rather than storing data in separate files for each application, data are stored physically to appear to users as being stored in only one location. A single database services multiple applications. For example, instead of a corporation storing employee data in separate information systems and separate files for personnel, payroll, and benefits, the corporation could create a single common human resources database. Figure 7-4 illustrates the database concept.

DATABASE MANAGEMENT SYSTEMS

A **database management system (DBMS)** is simply the software that permits an organization to centralize data, manage them efficiently, and provide access to the stored data by application programs. The DBMS acts as an interface between application programs and the physical data files. When the application program calls for a data item such as gross pay, the DBMS finds this item in the database and presents it to the application program. Using traditional data files the programmer would have to specify the size and format of each data element used in the program and then tell the computer where they were located. A DBMS eliminates most of the data definition statements found in traditional programs.

The DBMS relieves the programmer or end user from the task of understanding where and how the data are actually stored by separating the logical and physical views of the data. The **logical view** presents data as they would be perceived by end users or business specialists, whereas the **physical view** shows how data are actually organized and structured on physical storage media. There is only one physical view of the data, but there can be many different logical views. The database management software makes the physical database available for

---

program-data dependence
The close relationship between data stored in files and the software programs that update and maintain those files. Any change in data organization or format requires a change in all the programs associated with those files.

database (rigorous definition)
A collection of data organized to service many applications at the same time by storing and managing data so that they appear to be in one location.

database management system (DBMS)
Special software to create and maintain a database and enable individual business applications to extract the data they need without having to create separate files or data definitions in their computer programs.

logical view
A representation of data as they would appear to an application programmer or end user.

physical view
The representation of data as they would actually be organized on physical storage media.

Figure 7-4 The contemporary database environment. A single human resources database serves multiple applications and also allows a corporation to easily draw together all the information for various applications. The database management system acts as the interface between the application programs and the data.

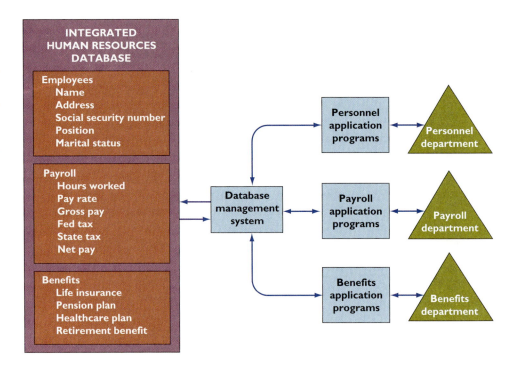

different logical views presented for various application programs. For example, an employee retirement benefits program might use a logical view of the human resources database illustrated in Figure 7-4 that requires only the employee's name, address, social security number, pension plan, and retirement benefits data.

A database management system has three components:

▮ A data definition language

▮ A data manipulation language

▮ A data dictionary

data definition language

The component of a database management system that defines each data element as it appears in the database.

The **data definition language** is the formal language programmers use to specify the content and structure of the database. The data definition language defines each data element as it appears in the database before that data element is translated into the forms required by application programs.

data manipulation language

A language associated with a database management system that end users and programmers use to manipulate data in the database.

Most DBMS have a specialized language called a **data manipulation language** that is used in conjunction with some conventional third- or fourth-generation programming languages to manipulate the data in the database. This language contains commands that permit end users and programming specialists to extract data from the database to satisfy information requests and develop applications. The most prominent data manipulation language today is **Structured Query Language,** or **SQL.** End users and information systems specialists can use SQL as an interactive query language to access data from databases, and SQL commands can be embedded in application programs written in conventional programming languages.

Structured Query Language (SQL)

The standard data manipulation language for relational database management systems.

The third element of a DBMS is a **data dictionary**. This is an automated or manual file that stores definitions of data elements and data characteristics such as usage, physical representation, ownership (who in the organization is responsible for maintaining the data), authorization, and security. Many data dictionaries can produce lists and reports of data use, groupings, program locations, and so on. Figure 7-5 illustrates a sample data dictionary report that shows the size, format, meaning, and uses of a data element in a human resources database. A **data element** represents a field. In addition to listing the standard name (AMT-PAY-BASE), the dictionary lists the names that reference this element in specific systems and identifies the individuals, business functions, programs, and reports that use this data element.

data dictionary

An automated or manual tool for storing and organizing information about the data maintained in a database.

By creating an inventory of data contained in the database, the data dictionary serves as an important data management tool. For instance, business users could consult the dictionary to find out exactly what pieces of data are maintained for the sales or marketing function or even to determine all the information maintained by the entire enterprise. The dic-

data element

A field.

```
NAME:  AMT-PAY-BASE
FOCUS NAME:  BASEPAY
PC NAME:     SALARY

DESCRIPTION:  EMPLOYEE'S ANNUAL SALARY

SIZE: 9 BYTES
TYPE: N      (NUMERIC)
DATE CHANGED: 01/01/95
OWNERSHIP: COMPENSATION
UPDATE SECURITY: SITE PERSONNEL
ACCESS SECURITY:  MANAGER, COMPENSATION PLANNING AND RESEARCH
                  MANAGER, JOB EVALUATION SYSTEMS
                  MANAGER, HUMAN RESOURCES PLANNING
                  MANAGER, SITE EQUAL OPPORTUNITY AFFAIRS
                  MANAGER, SITE BENEFITS
                  MANAGER, CLAIMS PAYING SYSTEMS
                  MANAGER, QUALIFIED PLANS
                  MANAGER, SITE EMPLOYMENT/EEO
BUSINESS FUNCTIONS USED BY:  COMPENSATION
                             HR PLANNING
                             EMPLOYMENT
                             INSURANCE
                             PENSION
                             401K

PROGRAMS USING:  PI01000
                 PI02000
                 PI03000
                 PI04000
                 PI05000

REPORTS USING:  REPORT 124 (SALARY INCREASE TRACKING REPORT)
                REPORT 448 (GROUP INSURANCE AUDIT REPORT)
                REPORT 452 (SALARY REVIEW LISTING)
                PENSION REFERENCE LISTING
```

Figure 7-5 Sample data dictionary report. The sample data dictionary report for a human resources database provides helpful information such as the size of the data element, which programs and reports use it, and which group in the organization is the owner responsible for maintaining it. The report also shows some of the other names that the organization uses for this piece of data.

tionary could supply business users with the name, format, and specifications required to access data for reports. Technical staff could use the dictionary to determine what data elements and files must be changed if a program is changed.

Most data dictionaries are entirely passive; they simply report. More advanced types are active; changes in the dictionary can be automatically used by related programs. For instance, to change ZIP codes from five to nine digits, one could simply enter the change in the dictionary without having to modify and recompile all application programs using ZIP codes.

In an ideal database environment, the data in the database are defined only once and used for all applications whose data reside in the database, thereby eliminating data redundancy and inconsistency. Application programs, which are written using a combination of the data manipulation language of the DBMS and a conventional programming language, request data elements from the database. Data elements called for by the application programs are found and delivered by the DBMS. The programmer does not have to specify in detail how or where the data are to be found.

A DBMS can reduce program-data dependence along with program development and maintenance costs. Access and availability of information can be increased because users and programmers can perform ad hoc queries of data in the database. The DBMS allows the organization to centrally manage data, their use, and security.

TYPES OF DATABASES

Contemporary DBMS use different database models to keep track of entities, attributes, and relationships. Each model has certain processing advantages and certain business advantages.

Relational DBMS

The most popular type of DBMS today for PCs as well as for larger computers and mainframes is the **relational DBMS**. The relational data model represents all data in the database

relational DBMS
A type of logical database model that treats data as if they were stored in two-dimensional tables. It can relate data stored in one table to data in another as long as the two tables share a common data element.

Figure 7-6 The relational data
model. Each table is a relation and
each row or record is a tuple.
Each column corresponds to a
field. These relations can easily be
combined and extracted to
access data and produce reports,
provided that any two share a
common data element. In this
example, the ORDER file shares
the data element "Part_Number"
with the PART file. The PART and
SUPPLIER files share the data element "Supplier_Number."

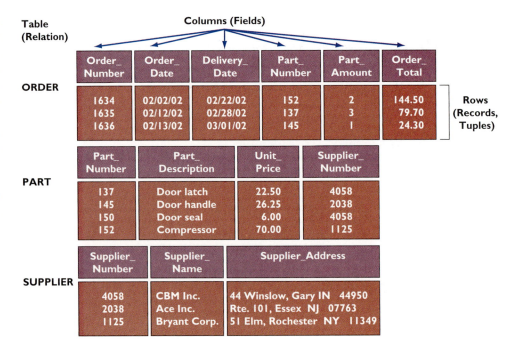

tuple

A row or record in a relational
database.

as simple two-dimensional tables called relations. The tables appear similar to flat files, but
the information in more than one file can be easily extracted and combined. Sometimes the
tables are referred to as files.

Figure 7-6 shows a supplier table, a part table, and an order table. In each table the rows
are unique records and the columns are fields. Another term for a row or record in a relation
is a **tuple**. Often a user needs information from a number of relations to produce a report.
Here is the strength of the relational model: It can relate data in any one file or table to data
in another file or table as long as both tables share a common data element.

To demonstrate, suppose we wanted to find in the relational database in Figure 7-6 the
names and addresses of suppliers who could provide us with part number 137 or part number 152. We would need information from two tables: the supplier table and the part table.
Note that these two files have a shared data element: Supplier_Number.

In a relational database, three basic operations as shown in Figure 7-7 are used to
develop useful sets of data: select, project, and join. The *select* operation creates a subset consisting of all records in the file that meet stated criteria. Select creates, in other words, a subset of rows that meet certain criteria. In our example, we want to select records (rows) from
the part table where the part number equals 137 or 152. The *join* operation combines relational tables to provide the user with more information than is available in individual tables.
In our example we want to join the now-shortened part table (only parts numbered 137 or
152 will be presented) and the supplier table into a single new result table.

The *project* operation creates a subset consisting of columns in a table, permitting the
user to create new tables (also called views) that contain only the information required. In
our example, we want to extract from the new result table only the following columns:
Part_Number, Supplier_Number, Supplier_Name, and Supplier_Address.

The SQL statements for producing the new result table in Figure 7-7 would be:

SELECT PART.Part_Number, SUPPLIER.Supplier_Number, SUPPLIER.Supplier_Name,
    SUPPLIER.Supplier_Address
FROM PART, SUPPLIER
WHERE PART.Supplier_Number = SUPPLIER.Supplier_Number AND Part_Number = 137 OR
    Part_Number = 152;

Leading mainframe relational database management systems include IBM's DB2 and
Oracle from the Oracle Corporation. DB2, Oracle, and Microsoft SQL Server are used as

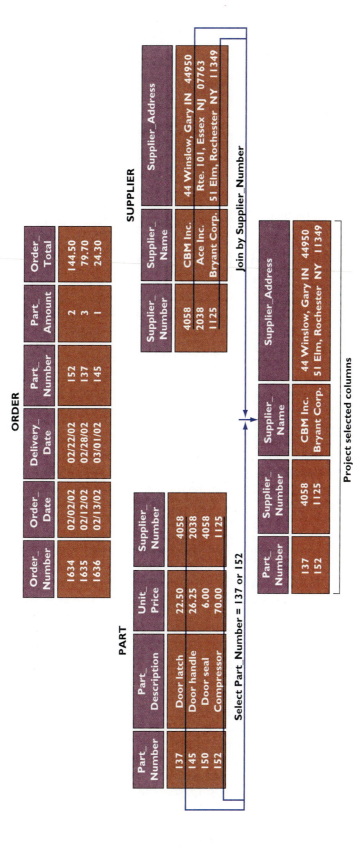

ORDER

Order_ Number	Order_ Date	Delivery_ Date	Part_ Number	Part_ Amount	Order_ Total
1634	02/02/02	02/22/02	152	2	144.50
1635	02/12/02	02/28/02	137	3	79.70
1636	02/13/02	03/01/02	145	1	24.30

PART

Part_ Number	Part_ Description	Unit_ Price	Supplier_ Number
137	Door latch	22.50	4058
145	Door handle	26.25	2038
150	Door seal	6.00	4058
152	Compressor	70.00	1125

Select Part_Number = 137 or 152

SUPPLIER

Supplier_ Number	Supplier_ Name	Supplier_Address
4058	CBM Inc.	44 Winslow, Gary IN 44950
2038	Ace Inc.	Rte. 101, Essex NJ 07763
1125	Bryant Corp.	51 Elm, Rochester NY 11349

Join by Supplier_Number

Part_ Number	Supplier_ Number	Supplier_ Name	Supplier_Address
137	4058	CBM Inc.	44 Winslow, Gary IN 44950
152	1125	Bryant Corp.	51 Elm, Rochester NY 11349

Project selected columns

Figure 7-7 The three basic operations of a relational DBMS. The select, project, and join operations allow data from two different tables to be combined and only selected attributes to be displayed.

227

Figure 7-8 A hierarchical database for a human resources system. The hierarchical database model looks like an organizational chart or a family tree. It has a single root segment (Employee) connected to lower level segments (Compensation, Job Assignments, and Benefits). Each subordinate segment, in turn, may connect to other subordinate segments. Here, Compensation connects to Performance Ratings and Salary History. Benefits connects to Pension, Life Insurance, and Health Care. Each subordinate segment is the child of the segment directly above it.

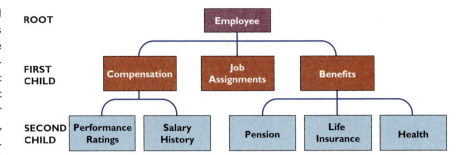

hierarchical DBMS

Older logical database model that organizes data in a treelike structure. A record is subdivided into segments that are connected to each other in one-to-many parent–child relationships.

network DBMS

An older logical database model that is useful for depicting many-to-many relationships.

DBMS for midrange computers. Microsoft Access is a PC relational database management system, and Oracle Lite is a DBMS for small, handheld computing devices.

Hierarchical and Network DBMS

One can still find older systems that are based on a hierarchical or network data model. The **hierarchical DBMS** presents data to users in a treelike structure. Within each record, data elements are organized into pieces of records called *segments*. To the user, each record looks like an organization chart with one top-level segment called the *root*. An upper segment is connected logically to a lower segment in a parent–child relationship. A parent segment can have more than one child, but a child can have only one parent.

Figure 7-8 shows a hierarchical structure that might be used for a human resources database. The root segment is Employee, which contains basic employee information such as name, address, and identification number. Immediately below it are three child segments: Compensation (containing salary and promotion data), Job Assignments (containing data about job positions and departments), and Benefits (containing data about beneficiaries and benefit options). The Compensation segment has two children below it: Performance Ratings (containing data about employees' job performance evaluations) and Salary History (containing historical data about employees' past salaries). Below the Benefits segment are child segments for Pension, Life Insurance, and Health, containing data about these benefit plans.

Whereas hierarchical structures depict one-to-many relationships, **network DBMS** depict data logically as many-to-many relationships. In other words, parents can have multiple children, and a child can have more than one parent. A typical many-to-many relationship for a network DBMS is the student–course relationship (see Figure 7-9). There are many courses in a university and many students. A student takes many courses and a course has many students.

Hierarchical and network DBMS are considered outdated and are no longer used for building new database applications. They are much less flexible than relational DBMS and do not support ad hoc, English language-like inquiries for information. All paths for accessing data must be specified in advance and cannot be changed without a major programming effort. For instance, if you queried the human resources database illustrated in Figure 7-8 to find out the names of the employees with the job title of administrative assistant, you would discover that there is no way that the system can find the answer in a reasonable amount of time. This path through the data was not specified in advance.

Relational DBMS, in contrast have much more flexibility in providing data for ad hoc queries, combining information from different sources, and providing capability to add new data and records without disturbing existing programs and applications. However, these sys-

Figure 7-9 The network data model. This illustration of a network data model showing the relationship the students in a university have to the courses they take represents an example of logical many-to-many relationships.

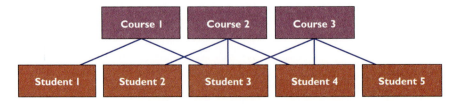

tems can be slowed down if they require many accesses to the data stored on disk to carry out the select, join, and project commands. Selecting one part number from among millions, one record at a time, can take a long time. Of course the database can be tuned to speed up prespecified queries.

Hierarchical DBMS can still be found in large legacy systems that require intensive high-volume transaction processing. A **legacy system** is a system that has been in existence for a long time and that continues to be used to avoid the high cost of replacing or redesigning it. Banks, insurance companies, and other high-volume users continue to use reliable hierarchical databases such as IBM's IMS (Information Management System), developed in 1969. Many organizations have converted to DB2, IBM's relational DBMS for new applications, while retaining IMS for traditional transaction processing. For example, Dallas-based Texas Instruments depends on IMS for its heavy processing requirements, including inventory, accounting, and manufacturing. As relational products acquire more muscle, firms will shift away completely from hierarchical DBMS, but this will happen over a long period of time.

legacy system
A system that has been in existence for a long time and that continues to be used to avoid the high cost of replacing or redesigning it.

Object-Oriented Databases

Conventional database management systems were designed for homogeneous data that can be easily structured into predefined data fields and records organized in rows or tables. But many applications today and in the future will require databases that can store and retrieve not only structured numbers and characters but also drawings, images, photographs, voice, and full-motion video. Conventional DBMS are not well suited to handling graphics-based or multimedia applications. For instance, design data in a computer-aided design (CAD) database consist of complex relationships among many types of data. Manipulating these kinds of data in a relational system requires extensive programming to translate these complex data structures into tables and rows. An **object-oriented DBMS**, however, stores the data and procedures as objects that can be automatically retrieved and shared.

Object-oriented database management systems (OODBMS) are becoming popular because they can be used to manage the various multimedia components or Java applets used in Web applications, which typically integrate pieces of information from a variety of sources. OODBMS also are useful for storing data types such as recursive data. (An example would be parts within parts as found in manufacturing applications.) Finance and trading applications often use OODBMS because they require data models that must be easy to change to respond to new economic conditions.

Although object-oriented databases can store more complex types of information than relational DBMS, they are relatively slow compared with relational DBMS for processing large numbers of transactions. Hybrid **object-relational DBMS** systems are now available to provide capabilities of both object-oriented and relational DBMS. A hybrid approach can be accomplished in three different ways: by using tools that offer object-oriented access to relational DBMS, by using object-oriented extensions to existing relational DBMS, or by using a hybrid object-relational database management system.

object-oriented DBMS
An approach to data management that stores both data and the procedures acting on the data as objects that can be automatically retrieved and shared; the objects can contain multimedia.

object-relational DBMS
A database management system that combines the capabilities of a relational DBMS for storing traditional information and the capabilities of an object-oriented DBMS for storing graphics and multimedia.

7.3 CREATING A DATABASE ENVIRONMENT

In order to create a database environment, one must understand the relationships among the data, the type of data that will be maintained in the database, how the data will be used, and how the organization will need to change to manage data from a company-wide perspective. We now describe important database design principles and the management and organizational requirements of a database environment.

DESIGNING DATABASES

To create a database, one must go through two design exercises: a conceptual design and a physical design. The conceptual, or logical, design of a database is an abstract model of the database from a business perspective, whereas the physical design shows how the database is actually arranged on direct access storage devices. Logical design requires a detailed description of the business information needs of the actual end users of the database. Ideally, database design will be part of an overall organizational data planning effort (see Chapter 12).

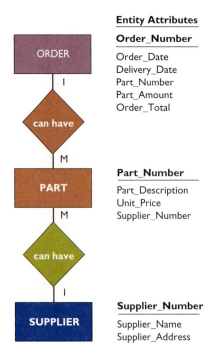

Entity Attributes

Order_Number

Order_Date
Delivery_Date
Part_Number
Part_Amount
Order_Total

Part_Number

Part_Description
Unit_Price
Supplier_Number

Supplier_Number

Supplier_Name
Supplier_Address

entity-relationship diagram

A methodology for documenting databases illustrating the relationship between various entities in the database.

normalization

The process of creating small stable data structures from complex groups of data when designing a relational database.

The conceptual database design describes how the data elements in the database are to be grouped. The design process identifies relationships among data elements and the most efficient way of grouping data elements together to meet information requirements. The process also identifies redundant data elements and the groupings of data elements required for specific application programs. Groups of data are organized, refined, and streamlined until an overall logical view of the relationships among all the data elements in the database emerges.

Database designers document the conceptual data model with an **entity-relationship diagram**, illustrated in Figure 7-10. The boxes represent entities and the diamonds represent relationships. The 1 or M on either side of the diamond represents the relationship among entities as either one-to-one, one-to-many, or many-to-many. Figure 7-10 shows that the entity ORDER can have more than one PART and a PART can only have one SUPPLIER. Many parts can be provided by the same supplier. The attributes for each entity are listed next to the entity and the key field is underlined.

To use a relational database model effectively, complex groupings of data must be streamlined to eliminate redundant data elements and awkward many-to-many relationships. The process of creating small, stable data structures from complex groups of data is called **normalization**. Figures 7-11 and 7-12 illustrate this process. In the particular business modeled here, an order can have more than one part but each part is provided by only one supplier. If we built a relation called ORDER with all the fields included here, we would have to repeat the name, description, and price of each part on the order and the name and address of each part vendor. This relation contains what are called repeating groups because there can be many parts and suppliers for each order, and it actually describes multiple entities—parts and suppliers as well as orders. A more efficient way to arrange the data is to break down ORDER into smaller relations, each of which describes a single entity. If we go step by step and normalize the relation ORDER, we emerge with the relations illustrated in Figure 7-12.

If a database has been carefully considered, with a clear understanding of business information needs and usage, the database model will most likely be in some normalized form. Many real-world databases are not fully normalized because this may not be the most sensible way to meet business information requirements. Note that the relational database illustrated in Figure 7-6 is not fully normalized because there could be more than one part for each order. The designers chose to not use the four relations described in Figure 7-12 because most of the orders handled by this particular business are only for one part. The designers might have felt that for this particular business it was inefficient to maintain four different tables.

DISTRIBUTING DATABASES

Database design also considers how the data are to be distributed. Information systems can be designed with a centralized database that is used by a single central processor or by multi-

ORDER

Order_Number	Part_Amount	Part_Number	Part_Description	Unit_Price	Supplier_Number	Supplier_Name	Supplier_Address	Order_Date	Delivery_Date	Order_Total

Figure 7-11 An unnormalized relation for ORDER. In an unnormalized relation there are repeating groups. For example, there can be many parts and suppliers for each order. There is only a one-to-one correspondence between Order_Number and Order_Date, Order_Total, and Delivery_Date.

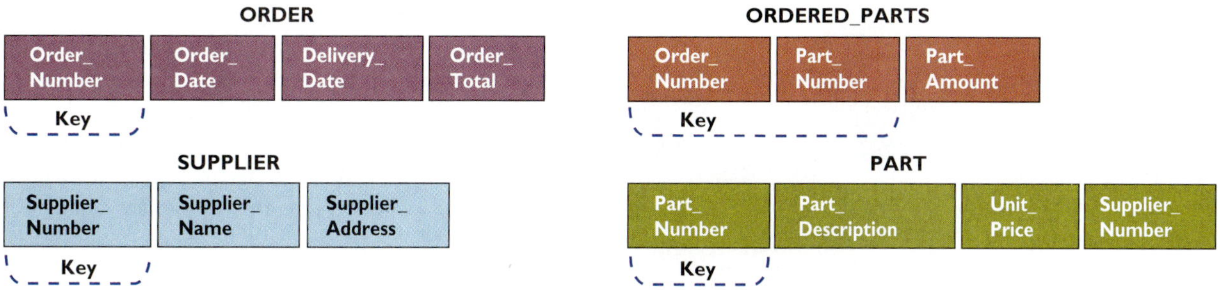

Figure 7-12 A normalized relation for ORDER. After normalization, the original relation ORDER has been broken down into four smaller relations. The relation ORDER is left with only three attributes and the relation ORDERED-PARTS has a combined, or concatenated, key consisting of Order_Number and Part_Number.

ple processors in a client/server network. Alternatively, the database can be distributed. A **distributed database** is one that is stored in more than one physical location. Parts of the database are stored physically in one location, and other parts are stored and maintained in other locations. There are two main ways of distributing a database (see Figure 7-13.) The central database can be partitioned (see Figure 7-13a) so that each remote processor has the necessary data to serve its local area. Changes in local files can be justified with the central database on a batch basis, often at night. Another strategy is to replicate the central database (Figure 7-13b) at all remote locations. For example, Lufthansa Airlines replaced its centralized mainframe database with a replicated database to make information more immediately available to flight dispatchers. Any change made to Lufthansa's Frankfort DBMS is automatically replicated in New York and Hong Kong. This strategy also requires updating of the central database on off hours.

Distributed systems reduce the vulnerability of a single, massive central site. They increase service and responsiveness to local users and often can run on smaller less expensive computers. Distributed systems, however, are dependent on high-quality telecommunications lines, which themselves are vulnerable. Moreover, local databases can sometimes depart from central data standards and definitions, and they pose security problems by widely distributing access to sensitive data. Database designers need to weigh these factors in their decisions.

distributed database
A database that is stored in more than one physical location. Parts or copies of the database are physically stored in one location, and other parts or copies are stored and maintained in other locations.

MANAGEMENT REQUIREMENTS FOR DATABASE SYSTEMS

Much more is required for the development of database systems than simply selecting a logical database model. The database is an organizational discipline, a method, rather than a

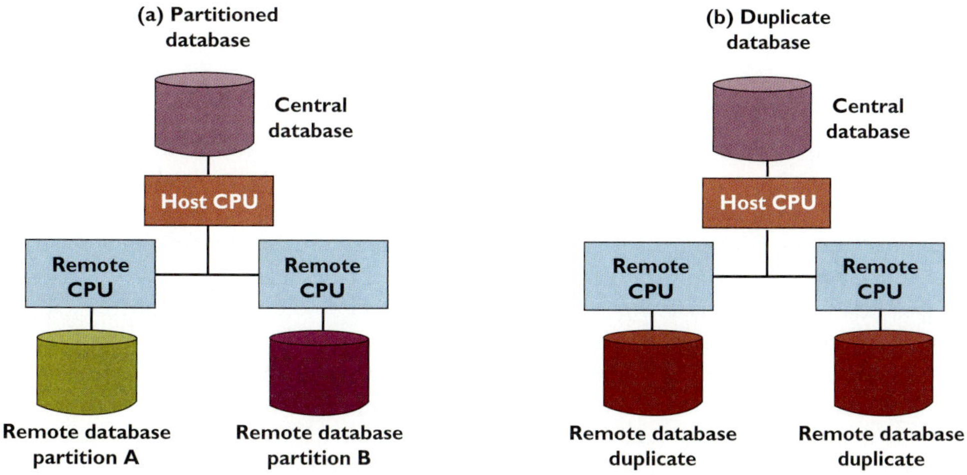

Figure 7-13 Distributed databases. There are alternative ways of distributing a database. The central database can be partitioned (a) so that each remote processor has the necessary data to serve its own local needs. The central database also can be duplicated (b) at all remote locations.

Figure 7-14 Key organizational elements in the database environment. For a database management system to flourish in any organization, data administration functions and data planning and modeling methodologies must be coordinated with database technology and management. Resources must be devoted to train end users to use databases properly.

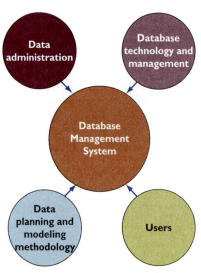

tool or technology. It requires organizational and conceptual change. Without management support and understanding, database efforts fail. The critical elements in a database environment are (1) data administration, (2) data planning and modeling methodology, (3) database technology and management, and (4) users. This environment is depicted in Figure 7-14.

Data Administration

data administration
A special organizational function for managing the organization's data resources, concerned with information policy, data planning, maintenance of data dictionaries, and data quality standards.

Database systems require that the organization recognize the strategic role of information and begin actively to manage and plan for information as a corporate resource. This means that the organization must develop a **data administration** function with the power to define information requirements for the entire company and with direct access to senior management. The chief information officer (CIO) or vice president of information becomes the primary advocate in the organization for database systems.

Data administration is responsible for the specific policies and procedures through which data can be managed as an organizational resource. These responsibilities include developing information policy, planning for data, overseeing logical database design and data dictionary development, and monitoring how information system specialists and end-user groups use data.

The fundamental principle of data administration is that all data are the property of the organization as a whole. Data cannot belong exclusively to any one business area or organizational unit. All data are to be made available to any group that requires them to fulfill its mission. An organization needs to formulate an **information policy** that specifies its rules for sharing, disseminating, acquiring, standardizing, classifying, and inventorying information throughout the organization. Information policy lays out specific procedures and accountabilities, specifying which organizational units share information, where information can be distributed, and who has responsibility for updating and maintaining the information. Although data administration is a very important organizational function, it has proved very challenging to implement.

information policy
Formal rules governing the maintenance, distribution, and use of information in an organization.

Data Planning and Modeling Methodology

The organizational interests served by the DBMS are much broader than those in the traditional file environment; therefore, the organization requires enterprise-wide planning for data. Enterprise analysis, which addresses the information requirements of the entire organization (as opposed to the requirements of individual applications), is needed to develop databases. The purpose of enterprise analysis is to identify the key entities, attributes, and relationships that constitute the organization's data. These techniques are described in greater detail in Chapter 12.

Database Technology, Management, and Users

database administration
Refers to the more technical and operational aspects of managing data, including physical database design and maintenance.

Databases require new software and a new staff specially trained in DBMS techniques, as well as new data management structures. Most corporations develop a database design and management group within the corporate information system division that is responsible for defining and organizing the structure and content of the database and maintaining the database. In close cooperation with users, the design group establishes the physical database, the logical relations among elements, and the access rules and procedures. The functions it performs are called **database administration**.

A database serves a wider community of users than traditional systems. Relational systems with fourth-generation query languages permit employees who are not computer specialists to access large databases. In addition, users include trained computer specialists. To optimize access for nonspecialists, resources must be devoted to training end users.

7.4 DATABASE TRENDS

Organizations are installing powerful data analysis tools and data warehouses to make better use of the information stored in their databases and are taking advantage of database technology linked to the World Wide Web. We now explore these developments.

MULTIDIMENSIONAL DATA ANALYSIS

Sometimes managers need to analyze data in ways that traditional database models cannot represent. For example, a company selling four different products—nuts, bolts, washers, and screws—in the East, West, and Central regions, might want to know actual sales by product for each region and might also want to compare them with projected sales. This analysis requires a multidimensional view of data.

To provide this type of information, organizations can use either a specialized multidimensional database or a tool that creates multidimensional views of data in relational databases. Multidimensional analysis enables users to view the same data in different ways using multiple dimensions. Each aspect of information—product, pricing, cost, region, or time period—represents a different dimension. So a product manager could use a multidimensional data analysis tool to learn how many washers were sold in the East in June, how that compares with the previous month and the previous June, and how it compares with the sales forecast. Another term for multidimensional data analysis is **on-line analytical processing (OLAP)**.

Figure 7-15 shows a multidimensional model that could be created to represent products, regions, actual sales, and projected sales. A matrix of actual sales can be stacked on top of a matrix of projected sales to form a cube with six faces. If you rotate the cube 90 degrees one way, the face showing will be product versus actual and projected sales. If you rotate the cube 90 degrees again, you can see region versus actual and projected sales. If you rotate 180 degrees from the original view, you can see projected sales and product versus region. Cubes can be nested within cubes to build complex views of data.

DATA WAREHOUSES AND DATAMINING

Decision makers need concise, reliable information about current operations, trends, and changes. What has been immediately available at most firms is current data only (historical data were available through special IS reports that took a long time to produce). Data often are fragmented in separate operational systems, such as sales or payroll, so that different managers make decisions from incomplete knowledge bases. Users and information system specialists may have to spend inordinate amounts of time locating and gathering data (Watson

on-line analytical processing (OLAP)
Capability for manipulating and analyzing large volumes of data from multiple perspectives.

WebFOCUS OLAP allows users to slice and dice data in many different ways to answer vital business questions such as "What's not selling and where?" or "What percent of my profits comes from what percent of my products?" On-line analytical processing (OLAP) gives users quick, unlimited views of multiple relationships in large quantities of data.

The intuitive OLAP control panel lets you directly interact with your WebFOCUS reports, slicing and dicing against any data – with or without a cube.

Figure 7-15 Multidimensional data model. The view that is showing is product versus region. If you rotate the cube 90 degrees, the face that will be showing is product versus actual and projected sales. If you rotate the cube 90 degrees again, you can see region versus actual and projected sales. Other views are possible. The ability to rotate the data cube is the main technique for multidimensional reporting. It is sometimes called "slice and dice."

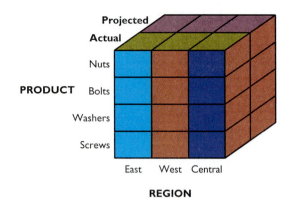

and Haley, 1998). Data warehousing addresses this problem by integrating key operational data from around the company in a form that is consistent, reliable, and easily available for reporting.

What Is a Data Warehouse?

data warehouse

A database, with reporting and query tools, that stores current and historical data extracted from various operational systems and consolidated for management reporting and analysis.

A **data warehouse** is a database that stores current and historical data of potential interest to managers throughout the company. The data originate in many core operational systems and external sources, including Web site transactions, each with different data models. They may include legacy systems, relational or object-oriented DBMS applications, and systems based on HTML or XML documents. The data from these diverse applications are copied into the data warehouse database as often as needed—hourly, daily, weekly, monthly. The data are standardized into a common data model and consolidated so that they can be used across the enterprise for management analysis and decision making. The data are available for anyone to access as needed but cannot be altered.

Figure 7-16 illustrates the data warehouse concept. The data warehouse must be carefully designed by both business and technical specialists to make sure it can provide the right information for critical business decisions. The firm may need to change its business processes to benefit from the information in the warehouse (Cooper, Watson, Wixom, and Goodhue, 2000). The Manager's Toolkit describes how to conduct a business analysis that addresses these issues.

data mart

A small data warehouse containing only a portion of the organization's data for a specified function or population of users.

Companies can build enterprise-wide data warehouses where a central data warehouse serves the entire organization, or they can create smaller, decentralized warehouses called data marts. A **data mart** is a subset of a data warehouse in which a summarized or highly focused portion of the organization's data is placed in a separate database for a specific population of

Figure 7-16 Components of a data warehouse. A data warehouse extracts current and historical data from operational systems inside the organization. These data are combined with data from external sources and reorganized into a central database designed for management reporting and analysis. The information directory provides users with information about the data available in the warehouse.

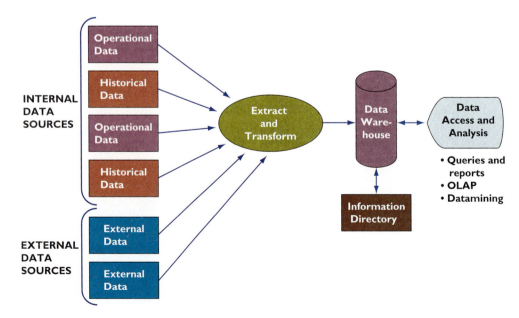

MIS IN ACTION   MANAGER'S TOOLKIT

HOW TO MAKE A DATA WAREHOUSE SERVE THE BUSINESS

The first steps in building a data warehouse involve conducting a thorough business analysis of the information requirements that could be satisfied by a data warehouse. Here are some of the questions managers should ask:

1. *Users:* Who are the primary users of the data warehouse? What levels of the organization and business functions do they represent?

2. *Ownership:* What organizational group or groups own the data? Who is responsible for maintaining the data? Who is authorized to access the data?

3. *Information requirements:* What types of reports and queries should the data warehouse support? What pieces of data are used in these reports and queries? Do the reports require the data to be detailed or summarized?

4. *Data sources:* What are the sources of data required by the reports? Which pieces come from internal TPS and other systems? Which come from sources outside the company? How can the company obtain the data for these reports?

5. *Currency:* How often do the data in the warehouse need to be updated? How long should historical data in the warehouse be maintained?

6. *Data standards:* Applications that were designed to support different functions or organizational units may use the same term in different ways. These discrepancies must be identified so that each data element is defined and used the same way in the data warehouse system. Does everyone agree on how each piece of data is defined and used?

7. *Quality expectations:* What level of accuracy and completeness of the data in the warehouse is sufficient to meet business needs?

8. *Benefits:* Precisely what are the business benefits of building this data warehouse? To what extent can these benefits be quantified? Are the benefits greater than the costs? (See Chapter 13.)

9. *Business process change:* Does the company need to change its business processes in order to use the information from the data warehouse effectively? How much change is required?

---

users. For example, a company might develop marketing and sales data marts to deal with customer information. A data mart typically focuses on a single subject area or line of business, so it usually can be constructed more rapidly and at lower cost than an enterprise-wide data warehouse. However, complexity, costs, and management problems will rise if an organization creates too many data marts.

Datamining

A data warehouse system provides a range of ad hoc and standardized query tools, analytical tools, and graphical reporting facilities, including tools for OLAP and datamining. **Datamining** uses a variety of techniques to find hidden patterns and relationships in large pools of data and infer rules from them that can be used to predict future behavior and guide decision making (Hirji, 2001). Datamining helps companies engage in one-to-one marketing where personalized or individualized messages can be created based on individual preferences. Table 7-1 describes how some organizations are benefiting from datamining. These systems can perform high-level analyses of patterns or trends, but they can also drill into more detail where needed.

datamining
Analysis of large pools of data to find patterns and rules that can be used to guide decision making and predict future behavior.

TABLE 7-1   HOW BUSINESSES ARE USING DATAMINING

Organization	Datamining Application
Nordstrom.com	Uses datamining to analyze data generated by visitors to its Web site. Uses the results to customize advertising and content to individual customers and to improve on-line customer service.
Carrier Corporation	Analyzes data generated by on-line purchasers and visitors to its Web site, combined with third-party demographic data to create profiles of on-line customers. Uses these profiles to target customers with appropriate products, such as multiroom air conditioners for suburban home owners or compact models for apartment dwellers.
American Express	Analyzes data from hundreds of billions of credit card purchases to create "one-to-one" marketing campaigns. Along with their credit card bills, customers receive personalized messages promoting goods and services in which they have shown interest.
Verizon Wireless	Analyzes Verizon's customer database to identify new customers so that customer-service representatives can determine whether they need special help or services. Also uses datamining to identify mobile phone customers who might benefit from switching calling plans and mails them special promotions. Verizon uses such initiatives to increase customer satisfaction and thus reduce customer churn.

LOUISE'S TRATTORIA MAKES A COMEBACK WITH DATAMINING

MIS In Action

When Barbra Streisand, Jim Carrey, and other Hollywood stars began patronizing a recently bankrupt low-priced restaurant, many wondered why. Yet that is precisely what happened to Louise's Trattoria, a 13-restaurant chain in Los Angeles serving inexpensive traditional Italian food. Louise's had been losing sales at an annual rate of 10 percent and had entered bankruptcy when it was purchased in December 1997 by LT Acquisition Corp. Fred LeFranc, who took over as LT president and CEO, had to find some way to boost customer satisfaction and increase sales.

LeFranc turned to datamining, enlisting the services of Gazelle Systems of Newton Upper Falls, Massachusetts. Charlotte Bogardus, the founder and chair of Gazelle Systems, explains that, "In the restaurant industry, everyone knows their labor and food costs, but what they haven't been able to do is measure their performance based on customer behavior." Gazelle matches its clients' historical credit card data with in-depth demographic and psychographic data gathered and sold to Gazelle by certain marketing companies. It then builds detailed profiles for each of Louise's customers by relating the purchased data to the credit card data. The profiles include many pieces of customer information, including customer frequency, buying patterns, educational level, and household location relative to the store locations of Gazelle's client. The data are given to Louise's with an ID number rather than a name to protect the privacy of the customers. Gazelle also provides its client with store and company indicators such as churn rates (the ratio of customers that have been lost to new customers plus existing customers). Finally Louise's receives analytical tools, enabling them to create the specific reports they need.

Louise's has a valuable database to work with because 85 percent of its customers pay by credit card. Gazelle decided only to examine Louise's top 500 customers using six months of data, and LeFranc was startled by the results. The majority of those examined turned out to be college educated, well-traveled single mothers with preteen children. They also owned 1.4 automobiles and bought fine wines. Clearly, LaFranc said, "they could afford to pay for quality." He "realized we had to create an image to make it cool to eat at Louise's—we couldn't be perceived as a spaghetti palace." The data also showed that customers were not returning often enough, that the churn rate was too high.

Management made several decisions based on this new understanding of customers. Knowing that quality was more important than price to its top customers, they introduced higher priced entrees, so that the average check size for each dinner rose from $12.50 to $16. They replaced some old-world Italian dishes with healthier vegetarian selections and added more expensive wines to the menu. They also introduced a new seafood section and an upgraded take-out service. Finally they refurbished each of the 13 restaurants, giving them a lighter, more modern ambiance. Annual sales have turned around from an annual decline of 10 percent to a rise of 9.5 percent in 2000. The frequency rate of returning patrons has climbed from two monthly visits to three-and-a-half. LeFranc believes that, although he might have been able to make the same changes on his own, the Gazelle data enabled him to do it much more rapidly.

To Think About: How did datamining help management make better decisions for Louise's Trattoria? Could LeFranc have made these changes without the Gazelle system? Explain your answer.

Sources: Beth Stackpole, "Uncorking a Business Recovery, Part I," itmanagement.earthweb.com, May 21, 2001 and "Uncorking a Business Recovery, Part II," itmanagement.earthweb.com, May 22, 2001 and Samuel Fromartz, "The Mystery of the Blood Red Ledger," Inc., April 1, 2001.

Datamining is both a powerful and profitable tool, but it poses challenges to the protection of individual privacy. Datamining technology can combine information from many diverse sources to create a detailed "data image" about each of us—our income, our driving habits, our hobbies, our families, and our political interests. The question of whether companies should be allowed to collect such detailed information about individuals is explored in Chapter 5.

Benefits of Data Warehouses

Data warehouses not only offer improved information but they also make it easy for decision makers to obtain it. They even include the ability to model and remodel the data. It has been estimated that 70 percent of the world's business information resides on mainframe databases, many of which are for older legacy systems. Many of these legacy systems are critical production applications that support the company's core business processes. As long as these systems can efficiently process the necessary volume of transactions to keep the company

MIS IN ACTION   DECISIONMAKING

CREATING COMPANY-WIDE DATA STANDARDS
Your industrial supply company wants to create a data warehouse where management can obtain a single corporate-wide view of critical sales information to identify best-selling products in specific geographic areas, key customers, and sales trends. Your sales and product

information are stored in two different systems: a divisional sales system running on a UNIX server and a corporate sales system running on an IBM mainframe. You would like to create a single standard format that consolidates these data from both systems. The following format has been proposed.

Product_ID	Product_Description	Cost_per_Unit	Units_Sold	Sales_Region	Division	Customer_ID

The following are sample files from the two systems that would supply the data for the data warehouse:

Mechanical Parts Division Sales System

Prod_No	Product_Description	Cost_per_Unit	Units_Sold	Sales_Region	Customer_ID
60231	4" Steel bearing	5.28	900,245	N.E.	Anderson
85773	SS assembly unit	12.45	992,111	M.W.	Kelly Industries

Corporate Sales System

Product_ID	Product_Description	Unit_Cost	Units_Sold	Sales_Territory	Division
60231	Bearing, 4"	5.28	900,245	Northeast	Parts
85773	SS assembly unit	12.02	992,111	Midwest	Parts

1. What business problems are created by not having these data in a single standard format?
2. How easy would it be to create a database with a single standard format that could store the data from both systems? Identify the problems that would have to be addressed.
3. Should the problems be solved by database specialists or general business managers? Explain.
4. Who should have the authority to finalize a single company-wide format for this information in the data warehouse?

running, firms are reluctant to replace them to avoid disrupting critical business functions and high system replacement costs. Many of these legacy systems use hierarchical DBMS or even older nondatabase files where information is difficult for users to access. Data warehouses enable decision makers to access data as often as they need without affecting the performance of the underlying operational systems. Many organizations are making access to their data warehouses even easier by using Web technology.

Organizations such as Chico's, described in the chapter opening vignette, and Louise's Trattoria, described in the Window on Management, have used the information gleaned from data warehouses and datamining to help them refocus their businesses.

DATABASES AND THE WEB

Database technology plays an important role in making organizations' information resources available on the World Wide Web. We now explore the role of hypermedia databases in the Web and the growing use of Web sites to access information stored in conventional databases inside the firm.

The Web and Hypermedia Databases

Web sites store information as interconnected pages containing text, sound, video, and graphics using a hypermedia database. The **hypermedia database** approach to information management stores chunks of information in the form of nodes connected by links the user specifies (see Figure 7-17). The nodes can contain text, graphics, sound, full-motion video, or executable computer programs. Searching for information does not have to follow a predetermined organization scheme. Instead, one can branch instantly to related information in any kind of relationship the author establishes. The relationship between records is less structured than in a traditional DBMS.

hypermedia database
An approach to data management that organizes data as a network of nodes linked in any pattern the user specifies; the nodes can contain text, graphics, sound, full-motion video, or executable programs.

Figure 7-17 A hypermedia database. In a hypermedia database, the user can choose his or her own path to move from node to node. Each node can contain text, graphics, sound, full-motion video, or executable programs.

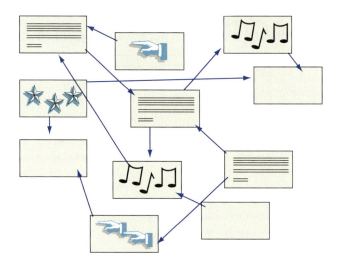

The hypermedia database approach enables users to access topics on a Web site in whatever order they wish. For instance, from the Web page from the U.S. National Oceanic and Atmospheric Administration (NOAA) illustrated on this page, one could branch to other Web pages by clicking on the topics in the left column. In addition to welcoming visitors to NOAA, these Web pages provide more information on NURP (National Undersea Research Program), News from the Deep, Undersea Research Centers, Funding Opportunities, Education, Research Highlights and Products, Undersea Technologies, and Undersea Web sites. The links from the on-screen page to the other related Web pages are highlighted in blue. We provide more detail on these and other features of Web sites in Chapter 9.

Linking Internal Databases to the Web

A series of middleware and other software products has been developed to help users gain access to organizations' legacy data through the Web. For example, a customer with a Web browser might want to search an on-line retailer's database for pricing information. Figure 7-18 illustrates how that customer might access the retailer's internal database over the Web. The user would access the retailer's Web site over the Internet using Web browser software on his or her client PC. The user's Web browser software would request data from the organization's database, using HTML commands to communicate with the Web server. Because

From the U.S. National Oceanic and Atmospheric Administration (NOAA) Web page, you can branch to other Web pages by clicking on the topics in the left column. Web sites store information as interconnected pages containing text, sound, video, and graphics using a hypermedia approach to data management.

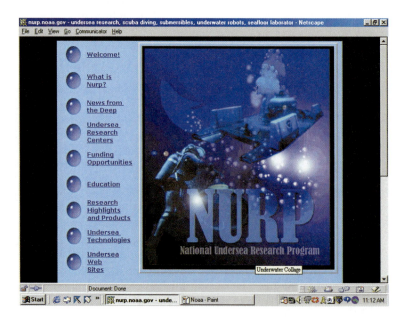

Figure 7-18 Linking internal databases to the Web. Users can access an organization's internal database through the Web using their desktop PCs and Web browser software.

many back-end databases cannot interpret commands written in HTML, the Web server would pass these requests for data to special software that would translate HTML commands into SQL so that they could be processed by the DBMS working with the database. In a client/server environment, the DBMS resides on a special dedicated computer called a **database server**. The DBMS receives the SQL requests and provides the required data. The middleware would transfer information from the organization's internal database back to the Web server for delivery in the form of a Web page to the user.

Figure 7-18 shows that the software working between the Web server and the DBMS could be an application server, a custom program, or a series of software scripts. An **application server** is a software program that handles all application operations, including transaction processing and data access, between browser-based computers and a company's back-end business applications or databases. The application server takes requests from the Web server, runs the business logic to process transactions based on those requests, and provides connectivity to the organization's back-end systems or databases. *Common Gateway Interface (CGI)* is a specification for transferring information between a Web server and a program designed to accept and return data. The program could be written in any programming language, including C, Perl, Java, or Visual Basic.

There are a number of advantages to using the Web to access an organization's internal databases. Web browser software is extremely easy to use, requiring much less training than even user-friendly database query tools. The Web interface requires no changes to the internal database. Companies leverage their investments in older systems because it costs much less to add a Web interface in front of a legacy system than to redesign and rebuild the system to improve user access.

database server

A computer in a client/server environment that is responsible for running a DBMS to process SQL statements and perform database management tasks.

application server

Software that handles all application operations between browser-based computers and a company's back-end business applications or databases.

The ThomasRegister.com Web site links to a database of more than 170,000 companies, 400,000 products, thousands of on-line catalogs, and millions of CAD drawings searchable by product, company, or brand name. More and more organizations are using the Web to provide an interface to internal databases.

ICELAND'S MEDICAL RECORDS DATABASE: MEDICAL PROGRESS OR THREAT TO PRIVACY?

DeCode Genetics, a U.S. genomics company headquartered in Reykjavik, Iceland, is something of a celebrity in this island nation of 280,000 people. In 2000, the Icelandic government granted this tiny start-up an exclusive 12-year license to design, build, and manage a national medical records database for Iceland. In addition to the centralization of medical records, the government has also granted DeCode the right to cross-reference that data with genetic and genealogical data on individual Icelanders.

Iceland's population is small, stable, and homogeneous, consisting primarily of descendents from a small group of ninth-century Norse and Celtic settlers. Obsessed with ancestry, Icelanders have maintained records tracing family ties to 80 percent of all Icelanders who have ever lived. Comprehensive medical records date back to 1915. Such well-documented genealogical and medical records on a relatively homogeneous group of people make it much easier for researchers to identify genetic mutations. DeCode has expressed confidence that using these two databases, along with genetic data collected from Icelanders voluntarily participating in research on 35 key diseases, it will be able to identify the genes or genetic variations that cause or contribute to many different illnesses. In particular they have targeted Alzheimer's disease, asthma, Parkinson's disease, lung and prostate cancer, and osteoporosis.

DeCode has develop sophisticated analytical software tools to locate genetic variations that may be found in a number of diseases so that it can market new drugs and diagnostic tests for these genetic ailments. DeCode has already discovered about 24 genes it believes are related to more than 15 diseases. Hoffman-La Roche, the giant Swiss pharmaceutical firm, has been working in partnership with DeCode, launching programs to develop new drugs for schizophrenia, stroke, and peripheral arterial occlusive disease.

DeCode's projects are not without controversy. As many as one-third of the physicians in the clinics around Iceland where medical data were previously stored have refused to submit their records until they have received the written consent of their patients. In fact, the Health Sector Database Act passed in 1998 (which enabled the Ministry of Health to grant a license to create and manage a national medical database) and the subsequent granting of the license to DeCode have been met with increasing resistance. A group called Mannvernd (Icelandic for human protection) was formed to try to overturn the act. Its founder, Dr. Petur Hauksson, is a psychiatrist who fears that his patients may face discrimination, as may people with DNA that reveals a predisposition to serious illness. Although DeCode has developed an automated encryption software program to keep participants' identities secret, Dr. Hauksson believes that in a small country such as Iceland a medical history alone could potentially reveal a person's identity.

Mannvernd members were particularly perturbed that the Health Sector Database Act assumed the consent of the citizenry. Under pressure, the government instituted a program in which Icelanders can elect not to have their medical records included in the database. However, if their records have already been entered, they cannot have them removed. DeCode's critics are also concerned that voluntary participants in disease studies must agree to allow their DNA to be used in any other research DeCode decides to undertake. Mannvernd has filed suit against DeCode for violating Icelanders' right to privacy.

To Think About: Should national medical and genetic databases be allowed? Why or why not? What management, organization, and technology issues should be addressed if such databases are created?

Sources: Stephanie Overby, "Iceland's Dilemma: Privacy vs. Progress," *CIO Magazine*, July 15, 2001; and "Mapping the Icelandic Genome," http://sunsite.berkeley.edu/biotech/Iceland.

TABLE 7-2	EXAMPLES OF WEB-ENABLED DATABASES

Organization	Use of Web-Enabled Database
IGo.com	Web site is linked to a giant relational database housing information about batteries and peripherals for computers and other portable electronic devices. Visitors can immediately find on-line information about each electronic device and the batteries and parts it uses and place orders for these parts over the Web.
Australian National University Bioinformatics Group	Web site links to a Universal Viral Database, which describes all viruses of animals and plants. Visitors can search the database for descriptions of viruses, images of viruses, and links to genomic and protein databanks.
Thomas Register Advanced Order Online	Web site links to Thomas's database of more than 170,000 companies, 400,000 products, thousands of product catalogs, and millions of CAD drawings searchable by product, part number, or brand name. Visitors can search for products, view a company's catalog, request price quotes, make purchases on-line using a credit card or company purchasing card, and track orders.

MAKE IT YOUR BUSINESS

FINANCE AND ACCOUNTING

Banks and financial services have benefited from a database approach to information management. Much of their data were traditionally organized along product lines in a number of different systems where it was difficult to provide a complete picture of a customer's transactions with the organization. Database management software and data warehouses have enabled these firms to organize their data more flexibly so that they can view information by customer, financial product, or other criteria. Financial firms are also intensive users of datamining for analyzing credit risk or for identifying profitable customers.

HUMAN RESOURCES

Companies typically maintain human resources databases enabling them to maintain data on employees, benefits plans, and training programs and to provide reports to the government concerning compliance with health, safety, and equal employment opportunity regulations. Since these human resources databases contain sensitive information such as salaries, job performance evaluations, and medical history, companies must be very careful about distributing this information. The security and data access rules for DBMS can help protect confidentiality and privacy. You can find examples of human resources applications on page 240.

MANUFACTURING AND PRODUCTION

Many manufacturing and production processes rely on database technology. Companies maintain large databases of finished goods, raw materials in inventory, and goods in transit that can be used for supply chain management. The manufacturing process makes use of numerous databases on suppliers, jobs in progress, product components, product quality, and costs. You can find examples of manufacturing and production applications on pages 244–247.

SALES AND MARKETING

Database, data warehouse, and datamining technologies have been powerful tools for marketers because they enable firms to assemble and analyze vast quantities of data about customers from many different sources. By querying these customer databases, analysts can identify customers most interested in specific products or highly profitable customers. They can target specialized products and promotions based on these detailed customer profiles. The sales function can benefit from allowing customers to access corporate databases linked to the Web to place orders or to find out product information. You can find examples of sales and marketing applications on pages 218–219 and 236.

Accessing corporate databases through the Web is creating new efficiencies and opportunities, in some cases even changing the way business is being done. Some companies have created new businesses based on access to large databases via the Web. Others are using Web technology to provide employees with integrated firmwide views of information. The major enterprise system vendors have enhanced their software so that users can access enterprise data through a Web interface. Table 7-2 describes some of these applications of Web-enabled databases.

Database technology has provided many organizational benefits, but it allows firms to maintain large databases with detailed personal information that pose a threat to individual privacy. The Window on Organizations describes the privacy issues surrounding the creation of a national medical records database for Iceland.

MANAGEMENT WRAP-UP

Selecting an appropriate data model and data management technology for the organization is a key management decision. Managers will need to evaluate the costs and benefits of implementing a database environment and the capabilities of various DBMS or file management technologies. Management should ascertain that organizational databases are designed to meet management information objectives and the organization's business needs.

The organization's data model should reflect its key business processes and decision-making requirements. Data planning may need to be performed to make sure that the organization's data model delivers information efficiently for its business processes and enhances organizational performance. Designing a database is an organizational endeavor.

Multiple database and file management options are available for organizing and storing information. Key technology decisions should consider the efficiency of accessing information, flexibility in organizing information, the type of information to be stored and arranged, compatibility with the organization's data model, and compatibility with the organization's hardware and operating systems.

For Discussion

1. It has been said that you do not need database management software to create a database environment. Discuss.

2. To what extent should end users be involved in the selection of a database management system and database design?

SUMMARY

1. *Why do businesses have trouble finding the information they need in their information systems?* A computer system organizes data in a hierarchy that starts with bits and bytes and progresses to fields, records, files, and databases. Traditional file management techniques make it difficult for organizations to keep track of all of the pieces of data they use in a systematic way or to organize these data so that they can be easily accessed. Different functional areas and groups were allowed to develop their own files independently. Over time, this traditional file environment creates problems such as data redundancy and inconsistency, program-data dependence, inflexibility, poor security, and lack of data-sharing and availability.

2. *How does a database management system help businesses improve the organization of their information?* A database management system (DBMS) consists of software that permits centralization of data and data management so that businesses have a single consistent source for all their data needs. A single database services multiple applications. A DBMS includes a data definition language, a data manipulation language, and a data dictionary capability. The most important feature of the DBMS is its ability to separate the logical and physical views of data. The user works with a logical view of data. The DBMS retrieves information so that the user does not have to be concerned with its physical location.

3. *How do the principal types of database models affect the way businesses can access and use their information?* The principal types of databases today are relational DBMS and object-oriented DBMS. Relational systems are very flexible for supporting ad hoc requests for information and for combining information from different sources. They support many-to-many relationships among entities and are efficient for storing alphanumeric data that can be organized into structured fields and records. This flexibility was not possible with the older hierarchical and network database models. Object-oriented DBMS can store graphics and other types of data in addition to conventional text data to support multimedia applications. Organizations should use the DBMS that is best suited for their data model.

Designing a database requires both a logical design and a physical design. The logical design models the database from a business perspective. The process of creating small, stable data structures from complex groups of data when designing a relational database is termed *normalization*. Database design also considers whether a complete database or portions of the database can be distributed to more than one location to increase responsiveness and reduce vulnerability and costs. There are two major types of distributed databases: replicated databases and partitioned databases.

4. *What are the management and organizational requirements of a database environment?* Developing a database environment requires much more than selecting database technology. It requires a formal information policy governing the maintenance, distribution, and use of information in the organization. The organization must also develop a data administration function and a data planning methodology. There is political resistance in organizations to many key database concepts, especially to sharing of information that has been controlled exclusively by one organizational group.

5. *What new tools and technologies can make databases more accessible and useful?* There are powerful tools available to analyze the information in databases and to take advantage of the information resources on the World Wide Web. Multidimensional data analysis, also known as on-line analytical processing (OLAP), can represent relationships among data as a multidimensional structure, which can be visualized as cubes of data and cubes within cubes of data, allowing for more sophisticated data analysis. Data can be more conveniently analyzed across the enterprise by using a data warehouse, in which current and historical data are extracted from many different operational systems and consolidated for management decision making. Datamining analyzes large pools of data, including the contents of data warehouses, to find patterns and rules that can be used to predict future behavior and guide decision making. Hypermedia databases allow data to be stored in nodes linked together in any pattern the user establishes and are used for storing information at Web sites. Conventional databases can be linked to the Web to facilitate user access to an organization's internal data.

KEY TERMS

Application server, 239

Attribute, 221

Data administration, 232

Data definition language, 224

Data dictionary, 224

Data element, 224

Data manipulation language, 224

Data mart, 234

Data redundancy, 222

Data warehouse, 234

Database, 221

Database (rigorous definition), 223

Database administration, 232

Database management system (DBMS), 223

Database server, 239

Datamining, 235

Distributed database, 231

Entity, 221

Entity-relationship diagram, 230

Field, 221

File, 221

Hierarchical DBMS, 228

Hypermedia database, 237

Information policy, 232

Key field, 221

Legacy system, 229

Logical view, 223

Network DBMS, 228

Normalization, 230

Object-oriented DBMS, 229

Object-relational DBMS, 229

On-line analytical processing (OLAP), 233

Physical view, 223

Program-data dependence, 223

Record, 221

Relational DBMS, 225

Structured Query Language (SQL), 224

Tuple, 226

REVIEW QUESTIONS

1. Why is file management important for overall system performance?

2. List and describe each of the components in the data hierarchy.

3. Define and explain the significance of entities, attributes, and key fields.

4. List and describe some of the problems of the traditional file environment.

5. Define a database and a database management system.

6. Name and briefly describe the three components of a DBMS.

7. What is the difference between a logical and a physical view of data?

8. List some benefits of a DBMS.

9. Describe the principal types of databases and the advantages and disadvantages of each.

10. What is normalization? How is it related to the features of a well-designed relational database?

11. What is a distributed database, and what are the two main ways of distributing data?

12. What are the four key organizational elements of a database environment? Describe each briefly.

13. Describe the capabilities of on-line analytical processing (OLAP) and datamining.

14. What is a data warehouse? How can it benefit organizations?

15. What is a hypermedia database? How does it differ from a traditional database? How is it used for the Web?

16. How can users access information from a company's internal databases via the Web?

APPLICATION SOFTWARE EXERCISE: DATABASE EXERCISE

BUILDING A RELATIONAL DATABASE FOR A SMALL BUSINESS

Sylvester's Bike Shop, located in San Francisco, California, sells road, mountain, hybrid, leisure, and children's bicycles. Currently, Sylvester's purchases bikes from three suppliers, but plans to add new suppliers in the near future. This rapidly growing business needs a database system to manage this information.

Initially, the database should house information about suppliers and products. The database will contain two tables: a supplier table and a product table. The reorder level refers to the number of items in inventory that triggers a decision to order more items to prevent a stockout. (In other words, if the number of units of a particular bicycle in inventory falls below the reorder level, the item should be reordered.) The user should be able to perform several queries and produce several managerial reports based on the data contained in the two tables.

Using the information found in the tables on the Laudon Web site for Chapter 7, build a simple relational database for Sylvester's. Once you have built the database, perform the following activities.

a) Prepare a report that identifies the five most expensive bicycles. The report should list the bicycles in descending order from most expensive to least expensive, the quantity on hand for each and the markup percentage for each.

b) Prepare a report that lists each supplier, its products, quantity on hand, and associated reorder levels. The report should be sorted alphabetically by supplier. Within each supplier category, the products should be sorted alphabetically.

c) Prepare a report listing only the bicycles that are low in stock and need to be reordered. The report should provide supplier information for the items identified.

b) Write a brief description of how the database could be enhanced to further improve management of the business. What tables or fields should be added? What additional reports would be useful?

GROUP PROJECT

Review Figure 7-4, which provides an overview of a human resources database. Some additional information that might be maintained in such a database are an employee's date of hire, date of termination, number of children, date of birth, educational level, sex code, Social Security tax, Medicare tax, year-to-date gross pay and net pay, amount of life insurance coverage, health-care plan payroll-deduction amount, life insurance plan payroll-deduction amount, and pension plan payroll-deduction amount.

Form a group with three or four of your classmates. Prepare two sample reports using the data in the database that might be of interest to either the employer or the employee. What pieces of information should be included on each report? In addition, prepare a data dictionary entry for one of the data elements in the database similar to the entry illustrated in Figure 7-5.

Your group's analysis should determine what business functions use this data element, which function has the primary responsibility for maintaining the data element, and which positions in the organization can access that data element. If possible, use electronic presentation software to present your findings to the class.

TOOLS FOR INTERACTIVE LEARNING

■ INTERNET

The Internet Connection for this chapter will direct you to a series of Web sites where you can complete an exercise to evaluate various commercial database management system products. You can also use the Interactive Study Guide to test your knowledge of the topics in this chapter and get instant feedback where you need more practice.

■ CD-ROM

If you use the Multimedia Edition CD-ROM with this chapter, you can find a video clip illustrating the THOR satellite tracking application based on a relational database management system, an audio overview of the major themes of this chapter, and bullet text summarizing the key points of the chapter.

■ ELECTRONIC COMMERCE PROJECT

At the Laudon Web site for Chapter 7, you will find an Electronic Commerce project for setting up a business in Australia that requires searches of on-line databases.

CASE STUDY—*Ford and Firestone's Tire Recall: The Costliest Information Gap in History*

On August 9, 2000, Bridgestone/Firestone Inc. announced it would recall more than 6.5 million tires, most of which had been mounted as original equipment on Ford Motor Co. Explorers and other Ford light trucks. Bridgestone/Firestone had become the subject of an intense federal investigation of 46 deaths and more than 300 incidents where Firestone tires allegedly shredded on the highway. The Firestone tires affected were 15-inch Radial ATX and Radial ATX II tires produced in North America and certain Wilderness AT tires manufactured at the firm's Decatur, Illinois, plant. This tire recall was the second biggest in history, behind only Firestone's recall of 14.5 million radial tires in 1978. The 1978 tire recall financially crippled the company for years to come and the August 2000 recall threatened to do the same. Consumers, the federal government, and the press wanted to know: Why didn't Ford and Firestone recognize this problem sooner? Let us look at the series of events surrounding the tire recall and the role of information management.

1988—Financially weakened from its 1978 tire recall, Firestone agreed to be acquired by Bridgestone Tires, a Japanese firm. To increase its sales, Firestone became a supplier of tires for Ford Motors' new sport-utility vehicle (SUV), the Explorer.

March 11, 1999—In response to a Ford concern about tire separations on the Explorer, Bridgestone/Firestone (Firestone) sent a confidential memo to Ford claiming that less than 0.1 percent of all Wilderness tires (which are used on the Explorer) had been returned under warranty for all kinds of problems. The note did not break out tread separations from other problems but did say this "rate of return is extremely low and substantiates [Firestone's] belief that this tire performs exceptionally well in the U.S. market."

August 1999—Ford Motors announced a recall in 16 foreign countries of all tires that had shown a tendency to fail mainly because of a problem of tread separation. The failures were primarily on the Ford Explorer, and the largest number of tires recalled was in Saudi Arabia. Firestone produced most of the tires. (A year earlier, Ford had noted problems with tread separation on Firestone tires mounted on Explorers in Venezuela and had sent samples of the failed tires to Bridgestone for analysis.) Ford did not report the recall to U.S. safety regulators because such reporting was not required.

May 2, 2000—Three days after another fatal accident involving Firestone/Ford Explorer tread separations, the National Highway Transportation Safety Administration (NHTSA) opened a full investigation into possible defects with the

Firestone ATX, ATX II, and Wilderness tires. The agency listed 90 complaints nationwide, including 34 crashes and 24 injuries or deaths. NHTSA also learned of the foreign recalls.

August 2000
August 9—At a news conference, Firestone announced that it would recall about 6.5 million tires that were then on light trucks and SUVs because they had been implicated in more than 40 fatalities. The company said it would replace all listed tires on any vehicle regardless of their condition or age. Firestone said it continued to stand by the tires. One Japanese analyst estimated the recall would cost the company as much as $500 million.

Firestone emphasized the importance of maintaining proper inflation pressure. Firestone recommended a pressure of 30 pounds–per–square inch (psi), whereas Ford recommended a range of 26 to 30 psi. Ford claimed its tests showed the tire performed well at 26 psi and that the lower pressure made for a smoother ride. However, Firestone claimed underinflation could put too much pressure on the tire, contributing to a higher temperature and causing the belts to separate. Ford pointed out that, although NHTSA had not closed its investigation, the two companies did not want to wait to act. NHTSA had by now received 270 complaints, including 46 deaths and 80 injuries, about these tires peeling off their casings when Ford SUVs and some trucks traveled at high speeds.

August 10—Press reports asked why Ford did not act within the United States when it took action to replace tires on more than 46,000 Explorers sold overseas.

August 13—The *Washington Post* reported that the Decatur, Illinois, Firestone plant, the source of many of the recalled tires, "was rife with quality-control problems in the mid-1990s." It said, "workers [were] using questionable tactics to speed production and managers [were] giving short shrift to inspections." The article cited former employees who were giving testimony in lawsuits against Firestone.

August 15—The NHTSA announced it had now linked 62 deaths to the recalled Firestone tires. It also had received more than 750 complaints on these tires.

September 2000
September 4—The U.S. Congress opened hearings on the Firestone and Ford tread separation problem. Congressional investigators released a memo from Firestone to Ford dated March 12, 1999, in which Firestone expressed "major reservations" about a Ford plan to replace Firestone tires overseas. A Ford representative at the hearing argued it had no need to report the replacement program because it was addressing a customer satisfaction problem and not a safety issue. The spokesperson added, "We are under no statutory obligations [to report overseas recalls] on tire actions."

Ford CEO Nasser testified before a joint congressional hearing that "this is clearly a tire issue and not a vehicle issue." He pointed out that "there are almost 3 million Goodyear tires on Ford Explorers that have not had a tread separation problem. So we know that this is a Firestone tire issue." However, he offered to work with the tire industry to develop and implement an

"early warning system" to detect signs of tire defects earlier, and he expressed confidence this would happen. He said, "This new system will require that tire manufacturers provide comprehensive real world data on a timely basis." He also said that in the future his company would advise U.S. authorities of safety actions taken in overseas markets and vice versa.

Nasser said his company did not know of the problem until a few days prior to the announcement of the recall because "tires are the only component of a vehicle that are separately warranted." He said his company had "virtually pried the claims data from Firestone's hands and analyzed it." Ford had not obtained warranty data on tires the same way it did for brakes, transmissions, or any other part of a vehicle. It was Firestone that had collected the tire warranty data. Ford thus lacked a database that could be used to determine whether reports of incidents with one type of tire could indicate a special problem relative to tires on other Ford vehicles. Ford only obtained the tire warranty data from Firestone on July 28. A Ford team with representatives of the legal, purchasing, and communication departments; safety experts; and Ford's truck group worked intensively with experts from Firestone to try to find a pattern in the tire incident reports. They finally determined that the problem tires originated in a Decatur, Illinois, plant during a specific period of production and that the bulk of tread separation incidents had occurred in Arizona, California, Texas, and Florida, all hot weather states. This correlated with the circumstances surrounding tire separations overseas.

Firestone's database on damage claims had been moved to Bridgestone's American headquarters in Nashville in 1988 after Firestone was acquired by Bridgestone. The firm's database in warranty adjustments, which was regularly used by Firestone safety staff, remained at Firestone's former headquarters in Akron, Ohio.

After the 1999 tire recalls in Saudi Arabia and other countries, Nasser asked Firestone to review data on U.S. customers. Firestone assured Ford "that there was no problem in this country," and, Nasser added, "our data, as well as government safety data, didn't show anything either." Nasser said Ford only became concerned when it "saw Firestone's confidential claims data." He added, "If I have one regret, it is that we did not ask Firestone the right questions sooner."

September 8—The *New York Times* released its own analysis of the Department of Transportation's Fatality Analysis Reporting System (FARS). FARS is one of the few tools available to the government to independently track defects that cause fatal accidents. The *Times* found "that fatal crashes involving Ford Explorers were almost three times as likely to be tire related as fatal crashes involving other sport utility vehicles." The newspaper's analysis also said, "The federal data shows no tire-related fatalities involving Explorers from 1991 to 1993 and a steadily increasing number thereafter which may reflect that tread separation becomes more common as tires age."

Their analysis brought to light difficulties in finding patterns in the data that would have alerted various organizations to a problem earlier. Ford and Firestone said they had not detected such a pattern in the data, and the NHTSA said they had looked at a variety of databases without finding the tire flaw pattern. According to the *Times,* without having a clear idea of what one is looking for makes it much harder to find the problem. The *Times* did have the advantage of hindsight when it analyzed the data.

The Department of Transportation databases independently track defects that contribute to fatal accidents, with data on about 40,000 fatalities each year. However, they no longer contain anecdotal evidence from garages and body shops because they no longer have the funding to gather this information. They only have information on the type of vehicle, not the type of tire, involved in a fatality. Tire involvement in fatal accidents is common because tires, in the normal course of their life, will contribute to accidents as they age, so that accidents where tires may be a factor are usually not noteworthy. In comparison, Sue Bailey, the administrator of highway safety, pointed out that accidents with seat belt failures stand out because seat belts should never fail. Safety experts note that very little data is collected on accidents resulting only in nonfatal injuries even though there are six to eight times more such accidents than fatal accidents. Experts also note that no data is collected on the even more common accidents with only property damage. If more data were collected, the *Times* concluded, "trends could be obvious sooner." Until Firestone announced its tire recall in August 2000, NHTSA had received only five complaints per year concerning Firestone's ATX, ATX II, and Wilderness AT tires out of 50,000 complaints of all kinds about vehicles.

Although Firestone executives had just testified that Firestone's warranty claim data did not show a problem with the tires, Firestone documents made public by congressional investigators showed that in February Firestone officials were already concerned with rising warranty costs for the now-recalled tires. September 12—Yoichiro Kaizaki, president of Bridgestone (parent of Firestone), acknowledged inadequate attention to quality control. "The responsibility for the problem lies with Tokyo," he said. "We let the U.S. unit use its own culture. There was an element of mistake in that."

September 19—*USA Today* reported that in more than 80 tire lawsuits against Firestone since 1991, internal Firestone documents and sworn testimony had been kept secret as part of the Firestone settlements. Observers noted that had these documents been made public at the time, many of the recent deaths might have been avoided.

September 22—The Firestone tires that were at the center of the recalled tires passed all U.S. government–required tests, causing NHTSA head Sue Bailey to say, "Our testing is clearly outdated."

During September, both Bridgestone and Firestone announced they would install supply chain information systems to prevent anything similar happening in the future. Firestone started spending heavily to make its claims database more usable for safety analysis.

January 2001—Yoichiro Kaizaki, the president and chief executive of the Bridgestone Corporation, resigned.

May 22, 2001—Bridgestone/Firestone ended its 100-year relationship as a supplier to Ford, accusing the automaker of refusing to acknowledge safety problems with the Explorer.

June 23, 2001—Sean Kane, a leading traffic safety consultant and a group of personal injury lawyers disclosed that in 1996 they had identified a pattern of failures of Firestone ATX tires on Ford Explorers but did not report the pattern to government safety regulators for four years. They did not inform the NHTSA, fearing a government investigation would prevent them from winning suits against Bridgestone/Firestone brought by their clients. Professor Geoffrey C. Hazard, Jr., a leading expert on legal ethics, said the lawyers had "a civic responsibility" to make their findings known but had not broken any laws by withholding this information.

June 27, 2001—Bridgestone/Firestone announced it planned to close its Decatur, Illinois, factory where many of the tires with quality problems had been produced.

October 4, 2001—Firestone announced it would replace an additional 3.5 million Wilderness AT tires made before 1998.

Sources: Kenneth N. Gilpin, "Firestone Will Recall an Additional 3.5 Million Tires," *The New York Times,* Octoer 5, 2001; Keith Bradsher, "S.U.V. Tire Defects Were Known in '96 but Not Reported," *New York Times,* June 24, 2001; David Barboza, "Bridgestone/Firestone to Close Tire Plant at Center of Huge Recall," *New York Times,* June 28, 2001; Mike Geyelin, "Firestone Quits as Tire Supplier to Ford," *Wall Street Journal,* May 22, 2001; Miki Tanikawa, "Chief of Bridgestone Says He Will Resign," *New York Times,* January 12, 2001; Kenneth N. Gilpin, "Firestone Will Recall an Additional 3.5 Million Tires," *The New York Times,* October 5, 2001; Matthew L. Wald and Josh Barbanel, "Link Between Tires and Crashes Went Undetected in Federal Data," *New York Times,* September 8, 2000; Robert L. Stimson, Karen Lundegaard, Norhiko Shirouzu, and Jenny Heller, "How the Tire Problem Turned into a Crisis for Firestone and Ford," *Wall Street Journal,* August 10, 2000; Mark Hall, "Information Gap," *Computerworld,* September 18, 2000; Keith Bradsher, "Documents Portray Tire Debacle as a Story of Lost Opportunities," *New York Times,* September 10, 2000; Ed Foldessy and Stephen Power, "How Ford, Firestone Let the Warnings Slide By as Debacle Developed," *Wall Street Journal,* September 6, 2000; Ford Motor Company, "Bridgestone/Firestone Announces Voluntary Tire Recall," August 9, 2000; Edwina Gibbs, "Bridgestone Sees $350 Million Special Loss, Stock Dives," Yahoo.com, August 10, 2000; John O'Dell and Edmund Sanders, "Firestone Begins Replacement of 6.4 Million Tires," *Los Angeles Times,* August 10, 2000; James V. Grimaldi, "Testimony Indicates Abuses at Firestone," *Washington Post,* August 13, 2000; Dina ElBoghdady, "Broader Tire Recall Is Urged," *Detroit News,* August 14, 2000; "Ford Report Recommended Lower Tire Pressure," *The Associated Press,* August 20, 2000; Caroline E. Mayer, James V. Grimaldi, Stephen Power, and Robert L. Simison, "Memo Shows Bridgestone and Ford Considered Recall over a Year Ago," *Wall Street Journal,* September 6, 2000; Timothy Aeppel, Clare Ansbery, Milo Geyelin, and Robert L. Simison, "Ford and Firestone's Separate Goals, Gaps in Communication Gave Rise to Tire Fiasco," *Wall Street Journal,* September 6, 2000; Matthew L. Wald, "Rancor Grows Between Ford and Firestone," *New York Times,* September 13, 2000; Keith Bradsher, "Questions Raised About Ford Explorer's Margin of Safety," *New York Times,* September 16, 2000; "Sealed Court Records Kept Tire Problems Hidden," *USA Today,* September 19, 2000; Tim Dobbyn, "Firestone Recall Exposes Flaws in

Government Tests," *New York Daily News*, September 22, 2000; Bridgestone/Firestone, Inc., "Statement of February 4, 2000," Tire-defects.com.

CASE STUDY QUESTIONS

1. Briefly summarize the problems and major issues in this case.

2. To what extent was this crisis an information management problem? What role did databases and data management play?

3. Explain why the growing trend of deaths was not spotted for a very long time. Why do you think it took so long for the issue to come to the attention of the general public?

4. List the different databases the parties had at their disposal as the problem grew, and list the data elements in those databases that were key to finding the tread separation problem earlier. Ignoring for the moment all other data problems, what critical data elements were these organizations not storing? For each one, why do you think it was critical and why it was not being stored?

5. Make a list of useful questions that these organizations might have asked of the databases but did not. Discuss why you think they did not ask these questions.

6. Evaluate the types of data collected and the questions asked in analyzing the data by each of the key organizations (Firestone, Ford, the U.S. government, and the legal community).

7. How did the relationships among Firestone, Ford, the U.S. government, and the legal community affect the development of the problem? The decisions on action that needed to be taken?

8. What data-related changes and improvements did the various parties and reporters suggest? Name other changes you believe should be made.

chapter

8 TELECOMMUNICATIONS AND NETWORKS

objectives

At many points in your career, you will need to make decisions about how to use telecommunications technology and services in your business. After completing this chapter, you will be able to answer the following questions:

1. *What technologies are used in telecommunications systems?*
2. *What telecommunications transmission media should our organization use?*
3. *How should our organization design its networks?*
4. *What alternative network services are available to our organization?*
5. *What telecommunications applications can be used for electronic commerce and electronic business?*

Scientific-Atlanta Creates Wireless Links to Its Supply Chain

Scientific-Atlanta provides state-of-the-art terrestrial and satellite network products and systems to cable operators, broadcasters, telephone companies, governments, and international corporations. The company's management and information systems specialists both agreed that the company needed an enterprise-wide inventory tracking system for its popular digital set-top boxes. The company had been batch downloading product serial numbers. Order entry was disconnected from the product tracking process, and real-time access to warehouse information was impossible. Errors in the shipping process were a natural result. Clerks had to spend considerable time tracking these errors down and correcting them.

Scientific-Atlanta believed the solution to this problem was a portable method of collecting serial numbers that could be used to access an enterprise system that recorded all product transactions in every warehouse. The company selected a SAP/R3 ERP system running UNIX on Hewlett-Packard hardware with an Oracle database. The data for the system would be collected using a wireless local area network (LAN) with portable handheld Janus 2020 terminals to scan assets and print barcode labels. InnoVision, an Alpharetta, Georgia, consulting firm, helped the company adapt its WinTrak for R3 software to integrate the automated data collection system with the new wide area network (WAN) for the enterprise system, which linked manufacturing plants in Norcross, Georgia, El Paso, Texas, and Juarez, Mexico. Scientific-Atlanta implemented the new system in stages and went live in June 1998.

The new system allows the company to validate all information related to product shipments and to track the serial numbers of set-top boxes, which is necessary when loaning set-top boxes to cable customers. Scientific-Atlanta tracks its products by serial number from receipt through inventory, shipment, and even repairs.

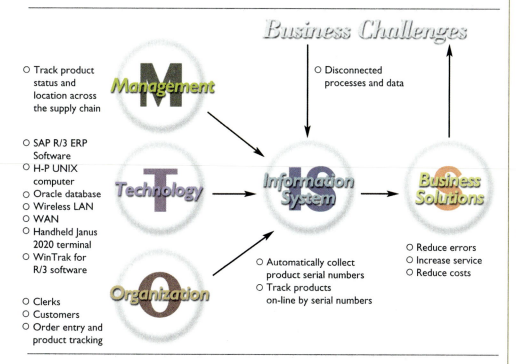

Business Challenges

- Track product status and location across the supply chain

Management

- SAP R/3 ERP Software
- H-P UNIX computer
- Oracle database
- Wireless LAN
- WAN
- Handheld Janus 2020 terminal
- WinTrak for R/3 software

Technology

- Clerks
- Customers
- Order entry and product tracking

Organization

- Disconnected processes and data

Information System

- Automatically collect product serial numbers
- Track products on-line by serial numbers

Business Solutions

- Reduce errors
- Increase service
- Reduce costs

The new portable system helped the company increase the accuracy of its inventory and data. High-volume orders are much easier to ship and track without error. Units scheduled for shipment are validated after they are scanned, and any problems with an order can be corrected on the spot. The handheld terminals force users to make corrections before the scanning process can continue. Management can make immediate inquiries on the status and location of products within the enterprise and across the supply chain.

Sources: "Software Links Supply Chain with SAP ERP at Scientific-Atlanta," *Enterprise Systems Journal*, June 2001; and "WinTrak Software Provides a Bridge Between Supply Chain Operations and SAP R/3 at Scientific-Atlanta," www.innovisionusa.com.

Scientific-Atlanta, like many organizations all over the world, has found ways to benefit from communications technology to coordinate its internal activities and to communicate more efficiently with other organizations. It would be virtually impossible to conduct business today without using communications technology, and applications of networks and communications technology for electronic business and electronic commerce are multiplying. However, incorporating communications technology into today's applications and information technology infrastructure raises several management challenges:

1. **Managing LANs.** Although local area networks (LANs) appear to be flexible and inexpensive ways of delivering computing power to new areas of the organization, they must be carefully administered and monitored. LANs are especially vulnerable to network disruption, loss of essential data, access by unauthorized users, and infection from computer viruses (see Chapter 14). Dealing with these problems requires special technical expertise that is not normally available in end-user departments and is in very short supply.

2. **Managing bandwidth.** Networks are the foundation of electronic commerce and the digital economy. Without network infrastructures that offer fast, reliable access, companies would lose many on-line customers and jeopardize relationships with suppliers and business partners as well. Although telecommunication transmission costs are rapidly dropping, total network transmission capacity (bandwidth) requirements have been growing by 40 percent each year. If more people use networks or the firm implements data-intensive applications that require high-capacity transmission, a firm's network costs can easily spiral upward. Balancing the need to ensure network reliability and availability against mushrooming network costs is a central management concern.

Most of the information systems we use today require networks and communications technology. Companies, large and small from all over the world, are using networked systems and the Internet to locate suppliers and buyers, to negotiate contracts with them, and to service their trades. Applications of networks are multiplying in research, organizational coordination, and control. Networked systems are fundamental to electronic commerce and electronic business.

Today's computing tasks are so closely tied to networks that some believe "the network is the computer." This chapter describes the components of telecommunications systems, showing how they can be arranged to create various types of networks and network-based applications that can increase an organization's efficiency and competitiveness.

8.1 THE TELECOMMUNICATIONS REVOLUTION

telecommunications
The communication of information by electronic means, usually over some distance.

Telecommunications is the communication of information by electronic means, usually over some distance. Previously, telecommunications meant voice transmission over telephone lines. Today, a great deal of telecommunications transmission is digital data transmission, using computers to transmit data from one location to another. We are currently in the middle of a telecommunications revolution that is spreading communications technology and telecommunications services throughout the globe.

THE MARRIAGE OF COMPUTERS AND COMMUNICATIONS

Telecommunications used to be a monopoly of either the state or a regulated private firm. In the United States, American Telephone and Telegraph (AT&T) provided virtually all telecommunications services. Telecommunications in Europe and in the rest of the world traditionally has been administered primarily by a state post, telephone, and telegraph authority (PTT). The U.S. monopoly ended in 1984 when the Justice Department forced AT&T

to give up its monopoly and allowed competing firms to sell telecommunications services and equipment. The 1996 Telecommunications Deregulation and Reform Act widened deregulation by freeing telephone companies, broadcasters, and cable companies to enter each other's markets. Other areas of the world are starting to open up their telecommunications services to competition as well.

Thousands of companies have sprung up to provide telecommunications products and services, including local and long-distance telephone services, cellular phones and wireless communication services, data networks, cable TV, communications satellites, and Internet services. Managers will be continually faced with decisions on how to incorporate these services and technologies into their information systems and business processes.

THE INFORMATION SUPERHIGHWAY

Deregulation and the marriage of computers and communications also has made it possible for the telephone companies to expand from traditional voice communications into new information services, such as those providing transmission of news reports, stock reports, television programs, and movies. These efforts are laying the foundation for the **information superhighway**, a vast web of high-speed digital telecommunications networks delivering information, education, and entertainment services to business, government, and homes. The networks comprising the highway are national or worldwide in scope and accessible by the general public rather than restricted to use by members of a specific organization or set of organizations, such as corporations. Some analysts believe this information superhighway will have as profound an impact on economic and social life in the twenty-first century as railroads and interstate highways did in the past.

The information superhighway concept is broad and rich, providing new ways for organizations and individuals to obtain and distribute information that virtually eliminate the barriers of time and place. Uses of this new superhighway for electronic commerce and electronic business are quickly emerging. The most well known and easily the largest implementation of the information superhighway is the Internet.

information superhighway
High-speed digital telecommunications networks that are national or worldwide in scope and accessible by the general public rather than restricted to specific organizations.

8.2   COMPONENTS AND FUNCTIONS OF A TELECOMMUNICATIONS SYSTEM

A **telecommunications system** is a collection of compatible hardware and software arranged to communicate information from one location to another. Figure 8-1 illustrates the components of a typical telecommunications system. Telecommunications systems can transmit

telecommunications system
A collection of compatible hardware and software arranged to communicate information from one location to another.

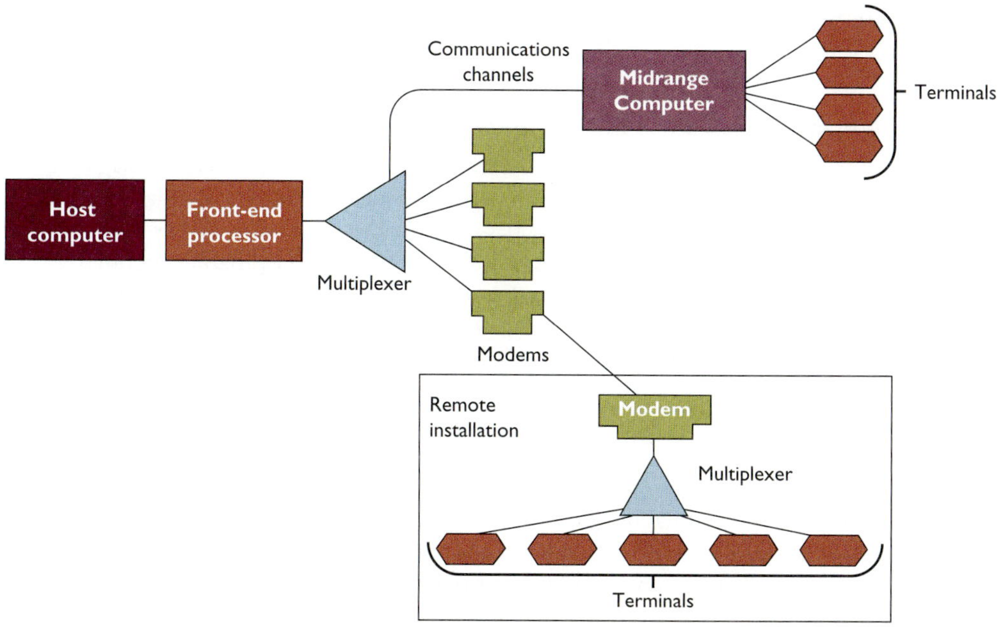

Figure 8-1 Components of a telecommunications system. This figure illustrates some of the hardware components that would be found in a typical telecommunications system. They include computers, terminals, communications channels, and communications processors, such as modems, multiplexers, and the front-end processor. Special communications software controls input and output activities and manages other functions of the communications system.

text, graphic images, voice, or video information. This section describes the major components of telecommunications systems. Subsequent sections describe how the components can be arranged into various types of networks.

TELECOMMUNICATIONS SYSTEM COMPONENTS

The following are essential components of a telecommunications system:

1. Computers to process information.

2. Terminals or any input/output devices that send or receive data.

3. Communications channels, the links by which data or voice are transmitted between sending and receiving devices in a network. Communications channels use various communications media, such as telephone lines, fiber-optic cables, coaxial cables, and wireless transmission.

4. Communications processors, such as modems, multiplexers, controllers, and front-end processors, which provide support functions for data transmission and reception.

5. Communications software, which controls input and output activities and manages other functions of the communications network.

FUNCTIONS OF TELECOMMUNICATIONS SYSTEMS

In order to send and receive information from one place to another, a telecommunications system must perform a number of separate functions. The system transmits information, establishes the interface between the sender and the receiver, routes messages along the most efficient paths, performs elementary processing of the information to ensure that the right message gets to the right receiver, performs editorial tasks on the data (such as checking for transmission errors and rearranging the format), and converts messages from one speed (say, the speed of a computer) into the speed of a communications line or from one format to another. Finally, the telecommunications system controls the flow of information. Many of these tasks are accomplished by computers.

A telecommunications network typically contains diverse hardware and software components that need to work together to transmit information. Different components in a network can communicate by adhering to a common set of rules that enable them to talk to each other. This set of rules and procedures governing transmission between two points in a network is called a **protocol**. Each device in a network must be able to interpret the other device's protocol. The principal functions of protocols in a telecommunications network are to identify each device in the communication path, to secure the attention of the other device, to verify correct receipt of the transmitted message, to verify that a message requires retransmission because it cannot be correctly interpreted, and to perform recovery when errors occur.

TYPES OF SIGNALS: ANALOG AND DIGITAL

Information travels through a telecommunications system in the form of electromagnetic signals. Signals are represented in two ways: analog and digital signals. An **analog signal** is represented by a continuous waveform that passes through a communications medium. Analog signals are used to handle voice communications and to reflect variations in pitch.

A **digital signal** is a discrete, rather than a continuous, waveform. It transmits data coded into two discrete states: 1-bits and 0-bits, which are represented as on—off electrical pulses. Most computers communicate with digital signals, as do many local telephone companies and some larger networks. However, if a traditional telephone network is set up to process analog signals, a digital signal cannot be processed without some alterations. All digital signals must be translated into analog signals before they can be transmitted in an analog system. The device that performs this translation is called a **modem** (Modem is an abbreviation for MOdulation/DEModulation.) A modem translates a computer's digital signals into analog form for transmission over ordinary telephone lines, or it translates analog signals back into digital form for reception by a computer (see Figure 8-2).

protocol
A set of rules and procedures that govern transmission between the components in a network.

analog signal
A continuous waveform that passes through a communications medium; used for voice communications.

digital signal
A discrete waveform that transmits data coded into two discrete states as 1-bits and 0-bits, which are represented as on–off electrical pulses; used for data communications.

modem
A device for translating digital signals into analog signals and vice versa.

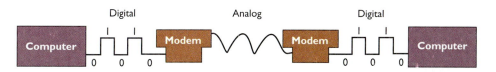

Figure 8-2 Functions of the modem. A modem is a device that translates digital signals from a computer into analog form so that they can be transmitted over analog telephone lines. The modem also is used to translate analog signals back into digital form for the receiving computer.

COMMUNICATIONS CHANNELS

Communications **channels** are the means by which data are transmitted from one device in a network to another. A channel can use different kinds of telecommunications transmission media: twisted wire, coaxial cable, fiber optics, terrestrial microwave, satellite, and other wireless transmission. Each has advantages and limitations. High-speed transmission media are more expensive in general, but they can handle higher volumes, which reduces the cost per bit. For instance, the cost per bit of data can be lower via satellite link than via leased telephone line if a firm uses the satellite link 100 percent of the time. There is also a wide range of speeds possible for any given medium depending on the software and hardware configuration.

channels
The links by which data or voice are transmitted between sending and receiving devices in a network.

Twisted Wire

Twisted wire consists of strands of copper wire twisted in pairs and is the oldest transmission medium. Most of the telephone systems in a building rely on twisted wires installed for analog communication, but they can be used for digital communication as well. Although it is low in cost and already is in place, twisted wire is relatively slow for transmitting data, and high-speed transmission causes interference called *crosstalk*. However, new software and hardware have raised the twisted-wire transmission capacity to make it useful for local- and wide-area computer networks as well as telephone systems.

twisted wire
A transmission medium consisting of pairs of twisted copper wires; used to transmit analog phone conversations but can be used for data transmission.

Coaxial Cable

Coaxial cable, like that used for cable television, consists of thickly insulated copper wire, which can transmit a larger volume of data than twisted wire. It often is used in place of twisted wire for important links in a telecommunications network because it is a faster, more interference-free transmission medium, with speeds of up to 200 megabits per second. However, coaxial cable is thick, is hard to wire in many buildings, and cannot support analog phone conversations. It must be moved when computers and other devices are moved.

coaxial cable
A transmission medium consisting of thickly insulated copper wire; can transmit large volumes of data quickly.

Fiber Optics and Optical Networks

Fiber-optic cable consists of thousands of strands of clear glass fiber, each the thickness of a human hair, which are bound into cables. Data are transformed into pulses of light, which are sent through the fiber-optic cable by a laser device at a rate from 500 kilobits to several trillion bits per second. Fiber-optic cable is considerably faster, lighter, and more durable than wire media and is well suited to systems requiring transfers of large volumes of data. However, fiber-optic cable is more difficult to work with, more expensive, and harder to install.

fiber-optic cable
A fast, light, and durable transmission medium consisting of thin strands of clear glass fiber bound into cables. Data are transmitted as light pulses.

Until recently, fiber-optic cable has been used primarily as the high-speed network **backbone**, whereas twisted wire and coaxial cable have been used to connect the backbone to individual businesses and households. A backbone is the part of a network that handles the major traffic. It acts as the primary path for traffic flowing to or from other networks. Telecommunications carriers are bringing fiber all the way into the basement of buildings so they can provide a variety of new services to business and eventually residential customers. These **optical networks** can transmit all types of traffic—voice, data, and video—over fiber cables and provide the massive bandwidth for new types of services and software. Using optical networks, on-demand video, software downloads, and high-quality digital audio can be accessed using set-top boxes and other information appliances without any degradation in quality or delays.

backbone
Part of a network handling the major traffic and providing the primary path for traffic flowing to or from other networks.

optical network
High-speed networking technologies for transmitting data in the form of light pulses.

For example, Bredbandsbolaget AB, a Swedish local telecommunications carrier, ran fiber to apartment blocks and wired buildings to give each household a dedicated 10 megabits per second connection upgradable to 100 megabits per second if required. Users pay 200 Swedish

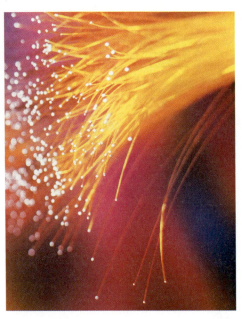

Fiber-optic cable can transmit data that have been transformed into pulses of light at speeds of up to 6 terabits per second. Fiber optic technology is used in high-capacity optical networks.

kroner ($25 per month) for the connection and Internet access, and an additional charge for hundreds of TV channels, programmable TV, video on demand, telephone services, games, and software rentals. Delays are so infrequent on the Bredbandsbolaget network that customers can't tell whether they are working with software programs delivered over the network or those running on their own hardware. Thus, Bredsbandsbolaget can offer games and software rental without the user downloading programs, and customers don't need high-powered PCs to use the services (Heywood, 2000).

Currently, fiber-optic networks are slowed down by the need to convert electrical data to optics to send it over a fiber line and then reconvert it back. The long-term goal is to create pure optical networks in which light packets shuttle digital data at tremendous speed without ever converting them to electrical signals. Many new optical technologies are in development for this purpose. Next-generation optical networks will also boost capacity by using **dense wavelength division multiplexing (DWDM).** DWDM boosts transmission capacity by using many different colors of light, or different wavelengths, to carry separate streams of data over the same fiber strand at the same time. DWDM combines up to 160 wavelengths per strand and can transmit up to 6.4 terabits per second over a single fiber. This technology will enable communications service providers to add bandwidth to an existing fiber-optic network without having to lay more fiber-optic cable. Before wavelength division multiplexing, optical networks could only use a single wavelength per strand.

Wireless Transmission

Wireless transmission that sends signals through air or space without any physical tether has become an increasingly popular alternative to tethered transmission channels, such as twisted wire, coaxial cable, and fiber optics. Today, common technologies for wireless data transmission include microwave transmission, communication satellites, pagers, cellular telephones, personal communication services (PCS), smart phones, personal digital assistants (PDAs), and mobile data networks.

The wireless transmission medium is the electromagnetic spectrum, illustrated in Figure 8-3. Some types of wireless transmission, such as microwave or infrared, by nature occupy specific spectrum frequency ranges (measured in megahertz). Other types of wireless transmissions are actually functional uses, such as cellular telephones and paging devices, that have been assigned a specific range of frequencies by national regulatory agencies and international agreements. Each frequency range has its own strengths and limitations, and these have helped determine the specific function or data communications niche assigned to it.

Microwave systems, both terrestrial and celestial, transmit high-frequency radio signals through the atmosphere and are widely used for high-volume, long-distance, point-to-point communication. Microwave signals follow a straight line and do not bend with the curvature of the earth; therefore, long-distance terrestrial transmission systems require that transmission stations be positioned 25 to 30 miles apart, adding to the expense of microwave.

This problem can be solved by bouncing microwave signals off **satellites,** enabling them to serve as relay stations for microwave signals transmitted from terrestrial stations. Communication satellites are cost effective for transmitting large quantities of data over very long distances. Satellites are typically used for communications in large, geographically dispersed organizations that would be difficult to tie together through cabling media or terrestrial microwave. For instance, Amoco uses satellites for real-time data transfer of oil field exploration data gathered from searches of the ocean floor. Exploration ships transfer these

dense wavelength division multiplexing (DWDM)

Technology for boosting transmission capacity of optical fiber by using many different wavelengths to carry separate streams of data over the same fiber strand at the same time.

microwave

A high-volume, long-distance, point-to-point transmission in which high-frequency radio signals are transmitted through the atmosphere from one terrestrial transmission station to another.

satellite

The transmission of data using orbiting satellites that serve as relay stations for transmitting microwave signals over very long distances.

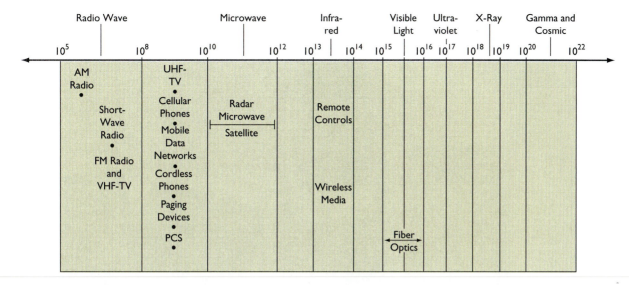

Figure 8-3 Frequency ranges for communications media and devices. Each telecommunications transmission medium or device occupies a different frequency range, measured in megahertz, on the electromagnetic spectrum.

data using geosynchronous satellites to central computing centers in the United States for use by researchers in Houston, Tulsa, and suburban Chicago. Figure 8-4 illustrates how this system works.

Conventional communication satellites move in stationary orbits approximately 22,000 miles above the earth. A newer satellite medium, the low-orbit satellite, is beginning to be deployed. These satellites travel much closer to the earth and are able to pick up signals from weak transmitters. They also consume less power and cost less to launch than conventional satellites. With such wireless networks, businesspeople will be able to travel virtually anywhere in the world and have access to full communication capabilities including videoconferencing and multimedia-rich Internet access.

Other wireless transmission technologies are being used in situations requiring remote access to corporate systems and mobile computing power. **Paging systems** have been used for several decades, originally by beeping when the user received a message and requiring the user to telephone an office to learn about the message. Today, paging devices can send and receive short alphanumeric messages that the user reads on the pager's screen. Paging is useful for communicating with mobile workers, such as repair crews; one-way paging also can provide an inexpensive way of communicating with workers in offices. For example, the law firm Paul, Hastings, Janofsky, & Walker equips its 800 attorneys with BlackBerry two-way pagers to help them keep in close contact with clients while traveling. The paging devices automatically alert the attorneys when they receive new e-mail, voice mail, or fax so that they do not need to constantly make long-distance calls to check their voice mail (Carr, 2001).

paging system
A wireless transmission technology in which the pager beeps when the user receives a message; used to transmit short alphanumeric messages.

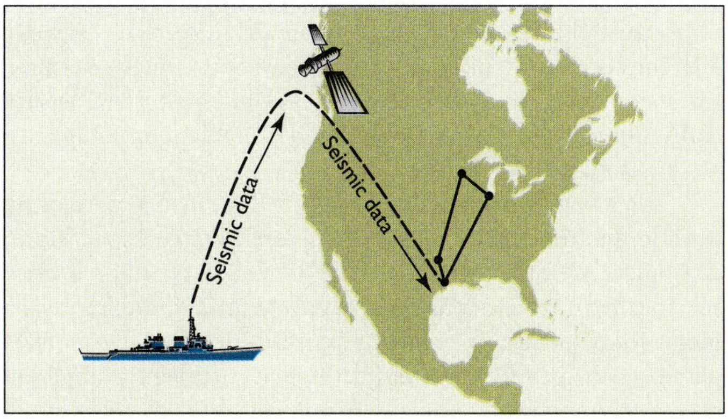

Figure 8-4 Amoco's satellite transmission system. Satellites help Amoco transfer seismic data between oil exploration ships and research centers in the United States.

The Palm VII PDA, Nokia 6360 mobile phone, and the BlackBerry wireless e-mail solution are examples of handheld devices for wireless communication. Some of these devices can provide wireless access to the Internet.

cellular telephone

A device that transmits voice or data, using radio waves to communicate with radio antennas placed within adjacent geographic areas called cells.

personal communication services (PCS)

A digital cellular technology that uses lower power, higher frequency radio waves than does analog cellular technology.

smart phone

Wireless phone with voice, text, and Internet capabilities.

personal digital assistants (PDA)

Small, pen-based, handheld computers with built-in wireless telecommunications capable of entirely digital communications transmission.

mobile data networks

Wireless networks that enable two-way transmission of data files.

Cellular telephones work by using radio waves to communicate with radio antennas (towers) placed within adjacent geographic areas called *cells*. A telephone message is transmitted to the local cell by the cellular telephone and then is handed off from antenna to antenna—cell to cell—until it reaches the cell of its destination, where it is transmitted to the receiving telephone. As a cellular signal travels from one cell into another, a computer that monitors signals from the cells switches the conversation to a radio channel assigned to the next cell. The radio antenna cells normally cover eight-mile hexagonal cells, although their radius is smaller in densely populated localities.

Older cellular systems are analog and newer cellular systems are digital. **Personal communication services (PCS)** are one popular type of digital cellular service. PCS are entirely digital. They can transmit both voice and data and operate in a higher frequency range than analog cellular telephones. PCS cells are much smaller and more closely spaced than analog cells, and can accommodate higher traffic demands.

In addition to handling voice transmission, newer models of digital cellular phones can handle voice mail, e-mail, and faxes, save addresses, access a private corporate network, and access information from the Internet. These **smart phones** are being equipped with Web browser software that lets digital cellular phones or other wireless devices access Web pages formatted to send text or other information that is suitable for tiny screens. Some smart phone models offer larger screens and keypads to make Internet access easier.

Personal digital assistants (PDA) are small, pen-based, handheld computers capable of entirely digital communications transmission. They have built-in wireless telecommunications capabilities as well as work-organization software. A well-known example is the Palm VII connected organizer. It can display and compose e-mail messages and can provide Internet access. The handheld device includes applications such as an electronic scheduler, address book, and expense tracker, and can accept data entered with a special stylus through an on-screen writing pad.

Wireless networks explicitly designed for two-way transmission of data files are called **mobile data networks**. These radio-based networks transmit data to and from handheld computers. One type of mobile data network is based on a series of radio towers constructed specifically to transmit text and data. Ardis is a publicly available network that uses such media for national two-way data transmission. Otis Elevators uses the Ardis network to dispatch repair technicians around the country from a single office in Connecticut and to receive their reports.

WIRELESS SYSTEMS MAKE FOR MEDICAL MOBILITY

Window on Technology

MIS In Action

If you become involved in a serious automobile accident, you may urgently need high-quality medical help on the spot. In Sweden such medical care may be possible through wireless communications. Sweden's National Board of Health and Welfare has installed mobile wireless communications between 51 ambulances and 7 related hospitals. The system, called IS Swede, can access the hospitals' databases and uses wireless LANs, WANs, and a global positioning system (GPS).

When an ambulance arrives at a medical scene, a paramedic can access a patient's stored medical records through IS Swede using a handheld device. She or he often will first transmit the patient's critical measurements, including blood pressure, pulse, and any medication already administered. These data, along with hospital medical records, are transmitted to a doctor who reviews the information and quickly transmits treatment directions back to the paramedic. With this system, the paramedic can treat the patient according to the patient's injury symptoms, allergies, and medical history. The transmitted data update the patient's medical records, and the paramedic attaches a barcode to the patient so the hospital staff will accurately identify that person and have a complete record of treatment already given, plus other treatment the doctor recommended but was impossible on the ambulance. The GPS enables the hospital's emergency room staff to estimate when the patient will arrive and to prepare necessary treatment.

A very different medical application using wireless mobile devices may be helping pharmaceutical companies improve the accuracy and efficiency of their research on potential new drugs. Clinical trials on human beings can take years to conclude, and recording complete and accurate records is difficult. Mobile devices, such as handheld computers and data-enabled cell phones, allow patients to enter their daily, weekly, and monthly data directly into a database. The data might include pulse and blood pressure readings as well as any drugs taken. The mobile devices can also be used to signal patients that it is time to take their measurements and medicine and to report the required data.

GlaxoSmithKline equipped clinical trial patients with Everex PDAs and diary-keeping software to capture data directly from the patients themselves. They sound an alarm when it is time for the patient to take medicine or to answer questions. The patient then touch-answers a series of questions that are displayed in text and graphics. The answers are transmitted weekly to GlaxoSmithKline's server through a wireless modem so that the company can make sure subjects are recording their diary entries each day. Most clinical trials have an attrition rate of 10 to 30 percent, and GlaxoSmithKline hopes that this system will reduce that rate for their study. According to MaryBeth Dalessandro, a GlaxoSmithKline clinical scientist, the wireless system saved the company time by providing data in a much cleaner format.

MAKE IT YOUR BUSINESS

To Think About: How can wireless communication benefit a medical-related company? The general public? What technology, management, and organizational issues need to be addressed when adopting mobile telecommunications systems?

Sources: John Edwards, "Clinical Trial by Mobility," www.mbusinessdaily.com, September 2001; and Jim Geier, "Saving Lives with Roving LANs," *Network World,* February 5, 2001.

Wireless networks and transmission devices can be more expensive, slower, and more error prone than transmission over wired networks (Varshney and Vetter, 2000), although the major digital cellular networks are upgrading the speed of their services. Bandwidth and energy supply in wireless devices require careful management from both hardware and software standpoints (Imielinski and Badrinath, 1994). Security and privacy will be more difficult to maintain because wireless transmission can be easily intercepted (see Chapter 14).

Data cannot be transmitted seamlessly between different wireless networks if they use incompatible standards. For example, digital cellular service in the United States is provided by different operators using one of several competing digital cellular technologies (CDMA, GSM 1900, and TDMA IS-136) that are incompatible. Many digital cellular handsets that use one of these technologies cannot operate in other countries outside North America, which operate at different frequencies with still another set of standards. We provide a detailed discussion of these standards and other standards for networking in Chapter 9.

Wireless communication has many applications, including the healthcare systems described in the Window on Technology.

TABLE 8-1	TYPICAL SPEEDS AND COSTS OF TELECOMMUNICATIONS TRANSMISSION MEDIA

Medium	Speed	Cost
Twisted wire	up to 100 Mbps	Low
Microwave	up to 200+ Mbps	
Satellite	up to 200+ Mbps	
Coaxial cable	up to 200 Mbps	
Fiber-optic cable	up to 6+ Tbps	High

bps = bits per second; Kbps = kilobits per second; Mbps = megabits per second; Gbps = gigabits per second; Tbps = terabits per second

Transmission Speed

The total amount of information that can be transmitted through any telecommunications channel is measured in bits per second (bps). Sometimes this is referred to as the baud rate. A **baud** is a binary event representing a signal change from positive to negative or vice versa. The baud rate is not always the same as the bit rate. At higher speeds a single signal change can transmit more than one bit at a time, so the bit rate generally will surpass the baud rate.

One signal change, or cycle, is required to transmit one or several bits per second; therefore, the transmission capacity of each type of telecommunications medium is a function of its frequency. The number of cycles per second that can be sent through that medium is measured in hertz (see Chapter 6). The range of frequencies that can be accommodated on a particular telecommunications channel is called its **bandwidth**. The bandwidth is the difference between the highest and lowest frequencies that can be accommodated on a single channel. The greater the range of frequencies, the greater the bandwidth and the greater the channel's transmission capacity. Table 8-1 compares the transmission speed and relative costs of the major types of transmissions media.

COMMUNICATIONS PROCESSORS AND SOFTWARE

Communications processors, such as front-end processors, concentrators, controllers, multiplexers, and modems, support data transmission and reception in a telecommunications network. In a large computer system, the **front-end processor** is a special purpose computer dedicated to communications management and is attached to the main, or host, computer. The front-end processor performs communications processing such as error control, formatting, editing, controlling, routing, and speed and signal conversion.

A **concentrator** is a programmable telecommunications computer that collects and temporarily stores messages from terminals until enough messages are ready to be sent economically. The concentrator bursts signals to the host computer.

A **controller** is a specialized computer that supervises communications traffic between the CPU and peripheral devices, such as terminals and printers. The controller manages messages from these devices and communicates them to the CPU. It also routes output from the CPU to the appropriate peripheral device.

A **multiplexer** is a device that enables a single communications channel to carry data transmissions from multiple sources simultaneously. The multiplexer divides the communications channel so that it can be shared by multiple data streams. The multiplexer may divide a high-speed channel into multiple channels of slower speed or may assign each transmission source a very small slice of time for using the high-speed channel.

Special telecommunications software residing in the host computer, front-end processor, and other processors in the network is required to control and support network activities. This software is responsible for functions such as network control, access control, transmission control, error detection/correction, and security. More detail on security software can be found in Chapter 14.

baud

A change in signal from positive to negative or vice versa that is used as a measure of transmission speed.

bandwidth

The capacity of a communications channel as measured by the difference between the highest and lowest frequencies that can be transmitted by that channel.

front-end processor

A special purpose computer dedicated to managing communications for the host computer in a network.

concentrator

Telecommunications computer that collects and temporarily stores messages from terminals for batch transmission to the host computer.

controller

A specialized computer that supervises communications traffic between the CPU and the peripheral devices in a telecommunications system.

multiplexer

A device that enables a single communications channel to carry data transmissions from multiple sources simultaneously.

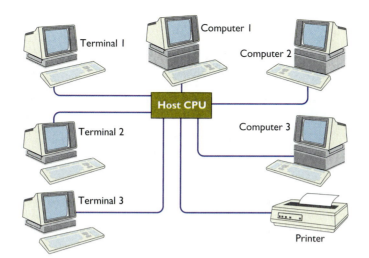

Figure 8-5 A star network topology. In a star network configuration, a central host computer acts as a traffic controller for all other components of the network. All communication between the smaller computers, terminals, and printers must first pass through the central computer.

8.3 COMMUNICATIONS NETWORKS

A number of different ways exist to organize telecommunications components to form a network and hence provide multiple ways of classifying networks. Networks can be classified by their shape, or **topology**. Networks also can be classified by their geographic scope and the type of services provided. This section describes different ways of looking at networks.

NETWORK TOPOLOGIES

One way of describing networks is by their shape, or topology. As illustrated in Figures 8-5 to 8-7, the three most common topologies are the star, bus, and ring.

The Star Network

The **star network** (see Figure 8-5) consists of a central host computer connected to a number of smaller computers or terminals. This topology is useful for applications where some processing must be centralized and some can be performed locally. One problem with the star network is its vulnerability. All communication between points in the network must pass through the central computer. Because the central computer is the traffic controller for the other computers and terminals in the network, communication in the network will come to a standstill if the host computer stops functioning.

The Bus Network

The **bus network** (see Figure 8-6) links a number of computers by a single circuit made of twisted wire, coaxial cable, or fiber-optic cable. All of the signals are broadcast in both directions to the entire network, with special software to identify which components receive each message (there is no central host computer to control the network). If one of the computers in the network fails, none of the other components in the network are affected. However, the channel in a bus network can handle only one message at a time, so performance can degrade if there is a high volume of network traffic. When two computers transmit messages simultaneously, a "collision" occurs, and the messages must be re-sent.

The Ring Network

Like the bus network, the **ring network** (see Figure 8-7) does not rely on a central host computer and will not necessarily break down if one of the component computers malfunctions. Each computer in the network can communicate directly with any other computer, and each processes its own applications independently. However, in a ring

topology
The shape or configuration of a network.

star network
A network topology in which all computers and other devices are connected to a central host computer. All communications between network devices must pass through the host computer.

bus network
Network topology linking a number of computers by a single circuit with all messages broadcast to the entire network.

ring network
A network topology in which all computers are linked by a closed loop in a manner that passes data in one direction from one computer to another.

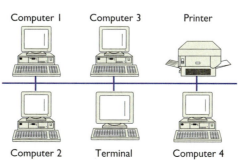

Figure 8-6 A bus network topology. This topology allows all messages to be broadcast to the entire network through a single circuit. There is no central host, and messages can travel in both directions along the cable.

Figure 8-7 A ring network topology. In a ring network configuration, messages are transmitted from computer to computer, flowing in a single direction through a closed loop. Each computer operates independently so that if one fails, communication through the network is not interrupted.

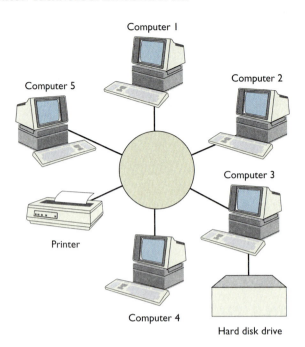

Computer 1

Computer 2

Computer 5

Computer 3

Printer

Computer 4

Hard disk drive

topology, the connecting wire, cable, or optical fiber forms a closed loop. Data are passed along the ring from one computer to another and always flow in one direction. Both ring and bus topologies are used in local area networks (LANs), which are discussed in the next section.

PRIVATE BRANCH EXCHANGES, LOCAL AREA NETWORKS (LANS), AND WIDE AREA NETWORKS (WANS)

Networks may be classified by geographic scope into local networks and wide area networks. Wide area networks encompass a relatively wide geographic area, from several miles to thousands of miles, whereas local networks link local resources, such as computers and terminals, in the same department or building of a firm. Local networks consist of private branch exchanges and local area networks.

Private Branch Exchanges

private branch exchange (PBX)

A central switching system that handles a firm's voice and digital communications.

A **private branch exchange (PBX)** is a special-purpose computer originally designed for handling and switching office telephone calls at a company site. Today's PBXs can carry voice and data to create local networks. PBXs can store, transfer, hold, and redial telephone calls, and they also can be used to switch digital information among computers and office devices. Using a PBX, you can write a letter on a PC in your office, send it to the printer, then dial up the local copying machine and have multiple copies of your letter created.

The advantage of digital PBXs over other local networking options is that they do not require special wiring. A PC connected to a network by telephone can be plugged or unplugged anywhere in a building, using the existing telephone lines. Commercial vendors support PBXs, so the organization does not need special expertise to manage them.

The geographic scope of PBXs is limited, usually to several hundred feet, although the PBX can be connected to other PBX networks or to packet switched networks (see the discussion of network services in this section) to encompass a larger geographic area. The primary disadvantages of PBXs are that they are limited to telephone lines and they cannot easily handle very large volumes of data.

Local Area Networks

local area network (LAN)

A telecommunications network that requires its own dedicated channels and that encompasses a limited distance, usually one building or several buildings in close proximity.

A **local area network (LAN)** encompasses a limited distance, usually one building or several buildings in close proximity. Most LANs connect devices located within a 2,000-foot radius,

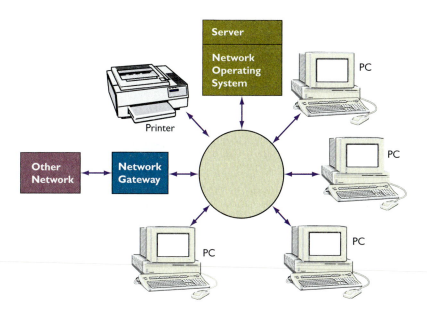

Figure 8-8 A local area network (LAN). A typical local area network connects computers and peripheral devices that are located close to each other, often in the same building.

and they have been widely used to link PCs. LANs require their own communications channels.

LANs generally have higher transmission capacities than PBXs, using bus or ring topologies. They are recommended for applications transmitting high volumes of data and other functions requiring high transmission speeds, including video transmissions and graphics. LANs often are used to connect PCs in an office to shared printers and other resources or to link computers and computer-controlled machines in factories.

LANs are more expensive to install than PBXs and are more inflexible, requiring new wiring each time a LAN is moved. One way to solve this problem is to create a wireless LAN. LANs are usually controlled, maintained, and operated by end users. This means that the user must know a great deal about telecommunications applications and networking.

Figure 8-8 illustrates one model of a LAN. The server acts as a librarian, storing programs and data files for network users. The server determines who gets access to what and in what sequence. Servers may be powerful PCs with large hard-disk capacity, workstations, midrange computers, or mainframes, although specialized computers are available for this purpose.

The network gateway connects the LAN to public networks, such as the telephone network, or to other corporate networks so that the LAN can exchange information with networks external to it. A **gateway** is generally a communications processor that can connect dissimilar networks by translating from one set of protocols to another. A **router** is used to route packets of data and to determine the next point in a network to which data should be sent.

LAN technology consists of cabling (twisted wire, coaxial, or fiber-optic cable) or wireless technology that links individual computer devices, network interface cards (which are special adapters serving as interfaces to the cable), and software to control LAN activities. The LAN network interface card specifies the data transmission rate, the size of message units, the addressing information attached to each message, and network topology (Ethernet uses a bus topology, for example).

LAN capabilities also are defined by the **network operating system (NOS)**. The network operating system can reside on every computer in the network, or it can reside on a single designated server for all the applications on the network. The NOS routes and manages communications on the network and coordinates network resources. Novell NetWare, Microsoft Windows 2000 Server, Windows 2000 Enterprise Server, and IBM's OS/2 Warp Server are popular network operating systems.

LANs may take the form of client/server networks, in which the server provides data and application programs to "client" computers on the network (see the Chapter 6 discussion of client/server computing) or they may use a peer-to-peer architecture. A **peer-to-peer** network treats all processors equally and is used primarily in small networks. Each computer on the network has direct access to each other's workstations and shared peripheral devices.

gateway
A communications processor that connects dissimilar networks by providing the translation from one set of protocols to another.

router
Device that forwards packets of data from one LAN or WAN to another.

network operating system (NOS)
Special software that routes and manages communications on the network and coordinates network resources.

peer-to-peer
Network architecture that gives equal power to all computers on the network; used primarily in small networks.

Wide Area Networks (WANs)

wide area network (WAN)
Telecommunications network that spans a large geographical distance. May consist of a variety of wired, satellite, and microwave technologies.

Wide area networks (WANs) span broad geographical distances, ranging from several miles to entire continents. WANs may consist of a combination of switched and dedicated lines, microwave, and satellite communications. **Switched lines** are telephone lines that a person can access from his or her terminal to transmit data to another computer, the call being routed or switched through paths to the designated destination. **Dedicated lines**, or non-switched lines, are continuously available for transmission, and the lessee typically pays a flat rate for total access to the line. The lines can be leased or purchased from common carriers or private communications media vendors. Most existing WANs are switched. Amoco's network for transmitting seismic data illustrated in Figure 8-4 is a WAN.

When individual business firms maintain their own wide area networks, the firm is responsible for telecommunications content and management. However, private wide area networks are expensive to maintain, or firms may not have the resources to manage their own wide area networks. In such instances, companies may choose to use commercial network services to communicate over vast distances.

switched lines
Telephone lines that a person can access from a terminal to transmit data to another computer, the call being routed or switched through paths to the designated destination.

dedicated lines
Telephone lines that are continuously available for transmission by a lessee. Typically conditioned to transmit data at high speeds for high-volume applications.

NETWORK SERVICES AND BROADBAND TECHNOLOGIES

In addition to topology and geographic scope, networks can be classified by the types of service they provide.

Value-Added Networks (VANs)

Value-added networks are an alternative to firms designing and managing their own networks. **Value-added networks (VANs)** are private, multipath, data-only, third-party-managed networks that can provide economies in the cost of service and in network management because they are used by multiple organizations. The value-added network is set up by a firm that is in charge of managing the network. That firm sells subscriptions to other firms wishing to use the network. Subscribers pay only for the amount of data they transmit plus a subscription fee. The network may use twisted-pair lines, satellite links, and other communications channels leased by the value-added carrier.

The term *value added* refers to the extra value added to communications by the telecommunications and computing services these networks provide to clients. Customers do not have to invest in network equipment and software or perform their own error checking, editing, routing, and protocol conversion. Subscribers may achieve savings in line charges and transmission costs because the costs of using the network are shared among many users. The resulting costs may be lower than if the clients had leased their own lines or satellite services. (Maintaining a private network may be most cost effective for organizations with a high communications volume.) International VANs have representatives with language skills and knowledge of various countries' telecommunications administrations and can arrange access to lines and equipment abroad.

value-added network (VAN)
Private, multipath, data-only, third-party-managed network that multiple organizations use on a subscription basis.

Other Network Services

packet switching
Technology that breaks blocks of text into small, fixed bundles of data and routes them in the most economical way through any available communications channel.

Traditional analog telephone service is based on circuit switching, where a direct connection must be maintained between two nodes in a network for the duration of the transmission session. **Packet switching** is a basic switching technique that can be used to achieve economies and higher speeds in long-distance transmission. VANs and the Internet use packet switching. Packet switching breaks up a lengthy block of text into small, fixed bundles of data called packets. (The X.25 packet switching standard uses packets of 128 bytes each.) The packets include information for directing the packet to the right address and for checking transmission errors along with the data. Data are gathered from many users, divided into small packets, and transmitted via various communications channels. Each packet travels independently through the network. Packets of data originating at one source can be routed through different paths in the network before being reassembled into the original message when they reach their destination. Figure 8-9 illustrates how packet switching works.

frame relay
A shared network service technology that packages data into bundles for transmission but does not use error-correction routines. Cheaper and faster than packet switching.

Frame relay is a shared network service that is faster and less expensive than packet switching and can achieve transmission speeds up to 1.544 megabits per second. Frame relay

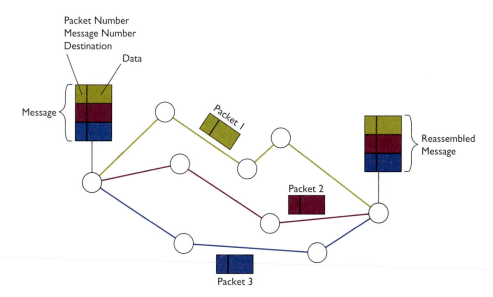

Figure 8-9 Packed-switched networks and packet communications. Data are grouped into small packets, which are transmitted independently via various communications channels and reassembled at their final destination.

packages data into frames that are similar to packets, but it does not perform error correction. It works well on reliable lines that do not require frequent retransmissions because of error.

Most corporations today use separate networks for voice, private-line services, and data, each of which is supported by a different technology. A service called **asynchronous transfer mode (ATM)** may overcome some of these problems because it can seamlessly and dynamically switch voice, data, images, and video between users. ATM also promises to tie LANs and WANs together more easily. (LANs generally are based on lower-speed protocols, whereas WANs operate at higher speeds.) ATM technology parcels information into uniform cells, each with 53 bytes, eliminating the need for protocol conversion. It can pass data between computers from different vendors and permits data to be transmitted at any speed the network handles. ATM can transmit up to 2.5 gigabits per second.

Integrated Services Digital Network (ISDN) is an international standard for dial-up network access that integrates voice, data, image, and video services in a single link. There are two levels of ISDN service: Basic Rate ISDN and Primary Rate ISDN. Each uses a group of B (bearer) channels to carry voice or data along with a D (delta) channel for signaling and control information. Basic Rate ISDN can transmit data at a rate of 128 kilobits per second on an existing local telephone line. Organizations and individuals requiring simultaneous voice or data transmission over one physical line might choose this service. Primary Rate ISDN offers transmission capacities in the megabit range and is designed for large users of telecommunications services.

Other high-capacity services include digital subscriber line (DSL) technologies, cable modems, and T1 lines. Like ISDN, **digital subscriber line (DSL)** technologies also operate over existing copper telephone lines to carry voice, data, and video, but they have higher transmission capacities than ISDN. There are several categories of DSL. Asymmetric digital subscriber line (ADSL) supports a transmission rate of 1.5 to 9 megabits per second when receiving data and up to 640 kilobits per second when sending data. Symmetric digital subscriber line (SDSL) supports the same transmission rate for sending and receiving data of up to 3 megabits per second. **Cable modems** are modems designed to operate over cable TV lines. They can provide high-speed access to the Web or corporate intranets of up to 4 megabits per second. However, cable modems use a shared line so that transmission will slow down if there are a large number of local users sharing the cable line. A cable modem at present has stronger capabilities for receiving data than for sending data. A **T1 line** is a dedicated telephone connection comprising 24 channels that can support a data transmission rate of 1.544 megabits per second. Each of these 64-kilobit-per-second channels can be configured to carry voice or data traffic. These services often are used for high-capacity Internet connections. Table 8-2 summarizes these network services.

asynchronous transfer mode (ATM)

A networking technology that parcels information into 53-byte cells, allowing data to be transmitted between computers from different vendors at any network speed.

Integrated Services Digital Network (ISDN)

International standard for transmitting voice, video, image, and data to support a wide range of service over the public telephone lines.

digital subscriber line (DSL)

A group of technologies providing high-capacity transmission over existing copper telephone lines.

cable modem

Modem designed to operate over cable TV lines to provide high-speed access to the Web or corporate intranets.

T1 line

A dedicated telephone connection comprising 24 channels that can support a data transmission rate of 1.544 megabits per second. Each channel can be configured to carry voice or data traffic.

TABLE 8-2   NETWORK SERVICES

Service	Description	Bandwidth
X.25	Packet-switching standard that parcels data into packets of 128 bytes	Up to 1.544 Mbps
Frame relay	Packages data into frames for high-speed transmission over reliable lines but does not use error-correction routines	Up to 1.544 Mbps
ATM (asynchronous transfer mode)	Parcels data into uniform cells to allow high-capacity transmission of voice, data, images, and video between different types of computers	25 Mbps–2.5 Gbps
ISDN	Digital dial-up network access standard that can integrate voice, data, and video services	Basic Rate ISDN: 128 Kbps; Primary Rate ISDN: 1.5 Mbps
DSL (digital subscriber line)	Series of technologies for high-capacity transmission over copper wires	ADSL–up to 9 Mbps for receiving and up to 640 Kbps for sending data; SDSL–up to 3 Mbps for both sending and receiving
T1	Dedicated telephone connection with 24 channels for high-capacity transmission	1.544 Mbps
Cable modem	Service for high-speed transmission of data over cable TV lines that are shared by many users	Up to 4 Mbps

broadband
High-speed transmission technology. Also designates a communications medium that can transmit multiple channels of data simultaneously.

High-speed transmission technologies are sometimes referred to as **broadband**. The term broadband is also used to designate transmission media that can carry multiple channels simultaneously over a single communications medium.

NETWORK CONVERGENCE

converged network
Network with technology to enable voice, video, and data to run over a single network

Most companies maintain separate networks for voice, data, and video, but products are now available to create **converged networks,** which can deliver voice, data, and video in a single network infrastructure. These multiservice networks can potentially reduce networking costs by eliminating the need to provide support services and personnel for each different type of network. Multiservice networks can be attractive solutions for companies running multime-

---

MIS IN ACTION   DECISIONMAKING

CHOOSING AN INTERNET CONNECTION SERVICE

You run a graphic design company with 15 employees that do page layout and illustrations for magazine and book publishers in many different parts of the United States. You want to take advantage of network services to send files of your illustrations and layout work to your clients for review. The average size of each graphics file you transmit is 4 megabytes and an average of 25 of these files are sent to clients each day. Schedules are tight and productivity can be impacted if all of your network resources are tied up transmitting files. You are also on a very tight budget. The following network services are available in your area. At its current size, your business could use one dedicated telephone line with software that enables up to 20 employees to share Internet use.

Option	Transmission Capacity	Cost
Dial-up service with 56 Kbps analog modems for each employee	56 Kbps	$40 per month for Internet service + basic $35 per month phone charge
ISDN line	128 Kbps	$100 per month + $300 installation fee
Cable modem	1–2 Mbps	$75 per month + $125 installation fee
Synchronous DSL	512 Kbps sending and receiving	$100 for DSL modem + $175 per month
T1 line	1.5 Mbps	$1,200 per month

1. What is the average amount of time your business would spend daily transmitting files for each of these options?
2. Which of these options is most appropriate for your company? Why?
3. If your business expanded and you had 60 employees and 100 files to transmit daily, which option would you choose?

dia applications such as video collaboration, voice-data call centers, distance learning (see the following section), or **unified messaging**. (Unified messaging systems combine voice mail, e-mail, and faxes so they can all be obtained from one system.)

8.4 Electronic Commerce and Electronic Business Technologies

Baxter International, described in Chapter 3, realized the strategic significance of telecommunications. The company placed its own computer terminals in hospital supply rooms. Customers could dial up a local VAN and send their orders directly to the company. Other companies also are achieving strategic benefits by developing electronic commerce and electronic business applications based on networking technologies.

Electronic mail (e-mail), groupware, voice mail, facsimile machines (fax), digital information services, teleconferencing, dataconferencing, videoconferencing, and electronic data interchange are key applications for electronic commerce and electronic business because they provide network-based capabilities for communication, coordination, and speeding the flow of purchase and sale transactions.

Electronic Mail and Groupware

We described the capabilities of electronic mail, or e-mail, in Chapter 6. E-mail eliminates telephone tag and costly long-distance telephone charges, expediting communication between different parts of an organization. Many organizations operate their own internal electronic-mail systems, but communications companies such as MCI and AT&T offer these services, as do commercial on-line information services such as America Online and public networks on the Internet (see Chapter 9). Employee use of e-mail and the Internet has become an important management issue, as described in the Window on Management, which examines whether monitoring employees using e-mail, the Internet, and other network facilities is ethical.

Although e-mail has become a valuable tool for communication, groupware provides additional capabilities for supporting enterprise-wide communication and collaborative work. Individuals, teams, and work groups at different locations in the organization can use groupware to participate in discussion forums and work on shared documents and projects. More details on the use of groupware for collaborative work can be found in Chapters 6 and 10.

Voice Mail and Fax

A **voice mail** system digitizes the sender's spoken message, transmits it over a network, and stores the message on disk for later retrieval. When the recipient is ready to listen, the messages are reconverted to audio form. Various store-and-forward capabilities notify recipients that messages are waiting. Recipients have the option of saving these messages for future use, deleting them, or routing them to other parties.

Facsimile (fax) machines can transmit documents containing both text and graphics over ordinary telephone lines. A sending fax machine scans and digitizes the document image. The digitized document is transmitted over a network and reproduced in hard copy form by a receiving fax machine. The process results in a duplicate, or facsimile, of the original.

Teleconferencing, Dataconferencing, and Videoconferencing

People can meet electronically, even though they are hundreds or thousands of miles apart, by using teleconferencing, dataconferencing, or videoconferencing. **Teleconferencing** allows a group of people to confer simultaneously via telephone or via electronic-mail group communication software. Teleconferencing that includes the ability of two or more people at distant locations to work on the same document or data simultaneously is called **dataconferencing**. With dataconferencing, users at distant locations are able to edit and

unified messaging
System combining voice messages, e-mail, and fax so that they can all be obtained from a single system.

voice mail
A system for digitizing a spoken message and transmitting it over a network.

facsimile (fax)
A machine that digitizes and transmits documents with both text and graphics over telephone lines.

teleconferencing
The ability to confer with a group of people simultaneously using the telephone or electronic-mail group communication software.

dataconferencing
Teleconferencing in which two or more users are able to edit and modify data files simultaneously.

MONITORING EMPLOYEES ON NETWORKS: UNETHICAL OR GOOD BUSINESS?

E-mail usage has exploded as hundreds of millions of people the world over turn to it for speedy, convenient, and inexpensive business and personal communications. Not surprisingly the use of e-mail and the Web for personal reasons at the workplace has also grown. A number of studies have concluded that at least 25 percent of employee on-line time is spent on non-work related Web surfing.

Many companies are starting to monitor their employees' use of e-mail and the Internet. A study by the American Management Association concluded that more than 75 percent of large U.S. companies are recording and reviewing employee communications and activities on the job, including e-mail, Internet connections, and computer files. Is monitoring employee network use unethical, or is it simply good business?

Managers worry about the loss of time and employee productivity when employees are focusing on personal rather than company business. If personal traffic on company networks is too high, it can also clog the company's network so that business work cannot be performed. Lockheed Martin Corporation's network was locked up for 6 hours when an employee sent an e-mail message to other employees concerning an upcoming religious holiday.

Too much time on personal business, Internet or not, can mean lost revenue or overcharges to clients. Some employees may be charging time they spend trading stocks over the Web or pursuing other personal business.

When employees use e-mail or the Web at employer facilities, anything they do, including anything illegal, carries the company's name. Therefore, the employer can be traced and held liable. Managements fear that racist, sexually explicit, or other potentially offensive material could result in adverse publicity and even lawsuits. Even if the company is found not to be liable, responding to lawsuits will cost the company tens of thousands of dollars at a minimum. Companies also fear e-mail leakage of trade secrets.

Some companies try to ban all personal activities on corporate networks—zero tolerance. Others block employee access to specific Web sites or limit personal time on the Web using software that allows them to track the Web sites their employees visit, the amount of time they spend at these sites, and the files they download. Some firms have fired employees that have stepped out of bounds. In July 2000 Dow Chemical fired 50 workers and disciplined 200 others when an e-mail investigation found that employees at all levels had sent pornography and violent images from company computers.

No solution is problem-free, but many consultants believe companies should have a written corporate policy on employee e-mail and Internet use. The policy should include explicit ground rules that state, by position or level, under what circumstances employees can use company facilities for personal e-mail or Internet use. The policy should also inform employees if these activities are monitored and explain why. The rules may need to be tailored to the specific organization because different companies may need to access different Web materials as part of their businesses. For example, although some companies may exclude anyone from visiting sites that have explicit sexual material, law firm or hospital employees may require access, whereas investment firms will need to allow many of their employees access to other investment sites.

To Think About: Should managers monitor employee e-mail and Internet usage? Why or why not? Describe an effective e-mail and Web use policy for a company.

Sources: Lou Hirsch, "The Boss Is Watching: Workplace Monitoring on the Rise," *NewsFactor Network,* June 29, 2001; Stephen Shankland, "Study: Web, E-Mail Monitoring Spreads," *CNET News,* July 8, 2001; "Dow Chemical Fires 50 Workers After E-Mail Investigation," SiliconValley.com, July 27, 2000; Jesse Berst, "How to Spy on Your Employees," *MSNBC Technology,* August 21, 2000; "U.S. Web Use Mostly at Work," Reuters, April 6, 2000; and Michael J. McCarthy, "Web Surfers Beware: The Company Tech May Be a Secret Agent," *Wall Street Journal,* January 10, 2000.

---

modify data (text, such as word processing documents; numeric, such as spreadsheets; and graphic) files. Teleconferencing in which participants see each other over video screens is termed *video teleconferencing,* or **videoconferencing**.

videoconferencing

Teleconferencing in which participants see each other over video screens.

These forms of electronic conferencing are growing in popularity because they save travel time and cost. Legal firms might use videoconferencing to take depositions and to convene meetings between lawyers in different branch offices. Videoconferencing can help companies promote remote collaboration from different locations or fill in personnel expertise gaps. Electronic conferencing is useful for supporting telecommuting, enabling home workers to meet with or collaborate with their counterparts working in the office or elsewhere.

Videoconferencing usually has required special videoconference rooms, videocameras, microphones, television monitors, and a computer equipped with a codec device that con-

With PC desktop videoconferencing systems, users can see each other and simultaneously work on the same document. Organizations are using videoconferencing to improve coordination and save travel time and costs.

verts video images and analog sound waves into digital signals and compresses them for transfer over communications channels. Another codec on the receiving end reconverts the digital signals back into analog for display on the receiving monitor. PC-based, desktop videoconferencing systems in which users can see each other and simultaneously work on the same document are reducing videoconferencing costs so that more organizations can benefit from this technology.

Desktop videoconferencing systems typically provide a local window, in which you can see yourself, and a remote window to display the individual with whom you are communicating. Most desktop systems provide audio capabilities for two-way, real-time conversations and a whiteboard. The whiteboard is a shared drawing program that lets multiple users collaborate on projects by modifying images and text on-line. Software products, such as Microsoft NetMeeting (a feature of the Windows operating system), Netscape Communicator's Conference, and CU-SeeMe (available in both shareware and commercial versions), provide low-cost tools for desktop videoconferencing over the Internet.

DIGITAL INFORMATION SERVICES, DISTANCE LEARNING AND E-LEARNING

Powerful and far-reaching digital electronic services enable networked PC and workstation users to obtain information from outside the firm instantly without leaving their desks.

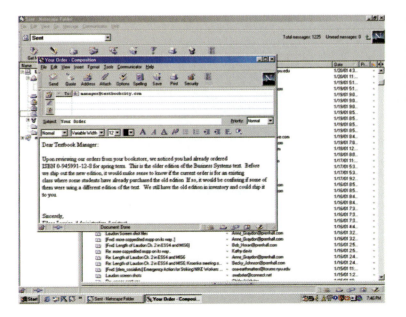

Netscape Communicator includes e-mail functions such as attaching files, displaying messages, and providing logs of all incoming and outgoing messages. E-mail has become an important tool for organizational communication.

| TABLE 8-3 | COMMERCIAL DIGITAL INFORMATION SERVICES |

Provider	Type of Service
America Online	General interest/business information
Prodigy	General interest/business information
Microsoft Network	General interest/business information
Dow Jones News Retrieval	Business/financial information
Dialog	Business/scientific/technical information
Lexis-Nexis	News/business/legal information

Stock prices, periodicals, competitor data, industrial supplies catalogs, legal research, news articles, reference works, and weather forecasts are some of the information that can be accessed on-line. Many of these services provide capabilities for electronic mail, electronic bulletin boards, on-line discussion groups, shopping, and travel reservations as well as Internet access. Table 8-3 describes the leading commercial digital information services. The following chapter describes how organizations can access even more information resources using the Internet.

Organizations can also use communications technology to run distance learning programs where they can train employees in remote locations without requiring the employees to be physically present in a classroom. **Distance learning** is education or training delivered over a distance to individuals in one or more locations. Although distance learning can be accomplished with print-based materials, the distance learning experience is increasingly based on information technology, including videoconferencing, satellite or cable television, or interactive multimedia, including the Web. The term **e-learning** is increasingly being used to describe instruction using purely digital technology delivered over the Internet or private networks. Some distance learning programs use *synchronous communication,* where teacher and student are present at the same time during the instruction, even if they are in different places. Other programs use *asynchronous communication,* where teacher and student don't have person-to-person interaction at the same time or place. For example, students might access a Web site to obtain their course materials and communicate with their instructors via e-mail.

distance learning

Education or training delivered over a distance to individuals in one or more locations.

e-learning

Instruction delivered through purely digital technology using the Internet or private networks.

America Online gives subscribers access to extensive information resources, including news reports, weather, education, financial services, and information on the Web. Companies and individuals can use such digital information services to obtain information instantly from their desktops.

Instructors can use Blackboard Web-based software to provide their students with course materials, virtual assessments, and a dedicated academic resource center on the Web. Such tools can be used to support distance learning.

ELECTRONIC DATA INTERCHANGE

Electronic data interchange (EDI) is a key technology for electronic commerce because it allows the computer-to-computer exchange between two organizations of standard transaction documents such as invoices, bills of lading, or purchase orders. EDI lowers transaction costs because transactions can be automatically transmitted from one information system to another through a telecommunications network, eliminating the printing and handling of paper at one end and the inputting of data at the other. EDI also may provide strategic benefits by helping a firm lock in customers, making it easier for customers or distributors to order from them rather than from competitors. EDI can curb inventory costs by minimizing the amount of time components are in inventory.

electronic data interchange (EDI)

The direct computer-to-computer exchange between two organizations of standard business transaction documents.

EDI differs from electronic mail in that it transmits an actual structured transaction (with distinct fields such as the transaction date, transaction amount, sender's name, and recipient's name) as opposed to an unstructured text message such as a letter. Figure 8-10 illustrates how EDI works.

Organizations can most fully benefit from EDI when they integrate the data supplied by EDI with applications such as accounts payable, inventory control, shipping, and production planning (Premkumar, Ramamurthy, and Nilakanta, 1994), and when they have carefully planned for the organizational changes surrounding new business processes. Management support and training in the new technology are essential (Raymond and Bergeron, 1996). Companies also must standardize the form of the transactions they use with other firms and comply with legal requirements for verifying that the transactions are authentic. Many organizations prefer to use private networks for EDI transactions but are increasingly turning to the Internet for this purpose (see Chapters 4 and 9).

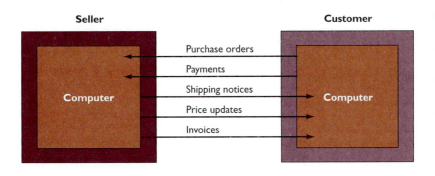

Figure 8-10 Electronic data interchange (EDI). Companies can use EDI to automate electronic commerce transactions. Purchase orders and payments can be transmitted directly from the customer's computer to the seller's computer. The seller can transmit shipping notices, price changes, and invoices electronically back to the customer.

MIS IN ACTION   MANAGER'S TOOLKIT

DEVELOPING A BUSINESS-DRIVEN TELECOMMUNICATIONS PLAN

Throughout your career you may be asked to find ways to use telecommunications technology to enhance your firm's competitive position. Here are the steps you need to take to develop a strategic telecommunications plan.

1. Determine the role of telecommunications in your firm's strategy. If your firm's long-range business plan requires increasing the scale and scope of operations, creating new products or services, or lowering operational costs, consider whether new telecommunications applications and services could promote these objectives.

2. Assess your firm's existing voice, data, and video communications capabilities. Are they sufficient to meet future business goals? What areas need improvement?

3. If additional telecommunications capabilities are required, establish the scope of these capabilities. You will need to consider:

   ▪ Distance: Are future communications needs primarily local or long distance?

   ▪ Services: What range of telecommunications services are needed: Do they include e-mail, EDI, voice mail, videoconferencing, graphics transmission, and internally generated transactions? Do these services need to be integrated?

   ▪ Points of access: How many different locations and users in the organization require access to new communications services and capabilities?

   ▪ Utilization: What frequency and volume of communications does your firm anticipate?

   ▪ Cost: How much do proposed telecommunications technology options cost? Which cost components are fixed? Which are variable?

   ▪ Security: What level of security and reliability do proposed networks have to maintain?

   ▪ Connectivity: How much time, money, and effort would be required to make sure all of the disparate components of a network or multiple networks can communicate with each other (see Chapter 9)?

MAKE IT YOUR BUSINESS

FINANCE AND ACCOUNTING

Telecommunications is widely used in specialized financial services firms and in other businesses to expedite funds transfer. Many non-financial companies use electronic data interchange (EDI) to transfer payments to suppliers and invoices to large corporate customers. Banks maintain networks to link their automated teller machines (ATMs) and branch offices to central computers that keep track of deposit, withdrawal, and fund transfer transactions occurring at remote locations. Financial services firms today depend on networked systems to provide their managers and clients with instant access to account information. These firms are heavy users of on-line digital information services, such as Dow Jones, to obtain data on firms' financial positions and on financial markets.

HUMAN RESOURCES

Contemporary human resources systems have realized great efficiencies by using communications technology to provide authorized human resources professionals and employees with direct on-line access to employee information. Employees can use telephone-based systems, the Web, or private corporate networks to review their employment records or make changes to their benefits plans. Managers can use e-mail and videoconferencing to communicate with employees and work teams. You can find examples of human resources applications on pages 257 and 266.

MANUFACTURING AND PRODUCTION

The manufacturing and production function has become highly networked and telecommunications-driven. Computers and computer-controlled machines on the factory floor are often linked in LANs. In companies with advanced manufacturing systems, each step in the manufacturing process uses networks to transmit data to the next step. Data from orders trigger transactions that can be transmitted via networks directly to manufacturing scheduling systems, to supply chain management systems, to the assembly line, and to systems for warehousing and delivery. You can find examples of manufacturing and production applications on pages 248–249 and 274–275.

SALES AND MARKETING

Many sales transactions today take place using point-of-sale systems that capture sales transaction data at the checkout counter using bar code scanners or other devices. These data are often transmitted via networks to the firm's central computer where they update the firm's order processing and inventory systems. Once consolidated in corporate systems, these data can be analyzed to identify high-performing and low-performing items, buying trends, and items needing rapid replenishment from suppliers. E-mail and call centers where customer telephone calls are directed to service representatives have become popular technologies for customer service and support. You can find examples of sales and marketing applications on pages 274–275.

MANAGEMENT WRAP-UP

Managers need to be continuously involved in telecommunications decisions because so many important business processes are based on telecommunications and networks. Management should identify the business opportunities linked to telecommunications technology and establish the business criteria for selecting the firm's telecommunications platform.

Telecommunications technology enables organizations to reduce transaction and coordination costs, promoting electronic commerce and electronic business. The organization's telecommunications infrastructure should support its business processes and business strategy.

Communications technology is intertwined with all the other information technologies and deeply embedded in contemporary information systems. Networks are becoming more pervasive and powerful, with capabilities to transmit voice, data, and video over long distances. Many alternative network designs, transmission technologies, and network services are available to organizations.

For Discussion

1. Network design is a key business decision as well as a technology decision. Why?

2. If you were an international company with global operations, what criteria would you use to determine whether to use a VAN service or a private WAN?

SUMMARY

1. *What technologies are used in telecommunications systems?* A telecommunications system consists of devices that create a network for communication from one location to another by electronic means. The essential components of a telecommunications system are computers, terminals, other input/output devices, communications channels, communications processors (such as modems, multiplexers, controllers, and front-end processors), and telecommunications software. Different components of a telecommunications network can communicate with each other with a common set of rules termed *protocols*. Data are transmitted throughout a telecommunications network using either analog signals or digital signals. A modem is a device that translates analog signals to digital signals and vice versa.

2. *What telecommunications transmission media should our organization use?* The capacity of a telecommunications channel is determined by the range of frequencies it can accommodate. The higher the range of frequencies, called bandwidth, the higher the capacity (measured in bits per second). The principal transmission media are twisted copper telephone wire, coaxial copper cable, fiber-optic cable, and wireless transmission using microwave, satellite, low-frequency radio waves, or infrared waves. The choice of transmission medium depends on the distance and volume of communication required by the organization and its financial resources. Fiber-optic and coaxial cable are used for high-volume transmission but are expensive to install. Twisted wire can only

transmit low volumes of data, but it is less expensive than other media, allowing companies to use the existing wiring for telephone systems for digital communication. Microwave and satellite are used for wireless communication over long distances.

3. *How should our organization design its networks?* Network design should be based on the organization's information requirements and the distance required for transmission. The three common network topologies are the star network, the bus network, and the ring network. In a star network, all communications must pass through a central computer, and star networks are primarily used when some centralized processing is required. The bus network links a number of devices to a single channel and broadcasts all of the signals to the entire network, with special software to identify which components receive each message. In a ring network, each computer in the network can communicate directly with any other computer but the channel is a closed loop. Data are passed along the ring from one computer to another. Network design should also consider geographic scope. Local area networks (LANs) and private branch exchanges (PBXs) are used to link offices and buildings in close proximity. LANs require special wiring, but PBXs are limited to existing telephone lines and low transmission speeds. Wide area networks (WANs) span a broad geographical distance, ranging from several miles to continents, and are private networks that are independently managed.

4. *What alternative network services are available to our organization?* A number of services are available to organizations for network management and Internet access. Value-added networks (VANs) sell wide area networking services to companies that do not want to build or maintain their own private networks. VANs (and the Internet) achieve economies and higher speeds in long-distance transmission by using packet switching, which breaks messages into small packets that are sent independently along different paths in a network and then reassembled at their destination.

Integrated Services Digital Network (ISDN) is an international standard for dial-up network access that integrates voice, data, image, and video services in a single link. Basic Rate ISDN can transmit data at a rate of 128 kilobits per second on an existing local telephone line.

Firms have the option of using frame relay, asynchronous transfer mode (ATM), digital subscriber line, cable modem, and T1 lines for high transmission capacity. Frame relay is a shared network service that is faster and less expensive than packet switching because it does not perform error correction routines. ATM can seamlessly and dynamically switch voice, data, images, and video between computers from different vendors and can tie LANs and wide area networks together. ATM can transmit up to 2.5 GBPS.

Digital subscriber line (DSL) technologies, cable modems, and T1 lines are often used for high-capacity Internet connections. Like ISDN, DSL technologies also operate over existing copper telephone lines to carry voice, data, and video, but they have higher transmission capacities than ISDN. Asymmetric digital subscriber line (ADSL) supports a transmission rate of 1.5 to 9 megabits per second when receiving data and up to 640 kilobits per second when sending data. Symmetric digital subscriber line (SDSL) supports the same transmission rate for sending and receiving data of up to 3 megabits per second. Cable modems are modems designed to operate over cable TV lines. They can provide high-speed access to the Web or corporate intranets of up to 4 megabits per second. A T1 line is a dedicated telephone connection comprising 24 channels that can support a data transmission rate of 1.544 megabits per second. Each of these 64-kilobit-per-second channels can be configured to carry voice or data traffic.

5. *What telecommunications applications can be used for electronic commerce and electronic business?* The principal telecommunications applications for electronic commerce and electronic business are electronic mail, voice mail, fax, digital information services, distance learning and e-learning, teleconferencing, dataconferencing, videoconferencing, electronic data interchange (EDI), and groupware. EDI is the computer-to-computer exchange between two organizations of standard transaction documents such as invoices, bills of lading, and purchase orders.

KEY TERMS

Analog signal, 252

Asynchronous transfer mode (ATM), 263

Backbone, 253

Bandwidth, 258

Baud, 258

Broadband, 264

Bus network, 259

Cable modem, 263

Cellular telephone, 256

Channels, 253

Coaxial cable, 253

Concentrator, 258

Controller, 258

Converged network, 264

Dataconferencing, 265

Dedicated lines, 262

Dense wavelength division multiplexing (DWDM), 254

Digital signal, 252

Digital subscriber line (DSL), 263

Distance learning, 268

E-learning, 268

Electronic data interchange (EDI), 269

Facsimile (fax), 265

Fiber-optic cable, 253

Frame relay, 262

Front-end processor, 258

Gateway, 261

Information superhighway, 251

Integrated Services Digital Network (ISDN), 263

Local area network (LAN), 260

Microwave, 254

Mobile data networks, 256

Modem, 252

Multiplexer, 258

Network operating system (NOS), 261

Optical network, 253

Packet switching, 262

Paging system, 255

Peer-to-peer, 261

Personal communication services (PCS), 256

Personal digital assistants (PDA), 256

Private branch exchange (PBX), 260

Protocol, 252

Ring network, 259

Router, 261

Satellite, 254

Smart phone, 256

Star network, 259

Switched lines, 262

T1 line, 263

Telecommunications, 250

Telecommunications system, 251

Teleconferencing, 265

Topology, 259

Twisted wire, 253

Unified messaging, 265

Value-added network (VAN), 262

Videoconferencing, 266

Voice mail, 265

Wide area network (WAN), 262

REVIEW QUESTIONS

1. What is the significance of telecommunications deregulation for managers and organizations?

2. What is a telecommunications system? What are the principal functions of all telecommunications systems?

3. Name and briefly describe each of the components of a telecommunications system.

4. Distinguish between an analog and a digital signal.

5. Name the different types of telecommunications transmission media and compare them in terms of speed and cost.

6. Name and describe the technologies used for wireless transmission.

7. What are optical networks? Why are they becoming important?

8. What is the relationship between bandwidth and a channel's transmission capacity?

9. Name and briefly describe the different kinds of communications processors.

10. Name and briefly describe the three principal network topologies.

11. Distinguish between a PBX and a LAN.

12. What are the components of a typical LAN? What are the functions of each component?

13. List and describe the various network services.

14. Distinguish between a WAN and a VAN.

15. Define the following: modem, baud, protocol, converged network, and broadband.

16. Name and describe the telecommunications applications that can support electronic commerce and electronic business.

APPLICATION SOFTWARE EXERCISE

SPREADSHEET EXERCISE: ANALYZING TELECOMMUNICATIONS COSTS

Your company is a moderately sized business headquartered in Albany, NY with satellite offices in four other locations. You have been asked to compare your current flat-rate, long-distance telephone plan with three sliding-rate, long-distance plans to see if you can reduce your communication costs. Table 1 provides the telephone usage statistics for all your company locations.

TABLE 1
CURRENT TELEPHONE SYSTEM USAGE

Location	No. of Calls/month (Day/Night)	Total Minutes/month (Day/Night)
Albany	300/20	1100/50
Philadelphia	200/15	500/30
Raleigh-Durham	200/15	500/30
Atlanta	300/20	1000/50
Miami	300/20	1000/50

Use this information and the table of telecommunications rates provided at the Laudon Web site for Chapter 8 to create a spreadsheet that will help your company select the least expensive telecommunications plan. You should assume that all of the alternative plans provide the same quality of service.

GROUP PROJECT

With a group of two or three of your fellow students, describe in detail the ways that telecommunications technology can provide a firm with competitive advantage. Use the companies described in Chapter 3 or other chapters you have read so far to illustrate the points you make, or select examples of other companies using telecommunications from business or computer magazines. If possible, use electronic presentation software to present your findings to the class.

TOOLS FOR INTERACTIVE LEARNING

INTERNET CONNECTION

The Internet Connection for this chapter will take you to the Rosenbluth Travel Web site where you can complete an exercise to analyze how Rosenbluth International uses the Web and communications technology in its daily operations. You can also use the Interactive Study Guide to test your knowledge of the topics in the chapter and get instant feedback where you need more practice.

ELECTRONIC BUSINESS PROJECT

At the Laudon Web site for Chapter 8, you can find an Electronic Business project to compare and evaluate the supply chain management services of Schneider National and J.B. Hunt.

CD-ROM

If you use the Multimedia Edition CD-ROM with this chapter, you can find a video demonstrating the capabilities of personal communication services, an audio overview of the major themes of this chapter, and bullet text summarizing the key points of the chapter.

CASE STUDY—*Schneider National Keeps on Trucking with Communications Technology*

Schneider National is far-and-away the largest trucking firm in the United States, with about 19,000 employees and a fleet of nearly 15,000 trucks (cabs) and 43,000 trailers. The company is so large that it is $1 billion larger than the next two largest trucking firms combined. Headquartered in Green Bay, Wisconsin, Schneider National services two-thirds of the Fortune 500 corporations, including such major clients as General Motors, Wal-Mart, Kimberly-Clark, Procter & Gamble, Chrysler, Sears Roebuck, and Staples. The company is privately owned and had annual sales in 2000 of about $3.1 billion, a growth of nearly 11 percent from the previous year.

Schneider National was a major trucking firm with Don Schneider as its CEO when, in the 1980s, the federal government deregulated the trucking industry, revolutionizing the business environment of the industry overnight. Interstate trucking firms no longer had to follow the rules of a regulatory bureaucracy about what kinds of freight to carry and where to take it. These rules had made it difficult for customers to change carriers because only certain trucking firms could meet these regulations. Competition for customers heated up. Schneider National responded to these demands with a multipronged strategy based on the use of information technology, so that computer systems were now playing a powerful role in Schneider National's operations. Moreover the company also began treating its employees differently, a major step toward democratizing the company. The company made a paradigm shift. Several other competitors responded to deregulation by merely lowering rates. They went bankrupt.

CEO Don Schneider's business philosophy emphasizes IT. Basic to his philosophy is Schneider National's communications with its customers. In its giant headquarters building, the ground floor contains its call center, a full acre in size, where 600 customer service representatives work. Using computers, they have easy access to any customer's history, enabling each customer service representative to answer customers' questions. The result is that the customer is satisfied and the jobs of Schneider National reps are eased. New customer service reps are given 4 to 6 weeks of training, much of it on the use of both the company's computer systems and the Web.

In 2000, 50 percent of Schneider National's customer orders were received either on the Web or on its electronic data interchange (EDI) system. Through the use of these electronic connections, the order automatically arrives in Schneider National's computer system, resulting in improved ordering accuracy and higher productivity, thus lowering the cost of the whole ordering operation. Moreover, within 15 to 30 minutes of sending an order electronically, customers know what truck will arrive and when. The system also includes electronic invoicing. The reason electronic orders encompass only 50 percent of the total orders received is because the Web system is new whereas EDI is an older technology, dating from the 1960s, that is very expensive, so the small companies cannot afford it. However, the Web is very inexpensive and easy to use, and Schneider is trying to get all of its customers to use the Web ordering system. In fact the goal for 2001 is to have 60 percent of Schneider orders arrive electronically, with the gain being through the Web.

Schneider's Web site was created by Schneider Logistics, a company spun off from Schneider to provide information technology and supply chain management services to Schneider and other companies. Its concept is for the transactions to be completely paperless. Ultimately, it will enable customers to enter their orders, check the status of their shipments—what truck or railroad car their goods are on, where they are now, and when they are scheduled to arrive—as well as check proof-of-delivery. All future services will be built to execute within a Web browser.

To make available the information that its customers require, and to plan its pickups, deliveries, and routes, Schneider National must gather a great deal of information about the trucks, both cabs and trailers. "Trucking companies are asset-intensive businesses," explained Donald Broughton, a senior transportation analyst at A. G. Edwards & Sons. He emphasized how crucial the use of the cabs and trailers can be when he added, "The guy who has the higher rate of asset utilization wins."

In 1998 Schneider National became the first fleet trucking company to use OmniTracs. OmniTracs is a satellite-based communications and positioning system produced by QualComm, the San Diego-based wireless communications company. Schneider National worked with QualComm in the development of the product. For it to operate, each tractor has a radio frequency identification tag, a computer with keyboard in the cab, and a satellite antenna with a GPS (global positioning system) on the back of the tractor. Using this system, the company knows where every truck is within 300 feet at all times. The driver and headquarters communicate as often as required. The dispatchers can send information to the driver on how to get to the delivery spot (if there is a problem), the location of the next pickup (usually from someplace nearby), directions to the pickup spot, the necessary papers (if any are required), and even traffic and road problems. The driver can respond with approval and raise any questions about the instructions, the truck, or the road. Schneider National sends and receives about four million messages per month.

The cost of OmniTracs system was $30 million. Schneider thought the drivers' response to the system might be negative, but he was wrong. "We thought drivers wouldn't know how to use it or want to use it," he said. "What we found was exactly the opposite," because they were frustrated at having to stop along the road and call headquarters at telephone booths every few hours. In fact the system has been such a success that by 2001 more than 1,250 fleet trucking companies had started using it.

Schneider National worked with QualComm again to develop SensorTracs in order to collect engine data, such as speed, RPMs, and oil pressure, via satellite. The data not only contribute to better maintenance of the engines but also help drivers to drive more safely and to take better care of the vehicles. The system can even increase the drivers' incomes. One element of a driver's monthly bonus is based on staying within certain key factor ranges when operating the vehicle.

Currently, Schneider National is working with QualComm to develop a trailer-tracking system. It too is wireless. Each trailer has a radio frequency identification tag, which is read by devices that are placed at various points along the rail lines and in the rail yards. The data are directly linked to Schneider National's fleet management and logistics systems. They tell the dispatchers and the customer reps if the trailers are empty or full and if they are hooked onto a cab, sitting in a yard, or rolling on a train. "Ultimately revenue is the measurement of how well we load and move these trailers, " said Paul Mueller, president of Schneider Technology Services, a unit of Schneider Logistics. "It is not uncommon to have to send drivers off-route to get [empty] trailers. When they arrive, the trailer isn't there or it might be loaded." Schneider National sees the new trailer-tracking system as a way to improve customer service through more on-time deliveries and better in-transit knowledge. It should increase drivers' satisfaction by increasing their billable miles and so their earnings. Ultimately it will increase trailer utilization and efficiency. The company does not intend to use it to reduce the number of trailers it owns because its orders are increasing. However, it does want to reduce the number of new trailers it needs to purchase so that it can use the saved funds elsewhere.

Schneider's Global Scheduling System (GSS) helps to optimize the use of both the company drivers and the loads throughout the country. The system processes about 7,000 load assignments daily, looking at all the possible combinations of drivers and loads on any one day. It accesses more than 7,000 possible combinations of drivers and loads per second, and of course the loads and trucks are at different locations each day. Its primary value is servicing customers by satisfying their requests to move freight. However, the GSS can also save the company money because fuel is expensive, and the system makes it more likely that when the trucker delivers his or her load, the next load to be picked up is close by.

Information technology is also being used to help Schneider retain drivers. There is an industry shortage of 80,000 to 100,000 drivers a year. The company's Touch Home program uses the existing in-cab computer technology to give the drivers e-mail access via satellite. The system thus enables drivers to stay in contact with their families.

The company is forging ahead. For example, currently it is working with *Network Computing* magazine on a Web site in which the entire logistics transaction will be accomplished electronically, including the order, its acceptance, pickup, delivery, billing, payment, and reporting. "Then order management will be a no-touch process from front to back," declared Steve Matheys, Schneider's vice president for application development. "That's a huge cost-saver and customer satisfaction play."

Sources: Todd Datz, "In IT for the Long Haul," *Darwin Magazine*, September 2001; Paul Musson, "Schneider National Partners with Sun for Service and Support," *Serverworld Magazine*, January 2001; "Schneider National Selects QualComm Trailer Tracking Solutions," www.qualcomm.com/pressroom, April 9, 2001; "Schneider National, Inc.," *The Industry Standard*, August 29, 2001; Bill Roberts, "Keep on Trackin'," *CIO Magazine*, June 15, 2000; Joel Conover, "Network Computing and Schneider National: Building an Enterprise Proving Grounds," *Network Computing*, July 20, 2000; Kelly Jackson Higgins, "Schneider National Rolls into the Web Age," *Network Computing*, February 7, 2000; Douglas Hubbard, "Try Simulation," *CIO Magazine*, June 15, 2000; and Esther Shein, "Smooth Operators," *CIO Magazine*, August 15, 2000.

CASE STUDY QUESTIONS

1. Analyze Schneider National and its business model using the value chain and competitive forces models.

2. What business strategy did Schneider National adopt? What is the role of telecommunications and information systems in that strategy?

3. How did Schneider's information systems change its business processes?

4. What management, organization, and technology issues did Schneider National have to address when information technology became so pervasive in its operations?

5. Has Schneider National's reliance upon information systems been successful? Is the company transforming itself into a digital firm? Why or why not?

9

THE INTERNET AND THE NEW INFORMATION TECHNOLOGY INFRASTRUCTURE

objectives

As a manager, you'll need to know how to maximize the benefits of Internet technology in your firm's information technology infrastructure. After completing this chapter, you will be able to answer the following questions:

1. *What is the new information technology (IT) infrastructure for business? Why is connectivity so important in this infrastructure?*

2. *How does the Internet work? What are its major capabilities?*

3. *How can organizations benefit from the Internet?*

4. *What are the principal technologies for supporting electronic commerce and electronic business?*

5. *What management problems are raised by the new information technology (IT) infrastructure? How can businesses solve these problems?*

MAKE **IT** YOUR BUSINESS

First Service Networks' Wireless Web Breakthrough

First Service Networks (FSN), based in Stamford, Connecticut, is a national maintenance contractor that works with more than 3,500 local firms throughout the United States to provide maintenance and repair services for more than 200 clients with 25,000 commercial sites. Coordinating thousands of local subcontractors often strained the company's 15-person customer service call center. If, for instance, clients phoned in 1,000 service requests, FSN representatives would have to pick up and answer 1,000 different incoming phone calls, then make 1,000 outgoing calls to local service contractors and finally call back each customer to inform them when the service contractor would arrive. These manual processes proved both cumbersome and expensive.

The company decided it required new business processes supported by more leading-edge information technology. Working with the PriceWaterhouse Coopers consulting firm, FSN decided to revamp its information technology infrastructure

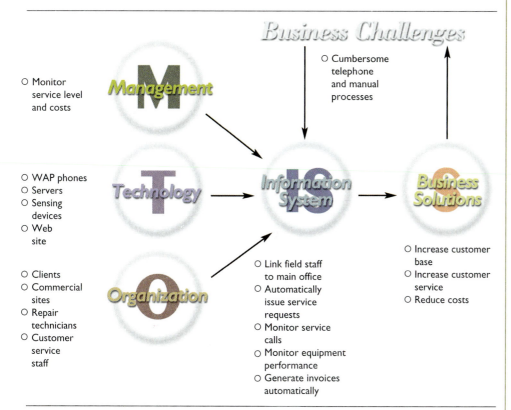

so that it could link directly with a customer's headquarters, individual commercial locations, and service contractors. In May 2001, FSN completed a $7.5 million project to link mobile phones to its customer relationship management (CRM) and financial applications. The phones were Web enabled using the Wireless Application Protocol (WAP).

Clients have three alternative ways of notifying FSN—via telephone by entering a service call, over the Internet, or by using a remote sensing device that automatically signals the system when there is a problem. Siebel Systems Field Service software automatically routes service requests accompanied by the history of the equipment being serviced to the WAP mobile phone of the appropriate local contractor. On receiving the service request as an electronic message on their mobile phones, the repair technicians enter their estimated arrival time using their mobile phone keypads. This information is immediately transmitted to FSN's main server for both FSN and its customers to view on the Web. Once the service technicians arrive on the job and determine the needed repairs, they use their phones to key in service status and service codes for transmittal to FSN's server and for on-line review and approval by the client and FSN. The customer can provide immediate on-line feedback if there is a dollar limit on the service cost. After the work is completed, the service technician electronically initiates an invoice, which is transmitted back to FSN's home office for approval.

FSN customers can use its Web site to monitor the status of the service calls and can generate reports comparing the performance of equipment throughout all their stores to identify problems. FSN can also use the system to monitor its subcontractors' performance and call center staffing levels as call volume rises.

Using this new system, bills can be collected more swiftly. With the old telephone-based system, FSN might not receive bills from subcontractors until 12 weeks after the work was finished. The new system passes information on the completed repair directly from the customer site to FSN's financial software, so that the contractor can be paid within 30 days. About 80 percent of service requests can now be handled without the old call center, so that each employee can handle five times more requests than in the past. FSN can keep its costs and prices low and handle additional service calls without any additional expense.

Sources: Robert Scheier, "The Wireless Workforce Pays Off," *mBusiness*, October 2001; and "First Service Networks: Clearing the Workflow Fog," PriceWaterhouse Coopers, 2001.

MANAGEMENT CHALLENGES

Like First Service Networks, many companies are extending their information technology infrastructures to include mobile computing devices, access to the Internet, and electronic links to other organizations. Electronic commerce, electronic business, and the emerging digital firm require a new information technology infrastructure that can integrate information from a variety of sources and applications. However, using Internet technology and this new IT infrastructure to digitally enable the firm raises the following management challenges:

1. **Taking a broader perspective on infrastructure development.**
   Electronic commerce and electronic business require an information technology infrastructure that can coordinate commerce-related transactions and operational activities across business processes and perhaps link the firm to others in its industry. The new IT infrastructure for the digitally enabled firm connects the whole enterprise and links with other infrastructures, including those of other organizations and the public Internet. Management can no longer think in terms of isolated networks and applications, or technologies confined to organizational boundaries.

2. **Selecting technologies for the new information technology (IT) infrastructure.** Internet technology, XML, and Java can only provide limited connectivity and application integration. Many firms have major applications where disparate hardware, software, and network components must be coordinated through other means. Networks based on one standard may not be able to be linked to those based on another without additional equipment, expense, and management overhead. Mobile computing devices may need to be integrated with corporate databases. Networks that meet today's requirements may lack the connectivity for domestic or global expansion in the future. Managers may have trouble choosing the right set of technologies for the firm's information technology (IT) infrastructure.

9.1 THE NEW INFORMATION TECHNOLOGY (IT) INFRASTRUCTURE FOR THE DIGITAL FIRM

Today's firms can use the information technologies we have described in previous chapters to create an information technology (IT) infrastructure capable of coordinating the activities of entire firms and even entire industries. By enabling companies to radically reduce their agency and transaction costs this new IT infrastructure provides a broad platform for electronic commerce, electronic business, and the emerging digital firm. This new IT infrastructure is based on powerful networks and Internet technology.

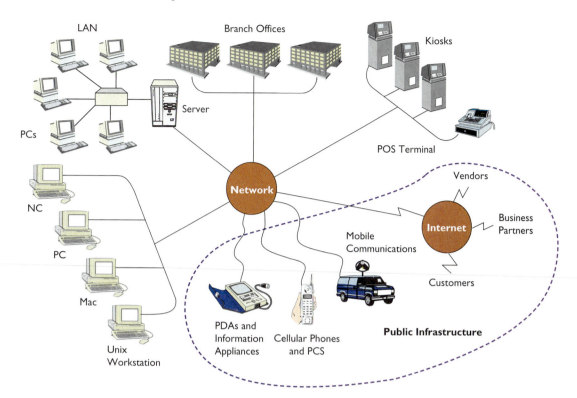

Figure 9-1   The new information technology (IT) infrastructure: The new IT infrastructure links desktop workstations, network computers, LANs, and server computers in an enterprise network so that information can flow freely between different parts of the organization. The enterprise network may also be linked to kiosks, point-of-sale (POS) terminals, PDAs, digital cellular telephones and PCS, and other mobile computing devices as well as to the Internet using public infrastructures. Customers, suppliers, and business partners may also be linked to the organization through this new IT infrastructure.

ENTERPRISE NETWORKING AND INTERNETWORKING

Figure 9-1 illustrates the new information technology (IT) infrastructure. The new IT infrastructure uses a mixture of computer hardware supplied by different vendors. Large, complex databases that need central storage are found on mainframes or specialized servers, whereas smaller databases and parts of large databases are loaded on PCs and workstations. Client/server computing often is used to distribute more processing power to the desktop. The desktop itself has been extended to a larger workspace that includes programmable cell phones, PDAs, pagers, and other mobile computing devices. This new IT infrastructure also incorporates public infrastructures, such as the telephone system, the Internet, and public network services. Internet technology plays a pivotal role in this new infrastructure as the principal communication channel with customers, employees, vendors, and distributors.

In the past, firms generally built their own software and developed their own computing facilities. As today's firms move toward this new infrastructure, their information systems departments are changing their roles to managers of software packages and software and networking services provided by outside vendors.

Through enterprise networking and internetworking, information flows smoothly between all of these devices within the organization and between the organization and its external environment. In **enterprise networking,** the organization's hardware, software, network, and data resources are arranged to put more computing power on the desktop and to create a company-wide network linking many smaller networks. The system is a network. In fact, for all but the smallest organizations the system is composed of multiple networks. A high-capacity backbone network connects many local area networks and devices.

The backbone may be connected to the networks of other organizations outside the firm, to the Internet, to the networks of public telecommunication service providers or to other public networks. The linking of separate networks, each of which retains its own identity, into an interconnected network is called **internetworking.**

enterprise networking

An arrangement of the organization's hardware, software, network, and data resources to put more computing power on the desktop and create a company-wide network linking many smaller networks.

internetworking

The linking of separate networks, each of which retains its own identity, into an interconnected network.

STANDARDS AND CONNECTIVITY FOR DIGITAL INTEGRATION

The new IT infrastructure is most likely to increase productivity and competitive advantage when digitized information can move seamlessly through the organization's web of electronic networks, connecting different kinds of machines, people, sensors, databases, functional divisions, departments, and work groups. This ability of computers and computer-based devices to communicate with one another and "share" information in a meaningful way without human intervention is called **connectivity.** Internet technology, XML, and Java software provide some of this connectivity, but these technologies cannot be used as a foundation for all of the organization's information systems. Most organizations still use proprietary networks. They need to develop their own connectivity solutions to make different kinds of hardware, software, and communications systems work together.

Achieving connectivity requires standards for networking, operating systems, and user interfaces. Open systems promote connectivity because they enable disparate equipment and services to work together. **Open systems** are built on public, nonproprietary operating systems, user interfaces, application standards, and networking protocols. In open systems, software can operate on different hardware platforms and in that sense can be "portable." Java and XML software, described in Chapter 6, can create an open system environment. The UNIX operating system supports open systems because it can operate on many different kinds of computer hardware. However, there are different versions of UNIX and no one version has been accepted as an open systems standard. Linux also supports open systems.

Models of Connectivity for Networks

There are different models for achieving connectivity in telecommunications networks. The **Transmission Control Protocol/Internet Protocol (TCP/IP)** model was developed by the U.S. Department of Defense in 1972 and is used in the Internet. Its purpose was to help scientists link disparate computers. Figure 9-2 shows that TCP/IP has a five-layer reference model.

1. *Application:* Provides end-user functionality by translating the messages into the user/host software for screen presentation.

2. *Transmission Control Protocol (TCP):* Performs transport, breaking application data from the end user down into TCP packets called datagrams. Each packet consists of a header with the address of the sending host computer, information for putting the data back together, and information for making sure the packets do not become corrupted.

3. *Internet Protocol (IP):* The Internet Protocol receives datagrams from TCP and breaks the packets down further. An IP packet contains a header with address information and carries TCP information and data. IP routes the individual datagrams from the sender

---

connectivity

A measure of how well computers and computer-based devices communicate and share information with one another without human intervention.

open systems

Software systems that can operate on different hardware platforms because they are built on public nonproprietary operating systems, user interfaces, application standards, and networking protocols.

Transmission Control Protocol/Internet Protocol (TCP/IP)

U.S. Department of Defense reference model for linking different types of computers and networks; used in the Internet.

Figure 9-2 The Transmission Control Protocol/Internet Protocol (TCP/IP) reference model. This figure illustrates the five layers of the TCP/IP reference model for communications.

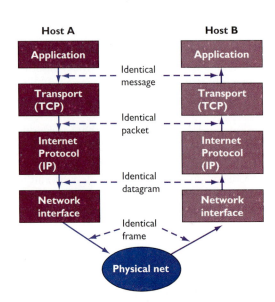

to the recipient. IP packets are not very reliable, but the TCP level can keep resending them until the correct IP packets get through.

4. *Network interface:* Handles addressing issues, usually in the operating system, as well as the interface between the initiating computer and the network.

5. *Physical net:* Defines basic electrical-transmission characteristic for sending the actual signal along communications networks.

Two computers using TCP/IP would be able to communicate even if they were based on different hardware and software platforms. Data sent from one computer to the other would pass downward through all five layers, starting with the sending computer's application layer and passing through the physical net. After the data reached the recipient host computer, they would travel up the layers. The TCP level would assemble the data into a format the receiving host computer could use. If the receiving computer found a damaged packet, it would ask the sending computer to retransmit it. This process would be reversed when the receiving computer responded.

The **Open Systems Interconnect (OSI)** model is an alternative model developed by the International Standards Organization for linking different types of computers and networks. It was designed to support global networks with large volumes of transaction processing. Like TCP/IP, OSI enables a computer connected to a network to communicate with any other computer on the same network or a different network, regardless of the manufacturer, by establishing communication rules that permit the exchange of information between dissimilar systems. OSI divides the telecommunications process into seven layers.

Equipment makers are starting to develop standards for small high-speed wireless networks to serve offices, campuses or homes. Two small wireless network standards are emerging. **802.11b** (also known as 802.11 High Rate or *Wi-Fi*) is a standard developed by the Institute of Electrical and Electronics Engineers (IEEE) for wireless LANs that can transmit up to 11 MBPS in the 2.4 GHz band within a 100 meter area. 802.11b networks are designed for workgroups that may need to handle a large number of simultaneous users. The **Bluetooth** standard allows low-power radio-based communication among wireless phones, pagers, computers, printers, and computing devices within any 10 meter area so that these devices could operate each other without direct user intervention. For example, a person could highlight a telephone number on a wireless Palm Pilot PDA and automatically activate a call on a digital telephone. Bluetooth can transmit up to 720 KBPS in the 2.4 GHz band and is designed primarily for small personal area networks linking up to 8 devices. Wireless digital cellular handset manufacturers are working on standards for wireless Internet access (see Section 9.3).

Other connectivity-promoting standards have been developed for graphical user interfaces, electronic mail, packet switching, and electronic data interchange (EDI). Any manager wishing to achieve some measure of connectivity in his or her organization should try to use these standards when designing networks, purchasing hardware and software, or developing information system applications.

Open Systems Interconnect (OSI)
International reference model for linking different types of computers and networks.

802.11b
Standard developed for wireless LANs for workgroups that can transmit up to 11 MBPS in the 2.4 GHz band within a 100 meter area. Also known as Wi-Fi.

bluetooth
Standard for wireless personal area networks that can transmit up to 720 KBPS within a 10 meter area.

9.2   THE INTERNET: INFORMATION TECHNOLOGY INFRASTRUCTURE FOR THE DIGITAL FIRM

The Internet is perhaps the most well-known, and the largest, implementation of internetworking, linking hundreds of thousands of individual networks all over the world. The Internet has a range of capabilities that organizations are using to exchange information internally or to communicate externally with other organizations. Internet technology provides the primary infrastructure for electronic commerce, electronic business, and the emerging digital firm.

WHAT IS THE INTERNET?

The Internet began as a U.S. Department of Defense network to link scientists and university professors around the world. Even today individuals cannot connect directly to the Net,

Internet Service Provider (ISP)

A commercial organization with a permanent connection to the Internet that sells temporary connections to subscribers.

although anyone with a computer, a modem, and the willingness to pay a small monthly usage fee can access it through an Internet Service Provider. An **Internet Service Provider (ISP)** is a commercial organization with a permanent connection to the Internet that sells temporary connections to subscribers. Individuals also can access the Internet through such popular on-line services as America Online and Microsoft Network (MSN).

No one owns the Internet and it has no formal management organization. As a creation of the Defense Department for sharing research data, this lack of centralization was purposeful to make it less vulnerable to wartime or terrorist attacks. To join the Internet, an existing network needs only to pay a small registration fee and agree to certain standards based on the TCP/IP reference model. Costs are low. Each organization, of course, pays for its own networks and its own telephone bills, but those costs usually exist independent of the Internet. Regional Internet companies have been established to which member networks forward all transmissions. These Internet companies route and forward all traffic anywhere in the world, and the cost is still only that of a local telephone call. The result is that the costs of e-mail and other Internet connections tend to be far lower than equivalent voice, postal, or overnight delivery, making the Net a very inexpensive communications medium. It is also a very fast method of communication, with messages arriving anywhere in the world in a matter of seconds, or a minute or two at most. We now briefly describe the most important Internet capabilities.

INTERNET TECHNOLOGY AND SERVICES

The Internet is based on client/server technology. Individuals using the Net control what they do through client applications, such as Web browser software. All the data, including e-mail messages and Web pages, are stored on servers. A client uses the Internet to request information from a particular Web server on a distant computer and the server sends the requested information back to the client via the Internet.

Client platforms today include not only PCs and other computers but also a wide array of handheld devices and information appliances, some of which can even provide wireless Internet access. An **information appliance** is a device such as an Internet-enabled cell phone or a television set-top box for Web-access and e-mail that has been customized to perform a few specialized computing tasks well with minimal user effort. Table 9-1 lists examples of some of these client platforms, most of which were described in Chapters 6 and 8. Experts believe that the role of the PC or desktop computer as the Internet client is diminishing as people turn to these easy-to-use specialized information appliances to connect to the Internet.

Servers dedicated to the Internet or even to specific Internet services are the heart of the information on the Net. Each Internet service is implemented by one or more software programs. All of the services may run on a single server computer, or different services may be allocated to different machines. There may be only one disk storing the data for these ser-

information appliance

Device that has been customized to perform a few specialized computing tasks well with minimal user effort.

TABLE 9-1   EXAMPLES OF INTERNET CLIENT PLATFORMS

Device	Description	Example
PC	General purpose computing platform that can perform many different tasks, but can be complex to use	Dell, Compaq, IBM PCs
Net PC	Network computer with minimal local storage and processing capability; designed to use software and services delivered over networks and the Internet	Sun Ray
Smart Phone	Has a small screen and keyboard for browsing the Web and exchanging e-mail in addition to providing voice communication	Nokia 6360
Game Machine	Game machine with a modem, keyboard, and capabilities to function as a Web access terminal	Sega Dreamcast (sega.com)
PDA	Wireless handheld personal digital assistant with e-mail and Internet service	Palm VII, Palm i705
E-mail machine	Tablet with keyboard that provides textual e-mail capabilities. Requires linking to an e-mail service	BlackBerry (blackberry.net)
Set-top box	Provides Web surfing and e-mail capabilities using a television set and a wireless keyboard	MSN TV (www.msntv.com)

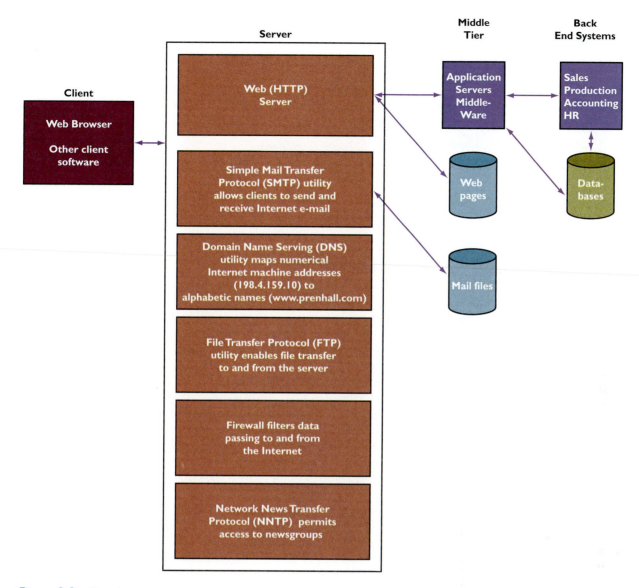

Figure 9-3 Client/server computing on the Internet. Client computers running Web browser and other software can access an array of services on servers via the Internet. These services may all run on a single server or on multiple specialized servers.

vices, or there may be multiple disks for each type, depending on the amount of information being stored. Figure 9-3 illustrates one way that these services might be arranged in a multi-tiered client/server architecture.

Web server software receives requests for Web pages from the client and accesses the Web pages from the disk where they are stored. Web servers can also access other information from an organization's internal information system applications and their associated databases and return that information to the client in the form of Web pages if desired. Specialized middleware, including application servers, is used to manage the interactions between the Web server and the organization's internal information systems for processing orders, tracking inventory, maintaining product catalogs, and other electronic commerce functions. For example, if a customer filled out an on-line form on a Web page to order a product such as a light fixture, the middleware would translate the request on the Web page into commands that could be used by the company's internal order processing system and customer database.

The most important Internet services for business include e-mail, Usenet newsgroups, LISTSERVs, chatting, Telnet, FTP, and the World Wide Web. They can be used to retrieve and offer information. Table 9-2 lists these capabilities and describes the functions they support.

TABLE 9-2   **MAJOR INTERNET SERVICES**

Capability	Functions Supported
E-mail	Person-to-person messaging; document sharing
Usenet newsgroups	Discussion groups on electronic bulletin boards
LISTSERVs	Discussion groups and messaging using e-mail mailing list servers
Chatting	Interactive conversations
Telnet	Log on to one computer system and do work on another
FTP	Transfer files from computer to computer
World Wide Web	Retrieve, format, and display information (including text, audio, graphics, and video) using hypertext links

Internet Tools for Communication

Electronic Mail (E-Mail).   The Net has become the most important e-mail system in the world because it connects so many people worldwide, creating a productivity gain that observers have compared to Gutenberg's development of movable type in the fifteenth century. Organizations use it to facilitate communication between employees and offices, and to communicate with customers and suppliers. Researchers use this facility to share ideas, information, even documents.

Figure 9-4 illustrates the components of an Internet e-mail address. The portion of the address to the left of the @symbol in a Net e-mail address is the name or identifier of the specific individual or organization. To the right of the @symbol is the domain name. The **domain name** is the name that identifies a unique node on the Internet. The domain name corresponds to a unique four-part numeric **Internet Protocol (IP) address** for each computer connected to the Internet. (For example, the domain name www.prenhall.com has the IP address 198.4.159.10) A **Domain Name System (DNS)** maps domain names to their IP addresses.

The domain name contains subdomains separated by a period. The domain that is farthest to the right is the top-level domain, and each domain to the left helps further define the domain by network, department, and even specific computer. The top-level domain name may be either a country indicator or a function indicator, such as *com* for a commercial organization or *gov* for a government institution. All e-mail addresses end with a country indicator except those in the United States, which ordinarily do not use one. In Figure 9-4, *it,* the top-level domain, is a country indicator, indicating that the address is in Italy. *Edu* indicates that the address is an educational institution; *univpisa* (in this case, University of Pisa) indicates the specific location of the host computer.

Usenet Newsgroups (Forums).   **Usenet** newsgroups are worldwide discussion groups in which people share information and ideas on a defined topic such as radiology or rock bands. Discussion takes place in large electronic bulletin boards where anyone can post messages for others to read. Many thousands of groups exist discussing almost all conceivable topics. Each Usenet site is financed and administered independently.

domain name
The unique name of a node on the Internet.

Internet Protocol (IP) address
Four-part numeric address indicating a unique computer location on the Internet.

domain name system (DNS)
A hierarchical system of servers maintaining databases enabling the conversion of domain names to their IP addresses.

Usenet
Forums in which people share information and ideas on a defined topic through large electronic bulletin boards where anyone can post messages on the topic for others to see and to which others can respond.

Figure 9-4 Analysis of an Internet address. In English, the e-mail address of physicist and astronomer Galileo Galilei would be translated as "G. Galileo University of Pisa, educational institution, Italy." The domain name to the right of the @ symbol contains a country indicator, a function indicator, and the location of the host computer.

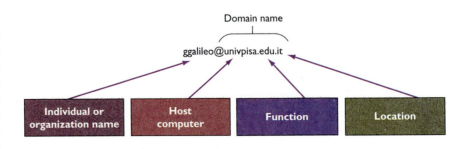

LISTSERV.   A second type of public forum, **LISTSERV,** allows discussions or messaging to be conducted through predefined groups but uses e-mail mailing list servers instead of bulletin boards for communications. If you find a LISTSERV topic you are interested in, you may subscribe. From then on, through your e-mail, you will receive all messages sent by others concerning that topic. You can, in turn, send a message to your LISTSERV and it will automatically be broadcast to the other subscribers. Many thousands of LISTSERV groups exist.

Chatting.   **Chatting** allows two or more people who are simultaneously connected to the Internet to hold live, interactive conversations. Chat groups are divided into channels, and each is assigned its own topic of conversation. The first generation of chat tools was for written conversations in which participants type their remarks using their keyboard and read responses on their computer screen. Systems featuring voice chat capabilities, such as those offered by Yahoo Chat, are now becoming popular.

A new enhancement to chat service called **instant messaging** even allows participants to create their own private chat channels. The instant messaging system alerts a person whenever someone on his or her private list is on-line so that the person can initiate a chat session with that particular individual. There are several competing instant messaging systems including Yahoo Messenger and America Online's Instant Messenger. Some of these systems can provide voice-based instant messages so that a user can click on a "talk" button and have an on-line conversation with another person.

Chatting and instant messaging can be effective business tools if people who can benefit from interactive conversations set an appointed time to "meet" and "talk" on a particular topic. For instance, UBS Warburg uses Web-based instant messaging systems to communicate news and market trends to employees on trading floors in Zurich, London, and New York and to clients (George and Swanson, 2001). Many on-line retailers are enhancing their Web sites with chat services to attract visitors, to encourage repeat purchases, and to improve customer service.

Telnet.   **Telnet** allows someone to be on one computer system while doing work on another. Telnet is the protocol that establishes an error-free, rapid link between the two computers, allowing you, for example, to log on to your business computer from a remote computer when you are on the road or working from your home. You can also log in and use third-party computers that have been made accessible to the public, such as using the catalog of the U.S. Library of Congress. Telnet will use the computer address you supply to locate the computer you want to reach and connect you to it.

Information Retrieval on the Internet

Information retrieval is a second basic Internet function. Many hundreds of library catalogs are on-line through the Internet, including those of such giants as the Library of Congress,

LISTSERV

On-line groups using e-mail broadcast from mailing list servers for discussions or messaging.

chatting

Live, interactive conversations over a public network.

instant messaging

Chat service that allows participants to create their own private chat channels so that a person can be alerted whenever someone on his or her private list is on-line to initiate a chat session with that particular individual.

Telnet

Network tool that allows someone to log on to one computer system while doing work on another.

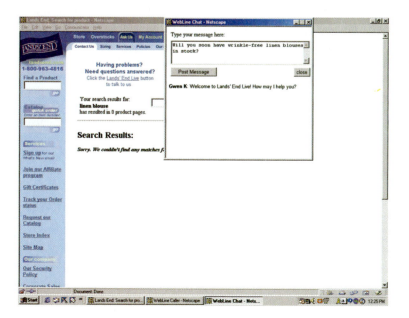

The Lands' End site provides on-line chat capabilities to answer visitors' questions and to help them find items for which they are looking. Chat services can help Web sites attract customers.

the University of California, and Harvard University. In addition, users are able to search many thousands of databases that have been opened to the public by corporations, governments, and nonprofit organizations. Individuals can gather information on almost any conceivable topic stored in these databases and libraries. Many use the Internet to locate and download some of the free, quality computer software that has been made available by developers on computers all over the world.

file transfer protocol (FTP)
Tool for retrieving and transferring files from a remote computer.

FTP.   **File transfer protocol (FTP)** is used to access a remote computer and retrieve files from it. FTP is a quick and easy method if you know the remote computer site where the file is stored. After you have logged on to the remote computer, you can move around directories that have been made accessible for FTP to search for the file(s) you want to retrieve. Once located, FTP makes transfer of the file to your own computer very easy.

THE NEXT GENERATION INTERNET AND INTERNET2

Internet2
Research network with new protocols and transmission speeds that provides an infrastructure for supporting high-bandwidth Internet applications.

The public Internet was not originally designed to handle massive quantities of data flowing through hundreds of thousands of networks. **Internet2** and Next Generation Internet (NGI) are consortia representing 180 universities, private businesses, and government agencies that are working on a new robust high-bandwidth version of the Internet. The Internet2 infrastructure is based on a series of interconnected *gigapops,* which are regional high-speed points-of-presence that serve as aggregation points for traffic from participating institutions. These gigapops in turn are connected to backbone networks with bandwidths exceeding 2.5 gigabits per second (GBPS). Internet2 connection speeds are in the hundreds of megabits per second range (MBPS), with at least 100 MBPS connections to servers and at least 10 MBPS to the desktop.

In addition to testing a more advanced version of the Internet Protocol and finding new ways to route broadcast messages, these research groups are developing protocols for permitting different quality-of-service levels. Today's Internet transmissions are "best effort"—packets of data arrive when they arrive without any regard to the priority of their contents. Different types of packets could be assigned different levels of priority as they travel over the network. For example, packets for applications such as videoconferencing, which need to arrive simultaneously without any break in service, could receive higher priority than e-mail messages, which do not have to be delivered instantaneously. The existing Internet is being enhanced to provide higher transmission speed, different levels of service, and increased security. The transition to the next generation Internet will be costly and ISPs will slowly make these changes (Weiser, 2001).

9.3   THE WORLD WIDE WEB

The World Wide Web (the Web) is at the heart of the explosion in the business use of the Net. The Web is a system with universally accepted standards for storing, retrieving, formatting, and displaying information using a client/server architecture. The Web combines text, hypermedia, graphics, and sound. It can handle all types of digital communication while making it easy to link resources that are half-a-world apart. The Web uses graphical user interfaces for easy viewing. It is based on a standard hypertext language called hypertext markup language (HTML), which formats documents and incorporates dynamic links to other documents stored in the same or remote computers. (We described HTML in Chapter 6.) Using these links, the user need only point at a highlighted key word or graphic, click on it, and immediately be transported to another document, probably on another computer somewhere else in the world. Users are free to jump from place to place following their own logic and interest.

Web browser software is programmed according to HTML standards (see Chapter 6). The standard is universally accepted, so anyone using a browser can access any of millions of Web sites. Browsers use hypertext's point-and-click ability to navigate or *surf*—move from site to site on the Web—to another desired site. The browser also includes an arrow or back button to enable the user to retrace his or her steps, navigating back, site by site.

home page
A World Wide Web text and graphical screen display that welcomes the user and explains the organization that has established the page.

Those who offer information through the Web must establish a **home page**—a text and graphical screen display that usually welcomes the user and explains the organization that has established the page. For most organizations, the home page will lead the user to other pages, with all the pages of a company being known as a Web site. For a corporation to establish a presence on the Web, therefore, it must set up a Web site of one or more pages. Most Web pages offer a way to contact the organization or individual. The person in charge of an organization's Web site is called a **Webmaster.**

To access a Web site, the user must specify a **uniform resource locator (URL),** which points to the address of a specific resource on the Web. For instance, the URL for Prentice Hall, the publisher of this text, is http://www.prenhall.com. *Http* stands for **hypertext transport protocol,** which is the communications standard used to transfer pages on the Web. Http defines how messages are formatted and transmitted and what actions Web servers and browsers should take in response to various commands. *Www.prenhall.com* is the domain name identifying the Web server storing the Web pages.

SEARCHING FOR INFORMATION ON THE WEB

Locating information on the Web is a critical function; more than 2 billion Web pages are in existence, and this number will quickly double. No comprehensive catalog of Web sites exists. The principal methods of locating information on the Web are Web site directories, search engines, and broadcast or "push" technology.

Several companies have created directories of Web sites and their addresses, providing search tools for finding information. Yahoo! is an example. People or organizations submit sites of interest, which then are classified. To search the directory, you enter one or more key words and then see displayed a list of categories and sites with those key words in the title.

Other search tools do not require Web sites to be preclassified and will search Web pages on their own automatically. Such tools, called **search engines,** can find Web sites that may be little known. They contain software that looks for Web pages containing one or more of the search terms; then they display matches ranked by a method that usually involves the location and frequency of the search terms. (Some search engine sites use human experts to help with the ranking.) These search engines create indexes of the Web pages they visit. The search engine software then locates Web pages of interest by searching through these indexes. Some search engines are more comprehensive or current than others, depending on how their components are tuned, and some also classify Web sites by subject categories. Google uses special software that indexes and ranks sites based on relevance measured by the number of users who access them and the number of outside links to a particular page. Specialized search engines are also available to help users locate specific types of information easily. For example, Moreover.com specializes in collecting and reporting news headlines from more than 1800 news sites. Some Web sites for locating information such as Yahoo! and AltaVista have become so popular and easy to use that they also serve as portals for the Internet (see Chapter 4).

Webmaster
The person in charge of an organization's Web site.

uniform resource locator (URL)
The address of a specific resource on the Internet.

hypertext transport protocol (http)
The communications standard used to transfer pages on the Web. Defines how messages are formatted and transmitted.

search engine
A tool for locating specific sites or information on the Internet.

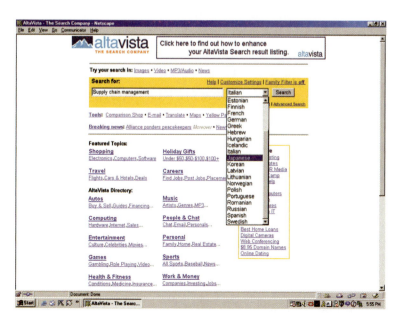

AltaVista provides a powerful search engine for accessing Web information resources and is a major Internet portal. Users can search for sites of interest by entering keywords or by exploring the categories.

MySimon is a shopping bot that can search Internet retailers for price and availability of products specified by the user. Displayed here are the results for a search of prices and sources for a popular children's book.

There are two ways of identifying Web pages to be tracked by search engines. One is to have Web page owners register their URLs with search engine sites. The other is to use software agents known as spiders, bots, and Web crawlers to traverse the Web and identify the Web pages for indexing. Chapter 10 details the capabilities of software agents with built-in intelligence, which can also help users search the Internet for shopping information. **Shopping bots** can help people interested in making a purchase filter and retrieve information about products of interest, evaluate competing products according to criteria they have established, and negotiate with vendors for price and delivery terms (Maes, Guttman, and Moukas, 1999). Many of these shopping agents search the Web for pricing and availability of products specified by the user and return a list of sites that sell the item along with pricing information and a purchase link. Table 9-3 compares various types of electronic commerce agents.

shopping bot
Software with varying levels of built-in intelligence to help electronic commerce shoppers locate and evaluate products or services they might wish to purchase.

Broadcast and "Push" Technology

Instead of spending hours surfing the Web, users can have the information they are interested in delivered automatically to their desktops through **"push" technology.** A computer broadcasts information of interest directly to the user, rather than having the user "pull" content from Web sites.

Special client software allows the user to specify the categories of information he or she wants to receive, such as news, sports, financial data, and so forth, and how often this infor-

"push" technology
Method of obtaining relevant information on networks by having a computer broadcast information directly to the user based on prespecified interests.

TABLE 9-3	EXAMPLES OF ELECTRONIC COMMERCE AGENTS
Agent	**Description**
MySimon	Real-time shopping bot searches more than 1,000 affiliated and unaffiliated merchants in 90 categories.
BestBookBuys.com	Shopping bot searches 26 on-line bookstores to help users find the lowest prices for titles they specify.
Bottom Dollar	Bot simultaneously queries many online retailers to obtain the best prices for products specified by the user.
Valuefind	Searches for the best deal from retail vendors, auctions, and classified ads. Users can limit the search to a specific price range and to certain Web sites. They can also create a "want list" that instructs bots to search for items on an ongoing basis and notify when they find the items specified at the price the user wants to pay.

Delivering information through "push" technology. Desktop News delivers a continuous stream of news and information from Web sites selected by users directly to their desktops as a customizable ticker toolbar.

mation should be updated. After finding the kind of information requested, push server programs serve it to the push client. The streams of information distributed through push technology are known as channels. Microsoft's Internet Explorer and Netscape Communicator include push tools that automatically download Web pages, inform the user of updated content, and create channels of user-specified sites. Using push technology to transmit information to a select group of individuals is one example of **multicasting.** (LISTSERVs sending e-mail to members of specific mailing lists is another.)

On-line marketplaces and exchanges can use push services to alert buyers to price changes and special deals. Companies are using internal push channels to broadcast important information, such as price updates or new competitor products, on their own private networks.

multicasting
Transmission of data to a selected group of recipients.

INTRANETS AND EXTRANETS

Organizations can use Internet networking standards and Web technology to create private networks called *intranets*. We introduced intranets in Chapter 1, explaining that an intranet is an internal organizational network that can provide access to data across the enterprise. It uses the existing company network infrastructure along with Internet connectivity standards and software developed for the World Wide Web. Intranets can create networked applications that can run on many different kinds of computers throughout the organization, including mobile handheld computers and wireless remote access devices.

Intranet Technology

Although the Web is open to anyone, the intranet is private and is protected from public visits by **firewalls**—security systems with specialized software to prevent outsiders from invading private networks. The firewall consists of hardware or software placed between an organization's internal network and an external network, including the Internet. The firewall is programmed to intercept each message packet passing between the two networks, examine its characteristics, and reject unauthorized messages or access attempts. We provide more detail on firewalls in Chapter 14.

firewall
Hardware or software placed between an organization's internal network and an external network to prevent outsiders from invading private networks.

Intranets require no special hardware and can run over any existing network infrastructure. Intranet software technology is the same as that of the World Wide Web. Intranets use HTML to program Web pages and to establish dynamic, point-and-click hypertext links to other pages. The Web browser and Web server software used for intranets are the same as those on the Web. A simple intranet can be created by linking a client computer with a Web browser to a computer with Web server software via a TCP/IP network. A firewall keeps unwanted visitors out.

Figure 9-5 Model of an extranet. In this model of an extranet, selected customers, suppliers, and business partners can access a company's private intranet from the public Internet. A firewall allows access only to authorized outsiders.

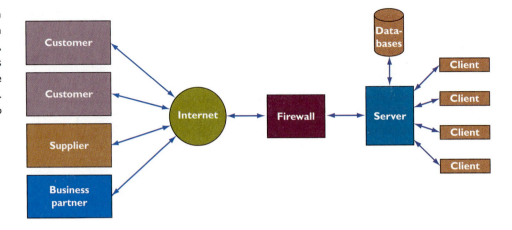

Extranets

Some firms are allowing people and organizations outside the firm to have limited access to their internal intranets. Private intranets that are extended to authorized users outside the company are called *extranets,* which we also introduced in Chapter 1. For example, authorized buyers could link to a portion of a company's intranet from the public Internet to obtain information about the cost and features of its products. The company can use firewalls to ensure that access to its internal data is limited and remains secure; firewalls can also authenticate users, making sure that only authorized people can access the site.

Extranets are especially useful for linking organizations with suppliers, customers, or business partners. They often are used for collaborating with other companies for supply chain management, product design and development, or training efforts. Private industrial networks are based on extranets. Figure 9-5 illustrates one way that an extranet might be set up.

THE WIRELESS WEB

Wireless Web

Web-based applications enabling users to access digital information from the Internet using wireless mobile computing devices.

Chapter 4 introduced *m-commerce,* the use of the Internet for purchasing goods and services as well as sending and receiving messages using handheld wireless devices. **Wireless Web** applications will enable users with Internet-enabled cell phones, PDAs, and other wireless computing devices to access digital information from the Internet and be connected anywhere, any time, any place. Web-enabled wireless devices will not replace the PC, but they will enable millions of people to access Web information services wherever they go. The Web will evolve into a vast pool of data resources that can be accessed in many different ways.

Businesses will increasingly incorporate wireless Internet access into their information technology infrastructures so that employees can access information wherever they are and make decisions instantly without being tethered to a desk or computer. Figure 9-6 illustrates how business processes using this wireless technology can become more efficient. First Service Networks, described in the chapter opening vignette, was hampered by its manual call center network, manual dispatch of independent service technicians, and manual invoicing process. Its new wireless Web application eliminates many time-consuming tasks.

Web content is being reformatted for wireless devices, and new content and services are being developed specifically for those devices. Specialized portals can steer users of Web-enabled wireless devices to the information they are most likely to need.

Table 9-4 describes what are likely to be the most popular categories of m-commerce services and applications. Location-based applications are of special interest because they take advantage of the unique capabilities of mobile technology. Whenever a user is connected to the Internet via a wireless device (cell phone, PDA, laptop), the transmission technology can be leveraged to determine that person's location and beam location-specific services or product information. For example, drivers could use this capability to obtain local weather data and local traffic information along with alternate route suggestions and descriptions of nearby restaurants.

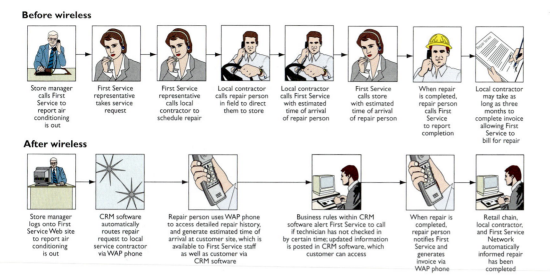

Figure 9-6 Before–after diagram of change in First Service Networks' business processes. By wirelessly automating most service requests, FSN can handle five times as many service requests without increasing its call center staff and respond more quickly to customers and contract repair staff. "Cutting Cost with Direct Customers," *mBusiness*, 10/01, pp. 36. Used with permission.

Although m-commerce is just starting up in the United States, millions of users in Japan and Europe already use cell phones to purchase goods, trade files, and obtain updated weather and sports reports. The Window on Organizations describes some of these m-commerce applications.

Wireless Web Standards

There are a plethora of standards governing every area of wireless communications. The two main standards for the Wireless Web are Wireless Application Protocol (WAP) and I-mode (see Figure 9-7).

Wireless Application Protocol (WAP) is a system of protocols and technologies that lets cell phones and other wireless devices with tiny display screens, low-bandwidth connections, and minimal memory access Web-based information and services. WAP uses **WML (Wireless Markup Language),** which is based on XML (see Chapter 6) and optimized for tiny displays. Like XML, WML describes data rather than only the way data are displayed. A person with a WAP-compliant phone uses the built-in microbrowser to make a request in WML. A **microbrowser** is an Internet browser with a small file size that can work with the low-memory constraints of handheld wireless devices and the low bandwidth of wireless networks. The request is passed to a WAP gateway, which retrieves the information from an Internet server in either standard HTML format or WML. The gateway translates HTML

Wireless Application Protocol (WAP)
System of protocols and technologies that lets cell phones and other wireless devices with tiny displays, low-bandwidth connections, and minimal memory access Web-based information and services.

WML (Wireless Markup Language)
Markup language for Wireless Web sites; based on XML and optimized for tiny displays.

microbrowser
Web browser software with a small file size that can work with low-memory constraints, tiny screens of handheld wireless devices, and low bandwidth of wireless networks.

TABLE 9-4	M-COMMERCE SERVICES AND APPLICATIONS

Type of M-Commerce Service	Applications
Information-based services	Instant messaging, e-mail, searching for a movie or restaurant using a cell phone or handheld PDA
Transaction-based services	Purchasing stocks, concert tickets, music, or games; searching for the best price of an item using a cell phone and buying it in a physical store or on the Web
Personalized services	Services that anticipate what you want based on your location or data profile, such as updated airline flight information or coupons for nearby restaurants

WILL M-COMMERCE TAKE OFF?

In parts of Europe and Asia, m-commerce is heating up. Consumers are using their cell phones as "electronic wallets" to shop, bank, and even pay their rent. For example, Terra Mobile, the wireless unit of Spain's Telefonica SA, is teaming up with Banco Bilbao Vizcaya Argentaria SA to provide a wireless payment system that enables users to purchase inexpensive products such as soft drinks or newspapers by pressing a few keys on their mobile phones. The cost of the purchase is automatically deducted from the customer's bank account. Subscribers to Italy's Omnitel, a unit of Vodafone Air Touch PLC, can use their cell phones to participate in wireless auctions for holiday packages, high-tech gear, and other products.

British shoppers can use ZagMe's location-based services to obtain discount coupons for shopping purchases. Subscribers first provide ZagMe with text messages via Short Message Service (SMS) indicating their phone number, date of birth, and gender. When the user arrives at a shopping location, she or he sends a text message indicting her or his location and the amount of time she or he plans to spend there. During that period of time, ZagMe sends a series of text messages with information about exclusive discounts and promotions from stores at that location. Participating retailers pay ZagMe a fee to broadcast their promotions.

Japan already has dozens of mobile phone services for which consumers are willing to pay. NTT DoCoMo Inc., the wireless arm of Nippon Telegraph and Telephone Co., offers a wireless Internet service that has already attracted 20 million subscribers. Subscribers receive an Internet-enabled cell phone with which they can send and receive e-mail and access numerous Web sites formatted for tiny screens. Subscribers can, for example, use a cell phone to send e-mail to friends, check train schedules, obtain movie listings, and read Japan's largest daily newspaper. They can also browse through restaurant guides, purchase tickets on Japan Airlines, trade stocks via DLJ Direct Inc., or view new cartoons.

The small keypads on mobile phones make it difficult for users to type in Web addresses. Subscribers to Japanese Web services can obtain menus of services tailored to their specific interests. Customers can sign onto a service with the click of a button without having to find and key in a complete Web address.

Some of these services are free; those that aren't, such as the newspaper, are bundled together and charged to users' monthly

telephone bills. The subscription fee for each Japanese wireless Internet service runs around $3 per month. Most Web sites for PCs in the United States have offered their contents for free and believe consumers will balk if they start charging for their services. They're still struggling to become profitable. But Japan's mobile phone–based Internet services are charging for content, adding their fees to subscribers' cellular telephone bills. People who would normally resist paying for Web services apparently are willing to subscribe to Wireless Web services because payment is so convenient.

The question is, how profitable? Many wireless services have yet to produce profits for their providers. U.S. businesses are watching wireless business models closely. It may be more difficult for the Wireless Web to flourish in the United States because the proportion of the population with cell phone service is much lower than that in Europe and Japan. Unlike Europe, which has standardized on GSM, the United States does not have a uniform national mobile technology standard, making it difficult for customers of one company to use their cell phones in areas where the local network standards are different.

To Think About: What types of businesses can benefit from supplying m-commerce services? Is m-commerce a good source of business models? Explain.

Sources: Simon Romero, "Weak Reception," *New York Times*, January 29, 2001; Jim Rendon, "Messaging Goes to the Mall," *mBusiness*, October 2001; John Blau, "Carriers, Banks Partner for Payments," *mBusiness*, April 2001; and Andrea Hamilton, "Coming to a Phone Near You," *Red Herring*, May 1 and 15, 2001.

I-mode

Standard developed by Japan's NTT DoCoMo mobile phone network for enabling cell phones to receive Web-based content and services.

content back into WML so that it can be received by the WAP client. The complexity of the translation process can affect the speed of information delivery. WAP supports most wireless network standards and operating systems for handheld computing devices such as PalmOS and Windows CE.

I-mode is a rival standard developed by Japan's NTT DoCoMo mobile phone network; it is widely used in Japan and is being introduced to Europe. I-mode uses compact HTML to

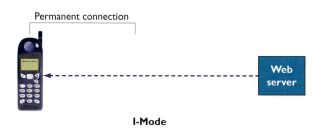

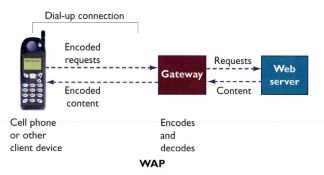

Figure 9-7 WAP versus I-Mode. WAP and I-mode are two competing standards for accessing information from the Wireless Web.

deliver content, making it easier for businesses to convert their HTML Web sites to mobile service. I-mode uses packet switching, which allows users to be constantly connected to the network and content providers to broadcast relevant information to users. (WAP users have to dial in to see if a site has changed.) I-mode can handle color graphics not available on WAP handsets, although WAP is being modified to handle color graphics.

M-Commerce Challenges

Rollout of m-commerce services has not been as rapid in the United States as in Japan and Europe. Keyboards and screens on cell phones are tiny and awkward to use. The data transfer speeds on existing wireless networks are very slow, ranging from 9.6 to 14.4 KBPS, compared to 56 KBPS for a dial-up connection to the Internet via a PC. Each second waiting for data to download costs the customer money. Most Internet-enabled phones have minimal memory and limited power supplies. Web content for wireless devices is primarily in the form of text with very little graphics. Not enough Web sites have reconfigured their services to display only the few lines of text that can be accommodated by cell phone screens.

Unlike Europe, U.S, wireless networks are based on several incompatible technologies. (Europe uses the GSM standard, whereas wireless carriers in the United States primarily use CDMA or TDMA standards.) For the Wireless Web to take off, more Web sites need to be designed specifically for wireless devices and wireless devices need to be more Web friendly.

Some of the limitations of m-commerce may be overcome by using voice recognition technology. **Voice portals** accept voice commands for accessing information from the Web. Voice portals offer customers a combination of content and services, with users accessing the content by speaking into a telephone. The user can orally request information, such as stock quotes, weather reports, airlines schedules, or news stories. For example, TellMe provides direct access to the Web using voice commands so that users can contact taxis, hotels, and friends as well as obtain weather reports, ski reports, and traffic information. Sophisticated voice recognition software processes the requests, which are translated back into speech for the customer.

M-commerce will also benefit from faster wireless networks. Cellular network providers are speeding up their services, preparing new versions of the three main digital standards to double their speed. Third-generation (3G) mobile communication networks will offer transmission speeds of up to 2 MBPS. Faster wireless networks will make it possible to stream high-quality video and audio to mobile devices along with new services. The Window on Technology describes other technology advances that will facilitate m-commerce and the opportunities they provide for entrepreneurs.

voice portal

Portal that can accept voice commands for accessing information from the Web.

M-COMMERCE INSPIRES NEW NETREPRENEURS

Building the Internet infrastructure has proven to be an extraordinary opportunity for entrepreneurship. New companies are popping up to develop the software and services needed to make the Wireless Web a success. Entrepreneurs are identifying segments of the wireless business in which they believe they can supply value.

More Magic is a mobile transaction platform company started by three Helsinki University students that provides more flexibility in mobile transaction processing than most of its competitors. It works on multiple mobile network systems, including Europe's GSM and the packet-switched Global Packet Radio Service (GPRS) networks. The technology makes it easy for vendors to change prices, which is essential for gas stations where prices change daily. Vendors, payment processors, and carriers can use this technology to allow consumers to select the payment options that suit them best, and the transaction-processing product can be installed vary rapidly. IBM, Norwegian carrier Netcom, and Finland's Benefon are using the More Magic platform for maps and other location-based information. Spring Toys, a Finnish wireless game company, is partnering with More Magic to provide billing services for its WAP games.

Webraska, a company of 30 employees located in Poissy, France, has identified geographic needs and makes available a service for WAP phones that provides real-time traffic data along with alternate route suggestions. Users originally had to enter their locations manually, but the company is switching to GPS (global positioning system) technology that automatically identifies the locations. Once that transition has been made, Webraska will be providing information about parking lots, gas stations, restaurants, hotels, and other services in the area. To achieve this, the company has joined with hotel networks, tourist guides, and auto clubs.

TJ.net is an Italian "mobile jukebox" service launched in May 2000, providing on-demand music, CD sales, chat, voice message boards, and promotional contests over mobile phones through a voice-activated menu. Instead of waiting for new songs to appear on the radio, TJ.net users dial into a voice-driven jukebox service to select songs from a list of featured tunes from nearly 300 record labels, listening to a 10-second ad before the songs play. Users can listen to an entire track or switch to another track or service after 15 seconds. They can then purchase CDs of the songs they like. About 70 percent of TJ.net revenue comes from advertisers and record company promotions. Marketers targeting teenage buyers find TJ.net valuable because it can collect detailed information about its teenage and young-adult audiences.

In Korea, employees are forbidden to trade stocks on office PCs. Seoul-based Infobank offers a secure wireless trading platform for mobile phone users. Infobank currently charges South Korean securities firms a flat monthly fee for using its technology but will soon charge fees for every stock trade. South Korean investors are taking advantage of this technology to trade stocks while driving, shopping, and eating, making South Korea the country with the highest percentage of mobile stock trading in the world.

To Think About: How do the technologies described here facilitate m-commerce? How could businesses use these technologies?

Sources: Jim Rendon, "Helsinki University Conjures Magic," *mBusiness,* May 2001; Margie Semilof, "French Firm Seeks Location, Dominance," *mBusiness,* May 2001; Sean Yokomizo, "Italian Teens Pay Up for M-Music," *mBusiness,* August 2001; Kristi Essick, Boris Grondahl, James Ledbetter, and Rick Wray, "Europe's Five Rising Stars," *The Industry Standard,* May 21, 2001; and Neel Chowdhury, "Infobank: Stock Trading on the Run," *Fortune,* October 9, 2000.

Businesses will need to review all of these issues when determining the role of Wireless Web technology in their business strategy. The Manager's Toolkit provides questions to guide management analysis.

ORGANIZATIONAL BENEFITS OF INTERNET AND WEB TECHNOLOGY

The Internet, intranets, and extranets are becoming the principal platforms for electronic commerce and electronic business because this technology provides so many benefits. The Internet's global connectivity, ease of use, low cost, and multimedia capabilities can be used to create interactive applications, services, and products. By using Internet technology, organizations can reduce communication and transaction costs, enhance coordination and collaboration, and accelerate the distribution of knowledge. Table 9-5 summarizes these benefits.

Connectivity and Global Reach

The value of the Internet lies in its ability to easily and inexpensively connect so many people from so many places all over the globe. Anyone who has an Internet address can log on to

MIS IN ACTION   MANAGER'S TOOLKIT

HOW TO INTEGRATE THE WIRELESS WEB INTO BUSINESS STRATEGY

Some businesses will benefit from incorporating the Wireless Web into their business strategy; others may not. Before investing heavily in Wireless Web technology and m-commerce, here are some key questions to ask

1. *Wireless value proposition:* Does adopting wireless technology enhance the company's existing business model? Can using wireless technology produce substantial gains in sales, customer loyalty, or customer service?

2. *User benefits:* Does the wireless technology provide a valuable service to the user? How valuable is this service? Does it save customers or employees substantial amounts of time?

3. *Rationale for switching:* Does the wireless technology create a product, service, or business process improvement that is so compelling that it will be enthusiastically adopted? How willing would users be to give up working at their desktops to use the new mobile technology?

4. *Business process change*: What business processes will change as a result of using wireless technology? What jobs and work practices will be affected? Will these changes be easy to make? Will employees require additional training in order to use the new technology? Will business processes of customers and suppliers have to change as well as those of the firm?

---

a computer and reach any other computer on the network, regardless of location, computer type, or operating system.

The Internet's global connectivity and ease of use can provide companies with access to businesses or individuals who normally would be outside their reach. Companies can link directly to suppliers, business partners, or individual customers at the same low cost, even if they are halfway around the globe. Internet technology provides a low-cost medium for forming global alliances and virtual organizations. The Web provides a standard interface and inexpensive global access, which can be used to create interorganizational systems among almost any organizations (Isakowitz, Bieber, and Vitali, 1998). Small companies who normally would find the cost of operating or selling abroad too expensive will find the Internet especially valuable.

Reduced Communication Costs

The Internet has made it easier and less expensive for companies to coordinate their staffs when opening new markets or working in isolated places because they do not have to build their own networks. For example, Schlumberger Ltd., the New York and Paris oil-drilling equipment and electronics producer, has reduced voice communication and overnight delivery charges by using Internet e-mail to keep managers in contact with employees in remote locations in 85 countries.

Hardware and software have been developed for **Internet telephony,** allowing companies to use the Internet for telephone voice transmission. (Internet telephony products sometimes are called IP telephony products.) **Voice over IP** technology, abbreviated VoIP, uses the Internet Protocol (IP) to deliver voice information in digital form using packet switching, avoiding the tolls charged by the circuit-switched telephone network (see Figure 9-8). IP telephony calls can be made and received with a desktop computer equipped with microphone and speakers or with a standard telephone or cell phone. New high-bandwidth networks will eliminate many of the early sound quality problems of this technology and enable the integration of voice with other Internet services. Companies with multiple sites

Internet telephony
Technologies that use the Internet Protocol's packet-switched connections for voice service.

voice over IP (VoIP)
Facilities for managing the delivery of voice information using the Internet Protocol (IP).

TABLE 9-5   INTERNET BENEFITS TO ORGANIZATIONS

Connectivity and global reach

Reduced communication costs

Lower transaction costs

Reduced agency costs

Interactivity, flexibility, and customization

Accelerated distribution of knowledge

Figure 9-8 How IP telephony works. An IP phone call digitizes and breaks up a voice message into data packets that may travel along different routes before being reassembled at their final destination. A server nearest the call's destination, called a gateway, arranges the packets in the proper order and directs them to the telephone number of the receiver or the IP address of the receiving computer.

"Using the Internet to Cut Phone Calls Down to Size" by David G. Wallace, The New York Times, July 19, 2001.

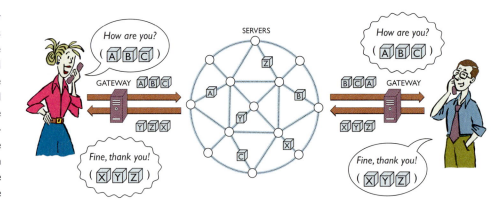

virtual private network (VPN)

A secure connection between two points across the Internet to transmit corporate data. Provides a low-cost alternative to a private network.

worldwide that are connected through a private or public IP network or that have seasonally variable demand for voice services are the most likely to benefit initially from this technology (Varshney, Snow, McGivern, and Howard, 2002).

Internet technology can also reduce communication costs by allowing companies to create virtual private networks as low-cost alternatives to private WANs. A **virtual private network (VPN)** is a secure connection between two points across the Internet, enabling private communications to travel securely over the public infrastructure. VPN services are available through Internet Service Providers (ISPs). The VPN provides many features of a private network at much lower cost than using private leased telephone lines or frame-relay connections. Companies can save on long-distance communication costs because workers can access remote locations for the cost of making a local call to an ISP.

There are several competing protocols used to protect data transmitted over the public Internet, including point-to-point tunneling protocol (PPTP). In a process called tunneling, packets of data are encrypted and wrapped inside IP packets so that non-IP data can travel through the Internet. By adding this "wrapper" around a network message to hide its content, organizations can create a private connection that travels through the public Internet.

Lower Transaction Costs

Businesses have found that conducting transactions electronically can be done at a fraction of the cost of paper-based processes. Using Internet technology reduces these transaction costs even further. For example, each time Federal Express clients use FedEx's Web site to track the status of their packages instead of inquiring by telephone, FedEx saves $8, amounting to a $2 million savings in operating costs each year. Table 4-1 in Chapter 4 provides more examples of Internet transaction cost savings.

Reduced Agency Costs

As organizations expand and globalization continues, the need to coordinate activities in remote locations is becoming more critical. The Internet reduces agency costs—the cost of managing employees and coordinating their work—by providing low-cost networks and inexpensive communication and collaboration tools that can be used on a global scale. Schlumberger, Cisco Systems, Nike, and Millipore are among many companies using the Net for this purpose.

Interactivity, Flexibility, and Customization

Internet tools can create interactive applications that can be customized for multiple purposes and audiences. Web pages have capabilities for interacting with viewers that cannot be found in traditional print media. Visitors attracted by alluring displays of text, graphics, video, and sound can click on hot buttons to make selections, take actions, or pursue additional information. Companies can use e-mail, chat rooms, and electronic discussion groups to create ongoing dialogues with their customers, using the information they gather to tailor communication precisely to fit the needs of each individual. They can create **dynamic pages** that reflect each customer's interests, based on information the customer has supplied to the

dynamic page

Web page with content that changes in response to information a visitor supplies to a Web site.

Web site. The content of a dynamic page changes in response to user input at a Web site. Internet applications can be scaled up or down as the size of their audience changes because the technology works with the firm's existing network infrastructure.

Accelerated Distribution of Knowledge

In today's information economy, rapid access to knowledge is critical to the success of many companies. Organizations are using the Internet to gain immediate access to information resources in key areas such as business, science, law, and government. With blinding speed, the Internet can link a lone researcher sitting at a computer screen to mountains of data (including graphics) all over the world, which would be otherwise too expensive and too difficult to tap. It has become easy and inexpensive for corporations to obtain the latest U.S. Department of Commerce statistics, current weather data, and laws of legal entities worldwide.

In addition to accessing public knowledge resources on the Internet and the Web, companies can create internal Web sites as repositories of their own organizational knowledge. Multimedia Web pages can organize this knowledge, giving employees easier access to information and expertise. Web browser software provides a universal interface for accessing information resources from internal corporate databases as well as from external information sources.

9.4 SUPPORT TECHNOLOGY FOR ELECTRONIC COMMERCE AND ELECTRONIC BUSINESS

Businesses seriously pursuing electronic commerce and electronic business need special tools for maintaining their Web sites. These tools include Web server and electronic commerce server software, customer tracking and personalization tools, Web content management tools, and Web site performance monitoring tools.

WEB SERVERS AND ELECTRONIC COMMERCE SERVERS

In Chapter 6 we introduced Web servers as the software necessary to run Web sites, intranets, and extranets. The core capabilities of Web server software revolve around locating and managing stored Web pages. Web server software locates the Web pages requested by client computers by translating the URL Web address into the physical file address for each requested Web page. The Web server then sends the requested pages to the client. Many Web servers also include tools for authenticating users, support for file transfer protocol (FTP), search engines and indexing programs, and capabilities for capturing Web site visitor information in log files. (Each request to the server for a file is recorded as an entry in the Web server log and is called a **hit**.) Apache HTTP Server and Microsoft's Internet Information Services (IIS) are currently the most popular Web servers. Management will have to examine carefully the servers available in order to determine which server offers the functionality that best fits the needs of the firm's Web site.

hit
An entry into a Web server's log file generated by each request to the server for a file.

Web server computers range in size from small desktop PCs to mainframes, depending on the size of the Web sites. The Web server computer must be large enough to handle the Web server software and the projected traffic of the particular site.

Servers differ in the number of simultaneous users they can handle, how quickly they can service their requests, and the technologies they support in Web applications. Server scalability is a major issue if a company is looking forward to rapid growth.

Specialized **electronic commerce server software** provides functions essential for e-commerce Web sites, often running on computers dedicated to this purpose. Functions the software must perform for both business-to-consumer and business-to-business e-commerce include:

electronic commerce server software
Software that provides functions essential for running e-commerce Web sites, such as setting up electronic catalogs and storefronts, and mechanisms for processing customer purchases.

- Setting up electronic storefronts and electronic catalogs to display product and pricing information.

- Designing electronic shopping carts so customers can collect the items they wish to purchase.

Open Market offers an integrated suite of applications for e-commerce management and content management. Business can use these tools to quickly develop full-function e-commerce sites.

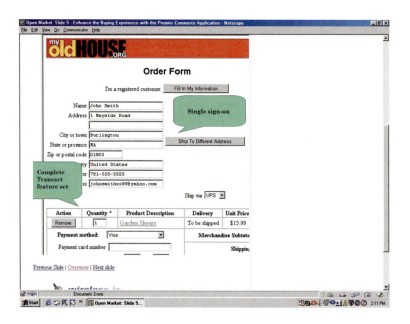

▌ Making shipping arrangements.

▌ Linking to electronic payment processing systems.

▌ Displaying product availability and tracking shipments.

▌ Connecting to back-office systems where necessary.

Systems designed for small business-to-consumer (B2C) e-commerce usually include wizards and templates to aid in the setting up of the storefronts and catalogs. However, high-end B2C and B2B systems such as Open Market Transact, Microsoft's Commerce Server, and IBM's WebSphere Commerce Suite require the help of IT professionals for installation and support.

Business-to-business (B2B) e-commerce software must support tasks that are more complex than those for B2C commerce. Although business-to-consumer prices are usually fixed, business-to-business prices are negotiable because they are affected by many contract factors, including volume, logistics preferences, and warranty coverages.

CUSTOMER TRACKING AND PERSONALIZATION TOOLS

Customer tracking and personalization tools have several main goals:

▌ Collecting and storing data on the behavior of on-line customers and combining that data with data already stored in the company's back-office systems.

▌ Analyzing the data in order better to understand the behavior of on-line customers.

▌ Identifying customer preferences and trends.

clickstream tracking

Tracking data about customer activities at Web sites and storing them in a log.

collaborative filtering

Tracking users' movements on a Web site, comparing the information gleaned about a user's behavior against data about other customers with similar interests to predict what the user would like to see next.

Chapter 4 described some of the benefits of personalizing Web sites to deliver content specific to each user. On-line personalization systems often use **clickstream tracking** tools to collect data on customer activities at Web sites and store them in a log. The tools record the site that users last visited before coming to your Web site and where these users go when they leave your site. They also record the specific pages visited on your site, the time spent on each page of the site, the types of pages visited, and what the visitors purchased. Web sites can also populate databases with explicit data gained when visitors fill out registration forms on the site or purchase products.

Collaborative filtering software tracks users' movements on a Web site, comparing the information it gains about a user's behavior against data about other customers with similar interests to predict what the user would like to see next. The software then makes recommendations to users based on their assumed interests. For example, Amazon.com uses collaborative filtering software to prepare personalized book recommendations: "Customers who bought this book also bought . . . . ."

Segmentation and rules-based systems use business rules to deliver certain types of information based on a user's profile, classifying users into smaller groups or segments based on these rules. The software uses demographic, geographic, income, or other information to divide, or segment, large populations into smaller groups for targeted content. Broadvision's electronic commerce system for offering personalized content to Web site visitors is a rules-based product.

Data collected from Web site visitors can be stored in a special data warehouse called a Webhouse. The process is known as **Webhousing.** Some Webhouses make it possible to combine the clickstream data with data from back-office systems and relevant external data to gain a fuller understanding of each customer. The goal of collecting all these data is to enable the company to unearth customer preferences and trends. Chapter 11 provides additional detail on Web customer data analysis.

Webhousing
Storing data collected from Web site visitors in a special data warehouse for this purpose.

WEB CONTENT MANAGEMENT TOOLS

Web content management tools exist because many companies have sites with thousands or hundreds of thousands of pages to manage, a task too great for a Webmaster. Web content management software has emerged to assist the Webmaster and other authorized staff in the collection, assembly, and management of content on a Web site, intranet, or extranet.

The materials on Web sites are often very complex and include many forms of data such as documents, graphics, and sound. Often the content must be dynamic, and parts of it must be capable of changing, depending on circumstances such as the identification of the visitor, the day of the month, the price of a product, or the requests of the visitor. Web content management tools help users organize and modify this material when needed and ensure that only those responsible for the specific content are able to update or change it.

Web content management tools
Software to facilitate the collection, assembly, and management of content on a Web site, intranet, or extranet.

WEB SITE PERFORMANCE MONITORING TOOLS

Most Web sites are plagued by problems such as slow performance, major outages, content errors, broken links between Web pages, transaction failures, and slow-loading pages. To address these problems, companies can use their own **Web site performance monitoring tools** or rely on Web site performance monitoring services.

Web site performance monitoring tools measure the response times of specific transactions such as inquiries, checking out purchases, or authorizing credit through a credit card. They can pinpoint the location of bottlenecks that slow down a Web site, such as performance problems at the Web or application server, a specific database, or a network router. Some tools test the site scalability through stressing the site by creating many test site visitors. Some tools also identify the causes for slow page loading speeds, such as loading too many banners, too many dense graphics files, or disk-space problems.

No single software tool exists that monitors all the functions we have described here. Companies that use these tools often purchase multiple packages or enlist external vendor specialists to do performance measurement for them.

Web site performance monitoring tools
Software tools for monitoring the time to download Web pages or perform Web transactions. These tools can identify broken links between Web pages and pinpoint other Web site problems and bottlenecks.

WEB HOSTING SERVICES

Companies that lack the financial or technical resources to operate their own Web sites or electronic commerce services can use Web hosting services. A **Web hosting service** maintains a large Web server computer or series of servers and provides fee-paying subscribers with space to maintain their Web sites. The subscribing companies may create their own Web pages or have the hosting service or a Web design firm create them. Some services offer *co-location,* in which the firm actually purchases and owns the server computer housing its Web site, but locates the server in the physical facility of the hosting service.

Companies can also use specialized e-commerce application service providers to set up and operate their e-commerce sites or intranets. Companies such as Freemerchant.com, Yahoo Store, and Bigstep.com provide low-cost e-commerce sites to small businesses with very simple e-commerce requirements that can use a predefined template for displaying and selling their wares.

Web hosting services offer solutions to small companies that do not have the resources to operate their own Web sites or to companies that still are experimenting with electronic

Web hosting service
Company with large Web server computers to maintain the Web sites of fee-paying subscribers.

WebTrends offers sophisticated Web site analysis and reporting tools for businesses of all sizes. Illustrated here is a report showing the most frequently viewed pages of a Web site.

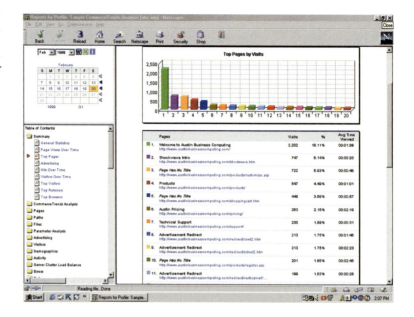

commerce. Such services cost much less than running one's own Web site, and the hosting services have technical staff who can design, develop, manage, and support the site.

Many large companies use Web hosting services because they offer highly experienced technical staff and servers in multiple global locations, along with backup server capacity to ensure 100 percent Web site availability. Companies such as IBM Global Services, LoudCloud, and Exodus Communications provide fully managed Web hosting services. High-end managed hosting can range from $50,000 to $1 million per month.

9.5   MANAGEMENT ISSUES AND DECISIONS

An information technology infrastructure for digitally enabling the enterprise requires coordinating many different types of computing and networking technologies, public and private infrastructures, and organizational processes. Careful management and planning are essential.

THE CHALLENGE OF MANAGING THE NEW INFORMATION TECHNOLOGY INFRASTRUCTURE

Implementing enterprise networking and the new information technology (IT) infrastructure has created problems as well as opportunities for organizations. Managers need to address these problems to create an IT infrastructure for digitally enabling their firms.

E-commerce and e-business are forcing companies to reassess their information technology infrastructures in order to remain competitive. Many organizations are saddled with a maze of old legacy applications, hardware, and networks that don't talk to each other. In order to support enterprise-wide business processes that can smoothly link to customers or suppliers via the Internet, they must rebuild their information architectures and information technology infrastructures. Five problems stand out: loss of management control over information systems, connectivity and application integration challenges, the need for organizational change, the hidden costs of enterprise computing, and the difficulty of ensuring infrastructure scalability, reliability, and security (see Table 9-6).

Loss of Management Control

Managing information systems technology and corporate data are proving much more difficult in a distributed environment because of the lack of a single, central point where needed management can occur. Distributed client/server networks, new mobile wireless networks, and Internet computing have empowered end users to become independent sources of computing power capable of collecting, storing, and disseminating data and software. Data and

TABLE 9-6	PROBLEMS POSED BY THE NEW INFORMATION TECHNOLOGY (IT) INFRASTRUCTURE

Loss of management control over systems

Connectivity and application integration challenges

Organizational change requirements

Hidden costs of enterprise computing

Scalability, reliability, security

software no longer are confined to the mainframe, under the management of the traditional information systems department, but reside on many different computing platforms throughout the organization.

An enterprise-wide information technology infrastructure requires that the business know where all of its data are located and ensure that the same piece of information, such as a product number, is used consistently throughout the organization (see Chapter 7). These data may not always be in a standard format or may reside on incompatible computing platforms. However, observers worry that excess centralization and management of information resources will reduce users' ability to define their own information needs. The dilemma posed by the enterprise networking and the new information technology infrastructure is one of central-management control versus end-user creativity and productivity.

Connectivity and Application Integration Challenges

We have already described the connectivity problems created by incompatible networks and standards, including connectivity problems for wireless networks. Digital firm organizations depend on enterprise-wide integration of their business processes and applications so that they can obtain their information from any point in the value chain. An order from a Web site should be able to trigger events automatically in the organization's accounting, inventory, and distribution applications to speed the product swiftly to the customer. This end-to-end process and application integration is extremely difficult to achieve and beyond the reach of many firms.

Organizational Change Requirements

Enterprise-wide computing is an opportunity to reengineer the organization into a more effective unit, but it will only create problems or chaos if the underlying organizational issues are not fully addressed (Duchessi and Chengalur-Smith, 1998). Behind antiquated legacy infrastructures are old ways of doing business, which must also be changed to work effectively in a new enterprise-wide IT infrastructure. Infrastructure and architecture for a business environment that can respond to rapidly changing marketplace and industry demands require changes in corporate culture and organizational structure that are not easy to make. It took several years of hard work and large financial investments for IBM to Web enable its business processes and convince disparate business units to adopt a "One IBM" mindset where everyone uses common tools. Sun Microsystems, the networking technology giant, experienced a painful two-year conversion of its own information systems to make them run on its own networks (Kanter, 2001).

Hidden Costs of Enterprise Computing

Many companies have found that the savings they expected from distributed client/server computing did not materialize because of unexpected costs. Hardware-acquisition savings resulting from downsizing often are offset by high annual operating costs for additional labor and time required for network and system management. Considerable time must be spent on tasks such as network maintenance; data backup; technical problem solving; and hardware, software, and software-update installations. Gains in productivity and efficiency from equipping employees with wireless mobile computing devices must be balanced against increased costs associated with integrating these devices into the firm's IT infrastructure and providing technical support.

Scalability, Reliability, and Security

Companies seeking to digitally enable their businesses require robust information technology infrastructures providing plentiful bandwidth and storage capacity for transmitting and maintaining all of the data generated by electronic commerce and electronic business transactions. Network infrastructures need not only to handle current e-commerce demands but also to scale rapidly to meet future demands while providing high levels of performance and availability for mission-critical applications.

Enterprise networking is highly sensitive to different versions of operating systems and network management software, with some applications requiring specific versions of each. It is difficult to make all of the components of large, heterogeneous networks work together as smoothly as management envisions. **Downtime**—periods of time in which the system is not operational—remains much more frequent in distributed systems than in established mainframe systems and should be considered carefully before taking essential applications off a mainframe.

Security is of paramount importance in firms with extensive networking and electronic transactions with individuals or other businesses outside organizational boundaries. Networks present end users, hackers, and thieves with many points of access and opportunities to steal or modify data. Systems linked to the Internet are even more vulnerable because the Internet was designed to be open to everyone. Wireless computing devices linked to corporate applications create new areas of vulnerability. We discuss these issues in greater detail in Chapter 14.

downtime
Period of time in which an information system is not operational.

SOME SOLUTIONS

Organizations can meet the challenges posed by the new IT infrastructure by planning for and managing business and organizational changes; increasing end-user training; asserting data administration disciplines; and considering connectivity, application integration, bandwidth, and cost in their technology planning.

Managing the Change

To gain the full benefit of any new technology, organizations must carefully plan for and manage the change. Business processes may need to be reengineered to accompany infrastructure changes (see Chapter 12). For example, equipping the sales force with wireless handheld devices for entering orders in the field provides an opportunity for management to review the sales process to see if redundant order entry activities or a separate order entry staff can be eliminated. Management must address the organizational issues that arise from shifts in staffing, function, power, and organizational culture attending a new information technology infrastructure.

Education and Training

A well-developed training program can help end users overcome problems resulting from the lack of management support and understanding of networked computing (Westin et al., 1985; Bikson et al., 1985). Technical specialists will need training in Web site, wireless, and client/server development and network support methods.

Data Administration Disciplines

The role of data administration (see Chapter 7) becomes even more important when networks link many different applications, business areas, and computing devices. Organizations must systematically identify where their data are located, which group is responsible for maintaining each piece of data, and which individuals and groups are allowed to access and use that data. They need to develop specific policies and procedures to ensure that their data are accurate, available only to authorized users, and properly backed up.

MAKE IT YOUR BUSINESS

FINANCE AND ACCOUNTING

Wireless Web technology has been the source of new financial services. Individual investors and investment professionals can use their mobile phones to obtain stock quotes and financial market news, to make stock trades, and to review their portfolios. Wireless Web and Internet technology are also making it possible to speed up fund flows by providing capabilities for immediate billing and invoicing. You can find examples of financial and accounting applications on pages 276–278, 292–294, and 308.

HUMAN RESOURCES

Internet technology has created new efficient and cost-effective tools for employee communication and coordination. Managers can use e-mail, chat, and instant messaging to communicate with employees that are in many different locations. Companies can use intranets to publish employee bulletins, policy manuals, directories, and other human resources documents. You can find examples of human resource applications on page 308.

MANUFACTURING AND PRODUCTION

Extranets are especially useful for collaborative commerce and supply chain management, and are the primary platform for private industrial networks. They are often used for providing product availability, pricing, and shipment data; for exchanging purchase orders and invoices; and for joint product development activities with other companies. You can find examples of manufacturing and production applications on pages 306–309.

SALES AND MARKETING

The Web is an especially powerful medium for sales and marketing because it provides capabilities for personalization and interacting with customers that cannot be found in other channels. Companies can engage in ongoing dialogues with customers using e-mail, chat, and electronic discussion groups to solidify their customer relationships. Wireless Web technology provides new information and location-based services for companies to sell, which could provide major new sources of revenue. You can find examples of sales and marketing applications on pages 276–278, 292, 294, and 306–309.

Planning for Connectivity and Application Integration

Senior management must take a long-term view of the firm's IT infrastructure and information architecture, making sure they can support the level of process and information integration for current and future needs. Infrastructure planning should consider how much connectivity would be required to digitally enable core strategic business processes. To what extent should network services be standardized throughout the organization? Will the firm be communicating with customers and suppliers using different technology platforms? How should wireless mobile computing networks be integrated with the rest of the firm?

Although some connectivity problems can be solved by using XML, intranets or the Internet, the firm will need to establish enterprise-wide standards for other systems and applications. Management can establish policies to keep networks and telecommunications services as homogeneous as possible, setting standards for data, voice, e-mail, and videoconferencing services along with hardware, software, and network operating systems.

An enterprise-wide architecture for integrated business applications and processes cannot be created through piecemeal changes. It represents a long-term endeavor that should be supported by top management and coordinated with the firm's strategic plans.

MANAGEMENT WRAP-UP

Planning the firm's IT infrastructure is a key management responsibility. Managers need to consider how the IT infrastructure supports the firm's business goals and whether the infrastructure should incorporate public infrastructures and links to other organizations. Planning should also consider the need to maintain some measure of management control as computing power becomes more widely distributed throughout the organization.

The new information technology infrastructure can enhance organizational performance by making information flow more smoothly between different parts of the organization and between the organization and its customers, suppliers, and other value partners. Organizations can use Internet technology and tools to reduce communication and coordination costs, create interactive products and services, and accelerate the distribution of knowledge.

Internet technology is providing the connectivity for the new information technology infrastructure and the emerging digital firm using the TCP/IP reference model and other standards for retrieving, formatting, and displaying information. Key technology decisions should consider the capabilities of the Internet, electronic commerce, and new wireless technologies along with connectivity, scalability, reliability, and requirements for application integration.

For Discussion

1. It has been said that developing an IT infrastructure for electronic commerce and electronic business is, above all, a business decision, as opposed to a technical decision. Discuss.

2. A fully integrated IT infrastructure is essential for business success. Do you agree? Why or why not?

Summary

1. *What is the new information technology (IT) infrastructure for business? Why is connectivity so important in this infrastructure?* The new information technology (IT) infrastructure uses a mixture of computer hardware supplied by different vendors, including mainframes, PCs, and servers, which are networked to each other. More processing power is available on the desktop through client/server computing and mobile personal information devices that provide remote access to the desktop from outside the organization. The new IT infrastructure also incorporates public infrastructures, such as the telephone system, the Internet, and public network services and electronic devices.

Connectivity is a measure of how well computers and computer-based devices can communicate with one another and "share" information in a meaningful way without human intervention. It is essential in enterprise networking in the new IT infrastructure, where different hardware, software, and network components must work together to transfer information seamlessly from one part of the organization to another. TCP/IP and OSI are important reference models for achieving connectivity in networks. Each divides the communications process into layers. UNIX is an operating system standard that can be used to create open systems, as can the Linux operating system. Connectivity also can be achieved by using Internet technology, XML, and Java.

2. *How does the Internet work? What are its major capabilities?* The Internet is a worldwide network of networks that uses the client/server model of computing and the TCP/IP network reference model. Using the Net, any computer (or computing appliance) can communicate with any other computer connected to the Net throughout the world. The Internet has no central management. The Internet is used for communications, including e-mail, public forums on thousands of topics, and live, interactive conversations. It also is used for information retrieval from hundreds of libraries and thousands of library, corporate, government, and nonprofit databases. It has developed into an effective way for individuals and organizations to offer information and products through a Web of graphical user interfaces and easy-to-use links worldwide. Major Internet capabilities include e-mail, Usenet, LISTSERV, chatting, Telnet, FTP, and the World Wide Web.

3. *How can organizations benefit from the Internet?* Many organizations use the Net to reduce communications costs when they coordinate organizational activities and communicate with employees. Researchers and knowledge workers are finding the Internet a quick, low-cost way to gather and disperse knowledge. The global connectivity and low cost of the Internet helps organizations lower transaction and agency costs, allowing them to link directly to suppliers, customers, and business partners and to coordinate activities on a global scale with limited resources. The Web provides interactive multimedia capabilities that can be used to create new products and services and closer relationships with customers. Communication can be customized to specific audiences.

4. *What are the principal technologies for supporting electronic commerce and electronic business?* Businesses need a series of software tools for maintaining a Web site. Web server software locates and manages Web pages stored on Web server computers. Electronic commerce server software provides capabilities for setting up electronic storefronts and arranging for payments and shipping. Customer tracking and personalization tools collect, store, and analyze data on Web site visitors. Content management tools facilitate the collection, assembly, and management of Web site content. Web site performance monitoring tools monitor the speed of Web site transactions and identify Web site performance problems. Businesses can use an external vendor's Web hosting service as an alternative to maintaining their own Web sites.

5. *What management problems are raised by the new information technology (IT) infrastructure? How can businesses solve these problems?* Problems posed by the new IT infrastructure include loss of management control over systems; the need to carefully manage organizational change; connectivity and application integration challenges; the difficulty of ensuring network scalability, reliability, and security; and controlling the hidden costs of enterprise computing.

Solutions include planning for and managing the business and organizational changes associated with enterprise-wide computing; increasing end-user training; asserting data administration disciplines; and considering connectivity, application integration, bandwidth, and cost controls when planning the IT infrastructure.

KEY TERMS

802.11b (Wi-Fi), 281

Bluetooth, 281

Chatting, 285

Clickstream tracking, 298

Collaborative filtering, 298

Connectivity, 280

Domain name, 284

Domain Name System (DNS), 284

Downtime, 302

Dynamic page, 296

Electronic commerce server software, 297

Enterprise networking, 279

File transfer protocol (FTP), 286

Firewall, 289

Hit, 297

Home page, 286

Hypertext transport protocol (http), 287

I-mode, 292

Information appliance, 282

Instant messaging, 285

Internet Protocol (IP) address, 284

Internet Service Provider (ISP), 282

Internet telephony, 295

Internet2, 286

Internetworking, 279

LISTSERV, 285

Microbrowser, 291

Multicasting, 289

Open systems, 280

Open Systems Interconnect (OSI), 281

"Push" technology, 288

Search engine, 287

Shopping bot, 288

Telnet, 285

Transmission Control Protocol/Internet Protocol (TCP/IP), 280

Uniform resource locator (URL), 287

Usenet, 284

Virtual private network (VPN), 296

Voice over IP (VoIP), 295

Voice portal, 293

Web content management tools, 299

Web hosting service, 299

Web site performance monitoring tools, 299

Webhousing, 299

Webmaster, 287

Wireless Application Protocol (WAP), 291

Wireless Web, 290

WML (Wireless Markup Language), 291

REVIEW QUESTIONS

1. What are the features of the new information technology infrastructure?

2. Why is connectivity so important for the digital firm? List and describe the major connectivity standards for networking and the Internet.

3. What is the Internet? List and describe alternative ways of accessing the Internet.

4. List and describe the principal Internet capabilities.

5. What are Internet2 and Next Generation Internet (NGI)? How does the next generation Internet differ from the first-generation Internet? What benefits does it provide?

6. Why is the World Wide Web so useful for individuals and businesses?

7. List and describe alternative ways of locating information on the Web.

8. What are intranets and extranets? How do they differ from the Web?

9. What is the Wireless Web? How does it differ from the conventional Web?

10. List and describe the types of m-commerce services and applications supported by the Wireless Web.

11. Compare the WAP and I-mode Wireless Web standards.

12. Describe the organizational benefits of Internet and Web technology.

13. List and describe the principal technologies for supporting electronic commerce and electronic business.

14. Under what conditions should firms consider Web hosting services?

15. Describe five problems posed by the new IT infrastructure.

16. Describe some solutions to the problems posed by the new IT infrastructure.

APPLICATION SOFTWARE EXERCISE

SPREADSHEET EXERCISE: ANALYZING WEB SITE VISITORS

Your firm, Marina Clothiers, sells casual pants, shirts, and other clothes for both men and women. Your firm has been attempting to increase the number of on-line customers by placing advertising banners for your Web site at other Web sites. When users click on these banner ads, they automatically are transported to your Web site. Data from your advertising campaign are summarized in the weekly Marketing Trends Reports (MTR) produced by your Web site analysis software, which appears on the Laudon Web site for Chapter 9.

❚ *Visitors*–are the number of people who visited your Web site by clicking on a banner ad for your site that was placed on an affiliated Web site.

❚ *Shoppers*–are the number of visitors referred by banner ads who reached a page in your Web site designated as a shopping page.

❚ *Attempted buyers*–are the number of potential buyers referred by banner ads who reached a Web page designated as a page for summarizing and paying for purchases.

❚ *Buyers*–are the number of buyers referred by banner ads who actually placed an order from your Web site.

❚ *Source*– indicates the specific Web site from which visitors came to your Web site.

In trying to increase the number of on-line customers, you must determine your Web site's success in converting visitors to actual buyers. You must also look at the abandonment rate–the percentage of attempted buyers who abandoned your Web site just as they were about to make a purchase. Low conversion rates and high abandonment rates are indicators that a Web site is not very effective. You also must identify likely Web site partners for a new advertising campaign. Use the MTR with your spreadsheet software to help you answer the questions below. Include a graphics presentation to support your findings:

1. What are the total number of visitors, shoppers, attempted buyers, and buyers at your Web site for this period?

2. Which sources provided the highest conversion rate to buyers at your Web site—that is, the percentage of visitors from a previous site that become buyers on your site? What is the average conversion rate for your Web site?

3. Which sources provided the highest abandonment rate at your Web site–that is, the percentage of attempted buyers that abandoned their shopping cart at your Web site before completing a purchase. What is the average abandonment rate for your Web site?

4. On which Web sites (or types of Web sites) should your firm purchase more banner ads?

GROUP PROJECT

Form a group with three or four of your classmates. Prepare evaluations of the wireless Internet capabilities of the Palm VII and the HP Jornada PocketPC handheld computing devices. Your analysis should consider the purchase cost of each device, any additional software required to make it Internet enabled, the cost of wireless Internet services, and what Internet services are available for each device. You should also consider other capabilities of each device, including the ability to integrate with existing corporate or PC applications. Which device would you select? What criteria would you use to guide your selection? If possible, use electronic presentation software to present your findings to the class.

TOOLS FOR INTERACTIVE LEARNING

■ INTERNET CONNECTION

The Internet Connection for this chapter will take you to a series of Web sites where you can evaluate tools for providing Wireless Web access. You can also use the Interactive Study Guide to test your knowledge of the topics in the chapter and get instant feedback where you need more practice.

■ CD-ROM

If you use the Multimedia Edition CD-ROM with this chapter, you can find a video demonstrating the Internet services provided by Apple Computer, an audio overview of the major themes of this chapter, and bullet text summarizing the key points of the chapter.

ELECTRONIC COMMERCE PROJECT

At the Laudon Web site for Chapter 9, you will find an Electronic Commerce Project where you can evaluate various Web search engines for business research.

CASE STUDY–*General Motors Takes a Test Drive on the Internet*

General Motors (GM) is the world's largest automaker, with 386,000 employees in 50 countries. GM vehicle brands include Chevrolet, Pontiac, Buick, Cadillac, Saturn, and GMC Trucks. GM also has vehicle production relationships with Opel, Vauxhall, Subaru, and Alfa Romeo. Its nonvehicle ventures include Allison Transmission (manufacturer of medium and heavy-duty transmissions), GM Locomotives, and a 35 percent share of Hughes Electronics (producer of satellites and communications). GM's subsidiary, GM Acceptance Corp. (GMAC) is a major financing organization that specializes in financing GM vehicle purchases and home mortgages.

GM's auto sales have been declining, from about 60 percent of the U.S. vehicle market in the 1970s, to only 28 percent today. The company continues to face stiff competition from Ford, Daimler Chrysler, and the Japanese, all of which have lower production costs than GM—and cars with better styling and quality.

GM's sheer size has proved to be one of its greatest burdens. For 70 years, GM operated along the lines laid down by CEO Alfred Sloan, who rescued the firm from bankruptcy in the 1920s. Sloan separated the firm into five separate operating groups and divisions (Chevrolet, Pontiac, Oldsmobile—which is being phased out—Buick, and Cadillac). Each division functioned as a semiautonomous company with its own marketing operations. GM remained a far-flung vertically integrated corporation that at one time manufactured up to 70 percent of its own parts. This model of top-down control and decentralized execution had once been a powerful source of competitive advantage, enabling GM to build cars at lower cost than its rivals. Over time, however, it worked against the company. Domestic competitors such as Chrysler were able to make vehicles at lower costs because they could purchase their parts from outside vendors and bargain on pricing. GM was not able to move quickly to update its selection and styling, and the quality of its cars lagged behind Japanese and even U.S. rivals. It took GM more time and money than competitors to produce a car because the firm was saddled with a lumbering bureaucracy and inefficient production processes.

GM's information systems reflected its welter of bureaucracies. At one time, GM had more than 100 mainframes and 34 computer centers but had no centralized system to link computer operations or to coordinate operations from one department to another. Each division and group had its own hardware and software so that the design group could not interact with production engineers via computer. GM had more than 16 different electronic mail systems, 28 different word processing systems, and a jumble of factory floor systems that could not communicate with management. Most of these systems were running on completely incompatible equipment.

Since the early 1980s GM's management has tried to standardize and integrate its systems. GM first used Electronic Data Systems (EDS) of Dallas (which it had briefly owned) to consolidate its computing centers into 21 uniform information-processing centers. EDS then consolidated 100 different GM networks into the world's largest private digital telecommunications network. In 1993, EDS replaced GM's hodgepodge of desktop models, network operating systems, and application development tools with standard hardware and software for office technology. GM has also been replacing 30 different materials and scheduling systems with one integrated system to handle inventory, manufacturing, and financial data.

GM's current chief information officer Ralph Szygenda has continued to work on streamlining the firm's information architecture and information technology infrastructure. Under his leadership, GM further trimmed the number of vendors of hardware, software, and services for its desktops and networks, and developed common business processes and systems. Szygenda's IS group replaced more than 50 systems with standard packaged software for personnel, payroll, and material management, including enterprise software to tie together human resources management and financial systems. GM replaced 26 different CAD/CAM systems with a single system. Customer data were fragmented among thousands of disparate databases maintained by GM's car and truck divisions and its leasing, home mortgage, and credit units. Szygenda initiated projects to integrate and standardize these data to provide a complete company-wide picture of the entire customer experience. Now GM can see which customers purchase vehicles frequently using GM financing and link each order to a customer's

entire car buying history. Before consolidating legacy systems and databases, this information would have been impossible to obtain.

In August 1999 GM added a new division devoted to the use of the Internet and e-commerce, known as eGM. Mark Hogan was named the head of the division and a corporate group vice president. In February 2000, 47-year-old Rick Wagoner was appointed CEO of GM, replacing Jack Smith. At that time Wagoner stated four main goals for the corporation, including his intention to focus on innovative products and services and the development of e-business. Wagoner's management team believes that by intensively weaving Internet technology into all of its business processes, GM can become a smarter, leaner, faster company, more in tune with customers. It also hopes this technology will help GM reduce from 24 to 12 months the time to design, engineer, and manufacture a new vehicle, cutting up to 10 percent of the cost of making a vehicle by eliminating supply chain inefficiencies. GM would use the savings produced from this skillful use of technology to increase spending on its vehicle designs. Although GM has the broadest vehicle lineup in the industry (49 models), it has lacked the resources to keep its models fresh.

Internet technology could be the catalyst for GM to reconstruct its entire value chain, transforming itself into a customer-focused business that provides many different electronic services to consumers, as well as cars. Indeed, more and more of GM's revenue comes from other sources, including the Internet. For instance, in April 2000 GM announced it would move into the world of on-line mortgages, cellular services, and information delivery, as well as selling its vehicle-based Internet technology. Ultimately, some think, all of this might make it the world's largest e-commerce company. Let us examine some of GM's Internet initiatives.

Selling vehicles on-line. The role of dealers is fundamental to the sale of automobiles. In fact, the laws in most states make it extremely difficult for anyone other than licensed auto dealerships to sell new vehicles, thanks to the lobbying power of the National Auto Dealers Association (NADA). Recently, GM has been experimenting with ways to sell vehicles on-line, although mostly with opposition from its dealers. They are concerned about GM trying to bypass them by selling vehicles on-line, a channel conflict. Hogan, however, describes GM's relationships with its dealers as "strong."

In March 1999, GM established GMBuyPower.com, a Web site where visitors can browse for GM cars; search by color, options, and availability; and find a dealer in their area that stocks the car they want. By autumn 2000, with the site receiving about 1 million hits per month, the company decided to use the site to make another try at selling vehicles on-line. This decision was partly in response to growing sales through such Web sites as Autobytel.com. GM is working on pilot programs to enable customers to purchase vehicles on-line through local dealerships. GMBuyPower.com attracted an average of 558,000 unique visitors per month between May 2000 and May 2001, more than double the volume of Ford's FordDirect.com dealer referral site. GM is now rolling out GMBuyPower.com to 45 global markets covering 95 percent of the car-driving world.

Dealers are vital to GM for several other reasons, including their close connection to their customers and to the automobile-purchasing public. "They understand what the on-line consumer is looking for," claims Scott McDonald, GM's director of e-sales. In addition, the dealers are essential because of their role in vehicle inventory. The process of making decisions about how many and which vehicles to produce requires a large inventory. The auto producers begin by making a guesstimate as to the number of each model to produce each year and in what color and with what options. The dealers in turn decide which of these vehicles they think they can sell and then make their purchases. Only then do customers begin to purchase, selecting from dealer inventories. To make the system work, the industry maintains about a two-month inventory of new vehicles. The value of GM's inventory is usually about $40 billion according to Hogan, making inventory costs very high. The dealer's' role is crucial, because dealers hold most of this inventory and so assume much of the risk and expense of owning the vehicles.

Building vehicles to order. One major weakness in the system of determining what to build is that if the manufacturers or the dealers guess wrong on total demand or on style, color, and other options, they must offer costly incentives to prod consumers to purchase these products. Auto producers are anxious to make cars that customers have actually ordered. "Build-to-order" has been around the auto industry for a long time, but only for very expensive cars, and it required a waiting period of two to three months before delivery. U.S. automakers have recently reduced wait time for ordered vehicles to six or seven weeks, and Toyota North America, the real leader, delivers a built-to-order vehicle in less than a month. Build-to-order would greatly reduce finished vehicle inventory costs as well as generate other production cost savings, potentially saving GM $20 billion per year. GM is so committed to build-to-order that it has assigned 200 people the goal of selling 80 percent of all GM new car purchases within three years.

Achieving this goal will require heavy reliance on GM's Internet infrastructure and extensive organizational change. The company will have to be able to take orders on-line, link its factories and suppliers on-line, change vehicle designs so they can be built more easily using modules, and greatly cut shipping times. Build-to-order requires producers to carry larger work-in-process inventories, a reversal of the 20-year trend of just-in-time component supply deliveries. According to James Mateyka, an automotive consultant at A. T. Kearney, "You would now need to hold, skillfully, inventories of certain kinds of parts [modules], such that you can be flexible enough to take a generically defined car, then at the last minute suddenly have a defined car."

In order to link factories to suppliers via cyberspace and reduce procurement and inventory costs, GM and other major auto manufacturers have established Covisint (see the Window on Organizations in Chapter 4), a massive net marketplace. GM spends $87 billion per year on raw materials and components and believes Covisint could cut the cost of producing each vehicle by perhaps $1,000 (estimates vary) as well as reduce the time from receiving a car order on-line to delivery from about 45 days to 10 days. Covisint is linked to GM's own private industrial

network, called GMSupplyPower. This extranet gives suppliers access to the latest information on production scheduling, inventory, and the quality of their parts.

Locate-to-order. Build-to-order is not yet a reality, and so the immediate problem is quickly finding the desired car, a strategy known as locate-to-order. To achieve this approach, GM must create a regional inventory of the pool of available vehicles using the Internet. The pool will be displayed on the Net so potential buyers can select the car they want regardless of its location. Customers then buy it through their local dealer According to Gary Dilts, Chrysler's senior vice president of e-commerce, 98 percent of the vehicles customers want are already available somewhere. Ultimately, however, GM will have to build-to-order because inventory cost savings are so compelling.

OnStar. Another information age venture GM has established is its wholly owned subsidiary, OnStar. It is a telematics system with onboard navigation, Internet, safety, and communications capabilities accessed through three buttons on the vehicle dashboard. A GPS (global positioning system) keeps the system constantly informed as to the location of the vehicle on the road. OnStar provides such services as emergency roadside assistance, stolen-vehicle tracking, and concierge support, such as making dinner reservations.

OnStar Personal Calling enables drivers to make and receive hands-free calls with voice-activated phones. The OnStar Virtual Advisor service allows users to retrieve personal data on the Web, including e-mail, news, stock quotes, and traffic and road-condition reports within a given radius of the driver's location. Whether the hardware is standard or an option, any user of OnStar will pay an annual subscription fee, ranging from $199 to $399 depending on the services taken.

With OnStar, GM cars become a platform that generates a continuous stream of high-margin revenue from drivers downloading and paying by the minute for Internet, data, and telecommunications services. With 70 percent of wireless telephone minutes logged in vehicles, GM could eventually become the largest reseller of cellular minutes in the United States. The service already has close to 1 million subscribers. GM has licensed OnStar to Honda and Toyota, and it will also be providing them such services as roadside assistance as well.

Internal uses. General Motors created an intranet portal called Socrates that enables users to search all of GM's internal sites from one starting point. Today 100,000 GM employees around the globe can access more than 500 internal GM sites through this portal. Employees can use Socrates to access their human resources information, participate in on-line training programs, and search through a repository of best practices. Socrates has capabilities for enabling employees to tailor the information they obtain to their own needs, making it easy for them to use. GM is even subsidizing the cost of home access for its employees because it wants to make the Internet a more integral part of their daily lives.

Ralph Szygenda has said that "The [automobile production] company that links design, procurement and sales—and puts it all together electronically—wins." Will his words be borne out? Can GM use the Internet to transform its hidebound bureaucracy? Two decades of restructuring and reorganization have brought about deep changes at GM, paring down the waste and overbloated organization. The company has cut down the time it takes to develop and produce a car from 48 to 18 months, eliminating $1 billion in engineering costs. Can these efforts stop the decline in GM's market share? GM has been losing money and market share in Europe, and risks falling behind Ford as the leader in U.S. sales. Foreign automakers are consolidating their grip on the U.S. auto market. Despite shedding tens of thousands of workers, chopping billions of dollars per year off of costs, and eliminating models, GM still struggles to earn net income of more than three cents on the dollar. (Other automakers generate net profit margins of 6 percent.) Although GM currently is not experiencing a financial crisis, it remains under heavy pressure to boost its mediocre profit margins.

Overall, GM has invested about $1.6 billion in streamlining its IT infrastructure and architecture along with various e-commerce and e-business initiatives. These changes have already reduced GM's IT budget by $800 million each year since 1996. But will this be enough to boost profits over the long run? If GM has the greatest technology and technology services, such as OnStar, but continues to build uninspired vehicles, how much can e-business help?

Sources: John Galvin, "Racing the Clock," *Smart Business Magazine,* May 2001; Antone Gonsalves, "IT's the Tiger in Their Tanks," *Information Week,* September 17, 2001; Jason Black, "Build Lasting Partnerships, " *Internet World,* August 1, 2001; Peter D. Henig, "The New Thin Client?" *Red Herring,* May 2001; Joseph B. White, Gregory L. White, and Horihiko Shirouzu, "Soon, the Big Three Won't Be, as Foreigners Make Inroads in U.S.," *Wall Street Journal,* August 13, 2001; Gregory L. White, "In Order to Grow, GM Finds That the Order of the Day Is Cutbacks," *Wall Street Journal,* December 18, 2000; Keith Bradsher, "G.M. Phaseout of Olds Is at Center of a Range of Cutbacks," *New York Times,* December 13, 2000; Dale Buss, "Custom Cars Stuck in Gridlock," *The Industry Standard,* October 16, 2000; Dale Buss, "The Race to Be Wired," *The Industry Standard,* September 4, 2000; Lee Copeland, "Automakers Put Workers Online," *Computerworld,* November 3, 2000; Lee Copeland, "General Motors' CIO Touts Corporate Benefits Portal," *Computerworld,* November 27, 2000; Lee Copeland, "GM Now Sells Web Technology, Not Just Cars," *Computerworld,* June, 5, 2000; Lee Copeland, "GM Shuts Doors on GMDriverSite.com," *Computerworld,* September 4, 2000; Sari Kalin, "Overdrive," *CIO Web Business Magazine,* July 1, 2000; Julia King and Lee Copeland, "GM Retools for E-Commerce That Goes Well Beyond Cars," *Computerworld,* April 17, 2000; Todd Lassa, "General Motors Is Making a Major Internet Play, and It's Put a Real 'Car Guy' Behind the Wheel. But Can He Drive an E-Business?" *Internet World Magazine,* March 1, 2000; Kathleen Melymuka, "GM Deal for Web-Based Dealership Software Falls Through," *Computerworld,* November 16, 2000; Robert L. Simison, "GM Retools to Sell Custom Cars Online," *Wall Street Journal,* February 22, 2000; Paul Strassmann, "GM's Info Gamble," *Computerworld,* June 5, 2000; Lauren Gibbons Paul, "The Biggest Gamble Yet," *CIO Magazine,* April 15, 2000; Todd Weiss, "GM to Begin Selling Oldsmobiles Online in Web-Site Pilot Program," *Computerworld,* September 19, 2000; Steve Ulfelder, "Internet Drag Race," *Computerworld,* March 6, 2000; Ken Yamada, "Shop Talk: Car Dealers, Customers Both Win on Web," *Red Herring,* September 26, 2000; Eric Young, "Stalled on the Digital Highway," *The Industry Standard,* September 4, 2000; and Jennifer Zaino, "OnStar Expands Services for Drivers," *Information Week,* November 14, 2000.

CASE STUDY QUESTIONS

1. Describe the competitive business environment in which GM is operating.

2. Describe the relationship between GM's organization and its information technology infrastructure. What management, organization, and technology factors influenced this relationship?

3. Evaluate the current business strategy of GM in response to its competitive environment. What is the role of Internet technology in that strategy? How successful is that strategy?

4. What management, organization, and technology issues do you think GM has had to face and will need to solve in implementing its Internet strategy?

5. How will GM have to redesign its business processes to be able to compete successfully and achieve a leading role in the new economy?

6. In GM's drive to sell cars on-line and to build-to-order, what are some of the problems that technology cannot address?

Part II Project

CREATING A NEW INTERNET BUSINESS

We have prepared a list of new businesses that could benefit from going on the Web. Select one of the businesses from the list and develop an Internet strategy for that business. You will need to identify the Internet business model to be pursued, use the Internet to research and analyze markets and competitors, and design part of the Web site for that business.

VIRTUAL TOUR OF ELECTRONIC COMMERCE SITES

To prepare for this project, review Internet business models by taking a virtual tour of the electronic commerce sites described in the following table. To take the tour, visit the Web site representing each business model. Explore the Web site so that you have a clear idea of how that business uses the Web for electronic commerce.

Virtual Tour of Electronic Commerce Sites

Business Model	Description	Organization	URL
Virtual Storefront	Sells physical goods on-line instead of through a physical storefront or retail outlet. The goods are then shipped to the customer.	Amazon.com	www.amazon.com
Information Broker	Provides primarily product, pricing, and availability information. The final purchase transaction is usually conducted elsewhere.	Edmunds.com	www.edmunds.com
Transaction Broker	Provides services that allow people to complete transactions, such as buying and selling securities.	E*Trade	www.etrade.com
On-line Marketplace	Provides digital environment where buyers and sellers can meet, search for products, display products, and establish prices for those products. Can provide on-line auctions or reverse auctions as well as negotiated or fixed pricing.	eBay	www.ebay.com
Content Provider	Creates revenue by providing digital content, such as digital news, music, photos, or video, over the Web.	Wall Street Journal Interactive	www.wsj.com
On-line Service Provider	Provides on-line hardware and software services for individuals and businesses.	Xdrive	www.xdrive.com
Portal	Provides an initial point of entry to the Web along with specialized content and other services.	Yahoo!	www.yahoo.com
Virtual Community	Provides on-line meeting place where people with similar interests can communicate and find useful information.	Geocities	www.geocities.com

SELECTING AN INTERNET BUSINESS MODEL AND DESIGNING A WEB STRATEGY

The five businesses we describe are fictitious but are based on real-world scenarios. Review each of them. Then select one business and answer the following questions:

1. What Internet business model would be appropriate for the company to follow in creating a Web site?

2. In what ways can the company benefit from a Web site? What functions should it perform for the company (marketing, sales, customer support, internal communications, etc.)?

3. In what other ways might the company use the Internet for its own benefit?

4. Prepare functional specifications for the company's use of the Web and the Internet. Include links to and from other sites or systems in your design.

5. Prepare a cost–benefit analysis of a proposal to implement the company's use of the Internet.

For each of the five businesses, we list a Web site of a real-world company in the same or a related business to help you understand that type of business. Visit the Web site related to the business you have selected and review it carefully.

Business 1: InfoInc.

InfoInc. is a start-up company that would like to provide a service by offering easy access to needed information in specialized fields such as accounting, finance, or medicine. Although its business plan calls for moving into a number of fields, InfoInc. would like to begin by addressing the needs of people in the accounting and tax fields. Its first two target groups are accounting professionals and the general public. For the general public, the plan is to provide a Web site with advice on various issues such as tax laws and IRA savings rules. The site would also contain links to other sites where visitors will be able to obtain advice on such issues as how to establish a new business. For accounting professionals, such as certified public accountants (CPAs) and corporate financial officers, InfoInc. would like to offer more detailed information services. In addition, the company wants to provide capabilities that might help the CPAs and financial officers manage their e-mail, voice mail, and fax.

Web reference: WebMD Inc. [http://webmd.com/]

Business 2: Aerospace Metal Alloys

Aerospace Metal is a distributor of exotic steel, aluminum, and titanium alloys to the aerospace industry and to other specialty industries. These metals, such as kovar and inconel, must meet exceptionally exacting standards because they become parts in airplanes, rockets, industrial furnaces, and other high-performance products. Aerospace sells raw materials produced in the form of bars, sheets, rings, and forgings. In turn, Aerospace customers use these materials to fabricate their final products. Many Aerospace customers are actually parts suppliers to end-product assemblers such as Boeing Aircraft. Aerospace Metal maintains a sales staff to sell these metals, and the company stores its products in seven warehouses throughout the country. They obtain their products from steel and metal manufacturers throughout North America. If a customer requests a product not carried by Aerospace, the company will special-order it from an appropriate supplier.

Web reference: Specialty Steel and Storage [http://www.steelforge.com]

Business 3: Columbiana

Columbiana is a small, independent island in the Caribbean. It is underdeveloped and is also off the tourist path for most visitors to that area despite its many attractions. The island has a unique history, with Indian ruins dating back 800 years and with many historical buildings, forts, and other sites built during its centuries as a British colony. A few first-class hotels have been built along some of its beautiful white beaches, and less expensive accommodations are also available along beaches, in several towns, and near several fishing villages. Its rain forests, rivers, striking mountains, and volcano cone all could be of interest to tourists. In addition, it has many restaurants that specialize in native dishes and fresh fish. The government not only wants to increase tourism but it also wants to increase trade by developing new markets for its tropical agricultural products. In addition, leaders hope to attract investment capital so that many of the unemployed residents can find jobs. Two major airlines have regular flights to Columbiana, as do several small Caribbean airlines. The island is on the tourist itinerary of only one cruise ship company. The Web site will not transact any business, but it will offer information and links to other appropriate sites.

Web reference: Dominica [http://dominica.dm]

Business 4: Home Do-It-Yourself Tools Inc.

As more and more people are turning to do-it-yourself home repairs, the market for tools of all kinds for home use has grown rapidly. The buyer has thousands of tools to choose from, and so the search can be time consuming and the prices paid can be very high. Home Do-It-Yourself Tools Inc. (Home Tools) was founded to capitalize on this trend. The founder initially opened a small store in Atlanta, Georgia, and soon thereafter established a catalog to try to expand the business. Home Tools uses a free 800 telephone number to take orders and to answer potential customers' technical and product questions, soliciting new customers through advertisements in magazines read by home repair enthusiasts. The owner now wants to make better use of the Internet to reach out to new customers, reduce Home Tools' cost per sale, and improve service quality. The heart of the business is a database listing several thousand tools and the tasks for which they are commonly used.

Web reference: iGo.com [http://www.igo.com].

Business 5: Low Cost Tires Inc.

Low Cost Tires Inc. (Tires Inc.) began as a small auto repair and tire shop in a small city outside of Chicago. While the original goal of the shop was to gain a reputation for quality repair, the owner also stressed meeting customer needs on the sale of tires. Low Cost Tires carries a very wide selection of tires so that customers can always be served on the spot. Its staff is highly trained and very knowledgeable about tires. Selling tires has turned out to be more profitable than auto repairs. Although the owner plans to maintain the auto repair business, he wants to use the Internet to expand tire sales and to capitalize on his staff's understanding of customer needs. Management believes the correct Web strategy could help Tires Inc. improve customer service locally, increase its customer base, and help it create retail outlets in new locations.

Web reference: The Luggage Factory [http://www.luggagefactoryoutlet.com/]

MANAGEMENT AND ORGANIZATIONAL SUPPORT SYSTEMS FOR THE DIGITAL FIRM

Chapter 10
Managing Knowledge for the Digital Firm

Chapter 11
Enhancing Management Decision-making for the Digital Firm

Part III Project
Designing an Enterprise Information Portal

chapter

10 MANAGING KNOWLEDGE FOR THE DIGITAL FIRM

As a manager, you'll want to know how your firm can benefit from information systems for knowledge management. After completing this chapter, you will be able to answer the following questions:

1. *Why do businesses today need knowledge management programs and systems for knowledge management?*

2. *Which information system applications are most useful for distributing, creating, and sharing knowledge in the firm?*

3. *What are the business benefits of using artificial intelligence technology for knowledge management?*

4. *How can businesses use expert systems and case-based reasoning to capture knowledge?*

5. *How can organizations benefit from using neural networks and other intelligent techniques?*

Knowledge Management: British Telecom's New Competitive Weapon

British Telecom (BT) plc is one of the world's leading telecommunications service providers, offering local, long distance, and international telecommunications services; mobile communications; and Internet services, primarily in the United Kingdom and Western Europe.

Until deregulation, BT held an unchallenged dominance of telecommunications services in the United Kingdom. Since the early 1990s, it has had to face competition from a wave of smaller, nimbler, newer companies. As of June 2000, BT's customer base had dwindled to 8.5 out of 10 million business lines in the United Kingdom, a far cry from total dominance of the market in 1992. The company had to find ways of responding more quickly to competitors and market changes.

The company's traditional library and research services could not provide business information and intelligence quickly enough for the company to respond to its new competitive pressures. British Telecom's corporate library was stuffed with unfiled paper and reports. Everything had to be checked in and out by hand. Librarians frantically tried to satisfy the research requests from several hundred

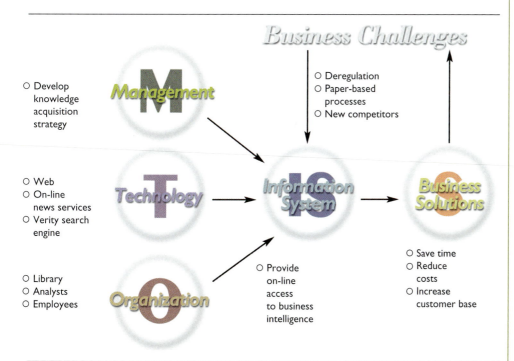

employees in sales, marketing, and strategy. Analysts who couldn't wait for the research to arrive by mail had to travel to London and do the work themselves—a 200-mile round trip for some. The company could only support a few hundred users with its traditional newspaper clipping service for competitive research.

Management realized the company needed a much quicker way to get competitive information into the field. BT converted its traditional paper clipping and research library services into a one-stop Web-based intelligence center called Intellact. Intellact puts many of the resources in BT's old research library on-line, where they can be accessed immediately by nearly 90,000 of the company's 137,000 worldwide employees in nearly every job function and every level of the firm. The system provides data, news, and research on almost every topic of concern to the company, incorporating sources such as the *New York Times*, the *Wall Street Journal*, proprietary industry research from firms such as Forrester Research and Gartner, and even obscure telecommunications journals. Its core news feed comes from Factiva's Reuters Business Briefing Select, which includes content from a large number of newspapers, magazines, and news wires, including Reuters and Dow Jones. The system provides 2,000 to 3,000 daily stories classified into 100 different topic "channels," including 40 competitor profile sites, 20 vertical market portals, and dozens of technology and regionally focused centers.

Every major topic, such as major competitors, industry customer groups, or wireless technology, has its own Web page populated by news feeds and BT's content management system. Intellact staff organize the pages, selecting and highlighting the most important stories for users. If users can't find what they need on the edited Web pages, Intellact provides a search tool powered by Verity where they can search on key words, timeframe, or information source.

The system handles about 7,000 user sessions per day, and its timely knowledge is credited with helping the company expedite sales deals and capture new customers.

Sources: Jason Compton, "Dial K for Knowledge," *CIO Magazine*, June 15, 2001; and www.groupbt.com.

MANAGEMENT CHALLENGES

British Telecom's Intellact is one example of how systems can be used to leverage organizational knowledge by making it more easily available. Collaborating and communicating with practitioners and experts and sharing ideas and information have become essential requirements in business, science, and government. In an information economy, capturing and distributing intelligence and knowledge and enhancing group collaboration have become vital to organizational innovation and survival. Special systems can be used for managing organizational knowledge, but they raise the following management challenges:

1. **Designing knowledge systems that genuinely enhance organizational performance.** Managers have encountered problems when attempting to transform their firms through knowledge management programs (Gold, Malhotra, and Segars, 2001). Information systems that truly enhance the productivity of knowledge workers may be difficult to build because the manner in which information technology can enhance higher-level tasks such as those performed by managers and professionals is not always clearly understood. Some aspects of organizational knowledge cannot be captured easily or codified, or the information that organizations finally manage to capture may become outdated as environments change. It is very difficult to integrate knowledge management programs with business strategy. Processes and interactions between information technology and social elements in organizations must be carefully managed (Grover and Davenport, 2001).

2. **Creating robust expert systems.** Expert systems must be changed every time there is a change in the organizational environment. Each time there is a change in the rules experts use, they must be reprogrammed. It is difficult to provide expert systems with the flexibility of human experts. Many thousands of businesses have undertaken experimental projects in expert systems, but only a small percentage have created expert systems that actually can be used on a production basis.

This chapter examines information system applications specifically designed to help organizations create, capture, distribute, and apply knowledge and information. First, we examine information systems for supporting information and knowledge work. Then we look at the ways that organizations can use artificial intelligence technologies for capturing and storing knowledge and expertise.

10.1 KNOWLEDGE MANAGEMENT IN THE ORGANIZATION

Chapter 1 described the emergence of the information economy and the digital firm in which the major source of wealth and prosperity is the production and distribution of information and knowledge, and firms increasingly rely on digital technology to enable business processes. For example, 55 percent of the U.S. labor force consists of knowledge and information workers, and 60 percent of the gross domestic product of the United States comes from the knowledge and information sectors, such as finance and publishing.

In an information economy, knowledge-based core competencies—the two or three things that an organization does best—are key organizational assets. Producing unique products or services or producing them at a lower cost than competitors is based on superior knowledge of the production process and superior design. Knowing how to do things effectively and efficiently in ways that other organizations cannot duplicate is a primary source of profit and a factor in production that cannot be purchased in external markets. Some management theorists believe that these knowledge assets are as important for competitive advantage and survival, if not more important, than physical and financial assets.

As knowledge becomes a central productive and strategic asset, organizational success increasingly depends on the firm's ability to produce, gather, store, and disseminate knowledge. With knowledge, firms become more efficient and effective in their use of scarce resources. Without knowledge, firms become less efficient and effective in their use of resources and ultimately fail.

Organizational Learning and Knowledge Management

How do firms obtain knowledge? Like humans, organizations create and gather knowledge through a variety of **organizational learning** mechanisms. Through trial and error, careful measurement of planned activities, and feedback from customers and the environment in general, organizations create new standard operating procedures and business processes that reflect their experience. This is called "organizational learning." Arguably organizations that can sense and respond to their environments rapidly will survive longer than organizations that have poor learning mechanisms.

Knowledge management increases the ability of the organization to learn from its environment and to incorporate knowledge into its business processes. **Knowledge management** refers to the set of processes developed in an organization to create, store, transfer, and apply knowledge. Information technology plays an important role in knowledge management as an enabler of business processes aimed at creating, storing, disseminating, and applying knowledge. Developing procedures and routines—business processes—to optimize the creation, flow, learning, protection, and sharing of knowledge in the firm is now a core management responsibility.

Companies cannot take advantage of their knowledge resources if they have inefficient processes for capturing and distributing knowledge, or if they fail to appreciate the value of the knowledge they already possess (Davenport and Prusak, 1998). Some corporations have created explicit knowledge management programs for protecting and distributing knowledge resources that they have identified and for discovering new sources of knowledge. These programs are often headed by a **chief knowledge officer (CKO)**. The chief knowledge officer is a senior executive who is responsible for the firm's knowledge management program. The CKO helps design programs and systems to find new sources of knowledge or to make better use of existing knowledge in organizational and management processes (Flash, 2001; Earl and Scott, 1999).

Systems and Infrastructure for Knowledge Management

All the major types of information systems described in this text facilitate the flow of information and the management of a firm's knowledge. Earlier chapters described systems that help firms understand and respond to their environments more effectively, notably enterprise and supply chain management systems, external and internal networks, databases, datamining, and communication-based applications. The concept of a "digital firm" refers to a firm with substantial use of information technology to enhance its ability to sense and respond to its environment.

Although all the information systems we have described help an organization sense and respond to its environment, some technologies uniquely and directly address the organizational learning and knowledge management task. Office systems, knowledge work systems (KWS), group collaboration systems, and artificial intelligence applications are especially useful for knowledge management because they focus on supporting information and knowledge work and on defining and capturing the organization's knowledge base. This knowledge base may include (1) structured internal knowledge (explicit knowledge), such as product manuals or research reports; (2) external knowledge of competitors, products, and

organizational learning
Creation of new standard operating procedures and business processes that reflect organizations' experience.

knowledge management
The set of processes developed in an organization to create, store, disseminate, and apply the firm's knowledge.

chief knowledge officer (CKO)
Senior executive in charge of the organization's knowledge management program.

Figure 10-1 Knowledge management requires an information technology (IT) infrastructure that facilitates the collection and sharing of knowledge as well as software for distributing information and making it more meaningful. The information systems illustrated here give close-in support to information workers at many levels in the organization.

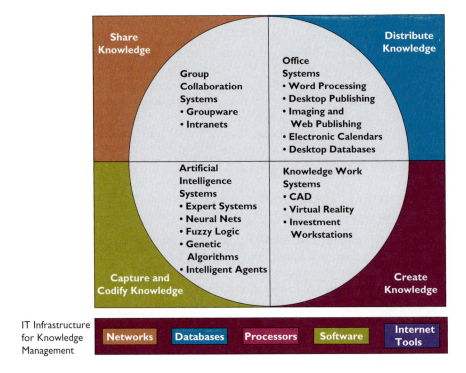

tacit knowledge
Expertise and experience of organizational members that has not been formally documented.

best practices
The most successful solutions or problem-solving methods that have been developed by a specific organization or industry.

organizational memory
The stored learning from an organization's history that can be used for decision making and other purposes.

information work
Work that primarily consists of creating or processing information.

data workers
People, such as secretaries or bookkeepers, who process and disseminate the organization's information and paperwork.

knowledge workers
People, such as engineers, scientists, or architects, who design products or services or create knowledge for the organization.

markets, including competitive intelligence; and (3) informal internal knowledge, often called **tacit knowledge**, which resides in the minds of individual employees but has not been formally documented in a structured form (Davenport, DeLong, and Beers, 1998).

Information systems can promote organizational learning by capturing, codifying, and distributing both explicit and tacit knowledge. Once information has been collected and organized in a system, it can be reused many times. Companies can use information systems to codify their best practices and make knowledge of these practices more widely available to employees. **Best practices** are the most successful solutions or problem-solving methods that have been developed by a specific organization or industry. In addition to improving existing work practices, the knowledge can be preserved as organizational memory to train future employees or to help them with decision making. **Organizational memory** is the stored learning from an organization's history that can be used for decision-making and other purposes. Information systems can also provide networks for linking people so that individuals with special areas of expertise can be easily identified and tacit knowledge can be shared.

Figure 10-1 illustrates the information systems and information technology (IT) infrastructure for supporting knowledge management. Office systems help disseminate and coordinate the flow of information in the organization. Knowledge work systems support the activities of highly skilled knowledge workers and professionals as they create new knowledge and try to integrate it into the firm. Group collaboration and support systems support the creation and sharing of knowledge among people working in groups. Artificial intelligence systems capture new knowledge and provide organizations and managers with codified knowledge that can be reused by others in the organization. These systems require an IT infrastructure that makes heavy use of powerful processors, networks, databases, software, and Internet tools.

10.2 INFORMATION AND KNOWLEDGE WORK SYSTEMS

Information work is work that consists primarily of creating or processing information. It is carried out by information workers who usually are divided into two subcategories: **data workers**, who primarily process and disseminate information; and **knowledge workers**, who primarily create knowledge and information.

Examples of data workers include secretaries, sales personnel, bookkeepers, and draftspeople. Researchers, designers, architects, writers, and judges are examples of knowledge

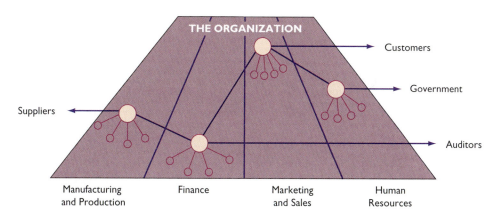

Figure 10-2 The three major roles of offices. Offices perform three major roles. (1) They coordinate the work of local professionals and information workers. (2) They coordinate work in the organization across levels and functions. (3) They couple the organization to the external environment.

workers. Data workers can be distinguished from knowledge workers because knowledge workers usually have higher levels of education and memberships in professional organizations. In addition, knowledge workers exercise independent judgment as a routine aspect of their work. Data and knowledge workers have different information requirements and different systems to support them.

DISTRIBUTING KNOWLEDGE: OFFICE AND DOCUMENT MANAGEMENT SYSTEMS

Most data work and a great deal of knowledge work takes place in offices, including most of the work done by managers. The office plays a major role in coordinating the flow of information throughout the entire organization. The office has three basic functions (see Figure 10-2):

▌ Managing and coordinating the work of data and knowledge workers.

▌ Connecting the work of the local information workers with all levels and functions of the organization.

▌ Connecting the organization to the external world, including customers, suppliers, government regulators, and external auditors.

Office workers span a very broad range: professionals, managers, sales, and clerical workers working alone or in groups. Their major activities include the following:

▌ Managing documents, including document creation, storage, retrieval, and dissemination.

▌ Scheduling for individuals and groups.

▌ Communicating, including initiating, receiving, and managing voice, digital, and document-based communications for individuals and groups.

▌ Managing data, such as on employees, customers, and vendors.

These activities can be supported by office systems (see Table 10-1). **Office systems** are any application of information technology that intends to increase productivity of information workers in the office. Fifteen years ago, office systems handled only the creation, processing, and management of documents. Today professional knowledge and information

office systems
Computer systems, such as word processing, voice mail, and imaging, that are designed to increase the productivity of information workers in the office.

TABLE 10-1 TYPICAL OFFICE SYSTEMS

Office Activity	Technology
Managing documents	Word processing, desktop publishing, document imaging, Web publishing, work flow managers
Scheduling	Electronic calendars, groupware, intranets
Communicating	E-mail, voice mail, digital answering systems, groupware, intranets
Managing data	Desktop databases, spreadsheets, user-friendly interfaces to mainframe databases

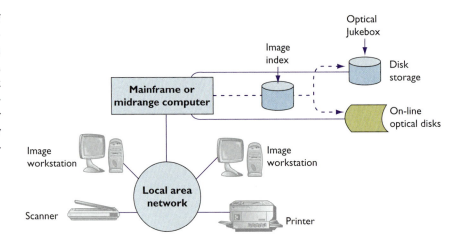

Figure 10-3 Components of an imaging system. A typical imaging system stores and processes digitized images of documents, using scanners, an optical disk system, an image index, workstations, and printers. A midrange or small mainframe computer may be required to control the activities of a large imaging system.

document imaging systems
Systems that convert documents and images into digital form so they can be stored and accessed by the computer.

jukebox
A device for storing and retrieving many optical disks.

work remains highly document centered. However, digital image processing—words and graphics—is also at the core of systems, as are high-speed digital communications services. Because office work involves many people jointly engaged in projects, contemporary office systems have powerful group assistance tools such as networked digital calendars. An ideal office environment would be based on a seamless network of digital machines linking professional, clerical, and managerial work groups and running a variety of types of software.

Although word processing and desktop publishing address the creation and presentation of documents, they only exacerbate the existing paper avalanche problem. Work flow problems arising from paper handling are enormous. It has been estimated that up to 85 percent of corporate information is stored on paper. Locating and updating information in that format is a great source of organizational inefficiency.

One way to reduce problems stemming from paper work flow is to employ document imaging systems. **Document imaging systems** are systems that convert documents and images into digital form so they can be stored and accessed by a computer. Such systems store, retrieve, and manipulate a digitized image of a document, allowing the document itself to be discarded. The system must contain a scanner that converts the document image into a bit-mapped image, storing that image as a graphic. If the document is not in active use, it usually is stored on an optical disk system. Optical disks, kept on-line in a **jukebox** (a device for storing and retrieving many optical disks), require up to a minute to retrieve the document automatically.

An imaging system also requires indexes that allow users to identify and retrieve a document when needed. Index data are entered so that a document can be retrieved in a variety of ways, depending upon the application. For example, the index may contain the document scan date, the customer name and number, the document type, and some subject information. Finally, the system must include retrieval equipment, primarily workstations capable of handling graphics, although printers usually are included. Figure 10-3 illustrates the components of a typical imaging system.

Traditional document-management systems can be expensive, requiring proprietary client/server networks, special client software, and storage capabilities. Intranets provide a low-cost and universally available platform for basic document publishing, and many companies are using them for this purpose. Employees can publish information using Web-page authoring tools and post it to an intranet Web server where it can be shared and accessed throughout the company with standard Web browsers. These Weblike "documents" can be multimedia objects combining text, graphics, audio, and video along with hyperlinks. After a document has been posted to the server, it can be indexed for quicker access and linked to other documents (see Figure 10-4).

For more sophisticated document-management functions, such as controlling changes to documents, maintaining histories of activity and changes in the managed documents, and the ability to search documents on either content or index terms, commercial Web-based systems such as those from IntraNet Solutions or Open Text are available. Vendors such as

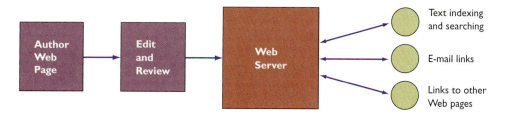

Figure 10-4 Web publishing and document management. An author can post information on an intranet Web server, where it can be accessed through a variety of mechanisms.

FileNet and Documentum have enhanced their traditional document-management systems with Web capabilities.

The Window on Management describes the benefits of Web-based systems for work flow management, document control, and project management in the architectural, engineering, and construction industries.

To achieve the large productivity gains promised by imaging technology, organizations must redesign their work flow. In the past, the existence of only one copy of a document largely shaped work flow. Work had to be performed serially; two people could not work on the same document at the same time. Significant staff time was devoted to filing and retrieving documents. After a document has been stored electronically, work flow management can change the traditional methods of working with documents (see Chapter 12).

CREATING KNOWLEDGE: KNOWLEDGE WORK SYSTEMS

Knowledge work is that portion of information work that creates new knowledge and information. For example, knowledge workers create new products or find ways to improve existing ones. Knowledge work is segmented into many highly specialized fields, and each field has a different collection of **knowledge work systems (KWS)** to support workers in that field. Knowledge workers perform three key roles that are critical to the organization and to the managers who work within the organization:

▮ Keeping the organization up-to-date in knowledge as it develops in the external world—in technology, science, social thought, and the arts.

▮ Serving as internal consultants regarding the areas of their knowledge, the changes taking place, and the opportunities.

▮ Acting as change agents evaluating, initiating, and promoting change projects.

Knowledge workers and data workers have somewhat different information systems support needs. Most knowledge workers rely on office systems, such as word processors, voice mail, and calendars, but they also require more specialized knowledge work systems.

knowledge work systems (KWS)

Information systems that aid knowledge workers in the creation and integration of new knowledge in the organization.

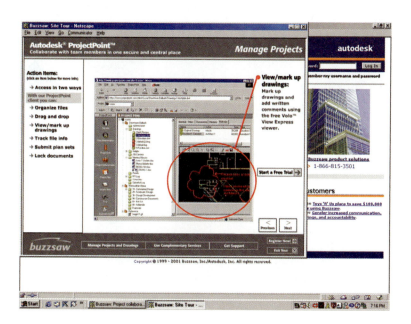

Buzzsaw.com provides tools for online project collaboration during all phases of the building life cycle. Users can manage, distribute, print, and share all project related documents and drawings in one secure location.

MANAGING CONSTRUCTION PROJECTS WITH THE INTERNET

Many people think that the most widely used tool in a construction project is a hammer, but it's probably a filing cabinet or fax machine. The $3.4 trillion U.S. construction industry is highly paper intensive. A complex project such as a large building requires the coordination of many different groups and hundreds of architectural drawings and design documents, which can change daily. Costly delays because of misplaced documents could make or break a company in an industry with razor-thin profit margins of 1 to 2 percent.

Web technology is starting to address this problem. New Web-based construction project management systems enable project managers to exchange documents and work on-line wherever they are using Web browser software. San Francisco-based Buzzsaw.com, for example, offers customers a shared space where project managers can exchange documents with engineers and architects, bid for subcontractor services, track scheduling and performance, and hold on-line meetings.

Toys R Us used Buzzsaw.com's services to better manage and speed up construction while reducing costs. In one project it remodeled two dilapidated theaters in New York's Times Square into the largest toy store in the world. This Times Square project, headed by Tracy LeBlanc, held weekly meetings with 15 project consultants, partly to decide on design changes. Once finished, agreements on changes were sent to the architects to integrate them into the plans, which were returned to the consultants who then made more detailed documents and passed them to the general construction contractor.

In the past all plans were hand drawn and then sent by mail or overnight express to the next person involved, who would have to have new plans drawn. The same process would be repeated until the final detailed documents were in the hands of the general contractor. This took a great deal of time and labor. Now,

changes can be uploaded to Buzzsaw.com for instant communication and immediate revision. Depending on the size of the project and the distance between the various individuals, using the Internet can save days or weeks and reduce the number of errors made in manual redrawing. Toys R Us paid $2,000 per month to subscribe to Buzzsaw.com but claimed the service would save $100,000 a year in messaging, printing, and photo processing costs alone. Figure 10-5 illustrates how the business processes for construction projects changed as a result of this system.

Even more significant savings result from using the service to keep a complicated project, such as the Toys R Us building, on time and within budget. For example, LeBlanc could use the system to monitor progress at the Times Square site from two Webcams installed at the construction site, controlling the rotation of the cameras from his computer keyboard. He and other members of the architectural, design, and construction team could also use Buzzsaw.com to view digital photos of the building.

Software also exists to enable construction companies to order and track construction supplies as needed. Management no longer must spend long hours ordering by telephone or using catalogs to select products. "This technology enables us to triple or quadruple the speed with which we can pull off a project," claims Randall Dolph, CIO of Gensler, a San Francisco-based architectural firm. It saves time and mail and overnight express expenses, while increasing speed and enabling managers to better control the processes.

To Think About: What are the management benefits of using Web-based construction management software? What are the possible drawbacks?

Sources: Mark Roberti, "Cutting Construction Chaos," *The Industry Standard,* June 11, 2001; and Matt Villano, "Building on I.T.," *CIO Magazine,* June 15, 2001.

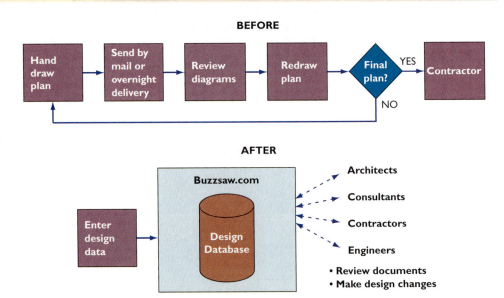

Figure 10-5 Changes in the construction project management process. Toys R Us replaced its multistep paper-based process for generating and revising construction design plans with a much simpler process, using Web-based project management tools for the construction industry.

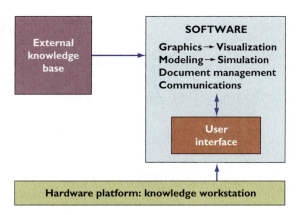

Figure 10-6 Requirements of knowledge work systems. Knowledge work systems require strong links to external knowledge bases in addition to specialized hardware and software.

Knowledge work systems are specifically designed to promote the creation of knowledge and to ensure that new knowledge and technical expertise are properly integrated into the business.

Requirements of Knowledge Work Systems

Knowledge work systems have characteristics that reflect the special needs of knowledge workers. First, knowledge work systems must give knowledge workers the specialized tools they need, such as powerful graphics, analytical tools, and communications and document-management tools. These systems require great computing power in order to handle rapidly the sophisticated graphics or complex calculations necessary to such knowledge workers as scientific researchers, product designers, and financial analysts. Because knowledge workers are so focused on knowledge in the external world, these systems also must give the worker quick and easy access to external databases.

A user-friendly interface is very important to a knowledge worker's system. User-friendly interfaces save time by allowing the user to perform needed tasks and get to required information without having to spend a lot of time learning how to use the computer. Saving time is more important for knowledge workers than for most other employees because knowledge workers are highly paid—wasting a knowledge worker's time is simply too expensive. Figure 10-6 summarizes the requirements of knowledge work systems.

Knowledge workstations often are designed and optimized for the specific tasks to be performed, so a design engineer will require a different workstation than a lawyer. Design engineers need graphics with enough power to handle three-dimensional computer-aided design (CAD) systems. However, financial analysts are more interested in having access to a myriad of external databases and in optical disk technology so they can access massive amounts of financial data very quickly.

Examples of Knowledge Work Systems

Major knowledge work applications include computer-aided design (CAD) systems, virtual reality systems for simulation and modeling, and financial workstations. **Computer-aided design (CAD)** automates the creation and revision of designs, using computers and sophisticated graphics software. Using a more traditional physical design methodology, each design modification requires a mold to be made and a prototype to be physically tested. That process must be repeated many times, which is very expensive and time-consuming. Using a CAD workstation, the designer only needs to make a physical prototype toward the end of the design process because the design can be easily tested and changed on the computer. The ability of CAD software to provide design specifications for the tooling and the manufacturing process also saves a great deal of time and money while producing a manufacturing process with far fewer problems. For example, The Maddox Design Group of Atlanta, Georgia, uses MicroArchitect CAD software from IdeaGraphix for architectural design. Designers can quickly put the architectural background in, pop in doors and windows, and then do the engineering layout. The software can generate door and window schedules, time accounting reports, and projected costs.

computer-aided design (CAD)

Information system that automates the creation and revision of designs using sophisticated graphics software.

A group of Chrysler Corporation engineers examines a new automobile design using a computer-aided design (CAD) tool. CAD systems improve the quality and precision of product design by performing much of the design and testing work on the computer.

virtual reality systems
Interactive graphics software and hardware that create computer-generated simulations that provide sensations that emulate real-world activities.

Virtual reality systems have visualization, rendering, and simulation capabilities that go far beyond those of conventional CAD systems. They use interactive graphics software to create computer-generated simulations that are so close to reality that users almost believe they are participating in a real-world situation. In many virtual reality systems, the user dons special clothing, headgear, and equipment, depending on the application. The clothing contains sensors that record the user's movements and immediately transmit that information back to the computer. For instance, to walk through a virtual reality simulation of a house, you would need garb that monitors the movement of your feet, hands, and head. You also would need goggles containing video screens and sometimes audio attachments and feeling gloves so that you can be immersed in the computer feedback.

Virtual reality is just starting to provide benefits in educational, scientific, and business work. For example, neuroradiologists at New York's Beth Israel Medical Center can use the Siemens Medical Systems 3D Virtuoso System to peek at the interplay of tiny blood vessels or take a fly-through of the aorta. Surgeons at New York University School of Medicine can use three-dimensional modeling to target brain tumors more precisely, thereby reducing bleeding and trauma.

Virtual reality applications are being developed for the Web using a standard called **Virtual Reality Modeling Language (VRML)**. VRML is a set of specifications for interactive, three-dimensional modeling on the World Wide Web that can organize multiple media types, including animation, images, and audio to put users in a simulated real-world environment. VRML is platform independent, operates over a desktop computer, and requires little bandwidth. Users can download a three-dimensional virtual world designed using VRML from a server over the Internet using their Web browser.

Virtual Reality Modeling Language (VRML)
A set of specifications for interactive three-dimensional modeling on the World Wide Web.

DuPont, the Wilmington, Delaware, chemical company, created a VRML application called HyperPlant, which allows users to access three-dimensional data over the Internet with Netscape Web browsers. Engineers can go through three-dimensional models as if they were physically walking through a plant, viewing objects at eye level. This level of detail reduces the number of mistakes they make during construction of oil rigs, oil plants, and other structures.

The Sharper Image (www.sharperimage.com) 3D Enhanced Catalog for Website visitors with high-speed Internet connections and powerful processors provides images of products in three dimensions. Visitors can rotate digitized images of many products so that they can examine them from any angle. The user could zoom in to see specific details and manipulate the object to see how the lid opens or how it folds for storage.

investment workstation
Powerful desktop computer for financial specialists, which is optimized to access and manipulate massive amounts of financial data.

The financial industry is using specialized **investment workstations** to leverage the knowledge and time of its brokers, traders, and portfolio managers. Firms such as Merrill Lynch and Paine Webber have installed investment workstations that integrate a wide range of data from both internal and external sources, including contact management data, real-time and historical market data, and research reports. Previously, financial professionals had to spend considerable time accessing data from separate systems and piecing together the

Women can create a VRML "personal model" that approximates their physical proportions to help them visualize how they will look in clothing sold at the Lands' End Web site. The digitized image can be rotated to show how the outfits will look from all angles and users can click to change the clothes' color.

information they needed. By providing one-stop information faster and with fewer errors, the workstations streamline the entire investment process from stock selection to updating client records. Table 10-2 summarizes the major types of knowledge work systems.

SHARING KNOWLEDGE: GROUP COLLABORATION SYSTEMS AND ENTERPRISE KNOWLEDGE ENVIRONMENTS

Although many knowledge and information work applications have been designed for individuals working alone, organizations have an increasing need to support people working in groups. Chapters 6 and 8 introduced key technologies that can be used for group coordination and collaboration: e-mail, teleconferencing, dataconferencing, videoconferencing, groupware, and intranets. Groupware and intranets are especially valuable for this purpose.

Groupware

Until recently, *groupware* (which we introduced in Chapter 6) was the primary tool for creating collaborative work environments. Groupware is built around three key principles: communication, collaboration, and coordination. It allows groups to work together on documents, schedule meetings, route electronic forms, access shared folders, develop shared databases, and send e-mail. Table 10-3 lists the capabilities of major commercial groupware products that make them such powerful platforms for capturing information and experiences, coordinating common tasks, and distributing work through time and place.

EXAMPLES OF KNOWLEDGE WORK SYSTEMS

Knowledge Work System	Function in Organization
CAD/CAM (Computer-aided design/ computer-aided manufacturing)	Provides engineers, designers, and factory managers with precise control over industrial design and manufacturing
Virtual reality systems	Provide retailers, architects, engineers, and medical workers with precise, photorealistic simulations of objects
Investment workstations	High-end PCs used in financial sector to analyze trading situations instantaneously and facilitate portfolio management

TABLE 10-3	KNOWLEDGE MANAGEMENT CAPABILITIES OF GROUPWARE
Capability	**Description**
Publishing	Posting documents as well as simultaneous work on the same document by multiple users along with a mechanism to track changes to these documents
Replication	Maintaining and updating identical data on multiple PCs and servers
Discussion tracking	Organizing discussions by many users on different topics
Document management	Storing information from various types of software in a database
Work flow management	Moving and tracking documents created by groups
Security	Preventing unauthorized access to data
Portability	Availability of the software for mobile use to access the corporate network from the road
Application development	Developing custom software applications with the software

Information-intensive companies, such as consulting firms, law firms, and financial management companies, have found groupware an especially powerful tool for leveraging their knowledge assets.

Intranets and Enterprise Knowledge Environments

Chapters 4 and 9 described how some organizations are using intranets and Internet technologies for group collaboration, including e-mail, discussion groups, and multimedia Web documents. Some of these intranets are providing the foundation for enterprise knowledge environments in which information from a variety of sources and media, including text, sound, video, and even digital slides, can be shared, displayed, and accessed across an enterprise through a single common interface. Examples of enterprise knowledge environments can be found in Table 10-4. These comprehensive intranets can transform decades-old processes, allowing people to disseminate information, share best practices, communicate, conduct research, and collaborate in ways that were never before possible.

TABLE 10-4	EXAMPLES OF ENTERPRISE KNOWLEDGE ENVIRONMENTS
Organization	**Knowledge Management Capabilities**
Ford Motor Company	Intranet delivers information about news, people, processes, products, and competition to 95,000 professional employees. Employees can access on-line libraries and a Web Center of Excellence with information on best practices, standards, and recommendations.
Roche Laboratories	Global Healthcare Intelligence Platform integrates documents from multiple sources to provide its professional services group with up-to-date information and expertise relating to new Hoffman-La Roche pharmaceutical products. The system gathers relevant information from global news sources, specialty publishers, healthcare Web sites, government sources, and the firm's proprietary internal information systems, indexing, organizing, linking, and updating the information as it moves through the system. Users can search multiple sources and drill down through layers of detail to see relationships among pieces of data.
Shell Oil Company	Knowledge Management System (KMS) provides a communications and collaboration environment where employees can learn about and share information about best practices. Includes information from internal sources and from external sources, such as universities, consultants, other companies, and research literature. A Lotus Domino groupware application allows employees to carry on dialogues through the company intranet. The author of a best practice in the repository might use this tool to talk with colleagues about his or her experiences.
Booz Allen Hamilton	Knowledge Online intranet provides an on-line repository of consultants' knowledge and experience, including a searchable database organized around the firm's best specialties and best practices; other intellectual capital such as research reports, presentations, graphs, images, and interactive training material; and links to resumes and job histories.

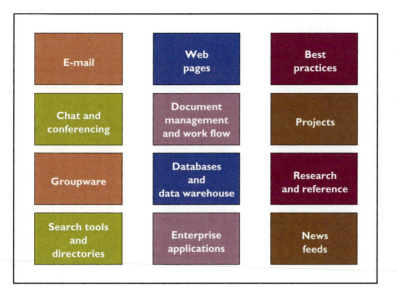

Figure 10-7 An enterprise information portal. The portal provides a single point of access to the firm's knowledge resources, and helps the firm coordinate information and people.

Enterprise knowledge environments are so rich and vast that many organizations have built specialized corporate portals to help individuals navigate through various knowledge resources. These **enterprise information portals**, also known as *enterprise knowledge portals* direct individuals to digital knowledge objects and information system applications, helping them make sense of the volume of information that is available and showing how organizational knowledge resources are interconnected. Figure 10-7 illustrates what an enterprise information portal might look like. It might include access to external sources of information, such as news feeds and research, as well as internal knowledge resources and capabilities for e-mail, chat, discussion groups, and videoconferencing. Software tools are available to build and personalize these portals.

enterprise information portal
Application that enables companies to provide users with a single gateway to internal and external sources of information.

A corporate portal can enhance employee productivity by presenting a seamless single point of access to all of the information resources employees need to do their jobs. Portals or portions of portals extended to customers, suppliers, and business partners can help these groups understand the company's business or unique value proposition. The Manager's Toolkit describes the business issues that must be addressed when developing a portal.

Another application for knowledge intranets is to provide a platform for *e-learning*, which we introduced in Chapter 8. For example, Johnson & Johnson created an Internet-based program called J&J Law School Online to help employees recognize and deal with legal issues they encounter in their daily work. A series of Web-based courses covers a variety of legal and ethical topics selected to match an employee's role within the company. APL Inc., the international subsidiary of the giant transportation firm NOL Group of Singapore, implemented a Web-based platform to train over 1500 sales representatives in more than 126 countries in Sibel System's customer relationship management software along with other key sales and financial software.

The collaborative and knowledge-sharing features of intranets, combined with their low cost, have made them attractive alternatives to proprietary groupware for collaborative work, especially among small and medium-size businesses. For simple tasks, such as sharing documents or document publishing, an intranet generally is less expensive to build and maintain than applications based on commercial groupware products, which require proprietary software and client/server networks.

For applications requiring extensive coordination and management, groupware software has important capabilities that intranets cannot yet provide. Groupware is more flexible when documents must be changed, updated, or edited on the fly. It can track revisions to a document as it moves through a collaborative editing process. Internal groupware-based networks are more secure than intranets. Web sites are more likely to crash or to have their servers overloaded when there are many requests for data. High-end groupware software such as Lotus Notes or OpenText LiveLink is thus more appropriate for applications requiring production and publication of documents by many authors, frequent updating and document

MIS IN ACTION · MANAGER'S TOOLKIT

ESTABLISHING THE BUSINESS REQUIREMENTS OF AN ENTERPRISE INFORMATION PORTAL

Portals can be viewed as electronic doorways into a company. They help users access essential information and collaborate with each other, and they can enhance business performance if they are carefully thought out. When designing a portal, here are some key questions business managers should ask:

1. *Content:* To what information should the portal point? How is this information used in the organization's business processes? Which sources of this information are internal? Which are external? Should the external sources be provided by a content aggregation service or gathered by the organization itself? Does any of this content have to be edited or repackaged to be used effectively?

2. *Users:* Who are the users of the portal? All employees or specific groups of employees? Should the portal or parts of the portal be accessible to people outside the organization?

3. *Personalization:* Does the portal page need to be personalized for specific users or groups in the organization? How much customization is required?

4. *Collaboration support:* Should the portal provide capabilities for communication and collaboration, such as e-mail, newsgroups, chat, or groupware?

5. *Ease of use:* How can the portal be designed so that it is easy to use and to navigate from one source of information to another? Do users need special search engines or knowledge maps to help them find information?

6. *Updating and editing:* How often does the information feeding the portal need to be updated? Which individuals in the organization will be responsible for updating this information or editing content?

7. *Management and administration:* Who is responsible for administering the portal and for approving and reviewing content?

8. *Benefits and costs:* What are the business benefits to be provided by the portal? Can they be quantified? Can these benefits justify the cost of building and maintaining the portal? (See the discussion of information system costs and benefits in Chapter 13.)

---

tracking, and high security and replication. Lotus Notes and other groupware products have been enhanced so they can be integrated with the Internet or private intranets and used for collaborative commerce and supply chain management. Groove Networks provides a peer-to-peer collaboration platform that enables workers on the fly to collaborate and share data without going through a central Web server.

Intranet technology works best as a central repository with a small number of authors and relatively static information that does not require frequent updating, although intranet tools for group collaboration are improving. Netscape Communications' Communicator software bundles a Web browser with messaging and collaboration tools, including e-mail, newsgroup discussions, a group scheduling and calendaring tool, and point-to-point conferencing.

Commercial software tools called teamware make intranets more useful for working in teams. **Teamware** consists of intranet-based applications for building a work team, sharing

teamware
Internet-based collaboration software that is customized for teamwork.

eRoom is a secure Web-based workplace and complete set of business collaboration tools that can be quickly tailored for specific buisiness initiatives and easily installed. Companies can use the eRoom solution to enable distributed work teams to work closely and creatively to plan, collaborate, strategize, and make decisions across the extended enterprise.

ABN AMRO BANKS ON ON-LINE KNOWLEDGE MANAGEMENT

Making vast amounts of company information available to employees so they can search and locate what they want or need should be easy, but ABN Amro North America, the North American subsidiary of ABN Amro Bank of the Netherlands found that is not the case. ABN Amro is Europe's eighth largest bank and the seventeenth largest bank in the world, with more than 110,000 employees and 3,500 branches worldwide. ABN Amro's New York regional office is responsible for codifying the bank's operating procedures for all bank departments in New York, as required by U.S. banking regulations. The procedures were published as a series of reports kept in ring binders. Updating these procedures was time consuming and expensive, because each new document had to be printed and then replaced in the binder by hand. Few employees ever used the documents because locating information in them was so difficult. Instead they queried their neighbors.

Isaac Kirzner, ABN Amro North America's senior vice president for information management and strategic technologies, found the solution was to create an easily searchable on-line version of each document. By using a data management product called Folio, employees could easily search for and find what they wanted. The software indexed every word in every document and highlighted every occurrence of that word so that users did not have to scan the entire document. Because every word was indexed, employees could search by name, phone number, name of city, or any other category they wished. Over time bulletins, newsletters, bank directories, and other documents were also made available electronically. Kirzner even got Harry Tempest, the CEO of ABN Amro North America, to become the executive sponsor of the project because Tempest understood the potential value of electronic publishing. The problem was that almost no one responded by using Folio.

Kirzner and his knowledge management team concluded that the difficulty was not that Folio was hard to use. Rather it was culture and custom, the perceived value of the documents, and even the introduction of the whole system. The knowledge management team decided to alter its approach by encouraging employees to locate information that was most familiar to them.

One product people did use widely was the telephone directory. Kirzner's team then added other documents people really wanted, such as the Chicago office cafeteria menu and information about visiting Amsterdam where corporate headquarters is located. Kirzner's expectation was that once employees became accustomed to using the system for information they personally valued, they might start using Folio to locate information found in strictly business documents, such as bank regulations. But Kirzner was not satisfied with only that approach. He also wanted to start marketing the product and its value so that this knowledge management capability would remain highly visible to all employees. The team used surveys, e-mail, advertising notices on pay stubs, and even a monthly column in the employee magazine to publicize the bank's knowledge management system and services.

In mid-2000 ABN Amro switched to LivePublish, a product of NextPage Inc. of Lehl, Utah, also the owner of Folio. LivePublish is a newer, totally Web compatible knowledge management system. Now ABN Amro employees can access commonly used lists, directories, forms, bank policy manuals, regulatory documents, and human resources materials as well as industry and market analyses and product and service information for developing customer proposals. The system enables the company to promote cross-selling by consolidating information about clients and the bank's product offerings. Use of the system has mushroomed. By early 2001 the knowledge system was experiencing about 2,000 hits per day, and this number is expected to double in 2002.

To Think About: How important do you think the use of ABN Amro's knowledge management system is to the organization? To management? What else do you think Kirzner might do to further increase the use of LivePublish at ABN Amro?

Sources: Karen Heyman, "Getting People to Read," *Knowledge Management,* April 2001; and www.abnamro.com.

---

ideas and documents, brainstorming, scheduling, tracking the status of tasks and projects, and archiving decisions made or rejected by project team members for future use. Teamware is similar to groupware, but it does not offer the powerful application development capabilities provided by sophisticated groupware products. However, it lets companies easily implement collaboration applications that can be accessed using a Web browser. eRoom Technology's eRoom and Lotus QuickPlace are examples of commercial teamware products.

Group collaboration and knowledge-sharing technologies alone cannot promote information sharing if team members do not believe it is in their interest to share, especially in organizations that encourage competition among employees. This technology can best enhance the work of a group if the applications are properly designed to fit the organization's needs and work practices and if management encourages a collaborative atmosphere. Successful knowledge sharing requires an appropriate knowledge sharing environment (Pan, Hsieh and Chen, 2001). The Window on Organizations describes how ABN Amro Bank grappled with this issue.

10.3 ARTIFICIAL INTELLIGENCE

Organizations are using artificial intelligence technology to capture individual and collective knowledge and to codify and extend their knowledge base.

WHAT IS ARTIFICIAL INTELLIGENCE?

artificial intelligence (AI)
The effort to develop computer-based systems that can behave like humans, with the ability to learn languages, accomplish physical tasks, use a perceptual apparatus, and emulate human expertise and decision making.

Artificial intelligence (AI) is the effort to develop computer-based systems (both hardware and software) that behave as humans. Such systems would be able to learn natural languages, accomplish coordinated physical tasks (robotics), use a perceptual apparatus that informs their physical behavior and language (visual and oral perception systems), and emulate human expertise and decision making (expert systems). Such systems also would exhibit logic, reasoning, intuition, and the just-plain-common-sense qualities that we associate with human beings. Figure 10-8 illustrates the elements of the artificial intelligence family. Another important element is intelligent machines, the physical hardware that performs these tasks.

Successful artificial intelligence systems are based on human expertise, knowledge, and selected reasoning patterns, but they do not exhibit the intelligence of human beings. Existing artificial intelligence systems do not come up with new and novel solutions to problems. Existing systems extend the powers of experts but in no way substitute for them or capture much of their intelligence. Briefly, existing systems lack the common sense and generality of naturally intelligent human beings.

Human intelligence is vastly complex and much broader than computer intelligence. A key factor that distinguishes human beings from other animals is their ability to develop associations and to use metaphors and analogies such as *like* and *as*. Using metaphor and analogy, humans create new rules, apply old rules to new situations, and, at times, act intuitively and/or instinctively without rules. Much of what we call common sense or generality in humans resides in the ability to create metaphor and analogy.

Human intelligence also includes a unique ability to impose a conceptual apparatus on the surrounding world. Metaconcepts such as cause-and-effect and time, and concepts of a lower order such as breakfast, dinner, and lunch, are all imposed by human beings on the world around them. Thinking in terms of these concepts and acting on them are central characteristics of intelligent human behavior.

WHY BUSINESS IS INTERESTED IN ARTIFICIAL INTELLIGENCE

Although artificial intelligence applications are much more limited than human intelligence, they are of great interest to business for the following reasons:

❙ To store information in an active form as organizational memory, creating an organizational knowledge base that many employees can examine and preserving expertise that might be lost when an acknowledged expert leaves the firm.

❙ To create a mechanism that is not subject to human feelings, such as fatigue and worry. This may be especially useful when jobs may be environmentally, physically, or mentally dangerous to humans. These systems also may be useful advisers in times of crisis.

Figure 10-8 The artificial intelligence family. The field of AI currently includes many initiatives: natural language, robotics, perceptive systems, expert systems, and intelligent machines.

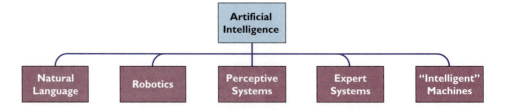

▮ To eliminate routine and unsatisfying jobs held by people.

▮ To enhance the organization's knowledge base by generating solutions to specific problems that are too massive and complex to be analyzed by human beings in a short period of time.

CAPTURING KNOWLEDGE: EXPERT SYSTEMS

In limited areas of expertise, such as diagnosing a car's ignition system or classifying biological specimens, the rules of thumb used by real-world experts can be understood, codified, and placed in a machine. Information systems that solve problems by capturing knowledge for a very specific and limited domain of human expertise are called **expert systems**. Expert systems capture the knowledge of skilled employees in the form of a set of rules. The set of rules in the expert system adds to the organizational memory, or stored learning of the firm. An expert system can assist decision making by asking relevant questions and explaining the reasons for adopting certain actions.

Expert systems lack the breadth of knowledge and the understanding of fundamental principles of a human expert. They are quite narrow, shallow, and brittle. They typically perform very limited tasks that can be performed by professionals in a few minutes or hours. Problems that cannot be solved by human experts in the same short period of time are far too difficult for an expert system. However, by capturing human expertise in limited areas, expert systems can provide benefits, helping organizations make high-quality decisions with fewer people.

expert system
Knowledge-intensive computer program that captures the expertise of a human in limited domains of knowledge.

How Expert Systems Work

Human knowledge must be modeled or represented in a way that a computer can process. The model of human knowledge used by expert systems is called the **knowledge base**. Two ways of representing human knowledge and expertise are rules and knowledge frames.

A standard structured programming construct (see Chapter 14) is the IF–THEN construct, in which a condition is evaluated. If the condition is true, an action is taken. For instance,

> IF INCOME > $45,000 (condition)
> THEN PRINT NAME AND ADDRESS (action)

A series of these rules can be a knowledge base. Any reader who has written computer programs knows that virtually all traditional computer programs contain IF–THEN statements. The difference between a traditional program and a **rule-based expert system** program is one of degree and magnitude. AI programs can easily have 200 to 10,000 rules, far more than traditional programs, which may have 50 to 100 IF–THEN statements. Moreover, in an AI program the rules tend to be interconnected and nested to a far greater degree than in traditional programs, as shown in Figure 10-9. Hence the complexity of the rules in a rule-based expert system is considerable.

Could you represent the knowledge in the Encyclopedia Britannica this way? Probably not, because the **rule base** would be too large, and not all the knowledge in the encyclopedia can be represented in the form of IF–THEN rules. In general, expert systems can be efficiently used only in those situations in which the domain of knowledge is highly restricted (such as in granting credit) and involves no more than a few thousand rules.

Knowledge frames can be used to represent knowledge by organizing information into chunks of interrelated characteristics. The relationships are based on shared characteristics rather than a hierarchy. This approach is grounded in the belief that humans use frames, or concepts, to make rapid sense out of perceptions. For instance, when a person is told, "Look for a tank and shoot when you see one," experts believe that humans invoke a concept, or frame, of what a tank should look like. Anything that does not fit this concept of a tank is ignored. In a similar fashion, AI researchers can organize a vast array of information into frames. The computer then is instructed to search the database of frames and list connections to other frames of interest. The user can follow the pathways pointed to by the system.

Figure 10-10 shows a part of a knowledge base organized by frames. A "CAR" is defined by characteristics or slots in a frame as a vehicle, with four wheels, a gas or diesel motor, and

knowledge base
Model of human knowledge that is used by expert systems.

rule-based expert system
An AI program that has a large number of interconnected and nested IF–THEN statements, or rules, that are the basis for the knowledge in the system.

rule base
The collection of knowledge in an AI system that is represented in the form of IF–THEN rules.

knowledge frames
A method of organizing expert system knowledge into chunks; the relationships are based on shared characteristics determined by the user.

Figure 10-9   Rules in an AI program. An expert system contains a number of rules to be followed when used. The rules themselves are interconnected; the number of outcomes is known in advance and is limited; there are multiple paths to the same outcome; and the system can consider multiple rules at a single time. The rules illustrated are for a simple credit-granting expert system.

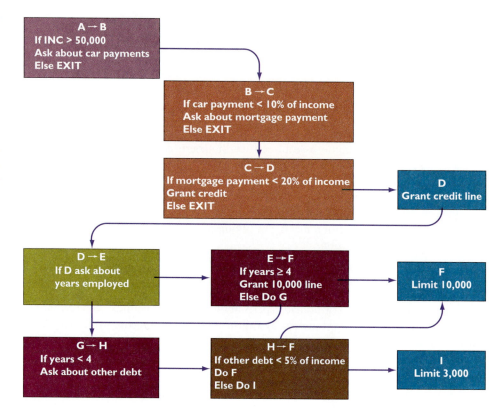

AI shell

The programming environment of an expert system.

inference engine

The strategy used to search through the rule base in an expert system; can be forward or backward chaining.

forward chaining

A strategy for searching the rule base in an expert system that begins with the information entered by the user and searches the rule base to arrive at a conclusion.

an action such as rolling or moving. This frame could be related to almost any other object in the database that shares any of these characteristics, such as the tank frame.

The **AI shell** is the programming environment of an expert system. In the early years of expert systems, computer scientists used specialized artificial intelligence programming languages, such as LISP or Prolog, that could process lists of rules efficiently. Today a growing number of expert systems use AI shells that are user-friendly development environments. AI shells can quickly generate user-interface screens, capture the knowledge base, and manage the strategies for searching the rule base.

The strategy to search through the rule base is called the **inference engine**. Two strategies are commonly used: forward chaining and backward chaining (see Figure 10-11).

In **forward chaining** the inference engine begins with the information entered by the user and searches the rule base to arrive at a conclusion. The strategy is to fire, or carry out,

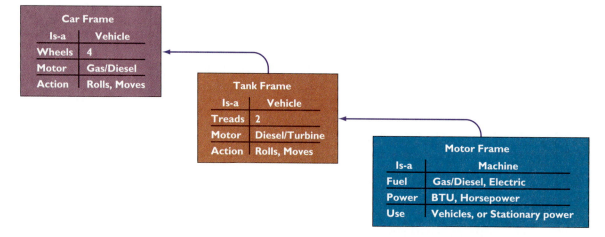

Figure 10-10   Frames to model knowledge. Knowledge and information can be organized into frames. Frames capture the relevant characteristics of the objects of interest. This approach is based on the belief that humans use "frames" or concepts to narrow the range of possibilities when scanning incoming information to make rapid sense out of perceptions.

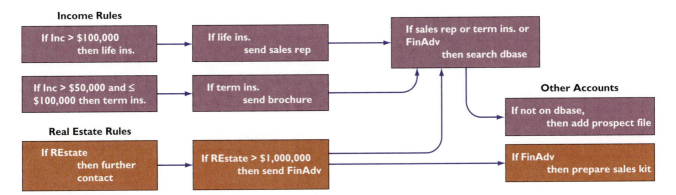

Figure 10-11   Inference engines in expert systems. An inference engine works by searching through the rules and "firing" those rules that are triggered by facts gathered and entered by the user.

the action of the rule when a condition is true. In Figure 10-11, beginning on the left, if the user enters a client with income greater than $100,000, the engine will fire all rules in sequence from left to right. If the user then enters information indicating that the same client owns real estate, another pass of the rule base will occur and more rules will fire. Processing continues until no more rules can be fired.

In **backward chaining** the strategy for searching the rule base starts with a hypothesis and proceeds by asking the user questions about selected facts until the hypothesis is either confirmed or disproved. In our example, in Figure 10-11, ask the question, "Should we add this person to the prospect database?" Begin on the right of the diagram and work toward the left. You can see that the person should be added to the database if a sales representative is sent, term insurance is granted, or a financial advisor visits the client.

backward chaining
A strategy for searching the rule base in an expert system that acts like a problem solver by beginning with a hypothesis and seeking out more information until the hypothesis is either proved or disproved.

Building an Expert System

Building an expert system is similar to building other information systems, but it is an iterative process with each phase possibly requiring several iterations before a full system is developed. Typically, the environment in which an expert system operates is continually changing so that the expert system must also continually change. Some expert systems, especially large ones, are so complex that in a few years the maintenance costs will equal the development costs.

An AI development team is composed of one or more experts, who have a thorough command of the knowledge base, and one or more knowledge engineers, who can translate the knowledge (as described by the expert) into a set of rules or frames. A **knowledge engineer** is similar to a traditional systems analyst but has special expertise in eliciting information and expertise from other professionals.

knowledge engineer
A specialist who elicits information and expertise from other professionals and translates it into a set of rules or frames for an expert system.

The team members must select a problem appropriate for an expert system. The project will balance potential savings from the proposed system against the cost. The team members will develop a prototype system to test assumptions about how to encode the knowledge of experts. Next, they will develop a full-scale system, focusing mainly on the addition of a very large number of rules. The complexity of the entire system grows with the number of rules, so the comprehensibility of the system may be threatened. Generally, the system will be pruned to achieve simplicity and power. The system is tested by a range of experts within the organization against the performance criteria established earlier. Once tested, the system will be integrated into the data flow and work patterns of the organization.

Examples of Successful Expert Systems

There is no accepted definition of a successful expert system. What is successful to an academic ("It works!") may not be successful to a corporation ("It costs a million dollars!"). The following are examples of expert systems that provide organizations with an array of benefits, including reduced errors, reduced costs, reduced training time, improved decisions, and improved quality and service.

Countrywide Funding Corporation developed an expert system called CLUES to evaluate the creditworthiness of loan applicants. Countrywide is using the rules in this system to answer inquiries from visitors to its Web site who want to know if they can qualify for a loan.

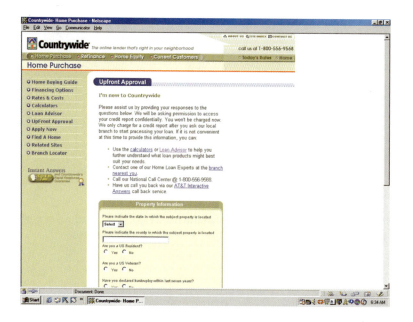

BlueCross BlueShield of North Carolina used Aion, an AI shell, to build an automated medical underwriting system (AMUS). AMUS links to an IBM IMS hierarchical database and to BlueCross BlueShield's in-house system for rate quoting, policy writing, and risk management. The system determines whether to underwrite applicants for health insurance after assessing their eligibility and medical risks. Underwriters can make changes to the rules as needed. This expert system enabled BlueCross BlueShield to reduce the time required to make an underwriting decision from one week to one day. The productivity gains from the system also enabled the company to eliminate or redeploy 8 underwriters and 15 support personnel, replacing them with 4 underwriting processors. Since adopting AMUS, the accuracy of underwriting decisions has improved (Kay, 2000).

Countrywide Funding Corp. in Pasadena, California, is a loan-underwriting firm with about 400 underwriters in 150 offices around the country. The company developed a PC-based expert system in 1992 to make preliminary creditworthiness decisions on loan requests. The company had experienced rapid, continuing growth and wanted the system to help ensure consistent, high-quality loan decisions. CLUES (Countrywide's Loan Underwriting Expert System) has about 400 rules. Countrywide tested the system by sending every loan application handled by a human underwriter to CLUES as well. The system was refined until it agreed with the underwriters in 95 percent of the cases.

Countrywide will not rely on CLUES to reject loans, because the expert system cannot be programmed to handle exceptional situations such as those involving a self-employed person or complex financial schemes. An underwriter will review all rejected loans and will make the final decision. CLUES has other benefits. Traditionally, an underwriter could handle six or seven applications a day. Using CLUES, the same underwriter can evaluate at least 16 per day. Countrywide now is using the rules in its expert system to answer e-mail inquiries from visitors to its Web site who want to know if they qualify for a loan.

The investment banking firm Goldman Sachs uses a rule-based expert system to keep unwanted stocks out of individual portfolios. Almost all of its client portfolios have restrictions specified by owners on which stocks or even entire sectors to exclude. Goldman wanted to make sure its global network of financial advisers respected these restrictions so that they did not make any purchases that clients didn't want. Goldman's business managers, compliance officers, and private wealth managers all play roles in deciding which stocks to purchase for a portfolio. The company developed a rule-based system that maintains rules for keeping a particular stock from entering a client's portfolio. By creating a centralized portfolio filtering system, Goldman is better able to catch mistakes before erroneous trades go through (Guerra, 2001).

Although expert systems lack the robust and general intelligence of human beings, they can provide benefits to organizations if their limitations are well understood. Only certain classes of problems can be solved using expert systems. Virtually all successful expert systems deal with problems of classification in which there are relatively few alternative outcomes and in which these possible outcomes are all known in advance. Many expert systems require large, lengthy, and expensive development efforts. Hiring or training more experts may be less expensive than building an expert system.

The knowledge base of expert systems is fragile and brittle; they cannot learn or change over time. In fast-moving fields, such as medicine or the computer sciences, keeping the knowledge base up to date is a critical problem. For example, Digital Equipment Corporation stopped using its XCON expert system for configuring VAX computers because its product line was constantly changing and it was too difficult to keep updating the system to capture these changes. Expert systems can only represent limited forms of knowledge. IF–THEN knowledge exists primarily in textbooks. There are no adequate representations for deep causal models or temporal trends. No expert system, for instance, can write a textbook on information systems or engage in other creative activities not explicitly foreseen by system designers. Many experts cannot express their knowledge using an IF–THEN format. Expert systems cannot yet replicate knowledge that is intuitive, based on analogy and on a sense of things.

Contrary to early promises, expert systems are most effective in automating lower-level clerical functions. They can provide electronic checklists for lower-level employees in service bureaucracies such as banking, insurance, sales, and welfare agencies. The applicability of expert systems to managerial problems is very limited. Managerial problems generally involve drawing facts and interpretations from divergent sources, evaluating the facts, and comparing one interpretation of the facts with another; they are not limited to simple classification. Expert systems based on the prior knowledge of a few known alternatives are unsuitable to the problems managers face on a daily basis.

ORGANIZATIONAL INTELLIGENCE: CASE-BASED REASONING

Expert systems primarily capture the knowledge of individual experts, but organizations also have collective knowledge and expertise that they have built up over the years. This organizational knowledge can be captured and stored using case-based reasoning. In **case-based reasoning (CBR)**, descriptions of past experiences of human specialists, represented as cases, are stored in a database for later retrieval when the user encounters a new case with similar parameters. The system searches for stored cases with problem characteristics similar to the new one, finds the closest fit, and applies the solutions of the old case to the new case. Successful solutions are tagged to the new case and both are stored together with the other cases in the knowledge base. Unsuccessful solutions also are appended to the case database along with explanations as to why the solutions did not work (see Figure 10-12).

case-based reasoning (CBR) Artificial intelligence technology that represents knowledge as a database of cases and solutions.

Expert systems work by applying a set of IF–THEN–ELSE rules against a knowledge base, both of which are extracted from human experts. Case-based reasoning, in contrast, represents knowledge as a series of cases, and this knowledge base is continuously expanded and refined by users.

Compaq Computer of Houston, Texas gave purchasers of its Pagemarq printer case-based reasoning software to help reduce customer service costs. The software knowledge base is a series of several hundred actual cases of Pagemarq printer problems—actual stories about smudged copies, printer memory problems, and jammed printers—all the typical problems people face with laser printers. Trained CBR staff entered case descriptions in textual format into the CBR system. They entered key words necessary to categorize the problem, such as smudge, smear, lines, streaks, and paper jam. They also entered a series of questions that might be needed to allow the software to further narrow the problem. Finally, solutions were attached to each case.

With the Compaq-supplied CBR system running on their computer, owners no longer need to call Compaq's service department. Instead, they run the software and describe the problem to the software. The system swiftly searches actual cases, discarding unrelated ones, selecting related ones. If necessary to further narrow the search results, the software will ask the user for more information. In the end, one or more cases relevant to the specific problem

Figure 10-12 How case-based reasoning works. Case-based reasoning represents knowledge as a database of past cases and their solutions. The system uses a six-step process to generate solutions to new problems encountered by the user.

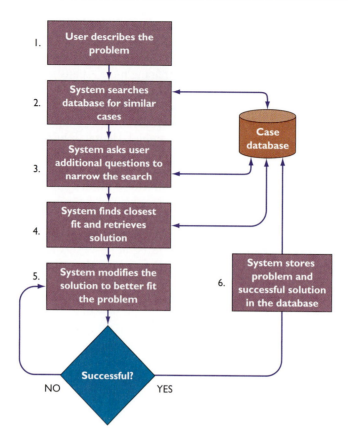

are displayed, along with their solutions. Now, customers can solve most of their own problems quickly without a telephone call, and Compaq has saved $10 million to $20 million annually in customer-support costs.

10.4 OTHER INTELLIGENT TECHNIQUES

Organizations are using other intelligent computing techniques to extend their knowledge base by providing solutions to problems that are too massive or complex to be handled by people with limited resources. Neural networks, fuzzy logic, genetic algorithms, and intelligent agents are developing into promising business applications.

NEURAL NETWORKS

There has been an exciting resurgence of interest in bottom-up approaches to artificial intelligence in which machines are designed to imitate the physical thought process of the bio-

Figure 10-13 Biological neurons of a leech. Simple biological models, like the neurons of a leech, have influenced the development of artificial or computational neural networks in which the biological cells are replaced by transistors or entire processors. *Source*: Defense Advance Research Projects Agency (DARPA), 1988. Unclassified.

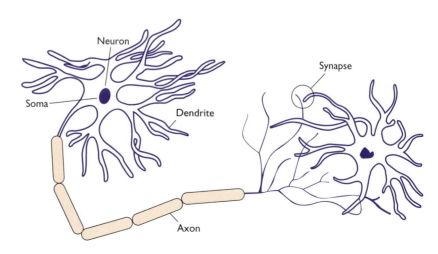

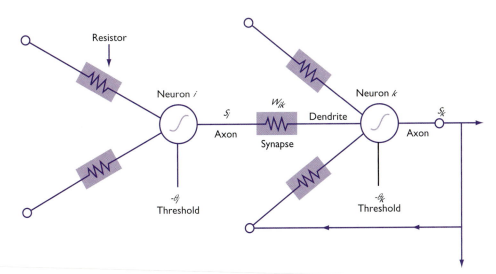

Figure 10-14 Artificial neural network with two neurons. In artificial neurons, the biological neurons become processing elements (switches), the axons and dendrites become wires, and the synapses become variable resistors that carry weighted inputs (currents) that represent data. *Source*: DARPA, 1988. Unclassified.

logical brain. Figure 10-13 shows two neurons from a leech's brain. The soma, or nerve cell, at the center acts like a switch, stimulating other neurons and being stimulated in turn. Emanating from the neuron is an axon, which is an electrically active link to the dendrites of other neurons. Axons and dendrites are the "wires" that electrically connect neurons to one another. The junction of the two is called a synapse. This simple biological model is the metaphor for the development of neural networks. A **neural network** consists of hardware or software that attempts to emulate the processing patterns of the biological brain.

The human brain has about 100 billion (10^{11}) neurons, each having about 1,000 dendrites, which form 100,000 billion (10^{14}) synapses. The brain's neurons operate in parallel, and the human brain can accomplish about 10^{16}, or ten million billion, interconnections per second. This far exceeds the capacity of any known machine or any machine planned or ever likely to be built with current technology.

However, complex networks of neurons have been simulated on computers. Figure 10-14 shows an artificial neural network with two neurons. The resistors in the circuits are variable and can be used to teach the network. When the network makes a mistake (i.e., chooses the wrong pathway through the network and arrives at a false conclusion), resistance can be raised on some circuits, forcing other neurons to fire. If this learning process continues for thousands of cycles, the machine learns the correct response. The neurons are highly interconnected and operate in parallel.

A neural net has a large number of sensing and processing nodes that continuously interact with each other. Figure 10-15 represents a neural network comprising an input layer, an output layer, and a hidden processing layer. The network is fed a training set of data for which the inputs produce a known set of outputs or conclusions. This helps the computer learn the correct solution by example. As the computer is fed more data, each case is

neural network
Hardware or software that attempts to emulate the processing patterns of the biological brain.

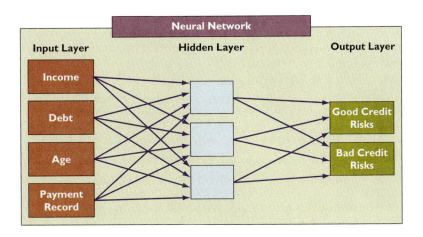

Figure 10-15 A neural network uses rules it "learns" from patterns in data to construct a hidden layer of logic. The hidden layer then processes inputs, classifying them based on the experience of the model. *Source*: Herb Edelstein, "Technology How-To: Mining Data Warehouses," *InformationWeek*, January 8, 1996. Copyright © 1996 CMP Media, Inc., 600 Community Drive, Manhasset, NY 11030. Reprinted with permission.

compared with the known outcome. If it differs, a correction is calculated and applied to the nodes in the hidden processing layer. These steps are repeated until a condition, such as corrections being less than a certain amount, is reached. The neural network in Figure 10-15 has "learned" how to identify a good credit risk.

The Difference Between Neural Networks and Expert Systems

What is different about neural networks? Expert systems seek to emulate or model a human expert's way of solving problems, but neural network builders claim that they do not model human intelligence, do not program solutions, and do not aim to solve specific problems per se. Instead, neural network designers seek to put intelligence into the hardware in the form of a generalized capability to learn. In contrast, the expert system is highly specific to a given problem and cannot be easily retrained.

Neural network applications are emerging in medicine, science, and business to address problems in pattern classification, prediction and financial analysis, and control and optimization. Papnet is a neural net-based system that distinguishes between normal and abnormal cells when examining Pap smears for cervical cancer that has far greater accuracy than visual examinations by technicians. The computer is not able to make a final decision, so a technician will review any selected abnormal cells. Using Papnet, a technician requires one-fifth the time to review a smear while attaining perhaps 10 times the accuracy of the existing manual method.

Neural networks are being used by the financial industry to discern patterns in vast pools of data that might help investment firms predict the performance of equities, corporate bond ratings, or corporate bankruptcies. VISA International Inc. is using a neural network to help detect credit card fraud by monitoring all VISA transactions for sudden changes in the buying patterns of cardholders.

Unlike expert systems, which typically provide explanations for their solutions, neural networks cannot always explain why they arrived at a particular solution. Moreover, they cannot always guarantee a completely certain solution, arrive at the same solution again with the same input data, or always guarantee the best solution (Trippi and Turban, 1989–1990). They are very sensitive and may not perform well if their training covers too little or too much data. In most current applications, neural networks are best used as aids to human decision makers instead of substitutes for them.

FUZZY LOGIC

Traditional computer programs require precision: on–off, yes–no, right–wrong. However, we human beings do not experience the world this way. We might all agree that +120 degrees is hot and -40 degrees is cold; but is 75 degrees hot, warm, comfortable, or cool? The answer depends on many factors: the wind, the humidity, the individual experiencing the temperature, one's clothing, and one's expectations. Many of our activities also are inexact. Tractor-trailer drivers would find it nearly impossible to back their rigs into spaces precisely specified to less than an inch on all sides.

fuzzy logic
Rule-based AI that tolerates imprecision by using nonspecific terms called membership functions to solve problems.

Fuzzy logic, a relatively new, rule-based development in AI, tolerates imprecision and even uses it to solve problems we could not have solved before. Fuzzy logic consists of a variety of concepts and techniques for representing and inferring knowledge that is imprecise, uncertain, or unreliable. Fuzzy logic can create rules that use approximate or subjective values and incomplete or ambiguous data. By expressing logic with some carefully defined imprecision, fuzzy logic is closer to the way people actually think than traditional IF–THEN rules.

Ford Motor Co. developed a fuzzy logic application that backs a simulated tractor-trailer into a parking space. The application uses the following three rules:

IF the truck is *near* jackknifing, THEN *reduce* the steering angle.

IF the truck is *far away* from the dock, THEN steer *toward* the dock.

IF the truck is *near* the dock, THEN point the trailer *directly* at the dock.

This logic makes sense to us as human beings, for it represents how we think as we back that truck into its berth.

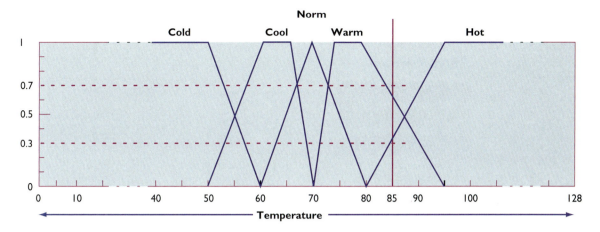

Figure 10-16   Implementing fuzzy logic rules in hardware. The membership functions for the input called temperature are in the logic of the thermostat to control the room temperature. Membership functions help translate linguistic expressions such as "warm" into numbers that the computer can manipulate.
Source: James M. Sibigtroth, "Implementing Fuzzy Expert Rules in Hardware," *AI Expert,* April 1992. © 1992 Miller Freeman, Inc. Reprinted with permission.

How does the computer make sense of this programming? The answer is relatively simple. The terms (known as membership functions) are imprecisely defined so that, for example, in Figure 10-16, cool is between 50 degrees and 70 degrees, although the temperature is most clearly cool between about 60 degrees and 67 degrees. Note that cool is overlapped by cold or norm. To control the room environment using this logic, the programmer would develop similarly imprecise definitions for humidity and other factors such as outdoor wind and temperature. The rules might include one that says: "If the temperature is cool or cold and the humidity is low while the outdoor wind is high and the outdoor temperature is low, raise the heat and humidity in the room." The computer would combine the membership function readings in a weighted manner and, using all the rules, raise and lower the temperature and humidity.

Fuzzy logic is widely used in Japan and is gaining popularity in the United States. Its popularity has occurred partially because managers find they can use it to reduce costs and shorten development time. Fuzzy logic code requires fewer IF–THEN rules, making it simpler than traditional code. The rules required in the previous trucking example, plus its term definitions, might require hundreds of IF–THEN statements to implement in traditional logic. Compact code requires less computer capacity, allowing Sanyo Fisher USA to implement camcorder controls without adding expensive memory to their product.

Fuzzy logic also allows us to solve problems not previously solvable, thus improving product quality. In Japan, Sendai's subway system uses fuzzy logic controls to accelerate so smoothly that standing passengers need not hold on. Mitsubishi Heavy Industries in Tokyo has been able to reduce the power consumption of its air conditioners by 20 percent by implementing control programs in fuzzy logic. The autofocus device in cameras is only possible because of fuzzy logic. Williams-Sonoma sells an "intelligent" steamer made in Japan that uses fuzzy logic. A variable heat setting detects the amount of grain, cooks it at the preferred temperature, and keeps the food warm up to 12 hours.

Management also has found fuzzy logic useful for decision making and organizational control. A Wall Street firm had a system developed that selects companies for potential acquisition, using the language stock traders understand. Recently, a system has been developed to detect possible fraud in medical claims submitted by healthcare providers anywhere in the United States.

GENETIC ALGORITHMS

Genetic algorithms (also referred to as adaptive computation) refer to a variety of problem-solving techniques that are conceptually based on the method that living organisms use to

genetic algorithms
Problem-solving methods that promote the evolution of solutions to specified problems using the model of living organisms adapting to their environment.

Figure 10-17 The components of a genetic algorithm. This example illustrates an initial population of "chromosomes," each representing a different solution. The genetic algorithm uses an iterative process to refine the initial solutions so that the better ones, those with the higher fitness, are more likely to emerge as the best solution.

Source: From *Intelligent Decision Support Methods: The Science of Knowledge Work* by Dhar/Stein, © 1997. Reprinted by permission of Pearson Education, Inc, Upper Saddle River, NJ.

		Color	Speed	Intelligence	Fitness
1 0 1 1 0 1	1	White	Medium	Dumb	40
0 1 0 1 0 1	2	Black	Slow	Dumb	43
1 1 0 1 1 0	3	White	Slow	Very Dumb	22
0 0 0 1 0 1	4	Black	Fast	Dumb	71
1 0 1 0 0 0	5	White	Medium	Very Smart	53
A population of chromosomes			**Decoding of chromosomes**	**Evaluation of chromosomes**	

adapt to their environments—the process of evolution. They are programmed to work the way populations solve problems—by changing and reorganizing their component parts using processes such as reproduction, mutation, and natural selection. Thus, genetic algorithms promote the evolution of solutions to particular problems, controlling the generation, variation, adaptation, and selection of possible solutions using genetically based processes. As solutions alter and combine, the worst ones are discarded and the better ones survive to go on to produce even better solutions. Genetic algorithms breed programs that solve problems even when no person can fully understand their structure (Holland, 1992).

A genetic algorithm works by representing information as a string of 0s and 1s. A possible solution can be represented by a long string of these digits. The genetic algorithm provides methods of searching all possible combinations of digits to identify the right string representing the best possible structure for the problem.

In one method, the programmer first randomly generates a population of strings consisting of combinations of binary digits (see Figure 10-17). Each string corresponds to one of the variables in the problem. One applies a test for fitness, ranking the strings in the population according to their level of desirability as possible solutions. After the initial population is evaluated for fitness, the algorithm then produces the next generation of strings, consisting of strings that survived the fitness test plus offspring strings produced from mating pairs of strings, and tests their fitness. The process continues until a solution is reached.

Solutions to certain types of problems in areas of optimization, product design, and the monitoring of industrial systems are especially appropriate for genetic algorithms. Many business problems require optimization because they deal with issues such as minimization of costs, maximization of profits, efficient scheduling, and use of resources. If these situations are very dynamic and complex, involving hundreds or thousands of variables or formulas, genetic algorithms can expedite the solution because they can evaluate many different solution alternatives quickly to find the best one. For example, General Electric engineers used genetic algorithms to help optimize the design for jet turbine aircraft engines, where each design change required changes in up to 100 variables. The supply chain management software from i2 Technologies incorporates genetic algorithms to optimize production scheduling models incorporating hundreds of thousands of details about customer orders, material and resource availability, manufacturing and distribution capability, and delivery dates. International Truck and Engine used this software to reduce costly schedule disruptions by 90 percent in five of its plants (Wakefield, 2001; Burtka, 1993).

Hybrid AI Systems

Genetic algorithms, fuzzy logic, neural networks, and expert systems can be integrated into a single application to take advantage of the best features of these technologies. Such systems are called **hybrid AI systems**. Hybrid applications in business are growing. In Japan, Hitachi, Mitsubishi, Ricoh, Sanyo, and others are starting to incorporate hybrid AI in products such as home appliances, factory machinery, and office equipment. Matsushita has developed a "neurofuzzy" washing machine that combines fuzzy logic with neural net-

hybrid AI systems
Integration of multiple AI technologies into a single application to take advantage of the best features of these technologies.

MAKE IT YOUR BUSINESS

FINANCE AND ACCOUNTING

Many expert system, neural network, and hybrid AI applications as well as knowledge work systems have been developed for the finance and accounting function. Rules-based expert systems have been widely used tools for evaluating the credit risk of loan applicants and for investment portfolio selection. A number of financial services firms use neural networks for stock and bond trading strategies, commodity trading, and detecting credit card fraud. Financial professionals use investment workstations that integrate a wide range of financial data from internal and external sources to support their research and analysis. You can find examples of finance and accounting applications on pages 324–325 and 334.

HUMAN RESOURCES

The human resources function uses Web publishing tools and intranets to communicate company policies to employees and to provide on-line directories of human resource policies and training programs. You can find examples of human resources applications on pages 326 and 329.

MANUFACTURING AND PRODUCTION

The manufacturing and production function is replete with knowledge system applications. Many companies are using intranets and group collaboration tools for sharing product design and manufacturing specifications among team members in many different locations and for project management. Robotic equipment now performs man-

ufacturing tasks such as welding or lifting heavy parts that are too difficult or tedious for humans. Expert systems have been used to guide the configuration of orders when products with many different parts or features are being assembled. Both expert systems and case-based reasoning systems are used for assisting diagnostic and repair work on malfunctioning products and equipment. Fuzzy logic helps improve the performance of products such as camcorders, air conditioners, washing machines, and subway cars. Genetic algorithms have generated solutions for problems in optimizing scheduling or design. You can find examples of manufacturing and production applications on pages 322–324 and 340.

SALES AND MARKETING

Specialized corporate portals and knowledge repositories have been created for sales and marketing staff to help them access and share information about customers, sales leads, competitors, and changes in product pricing and specifications. Virtual reality and VRML simulations can help customers experience the "look and feel" of products and even tailor some of these products more precisely to their needs. Case-based reasoning systems have been widely used for customer service and support. Many on-line intelligent agent tools and services have been developed to search the Web for products and services specified by users and to assist them in comparing prices and features. You can find examples of sales and marketing applications on pages 314–316, 324, and 345–347.

---

works. Nikko Securities has been working on a neurofuzzy system to forecast convertible-bond ratings.

INTELLIGENT AGENTS

Intelligent agents are software programs that work in the background to carry out specific, repetitive, and predictable tasks for an individual user, business process, or software application. The agent uses a built-in or learned knowledge base to accomplish tasks or make decisions on the user's behalf. Intelligent agents can be programmed to make decisions based on the user's personal preferences—for example, to delete junk e-mail, schedule appointments, or travel over interconnected networks to find the cheapest airfare to California. The agent can be likened to a personal digital assistant collaborating with the user in the same work environment. It can help the user by performing tasks on the user's behalf, training or teaching the user, hiding the complexity of difficult tasks, helping the user collaborate with other users, or monitoring events and procedures.

There are many intelligent agent applications today in operating systems, application software, e-mail systems, mobile computing software, and network tools. For example, the Wizards found in Microsoft Office software tools have built-in capabilities to show users how to accomplish various tasks, such as formatting documents or creating graphs, and to anticipate when users need assistance. Of special interest to business are intelligent agents for cruising networks, including the Internet, in search of information. Chapter 9 described how these *electronic commerce bots* can help consumers find products they want and assist them in comparing prices and other features. Because these mobile agents are personalized, semiautonomous, and continuously running, they can help automate several of the most time-consuming stages of the buying process and thus reduce transaction costs. Agent-based electronic commerce will become even more widespread as agent and Web technology become more powerful and flexible.

intelligent agent
Software program that uses a built-in or learned knowledge base to carry out specific, repetitive, and predictable tasks for an individual user, business process, or software application.

MANAGEMENT WRAP-UP

Leveraging and managing organizational knowledge have become core management responsibilities. Managers need to identify the knowledge assets of their organizations and make sure that appropriate systems and processes are in place to maximize their use.

Systems for knowledge and information work and artificial intelligence can enhance organizational processes in a number of ways. They can facilitate communication, collaboration, and coordination, bring more analytical power to bear in the development of solutions, or reduce the amount of human intervention in organizational processes.

An array of technologies is available to support knowledge management, including artificial intelligence technologies and tools for knowledge and information work and group collaboration. Managers should understand the costs, benefits, and capabilities of each technology and the knowledge management problem for which each is best suited.

For Discussion

1. Discuss some of the ways that knowledge management provides organizations with strategic advantage. How strategic are knowledge management systems?

2. How much can the use of artificial intelligence change the management process?

SUMMARY

1. *Why do businesses today need knowledge management programs and systems for knowledge management?* Businesses need knowledge management programs because knowledge has become a central productive and strategic asset in today's information economy and a potential source of strategic advantage. Knowledge management is a set of processes for systematically and actively managing and leveraging the stores of knowledge in an organization. Information systems can play a valuable role in knowledge management, helping the organization create, store, disseminate, and apply knowledge and capture its knowledge base. Office systems, knowledge work systems (KWS), group collaboration systems, and artificial intelligence applications are especially useful for knowledge management because they focus on supporting information and knowledge work and on defining and codifying the organization's knowledge base.

2. *Which information system applications are most useful for distributing, creating, and sharing knowledge in the firm?* Offices coordinate information work in the organization, link the work of diverse groups in the organization, and couple the organization to its external environment. Office systems support these functions by automating document management, communications, scheduling, and data management. Word processing, desktop publishing, Web publishing, and digital imaging systems support document management activities. Electronic-mail systems and groupware support communications activities. Electronic calendar applications and groupware support scheduling activities. Desktop data-management systems support data-management activities.

Knowledge work systems (KWS) support the creation of knowledge and its integration into the organization. KWS require easy access to an external knowledge base; powerful computer hardware that can support software with intensive graphics, analysis, document management, and communications capabilities; and a user-friendly interface. KWS often run on workstations that are customized for the work they must perform. Computer-aided design (CAD) systems and virtual reality systems, which create interactive simulations that behave like the real world, require graphics and powerful modeling capabilities. KWS for financial professionals provide access to external databases and the ability to analyze massive amounts of financial data very quickly.

Groupware is special software to support information-intensive activities in which people work collaboratively in groups. Intranets can perform many group collaboration and support functions and allow organizations to use Web publishing capabilities for document management.

3. *What are the business benefits of using artificial intelligence technology for knowledge management?* Artificial intelligence is the development of computer-based systems that behave like humans. There are five members of the artificial intelligence family tree: natural language, robotics, perceptive systems, expert systems, and intelligent machines. Artificial intelligence lacks the flexibility, breadth, and generality of human intelligence, but it can be used to capture and codify organizational knowledge. Businesses can use artificial intelligence to help them create an organizational knowledge base to preserve expertise; to perform routine, unsatisfying, or danger-

ous jobs; and to generate solutions to specific problems that are too massive and complex to be analyzed by human beings in a short period of time.

4. *How can businesses use expert systems and case-based reasoning to capture knowledge?* Expert systems are knowledge-intensive computer programs that solve problems that heretofore required human expertise. The systems capture a limited domain of human knowledge using rules or frames. The strategy to search through the knowledge base, called the *inference engine,* can use either forward or backward chaining. Expert systems are most useful for problems of classification or diagnosis. Case-based reasoning represents organizational knowledge as a database of cases that can be continually expanded and refined. When the user encounters a new case, the system searches for similar cases, finds the closest fit, and applies the solutions of the old case to the new case. The new case is stored with successful solutions in the case database.

5. *How can organizations benefit from using neural networks and other intelligent techniques?* Neural networks consist of hardware and software that attempt to mimic the thought processes of the human brain. Neural networks are notable for their ability to learn without programming and to recog-

nize patterns that cannot be easily discerned by humans. They are being used in science, medicine, and business primarily to discriminate patterns in massive amounts of data.

Fuzzy logic is a software technology that expresses logic with some carefully defined imprecision so that it is closer to the way people actually think than traditional IF–THEN rules. Fuzzy logic has been used for controlling physical devices and is starting to be used for limited decision-making applications.

Genetic algorithms develop solutions to particular problems using genetically based processes such as fitness, crossover, and mutation. Genetic algorithms are beginning to be applied to problems involving optimization, product design, and monitoring industrial systems where many alternatives or variables must be evaluated to generate an optimal solution.

Intelligent agents are software programs with built-in or learned knowledge bases that carry out specific, repetitive, and predictable tasks for an individual user, business process, or software application. Intelligent agents can be programmed to search for information or conduct transactions on networks, including the Internet.

KEY TERMS

AI shell, 332

Artificial intelligence (AI), 330

Backward chaining, 333

Best practices, 318

Case-based reasoning (CBR), 335

Chief knowledge officer (CKO), 317

Computer-aided design (CAD), 323

Data workers, 318

Document imaging systems, 320

Enterprise information portal, 327

Expert system, 331

Forward chaining, 332

Fuzzy logic, 338

Genetic algorithms, 339

Hybrid AI systems, 340

Inference engine, 332

Information work, 318

Intelligent agent, 341

Investment workstation, 324

Jukebox, 320

Knowledge base, 331

Knowledge engineer, 333

Knowledge frames, 331

Knowledge management, 317

Knowledge workers, 318

Knowledge work systems (KWS), 321

Neural network, 337

Office systems, 319

Organizational learning, 317

Organizational memory, 318

Rule base, 331

Rule-based expert system, 331

Tacit knowledge, 318

Teamware, 328

Virtual Reality Modeling Language (VRML), 324

Virtual reality systems, 324

REVIEW QUESTIONS

1. What is knowledge management? List and briefly describe the information systems that support it and the kind of information technology (IT) infrastructure it requires.

2. How does knowledge management promote organizational learning?

3. Describe the roles of the office in organizations. What are the major activities that take place in offices?

4. What are the principal types of information systems that support information worker activities in the office?

5. What are the generic requirements of knowledge work systems? Why?

6. Describe how the following systems support knowledge work: computer-aided design (CAD), virtual reality, and investment workstations.

7. How does groupware support information work? Describe its capabilities and Internet and intranet capabilities for collaborative work.

8. What is artificial intelligence? Why is it of interest to business?

9. What is the difference between artificial intelligence and natural or human intelligence?

10. Define an expert system and describe how it can help organizations use their knowledge assets.

11. Define and describe the role of the following in expert systems: rule base, frames, inference engine.

12. What is case-based reasoning? How does it differ from an expert system?

13. Describe three problems of expert systems.

14. Describe a neural network. With what kinds of tasks would a neural network excel?

15. Define and describe fuzzy logic. For what kinds of applications is it suited?

16. What are genetic algorithms? How can they help organizations solve problems? For what kinds of problems are they suited?

17. What are intelligent agents? How can they be used to benefit businesses?

APPLICATION SOFTWARE EXERCISE

EXPERT SYSTEM EXERCISE: BUILDING A SIMPLE EXPERT SYSTEM FOR RETIREMENT PLANNING

When employees at your company retire, they are given cash bonuses. These cash bonuses are based on the length of employment and the retiree's age. In order to receive a bonus, an employee must be at least 50 years of age and have worked for the company for 5 years. The following table summarizes the criteria for determining bonuses.

Using the information provided, build a simple expert system. Try to find a demonstration copy of an expert system software tool on the Web that you can download. Alternatively, use your spreadsheet software to build the expert system.

Length of Employment	Bonus
< 5 years	No bonus
6 – 10 years	20 percent of current annual salary
11 – 15 years	30 percent of current annual salary
16 – 20 years	40 percent of current annual salary
20 – 25 years	50 percent of current annual salary
26 or more years	100 percent of current annual salary

GROUP PROJECT

With a group of classmates, select two groupware products such as Lotus Notes, OpenText LiveLink, or Groove and compare their features and capabilities. To prepare your analysis, use articles from computer magazines and the Web sites for the groupware vendors. If possible, use electronic presentation software to present your findings to the class.

TOOLS FOR INTERACTIVE LEARNING

◾ INTERNET CONNECTION

The Internet Connection for this chapter will take you to the National Aeronautics and Space Administration (NASA) Web site, where you can complete an exercise showing how this Web site can be used by knowledge workers. You can also use the Interactive Study Guide to test your knowledge of the topics in this chapter and get instant feedback where you need more practice.

◾ CD-ROM

If you use the Multimedia Edition CD-ROM with this chapter, you can find a video clip illustrating how the Papnet neural network is used for medical testing, an audio overview of the major themes of this chapter, and bullet text summarizing the key points of the chapter.

◾ ELECTRONIC COMMERCE PROJECT

The Electronic Commerce project for this chapter will direct you to Web sites where you can compare the capabilities of two shopping bots for the Web.

CASE STUDY—*Frito-Lay's Drive to Repackage Knowledge*

Frito-Lay is well known to the general public, with products such as Fritos, Lay potato chips, Doritos chips, Cheetos, Ruffles, Cracker Jacks, SunChips, Grandma's Cookies, and even Tropicana. It is the largest snack-food maker in the world, selling 40 percent of the world's salty snacks in about 120 countries and reaching 60 percent of this market in the United States. Headquartered in Plano, Texas, and with more than 37,000 employees, Frito-Lay had sales reaching nearly $13 billion in 2000, representing about two-thirds of the sales and profits of PepsiCo, its parent company.

The company also enjoys a very good reputation both for its management and its use of computer technology. In 1989, the company installed a data warehouse so it would know the location and price of each bag of chips that was sold throughout the United States. In 1991 Frito-Lay gave its sales reps handheld computers, and pricing and product decision making began to move down the chain of command. The company was one of the first to do so and many companies followed suit. In 1995 Frito-Lay spent $130 million to purchase 15,000 new handheld computers that would enable the company to make even better use of information technology. As technology continued to improve, the decisions moved further down the organization, finally reaching the sales staff working at the individual store level.

Frito-Lay's main goal for its handhelds was to offer its customers, and through them the consumers, as much choice as possible by empowering its field staff, who had the closest contact with its customers. Management also wanted to improve Frito-Lay's product forecasting and improve its inventory management. Using handhelds, the sales staff was better able to track inventories and to improve communication with their retailers. Using handhelds, the sales reps were even able to agree to and lock in specific prices for given products—such decisions no longer needed to be bumped up to regional or national management.

Despite highly acclaimed information systems, Frito-Lay had serious problems managing its data. Data were fragmented among separate national databases for functions such as marketing and accounting. Both its sales staff and sales information were widely scattered around the country. Data about company policies, experiences, and customers were stored in separate systems geographically spread throughout the United States, some being stored in Plano. The scattered data were even captured and stored using an array of disparate technologies. The Frito-Lay sales force found it nearly impossible to gather such data when they were needed. Nor could they easily assemble sales data along with profitability data from the customer's system and competitive and industry information from the Web.

The sales staff also had serious problems sharing information with each other—those assigned to the same company had no easy way to share their knowledge about their customers. Salespeople in different locations would have to do similar research or ask or similar questions of corporate sales, marketing, and operations staffs, a waste of everyone's time and energy. Those questions might include

- What are the current consumer trends in this snack?
- How do the retail customers of this chain of stores behave compared to other customers?
- Why does Frito-Lay want to display some products in different areas of the store?
- What stimulates shoppers to select specific products while walking through the store?

Sales staff working with the same customer did not have a way to brainstorm together or collaborate on a particular challenge. Nor did staff members even have ways to identify and consult with internal experts on particular companies or issues. Performance suffered.

In the late 1990s Frito-Lay found itself serving fewer, larger customers who expected suppliers to provide more service. One of the biggest customers reorganized and centralized its purchasing decision making. This unnamed company is a multibillion dollar supermarket chain that is considered a leading marketer and merchandiser. It quickly began making new demands on Frito-Lay, such as wanting to see study results supporting a marketing idea suggested by a Frito-Lay salesperson. "They were pushing us to support [the suggestion] with quantitative and qualitative research," explained Mike Marino, Frito-Lay vice president of customer development "and we had no simple way to obtain that information." Frito-Lay quickly created a few national sales teams to work with this and other such customers on a national basis. Its goal was to provide more information to these large, centralized customers. The members of the new national teams came from the regional teams and remained scattered around the country. They had no experience in working with a customer's national office and found the challenge particularly rough because of the dispersed data. The company simply had not built the information technology infrastructure needed to access that data from other locations. The difficulties became evident in 1998 when, because of strong pressure, the turnover in the new national sales teams reached 25 percent. Frito-Lay had to make its information easily available by building a knowledge management portal.

Frito-Lay's portal would primarily operate on the corporate intranet. The three stated Frito-Lay goals for the portal were to organize knowledge and make it fairly easy to obtain; to utilize customer-specific data; and to increase team collaboration. In 1999 Marino hired Navigator Systems Inc., a Dallas, Texas, consulting firm that focused on business intelligence, enterprise collaboration, and e-commerce applications. A Frito-Lay project team was appointed to work with Navigator Systems in creating the portal.

The portal had to be able to locate information requested by the sales team members. The system would have to search central databases of such departments as marketing, sales, and operations, as well as databases at other locations. Sales team members also had to be able to turn to in-house experts on each topic, and so the project team developed profiles of 100 identified experts on the portal. Once it was created, the project team decided to pilot the portal using the national team assigned to the unnamed national customer whose requests had initiated Frito-Lay's changes. The choice was ideal both because of the size and quality of the customer, and because the 15-member sales team was scattered in 10 locations throughout the country. Marino said, "We knew if we could deliver there, we could satisfy any customer."

Security was also a key function of the portal. The team that worked with the large customer was forbidden to communicate that client's proprietary information about sales performance to anyone outside the group serving that customer. The project built in password protections so that portal users could only access appropriate data. The software the team worked with included Lotus Domino groupware, IBM's DB2 database management software, PowerPoint electronic presentation software and the Autonomy search engine. Navigator used Lotus Domino to build an application that placed descriptions of important documents (promotion strategies, budgets for marketing projects, product displays), stored as spreadsheets, electronic presentations, and desktop publishing files, in a searchable index and made some of these documents available on-line. The Autonomy search engine searches specific Web sites identified by Frito-Lay sales staff as primary sources of industry news and competitive intelligence, and enables the user to obtain information from all of these sites in a single search.

The project team completed the prototype in three months, and in October 1999 they demonstrated it to select members of the pilot sales team. The sales team liked much about the system but found that the pilot contained unacceptable errors. The problems stemmed from the failure of the project team to include the sales team in the prototype design. Testing the prototype had to be delayed—it took four more months of working with salespeople. The system had to be redesigned to make it easier to use. It also had to add some missing key features. "You have to understand and even redesign work processes," said Tom Davenport, director of the Accenture Institute for Strategic Change, "so it's baked in as part of their day-to-day work." Features that were added included required call-in reporting because many people want to know what happened on a sales call. An account manager could be on the phone for days explaining what happened. Now, the company can post that information to a Web site, freeing up the account manager to document the call once and move on. One change allowed users to manipulate and analyze the data instead of simply looking at it. Another allowed salespeople to produce reports fashioned to customer requests.

The sales force had been alienated by the original prototype and was dubious about the success or even the value of the whole project. They had to be persuaded to support the new prototype when it was going to be demonstrated again. Many believed it would simply add more work. The project team addressed the problem in several ways. The sales staff worked closely with the project staff to design the changes. When the new prototype was finished, Frito-Lay sales team leader Joe Ackerman became the rollout team leader. "If it comes from the field," he said, "it's really better-received than if it's from headquarters."

The new Frito-Lay portal, named Customer Community Portal (CCP), went live in January 2000. To the customers, the salespersons now became respected consultants with important information. National staff turnover fell to zero in 2000 (except for positions that became open when a team member was promoted). "The tool has become extremely valuable for communication," Ackerman said. It is now used for daily contact management, call reporting, weekly cross-country meetings, training, document sharing, and access to data and industry news. As a result team members no longer need to fax documents around the country in order to share information or physically travel to the retail customer.

In addition sales for the pilot sales team increased almost twice as fast as for other customer teams. The use of the portal is being spread to three other Frito-Lay customer sales teams and is also starting to be tried in several other PepsiCo divisions. However, difficulties remain, including the need for employees to learn how to work differently.

Sources: Esther Shein, "The Knowledge Crunch," *CIO Magazine*, May 1, 2001; Larry Stevens, "Food Supplier Repackages Knowledge," *Knowledge Management*, January 2001; Kathleen Melymuka, "Profiting from Mistakes," *Computerworld*, April 30, 2001; "Frito-Lay, Inc." *The Industry Standard*, July 30, 2001; Primm Fox, "Premier 100: IT Leaders Must Provide 'Extraordinary Leadership,'" *Computerworld*, June 20, 2000; Julia King and Thomas Hoffman, "The Next IT Generation," *Computerworld*, April 6, 1998; and Keith Shaw, "Smithsonian Awards: 10 Years of Heroes," *Computerworld*, June 8, 1998.

CASE STUDY QUESTIONS

1. Summarize Frito-Lay's business and its business strategy. Then explain how knowledge management is related to the company's business strategy.

2. Describe the company's knowledge management problems in the early 1990s and the relationship of its existing systems to those problems. What management, organization, and technology factors were responsible for those problems?

3. How well does the Customer Community Portal support Frito-Lay's business strategy? What management, organization, and technology issues did the project team building the portal have to address?

4. In the long run, how successful will CCP be? Describe what you think might cause it to fail or succeed, and explain why.

11 ENHANCING MANAGEMENT DECISION-MAKING FOR THE DIGITAL FIRM

objectives

As a manager, you will be asked to make many different kinds of decisions. You will want to know how you can use information systems to improve your decision-making, whether you are working alone or in a group. After completing this chapter, you will be able to answer the following questions:

1. *How can information systems help individual managers make better decisions when the problems are nonroutine and constantly changing?*

2. *How can information systems help people working in a group make decisions more efficiently?*

3. *Are there any special systems that can facilitate decision-making among senior managers? Exactly what can these systems do to help high-level management?*

4. *What benefits can systems to support management decision-making provide for the organization as a whole?*

Air Canada Optimizes Flight Crew Scheduling—and Keep Employees Happy

When Air Canada acquired Canadian Airlines in 2000 it found itself with a new set of complex scheduling and management problems. The number of pilots it had to schedule for flights jumped from 2200 to 3600, an instant increase of 60 percent. Air Canada turned to Altitude PBS, a preferential bidding system developed by Montreal's AD OPT Technologies to help it with scheduling decisions. Altitude is a suite of advanced planning and scheduling applications used by airlines for workforce planning, scheduling, and management.

Air Canada now uses Altitude PBS to generate the flight schedules of its pilots from Canadian Airlines. The system has three components: a Bidder Interface, a Scheduler Interface, and an Optimizer. Flight crew members use the Bidder interface to specify the schedules they prefer from an extensive menu of choices.

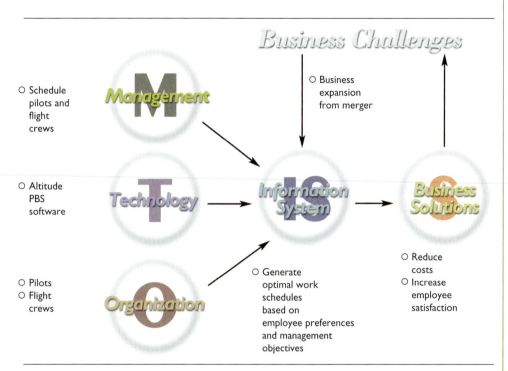

Employees can submit their bids from their home or on the road using an e-Scheduling module that can be accessed on the Internet or from designated terminals in airport pilot lounges. The system will take these personal preferences into account when making work assignments. The system also considers factors such as type of aircraft; crew seniority; crew locations; employee time for vacations, illness, and training; and company, union and government regulations when making scheduling assignments. The system then applies mathematical models to generate optimum flight schedules that address the business needs of management, industry and government rules and regulations, and the personal needs of flight crews. Altitude determines the optimal way to accommodate the preferences of crew members and the objectives of airline management.

By helping airline management make crew scheduling more efficient, Altitude is capable of producing annual savings of 5 percent and more in total labor and related expenses. This can be worth millions of dollars a year.

Sources: Jacques Desrosiers, "Air Canada Reaches 'Altitude'," *OR/MS Today*, April 2001; "Altitude Airline Crew Management Solutions," www.ad-opt.com and www.aircanada.com.

Air Canada's flight crew scheduling system is an example of a decision-support system (DSS). Such systems have powerful analytic capabilities to support managers during the process of arriving at a decision. Other systems in this category are group decision-support systems (GDSS), which support decision-making in groups, and executive support systems (ESS), which provide information for making strategic-level decisions. These systems can enhance organizational performance, but they raise the following management challenges:

MANAGEMENT CHALLENGES

1. **Building information systems that can actually fulfill executive information requirements.** Even with the use of critical success factors and other information requirements determination methods, it may still be difficult to establish information requirements for ESS and DSS serving senior management. Chapter 3 has already described why certain aspects of senior management decision-making cannot be supported by information systems because the decisions are too unstructured and fluid. Even if a problem can be addressed by an information system, senior management may not fully understand its actual information needs. For instance, senior managers may not agree on the firm's critical success factors, or the critical success factors they describe may be inappropriate or outdated if the firm is confronting a crisis requiring a major strategic change.

2. **Creating meaningful reporting and management decision-making processes.** Enterprise systems and data warehouses have made it much easier to supply DSS and ESS with data from many different systems than in the past. The remaining challenge is changing management thinking to use the data that are available to maximum advantage, to develop better reporting categories for measuring firm performance, and to inform new types of decisions. Many managers use the new capabilities in DSS and ESS to obtain the same information as before. Major changes in management thinking will be required to get managers to ask better questions of the data.

M ost information systems described throughout this text help people make decisions in one way or another, but DSS, GDSS, and ESS are part of a special category of information systems that are explicitly designed to enhance managerial decision-making. By taking advantage of more accurate firm-wide data provided by enterprise systems and the new information technology infrastructure, these systems can support very fine-grained decisions for guiding the firm, coordinating work activities across the enterprise, and responding rapidly to changing markets and customers. Many of these managerial decision-making applications are now Web-enabled. This chapter describes the characteristics of each of these types of information systems, showing how each enhances the managerial decision-making process and ultimately the performance of the organization.

DSS, GDSS, and ESS can support decision-making in a number of ways. They can automate certain decision procedures (for example, determining the highest price that can be charged for a product to maintain market share or the right amount of materials to maintain in inventory to maximize efficient customer response and product profitability). They can provide information about different aspects of the decision situation and the decision process, such as what opportunities or problems triggered the decision process, what solution alternatives were generated or explored, and how the decision was reached. Finally, they can stimulate innovation in decision-making by helping managers question existing decision procedures or explore different solution designs (Dutta, Wierenga, and Dalebout, 1997). The ability to explore the outcomes of alternative organizational scenarios, use precise firm-wide information, and provide tools to facilitate group decision processes can help managers make decisions that help the firm achieve its strategic objectives (Forgionne and Kohli, 2000).

decision-support system (DSS)

Computer system at the management level of an organization that combines data, analytical tools, and models to support semistructured and unstructured decision-making.

11.1 DECISION-SUPPORT SYSTEMS (DSS)

As noted in Chapter 2, a **decision-support system (DSS)** assists management decision-making by combining data, sophisticated analytical models and tools, and user-friendly software into a single powerful system that can support semistructured or unstructured decision-making. A DSS provides users with a flexible set of tools and capabilities for analyzing important blocks of data.

MIS AND DSS

Some of the earliest applications for supporting management decision-making were *management information systems (MIS)*, which we introduced in Chapter 2. MIS primarily provide information on the firm's performance to help managers in monitoring and controlling the business. They typically produce fixed, regularly scheduled reports based on data extracted and summarized from the organization's underlying transaction processing systems (TPS). The format for these reports is often specified in advance. A typical MIS report might show a summary of monthly sales for each of the major sales territories of a company. Sometimes MIS reports are exception reports, highlighting only exceptional conditions, such as when the sales quotas for a specific territory fall below an anticipated level or employees who have exceeded their spending limit in a dental care plan. Traditional MIS produced primarily hard copy reports. Today these reports might be available on-line through an intranet, and more MIS reports can be generated on-demand. Table 11-1 provides some examples of MIS applications.

DSS provide new sets of capabilities for nonroutine decisions and user control. An MIS provides managers with reports based on routine flows of data and assists in the general control of the organization, whereas a DSS emphasizes change, flexibility, and a rapid response. With a DSS there is less of an effort to link users to structured information flows and a correspondingly greater emphasis on models, assumptions, ad hoc queries, and display graphics.

Chapter 3 introduced the distinction between structured, semistructured, and unstructured decisions. Structured problems are repetitive and routine, for which known algorithms provide solutions. Unstructured problems are novel and nonroutine, for which there are no algorithms for solutions. One can discuss, decide, and ruminate about unstructured problems, but they are not solved in the sense that one finds an answer to an equation. Semistructured problems fall between structured and unstructured problems. While MIS primarily address structured problems, DSS support semistructured and unstructured problem analysis. Chapter 3 also introduced Simon's description of decision-making, which consists of four stages: intelligence, design, choice, and implementation. Decision-support systems are intended to help design and evaluate alternatives and monitor the adoption or implementation process.

TYPES OF DECISION-SUPPORT SYSTEMS

The earliest DSS tended to draw on small subsets of corporate data and were heavily model driven. Recent advances in computer processing and database technology have expanded the definition of a DSS to include systems that can support decision-making by analyzing vast

TABLE 11-1	EXAMPLES OF MIS APPLICATIONS
Organization	**MIS Application**
California Pizza Kitchen	Inventory Express application "remembers" each restaurant's ordering patterns, and compares the amount of ingredients used per menu item to predefined portion measurements established by management. The system identifies restaurants with out-of-line portions and notifies their management so that corrective action can be taken.
PharMark	Extranet MIS identifies patients with drug-use patterns that place them at risk for adverse outcomes.
Black & Veatch	Intranet MIS tracks construction costs for its various projects across the United States.
Taco Bell	TACO (Total Automation of Company Operations) system provides information on food cost, labor cost, and period-to-date costs for each restaurant.

quantities of data, including firm-wide data from enterprise systems and transaction data from the Web.

Today there are two basic types of decision-support systems, model-driven and data-driven (Dhar and Stein, 1997). **Model-driven DSS** were primarily stand-alone systems isolated from major organizational information systems that used some type of model to perform "what-if" and other kinds of analyses. Such systems were often developed by end-user divisions or groups not under central IS control. Their analysis capabilities were based on a strong theory or model combined with a good user interface that made the model easy to use. Air Canada's flight crew scheduling system described in the chapter-opening vignette and the voyage-estimating DSS described in Chapter 2 are examples of model-driven DSS.

The second type of DSS is a **data-driven DSS**. These systems analyze large pools of data found in major organizational systems. They support decision-making by allowing users to extract useful information that was previously buried in large quantities of data. Often data from transaction processing systems (TPS) are collected in data warehouses for this purpose. On-line analytical processing (OLAP) and datamining can then be used to analyze the data. Companies are starting to build data-driven DSS to mine customer data gathered from their Web sites as well as data from enterprise systems.

Traditional database queries answer such questions as, "How many units of product number 403 were shipped in November 2001?" OLAP, or multidimensional analysis, supports much more complex requests for information, such as, "Compare sales of product 403 relative to plan by quarter and sales region for the past two years." We described OLAP and multidimensional data analysis in Chapter 7. With OLAP and query-oriented data analysis, users need to have a good idea about the information for which they are looking.

Datamining is more discovery driven. *Datamining,* which was introduced in Chapter 7, provides insights into corporate data that cannot be obtained with OLAP by finding hidden patterns and relationships in large databases and inferring rules from them to predict future behavior. The patterns and rules then can be used to guide decision-making and forecast the effect of those decisions. The types of information that can be yielded from datamining include associations, sequences, classifications, clusters, and forecasts.

Associations are occurrences linked to a single event. For instance, a study of supermarket purchasing patterns might reveal that when corn chips are purchased, a cola drink is purchased 65 percent of the time, but when there is a promotion, cola is purchased 85 percent of the time. With this information, managers can make better decisions because they have learned the profitability of a promotion.

In *sequences*, events are linked over time. One might find, for example, that if a house is purchased, then a new refrigerator will be purchased within two weeks 65 percent of the time, and an oven will be bought within one month of the home purchase 45 percent of the time.

Classification recognizes patterns that describe the group to which an item belongs by examining existing items that have been classified and by inferring a set of rules. For example, businesses such as credit card or telephone companies worry about the loss of steady customers. Classification can help discover the characteristics of customers who are likely to leave and can provide a model to help managers predict who they are so that they can devise special campaigns to retain such customers.

Clustering works in a manner similar to classification when no groups have yet been defined. A datamining tool will discover different groupings within data, such as finding affinity groups for bank cards or partitioning a database into groups of customers based on demographics and types of personal investments.

Although these applications involve predictions, *forecasting* uses predictions in a different way. It uses a series of existing values to forecast what other values will be. For example, forecasting might find patterns in data to help managers estimate the future value of continuous variables such as sales figures.

Datamining uses statistical analysis tools as well as neural networks, fuzzy logic, genetic algorithms, or rule-based and other intelligent techniques (described in Chapter 10).

As noted in Chapter 3, it is a mistake to think that only individuals in large organizations make decisions. In fact, most decisions are made collectively. Frequently, decisions must be coordinated with several groups before being finalized. In large organizations,

---

model-driven DSS

Primarily stand-alone system that uses some type of model to perform "what-if" and other kinds of analyses.

---

data-driven DSS

A system that supports decision-making by allowing users to extract and analyze useful information that was previously buried in large databases.

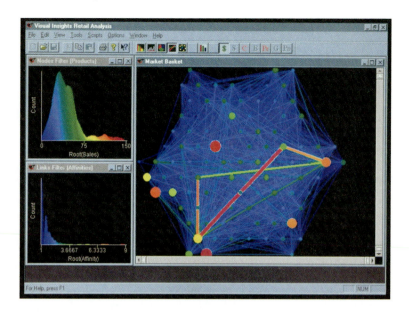

Lucent Technologies Visual Insights software can help businesses detect patterns in their data. Each dot in this example represents items purchased at one supermarket, with lines drawn between purchases of individual shoppers. The software shows links between different purchase items, such as cookies and milk.

decision-making is inherently a group process, and a DSS can be designed to facilitate group decision-making. Section 11.2 deals with this issue.

COMPONENTS OF DSS

Figure 11-1 illustrates the components of a DSS. They include a database of data used for query and analysis, a software system with models, datamining, and other analytical tools and a user interface.

The **DSS database** is a collection of current or historical data from a number of applications or groups. It may be a small database residing on a PC that contains a subset of corporate data that has been downloaded and possibly combined with external data. Alternatively, the DSS database may be a massive data warehouse that is continuously updated by major organizational TPS (including enterprise systems and data generated by Web site transactions). The data in DSS databases are generally extracts or copies of production databases so that using the DSS does not interfere with critical operational systems.

The **DSS software system** contains the software tools that are used for data analysis. It may contain various OLAP tools, datamining tools, or a collection of mathematical and analytical models that easily can be made accessible to the DSS user. A **model** is an abstract representation that illustrates the components or relationships of a phenomenon. A model can be a physical model (such as a model airplane), a mathematical model (such as an equation), or a verbal model (such as a description of a procedure for writing an order). Each decision-support system is built for a specific set of purposes and will make different collections of models available depending on those purposes.

Perhaps the most common models are libraries of statistical models. Such libraries usually contain the full range of expected statistical functions including means, medians, deviations, and scatter plots. The software has the ability to project future outcomes by analyzing a series of data. Statistical modeling software can be used to help establish relationships, such as relating product sales to differences in age, income, or other factors between communities. Optimization models, often using linear programming, determine optimal resource allocation to maximize or minimize specified variables

DSS database
A collection of current or historical data from a number of applications or groups. Can be a small PC database or a massive data warehouse.

DSS software system
Collection of software tools that are used for data analysis, such as OLAP tools, datamining tools, or a collection of mathematical and analytical models.

model
An abstract representation that illustrates the components or relationships of a phenomenon.

Figure 11-1 Overview of a decision-support system (DSS). The main components of the DSS are the DSS database, the DSS software system, and the user interface. The DSS database may be a small database residing on a PC or a massive data warehouse.

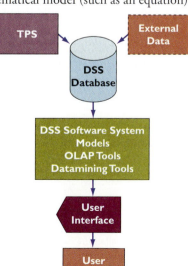

Figure 11-2 Sensitivity analysis. This table displays the results of a sensitivity analysis of the effect of changing the sales price of a necktie and the cost per unit on the product's breakeven point. It answers the question "What happens to the breakeven point if the sales price and the cost to make each unit increase or decrease?"

Total fixed costs	19000					
Variable cost per unit	3					
Average sales price	17					
Contribution margin	14					
Breakeven point	1357					
			Variable Cost per Unit			
Sales	1357	2	3	4	5	6
Price	14	1583	1727	1900	2111	2375
	15	1462	1583	1727	1900	2111
	16	1357	1462	1583	1727	1900
	17	1267	1357	1462	1583	1727
	18	1188	1267	1357	1462	1583

sensitivity analysis
Models that ask "what-if" questions repeatedly to determine the impact of changes in one or more factors on the outcomes.

such as cost or time. A classic use of optimization models is to determine the proper mix of products within a given market to maximize profits.

Forecasting models often are used to forecast sales. The user of this type of model might supply a range of historical data to project future conditions and the sales that might result from those conditions. The decision-maker could vary those future conditions (entering, for example, a rise in raw materials costs or the entry of a new, low-priced competitor in the market) to determine how these new conditions might affect sales. Companies often use this software to predict the actions of competitors. Model libraries exist for specific functions, such as financial and risk analysis models.

Among the most widely used models are **sensitivity analysis** models that ask "what-if" questions repeatedly to determine the impact of changes in one or more factors on the outcomes. "What-if" analysis—working forward from known or assumed conditions—allows the user to vary certain values to test results in order to better predict outcomes if changes occur in those values. "What happens if" we raise the price by 5 percent or increase the advertising budget by $100,000? What happens if we keep the price and advertising budget the same? Desktop spreadsheet software, such as Microsoft Excel or Lotus 1-2-3, is often used for this purpose (see Figure 11-2). Backward sensitivity analysis software is used for goal seeking: If I want to sell one million product units next year, how much must I reduce the price of the product?

The DSS user interface permits easy interaction between users of the system and the DSS software tools. A graphic, easy-to-use, flexible user interface supports the dialogue between the user and the DSS. The DSS users can be managers or employees with no patience for learning a complex tool, so the interface must be relatively intuitive. Many DSS today are being built with Web-based interfaces to take advantage of the Web's ease of use, interactivity, and capabilities for personalization and customization. Building successful DSS requires a high level of user participation to make sure the system provides the information managers need. The Manager's Toolkit provides some guidelines for developing DSS solutions.

MIS IN ACTION MANAGER'S TOOLKIT

HOW TO EVALUATE A DSS PROJECT

If your company is interested in using a DSS to support management decision-making, here are some key questions to ask:

1. What kind of problem do you expect this system to solve?
2. Does the solution require the use of models? If so, which ones? What are the variables in the problem?
3. Does the solution require the use of query and data analysis tools? If so, which ones?
4. What data do you need to arrive at a solution? Can all of the data be found from within the company or does some data come from

external sources? Can you obtain the data automatically from corporate and external databases or must the data be entered separately? How much effort would be required to assemble the required data for the system?

5. What type of user interface is required? Must users use it to input data as well as ask questions of the data? Is the interface easy to use?
6. What computer hardware and operating system are required to run this system?
7. How long does it take to get answers from the data? How clear are the results?

TABLE 11-2

EXAMPLES OF DECISION-SUPPORT SYSTEMS

Organization	DSS Application
General Accident Insurance	Customer buying patterns and fraud detection
Bank of America	Customer profiles
Frito-Lay, Inc.	Price, advertising, and promotion selection
Burlington Coat Factory	Store location and inventory mix
KeyCorp	Targeting direct mail marketing customers
National Gypsum	Corporate planning and forecasting
Southern Railway	Train dispatching and routing
Texas Oil and Gas Corporation	Evaluation of potential drilling sites
United Airlines	Flight scheduling, passenger demand forecasting
U.S. Department of Defense	Defense contract analysis

DSS APPLICATIONS AND THE DIGITAL FIRM

There are many ways in which DSS can be used to support decision-making. Table 11-2 lists examples of DSS in well-known organizations. Both data-driven and model-driven DSS have become very powerful and sophisticated, providing fine-grained information for decisions that enable the firm to coordinate both internal and external business processes much more precisely. Some of these DSS are helping companies improve supply chain management or plan scenarios for changing business conditions. Some can be used to fine-tune relationships with customers. Some take advantage of the company-wide data provided by enterprise systems. DSS today can also harness the interactive capabilities of the Web to provide decision-support tools to both employees and customers.

To illustrate the range of capabilities of a DSS, we now describe some successful DSS applications. San Miguel's and IBM's supply chain management systems, Pioneer Natural Resources' business simulation system, ShopKo Stores' pricing system described in the Window on Technology, and Air Canada's flight crew scheduling system described in the chapter opening vignette are examples of model-driven DSS. Royal Bank of Canada's customer segmentation system and Kinki Nippon Tourist's customer analysis system are examples of data-driven DSS. We will also examine some applications of geographic information systems (GIS), a special category of DSS for visualizing data geographically.

DSS for Supply Chain Management

Supply chain decisions involve determining "who, what, when, and where" from purchasing and transporting materials and parts through manufacturing products and distributing and delivering those products to customers. DSS can help managers examine this complex chain comprehensively and search among a huge number of alternatives for the combinations that are most efficient and cost-effective. The prime management goal might be to reduce overall costs while increasing the speed and accuracy of filling customer orders.

In 1994 IBM Research developed an advanced supply chain optimization and simulation tool called the Asset Management Tool (AMT) to reduce inventory levels yet maintain enough inventory in the supply chain to respond quickly to customer demands. AMT deals with a range of entities in the supply chain, including targets for inventory and customer service levels, product structure, channel assembly, supplier terms and conditions, and lead-time reduction. Users of AMT can evaluate supply chains in terms of financial tradeoffs associated with various configurations and operational policies.

The IBM Personal Systems Group (PSG) used AMT to reduce supply chain costs to cope with the large volumes, dropping prices, and slim profit margins in the personal computer market. PSG was able to reduce overall pipeline inventory by over 50 percent in 1997 and 1998. The system helped PSG reduce payments made to distributors and resellers to compensate for product price reductions by more than $750 million in 1998. PSG's cycle

SHOPKO'S DSS MAKES A SCIENCE OF MARKDOWNS

Like many retailers, discount chain ShopKo Stores Inc. hates markdowns. If the item such as a pair of running shorts did not sell at $7.99, the store would keep lowering the price again and again to $6.99, $5.99 and even $2.99 until it found the price that customers were willing to pay. But ShopKo was losing millions of dollars this way because its price markdowns were "best guesses." If it discounted an item too late, it would be stuck with truckloads of inventory. If it discounted too early, it would lose profits because people rushed in to buy goods they might have bought at a higher price. ShopKo's retail operations encompass 162 ShopKo discount stores in large and mid-sized cities and 165 Pamida discount stores in smaller rural communities, so knowing the best price to charge for items at each store has an enormous impact on profits.

ShopKo, along with other retailers such as J.C. Penney Co., L.L. Bean and Gymboree Corp. turned to information systems to help make markdowns more scientific. They are using software from Spotlight Solutions Inc. that works similar to the "yield management" practiced by airlines which can calculate precisely just how many seats to hold open at premium prices for last-minute passengers and how many to sell ahead of time at lower prices. The Spotlight Markdown Optimizer uses mathematical models and three years of ShopKo sales data to pinpoint exactly when and how much to mark down the price of an item to maximize gross profit margins. By analyzing several years of sales data for similar items, the software estimates a "seasonal demand curve" for each item and predicts how many units would sell each week at various prices. The software also uses sales history to predict how sensitive customer demand will be to price changes.

In August 2000 ShopKo started testing the Markdown Optimizer, which predicted that the sale of boys' fleece vests would peak in mid-August. Instead of taking its typical markdowns of 10 percent or 20 percent again and again, Shopko took a single 20 percent markdown in November 2000. It made a 30.2 percent gross profit margin on the vests during the three-month clearance period, a vast improvement over the conventional markdown approach used the previous year. When the pilot project was completed, sales for the 300 products in the test, including sheets and baby bottles, were 14 percent higher than a year earlier, while their gross profit margin percentage rose 24 percent. ShopKo sold 13 percent more of each product at the regular price than it would have in the past. The company is now rolling the system out to all of its stores and plans to create a separate markdown schedule for each location.

Before implementing Spotlight, ShopKo store buyers would sift through piles of weekly reports showing sales and inventory levels for thousands of different products in over 100 stores. Overwhelmed with the data and paperwork, they would have had to plan most markdowns before each selling season began and mark down an item at the same time at all of the stores. With the new system, they can adjust each markdown to the sales patterns of each of its stores so that a high-volume superstore and a low-volume store would benefit most by making the respective markdowns of 25 percent and 45 percent for the same item. Spotlight is also helping ShopKo trim labor costs as well, since clerks do not have to spend so much time changing price tags each time they mark down an item. Before using the software, ShopKo often marked down items three or four times. Now it only needs to make one or two markdowns to sell items out.

To Think About: What are the business benefits of using this DSS? How is Spotlight Markdown Optimizer changing the way ShopKo runs its business?

Sources: Amy Merrick, "Retailers Attempt to Get a Leg Up on Markdowns with New Software," *The Wall Street Journal,* August 7, 2001 and "ShopKo Stores Inc.," www.spotlightsolutions.com.

---

time from component procurement to product sale was reduced by four to six weeks, bringing reductions of 5 to 7 percent in overall product cost.

IBM's AS/400 midrange computer division used AMT to analyze and quantify the impact of product complexity. Information from the system helped IBM reduce the number of product features, substitute alternate parts, and delay customization. AMT also provided an analysis of the tradeoff between serviceability and inventory in IBM's QuickShip Program, helping the company reduce operational cost by up to 50 percent. IBM has also been able to use AMT to help its business partners improve management of their supply chains. For instance, supply chain analysis helped Piancor, one of IBM's major distributors, identify opportunities for optimizing the product flow between the two companies (Dietrich et al., 2000).

San Miguel Corporation uses DSS for supply chain management to help it distribute more than 300 products, such as beer, liquor, dairy products, and feedgrains to every corner of the Philippine archipelago. A Production Load Allocation system determines the quantity

Questions

1. Who are our most frequent customers?

2. Do they live close to our retail outlets?

3. How can we re-segment those customers?

4. How can we better reach those segments?

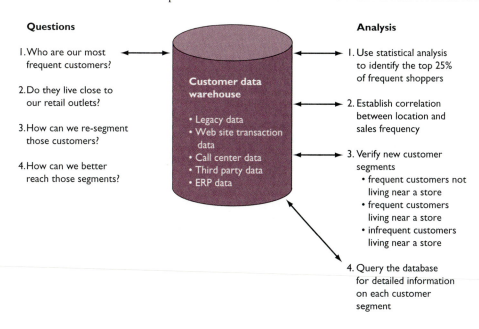

Customer data warehouse

- Legacy data
- Web site transaction data
- Call center data
- Third party data
- ERP data

Analysis

1. Use statistical analysis to identify the top 25% of frequent shoppers

2. Establish correlation between location and sales frequency

3. Verify new customer segments
   - frequent customers not living near a store
   - frequent customers living near a store
   - infrequent customers living near a store

4. Query the database for detailed information on each customer segment

Figure 11-3 DSS for customer analysis and segmentation. This DSS allows companies to segment their customer base with a high level of precision where it can be used to drive a marketing campaign. Based on the results of datamining, a firm can develop specific marketing campaigns for each customer segment. For example, it could target frequent customers living near a store with coupons for products of interest and with rewards for frequent shoppers.

of products to produce for each bottling line and how production output should be assigned to warehouses. It balances ordering, carrying, and stock-out costs while considering frequency of deliveries and minimum order quantities, saving the company $180,000 in inventory costs in one year. The DSS can generate optimal production allocation plans based on either minimizing cost or maximizing profit. San Miguel's system also helps it reassign deliveries and warehouse facilities to counter imbalances in capacity and demand. Managers used information from the system to move more of San Miguel delivery business to third-party logistics providers so that its own delivery trucks could be used more efficiently. The company found that it could reduce the number of routes serving sales districts in metropolitan Manila alone by 43 percent (Del Rosario, 1999).

DSS for Customer Relationship Management

DSS for customer relationship management use data mining to guide decisions about pricing, customer retention, market share, and new revenue streams. These systems typically consolidate customer information from a variety of systems into massive data warehouses and use various analytical tools to slice it into tiny segments for one-to-one marketing (see Figure 11-3).

Instead of sending customers the same marketing information, Royal Bank has developed a DSS for customer segmentation that can tailor messages to very small groups of people and offer them products, services, and prices that are more likely to appeal to them. This DSS consolidates data from various systems in the organization into a data warehouse. The Royal Bank's main customer database is its marketing information file (MIF) which also contains data from every document a customer fills out as well as data from checking accounts and credit cards, and the Royal Bank's enterprise and billing systems.

By querying the database, analysts can identify customers based on the products they might buy and the likelihood they will leave the bank and combine these data with demographic data from external sources. Royal Bank can then identify one or a group of profitable customers who appear to be getting ready to leave the bank. To identify such customers, the bank will look at the customer's bank balance (if it was recently kept low), credit card payments (if they were reduced in amount and perhaps paid later than in the past), and deposits (if they have become sporadic). These signs could indicate a customer who is recently unemployed, but they could also highlight a profitable customer preparing to switch to another bank. The Royal Bank, using its vast stored data, can quickly learn whether it has profited from this customer's business. They measure profitability looking at the customer's past ongoing balances, his or her use of his Royal Bank's line of credit, and the car loan and/or mortgage that person holds from the bank. The bank can also deduce from personal data whether the customer is at a stage in life when he or she will need more bank loans and other bank services.

Having identified such customer(s), the bank's marketing department might put together a tempting package of banking services at a low price, such as Internet banking, bill payment, unlimited ATM access, and a limited number of branch transactions, all for a fee of $9.95 per month. The bank knows that customers who use such service packages stay with the bank for about three years longer than do those who have no such package. If the customer is not satisfied with the specific package, marketing can even tailor a package specifically for that individual. Royal Bank is linking its customer database and legacy systems to the Web so that it can offer customers service packages instantly on-line as they access their accounts over the Internet. Royal Bank's customer segmentation is so effective that it can achieve a response rate as high as 30 percent to its marketing campaigns, compared to an average of 3 percent for the banking industry (Wilson, 2000 and Radding, 2000.)

Kinki Nippon Tourist (KNT), Japan's second largest travel agency, revolutionized Japanese tourism in the early 1980s by providing newspaper advertising and magazines explicitly customized for repeat customers that would allow them to purchase trips over the telephone. (Until KNT opened these new channels, tourists had to arrange their trips through a travel agency.) When competitors followed, KNT tried to develop a one-to-one marketing strategy to retain core customers and increase customer loyalty. To store and analyze detailed information on customer preferences, behavior, and opinions of tours, KNT implemented a massive data warehouse based on a Teradata relational database. The system runs on a WorldMark massively parallel processor and includes data on 1.5 million customers. The data come from telephone calls, conversations with tour operators, and customer questionnaires as well as transactions. Nearly 500 users can access the system directly through individual workstations.

By analyzing the detailed customer data, KNT uncovered new patterns that were previously undetectable in its old legacy systems. For example, it found that customers whose first tour was made by bus were likely to be repeat bus customers. The company can use this finding to target appropriate tours, events, and hospitality to these customers. KNT can also use the data warehouse to determine which newspaper ads work the best for certain tours and which tours are better promoted through direct mail. KNT's call center operators can use the information from the data warehouse to improve customer service. And KNT uses data from the system to customize its magazines to specific customer segments (NCR, 2001).

Some of these DSS for customer relationship management use data gathered from the Web. Chapter 9 has described how each action a visitor has taken when visiting a particular Web site can be captured on that Web site's log. Companies can mine these data to answer questions such as what customers are purchasing and what promotions are generating the most traffic. The results can help companies tailor marketing programs more effectively, redesign Web sites to optimize traffic, and create personalized buying experiences for Web site visitors. Other DSS combine Web site transaction data with data from enterprise systems.

DSS for Simulating Business Scenarios

We have already described the capabilities of model-driven DSS for performing "what-if" analyses of problems in specific areas of the firm. DSS with very powerful "what-if" and modeling capabilities have been developed for modeling entire business scenarios. Such DSS use information from both internal and external sources to help managers tune strategy to a constantly changing array of conditions and variables.

In the oil and gas industry, for example, there are many variables associated with running an energy company, including development and production costs and the ratio of gas and oil in a field. The number and complex relationship among these variables makes it difficult for managers to determine the cost-effectiveness of their business decisions. Pioneer Natural Resources (PNR) in Las Colinas, Texas, decided to create a DSS that could provide more precise information for those decisions.

In 1995, PNR executives started identifying all of the management variables and diagrammed all of the business processes in their company to create a model that could show the impact on the business when one or more of those variables changed. The company built a prototype DSS using Powersim, a simulation development tool from Powersim Corporation in Herndon, Virginia. PNR executives first tested the prototype to simulate PNR's volatile Gulf Coast division, which had very long production time lines.

The company primarily uses Powersim to create a model for scenario planning and "what-if" analyses. For example, by modeling different scenarios with Powersim, PNR management can determine how much more to pay a service company to put a well into production earlier, yet still earn a profit. Powersim runs on a Windows-based PC and uses Microsoft Excel spreadsheet software and Access database software for the input and output of business variables.

The company believes that each of its five divisions could potentially raise revenues by 25 to 40 percent using Powersim to model scenarios and adjust business variables. In addition, the simulation technology provides management with more control by helping managers determine the specific actions necessary to arrive at a desired business result or model the result of each business decision under consideration (Baldwin, 1998).

Geographic Information Systems (GIS)

Geographic information systems (GIS) are a special category of DSS that can analyze and display data for planning and decision-making using digitized maps. The software can assemble, store, manipulate, and display geographically referenced information, tying data to points, lines, and areas on a map. GIS can thus be used to support decisions that require knowledge about the geographic distribution of people or other resources in scientific research, resource management, and development planning. For example, GIS might be used to help state and local governments calculate emergency response times to natural disasters or to help banks identify the best locations for installing new branches or ATM terminals. GIS tools have become affordable even for small businesses and some can be used on the Web.

GIS have modeling capabilities, allowing managers to change data and automatically revise business scenarios to find better solutions. Johanna Dairies of Union, New Jersey, used GIS software to display its customers on a map and then design the most efficient delivery routes, saving the company $100,000 annually for each route that was eliminated. Sonny's Bar-B-Q, the Gainesville, Florida-based restaurant chain, used GIS with federal and local census data on median age, household income, total population, and population distribution to help management decide where to open new restaurants. The company's growth plan specifies that it will only expand into regions where barbecue food is very popular but where the number of barbecue restaurants is very small. Sonny's restaurants must be at least seven miles away from each other. Quaker Oats has used GIS to display and analyze sales and customer data by store locations. This information helps the company determine the best product mix for each retail store that carries Quaker Oats products and design advertising

geographic information system (GIS)

System with software that can analyze and display data using digitized maps to enhance planning and decision-making.

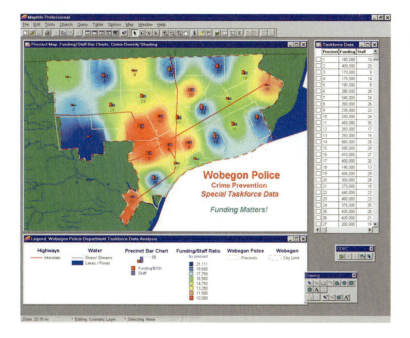

Geographic information system (GIS) software presents and analyzes data geographically, tying data to points, lines, and areas on a map. This map can help decision makers with crime analysis by mapping each incident and relating crime hotspots to distribution of police staff.

360 Part III I Management and Organizational Support Systems for the Digital Firm

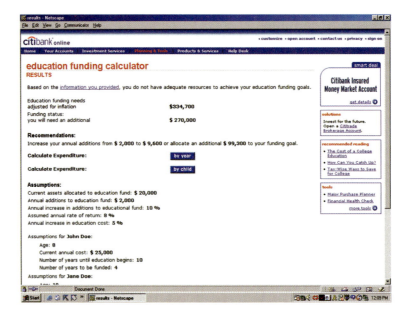

Citibank's Web site features on-line tools to help visitors make decisions about college education funding. DSS based on the Web can provide information from multiple sources and analytical tools to help potential customers select products and services.

campaigns targeted specifically to each store's customers. The chapter ending case study explores GIS in greater detail.

WEB-BASED CUSTOMER DECISION-SUPPORT SYSTEMS

The growth of electronic commerce has encouraged many companies to develop DSS where customers and employees can take advantage of Internet information resources and Web capabilities for interactivity and personalization. DSS based on the Web and the Internet can support decision-making by providing on-line access to various databases and information pools along with software for data analysis. Some of these DSS are targeted toward management, but many have been developed to attract customers by providing information and tools to assist their decision-making as they select products and services. Companies are finding that deciding which products and services to purchase has become increasingly information-intensive. People are now using more information from multiple sources to make purchasing decisions (such as purchasing a car or computer) before they interact with the product or sales staff. **Customer decision-support systems (CDSS)** support the decision-making process of an existing or potential customer.

customer decision-support system (CDSS)

System to support the decision-making process of an existing or potential customer.

People interested in purchasing a product or service can use Internet search engines, intelligent agents, on-line catalogs, Web directories, newsgroup discussions, e-mail, and other tools to help them locate the information they need to help with their decision. Information brokers, such as InsWeb.com, described in Chapter 4, are also sources of summarized, structured information for specific products or industries and may provide models for evaluating the information. Companies also have developed specific customer Web sites where all the information, models, or other analytical tools for evaluating alternatives are concentrated in one location. Web-based DSS have become especially popular in the financial services area because so many people are trying to manage their own assets and retirement savings. Table 11-3 lists some examples.

11.2 GROUP DECISION-SUPPORT SYSTEMS (GDSS)

Early DSS focused largely on supporting individual decision-making. However, because so much work is accomplished through groups within organizations, system developers and scholars began to focus on how computers can support group and organizational decision-making. A new category of systems developed known as group decision-support systems (GDSS).

TABLE 11-3	EXAMPLES OF WEB-BASED DSS
DSS	**Description**
General Electric Plastics	Web site provides a Design Solutions Center with a Web-based suite of on-line engineering tools for materials developers in the plastics industry. Visitors can select plastics materials, perform production costs estimates, search for product-specification information, and take on-line training.
Fidelity Investments	Web site features an on-line, interactive decision-support application to help clients make decisions about investment savings plans and investment portfolio allocations. The application allows visitors to experiment with numerous "what-if" scenarios to design investment savings plans for retirement or a child's college education. If the user enters information about his or her finances, time horizon, and tolerance for risk, the system will suggest appropriate portfolios of mutual funds. The application performs the required number-crunching and displays the changing return on investment as the user alters these assumptions.
Homes.com	Provides a nationwide listing of homes for sale, apartments for rent, and mortgages available. Visitors can find out what mortgages they qualify for and calculate the maximum mortgage they can afford and alternative monthly mortgage payments. They can also use tools to help them determine whether they should rent or buy.

WHAT IS A GDSS?

A **group decision-support system (GDSS)** is an interactive computer-based system to facilitate the solution of unstructured problems by a set of decision makers working together as a group (DeSanctis and Gallupe, 1987).

Groupware and Web-based tools for videoconferencing and electronic meetings described earlier in this text can support some group decision processes, but their focus is primarily on communication. This section focuses on the tools and technologies geared explicitly toward group decision-making. GDSS were developed in response to a growing concern over the quality and effectiveness of meetings. The underlying problems in group decision-making have been the explosion of decision-maker meetings, the growing length of those meetings, and the increased number of attendees. Estimates on the amount of a manager's time spent in meetings range from 35 percent to 70 percent.

Meeting facilitators, organizational development professionals, and information systems scholars have been focusing on this issue and have identified a number of discrete meeting elements that need to be addressed (Grobowski et al., 1990; Kraemer and King, 1988; Nunamaker et al., 1991). Among these elements are the following:

1. *Improved preplanning,* to make meetings more effective and efficient.

2. *Increased participation,* so that all attendees will be able to contribute fully even if the number of attendees is large. Free riding (attending the meeting but not contributing) must also be addressed.

3. *Open, collaborative meeting atmosphere,* in which attendees from various organizational levels feel able to contribute freely. The lower level attendees must be able to participate without fear of being judged by their management; higher status participants must be able to participate without having their presence or ideas dominate the meeting and result in unwanted conformity.

4. *Criticism-free idea generation,* enabling attendees to contribute without undue fear of feeling personally criticized.

5. *Evaluation objectivity,* creating an atmosphere in which an idea will be evaluated on its merits rather than on the basis of the source of the idea.

6. *Idea organization and evaluation,* which require keeping the focus on the meeting objectives, finding efficient ways to organize the many ideas that can be generated in a brainstorming session, and evaluating those ideas not only on their merits but also within appropriate time constraints.

7. *Setting priorities and making decisions,* which require finding ways to encompass the thinking of all the attendees in making these judgments.

group decision-support system (GDSS)
An interactive computer-based system to facilitate the solution to unstructured problems by a set of decision makers working together as a group.

8. *Documentation of meetings,* so that attendees will have as complete and organized a record of the meeting as may be needed to continue the work of the project.

9. *Access to external information,* which will allow significant, factual disagreements to be settled in a timely fashion, thus enabling the meeting to continue and be productive.

10. *Preservation of "organizational memory,"* so that those who do not attend the meeting can also work on the project. Often a project will include teams at different locations who will need to understand the content of a meeting at only one of the affected sites.

One response to the problems of group decision-making has been the adoption of new methods of organizing and running meetings. Techniques such as facilitated meetings, brainstorming, and criticism-free idea generation have become popular and are now accepted as standard. Another response has been the application of technology to the problems resulting in the emergence of group decision-support systems.

CHARACTERISTICS OF GDSS

How can information technology help groups arrive at decisions? Scholars have identified at least three basic elements of a GDSS: hardware, software tools, and people. Hardware refers to the conference facility itself, including the room, the tables, and the chairs. Such a facility must be physically laid out in a manner that supports group collaboration. It also must include some electronic hardware, such as electronic display boards, as well as audiovisual, computer, and networking equipment.

A wide range of *software tools,* including tools for organizing ideas, gathering information, ranking and setting priorities, and other aspects of collaborative work are being used to support decision-making meetings. We describe these tools in the next section. People refer not only to the participants but also to a trained facilitator and often to a staff that supports the hardware and software. Together these elements have led to the creation of a range of different kinds of GDSS, from simple electronic boardrooms to elaborate collaboration laboratories. In a collaboration laboratory, individuals work on their own desktop PCs or workstations. Their input is integrated on a file server and is viewable on a common screen at the front of the room; in most systems the integrated input is also viewable on the individual participant's screen.

GDSS SOFTWARE TOOLS

Some features of groupware tools for collaborative work described in Chapters 6 and 10 can be used to support group decision-making. There also are specific GDSS software tools for supporting group meetings. These tools were originally developed for meetings in which all participants are in the same room, but they also can be used for networked meetings in which participants are in different locations. Specific GDSS software tools include the following:

▮ *Electronic questionnaires* aid the organizers in pre-meeting planning by identifying issues of concern and by helping to ensure that key planning information is not overlooked.

▮ *Electronic brainstorming tools* allow individuals both simultaneously and anonymously, to contribute ideas on the topics of the meeting.

▮ *Idea organizers* facilitate the organized integration and synthesis of ideas generated during brainstorming.

▮ *Questionnaire tools* support the facilitators and group leaders as they gather information before and during the process of setting priorities.

▮ *Tools for voting or setting priorities* make available a range of methods from simple voting, to ranking in order, to a range of weighted techniques for setting priorities or voting (see Figure 11-4).

▮ *Stake holder identification and analysis tools* use structured approaches to evaluate the impact of an emerging proposal on the organization and to identify stakeholders and evaluate the potential impact of those stakeholders on the proposed project.

Figure 11-4 GDSS software tools. The Ventana Corporation's GroupSystems electronic meeting software helps people create, share, record, organize, and evaluate ideas in meetings, between offices, or around the world.

▌ *Policy formation tools* provide structured support for developing agreement on the wording of policy statements.

▌ *Group dictionaries* document group agreement on definitions of words and terms central to the project.

Additional tools are available, such as group outlining and writing tools, software that stores and reads project files, and software that allows the attendees to view internal operational data stored by the organization's production computer systems.

Overview of a GDSS Meeting

An **electronic meeting system (EMS)** is a type of collaborative GDSS that uses information technology to make group meetings more productive by facilitating communication as well as decision-making. It supports any activity in which people come together, whether at the same place at the same time or in different places at different times (Dennis et al., 1988; Nunamaker et al., 1991). IBM has a number of EMSs installed at various sites. Each attendee has a workstation. The workstations are networked and are connected to the facilitator's console, which serves as both the facilitator's workstation and control panel and the meeting's file server. All data that the attendees forward from their workstations to the group are collected and saved on the file server. The facilitator is able to project computer images onto the projection screen at the front center of the room. The facilitator also has an

electronic meeting system (EMS)

A collaborative GDSS that uses information technology to make group meetings more productive by facilitating communication as well as decision-making. Supports meetings at the same place and time or at different places and times.

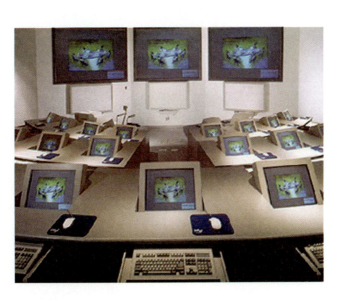

An electronic meeting system provides capabilities for group decision support such as networked workstations, projection screens, whiteboards, and software tools.

overhead projector available. Whiteboards are visible on either side of the projection screen. Many electronic meeting rooms are arranged in a semicircle and are tiered in legislative style to accommodate a large number of attendees.

The facilitator controls the use of tools during the meeting, often selecting from a large toolbox that is part of the organization's GDSS. Tool selection is part of the pre-meeting planning process. Which tools are selected depends on the subject matter, the goals of the meeting, and the facilitation methodology the facilitator will use.

Attendees have full control over their own desktop computers. An attendee is able to view the agenda (and other planning documents), look at the integrated screen (or screens as the session progresses), use ordinary desktop PC tools (such as a word processor or a spreadsheet), tap into production data that have been made available, or work on the screen associated with the current meeting step and tool (such as a brainstorming screen). However, no one can view anyone else's screens so participants' work is confidential until it is released to the file server for integration with the work of others. All input to the file server is anonymous—at each step everyone's input to the file server (brainstorming ideas, idea evaluation and criticism, comments, voting, etc.) can be seen by all attendees on the integrated screens, but no information is available to identify the source of specific inputs. Attendees enter their data simultaneously rather than in round-robin fashion as is done in meetings that have little or no electronic systems support.

Figure 11-5 shows the sequence of activities at a typical EMS meeting. For each activity it also indicates the type of tools used and the output of those tools. During the meeting all input to the integrated screens is saved on the file server. As a result, when the meeting is completed, a full record of the meeting (both raw material and resultant output) is available to the attendees and can be made available to anyone else with a need for access.

HOW GDSS CAN ENHANCE GROUP DECISION-MAKING

GDSS are being used more widely, so we are able to understand some of their benefits and evaluate some of the tools. We look again at how a GDSS affects the 10 group meeting issues raised earlier.

1. *Improved preplanning.* Electronic questionnaires, supplemented by word processors, outlining software, and other desktop PC software, can structure planning, thereby improving it. The availability of the planning information at the actual meeting can

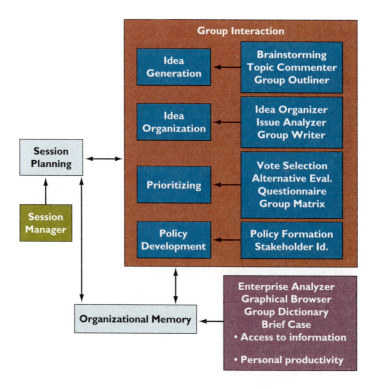

Figure 11-5 Group system tools. The sequence of activities and collaborative support tools used in an electronic meeting system (EMS) facilitates communication among attendees and generates a full record of the meeting.
Source: From Nunamaker et al., "Electronic Meeting Systems to Support Group Work" in *Communications of the ACM,* July 1991. Reprinted by permission.

also serve to enhance the quality of the meeting. Experts seem to feel that these tools add significance and emphasis to meeting preplanning.

2. *Increased participation.* Studies show that in traditional decision-making meetings without GDSS support the optimal meeting size is three to five attendees. Beyond that size, the meeting process begins to break down. Using GDSS software, studies show the meeting size can increase while productivity also increases. One reason for this is that attendees contribute simultaneously rather than one at a time, which makes more efficient use of the meeting time. Interviews of GDSS meeting attendees indicate that the quality of participation is higher than in traditional meetings.

3. *Open, collaborative meeting atmosphere.* A GDSS contributes to a more collaborative atmosphere in several ways. First, anonymity of input is essentially guaranteed. Individuals need not be afraid of being judged by their boss for contributing a possibly offbeat idea. Second, anonymity reduces or eliminates the deadening effect that often occurs when high-status individuals contribute. And third, the numbing pressures of social cues are reduced or eliminated.

4. *Criticism-free idea generation.* Anonymity ensures that attendees can contribute without fear of personally being criticized or of having their ideas rejected because of the identity of the contributor. Several studies show that interactive GDSS meetings generate more ideas and more satisfaction with those ideas than verbally interactive meetings (Nunamaker et al., 1991). GDSS can help reduce unproductive interpersonal conflict (Miranda and Bostrum, 1993–1994).

5. *Evaluation objectivity.* Anonymity prevents criticism of the source of ideas, thus supporting an atmosphere in which attendees focus on evaluating the ideas themselves. The same anonymity allows participants to detach from their own ideas so they are able to view them from a critical perspective. Evidence suggests that evaluation in an anonymous atmosphere increases the free flow of critical feedback and even stimulates the generation of new ideas during the evaluation process.

6. *Idea organization and evaluation.* GDSS software tools used for this purpose are structured and are based on methodology. They usually allow individuals to organize and then submit their results to the group (still anonymously). The group then iteratively modifies and develops the organized ideas until a document is completed. Attendees generally have viewed this approach as productive.

7. *Setting priorities and making decisions.* Anonymity helps lower level participants have their positions taken into consideration along with the higher level attendees.

8. *Documentation of meetings.* Evidence at IBM indicates that postmeeting use of the data is crucial. Attendees use the data to continue their dialogues after the meetings, to discuss the ideas with those who did not attend, and even to make presentations (Grobowski et al., 1990). Some tools enable the user to zoom in to more details on specific information.

9. *Access to external information.* Often a great deal of meeting time is devoted to factual disagreements. More experience with GDSS will indicate whether GDSS technology reduces this problem.

10. *Preservation of "organizational memory."* Specific tools have been developed to facilitate access to the data generated during a GDSS meeting, allowing non-attendees to locate needed information after the meeting. The documentation of a meeting by one group at one site has also successfully been used as input to another meeting on the same project at another site. GDSS could be further enhanced to integrate meeting memory with other organizational memory and supply this information to other parts of the organization (Schwabe, 1999).

If properly designed and supported, GDSS meetings can increase the number of ideas generated and the quality of decisions while producing the desired results in fewer meetings. However, their outcomes are not necessarily better than face-to-face meetings. GDSS seem most useful for tasks involving idea generation, complex problems, and large groups (Fjermestad and Hiltz, 2000–2001; 1998–1999). One problem with understanding the value of GDSS is their complexity. A GDSS can be configured in an almost infinite variety of ways. The effectiveness of the tools will partially depend upon the facilitator's effectiveness, the quality of the planning, the cooperation of the attendees, and the appropriateness of tools selected for different types of meetings and decision problems (Dennis, Wixom, and Vandenberg, 2001). GDSS can enable groups to exchange more information, but can't always help participants process the information effectively or reach better decisions (Dennis, 1996).

Researchers have noted that the design of an electronic meeting system and its technology is only one of a number of contingencies that affect the outcome of group meetings. Other factors, including the composition of the group, the task, the manner in which the problem is presented to the group, and the organizational context (including the organization's culture and environment) also affect the process of group meetings and meeting outcomes (Dennis and Wixom, 2001–2002; Hilmer and Dennis, 2000–2001; Dennis et al., 1999; Fjermestad, 1998).

11.3 Executive Support in the Enterprise

We have described how DSS and GDSS help managers make unstructured and semistructured decisions. **Executive support systems (ESS)** also help managers with unstructured problems, focusing on the information needs of senior management. Combining data from internal and external sources, ESS create a generalized computing and communications environment that can be focused and applied to a changing array of problems. ESS help senior executives monitor organizational performance, track activities of competitors, spot problems, identify opportunities, and forecast trends.

The Role of Executive Support Systems in the Organization

Before ESS, it was common for executives to receive numerous fixed-format reports, often hundreds of pages every month (or even every week). Today, an ESS can bring together data from all parts of the organization and allow managers to select, access, and tailor them as needed using easy-to-use desktop analytical tools and on-line data displays. Use of the systems has migrated down several organizational levels so that the executive and any designated subordinates are able to look at the same data in the same way.

Today's systems try to avoid the problem of data overload so common in paper reports because the data can be filtered or viewed in graphic format (if the user so chooses). ESS systems have the ability to **drill down,** moving from a piece of summary data to lower and lower levels of detail. The ability to drill down is useful not only to senior executives but to employees at lower levels of the organization who need to analyze data. OLAP tools for analyzing large databases provide this capability.

A major challenge of building executive support systems has been to integrate data from systems designed for very different purposes so that senior executives can review organizational performance from a firm-wide perspective. Often data critical to the senior executive had been unavailable. For example, sales data coming from an order-entry transaction processing system might not be linked to marketing information, a linkage the executive would find useful. In the traditional firm, which typically had hundreds or even thousands of incompatible systems, pulling such information together and making sense out of it was a major task. When the information was assembled, it was likely to be out of date, incomplete and inaccurate. Making decisions under these conditions was like a dart game with the bulls-eye swinging on a pendulum. Today, properly configured and implemented enterprise systems can provide managers with timely, comprehensive, and accurate firm-wide information. Executive support systems based on such data can be considered logical extensions of enterprise system functionality.

External data, including data from the Web, now are more easily available in many ESS as well. Executives need a wide range of external data from current stock market news to competitor information, industry trends, and even projected legislative action. Through

executive support system (ESS)

Information system at the strategic level of an organization designed to address unstructured decision-making through advanced graphics and communications.

drill down

The ability to move from summary data to lower and lower levels of detail.

their ESS, many managers have access to news services, financial market databases, economic information, and whatever other public data they may require.

Contemporary ESS include tools for modeling and analysis. With only a minimum of experience, most managers find they can use these tools to create graphic comparisons of data by time, region, product, price range, and so on. (Whereas DSS use such tools primarily for modeling and analysis in a fairly narrow range of decision situations, ESS use them primarily to provide status information about organizational performance.)

Developing ESS

ESS are executive systems, and must be designed so that high-level managers and others can use them without much training. One area that merits special attention is the determination of executive information requirements. ESS needs to have some facility for environmental scanning. A key information requirement of managers at the strategic level is the capability to detect signals of problems in the organizational environment that indicate strategic threats and opportunities (Walls et al., 1992). The ESS needs to be designed so that both external and internal sources of information can be used for environmental scanning purposes.

ESS potentially could give top executives the capability of examining other managers' work without their knowledge, so there may be some resistance to ESS at lower levels of the organization. Implementation of ESS should be carefully managed to neutralize such opposition (see Chapter 13).

Cost justification presents a different type of problem with an ESS. Because much of an executive's work is unstructured, how does one quantify benefits for a system that primarily supports such unstructured work? An ESS often is justified in advance by the intuitive feeling that it will pay for itself (Watson et al., 1991). If ESS benefits can ever be quantified, it is only after the system is operational.

BENEFITS OF EXECUTIVE SUPPORT SYSTEMS

Much of the value of ESS is found in their flexibility. These systems put data and tools in the hands of executives without addressing specific problems or imposing solutions. Executives are free to shape the problems as necessary, using the system as an extension of their own thinking processes. These are not decision-making systems; they are tools to aid executives in making decisions.

The most visible benefit of ESS is their ability to analyze, compare, and highlight trends. The easy use of graphics allows the user to look at more data in less time with greater clarity and insight than paper-based systems can provide. In the past, executives obtained the same information by taking up days and weeks of their staffs' valuable time. By using ESS, those staffs and the executives themselves are freed up for the more creative analysis and decision-making in their jobs. ESS capabilities for drilling down and highlighting trends also may enhance the quality of such analysis and can speed up decision-making (Leidner and Elam, 1993–1994).

Executives are using ESS to monitor performance more successfully in their own areas of responsibility. Some companies are using these systems to monitor key performance indicators for the entire firm and to measure firm performance against changes in the external environment (see the Window on Management). The timeliness and availability of the data result in needed actions being identified and taken earlier. Problems can be handled before they become too damaging; opportunities can also be identified earlier. These systems can thus help organizations move toward a "sense and respond" strategy.

A well-designed ESS could dramatically improve management performance and increase upper management's span of control. Immediate access to so much data allows executives to better monitor activities of lower units reporting to them. That very monitoring ability could allow decision-making to be decentralized and to take place at lower operating levels. Executives are often willing to push decision-making further down into the organization as long as they can be assured that all is going well. Alternatively, executive support systems based on enterprise-wide data could potentially increase management centralization, enabling senior executives to monitor the performance of subordinates across the company and direct them to take appropriate action when conditions change.

DIGITAL DASHBOARDS HELP UNION PACIFIC MANAGE

The Union Pacific Railroad is the largest railroad company in the United States, operating 33,500 miles of railroad track for hauling coal, automobiles, and other commodities across the country. It is a data-driven business, generating 10 gigabytes of track maintenance data daily as 4000 workers monitor and manage track upkeep and input data from hand and visual tests. All of these data were maintained on many different information systems using 25 different databases running on Oracle, IBM DB2, Teradata, Microsoft Access, and Microsoft SQL Server database software and Sun, IBM, Hewlett-Packard, and NCR computers.

Management could not easily access and analyze the data in its systems across the company to see where the railroad would best benefit from spending money and performing maintenance. It had created a multi-terabyte data warehouse for the data, but needed to use professional programmers to write queries to obtain the data needed by managers and field workers. Then in May of 2000, Union Pacific installed business intelligence software from nQuire Software Inc. in Minnetonka, Minnesota. This software was used to create a Web-based system that enables managers and workers to create their own personalized "digital dashboards" of critical information and access this information using Web browser software over a corporate intranet.

NQuire brought together data from 45 different sources to provide Union Pacific users with different views of real-time company-wide track condition data based on each individual's business information needs. Queries from both managers and workers can be answered in numerous ways to help them make better business decisions and plan projects.

There are many different ways in which reports can be "sliced and diced." For example, if managers want to take a snapshot of the railroad in Union Pacific's southern region, they can query the system, create a list of worst and best areas of track, and generate data that can be used for planning maintenance programs and deploying resources. If managers need to find the sections of rail with the most "curve wear" and "head wear" deterioration, nQuire can search company databases and come up with a list based on different criteria, such as the degree of curve in the tracks, rail location, when the rail was laid, or vertical wear of the tracks.

While the nQuire system was first used by 600 managers and workers, it has been extended to over 4000 Union Pacific employees. The company hopes it will eventually be used by its entire 65,000-person work force. Employees can access the information they need without paying information systems specialists to write special queries and reports. Union Pacific claims its investment in this system is paying off by enabling it to better manage its stock and replacement track.

To Think About: How did implementing the digital dashboard system benefit Union Pacific managers and employees? What are the benefits to the organization as a whole? What management, organization, and technology issues did Union Pacific have to consider when implementing its digital dashboard system?

Sources: David Aponovich, "Case Study: Union Pacific Keeps Data on Track," *Datamation,* July 2, 2001 and David Lewis, "Union Pacific Plans Major Analytics Rollout," *Internet Week,* February 26, 2001.

EXECUTIVE SUPPORT SYSTEMS AND THE DIGITAL FIRM

To illustrate the different ways in which an ESS can enhance management decision-making, we now describe important types of ESS applications for gathering business intelligence and monitoring corporate performance, including ESS based on enterprise systems.

ESS for Business Intelligence

Today, customer expectations, Internet technology, and new business models can alter the competitive landscape so rapidly that managers need special capabilities for competitive intelligence-gathering. ESS can help managers identify changing market conditions, formulate responses, track implementation efforts, and learn from feedback.

BP Sony NV, the Netherlands branch of the multinational electronics giant, wanted more insight from the marketplace to drive its competitive strategy. Until recently, its management reports were based primarily on financial and administrative data that took at least 24 hours to generate. Management wanted to be able to make meaningful decisions based on marketing and sales data as well so it could respond quickly to marketplace changes.

Sony Netherlands constructed a data warehouse and Executive Information System for this purpose.

The system is now available to 78 users in management, marketing, and sales. They can use the system to help them define strategies, search for opportunities, identify problems, and substantiate actions. Using a drill-down function, they can examine the underlying numbers behind the total result. For instance, while senior management can obtain sales results by business unit or product group, a marketing manager can use the system to look only at the group of products he or she was responsible for. The manager can produce a report to indicate exactly which products are strong or weak performers or to rank dealers by performance. The system is flexible, easy to use, and can provide much of this information to the user on-line (Information Builders, 2000).

Cookson Electronics of Foxborough, Massachusetts, a supplier of materials used in printed circuit boards and semiconductor packaging, has 14 divisions around the world. Each is responsible for a different point in the electronics life cycle, providing parts for computers, cell phones, and other consumer electronics. The semiconductor field has highly cyclical fluctuations in business and Cookson divisions responsible for this part of the business can help the entire firm predict demand by anticipating industry cycles. Working with senior managers, Cookson's senior intelligence officer Yann Morvan developed a list of key intelligence topics (KITs) linked to strategic decisions. For example, a KIT might cover the firm's top five competitors, suppliers, customers, or technologies.

The Cookson Electronic Business Intelligence System (CEBIS), based on Lotus Notes, enables Cookson's 6000 worldwide employees to access and contribute competitive intelligence information, such as competitor strategic alliances or geographic extensions or significant investments in research and development. Senior managers can use CEBIS to subscribe to the latest information on a specific KIT and receive news and analysis via e-mail or fax. Cookson expects the information from CEBIS will help managers counter threats and anticipate changes (Shand, 2000).

Monitoring Corporate Performance: Balanced Scorecard Systems

Companies have traditionally measured value using financial metrics such as return on investment (ROI), which we describe in Chapter 13. Many firms are now implementing a **balanced scorecard** model which supplements traditional financial measures with measurements from additional perspectives, such as customers, internal business processes, and learning and growth. Managers can use balanced scorecard systems to see how well the firm is meeting its strategic goals. The goals and measures for the balanced scorecard vary from company to company. Companies are setting up information systems to populate the scorecard for management.

Aurora Consolidated Laboratories, a division of Aurora Health Care, is Wisconsin's largest private employer, with 13 hospitals, dozens of clinics and health centers, and 3500 physicians reporting through over 100 cost centers. In addition to monitoring costs closely, management wanted to measure customer satisfaction, the efficiency of Aurora's lab processes, satisfaction of key partners and suppliers, and employee motivation and productivity. The company implemented a Web-based reporting and communications system based on WebFOCUS from Information Builders Inc. which uses data from more than 35 databases consolidated in a data warehouse to give managers a scorecard on how well they are progressing. The system provides up-to-date data on corporate performance, graphs and charts to spot trends and anomalies, and the capability to drill down to see detailed data behind the trends. Users can save reports from the system as HTML files for later viewing with their Web browsers. The system was initially available to 25 users, including senior managers, vice presidents, and selected supervisors but is being gradually opened to other managers (Information Builders, 2000).

Amsterdam-based ING Bank, which is part of the ING Group global financial services firm, adopted a balanced scorecard approach when it reorganized. Management wanted to shift from a product to a client orientation and develop appropriate performance indicators to measure progress in this new direction. In 1997 the bank built a Web-based balanced scorecard application using SAS tools for data warehousing and statistical analysis to measure

balanced scorecard
Model for analyzing firm performance which supplements traditional financial measures with measurements from additional business perspectives, such as customers, internal business processes, and learning and growth.

| TABLE 11-4 | STRATEGIC PERFORMANCE MANAGEMENT TOOLS FOR ENTERPRISE SYSTEMS |

Enterprise System Vendor	Description
SAP	Web-enabled mySAP.com™ Strategic Enterprise Management™ module provides reports giving managers a comprehensive view of firm performance. Features corporate performance metrics, simulation, and planning tools. Managers can model and communicate key performance indicators for a Balanced Scorecard. Another measurement tool called the Management Cockpit can be used to monitor strategic performance indicators using internal and external benchmarks.
PeopleSoft	Web-enabled Enterprise Performance Management (EPM) features modules for workforce analytics, customer relationship analytics, financial analytics, supply chain analytics, and profitability management for financial services. The Financial Analytics module supports Activity-Based Management and the Balanced Scorecard.
Oracle	Strategic Enterprise Management includes support for the Balanced Scorecard, activity-based management, and budgeting. A value-based management module under development will help companies develop and apply new accounting methods for quantifying intellectual capital.

progress with 21 indicators. Data to fill out the scorecard, from sources such as financial ledger applications and client retention and market penetration ratios feed a central data warehouse. The data come from systems running on Lotus Notes, Microsoft Excel spreadsheets, and Oracle and DB2 databases. The data warehouse and balanced scorecard software run on IBM RS/6000 servers. ING initially made the balanced scorecard system available only to midrange executives in sales, but later extended it to 3000 users, including people at nearly every level of its relationship management group. Users regularly check progress with the scorecard. For example, by comparing how many visits they have made to different clients, sales people can make better decisions about how to allocate their time (McCune, 2000).

Enterprise Wide Reporting and Analysis

Enterprise system vendors are now providing capabilities to extend the usefulness of data captured in operational systems to give management a picture of the overall performance of the firm. Some provide reporting of metrics for balanced scorecard analysis as well as more traditional financial and operating metrics. Table 11-4 describes strategic performance management tools for each of the major enterprise system vendors.

Companies can use these new enterprise reporting capabilities to create measures of firm performance that were not previously available. The head of Strategic Planning at Dow Chemical led a cross-functional steering team to develop a set of measures and reports based on data from the company's SAP enterprise system. Process experts in different areas of the company defined reporting categories such as expense management, inventory management, and sales. Dow then developed a data mart for each type of data, amounting to over twenty data marts. The data marts are integrated so that the numbers for the "business results" mart balance with numbers in the expenses and sales marts. Dow also implemented a new set of performance measures based on shareholder value and activity-based costing. **Activity-based costing** is a budgeting and analysis model that identifies all the resources, processes, and costs, including overhead and operating expenses, required to produce a specific product or service. It focuses on determining firm activities that cause costs to occur rather than on merely tracking what has been spent. It allows managers to see which products or services are profitable or losing money so they can determine the changes required to maximize firm profitability. Instead of reporting in terms of product and income, the system can focus on contribution margins and customer accounts, with the ability to calculate the current and lifetime value of each account. The system is used by over 5000 people, ranging from Dow's CEO to plant floor workers. (Davenport, 2000).

activity-based costing
Model for identifying all the company activities that cause costs to occur while producing a specific product or service so that managers can see which products or services are profitable or losing money and make changes to maximize firm profitability.

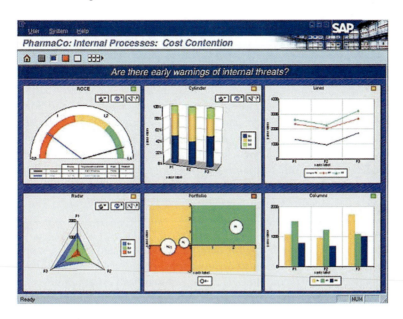

The Management Cockpit is an ergonomic concept for structuring and visualizing firm performance indicators using easy-to-understand displays. This display is based on SAP's Strategic Enterprise Management module, which uses Web technology to provide management with a comprehensive view of firm performance.

Management of Nissan Motor Company of Australia must oversee the activities of 550 people in 23 sites across the Australian continent. The company is primarily involved in Nissan's import and distribution activities for 35,000 automobiles each year. Like other automotive companies, Nissan Australia has extensive reporting requirements, including detailed controlling reports for financial accounts and monthly accounts. Managers need detailed

MAKE **IT** YOUR BUSINESS

FINANCE AND ACCOUNTING

The finance and accounting function is replete with DSS and ESS applications. Many DSS are based on financial models for breakeven analysis, profitability analysis, capital budgeting, and financial forecasting. Retail financial service firms depend on model-based DSS for client portfolio analysis and investment recommendations. ESS often provide overviews of firmwide financial performance, including activity-based costing and financial measures for balanced scorecard reporting. Reporting monthly or yearly cash flows and balances is a typical MIS for the finance and accounting function. You can find examples of finance and accounting applications on pages 359 and 369–370.

HUMAN RESOURCES

The human resources function uses model-based decision support systems for analysis of labor contract costs or alternative compensation plans for non-union employees. Executive information systems are used for human resources planning to project the firm's long-term labor force requirements. Comparing employee salaries to budgeted compensation amounts is a typical MIS for human resources.

MANUFACTURING AND PRODUCTION

The manufacturing and production function requires many decisions about the optimization of production, logistics, and maintenance that must evaluate many interrelated variables. Model-based DSS have been guiding decisions about supply chain management, including the development of optimal production plans, delivery schedules, and

inventory allocations. Recommending optimal plans for dispatching and routing vehicles and for facilities management are popular GIS applications. ESS can provide overviews of the firm's production resources. Comparing actual production amounts to targeted amounts for a monthly or yearly period is a typical MIS for manufacturing and production. You can find examples of manufacturing and production applications on pages 348–349, 355–357, 368–369, and 375–377.

SALES AND MARKETING

DSS applications abound in sales and marketing. Model driven DSS support decisions about product pricing, sales forecasting, and advertising and promotional campaigns. Companies increasingly use data-driven DSS for customer relationship management (CRM) to analyze customer purchasing patterns, detect customer retention problems, identify profitable customers, and develop targeted marketing campaigns. Some of these DSS for CRM combine customer data from Web transactions with customer transaction data from off-line sources. Many Web-based DSS provide access to information and products to influence customer purchasing decisions. ESS can be used for competitor analysis and identification of opportunities for new products or sales channels. GIS can analyze sales patterns and market data by location, supporting decisions on where to locate retail outlets or target marketing campaigns. Listing the best and worst-performing sales territories for a monthly or yearly period is a typical MIS for sales and marketing. You can find examples of sales and marketing applications on pages 356–358, 360–361, 369, and 375–377.

reports down to the model level, with controlling reports for each department. When Nissan used an old legacy mainframe system, it would take up to two weeks to create and distribute reports to the company's board of directors.

In 1997, Nissan Australia installed SAP's R/3 enterprise software, serving as a pilot for the rest of the Nissan organization. The company also installed Information Builders' SNAPpack Power Reporter to create custom reports with a Web interface and powerful drill-down capabilities that did not require extensive programming to produce. These reports can be generated immediately and include profit-and-loss reports, gross margin analysis, balance sheets, and wholesale and retail vehicles. Management requests for more profit analysis reports by model, state, and other variables can be easily satisfied (Information Builders, 2000).

MANAGEMENT WRAP-UP

Management is responsible for determining where management support systems can make their greatest contribution to organizational performance and for allocating the resources to build them. Management needs to work closely with system builders to make sure that these systems effectively capture the right set of information requirements and decision processes for guiding the firm.

Management support systems can improve organizational performance by speeding up decision-making or improving the quality of management decisions. However, some of these decision processes may not be clearly understood. A management support system will be most effective when system builders have a clear idea of its objectives, the nature of the decisions to be supported, and how the system will actually support decision-making.

Systems to support management decision-making can be developed with a range of technologies, including the use of large databases, modeling tools, graphics tools, datamining and analysis tools, and electronic meeting technology. Identifying the right technology for the decision or decision process to be supported is a key technology decision.

For Discussion
1. As a manager or user of information systems, what would you need to know to participate in the design and use of a DSS or an ESS? Why?
2. If businesses used DSS, GDSS, and ESS more widely, would they make better decisions? Explain.

SUMMARY

1. *How can information systems help individual managers make better decisions when the problems are non-routine and constantly changing?* A special category of systems called decision-support systems (DSS) combines data, sophisticated analytical models and tools, and user-friendly software into a single powerful system that can support semistructured or unstructured decision-making. There are two kinds of DSS: model-driven DSS and data-driven DSS. A DSS provides results of model-based or data-driven analysis that help managers design and evaluate alternatives and monitor the progress of the solution that was adopted. DSS can help support decisions for supply chain management and customer analysis as well as model alternative business scenarios. DSS targeted toward customers as well as managers are becoming available on the Web. A special category of DSS called geographic information systems (GIS) can analyze and display data for planning and decision-making using digitized maps. The components of a DSS are the DSS database, the DSS software system, and the user interface. The DSS database is a collection of current or historical data from a number of applications or groups that can be used for analysis. The data can come from both internal and external sources including enterprise systems and the Web. The DSS software system consists of OLAP and datamining tools or mathematical and analytical models that are used for analyzing the data in the database. The user interface allows users to interact with the DSS software tools directly.

2. *How can information systems help people working in a group make decisions more efficiently?* People working together in a group can use group decision-support systems to help them in the process of arriving at a decision. A group decision-support system (GDSS) is an interactive computer-based system to facilitate the solution of unstructured problems by a set of decision makers working together as a group rather than individually. Group decision-support systems (GDSS) have hardware, software, and people components. Hardware components consist of the conference room facilities, including seating arrangements and computer and other electronic hardware. Software components include tools for organizing ideas, gathering information, ranking and setting priorities, and documenting meeting sessions. People components include participants, a trained facilitator, and staff to support the hardware and software.

A GDSS helps decision makers meeting together to arrive at a decision more efficiently and is especially useful for increasing the productivity of meetings larger than four or five people. However, the effectiveness of GDSS is contingent on the composition of the group, the task, appropriate tool selection and meeting support, and the organizational context of the meeting.

3. *Are there any special systems that can facilitate decision-making among senior managers? Exactly what can these systems do to help high-level management?* Executive support systems help senior managers with unstructured problems that occur at the strategic level of the organization. ESS provide data from both internal and external sources and provide a generalized computing and communications environment that can be focused and applied to a changing array of problems. ESS helps senior executives monitor firm performance, spot problems, identify opportunities, and forecast trends. These systems can filter out extraneous details for high-level overviews, or they can drill down to provide senior managers with detailed transaction data if required. ESS are starting to take advantage of firm-wide data provided by enterprise systems. ESS help senior managers analyze, compare, and highlight trends so that they may more easily monitor organizational performance or identify strategic problems and opportunities. They are very useful for environmental scanning, providing business intelligence to help management detect signals of strategic threats or opportunities from the organization's environment. ESS can increase the span of control of senior management, allowing them to oversee more people with fewer resources.

4. *What benefits can systems to support management decision-making provide for the organization as a whole?* DSS, GDSS, and ESS are starting to take advantage of more accurate firm-wide data provided by enterprise systems and the new information technology infrastructure to support very fine-grained decisions for guiding the firm, coordinating work activities across the enterprise, and responding rapidly to changing markets and customers. DSS can be used to guide company-wide decisions in supply chain management, customer relationship management, and planning business scenarios. ESS can be used to monitor company-wide performance using both traditional financial metrics and the balanced scorecard model. The ability to explore the outcomes of alternative organizational scenarios, use precise firm-wide information, and provide tools to facilitate group decision processes can help managers make decisions that help the firm achieve its strategic objectives.

KEY TERMS

Activity-based costing, 370	Decision-support system (DSS), 350	Electronic meeting system (EMS), 363	Group decision-support system (GDSS), 361
Balanced scorecard, 369	Drill down, 366	Executive support system (ESS), 366	Model, 353
Customer decision-support system (CDSS), 360	DSS database, 353	Geographic information system (GIS), 359	Model-driven DSS, 352
Data-driven DSS, 352	DSS software system, 353		Sensitivity analysis, 354

REVIEW QUESTIONS

1. What is a decision-support system (DSS)? How does it differ from a management information system (MIS)?

2. How can a DSS support unstructured or semistructured decision-making?

3. What is the difference between a data-driven DSS and a model-driven DSS? Give examples.

4. What are the three basic components of a DSS? Briefly describe each.

5. How can DSS help firms with supply chain management and customer relationship management?

6. What is a geographic information system (GIS)? How can it support decision-making?

7. What is a customer decision-support system? How can the Internet be used for this purpose?

8. What is a group decision-support system (GDSS)? How does it differ from a DSS?

9. What are the underlying problems in group decision-making that have led to the development of GDSS?

10. Describe the three elements of a GDSS.

11. Name and describe five GDSS software tools.

12. What is an electronic meeting system (EMS)? Describe its capabilities.

13. For each of the underlying problems in group decision-making referred to in question 9, describe one or two ways GDSS can contribute to a solution.

14. Define and describe the capabilities of an executive support system (ESS).

15. How can the Internet and enterprise systems provide capabilities for executive support systems?

16. What are the benefits of ESS? How do these systems enhance managerial decision-making?

APPLICATION SOFTWARE EXERCISE

SPREADSHEET EXERCISE: PERFORMING BREAKEVEN ANALYSIS AND SENSITIVITY ANALYSIS

Selmore Collectible Toy Company (SCTC) makes toy sets consisting of collectible trucks, vans, and cars for the retail market. The firm is developing a new toy set that includes a battery-powered tractor trailer, complete with cab and trailer, sports car, and motorcycle. Each set sells for $100. Table 1 shows the major components of SCTC's annual fixed costs for a toy set. Each component includes the cost of purchases, depreciation, and operating expenses. Table 2 shows the major components of SCTC's variable costs per unit.

TABLE 1

SCTC FIXED COSTS

Category	Amount
Land	$42,500
Buildings	$332,500
Manufacturing machinery	$532,000
Office equipment	$212,800
Utilities	$30,500
Insurance	$99,700
Total	**$1,250,000**

TABLE 2

SCTC VARIABLE COSTS

	Current Plant
Labor	$15.00
Advertising	$1.00
Shipping & Receiving	$5.00
Total	**$21.00**

Prepare a spreadsheet to support the decision-making needs of SCTC's managers. The spreadsheet should show the fixed costs, variable costs per unit, the contribution margin, and the breakeven point for this new product. How many sets does SCTC have to sell before it can start turning a profit? Include a data table to show alternative breakeven points, assuming variations in insurance costs and labor costs. How would increasing the sale price to $125 affect the breakeven point? The Laudon Web site for Chapter 11 provides more detail on the range of costs to include in your sensitivity analysis and on the calculations required for a simple breakeven analysis.

GROUP PROJECT

With three or four of your classmates, identify several groups in your university that could benefit from a GDSS. Design a GDSS for one of those groups, describing its hardware, software, and people elements. If possible, use electronic presentation software to present your findings to the class.

TOOLS FOR INTERACTIVE LEARNING

■ **INTERNET CONNECTION**

The Internet Connection for this chapter will take you to a series of Web sites where you can complete an exercise using Web-based DSS. You can also use the Interactive Study Guide to test your knowledge of the topics in this chapter and get instant feedback where you need more practice.

■ **ELECTRONIC COMMERCE PROJECT**

At the Laudon Web site for Chapter 11, you will find an Electronic Commerce project that will use the interactive software at the Fidelity Investments Web site for investment portfolio analysis.

■ **CD-ROM**

If you use the Multimedia Edition CD-ROM with this chapter, you can find a video clip illustrating the use of Intel video-conferencing technology, an audio overview of the major themes of this chapter, and bullet text summarizing the key points of the chapter.

CASE STUDY—*BC Hydro Systems Electrify the Utilities Field*

Canada's third-largest electricity utility, BC Hydro, serves more than 1.6 million customers and is connected to 94 percent of British Columbia's population. British Columbia is a geographically large province in Western Canada, and BC Hydro has over 72,000 kilometers of transmission and distribution lines. Its power is overwhelmingly hydro-electric, and so it has 61 dams and 32 hydroelectric power stations. It has an outstanding record of 99.97 percent reliability. The average time for it to repair an outage is two hours, despite the enormous geographic challenges faced by the province due to its size and the many large mountains including both the Coast Mountains and the Canadian Rockies.

BC Hydro is part of a large grid that extends from western Canada, through the western United States and into Northern Mexico. This grid connects to others that altogether cover all of North America. A failure in one grid has the potential of cutting off power throughout the whole grid, which happened one evening in 1967 when all of northeast United States was blacked out.

Electric utilities traditionally have faced many challenges. The company must have not only the ability to generate the electricity, but also the means to transmit it to customers. Transmission involves complex issues including access rights to properties; vegetation maintenance; environmental protection; and management of the hydroelectric reservoir, which in turn involved such problems as downstream flood inundation. The company must know the location of every customer and of each outage, and it must be able to correct every one quickly. Similar problems exist for companies with major distribution requirements, such as gas and water distribution, telephone companies, and transportation facilities such as roads and railway tracks. Traditionally all aspects of these services require mapping, and prior to the use of computers, all mapping was done on paper by hand. Any changes required redrawing the map with the new details. Use of a specific map by more than one person (or more than one site) meant very slow addressing of the issues. Maps had to be passed around, copied, or even ignored. Similar problems existed when designing a facility.

Automated mapping for facilities management began in the 1970s with the development of geographic information systems (GIS). Originally GIS were used only to draw maps and record locations of assets and then of customers. In time such systems began to be used for basic modeling of real-world networks. However, BC Hydro systems were developed within specific departments and no company-wide system existed. Nor did different stations or departments share their data. Some departments continued to rely on paper maps and so hired consultants who used GIS to draw and print paper maps—computers were only easy-to-use printing devices.

In the early 1990s BC Hydro began using more sophisticated geospatial information technology (GIT). Geospatial information is based upon spatial data, which is data with location, including using lines, points, and areas. 80 percent of utility assets work is geospatial—that is, it is related to a position either on a map or in actual space. GIT systems store everything about a company's assets starting with its location. They contain rules of connectivity between assets, so that, for example, they will indicate when low and high voltage cables will be carried on the same towers or when a project includes plans to connect them (GIT rules will forbid such a mistake). The two- and three-dimensional models show land features, structures, and conductors. The software enables the use of computer drawings rather than paper drawings with all the benefits (faster, easier to modify, can be used by many people simultaneously, saves the company money, etc.).

Geospatial software enables users to store, relate, manipulate and analyze spatial data. For example it is used to locate a gas leak, and to plan and develop a new highway or new telecommunication cables. Users can query the data using a wide variety of query predicates, such as on, near, inside, touches, connected to, and adjacent. They can ask such questions as:

- Which buildings will be affected if I release . . . . . gallons of water per minute through the dam over the normal maximum allowed?
- Which customers are affected if I bypass this cable to make repairs?
- What is the shortest way to connect A with B?
- What are the problems if I do connect A and B?
- Where does my signal become so weak that I need to install a booster?

Using the software one can display and analyze the connectivity of the real world objects stored in its database. For example it can show who is affected if a coaxial cable is damaged or new electric lines are going to be laid. The software offers more efficient and effective planning, design, construction, operation, and maintenance, while customers are more satisfied.

In the 1990s BC Hydro developed many computer programs itself as well as using software from a number of companies, including GE Smallworld, headquartered in Cambridge, England. GE Smallworld produces software that is used in 40 countries by utility and communication companies. GE Smallworld uses an open architecture which enables its programs to communicate with other software such as the corporate systems BC Hydro has developed. Smallworld claims that its software models "real world assets and services, allowing organizations to understand where their facilities and customers are located, how they connect to one another, and provides for the seamless integration of the information across the enterprise."

The Smallworld software stores location information of BC Hydro customers, assets and other locations affected by the company's activities. BC Hydro uses its asset records to understand where its customers are as well as the location of its own facilities in relation to its customers and the location of facilities of others directly affected by its activities. Its systems automate the storage and easy retrieval of the current state of recorded properties. For example when an installation or repair job is finished, someone working on the job marks it as completed and all related records are automatically updated. This eliminates the need to make changes to the property, project or process more than once. Modeling is also central to the use of GIT software because BC Hydro reports that it improves their decision-making and then speeds up the execution of those decisions.

One important use of the geographic software is for corridor management. Many companies must develop, lay and service corridors for electric or cable wires and water or oil pipes. Corridor installation issues for BC Hydro include transmission and access rights-of-way, property issues, corridor maintenance,

line clearances, environmental protection, and hydroelectric reservoir management, involving such problems as downstream flood inundation. BC Hydro developed a suite of applications called PowerGrid for each of these areas. It claims that PowerGrid saves the company lots of money when it uses older two-dimensional GIS data, but the savings are even greater when the model is three-dimensional. As a result it is making three-dimensional data available for many more applications, and it is also making three-D data available on laptops for use in the field.

The software can also search geographic data to locate possible encroachments by BC Hydro on land belonging to others or by others onto land owned by BC Hydro. This enables BC Hydro to locate the worst-case possibilities when planning for needed clearances, corridors or installations. The system also is used to catalogue the vegetation, by their variety, in a corridor where some specific action is required depending upon the local climate, growth patterns, and danger from the plant. It is also used to help plan for specific ground covers that will reduce or eliminate the need to manage or avoid problems. The three-D data enable BC Hydro to identify downstream effects of any water that needs to be released due to extra heavy rainfalls. The system contains data on downstream property owners (whether customers or not) who will need to be notified or even evacuated in case of unavoidable large water releases.

If a customer calls to report an outage, BC Hydro's system recognizes the customer by the caller's telephone number. If the problem has already been reported, the customer is given an automated message to that effect. Otherwise, BC Hydro's dispatch software immediately assigns someone to solve the problem. Thus the crew is dispatched more quickly. Moreover, each crew vehicle carries a PC that is linked to the outage management system through a mobile data system. The same software is used to predict the probable cause of the outage, enabling the crews to work more efficiently in making the repair. During the crisis BC Hydro management, its customers and the media, can all check on the status of the repair at any time using the Web. When the repair is completed, all locations that have been affected by the problem are automatically notified. In addition the system automatically polls the affected customers to make sure the problem is solved, that their lights are in fact back on. Thus, only a small number of calls ever require the customer to be connected to a call-center agent, while the effectiveness of the software helps the company to maintain its two-hour repair record.

The company is running many other systems, such as Enterprise Land Base, which runs with and relates to all BC Hydro geospatial applications. This software is very valuable, for example, in keeping electric systems working and accessible for use even under peak demand. In addition the company has systems for distribution planning, for design changes and updates, and even for taxation.

Sources: Dan Bowditch, "BC Hydro Reaps GIS Benefits Across the Enterprise," *GEOWorld*, May 2001; "BC Hydro," http://oscar. cprost.sfu.ca/; *GE Smallworld*, "GE Smallworld Business Partner," http://geomantics.ncl.ac.uk/; *GE Smallworld*, "GE Smallworld," http://ecat.dacafe.com.

CASE STUDY QUESTIONS

1. Analyze BC Hydro's unusual competitive position using the competitive forces and value chain models. Keep in mind that competition in the electric utilities field has been growing rapidly since deregulation has begun to spread within the United States and will likely appear in Canada as well.

2. What is BC Hydro's business strategy? How did BC Hydro redesign its information systems to support that strategy?

3. What kinds of decision-support systems is BC Hydro using? What types of decisions do these systems support? What kinds of problems do they solve?

4. How effective have BC Hydro's DSS been in helping the company pursue its goals?

Part III Project

DESIGNING AN ENTERPRISE INFORMATION PORTAL

You are the CIO of a major corporation that researches, develops, manufactures, and distributes pharmaceuticals. Your company, United States Pharma Corp., is headquartered in the state of New Jersey in the United States, but it has sites in many countries around the world. Many of the research sites are in the United States, Germany, France, Great Britain, Australia, and Switzerland. Distribution sites are not only in the United States and Europe but also in a number of countries in East and South Asia, Africa, Australia, Latin America, and the Middle East.

Your company is involved with much more than research and development of new drugs. For example, it owns two companies that produce and sell generic drugs (drugs that are no longer protected by a patent and so are copied and sold under other names). It also produces many over-the-counter drugs to combat such problems as headaches, pain, athlete's foot, and allergic reactions. The company also produces and sells some drugs that help cure or improve some animal diseases such as heartworms and fleas.

The key to the ongoing profits of the company is the research and development of new pharmaceuticals. The company researches thousands of possible drugs in order to finally develop and patent only one that is successful and becomes a widely sold pharmaceutical product. Such products take 8 to 15 years to research, develop, and test, followed by clinical trials and finally approval by the U.S. Food and Drug Administration (FDA). The staff must research both diseases and their treatments, and the potential pharmaceuticals that could become innovative new drugs. Experts who are working on the cutting edge of medical, chemical, and other fields are carrying out research in order to develop possible new drugs and medical treatments.

To undertake the research and eventually test the new products and obtain FDA approval, the researchers and other scientists must test all the possible pharmaceuticals. They must also turn to many places to obtain and share information with others both inside and outside of the company. For example, they will want to communicate with the World Health Organization, the FDA, and the Centers for Disease Control and Prevention. In addition they will need to connect to the pharmaceutical industry's organizations, such as the International Federation of Pharmaceutical Manufacturers Associations (IFPMA). Health education and information sites are also critical, such as the U.S.

National Library of Medicine and such private organizations as the Mayo Clinic Health Oasis.

As the CIO, you have concluded that your company needs a corporate knowledge environment portal that can enable many of the corporate employees easily to access the information they need. The users of the portal would primarily be chemical, biological, and pharmaceutical researchers as well as medical personnel involved in research, tests, and eventually clinical trials.

1. Write a brief description of the company, its key functions, and systems.

2. Design the corporate portal, providing a description that can be reviewed and approved by your senior executive committee. Your design specifications should include the following:

   ▮ Internal systems and databases that users of the portal would need to access.

   ▮ External sources researchers would need to access to further their research.

   ▮ Internal and external communication and collaboration facilities the researchers would need to develop their ideas, pursue their research, and share their research and ideas with others.

   ▮ Intranet and Internet search tools to support research.

   ▮ Sources for relevant news relating to the company and research.

   ▮ U.S. FDA rules and regulations regarding clinical programs, clinical trials, and patent applications.

   ▮ Connections to pharmaceutical conferences and forums as well as professional organizations and appropriate professional journals.

   ▮ Any additional sources of information that would prove helpful to users.

   Use the Web to research these features. Your analysis should include the qualities of a good corporate portal and a description of commercially available tools for building your portal.

3. Design a home page for your portal that you can present to management.

PART IV

BUILDING INFORMATION SYSTEMS IN THE DIGITAL FIRM

Chapter 12
Redesigning the Organization with Information Systems

Chapter 13
Understanding the Business Value of Systems and Managing Change

Chapter 14
Information Systems Security and Control

Part IV Project
Redesigning Business Processes for Healthlite Yogurt Company

chapter

12 REDESIGNING THE ORGANIZATION WITH INFORMATION SYSTEMS

objectives

During your career, you will undoubtedly be looking for ways to use new information systems to improve the performance of your firm. You may be asked to help your organization build a new information system. After completing this chapter, you will be able to answer the following questions:

1. *How could building a new system change the way an organization works?*
2. *How can a company make sure that the new information systems it builds fit its business plan?*
3. *What are the steps required to build a new information system?*
4. *What alternative methods for building information systems are available?*
5. *Are there any techniques or system-building approaches to help us build e-commerce and e-business applications more rapidly?*

Land Information New Zealand Builds an On-Line Title Service

Land Information New Zealand (LINZ) is the government organization responsible for maintaining land title and survey information, handling about 800,000 title transactions each year. It recently developed Landonline, the first nationwide automated land survey and title service that can be accessed on-line.

Work on the system began in 1996 and should be completed in 2002. When the system is completed, 3 million title records, 2 million title instruments, 1.2 million plans, 1.3 million land parcels, and 40,000 geodetic survey marks will have been converted from paper documents to digital form.

The system integrates several different types of data such as text documents and cadastral survey maps into a single database. These data are also linked to dynamic geodetic data. New Zealand's land masses overlap two tectonic plates moving in opposite directions at a rate of 5 centimeters per year, so that survey coordinates become rapidly outdated.

Before the new system was built, each LINZ office was responsible for the records pertaining to the district it served. LINZ staff and customers could only obtain documents from the office in the district where the paper records were kept. The agency could not shift work between different locations, so that if real estate activity was booming in one part of New Zealand, that district office would be

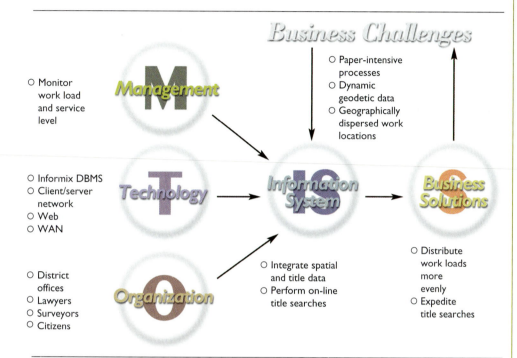

overwhelmed with transactions to record, whereas another district office might have too little work to do. Paperwork was piling up, requiring an additional kilometer of shelving each year to store new records.

With Landonline, title documents are stored in one central database that can be accessed by LINZ staff at all district offices and by lawyers, surveyors, and citizens from any location in the country. The system shows what information is current and what is historical so that users no longer need to sift through entries that no longer apply. Records are instantly updated as land title transactions are registered.

To develop the new system, LINZ management decided to work with the consulting firm of PriceWaterhouse Coopers for project planning and development, and with EDS New Zealand for converting the data from paper to computerized format for the system and for implementing a wide area network (WAN).

Working with its consultants, LINZ evaluated alternative DBMS to find one that could handle spatial data as well as conventional text data such as title information. The title information, which includes details on ownership and the legal description of each piece of property, must be tied to the survey data using parcel identification numbers. The survey data are images of plans originally drafted by surveyors on paper. They contain the spatial layout of property boundaries, corner points, coordinates, and bearings that tie their data to the geodetic data for the land masses. The DBMS also had to be able to adjust this survey data to keep it synchronized with the shifting land masses. The project team found that the Informix Dynamic Server was the only DBMS that could meet these requirements.

Landonline users can perform standard SQL queries across all elements of the business, including queries based on spatial data. For example, a LINZ official can query the system to see all the titles for properties with easements, incorporating easements within 15 meters of a specific fire hydrant.

Landonline was first implemented in one New Zealand land district and is being phased into the country's 11 other districts. Each LINZ office will have client/server access to the system and will be able to query data from all 12 land districts using the WAN. Once EDS finishes converting title records in each land district, registered users will be able to access the system via the Web.

Sources: Kevin P. Corbley, "Upping the Ante," *GEOWorld,* May 2001; and www.landonline.govt.nz.

MANAGEMENT CHALLENGES

Land Information New Zealand's Landonline system illustrates the many factors at work in the development of a new information system. Building the new system entailed analyzing the company's problems with existing information systems, assessing people's information needs, selecting appropriate technology, and redesigning business processes and jobs. Management had to monitor the system-building effort and evaluate its benefits and costs. The new information system represented a process of planned organizational change. However, building information systems, especially those on a large scale, presents many challenges. Here are several challenges to consider:

1. **Major risks and uncertainties in systems development.** Information systems development has major risks and uncertainties that make it difficult for systems to achieve their goals. One problem is the difficulty of establishing information requirements, both for individual end users and for the organization as a whole. The requirements may be too complex or subject to change. Another problem is that the time and cost factors to develop an information system are very difficult to analyze, especially in large projects. A third problem is the difficulty of managing the organizational change associated with a new system. Although building a new information system is a process of planned organizational change, this does not mean that change can always be planned or controlled. Individuals and groups in organizations have varying interests, and they may resist changes in procedures, job relationships, and technologies. Although this chapter describes some ways of dealing with these risks and uncertainties, the issues remain major management challenges.

2. **Controlling information systems development outside the information systems department.** There may not be a way to establish standards and controls for systems development that is not managed by the information systems department, such as end-user development or outsourcing. Standards and controls that are too restrictive may not only generate user resistance but also may stifle end-user innovation. If controls are too weak, the firm may encounter serious problems with data integrity and connectivity. It is not always possible to find the right balance.

This chapter describes how new information systems are conceived, built, and installed, with special attention to the issues of organizational design, business process reengineering, and total quality management. It describes the core systems development activities and how to ensure that new systems are linked to the organization's business plan and information requirements. This chapter also examines alternative approaches for building systems.

12.1 SYSTEMS AS PLANNED ORGANIZATIONAL CHANGE

This text has emphasized that an information system is a sociotechnical entity, an arrangement of both technical and social elements. The introduction of a new information system involves much more than new hardware and software. It also includes changes in jobs, skills, management, and organization. In the sociotechnical philosophy, one cannot install new technology without considering the people who must work with it (Bostrom and Heinen, 1977). When we design a new information system, we are redesigning the organization.

One important thing to know about building a new information system is that this process is one kind of planned organizational change. System builders must understand how a system will affect the organization as a whole, focusing particularly on organizational conflict and changes in the locus of decision making. Builders must also consider how the nature of work groups will change under the new system. Systems can be technical successes but organizational failures because of a failure in the social and political process of building the system. Analysts and designers are responsible for ensuring that key members of the organization participate in the design process and are permitted to influence the system's ultimate shape.

LINKING INFORMATION SYSTEMS TO THE BUSINESS PLAN

Deciding which new systems to build should be an essential component of the organizational planning process. Organizations need to develop an information systems plan that supports their overall business plan and in which strategic systems are incorporated into top-level planning. Once specific projects have been selected within the overall context of a strategic plan for the business and the systems area, an **information systems plan** can be developed. The plan serves as a road map indicating the direction of systems development, the rationale, the current situation, the management strategy, the implementation plan, and the budget (see the Manager's Toolkit.)

information systems plan
A road map indicating the direction of systems development: the rationale, the current situation, the management strategy, the implementation plan, and the budget.

MIS IN ACTION   MANAGER'S TOOLKIT

HOW TO DEVELOP AN INFORMATION SYSTEMS PLAN

A good information systems plan should address the following topics:

1. **Purpose of the Plan**
   Overview of plan contents
   Changes in firm's current situation
   Firm's strategic plan
   Current business organization and future organization
   Key business processes
   Management strategy
2. **Strategic Business Plan**
   Current situation
   Current business organization
   Changing environments
   Major goals of the business plan
3. **Current Systems**
   Major systems supporting business functions and processes
   Current infrastructure capabilities
   　Hardware
   　Software
   　Database
   　Telecommunications and Internet
   Difficulties meeting business requirements
   Anticipated future demands
4. **New Developments**
   New system projects
   　Project descriptions
   　Business rationale
   New infrastructure capabilities required
   　Hardware
   　Software

   　Database
   　Telecommunications and Internet
5. **Management Strategy**
   Acquisition plans
   Milestones and timing
   Organizational realignment
   Internal reorganization
   Management controls
   Major training initiatives
   Personnel strategy
6. **Implementation Plan**
   Anticipated difficulties in implementation
   Progress reports
7. **Budget Requirements**
   Requirements
   Potential savings
   Financing
   Acquisition cycle

The plan contains a statement of corporate goals and specifies how information technology supports the attainment of those goals. The report shows how general goals will be achieved by specific systems projects. It lays out specific target dates and milestones that can be used later to evaluate the plan's progress in terms of how many objectives were actually attained in the time frame specified in the plan. The plan indicates the key management decisions concerning hardware acquisition; telecommunications; centralization/decentralization of authority, data, and hardware; and required organizational change. Organizational changes are also usually described, including management and employee training requirements; recruiting efforts; changes in business processes; and changes in authority, structure, or management practice.

ESTABLISHING ORGANIZATIONAL INFORMATION REQUIREMENTS

In order to develop an effective information systems plan, the organization must have a clear understanding of both its long- and short-term information requirements. Two principal methodologies for establishing the essential information requirements of the organization as a whole are enterprise analysis and critical success factors.

Enterprise Analysis (Business Systems Planning)

enterprise analysis
An analysis of organization-wide information requirements that examines the entire organization in terms of organizational units, functions, processes, and data elements; helps identify the key entities and attributes in the organization's data.

Enterprise analysis (also called *business systems planning*) argues that the firm's information requirements can only be understood by looking at the entire organization in terms of organizational units, functions, processes, and data elements. Enterprise analysis can help identify the key entities and attributes of the organization's data.

The central method used in the enterprise analysis approach is to take a large sample of managers and ask them how they use information, where they get the information, what their environments are like, what their objectives are, how they make decisions, and what their data needs are. The results of this large survey of managers are aggregated into subunits, functions, processes, and data matrices. Data elements are organized into logical application groups—groups of data elements that support related sets of organizational processes. Figure 12-1 is an output of enterprise analysis conducted by the Social Security Administration as part of a massive systems redevelopment effort. It shows what information is required to support a particular process, which processes create the data, and which use them. The shaded boxes in the figure indicate a logical application group. In this case, actuarial estimates, agency plans, and budget data are created in the planning process, suggesting that an information system should be built to support planning.

The weakness of enterprise analysis is that it produces an enormous amount of data that is expensive to collect and difficult to analyze. Most of the interviews are conducted with senior or middle managers, but there is little effort to collect information from clerical workers and supervisory managers. Moreover, the questions frequently focus not on management's critical objectives and where information is needed but rather on what existing information is used. The result is a tendency to automate whatever exists. But in many instances, entirely new approaches to how business is conducted are needed, and these needs are not addressed.

Strategic Analysis or Critical Success Factors

critical success factors (CSFs)
A small number of easily identifiable operational goals shaped by the industry, the firm, the manager, and the broader environment that are believed to assure the success of an organization. Used to determine the information requirements of an organization.

The strategic analysis, or critical success factors, approach argues that an organization's information requirements are determined by a small number of **critical success factors (CSFs)** of managers. If these goals can be attained, the firm's or organization's success is assured (Rockart, 1979; Rockart and Treacy, 1982). CSFs are shaped by the industry, the firm, the manager, and the broader environment. An important premise of the strategic analysis approach is that there are a small number of objectives that managers can easily identify and on which information systems can focus.

The principal method used in CSF analysis is personal interviews—three or four—with a number of top managers to identify their goals and the resulting CSFs. These personal CSFs are aggregated to develop a picture of the firm's CSFs. Then systems are built to deliver information on these CSFs. (See Table 12-1 for an example of CSFs. For the method of developing CSFs in an organization, see Figure 12-2.)

The strength of the CSF method is that it produces a smaller data set to analyze than does enterprise analysis. Only top managers are interviewed, and the questions focus on a small number of CSFs rather than a broad inquiry into what information is used or needed. The CSF method takes into account the changing environment with which organizations and managers must deal. This method explicitly asks managers to look at the environment and consider how their analysis of it shapes their information needs. It is especially suitable for top management and for the development of DSS and ESS. Unlike enterprise analysis, the CSF method focuses organizational attention on how information should be handled.

The method's primary weakness is that the aggregation process and the analysis of the data are art forms. There is no particularly rigorous way in which individual CSFs can be

Figure 12-1 Process/data class matrix. This chart depicts which data classes are required to support particular organizational processes and which processes are the creators and users of data.

LOGICAL APPLICATION GROUPS — DATA CLASSES

Data classes (columns, left to right): Actuarial estimates, Agency plans, Budget, Program regs./policy, Admin. regs./policy, Labor agreements, Data standards, Procedures, Automated systems documentation, Educational media, Public agreements, Intergovernmental agreements, Grants, External, Exchange control, Administrative accounts, Program expenditures, Audit reports, Organization/position, Employee identification, Recruitment/placement, Complaints/grievances, Training resources, Security, Equipment utilization, Space utilization, Supplies utilization, Workload schedules, Work measurement, Enumeration I.D., Enumeration control, Earnings, Employer I.D., Earnings control, Claims characteristics, Claims control, Decisions, Payment, Collection/waiver, Notice, Inquiries control, Quality appraisal

PROCESSES	Actuarial estimates	Agency plans	Budget	Program regs./policy	Admin. regs./policy	Labor agreements	Data standards	Procedures	Automated systems documentation	Educational media	Public agreements	Intergovernmental agreements	Grants	External	Exchange control	Administrative accounts	Program expenditures	Audit reports	Organization/position	Employee identification	Recruitment/placement	Complaints/grievances	Training resources	Security	Equipment utilization	Space utilization	Supplies utilization	Workload schedules	Work measurement	Enumeration I.D.	Enumeration control	Earnings	Employer I.D.	Earnings control	Claims characteristics	Claims control	Decisions	Payment	Collection/waiver	Notice	Inquiries control	Quality appraisal
PLANNING																																										
Develop agency plans	C	C	C	U	U								U																													
Administer agency budget	C	C	C	U	U						U	U	U		U	U	U		U	U					U	U	U		U		U		U		U			U			U	U
Formulate program policies	U	U		C			U						U			U			U		U												U									U
Formulate admin. policies		U		U	C	C	U						U			U	U		U		U																					
Formulate data policies		U	U		U		C	U	U																					U	U	U	U									
Design work processes		U		U	U			C	C		U	U							U																			U				U
GENERAL MANAGEMENT																																										
Manage public affairs		U		U	U			U		C	C	C																														
Manage intrgovt. affairs	U	U		U	U			U		U	C	C	C												U	U		U	U		U		U		U							
Exchange data				U						U	U	U	U	U	C	U	U								U																	
Maintain admin. accounts		U		U				U		U	U					C			U						U	U	U								U		U					
Maintain prog. accounts		U	U					U		U	U						C											U				U		U	U	U	U	U		U		
Conduct audits		U		U				U	U						U	U	C		U									U														
Establish organizations		U		U				U											C	U					U	U																U
Manage human resources		U		U	U	U		U											C	C	C	C	C																			
Provide security				U	U		U	U	U															C	C	C	C		U													
Manage equipment		U		U			U	U	U															C	C	C	C															
Manage facilities		U		U				U																U	U	C																
Manage supplies		U		U				U																C	U	U	C															
Manage workloads	U		U	U	U			U					U											U	U	U	U	C	C		U		U		U						U	U
PROGRAM ADMIN.																																										
Issue Social Security nos.								U			U		U																	C	C											
Maintain earnings								U			U	U	U																	U		C	C	C	U							
Collect claims information				U	U			U					U																	U	U				C	C	U	U	U			
Determine elig./entlmt.								U																						U	U	U			U		C	U	U			
Compute payments				U				U									U													U		U			U		U	C	C			
Administer debt mgmt.				U				U									U																		U				C			
SUPPORT																																										
Generate notices								U					U																	U		U			U		U	U	U	C		
Respond to prog. inquiries				U				U		U																				U		U	U		U		U	U	U	U	C	
Provide quality assessment				U	U			U	U																					U		U			U		U				U	C

KEY
C = creators of data   U = users of data

TABLE 12-1

CRITICAL SUCCESS FACTORS AND ORGANIZATIONAL GOALS

Example	Goals	CSF
Profit concern	Earnings/share	Automotive industry
	Return on investment	Styling
	Market share	Quality dealer system
	New product	Cost control
		Energy standards
Nonprofit	Excellent healthcare	Regional integration with other hospitals
	Meeting government regulations	Improved monitoring of regulations
	Future health needs	Efficient use of resources

Source: Rockart (1979).

Figure 12-2 Using CSFs to develop systems. The CSF approach relies on interviews with key managers to identify their CSFs. Individual CSFs are aggregated to develop CSFs for the entire firm. Systems can then be built to deliver information on these CSFs.

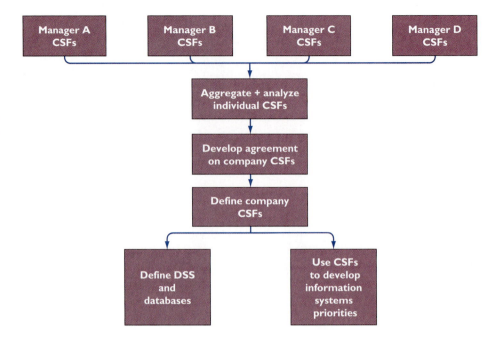

aggregated into a clear company pattern. Second, there is often confusion among interviewees (and interviewers) between *individual* and *organizational* CSFs. They are not necessarily the same. What can be critical to a manager may not be important for the organization. Moreover, this method is clearly biased toward top managers because they are the ones (generally the only ones) interviewed.

SYSTEMS DEVELOPMENT AND ORGANIZATIONAL CHANGE

New information systems can be powerful instruments for organizational change, enabling organizations to redesign their structure, scope, power relationships, work flows, products, and services. Table 12-2 describes some of the ways that information technology is being used to transform organizations and business processes.

TABLE 12-2 **HOW INFORMATION TECHNOLOGY CAN TRANSFORM ORGANIZATIONS**

Information Technology	Organizational Change
Global networks	International division of labor: The operations of a firm and its business processes are no longer determined by location; the global reach of firms is extended; costs of global coordination decline. Transaction costs decline.
Enterprise networks	Collaborative work and teamwork: The organization of work can now be coordinated across divisional boundaries; the costs of management (agency costs) decline. Multiple tasks can be worked on simultaneously from different locations.
Distributed computing	Empowerment: Individuals and work groups now have the information and knowledge to act. Business processes can be streamlined. Management costs decline. Hierarchy and centralization decline.
Portable computing	Virtual organizations: Work is no longer tied to physical location. Knowledge and information can be delivered anywhere they are needed, anytime. Work becomes portable.
Multimedia and graphical interfaces	Accessibility: Everyone in the organization—even senior executives—can access information and knowledge. Organizational costs decline as work flows move from paper to digital image, documents, and voice. Complex knowledge objects can be stored and represented as objects containing graphics, audio, video, or text.

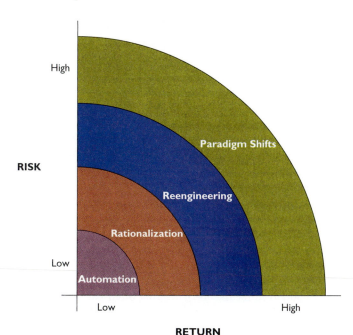

High

RISK

Paradigm Shifts

Reengineering

Rationalization

Low

Automation

Low   High

RETURN

Figure 12-3 Organizational change carries risks and rewards. The most common forms of organizational change are automation and rationalization. These relatively slow moving and slow changing strategies present modest returns but little risk. Faster and more comprehensive change—like reengineering and paradigm shifts—carries high rewards but offers substantial chances of failure.

The Spectrum of Organizational Change

Information technology can promote various degrees of organizational change, ranging from incremental to far-reaching. Figure 12-3 shows four kinds of structural organizational change that are enabled by information technology: (1) automation, (2) rationalization, (3) reengineering, and (4) paradigm shifts. Each carries different rewards and risks.

The most common form of IT-enabled organizational change is **automation.** The first applications of information technology involved assisting employees with performing their tasks more efficiently and effectively. Calculating paychecks and payroll registers, giving bank tellers instant access to customer deposit records, and developing a nationwide network of airline reservation terminals for airline reservation agents are all examples of early automation.

A deeper form of organizational change—one that follows quickly from early automation—is **rationalization of procedures**. Automation frequently reveals new bottlenecks in production and makes the existing arrangement of procedures and structures painfully cumbersome. Rationalization of procedures is the streamlining of standard operating procedures, eliminating obvious bottlenecks, so that automation can make operating procedures more efficient. For example, Land Information New Zealand's new system is effective not only because it uses computer technology but also because its design allows the organization to operate more efficiently. The procedures of Land Information New Zealand (LINZ), or any organization, must be rationally structured to achieve this result. LINZ had to have standard identification numbers for land parcels and standard rules for matching title information with drawings and other documents. Without a certain amount of rationalization in LINZ's organization, its computer technology would have been useless.

A more powerful type of organizational change is **business process reengineering,** in which business processes are analyzed, simplified, and redesigned. Using information technology, organizations can rethink and streamline their business processes to improve speed, service, and quality. Business reengineering reorganizes work flows, combining steps to cut waste and eliminating repetitive, paper-intensive tasks (sometimes the new design eliminates jobs as well). It is much more ambitious than rationalization of procedures, requiring a new vision of how the process is to be organized.

A widely cited example of business reengineering is Ford Motor Company's *invoiceless processing*. Ford employed more than 500 people in its North American Accounts Payable organization. The accounts payable clerks spent most of their time resolving discrepancies between purchase orders, receiving documents, and invoices. Ford reengineered its accounts

automation

Using the computer to speed up the performance of existing tasks.

rationalization of procedures

The streamlining of standard operating procedures, eliminating obvious bottlenecks, so that automation makes operating procedures more efficient.

business process reengineering

The radical redesign of business processes, combining steps to cut waste and eliminating repetitive, paper-intensive tasks in order to improve cost, quality, and service, and to maximize the benefits of information technology.

payable process, instituting a system wherein the purchasing department enters a purchase order into an on-line database that can be checked by the receiving department when the ordered items arrive. If the received goods match the purchase order, the system automatically generates a check for accounts payable to send to the vendor. There is no need for vendors to send invoices. After reengineering, Ford was able to reduce headcount in accounts payable by 75 percent and produce more accurate financial information (Hammer and Champy, 1993).

Rationalizing procedures and redesigning business processes are limited to specific parts of a business. New information systems can ultimately affect the design of the entire organization by transforming how the organization carries out its business or even the nature of the business itself. For instance, Schneider National, described in the Chapter 8 case study, used new information systems to change its business model. Schneider created a new business managing the logistics for other companies. Baxter International's stockless inventory system (described in Chapter 3) transformed Baxter into a working partner with hospitals and into a manager of its customers' supplies. This more radical form of business change is called a **paradigm shift.** A paradigm shift involves rethinking the nature of the business and the nature of the organization itself.

Paradigm shifts and reengineering often fail because extensive organizational change is so difficult to orchestrate (see Chapter 13). Why then do so many corporations entertain such radical change? Because the rewards are equally high (see Figure 12-3). In many instances firms seeking paradigm shifts and pursuing reengineering strategies achieve stunning, order-of-magnitude increases in their returns on investment (or productivity). Some of these success stories, and some failure stories, are included throughout this book.

paradigm shift

Radical reconceptualization of the nature of the business and the nature of the organization.

12.2 BUSINESS PROCESS REENGINEERING AND TOTAL QUALITY MANAGEMENT (TQM)

Many companies today are focusing on building new information systems that will improve their business processes. Some of these system projects represent radical restructuring of business processes, whereas others entail more incremental change.

BUSINESS PROCESS REENGINEERING

If organizations rethink and radically redesign their business processes before applying computing power, they can potentially obtain very large payoffs from their investments in information technology. The home mortgage industry is a leading example in the United States of how major corporations have implemented business process reengineering. The application process for a home mortgage traditionally took about six to eight weeks and cost about $3,000. The goal of many mortgage banks has been to lower that cost to $1,000 and the time to obtain a mortgage to about one week. Leading mortgage banks such as BankBoston, Countrywide Funding Corporation, and Banc One Corporation have redesigned the mortgage application process.

The mortgage application process is divided into three stages: origination, servicing, and secondary marketing. Figure 12-4 illustrates how business process redesign has been used in each of these stages.

In the past, a mortgage applicant filled out a paper loan application. The bank entered the application into its computer system. Specialists, such as credit analysts and underwriters from perhaps eight different departments, accessed and evaluated the application individually. If the loan application was approved, the closing was scheduled. After the closing, bank specialists dealing with insurance or funds in escrow serviced the loan. This "desk-to-desk" assembly-line approach might take up to 17 days.

Leading banks have replaced the sequential desk-to-desk approach with a speedier "work cell" or team approach. Now, loan originators in the field enter the mortgage application directly into laptop computers. Software checks the application transaction to make sure that all of the information is correct and complete. The loan originators transmit the loan applications using a dial-up network to regional production centers. Instead of working on the

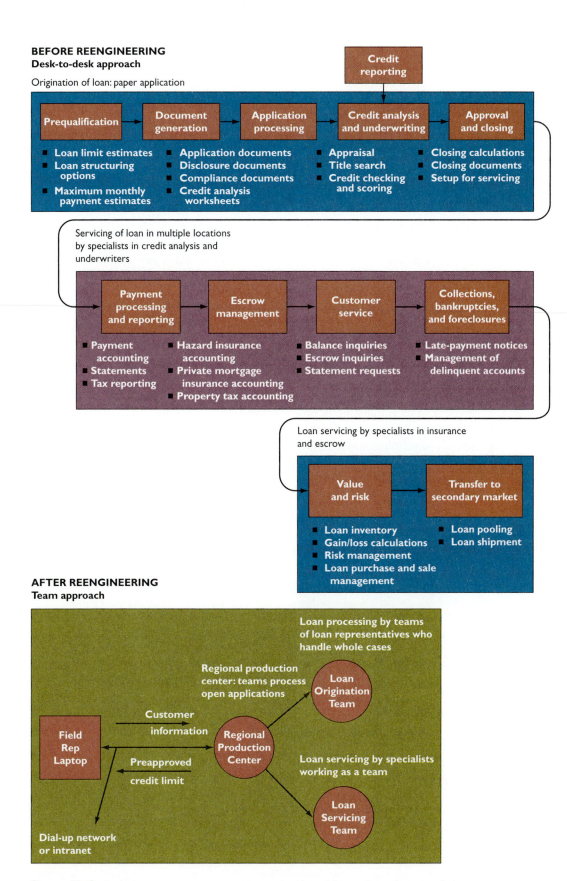

BEFORE REENGINEERING
Desk-to-desk approach

Origination of loan: paper application

Credit reporting

| Prequalification | Document generation | Application processing | Credit analysis and underwriting | Approval and closing |

- Loan limit estimates
- Loan structuring options
- Maximum monthly payment estimates

- Application documents
- Disclosure documents
- Compliance documents
- Credit analysis worksheets

- Appraisal
- Title search
- Credit checking and scoring

- Closing calculations
- Closing documents
- Setup for servicing

Servicing of loan in multiple locations by specialists in credit analysis and underwriters

| Payment processing and reporting | Escrow management | Customer service | Collections, bankruptcies, and foreclosures |

- Payment accounting
- Statements
- Tax reporting

- Hazard insurance accounting
- Private mortgage insurance accounting
- Property tax accounting

- Balance inquiries
- Escrow inquiries
- Statement requests

- Late-payment notices
- Management of delinquent accounts

Loan servicing by specialists in insurance and escrow

| Value and risk | Transfer to secondary market |

- Loan inventory
- Gain/loss calculations
- Risk management
- Loan purchase and sale management

- Loan pooling
- Loan shipment

AFTER REENGINEERING
Team approach

Loan processing by teams of loan representatives who handle whole cases

Regional production center: teams process open applications

Loan Origination Team

Field Rep Laptop

Customer information

Regional Production Center

Preapproved credit limit

Loan servicing by specialists working as a team

Loan Servicing Team

Dial-up network or intranet

Figure 12-4 Redesigning mortgage processing in the United States. By redesigning their mortgage processing systems and the mortgage application process, mortgage banks can reduce the costs of processing the average mortgage from $3,000 to $1,000, and reduce the time of approval from six weeks to one week or less. Some banks are even preapproving mortgages and locking interest rates on the same day the customer applies.

application individually, the credit analysts, loan underwriters, and other specialists convene electronically, working as a team to approve the mortgage. Some banks provide customers with a nearly instant credit lock-in of a guaranteed mortgage so they can find a house that meets their budget immediately. Such preapproval of a credit line is truly a radical reengineering of the traditional business process.

After closing, another team of specialists sets up the loan for servicing. The entire loan application process can take as little as two days. Loan information is easier to access than before, when the loan application could be in eight or nine different departments. Loan originators also can dial into the bank's network to obtain information on mortgage loan costs or to check the status of a loan for the customer.

By redesigning their approach to mortgage processing, mortgage banks have achieved remarkable efficiencies. They have not focused on redesigning a single business process but instead they have reexamined the entire set of logically connected processes required to obtain a mortgage. Instead of automating the previous method of mortgage processing, the banks have completely rethought the entire mortgage application process.

Work Flow Management

work flow management
The process of streamlining business procedures so that documents can be moved easily and efficiently from one location to another.

To streamline the paperwork in the mortgage application process, banks have turned to work flow and document management software. By using this software to store and process documents electronically, organizations can redesign their work flows so that documents can be worked on simultaneously or moved more easily and efficiently from one location to another. The process of streamlining business procedures so that documents can be moved easily and efficiently is called **work flow management.** Work flow and document management software automates processes such as routing documents to different locations, securing approvals, scheduling, and generating reports. Two or more people can work simultaneously on the same document, allowing much quicker completion time. Work need not be delayed because a file is out or a document is in transit. And with a properly designed indexing system, users will be able to retrieve files in many different ways, based on the content of the document.

STEPS IN EFFECTIVE REENGINEERING

To reengineer effectively, senior management needs to develop a broad strategic vision that calls for redesigned business processes. For example, Mitsubishi Heavy Industries management looked for breakthroughs to lower costs and accelerate product development that would enable the firm to regain world market leadership in shipbuilding. The company redesigned its entire production process to replace expensive labor-intensive tasks with robotic machines and computer-aided design tools. Companies should identify a few core business processes to be redesigned, focusing on those with the greatest potential payback (Davenport and Short, 1990).

Management must understand and measure the performance of existing processes as a baseline. If, for example, the objective of process redesign is to reduce time and cost in developing a new product or filling an order, the organization needs to measure the time and cost consumed by the unchanged process. For example, before reengineering, it cost C. R. England & Sons Inc. $5.10 to send an invoice; after processes were reengineered the cost per invoice dropped to 15 cents (Davidson, 1993).

The conventional method of designing systems establishes the information requirements of a business function or process and then determines how they can be supported by information technology. However information technology can create new design options for various processes because it can be used to challenge long-standing assumptions about work arrangements that used to inhibit organizations. Table 12-3 provides examples of innovations that have overcome these assumptions using companies discussed in the text. Information technology should be allowed to influence process design from the start.

Following these steps does not automatically guarantee that reengineering will always be successful. The organization's IT infrastructure should have capabilities to support business process changes that span boundaries between functions, business units, or firms (Broadbent, Weill, and St. Clair, 1999). The majority of reengineering projects do not

TABLE 12-3	NEW PROCESS DESIGN OPTIONS WITH INFORMATION TECHNOLOGY		
Assumption	**Technology**	**Options**	**Examples**
Field personnel need offices to receive, store, and transmit information	Wireless communications	People can send and receive information from wherever they are	Swedish National Board of Health and Welfare GlaxoSmithKline
Information can appear only in one place at one time	Shared databases	People can collaborate on the same project from scattered locations; information can be used simultaneously wherever it is needed	Banc One
People are needed to ascertain where things are located	Automatic identification and tracking technology	Things can tell people where they are	United Parcel Service
Businesses need reserve inventory to prevent stockouts	Networks, extranets, and EDI	Just-in-time delivery and stockless supply	Baxter International Wal-Mart

achieve breakthrough gains in business performance. A reengineered business process or a new information system inevitably affects jobs, skill requirements, work flows, and reporting relationships (Teng, Jeong, and Grover, 1998). Fear of these changes breeds resistance, confusion, and even conscious efforts to undermine the change effort. We examine these organizational change issues more carefully in Chapter 13. Managing change is neither simple nor intuitive.

PROCESS IMPROVEMENT AND TOTAL QUALITY MANAGEMENT (TQM)

In addition to increasing organizational efficiency, companies are also changing their business processes to improve the quality in their products, services, and operations. Many are using the concept of **total quality management (TQM)** to make quality the responsibility of all people and functions within an organization. TQM holds that the achievement of quality control is an end in itself. Everyone is expected to contribute to the overall improvement of quality—the engineer who avoids design errors, the production worker who spots defects, the sales representative who presents the product properly to potential customers, and even the secretary who avoids typing mistakes. TQM derives from quality management concepts developed by American quality experts such as W. Edwards Deming and Joseph Juran, but it was popularized by the Japanese. Studies have repeatedly shown that the earlier in the business cycle a problem is eliminated, the less it costs the company. Thus quality improvements cannot only raise the level of product and service quality but they can also lower costs.

total quality management (TQM)
A concept that makes quality control a responsibility to be shared by all people in an organization.

How Information Systems Contribute to Total Quality Management

TQM is considered to be more incremental than business process reengineering (BPR) because its efforts often focus on making a series of continuous improvements rather than dramatic bursts of change. Sometimes, however, processes may have to be fully reengineered to achieve a specified level of quality. Information systems can help firms achieve their quality goals by helping them simplify products or processes, meet benchmarking standards, make improvements based on customer demands, reduce cycle time, and increase the quality and precision of design and production.

> **Simplifying the product or the production process.** The fewer steps in a process, the less time and opportunity for an error to occur. Ten years ago, 1-800-FLOWERS, a multimillion-dollar telephone and Web-based floral service with a global reach, was a much smaller company that spent too much on advertising because it could not retain its customers. It had poor service, inconsistent quality, and a cumbersome manual order-taking process. Telephone representatives had to write the order, obtain credit card approval, determine which participating florist was closest

to the delivery location, select a floral arrangement, and forward the order to the florist. Each step in the manual process increased the chance of human error, and the whole process took at least a half hour. Owners Jim and Chris McCann installed a new computer system that downloads orders taken at telecenters into a central computer and electronically transmits them to local florists. Orders are more accurate and arrive at the florist within one to two minutes (Gill, 1998).

Benchmarking. Many companies have been effective in achieving quality by setting strict standards for products, services, and other activities, and then measuring performance against those standards. This procedure is called **benchmarking**. Companies may use external industry standards, standards set by other companies, internally developed high standards, or some combination of the three. L L. Bean, Inc., the Freeport, Maine, outdoor catalog company, used benchmarking to achieve an order shipping accuracy of 99.9 percent. Its old batch order fulfillment system could not handle the surging volume and variety of items to be shipped. After studying German and Scandinavian companies with leading-edge order fulfillment operations, L. L. Bean carefully redesigned its order fulfillment process and information systems so that orders could be processed as soon as they were received and shipped out within 24 hours.

Use customer demands as a guide to improving products and services. Improving customer service, making customer service the number one priority, will improve the quality of the product itself. Delta Airlines decided to focus more on its customers, installing a customer care system at its airport gates. For each flight, the airplane seating chart, reservations, check-in information, and boarding data are linked in a central database. Airline personnel can track which passengers are on board regardless of where they checked in and use this information to help passengers reach their destinations quickly even if delays cause them to miss connecting flights.

Reduce cycle time. Reducing the amount of time from the beginning of a process to its end (cycle time) usually results in fewer steps. Shorter cycles mean that errors are often caught earlier in production (or logistics or design or whatever the function), often before the process is complete, eliminating many hidden costs. Iomega Corporation in Roy, Utah, a manufacturer of disk drives, was spending $20 million a year to fix defective drives at the end of its 28-day production cycle. Reengineering the production process allowed the firm to reduce cycle time to a day and a half, eliminating this problem and winning the prestigious Shingo Prize for Excellence in American Manufacturing.

benchmarking
Setting strict standards for products, services, or activities and measuring organizational performance against those standards.

Delta Airlines developed information systems to improve service to customers when they are checking in and connecting flights. Improving customer service is one way that information systems can support Total Quality Management (TQM).

Improve the quality and precision of the design. Computer-aided design (CAD) software has made dramatic quality improvements possible in a wide range of businesses from aircraft manufacturing to production of razor blades. Alan R. Burns, head of the Airboss Company in Perth, Australia, used CAD to invent and design a new modular tire made up of a series of replaceable modules or segments so that if one segment were damaged, only that segment, not the whole tire, would need replacing. Burns established quality performance measurements for such key tire characteristics as load, temperature, speed, wear life, and traction. He entered these data into a CAD software package, which he used to design the modules. Using the software, he was able iteratively to design and test until he was satisfied with the results. He did not need to develop an actual working model until the iterative design process was almost complete. Because of the speed and accuracy of the CAD software, the product he produced was of much higher quality than would have been possible through manual design and testing.

Increase the precision of production. For many products, one key way to achieve quality is to make the production process more precise, thereby decreasing the amount of variation from one part to another. GE Medical Systems performed a rigorous quality analysis to improve the reliability and durability of its Lightspeed diagnostic scanner. It broke the processes of designing and producing the scanner into many distinct steps and established optimum specifications for each component part. By understanding these processes precisely, engineers learned that a few simple changes would significantly improve the product's reliability and durability.

12.3 OVERVIEW OF SYSTEMS DEVELOPMENT

Whatever their scope and objectives, new information systems are an outgrowth of a process of organizational problem solving. A new information system is built as a solution to some type of problem or set of problems the organization perceives it is facing. The problem may be one where managers and employees realize that the organization is not performing as well as expected, or it may come from the realization that the organization should take advantage of new opportunities to perform more successfully.

The activities that go into producing an information system solution to an organizational problem or opportunity are called **systems development.** Systems development is a structured kind of problem solving with distinct activities. These activities consist of systems analysis, systems design, programming, testing, conversion, and production and maintenance.

Figure 12-5 illustrates the systems development process. The systems development activities depicted here usually take place in sequential order. But some of the activities may need

systems development
The activities that go into producing an information system solution to an organizational problem or opportunity.

Figure 12-5 The systems development process. Each of the core systems development activities entails interaction with the organization.

Organization

to be repeated or some may be taking place simultaneously, depending on the approach to system building that is being employed (see Section 12.4). Note also that each activity involves interaction with the organization. Members of the organization participate in these activities and the systems development process creates organizational changes.

SYSTEMS ANALYSIS

systems analysis

The analysis of a problem that the organization will try to solve with an information system.

Systems analysis is the analysis of the problem that the organization will try to solve with an information system. It consists of defining the problem, identifying its causes, specifying the solution, and identifying the information requirements that must be met by a system solution.

The systems analyst creates a road map of the existing organization and systems, identifying the primary owners and users of data in the organization. These stakeholders have a direct interest in the information affected by the new system. In addition to these organizational aspects, the analyst also briefly describes the existing hardware and software that serve the organization.

From this organizational analysis, the systems analyst details the problems of existing systems. By examining documents, work papers, and procedures; observing system operations; and interviewing key users of the systems, the analyst can identify the problem areas and objectives a solution would achieve. Often the solution requires building a new information system or improving an existing one.

feasibility study

As part of the systems analysis process, the way to determine whether the solution is achievable, given the organization's resources and constraints.

The systems analysis would include a **feasibility study** to determine whether that solution was feasible, or achievable, from a financial, technical, and organizational standpoint. The feasibility study would determine whether the proposed system was a good investment, whether the technology needed for the system was available and could be handled by the firm's information systems specialists, and whether the organization could handle the changes introduced by the system.

Normally, the systems analysis process will identify several alternative solutions that the organization can pursue. The process then will assess the feasibility of each. A written systems proposal report will describe the costs and benefits, advantages and disadvantages of each alternative. It is up to management to determine which mix of costs, benefits, technical features, and organizational impacts represents the most desirable alternative.

Establishing Information Requirements

Perhaps the most challenging task of the systems analyst is to define the specific information requirements that must be met by the system solution selected. At the most basic level, the **information requirements** of a new system involve identifying who needs what information, where, when, and how. Requirements analysis carefully defines the objectives of the new or modified system and develops a detailed description of the functions that the new system must perform. Faulty requirements analysis is a leading cause of systems failure and high systems development costs (see Chapter 13). A system designed around the wrong set of requirements will either have to be discarded because of poor performance or will need to undergo major modifications. Section 12.4 describes alternative approaches to eliciting requirements that help minimize this problem.

information requirements

A detailed statement of the information needs that a new system must satisfy; identifies who needs what information, and when, where, and how the information is needed.

In many instances, building a new system creates an opportunity to redefine how the organization conducts its daily business. Some problems do not require an information system solution but instead need an adjustment in management, additional training, or refinement of existing organizational procedures. If the problem is information related, systems analysis still may be required to diagnose the problem and arrive at the proper solution.

SYSTEMS DESIGN

systems design

Details how a system will meet the information requirements as determined by the systems analysis.

Systems analysis describes what a system should do to meet information requirements, and **systems design** shows how the system will fulfill this objective. The design of an information system is the overall plan or model for that system. Like the blueprint of a building or house, it consists of all the specifications that give the system its form and structure.

The systems designer details the system specifications that will deliver the functions identified during systems analysis. These specifications should address all of the managerial,

TABLE 12-4   DESIGN SPECIFICATIONS

Output	Controls
Medium	Input controls (characters, limit, reasonableness)
Content	Processing controls (consistency, record counts)
Timing	Output controls (totals, samples of output)
Input	Procedural controls (passwords, special forms)
Origins	Security
Flow	Access controls
Data entry	Catastrophe plans
User interface	Audit trails
Simplicity	Documentation
Efficiency	Operations documentation
Logic	Systems documents
Feedback	User documentation
Errors	Conversion
Database design	Transfer files
Logical data relations	Initiate new procedures
Volume and speed requirements	Select testing method
File organization and design	Cut over to new system
Record specifications	Training
Processing	Select training techniques
Computations	Develop training modules
Program modules	Identify training facilities
Required reports	Organizational changes
Timing of outputs	Task redesign
Manual procedures	Job design
What activities	Process design
Who performs them	Office and organization structure design
When	Reporting relationships
How	
Where	

organizational, and technological components of the system solution. Table 12-4 lists the types of specifications that would be produced during systems design.

Like houses or buildings, information systems may have many possible designs. Each design represents a unique blend of technical and organizational components. What makes one design superior to others is the ease and efficiency with which it fulfills user requirements within a specific set of technical, organizational, financial, and time constraints.

The Role of End Users

User information requirements drive the entire system-building effort. Users must have sufficient control over the design process to ensure that the system reflects their business priorities and information needs, not the biases of the technical staff (Hunton and Beeler, 1997). Working on design increases users' understanding and acceptance of the system, reducing problems caused by power transfers, intergroup conflict, and unfamiliarity with new system functions and procedures. As we describe in Chapter 13, insufficient user involvement in the design effort is a major cause of system failure. However, some types systems require more user participation in design than others and Section 12.4 shows how alternative systems development methods address the user participation issue.

Building successful information systems requires close cooperation among end users and information systems specialists throughout the systems development process.

COMPLETING THE SYSTEMS DEVELOPMENT PROCESS

The remaining steps in the systems development process translate the solution specifications established during systems analysis and design into a fully operational information system. These concluding steps consist of programming, testing, conversion, production, and maintenance.

Programming

During the **programming** stage, system specifications that were prepared during the design stage are translated into software program code. On the basis of detailed design documents for files, transaction and report layouts, and other design details, specifications for each program in the system are prepared. Organizations write the software programs themselves or purchase application software packages for this purpose.

Testing

Exhaustive and thorough **testing** must be conducted to ascertain whether the system produces the right results. Testing answers the question, "Will the system produce the desired results under known conditions?"

   The amount of time needed to answer this question has been traditionally underrated in systems project planning (see Chapter 14). Testing is time consuming: Test data must be carefully prepared, results reviewed, and corrections made in the system. In some instances parts of the system may have to be redesigned. The risks of glossing over this step are enormous.

   Testing an information system can be broken down into three types of activities: unit testing, system testing and acceptance testing. **Unit testing,** or program testing, consists of testing each program separately in the system. It is widely believed that the purpose of such testing is to guarantee that programs are error free, but this goal is realistically impossible. Testing should be viewed instead as a means of locating errors in programs, focusing on finding all the ways to make a program fail. Once pinpointed, problems can be corrected.

   System testing tests the functioning of the information system as a whole. It tries to determine if discrete modules will function together as planned and whether discrepancies exist between the way the system actually works and the way it was conceived. Among the areas examined are performance time, capacity for file storage and handling peak loads, recovery and restart capabilities, and manual procedures.

   Acceptance testing provides the final certification that the system is ready to be used in a production setting. Systems tests are evaluated by users and reviewed by management. When all parties are satisfied that the new system meets their standards, the system is formally accepted for installation.

   The systems development team works with users to devise a systematic test plan. The **test plan** includes all of the preparations for the series of tests we have just described.

---

programming
The process of translating the system specifications prepared during the design stage into program code.

testing
The exhaustive and thorough process that determines whether the system produces the desired results under known conditions.

unit testing
The process of testing each program separately in the system. Sometimes called program testing.

system testing
Tests the functioning of the information system as a whole in order to determine if discrete modules will function together as planned.

acceptance testing
Provides the final user and management certification that the system is ready to be used in a production setting.

test plan
Prepared by the development team in conjunction with the users; it includes all of the preparations for the series of tests to be performed on the system.

Procedure	Address and Maintenance "Record Change Series"		Test Series 2			
Prepared By:		Date:		Version:		
Test Ref.	Condition Tested	Special Requirements	Expected Results	Output On	Next Screen	
2	Change records					
2.1	Change existing record	Key field	Not allowed			
2.2	Change nonexistent record	Other fields	"Invalid key" message			
2.3	Change deleted record	Deleted record must be available	"Deleted" message			
2.4	Make second record	Change 2.1 above	OK if valid	Transaction file	V45	
2.5	Insert record		OK if valid	Transaction file	V45	
2.6	Abort during change	Abort 2.5	No change	Transaction file	V45	

Figure 12-6 A sample test plan to test a record change. When developing a test plan, it is imperative to include the various conditions to be tested, the requirements for each condition tested, and the expected results. Test plans require input from both end users and information system specialists.

Figure 12-6 shows an example of a test plan. The general condition being tested is a record change. The documentation consists of a series of test-plan screens maintained on a database (perhaps a PC database) that is ideally suited to this kind of application.

Conversion

Conversion is the process of changing from the old system to the new system. Four main conversion strategies can be employed: the parallel strategy, the direct cutover strategy, the pilot study strategy, and the phased approach strategy.

In a **parallel strategy** both the old system and its potential replacement are run together for a time until everyone is assured that the new one functions correctly. This is the safest conversion approach because, in the event of errors or processing disruptions, the old system can still be used as a backup. However, this approach is very expensive, and additional staff or resources may be required to run the extra system.

The **direct cutover** strategy replaces the old system entirely with the new system on an appointed day. At first glance, this strategy seems less costly than the parallel conversion strategy. However, it is a very risky approach that can potentially be more costly than parallel activities if serious problems with the new system are found. There is no other system to fall back on. Dislocations, disruptions, and the cost of corrections may be enormous.

The **pilot study** strategy introduces the new system to only a limited area of the organization, such as a single department or operating unit. When this pilot version is complete and working smoothly, it is installed throughout the rest of the organization, either simultaneously or in stages.

The **phased approach** strategy introduces the new system in stages, either by functions or by organizational units. If, for example, the system is introduced by functions, a new payroll system might begin with hourly workers who are paid weekly, followed six months later by adding salaried employees (who are paid monthly) to the system. If the system is introduced by organizational units, corporate headquarters might be converted first, followed by outlying operating units four months later.

Moving from an old system to a new one requires that end users be trained to use the new system. Detailed **documentation** showing how the system works from both a technical and end-user standpoint is finalized during conversion time for use in training and everyday operations. Lack of proper training and documentation contributes to system failure, so this portion of the systems development process is very important.

Production and Maintenance

After the new system is installed and conversion is complete, the system is said to be in **production.** During this stage the system will be reviewed by both users and technical

conversion
The process of changing from the old system to the new system.

parallel strategy
A safe and conservative conversion approach where both the old system and its potential replacement are run together for a time until everyone is assured that the new one functions correctly.

direct cutover
A risky conversion approach whereby the new system completely replaces the old one on an appointed day.

pilot study
A strategy to introduce the new system to a limited area of the organization until it is proven to be fully functional; only then can the conversion to the new system across the entire organization take place.

phased approach
Introduces the new system in stages either by functions or by organizational units.

documentation
Descriptions of how an information system works from both a technical and an end-user standpoint.

TABLE 12-5	SYSTEMS DEVELOPMENT
Core Activity	**Description**
Systems analysis	Identify problem(s)
	Specify solution
	Establish information requirements
Systems design	Create design specifications
Programming	Translate design specifications into program code
Testing	Unit test
	Systems test
	Acceptance test
Conversion	Plan conversion
	Prepare documentation
	Train users and technical staff
Production and maintenance	Operate the system
	Evaluate the system
	Modify the system

production

The stage after the new system is installed and the conversion is complete; during this time the system is reviewed by users and technical specialists to determine how well it has met its original goals.

maintenance

Changes in hardware, software, documentation, or procedures to a production system to correct errors, meet new requirements, or improve processing efficiency.

specialists to determine how well it has met its original objectives and to decide whether any revisions or modifications are in order. Changes in hardware, software, documentation, or procedures to a production system to correct errors, meet new requirements, or improve processing efficiency are termed **maintenance.**

Studies of maintenance have examined the amount of time required for various maintenance tasks (Lientz and Swanson, 1980). Approximately 20 percent of the time is devoted to debugging or correcting emergency production problems; another 20 percent is concerned with changes in data, files, reports, hardware, or system software. But 60 percent of all maintenance work consists of making user enhancements, improving documentation, and recoding system components for greater processing efficiency. The amount of work in the third category of maintenance problems could be reduced significantly through better systems analysis and design practices. Table 12-5 summarizes the systems development activities.

12.4 ALTERNATIVE SYSTEM-BUILDING APPROACHES

Systems differ in terms of their size and technological complexity, and in terms of the organizational problems they are meant to solve. Because there are different kinds of systems, a number of methods have been developed to build systems. This section describes these alternative methods: the traditional systems lifecycle, prototyping, application software packages, end-user development, and outsourcing.

systems lifecycle

A traditional methodology for developing an information system that partitions the systems development process into formal stages that must be completed sequentially with a very formal division of labor between end users and information systems specialists.

TRADITIONAL SYSTEMS LIFECYCLE

The **systems lifecycle** is the oldest method for building information systems and is still used today for medium or large complex systems projects. The lifecycle methodology is a very formal approach to building a system, dividing systems development into formal stages that must take place in sequential order. All the activities in each stage must be completed before the next stage can begin. The systems lifecycle methodology also maintains a very formal division of labor between end users and information systems specialists. Technical specialists, such as systems analysts and programmers, are responsible for much of the systems analysis, design, and implementation work; end users are limited to providing information requirements and reviewing the technical staff's work. The lifecycle emphasizes formal specifications

TABLE 12-6   THE SYSTEMS LIFECYCLE

Stage	Division of Labor	End Product
Systems analysis	Technical specialists identify the problem, gather information requirements, develop alternative solutions, and establish a project management plan. Business users provide information requirements, establish financial or operational constraints on the solution, and select the solution.	Systems proposal report
Systems design	Technical specialists model and document design specifications and select the hardware and software technologies for the solution. Business users approve the design specifications.	Design specifications
Programming	Technical specialists write program code.	Program specifications and code
Testing	Technical specialists develop test plans and conduct unit, system, and acceptance tests. Business users provide test data and scenarios and validate test results.	System performance tests
Conversion	Technical specialists prepare a conversion plan and supervise conversion. Business users evaluate the new system and decide when the new system can be put into production.	User sign-off
Production and maintenance	Technical specialists evaluate the technical performance of the system and perform maintenance. Business users use the system and evaluate its functional performance.	Postimplementation audit

and paperwork, so many documents are generated during the course of a systems project. Table 12-6 provides more detail on this system-building approach.

After the system is installed and in production, users and technical specialists will go through a formal **postimplementation audit** that determines how well the new system has met its original objectives and whether any revisions or modifications are required. After the system has been fine-tuned, it will need to be maintained while it is in production to correct errors, meet requirements, or improve processing efficiency. Over time, the system may require so much maintenance to remain efficient and meet user objectives that it will come to the end of its useful life span. Once the system's lifecycle comes to an end, a completely new system is called for and the lifecycle may begin again.

The systems lifecycle is still used for building large complex systems that require a rigorous and formal requirements analysis, predefined specifications, and tight controls over the systems-building process. However, the systems lifecycle approach is costly, time consuming, and inflexible. Volumes of new documents must be generated and steps repeated if requirements and specifications need to be revised. Because of the time and cost to repeat the sequence of lifecycle activities, the methodology encourages freezing of specifications early in the development process, discouraging change. The lifecycle approach is also not suitable for many small desktop systems, which tend to be less structured and more individualized.

PROTOTYPING

Prototyping consists of building an experimental system rapidly and inexpensively for end users to evaluate. By interacting with the prototype, users can get a better idea of their information requirements. The prototype endorsed by the users can be used as a template to create the final system.

The **prototype** is a working version of an information system or part of the system, but it is meant to be only a preliminary model. Once operational, the prototype will be further refined until it conforms precisely to users' requirements. Once the design has been finalized, the prototype can be converted to a polished production system.

The process of building a preliminary design, trying it out, refining it, and trying again has been called an **iterative** process of systems development because the steps required to build a system can be repeated over and over again. Prototyping is more explicitly iterative than the conventional lifecycle, and it actively promotes system design changes. It has been

postimplementation audit
Formal review process conducted after a system has been placed in production to determine how well the system has met its original objectives.

prototyping
The process of building an experimental system quickly and inexpensively for demonstration and evaluation so that users can better determine information requirements.

prototype
The preliminary working version of an information system for demonstration and evaluation purposes.

iterative
A process of repeating over and over again the steps to build a system.

Figure 12-7 The protoyping process. The process of developing a prototype can be broken down into four steps. Because a prototype can be developed quickly and inexpensively, system builders can go through several iterations, repeating steps 3 and 4, to refine and enhance the prototype before arriving at the final operational one.

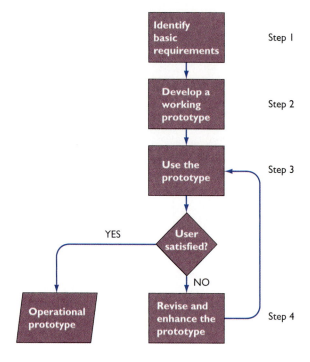

said that prototyping replaces unplanned rework with planned iteration, with each version more accurately reflecting users' requirements.

Steps in Prototyping

Figure 12-7 shows a four-step model of the prototyping process, which consists of the following:

Step 1: *Identify the user's basic requirements.* The system designer (usually an information systems specialist) works with the user only long enough to capture his or her basic information needs.

Step 2: *Develop an initial prototype.* The system designer creates a working prototype quickly, using fourth-generation software, interactive multimedia, or computer-aided software engineering (CASE) tools described in Chapter 14.

Step 3: *Use the prototype.* The user is encouraged to work with the system in order to determine how well the prototype meets his or her needs and to make suggestions for improving the prototype.

Step 4: *Revise and enhance the prototype.* The system builder notes all changes the user requests and refines the prototype accordingly. After the prototype has been revised, the cycle returns to step 3. Steps 3 and 4 are repeated until the user is satisfied.

When no more iterations are required, the approved prototype then becomes an operational prototype that furnishes the final specifications for the application. Sometimes the prototype itself is adopted as the production version of the system.

Advantages and Disadvantages of Prototyping

Prototyping is most useful when there is some uncertainty about requirements or design solutions. Prototyping is especially useful in designing an information system's **end-user interface** (the part of the system that end users interact with, such as on-line display and data-entry screens, reports, or Web pages). Because prototyping encourages intense end-user involvement throughout the systems development process, it is more likely to produce systems that fulfill user requirements.

However, rapid prototyping can gloss over essential steps in systems development. If the completed prototype works reasonably well, management may not see the need for reprogramming, redesign, or full documentation and testing to build a polished production sys-

end-user interface

The part of an information system through which the end user interacts with the system, such as on-line screens and commands.

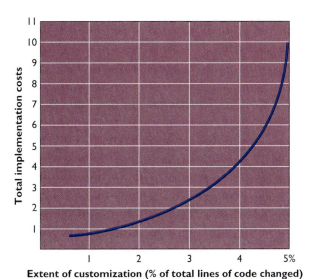

Figure 12-8 The effects of customizing a software package on total implementation costs. As the modifications to a software package rise, so does the cost of implementing the package. Savings promised by the package can be whittled away by excessive changes.

tem. Some of these hastily constructed systems may not easily accommodate large quantities of data or a large number of users in a production environment.

APPLICATION SOFTWARE PACKAGES

Information systems can be built using software from **application software packages,** which we introduced in Chapter 6. There are many applications that are common to all business organizations—for example, payroll, accounts receivable, general ledger, or inventory control. For such universal functions with standard procedures, a generalized system will fulfill the requirements of many organizations.

If a software package can fulfill most of an organization's requirements, the company does not have to write its own software. The company can save time and money by using the prewritten, predesigned, pretested software programs from the package. Package vendors supply much of the ongoing maintenance and support for the system, including enhancements to keep the system in line with ongoing technical and business developments.

If an organization has unique requirements that the package does not address, many packages include capabilities for customization. **Customization** features allow a software package to be modified to meet an organization's unique requirements without destroying the integrity of the package software. If a great deal of customization is required, additional programming and customization work may become so expensive and time consuming that they eliminate many of the advantages of software packages. Figure 12-8 shows how package costs in relation to total implementation costs rise with the degree of customization. The initial purchase price of the package can be deceptive because of these hidden implementation costs.

Selecting Software Packages

When a system is developed using an application software package, systems analysis will include a package evaluation effort. The most important evaluation criteria are the functions provided by the package, flexibility, user-friendliness, hardware and software resources, database requirements, installation and maintenance effort, documentation, vendor quality, and cost. The package evaluation process often is based on a **Request for Proposal (RFP),** which is a detailed list of questions submitted to packaged software vendors.

When a software package solution is selected, the organization no longer has total control over the system design process. Instead of tailoring the system design specifications directly to user requirements, the design effort will consist of trying to mold user requirements to conform to the features of the package. If the organization's requirements conflict with the way the package works and the package cannot be customized, the organization will have to adapt to the package and change its procedures.

A new company that was just being set up, such as the one described in the Window on Organizations, could adopt the business processes and information flows provided by the

application software package
A set of prewritten, precoded application software programs that are commercially available for sale or lease.

customization
The modification of a software package to meet an organization's unique requirements without destroying the package software's integrity.

Request for Proposal (RFP)
A detailed list of questions submitted to vendors of software or other services to determine how well the vendor's product can meet the organization's specific requirements.

INDIAN MOTORCYCLES IS REBORN WITH NEW INFORMATION SYSTEMS

Window on

Organizations

MIS In Action

Indian Motorcycles built the first American-made motorcycle in 1901. Until the early 1950s, the company had a devoted following and a reputation for quality motorcycles with character. Looking at their dark, skirted fenders, flowing lines, and beautifully painted metal, some devotees believed they were the best motorcycles ever made. But in 1953, the company had to close its doors, crippled by excessive reliance on army contracts and a crumbling dealer network. Today, the company has come roaring back, and its management credits new information systems for its rebirth.

Indian's brand image was so strong that investors thought it worthwhile to revive the company. In 1998 a Canadian firm teamed up with the California Motorcycle Company, a small builder of Harley Davidson clone bikes, to make motorcycles in the old classic Indian style and a broad range of related parts, accessories, riding gear, and lifestyle apparel. Under this new leadership, Indian Motorcycle Company of America was reborn. The new company is headquartered in Gilroy, California.

One of the company's first steps was to invest $1.3 million in Oracle 11.03, a full-function enterprise resource planning package. Indian's management decided to use the enterprise package as a template for the new company's business processes. In other words, instead of defining the organization's business processes first and then finding software that worked with them, Indian's management immediately adopted the business processes and information flows dictated by the package as those for the new company. How the new company would move items in the work line, open and close work orders, receive products, and treat suppliers was thus determined at the outset by the software. The company's organizational culture would have to change to accept these ways of doing business.

By using an enterprise system from the outset with a centralized database and centralized demand planning, the company could react more quickly to demand and make changes to forecasts and sales orders right from the start. Integrated processes could help it reduce lead times, inventory, and other costs, and provide the flexibility to assemble the bikes that consumers wanted without being strapped with huge manufacturing and tooling facilities.

Indian Motorcycles also established an extranet based on Oracle's Web Customer software to link its dealers to the system. More than half of the company's dealers use it regularly to check product availability, manage orders and accounts, and review new specifications. They can also use it to import data into their own Excel spreadsheets for further analysis.

The new Indian Motorcycles produced its first motorcycles in 2000. Although they had styling reminiscent of the classic 1948 Indian Chief model, they initially received a lukewarm reception from the motorcycle crowd. Indian's management believes it has the right organization and know-how to turn this situation around. Instead of building a mammoth vehicle manufacturing structure, it spent its dollars on building brand awareness and on technology that can precisely track which bikes are selling in which markets and how quickly they sell.

MAKE IT YOUR BUSINESS

To Think About: Not many companies think of systems first and then build the way they do business around software packages from the start. What are the advantages and disadvantages of using this approach?

Sources: Stewart Deck, "How Indian Got Its Vroom Back," *CIO Magazine,* June 15, 2001; and "Indian Motorcycles Builds Management Team," www.indianmotorcycle.com.

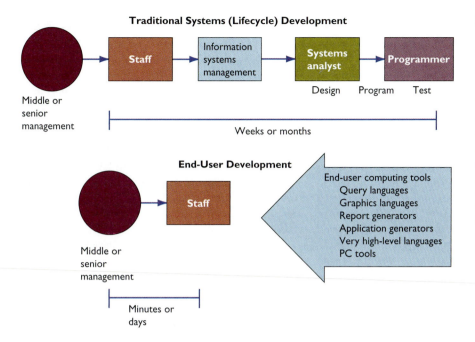

Figure 12-9 End-user versus system lifecycle development. End users can access computerized information directly or develop information systems with little or no formal technical assistance. On the whole, end-user-developed systems can be completed more rapidly than those developed through the conventional systems lifecycle. *Source:* From *Application Development Without Programmers,* by James Martin, © 1982. Reprinted by permission of Prentice Hall Inc., Upper Saddle River, NJ.

package as its own business processes. But organizations that have been in existence for some time will not be able to easily change the way they work to conform to the package.

END-USER DEVELOPMENT

Some types of information systems can be developed by end users with little or no formal assistance from technical specialists. This phenomenon is called **end-user development.** Using fourth-generation languages, graphics languages, and PC software tools, end users can access data, create reports, and develop entire information systems on their own, with little or no help from professional systems analysts or programmers. Many of these end-user developed systems can be created much more rapidly than with the traditional systems lifecycle. Figure 12-9 illustrates the concept of end-user development.

end-user development
The development of information systems by end users with little or no formal assistance from technical specialists.

Benefits and Limitations of End-User Development

Many organizations have reported gains in application development productivity by using fourth-generation tools that in a few cases have reached 300 to 500 percent (Glass, 1999; Green, 1984–85). Allowing users to specify their own business needs improves requirements gathering and often leads to a higher level of user involvement and satisfaction with the system. However, fourth-generation tools still cannot replace conventional tools for some business applications because they cannot easily handle the processing of large numbers of transactions or applications with extensive procedural logic and updating requirements.

End-user computing also poses organizational risks because it occurs outside of traditional mechanisms for information system management and control. When systems are created rapidly without a formal development methodology, testing and documentation may be inadequate. Control over data can be lost in systems outside the traditional information systems department (see Chapter 7).

Managing End-User Development

To help organizations maximize the benefits of end-user applications development, management should control the development of end-user applications by requiring cost justification of end-user information system projects and by establishing hardware, software, and quality standards for user-developed applications.

When end-user computing first became popular, organizations used information centers to promote standards for hardware and software so that end users could not introduce many disparate and incompatible technologies into the firm (Fuller and Swanson, 1992).

HARVARD PILGRIM HEALTHCARE OUTSOURCES TO SAVE ITS LIFE

Harvard Pilgrim Healthcare is New England's oldest and most prestigious health maintenance organization (HMO), providing healthcare coverage in Massachusetts, Maine, Vermont, and New Hampshire. The company is also the product of many health plan mergers. In 1986 (when the company was called the Harvard Community Health Plan and had 240,000 members), it acquired MultiGroup, a regional New England HMO with 105,000 members. Management chose not to integrate the combining companies' health plan claims and enrollment systems. Over the next 11 years, this HMO continued to acquire other regional health plans, including Rhode Island Group Health Association and Neighborhood Health Plan, and Pilgrim Health Care. Because senior management failed to appreciate the importance of information systems, Harvard Pilgrim never fully integrated all of the different systems of the companies it acquired.

In April 1999 Harvard Pilgrim reported a devastating $54 million net loss and an operating loss of $94 million for the previous year. The company's CEO and other senior managers all resigned. Charles Baker, the new CEO, appointed Louis Gutierrez, deputy director of information technology at the Federal Reserve Bank, as the company's new CIO. The company had made incorrect estimates of how revenue and claims accounting were handled, and such errors were largely attributable to its mishmash of information systems.

Gutierrez was charged with untangling a mess of more than 55 core application systems including four claims processing systems, which prevented Harvard Pilgrim from tracking claims or setting accurate healthcare premiums. The company could not develop accurate consolidated financial reports using these redundant systems.

Senior management asked Gutierrez to decide whether to outsource Harvard Pilgrim's claims processing or its entire information technology function, including computer center operations, network infrastructure, and programming. Gutierrez decided to outsource both in order to obtain a "common accountability of IT and claims processing." He believed that the company had to change the way both the technology and its employees worked so that claims processing and information systems worked together as a cohesive unit with common goals.

Gutierrez and his team selected Perot Systems as their outsourcing vendor in October 1999 because it fulfilled most of their requirements and also had more consultants with expertise in Amisys than their competitors. (Amisys was Harvard Pilgrim's primary operating software.) The outsourcing deal did not produce any layoffs. Harvard Pilgrim's 826 claims processing and information systems staff members continued working at their desks but became Perot Systems employees. Gutierrez kept Harvard Pilgrim's 40 staff members in charge of data warehousing, e-commerce strategy, security policy, and technology process engineering under his direct control.

To Think About: What were the management benefits of outsourcing for Harvard Pilgrim Healthcare? What management, organization, and technology issues did it have to address in its outsourcing decision and information systems plans?

Sources: Angela Genusa, "Blood, Sweat and Systems Integration," *CIO Magazine,* June 15, 2001; and www.harvardpilgrim.org.

---

information center

A special facility within an organization that provides training and support for end-user computing.

Information centers are special facilities housing hardware, software, and technical specialists to supply end users with tools, training, and expert advice so they can create information system applications on their own or increase their productivity. The role of information centers is diminishing as end-users become more computer literate, but organizations still need to closely monitor and manage end-user development.

OUTSOURCING

outsourcing

The practice of contracting computer center operations, telecommunications networks, or applications development to external vendors.

If a firm does not want to use its internal resources to build or operate information systems, it can hire an external organization that specializes in providing these services to do the work. The process of turning over an organization's computer center operations, telecommunications networks, or applications development to external vendors is called **outsourcing.** The application service providers (ASPs) described in Chapter 6 are one form of outsourcing. Subscribing companies would use the software and computer hardware provided by the ASP as the technical platform for their system. In another form of outsourcing, a company would hire an external vendor to design and create the software for its system, but that company would operate the system on its own computer.

TABLE 12-7 COMPARISON OF SYSTEMS-DEVELOPMENT APPROACHES

Approach	Features	Advantages	Disadvantages
Systems lifecycle	Sequential step-by-step formal process Written specification and approvals Limited role of users	Necessary for large complex systems and projects	Slow and expensive Discourages changes Massive paperwork to manage
Prototyping	Requirements specified dynamically with experimental system Rapid, informal, and iterative process Users continually interact with the prototype	Rapid and relatively inexpensive Useful when requirements uncertain or when end-user interface is very important Promotes user participation	Inappropriate for large, complex systems Can gloss over steps in analysis, documentation, and testing
Applications software package	Commercial software eliminates need for internally developed software programs	Design, programming, installation, and maintenance work reduced Can save time and cost when developing common business applications Reduces need for internal information systems resources	May not meet organization's unique requirements May not perform many business functions well Extensive customization raises development costs
End-user development	Systems created by end users using fourth-generation software tools Rapid and informal Minimal role of information systems specialists	Users control systems-building Saves development time and cost Reduces application backlog	Can lead to proliferation of uncontrolled information systems and data Systems do not always meet quality assurance standards
Outsourcing	Systems built and sometimes operated by external vendor	Can reduce or control costs Can produce systems when internal resources are not available or technically deficient	Loss of control over the information systems function Dependence on the technical direction and prosperity of external vendors

Outsourcing has become popular because some organizations perceive it as more cost effective than maintaining their own computer center or information systems staff (see the Window on Management). The provider of outsourcing services benefits from economies of scale (the same knowledge, skills, and capacity can be shared with many different customers) and is likely to charge competitive prices for information systems services. Outsourcing allows a company with fluctuating needs for computer processing to pay for only what it uses rather than to build its own computer center, which would be underutilized when there is no peak load. Some firms outsource because their internal information systems staff cannot keep pace with technological change or innovative business practices or because they want to free up scarce and costly talent for activities with higher payback.

Not all organizations benefit from outsourcing, and the disadvantages of outsourcing can create serious problems for organizations if they are not well understood and managed (Earl, 1996). Many firms underestimate costs for identifying and evaluating vendors of information technology services, for transitioning to a new vendor, and for monitoring vendors to make sure they are fulfilling their contractual obligations. These "hidden costs" can easily undercut anticipated benefits from outsourcing (Barthelemy, 2001). When a firm allocates the responsibility for developing and operating its information systems to another organization, it can lose control over its information systems function. If the organization lacks the expertise to negotiate a sound contract, the firm's dependency on the vendor could result in high costs or loss of control over technological direction (Lacity, Willcocks, and Feeny, 1996). Firms should be especially cautious when using an outsourcer to develop or to operate applications that give it some type of competitive advantage.

Table 12-7 compares the advantages and disadvantages of each of the system-building alternatives.

12.5 Application Development for the Digital Firm

Electronic commerce, electronic business, and the emerging digital firm pose new challenges for system building. Technologies and business conditions are changing so rapidly that agility and scalability have become a critical success factor and primary goal of system design. Businesses need software components that can be added, modified, replaced, or reconfigured to enable them to respond rapidly to new opportunities. Systems must be scalable to accommodate growing numbers of users and to deliver data over multiple platforms—client/server networks, desktop computers with Web browsers, cell phones, and other mobile devices. E-Commerce and e-business systems may also need to be designed so that they can run in hosted environments as well as on the company's own hardware and software platforms. To remain competitive, some firms feel pressured to design, develop, test, and deploy Internet or intranet applications in a matter of weeks or months (Earl and Khan, 2001).

Older development methods were based on a much more static view of systems. In the past, systems development would be based on a formal design document with functional specifications that was handed off to a development team. Alternatively, applications might be loosely designed and iteratively developed with multiple passes going to users for review and revision. Such development processes often took months or years and were ill suited to the pace and profile of Internet or intranet projects. Traditional methods did not address the new features of Internet-based applications, which might have multiple tiers of clients and servers with different operating systems linked to transaction processing systems, as well as business processes that had to be coordinated with those of customers or suppliers.

In the digital firm environment, organizations need to be able to add, change, and retire their technology capabilities very rapidly. Companies are adopting shorter, more informal development processes for many of their e-commerce and e-business applications, processes that provide fast solutions that do not disrupt their core transaction processing systems and organizational databases. They are relying more heavily on fast-cycle techniques such as rapid application development (RAD), prototypes, and reusable standardized software components that can be assembled into a complete set of services for e-commerce and e-business.

Object-Oriented Software Development

object-oriented software development

An approach to software development that shifts the focus from modeling processes and data to combining data and procedures to create objects.

Organizations are increasingly turning to object-oriented software development for creating systems that are more flexible and easier to build and maintain. Chapter 6 introduced object-oriented programming, which combines data and the specific procedures that operate on those data into one object. **Object-oriented software development** differs from traditional system-building approaches by shifting the focus from separately modeling processes and data to combining data and procedures into unified objects. The system is modeled as a collection of classes and objects and includes the relationships among them. The objects are defined, programmed, documented, and saved as building blocks for future applications. Information requirements are specifed through *use cases* that describe the interactions between the system and its users. Objects are reusable, so object-oriented software development could reduce the time and cost of writing software because organizations can reuse software objects that have already been created as building blocks for other applications. New systems can be created by using some existing objects, changing others, and adding a few new objects. Object-oriented development is very useful for creating Web applications.

In theory, design and programming can begin as soon as requirements are completed through the use of iterations of rapid prototyping. Object-oriented frameworks have been developed to provide reusable, semicomplete applications that the organization can further customize into finished applications (Fayad and Schmidt, 1997). However, information systems specialists must learn a completely new way of modeling a system (Sircar, Nerur, and Mahapatra, 2001), and object-oriented models of systems aren't always more usable than process-oriented models (Agarwal, De, Sinha, and Tanniru, 2000). Conversion to an object-oriented approach may require large-scale organizational investments, which management must balance against the anticipated payoffs. No organization will see savings from reusability until it builds up a library of objects to draw on and understands which objects have broad use (Pancake, 1995).

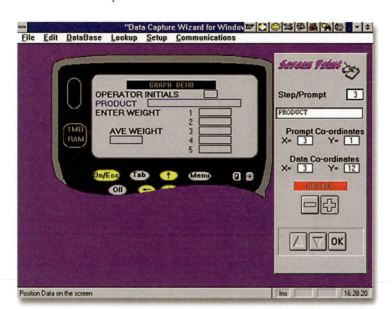

Intava Gravity Professional is a visual development tool for rapid creation of multi-platform mobile Web applcations. RAD tools enable companies to create rapid solutions without extensive programming.

RAPID APPLICATION DEVELOPMENT (RAD)

Object-oriented software tools, reusable software, prototyping, and fourth-generation tools are helping system builders create working systems much more rapidly than they could using traditional system-building methods and software tools. The term **rapid application development (RAD)** is used to describe this process of creating workable systems in a very short period of time. RAD can include the use of visual programming and other tools for building graphical user interfaces, iterative prototyping of key system elements, the automation of program code generation, and close teamwork among end users and information systems specialists. Simple systems often can be assembled from prebuilt components. The process does not have to be sequential, and key parts of development can occur simultaneously.

Sometimes a technique called **JAD (joint application design)** is used to accelerate the generation of information requirements and to develop the initial systems design. JAD brings end users and information systems specialists together in an interactive session to discuss the system's design. Properly prepared and facilitated, JAD sessions can significantly speed the design phase while involving users at an intense level.

WEB SERVICES

We have already described how firms are basing portions of their information technology infrastructure on services supplied by external vendors. Increasingly, new information system applications will be built using Web services. **Web services** are software components deliverable over the Internet that enable one application to communicate with another with no translation required. By allowing applications to communicate and share data regardless of operating system, programming language, or client device, Web services can provide significant cost savings over traditional in-house systems while opening up new opportunities for collaboration with other companies (Hagel and Brown, 2001). For example, Dollar Rent a Car Systems uses Web services to integrate its on-line booking system with Southwest Airlines Co.'s Web site. Although both companies' systems are based on different technology platforms, a person booking a flight on Southwestair.com can reserve a car from Dollar without leaving the airline's Web site (McDougall, 2001). IBM has included Web service tools in its WebSphere e-business software, and Microsoft has incorporated Web services tools in its .NET platform.

Web services use an open "plug and play" architecture rather than a proprietary architecture. This architecture has three layers. The first consists of software standards and communication protocols such as XML, SOAP, WSDL, and UDDI, that allow information to be exchanged easily among different applications. XML, introduced in Chapter 6, provides a standard description of data in Web pages and databases. *SOAP*, which stands for Simple

rapid application development (RAD)
Process for developing systems in a very short time period by using prototyping, fourth-generation tools, and close teamwork among users and systems specialists.

joint application design (JAD)
Process to accelerate the generation of information requirements by having end users and information systems specialists work together in intensive interactive design sessions.

Web services
Software components deliverable over the Internet that enable one application to communicate with another with no translation required.

Object Access Protocol, allows applications to pass data and instructions to one another. *WSDL* stands for Web Services Description Language and allows a Web service to be described so that it can be used by other applications. *UDDI,* standing for Universal Description, Discovery, and Integration, allows a Web service to be listed in a directory of Web services so that it can be easily located. Using these standards and protocols, a software application can connect freely to other applications without custom programming for each different application with which it wants to communicate. Everyone shares the same standards.

The middle layer of Web services consists of a service grid to create environments essential for carrying out critical business activities. This middle layer provides a set of shared utilities, such as security, third-party billing and payment that are used for critical business functions and transactions over the Internet. The service grid also includes utilities for transporting messages and identifying available services.

The third layer consists of application services, such as credit card processing or production scheduling, that automate specific business functions. Some application services will be proprietary to a particular company and others will be shared among all companies. A company may also develop its own application services and then sell them to other companies on a subscription basis. For instance, Citibank developed and markets CitiConnect, an XML-based payment processing service that plugs into existing B2B net marketplaces.

Companies can use Web services in conjunction with their existing systems, connecting their traditional applications to outside services one by one as the need arises. Instead of building and maintaining unique home-grown systems, firms can pay for only the pieces of software functionality they need. Web services should help firms reduce their investments in large fixed information technology assets and large in-house information systems staff.

Looking Beyond the Organization

Building new systems for a digital firm environment requires more than innovative development approaches. E-commerce and e-business require systems planning and systems analysis based on a broader view of the organization, one that encompasses business processes extended beyond firm boundaries (Fingar, 2000). Firms can no longer execute their business and system plans alone because they need to forge new electronic relationships with suppliers, distributors, and customers. Their business processes often need to be integrated with customer and supplier business processes.

MAKE IT YOUR BUSINESS

FINANCE AND ACCOUNTING

The finance and accounting function helps system builders identify the costs and benefits of new information system projects and assess their economic feasibility. It also assists with the financial analysis of system-building alternatives, comparing the costs of custom in-house development to the costs of developing with application software packages or outsourcing to external vendors. You can find examples of finance and accounting applications on pages 404 and 412–413.

HUMAN RESOURCES

The human resources function assists with the analysis of changes in work flows and job responsibilities resulting from new information systems. Human resources specialists may also be involved with corporate programs to educate employees in Total Quality Management (TQM) principles as well as efforts to train employees to use new information systems.

MANUFACTURING AND PRODUCTION

Manufacturing and production have been a focal point for process improvements to improve quality. Information systems have been used to identify defects and variances from quality standards, to reduce cycle time, and to increase precision in design and production. When firms are installing new enterprise systems, one of their major objectives is to improve coordination of business processes for manufacturing and production and between manufacturing and production and the other functional areas. You can find examples of manufacturing and production applications on pages 380–382, 391–393, and 402.

SALES AND MARKETING

Information systems have supported quality improvements in sales and marketing that provide better customer service as well as products and sales experiences that increase customer satisfaction. Web-based information systems for on-line sales and marketing have become a high priority for corporate system-building during the last few years. You can find examples of sales and marketing applications on pages 391–393, 402, and 412–413.

MANAGEMENT WRAP-UP

Selection of a systems-building approach can have a big impact on the time, cost, and end product of systems development. Managers should be aware of the strengths and weaknesses of each systems-building approach and the types of problems for which each is best suited.

Organizational needs should drive the selection of a systems-building approach. The impact of application software packages and of outsourcing should be carefully evaluated before they are selected because these approaches give organizations less control over the systems-building process.

Various software tools are available to support the systems-building process. Key technology decisions should be based on the organization's familiarity with the technology and its compatibility with the organization's information requirements, IT infrastructure, and information architecture.

For Discussion

1. Why is selecting a systems development approach an important business decision? Who should participate in the selection process?

2. Some have said that the best way to reduce systems development costs is to use application software packages or fourth-generation tools. Do you agree? Why or why not?

SUMMARY

1. *How could building a new system change the way an organization works?* Building a new information system is a form of planned organizational change that involves many different people in the organization. Because information systems are sociotechnical entities, a change in information systems involves changes in work, management, and the organization. Four kinds of technology-enabled change are (1) automation, (2) rationalization of procedures, (3) business process reengineering, and (4) paradigm shift, with far-reaching changes carrying the greatest risks and rewards. Many organizations are attempting business process reengineering to redesign work flows and business processes in the hope of achieving dramatic productivity breakthroughs.

2. *How can a company make sure that the new information systems it builds fit its business plan?* Organizations should develop information systems plans that describe how information technology supports the attainment of their business goals. The plans indicate the direction of systems development, the rationale, implementation strategy, and budget. Enterprise analysis and critical success factors (CSFs) can be used to elicit organization-wide information requirements that must be addressed by the plans.

3. *What are the steps required to build a new information system?* The core activities in systems development are systems analysis, systems design, programming, testing, conversion, production, and maintenance. Systems analysis is the study and analysis of problems of existing systems and the identification of requirements for their solutions. Systems design provides the specifications for an information system solution, show-

ing how its technical and organizational components fit together.

4. *What alternative methods for building information systems are available?* There are a number of alternative methods for building information systems, each suited to different types of problems. The oldest method for building systems is the systems lifecycle, which requires that information systems be developed in formal stages. The stages must proceed sequentially and have defined outputs; each requires formal approval before the next stage can commence. The system lifecycle is useful for large projects that need formal specifications and tight management control over each stage of system building. However, this approach is very rigid and costly and is not well suited for unstructured, decision-oriented applications where requirements cannot be immediately visualized.

Prototyping consists of building an experimental system rapidly and inexpensively for end users to interact with and evaluate. The prototype is refined and enhanced until users are satisfied that it includes all of their requirements and can be used as a template to create the final system. Prototyping encourages end-user involvement in systems development and iteration of design until specifications are captured accurately. The rapid creation of prototypes can result in systems that have not been completely tested or documented or that are technically inadequate for a production environment.

Developing an information system using an application software package eliminates the need for writing software programs when developing the system. Using a software package reduces the amount of design, testing, installation, and maintenance work required to build a system. Application software packages are helpful if a firm does not have the internal information systems staff or financial resources to custom-develop a system. To meet an organization's unique requirements, packages may require extensive modifications that can substantially raise development costs.

End-user development is the development of information systems by end users, either alone or with minimal assistance from information systems specialists. End-user-developed systems can be created rapidly and informally using fourth-generation software tools. The primary benefits of end-user development are improved requirements determination; reduced application backlog; and increased end-user participation in, and control of, the systems development process. However, end-user development, in conjunction with distributed computing, has introduced new organizational risks by propagating information systems and data resources that do not necessarily meet quality assurance standards and that are not easily controlled by traditional means.

Outsourcing consists of using an external vendor to build (or operate) a firm's information systems. The work is done by the vendor rather than by the organization's internal infor-

mation systems staff. Outsourcing can save application development costs or allow firms to develop applications without an internal information systems staff. However, firms risk losing control over their information systems and becoming too dependent on external vendors.

5. *Are there any techniques or system-building approaches to help us build e-commerce and e-business applications more rapidly?* Businesses today are often required to build e-commerce and e-business applications very rapidly in order to remain competitive. They are relying more heavily on rapid application development (RAD), joint application design (JAD), and reusable software components to speed up the systems development process. Object-oriented software development is expected to reduce the time and cost of writing software and of making maintenance changes because it models a system as a series of reusable objects that combine both data and procedures. Rapid application development (RAD) uses object-oriented software, visual programming, prototyping, and fourth-generation tools for very rapid creation of systems. Web services will enable organizations to build and enhance systems by obtaining the functionality they need as software application components delivered over the Internet.

KEY TERMS

Acceptance testing, 396	End-user interface, 400	Paradigm shift, 388	Request for Proposal (RFP), 401
Application software package, 401	Enterprise analysis, 384	Parallel strategy, 397	Systems analysis, 394
Automation, 387	Feasibility study, 394	Phased approach, 397	Systems design, 394
Benchmarking, 392	Information center, 404	Pilot study, 397	Systems development, 393
Business process reengineering, 387	Information requirements, 394	Postimplementation audit, 399	Systems lifecycle, 398
Conversion, 397	Information systems plan, 383	Production, 398	System testing, 396
Critical success factors (CSFs), 384	Iterative, 399	Programming, 396	Test plan, 396
Customization, 401	Joint application design (JAD), 407	Prototype, 399	Testing, 396
Direct cutover, 397	Maintenance, 398	Prototyping, 399	Total quality management (TQM), 391
Documentation, 397	Object-oriented software development, 406	Rapid application development (RAD), 407	Unit testing, 396
End-user development, 403	Outsourcing, 404	Rationalization of procedures, 387	Web services, 407
			Work flow management, 390

REVIEW QUESTIONS

1. Why can an information system be considered planned organizational change?

2. What are the major categories of an information systems plan?

3. How can enterprise analysis and critical success factors be used to establish organization-wide information system requirements?

4. Describe each of the four kinds of organizational change that can be promoted with information technology.

5. What is business process reengineering? What steps are required to make it effective?

6. What is the difference between systems analysis and systems design? What activities do they comprise?

7. What are information requirements? Why are they difficult to determine correctly?

8. Why is the testing stage of systems development so important? Name and describe the three stages of testing for an information system.

9. What role do programming, conversion, production, and maintenance play in systems development?

10. What is the traditional systems lifecycle? Describe each of its steps and its advantages and disadvantages for system building.

11. What do we mean by information system prototyping? What are its benefits and limitations? List and describe the steps in the prototyping process.

12. What is an application software package? What are the advantages and disadvantages of developing information systems based on software packages?

13. What do we mean by end-user development? What are its advantages and disadvantages? Name some policies and procedures for managing end-user development.

14. What is outsourcing? Under what circumstances should it be used for building information systems?

15. What is the difference between object-oriented software development and traditional software development? What are the advantages of using object-oriented software development in building systems?

16. What is rapid application development (RAD)? How can it help system builders?

17. What are Web services? How can they help firms build and enhance their information systems?

APPLICATION SOFTWARE EXERCISE

DATABASE AND WEB PAGE DEVELOPMENT TOOL EXERCISE: BUILDING A JOB DATABASE AND WEB PAGE FOR A CONSULTING FIRM

KTP Consulting operates in various locations around the world. KTP specializes in designing, developing, and implementing enterprise systems for medium to large-size companies. KTP offers its employees opportunities to travel, live, and work in various locations throughout the United States, Europe, and Asia. The firm's human resources department has a simple database that enables its staff to track job vacancies. When an employee is interested in relocating, she or he contacts the human resources department for a list of KTP job vacancies. KTP also posts its employment opportunities on the company Web site.

What type of data should be included in the KTP job vacancies database? What information should not be included in this database? Based on your answers to these questions, build a job vacancies database for KTP. Populate the database with at least 20 records. You should also build a simple Web page that incorporates job vacancy data from your newly created database. Submit a disk containing a copy of the KTP database and Web page to your professor.

GROUP PROJECT

With three or four of your classmates, select a system described in this text that uses the Web. Examples might include the Cisco Systems Web site in Chapter 1, the GE Web site in Chapter 3, the Schneider National Web site in Chapter 8, and the GM Web site in Chapter 9. Review the Web site for the system you select.

Use what you have learned from the Web site and the description in this book to prepare a report describing some of the design specifications for the system you select. Present your findings to the class.

TOOLS FOR INTERACTIVE LEARNING

◼ INTERNET CONNECTION

The Internet Connection for this chapter will direct you to the SAP Web site where you can complete an exercise to evaluate the capabilities of this major multinational software package and learn more about enterprise resource planning. You can also use the Interactive Study Guide to test your knowledge of the topics in this chapter and get instant feedback where you need more practice.

◼ ELECTRONIC BUSINESS PROJECT

At the Laudon Web site for Chapter 12, you can complete an Electronic Business project to redesign business processes to participate in a net marketplace.

◼ CD-ROM

If you use the Multimedia Edition CD-ROM with this chapter, you can find a video clip on Andersen Consulting's Smart Store and Retail Place illustrating the innovative use of technology to rethink the delivery of goods and services, an audio overview of the introduction to this chapter, and bullet text summarizing the key points of the chapter.

CASE STUDY—*Can APCO Insure Its Future with a New System?*

APCO, short for the Automobile Protection Corp., is a little-known company whose field is automotive service insurance and whose goal is to market and administer contracts that cover both automobile warranties and service contracts. Headquartered in Atlanta, Georgia, the company was launched in 1984 and was acquired by Ford in 1999 for $165 million. Its contracts are actually insurance policies that cover the costs of repairing vehicles—contracts that dealers offer when customers purchase a vehicle. Although some dealers insure for repairs themselves, usually these contracts are actually offered by insurance companies in the name of the dealers, and they are usually sold through the dealers.

APCO is not a dealer, a service organization, or an insurer but instead arranges for warranting and servicing insurance with various insurance companies. It then markets these policies as service contracts or warranties through the automobile dealers. Once these contracts are sold to the vehicle purchasers, APCO administers them through the dealers. It also handles private-label service contracts for partners who finance and sell their own contracts and then engage APCO to administer them. Its private-label partners include such well-known companies as Allstate, American Honda Finance, Banc One, Manhein Auto Auctions, Mazda USA, and Volvo Canada.

Although APCO had only $8 million in sales in 1989, its fifth year, by the year 2000, its sales had grown to $165 million, and sales were expected to grow 9 to 10 percent in 2001. In the year 2000 APCO had about 1,200 dealer–customers in the United States. About 2 percent of all extended automobile service contracts sold in the United States are sold through dealers. This leaves a huge potential market for APCO to expand into as well as into markets in Canada and Europe. APCO's main competitors are vehicle manufacturers, many of which also offer factory-backed warranties although at a higher price.

APCO now has a major problem, one that many companies would love to have—a massive expansion of customers that has already occurred and is likely to continue. APCO experienced a dramatic upsurge in sales, increasing more than 20 times in only 11 years. The result is that both dealer–customer applications for its policies and the submission of repair claims have become almost unmanageable as well as extremely costly. A significant element of that problem is that APCO issues and administers hundreds of different policies to thousands of policyholders, each of which is complex. Different dealers offer different types and amounts of service in those contracts, and all customers must select the level and type of service they will pay for when they purchase the contracts. APCO faces many of the same problems with the thousands of private-label contracts it administers.

APCO's work is highly document intensive and time consuming. All of this time and manual work is inefficient and makes the process very costly. The first step in the process is for the company to design and create many different documents, one for each type of contract the dealers require. Given the hundreds of different dealer contracts and all their possible options, this is extremely complex. Currently, APCO minimizes the number of contracts it must support by creating a large number of generic contracts that, when issued to the auto purchaser, must be adjusted both to each specific dealer and to each customer. These adjustments are done in the contract's declaration section, where the dealer records which other contract sections apply to a specific customer's contract and which do not, depending on what the dealer wants to offer and what specific coverage the customer has agreed to pay for. Once the dealer has filled out the declaration section, it must be approved by APCO, and only after that can it be issued to the auto purchaser.

With the current system, this whole process is very slow and costly. After a dealer fills out the declaration section, it is mailed to APCO where the data are manually entered into APCO's computers. Next the computer processes the application, after which it is forwarded to the underwriters where it is manually entered into the underwriters' computers. It is then approved or rejected and mailed back to the dealer. Finally, assuming the document has been approved, the customer must return to sign it. The whole process usually takes between five and ten days to be completed.

Being heavily manual and requiring the data to be entered several times, the process is also quite error prone, requiring many corrections and resulting in many improper contract applications. For instance, between one-half and three-quarters of the applications received by APCO under the current system are rejected because required information is missing. This adds to the expense and the wasted time. In addition, the errors and the slowness of approval seriously damage APCO's relations with its customers—the dealers—as well as the dealers' relations with their customers—the automobile purchasers. The same problems exist when private-label (partner) vehicle customers decide to sign an APCO contract.

Claims processing uses systems similar to the contract systems, and they are also time consuming, error-prone, and expensive. Such expensive and time-consuming processes seriously interfere with APCO's ability to retain current customers and to acquire new customers. In fact, the cost and time for contract creation and approval, along with claims administration, have caused the company almost to lose control over both processes. Unless a way is found to better manage it all, expanding further into the United States and into foreign markets will only greatly increase the problems, creating even more difficulties for APCO's and the dealers' customers. That is the problem APCO faces, and something must be done.

At the time the customer buys the automobile, APCO would "ultimately like the customer to leave the dealership with the [APCO] contract in hand," explained Brian Kohrman, APCO's MIS director. With a proper system, "We'd be able to do approval and denial almost immediately," he said, "and ultimately fire the contract right back to the dealership and have them print [it] out and have it signed, right there." Dan Walsh, APCO's vice president and creative director, believes that, with the right package, APCO "can start providing customers with coverage information that's more specific to whatever they purchased. It becomes more personalized and gives the customer more accurate information."

Automobile dealers maintain that the buying experience must become friendlier because today's shoppers are too startled and even frightened when they first see the vehicle sticker price. As a result dealers are searching for ways to reduce the tensions and fears throughout the entire sales process, including warrantees and servicing. Moreover, servicing is extremely important to dealers for another reason—it is very profitable. Dealers usually make more profit from servicing than from vehicle sales. Almost all service customers have purchased their vehicles from that dealer, and dealers must find ways to sign them up as service customers and then to hold on to them. Auto industry service retention rates are currently at or below 30 percent when the vehicle is under warranty and fall even further after the warranty expires. Making the whole service contract process friendlier and quicker is one way to help gain more service customers because it should result in the sale of more of these contracts.

APCO's existing information systems store most of their data in old-fashioned flat files rather than in more modern relational database management systems. As a result, in several steps each contract document, along with its data and other key pieces of information, must be transmitted to the next application where it has to be reformatted for that application. For several steps the data must be reentered manually into the next system. Contracts and paper reports are physically handed to the APCO underwriters.

Although the creation of each contract document requires the approval of the compliance department, in reality contract design and creation should be the responsibility of compliance. APCO's systems run on IBM RS/6000 workstations using the UNIX operating system, Windows NT for the network operating system, and Microsoft SQL Server as the database management software. APCO's client workstations use the Microsoft Windows operating system along with Office desktop productivity tools and the Internet Explorer Web browser. Although APCO does use some modern software packages, such as an Adobe PageMaker package to create the contract forms, its systems are based primarily on homegrown pieces of software.

The company wants to automate its entire application process to speed up everything for both APCO and its customers and to eliminate much of the reliance on paper documents. For instance if a new, more modern system were running, according to Kohrman, compliance will need to "extract the information as easily as possible, without a lot of IT overhead," an improvement that can be achieved if APCO begins to use a relational DBMS.

APCO has moved to solve this problem by issuing a Request for Proposal (RFP) for the first of a series of changes that its systems require. Its goal is to create for APCO and its customers a Web-based system for the creation and approval of contracts and for the administration of vehicle servicing. The system must simplify and speed up the business processes in order to support the planned growth of the company, increase customer service, and reduce costs.

The first step is to create a comprehensive electronic document-management (or content-management) system. The company wants the final content-management system to be highly automated so it can handle the whole process from the creation of all documents to the handling of an automobile purchaser's application for the insurance to final approval. The new system must decrease the amount of content APCO must handle by replacing its method of storing a separate document for each program and level of coverage. The new system should enable specific contracts to be assembled from many stored components, some of which will be unique to that particular document. However, most, if not all, of the components of the documents will be shared with many other contracts. The system will have to collect all the required components according to the rules for that particular program and state requirements.

APCO is wondering how the Web could be used to speed up the whole process and provide a new channel for enrolling and servicing customers and whether Internet technology could help it lower its (and dealers') costs. Kohrman's goal is to have the customers of the dealers leave the dealers' premises not only with the automobile they have just purchased but also with a warranty and/or service contract signed and in hand.

Sources: Ron Copeland, "Wanted: E-Document Strategy," *Information Week,* March 19, 2001; Kristin Hooper, "Building a Content-Management System, Soup to Nuts," *Information Week,* March 19, 2001; and Bob Wallace, "Software Will Let Customers Book That Oil Change Online," *Computerworld,* February 8, 1999.

CASE STUDY QUESTIONS

1. Analyze APCO and its business model using the competitive forces and value chain models.

2. How well did APCO's systems support its business model? What management, organization, and technology factors were responsible for its problems?

3. Propose a system solution for APCO. Your analysis should describe the objectives of the solution, the requirements to be met by the new system (or series of systems), and the feasibility of your proposal. Include an overview of the systems you would recommend and explain how those systems would address the problems listed in your goals. Your analysis should consider organizational and management issues to be addressed by the solution as well as technology issues.

4. If you were the systems analyst for this project, list five questions you would ask during interviews to elicit the information you need for your systems study report.

5. What method would you use to develop your system solution? Why?

chapter 13

UNDERSTANDING THE BUSINESS VALUE OF SYSTEMS AND MANAGING CHANGE

objectives

At many points during your career, you will be involved in projects to build new information systems. You will need to know how to measure the business benefits of these investments and how to make sure that these systems work successfully in your organization. After completing this chapter, you will be able to answer the following questions:

1. *How can our company measure the business benefits of our information systems? What models should be used to measure that business value?*

2. *Why do so many system projects fail? What are the principal reasons for system failures?*

3. *How should the organizational change surrounding a new system be managed to ensure success?*

4. *Are there any special challenges in implementing international information systems?*

5. *What strategies can our organization use to manage the system implementation process more effectively?*

The Rise and Fall of Boo.com

Boo.com was one of the most widely anticipated e-commerce sites in history. The company planned to sell trendy fashion products at full retail price over the Web, offering such brands as North Face, Adidas, Fila, Vans, Cosmic Girl, and Donna Karan. Boo's Web site enabled shoppers to view every product in full color, three-dimensional images from any angle. An advanced search engine helped customers search for items by color, brand, price, style, and even sport. The site featured a universal sizing system based on size variations among brands and countries. Visitors were able to question Miss Boo, an animated figure offering fashion advice based on locale or on a specific activity (such as trekking in Nepal). Boo.com also offered free delivery within one week and free returns for dissatisfied customers.

Boo.com's founders were two 28-year-old Swedish friends, Ernst Malmsten and Kajsa Leander, who had already established and later sold the on-line bookstore

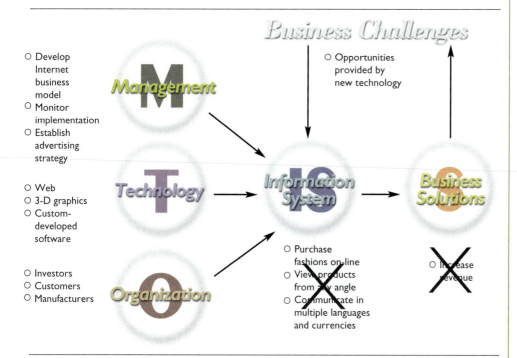

Bokus.com, and Patrik Hedelin, an investment banker at HSBC Holdings. They obtained financial backing from a string of prestigious investors, including the investment bank of J. P. Morgan.

Malmsten and Leander set a target date of May 1999 for launching the Web site. Boo planned to develop both its complex Internet platform and customer-fulfillment systems from scratch. Management committed $25 million to advertisements in expensive, trendy, fashion magazines, such as Vanity Fair, and on cable television and the Internet before the Web site had been launched.

There was so much unfinished technical development work that the Web site launching was pushed back several times. With the original advertising campaign long over, observers commented that by raising people's interest while delaying its opening, Boo.com disappointed and alienated potential customers. Boo's Web site was finally launched in early November, but the promised mass marketing blitz never materialized.

Developing Boo's own software proved slow and expensive. The plan required rich, complex graphics so visitors could view products from any angle. The technicians also had to develop an intricate virtual inventory system because Boo maintained very little inventory of its own. Items in Boo's order basket were actually ordered from the manufacturer, not from Boo, so one customer might have a basket containing items from four or five different sources. The site also had to allow its customers to communicate in any one of seven languages and to convert 18 different currencies and calculate taxes from 18 different countries.

To connect to Boo.com, visitors had to have a minimum 56K connection, but even this was too low for most U.S. and European users to handle all the Boo graphics. Product descriptions were displayed in tiny one-inch square windows, making descriptions not only difficult to read but also difficult to scroll through. The Boo hierarchical menus required patience and precision; visitors making a wrong choice had no alternative but to return to the top to start over again. An especially annoying feature of the site was the constant presence of Miss Boo. She was constantly injected regardless of whether the visitor desired her style advice. Many visitors reacted as they might if they were shopping in a bricks-and-mortar store and had a live clerk hovering over them, commenting without stop. Boo's Web site performance was terrible. At launch time, 40 percent of the site's visitors could not even gain access. The site was buggy, even causing visitors' computers to freeze.

With sales lagging badly and the company running out of cash, Boo began selling clothing at a 40 percent discount and laying off employees. On May 17, 2000, Malmsten hired a firm to liquidate the company. Fashionmall.com purchased the remnants of Boo.com the following month, including its brand name, Web address, advertising materials, and on-line content. Investors had lost an estimated $135 million to $185 million. Many people are still wondering how it could have all gone so wrong so swiftly.

Sources: Michelle Slatalla, "Boo.com Tries Again, Humbled and Retooled," *New York Times*, January 11, 2001; "Life and Death: Private Dot-Coms," *The Industry Standard*, July 2, 2001; and Andrew Ross Sorkin, "From Big Idea to Big Bust: The Wild Ride of Boo.com," *New York Times*, December 13, 2000.

MANAGEMENT CHALLENGES

One of the principal challenges posed by information systems is ensuring they can deliver genuine business benefits. Organizations need to find ways of measuring the business value of their information systems and to ensure that these systems actually deliver the benefits they promise. There is a very high failure rate among information systems projects because organizations have incorrectly assessed their business value or because firms have failed to manage the organizational change process surrounding the introduction of new technology. What happened to Boo.com is actually very common among traditional information systems projects as well as for dot.com Web sites. Successful system-building requires skillful planning and change management, and you should be aware of the following management challenges:

1. **Determining benefits of a system when they are largely intangible.** As the sophistication of systems grows, they produce fewer tangible and more intangible benefits. By definition, there is no solid method for pricing intangible benefits. Organizations could lose important opportunities if they only use strict financial criteria for determining information systems benefits. However, organizations could make very poor investment decisions if they overestimate intangible benefits.

2. **Dealing with the complexity of large-scale systems projects.** Large-scale systems, including enterprise systems, that affect large numbers of organizational units and staff members and that have extensive information requirements and business process changes are difficult to oversee, coordinate, and plan for. Implementing such systems, which have multiyear development periods, is especially problematic because the systems are so complex. In addition, there are few reliable techniques for estimating the time and cost to develop large-scale information systems. Guidelines presented in this chapter are helpful but cannot guarantee that a large information system project can be precisely planned with accurate cost figures.

I n this chapter we examine various ways of measuring the business value provided by information systems, describing both financial and nonfinancial models. We then examine the role of change management in successful system implementation. Finally we present strategies for reducing the risks in systems projects and improving project management.

13.1 UNDERSTANDING THE BUSINESS VALUE OF INFORMATION SYSTEMS

Information systems can have several different values for business firms. A consistently strong information technology infrastructure can, over the long term, play an important strategic role in the life of the firm. Considered less grandly, information systems can simply facilitate a firm's survival.

It is important also to realize that systems can have value but that the firm may not capture all or even some of the value. Although system projects can result in firm benefits, such as profitability and productivity, some or all of the benefits can go directly to the consumer in the form of lower prices or more reliable services and products (Hitt and Brynjolfsson, 1996). Society can reward firms that enhance consumer surplus by allowing them to survive or by rewarding them with increases in business revenues. But from a management point of view, the challenge is to retain as much of the benefit of systems investments as is feasible in current market conditions.

The worth of systems from a financial perspective essentially revolves around the question of return on invested capital. The value of systems comes down to one question: Does a particular IT investment produce sufficient returns to justify its costs? There are many problems with this approach, not the least of which is how to estimate benefits and count the costs.

TRADITIONAL CAPITAL BUDGETING MODELS

Capital budgeting models are one of several techniques used to measure the value of investing in long-term capital investment projects. The process of analyzing and selecting various proposals for capital expenditures is called **capital budgeting.** Firms invest in capital projects to expand production to meet anticipated demand or to modernize production equipment to reduce costs. Firms also invest in capital projects for many noneconomic reasons, such as installing pollution control equipment, converting to a human resources database to meet some government regulations, or satisfying nonmarket public demands. Information systems are considered long-term capital investment projects. Six capital budgeting models are used to evaluate capital projects:

> **capital budgeting**
>
> The process of analyzing and selecting various proposals for capital expenditures.

The payback method

The accounting rate of return on investment (ROI)

The cost–benefit ratio

The net present value

The profitability index

The internal rate of return (IRR)

All capital budgeting methods rely on measures of cash flows into and out of the firm. Capital projects generate cash flows into and out of the firm. The investment cost is an immediate cash outflow caused by the purchase of the capital equipment. In subsequent years, the investment may cause additional cash outflows that will be balanced by cash inflows resulting from the investment. Cash inflows take the form of increased sales of more products (for reasons such as new products, higher quality, or increasing market share) or reduced costs in production and operations. The difference between cash outflows and cash inflows is used for calculating the financial worth of an investment. Once the cash flows have been established, several alternative methods are available for comparing different projects and deciding about the investment.

Financial models assume that all relevant alternatives have been examined, that all costs and benefits are known, and that these costs and benefits can be expressed in a common

TABLE 13-1 COSTS AND BENEFITS OF INFORMATION SYSTEMS

Costs	Intangible Benefits
Hardware	Improved asset utilization
Telecommunications	Improved resource control
Software	Improved organizational planning
Services	Increased organizational flexibility
Personnel	More timely information
	More information
Tangible Benefits (cost savings)	Increased organizational learning
Increased productivity	Legal requirements attained
Lower operational costs	Enhanced employee goodwill
Reduced workforce	Increased job satisfaction
Lower computer expenses	Improved decision making
Lower outside vendor costs	Improved operations
Lower clerical and professional costs	Higher client satisfaction
Reduced rate of growth in expenses	Better corporate image
Reduced facility costs	

metric, specifically, money. When one has to choose among many complex alternatives, these assumptions are rarely met in the real world, although they may be approximated. Table 13-1 lists some of the more common costs and benefits of systems. **Tangible benefits** can be quantified and assigned a monetary value. **Intangible benefits,** such as more efficient customer service or enhanced decision making, cannot be immediately quantified but may lead to quantifiable gains in the long run.

tangible benefits
Benefits that can be quantified and assigned a monetary value; they include lower operational costs and increased cash flows.

intangible benefits
Benefits that are not easily quantified; they include more efficient customer service or enhanced decision making.

Limitations of Financial Models

Many well-known problems emerge when financial analysis is applied to information systems (Dos Santos, 1991). Financial models do not express the risks and uncertainty of their own cost and benefits estimates. Costs and benefits do not occur in the same time frame—costs tend to be upfront and tangible, whereas benefits tend to be back loaded and intangible. Inflation may affect costs and benefits differently. Technology—especially information technology—can change during the course of the project, causing estimates to vary greatly. Intangible benefits are difficult to quantify. These factors play havoc with financial models.

The difficulties of measuring intangible benefits give financial models an application bias: Transaction and clerical systems that displace labor and save space always produce more measurable, tangible benefits than management information systems, decision-support systems, or computer-supported collaborative work systems (see Chapters 10 and 11)

There is some reason to believe that investment in information technology requires special consideration in financial modeling. Capital budgeting historically concerned itself with manufacturing equipment and other long-term investments, such as electrical generating facilities and telephone networks. These investments had expected lives of more than one year and up to 25 years. However, information systems differ from manufacturing systems in that their life expectancy is shorter. The very high rate of technological change in computer-based information systems means that most systems are seriously out of date in five to eight years. The high rate of technological obsolescence in budgeting for systems means simply that the payback period must be shorter and the rates of return higher than typical capital projects with much longer useful lives.

The bottom line with financial models is to use them cautiously and to put the results into a broader context of business analysis. Let us look at an example to see how these problems arise and can be handled. The following case study is based on a real-world scenario, but the names have been changed.

CASE EXAMPLE: PRIMROSE, MENDELSON, AND HANSEN

Primrose, Mendelson, and Hansen is a 250-person law partnership on Manhattan's West Side with branch offices in London, Los Angeles, and Paris. Founded in 1923, Primrose has excelled in corporate, taxation, environmental, and health law. Its litigation department is also well known.

The Problem

The firm occupies three floors of a new building. Many partners still have five-year-old PCs on their desktops but rarely use them except to read e-mail. Virtually all business is conducted face-to-face in the office, or when partners meet directly with clients on the clients' premises. Most of the law business involves marking up (editing), creating, filing, storing, and sending documents. In addition, the tax, pension, and real estate groups do a considerable amount of spreadsheet work.

With overall business off 15 percent since 2000, the chair, Edward W. Hansen, III, is hoping to use information systems to cope with the flood of paperwork, enhance service to clients, and slow the growth in administrative costs.

First, the firm's income depends on billable hours, and every lawyer is supposed to keep a diary of his or her work for specific clients in 30-minute intervals. Generally, senior lawyers at this firm charge about $500 an hour for their time. Unfortunately, lawyers often forget what they have been working on and must reconstruct their time diaries. The firm hopes that there will be some automated way of tracking billable hours.

Second, much time is spent communicating with clients around the world, with other law firms both in the United States and overseas, and with the Primrose branch offices. The fax machine has become the communication medium of choice, generating huge bills and developing lengthy queues. The firm looks forward to using some sort of secure e-mail, or even the Internet, for communication. Law firms are wary of breaches in the security of confidential client information.

Third, Primrose has no client database! A law firm is a collection of fiefdoms—each lawyer has his or her own clients and keeps the information about them private. This, however, makes it impossible for management to find out who is a client of the firm, who is working on a deal with whom, and so forth. The firm maintains a billing system, but the information in the system is too difficult to search. What Primrose needs is an integrated client management system that will take care of billing, monitor hourly charges, and make client information available to others in the firm. Even overseas offices want to have information on who is taking care of a particular client in the United States.

Fourth, there is no system to track costs. The head of the firm and the department heads who compose the executive committee cannot identify what the costs are, where the money is being spent, who is spending it, and how the firm's resources are being allocated. A decent accounting system that could identify the cash flows and the costs a bit more clearly than the firm's existing journal would be a big help.

The Solution

Information systems could obviously have some survival value and perhaps could grant a strategic advantage to Primrose if a system were correctly built and implemented. We can detail the costs of a new system solution by department and estimated benefits.

The technical solution adopted was to create a local area network composed of 300 fully configured Pentium 4 multimedia desktop PCs, three Windows.NET servers, and an Ethernet 10 megabit per second (Mbps) local area network on a coaxial cable. The network connects all the lawyers and their secretaries to a single, integrated system yet permits each lawyer to configure his or her desktop with specialized software and hardware. The older machines were given away to charity.

All desktop machines were configured with Windows XP Professional and Office XP software, and the servers ran Windows.NET Server. Lotus Notes was chosen to handle client accounting, document management, group collaboration, and e-mail because it provided an easy-to-use interface and secure links to external networks (including the Internet). The

Internet was rejected as an e-mail technology because of its uncertain security. The Primrose local area network is linked to external networks so that the firm can obtain information online from Lexis (a legal database) and several financial database services.

The new system required Primrose to hire a director of systems—a new position for most law firms. Two systems personnel were required to operate the system and train lawyers. An outside trainer was also hired for a short period.

Figure 13-1 shows the estimated costs and benefits of the system. The system had an actual investment cost of $1,733,100 in the first year (Year 0) and a total cost over six years of $3,690,600. The estimated benefits total $6,420,000 after six years. Was the investment worthwhile? If so, in what sense? There are financial and nonfinancial answers to these questions. Let us look at the financial models first. They are depicted in Figure 13-2.

The Payback Method

payback method

A measure of the time required to pay back the initial investment on a project.

The **payback method** is quite simple: It is a measure of the time required to pay back the initial investment of a project. The payback period is computed as

$$\frac{\text{Original investment}}{\text{Annual net cash inflow}} = \text{Number of years to pay back}$$

In the case of Primrose, it will take more than two years to pay back the initial investment. (Because cash flows are uneven, annual cash inflows are summed until they equal the original investment in order to arrive at this number.) The payback method is a popular method because of its simplicity and power as an initial screening method. It is especially good for high-risk projects in which the useful life of a project is difficult to determine. If a project pays for itself in two years, then it matters less how long after two years the system lasts.

Estimated Costs and Benefits 2001-2006

	A	B	C	D	E	F	G	H	I	J	K	L
1	Year :				0	1	2	3	4	5		
2					2001	2002	2003	2004	2005	2006		
3	**Costs Hardware**											
4		Servers		3@ 20000	60,000	10,000	10,000	10,000	10,000	10,000		
5		PCs		300@3000	900,000	10,000	10,000	10,000	10,000	10,000		
6		Network cards		300@100	30,000	0	0	0	0	0		
7		Scanners		6@100	600	500	500	500	500	500		
8												
9	Telecommunications											
10		Routers		10@500	5,000	1,000	1,000	1,000	1,000	1,000		
11		Cabling		150,000	150,000	0	0	0	0	0		
12		Telephone connect costs		50,000	50,000	50,000	50,000	50,000	50,000	50,000		
13												
14	Software											
15		Database		15,000	15,000	15,000	15,000	15,000	15,000	15,000		
16		Network		10,000	10,000	2,000	2,000	2,000	2,000	2,000		
17		Groupware		300@500	150,000	3,000	3,000	3,000	3,000	3,000		
18												
19	Services											
20		Lexis		50,000	50,000	50,000	50,000	50,000	50,000	50,000		
21		Training		300hrs@75/hr	22,500	10,000	10,000	10,000	10,000	10,000		
22		Director of Systems		100,000	100,000	100,000	100,000	100,000	100,000	100,000		
23		Systems Personnel		2@70000	140,000	140,000	140,000	140,000	140,000	140,000		
24		Trainer		1@50000	50,000	0	0	0	0	0		
25												
26	**Total Costs**				1,733,100	391,500	391,500	391,500	391,500	391,500	3,690,600	
27	Benefits											
28			1. Billing enhancements		300,000	500,000	600,000	600,000	600,000	500,000		
29			2. Reduced paralegals		50,000	100,000	150,000	150,000	150,000	150,000		
30			3. Reduced clerical		50,000	100,000	100,000	100,000	100,000	100,000		
31			4. Reduced messenger		15,000	30,000	30,000	30,000	30,000	30,000		
32			5. Reduced telecommunications		5,000	10,000	10,000	10,000	10,000	10,000		
33			6. Lawyer efficiencies		120,000	240,000	360,000	360,000	360,000	360,000		
34												
35	**Total Benefits**				540,000	980,000	1,250,000	1,250,000	1,250,000	1,150,000	6,420,000	

Sheet1 / Sheet2 / Sheet3

Figure 13-1 Costs and benefits of the Legal Information System. This spreadsheet analyzes the basic costs and benefits of implementing an information system for the law firm. The costs for hardware, telecommunications, software, services, and personnel are analyzed over a six-year period.

	Estimated Costs and Benefits 2001-2006											
	A	B	C	D	E	F	G	H	I	J	K	L
1	Year :			0	1	2	3	4	5			
2	Net Cash Flow (not including orig. investment)	540,000			588,500	858,500	858,500	858,500	758,500			
3	Net Cash Flow (including orig. investment)			-1,193,100	588,500	858,500	858,500	858,500	758,500			
4												
5	(1) Payback Period = 2.5 years					Cumulative Cash Flow						
6	Initial investment = 1,733,100			Year 0	540,000	540,000						
7				Year 1	588,500	1,128,500						
8				Year 2	858,500	1,987,000						
9				Year 3	858,500	2,845,500						
10				Year 4	858,500	3,704,000						
11				Year 5	758,500	4,462,500						
12												
13	(2) Accounting rate of return											
14												
15	(Total benefits-Total Costs-Depreciation)/Useful life				Total Benefits	6,420,000						
16	---				Total Costs	3,690,600						
17	Total initial investment				Depreciation	1,733,100						
18				Tot. benefits-tot. costs-depreciation		996,300						
19					Life	6 years						
20												
21					Initial investment		1,733,100					
22	ROI =	(996,300/6)	9.58%									
23		1,733,100										
24												
25	(3) Cost-Benefit Ratio	Total Benefits		6,420,000	1.74							
26		Total Costs		3,690,600								
27												
28	(4) Net Present Value											
29		= NPV (0.05,D2:I2)-1,733,100				2,001,529						
30												
31	(5) Profitability Index											
32		PV/Investment	3,734,629/1,733,100		2.15							
33												
34	(6) Internal Rate of Return											
35												
36		= IRR(D3:I3)			55%							

Sheet1 \ **Sheet2** / Sheet3

Figure 13-2 Financial models. To determine the financial basis for a project a series of financial models helps determine the return on invested capital. These calculations include the payback period, the accounting rate of return (ROI), the cost–benefit ratio, the net present value, the profitability index, and the internal rate of return (IRR).

The weakness of this measure is its virtues: The method ignores the time value of money, the amount of cash flow after the payback period, the disposal value (usually zero with computer systems), and the profitability of the investment.

Accounting Rate of Return on Investment (ROI)

Firms make capital investments to earn a satisfactory rate of return. Determining a satisfactory rate of return depends on the cost of borrowing money, but other factors can enter into the equation. Such factors include the historic rates of return expected by the firm. In the long run, the desired rate of return must equal or exceed the cost of capital in the marketplace. Otherwise, no one will lend the firm money.

The **accounting rate of return on investment (ROI)** calculates the rate of return from an investment by adjusting the cash inflows produced by the investment for depreciation. It gives an approximation of the accounting income earned by the project.

To find the ROI, first calculate the average net benefit. The formula for the average net benefit is as follows:

$$\frac{(\text{Total benefits } - \text{ Total cost } - \text{ Depreciation})}{\text{Useful life}} = \text{Net benefit}$$

This net benefit is divided by the total initial investment to arrive at ROI. The formula is

$$\frac{\text{Net benefit}}{\text{Total initial investment}} = \text{ROI}$$

accounting rate of return on investment (ROI)

Calculation of the rate of return on an investment by adjusting cash inflows produced by the investment for depreciation. Approximates the accounting income earned by the investment.

In the case of Primrose, the average rate of return on the investment is 9.58 percent, which could be a good return on investment if the cost of capital (the prime rate) has been hovering around 6 to 8 to percent.

The weakness of ROI is that it can ignore the time value of money. Future savings are simply not worth as much in today's dollars as are current savings. However, ROI can be modified (and usually is) so that future benefits and costs are calculated in today's dollars. (The present value function on most spreadsheets will perform this conversion.)

Net Present Value

Evaluating a capital project requires that the cost of an investment (a cash outflow usually in year 0) be compared with the net cash inflows that occur many years later. But these two kinds of inflows are not directly comparable because of the time value of money. Money you have been promised to receive three, four, and five years from now is not worth as much as money received today. Money received in the future has to be discounted by some appropriate percentage rate—usually the prevailing interest rate, or sometimes the cost of capital. **Present value** is the value in current dollars of a payment or stream of payments to be received in the future. It can be calculated by using the following formula:

present value

The value, in current dollars, of a payment or stream of payments to be received in the future.

$$\text{Payment} \times \frac{1 - (1 + \text{interest})^{-n}}{\text{Interest}} = \text{Present value}$$

Thus, to compare the investment (made in today's dollars) with future savings or earnings, you need to discount the earnings to their present value and then calculate the net present value of the investment. The **net present value** is the amount of money an investment is worth, taking into account its cost, earnings, and the time value of money. The formula for net present value is

net present value

The amount of money an investment is worth, taking into account its cost, earnings, and the time value of money.

Present value of expected cash flows − Initial investment cost = Net present value

In the case of Primrose, the present value of the stream of benefits is $3,734,629, and the cost (in today's dollars) is $1,733,100, giving a net present value of $2,001,529. In other words, for a $1.7 million investment today, the firm will receive more than $2 million. This is a fairly good rate of return on an investment.

Cost–Benefit Ratio

A simple method for calculating the returns from a capital expenditure is to calculate the **cost–benefit ratio**, which is the ratio of benefits to costs. The formula is

cost–benefit ratio

A method for calculating the returns from a capital expenditure by dividing total benefits by total costs.

$$\frac{\text{Total benefits}}{\text{Total costs}} = \text{Cost–benefit ratio}$$

In the case of Primrose, the cost–benefit ratio is 1.74, meaning that the benefits are 1.74 times greater than the costs. The cost–benefit ratio can be used to rank several projects for comparison. Some firms establish a minimum cost–benefit ratio that must be attained by capital projects. The cost–benefit ratio can, of course, be calculated using present values to account for the time value of money.

Profitability Index

One limitation of net present value is that it provides no measure of profitability. Neither does it provide a way to rank order different possible investments. One simple solution is provided by the profitability index. The **profitability index** is calculated by dividing the present value of the total cash inflow from an investment by the initial cost of the investment. The result can be used to compare the profitability of alternative investments.

profitability index

Used to compare the profitability of alternative investments; it is calculated by dividing the present value of the total cash inflow from an investment by the initial cost of the investment.

$$\frac{\text{Present value of cash inflows}}{\text{Investment}} = \text{Profitability index}$$

In the case of Primrose, the profitability index is 2.15. The project returns more than its cost. Projects can be rank ordered on this index, permitting firms to focus on only the most profitable projects.

Internal Rate of Return (IRR)

Internal rate of return is a variation of the net present value method. It takes into account the time value of money. **Internal rate of return (IRR)** is defined as the rate of return or profit that an investment is expected to earn. IRR is the discount (interest) rate that will equate the present value of the project's future cash flows to the initial cost of the project (defined here as a negative cash flow in year 0 of $1,193,100). In other words, the value of R (discount rate) is such that Present value − Initial cost = 0. In the case of Primrose, the IRR is 55 percent.

internal rate of return (IRR)
The rate of return or profit that an investment is expected to earn.

Results of the Capital Budgeting Analysis

Using methods that take into account the time value of money, the Primrose project is cash-flow positive over the time period and returns more benefits than it costs. Against this analysis, one might ask what other investments would be better from an efficiency and effectiveness standpoint? Also, one must ask if all the benefits have been calculated. It may be that this investment is necessary for the survival of the firm, or necessary to provide a level of service demanded by its clients. What are other competitors doing? In other words, there may be other intangible and strategic business factors to take into account.

STRATEGIC CONSIDERATIONS

Other methods of selecting and evaluating information system investments involve strategic considerations that are not addressed by traditional capital budgeting methods. When the firm has several alternative investments from which to select, it can employ portfolio analysis and scoring models. It can apply real options pricing models to IT investments that are highly uncertain or use a knowledge value-added approach to measure the benefits of changes to business processes. Several of these methods can be used in combination.

Portfolio Analysis

Rather than using capital budgeting, a second way of selecting among alternative projects is to consider the firm as having a portfolio of potential applications. Each application carries risks and benefits. The portfolio can be described as having a certain profile of risk and benefit to the firm (see Figure 13-3). Although there is no ideal profile for all firms, information-intensive industries (e.g., finance) should have a few high-risk, high-benefit projects to ensure that they stay current with technology. Firms in non-information-intensive industries should focus on high-benefit, low-risk projects.

Risks are not necessarily bad. They are tolerable as long as the benefits are commensurate. Section 13.2 describes the factors that increase the risks of systems projects.

Once strategic analyses have determined the overall direction of systems development, a **portfolio analysis** can be used to select alternatives. Obviously, one can begin by focusing on systems of high benefit and low risk. These promise early returns and low risks. Second, high-benefit, high-risk systems should be examined; low-benefit, high-risk systems should be totally avoided; and low-benefit, low-risk systems should be reexamined for the possibility of rebuilding and replacing them with more desirable systems having higher benefits. The Window on Management describes how ING Americas benefited from using this approach.

portfolio analysis
An analysis of the portfolio of potential applications within a firm to determine the risks and benefits, and to select among alternatives for information systems.

scoring model
A quick method for deciding among alternative systems based on a system of ratings for selected objectives.

Scoring Models

A quick and sometimes compelling method for arriving at a decision on alternative systems is a **scoring model.** Scoring models give alternative systems a single score based on the extent to which they meet selected objectives (Matlin, 1989; Buss, 1983).

In Table 13-2 the firm must decide among three alternative office systems: (1) an IBM AS/400 client/server system with proprietary software, (2) a UNIX-based client/server system using an Oracle database, and (3) a Windows client/server system using Windows XP, Windows.NET Server, and Lotus Notes. Column 1 lists

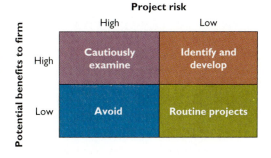

Figure 13-3 A system portfolio. Companies should examine their portfolio of projects in terms of potential benefits and likely risks. Certain kinds of projects should be avoided altogether and others developed rapidly. There is no ideal mix. Companies in different industries have different profiles.

Window on Management

MIS In Action

PORTFOLIO ANALYSIS BRINGS BENEFITS TO ING BANK

Instead of calculating returns on each information systems project, some companies are realizing millions of dollars in annual savings by using portfolio analysis. They are treating their investments in hardware, software, and information technology services as if they were a collection of "retirement" investments. For example, some projects, such as an e-commerce project, are high-risk, high-return investments similar to aggressive stocks, whereas others are lower-risk, lower-return investments, similar to U.S. Treasury bonds. Management can then look at this information system portfolio and ask: "What is the real cash flow or profitability impact from each investment?"

ING Americas, an arm of the Netherlands financial services giant ING Group NV, saved $16 million in 1999, the first year it used portfolio analysis. ING Americas has annual information technology costs of about $475 million and was able to use the results of its portfolio analysis to eliminate redundant projects and to cut the costs of others. The company found, for instance, that it had three competing information systems projects that would allow people to gain access to multiple applications by signing on only once to the corporate computer system. The projects were consolidated.

ING's portfolio analysis also showed that several of its units were planning to upgrade similar information system applications used for making payments to agents and customers. Management then eliminated some of the overlapping projects and turned the surviving projects into "centers of excellence" that could share systems and expertise with the rest of the company.

One factor in ING's successful use of portfolio analysis was its commitment to using a company-wide program management office to evaluate the costs, risks, and benefits of information system projects costing more than $500,000. (Projects costing less than that amount are under the control of the CEOs of ING's individual business units.) The program management office then passes its reviews of projects to a high-level committee of business and information systems managers. This committee reviews the status of each project in light of corporate performance, changing market conditions, and new strategic initiatives and makes the final decision on which projects to fund. This program management office also helped ING merge the information systems units of the companies it acquired into a centralized information technology service that could be shared by all of ING's business units.

ING uses a common set of metrics to evaluate all of its information system projects. The program office specifies the nature of the benefit to be obtained from a new system, such as improving operating efficiencies or reducing staff levels, and reviews each system after it is implemented to make sure the benefits identified are actually realized.

Although ING's portfolio analysis effort has proved effective for traditional systems, ING is struggling with ways to apply it to new Internet-based systems.

To Think About: What were the management benefits of using portfolio analysis for ING's systems? Can you think of any disadvantages to this approach?

Sources: Robert L. Scheier, "Stabilizing Your Risk," *Computerworld ROI*, May/June 2001; and Beth Gold-Bernstein, "Determining the ROI for e-Business Integration," *AnalystQ*, August 3, 2001.

---

the criteria that decision makers may apply to the systems. These criteria are usually the result of lengthy discussions among the decision-making group. Often the most important outcome of a scoring model is not the score but simply agreement on the criteria used to judge a system (Ginzberg, 1979; Nolan, 1982). Column 2 lists the weights that decision makers attach to the decision criterion. The scoring model helps to bring about agreement among participants concerning the rank of the criteria. Columns 3 to 5 use a 1-to-5 scale (lowest to highest) to express the judgments of participants on the relative merits of each system. For example, concerning the percentage of user needs that each system meets, a score of 1 for a system argues that this system, when compared with others being considered, will be low in meeting user needs.

As with all objective techniques, there are many qualitative judgments involved in using the scoring model. This model requires experts who understand the issues and the technology. It is appropriate to cycle through the scoring model several times, changing the criteria and weights, to see how sensitive the outcome is to reasonable changes in criteria. Scoring models are used most commonly to confirm, to rationalize, and to support decisions, rather than as the final arbiters of system selection.

TABLE 13-2 colspan	**SCORING MODEL USED TO CHOOSE AMONG ALTERNATIVE OFFICE SYSTEMS[a]**					
Criterion	Weight	AS/400		Unix		Windows XP
Percentage of user needs met	0.40	2	0.8	3	1.2	4	1.6
Cost of the initial purchase	0.20	1	0.2	3	0.6	4	0.8
Financing	0.10	1	0.1	3	0.3	4	0.4
Ease of maintenance	0.10	2	0.2	3	0.3	4	0.4
Chances of success	0.20	3	0.6	4	0.8	4	0.8
Final score			1.9		3.2		4.0

Scale: 1 = low, 5 = high

[a]One of the major uses of scoring models is in identifying the criteria of selection and their relative weights. In this instance, an office system based on Windows XP appears preferable.

If Primrose had other alternative systems projects to select from, it could have used the portfolio and scoring models as well as financial models to establish the business value of its systems solution.

Primrose did not have a portfolio of applications that could be used to compare the proposed system. Senior lawyers believed the project was low in risk using well-understood technology. They believed the rewards were even higher than the financial models stated because the system might enable the firm to expand its business. For instance, the ability to communicate with other law firms, with clients, and with the international staff of lawyers in remote locations was not even considered in the financial analysis.

Real Options Pricing Models

Some information system projects are highly uncertain. Their future revenue streams are unclear and their up-front costs are high. Suppose, for instance, that a firm is considering a $20 million investment to upgrade its information technology infrastructure. If this infrastructure were available, the organization would have the technology capabilities to respond to future problems and opportunities. Although the costs of this investment can be calculated, not all of the benefits of making this investment can be established in advance. But if the firm waits a few years until the revenue potential becomes more obvious, it might be too late to make the infrastructure investment. In such cases, managers might benefit from using real options pricing models to evaluate information technology investments.

Real options pricing models use the concept of options valuation borrowed from the financial industry. An option is essentially the right, but not the obligation, to act at some future date. A typical call option, for instance, is a financial option in which a person buys the right (but not the obligation) to purchase an underlying asset (usually a stock) at a definite price (strike price) for a limited period of time. For instance, on January 22, 2002, for $1.50 one could purchase the right (a call option) to buy 100 shares of Wal-Mart common stock at $60 per share in March 2002. If, by March 2002, the price of Wal-Mart stock did not rise above $60, you would not exercise the option, and the value of the option would fall to zero on the strike date. If, however, the price of Wal-Mart common stock rose to, say, $100 per share, you could purchase the stock for the strike price of $60, and retain the profit of $40 per share.

Real options involving investments in capital projects are different from financial options in that they cannot be traded on a market and they differ in value based on the firm in which they are made. Thus, an investment in an enterprise system will have very different real option values in different firms because the ability to derive value from even identical enterprise systems depends on firm factors, for example, prior expertise, skilled labor force, market conditions, and other factors. Nevertheless, several scholars have argued that the real options theory can be useful when considering highly uncertain IT investments, and potentially the same techniques for valuing financial options can be used (Benaroch and Kauffman, 2000; Taudes, Feurstein, and Mild, 2000). (Calculation of real options values for IT projects is beyond the scope of this text.)

real options pricing models Models for evaluating information technology investments with uncertain returns by using techniques for valuing financial options.

MIS IN ACTION   DECISIONMAKING

EVALUATING ERP SYSTEMS WITH A SCORING MODEL

Your company, Audio Direct, sells parts used in audio systems for cars and trucks and is growing very fast. Your management team has decided that the firm can speed up product delivery to customers and lower inventory and customer support costs by installing an enterprise resource planning (ERP) system. Two enterprise software vendors have responded to your request for proposals (RFP) and have submitted reports showing which of your detailed list of requirements can be

supported by their systems. Audio Direct attaches the most importance to capabilities for sales order processing, inventory management, and warehousing. The information systems staff prepared the following matrix comparing the vendors' capabilities for these functions. It shows the percentage of requirements for each function that each alternative ERP system can provide. It also shows the weight, or relative importance, the company attaches to each of these functions.

Function	Weight	ERP System A %	ERP System A Score	ERP System B %	ERP System B Score
1.0 Order Processing					
1.1 On-line order entry	4	67		73	
1.2 On-line pricing	4	81		87	
1.3 Inventory check	4	72		81	
1.4 Customer credit check	3	66		59	
1.5 Invoicing	4	73		82	
Total Order Processing					
2.0 Inventory Management					
2.1 Production forecasting	3	72		76	
2.2 Production planning	4	79		81	
2.3 Inventory control	4	68		80	
2.4 Reports	3	71		69	
Total Inventory Management					
3.0 Warehousing					
3.1 Receiving	2	71		75	
3.2 Picking/packing	3	77		82	
3.3 Shipping	4	92		89	
Total Warehousing					
Grand Total					

1. Calculate each ERP vendor's score by multiplying the percentage of requirements for each function by the weight for that function.

2. Calculate each ERP vendor's total score for each of the three major functions (order processing, inventory management, and warehousing.) Then calculate the grand total for each vendor.

3. On the basis of vendor scores, which ERP vendor would you select?

4. Are there any other factors, including intangible benefits, that might affect your decision?

Real options pricing models (ROPM) offer an approach to thinking about information technology projects that takes into account the value of management learning over time and the value of delaying investment. In real options theory, the value of the IT project (real option) is a function of the value of the underlying IT asset (present value of expected revenues from the IT project), the volatility of the value in the underlying asset, the cost of converting the option investment into the underlying asset (the exercise price), the risk free interest rate, and the option time to maturity (length of time the project can be deferred).

The real options model addresses some of the limitations of the discounted cash flow models described earlier, which essentially call for investing in an information technology project only when the value of the discounted cash value of the investment is greater than zero. The ROPM allows managers to systematically take into account the volatility in the value of IT projects over time, the optimal timing of the investment, and the changing cost of implementation as technology prices fall over time. Briefly, the ROPM places a value on management learning, and the use of an unfolding investment technique (investing in chunks) based on learning over time.

The disadvantages of this model are primarily in estimating all the key variables, especially the expected cash flows from the underlying asset, and changes in the cost of implementation. Several rule-of-thumb approaches are being developed (McGrath and MacMillan, 2000). ROPM can be useful when there is no experience with a technology and its future is highly uncertain.

Knowledge Value–Added Approach

A different approach to traditional capital budgeting is to focus on the knowledge input into a business process as a way of determining the costs and benefits of changes in business processes from new information systems. Any program that uses information technology to change business processes requires knowledge input. The value of the knowledge used to produce improved outputs of the new process can be used as a measure of the value added. Knowledge inputs can be measured in terms of learning time to master a new process and a return on knowledge can be estimated. This method makes certain assumptions that may not be valid in all situations, especially product design and research and development, where processes do not have predetermined outputs (Housel, El Sawy, Zhong, and Rodgers, 2001).

INFORMATION TECHNOLOGY INVESTMENTS AND PRODUCTIVITY

Information technology now accounts for more than 40 percent of total business expenditures on capital equipment in the United States. Whether this investment has translated into genuine productivity gains remains open to debate. Productivity is a measure of the firm's efficiency in converting inputs to outputs. It refers to the amount of capital and labor required to produce a *unit of output*. For over a decade, researchers have been trying to quantify the benefits from information technology investments by analyzing data collected at the economy level, industry level, firm level, and information system application level. The results of these studies have been mixed and the term "productivity paradox" was coined to describe such findings.

Although information technology has increased productivity in manufacturing, especially the manufacture of information technology products, the extent to which computers have enhanced the productivity of the service sector is unclear. Some studies show that investment in information technology has not led to any appreciable growth in productivity among office workers. Corporate downsizings and cost-reduction measures have increased worker efficiency but have not yet led to sustained enhancements signifying genuine productivity gains (Roach, 2000, 1996, and 1988). Cell phones, home fax machines, laptop computers, and information appliances allow highly-paid knowledge workers to get more work done by working longer hours and bringing their work home, but they are not necessarily getting more work done in a specified unit of time.

The contribution of information technology to productivity in information and knowledge industries may be difficult to measure because of the problems of identifying suitable units of output for information work (Panko, 1991). How does one measure the output of a law office? Should one measure productivity by examining the number of forms completed per employee (a measure of physical unit productivity) or by examining the amount of revenue produced per employee (a measure of financial unit productivity) in an information- and knowledge-intense industry? Earlier studies used data that are more than 10 years old, when computers were not as intensively used as they are today.

Other studies have focused on the value of outputs (essentially revenues), profits, ROI, and stock market capitalization as the ultimate measures of firm efficiency. These studies found that information technology investment started to generate a productivity payback in the 1990s (Brynjolfsson and Hitt, 1999 and 1993). Banker (2001) and others (Brynjolfsson, Hitt, and Yang, 1999) found that higher investment in information technology produces higher stock valuations for the entire industry. Moreover, several authors have argued that IT-induced growth in firm efficiency accelerated in the 1990s because of organizational learning and changes required in business processes to effectively unleash the potential of new information technology.

In addition to reducing costs, computers may increase the quality of products and services for consumers or may create entirely new products and revenue streams. These intangible benefits are difficult to measure and consequently are not addressed by conventional productivity measures. Moreover, because of competition, the value created by computers may primarily flow to customers rather than to the company making the investments (Brynjolfsson, 1996). For instance, the investment in ATM machines by banks has not resulted in higher profitability for any single bank, although the industry as a whole has prospered and consumers enjoy the benefits without paying higher fees.

Researchers focusing on the interaction of production efficiency and product quality have found that investments that increase production efficiency and improve product quality can increase profits while decreasing productivity. IT investments that reduce variable costs of designing, developing, and manufacturing a product enable a firm to improve product quality and charge a higher price, but may also increase total production costs and under a range of conditions, decrease firm productivity (Thatcher and Oliver, 2001). Hence, the returns of information technology investments should be analyzed within the competitive context of the firm, the industry, and the specific way in which information technology is being applied.

13.2 THE IMPORTANCE OF CHANGE MANAGEMENT IN INFORMATION SYSTEM SUCCESS AND FAILURE

Benefits from information technology investments will be reduced if firms do not consider the costs of organizational change associated with a new system or make these changes effectively (Ryan and Harrison, 2000; Irani and Love, 2000–2001). The introduction or alteration of an information system has a powerful behavioral and organizational impact. It transforms how various individuals and groups perform and interact. Changes in the way that information is defined, accessed, and used to manage the organization's resources often lead to new distributions of authority and power. This internal organizational change breeds resistance and opposition and can lead to the demise of an otherwise good system.

A very large percentage of information systems fail to deliver benefits or to solve the problems for which they were intended because the process of organizational change surrounding system-building was not properly addressed. Successful system-building requires careful change management.

INFORMATION SYSTEM PROBLEM AREAS

The problems causing information **system failure** fall into multiple categories, as illustrated by Figure 13-4. The major problem areas are design, data, cost, and operations.

Design

The actual design of the system may fail to capture essential business requirements or improve organizational performance. Information may not be provided quickly enough to be helpful; it may be in a format that is impossible to digest and use; or it may represent the wrong pieces of data.

The way in which nontechnical business users must interact with the system may be excessively complicated and discouraging. A system may be designed with a poor **user interface.** The user interface is the part of the system with which end users interact. For example, an input form or an on-line data entry screen may be so poorly arranged that no one wants to submit data. The procedures to request on-line information

---

system failure

An information system that either does not perform as expected, is not operational at a specified time, or cannot be used in the way it was intended.

user interface

The part of the information system through which the end user interacts with the system; type of hardware and the series of on-screen commands and responses required for a user to work with the system.

Figure 13-4 Information system problem areas. Problems with an information system's design, data, cost, or operations can be evidence of a system failure.

The Metropolitan Museum of Art's Web site has been praised for presenting a wealth of information about the museum's collection that can be browsed quickly and intuitively. A well-designed user inteface contributes to system success.

retrieval may be so unintelligible that users are too frustrated to make requests. Web sites may discourage visitors from exploring further if Web pages are cluttered and poorly arranged or users can't easily find the information they are seeking. The Manager's Toolkit provides some guidelines for effective Web page design.

An information system will be judged a failure if its design is not compatible with the structure, culture, and goals of the organization as a whole. Historically, information system design has been preoccupied with technical issues at the expense of organizational concerns. The result has often been information systems that are technically excellent but incompatible with their organization's structure, culture, and goals. Without a close organizational fit, such systems create tensions, instability, and conflict.

MIS IN ACTION MANAGER'S TOOLKIT

DESIGNING A USER-FRIENDLY WEB SITE

The design and user friendliness of a Web site can mean the difference between e-commerce and e-business success and failure. Studies have found that poor design is more common than good design and that close to 50 percent of Web shoppers gave up purchasing items on-line because they could not easily locate the products they wanted on a Web site. Here are the most important factors to consider when designing an effective Web site:

Content: Content should be appropriate to the purpose of the site and its intended audience. Short sentences and paragraphs and bulleted lists should be used so that content can be scanned easily. A search function should be available if the site has large amounts of information.

Page design and layout: Graphics and design convey function and meaning and are an integral part of the user's Web site experience. Page design and layout, including color, fonts, and images, should be balanced, clean, and uncluttered. Both graphic and text elements should be clearly legible and pages should be short enough so that users don't have to do a great deal of vertical scrolling.

Navigation: Most user interactions with Web sites require navigating hypertext links between Web pages. Web sites should

be designed so that users have a clear sense of where they are within the local organization of information. Navigating from page to page should be simple. Users should be able to easily backtrack or return to the home page. Basic navigation links should be present on every page of the Web site.

Accessibility: Users should be able to obtain the information they want with the fewest possible steps in the shortest time. Information on Web sites should be organized to minimize the number of steps through menu pages.

Load factors: Users are frustrated by long delays, so Web pages should load quickly. The loading time for a Web page will be slowed down by large numbers of simultaneous visitors to a Web site and extensive multimedia graphics and dynamic content. Therefore, Web page designs need to be "tuned" to the network access speeds of most users as well as the capabilities of systems where they are hosted.

Standards: The Web site should work with the most popular Web browser software, including Microsoft Internet Explorer and Netscape Navigator, and with Macintosh computers as well as computers using the Intel hardware standard and Windows operating systems.

Data

The data in the system may have a high level of inaccuracy or inconsistency. The information in certain fields may be erroneous or ambiguous; or it may not be organized properly for business purposes. Information required for a specific business function may be inaccessible because the data are incomplete.

Cost

Some systems operate quite smoothly, but their cost to implement and run on a production basis may be way over budget. Other system projects may be too costly to complete. In both cases, the excessive expenditures cannot be justified by the demonstrated business value of the information they provide.

Operations

The system does not run well. Information is not provided in a timely and efficient manner because the computer operations that handle information processing break down. Jobs that abort too often lead to excessive reruns and delayed or missed schedules for delivery of information. An on-line system may be operationally inadequate because the response time is too long.

Some of these problems can be attributed to technical features of information systems but most stem from organizational factors (Keil, Cule, Lyytinen, and Schmidt, 1998). System builders need to understand these organizational issues and learn how to manage the change associated with a new information system.

CHANGE MANAGEMENT AND THE CONCEPT OF IMPLEMENTATION

To effectively manage the organizational change surrounding the introduction of a new information system, one must examine the process of implementation. **Implementation** refers to all organizational activities working toward the adoption, management, and routinization of an innovation such as a new information system. In the implementation process, the systems analyst is a **change agent.** The analyst not only develops technical solutions but also redefines the configurations, interactions, job activities, and power relationships of various organizational groups. The analyst is the catalyst for the entire change process and is responsible for ensuring that the changes created by a new system are accepted by all parties involved. The change agent communicates with users, mediates between competing interest groups, and ensures that the organizational adjustment to such changes is complete.

One model of the implementation process is the Kolb/Frohman model of organizational change. This model divides the process of organizational change into a seven-stage relationship between an organizational *consultant* and his or her *client*. (The consultant corresponds to the information system designer and the client to the user.) The success of the change effort is determined by how well the consultant and client deal with the key issues at each stage (Kolb and Frohman, 1970). Other models of implementation describe the relationship as one between designers, clients, and decision makers, who are responsible for managing the implementation effort to bridge the gap between design and utilization (Swanson, 1988). Recent work on implementation stresses the need for flexibility and improvisation with organizational actors not limited to rigid prescribed roles (Markus and Benjamin, 1997; Orlikowski and Hofman, 1997).

CAUSES OF IMPLEMENTATION SUCCESS AND FAILURE

Implementation outcome can be largely determined by the following factors:

┃ The role of users in the implementation process
┃ The degree of management support for the implementation effort
┃ The level of complexity and risk of the implementation project
┃ The quality of management of the implementation process

These are largely behavioral and organizational issues and are illustrated in Figure 13-5.

---

implementation
All organizational activities working toward the adoption, management, and routinization of an innovation.

change agent
In the context of implementation, the individual acting as the catalyst during the change process to ensure successful organizational adaptation to a new system or innovation.

User Involvement and Influence

User involvement in the design and operation of information systems has several positive results. First, if users are heavily involved in systems design, they have more opportunities to mold the system according to their priorities and business requirements, and more opportunities to control the outcome. Second, they are more likely to react positively to the completed system because they have been active participants in the change process itself. It is often difficult to get users involved in a development project if they are pressed for time. Even when such involvement is limited, hands-on experience with the system helps users appreciate its benefits, and users often provide useful suggestions for improvement (De and Ferrat, 1998). The Window on Organizations illustrates the importance of involving users for implementation success.

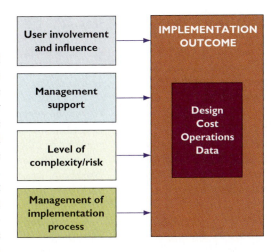

Figure 13-5 Factors in information system success or failure. The implementation outcome can be largely determined by the role of users; the degree of management support; the level of risk and complexity in the implementation project; and the quality of management of the implementation process. Evidence of success or failure can be found in the areas of design, cost, operations, or data of the information system.

Incorporating the user's knowledge and expertise leads to better solutions. However, users often take a very narrow and limited view of the problem to be solved and may overlook important opportunities for improving business processes or innovative ways to apply information technology. The skills and vision of professional system designers are still required much the same way that the services of an architect are required when building a new house (Markus and Keil, 1994).

The relationship between consultant and client has traditionally been a problem area for information system implementation efforts. Users and information systems specialists tend to have different backgrounds, interests, and priorities. This is referred to as the **user–designer communications gap**. These differences lead to divergent organizational loyalties, approaches to problem solving, and vocabularies. Information systems specialists, for example, often have a highly technical, or machine, orientation to problem solving. They look for elegant and sophisticated technical solutions in which hardware and software efficiency is optimized at the expense of ease of use or organizational effectiveness. Users prefer systems that are oriented to solving business problems or facilitating organizational tasks. Often the orientations of both groups are so at odds that they appear to speak in different tongues. These differences are illustrated in Table 13-3, which depicts the typical concerns of end users and technical specialists (information system designers) regarding the development of a new information system. Communication problems between end users and designers are a major reason why user requirements are not properly incorporated into information systems and why users are driven out of the implementation process.

user–designer communications gap
The difference in backgrounds, interests, and priorities that impede communication and problem solving among end users and information systems specialists.

TABLE 13-3

THE USER–DESIGNER COMMUNICATIONS GAP

User Concerns	Designer Concerns
Will the system deliver the information I need for my work?	How much disk storage space will the master file consume?
How quickly can I access the data?	How many lines of program code will it take to perform this function?
How easily can I retrieve the data?	How can we cut down on CPU time when we run the system?
How much clerical support will I need to enter data into the system?	What is the most efficient way of storing these data?
How will the operation of the system fit into my daily business schedule?	What database management system should we use?

INVOLVING THE USERS AT BRITISH AIRWAYS

British Airways is the world's biggest international airline, serving 535 destinations in 160 countries. More than 3,000 of its 65,000 employees work in North America. In 1999 the North American division of British Airways wanted to replace its outdated paper-based time and attendance system with more up-to-date on-line software. The primary users of the system were the customer service and human resources departments.

The target date for implementing the new system was March 2001. But after a year of uncoordinated effort evaluating various software packages, no vendor had been selected. The human resources department wanted an employee "self-service" time and attendance system that could free up staff time for employee recruiting and training. The customer service department, however, wanted an automated capability for calculating manpower requirements per work shift based on historical data.

To provide leadership to carry the project forward, Irv Rudowitz, British Airways' senior vice president for people and organizational delivery, enlisted Georgia LaBarge, the manager of employee services for British Airways North America in New York. LaBarge realized that the two departments needed to collaborate more closely and to compromise to find a common system on which they could agree. She called on both departments to share data about their information requirements and their evaluations of package vendors.

By opening lines of communication, LaBarge was able to persuade the customer service department to compromise on the scheduling module. Because most scheduling modules are written for a specific use, a scheduling module that could calculate manpower needs for customer service centers could not be used by other British Airways departments. LaBarge pointed out that installing a module that could only be used by one department ran counter to the corporate goal of installing applications that could be used by multiple departments. The most important requirements for the system to fulfill were tracking time and attendance according to the company's business rules for different groups of employees.

Neither department had found a suitable software package. A partner airline recommended the Employee Relationship Management package from WorkBrain Inc. in Toronto.

WorkBrain was able to demonstrate that its software could support British Airways' most complex business rules regarding time and attendance, such as multiple union contract rules regarding scheduling and pay for employees on holidays. WorkBrain added a generic scheduling module that could be tailored to the specific needs of the customer service department and to other British Airways departments.

British Airways employees in North America can access the WorkBrain system from desktop computers and kiosks to track their attendance and hours worked, to bid on preferred work and vacation schedules, and to trade shifts and vacations.

After vendor selection was completed, Steve Pruneau, project manager for customer service for British Airways North America, became the project manager to oversee the implementation. By opening up channels of communication and listening to all of its key user groups, British Airways was able to implement the WorkBrain system in limited parts of the company by its March 2001 deadline.

To Think About: What implementation problems did British Airways encounter? What management, organization, and technology issues did it have to address to arrive at an appropriate system solution? How critical was user involvement in implementing the solution?

Sources: Peter Lucas, "Collaboration Deadline," *Knowledge Management*, May 2001; and "Creating Value Across the Enterprise," www.workbrain.com, accessed August 24, 2001.

Systems development projects run a very high risk of failure when there is a pronounced gap between users and technicians and when these groups continue to pursue different goals. Under such conditions, users are often driven out of the implementation process. Because they cannot comprehend what the technicians are saying, users conclude that the entire project is best left in the hands of the information specialists alone. With so many implementation efforts guided by purely technical considerations, it is no wonder that many systems fail to serve organizational needs.

Management Support and Commitment

If an information systems project has the backing and commitment of management at various levels, it is more likely to be perceived positively by both users and the technical information services staff. Both groups will believe that their participation in the development process will receive higher-level attention and priority. They will be recognized and rewarded for the time and effort they devote to implementation. Management backing also ensures that a systems project will receive sufficient funding and resources to be successful. Furthermore, all the changes in work habits and procedures and any organizational realignments associated with a new system depend on management backing to be enforced effectively. If a manager considers a new system a priority, the system will more likely be treated that way by his or her subordinates (Doll, 1985; Ein-Dor and Segev, 1978).

Level of Complexity and Risk

Systems differ dramatically in their size, scope, level of complexity, and organizational and technical components. Some systems development projects are more likely to fail or suffer delays because they carry a much higher level of risk than others. The level of project risk is influenced by project size, project structure, and the level of technical expertise of the information systems staff and project team.

- **Project size** The larger the project—as indicated by the dollars spent, the size of the implementation staff, the time allocated for implementation, and the number of organizational units affected—the greater the risk. Very large-scale system projects have a failure rate that is 50 to 75 percent higher than for other projects because such projects are so complex and difficult to control. The behavioral characteristics of the system—who owns the system and how much it influences business processes—contribute to the complexity of large-scale system projects just as much as technical characteristics, such as the number of lines of program code, length of project, and budget (The Concours Group, 2000; Laudon, 1989; U.S. General Services Administration, 1988).

- **Project structure** Some projects are more highly structured than others. Their requirements are clear and straightforward so the outputs and processes can be easily defined. Users know exactly what they want and what the system should do; there is almost no possibility of the users changing their minds. Such projects run a much lower risk than those with relatively undefined, fluid, and constantly changing requirements; with outputs that cannot be fixed easily because they are subject to users' changing ideas; or with users who cannot agree on what they want.

- **Experience with technology** The project risk will rise if the project team and the information system staff lack the required technical expertise. If the team is unfamiliar with the hardware, system software, application software, or database management system proposed for the project, it is highly likely that the project will experience technical problems or take more time to complete because of the need to master new skills.

Management of the Implementation Process

The development of a new system must be carefully managed and orchestrated. Often basic elements of success are forgotten. Training to ensure that end users are comfortable with the new system and fully understand its potential uses is often sacrificed or forgotten in systems development projects. If the budget is strained at the very beginning, toward the end of a project there will likely be insufficient funds for training and documentation (Bikson et al., 1985).

The conflicts and uncertainties inherent in any implementation effort will be magnified when an implementation project is poorly managed and organized. As illustrated in Figure 13-6, a systems development project without proper management will most likely suffer these consequences:

- Cost overruns that vastly exceed budgets
- Unexpected time slippage

Figure 13-6 Consequences of poor project management. Without proper management, a systems development project will take longer to complete and most often will exceed the allocated budget. The resulting information system will most likely be technically inferior and may not be able to demonstrate any benefits to the organization.

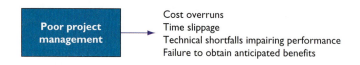

- Technical shortfalls resulting in performance that is significantly below the estimated level
- Failure to obtain anticipated benefits

How badly are projects managed? On average, private sector projects are underestimated by one-half in terms of budget and time required to deliver the complete system promised in the system plan. A very large number of projects are delivered with missing functionality (promised for delivery in later versions). Between 30 and 40 percent of all software projects are "runaway" projects that far exceed the original schedule and budget projections, and fail to perform as originally specified (Keil, Mann, and Rai, 2000). Why are projects managed so poorly and what can be done about it? Here we discuss some possibilities.

Ignorance and optimism The techniques for estimating the length of time required to analyze and design systems are poorly developed. Most applications are "first time" (i.e., there is no prior experience in the application area). The larger the scale of systems, the greater the role of ignorance and optimism. The net result of these factors is that estimates tend to be optimistic, "best case," and wrong. It is assumed that all will go well when in fact it rarely does.

The mythical man-month The traditional unit of measurement used by systems designers to project costs is the **man-month.** Projects are estimated in terms of how many man-months will be required. However, adding more workers to projects does not necessarily reduce the elapsed time needed to complete a systems project (Brooks, 1974). Unlike cotton picking—when tasks can be rigidly partitioned, communication between participants is not required, and training is unnecessary—systems analysis and design involves *tasks that are sequentially linked, cannot be performed in isolation, and require extensive communications and training.* Adding labor to software projects can often slow down delivery as the communication, learning, and coordination costs escalate and detract from the output of participants. For comparison, imagine what would happen if five amateur spectators were added to one team in a championship professional basketball game? The team composed of five professional basketball players would probably do much better in the short run than the team with five professionals and five amateurs.

Falling behind: bad news travels slowly upward Among projects in all fields, slippage in projects, failure, and doubts are often not reported to senior management until it is too late (Smith, Keil and Depledge, 2001; Keil and Robey, 2001). The CON-FIRM project, a very large-scale information systems project to integrate hotel, airline, and rental car reservations, is a classic example. It was sponsored by Hilton Hotels, Budget Rent-A-Car, and Marriott Corporation and developed by AMR Information Services, Inc., a subsidiary of American Airlines Corporation. The project was very ambitious and technically complex, employing a staff of 500. Members of the CONFIRM project management team did not immediately come forward with accurate information when the project started encountering problems coordinating various transaction processing activities. Clients continued to invest in a project that was faltering because they were not informed of its problems with database, decision-support, and integration technologies (Oz, 1994).

man-month

The traditional unit of measurement used by systems designers to estimate the length of time to complete a project. Refers to the amount of work a person can be expected to complete in a month.

CHANGE MANAGEMENT CHALLENGES FOR ENTERPRISE APPLICATIONS, BUSINESS PROCESS REENGINEERING (BPR), AND MERGERS AND ACQUISITIONS

Given the challenges of innovation and implementation, it is not surprising to find a very high failure rate among enterprise system and business process reengineering (BPR) projects, which typically require extensive organizational change and which may require replacing old technologies and legacy systems that are deeply rooted in many interrelated business processes. A number of studies have indicated that 70 percent of all business process reengineering projects fail to deliver promised benefits. Likewise, a high percentage of enterprise resource planning projects fail to be fully implemented or to meet the goals of their users even after three years of work (Gillooly, 1998).

Many enterprise system and reengineering projects have been undermined by poor implementation and change management practices that failed to address employees' concerns about change. Dealing with fear and anxiety throughout the organization; overcoming resistance by key managers; changing job functions, career paths, and recruitment practices; and training have posed greater threats to reengineering than the difficulties companies faced visualizing and designing breakthrough changes to business processes.

Enterprise systems create myriad interconnections among various business processes and data flows to ensure that information in one part of the business can be obtained by any other unit, to help people eliminate redundant activities, and to make better management decisions. Massive organizational changes are required to make this happen. Information that was previously maintained by different systems and different departments or functional areas must be integrated and made available to the company as a whole. Business processes must be tightly integrated, jobs must be redefined, and new procedures must be created throughout the company. Employees are often unprepared for new procedures and roles (Davenport, 2000 and 1998).

Customer relationship management (CRM) and supply chain management systems are also very difficult to implement successfully. Most firms embracing CRM need to transform their focus from a product-centric view to a customer-centric view, which requires some fundamental changes in organizational culture and business processes as well as closer cooperation between the information systems and sales and maketing groups. [The median CRM budget is around $1 million, with an implementation time of four years. Between 55% and 75% of CRM projects fail to meet their objectives (McDonnell, 2001; Yu, 2001).] Supply chain management also requires closer coordination among different functional groups and different organizations as well as extensive business process change.

System Challenges of Mergers and Acquisitions

Mergers and acquisitions (M&As) have been proliferating because they are major growth engines for businesses. Potentially, firms can cut costs significantly by merging with competitors, reduce risks by expanding into different industries (e.g., conglomerating), and create larger pools of competitive knowledge and expertise by joining forces with other players. There are also economies of time: A firm can gain market share and expertise very quickly through acquisition rather than building over the long term.

Although some firms, such as General Electric, are quite successful in carrying out mergers and acquisitions, research has found that more than 70 percent of all M&As result in a decline in shareholder value, and often lead to divestiture at a later time (Braxton Associates, 1997; Economist, 1997). A major reason why mergers and acquisitions fail is the difficulty of integrating the systems of different companies. Mergers and acquisitions are deeply affected by the organizational characteristics of the merging companies as well as by their information technology (IT) infrastructures. Combining the information systems of two different companies usually requires considerable organizational change and complex system projects to manage. If the integration is not properly managed, firms can emerge with a tangled hodgepodge of inherited legacy systems built by aggregating the systems of one firm after another. Without a successful systems integration, the benefits anticipated from the merger cannot be realized, or, worse, the merged entity cannot execute its business processes and loses customers.

When a company targeted for acquisition has been identified, information systems managers will need to identify the realistic costs of integration; the estimated benefits of economies in operation, scope, knowledge, and time; and any problematic systems that require major investments to integrate. In addition, IT managers can critically estimate any likely costs and organizational changes required to upgrade the IT infrastructure or make major system improvements to support the merged companies.

THE CHALLENGE OF IMPLEMENTING GLOBAL SYSTEMS

Firms seeking to develop global systems face the same problems as any large, domestic, systems development effort, but the problems are more complex because of the international environment.

Disparate Information Requirements and Business Processes

Most multinational companies trying to develop transnational systems (see Chapter 2) have a hodgepodge of disparate local systems based on many different—and often incompatible—technology platforms and business processes. Each local production facility might use different manufacturing resources planning, marketing, sales, and human resource systems. The information systems for each country would reflect local cultural, political, and social conditions, which may not be compatible with global business processes and information flows. There are different national laws governing accounting practices, the movement of information, information privacy of citizens, origins of software and hardware in systems, and radio and satellite telecommunications. Cultural and political differences profoundly affect organizations' standard operating procedures and business processes.

European countries have very strict laws concerning transborder data flow and privacy. **Transborder data flow** is defined as the movement of information across international boundaries in any form. Some European countries prohibit the processing of financial information outside their boundaries or the movement of personal information to foreign countries. The European Directive on Data Protection, which went into effect in October 1998, restricts the flow of any information to countries (such as the United States) that do not meet strict European Union standards protecting personal information. In response, most multinational firms develop information systems within each European country to avoid the cost and uncertainty of moving information across national boundaries.

Language remains a significant barrier. Although English has become a kind of standard business language, this is truer at higher levels of companies but not throughout the middle and lower ranks. Software may have to be built with local language interfaces before a new information system can be successfully implemented.

Technology Hurdles: Lack of Standards and Connectivity

Hardware, software, and telecommunications pose special technical challenges in an international setting. The major hardware challenge is finding some way to standardize the firm's computer hardware platform when there is so much variation from operating unit to operating unit and from country to country. The major global software challenge is finding applications that are user friendly and that truly enhance the productivity of international work teams. The major telecommunications challenge is making data flow seamlessly across networks shaped by disparate national standards. Overcoming these challenges requires systems integration and connectivity on a global basis.

transborder data flow
The movement of information across international boundaries in any form.

Software interfaces may have to be translated to accommodate users in non-English speaking countries.

Integrated global networks are extremely difficult to create. The lack of a reliable communications infrastructure and the high costs of installing one are widespread in the much of the world. Where an infrastructure exists in less-developed countries, it is often outdated, lacks digital circuits, and has very noisy lines.

Existing standards for networking and electronic data interchange (EDI) are very industry specific and country specific. The Open Systems Interconnect (OSI) reference model for linking networks is more popular in Europe than it is in the United States. Various industry groups have standardized on other networking architectures, such as Transmission Control Protocol/Internet Protocol (TCP/IP) or IBM's proprietary Systems Network Architecture (SNA). Even standards such as ISDN (Integrated Services Digital Network) vary from country to country.

If new software must be created, another challenge is to build software that can be realistically used by multiple business units from different countries, because these business units are accustomed to their own unique business processes and definitions of data. Special interfaces may need to be built to accommodate different languages.

Increasingly, firms are turning to enterprise systems to standardize their business processes on a global basis and to create coordinated global supply chains. However, enterprise systems are not always compatible with differences in languages and business practices (Soh, Kien, and Tay-Yap, 2000). Company units in countries that are not technically sophisticated may also encounter problems trying to manage the technical complexities of enterprise software.

Local User Resistance to Global Systems

It is difficult to convince local managers anywhere in the world that they should change their business processes to coordinate with the rest of the company, especially if this might interfere with their local performance. (Local managers generally are rewarded for meeting local objectives of their division or plant.) Moreover, it is difficult to coordinate development of projects around the world in the absence of a powerful telecommunications network and, therefore, difficult to encourage local users to take on ownership in the systems developed.

13.3 Managing Implementation

Not all aspects of the implementation process can be easily controlled or planned (Alter and Ginzberg, 1978). However, the chances for system success can be increased by anticipating potential implementation problems and applying appropriate corrective strategies. Various project management, requirements gathering, and planning methodologies have been developed for specific categories of problems. Strategies have also been devised for ensuring that users play an appropriate role throughout the implementation period and for managing the organizational change process.

Controlling Risk Factors

The first step in managing project risk is to identify the nature and level of risk confronting the project (Schmidt, Lyytinen, Keil, and Cule, 2001). Implementers can then adopt a contingency approach to project management, handling each project with the tools, project management methodologies, and organizational linkages geared to its level of risk (Barki, Rivard, and Talbot, 2001; McFarlan, 1981).

Managing Technical Complexity

Projects with *challenging and complex technology* to master benefit from **internal integration tools.** The success of such projects depends on how well their technical complexity can be managed. Project leaders need both heavy technical and administrative experience. They must be able to anticipate problems and develop smooth working relationships among a predominantly technical team. The team should be under the leadership of a manager with a strong technical and project management background and team members should be highly experienced. Team meetings should take place frequently. Essential technical skills or expertise not available internally should be secured from outside the organization.

internal integration tools
Project management technique that ensures that the implementation team operates as a cohesive unit.

This project team of professionals is using computing tools to enhance communication, analysis, and decision-making.

Formal Planning and Control Tools

formal planning tools

Project management technique that structures and sequences tasks, budgeting time, money, and technical resources required to complete the tasks.

formal control tools

Project management technique that helps monitor the progress toward completion of a task and fulfillment of goals.

external integration tools

Project management technique that links the work of the implementation team to that of users at all organizational levels.

Large projects will benefit from appropriate use of **formal planning** and **formal control tools.** With project management techniques, such as Program Evaluation and Review Technique (PERT) or Gantt charts, a detailed plan can be developed. (PERT lists the specific activities that make up a project, their duration, and the activities that must be completed before a specific activity can start. A Gantt chart such as that illustrated in Figure 13-7 visually represents the sequence and timing of different tasks in a development project as well as their resource requirements.) Tasks can be defined and resources budgeted.

These project management techniques can help managers identify bottlenecks and determine the impact that problems will have on project completion times. They can also help system developers partition implementation into smaller, more manageable segments with defined, measurable business results (Fichman and Moses, 1999). Standard control techniques will successfully chart the progress of the project against budgets and target dates, so deviations from the plan can be spotted.

Increasing User Involvement and Overcoming User Resistance

Projects with relatively *little structure and many undefined requirements* must involve users fully at all stages. Users must be mobilized to support one of many possible design options and to remain committed to a single design. **External integration tools** consist of ways to link the work of the implementation team to users at all organizational levels. For instance, users can become active members of the project team, take on leadership roles, and take charge of installation and training.

Unfortunately, systems development is not an entirely rational process. Users leading design activities have used their positions to further private interests and to gain power rather than to promote organizational objectives (Franz and Robey, 1984). Users may not always be involved in systems projects in a productive way.

Participation in implementation activities may not be enough to overcome the problem of user resistance. The implementation process demands organizational change. Such change may be resisted because different users may be affected by the system in different ways. Whereas some users may welcome a new system because it brings changes they perceive as beneficial to them, others may resist these changes because they believe the shifts are detrimental to their interests (Joshi, 1991).

If the use of a system is voluntary, users may choose to avoid it; if use is mandatory, resistance will take the form of increased error rates, disruptions, turnover, and even sabotage. Therefore, the implementation strategy must not only encourage user participation and

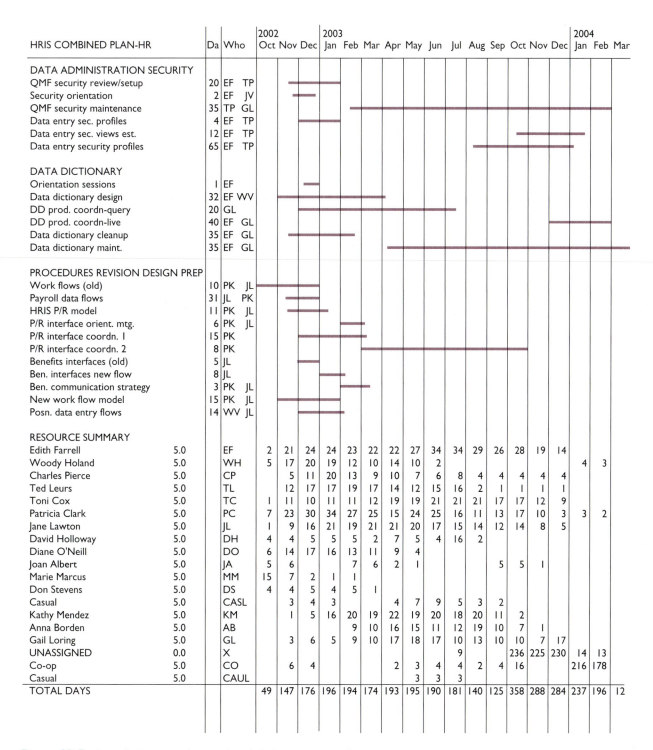

HRIS COMBINED PLAN-HR

Timeline columns: 2002 (Oct Nov Dec) · 2003 (Jan Feb Mar Apr May Jun Jul Aug Sep Oct Nov Dec) · 2004 (Jan Feb Mar)

Task	Da	Who
DATA ADMINISTRATION SECURITY		
QMF security review/setup	20	EF TP
Security orientation	2	EF JV
QMF security maintenance	35	TP GL
Data entry sec. profiles	4	EF TP
Data entry sec. views est.	12	EF TP
Data entry security profiles	65	EF TP
DATA DICTIONARY		
Orientation sessions	1	EF
Data dictionary design	32	EF WV
DD prod. coordn-query	20	GL
DD prod. coordn-live	40	EF GL
Data dictionary cleanup	35	EF GL
Data dictionary maint.	35	EF GL
PROCEDURES REVISION DESIGN PREP		
Work flows (old)	10	PK JL
Payroll data flows	31	JL PK
HRIS P/R model	11	PK JL
P/R interface orient. mtg.	6	PK JL
P/R interface coordn. 1	15	PK
P/R interface coordn. 2	8	PK
Benefits interfaces (old)	5	JL
Ben. interfaces new flow	8	JL
Ben. communication strategy	3	PK JL
New work flow model	15	PK JL
Posn. data entry flows	14	WV JL

RESOURCE SUMMARY

Name		Who	Oct	Nov	Dec	Jan	Feb	Mar	Apr	May	Jun	Jul	Aug	Sep	Oct	Nov	Dec	Jan	Feb	Mar
Edith Farrell	5.0	EF	2	21	24	24	23	22	22	27	34	34	29	26	28	19	14			
Woody Holand	5.0	WH	5	17	20	19	12	10	14	10	2							4	3	
Charles Pierce	5.0	CP		5	11	20	13	9	10	7	6	8	4	4	4	4	4			
Ted Leurs	5.0	TL		12	17	17	19	17	14	12	15	16	2	1	1	1	1			
Toni Cox	5.0	TC	1	11	10	11	11	12	19	19	21	21	21	17	17	12	9			
Patricia Clark	5.0	PC	7	23	30	34	27	25	15	24	25	16	11	13	17	10	3	3	2	
Jane Lawton	5.0	JL	1	9	16	21	19	21	21	20	17	15	14	12	14	8	5			
David Holloway	5.0	DH	4	4	5	5	5	2	7	5	4	16	2							
Diane O'Neill	5.0	DO	6	14	17	16	13	11	9	4										
Joan Albert	5.0	JA	5	6			7	6	2	1				5	5	1				
Marie Marcus	5.0	MM	15	7	2	1	1													
Don Stevens	5.0	DS	4	4	5	4	5	1												
Casual	5.0	CASL		3	4	3			4	7	9	5	3	2						
Kathy Mendez	5.0	KM		1	5	16	20	19	22	19	20	18	20	11	2					
Anna Borden	5.0	AB					9	10	16	15	11	12	19	10	7	1				
Gail Loring	5.0	GL		3	6	5	9	10	17	18	17	10	13	10	10	7	17			
UNASSIGNED	0.0	X											9		236	225	230	14	13	
Co-op	5.0	CO	6	4					2	3	4	4	2	4	16			216	178	
Casual	5.0	CAUL									3	3	3							
TOTAL DAYS			49	147	176	196	194	174	193	195	190	181	140	125	358	288	284	237	196	12

Figure 13-7 Formal planning and control tools help to manage information systems projects successfully. The Gantt chart in this figure was produced by a commercially available project management software package. It shows the task, person-days, and initials of each responsible person, as well as the start and finish dates for each task. The resource summary provides a good manager with the total person-days for each month and for each person working on the project to successfully manage the project. The project described here is a data administration project.

counterimplementation

A deliberate strategy to thwart the implementation of an information system or an innovation in an organization.

involvement, it must also address the issue of counterimplementation (Keen, 1981). **Counterimplementation** is a deliberate strategy to thwart the implementation of an information system or an innovation in an organization.

Strategies to overcome user resistance include user participation (to elicit commitment as well as to improve design), user education and training, management edicts and policies, and providing better incentives for users who cooperate. The new system can be made more user friendly by improving the end-user interface. Users will be more cooperative if organizational problems are solved prior to introducing the new system.

DESIGNING FOR THE ORGANIZATION

Because the purpose of a new system is to improve the organization's performance, the systems development process must explicitly address the ways in which the organization will change when the new system is installed, including installation of intranets, extranets, and Internet applications. In addition to procedural changes, transformations in job functions, organizational structure, power relationships, and behavior will all have to be carefully planned. When technology-induced changes produce unforeseen consequences, the organization can benefit by improvising to take advantage of new opportunities. Information systems specialists, managers, and users should remain open-minded about their roles in the change management process and not adhere to rigid, narrow perceptions (Orlikowski and Hofman, 1997; Markus and Benjamin, 1997). Table 13-4 lists the organizational dimensions that would need to be addressed for planning and implementing many systems.

organizational impact analysis

Study of the way a proposed system will affect organizational structure, attitudes, decision making, and operations.

Although systems analysis and design activities are supposed to include an organizational impact analysis, this area has traditionally been neglected. An **organizational impact analysis** explains how a proposed system will affect organizational structure, attitudes, decision making, and operations. To integrate information systems successfully with the organization, thorough and fully documented organizational impact assessments must be given more attention in the development effort.

Allowing for the Human Factor

The quality of information systems should be evaluated in terms of user criteria rather than the criteria of the information systems staff. In addition to targets such as memory size, access rates, and calculation times, systems objectives should include standards for user performance. For example, an objective might be that data entry clerks learn the procedures and codes for four new on-line data entry screens in a half-day training session.

ergonomics

The interaction of people and machines in the work environment, including the design of jobs, health issues, and the end-user interface of information systems.

Areas where users interface with the system should be carefully designed, with sensitivity to ergonomic issues. **Ergonomics** refers to the interaction of people and machines in the work environment. It considers the design of jobs, health issues, and the end-user interface of information systems. The impact of the application system on the work environment and job dimensions must be carefully assessed.

TABLE 13-4	ORGANIZATIONAL FACTORS IN SYSTEMS PLANNING AND IMPLEMENTATION

Employee participation and involvement

Job design

Standards and performance monitoring

Ergonomics (including equipment, user interfaces, and the work environment)

Employee grievance resolution procedures

Health and safety

Government regulatory compliance

Sociotechnical Design

Most contemporary systems-building approaches tend to treat end users as essential to the systems-building process but playing a largely passive role relative to other forces shaping the system, such as the specialist system designers and management. A different tradition rooted in the European social democratic labor movement assigns users a more active role, one that empowers them to codetermine the role of information systems in their workplace (Clement and Van den Besselaar, 1993).

This tradition of participatory design emphasizes participation by the individuals most affected by the new system. It is closely associated with the concept of sociotechnical design. A **sociotechnical design** plan establishes human objectives for the system that lead to increased job satisfaction. Designers set forth separate sets of technical and social design solutions. The social design plans explore different work group structures, allocation of tasks, and the design of individual jobs. The proposed technical solutions are compared with the proposed social solutions. Social and technical solutions that can be combined are proposed as sociotechnical solutions. The alternative that best meets both social and technical objectives is selected for the final design. The resulting sociotechnical design is expected to produce an information system that blends technical efficiency with sensitivity to organizational and human needs, leading to high job satisfaction (Mumford and Weir, 1979). Systems with compatible technical and organizational elements are expected to raise productivity without sacrificing human and social goals.

sociotechnical design
Design to produce information systems that blend technical efficiency with sensitivity to organizational and human needs.

MANAGING GLOBAL IMPLEMENTATIONS

Companies striving to implement global systems should realize that not all systems should be coordinated on a transnational basis. There are only some core systems that are truly worth sharing from a cost and feasibility point of view. **Core systems** are systems that support functions that are absolutely critical to the organization. Other systems should be partially coordinated because they share key elements, but they do not have to be totally common across national boundaries. For such systems, a good deal of local variation is possible and desirable. A final group of systems are peripheral, truly provincial, and are needed to suit local requirements only (see Figure 13-8).

Core systems can be identified by creating a short list of 10 business processes that are absolutely critical for the firm. Management then can decide which processes should be captured in core systems, centrally coordinated, designed, and implemented around the globe, and which should be regional and local. By limiting transnational development to a small

core systems
Systems that support functions that are absolutely critical to the organization.

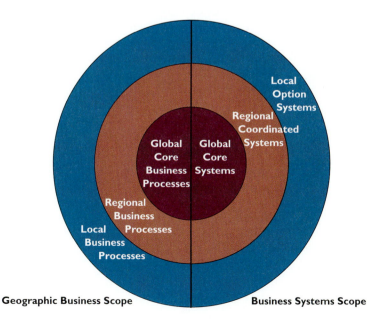

Geographic Business Scope   **Business Systems Scope**

Figure 13-8 Agency and other coordination costs increase as the firm moves from local option systems toward regional and global systems. However, transaction costs of participating in global markets probably decrease as firms develop global systems. A sensible strategy is to reduce agency costs by developing only a few core global systems that are vital for global operations, leaving other systems in the hands of regional and local units.
Source: From *Managing Information Technology in Multinational Corporations* by Edward M. Roche, © 1993. Adapted by permission of Prentice Hall, Inc., Upper Saddle River, NJ.

group of absolutely critical systems, management can divide opposition to a transnational strategy. At the same time, it can appease those who oppose global worldwide coordination by permitting some local systems development to continue.

Implementation Tactics: Cooptation

cooptation

Bringing the opposition into the process of designing and implementing a solution without giving up control of the direction and nature of the change.

Involving people in change, assuring them that change is in the best interests of the company and their local units, is a key tactic. Management can use cooptation to encourage user participation in a new system design without giving up control over the development of the project to local interests. **Cooptation** is defined as bringing the opposition into the process of designing and implementing the solution without giving up control over the direction and nature of the change. Minimally, however, local units must agree on a short list of transnational systems, and some pressure from senior management may be required to solidify support of this idea.

Management could give each country unit the opportunity to develop one transnational application first in its home territory, and then throughout the world. In this manner, each major country systems group is given a piece of the action in developing a transnational system, and local units feel a sense of ownership in the transnational effort.

Recruiting a wide range of local individuals to transnational centers of excellence also helps send the message that all significant groups are involved in the design and will have an influence. These centers of excellence in key locations around the world could perform the initial identification and specification of core business processes and the core systems development. New systems would first be installed and tested in designated pilot regions before they would be rolled out to other parts of the globe.

Creating a Global Technology Infrastructure

Firms have several options for providing the international connectivity required for their global systems: They can build their own international private network, rely on a value-added network service (VAN, see Chapter 8) based on the public switched networks throughout the world, or use Internet technology. Firms can build global intranets and use Virtual Private Networks (VPNs) from Internet service providers (see Chapter 9). VPNs can

MAKE **IT** YOUR BUSINESS

FINANCE AND ACCOUNTING

A series of financial models are used to justify capital investments in new information systems. The finance and accounting function is responsible for supervising the financial analysis of information systems investments and for providing information on corporate cash flows used in capital budgeting calculations. You can find examples of finance and accounting applications on page 424.

HUMAN RESOURCES

The human resources function can play a valuable role in system implementation by helping with change management. When a new system is proposed, human resources staff can assist with the organizational impact analysis and locate new positions for employees whose jobs would be eliminated. Human resources could also arrange for employee training in the new system. You can find examples of human resources applications on page 432.

MANUFACTURING AND PRODUCTION

Supply chain management systems and enterprise resource planning systems can provide significant tangible benefits such as reductions in

inventory costs and intangible benefits such as faster response to customer demands. However, both types of systems are among the most difficult systems to implement successfully because they require major business process changes as well as new technology. You can find examples of manufacturing and production applications on pages 446–448.

SALES AND MARKETING

Customer relationship management systems can provide tangible benefits such as reduced direct marketing costs and intangible benefits such as better customer service and support. These systems can be difficult to implement because they may require integrating customer information from multiple sources and changes to the firm's business processes for interacting with customers and gathering customer data. User interface design is especially important for customer-facing Web applications. You can find examples of sales and marketing applications on pages 414–416.

provide many features of a private network to firms operating internationally although they may not provide the same level of quick and predictable response as private networks.

"Fourth-Generation" Project Management

Traditional techniques for managing projects deal with problems of size and complexity by breaking large projects into subprojects; assigning teams, schedules, and milestones to each; and focusing primarily on project mechanics rather than business results. These techniques are inadequate for enterprise systems and other large-scale system projects with extremely complex problems of organizational coordination and change management, complex and sometimes unfamiliar technology, and continually changing business requirements. A new "fourth-generation" of project management techniques is emerging to address these challenges.

In this model, project planning assumes an enterprise-wide focus, driven by the firm's strategic business vision and technology architecture. Project and subproject managers focus on solving problems and meeting challenges as they arise rather than simply meeting formal project milestones. It may be useful for organizations to establish a separate program office to manage subprojects, coordinate the entire project effort with other ongoing projects, and coordinate the project with ongoing changes in the firm's business strategy, information technology architecture and infrastructure, and business processes (The Concours Group, 2000).

Management Wrap-Up

Managers must link systems development to the organization's strategy and identify precisely which systems should be changed to achieve large-scale benefits for the organization as a whole. Two principal reasons for system failure are inadequate management support and poor management of the implementation process. Managers should fully understand the level of complexity and risk in new systems projects as well as their potential business value.

Building an information system is a process of planned organizational change. Many levels of organizational change are possible. Global systems, enterprise systems, supply chain and customer relationship management systems, and business process reengineering projects are high-risk implementations because they require far-reaching organizational changes that are often resisted by members of the organization. Eliciting user support and maintaining an appropriate level of user involvement at all stages of system building are essential.

Selecting the right technology for a system solution that fits the problem's constraints and the organization's information technology infrastructure is a key business decision. Systems sometimes fail because the technology is too complex or sophisticated to be easily implemented or because system builders lack the requisite skills or experience to work with it. Managers and systems builders should be fully aware of the risks and rewards of various technologies as they make their technology selections.

For Discussion
1. It has been said that when we design an information system we are redesigning the organization. What are the ramifications of this statement?
2. It has been said that most systems fail because system builders ignore organizational behavior problems. Why?

Summary

1. *How can our company measure the business benefits of our information systems? What models should be used to measure that business value?* There are many different ways in which information systems can provide business value for a firm, including increased profitability and productivity. Some, but not all of these business benefits can be quantified and measured.

Capital budgeting models are used to determine whether an investment in information technology produces sufficient returns to justify its costs. The principal capital budgeting models are the payback method, accounting rate of return on investment (ROI), cost–benefit ratio, net present value, profitability index, and internal rate of return (IRR).

Other models for evaluating information system investments involve nonfinancial and strategic considerations. Portfolio analysis and scoring models can be used to evaluate alternative information systems projects. Real options pricing models, which apply the same techniques for valuing financial options to systems investments, can be useful when considering highly uncertain IT investments.

Although information technology has increased productivity in manufacturing, especially the manufacture of information technology products, the extent to which computers have enhanced the productivity of the service sector remains under debate. In addition to reducing costs, computers may increase the quality of products and services for consumers or may create entirely new products and revenue streams. These intangible benefits are difficult to measure and consequently are not addressed by conventional productivity measures.

2. *Why do so many system projects fail? What are the principal reasons for system failures?* A very large percentage of information systems fail to deliver benefits or solve the problems for which they were intended because the process of organizational change surrounding system-building was not properly addressed. The principal causes of information system failure are (1) insufficient or improper user participation in the systems development process, (2) lack of management support, (3) high levels of complexity and risk in the systems development process, and (4) poor management of the implementation process. There is a very high failure rate among business process reengineering and enterprise system projects because they require extensive organizational change. Customer relationship management and supply chain management system projects as well as system changes resulting from mergers and acquisitions are also difficult to implement successfully because they usually require fundamental changes to business processes.

3. *How should the organizational change surrounding a new system be managed to ensure success?* Building an information system is a process of planned organizational change that must be carefully managed. The term implementation refers to the entire process of organizational change surrounding the introduction of a new information system. One can better understand system success and failure by examining different patterns of implementation. Especially important is the relationship between participants in the implementation process, notably the interactions between system designers and users. Conflicts between the technical orientation of system designers and the business orientation of end users must be resolved. The success of organizational change can be determined by how well information systems specialists, end users, and decision makers deal with key issues at various stages in implementation.

4. *Are there any special challenges in implementing international information systems?* International system implementations are more complex because of the challenge of coordinating disparate business processes and technologies among many different business units in different countries. The information system portfolios in most multinational corporations have evolved without a conscious plan. The information systems for each country would reflect local cultural, political and social conditions, which may not be compatible with global business processes and information flows. The technology platforms for each of the business units are often incompatible. Networking standards and availability differ from country to country, making it difficult to create global networks for seamlessly exchanging information. Overcoming these challenges requires systems integration and connectivity on a global basis.

5. *What strategies can our organization use to manage the system implementation process more effectively?* Management support and control of the implementation process are essential, as are mechanisms for dealing with the level of risk in each new systems project. Some companies experience organizational resistance to change. Project risk factors can be brought under some control by a contingency approach to project management. The level of risk in a systems development project is determined by three key dimensions: (1) project size, (2) project structure, and (3) experience with technology. The risk level of each project will determine the appropriate mix of external integration tools, internal integration tools, formal planning tools, and formal control tools to be applied.

Appropriate strategies can be applied to ensure the correct level of user participation in the systems development process and to minimize user resistance. Information system design and the entire implementation process should be managed as planned organizational change. Participatory design emphasizes the participation of the individuals most affected by a new system. Sociotechnical design aims for an optimal blend of social and technical design solutions.

An implementation strategy for global systems requires defining a small subset of core business processes and focusing on building core systems that could support these

processes. Cooptation tactics may be necessary to help ensure that widely dispersed foreign units participate in the operation of new global systems while global headquarters continues to maintain overall control. To provide the international connectivity required for global systems, firms can build their own international private network, rely on a network service based on the public switched networks throughout the world, or use the Internet and intranets.

KEY TERMS

Accounting rate of return on investment (ROI), 421

Capital budgeting, 417

Change agent, 430

Cooptation, 442

Core systems, 441

Cost–benefit ratio, 422

Counterimplementation, 440

Ergonomics, 440

External integration tools, 438

Formal control tools, 438

Formal planning tools, 438

Implementation, 430

Intangible benefits, 418

Internal integration tools, 437

Internal rate of return (IRR), 423

Man-month, 434

Net present value, 422

Organizational impact analysis, 440

Payback method, 420

Portfolio analysis, 423

Present value, 422

Profitability index, 422

Real options pricing models, 425

Scoring model, 423

Sociotechnical design, 441

System failure, 428

Tangible benefits, 418

Transborder data flow, 436

User–designer communications gap, 431

User interface, 428

REVIEW QUESTIONS

1. Name and describe the principal capital budgeting methods used to evaluate information system projects.

2. What are the limitations of financial models for establishing the value of information systems?

3. Describe how portfolio analysis and scoring models can be used to establish the worth of systems.

4. How can real options pricing models be used to help evaluate information technology investments?

5. Have information systems enhanced productivity in businesses? Explain your answer.

6. Why do builders of new information systems need to address change management?

7. What kinds of problems provide evidence of information system failure?

8. Why is it necessary to understand the concept of implementation when managing the organizational change surrounding a new information system?

9. What are the major causes of implementation success or failure?

10. What is the user–designer communications gap? What kinds of implementation problems can it create?

11. Why is there such a high failure rate among enterprise resource planning (ERP) and business process reengineering (BPR) projects? Why are customer relationship management and supply chain management systems often difficult to implement?

12. What role do information systems play in the success or failure of mergers and acquisitions?

13. What are the challenges of implementing global systems?

14. What dimensions influence the level of risk in each systems development project?

15. What project management techniques can be used to control project risk?

16. What strategies can be used to overcome user resistance to systems development projects?

17. What organizational considerations should be addressed by information system design?

18. What strategies can be used to make implementation of global systems more successful?

APPLICATION SOFTWARE EXERCISE:

SPREADSHEET EXERCISE: CAPITAL BUDGETING FOR A NEW CAD SYSTEM

Your company would like to invest in a new computer-aided-design (CAD) system, requiring purchases of hardware, software, and networking technology as well as expenditures for installation, training, and support. The Laudon Web site for Chapter 13 contains tables showing each cost component for the new system as well as annual maintenance costs over a five-year period. You believe the new system will produce annual sav-

ings by reducing the amount of labor required to generate designs and design specifications and thus increase your firm's annual cash flow. Using the data provided and instructions on the Laudon Web site for Chapter 13, create a worksheet that calculates the costs and benefits of the investment over a five-year period and analyzes the investment using the six capital budgeting models presented in this chapter. Is this investment worthwhile? Why or why not?

GROUP PROJECT

Form a group with two or three other students. Write a description of the implementation problems you might expect to encounter for the information system you designed for the business process redesign project that follows Chapter 14. Write an analysis of the steps you would take to solve or prevent these

problems. Alternatively, you could describe the implementation problems that might be expected for one of the systems discussed in the Window On boxes or chapter ending cases in this text. If possible, use electronic presentation software to present your findings to the class.

TOOLS FOR INTERACTIVE LEARNING

■ INTERNET CONNECTION

The Internet Connection for this chapter will direct you to a series of Web sites where you can complete an exercise to evaluate user interfaces and user–system interactions. You can also use the Interactive Study Guide to test your knowledge of the topics in this chapter and get instant feedback when you need more practice.

■ CD-ROM

If you use the Multimedia Edition CD-ROM with this chapter, you can find an audio overview of the major themes of this chapter and bullet text summarizing the key points of the chapter.

■ ELECTRONIC COMMERCE PROJECT

At the Laudon Web site for Chapter 13, you can find an Electronic Commerce project for buying and financing a home purchase.

CASE STUDY—*A New Supply Chain Project Has Nike Running for Its Life*

Nike, Inc., is the world's number one athletic shoemaker, with 500,000 workers in 55 countries and sales topping 40 percent of the athletic shoe market. The company went through a phenomenal growth spurt from 1996 through 1999, with its annual sales reaching $9 billion in 2000. And yet during 2000 and 2001 the company encountered financial problems and its reputation was seriously damaged.

Many reasons have been suggested for Nike's recent decline. One, in the minds of many, is Michael Jordan's final retirement as a basketball player (Jordan had been a Nike spokesperson.) Many also believe that the slowing economy in 2000–2001 hurt Nike. However, John Shanley, an analyst at Wells Fargo Van Kaspar, points out that, "Athletic footwear remains hot as a pis-

tol." When Nike's stock value fell by more than 15 percent, Reebok's stock skyrocketed by more than 250 percent. Analysts blame poor shoe design and note that New Balance's market share climbed from 7 percent in 1999 to 9 percent in 2000, whereas Nike's share dropped from 43 percent to 40 percent. (New Balance is successfully placing greater emphasis on more subtle designs.)

Nike may have been hurt by the severe public relations problems it faced in recent years. The company was the object of intensive public accusations of exploiting foreign labor, particularly in Indonesia.

One reason for Nike's problems that everyone, including Nike, agrees on, has been the overproduction of some unpopular shoes and the underproduction of other popular designs. Nike blames both the new supply-chain software it installed and i2 Technologies Inc., the maker of that software, for these production errors.

Dallas, Texas-based i2 is a major supply-chain software vendor. The company has been highly successful, with many customers both large and small. I2's supply-chain software is designed to improve the management of inventory, production, shipping, and sales forecasting. Nike turned to i2 because it wanted to be able to respond more quickly to shoe market changes by being able to plan production schedules and begin production of a new line of shoes in one week rather than taking a full month after demand shifts. The system is supposed to help predict demand so that the company could better plan and control the production of existing products. Thus, Nike would be able more quickly to reduce the production of shoes that have gone out of style, leaving the company with fewer unwanted shoes, while increasing its production of shoe styles that are rising in demand.

Nike had previously made a major commitment to this type of software by installing an SAP supply-chain management system in the late 1990s. However, the system was problem ridden and, in Nike's view, inadequate, leading to Nike's second attempt, this time with i2. Nike, like most big corporations, has experience with major information technology projects, the previous one being the installation of an intranet in mid-1997. That project was meant to bring key people in many countries into close contact with the headquarters in order to improve global collaboration and so significantly reduce the time it took to make product design decisions. In that case also, Nike's goal was to respond rapidly to changes in style demands. But many vital employees seldom used the intranet. A later evaluation of the project showed that Nike had planned the project poorly, that key people had been left out, and that the staff was inadequately trained on both the system and its business value.

The key element of the i2 project was to aid in speedily forecasting market changes. In addition it was also to automate and so make efficient the way Nike manufactures, ships, and sells its shoes, and thereby lowering operating costs. Even Federal Reserve Chairman Alan Greenspan recognized the potential of that type of software when he said, "New technologies for supply-chain management can perceive imbalances in inventories at a very early stage—virtually in real time." He added it "can cut production promptly in response to the developing signs of unintended inventory building."

However, that type of software raises many questions. Very few companies can prove any real payoffs from supply-chain management systems. "Documenting the ROI from supply-chain management is difficult," claims Vinod Singhal, an associate professor of operations management at the Georgia Institute of Technology in Atlanta. Moreover, supply-chain projects are costly and time consuming. In one study by Singhal, supply-

change project blunders resulted in an average stock price drop of 8.62 percent.

Not only did Nike recognize that the project would be difficult after its SAP experience, but so did i2. "We knew going in that it was going to be a tough implementation," said Katrina Roche, i2's chief marketing officer, "because the apparel industry tends to be very complex and because Nike had tried other [supply chain tool] vendors and they didn't work out." The $400 million project, part of which was to install the i2 software, began in June 2000.

The problems became public when Nike miscalculated future demand for its shoes, and Nike officials blamed the i2 supply-and-demand-planning (supply-chain) software, claiming that it did not perform as expected. Nike made the problem public on February 27, 2001, when it warned of a profit drop at the end of its fiscal third quarter (the next day). A Nike spokeswoman said the i2 software "didn't deliver on performance or functionality." Philip Knight, the Nike chairman and CEO, commented that Nike "experienced complications arising from the impact of implementing our new demand and supply planning systems and processes." However Knight did insist that his company would fix the problem and achieve big savings. Pierre Mitchell, an analyst and supply-chain expert at AMR Research, wondered why Nike couldn't predict the disaster. He said, "Blaming the software vendor is a very old practice." Criticizing Nike's CEO, he said, "Phil Knight makes it sound like it's a surprise to him." Commenting on Knight's management, Mitchell added, "If he doesn't have checkpoints for these kinds of [giant] projects, if he doesn't know where $400 million of his company's money is going, then he doesn't have control of his company." He also pointed out that the system was not designed specifically for the shoe and apparel business, and "that increases the risk that something is going to go terribly wrong."

Nike ran into financial problems when it ordered suppliers to produce too many shoe styles which were declining in popularity, and it did not order enough of the newer models for which the popularity had sharply increased. Orders for some of the less popular shoes were sent to the factories twice—once by the old order-management system and once by the new system—whereas orders for the newer models "fell through the cracks." Foot Locker, the largest Nike shoes retailer in the United States, had to reduce prices on such shoes as Nike's Air Garnett III, which had become a slow-selling shoe and now had to be sold at about $90 instead of about $140. Similarly, the price of Air Terra Human 2 was lowered to $49.99 when it should have been selling at about $100. The company also was late in delivering many of its more popular shoes because of their late production. As a result Nike had to ship them by plane at $4 to $8 a pair compared to 75 cents for shipping by boat.

At the February 27 informational meeting, Nike said their estimated profit for the quarter would decline from about 50 to 55 cents per share to about 35 to 40 cents. It also announced that the inventory problems would persist for the next six to nine months while the company sold off the overproduction. It further announced that the problems would cost $80 million to $100 million in sales for that quarter.

As to the future of the project, Knight said, "We believe that we have addressed the issues around this implementation and that over the long term, we will achieve significant financial and organizational benefit from our global supply-chain initiative." A Nike spokeswoman said that Nike is working with i2 to solve the problems and added that i2 had "created some technical and operational workarounds," and the implementation is now stable.

I2 had a very different view on the source of Nike's problems. I2's initial response, on February 27, was that there had been implementation problems, but they "are behind us," according to an i2 spokesperson. He said further that it is a very large and difficult project, but insisted the two companies have "a strong partnership." However, the company also answered directly Nike's finger pointing. Greg Brady, the president of i2 Technologies Inc. and a person who had been highly involved with the project, said that he and his company only learned that Nike blamed them when Knight made his public statement that day. "If our deployment was creating a business problem for them, why were we never informed?" Lee Geishecker, a Gartner analyst, commented on Brady's statement saying she does not understand why a company losing so much money because of deployment would not inform the principals. "How can you let the problems not be solved?" Nike never responded to that allegation.

An i2 spokesman said, "Think of all the possible permutations, and it becomes a complex and challenging job to get the system implemented." He claimed that i2 software accounts for only about 10 percent of Nike's $400 million supply-chain project. He pointed out that SAP and Siebel Systems Inc. are also involved with the system, and Nike's stated cost ($400 million) also includes hardware. Brady added, "There is no way that software is responsible for Nike's earnings problem." The company claimed the major problem with the software was Nike's customization. I2 said it did all the required specialized customization work that Nike requested. The customized software then had to be linked with Nike's other back-end systems. However, Roche maintained, "We recommend that customers follow our guidelines for implementation—we have a specific methodology and templates for customers to use—but Nike chose not to use our implementation methodology." She believed Nike saw the i2 methodology as too rigid and so did not use it. Jennifer Tejada, i2's vice president of marketing, also said that i2's software had been too heavily customized.

Tejada raised another issue when she said her company always urges its customers to deploy the system in stages, but Nike went live to thousands of suppliers and distributors simul-taneously. Roche claimed this is "an isolated incident." She contended that, "We've got over 1,000 customers up and running, and some of them are in the apparel industry as well. This is the first time any of them have made this kind of announcement." According to Geishecker, Nike went live a little more than a year after launching the project, yet this large a project customarily takes two years, and the system is often deployed in stages. Brent Thrill, an analyst at Credit Suisse First Boston, sent a note to his clients saying that because of the complexities he would not have been surprised if to test the system Nike had run the i2 system for three years while keeping the older system running. Larry Lapide, a research analyst at AMR and a supply-chain expert, jumped in saying, "Whenever you put software in, you don't go big-bang and you don't go into production right away. Usually you get these bugs worked out . . . before it goes live across the whole business." However, Karen Peterson, a research director in the Gartner Group, disagreed, noting that Kmart, which also has major complexities in its forecasting and managing of the supply chain, also reported problems with i2 software. She asserted that, "i2 excels at sales but its execution isn't always flawless. The salespeople make bold promises that their software doesn't always live up to." Roche also said that Nike converted to the new software too early. She claimed Nike started to enter data for its forthcoming spring 2001 line before the cutover to the i2 software was completed. "The solution wasn't stable at the time they started using it."

Sources: Tim Wilson, "Nike: I2 Software Just Didn't Do It," *Techweb,* March 1, 2001; Eric Young and Mark Roberti, "The Swoosh Stumbles," *The Industry Standard,* March 12, 2001; Marc L. Songini, "Nike Blames Financial Snag on Supply-Chain Project," *Computerworld,* February 27, 2001; "Disaster of the Day: Nike," *Forbes,* February 22, 2001; "Dog of the Day: I2 Technologies," *Forbes,* February 27, 2001; "Forbes Forecast: Nike Gets the Boot," *Forbes,* February 27, 2001; Alorie Gilbert, "I2 Forecasts Slow Growth, Losses," *Information Week,* April 19, 2001; Sari Kalin, "SneakerNet," *CIO Web Business Magazine,* August 1, 1999; Steve Konicki, "I2 Says: 'You Too, Nike,'" *Information Week,* March 1, 2001, "Lower Profit at Nike Blamed on i2 Software," *Information Week,* February 28, 2001, and "Nike Just Didn't Do It Right, Says I2 Technologies," *Information Week,* March 5, 2001; Mark Roberti, "I2 Names a New CEO," *The Standard,* May 2, 2001; David Shook, "Why Nike Is Dragging Its Feet," *Business Week Online,* March 19, 2001; Tom Smith, "Supply Chain Isn't Place to Experiment," *Internet Week,* March 6, 2001; "Swoosh Suits," *Forbes,* April 16, 2001; Marc Songini, "Supply-Chain ROI Is Elusive," *Computerworld,* January 1, 2001; and Tim Wilson, "Errors Aren't Always the Computer's Fault," *Internet Week,* March 26, 2001.

CASE STUDY QUESTIONS

1. Analyze Nike's business model and business strategy using the value chain and competitive forces models.

2. Classify and describe the problems Nike encountered when it installed the i2 supply chain software. What organizational, management, and technology factors caused these problems?

3. What role did the i2 software play in the failure of Nike's new supply-chain management system?

4. Did Nike manage the i2 project well? Explain your response.

5. Who or what do you blame for the failures of the project? Explain your response.

6. Evaluate the risks of Nike's supply-chain project from the outset, identifying its key risk factors. Describe the steps you would have taken to prevent supply-chain management problems from occurring at Nike.

7. What did you learn from this case study about solving business problems with software? About project management? About selecting a software company?

chapter

14 INFORMATION SYSTEMS SECURITY AND CONTROL

As a manager, you'll want to ensure that your firm's systems are reliable and secure. After completing this chapter, you will be able to answer the following questions:

objectives

1. *Why are information systems so vulnerable to destruction, error, abuse, and system quality problems?*
2. *What types of controls are available for information systems?*
3. *What special measures must be taken to ensure the reliability, availability and security of electronic commerce and digital business processes?*
4. *What are the most important software quality assurance techniques?*
5. *Why are auditing information systems and safeguarding data quality so important?*

September 11th, 2001: No More "Business as Usual" for Supply Chain Systems

On September 11th, 2001, two airplanes commandeered by terrorists crashed into the World Trade Center and a third crashed into the Pentagon, taking the lives of over 3000 people. In addition to damaging financial industry firms, these horrific attacks created serious supply chain disruptions throughout the United States. All air and ground transportation across U.S. borders was halted for several days, causing extensive delays in the arrival of production materials.

Companies using lean-inventory management were seriously impacted. Lean inventory requires many parts to be delivered in small batches only minutes before they are needed, resulting in little or no inventory storage. In the days following September 11th, parts shipments were interrupted and these deliveries could not be made on time. Assembly line shutdowns can cost some manufacturers as much as $10,000 per minute.

Ford had to close five North American plants for several days when the grounding of all aircraft meant that parts were not available. Chrysler experienced 18-hour delays just for trucks crossing the

450

Canadian-U.S. borders. The company immediately responded to the WTC attacks by assessing which parts were critical at each plant. It then closed all U.S. plants for the next day (September 12) and added a second driver to many trucks so time would not be wasted as drivers stopped to rest. DaimlerChrysler was already using its extranet to

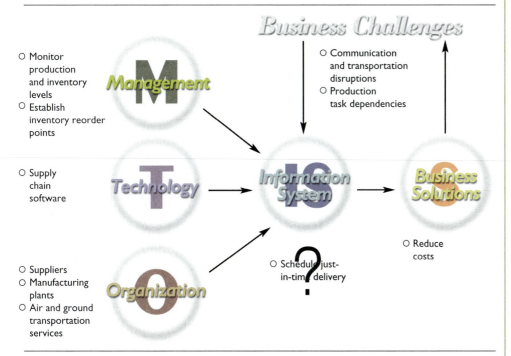

Business Challenges

- Monitor production and inventory levels
- Establish inventory reorder points

Management

- Supply chain software

Technology

- Suppliers
- Manufacturing plants
- Air and ground transportation services

Organization

- Communication and transportation disruptions
- Production task dependencies

Information System

Business Solutions

- Reduce costs

- Schedule just-in-time delivery

?

send alerts to its suppliers up to five times daily, and by the evening of September 11th it had notified its 150 largest suppliers to ship 12 hours' worth of parts, a dramatic increase in buffer stock. "If you don't put that extra float in the system," said David Hodgson, who oversees the timeliness of parts deliveries for DaimlerChrysler plants, "you're going to run out of parts." It also informed its suppliers to adjust delivery plans based on anticipated delays. The Canadian Pacific Railway agreed to activate its emergency shuttle service to speed deliveries from Canada. When commercial flights resumed on September 13, Chrysler ordered many of its drivers to their closest airports where Chrysler-chartered planes would be waiting to pick up their loads.

Some companies are considering stockpiling critical parts to put more float into their production systems. Ford, GM, and others that have invested heavily in warehouses and systems designed specifically for lean inventory are re-evaluating these systems. Ford is stockpiling critical parts to make sure its production lines keep moving, and GM has developed a contingency plan for stockpiling parts as well. Both believe that September 11th changed the meaning of "business as usual" and that the shipment of parts from around the world could be subject to unpredictable disruptions and delays for many years to come.

Supply chain software systems will have to change as well. They may need to introduce more flexibility in lead times for production planning so that the software can dynamically handle the "surge and ebb" of lead times in unusual situations. Supply chain software must also reflect longer delivery times when companies must switch from air to ground transportation.

Sources: Jeffrey Ball, "Chrysler Averts a Parts Crisis," *The Wall Street Journal*," September 24, 2001; Steve Konicki, "Automakers Look to Reconstruct Supply Chains," *Information Week*, September 24, 2001; Richard Karpinski, "E-Business Aftermath," *Transformation Today*, September 24, 2001; and Jim Ericson, "Addressing Supply-Chain Disruptions," *Line56*, October 4, 2001.

The experience of DaimlerChrysler and other U.S. automakers depending on just-in-time delivery and supply chain management systems illustrates the need for organizations to take special measures to protect their information systems and ensure their continued operation. Communication disruptions, use by unauthorized people, software failures, hardware failures, natural disasters, employee errors—and terrorist attacks— can prevent information systems from running properly or running at all. As you read this chapter, you should be aware of the following management challenges.

1. **Designing systems that are neither over-controlled nor under-controlled.** While security breaches and damage to information systems still come from organizational insiders, security breaches from outside the organization are increasing because firms pursuing electronic commerce are open to outsiders through the Internet. It is difficult for organizations to determine how open or closed they should be to protect themselves. If a system requires too many passwords, authorizations, or levels of security to access information, the system will go unused. Controls that are effective but that do not prevent authorized individuals from using a system are difficult to design.

2. **Applying quality assurance standards in large systems projects.** This chapter explains why the goal of zero defects in large, complex pieces of software is impossible to achieve. If the seriousness of remaining bugs cannot be ascertained, what constitutes acceptable—if not perfect—software performance? And even if meticulous design and exhaustive testing could eliminate all defects, software projects have time and budget constraints that often prevent management from devoting as much time to thoroughly testing them as it should. Under such circumstances it would be difficult for managers to define a standard for software quality and to enforce it.

Computer systems play such a critical role in business, government, and daily life that organizations must take special steps to protect their information systems and to ensure that they are accurate, reliable, and secure. This chapter describes how information systems can be controlled and made secure so that they serve the purposes for which they are intended.

14.1 SYSTEM VULNERABILITY AND ABUSE

Before computer automation, data about individuals or organizations were maintained and secured as paper records dispersed in separate business or organizational units. Information systems concentrate data in computer files that could potentially be accessed easily by large numbers of people and by groups outside of the organization. Consequently, automated data are more susceptible to destruction, fraud, error, and misuse.

When computer systems fail to run or work as required, firms that depend heavily on computers experience a serious loss of business function. The longer computer systems are down, the more serious the consequences for the firm. Firms which need Web sites continuously on-line for electronic commerce stand to lose millions of dollars for every business day that the sites are not working. For example, an on-line brokerage Web site stands to lose $5 million for every eight-hour trading day that it is not operational. Amazon.com lost $244,000 for every hour it was out of service during a hacker attack in February 2000 (Bertin, 2001; The Industry Standard, 1999). Some firms relying on computers to process their critical business transactions might experience a total loss of business function if they lose computer capability for more than a few days.

WHY SYSTEMS ARE VULNERABLE

When large amounts of data are stored in electronic form they are vulnerable to many more kinds of threats than when they exist in manual form. Table 14-1 lists the most common threats against computerized information systems. They can stem from technical, organizational, and environmental factors compounded by poor management decisions.

TABLE 14-1	**THREATS TO COMPUTERIZED INFORMATION SYSTEMS**

Hardware failure	Fire
Software failure	Electrical problems
Personnel actions	User errors
Terminal access penetration	Program changes
Theft of data, services, equipment	Telecommunication problems

Advances in telecommunications and computer software have magnified these vulnerabilities. Through telecommunication networks, information systems in different locations can be interconnected. The potential for unauthorized access, abuse, or fraud is not limited to a single location but can occur at any access point in the network.

Additionally, more complex and diverse hardware, software, organizational, and personnel arrangements are required for telecommunication networks, creating new areas and opportunities for penetration and manipulation. Wireless networks using radio-based technology are even more vulnerable to penetration because radio frequency bands are easy to scan. The Internet poses special problems because it was explicitly designed to be accessed easily by people on different computer systems. The vulnerabilities of telecommunication networks are illustrated in Figure 14-1.

Hackers and Computer Viruses

The explosive growth of Internet use by businesses and individuals has been accompanied by rising reports of Internet security breaches. The main concern comes from unwanted intruders, or hackers, who use the latest technology and their skills to break into supposedly secure computers or to disable them. A **hacker** is a person who gains unauthorized access to a computer network for profit, criminal mischief, or personal pleasure. There are many ways that hacker break-ins can harm businesses. Some malicious intruders have planted logic bombs, Trojan horses, and other software that can hide in a system or network until executing at a

hacker

A person who gains unauthorized access to a computer network for profit, criminal mischief, or personal pleasure.

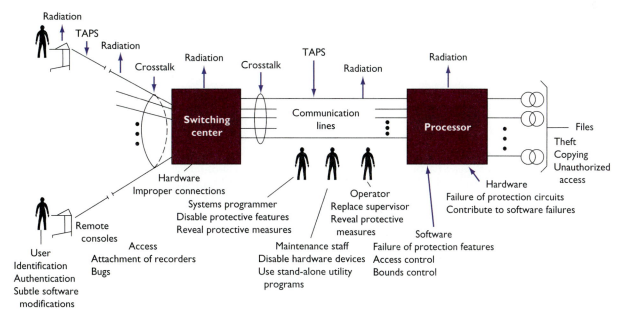

Figure 14-1   Telecommunication network vulnerabilities. Telecommunication networks are highly vulnerable to natural failure of hardware and software and to misuse by programmers, computer operators, maintenance staff, and end users. It is possible to tap communication lines and illegally intercept data. High-speed transmission over twisted wire communication channels causes interference called crosstalk. Radiation can disrupt a network at various points as well.

Window on

Organizations

MIS In Action

Hackers, Cyber-terrorists, and Information Warfare: An Electronic Pearl Harbor in the Making?

First they attack the computer networks for the Nasdaq and New York Stock Exchange (NYSE), disrupting trading. Next, the computer networks for major retail banks such as Citibank and Chase go down. Then a "worm" program shuts down the electrical grid in Chicago and the air traffic control operations in Atlanta, diverting hundreds of flights. At the same time, a "logic bomb" program opens the floodgates for the Hoover Dam. If well timed and placed, a series of such attacks on power, transportation, communications, and financial systems could cripple the infrastructure that keeps the United States running in a matter of hours and leave it paralyzed for days.

Who could plan and carry off this digital blitzkrieg? It could be anyone with a computer and an Internet connection—a disgruntled employee, a group of malicious hackers or a well-funded, well-organized group such as Osama Bin Laden's Al Qaeda terrorist network or the government of Iraq. Many experts believe the United Sates is widely exposed to this kind of attack. Groups from a number of countries, including China, are probing and mapping U.S. networks and at least 20 countries are developing offensive and defensive cyber-warfare capabilities.

U.S. military networks are also vulnerable to cyber-warfare and cyber-terrorism attacks, with 95 percent of all Pentagon communications carried over unclassified commercial networks. In 2000, 413 intruders broke into U.S military networks. That same year, 155 systems at 32 U.S. federal government agencies suffered attacks where hackers were able to take full root-privilege control of systems with sensitive information. (An attacker that acquires root privileges has the power to do anything a system administrator could do, including copying files or installing software to monitor the activities of end users.) Since March 1998 a group of hackers based in Russia has broken into Pentagon and other government computer networks and stolen thousands of unclassified technical files. The U.S. General Accounting Office (GAO) has identified significant security weaknesses at 24 federal agencies that put sensitive data at risk.

The U.S. government has taken some steps to deal with the potential threat. In February 1998 President Clinton created the National Infrastructure Protection Center to provide an early warning system for cyber-attacks and liaison between the U.S. government and corporations. The Pentagon has formed a Joint Task Force for Computer Network Operations to coordinate defensive and offensive information warfare programs.

MAKE **IT** YOUR BUSINESS

To Think About: Assess the potential business and military impact of the cyber-attacks described here. What management, organization, and technology factors should be considered in an Internet security plan?

Sources: John Galvin, "Info War," *Smart Business Magazine,* June 2001 and "Radar: The Real Online Battleground," *Smart Business Magazine,* March 2001; Andrea Stone, "Cyberspace Is the Next Battlefield," *USA Today,* June 18, 2001; Eva Marer, "Companies Confront Rising Network Threats," *Datamation,* September 2, 2001; and Patrick Thibodeau, "Federal Systems Increasingly Falling Prey to Hackers," *Computerworld,* April 9, 2001.

---

denial of service attack
Overwhelming a Web server with requests for data in order to cripple the network.

specified time. (A Trojan horse is a software program that appears legitimate but contains a second hidden function that may cause damage.) In **denial of service attacks,** hackers flood a network server or Web server with requests for information or other data in order to crash the network. A high-profile denial of service attack launched in February 2000 against major e-commerce sites such as Yahoo, E*TRADE, eBay, and Amazon.com had a financial impact of over $1.2 billion. Researchers have found denial-of-service attacks occurring 4000 times every week, often targeting individuals and small businesses (Bertin, 2001; Marer, 2001). The Window on Organizations describes what could happen in a worst case scenario in which on-line intruders could disable a power grid, alter medical databases, or cripple several of the high-level servers running the Internet.

computer virus
Rogue software programs that are difficult to detect which spread rapidly through computer systems, destroying data or disrupting processing and memory systems.

Serious system disruptions have been caused by hackers propagating **computer viruses.** These are rogue software programs that spread rampantly from system to system, clogging computer memory or destroying programs or data. Many thousands of viruses are known to exist, with 200 or more new viruses created each month. Table 14-2 describes the characteristics of the most common viruses.

Many viruses today are spread through the Internet, from files of downloaded software or from files attached to e-mail transmissions. Viruses can also invade computerized information systems from other computer networks as well as from "infected" diskettes from an outside source or infected machines. The potential for massive damage and loss from future computer viruses remains. The Chernobyl, Melissa, and ILOVEYOU viruses caused exten-

TABLE 14-2   EXAMPLES OF COMPUTER VIRUSES

Virus Name	Description
Concept, Melissa	Macro viruses that exist inside executable programs called macros, which provide functions within programs such as Microsoft Word. Can be spread when Word documents are attached to e-mail. Can copy from one document to another and delete files.
Code Red, Nimda	"Worm" type viruses that arrive attached to e-mail and spread from computer to computer. When launched they e-mail themselves to computers running Microsoft operating systems and software, slowing Internet traffic as they propagate and circulate.
ILOVEYOU (Love Bug)	Script virus written in script programming language such as VBScript or JavaScript. Overwrites.jpg and .mp3 files. Uses Microsoft Outlook and Internet Relay Chat to spread to other systems.
Monkey	Makes the hard disk look like it has failed because Windows will not run.
Chernobyl	File infecting virus. Erases a computer's hard drive and ROM BIOS (Basic Input/Output System).
Junkie	A "multipartite" virus that can infect files as well as the boot sector of the hard drive (the section of a PC hard drive that the PC first reads when it boots up). May cause memory conflicts.
Form	Makes a clicking sound with each keystroke but only on the eighteenth day of the month. May corrupt data on the floppy disks it infects.

sive PC damage worldwide after spreading around the world through infected e-mail. Now viruses are spreading to wireless computing devices. Mobile device viruses could pose a serious threat to enterprise computing because so many wireless devices are now linked to corporate information systems.

Organizations can use antivirus software and screening procedures to reduce the chances of infection. **Antivirus software** is special software designed to check computer systems and disks for the presence of various computer viruses. Often the software can eliminate the virus from the infected area. However, most antivirus software is only effective against viruses already known when the software is written—to protect their systems, management must continually update their antivirus software.

antivirus software
Software designed to detect, and often eliminate, computer viruses from an information system.

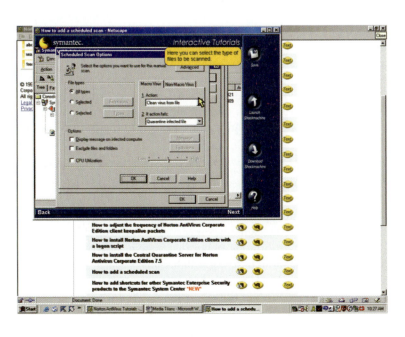

Many organizations use antivirus software to check computer systems and disks for the presence of various computer viruses. Symantec's antivirus software illustrated here identifies viruses that have infected a system and provides tools for eradicating them.

CONCERNS FOR SYSTEM BUILDERS AND USERS

The heightened vulnerability of automated data has created special concerns for the builders and users of information systems. These concerns include disaster, security, and administrative error.

Disaster

Computer hardware, programs, data files, and other equipment can be destroyed by fires, power failures, or other disasters. It may take many years and millions of dollars to reconstruct destroyed data files and computer programs and some may not be able to be replaced. If an organization needs them to function on a day-to-day basis, it will no longer be able to operate. This is why companies such as VISA USA Inc. and National Trust employ elaborate emergency backup facilities. VISA USA Inc. has duplicate mainframes, duplicate network pathways, duplicate terminals, and duplicate power supplies. VISA even uses a duplicate data center in McLean, Virginia, to handle half of its transactions and to serve as an emergency backup to its primary data center in San Mateo, California. National Trust, a large bank in Ontario, Canada, uses uninterruptable power supply technology provided by International Power Machines (IPM) because electrical power at its Mississauga location fluctuates frequently.

Rather than build their own backup facilities, many firms contract with disaster recovery firms, such as Comdisco Disaster Recovery Services in Rosemont, Illinois, and SunGard Recovery Services headquartered in Wayne, Pennsylvania. These disaster recovery firms provide hot sites housing spare computers at locations around the country where subscribing firms can run their critical applications in an emergency. Disaster recovery services offer backup for client/server systems as well as traditional mainframe applications. As firms become increasingly digital and depend on systems that must be constantly available, disaster recovery planning has taken on new importance.

Security

security

Policies, procedures, and technical measures used to prevent unauthorized access, alteration, theft, or physical damage to information systems.

Security refers to the policies, procedures, and technical measures used to prevent unauthorized access, alteration, theft, or physical damage to information systems. Security can be promoted with an array of techniques and tools to safeguard computer hardware, software, communication networks, and data. We have already discussed some disaster protection measures. Other tools and techniques for promoting security will be discussed in subsequent sections.

Errors

Computers also can serve as instruments of error, severely disrupting or destroying an organization's record keeping and operations. For instance, poor software caused the crash of a Mars polar lander operated by the U.S. National Aeronautics and Space Administration (NASA) in December 1999. One sensor erroneously detected that the craft's legs had popped out and shut down its rocket engines prematurely, even though another sensor designed to alert the craft when it touched ground did not show this happening. The landing system software had not been programmed to compare the feedback from both sensors (Wessel, 2001). Errors in automated systems can occur at many points in the processing cycle: through data entry, program error, computer operations, and hardware. Figure 14-2 illustrates all of the points in a typical processing cycle where errors can occur.

SYSTEM QUALITY PROBLEMS: SOFTWARE AND DATA

In addition to disasters, viruses, and security breaches, defective software and data also pose a constant threat to information systems, causing untold losses in productivity. An undiscovered error in a company's credit software or erroneous financial data can result in millions of dollars of losses (see the Window on Management). A hidden software problem in AT&T's long distance system brought down that system, bringing the New York-based financial exchanges to a halt and interfering with billions of dollars of business around the country for a number of hours. Modern passenger and commercial vehicles are increasingly dependent on computer programs for critical functions. A hidden software defect in a braking system could result in the loss of lives.

Bugs and Defects

A major problem with software is the presence of hidden **bugs** or program code defects. Studies have shown that it is virtually impossible to eliminate all bugs from large programs. The main source of bugs is the complexity of decision-making code. Even a relatively small program of several hundred lines will contain tens of decisions leading to hundreds or even thousands of different paths. Important programs within most corporations are usually much larger, containing tens of thousands or even millions of lines of code, each with many times the choices and paths of the smaller programs. Such complexity is difficult to document and design—designers document some reactions wrongly or fail to consider some possibilities. Studies show that about 60 percent of errors discovered during testing are a result of specifications in the design documentation that were missing, ambiguous, in error, or in conflict.

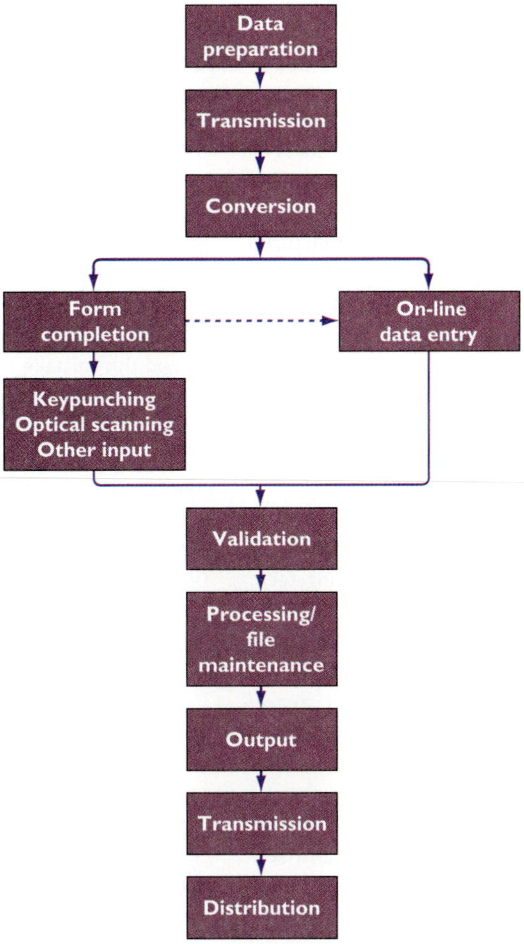

Zero defects, a goal of the total quality management movement, cannot be achieved in larger programs. Complete testing simply is not possible. Fully testing programs that contain thousands of choices and millions of paths would require thousands of years. Eliminating software bugs is an exercise in diminishing returns, because it would take proportionately longer testing to detect and eliminate obscure residual bugs (Littlewood and Strigini, 1993). Even with rigorous testing, one could not know for sure that a piece of software was dependable until the product proved itself after much operational use. The message? We cannot eliminate all bugs, and we cannot know with certainty the seriousness of the bugs that do remain.

Figure 14-2 Points in the processing cycle where errors can occur. Each of the points illustrated in this figure represents a control point where special automated or manual procedures should be established to reduce the risk of errors during processing.

bugs
Program code defects or errors.

The Maintenance Nightmare

Another reason that systems are unreliable is that computer software traditionally has been a nightmare to maintain. Maintenance, the process of modifying a system in production use, is the most expensive phase of the systems development process. In most organizations nearly half of information systems staff time is spent in the maintenance of existing systems.

Why are maintenance costs so high? One major reason is organizational change. The firm may experience large internal changes in structure or leadership, or change may come from its surrounding environment. These organizational changes affect information requirements. Another reason appears to be software complexity, as measured by the number and size of interrelated software programs and subprograms and the complexity of the flow of program logic between them (Banker, Datar, Kemerer, and Zweig, 1993). A third common cause of long-term maintenance problems is faulty systems analysis and design, especially analysis of information requirements. Some studies of large TPS systems by TRW, Inc., have found that a majority of system errors—64 percent—result from early analysis errors (Mazzucchelli, 1985).

Figure 14-3 illustrates the cost of correcting errors based on the experience of consultants reported in the literature. If errors are detected early, during analysis and design, the cost to the systems development effort is small. But if they are not discovered until after

NATIONAL AUSTRALIA BANK WRITES OFF LOSSES FROM COMPUTER ERRORS

In 1998 the largest bank in Australia, the National Australia Bank (NAB), bought HomeSide Lending, Inc. for around $1.2 billion. HomeSide, which is headquartered in Jacksonville, Florida, is the sixth largest home loan servicing company in the United States with about two million loans. When NAB purchased it, the bank saw HomeSide's processing and servicing systems as so useful that it planned to use its software throughout its worldwide organization. Trouble began to appear publicly on June 1, 2001, when NAB's CEO, Frank Cicutto, verified the rumor that the bank was considering selling HomeSide. What had gone wrong?

HomeSide ran into trouble earlier that year when the United States Federal Reserve lowered short-term interest rates a number of times, and that indirectly caused long-term rates to fall, including mortgage rates. A large number of mortgagers refinanced their mortgages at lower rates, including many mortgages held by HomeSide. Clearly HomeSide and NAB management had not understood the situation clearly enough and saw its stream of income fall as the number and interest rate of mortgages it was servicing declined. These miscalculations prompted a $288 million after-tax write-down.

A more long-standing and fundamental problem could be traced to an error in HomeSide's vaunted processing and servicing software. Homeside had developed a computer model that was designed to forecast the income it would receive from loan servicing. This forecast model was linked to another model it had developed which fed critical information to the forecast. Both models required that an interest rate be plugged into the systems. Central to the success of the forecasting model was that both models use the same set of rates—both had to be gross interest or both had to be net interest. But in fact from the beginning the company used a gross rate for one model and a net rate for the other. The result was that the income-

forecasting model projected severely overstated fees the company expected to collect.

Soon after HomeSide announced a write-down of $400 million because of its failure to handle the fall in its stream of income, the company hired Cohane Rafferty Securities consultants to investigate. On about September 1st the consultants discovered the contradiction in the interest rates plugged into the two models used to project HomeSide's future fees. They found this mistake cost the company about $400 million in two years. Further examination uncovered another even more expensive error in the models because they were based on assumptions that failed to foresee the "continued unprecedented uncertainty and turbulence" in the mortgage servicing markets. According to the consultants, that error forced the company to swallow another $760 million charge.

It has become clear that the forecasting system had an error in its design. Even more, the flaw had not been noticed for two years. Nor was management aware of the failed projection of HomeSide issues from the turbulent mortgage market. The systems were not properly controlled and not even the auditors had uncovered the discrepancies and failures.

To Think About: To what extent were NAB's losses management problems or technology problems? What should management have done differently to have prevented these problems and the company's financial losses?

Source: Becky Gaylord, "Oops! Bank Will Write Off $1.75 Billion," *The New York Times,* September 8, 2001; Simon Barker-Benfield, "Publications Say HomeSide Lending for Sale," *The Florida Times-Union,* June 6, 2001; Mark Basch, "First Coast Ticker: HomeSide Only Part of NAB's Problems," *The Florida Times-Union,* September 24, 2001; "Fitch Places HomeSide Lending, Inc. On RTG Watch Negative," *Fitch Australia Press Release,* July 6, 2001; Lisa R. Schoolcraft, "Australians May Sell HomeSide Lending," *The Business Journal of Jacksonville,* June 1, 2001.

programming, testing, or conversion has been completed, the costs can soar astronomically. A minor logic error, for example, that could take 1 hour to correct during the analysis and design stage could take 10, 40, and 90 times as long to correct during programming, conversion, and post-implementation, respectively.

Data Quality Problems

The most common source of information system failure is poor data quality. Data that are inaccurate, untimely, or inconsistent with other sources of information can create serious operational and financial problems for businesses. When bad data go unnoticed, they can lead to bad decisions, product recalls, and even financial losses (Redman, 1998). Companies cannot pursue aggressive marketing and customer relationship management strategies unless they have high-quality data about their customers. Table 14-3 describes examples of data quality problems.

Poor data quality may stem from errors during data input or faulty information system and database design (Wand and Wang, 1996; Strong, Lee, and Wang, 1997). In the follow-

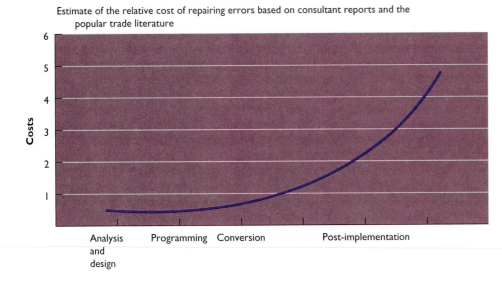

Estimate of the relative cost of repairing errors based on consultant reports and the popular trade literature

Figure 14-3 The cost of errors over the systems development cycle. The most common, most severe, and most expensive system errors develop in the early design stages. They involve faulty requirements analysis. Errors in program logic or syntax are much less common, less severe, and less costly to repair than design errors.
Source: Alberts, 1976.

ing sections we examine how organizations can deal with data and software quality problems as well as other threats to information systems.

14.2 CREATING A CONTROL ENVIRONMENT

To minimize errors, disasters, interruptions of service, computer crimes, and breaches of security, special policies and procedures must be incorporated into the design and implementation of information systems. The combination of manual and automated measures that safeguard information systems and ensure that they perform according to management standards is termed controls. **Controls** consist of all the methods, policies, and organizational procedures that ensure the safety of the organization's assets, the accuracy and reliability of its accounting records, and operational adherence to management standards.

In the past, the control of information systems was treated as an afterthought, addressed only toward the end of implementation, just before the system was installed. Today, however, organizations are so critically dependent on information systems that vulnerabilities and control issues must be identified as early as possible. The control of an information system must

controls
All of the methods, policies, and procedures that ensure protection of the organization's assets, accuracy and reliability of its records, and operational adherence to management standards.

TABLE 14-3 | EXAMPLES OF DATA QUALITY PROBLEMS

Organization	Data Quality Problem
Royal Bank of Canada	Databases contained "garbage" character strings entered by employees lacking correct client addresses instead of the correct postal code. When the bank tried to target a particular geographic area to promote a popular Christmas loan, a notable percentage of clients came up with the postal code HOHOHO and the bank could not obtain accurate information for mailings.
Sears Roebuck	Could not effectively pursue cross-selling among its customers because each of its businesses, including retail, home services, credit, and Web site had their own information systems with conflicting customer data. Sears needed to develop a massive data warehouse that consolidated and cleansed the data from all of these systems in order to create a single customer list.
Paint Bull	Found that nearly half the names in its purchased mailing lists of prospective customers were inaccurate or out of date. Lost $10 for every promotional package of videos and catalogs that was returned as undeliverable.
FBI	A study of the FBI's computerized criminal record systems found a total of 54.1 percent of the records in the National Crime Information Center System were inaccurate, ambiguous, or incomplete. The FBI has taken some steps to correct these problems, but computerized criminal history records are used to screen employees in both the public and private sectors. Inaccurate records could unjustly deny people employment.
Supermarkets	Several studies have established that 5 to 12 percent of bar-code sales at retail supermarkets are erroneous and that the average ratio of overcharges to undercharges runs 4:1.

be an integral part of its design. Users and builders of systems must pay close attention to controls throughout the system's life span.

GENERAL CONTROLS AND APPLICATION CONTROLS

Computer systems are controlled by a combination of general controls and application controls. **General controls** govern the design, security, and use of computer programs and the security of data files in general throughout the organization's information technology infrastructure. On the whole, general controls apply to all computerized applications and consist of a combination of hardware, software and manual procedures that create an overall control environment. **Application controls** are specific controls unique to each computerized application, such as payroll or order processing. They consist of controls applied from the business functional area of a particular system and from programmed procedures.

General Controls and Data Security

General controls include software controls, physical hardware controls, computer operations controls, data security controls, controls over the systems implementation process, and administrative controls. Table 14-4 describes the function of each of these controls.

Although most of these general controls are designed and maintained by information systems specialists, **data security controls** and **administrative controls** require input and oversight from end users and business managers. For example, information systems specialists would be responsible for certain aspects of data security controls, such as making computer terminals available only to authorized users or using system software and application software to create a series of passwords that users would need in order to access systems. Users, however, would specify the business rules for accessing data, such as what positions in the organization have rights to view and update the data.

Figure 14-4 illustrates the security allowed for two sets of users of an on-line personnel database with sensitive information such as employees' salaries, benefits, and medical histories. One set of users consists of all employees who perform clerical functions such as inputting employee data into the system. All individuals with this type of profile can update the system but can neither read nor update sensitive fields such as salary, medical history, or

general controls
Overall controls that establish a framework for controlling the design, security, and use of computer programs throughout an organization.

application controls
Specific controls unique to each computerized application.

data security controls
Controls to ensure that data files on either disk or tape are not subject to unauthorized access, change, or destruction.

administrative controls
Formalized standards, rules, procedures, and disciplines to ensure that the organization's controls are properly executed and enforced.

TABLE 14-4   GENERAL CONTROLS

Type of General Control	Description
Software controls	Monitor the use of system software and prevent unauthorized access of software programs, system software, and computer programs. System software is an important control area because it performs overall control functions for the programs that directly process data and data files.
Hardware controls	Ensure that computer hardware is physically secure, and check for equipment malfunction. Computer equipment should be specially protected against fires and extremes of temperature and humidity. Organizations that are critically dependent on their computers also must make provisions for backup or continued operation to maintain constant service.
Computer operations controls	Oversee the work of the computer department to ensure that programmed procedures are consistently and correctly applied to the storage and processing of data. They include controls over the setup of computer processing jobs and computer operations, and backup and recovery procedures for processing that ends abnormally.
Data security controls	Ensure that valuable business data files on either disk or tape are not subject to unauthorized access, change, or destruction while they are in use or in storage.
Implementation controls	Audit the systems development process at various points to ensure that the process is properly controlled and managed. The systems development audit looks for the presence of formal reviews by users and management at various stages of development; the level of user involvement at each stage of implementation; and the use of a formal cost/benefit methodology in establishing system feasibility. The audit should look for the use of controls and quality assurance techniques for program development, conversion, and testing and for complete and thorough system, user, and operations documentation.
Administrative controls	Formalized standards, rules, procedures, and control disciplines to ensure that the organization's general and application controls are properly executed and enforced.

SECURITY PROFILE 1

User: Personnel Dept. Clerk

Location: Division 1

Employee Identification
Codes with This Profile: 00753, 27834, 37665, 44116

Data Field Restrictions	Type of Access
All employee data for Division 1 only	Read and Update
• Medical history data	None
• Salary	None
• Pensionable earnings	None

SECURITY PROFILE 2

User: Divisional Personnel Manager

Location: Division 1

Employee Identification
Codes with This Profile: 27321

Data Field Restrictions	Type of Access
All employee data for Division 1 only	Read Only

Figure 14-4 Security profiles for a personnel system. These two examples represent two security profiles or data security patterns that might be found in a personnel system. Depending on the security profile, a user would have certain restrictions on access to various systems, locations, or data in an organization.

earnings data. Another profile applies to a divisional manager, who cannot update the system but who can read all employee data fields for his or her division, including medical history and salary. These profiles would be established and maintained by a data security system based on access rules supplied by business groups. The data security system illustrated in Figure 14-4 provides very fine-grained security restrictions, such as allowing authorized personnel users to inquire about all employee information except in confidential fields such as salary or medical history.

Business users would be responsible for establishing administrative controls, which are formal organizational procedures to make sure that all of the other general and application controls are properly enforced. These controls ensure that job functions are designed to minimize the risk of errors or fraudulent manipulation of the organization's assets. For instance, individuals responsible for operating systems (who typically belong to the information systems department) would not be the same ones who could initiate transactions that change the assets held in these systems. Administrative controls would include written policies and procedures establishing formal standards for information system operations and clearly specified accountabilities and responsibilities. Administrative controls include mechanisms for supervising personnel involved in control procedures to make sure that the controls for an information system are performing as intended.

Application Controls

Application controls include both automated and manual procedures that ensure that only authorized data are completely and accurately processed by that application. Application controls can be classified as (1) input controls, (2) processing controls, and (3) output controls.

Input controls check data for accuracy and completeness when they enter the system. There are specific input controls for input authorization, data conversion, data editing, and error handling. **Processing controls** establish that data are complete and accurate during updating. Run control totals, computer matching, and programmed edit checks are used for this purpose. **Output controls** ensure that the results of computer processing are accurate, complete, and properly distributed.

Table 14-5 provides more detailed examples of each type of application control. Not all of the application controls discussed here are used in every information system. Some systems require more of these controls than others, depending on the importance of the data and the nature of the application.

input controls
The procedures to check data for accuracy and completeness when they enter the system.

processing controls
The routines for establishing that data are complete and accurate during updating.

output controls
Measures that ensure that the results of computer processing are accurate, complete, and properly distributed.

TABLE 14-5   APPLICATION CONTROLS

Name of Control	Type of Application Control	Description
Control totals	Input, processing	Totals established beforehand for input and processing transactions. These totals can range from a simple document count to totals for quantity fields such as total sales amount (for a batch of transactions). Computer programs count the totals from transactions input or processed.
Edit checks	Input	Programmed routines that can be performed to edit input data for errors before they are processed. Transactions that do not meet edit criteria will be rejected. For example, data might be checked to make sure they were in the right format (a 9-digit Social Security number should not contain any alphabetic characters).
Computer matching	Input, processing	Matches input data with information held on master or suspense files, with unmatched items noted for investigation. For example, a matching program might match employee time cards with a payroll master file and report missing or duplicate time cards.
Run control totals	Processing, output	Balance the total of transactions processed with total number of transactions input or output.
Report distribution logs	Output	Documentation specifying that authorized recipients have received their reports, checks, or other critical documents.

PROTECTING THE DIGITAL FIRM

As companies increasingly rely on digital networks for their revenue and operations, they need to take additional steps to ensure that their systems and applications are always available to support their digital business processes.

High-Availability Computing

In a digital firm environment, information technology infrastructures must provide a continuous level of service availability across distributed computing platforms. Many factors can disrupt the performance of a Web site, including network failure, heavy Internet traffic, and exhausted server resources. Computer failures, interruptions, and downtime can translate into disgruntled customers, millions of dollars in lost sales, and the inability to perform critical internal transactions. Firms such as those in the airline and financial service industries with critical applications requiring on-line transaction processing have traditionally used fault-tolerant computer systems for many years to ensure 100 percent availability. In **on-line transaction processing,** transactions entered on-line are immediately processed by the computer. Multitudinous changes to databases, reporting, or requests for information occur each instant. **Fault-tolerant computer systems** contain redundant hardware, software, and power supply components that can back the system up and keep it running to prevent system failure. Fault-tolerant computers contain extra memory chips, processors, and disk storage devices. They can use special software routines or self-checking logic built into their circuitry to detect hardware failures and automatically switch to a backup device. Parts from these computers can be removed and repaired without disruption to the computer system. E-Smart Direct Services, Inc. of Etobicoke, Ontario in Canada, a provider of electronic payment processing and authorization services for retailers and financial institutions, needs a technology platform with 100 percent 24 hour system availability. The company uses fault-tolerant systems from Stratus for this purpose.

Fault tolerance should be distinguished from **high-availability computing.** Both fault tolerance and high-availability computing are designed to maximize application and system availability. Both use backup hardware resources. However, high-availability computing helps firms recover quickly from a crash, while fault tolerance promises continuous availability and the elimination of recovery time altogether. High-availability computing environments are a minimum requirement for firms with heavy electronic commerce processing or that depend on digital networks for their internal operations. High availability computing requires an assortment of tools and technologies to ensure maximum performance of com-

on-line transaction processing
Transaction processing mode in which transactions entered on-line are immediately processed by the computer.

fault-tolerant computer systems
Systems that contain extra hardware, software, and power supply components that can back a system up and keep it running to prevent system failure.

high-availability computing
Tools and technologies, including backup hardware resources, to enable a system to recover quickly from a crash.

MIS IN ACTION   MANAGER'S TOOLKIT

HOW TO DEVELOP A DISASTER RECOVERY PLAN

1. Conduct a business impact analysis to identify the firm's most critical systems and the impact a systems outage would have on the business. Managers need to determine the maximum amount of time the business can survive with its systems down and what parts of the business need to be restored first.

2. Assess the risk of particular disasters such as floods, power outages, or terrorist attacks occurring at your specific company. (See the discussion of risk analysis in the following section.)

3. Identify the most mission-critical applications, the files they use, and where these files and applications are located.

4. Develop an action plan for handling mission critical applications, such as using manual processes or running these applications at a disaster recovery service or backup computer system at another location.

5. Outline responsibilities of individual staff members and procedures to follow during a disaster, including how to locate and communicate with employees.

6. Test the disaster recovery plan at least once a year.

7. Use a consistent planning process and methodology so that all business groups understand the ground rules and how disaster planning will be funded.

8. Make sure you have the backing and support of senior management to ensure compliance.

---

puter systems and networks, including redundant servers, mirroring, load balancing, clustering, storage area networks (see Chapter 6), and a good **disaster recovery plan.** The firm's computing platform must be extremely robust with scalable processing power, storage, and bandwidth.

Disaster recovery planning devises plans for the restoration of computing and communication services after they have been disrupted by an event such as an earthquake, flood, or terrorist attack. Business managers and information technology specialists need to work together to determine what kind of plan is necessary and which systems and business functions are most critical to the company. The Manager's Toolkit describes the major elements of a disaster recovery plan.

Load balancing distributes large numbers of access requests across multiple servers. The requests are directed to the most available server so that no single device is overwhelmed. If one server starts to get swamped, requests are forwarded to another server with more capacity. **Mirroring** uses a backup server that duplicates all the processes and transactions of the primary server. If the primary server fails, the backup server can immediately take its place without any interruption in service. However, server mirroring is very expensive because each server must be mirrored by an identical server whose only purpose is to be available in the event of a failure. Clustering is a less expensive technique for ensuring continued availability. High-availability **clustering** links two computers together so that the second computer can act as a backup to the primary computer. If the primary computer fails, the second computer picks up its processing without any pause in the system. (Computers can also be clustered together as a single computing resource to speed up processing.) High-availability computing also requires a security infrastructure that can support electronic commerce and electronic business, as described in the following section.

Internet Security Challenges

Linking to the Internet or transmitting information via intranets and extranets require special security measures. Large public networks, including the Internet, are more vulnerable because they are virtually open to anyone and because they are so huge that when abuses do occur, they can have an enormously widespread impact. When the Internet becomes part of the corporate network, the organization's information systems can be vulnerable to actions from outsiders. The architecture of a Web-based application typically includes a Web client, a server, and corporate information systems linked to databases. Each of these components presents security challenges and vulnerabilities, which are illustrated in Figure 14-5 (Joshi, Aref, Ghafoor, and Spafford, 2001).

Computers that are constantly connected to the Internet via cable modem or DSL line are more open to penetration by outsiders because they use a fixed Internet address where they can be more easily identified. (With dial-up service, a temporary Internet address is assigned for each session.) A fixed Internet address creates a fixed target for hackers.

disaster recovery plan
Plan for running the business in the event of a computer outage. Includes organizational procedures as well as backup processing, storage, and database capabilities.

load balancing
Distribution of large numbers of requests for access among multiple servers so that no single device is overwhelmed.

mirroring
Duplicating all the processes and transactions of a server on a backup server to prevent any interruption in service if the primary server fails.

clustering
Linking two computers together so that the second computer can act as a backup to the primary computer or speed up processing.

Figure 14-5 Internet security challenges. There are security challenges at each of the layers of an Internet computing environment and in the communications between the client and server layers.

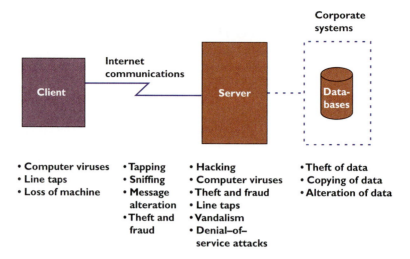

Client

Internet communications

Server

Corporate systems

Databases

- • Computer viruses
- • Line taps
- • Loss of machine

- • Tapping
- • Sniffing
- • Message alteration
- • Theft and fraud

- • Hacking
- • Computer viruses
- • Theft and fraud
- • Line taps
- • Vandalism
- • Denial–of–service attacks

- • Theft of data
- • Copying of data
- • Alteration of data

Both electronic commerce and electronic business require companies to be both more open and more closed at the same time. To benefit from electronic commerce, supply chain management, and other digital business processes, companies need to be open to outsiders such as customers, suppliers, and trading partners. Corporate systems must also be extended outside the organization so that they can be accessed by employees working with wireless and other mobile computing devices. Yet these systems also must be closed to hackers and other intruders. The new information technology infrastructure requires a new security culture and infrastructure that allows businesses to straddle this fine line. Corporations need to extend their security policies to include procedures for suppliers and other business partners.

Chapter 9 described the use of *firewalls* to prevent unauthorized users from accessing private networks. As growing numbers of businesses expose their networks to Internet traffic, firewalls are becoming a necessity.

A firewall is generally placed between internal LANs and WANs and external networks such as the Internet. The firewall controls access to the organization's internal networks by acting like a gatekeeper that examines each user's credentials before they can access the network. The firewall identifies names, Internet Protocol (IP) addresses, applications, and other characteristics of incoming traffic. It checks this information against the access rules that have been programmed into the system by the network administrator. The firewall prevents unauthorized communication into and out of the network, allowing the organization to enforce a security policy on traffic flowing between its network and the Internet (Oppliger, 1997).

Elron Software's Internet Manager Firewall Network Security Software includes tools to protect organizations against unauthorized access and malicious acts from both Internet and intranet sources.

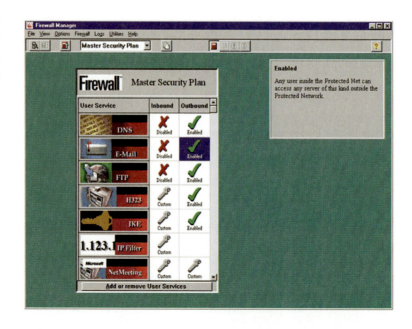

There are essentially two major types of firewall technologies: proxies and stateful inspection. *Proxies* stop data originating outside the organization at the firewall, inspect them, and pass a proxy to the other side of the firewall. If a user outside the company wants to communicate with a user inside the organization, the outside user first "talks" to the proxy application and the proxy application communicates with the firm's internal computer. Likewise a computer user inside the organization goes through the proxy to "talk" with computers on the outside. Because the actual message doesn't pass through the firewall, proxies are considered more secure than stateful inspection. However, they have to do a lot of work and can consume system resources, degrading network performance. The Raptor Firewall product is primarily a proxy-based firewall.

In *stateful inspection,* the firewall scans each packet of incoming data, checking its source, destination addresses, or services. It sets up state tables to track information over multiple packets. User-defined access rules must identify every type of packet that the organization does not want to admit. Although stateful inspection consumes fewer network resources than proxies, it is theoretically not as secure because some data pass through the firewall. Cisco Systems' firewall product is an example of a stateful inspection firewall. Hybrid firewall products are being developed. For instance, Check Point is primarily a stateful inspection product but it has incorporated some proxy capabilities for communication.

To create a good firewall, someone must write and maintain the internal rules identifying the people, applications, or addresses that are allowed or rejected in very fine detail. Firewalls can deter, but not completely prevent, network penetration from outsiders and should be viewed as one element in an overall security plan. In order to deal effectively with Internet security, broader corporate policies and procedures, user responsibilities, and security awareness training may be required (Segev, Porra, and Roldan, 1998).

In addition to firewalls, commercial security vendors now provide intrusion detection tools and services to protect against suspicious network traffic. **Intrusion detection systems** feature full-time monitoring tools placed at the most vulnerable points or "hot spots" of corporate networks to continually detect and deter intruders. Scanning software looks for known problems such as bad passwords, checks to see if important files have been removed or modified, and sends warnings of vandalism or system administration errors. Monitoring software examines events as they are happening to look for security attacks in progress. The intrusion detection tool can also be customized to shut down a particularly sensitive part of a network if it receives unauthorized traffic.

intrusion detection system
Tools to monitor the most vulnerable points in a network to detect and deter unauthorized intruders.

Security and Electronic Commerce

Security of electronic communications is a major control issue for companies engaged in electronic commerce. It is essential that commerce-related data of buyers and sellers be kept private when they are transmitted electronically. The data being transmitted also must be protected against being purposefully altered by someone other than the sender, so that, for example, stock market execution orders or product orders accurately represent the wishes of the buyer and seller.

Much on-line commerce continues to be handled through private EDI networks usually run over VANs. VANs (value-added networks) are relatively secure and reliable. However, because they have to be privately maintained and run on high-speed private lines, VANs are expensive, easily costing a company $100,000 per month. They also are inflexible, being connected only to a limited number of sites and companies. As a result, the Internet is emerging as the network technology of choice. EDI transactions on the Internet run from one-half to one-tenth the cost of VAN-based transactions.

Many organizations rely on encryption to protect sensitive information transmitted over the Internet and other networks. **Encryption** is the coding and scrambling of messages to prevent unauthorized access to or understanding of the data being transmitted. A message can be encrypted by applying a secret numerical code called an encryption key so that it is transmitted as a scrambled set of characters. (The key consists of a large group of letters, numbers, and symbols.) In order to be read, the message must be decrypted (unscrambled) with a matching key.

encryption
The coding and scrambling of messages to prevent their being read or accessed without authorization.

There are several alternative methods of encryption, but "public key" encryption is becoming popular. Public key encryption, illustrated in Figure 14-6, uses two different keys,

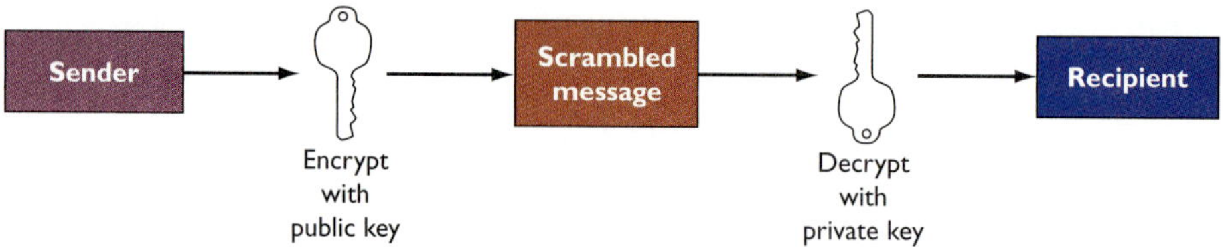

Figure 14-6   Public key encryption. A public key encryption system can be viewed as a series of public and private keys that lock data when they are transmitted and unlock the data when they are received. The sender locates the recipient's public key in a directory and uses it to encrypt a message. The message is sent in encrypted form over the Internet or a private network. When the encrypted message arrives, the recipient uses his or her private key to decrypt the data and read the message.

one private and one public. The keys are mathematically related so that data encrypted with one key only can be decrypted using the other key. To send and receive messages, communicators first create separate pairs of private and public keys. The public key is kept in a directory and the private key must be kept secret. The sender encrypts a message with the recipient's public key. On receiving the message, the recipient uses his or her private key to decrypt it.

Encryption is especially useful to shield messages on the Internet and other public networks because they are less secure than private networks. Encryption helps protect transmission of payment data, such as credit card information, and addresses the problems of authentication and message integrity. **Authentication** refers to the ability of each party to know that the other parties are who they claim to be. In the nonelectronic world, we use our signatures. (Bank-by-mail systems avoid the need for signatures on checks they issue for their customers by using well-protected private networks where the source of the request for payment is recorded and can be proven. Microsoft provides an on-line identification service called Passport for this purpose, authenticating user identification when any Microsoft Web service is accessed.) **Message integrity** is the ability to be certain that the message being sent arrives without being copied or changed.

Digital signatures and digital certificates help with authentication. The Electronic Signatures in Global and National Commerce Act of 2000 has given digital signatures the same legal status as those written on ink or paper. A **digital signature** is a digital code attached to an electronically transmitted message that is used to verify the origins and contents of a message. It provides a way to associate a message with the sender, performing a function similar to a written signature. For an electronic signature to be legally binding in court, someone must be able to verify that the signature actually belongs to whoever sent the data and that the data were not altered after being "signed."

Digital certificates are data files used to establish the identity of people and electronic assets for protection of on-line transactions (see Figure 14-7). A digital certificate system uses a trusted third party known as a certificate authority (CA) to validate a user's identity. The CA system can be run as a function inside an organization or by an outside company such as VeriSign Inc. in Mountain View, California. The CA verifies a digital certificate user's identity off-line. This information is put into a CA server, which generates an encrypted digital certificate containing owner identification information and a copy of the owner's public key. The certificate authenticates that the public key belongs to the designated owner. The CA makes its own public key available publicly either in print or perhaps on the Internet. The recipient of an encrypted message uses the CA's public key to decode the digital certificate attached to the message, verifies it was issued by the CA, and then obtains the sender's public key and identification information contained in the certificate. Using this information, the recipient can send an encrypted reply. The digital certificate system would enable, for example, a credit card user and merchant to validate that their digital certificates were issued by an authorized and trusted third party before they exchange data.

SSL (Secure Sockets Layer) and S-HTTP (Secure Hypertext Transport Protocol) are protocols used for secure information transfer over the Internet. They allow client and server computers to manage encryption and decryption activities as they communicate with each other during a secure Web session. Some credit card payment systems use the Secure Sockets

---

authentication

The ability of each party in a transaction to ascertain the identity of the other party.

message integrity

The ability to ascertain that a transmitted message has not been copied or altered.

digital signature

A digital code that can be attached to an electronically transmitted message to uniquely identify its contents and the sender.

digital certificate

An attachment to an electronic message to verify the identity of the sender and to provide the receiver with the means to encode a reply.

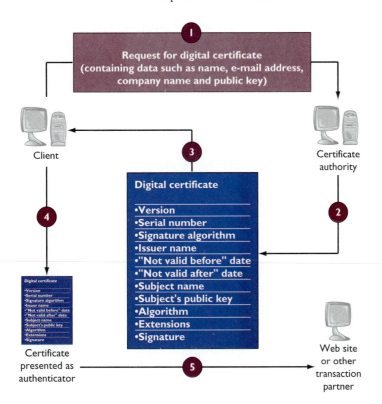

Figure 14-7 Digital certificates. Digital certificates can be used to establish the identity of people or electronic assets. They protect on-line transactions by providing secure, encrypted on-line communication.

Layer (SSL) protocol for encrypting the credit card payment data. VISA International, MasterCard International, American Express, and other major credit card companies and banks have adopted a more secure protocol using digital certificates and digital wallets called the **Secure Electronic Transaction (SET)** protocol for encrypting credit card payment data over the Internet and other open networks.

DEVELOPING A CONTROL STRUCTURE: COSTS AND BENEFITS

Information systems can make exhaustive use of all the control mechanisms previously discussed. But they may be so expensive to build and so complicated to use that the system is economically or operationally unfeasible. Some cost/benefit analysis must be performed to determine which control mechanisms provide the most effective safeguards without sacrificing operational efficiency or cost.

One of the criteria that determines how much control is built into a system is the importance of its data. Major financial and accounting systems, for example, such as a payroll system or one that tracks purchases and sales on the stock exchange, must have higher standards of control than a tickler system to track dental patients and remind them that their six-month checkup is due. For instance, Swissair invested in additional hardware and software to increase its network reliability because it was running critical reservation and ticketing applications.

The cost-effectiveness of controls will also be influenced by the efficiency, complexity, and expense of each control technique. For example, complete one-for-one checking may be time consuming and operationally impossible for a system that processes hundreds of thousands of utilities payments daily. But it might be possible to use this technique to verify only critical data such as dollar amounts and account numbers, while ignoring names and addresses.

A third consideration is the level of risk if a specific activity or process is not properly controlled. System builders can undertake a **risk assessment,** determining points of vulnerability, the likely frequency of a problem and the potential damage if it were to occur. For example, if an event is likely to occur no more than once a year, with a maximum of $1000 loss to the organization, it would not be feasible to spend $20,000 on the design and maintenance of a control to protect against that event. However, if that same event could occur at

Secure Electronic Transaction (SET)
A standard for securing credit card transactions over the Internet and other networks.

risk assessment
Determining the potential frequency of the occurrence of a problem and the potential damage if the problem were to occur. Used to determine the cost/benefit of a control.

TABLE 14-6	ON-LINE ORDER PROCESSING RISK ASSESSMENT		
Exposure	Probability of Occurrence (%)	Loss Range/ Average ($)	Expected Annual Loss ($)
Power failure	30	5000–200,000 (102,500)	30,750
Embezzlement	5	1000–50,000 (25,500)	1275
User error	98	200–40,000 (20,100)	19,698

This chart shows the results of a risk assessment of three selected areas of an on-line order processing system. The likelihood of each exposure occurring over a one-year period is expressed as a percentage. The next column shows the highest and lowest possible loss that could be expected each time the exposure occurred and an average loss calculated by adding the highest and lowest figures together and dividing by 2. The expected annual loss for each exposure can be determined by multiplying the average loss by its probability of occurrence.

least once a day, with a potential loss of more than $300,000 a year, $100,000 spent on a control might be entirely appropriate.

Table 14-6 illustrates sample results of a risk assessment for an on-line order processing system that processes 30,000 orders per day. The probability of a power failure occurring in a one-year period is 30 percent. Loss of order transactions while power is down could range from $5000 to $200,000 for each occurrence, depending on how long processing was halted. The probability of embezzlement occurring over a yearly period is about 5 percent, with potential losses ranging from $1000 to $50,000 for each occurrence. User errors have a 98 percent chance of occurring over a yearly period, with losses ranging from $200 to $40,000 for each occurrence. The average loss for each event can be weighted by multiplying it by the probability of its occurrence annually to determine the expected annual loss. Once the risks have been assessed, system builders can concentrate on the control points with the greatest vulnerability and potential loss. In this case, controls should focus on ways to minimize the risk of power failures and user errors. Increasing management awareness of the full range of actions they can take to reduce risks can substantially reduce system losses (Straub and Welke, 1998).

In some situations, organizations may not know the precise probability of threats occurring to their information systems, and they may not be able to quantify the impact of such events. In these instances, management may choose to describe risks and their likely impact in a qualitative manner (Rainer, Snyder, and Carr, 1991).

To decide which controls to use, information system builders must examine various control techniques in relation to each other and to their relative cost-effectiveness. A control weakness at one point may be offset by a strong control at another. It may not be cost-effective to build tight controls at every point in the processing cycle if the areas of greatest risk are secure or if compensating controls exist elsewhere. The combination of all of the controls developed for a particular application will determine its overall control structure.

THE ROLE OF AUDITING IN THE CONTROL PROCESS

MIS audit
Identifies all the controls that govern individual information systems and assesses their effectiveness.

How does management know that information systems controls are effective? To answer this question, organizations must conduct comprehensive and systematic audits. An **MIS audit** identifies all of the controls that govern individual information systems and assesses their effectiveness. To accomplish this, the auditor must acquire a thorough understanding of operations, physical facilities, telecommunications, control systems, data security objectives, organizational structure, personnel, manual procedures, and individual applications.

The auditor usually interviews key individuals who use and operate a specific information system concerning their activities and procedures. Application controls, overall integrity controls, and control disciplines are examined. The auditor should trace the flow of sample

MIS IN ACTION   DECISIONMAKING

ANALYZING SECURITY VULNERABILITIES

A survey of your firm's information technology infrastructure has produced the following security analysis statistics:

Security Vulnerabilities by Type of Computing Platform

Platform	Number of Computers	High Risk	Medium Risk	Low Risk	Total Vulnerabilities
Windows.NET Server (corporate applications)	1	11	37	19	
Windows XP Professional (high-level administrators)	3	56	242	87	
Linux (e-mail and printing services)	1	3	154	98	
Sun Solaris (Unix) (E-commerce and Web servers)	2	12	299	78	
Windows XP Professional User desktops and laptops with office productivity tools that can also be linked to the corporate network running corporate applications and intranet	195	14	16	1237	

High risk vulnerabilities include non-authorized users accessing applications, guessable passwords, user name matching the password, active user accounts with missing passwords, and the existence of unauthorized programs in application systems.

Medium risk vulnerabilities include the ability of users to shut down the system without being logged on, passwords and screen saver settings that were not established for PCs, and outdated versions of software still being stored on hard drives.

Low risk vulnerabilities include the inability of users to change their passwords, user passwords that have not been changed periodically, and passwords that were smaller than the minimum size specified by the company.

1. Calculate the total number of vulnerabilities for each platform. What is the potential impact of the security problems for each computing platform on the organization?
2. If you only have one information systems specialist in charge of security, which platforms should you address first in trying to eliminate these vulnerabilities? Second? Third? Last? Why?
3. Identify the types of control problems illustrated by these vulnerabilities and explain the measures that should be taken to solve them.
4. What does your firm risk by ignoring the security vulnerabilities identified?

---

transactions through the system and perform tests, using, if appropriate, automated audit software.

The audit lists and ranks all control weaknesses and estimates the probability of their occurrence. It then assesses the financial and organizational impact of each threat. Figure 14-8 is a sample auditor's listing of control weaknesses for a loan system. It includes a section for notifying management of such weaknesses and for management's response. Management is expected to devise a plan for countering significant weaknesses in controls.

14.3 ENSURING SYSTEM QUALITY

Organizations can improve system quality by using software quality assurance techniques and by improving the quality of their data.

SOFTWARE QUALITY ASSURANCE METHODOLOGIES AND TOOLS

Solutions to software quality problems include using an appropriate systems development methodology, proper resource allocation during systems development, the use of metrics, and attention to testing.

Structured Methodologies

Various tools and development methodologies have been employed to help system builders document, analyze, design, and implement information systems. A **development methodology** is a collection of methods, one or more for every activity within every phase of a systems development project. The primary function of a development methodology is to provide discipline to the entire development process. A good development methodology establishes

development methodology
A collection of methods, one or more for every activity within every phase of a development project.

Function: Personal Loans _____   Prepared by: _____ J. Ericson _____   Received by: _____ T. Barrow _____
Location: Peoria, Ill. _____   Preparation date: __ June 16, 2002 _____   Review date: _____ June 28, 2002 _____

Nature of Weakness and Impact	Chance for Substantial Error		Effect on Audit Procedures	Notification to Management	
	Yes/ No	Justification	Required Amendment	Date of Report	Management Response
Loan repayment records are not reconciled to borrower's records during processing.	Yes	Without a detection control, errors in individual client balances may remain undetected.	Confirm a sample of loans.	5/10/02	Interest Rate Compare Report provides this control.
There are no regular audits of computer-generated data (interest charges).	Yes	Without a regular audit or reasonableness check, widespread miscalculations could result before errors are detected.		5/10/02	Periodic audits of loans will be instituted.
Programs can be put into production libraries to meet target deadlines without final approval from the Standards and Controls group.	No	All programs require management authorization. The Standards and Controls group controls access to all production systems, and assigns such cases to a temporary production status.			

Figure 14-8   Sample auditor's list of control weaknesses. This chart is a sample page from a list of control weaknesses that an auditor might find in a loan system in a local commercial bank. This form helps auditors record and evaluate control weaknesses and shows the results of discussing those weaknesses with management, as well as any corrective actions taken by management.

organization-wide standards for requirements gathering, design, programming, and testing. To produce quality software, organizations must select an appropriate methodology and then enforce its use. The methodology should call for systems requirement and specification documents that are complete, detailed, accurate, and documented in a format the user community can understand before they approve it. Specifications also must include agreed on measures of system quality so that the system can be evaluated objectively while it is being developed and once it is completed.

Development methodologies reflect different philosophies of systems development. Chapter 12 has already described object-oriented software development. The traditional structured methodologies and computer-aided software engineering (CASE) are other important methodologies and tools for producing quality software. Structured methodologies have been used to document, analyze, and design information systems since the 1970s. **Structured** refers to the fact that the techniques are step-by-step, with each step building on the previous one. Structured methodologies are top-down, progressing from the highest, most abstract level to the lowest level of detail—from the general to the specific. For example, the highest level of a top-down description of a human resources system would show the main human resources functions: personnel, benefits, compensation, and Equal Employment Opportunity (EEO). Each of these would be broken down into the next layer. Benefits, for instance, might include pension, employee savings, healthcare, and insurance. Each of these layers in turn would be broken down until the lowest level of detail could be depicted.

The traditional structured methodologies are process-oriented rather than data-oriented. Although data descriptions are part of the

structured

Refers to the fact that techniques are carefully drawn up, step by step, with each step building on a previous one.

An auditor interviews key individuals who use and operate a specific information system concerning their activities and procedures. The auditor often traces the flow of sample transactions through the system and performs tests using automated audit software.

methods, the methodologies focus on how the data are transformed rather than on the data themselves. These methodologies are largely linear; each phase must be completed before the next one can begin. Structured methodologies include structured analysis, structured design, and the use of flowcharts.

Structured Analysis

Structured analysis is widely used to define system inputs, processes, and outputs. It offers a logical graphic model of information flow, partitioning a system into modules that show manageable levels of detail. It rigorously specifies the processes or transformations that occur within each module and the interfaces that exist between them. Its primary tool is the **data flow diagram (DFD),** a graphic representation of a system's component processes and the interfaces (flow of data) between them.

Figure 14-9 shows a simple data flow diagram for a mail-in university course registration system. The rounded boxes represent processes, which portray the transformation of data. The square box represents an external entity, which is an originator or receiver of information located outside the boundaries of the system being modeled. The open rectangles represent data stores, which are either manual or automated inventories of data. The arrows represent data flows, which show the movement between processes, external entities, and data stores. They always contain packets of data with the name or content of each data flow listed beside the arrow.

This data flow diagram shows that students submit registration forms with their name, identification number, and the numbers of the courses they wish to take. In process 1.0 the system verifies that each course selected is still open by referencing the university's course file. The file distinguishes courses that are open from those that have been canceled or filled. Process 1.0 then determines which of the student's selections can be accepted or rejected. Process 2.0 enrolls the student in the courses for which he or she has been accepted. It updates the university's course file with the student's name and identification number and recalculates the class size. If maximum enrollment has been reached, the course number is flagged as closed. Process 2.0 also updates the university's student master file with information about new students or changes in address. Process 3.0 then sends each student applicant a confirmation-of-registration letter listing the courses for which he or she is registered and noting the course selections that could not be fulfilled.

The diagrams can be used to depict higher level processes as well as lower level details. Through leveled data flow diagrams, a complex process can be broken down into successive levels of detail. An entire system can be divided into subsystems with a high-level data flow diagram. Each subsystem, in turn, can be divided into additional subsystems with second-level data flow diagrams, and the lower level subsystems can be broken down again until the lowest level of detail has been reached.

structured analysis

A method for defining system inputs, processes, and outputs and for partitioning systems into subsystems or modules that show a logical graphic model of information flow.

data flow diagram (DFD)

Primary tool for structured analysis that graphically illustrates a system's component processes and the flow of data between them.

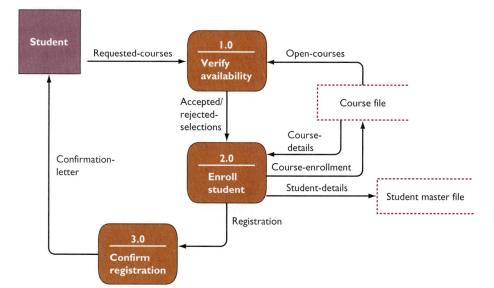

Figure 14-9 Data flow diagram for mail-in university registration system. The system has three processes: Verify availability (1.0), Enroll student (2.0), and Confirm registration (3.0). The name and content of each of the data flows appear adjacent to each arrow. There is one external entity in this system: the student. There are two data stores: the student master file and the course file.

process specifications
Describe the logic of the processes occurring within the lowest levels of a data flow diagram.

structured design
Software design discipline encompassing a set of design rules and techniques for designing systems from the top down in a hierarchical fashion.

structure chart
System documentation showing each level of design, the relationship among the levels, and the overall place in the design structure; can document one program, one system, or part of one program.

structured programming
A discipline for organizing and coding programs that simplifies the control paths so that the programs can be easily understood and modified; uses the basic control structures and modules that have only one entry point and one exit point.

module
A logical unit of a program that performs one or several functions.

sequence construct
The sequential single steps or actions in the logic of a program that do not depend on the existence of any condition.

Another tool for structured analysis is a data dictionary, which contains information about individual pieces of data and data groupings within a system (see Chapter 7). The data dictionary defines the contents of data flows and data stores so that system builders understand exactly what pieces of data they contain. **Process specifications** describe the transformation occurring within the lowest level of the data flow diagrams. They express the logic for each process.

Structured Design

Structured design encompasses a set of design rules and techniques that promotes program clarity and simplicity, thereby reducing the time and effort required for coding, debugging, and maintenance. The main principle of structured design is that a system should be designed from the top down in hierarchical fashion and refined to greater levels of detail. The design should first consider the main function of a program or system, then break this function into subfunctions and decompose each subfunction until the lowest level of detail has been reached. The lowest level modules describe the actual processing that will occur. In this manner all high-level logic and the design model are developed before detailed program code is written. If structured analysis has been performed, the structured specification document can serve as input to the design process. Our earlier human resources top-down description provides a good overview example of structured design.

As the design is formulated, it is documented in a structure chart. The **structure chart** is a top-down chart, showing each level of design, its relationship to other levels, and its place in the overall design structure. Figure 14-10 shows a high level structure chart for a payroll system. If a design has too many levels to fit onto one structure chart, it can be broken down further on more detailed structure charts. A structure chart may document one program, one system (a set of programs), or part of one program.

Structured Programming

Structured programming extends the principles governing structured design to the writing of programs to make software programs easier to understand and modify. It is based on the principle of modularization, which follows from top-down analysis and design. Each of the boxes in the structure chart represents a component **module** that is usually directly related to a bottom-level design module. It constitutes a logical unit that performs one or several functions. Ideally, modules should be independent of each other and should have only one entry to and exit point. They should share data with as few other modules as possible. Each module should be kept to a manageable size. An individual should be able to read and understand the program code for the module and easily keep track of its functions.

Proponents of structured programming have shown that any program can be written using three basic control constructs, or instruction patterns: (1) simple sequence, (2) selection, and (3) iteration. These control constructs are illustrated in Figure 14-11.

The **sequence construct** executes statements in the order in which they appear, with control passing unconditionally from one statement to the next. The program will execute statement A and then statement B.

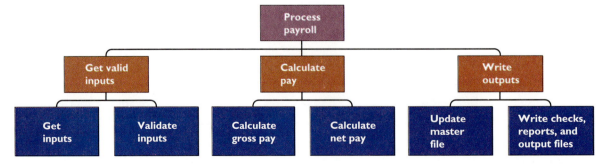

Figure 14-10 High-level structure chart for a payroll system. This structure chart shows the highest or most abstract level of design for a payroll system, providing an overview of the entire system.

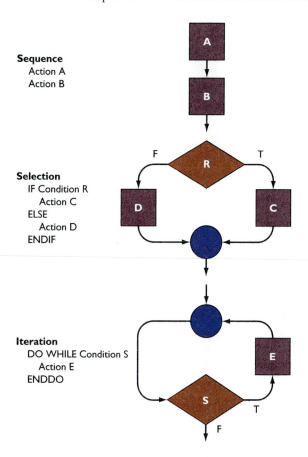

Sequence
  Action A
  Action B

Selection
  IF Condition R
    Action C
  ELSE
    Action D
  ENDIF

Iteration
  DO WHILE Condition S
    Action E
  ENDDO

Figure 14-11 Basic program control constructs. The three basic control constructs used in structured programming are sequence, selection, and iteration.

The **selection construct** tests a condition and executes one of two alternative instructions based on the results of the test. Condition R is tested. If R is true, statement C is executed. If R is false, statement D is executed. Control then passes to the next statement.

The **iteration construct** repeats a segment of code as long as a conditional test remains true. Condition S is tested. If S is true, statement E is executed and control returns to the test of S. If S is false, E is skipped and control passes to the next statement.

Flowcharts

Flowcharting is an old design tool that is still in use. **System flowcharts** detail the flow of data throughout an entire information system. Flowcharting is no longer recommended for program design because it does not provide top-down modular structure as effectively as other techniques. However, system flowcharts still may be used to document physical design specifications because they can show all inputs, major files, processing, and outputs for a system, and they can document manual procedures.

Using specialized symbols and flow lines, the system flowchart traces the flow of information and work in a system, the sequence of processing steps, and the physical media on which data are input, output, and stored. Figure 14-12 shows some of the basic symbols for system flowcharting used in a high-level system flowchart for a payroll system. The plain rectangle is a general symbol for a process. Flow lines show the sequence of steps and the direction of information flow. Arrows are employed to show direction if it is not apparent in the diagram.

Limitations of Traditional Methods

Although traditional methods are valuable, they can be inflexible and time-consuming. Completion of structured analysis is required before design can begin, and programming must await the completed deliverables from design. A change in specifications requires that first the analysis documents and then the design documents must be modified before the programs

selection construct
The logic pattern in programming where a stated condition determines which of two alternative actions can be taken.

iteration construct
The logic pattern in programming where certain actions are repeated while a specified condition occurs or until a certain condition is met.

system flowchart
A graphic design tool that depicts the physical media and sequence of processing steps used in an entire information system.

Figure 14-12 System flow-chart for a payroll system. This is a high-level system flowchart for a batch payroll system. Only the most important processes and files are illustrated. Data are input from two sources: time cards and payroll-related data (such as salary increases) passed from the human resources system. The data are first edited and validated against the existing payroll master file before the payroll master is updated. The update process produces an updated payroll master file, various payroll reports (such as the payroll register and hours register), checks, a direct deposit tape, and a file of payment data that must be passed to the organization's general ledger system. The direct deposit tape is sent to the automated clearinghouse that serves the banks offering direct deposit services to employees.

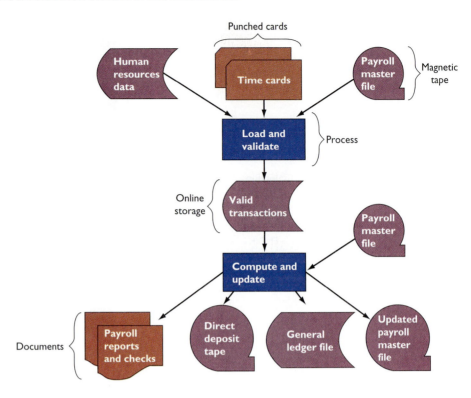

can be changed to reflect the new requirement. Structured methodologies are function-oriented, focusing on the processes that transform the data. Chapter 12 described how object-oriented development addresses this problem. System builders can also use computer-aided software engineering (CASE) tools to make structured methods more flexible.

Computer-Aided Software Engineering (CASE)

computer-aided software engineering (CASE)

The automation of step-by-step methodologies for software and systems development to reduce the amount of repetitive work the developer needs to do.

Computer-aided software engineering (CASE)—sometimes called *computer-aided systems engineering*—is the automation of step-by-step methodologies for software and systems development to reduce the amount of repetitive work the developer needs to do. Its adoption can free the developer for more creative problem-solving tasks. CASE tools also facilitate the creation of clear documentation and the coordination of team development efforts. Team members can share their work easily by accessing each other's files to review or modify what has been done. Some studies have found that systems developed with CASE and the newer methodologies are more reliable, and they require repairs less often (Dekleva, 1992). Modest productivity benefits can also be achieved if the tools are used properly. Many CASE tools are PC-based, with powerful graphical capabilities.

CASE tools provide automated graphics facilities for producing charts and diagrams, screen and report generators, data dictionaries, extensive reporting facilities, analysis and checking tools, code generators, and documentation generators. Most CASE tools are based on one or more of the popular structured methodologies. Some support object-oriented development. In general, CASE tools try to increase productivity and quality by doing the following:

▌ Enforce a standard development methodology and design discipline.

▌ Improve communication between users and technical specialists.

▌ Organize and correlate design components and provide rapid access to them via a design repository.

▌ Automate tedious and error-prone portions of analysis and design.

▌ Automate code generation, testing, and control rollout.

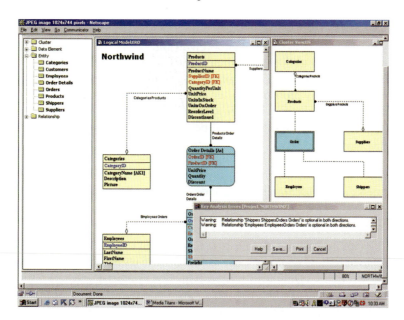

CASE tools include capabilities for generating and validating entity-relationship diagrams and data flow diagrams. Such tools facilitate the creation of clear and accurate design specifications and the coordination of team development efforts.

Many CASE tools have been classified in terms of whether they support activities at the front end or the back end of the systems development process. Front-end CASE tools focus on capturing analysis and design information in the early stages of systems development, whereas back-end CASE tools address coding, testing, and maintenance activities. Back-end tools help convert specifications automatically into program code.

CASE tools automatically tie data elements to the processes where they are used. If a data flow diagram is changed from one process to another, the elements in the data dictionary would be altered automatically to reflect the change in the diagram. CASE tools also contain features for validating design diagrams and specifications. CASE tools thus support iterative design by automating revisions and changes and providing prototyping facilities.

A CASE information repository stores all the information defined by the analysts during the project. The repository includes data flow diagrams, structure charts, entity-relationship diagrams, data definitions, process specifications, screen and report formats, notes and comments, and test results. CASE tools now have features to support client/server applications, object-oriented programming, and business process redesign. Methodologies and tool sets are being created to leverage organizational knowledge of business process reengineering (Nissen, 1998).

To be used effectively, CASE tools require organizational discipline. Every member of a development project must adhere to a common set of naming conventions and standards as well as a development methodology. The best CASE tools enforce common methods and standards, which may discourage their use in situations where organizational discipline is lacking.

Resource Allocation during Systems Development

Views on **resource allocation** during systems development have changed significantly over the years. Resource allocation determines the way the costs, time, and personnel are assigned to different phases of the project. In earlier times, developers focused on programming, with only about 1 percent of the time and costs of a project being devoted to systems analysis (determining specifications). More time should be spent in specifications and systems analysis, decreasing the proportion of programming time and reducing the need for so much maintenance time. Documenting requirements so that they can be understood from their origin through development, specification, and continuing use can also reduce errors as well as time and costs (Domges and Pohl, 1998). Current literature suggests that about one-quarter of a project's time and cost should be expended in specifications and analysis, with perhaps 50 percent of its resources being allocated to design and programming. Installation and post-implementation ideally should require only one-quarter of the project's resources. Investments in software quality initiatives early in a project are likely to provide the greatest payback (Slaughter, Harter, and Krishnan, 1998).

resource allocation
The determination of how costs, time, and personnel are assigned to different phases of a systems development project.

Software Metrics

Software metrics can play a vital role in increasing system quality. **Software metrics** are objective assessments of the system in the form of quantified measurements. Ongoing use of metrics allows the IS department and the user to jointly measure the performance of the system and identify problems as they occur. Examples of software metrics include the number of transactions that can be processed in a specified unit of time, on-line response time, the number of payroll checks printed per hour, and the number of known bugs per hundred lines of code.

For metrics to be successful, they must be carefully designed, formal, and objective. They must measure significant aspects of the system. In addition, metrics are of no value unless they are used consistently and users agree to the measurements in advance.

Testing

Chapter 12 described the stages of testing required to put an information system in operation—program testing, system testing, and acceptance testing. Early, regular, and thorough testing will contribute significantly to system quality. In general, software testing is often misunderstood. Many view testing as a way to prove the correctness of work they have done. In fact, we know that all sizable software is riddled with errors, and we must test to uncover these errors.

Testing begins at the design phase. Because no coding exists yet, the test normally used is a **walkthrough**—a review of a specification or design document by a small group of people carefully selected based on the skills needed for the particular objectives being tested. Once coding begins, coding walkthroughs also can be used to review program code. However, code must be tested by computer runs. When errors are discovered, the source is found and eliminated through a process called **debugging.**

Electronic commerce and electronic business applications introduce new levels of complexity for testing to ensure high-quality performance and functionality. Behind each large Web site such as Amazon.com, eBay, or E*Trade are hundreds of servers, thousands of miles of network cable, and hundreds of software programs, creating numerous points of vulnerability. These Web sites must be built and tested to make sure that they can withstand expected—and unexpected—spikes and peaks in their load. Both Web site traffic and technical components such as hardware, software, and networks must be taken into consideration during application development and during testing.

To test a Web site realistically, companies need to find a way to subject the Web site to the same number of concurrent users as would actually be visiting the site at one time and to devise test plans that reflect what these people would actually be doing. For example, a retail e-commerce site should create a test scenario where there are many visitors just browsing and some are making purchases.

Testing wireless applications poses additional challenges. Many wireless and conventional Web applications are linked to the same back-end systems so the total load on those systems will increase dramatically as wireless users are added. Automated load testing tools that simulate thousands of simultaneous wireless Web and conventional Web browser sessions can help companies measure the impact on system performance.

Many companies delay testing until the end of the application development phase, when design decisions have been finalized and most of the software program code has been written. Leaving Web site performance and scalability tests until the end of the application development cycle is extremely risky because such problems often stem from the fundamental workings of the system. To minimize the chance of discovering major structural problems late in the systems development process, companies should perform this testing well before the system is complete. This makes it possible to address performance bottlenecks and other issues in each application level or system component before everything is integrated.

DATA QUALITY AUDITS AND DATA CLEANSING

Information system quality can also be improved by identifying and correcting faulty data, making error detection a more explicit organizational goal (Klein, Goodhue, and Davis,

MAKE IT YOUR BUSINESS

FINANCE AND ACCOUNTING

Security and reliability are absolutely critical in systems for banking and financial services because errors, fraud, and disruption of service can lead to large monetary losses and the erosion of consumer confidence in these companies and even the entire financial industry. Prevention of fraud, errors, and manipulation of assets in financial and accounting systems are key objectives of application and general controls. The accounting function is often involved in information system audits and in the design of information system controls. You can find examples of finance and accounting applications on pages 454, 458, and 480–483.

HUMAN RESOURCES

"People factors" are as important as technology in establishing the security and reliability of the firm's information systems. Many security breaches and system errors are caused by legitimate company "insiders." Software quality depends on the commitment to quality of the people designing the software. Establishing quality and security-consciousness among employees has become an important human resources function. Human resources data include confidential pieces of information such as salary or illnesses that require tight data security safeguards. You can find examples of human resources applications on pages 480–483.

MANUFACTURING AND PRODUCTION

Manufacturing systems today are more vulnerable than in the past because they have become increasingly networked and integrated with each other as well as with the manufacturing systems of other firms. Supply chain management systems can be deeply affected by network outages or software quality problems because interrupted flows of information can adversely impact so many members of the supply chain. Security and reliability are thus very high priorities in the design of intranets and extranets for manufacturing and production. You can find examples of manufacturing and production applications on pages 450–451.

SALES AND MARKETING

Electronic commerce requires secure payment systems for on-line purchases as well as fault-tolerant or high-availability systems that prevent interruptions of service. Encryption, digital signatures, digital certificates, and technologies for scalability and high-availability computing are important technologies for creating such systems.

1997). The analysis of data quality often begins with a **data quality audit,** which is a structured survey of the accuracy and level of completeness of the data in an information system. Data quality audits are accomplished by the following methods:

| Surveying end users for their perceptions of data quality

| Surveying entire data files

| Surveying samples from data files

> **data quality audit**
> A survey and/or sample of files to determine accuracy and completeness of data in an information system.

Unless regular data quality audits are undertaken, organizations have no way of knowing to what extent their information systems contain inaccurate, incomplete, or ambiguous information.

Until recently, many organizations were not giving data quality the priority it deserves (Tayi and Ballou, 1998). Now electronic commerce and electronic business are forcing more companies to pay attention to data quality because a digitally enabled firm cannot run efficiently without accurate data about customers and business partners. **Data cleansing** has become a core requirement for data warehousing, customer relationship management, and Web-based commerce. Companies implementing data warehousing often find inconsistencies in customer or employee information as they try to integrate information from different business units. Companies are also finding mistakes in the data provided by customers or business partners through a Web site. On-line net marketplaces (see Chapter 4) are especially problematic because they use catalog data from dozens to thousands of suppliers and these data are often in different formats, with different classification schemes for product numbers, product descriptions, and other attributes. Data cleansing tools can be used to correct errors in these data and to integrate these data in a consistent company-wide format. For example, Prudential Insurance Co. of America was able to build a giant data warehouse with a company-wide view of customers across 8 lines of business by creating company-wide standards for nearly 3000 data elements such as customer name, product code, and policy number. Prudential conducts regular data cleansing and audits to ensure that data remain accurate and that naming standards are strictly enforced (Stackpole, 2001).

> **data cleansing**
> Correcting errors and inconsistencies in data to increase accuracy so that they can be used in a standard company-wide format.

MANAGEMENT WRAP-UP

Management is responsible for developing the control structure and quality standards for the organization. Key management decisions include establishing standards for systems accuracy and reliability, determining an appropriate level of control for organizational functions, and establishing a disaster recovery plan.

The characteristics of the organization play a large role in determining its approach to quality assurance and control issues. Some organizations are more quality and control conscious than others. Their cultures and business processes support high standards of quality and performance. Creating high levels of security and quality in information systems can be a process of lengthy organizational change.

A number of technologies and methodologies are available for promoting system quality and security. Technologies such as antivirus and data security software, firewalls, fault-tolerant and high-availability computing technology, and programmed procedures can be used to create a control environment, whereas software metrics, systems development methodologies, and automated tools for systems development can be used to improve software quality. Organizational discipline is required to use these technologies effectively.

For Discussion

1. It has been said that controls and security should be one of the first areas to be addressed in the design of an information system. Do you agree? Why or why not?
2. How much software testing is "enough"? What management, organization, and technology issues should you consider in answering this question?

SUMMARY

1. *Why are information systems so vulnerable to destruction, error, abuse, and system quality problems?* With data concentrated into electronic form and many procedures invisible through automation, computerized information systems are vulnerable to destruction, misuse, error, fraud, and hardware or software failures. On-line systems and those utilizing the Internet are especially vulnerable because data and files can be immediately and directly accessed through computer terminals or at many points in the network. Hackers can penetrate corporate networks and cause serious system disruptions. Computer viruses can spread rampantly from system to system, clogging computer memory or destroying programs and data. Software presents problems because of the high costs of correcting errors and because software bugs may be impossible to eliminate. Data quality can also severely impact system quality and performance.

2. *What types of controls are available for information systems?* Controls consist of all the methods, policies, and organizational procedures that ensure the safety of the organization's assets, the accuracy and reliability of its accounting records, and adherence to management standards. There are two main categories of controls: general controls and application controls.

    General controls handle the overall design, security, and use of computers, programs and files for the organization's information technology infrastructure. They include physical hardware controls, system software controls, data file security controls, computer operations controls, controls over the system implementation process, and administrative disciplines.

    Application controls are those unique to specific computerized applications. They focus on the completeness and accuracy of input, updating and maintenance, and the validity of the information in the system. Application controls consist of (1) input controls, (2) processing controls, and (3) output controls.

    To determine which controls are required, designers and users of systems must identify all of the control points and control weaknesses and perform risk assessment. They must also perform a cost/benefit analysis of controls and design controls that can effectively safeguard systems without making them unusable.

3. *What special measures must be taken to ensure the reliability, availability, and security of electronic commerce and digital business processes?* Companies require special measures to support electronic commerce and digital business processes. They can use fault-tolerant computer systems or create high-availability computing environments to make sure that their information systems are always available and performing without interruptions. Disaster recovery plans provide procedures and facilities for restoring computing and commu-

nication services after they have been disrupted. Firewalls and intrusion detection systems help safeguard private networks from unauthorized access when organizations use intranets or link to the Internet. Encryption is a widely used technology for securing electronic transmissions over the Internet. Digital certificates provide further protection of electronic transactions by authenticating a user's identity.

4. *What are the most important software quality assurance techniques?* The quality and reliability of software can be improved by using a standard development methodology, software metrics, thorough testing procedures, and by allocating resources to put more emphasis on the analysis and design stages of systems development.

Structured methodologies have been used to increase software quality since the 1970s. Structured analysis highlights the flow of data and the processes through which data are transformed. Its principal tool is the data flow diagram. Structured design and programming are software design disciplines that produce reliable, well-documented software with a simple, clear structure that is easy for others to understand and maintain. System flowcharts are useful for documenting the physical aspects of system design.

Computer-aided software engineering (CASE) automates methodologies for systems development. It promotes standards and improves coordination and consistency during systems development. CASE tools help system builders construct a better model of a system and facilitate revision of design specifications to correct errors.

5. *Why are auditing information systems and safeguarding data quality so important?* Comprehensive and systematic MIS auditing can help organizations to determine the effectiveness of the controls in their information systems. Regular data quality audits should be conducted to help organizations ensure a high level of completeness and accuracy of the data stored in their systems. Data cleansing should also be performed to create consistent and accurate data for company-wide use in electronic commerce and electronic business.

KEY TERMS

Administrative controls, 460	Debugging, 476	Intrusion detection system, 465	Secure Electronic Transaction (SET), 467
Antivirus software, 455	Denial of service attack, 454	Iteration construct, 473	
Application controls, 460	Development methodology, 469	Load balancing, 463	Security, 456
Authentication, 466	Digital certificate, 466	Message integrity, 466	Sequence construct, 472
Bugs, 457	Digital signature, 466	Mirroring, 463	Selection construct, 473
Clustering, 463	Disaster recovery plan, 463	MIS audit, 468	Software metrics, 476
Computer-aided software engineering (CASE), 474	Encryption, 465	Module, 472	Structure chart, 472
	Fault-tolerant computer system, 462	On-line transaction processing, 462	Structured, 470
Computer virus, 454			Structured analysis, 471
Controls, 459	General controls, 460	Output controls, 461	Structured design, 472
Data cleansing, 477	Hacker, 453	Process specifications, 472	Structured programming, 472
Data flow diagram (DFD), 471	High-availability computing, 462	Processing controls, 461	System flowchart, 473
Data quality audit, 477		Resource allocation, 475	Walkthrough, 476
Data security controls, 460	Input controls, 461	Risk assessment, 467	

REVIEW QUESTIONS

1. Why are computer systems more vulnerable than manual systems to destruction, fraud, error, and misuse? Name some of the key areas where systems are most vulnerable.

2. Name some features of on-line information systems that make them difficult to control.

3. How can bad software and data quality affect system performance and reliability? Describe two software quality problems.

4. What are controls? Distinguish between general controls and application controls.

5. Name and describe the principal general and application controls for computerized systems.

6. What is security? List and describe controls that promote security for computer hardware, computer networks, computer software, and computerized data.

7. What special security measures must be taken by organizations linking to the Internet?

8. Distinguish between fault-tolerant and high-availability computing.

9. Describe the role of firewalls, intrusion detection systems, and encryption systems in promoting security.

10. Why are digital signatures and digital certificates important for electronic commerce?

11. What is the function of risk assessment?

12. How does MIS auditing enhance the control process?

13. Name and describe four software quality assurance techniques.

14. What is structured analysis? What is the role of the data flow diagram in structured analysis?

15. How is structured design related to structured programming? How can both promote software quality?

16. Why are data quality audits and data cleansing essential?

APPLICATION SOFTWARE EXERCISE

SPREADSHEET EXERCISE: PERFORMING A SECURITY RISK ASSESSMENT

Mercer Paints is a small but highly regarded paint manufacturing company located in Alabama. The company has a network in place, linking many of its business operations. While the firm feels that its security is adequate, the recent addition of a Web site has been an open invitation to hackers. Management requested a risk assessment. The risk assessment identified several potential exposures; these exposures, associated probabilities, and average losses are summarized in the table that can be found on the Laudon Web site for Chapter. 14. In addition to the potential exposures listed, you should identify at least three other potential threats to Mercer Paints, assign probabilities, and estimate a loss range.

Using a spreadsheet product and the risk assessment data provided on the Laudon Web site, calculate the expected annual loss for each exposure. Which control points have the greatest vulnerability? What recommendations would you make to Mercer Paints? Prepare a written report that summarizes your findings and recommendations.

GROUP PROJECT

Form a group with two or three other students. Select a system described in one of the chapter ending cases. Write a description of the system, its functions, and its value to the organization. Then write a description of both the general and application controls that should be used to protect the organization. If possible, use electronic presentation software to present your findings to the class.

TOOLS FOR INTERACTIVE LEARNING

■ INTERNET CONNECTION

The Internet Connection for this chapter will take you to a series of Web sites where you can complete an exercise to evaluate various secure electronic payment systems for the Internet. You can also use the Interactive Study Guide to test your knowledge of the topics in this chapter and get instant feedback where you need more practice.

■ CD-ROM

If you use the Multimedia Edition CD-ROM with this chapter, you can find a video clip illustrating the Comdisco disaster recovery service, an audio overview of the major themes of this chapter, and bullet text summarizing the key points of the chapter.

■ ELECTRONIC BUSINESS PROJECT

At the Laudon Web site for Chapter 14, you will find an Electronic Business project to evaluate security outsourcing services.

CASE STUDY—*The World Trade Center Disaster: Who Was Prepared?*

A little after 8AM on Tuesday morning, September 11th, 2001, four cross-country passenger jetliners were hijacked with loaded fuel tanks. One was crashed into a section of the Pentagon, another plunged into the Pennsylvania countryside when passengers prevented the hijackers from hitting their target. The other two planes were crashed into New York City's two World Trade Center (WTC) towers, ultimately causing them to implode and kill 3,000 people.

All WTC offices were destroyed, a total of over 15 million square feet of office space. Some of the nearby buildings, includ-ing the World Financial Center (WFC), the American Express Building, and 1 Liberty Plaza, were badly damaged and were immediately evacuated. With the New York Stock Exchange (NYSE) located so very close, the WTC area was the center of global finance and many nearby financial firms were also adversely affected.

The financial industry's equipment loss was immense. The Tower Group, a technology research company, estimated that securities firms alone will spend up to $3.2 billion just to replace computer equipment. Much of the WTC IT and telecommunications equipment was underground and was destroyed by the collapsing debris. Tower calculates replacements will include 16,000 trading-desk workstations, 34,000 PCs, 8,000 servers, plus large numbers of computer terminals, printers, storage devices, and network hubs and switches. Setting up this equipment will cost an additional $1.5 billion.

The most vital issue for many companies was their loss of staff. Few recovery plans anticipated such a catastrophe. Organizations that were directly hit did not even know who in their companies had survived or where they were because hardly any kept secure, accessible lists of employees or contact information. The New York Board of Trade (NYBT), which had its trading floor in the WTC to deal in such commodities as coffee, orange juice, cocoa, sugar and cotton, had to call all employees, one by one. Often survivors couldn't be reached because area telephone facilities were destroyed while any working circuits were overloaded. A few companies had considered some staff problems. Disaster recovery companies did provide some workspace for their customers. Comdisco had seven WTC customers, and it made space available for 3,000 customer employees, enabling those companies to continue operations. Some recovery companies, including SunGard, made available tractor-trailers equipped with portable data centers. Not all plans worked. Barclays Bank had planned for evacuating its 1,200-person investment-banking unit to its disaster recovery site in New Jersey, but the site proved to be too small for so many employees. Moreover, the bridges and tunnels crossing the Hudson River were immediately closed so most employees could not get there. Fortunately Barclays was able to shift much of its work to its London, Hong Kong, and Tokyo offices, although the time differences forced those workers to do double shifts.

Data loss is extremely critical, often requiring extensive planning. Many organizations already relied on disaster recovery companies such as SunGard, Comdisco, and Recall, which offer office space, computers, and telecommunications equipment when disasters occur. "Cold site" recovery requires the companies to back up their own data onto tapes, storing them offsite. If a disaster occurs, the organizations transport their backup tapes to the recovery sites where they load and boot their applications from scratch using their backup tapes. Although the cold site approach is relatively inexpensive, restoring data can be slow, often taking up to 24 hours. If the tapes are stored at the affected site or relatively close by, all data may be permanently lost, which could put some companies out of business. Moreover, the data for all activity since the last backup will be lost.

"Hot site" backups can solve some problems, but may cost some companies as much as $1 million monthly. A hot site is located offsite where a reserve computer continually creates a mirror image of the production computer's data. Should a data disaster occur, the company can quickly switch over to the back up computer and continue to operate. If the production site itself is destroyed, the staff will actually go to the hot site to operate.

While many companies lost a great deal of data in the attack, a recent Morgan Stanley technology team report said the WTC was "probably one of the best-prepared office facilities from a systems and data recovery perspective." Lower Manhattan's extraordinary data security concern erupted in 1993 when a large bomb exploded in the subterranean parking area of the WTC in a terrorist attack. Six people were killed and more than 1,000 were injured. Realizing how vulnerable they were, many companies took steps to protect themselves. Pressures for emergency planning further increased as companies faced the feared Y2K problems. As a result, the data for many organizations were relatively well protected when the recent WTC attack occurred. Let us look at how some organizations responded to the attack.

Prior to 1993, to protect itself, the NYBT had contracted with SunGard Data Systems Inc. for "cold site" disaster recovery. After the 1993 bombing it decided to establish its own hot site. It rented a computer and trading floor space in Queens for $300,000 annually. It hired Comdisco to help it set up the hot backup site, which it hoped to never have to use despite the expense. After the attack the NYBT quickly moved its operations to Queens and began trading on September 17, along with the NYSE, Nasdaq, and the other exchanges that had not suffered direct hits.

Sometimes backups are too limited. Most disaster recovery companies and their clients have been too focused on recovery of mainframes and have insufficient capabilities for recovering midrange systems and servers. Moreover, backups are often stored in the same office or site and so are useless if the location is destroyed. For example the Board of Trade backed up only some servers and PCs, and those backups were stored in a fireproof safe in the WTC where they were buried beneath many thousands of tons of rubble.

Giant bond trader Cantor Fitzgerald occupied several top floors in one of the WTC buildings and lost its offices and nearly 700 of its 1000 American staff. No company could have adequately planned for the magnitude of this disaster. However Cantor was almost immediately able to shift its functions to its Connecticut and London offices, and its surviving U.S. traders began settling trades by telephone. Despite its enormous losses, the company amazingly resumed operations in just two days, partly with the help of backup companies, software, and computer systems. One reason for its rapid recovery was Recall, Cantor's disaster recovery company. Recall had up-to-date Cantor data because it had been picking up Cantor backup tapes three to five times daily. Moreover, in 1999 Cantor had started switching much of its trading to eSpeed, a fully automated on-line system. After the WTC disaster Peter DaPuzzo, a founder and head of Cantor Fitzgerald, decided that the company would not replace any of the over 100 lost bond traders. Instead the company switched its entire bond trading to eSpeed.

America's oldest bank, the Bank of New York (BONY), is a critical hub for securities processing because it is one of the largest custodians and clearing institutions in the United States. Half the trading in U.S. government bonds moves through its settlement system. The bank also handles around 140,000 fund transfers totaling $900 billion every day. Since the bank facilitates the transfer of cash between buyers and sellers, any outage or disruption of its systems would leave some firms short of anticipated cash already promised to others. BONY was under extraordinary pressure to keep running at full speed.

BONY operations were heavily concentrated in downtown Manhattan, very close to the World Trade Center. The bank is headquartered at 1 Wall Street, almost adjoining the WTC and had two other sites on Barclay and Church Streets that were even closer. These buildings housed 5,300 employees plus the bank's main computer center. On September 11th, the bank lost the two closest sites and their equipment. The bank had arranged for its computer processing to revert to centers outside New York in case of emergency, but it was not able to follow its plan. The World Trade Center attack had heavily damaged a major Verizon switching station at 140 West Street serving 3 million data circuits in lower Manhattan. The loss of this switching station left BONY without any bandwidth for transmitting voice and data communications to downtown New York, and the bank struggled to find ways to connect with customers.

The bank's disaster recovery plan called for paper check processing to be moved from its financial district computer center to its Cherry Hill, New Jersey facility. With communication so disrupted, BONY management decided Cherry Hill was too distant and moved the functions to its closer center in Lodi, New Jersey. However, that center lacked machines for its lockbox business, in which it opens envelopes that contain bill payments, deposits checks, and reads payment stubs to credit the right accounts.

The bank had deliberately planned to have different levels of backup for different functions. The bank's government bond processing was backed up by a second computer that could take over on a moment's notice. No such backup existed for the bank's 350 automated teller machines. The bank rationalized that its customers could use other banks' machines in case of a problem and its customers were forced to do that. Even the backup system for the government bond business did not work properly because the communication lines between its backup sites and clients' backup sites were often of low capacity and had not been fully tested and debugged. For example, BONY's required connection to the Government Securities Clearing Corporation, a central component of the government bond market, failed, so tapes had to be driven to that organization for several days. Trades were properly posted but clients could not obtain timely reports on their positions. The bank had also established redundant telecommunication facilities in case of problems with one line, but they turned out to be routed through the same physical phone facilities. John Costas, the president and COO of UBS Warburg, explained "We've all learned that when we have backup lines, we should know a lot more about where they run."

As a result, the Bank of New York's customers expecting funds from the Bank of New York didn't receive them on time and had to borrow emergency cash for the Federal Reserve. Yet Thomas A. Renyi, the Bank of New York's chairman, expressed pride in how the bank had responded. He said "Our longstanding disaster recovery plans worked, and they worked in the extreme." It will be months before BONY can return to its computer center at 101 Barclay Street and the bank is working with IBM on locating an interim computer center and on improving its backup systems.

The Nasdaq stock exchange seems to have had more success. It has no trading floor anywhere but instead is a vast distributed network with over 7,000 workstations at about 2,500 sites, all connected to its network through at least 20 points of presence (POPs). The POPs in turn are doubly or triply connected to its main network and data centers in Connecticut and Maryland. Nasdaq's headquarters at 1 Liberty Plaza were heavily damaged. Its operational staff and its press and broadcast functions are housed in its Times Square building. On September 11th (Tuesday), Nasdaq opened as usual, at 8AM but it closed at 9:15AM, and did not open again until the following Monday when the NYSE and other exchanges resumed trading. Nasdaq was well prepared for the disaster with its highly redundant setup. Nasdaq had required many managers to carry two cell phones in case both the telephone and one cell phone did not work and required every employee from the chairman on down to carry a crisis line number card. It had many cameras and monitoring systems so that the company would know what actually happened if a disaster or other crisis should strike. Nasdaq had even purposely established a very close relationship with Worldcom, its telecommunications provider, and it had made sure Worldcom had access to different networks for the purpose of redundancy.

At first Nasdaq established a command center at its Times Square office, but the implosion of the WTC buildings destroyed Nasdaq's telephone switches connected to that office, and so the essential staff members were quickly moved to a nearby hotel. Management immediately addressed the personnel situation, creating an executive locator system in Maryland with everyone's names and telephone numbers and a list of the still missing. Next it evaluated the physical situation—what was destroyed, what ceased to work, where work could proceed—while finding offices for the 127 employees who worked near the WTC. Then it started to evaluate the regulatory and trading industry situations and the conditions of Nasdaq's trading companies. The security staff was placed on high alert to search for attempted penetration of the building or the network.

On Wednesday, September 12, Nasdaq management determined that 30 of the 300 firms it called would not be able to open the next day, 10 of which needed to operate out of backup centers. Management assigned some of its own staff to work with all 30 firms to help solve their problems. The next day it learned that the devastated lower Manhattan telecommunications would not be ready to support Nasdaq opening the following day. It decided to postpone Nasdaq's opening until Monday, September 17. On Saturday and again on Sunday Nasdaq successfully ran industry-wide testing. On Monday, only six days after the attack, Nasdaq opened and successfully processed 2.7 billion shares, by far its largest volume ever.

Nasdaq found its distributed systems worked very well, while its rapid recovery validated the necessity for two network topologies. Moreover, while Nasdaq lost no senior staff, the company had three dispersed management sites, and had it lost one, the company could still operate because of the leadership at its two remaining sites. Nasdaq also realized its extensive crisis management rehearsals for both Y2K and the conversion to decimals had proven vital, verifying the need to schedule more rehearsals regularly. The company even recognized how critical ongoing communications were, and so it formalized regular nationwide company telecommunication forums. It even established automatic triggers for regular communication forums with the Securities and Exchange Commission (SEC).

Sources: Anthony Guerra, "The Buck Stopped Here: BONY's Disaster Recovery Comes Under Attack, " *Wall Street and Technology,* November 2001; Saul Hansell with Riva D. Atlas, "Disruptions Put Bank of New York to the Test," *The New York Times,* October 6, 2001; Tom Field, "How Nasdaq Bounced Back," *CIO Magazine,* November 1, 2001; Dennis K. Berman and Calmetta Coleman, "Companies Test System-Backup Plans as They Struggle to Recover Lost Data," *The Wall Street Journal,* September 13, 2001; Jayson Blair, "A Nation Challenged: The Computers," *The New York Times,* September 20, 2001; Debra Donston, "Disaster Recovery's Core Component: People," *eWeek,* September 13, 2001; Tom Field, "Disaster Recovery: Nasdaq," *CIO,* October 12, 2001; John Foley, "Ready for Anything?" *Information Week,* September 24, 2001; Sharon Gaudin, "Protecting a Net in a Time of Terrorism," *Network World Fusion,* September 24, 2001; Stan Gibson, "Mobilizing IT," *eWeek,* September 17, 2001; Eugene Grygo and Jennifer Jones, "U.S. Recovery: Cost of Rebuilding N.Y. IT Infrastructures Estimated at $3.2 Billion," *InfoWorld,* September 19, 2001; Edward Iwata and Jon Schwartz, "Tech Firms Jump In to Help Companies Mobilize to Rebuild Systems, Reclaim Lost Data," *USA Today,* September 19, 2001; April Jacobs, "Good Planning Kept NAS-DAQ Running During Attacks," *Network World Fusion,* September 24, 2001; Suzanne Kapner, "Wall Street Runs Through London," *The New York Times,* September 27, 2001; Richard Karpinski, "E-Business Aftermath," *InternetWeek,* September 24, 2001; Diane Rezendes Khirallah, "Disaster Takes Toll on Public Network," *Information Week,* September 17, 2001; Daniel Machalaba and Carrick Mollenkamp, "Companies Struggle to Cope with Chaos, Breakdowns and Trauma," *The Wall Street Journal,* September 13, 2001; Paul McDougall and Rick Whiting, "Assessing the Impact (Part One)," *Information Week,* September 17, 2001; Patrick McGeehan, "A Nation Challenged: Wall Street," *The New York Times,* September 21, 2001; Paula Musich, "Rising From the Rubble," *eWeek,* September 24, 2001; Kathleen Ohlson, "Businesses Start the Recovery Process," *Network World Fusion,* September 12, 2001; Julia Scheeres, "Attack Can't Erase Stored Data," *wired.com,* September 21, 2001; Carol Sliwa, "New York Board of Trade Gets Back to Business," *Computerworld,* September 24, 2001; Marc L. Songini, "Supply Chains Face Changes After Attacks," *Computerworld,* October 1, 2001; Bob Tedeschi, "More Web Spending with a Focus," *The New York Times,* October 8, 2001; Dan Verton, "IT Operations Damaged in Pentagon Attack," *Computerworld,* September 24, 2001; Shawn Tully, "Rebuilding Wall Street," *Fortune,* October 1, 2001; and "WTC Technology Replacement Costs Billions," *excite.com,* September 14, 2001.

CASE STUDY QUESTIONS:

1. Summarize the business and technology problems created by the September 11th, 2001 attack on the World Trade Center.

2. How well prepared were companies described in this case for the problems resulting from the WTC disaster?

3. Compare the responses of NASDAQ and the Bank of New York to September 11th. What management, organization, and technology factors affected their disaster recoveries?

4. Were there any security problems that companies had failed to anticipate when the WTC attacks occurred? How well did companies deal with them?

5. Explain some effective actions taken because of creative management responses which were not in company disaster plans.

6. Select a major financial company and write a summary description of its operations. Then develop an outline of a security plan for that company.

Redesigning Business Processes for Healthlite Yogurt Company

Healthlite Yogurt Company, a U.S. market leader in yogurt and related health products, is experiencing sharp growing pains. Healthlite's sales have tripled during the past five years. However, new local competitors, offering fast delivery from local production centers and lower prices, are challenging Healthlite for retail shelf space with a bevy of new products. Healthlite needs to justify its share of shelf space to grocers and is seeking additional shelf space for its new yogurt-based products such as frozen desserts and low-fat salad dressings. Yogurt has a very short shelf life measured in days, and it must be moved very quickly.

Healthlite's corporate headquarters is in Danbury, Connecticut. Corporate has a central mainframe computer that maintains most of the major business databases. All production takes place in processing plants that are located in New Jersey, Massachusetts, Tennessee, Illinois, Colorado, Washington, and California. Each processing plant has its own minicomputer, which is linked to the corporate mainframe. Customer credit verification is maintained at corporate headquarters, where customer master files are maintained and order verification or rejection is determined. Once processed centrally, order data are then fed to the appropriate local processing plant minicomputer.

Healthlite has 20 sales regions, each with approximately 30 sales representatives and a regional sales manager. Healthlite has a 12-person marketing group at corporate headquarters. Each salesperson is able to store and retrieve data for assigned customer accounts using a terminal in the regional office linked to the corporate mainframe. Reports for individual salespeople (printouts of orders, rejection notices, customer account inquiries, etc.) and for sales offices are printed in the regional offices and mailed to them.

Sometimes, the only way to obtain up-to-date sales data is for managers to make telephone calls to subordinates and then piece the information together. Data about sales and advertising expenses, promotional campaigns, and customer shelf space devoted to Healthlite products are maintained manually at the regional offices. The central computer contains only consolidated, company-wide files for customer account data and order and billing data.

The existing order processing system requires sales representatives to write up hard-copy tickets to place orders through the mail or by fax. Each ticket lists the amount and kind of product ordered by the customer account. Approximately 20 workers at

Healthlite corporate headquarters open, sort, and enter 500,000 order tickets per week into the system. Frequently, orders are delayed when the fax machines break down. Order information is transmitted every evening from the mainframe to a minicomputer at each of Healthlite's processing sites. The daily order specifies the total yogurt and yogurt product demand for each processing center. The processing center then produces the amount and type of yogurt and yogurt-related products ordered and ships out the orders. Shipping managers at the processing centers assign the shipments to various transportation carriers, who deliver the products to receiving warehouses located in the regions.

A year ago, growth in new products and sales had reached a point where the firm was choking on paper. For each order, a salesperson filled out at least two forms per account. Some sales representatives have more than 80 customers. As it became bogged down in paper, Healthlite saw increased delays in the processing of its orders. Because yogurt is a fresh food product, it could not be held long in inventory. Yet Healthlite had trouble shipping the right goods to the right places on time. It was taking between 4 and 14 days to process and ship an order, depending on mail delivery rates. Healthlite also found accounting discrepancies of $1.5 million annually between the sales force and headquarters.

Communication between sales managers and sales representatives has been primarily through the mail or by telephone. For example, regional sales managers have to send representatives letters with announcements of promotional campaigns or pricing discounts. Sales representatives have to write up their monthly reports of sales calls and then mail this information to regional headquarters.

Healthlite is considering new information system solutions. First of all, the firm would like to solve the current order entry crisis and develop immediately a new order processing system. Management would also like to make better use of information systems to support sales and marketing activities and to take advantage of new Web-based information technologies. In particular, management wants a sales-oriented Web site to help market the products but is unsure how this will fit into the sales effort. Management wants to know how these new technologies can assist the local groceries and large chains who sell the product to the actual consumer.

Senior management is looking for a modest reduction in employee head count as new, more effective systems come on-line to help pay for the investment in new systems. Although senior management wants the company to deploy contemporary systems, they do not want to experiment with new technologies and are only comfortable using technology that has proven itself in real-world applications.

SALES AND MARKETING INFORMATION SYSTEMS: BACKGROUND

Sales orders must be processed and related to production and inventory. Sales of products in existing markets must be monitored, and new products must be developed for new markets. Firms need sales and marketing information in order to do product planning, make pricing decisions, devise advertising and other promotional campaigns, and forecast market potential for new and existing products. They must also monitor the efficiency of the distribution of their products and services. The sales function of a typical business captures and processes customer orders which are used to produce invoices for customers and data for inventory and production. A typical invoice is illustrated here.

Healthlite Yogurt Inc.

Customer:

Highview Supermarket
223 Highland Avenue
Ossining, New York 10562

Order Number: 679940
Customer Number: #00395
Date: 04/15/02

Quantity	SKU#	Description	Unit Price	Amount
100	V3392	8 oz Vanilla	.44	44.00
50	S4456	8 oz Strawberry	.44	22.00
65	L4492	8 oz Lemon	.44	28.60

Shipping	*10.00*
Total Invoice:	*$104.60*

Data from order entry are used by a firm's accounts receivable system and by the firm's inventory and production systems. The production planning system, for instance, builds its daily production plans based on the prior day's sales. The number and type of product sold determines how many units to produce and when.

Sales managers need information to plan and monitor the performance of the sales force. Management also needs information on the performance of specific products, product lines, or brands. Price, revenue, cost, and growth information can be used for pricing decisions, for evaluating the performance of current products, and for predicting the performance of future products.

From basic sales and invoice data, a firm can produce a variety of reports with valuable information to guide sales and marketing work. For weekly, monthly, or annual time periods, information can be gathered on which retail outlets order the most, on what the average order amount is, on which products move slowest and fastest, on which salespersons sell the most and least, on which geographic areas purchase the most (and least) of a given product, and on how current sales of a product compare to last year's sales.

THE ASSIGNMENT

Either alone, or with a group of three or four of your classmates, develop a proposal for redesigning Healthlite's business processes for sales, marketing, and order processing that would make the company more competitive. Your report should include the following:

- An overview of the organization—its structure, products, and major business processes for sales, marketing, and order processing.

- An analysis of Healthlite's problems: What are Healthlite's problems? How are these problems related to existing business processes and systems? What management, organization, and technology factors contributed to these problems?

- An overall management plan for improving Healthlite's business and system situation. This would include a list of objectives, a time frame, major milestones, and an assessment of the costs and benefits of implementing this plan.

- Identification of the major changes in business processes required to achieve your plan.

- Identification of the major new technology components of your plan that are required to support the new business processes. If your solution requires a new system or set of systems, describe the functions of these systems; what pieces of information these systems should contain; and how this information should be captured, organized, and stored.

- A sample data entry screen or report for one of the new systems, if proposed.

- A description of the steps you would take as a manager to handle the conversion from the old system to the new.

- Quality assurance measures.

Your report should also describe the organizational impact of your solution. Consider human interface issues, the impact on jobs and interest groups, and any risks associated with implementing your solution. How will you implement your solution to take these issues into account?

It is important to establish the scope of the system project. It should be limited to order processing and related sales and marketing business processes. You do not have to redesign Healthlite's manufacturing, accounts receivable, distribution, or inventory control systems for this project.

INTERNATIONAL CASE STUDY

CASE STUDY 1: GINORMOUS LIFE INSURANCE COMPANY

Len Fertuck, University of Toronto (Canada)

Ginormous Life is an insurance company with a long tradition. The company has four divisions that each operate their own computers. The IS group provides analysis, design, and programming services to all of the divisions. The divisions are actuarial, marketing, operations, and investment. All divisions are located at the corporate headquarters building. Marketing also has field offices in 20 cities across the country.

- **The Actuarial Division** is responsible for the design and pricing of new kinds of policies. They use purchased industry data and weekly summaries of data obtained from the Operations Division. They have their own DEC VAX minicomputer, running the Unix operating system, to store data files. They do most of their analysis on PCs and Sun workstations, either on spreadsheets or with a specialized interactive language called APL.

- **The Marketing Division** is responsible for selling policies to new customers and for follow-up of existing customers in case they need changes to their current insurance. All sales orders are sent to the Operations Division for data entry and billing. They use purchased external data for market research and weekly copies of data from operations for follow-ups. They have their own IBM AS/400 minicomputer with dumb terminals for clerks to enter sales data. There are also many PCs used to analyze market data using statistical packages like SAS.

- **The Operations Division** is responsible for processing all mission-critical financial transactions including payroll. They record all new policies, send regular bills to customers, evaluate and pay all claims, and cancel lapsed policies. They have all their data and programs on two IBM ES/9000 mainframes running under the OS/390 operating system. The programs are often large and complex because they must service not only the 15 products currently being sold but also the 75 old kinds of policies that are no longer being sold but still have existing policy holders. Clerks use dumb terminals to enter and update data. Applications written in the last five years have used an SQL relational database to store data, but most programs are still written in COBOL. The average age of the transaction processing programs is about 10 years.

- **The Investment Division** is responsible for investing premiums until they are needed to pay claims. Their data consist primarily of internal portfolio data and research data obtained by direct links to data services. They have a DEC minicomputer to store their data. The internal data are received by a weekly download of cash flows from the Operations Division. External data are obtained as needed. They use PCs to analyze data obtained either from the mini or from commercial data services.

A controlling interest in Ginormous Life has recently been purchased by Financial Behemoth Corp. The management of Financial Behemoth has decided that the firm's efficiency and profitability must be improved. Their first move has been to put Dan D. Mann, a hotshot information systems specialist from Financial Behemoth, in charge of the Information Systems Division. He has been given the objective of modernizing and streamlining the computer facilities without any increase in budget.

In the first week on the job, Dan discovered that only seven junior members of the staff of 200 information systems specialists know anything about CASE tools, End-User Computing, or LANs. They have no experience in implementing PC systems. There is no evidence of any formal decision-support systems or executive information systems in the organization. New applications in the last five years have been implemented in COBOL on DB2, a relational database product purchased from IBM. Over two-thirds of applications are still based on COBOL flat files. One of the benefits of using DB2 is that it is now possible to deliver reports quickly based on ad hoc queries. This is creating a snowballing demand for conversion of more systems to a relational database so that other managers can get similar service.

There have been some problems with the older systems. Maintenance is difficult and costly because almost every change to the data structure of applications in operations requires corresponding changes to applications in the other divisions. There has been a growing demand in other divisions for faster access to operations data. For instance the Investment Division claims that they could make more profitable investments if they had continuous access to the cash position in operations. Marketing complains that they get calls from clients about claims and cannot answer them because they do not have current access to the status of the claim. Management wants current access to a wide variety of data in summary form so they can get a better understanding of the business. The IS group says that it would be difficult to provide access to data in operations because of security considerations. It is difficult to ensure that users do not make unauthorized changes to the COBOL files.

The IS group complains that they cannot deliver all the applications that users want because they are short-staffed. They spend 90 percent of their time maintaining the existing systems. The programmers are mostly old and experienced and employee turnover is unusually low, so there is not likely to be much room for improvement by further training in programming. Employees often remark that the company is a very pleasant and benevolent place to work. At least they did until rumors of deregulation and foreign competition started to sweep the industry.

Dan foresees that there will be an increasing need for computer capacity as more and more applications are converted to on-line transaction processing and more users begin to make ad hoc queries. Dan is also wondering if intranets or the Internet should become part of any new software.

Dan began to look for ways to solve the many problems of the Information Systems Division. He solicited proposals from various vendors and consultants in the computer industry. After a preliminary review of the proposals, Dan was left with three broad options suggested by IBM, Oracle Corp., and Datamotion, a local consulting firm. The proposals are briefly described below.

IBM proposes an integrated solution using IBM hardware and software. The main elements of the proposal are:

▐ **Data and applications will remain on a mainframe.** The IBM ES/9000 series of hardware running their OS/390 operating system will provide mainframe services. Mainframe hardware capacity will have to be approximately doubled by adding two more ES/9000 series machines. The four machines will run under OS/390 with Parallel Sysplex clustering technology that allows for future growth. The Parallel Sysplex system can be scaled by connecting up to 32 servers to work in parallel and be treated as a single system for scheduling and system management. The OS/390 operating system can also run Unix applications.

▐ **AS/400 minicomputers running under the OS/400 operating system** will replace DEC minicomputers.

▐ **RS/6000 workstations running AIX**—a flavor of the Unix operating system—can be used for actuarial computations. All hardware will be interconnected with IBM's proprietary SNA network architecture. PCs will run under the OS/2 operating system and the IBM LAN Server to support both Microsoft Windows applications and locally designed applications that communicate with mainframe databases.

▐ **A DB2 relational database will store all data on-line.** Users will be able to access any data they need through their terminals or through PCs that communicate with the mainframe.

▐ **Legacy systems will be converted using reengineering tools,** like Design Recovery and Maintenance Workbench from Intersolv, Inc. These will have the advantage that they will continue to use the COBOL code that the existing programmers are familiar with. New work will be done using CASE tools with code generators that produce COBOL code.

▐ **Proven technology.** The IBM systems are widely used by many customers and vendors. Many mission-critical application programs are available on the market that address a wide variety of business needs.

Oracle Corp. proposed that all systems be converted to use their Oracle database product and its associated screen and report generators. They said that such a conversion would have the following advantages:

▐ **Over 90 hardware platforms are supported.** This means that the company is no longer bound to stay with a single hardware vendor. Oracle databases and application programs can be easily moved from one manufacturer's machine to another manufacturer's machine by a relatively simple export and import operation as long as applications are created with

Oracle tools. Thus the most economical hardware platform can be used for the application. Oracle will also access data stored in an IBM DB2 database.

▐ **Integrated CASE tools and application generators.** Oracle has its own design and development tools called Designer/2000 and Developer/2000. Applications designed with Designer/2000 can be automatically created for a wide variety of terminals or for the World Wide Web. The same design can be implemented in Windows, on a Macintosh, or on X-Windows in Unix. Applications are created using graphic tools that eliminate the need for a language like COBOL. The designer works entirely with visual prototyping specifications.

▐ **Vertically integrated applications.** Oracle sells a number of common applications, like accounting programs, that can be used as building blocks in developing a complete system. These applications could eliminate the need to redevelop some applications.

▐ **Distributed network support.** A wide variety of common network protocols like SNA, DecNet, Novell, and TCP/IP are supported. Different parts of the database can be distributed to different machines on the network and accessed or updated by any application. All data are stored on-line for instant access. The data can be stored on one machine and the applications can be run on a different machine, including a PC or workstation, to provide a client/server environment. The ability to distribute a database allows a large database on an expensive mainframe to be distributed to a number of cheaper minicomputers.

Datamotion proposed a data warehouse approach using software tools from Information Builders Inc. Existing applications would be linked using EDA, a middleware data warehouse server that acts as a bridge between the existing data files and the users performing enquiries. New applications would be developed using an application tool called Cactus. The advantages of this approach are:

▐ **Data Location Transparency.** EDA Hub Server provides a single connection point from which applications can access multiple data sources anywhere in the enterprise. In addition, users can join data between any supported EDA database—locally, cross-server, or cross-platform. Users can easily access remote data sources for enhanced decision-making capabilities.

▐ **The EDA server can reach most nonrelational databases** and file systems through its SQL translation engine. EDA also supports 3GL, 4GL, static SQL, CICS, IMS/TM, and proprietary database-stored procedure processing.

▐ **Extensive network and operating system support.** EDA supports 14 major network protocols and provides protocol translation between dissimilar networks. EDA also runs on 35 different processing platforms. EDA servers support optimized SQL against any RDBMS. And the EDA server can automatically generate the dialect of SQL optimal for the targeted data source. It is available on Windows 3.x, Windows 95/98, Windows NT, OS/2, MVS, Unix, CICS, VM, OpenVMS, Tandem, and AS/400.

- **Comprehensive Internet Support.** With EDA's Internet services, users can issue requests from a standard Web browser to any EDA-supported data source and receive answer sets formatted as HTML pages.

- **Cactus promotes modern development methods.** Cactus allows the developer to partition an application, keeping presentation logic, business logic, and data access logic separate. This partitioning of functionality can occur across a large number of enterprise platforms to allow greater flexibility in achieving scalability, performance, and maintenance. Cactus provides all the tools needed to deal with every aspect of developing, testing, packaging, and deploying client/server traditional applications or Web-based applications.

Dan is not sure which approach to take for the future of Ginormous Life. Whichever route he follows, the technology will have an enormous impact on the kinds of applications his staff will be able to produce in the future and the way in which they will produce them. While industry trends toward downsizing and distribution of systems may eventually prove to be more efficient, Dan's staff does not have much experience with the new technologies that would be required. He is uncertain about whether there will be a sufficient payoff to justify the organizational turmoil that will result from a major change in direction. Ideally he would like to move quickly to a modern client/server system with minimal disturbance to existing staff and develop-

ment methods, but he fears that both of these are not simultaneously possible.

Source: Reprinted by permission of Len Fertuck, University of Toronto, Canada.

CASE STUDY QUESTIONS

Dan must prepare a strategy for the renewal of the Information Systems Division over the next three years. As his assistant, prepare an outline, in point form, containing the following items:

1. A list of factors or issues that must be considered in selecting a technology platform for the firm.

2. Weights for each factor obtained by dividing up 100 points among the factors in proportion to their importance.

3. A score from 0 to 10 of how each of the three proposals performs on each factor.

4. A grand score for each proposal obtained by summing the product of the proposal score times the factor weight for each proposal.

5. The technology that you would recommend that Dan adopt and the reason for choosing the particular technology that you recommend.

6. The order in which each component of the technology should be introduced and the reason for selecting the order.

INTERNATIONAL CASE STUDY

CASE STUDY 2: FROM ANALYSIS TO EVALUATION—
THE EXAMPLE OF CUPARLA

Gerhard Schwabe, University of Koblenz—Landau (Germany)

Analysis and Design

Just like in other towns, members of the Stuttgart City Council have a large workload: In addition to their primary profession (e.g., as an engineer at Daimler Benz) they devote more than 40 hours a week to local politics. This extra work has to be done under fairly unfavorable conditions. Only council sessions and party meetings take place in the city hall; the deputies of the local council do not have an office in the city hall to prepare or coordinate their work. This means, for example, that they have to read and file all official documents at home. In a city with more than 500,000 inhabitants they receive a very large number of documents. Furthermore, council members feel that they could be better informed by the administration and better use could be made of their time. Therefore Hohenheim University and partners* launched the Cuparla project to improve the information access and collaboration of council members.

A detailed analysis of their work revealed the following characteristics of council work:

▌ Since council members are very mobile, support has to be available to them any time and in any place.

▌ Council members collaborate and behave differently in different contexts: While they act informally and rather openly in the context of their own party, they behave more controlled and formal in official council sessions.

▌ A closer investigation of council work reveals a low degree of process structure. Every council member has the right of initiative and can inform and involve other members and members of the administration in any order.

▌ Council members rarely are power computer users. Computer support for them has to be very straightforward and intuitive to use.

When designing computer support we initially had to decide on the basic orientation of our software. We soon abandoned a workflow model as there are merely a few steps and there is little order in the collaboration of local politicians. Imposing a new structure into this situation would have been too restrictive for the council members. We then turned to pure document-orientation, imposing no structure at all on the council members' work. We created a single large database with all the documents any member of the city council ever needs. However, working with this database turned out to be too complex for the council members. In addition, they need to control the access to certain documents at all stages of the decision-making process. For example, a party may not want to reveal a proposal to other parties before

it has officially been brought up in the city council. Controlling access to each document individually and changing the access control list was not feasible.

Therefore, the working context was chosen as a basis of our design. Each working context of a council member can be symbolized by a "room." A private office corresponds to the council member working at home; there is a party room, where he collaborates with his party colleagues, and a committee room symbolises the place for committee meetings. In addition, there is a room for working groups, a private post office, and a library for filed information. All rooms hence have an electronic equivalent in the Cuparla software. When a council member opens the Cuparla software, he sees all the rooms from the entrance hall (Figure 1).

The council member creates a document in one room (e.g., his private office) and then shares it with other council members in other rooms. If he moves a document into the room of his party, he shares it with his party colleagues; if he hands it on to the administration, he shares it with the mayors, administration officials, and all council members.

The interface of the electronic rooms resembles the setup of the original rooms. Figure 2 shows the example of the room for a parliamentary party. On the left hand side of the screen there are document locations, whereas, on the right hand side, the documents of the selected location are presented. Documents that are currently being worked on are displayed on the "desk." These documents have the connotation that they need to be worked on without an additional outside trigger. If a document is in the files, it belongs to a topic that is still on the political agenda. However, a trigger is necessary to move it off of the shelf. If a topic is not on the political agenda any more, all documents belonging to it are moved to the archive.

The other locations support the collaboration within the party. The conference desk contains all documents for the next (weekly) party meeting. Any council member of the party can put documents there. When a council member prepares for the meeting, he or she merely has to check the conference desk for relevant information. The mailbox for the chairman contains all documents that the chairman needs to decide on. In contrast to his e-mail account all members have access to the mailbox. Double work is avoided as every council member is aware of the chairman's agenda. The mailbox of the assistant contains tasks for the party assistants; the mailbox for the secretary, assignments for the secretary (e.g., a draft for a letter). The inbox contains documents that have been moved from other rooms into this room.

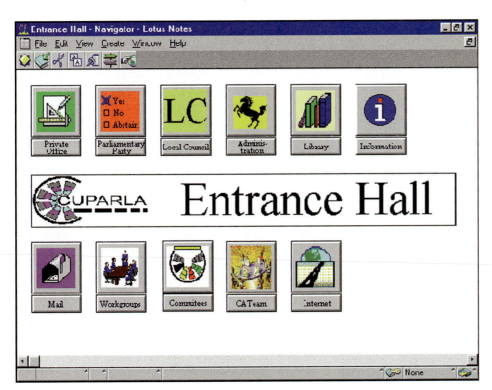

Figure 1   Entrance hall

Thus, in the electronic room all locations correspond to the current manual situation. Council members do not have to relearn their work. Instead, they collaborate in the shared environment they are accustomed to with shared expectations about the other peoples' behaviour. Feedback from the pilot users indicates that this approach is appropriate.

Some specific design features make the software easy to use. The software on purpose does not have a fancy three-dimensional interface that has the same look as a real room. Buttons (in the entrance hall) and lists (in the rooms) are much easier to use and do not distract the user from the essential parts. Each location (e.g., the desk) has a little arrow. If a user clicks on this arrow, a document is moved to the location. This operation is much easier for a beginner than proceeding by "drag and drop."

Furthermore, software design is not restricted to building an electronic equivalent of a manual situation. If one wants to truly

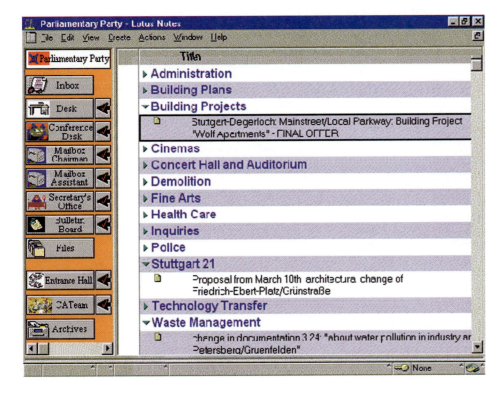

Figure 2   Parliamentary party room

benefit from the opportunities of electronic collaboration support systems, one has to include new tools that are not possible in the manual setting. For example, additional cross-location and room search features are needed to make it easy for the council member to retrieve information. The challenge of interface design is to give the user a starting point that is close to the situation he is used to. A next step is to provide the user with options to improve and adjust his working behavior to the opportunities offered by the use of a computer.

Organizational Implementation

Building the appropriate software is only one success factor for a groupware project. Organizational implementation typically is at least as difficult. Groupware often has a free rider problem: All want to gain the benefit and nobody wants to do the work. Furthermore, many features are only beneficial if all participate actively. For example, if a significant part of a council faction insists on using paper documents for their work, providing and sharing electronic documents actually means additional work for the others. This can easily lead to the situation that groupware usage never really gets started. To "bootstrap" usage we started with the (socially) simple activities and ended with the (socially) complex activities (Figure 3).

In the first step we provided the basic council information in digital form. The city council has the power to demand this initial organizational learning process from the administration. Once there is sufficient information the individual council member can already benefit from the system without relying on the usage of his fellow councillors. The usage conventions are therefore socially simple. As better information is a competitive advantage for a council member, there was an incentive for the individual effort required to learn the system. Communication support (e-mail, fax) is a more complex process, because its success depends on reliable usage patterns by all communication partners. The usage patterns are straightforward and easy to learn. We therefore implemented them in a second phase. Coordination activities (sharing to-do lists, sharing calendars) and cooperation activities (sharing documents and room locations, electronic meetings) depend on the observance of socially complex usage conventions by all group members. For example, the council member had to learn that her activities had effects on the documents and containers of all others and that "surprises" typically resulted from ill-coordinated activities of several group members. The council has to go through an intensive organizational learning process to benefit from the features. For example, the party's business processes had to be reorganized.

We offered collaboration and coordination support in the same phase to the council members. Their appropriation depended on the party's culture: A hierarchically organized party preferred to use the coordination features and requested to turn off many collaborative features. In another party most councillors had equal rights. This party preferred the collaborative features.

Economic Benefits

The ultimate success of any IS project is not only determined by the quality of the developed technology but also by its economic benefits. Thus, the economic benefit of Cuparla was evaluated in the first quarter of 1998 after about four months of use by the whole city council (pilot users had been using the system for more than a year). Evaluating the economic benefits of innovative software is notoriously difficult. Reasons for that include

1. It is difficult to attribute costs to a single project. For example, the city of Stuttgart had to wire part of their city hall for Cuparla—is this a cost of the project? And how about the servers bought for Cuparla and co-used for other purposes? And the cost for the information that was collected for the city council and is now being used in the administration's intranet?

2. Many benefits cannot be quantified in monetary terms. For instance, how much is it worth if the council members make better informed decisions? Or, how much is it worth if council membership becomes more attractive?

3. What is the appropriate level of aggregation for economic benefits? Should it be the cost and benefit for the individual council member? Or the parties? Or the whole city council? Or even the whole city of Stuttgart? Or should the improved processes be measured?

The evaluation of Cuparla was therefore not based on purely monetary terms; rather evaluation results were aggregated on five sets of criteria (cost, time, quality, flexibility, and human situation) and four levels of aggregation (individual, group, process, organization) resulting in a 4×5 matrix (Figure 4).

The trick is to attribute the effects only to the lowest possible level, e.g., if one can attribute the cost of an individual PC to an individual council member, it counts only there and not on the group level. On the other hand, a server probably can only be attributed to the group of all council members and so on. We will now briefly go through the major effects:

Costs: Both on the individual and the group level costs have gone up significantly (notebooks, ISDN, printer, server, etc.).

Figure 3   Steps of groupware implementation

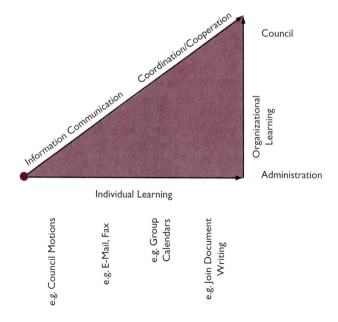

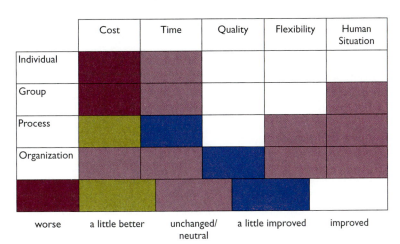

Figure 4 Aggregated evaluation of Cuparla (March 1998)

There is a potential for cost savings if the council members forgo the delivery of paper copies of the documents. There have been some additional costs on the process level, but not as much as on the two levels below. There may have been direct cost savings by the provision of electronic documents in the council-related business processes, but we were not able to identify them. As the administration was reluctant to really reorganize its internal business processes, many potential cost savings could not be realized. As all costs could be attributed to the levels business process, group or individual, we noted a cost neutrality for the level "organization" (the costs for provisionally wiring the city hall were negligible).

Time: During the pilot phase, the system did not save time for the councillors; to the contrary, the individual councillors had to work longer in order to learn how to use the Cuparla system. However, the councillors also indicated that they used their time more productively, i.e., the overtime was well invested. Thus, we decided to summarize the effects on the individual level as "neutral." Cuparla had also not yet led to faster or more efficient decisions in the council or its subgroups. Therefore the effects are graded "unchanged." The council members see potential here, but the speed of decisions is not only a matter of work efficiency but also has a political dimension and politics does not change that fast. Some business processes were rated as being faster, particularly the processes at the interface between council and administration (e.g., the process of writing the meeting minutes). There was no effect on the organization as a whole; i.e., the city of Stuttgart was not faster at reacting to external challenges and opportunities.

Quality: The council members reported a remarkable improvement of quality of their work. The council members feel that the quality of their decisions has been improved by the much better access to information. The work of the parties has benefited from the e-mail and the collaboration features of Cuparla as well as the computer support of strategic party meetings. As the interface between different subprocesses of council work has fewer media changes and the (partially erroneous) duplication of information has been reduced, the council members and members of the administration also reported an improved quality of their business processes. The

creation of an organization-wide database of council-related information even contributed to a somewhat better work in the whole administration.

Flexibility: Improved individual flexibility was the most important benefit of Cuparla. This holds true for spatial, temporal, and interpersonal flexibility. People can work and access other people any place and any time they want. On the group level Cuparla has enhanced the flexibility within parties as it has become easier to coordinate the actions of the council members. There have not been any significant changes to the flexibility on the process or organizational levels.

Human situation: Cuparla has made council membership more attractive because it has become easier to reconcile one's primary job, council work, and private life. Furthermore Cuparla is regarded as an opportunity for the council member's individual development. There were no significant changes to the human situation on the group, process, or organizational levels.

As mentioned above, these effects were measured after a relatively short period of usage. By the time of writing this case study, (January 2000), Cuparla had become an indispensable part of council work. When the system was down for a week in the beginning of 2000 because of router problems, the council members were so annoyed that the local newspaper reported their unanimous complaint in a committee meeting.

Additional English Literature

Schwabe, G., and Krcmar, H. "Digital Material in a Political Work Context—The Case of Cuparla." Appears in the *Proceedings of the European Conference on Information Systems,* ECIS 2000 in Vienna.

Schwabe, G., and Krcmar, H. "Piloting a Sociotechnical Innovation." Appears in the *Proceedings of the European Conference on Information Systems,* ECIS 2000 in Vienna.

Schwabe, G. "Understanding and Supporting Knowledge Management and Organizational Memory in a City Council." In Hawaii International Conference on System Sciences 1999 (HICSS99), CD-ROM, 12 pages.

Schwabe, G., and Krcmar, H. "Electronic Meeting Support for Councils." Appears in *Journal of AI and Society,* 1999.

CASE STUDY QUESTIONS

1. Analyze the management, organization, and technology issues that had to be addressed by the Cuparla project.

2. Analyze the interface and design of the Cuparla system. What problems does it solve? What organizational processes does it support? How effective is it?

3. How successful was the Cuparla project? Describe the implementation issues, costs, and benefits.

Source: From "Analysis to Interface Design—The Example of Cuparla," by Gerhard Schwabe, Stephen Wilczek, and Helmut Krcmar. Reprinted by permission.

*The project partners were Hohenheim University (Coordinator), Datenzentrale Baden-Württemberg and GroupVision Software-systeme GmbH. The project was funded as part of its R&D program by DeTeBerkom GmbH, a 100% subsidiary of German Telekom.

INTERNATIONAL CASE STUDY

CASE STUDY 3: SKANDIABANKEN: DEVELOPING INFORMATION CAPABILITIES FOR AN EFFECTIVE E-BUSINESS STRATEGY (ABRIDGED)

Professor Donald A. Marchand and Katarina Paddack, International Institute for Management Development, Lausanne, Switzerland

SkandiaBanken is better than other banks in every subcategory. Its Internet service is simpler to use and easier to understand, its interest rates are better, its fees are lower, and its offering of services is immense. For people who have the opportunity to use the Internet as a tool for handling their banking business, SkandiaBanken is unbeatable.

Jury, Best Bank of the Year, *Privata Affärer* (2000)

In December 2000, SkandiaBanken heard that it had been awarded Best Bank of the Year for the third year in a row by Sweden's personal finance magazine, *Privata Affärer*. SkandiaBanken was the only bank to have been awarded the honor more than once in the competition's 10-year history. Earlier in the year, *Internetworld* magazine had also chosen SkandiaBanken as Sweden's best Internet bank, and its Norwegian operations, which had begun in April, had been recognized as Norway's Best Bank of the Year by the Norwegian computer association.

Surprised and honored that SkandiaBanken—a "niche" bank—had beaten all major competitors in both customer service satisfaction and value, CEO Göran Lenkel and CIO Kent Nilsson pondered whether the next several years would prove equally rewarding. Defying competitors' predictions that a pure direct bank could not be profitable, SkandiaBanken had been successful from the start. However, large banking competitors and other new entrants with deep pockets had begun to catch up, with improvements to their own Internet services. In addition, the opening of the European market would allow companies with similar banking models to compete on interest rates and fees—areas in which SkandiaBanken had been the most competitive in the Swedish and Norwegian markets. Which of their company's business capabilities would ensure future e-business success?

SkandiaBanken Overview

SkandiaBanken, Sweden's first "branchless" bank, was created in October 1994, marking the first successful entry of a "nonbank" into the Swedish banking market. Relying solely on Internet and telephone channels, SkandiaBanken had grown to become Sweden's fifth largest bank in personal banking by 2000 and its fourth largest bank in terms of Internet customers.[1] By the end of 2000, eight months after beginning its Norway operations, SkandiaBanken had also captured 6% of the Norwegian Internet banking market, surpassing expectations.

A business unit of the Skandia Group, Sweden's largest and best known insurance company, SkandiaBanken offered products and services targeted primarily at the personal banking market (*see* Figure 1). These services supplemented Skandia's existing long-term savings, asset management, and P&C insurance products. SkandiaBanken would eventually serve as an alternative distribution channel for all Skandia insurance products.

SkandiaBanken's 380 employees served over 400,000 customers from its two offices in Stockholm, Sweden and Bergen, Norway. From 1995 to 2000, SkandiaBanken averaged yearly increases of 26% in new customers and anticipated a customer base of 500,000 in 2001.[2] During the same period, deposits had risen from SKr 4.3 to SKr 15.2 billion[3] (five-year annual average growth rate of 30%), while lending had risen from SKr 3.7 to SKr 15.3 billion (five-year annual average growth rate of 37%). Since 1995, in spite of competitors' predictions, SkandiaBanken had boasted six profitable years, with operating income at SKr 63 million for 2000 (*refer to* Exhibit 1), becoming one of the few profitable niche banks in Europe. By 2000, SkandiaBanken averaged 1.8 million visits per month to its website (www.skandiabanken.se).

SkandiaBanken's e-Business Strategy

SkandiaBanken's e-business model was based on three principles to guide value creation for the customer and the company: truthfulness, simplicity, and high interest.

Truthfulness

Truthfulness guided all interactions with customers and with employees. To build its reputation as the "truthful bank," SkandiaBanken set up a transparent and straightforward service fee schedule. Account interest was capitalized every month—in contrast to traditional banking accounts that calculated annual interest based on average and minimum totals.

In 1999, following increasingly high ATM costs, Lenkel sent customers a letter that drew media criticism. He asked customers to help SkandiaBanken keep its costs down by increasing the average ATM withdrawal amount and decreasing the frequency of withdrawals. Despite the negative press, SkandiaBanken was able to avoid charging ATM fees by telling its customers the truth and soliciting their involvement.

Figure 1
SkandiaBanken
Products

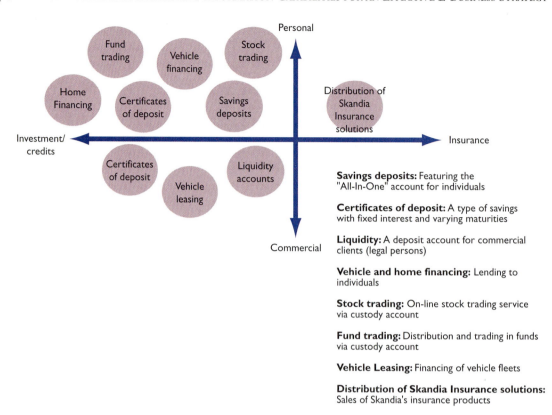

Savings deposits: Featuring the "All-In-One" account for individuals

Certificates of deposit: A type of savings with fixed interest and varying maturities

Liquidity: A deposit account for commercial clients (legal persons)

Vehicle and home financing: Lending to individuals

Stock trading: On-line stock trading service via custody account

Fund trading: Distribution and trading in funds via custody account

Vehicle Leasing: Financing of vehicle fleets

Distribution of Skandia Insurance solutions: Sales of Skandia's insurance products

Simplicity

Simplicity ruled all aspects of the e-business model: customer relationships, products and services, business processes, development of IT solutions, and organizational structure.

Striving for simplicity, SkandiaBanken offered an "All-in-One" (Allt I Ett) account: savings deposits could easily be moved between funds, stock trading, and certificates of deposits. Bills could automatically be paid from the account, and salary deposited directly into the account. For the first time in Sweden's banking system, money could be easily transferred between SkandiaBanken accounts and accounts in other banks. Customers could also benefit from auto, home mortgage, or Skandia insurance products and pay for them directly from their account. By 2000, all account fees had been dropped, making SkandiaBanken the most competitive personal banking service in the market.[4]

High Interest Rates

SkandiaBanken offered the most competitive interest rates in the market, initially averaging 2% to 3% more than competitors' rates. To support higher-than-market interest rates, SkandiaBanken needed to cover account deposit rates in two ways. First, customers were encouraged to channel savings deposits into revenue-creating areas such as multi-investment funds and equities.

Second, SkandiaBanken focused on increasing the bank's high-interest, long-term lending avenues such as home mortgages and high-margin car financing businesses.[5] To manage deposits and lending levels, SkandiaBanken had to carefully manage three business areas that did not always share the same customer base. For example, personal banking services (including fund management and stock trading) and home

mortgages were marketed both to Skandia customers and the general public, whereas auto financing worked through 500 auto dealers and included Skandia insurance products in its financing packages.

Behind the Scenes: Developing Capabilities for E-Business Success

To manage this direct model, first as a telephone bank and then as an Internet bank with telephone support, SkandiaBanken's senior managers had developed a management philosophy to guide the development of the business capabilities needed to be successful.

Nilsson described:

> We wanted to create the bank of the future—an organization that could easily change with new market trends and that would be totally responsive to customer needs. We tried to create a view of outside, looking in—from the customer's perspective.

The first part of this philosophy involved developing a company culture that supported personal responsibility and action. Lenkel explained:

> Our people are the bank. The way that we compete with information is not just through IT—we focus heavily on our people and their behaviors. We want our employees to have an intimate experience with our customers and establish relationships with them.

Nilsson added:

> This means that our employees do not just learn *about* customers, but need to listen and learn *from* customers.

Figure 2   The Customer Viewpoint

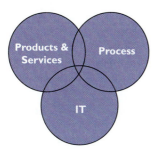

The second part of this philosophy involved getting both business and IT people to adopt a "customer viewpoint" of the organization. Nilsson explained:

> I use what people at SkandiaBanken now call the "mickey mouse" diagram, which to me represents the customer viewpoint, to get people to think more holistically about our business [see Figure 2]. A customer does not just "see" the products and services being offered to him, but also evaluates us on the processes, or routines, we set up to deliver these products. The customer might not evaluate us directly on the IT that we have, but it is a necessary part of the entire model because it allows us to create the customer experience.

> In the past, these three areas were separate, with people thinking only about their own area. For example, IT people would only worry about IT systems and databases, without understanding either the business processes or customer needs. Product development people would only think about what new products to develop, with no thought to delivery processes or knowledge of IT. One of the biggest problems we had was getting our well-educated, super-technical people to understand the other two circles.

> I believe this is the e-business problem. People only talk about IT, without thinking of the concept more holistically in all three circles. People are looking for a technical solution. But it is not a technical solution, it is a philosophical solution, a way of business thinking. IT is not "alive"—it is not thinking, setting the rules, responding to customer needs. People are the ones who create value in the company and think of new ways to use the technology to better the customer experience.

"Our Bank is Our People": Developing Information Behaviors and Values

Towards a Bias for Action: Information Proactiveness
Lenkel noted:

> Motivating our employees to take responsibility and act on the information provided to them and gathered from our customers is a key factor in managing this type of operation. Every time a customer calls or writes an e-mail, he or she is in direct contact with one of our employees. We have a very small call center and back office support so it is imperative that each employee knows how to get a solution for the customer.

Catrina Ingelstam, manager of Stock Brokering Services, commented:

> Göran makes it clear that he wants us to act rather than stand on the sidelines. We are expected to take the initiative and are expected to inform ourselves about things that we need to know.

To emphasize the importance of individual initiative and responsibility, Lenkel refused to publish or talk about an organizational chart or formal reporting hierarchy. Nilsson explained:

> When you talk about organization, people tend to get complacent and think that things can't be done in a different way. We wanted to maintain an atmosphere of creativity and action.

To stress the importance of prompt action, Lenkel discouraged formal management meetings to ensure that problems were dealt with immediately. He also instituted an open door policy, rather than an appointment-setting culture. Anyone needing to speak with him was encouraged to stop by his office at any time, and he encouraged this behavior with all members of the organization.

Developing Mature Information Behaviors to Support a Proactive Culture
Despite the informal working environment, the way information was distributed in the company was extremely formal to make sure that the information people needed to make decisions and solve customer problems was accessible, easy to understand, and complete. Lenkel noted:

> We are a direct bank with very few employees. We need to make sure that people understand that it is critical that all information be made available for everyone to use.

To discourage information hoarding, Lenkel insisted that people get rid of paper sitting on their desks and enter it into the system. One employee commented:

> I can find almost any type of information I need on our information system. The information is updated weekly and each unit takes responsibility for updating the information pertaining to its area. There are no written instructions about this; people just do it.

Several years later, Lenkel pushed this concept further by removing all bookcases from management offices.

Transparency was also encouraged by sharing performance information and goals throughout the organization. In addition to articulating a clear, simple business model, precise organizational, team, and personal goals were set and shared throughout the company. Organizational targets were publicized: for increases in fund distribution and worth, number of new customers, movement of customers, to the Internet, stock broking customers, fund customers and revenues. Within each business unit, additional goals were set relating to income targets, customer satisfaction, and quality. "We have no set budgets, but rely on constantly updated working plans," described one employee. Lenkel expanded on this:

> We are very transparent with setting goals for the group. Everyone knows who is doing what. Everyone knows his or her targets and calculations for revenues and costs. Employees understand this connection."

In the call center, a computer-based monitoring system tracked—in real time—service levels, average call times, down times, and customer response rates for both individuals and teams. Customer Service director Anna-Karin Laurell described:

> Anyone can check how he or she is doing at any time. We try and use the system as a tool for setting and attaining goals, rather than as a watch-dog system.

In addition, innovation and action were reinforced by a management team that expected mistakes to happen. Nilsson explained:

> We have a saying in our IT group: "Success depends on making a carefully planned series of small mistakes in order to avoid making unplanned large ones." We have one person who is in charge of keeping track of the mistakes and passing on good problem solving solutions to the rest of the group. We can't be afraid to change the path if we see that we are going the wrong way. We want to encourage people not to be afraid of making mistakes and to try to do things in different ways.

In the words of one employee:

> I think we are different from many other companies because Göran really trusts us and lets us make mistakes.

In the call center, customer representatives were hired based on their energy and their ability to listen and make quick decisions. Employees were not given telephone scripts, but were encouraged to develop their own style to deal with customers. During the first four years of operation, customer representatives were divided into teams, each with a team leader. By 2000, Lenkel had pushed the model further by eliminating all team "managers," moving to a totally self-monitoring call center system. At this time, too, service levels were among the highest in the on-line banking industry, with an average call pick-up of nine seconds and e-mail response rates of five minutes.[6]

"Knowing the Customer": Developing Information Management Practices

Sensing Customer Needs

Lenkel insisted on having no secretaries in the organization to ensure that information did not get filtered through a middle person:

> Our ultimate goal is to succeed in listening to our customers, and to change based on what they tell us that they want. Customer needs change constantly. If we do not know what they are thinking, what they expect from us, we will fail as a company.

Knowing the customer also meant developing simple processes to collect customer complaints and sense customer needs:

> We receive 5,000 e-mails a month with customer suggestions. And we take these suggestions very seriously. We like to think of our customers as employees that are developing the future of our bank. Unless we know them, we cannot respond to their needs.

Regular customer surveys also helped to monitor changes in customer needs and expectations. SkandiaBanken managers stressed customer sensitivity through a policy on new products

or IT services: No new product or service would be introduced to customers unless they first requested it, even if the system had already been developed. Nilsson observed:

> What does this policy do? It forces our employees to constantly listen to the customer, rather than telling the customer what we think he wants or needs.

Collecting, Organizing, and Maintaining Customer Information

Responding to customers also required information to be organized in a simple, straightforward format—information not only had to be easy to access but also carefully and deliberately chosen so as not to overload the customer. Nilsson commented:

> Keeping it simple—especially in terms of providing information—is not an easy task. This is especially crucial for our business model that intends to provide customers with the information they need for self-service.

Lenkel explained:

> The key to our business is not to provide all the information, but the relevant information. You can get too much information. Part of our challenge is to decide which information to provide to the customer that makes sense to him or her. For example, based on our knowledge and expertise, we have chosen the best 80 to 90 mutual funds—out of the 1,400 available in Sweden—to offer our customers. Similarly, we filter information about equities and all other information on our website.

One litmus test of the information provided to customers occurred in the call center:

> If our customer representatives cannot easily explain our services and find the information they need, there is no way the customers are going to be able to do so on their own. We spend an enormous amount of time thinking about how to provide the information customers ask for in a logical, convenient and straightforward way. This not only involves filtering information but also thinking through the entire information process and getting it down to as simple a form as possible.

To maintain the customer viewpoint of the information process and test its convenience, relevance, and quality, customer representatives in the call center worked from the same web interface seen and used by the customer. Nilsson noted:

> I get at least one call a day from IT vendors telling me they have the CRM (customer relationship management) solution. They believe the machine, the technology, constitutes a customer relationship system. I think it is instead about the process and the people. The computer or IT system doesn't do anything. It is the people and the information processes set up to provide the information that drive the real customer relationship.

Developing Mature Information Management Practices

When designing a new product, adding information to the website or developing a new information system, SkandiaBanken managers always approached the issue in the same way: first and foremost from the customer's point of view. Nilsson explained:

> Whenever the business comes up with a new product or service suggestion, we have a detailed discussion about the mickey mouse diagram. We get together a cross-functional group of people who will be involved—business managers, IT developers and product managers. Then we always start the conversation about the customer: What information does the customer need to have or what is the decision the customer needs to make?

> Once this is clarified we move on to the specific process questions. Why do we want to add this information service? Is it based on just a "feeling" or are there facts and a business case? What are the business decision needs?

> Then we start to outline the process. Where does the information come from? What are we going to do with the information? Who needs to have access to this information—within the business unit and across the entire company? Who is going to maintain the information? What information do other departments add to the process? What format will provide the most convenient access and use?

> Next, we constantly think about the information process and how to simplify it. We want to keep the information process simple, eliminating as many sub-processes and instructions as possible to satisfy the largest number of customers.

> The last step is determining the appropriate technology application for the specific process. By the time the IT people get their hands on the project, we have already clarified customer needs, business unit needs and clearly defined a simple information process. The one thing I have learned is that if the process is not good, forget about doing IT.

Using Information Capabilities to Save on Resources and Enhance the Customer Experience

In 1998, SkandiaBanken supported four separate call centers: for savings accounts, car leasing accounts, mortgage accounts, and equities advice. By 2000, the business units had succeeded in transferring specific knowledge and information into one call center, despite the differences in business needs and expertise.[7] On-line applications and automatic approval tools for home mortgage and auto financing requests also helped to improve decisions and reduce risk in these lending areas, allowing less technical customer representatives to handle other customer issues.

A well-managed customer database also allowed SkandiaBanken to know its customers from a transaction and data point of view. Lenkel observed:

> We know from being able to link with the national database that holds salary information that we have attracted the top 10% to 15% of preferred banking customers in the country. From this information and from customer profiles, we are able to offer "preferred" customers some service advantages that make their customer experience the best it could be. For example, a telephone call from a preferred customer will bump his or her call ahead of the waiting queue to a customer representative without his or her knowing the reason.

Information about website use is also tracked and analyzed to determine the optimal way to present and organize information. Some of the most important information we get from this analysis is not what information the customer is using, but what the customer is *not* using.

Developing IT Practices

Three principles guided development of SkandiaBanken's IT systems: low cost, practicality and simplicity, and the outsourcing of non-value-adding systems.

▌ Low cost: "What does the customer want to pay for?"

One of the first principles that guided IT investment at SkandiaBanken was what the customer was willing to pay for. Nilsson explained:

> At what point will the customer be willing to pay more for the service provided by a new system? It is sometimes hard to keep enthusiastic IT developers and managers focused on this issue—they are constantly coming up with great new ideas. However, we have to always keep coming back to the question: What is the gain for the customer and at what cost?

▌ Practicality and simplicity: "Do what works"

SkandiaBanken's management team also insisted on simplicity and practicality in developing IT systems. Nilsson described:

> I am not an engineer or computer technician. My role in this was to help come up with the ideas behind the actual IT tools. A company needs to have insight into what you want to provide to the customer, independent from the technical details.

First, projects were kept small, simple, and practical. Second, "group think" excluding technical people was often used to encourage creativity, especially during the first several years of operation. Nilsson explained:

> It is *difficult* to create easy, small solutions—it is much easier to complicate things. It is the people who use the system that are the real developers. They may not know exactly how the technology works, but they know what they want to be able to do with it.

▌ Adding value: "Outsource the rest"

The last guiding principle for IT development was developing and managing value-added systems while outsourcing the rest. As a result, SkandiaBanken had only a small IT group—25 IT employees in 2000.

Building a Solid IT Operational and Process Foundation

One of the first challenges SkandiaBanken faced was to create an IT infrastructure that would be able to "talk" with any system and provide a total integrated solution. Nilsson noted:

> We were not concerned about owning all the databases we would need to run a low-cost operation, but instead about how to create an integrated interface with the customer and the business.

Customer Channels

(one PIN number)

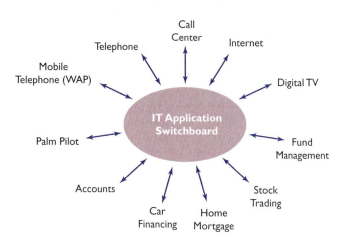

Business Interfaces

Figure 3   Customer and Business Integration

The outcome was the development of an IT application "switchboard" that allowed SkandiaBanken not only to link all of its databases and systems into one integrated structure but also to add new databases or remove old ones quickly and easily.

Integration of business operations at SkandiaBanken provided a unified customer interface, regardless of channel, that could be supported by a single pin number and provide information in a consistent manner (*see* Figure 3).

Pär Lundkvist, IT manager, described:

> When we were deciding how to create the bank from a technical standpoint, we knew we wanted it to be independent of the device or channel the customer was using. Today, we can easily integrate and operationalize a new customer channel—such as WAP or digital TV—within a day or two. As soon as the customer asks for it, we can have it up and running. The same applies to business systems. The new car finance system in Norway took us only four weeks to get up and running.

By 2000, in addition to its reputation for responsiveness, SkandiaBanken had built a reputation for system quality. That year, Microsoft wrote a case study on the reliability of SkandiaBanken's Internet site that it used in its European operations. Lundkvist noted:

> Customers need to be sure that our systems are up and running 24/7. We are working very hard on the quality of our systems and on maintaining quality service.

Business integration on the operational level also had several outcomes. In a joint venture with Ericsson and IBM, SkandiaBanken became the first bank in Europe to develop an application link for telephone-activated pop-up screens in the call center, greatly improving customer service. A call center monitoring system helped to reduce down time, increase efficiency, and raise service levels to among the highest in the banking industry. Separating back office and administrative functions

from call center activities freed customer representatives to provide better customer service. In 2000, excellence in operational systems allowed SkandiaBanken to integrate its four call centers into one, despite different customers among business units.

Developing the IT application switchboard allowed SkandiaBanken to interface directly with the existing banking industry infrastructure, eliminating the need for banking middlemen and reducing cost though streamlined information processes (*see* Figure 4).

SkandiaBanken's ability to link directly into these databases gave customers a number of service options, provided free of charge by the bank: electronic or manual bill payments either through SkandiaBanken or the national bill payment system (Post Giro); Visa card payments; foreign bill payments; and electronic transfers between accounts within SkandiaBanken or with another bank.

Developing IT Maturity: Support for Innovation and Management Decision Making

In 2001, two innovations would also have both business and customer benefits: on-line credit application and approval within 15 seconds for home mortgages and 4 seconds for car loans.

In the car financing business unit, IT innovation created an auto dealer portal, to be launched in late 2001. To move dealers to the Internet, SkandiaBanken began an education program—teaching them how to use the Internet and access SkandiaBanken's website—and often also installed software for them.

The portal, personalized for each of its 500 dealers, provided information that would help dealers perform their jobs better. Portal services and tools included: on-line credit application, on-line insurance application (Skandia), dealer news, interest rate information, on-line car registration, tax calculator and e-learning (financing training site for new dealer employees). The portal also provided access to three types of customized dealer information:

▌ **Sales statistics:** personalized sales statistics for each car dealer (e.g., six months sales report).

▌ **Customer reports:** personalized customer reports for follow-up business. Roger Alm, manager of Car Financing, explained:

> We provide our dealers with sales tips. For example, if we know that someone has only six months left on a car loan that was purchased three years earlier, we can provide the dealer with information on the customer and the car. The dealer then calls the customer, tells him that he has a huge demand for that type of used car and asks if the customer would like to come in and see any of his new models? We are trying to provide tools that make the dealer's life a little easier.

▌ **Auto Auction:** gave dealers the opportunity to bid for SkandiaBanken cars for sale as a result of defaulted loans. Eventually, the site would allow dealers to buy and sell vehicles from each other.

Business analytics systems such as click-through tracking allowed SkandiaBanken to track customer use of information on the web, enabling it to test new information and decide which information to remove from the website and which was most useful to customers. In 2001, SkandiaBanken would give customers the ability to personalize their interface. It employed

Figure 4 SkandiaBanken Banking Infrastructure and System Linkages

some customer data mining techniques and planned to tap this information source in the future.

Finally, excellence in IT would allow savings and lending levels across all business units to be easily monitored to maintain the needed balance in savings and lending products to remain profitable and reduce risk. Lenkel warned:

> We have to be careful not to grow too quickly in savings accounts without comparable growth levels in the higher interest lending products to offset the higher than market interest rates on savings accounts. Our business is all about balance and managed growth.

Regional Expansion: Creating a Nordic Bank

In April 2000, SkandiaBanken began its first cross-border expansion into neighboring Norway. Mimicking its development in Sweden, SkandiaBanken took over the house and car financing operations of the Norwegian insurer Vesta, which had been purchased by the Skandia Group. The new business unit in Bergen, Norway was a copy of SkandiaBanken's Swedish operations, supporting a call center and business staff. By year-end 2000 SkandiaBanken Norge had attracted 65,000 customers, surpassing expectations, and jumped to be the leading online bank in Norway with a 6% market share. SkandiaBanken hoped to attain 135,000 customers by year-end 2001.

SkandiaBanken also planned to expand services into Denmark in 2001 with the acquisition of Din Bank, a pure-play Internet and telephone bank with products and services similar to those of SkandiaBanken. Din Bank, the leading niche bank in Denmark, had approximately 30,000 customers, deposits of DKr 1.7 billion[8], lending of DKr 0.6 billion and shareholders' equity of DKr 171 million.

SkandiaBanken's Competitive Advantage

Despite SkandiaBanken's current success and Nordic expansion plans, Lenkel and Nilsson were aware that it would face even greater competition in the future as traditional European banks grew better at offering Internet service and as other niche banks entered the Nordic market.

Nilsson commented:

> Even though our business model is based on e-business, our competitive advantage does not lie in the technology. Technology is extremely easy to copy. It is our philosophy, the way that we think, how we listen to customers to find out their needs and our willingness to respond quickly to the information provided by the customer that make us different from our competitors.

Lenkel added:

> Our competitive advantage? We may not have as many customers as the big four competitors in Sweden but we definitely know our customers better than they know theirs. Our competitors have a lot of baggage and legacies in terms of culture, structure, IT and the way they have traditionally worked. It is very difficult to change that type of organization.

Nilsson explained:

> We really do not think of ourselves as a "bank." The way that we need to define ourselves is based on the financial services customers want and what we can deliver. Who knows where our customers will lead us? We can't predict what will happen in the next five years. But we need to be ready and willing to respond as best we can to the changes the future will bring.

EXHIBIT 1   SKANDIABANKEN BALANCE SHEET

(SKr million)	2000	1999	1998	1997	1996	1995
Interest income	1,065	857	787	654	619	501
Interest expense	(617)	(504)	(485)	(395)	(370)	(283)
Commissions (net)	150	96	128	143	97	73
Net result of financial transactions	1	0	(1)	(6)	20	2
Other operating income	49	12	12	2	7	58
Operating income total	**648**	**461**	**441**	**398**	**373**	**351**
Administrative overheads	(547)	(357)	(319)	(255)	(241)	(226)
Other operating expenses	(33)	(24)	(34)	(29)	(42)	(41)
Depreciation and write-downs of tangible fixed assets	(18)	(13)	(9)	(9)	—	—
Total expenses	**(598)[9]**	**(394)[10]**	**(362)[11]**	**(293)**	**(283)**	**(267)**
Credit loss, net	**13**	**(4)**	**(3)**	**(1)**	**(4)**	**1**
Operating income	**63**	**63**	**75**	**104**	**86**	**85**

Source: Company information

Lenkel laughed:

We are definitely a small fish in a big sea with many larger fish. But we know what our customers want, and we are determined to give it to them. That is our competitive advantage.

CASE STUDY QUESTIONS

1. Analyze SkandiaBanken using the competitive forces and value chain models.

2. What is SkandiaBanken's business model and business strategy? How do information systems support this strategy?

3. Describe the relationship between SkandiaBanken's systems and its management, organizational structure, and culture.

4. Is SkandiaBanken's competitive advantage sustainable? Explain your answer.

Research Associate Katarina Paddack prepared this case under the supervision of Professor Donald A. Marchand as a basis for class discussion rather than to illustrate either effective or ineffective handling of a business situation. Copyright © 2001 by IMD - International Institute for Management Development, Lausanne, Switzerland. Not to be used or reproduced without written permission directly from IMD.

[1] The top three banks in numbers of Internet customers included Nordea (formerly MeritaNordbanken), ForeningsSparbanken, and Skandinaviska Enskida Banken.

[2] 40% of SkandiaBanken's customer base were Skandia customers; the remaining 60% of customers came from the general public.

[3] 1 Swedish krona, SKr 1 = US$0.10 = ε0.11 (December 2000)

[4] In 2000, yearly fees were charged for Visa credit cards, international bank cards, and the use of Skandia Giro, a manual bill payment service.

[5] Home mortgages made up 64% of all lending, followed by car lending at 26%.

[6] Call center customer representatives were trained to respond to both telephone and Internet information requests and problems. In 2000, SkandiaBanken serviced 1 million calls and 60,000 e-mail requests.

[7] The call center acted as a cost center, charging each BU for services associated with its business.

[8] 1 Danish krone, DKr 1 = US$0.12 = ε0.13 (December 2001)

[9] Included investment in Norwegian operations.

[10] Included investment in Norwegian operations.

[11] Included fully expensed development costs of SKr 26 million for Internet equities trading service and a customer investment marketplace.

INTERNATIONAL CASE STUDY

CASE STUDY 4: JAPAN AIRLINES:
IMPACT OF E-TICKETING*

Amir Hoosain, Shamza Khan, Dr. Dennis Kira, and Dr. Ali Farhoomand,

The University of Hong Kong

During the 1990s, Internet usage doubled every 100 days and inspired the 'e-commerce revolution,' bringing changes to business fundamentals and sources of competitive advantage. Electronic commerce radically altered the way companies conducted business and provided services to customers. Firms could enter markets globally to expand their customer and supplier base by positioning businesses on-line. e-Commerce, effectively implemented, resulted in lower costs and increased direct interaction between a business and its customers, suppliers, service providers, employees, and other parties in the value-chain.

Since privatising in 1987, Japan Airlines (JAL) faced many difficulties including image problems and intense domestic and global competition. In addition to competitive pressures and increased airport charges, fuel taxes increased while the domestic downturn affected JAL's prospects throughout the 1990s. A restructuring strategy achieved some success in JAL's cost-cutting objectives but such savings through traditional means were nearing their potential.

In the meantime, many major international carriers were making headlines with aggressive efforts to achieve the reality of electronic travel services, including electronic ticketing (e-ticketing) and smart cards. However, JAL was so busy managing its financial situation that it overlooked competing foreign carriers that were introducing e-ticketing to the Japanese market.

Airlines that had implemented e-ticketing, primarily in North America, experienced considerable savings in distribution costs through Internet sales and by automating many selling processes. The JAL management wondered, to what extent might this success be replicated by a Japanese major and what would be the best approach for pursuing e-ticketing implementation in Japan?

JAL's Growth

The precursor to Japan Airlines (JAL) was the Japan Air Transport Company, the Japanese national airline dissolved by the allies after World War II. During the US occupation, Japan was not permitted to establish its own airline, but in 1951; a group of bankers founded JAL, in essence a revival of the Japan Air Transport Company. Under the Allied Peace Treaty, JAL was forbidden from using Japanese flight crew and therefore, leased pilots and a small fleet of aircraft from Northwest Airlines. By 1953, the fledgling airline had its own aircraft and crew, with government and the public sharing ownership. Under the Japan Air Lines Company Limited Law, JAL was granted special status

as the 'flag carrier' and the only domestic airline allowed to operate international routes.

As the airline grew, its operations received heavy scrutiny from the government, its largest stockholder. Government involvement placed certain limitations on managerial independence and created a highly bureaucratic and complex organisational structure.[1]

In the late 1970s, deregulation revolutionised the US airline industry and the movement inevitably forced the Japanese airline sector to abolish the Japan Air Lines Company Limited Law in November 1987; the government relinquished its stake in JAL and divested its shares to the public. JAL became fully privatised and acquired greater freedom to expand into new areas and to exercise autonomy in corporate decision making. In the new environment, Japanese civil aviation companies were better able to respond and adapt to changing market demands and competitor actions. Perhaps due to the legacy of government protectionism, JAL was not known for its customer orientation and when surveyed in 1986, domestic travellers rated the company's service as bureaucratic and unfriendly relative to its domestic competitors.[2] Also, as a consequence of privatisation, air transport was no longer nationalised and JAL's chief domestic rival, All Nippon Airways (ANA) was permitted to enter the domain of overseas service.

During the 1990s, JAL experienced a financial downturn due to high labour costs and over expansion of its fleet and facilities, coupled with the slowing Japanese economic growth as a result of over-investments in the late 1980s. In recognition of these problems, JAL announced a US$4.8 billion cost-cutting plan.

The company's restructuring agenda fell under four classifications as follows:

- Outsourcing secondary services.
- Overall staff reduction/making wages competitive within industry norms.
- Disposing of non-core assets.
- Creating lower cost subsidiary airlines such as Japan Air Charter (for short-haul international flights) and Japan Express (for short-haul domestic flights).

By 1994, passenger counts for JAL were higher, but the airline had been pressured to cut prices to match the competition's lower fares. In the same year, Osaka's new airport gave a boost to JAL's overseas traffic, but brought intense competition by allowing

503

more flights into Japan. In 1995, JAL and American Airlines (AA) formed an alliance, agreeing to link their computerised reservations systems (AXESS and Sabre respectively) and to serve as agents for each other's cargo businesses. This partnership was the first of several in years to come and characteristic of a rapidly evolving industry where cost-cutting and strategic alliances were critical for sustained growth.

Developments within the Travel Industry

Throughout the 1990s, major structural changes in the airline industry were instigated through e-commerce. The use of the Internet created several advantages for airlines including direct access to customers and cost-effective methods of conducting business processes on-line. On the other hand, growing e-commerce activity and the Internet's globalisation effect increased competitive business pressures and created a rapidly changing business landscape. The airline industry was pressured to transform organisational processes to adapt to the changing environment by becoming more competitive. The Internet provided airlines with the ability to do business on a global basis, to react quickly, differentiate services, monitor changes, and customise services with a view to winning customer loyalty. This was only attainable through the implementation of the appropriate mix of technology, process management, and corporate strategy.

Disintermediation and Reintermediation

The nature of e-commerce could reap major benefits for Japan, with its bureaucratic tangle of middlemen in a complex market distribution system. In the air travel industry, travel agents were the traditional intermediaries between airlines and travellers, and were compensated for services through commissions paid by airlines. Through the advent of e-commerce, the very survival of the traditional travel agent was threatened by disintermediation through airline direct services and travel cybermediaries.

e-Commerce observers predicted the displacement of the traditional intermediary—the travel agent. This 'disintermediation' process was achieved through direct access to airlines. However, cutting out the middleman caused new problems, ranging from fulfilment of single transactions from individual consumers, to setting up new customer service centres.

Travel agents needed to provide new value. Additional pressure was placed on travel agents with the airlines imposing commission caps. The emergence of e-ticketing weakened the travel agent's role in the distribution chain as their principal role of putting tickets into the travellers' hands could be eliminated by airlines and Websites offering e-ticketing.

Most travel agents, however, demonstrated strong survival skills. According to the American Society of Travel Agents, 49 percent of travel agencies had Websites of their own, compared with 37 percent in 1998. Studies showed that many people who surfed the Internet for deals then turned to travel agents to make their bookings.

Internet travel agents began refocusing on the leisure travel market by offering a variety of broad travel packages at competitive prices. At the same time, airlines in many cases expanded by acquiring travel sites. UA had a minority stake in GetThere.com (formerly Internet Travel Network) and Continental held a stake in Rosenbluth Interactive, owners of Biztravel.com. To some

observers, however, airlines failed to fully exploit the potential of the Internet and invest continuously in their Websites. As a result, they lagged behind on-line agents in innovation and the provision of integrated travel services.

Industry experts observed that while there were disintermediation forces, an equally vibrant industry of intermediaries emerged to serve the needs of airlines and customers. These new intermediaries, known as 'cybermediaries', reintermediated services in the airline industry. Cybermediaries competed with the traditional travel agents and an airline's direct services. They staked territory in cyberspace between the airlines and the traveller. Cybermediaries offered several advantages over an airline's direct services:

❚ Permitting travellers to book flights on almost any airline.

❚ Providing features to assist travellers in searching for the lowest prices.

❚ Notifying travellers by e-mail when a discount fare was posted for a particular destination of interest.

The concept of e-ticketing and its impact on the ticketing process was of prime importance in enabling the development of self-service technologies and electronic travel innovations. According to a study by Jupiter Communications, travel had become the number one product purchased on-line, netting US$911 million in 1997.[3] On-line travel sales are expected to account for 35 percent of all on-line sales globally by 2002 and travel purchases are expected to range from US$5 billion to US$30 billion by 2003.[4] Much of these purchases, however, were made through innovative 'virtual travel agencies'.

On one hand, airlines welcomed the creation of new channels to sell and promote their products, especially those that challenged the costly travel agent system. However, these new entrants also pre-empted the airlines' own efforts to implement direct sales and minimise distribution costs. In response, some airlines imposed tighter restrictions on commissions paid through such channels, but these new industry dynamics remained a cause for concern.

Computerised Reservation Systems

With the deregulation of the US airline industry in the late 1970s, American carriers had experienced similar competitive pressures and invested heavily in the innovation and development of computerised reservation systems (CRS)[5] to seek a competitive advantage. The advent of CRSs revolutionised airline business dynamics and the broader travel industry, elevating the role of information technology (IT). In 1987, JAL formed its newest subsidiary, AXESS International Network Inc., in a bid to develop its own computerised reservation system. JAL's management witnessed increased competitiveness resulting from the development of CRS (Sabre and Apollo) by its American counterparts and felt it necessary to develop a system of their own to seek a competitive advantage in the evolving CRS market.

JAL's CRS project was originally established as a marketing initiative, receiving full managerial support and huge capital and human resource investments. The resulting system—AXESS, was an integrated travel information and reservation system linked to hotel chains as well as other CRSs. The Sabre Group CRS (which had spun off from its originator, AA) bought a 25 percent stake in AXESS. AXESS became a cornerstone of JAL's strategy and was noted for its superior functionality as compared to other domestic reservation systems. This system was tightly integrated with other JAL information systems and offered enhanced services such as Japanese/English bilingual information retrieval. To ensure target users, such that travel agents and corporate inhouse travel departments would adopt AXESS, several value-adding features were incorporated, such as back office accounting and customer profile management systems. AXESS also reduced the ticket-processing time from 15 minutes to five seconds.

Introduction of e-Ticketing[6]

Airline deregulation triggered major changes including the privatisation of national carriers and the proliferation of start-ups throughout the airline industry. In 1993, Valujet, an Atlanta-based no-frills carrier, pioneered a revolutionary innovation with low fares, no traditional paper tickets, and a proprietary reservation system, its comprehensive route structure and direct sales channel translated into simple accounting needs and made it especially well suited for the 'e-ticketing' initiative [refer to **Appendix 1** for an illustration of the e-ticketing process].[7] In the same year, Morris Air, a small carrier based in Salt Lake City, introduced e-ticketing to increase its distribution potential; it was later acquired by Southwest Airlines. Southwest elected to implement the e-ticketing software and systems that came with the purchase, following a dispute with the Apollo/Galileo and System One systems.

Both e-ticketing pioneers, Morris Air and Valujet, gained tremendous value from the implementation. Morris Air's sales through travel agents decreased to around 33 percent and the carrier observed further benefits in check-in time and accounting labour savings; Valujet estimated that e-ticketing had cut costs by around ten percent. Soon, major US carriers were rapidly adopting e-ticketing.

Industry experts believed that e-ticketing would inevitably succeed traditional ticketing as the *de facto* standard because of the following obvious benefits for firms:[8]

▌ Acceptance by the airline carrier's target customers because of enhanced customer service and improved travel efficiency.

▌ High proportion of direct sales. By eliminating the middle-man, airlines could save on agent commission costs and agency fees.

▌ High proportion of business/corporate customers. Repeat business allowed airlines to monitor travelling trends and offer personalised service.

▌ Existence of advanced credit card payment systems. e-Ticketing could be integrated easily into existing payment systems to provide 'one-stop' shopping.

▌ Prevalence of carry-on baggage. Many customers liked to travel with minimum luggage, making e-ticketing and seamless travel attractive. Business travel was usually restricted to a short timeframe; the elimination of luggage check-in improved efficiency.

▌ Air travel consists primarily of point-to-point passengers. The existence of self-service check-in equipment reduced check-in times, thus improving efficiency and customer service.

▌ Airlines controlled the check-in environment. A simple network structure without connecting flights and multi-carrier itineraries give rise to 'seamless' travel.

▌ Ability to adapt computer systems. Airlines preferred to use their own systems, equipment, and personnel to avoid the need to develop additional interfaces with other systems.

The earlier e-ticketing pioneers approached systems development through in-house innovation. Major US and European airlines also came under pressure to respond and develop their own systems [refer to **Appendix 2** for an overview of the impact of e-ticketing on various airline functions]. Other airlines adopting e-ticketing technology took a 'fast follow' approach by seeking existing technology and customising it to their requirements. Indeed, airlines opting for the 'fast follow' method benefited from the standardisation efforts.

Ron LeRadza, the General Manager of product distribution at Air Canada, conveyed the essence of this approach:

> We don't want to be leaders in the field. By waiting to see what problems and successes other carriers experience, we can make good progress with the introduction of our own systems.[9]

e-Ticketing in North America and Asia

Before the introduction of e-ticketing, distribution costs ranging from travel agent commissions to ticket stock, were high across the airline industry. By the mid-1990s, distribution costs represented an average of 24 percent of total costs, ranking even higher than airlines' fuel costs. Although the concept of e-ticketing emerged in 1993, it was only after initiatives by new airline entrants that major airlines overcame reservations concerning adoption and implementation. Improved value through enhanced customer service, personalised information and other integrated travel information, was difficult to resist once e-ticketing benefits for customers and companies were clear. [Refer to **Appendix 3** for an illustration of some advantages and disadvantages of e-ticketing for the various parties in the air travel process.]

The main benefit of e-ticketing for airlines included transferring a portion of the airlines' travel agency sales, rife with commissions and segment booking fees, to direct sales channels. This opened up the potential for non-traditional channels of distribution that continued to arise with the advances of modern telecommunications.

As a result of these benefits, by early 2000, e-ticketing had become universal in North America and represented over 40 percent of total bookings for main carriers. In May 1999, UA announced that 51 percent of the seven million tickets it sold that month were e-tickets—the first time that e-ticketing use had achieved such a majority. By year's end, UA's e-ticketing service was 100 percent available to all 259 destinations in its worldwide network. Within five years, its e-ticket strategy had gone from conception to setting world standards in implementation.[10] With growing acceptance of e-ticketing, a number of basic interline e-ticketing (described later) implementations were under establishment.

Although e-ticketing was widely adopted by North American carriers, relatively few Asian carriers provided this service. e-Ticketing services in Asia were first experienced in Hong Kong in 1999. By early 2000, only Singapore Airlines had introduced e-ticketing to limited destinations; Cathay Pacific offered e-ticketing to Hong Kong, Australia, Singapore and Manchester and had further plans to include Japan, the US, Canada, Taiwan, and London Heathrow. Airline Websites offered features such as direct ticket sales, frequent flier programme administration, flight-tracking, promotional releases, and on-line gift catalogues and on-line ticket auctions.[11]

In Japan, American carriers were pulling ahead of JAL and its domestic counterparts; UA and Delta had introduced e-ticketing and Northwest had imminent plans to follow suit. The Australian carrier, Qantas, was also set to extend its e-ticket offering to the Japanese market. A 1999 study commissioned by SITA, the leading provider of integrated telecommunications and information support to the air transport industry, revealed a possible root of this disparity—the average planned IT investment by Asia-Pacific airlines lagged far behind that of American and European carriers.

Interline e-Travel

Interline e-ticketing referred to travelling by an e-ticket with an itinerary spanning multiple carriers; this service provided great value to customers but could pose considerable complications for airlines offering the service. So far, most airlines that offered on-line e-ticket bookings only facilitated point-to-point tickets between certain stated destinations. On-line booking facilities could not handle fares permitting stopovers and such requests had to be made at appropriate reservation offices either in person or via telephone.

In October 1996, a resolution addressing interline e-ticketing was adopted at the IATA/ATA Joint Passenger Services Conference and was made effective from January 1997.[12] These resolutions contained specifications for the eventual introduction of interline e-ticketing. However, interline e-ticketing development was progressing relatively slowly.

JAL Alliances

In January 1998, an agreement was signed between Japan and the US, granting JAL, Northwest Airlines, United Airlines (UA), and ANA, unlimited flying rights between the two countries. Additionally, new service opportunities were provided to Continental, American, Delta, TWA, and USAirways. The agreement was immediately criticised by JAL executives as favouring the American carriers.

However, by 1998, JAL improved profitability with proceeds from the sale of assets and managed to pay dividends for the first time in seven years; economic conditions had also improved. The number of passengers from Japan was expected to pick up, but questions still remained about JAL's ability to compete with its American and European counterparts, particularly with the opening of a new runway at Narita, which could prompt more aggressive pricing. The reduction in labour costs and the disposal of assets were nearing their limits and the airline found it difficult to make further savings in this area.

With the multitude of one-to-one code sharing and collaborative agreements JAL had accumulated, industry observers began to wonder if the airline had eventual plans to be a formal member of one of the increasing number of alliances among the international carriers. The larger American and European airlines had taken leading roles in pushing for alliances centred on code sharing and joint marketing (including shared frequent flier programmes) to benefit from the economies of scale.

Multi-carrier groups were created to address the pressures of heightened competition. Other alliances, such as UA's Star Alliance had grown to a considerable prominence. Although JAL had entered individual agreements with several Oneworld alliance members, including AA, British Airways, Cathay Pacific, and Iberia Airlines, it insisted on pursuing collaborations on a one-to-one basis. Nonetheless, by mid-1999, JAL announced the introduction of a task force to study the advantages and disadvantages of joining an alliance.

The Japan-US Civil Aviation Agreement (1998)

"The purpose of the negotiations was to narrow the imbalance between Japan and the US, which has favoured the US since 1952 [when the original US-Japan pact was signed]. Instead, the gap has been widened," said JAL president Akira Kondo.

To some industry observers however, the implications of the Japan-US civil aviation agreement were not so bleak — Japanese carriers still had better access to the domestic corporate market and increased competition would boost overall traffic in the region, potentially to the benefit of all carriers serving Japan.

Despite the deregulation of the Japanese aviation industry, US carriers did not enjoy complete freedom to undercut fares offered by Japanese airlines. While the Japanese government offered assurances that demand would determine prices on trans-Pacific routes, it was thought that JAL's fares would serve as a benchmark for other airlines. More worrisome was the threat of excess capacity across the industry and the loss of control at JAL's hubs as a result. Also on the horizon was further cause for concern—the opening of a second runway at Narita, anticipated in 2002. The new runway would dramatically increase the access that foreign carriers had to the Japanese market, with annual slots going up by as much as 70 percent.[13] Another warning came in a Standard & Poor's report on the airline, where it was suggested that with increased competition, any cost savings that would result from JAL's efforts could be offset by a necessary increase in promotional expenses.[14]

One of the more positive terms of the Japan-US civil aviation agreement was the provision permitting JAL to pursue a code-sharing alliance with a major American airline. Such an alliance was formed with its marketing partner of three years, AA. This alliance provided JAL with access to AA's extensive feeder network within the US, resulting in a vast increase to the booking options available for clients departing to Asia. The partnership with AA also increased JAL's appeal to passengers unfamiliar with the airline, who might otherwise prefer to make arrangements with a US carrier.[15] Over the next year, JAL announced further code-sharing partnerships with Cathay Pacific, Swissair, Alitalia and Iberia Airlines and formed an alliance with Lufthansa and Scandinavian Airlines System for a cargo route between Japan and Northern Europe.

As the competitive environment grew complicated in the area of international service, Japan's domestic market showed signs of change. By the late 1990s, JAL's domestic market share had made some headway against leaders ANA and Japan Air System (JAS). JAL benefited from the abolition of traffic thresholds on internal routes in Japan that had prohibited it from encroaching on ANA's realm of service. With internal expansion, JAL was able to provide a more extensive international feed than the other two majors and the success of its frequent flier programme contributed further to customer loyalty. This is not to say that the domestic market was devoid of developments—a number of up-start airlines, Hokkaido International Airlines (Air Do), Skymark Airlines and Pan Asia Airways were granted operating authority by the Ministry of Transport and were making a modest emergence. While these start-ups were in their infancies, JAL and ANA implemented aggressive pricing on domestic routes in an attempt to stifle the new threat.[16]

In August 1999, JAL and JAS announced an agreement to code share certain international flights for a trial period — from October 1999 to March 2000. This was the first such plan announced by Japanese carriers and called for the use of JAL equipment and flight personnel at the JAS arrival and departure berths at Narita. Each airline maintained its own flight number and tickets continued to be sold through their separate marketing channels. At the time, JAS was also in the process of negotiating a code-sharing agreement with ANA. These developments unfolded amid some speculation that Japan's airlines may one day combine to form a 'super carrier' for cost-saving and competitive purposes.[17]

Process Integration

With deregulation, JAL recognised the pressing need to advance customer service and improve profitability. To some extent, these objectives were attained through traditional modes of restructuring. Management's desire to reduce the volume of paper-based transactions led to the swift development of electronic data interchange (EDI) applications for cost reduction and logistical coordination.[18] A proprietary EDI system provided JAL with accurate and timely information to manage their complex network of relationships and to enable procurement, just-in-time delivery, and joint-venture operations. This network, developed by the Multi-Japan Network, was a JAL group member; JAL readily accepted the EDI implementation. The network's proprietary nature gave JAL confidence in information security and accuracy. EDI encouraged cost reduction by facilitating functions ranging from fuel procurement, aircraft maintenance parts delivery as well as improving the overall communication throughout the group.

For a period in 1997, JAL's Website was the second most popular site in Japan, receiving 60,000 visitors a day, second only to *Asahi Shimbun* daily newspaper's Website.[19] A Website was also created to serve the American region, in conjunction with the company's efforts to expand its North American business. JAL had begun accepting reservations via the Internet in July 1996. Travel reservations were implemented through collaboration with the Travelocity system, belonging to the Sabre Group. E-Ticketing was not available, but customers could make travel arrangements through a customised version of Travelocity and traditional tickets were later sent by mail from the Travelocity service centre. Initially, this service was exclusive to domestic flights, but it was expanded to include international service in January 1997. The reservation system generated US$4 million in revenue.[20]

According to JAL spokesman Akihiko Sato, most people who made reservations via the Internet were business passengers using domestic services and the proportion of repeat users was high.[21] The volume of on-line bookings for international travel was considerably smaller because many Japanese travellers purchased package tours for overseas travel. Direct ticket sales saved JAL the high travel agent commissions, ranging from five to nine percent of ticket price.

By the late 1990s, e-ticket sales represented approximately ten percent of all airline tickets worldwide. Many major airlines offered on-line booking with e-ticketing facilities. Websites were user-friendly, self-explanatory, with step-by-step instructions on booking on-line. Some airlines even gave on-line booking rewards in the form of bonus air miles to create customer loyalty. In fact, firms realised that on-line Website management should produce the ultimate goal of creating customer satisfaction and customer loyalty. During this period, there was growing popularity of the integrated front-end management process, which referred to firms creating seamless and tightly integrated management of customer order acquisition strategies. This meant that Websites were points of entry for customers and that a customer visit on-line should result in the purchase of a good/service and in return, firms manage the purchase in an integrated fashion with the use of appropriate technology, process management, and strategy to execute all the functions involved.

For some, e-ticketing was seen as a source of competitive advantage, but JAL adopted a more traditional approach in their business re-engineering process rather than radically changing their business strategy. In response to the impending changes in their competitive environment, JAL formed horizontal alliances with other service providers such as car hire companies, hotels and leisure service providers as a means of improving customer service. They also vertically integrated by establishing value-added services to core activities such as:

- Provision of airport transportation services.
- Provision of airport lounges.
- Provision of advance seat selection services.
- Provision of a baggage delivery service.
- Provision of priority guest services.
- Provision of a strong US and European network by forming alliances with other major air carriers.

However, these had become commoditised services which most major airlines provided. In addition, other airline Websites such as UA's provided customers with one-stop services for all airline booking and vacation requirements. All customers had to do was to get on-line, and UA would manage any requirements thereafter. It created customer satisfaction and entrenched customer loyalty. This was a management philosophy most firms were moving towards. However, JAL, while making small innovations, still had a fragmented strategy with regard to managing passengers' on-line bookings. Domestic passengers could only book through traditional travel agents while North American customers could book JAL seats through Travelocity.

With the expanding interconnection of customers and suppliers, e-commerce will facilitate the creation of electronic 'supply Webs' surpassing the capability of a simple supply-chain. As a result, value will be added as transactions pass between participants, while costly human intervention will be kept at a minimum.

UA was one of the first among the major international airlines to implement e-commerce to enhance its value-chain. UA adopted a management philosophy with a process methodology that took into consideration every aspect of the firm and its environment. They focused on the consumer to improve interactions and streamlined operations by adding value internally to deliver superior customer service. UA carried this out by creating a new Website that provided a new look and improved navigation. They added quick-search features that allowed customers to check schedules and flight information from the homepage as well as the ability to check their Mileage Plus account summary. To make navigation easier, the homepage was presented in four categories:

▌ *Planning Travel*—view schedules, compare fares, purchase travel, request upgrades, redeem award miles or update customer profile.

▌ *Travel Support*—locate information about services, baggage guidelines, onboard entertainment, and airport maps.

▌ *Mileage Plus*—review frequent flier accounts and the latest promotion updates to earn bonus points.

▌ *About United*—product information, alliances, and commitment to improving customer satisfaction.

This philosophy of integrated selling-chain management was gaining a lot of popularity among firms because it created added value for them and was touted as becoming a critical facet of conducting on-line business effectively. The idea was to create added value, for example, through information sharing. By sharing information along each link in an airline's process, airlines created value for customers by providing updated information on schedules and personalised customer services. Such integrated chains required firms to re-engineer their fundamental business processes to adapt their line of business to an e-commerce framework.

JAL's Future

Within a few years, on-line booking volumes skyrocketed and airlines scrambled with competing virtual distribution channels. Airlines offered various incentives to lure customers, and stood at fairly even market share with the on-line agents. Sales in 1999 were predicted to be at least US$8 billion and the market was expected to go up to US$20 billion in 2001.[22]

Japan's economy, however, remained largely under the influence of government ministries and *keiretsu* affiliations, resulting in a general preference for Japanese developed technology rather than the adoption of systems and technologies from abroad.[23]

In the airline industry, smart cards[24] followed on the heels of e-ticketing as a major component in companies' visions of seamless travel. With the full implementation of such technologies, customers would be able to transfer funds from a bank onto the card and make travel purchases on-line by transferring value from the smart card through a smart card reader installed in a personal computer. In addition, a customer's frequent flier information, mileage record as well as seating and meal preferences would already be stored in the card, thus expediting the on-line purchasing process. Once completed, an e-ticket and any necessary legal notices would then be transmitted and stored in the smart card. At the airport, the card would accelerate the check-in process, enable the use of automated kiosks, store other travel documentation and serve as a boarding pass and baggage receipt as well as provide access to club lounges and other benefits. With potentially vast linkages to other service partners, the additional functions of the smart card were left to one's imagination.

Using technology as an enabler, airlines were rapidly adopting strategies and re-engineering their businesses to focus on adding more value to customers. Smart card technology, for example, was a vision which companies thought they could soon implement and offer as a service to customers. Airlines were experimenting with new dimensions in ticket distribution technology with the introduction of speech recognition systems capable of performing reservations, sales, and schedule and flight information functions. Some airlines viewed this as a mere supplement to the existing distribution methods, but others felt it would dramatically impact the industry when used in conjunction with e-ticketing and Internet sales.

Japan's traditionally complex bureaucratic organisational structures, coupled with heavy government regulation, seemed to hinder the development of the Japanese airline industry since its infancy and also affected its ability to innovate. JAL's strategy over the past decade focused on cost savings and efficiency improvement; however, changes remained within the realm of traditional business management practices. No major management effort was initiated to capture the opportunities offered by e-commerce and no dramatic business re-engineering processes were undertaken. At best, efforts to grow JAL's business on-line and seek alternative methods of growth remained fragmented; JAL's management philosophy seemed submerged by heavy cultural and regulatory influences.

JAL President and CEO Isao Kaneko could only express 'cautious optimism' for a turnaround in 1999 on the recent news that Japan's economic growth was accelerating. However, JAL was under pressure despite increasing consumer spending and passenger traffic. Was this costly short-sightedness on the part of management, or was it in fact wiser in the long run for Japan's largest airline to consolidate internally and take a 'fast follow' approach to e-ticketing in the light of vast implementation hurdles and uncertainties over eventual standards? Could it catch up with international airlines and compete effectively in the domestic and international market under the current management? What was the appropriate strategy to compete in the globalised and competitive environment that e-commerce posed?

CASE STUDY QUESTIONS

1. Evaluate Japan Airlines using the competitive forces and value chain models.

2. What is JAL's business strategy? How does it use information systems to support that strategy? What role do the Web and e-ticketing play in that strategy?

3. How does JAL's use of information technology differ from other major airlines?

4. How much has information technology been an enabler for Japan Airlines? Explain your answer.

Source: Amir Hoosain and Shamza Khan prepared this case under the supervision of Dr. Dennis Kira and Dr. Ali Farhoomand. Copyright © 2000 The University of Hong Kong. Ref. 00/78C

[1]Chatfield, A.T. & Bjorn-Andersen, N. (1997), *Journal of Management Information Systems,* Vol. 14, No. 1, Summer, pp. 13–40.

[2]Wataname, K. (1995), "Challenges for Japanese Airlines", *Nihon Koku no Chosen,* Tokyo: Nohon Noritsu Kyokai Management Center.

[3]"On-line Travel Purchases Steadily Increase; Airlines Position to Get a Piece of the Pie", *World Airline News,* 9 April 1999.

[4]"Web@ Work: E Travel Sales on the Rise", *Asia Computer Weekly,* 4 October 1999.

[5]Computerised reservation systems facilitate on-line reservations with a variety of suppliers and enable prior bookings up to one year in advance.

[6]Wauthy, Y. (1997), "Business Research Project: Electronic Ticketing in the Airline Industry, History, Implementation, Consequences and Impact for the Future", Concordia University, October.

[7]e-Ticketing is the process when a ticket is booked either via an agent or on-line, the information is transmitted directly to the airline's database and once the information is sent, one can access the database to check, modify or cancel the details of the booking. After making a reservation or booking through an agent or on-line, the customer needs only a confirmation number and itinerary, both of which can be issued immediately over the telephone or through the airline's Website. At the airport all that is needed is the confirmation number, photograph ID and credit card where necessary.

[8]Orla, K. (1996), "Strategic Technology Assessment: Aer Lingus and Electronic Ticketing", December. URL:http//www.cs.ted.ie/courses/ism/strechs/ind1/as/msg00011.html

[9]"Electronic Ticketing Without Frontiers", Airlines International.

[10]"United Airline's e-Ticket (SM) Service Now Available Worldwide", *PR Newswire,* 17 November 1999.

[11]On-line ticket auction is where an airline will post a travel offer on its Website which is then open for surfers to bid against each other until the highest price is reached or bidding has closed.

[12]Resolution 722f for airlines and 722g for travel agents in neutral ticketing environments.

[13]Hayashi, D. *et al.* (1998), *HSBC James Capel Report: Japan Airlines,* 29 May.

[14]Jones, D. (1998), "From One Crisis to Another", *Air Finance Journal,* September.

[15]Jones, D. (1998).

[16]"Japanese Carriers Defend Domestic Pricing Structures" *World Airlines News,* 17 December 1999.

[17]Laterman, K. (1999), "Japanese Airlines Need Restructuring to Keep Their Heads Above the Clouds", TheStreet.com, 26 September, URL: http://www.thestreet.com/int/asia/787066.html, January 2000.

[18]Chatfield, A.T. & Bjorn-Andersen, N. (1997), *Journal of Management Information Systems,* Vol. 14, No. 1, Summer, pp. 13–40.

[19]"JAL Internet Site Proves Popular", *Travel Trade Gazette UK & Ireland,* 15 January 1997

[20]Hirao, S. (1998), "Japan's Electronic Commerce: Companies Learn By Trial and Error to Sell on the Net", *Japan Times Weekly International Edition,* 11 May.

[21]*Japan Times Weekly International Edition,* 11 May 1998.

[22]"Gomez Advisors Release First Internet Airline Scorecard", *Business Wire,* 8 September 1999.

[23]"Smart Cards Come to Japan", *Credit Card Management,* September 1998.

[24]Smart cards are standard plastic cards containing an integrated circuit, systems and applications software and permanent data.

THE E-TICKETING PROCESS

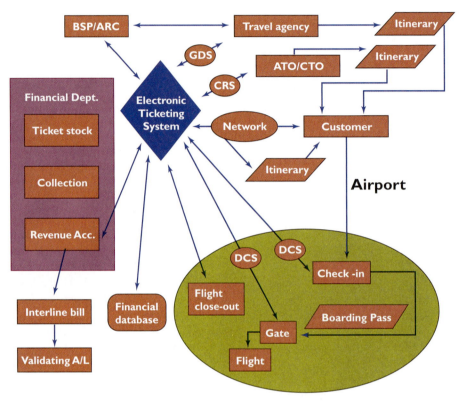

* e-Ticketing process diagram, e.g. Yves Wauthy, Electronic Ticketing in the airline industry.

APPENDIX 2

AN OVERVIEW OF THE IMPACT OF E-TICKETING ON VARIOUS AIRLINE FUNCTIONS

Computerised reservation systems	With the creation of an e-ticket at a CRS terminal, a record is entered into the airline's e-ticketing database according to ATA/IATA standards.
Departure control systems	This system must be adapted to allow airline check-in and gate agents access to the e-ticketing database and enable them to update the passenger's status over the course of passenger handling operations.
Accounting systems	In addition to its function as a travel document, the e-ticket serves a financial function and must be under the auspices of the accounting systems throughout the course of its use. The e-ticket is used for billing and revenue accounting purposes.
Settlement systems	Known as the Airline Reporting Corporation (ARC) in the US and Bank Settlement Plan (BSP) in other countries, settlement systems are in use in travel agencies to expedite ticket and accounting functions. The systems are comprised of a neutral ticket issue to serve travel on multiple providers. The billing function is centralised by ARC/BSP, which then 'settles' the transactions with the airlines. With the advent of e-ticketing, paper ticket settlement systems are no longer applicable, but new settlement systems must be implemented.

APPENDIX 3

THE ADVANTAGES AND DISADVANTAGES OF E-TICKETING FOR VARIOUS PARTIES WITHIN THE TRAVEL INDUSTRY

	Advantages	**Disadvantages**
Airlines	• Enables new distribution channels • Benefits direct sales over costly intermediaries • Eliminates paper ticket production • Simplifies modification and refunds • Reduction in check-in time and possibility of self-check-in • Eliminates data-entry redundancy • Accelerated revenue processing • Labour savings in terms of sales, passenger handling, and accounting functions.	• Uncertainty over acceptance by the travelling public • The matter of implementing interline e-ticketing and similarly, of supporting last minute schedule changes • Display of legal information, such as the Warsaw Convention on liability • Verifying customer identification • Threat of fraud—in terms of unauthorised issuance of e-tickets and fraudulent payment via credit card
Customers	• Greater flexibility in ticket purchasing • Convenience of travelling without physical documentation that can be lost, stolen, or destroyed • Ability to modify itinerary and make cancellations without adjusting a paper ticket • Added efficiency with check-in or possibility of self-check-in • Automated access to customer profile/frequent flier information	• Complications resulting from user or system error, such as double booking, neglecting to cancel a ticket • Increased risk of letting tickets go unused, especially by corporate travellers • At the early stages of e-ticket implementation, complications might arise due to system shortcomings—particularly in making last minute changes
Travel Agents	• Higher productivity resulting from the streamlined ticketing process • Simplified modification of itineraries • Savings on ticket delivery costs • Reduced importance of geographic position of the travel agency—allowing it to cater to a broader clientele and perhaps to experience rental savings	• Large loss of agency fees due to booking by direct channels is a threat to agencies • Initial training required to become familiar with ticketing procedures • Subject to added constraints on CRS as airlines push for e-ticketing standardisation across the board • e-Ticketing still unsuited for complex itineraries and interlining

REFERENCES

CHAPTER 1

Ackoff, R. L. "Management Misinformation System." *Management Science* 14, no. 4 (December 1967), B140–B116.

Allen, Brandt R., and **Andrew C. Boynton.** "Information Architecture: In Search of Efficient Flexibility." *MIS Quarterly* 15, no. 4 (December 1991).

Bakos, J. Yannis. "The Emerging Role of Electronic Marketplaces on the Internet." *Communications of the ACM* 41, no. 8 (August 1998).

Barrett, Stephanie S. "Strategic Alternatives and Interorganizational System Implementations: An Overview." *Journal of Management Information Systems* (Winter 1986–1987).

Benjamin, Robert, and **Rolf Wigand.** "Electronic Markets and Virtual Value Chains on the Information Superhighway." *Sloan Management Review* (Winter 1995).

Brynjolfsson, E. T., T. W. Malone, V. Gurbaxani, and **A. Kambil.** "Does Information Technology Lead to Smaller Firms?" *Management Science* 40, no. 12 (1994).

Davis, Gordon B., and **Margrethe H. Olson.** *Management Information Systems: Conceptual Foundations, Structure, and Development,* 2nd ed. New York: McGraw-Hill (1985).

Deans, Candace P., and **Michael J. Kane.** *International Dimensions of Information Systems and Technology.* Boston, MA: PWS-Kent (1992).

Dickson, Gray W. and **Gerardine DeSanctis.** *Information Technology and Future Enterprise.* Upper Saddle River, NJ: Prentice-Hall (2001).

"Eastman is Keen on E-Commerce." *Information Week* (August 2, 2000).

Fedorowicz, Jane, and **Benn Konsynski.** "Organization Support Systems: Bridging Business and Decision Processes." *Journal of Management Information Systems* 8, no. 4 (Spring 1992).

Feeny, David E., and **Leslie P. Willcocks.** "Core IS Capabilities for Exploiting Information Technology." *Sloan Management Review* 39, no. 3 (Spring 1998).

Gallupe, R. Brent. "Images of Information Systems in the Early 21st Century." *Communications of the Association for Information Systems* 3, no. 3 (February 2000).

Gilmore, James H., and **B. Joseph Pine, II.** "The Four Faces of Mass Customization." *Harvard Business Review* (January–February 1997).

Gorry, G. A., and **M. S. Scott Morton.** "A Framework for Management Information Systems." *Sloan Management Review* 13, no. 1 (1971).

Johnston, Russell, and **Michael J. Vitale.** "Creating Competitive Advantage with Interorganizational Information Systems." *MIS Quarterly* 12, no. 2 (June 1988).

Keen, Peter G. W. *Shaping the Future: Business Design Through Information Technology.* Cambridge, MA: Harvard Business School Press (1991).

King, John. "Centralized vs. Decentralized Computing: Organizational Considerations and Management Options." *Computing Surveys* (October 1984).

Kling, Rob, and **William H. Dutton.** "The Computer Package: Dynamic Complexity." In *Computers and Politics,* edited by James Danziger, William H. Dutton, Rob Kling, and Kenneth Kraemer. New York: Columbia University Press (1982).

Konicki, Steve. "Lockheed Martin Jet Fighter Win Ushers in New Era of Real Time Project Management." *Information Week* (November 12, 2001).

Leonard-Barton, Dorothy. *Wellsprings of Knowledge.* Boston, MA: Harvard Business School Press (1995).

Liker, Jeffrey K., David B. Roitman, and **Ethel Roskies.** "Changing Everything All at Once: Work Life and Technological Change." *Sloan Management Review* (Summer 1987).

Malone, T. W., and **J. F. Rockart.** "Computers, Networks and the Corporation." *Scientific American* 265, no. 3 (September 1991).

Malone, Thomas W., JoAnne Yates, and **Robert I. Benjamin.** "Electronic Markets and Electronic Hierarchies." *Communications of the ACM* (June 1987).

———. "The Logic of Electronic Markets." *Harvard Business Review* (May–June 1989).

McFarlan, F. Warren, James L. McKenney, and **Philip Pyburn.** "The Information Archipelago—Plotting a Course." *Harvard Business Review* (January–February 1983).

———. "Governing the New World." *Harvard Business Review* (July–August 1983).

McKenney, James L., and **F. Warren McFarlan.** "The Information Archipelago—Maps and Bridges." *Harvard Business Review* (September–October 1982).

Orlikowski, Wanda J., and **Stephen R. Bailey.** "Technology and Institutions: What Can Research on Information Technology and Research on Organizations Learn from Each Other?" *MIS Quarterly* 25, no. 2 (June 2001).

Orlikowski, Wanda J., and **Jack J. Baroudi.** "Studying Information Technology in Organizations: Research Approaches and Assumptions." *Information Systems Research* 2, no. 1 (March 1991).

Quinn, James Brian. "Strategic Outsourcing: Leveraging Knowledge Capabilities." *Sloan Management Review* 40, no. 4 (Summer 1999).

Roche, Edward M. "Planning for Competitive Use of Information Technology in Multinational Corporations." AIB UK Region, Brighton Polytechnic, Brighton, UK, Conference Paper (March 1992). Edward M. Roche, W. Paul Stillman School of Business, Seton Hall University.

Rockart, John F., and **James E. Short.** "IT in the 1990s: Managing Organizational Interdependence." *Sloan Management Review* 30, no. 2 (Winter 1989).

Sambamurthy, V., and **Robert W. Zmud.** "Research Commentary: The Organizing Logic for an Enterprise's IT Activities in the Digital Era-A Prognosis of Practice and a Call to Research." *Information Systems Research* 11, No. 2 (June 2000).

Scott Morton, Michael, ed. *The Corporation in the 1990s.* New York: Oxford University Press (1991).

Slywotzky, Adrian J., and **David J. Morrison.** *How Digital Is Your Business?* New York: Crown Business (2001).

Tornatsky, Louis G., J. D. Eveland, Myles G. Boylan, W. A. Hertzner, E. C. Johnson, D. Roitman, and **J. Schneider.** "The Process of Technological Innovation: Reviewing the Literature." Washington, DC: National Science Foundation (1983).

Tuomi, Ilkka. "Data Is More Than Knowledge." *Journal of Management Information Systems* 16, no. 3 (Winter 1999-2000).

Weill, Peter, and **Marianne Broadbent.** *Leveraging the New Infrastructure.* Cambridge, MA: Harvard Business School Press (1998).

———. "Management by Maxim: How Business and IT Managers Can Create IT Infrastructures." *Sloan Management Review* (Spring 1997).

Zipkin, Paul. "The Limits of Mass Customization." *Sloan Management Review* 42, no. 3 (Spring 2001).

CHAPTER 2

Anthony, R. N. *Planning and Control Systems: A Framework for Analysis.* Cambridge, MA: Harvard University Press (1965).

Bensaou, M. "Portfolios of Buyer-Supplier Relationships. " *Sloan Management Review* 40, no. 4 (Summer 1999).

Berry, Leonard L., and **A. Parasuraman.** "Listening to the Customer—the Concept of a Service-Quality Information System." *Sloan Management Review* (Spring 1997).

Chismar, William G., and **Laku Chidambaram.** "Telecommunications and the Structuring of U.S. Multinational Corporations." *International Information Systems* 1, no. 4 (October 1992).

Choi, **Soong-Yong,** and **Andrew B. Whinston,** "Communities of Collaboration." *IQ Magazine.* (July/August 2001).

Concours Group. "ESII: Capitalizing on Enterprise Systems and Infrastructure." (1999).

Cox, Butler. *Globalization: The IT Challenge.* Sunnyvale, CA: Amdahl Executive Institute (1991).

Culnan, Mary J. "Transaction Processing Applications as Organizational Message Systems: Implications for the Intelligent Organization." Working paper no. 88-10, Twenty-second Hawaii International Conference on Systems Sciences (January 1989).

Davenport, Tom. *Mission Critical: Realizing the Promise of Enterprise Systems.* Boston, MA: Harvard Business School Press (2000).

———. "Putting the Enterprise into Enterprise Systems." *Harvard Business Review* (July–August 1998).

Deans, Candace P., and **Michael J. Kane.** *International Dimensions of Information Systems and Technology.* Boston, MA: PWS-Kent (1992).

Deans, Candace P., Kirk R. Karwan, Martin D. Goslar, David A. Ricks, and **Brian Toyne.** "Key International Issues in U.S.-Based Multinational Corporations." *Journal of Management Information Systems* 7, no. 4 (Spring 1991).

Handfield, Robert B., and **Ernest L. Nichols, Jr.** *Introduction to Supply Chain Management.* Upper Saddle River, NJ: Prentice-Hall (1999).

Houdeshel, George, and **Hugh J. Watson.** "The Management Information and Decision Support (MIDS) System at Lockheed Georgia." *MIS Quarterly* 11, no. 1 (March 1987).

Huber, George P. "Organizational Information Systems: Determinants of Their Performance and Behavior." *Management Science* 28, no. 2 (1984).

Ives, Blake, and **Sirkka Jarvenpaa.** "Applications of Global Information Technology: Key Issues for Management." *MIS Quarterly* 15, no. 1 (March 1991).

———. "Global Business Drivers: Aligning Information Technology to Global Business Strategy. *IBM Systems Journal* 32, no. 1 (1993).

———. "Global Information Technology: Some Lessons from Practice." *International Information Systems* 1, no. 3 (July 1992).

Kalakota, Ravi, and **Marcia Robinson.** *e-Business 2.0: Roadmap for Success.* Reading, MA: Addison-Wesley (2001).

Keen, Peter G. W. *The Process Edge.* Boston, MA: Harvard Business School Press (1997).

Keen, Peter G. W., and **M. S. Morton.** *Decision Support Systems: An Organizational Perspective.* Reading, Ma: Addison-Wesley (1978).

King, William R., and **Vikram Sethi.** "An Empirical Analysis of the Organization of Transnational Information Systems." *Journal of Management Information Systems* 15, no. 4 (Spring 1999).

King, John. "Centralized vs. Decentralized Computing: Organizational Considerations and Management Options." *Computing Surveys* (October 1984).

Kumar, Kuldeep. "Technology for Supporting Supply Chain Management." *Communications of the ACM* 44, no. 6 (June 2001).

Lee, Hau, L., V. Padmanabhan, and **Seugin Whang.** "The Bullwhip Effect in Supply Chains." *Sloan Management Review* (Spring 1997).

Levy, David. "Lean Production in an International Supply Chain." *Sloan Management Review* (Winter 1997).

Malone, Thomas M., Kevin Crowston, Jintae Lee, and **Brian Pentland**. "Tools for Inventing Organizations: Toward a Handbook of Organizational Processes." *Management Science* 45, no. 3 (March 1999).

Palaniswamy, Rajagopal, and **Tyler Frank**. "Enhancing Manufacturing Performance with ERP Systems." *Information Systems Management* (Summer 2000).

Palvia, Shailendra, Prashant Palvia, and **Ronald Zigli,** eds. *The Global Issues of Information Technology Management.* Harrisburg, PA: Idea Group Publishing (1992).

Patton, Susannah. "The Truth About CRM." *CIO Magazine* (May 1, 2001).

Roche, Edward M. *Managing Information Technology in Multinational Corporations.* New York: Macmillan (1992).

Rockart, John F., and **Michael E. Treacy.** "The CEO Goes On-line." *Harvard Business Review* (January–February 1982).

Seybold, Patricia B. "Get Inside the Lives of Your Customers." *Harvard Business Review* (May 2001).

Sprague, Ralph H., Jr., and **Eric D. Carlson.** *Building Effective Decision Support Systems.* Englewood Cliffs, NJ: Prentice Hall (1982)

Tractinsky, Noam, and **Sirkka L. Jarvenpaa.** "Information Systems Design Decisions in a Global Versus Domestic Context." *MIS Quarterly* 19, no. 4 (December 1995).

Watson, Richard T., Gigi G. Kelly, Robert D. Galliers, and **James C. Brancheau.** "Key Issues in Information Systems Management: An International Perspective." *Journal of Management Information Systems* 13, no. 4 (Spring 1997).

Welty, Bill, and **Irma Becerra-Fernandez**. "Managing Trust and Commitment in Supply Chain Relationships." *Communications of the ACM* 44, no. 6 (June 2001).

CHAPTER 3

Allison, Graham T. *Essence of Decision-Explaining the Cuban Missile Crisis.* Boston: Boston: Little Brown (1971).

Alter, Steven, and **Michael Ginzberg.** "Managing Uncertainty in MIS Implementation." *Sloan Management Review* 20, no. 1 (Fall 1978).

Anthony, R. N. *Planning and Control Systems: A Framework for Analysis.* Cambridge, MA: Harvard University Press (1965).

Attewell, Paul, and **James Rule.** "Computing and Organizations: What We Know and What We Don't Know." *Communications of the ACM* 27, no. 12 (December 1984).

Beer, Michael, Russell A. Eisenstat, and **Bert Spector.** "Why Change Programs Don't Produce Change." *Harvard Business Review* (November–December 1990).

Bakos, J. Yannis, and **Michael E. Treacy.** "Information Technology and Corporate Strategy: A Research Perspective." *MIS Quarterly* (June 1986).

Bikson, T. K., and **J. D. Eveland.** "Integrating New Tools into Information Work." The Rand Corporation (1992). RAND/RP-106.

Blau, Peter, and **W. Richard Scott.** *Formal Organizations.* San Francisco: Chandler Press (1962).

Brancheau, James C., Brian D. Janz, and **James C. Wetherbe.** "Key Issues in Information Systems Management: 1994–1995 SIM Delphi Results." *MIS Quarterly* 20, no. 2 (June 1996).

Caldwell, Bruce. "A Cure for Hospital Woes." *Information Week* (September 9, 1991).

Camuffo, Arnaldo, Pietro Romano, and **Andrea Vinelli.** "Benetton Transforms Its Global Network," *Sloan Management Review* 43, no. 1 (Fall 2001).

Cash, J. I., and **Benn R. Konsynski.** "IS Redraws Competitive Boundaries." *Harvard Business Review* (March–April 1985).

Chan, Yolande E., Sid L. Huff, Donald W. Barclay, and **Duncan G. Copeland.** "Business Strategic Orientation, Information Systems Strategic Orientation, and Strategic Alignment." *Information Systems Research* 8, no. 2 (June 1997).

Christensen, Clayton. "The Past and Future of Competitive Advantage." *Sloan Management Review* 42, no. 2 (Winter 2001).

Christensen, Clayton M., Michael Raymor, and **Matthew Verlinden.** "Skate to Where the Money Will Be." *Harvard Business Review* (November 2001).

Clemons, Eric K. "Evaluation of Strategic Investments in Information Technology." *Communications of the ACM* (January 1991).

Clemons, Eric K., and **Bruce W. Weber.** "Segmentation, Differentiation, and Flexible Pricing: Experience with Information Technology and Segment-Tailored Strategies." *Journal of Management Information Systems* 11, no. 2 (Fall 1994).

Clemons, Eric K., and **Michael Row.** "McKesson Drug Co.: Case Study of a Strategic Information System." *Journal of Management Information Systems* (Summer 1988).

———. "Sustaining IT Advantage: The Role of Structural Differences." *MIS Quarterly* 15, no. 3 (September 1991).

———. "Limits to Interfirm Coordination through IT." *Journal of Management Information Systems* 10, no. 1 (Summer 1993).

——— and **Il-Horn Hann.** "Rosenbluth International: Strategic Transformation." *Journal of Management Information Systems* 16, no. 2 (Fall 1999).

Coase, Ronald H. "The Nature of the Firm."(1937) in Putterman, Louis, and Randall Kroszner. *The Economic Nature of the Firm: A Reader*, Cambridge University Press (1995).

Cohen, Michael, James March, and **Johan Olsen.** "A Garbage Can Model of Organizational Choice." *Administrative Science Quarterly* 17 (1972).

Copeland, Duncan G., and **James L. McKenney.** "Airline Reservations Systems: Lessons from History." *MIS Quarterly* 12, no. 3 (September 1988).

Davenport, Thomas H., and **Keri Pearlson.** "Two Cheers for the Virtual Office." *Sloan Management Review* 39, no. 4 (Summer 1998).

———, **Jeanne G. Harris,** and **Ajay K. Kohli.** "How Do They Know Their Customers So Well?" *Sloan Management Review* 42, no. 2 (Winter 2001).

Drucker, Peter. "The Coming of the New Organization." *Harvard Business Review* (January–February 1988).

Eardley, Alan, David Avison, and **Philip Powell.** "Developing Information Systems to Support Flexible Strategy." *Journal of Organizational Computing and Electronic Commerce* 7, no. 1 (1997).

Earl, Michael J., and **Jeffrey L. Sampler.** "Market Management to Transform the IT Organization." *Sloan Management Review* 39, no. 4 (Summer 1998).

El Sawy, Omar A. "Implementation by Cultural Infusion: An Approach for Managing the Introduction of Information Technologies." *MIS Quarterly* (June 1985).

Etzioni, Amitai. *A Comparative Analysis of Complex Organizations.* New York: Free Press (1975).

Fayol, Henri. *Administration industrielle et generale.* Paris: Dunods (1950, first published in 1916).

Feeny, David E., and **Blake Ives.** "In Search of Sustainability: Reaping Long-Term Advantage from Investments in Information Technology." *Journal of Management Information Systems* (Summer 1990).

Feeny, David. "Making Business Sense of the E-Opportunity." *Sloan Management Review* 42, no. 2 (Winter 2001).

Fisher, Marshall L., Ananth Raman, and **Anne Sheen McClelland.** "Rocket Science Retailing Is Almost Here: Are You Ready?" *Harvard Business Review* (July–August 2000).

Freeman, John, Glenn R. Carroll, and **Michael T. Hannan.** "The Liability of Newness: Age Dependence in Organizational Death Rates." *American Sociological Review* 48 (1983).

Fritz, Mary Beth Watson, Sridhar Narasimhan, and **Hyeun-Suk Rhee.** "Communication and Coordination in the Virtual Office." *Journal of Management Information Systems* 14, no. 4 (Spring 1998).

Fulk, Janet, and **Geraldine DeSanctis.** "Electronic Communication and Changing Organizational Forms." *Organization Science* 6, no. 4 (July–August 1995).

Garvin, David A. "The Processes of Organization and Management." *Sloan Management Review* 39, no. 4 (Summer 1998).

Glazer, Rashi. "Winning in Smart Markets." *Sloan Management Review* 40, no. 4 (Summer 1999).

Gorry, G. Anthony, and **Michael S. Scott Morton.** "A Framework for Management Information Systems." *Sloan Management Review* 13, no. 1 (Fall 1971).

Gurbaxani, V., and **S. Whang.** "The Impact of Information Systems on Organizations and Markets." *Communications of the ACM* 34, no. 1 (Jan. 1991).

Henderson, John C., and **John J. Sifonis.** "The Value of Strategic IS Planning: Understanding Consistency, Validity, and IS Markets." *MIS Quarterly* 12, no. 2 (June 1988).

Hopper, Max. "Rattling SABRE-New Ways to Compete on Information." *Harvard Business Review* (May–June 1990).

Hinds, Pamela, and **Sara Kiesler.** "Communication across Boundaries: Work, Structure, and Use of Communication Technologies in a Large Organization." *Organization Science* 6, no. 4 (July–August 1995).

Hitt, Lorin M. "Information Technology and Firm Boundaries: Evidence from Panel Data." *Information Systems Research* 10, no. 2 (June 1999).

Hitt, Lorin M., and **Erik Brynjolfsson.** "Information Technology and Internal Firm Organization: An Exploratory Analysis." *Journal of Management Information Systems* 14, no. 2 (Fall 1997).

Holweg, Matthias and **Frits K. Pil.** "Successful Build-to-Order Strategies Start with the Customer." *Sloan Management Review* 43, no. 1 (Fall 2001).

Huber, George P. "Cognitive Style as a Basis for MIS and DSS Designs: Much Ado About Nothing?" *Management Science* 29 (May 1983).

Huber, George. "Organizational Learning: The Contributing Processes and Literature." *Organization Science,* 2 (1991), pp. 88–115.

———. "The Nature and Design of Post-Industrial Organizations." *Management Science* 30, no. 8 (August 1984).

Isenberg, Daniel J. "How Senior Managers Think." *Harvard Business Review* (November–December 1984).

Jensen, Michael C., and **William H. Meckling.** "Theory of the Firm: Managerial Behavior, Agency Costs, and Ownership Structure." *Journal of Financial Economics* 3 (1976).

Jensen, Michael C., and **William H. Meckling.** "Specific and General Knowledge and Organizational Science." In *Contract Economics,* edited by L. Wetin and J. Wijkander. Oxford: Basil Blackwell (1992).

Kanter, Rosabeth Moss. "The New Managerial Work." *Harvard Business Review* (November–December 1989).

Johnston, Russell, and **Michael R. Vitale.** "Creating Competitive Advantage with Interorganizational Information Systems." *MIS Quarterly* 12, no. 2 (June 1988).

Kambil, Ajit, and **James E. Short.** "Electronic Integration and Business Network Redesign: A Roles-Linkage Perspective." *Journal of Management Information Systems* 10, no. 4 (Spring 1994).

Keen, Peter G.W. "Information Systems and Organizational Change." *Communications of the ACM* 24, no. 1 (January 1981).

Kettinger, William J., Varun Grover, Subashish Guhan, and **Albert H. Segors.** "Strategic Information Systems Revisited: A Study in Sustainability and Performance." *MIS Quarterly* 18, no. 1 (March 1994).

King, J. L., V. Gurbaxani, K. L. Kraemer, F. W. McFarlan, K. S. Raman, and **C. S. Yap.** "Institutional Factors in Information Technology Innovation." *Information Systems Research* 5, no. 2 (June 1994).

King, W. R. "Creating a Strategic Capabilities Architecture." *Information Systems Management* 12, no. 1 (Winter 1995).

Kling, Rob. "Social Analyses of Computing: Theoretical Perspectives in Recent Empirical Research." *Computing Survey* 12, no. 1 (March 1980).

Kling, Rob, and **William H. Dutton.** "The Computer Package: Dynamic Complexity." In *Computers and Politics,* edited by James Danziger, William Dutton, Rob Kling, and Kenneth Kraemer. New York: Columbia University Press (1982).

Kolb, D. A., and **A. L. Frohman.** "An Organization Development Approach to Consulting." *Sloan Management Review* 12, no. 1 (Fall 1970).

Konsynski, Benn R., and **F. Warren McFarlan.** "Information Partnerships—Shared Data, Shared Scale." *Harvard Business Review* (September–October 1990).

Kotter, John T. "What Effective General Managers Really Do." *Harvard Business Review* (November–December 1982).

Kraemer, Kenneth, John King, Debora Dunkle, and **Joe Lane.** *Managing Information Systems.* Los Angeles: Jossey-Bass (1989).

Kraut, Robert, Charles Steinfield, Alice P Chan, Brian Butler, and **Anne Hoag.** "Coordination and Virtualization: The Role of Electronic Networks and Personal Relationships." *Organization Science* 10, no. 6 (November–December 1999).

Kumar, Kuldeep, and **Jos Van Hillegersberg.** "ERP Experiences and Revolution." *Communications of the ACM* 43, no. 4 (April 2000).

Laudon, Kenneth C. *Computers and Bureaucratic Reform.* New York: Wiley (1974).

———. *Dossier Society: Value Choices in the Design of National Information Systems.* New York: Columbia University Press (1986).

———. "Environmental and Institutional Models of Systems Development." *Communications of the ACM* 28, no. 7 (July 1985).

———. "A General Model of the Relationship Between Information Technology and Organizations." Center for Research on Information Systems, New York University. Working paper, National Science Foundation (1989).

———. "The Promise and Potential of Enterprise Systems and Industrial Networks." Working paper, The Concours Group. Copyright Kenneth C. Laudon (1999).

Lawrence, Paul, and **Jay Lorsch.** *Organization and Environment.* Cambridge, MA: Harvard University Press (1969).

Leavitt, Harold J. "Applying Organizational Change in Industry: Structural, Technological, and Humanistic Approaches." In *Handbook of Organizations,* edited by James G. March. Chicago: Rand McNally (1965).

Leavitt, Harold J., and **Thomas L. Whisler.** "Management in the 1980s." *Harvard Business Review* (November–December 1958).

Lee, Ho-Geun. "Do Electronic Marketplaces Lower the Price of Goods?" *Communications of the ACM* 41, no. 1 (January 1998).

Lindblom, C. E. "The Science of Muddling Through." *Public Administration Review* 19 (1959).

McFarlan, F. Warren. "Information Technology Changes the Way You Compete." *Harvard Business Review* (May–June 1984).

Main, Thomas J., and **James E. Short.** "Managing the Merger: Building Partnership Through IT Planning at the New Baxter." *MIS Quarterly* 13, no. 4 (December 1989).

Mata, Franciso J., William L. Fuerst, and **Jay B. Barney.** "Information Technology and Sustained Competitive Advantage: A Resource-Based Analysis." *MIS Quarterly* 19, no. 4 (December 1995).

Machlup, Fritz. *The Production and Distribution of Knowledge in the United States.* Princeton, NJ: Princeton University Press (1962).

McKenney, James L., and **Peter G. W. Keen.** "How Managers' Minds Work." *Harvard Business Review* (May–June 1974).

Maier, Jerry L., R. Kelly Rainer, Jr., and **Charles A. Snyder.** "Environmental Scanning for Information Technology: An Empirical Investigation." *Journal of Management Information Systems* 14, no. 2 (Fall 1997).

Malone, Thomas W. "Is Empowerment Just a Fad? Control, Decision-Making, and IT." *Sloan Management Review* (Winter 1997).

March, James G., and **Herbert A. Simon.** *Organizations.* New York: Wiley (1958).

March, James G., and **G. Sevon.** "Gossip, Information, and Decision Making." In *Advances in Information Processing in Organizations,* edited by Lee S. Sproull and J. P. Crecine. vol. 1. Hillsdale, NJ: Erlbaum (1984).

Markus, M. L. "Power, Politics, and MIS Implementation." *Communications of the ACM* 26, no. 6 (June 1983).

Mendelson, Haim, and **Ravindra R. Pillai.** "Clock Speed and Informational Response: Evidence from the Information Technology Industry." *Information Systems Research* 9, no. 4 (December 1998).

Mintzberg, Henry. "Managerial Work: Analysis from Observation." *Management Science* 18 (October 1971).

Mintzberg, Henry. *The Structuring of Organizations.* Englewood Cliffs, NJ: Prentice Hall (1979).

———. *The Nature of Managerial Work.* New York: Harper & Row (1973).

Mintzberg, Henry, and **Frances Westley.** "Decision Making: It's Not What You Think." *Sloan Management Review* (Spring 2001).

Orlikowski, Wanda J., and **Daniel Robey.** "Information Technology and the Structuring of Organizations." *Information Systems Research* 2, no. 2 (June 1991).

Pindyck, Robert S., and **Daniel L. Rubinfeld.** *Microeconomics, Fifth Ed.* Upper Saddle River, NJ: Prentice Hall (2001).

Porter, Michael. *Competitive Strategy.* New York: Free Press (1980).

———. *Competitive Advantage.* New York: Free Press (1985).

———. "How Information Can Help You Compete." *Harvard Business Review* (August–September 1985a).

———. "Strategy and the Internet." *Harvard Business Review* (March 2001).

Porter, Michael E., and Scott Stern. "Location Matters." *Sloan Management Review* 42, no. 4 (Summer 2001).

Rebello, Joseph. "State Street Boston's Allure for Investors Starts to Fade." *The Wall Street Journal* (January 4, 1995).

Reich, Blaize Horner, and Izak Benbasat. "Factors that Influence the Social Dimension of Alignment between Business and Information Technology Objectives." *MIS Quarterly 24,* no. 1 (March 2000).

Robey, Daniel, and Marie-Claude Boudreau. "Accounting for the Contradictory Organizational Consequences of Information Technology: Theoretical Directions and Methodological Implications." *Information Systems Research* 10, no. 42 (June 1999).

Robey, Daniel, and Sundeep Sahay. "Transforming Work through Information Technology: A Comparative Case Study of Geographic Information Systems in County Government." *Information Systems Research* 7, no. 1 (March 1996).

Sauter, Vicki L. "Intuitive Decision-Making." *Communications of the ACM* 42, no 6 (June 1999).

Schein, Edgar H. *Organizational Culture and Leadership.* San Francisco: Jossey-Bass (1985).

Schwenk, C. R. "Cognitive Simplification Processes in Strategic Decision Making." *Strategic Management Journal,* 5 (1984).

Shapiro, Carl, and Hal R. Varian. *Information Rules.* Boston, MA: Harvard Business School Press (1999).

Shore, Edwin B. "Reshaping the IS Organization." *MIS Quarterly* (December 1983).

Short, James E., and N. Venkatraman. "Beyond Business Process Redesign: Redefining Baxter's Business Network." *Sloan Management Review* (Fall 1992).

Simon, H. A. *The New Science of Management Decision.* New York: Harper & Row (1960).

Simon, Herbert A. "Applying Information Technology to Organization Design." *Public Administration Review* (May–June 1973).

Starbuck, William H. "Organizations as Action Generators." *American Sociological Review* 48 (1983).

Starbuck, William H., and Frances J. Milliken. "Executives' Perceptual Filters: What They Notice and How They Make Sense." In *The Executive Effect: Concepts and Methods for Studying Top Managers,* edited by D. C. Hambrick. Greenwich, CT: JAI Press (1988).

Staples, D. Sandy, John S. Hulland, and Christopher A. Higgins. "A Self-Efficacy Theory Explanation for the Management of Remote Workers in Virtual Organizations." *Organization Science* 10, no. 6 (November–December 1999).

Straub, Detmar, and James C. Wetherbe. "Information Technologies for the 1990s: An Organizational Impact Perspective." *Communications of the ACM* 32, no. 11 (November 1989).

Turner, Jon A. "Computer Mediated Work: The Interplay Between Technology And Structured Jobs." *Communications Of The ACM* 27, No. 12 (December 1984).

Turner, Jon A., and Robert A. Karasek, Jr. "Software Ergonomics: Effects of Computer Application Design Parameters on Operator Task Performance and Health." *Ergonomics* 27, no. 6 (1984).

Tushman, Michael L., and Philip Anderson. "Technological Discontinuities and Organizational Environments." *Administrative Science Quarterly* 31 (September 1986).

Tversky, A., and D. Kahneman. "The Framing of Decisions and the Psychology of Choice." *Science* 211 (January 1981).

Uslaner, Eric M. "Social Capital and the Net." *Communications of the ACM* 43, no. 12 (December 2000).

Weber, Max. *The Theory of Social and Economic Organization.* Translated by Talcott Parsons. New York: Free Press (1947).

Williamson, Oliver E. *The Economic Institutions of Capitalism.* New York: Free Press (1985).

Wiseman, Charles. *Strategic Information Systems.* Homewood, IL: Richard D. Irwin (1988).

Wrapp, H. Edward. "Good Managers Don't Make Policy Decisions." *Harvard Business Review* (July–August 1984).

CHAPTER 4

Andrew, James P., Andy Blackburn, and Harold L. Sirkin. "The Business-to-Business Opportunity." *Boston Consulting Group* (October 2000).

Armstrong, Arthur, and John Hagel, III. "The Real Value of On-line Communities." *Harvard Business Review* (May–June 1996).

Bakos, Yannis. "The Emerging Role of Electronic Marketplaces and the Internet." *Communications of the ACM* 41, no. 8 (August 1998).

Bannan, Karen J. "Chatting Up a Sale." *The Wall Street Journal* (October 23, 2000).

Baron, John P., Michael J. Shaw, and Andrew D. Bailey, Jr. "Web-based E-catalog Systems in B2B Procurement." *Communications of the ACM* 43, no.5 (May 2000).

Barua, Anitesh, Sury Ravindran, and Andrew B. Whinston. "Efficient Selection of Suppliers over the Internet." *Journal of Management Information Systems* 13, no. 4 (Spring 1997).

Barua, Anitesh, Prabhudev Konana, Andrew B. Whinston, and Fang Yin. "Driving E-Business Excellence," *Sloan Management Review* 43, no. 1 (Fall 2001).

Chaudhury, Abhijit, Debasish Mallick, and H. Raghav Rao. "Web Channels in E-Commerce." *Communications of the ACM* 44, No. 1 (January 2001).

Christensen, Clayton M. *The Innovator's Dilemma.* New York: HarperCollins (2000).

Choi, Soon-Yong, Dale O. Stahl, and Andrew B. Whinston. *The Economics of Electronic Commerce.* Indianapolis, IN: Macmillan Technical Publishing (1997).

Cronin, Mary. *The Internet Strategy Handbook.* Boston, MA: Harvard Business School Press (1996).

Downes, Larry, and Chunka Mui. *Unleashing the Killer App: Digital Strategies for Market Dominance.* Boston, MA: Harvard Business School Press (1998).

El Sawy, Omar A., Arvind Malhotra, Sanjay Gosain, and Kerry M. Young. "IT-Intensive Value Innovation in the Electronic Economy: Insights from Marshall Industries." *MIS Quarterly* 23, no. 3, (September 1999).

Elofson, Greg, and William N. Robinson. "Creating a Custom Mass Production Channel on the Internet." *Communications of the ACM* 41, no. 3 (March 1998).

Evans, Philip, and Thomas S. Wurster. *Blown to Bits: How the New Economics of Information Transforms Strategy.* Boston, MA: Harvard Business School Press (2000).

Evans, Philip, and Thomas S. Wurster. "Getting Real about Virtual Commerce." *Harvard Business Review* (November–December 1999).

———. "Strategy and the New Economics of Information." *Harvard Business Review* (September–October 1997).

Farhoomand, Ali with Peter Lovelock. *Global E-Commerce.* Singapore: Pearson Education Asia (2001).

Ghosh, Shikhar. "Making Business Sense of the Internet." *Harvard Business Review* (March–April 1998).

Gopal, Ram D., Zhiping Walter, and **Arvind K. Tripathi**. "Amediation: New Horizons In Effective Email Advertising." *Communications of the ACM* 44, no. 12 (December 2001).

Grover, Varun, and **Pradipkumar Ramanlal.** "Six Myths of Information and Markets: Information Technology Networks, Electronic Commerce, and the Battle for Consumer Surplus." *MIS Quarterly* 23, no. 4 (December 1999).

————— and **James T.C. Teng.** "E-Commerce and the Information Market." *Communications of the ACM* 44, no. 4 (April 2001).

Gulati, Ranjay, and **Jason Garino.** "Get the Right Mix of Bricks and Clicks." *Harvard Business Review* (May–June 2000).

Hagel, John III, and **Marc Singer.** *Net Worth.* Boston, MA: Harvard Business School Press (1999).

—————. "Unbundling the Corporation." *Harvard Business Review* (March–April 1999).

Jones, Sara, Marc Wilikens, Philip Morris, and **Marcelo Masera.** "Trust Requirements in E-Business." *Communications of the ACM* 43, no. 12 (December 2000).

Kalakota, Ravi, and **Andrew B. Whinston.** *Electronic Commerce: A Manager's Guide.* Reading MA: Addison-Wesley (1997).

Kanan, P. K., Ai-Mei Chang, and **Andrew B. Whinston.** "Marketing Information on the I-Way." *Communications of the ACM* 41, no. 3 (March 1998).

Kaplan, Steven, and **Mohanbir Sawhney.** "E-Hubs: the New B2B Marketplaces." *Harvard Business Review* (May–June 2000).

Kauffman, Robert J., and **Bin Wang.** "New Buyers' Arrival Under Dynamic Pricing Market Microstructure: The Case of Group-Buying Discounts on the Internet." *Journal of Management Information Systems* 18, no. 2 (Fall 2001).

Kenny, David, and **John F. Marshall.** "Contextual Marketing." *Harvard Business Review* (November–December 2000).

Lai, Vincent S. "Intraorganizational Communication with Intranets." *Communications of the ACM* 44, no. 7 (July 2001).

Laudon, Kenneth C., and **Carol Guercio Traver.** *E-Commerce: Business, Technology, Society.* Boston: Addison-Wesley (2002).

Lee, Hau L., and **Seungin Whang.** "Winning the Last Mile of E-Commerce." *Sloan Management Review* 42, no. 4 (Summer 2001).

Lee, Ho Geun, and **Theodore H. Clark.** "Market Process Reengineering through Electronic Market Systems: Opportunities and Challenges." *Journal of Management Information Systems* 13, no. 3 (Winter 1997).

Lee, Ho Geun. "Do Electronic Marketplaces Lower the Price of Goods?" *Communications of the ACM* 41, no. 1 (January 1998).

McWilliam, Gil. "Building Stronger Brands through Online Communities." *Sloan Management Review* 41, no. 3 (Spring 2000).

Mougayar, Walid. *Opening Digital Markets,* 2nd ed. New York: McGraw-Hill (1998).

O'Leary, Daniel E., Daniel Koukka, and **Robert Plant.** "Artificial Intelligence and Virtual Organizations." *Communications of the ACM* 40, no. 1 (January 1997).

Palmer, Jonathan W., and **David A. Griffith.** "An Emerging Model of Web Site Design for Marketing." *Communications of the ACM* 41, no. 3 (March 1998).

Prahalad, C.K., and **Venkatram Ramaswamy.** "Coopting Consumer Competence." *Harvard Business Review* (January–February 2000).

Quelch, John A., and **Lisa R. Klein.** "The Internet and International Marketing." *Sloan Management Review* (Spring 1996).

Rayport, J. F., and **J. J. Sviokla.** "Managing in the Marketspace." *Harvard Business Review* (November–December 1994).

Redburn, Tom. "How Much Am I Bid for this Imperfect Marketplace?" *The New York Times E-Commerce Section* (December 13, 2000).

Reichheld, Frederick E., and **Phil Schefter.** "E-Loyalty: Your Secret Weapon on the Web." *Harvard Business Review* (July–August 2000).

Schoder, Detlef, and **Pai-ling Yin.** "Building Firm Trust Online." *Communications of the ACM* 43, no. 12 (December 2000).

Singh, Surendra N., and **Nikunj P. Dalal.** "Web Home Pages as Advertisements." *Communications of the ACM* 42, no. 8 (August 1999).

Smith, Michael D., Joseph Bailey, and **Erik Brynjolfsson.** "Understanding Digital Markets: Review and Assessment" in Erik Brynjolfsson and Brian Kahin, ed. *Understanding the Digital Economy.* Cambridge, MA: MIT Press (1999).

Steinfield, Charles. "The Impact of Electronic Commerce on Buyer-Seller Relationships." *JCMC* 1, no. 3 (December 1995).

Subramanian, Rangan, and **Ron Adner.** "Profits and the Internet: Seven Misconceptions." *Sloan Management Review* 42, no. 4 (Summer 2001).

Venkatraman, N. "Five Steps to a Dot-Com Strategy: How to Find Your Footing on the Web." *Sloan Management Review* 41, no. 3 (Spring 2000).

Weill, Peter and **Michael Vitale.** *Place to Space: Migrating to E-Business Models.* Boston, MA: Harvard Business School Press (2001).

Werbach, Kevin. "Syndication: The Emerging Model for Business in the Internet Era." *Harvard Business Review* (May–June 2000).

Wigand, Rolf T., and **Robert Benjamin.** "Electronic Commerce: Effects on Electronic Markets." *JCMC* 1, no. 3 (December 1995).

Willcocks, Leslie, and **Robert Plant.** "Pathways to E-Business Leadership." *Sloan Management Review* (Spring 2001).

Wise, Richard, and **David Morrison.** "Beyond the Exchange: The Future of B2B." *Harvard Business Review* (November–December 2000).

CHAPTER 5

Angwin, Julia. "How an E-Posse Led to Arrests in Online Fraud." *The Wall Street Journal* (May 4, 2000).

Association of Computing Machinery. "ACM's Code of Ethics and Professional Conduct." *Communications of the ACM* 36, no. 12 (December 1993).

Ball, Kirstie S. "Situating Workplace Surveillance: Ethics and Computer-based Performance Monitoring." *Ethics and Information Technology* 3, no. 3 (2001).

Bellman, Steven, Eric J. Johnson, and **Gerald L. Lohse.** "To Opt-in or Opt-out? It Depends on the Question." *Communications of the ACM* 44, no. 2 (February 2001).

Bennett, Colin J. "Cookies, Web Bugs, Webcams, and Cue Cats: Patterns of Surveillance on the World Wide Web." *Ethics and Information Technology* 3, no. 3 (2001).

Berdichevsky, Daniel, and **Erik Neunschwander.** "Toward an Ethics of Persuasive Technology." *Communications of the ACM* 42, no. 5 (May 1999).

Bowen, Jonathan. "The Ethics of Safety-Critical Systems." *Communications of the ACM* 43, no. 3 (April 2000).

Brod, Craig. *Techno Stress—The Human Cost of the Computer Revolution.* Reading MA: Addison-Wesley (1982).

Brown Bag Software vs. Symantec Corp. 960 F2D 1465 (Ninth Circuit, 1992).

Burk, Dan L. "Copyrightable Functions and Patentable Speech." *Communications of the ACM* 44, no. 2 (February 2001).

Cavazos, Edward A. "The Legal Risks of Setting up Shop in Cyberspace." *Journal of Organizational Computing* 6, no. 1 (1996).

Chabrow, Eric R. "The Internet: Copyrights." *Information Week* (March 25, 1996).

Cheng, Hsing K., Ronald R. Sims, and **Hildy Teegen.** "To Purchase or to Pirate Software: An Empirical Study." *Journal of Management Information Systems* 13, no. 4 (Spring 1997).

Clarke, Roger. "Internet Privacy Concerns Confirm the Case for Intervention." *Communications of the ACM* 42, no. 2 (February 1999).

Collins, W. Robert, Keith W. Miller, Bethany J. Spielman, and **Phillip Wherry.** "How Good Is Good Enough? An Ethical Analysis of Software Construction and Use." *Communications of the ACM* 37, no. 1 (January 1994).

Computer Systems Policy Project. "Perspectives on the National Information Infrastructure." (January 12, 1993).

Cranor, Lorrie Faith, and **Brian A. LaMacchia.** "Spam!" *Communications of the ACM* 41, no. 8 (August 1998).

Davis, Randall. "The Digital Dilemma." *Communications of the ACM* 44, no. 2 (February 2001).

Dejoie, Roy, George Fowler, and **David Paradice,** eds. *Ethical Issues in Information Systems.* Boston: Boyd & Fraser (1991).

Denning, Dorothy E., et al., "To Tap or Not to Tap." *Communications of the ACM* 36, no. 3 (March 1993).

Friedman, Batya, Peter H. Kahn, Jr., and **Daniel C. Howek.** "Trust Online." *Communications of the ACM* 43, no. 12 (December 2000).

Froomkin, A. Michael. "The Collision of Trademarks, Domain Names, and Due Process in Cyberspace." *Communications of the ACM* 44, no. 2 (February 2001).

Gattiker, Urs E., and **Helen Kelley**. "Morality and Computers: Attitudes and Differences in Judgments." *Information Systems Research* 10, no. 3 (September 1999).

Gopal, Ram D., and **G. Lawrence Sanders.** "Preventive and Deterrent Controls for Software Piracy." *Journal of Management Information Systems* 13, no. 4 (Spring 1997).

———. "Global Software Piracy: You Can't Get Blood Out of a Turnip." *Communications of the ACM* 43, no. 9 (September 2000).

Graham, Robert L. "The Legal Protection of Computer Software." *Communications of the ACM* (May 1984).

Green, R. H. *The Ethical Manager.* New York: Macmillan (1994).

Harrington, Susan J. "The Effect of Codes of Ethics and Personal Denial of Responsibility on Computer Abuse Judgments and Intentions." *MIS Quarterly* 20, no. 2 (September 1996).

Harmon, Amy. "Software that Tracks E-Mail is Raising Privacy Concerns." *The New York Times* (November 22, 2000).

Huff, Chuck, and **C. Dianne Martin.** "Computing Consequences: A Framework for Teaching Ethical Computing." *Communications of the ACM* 38, no. 12 (December 1995).

Joes, Kathryn. "EDS Set to Restore Cash-Machine Network." *The New York Times* (March 26, 1993).

Johnson, Deborah G. "Ethics Online." *Communications of the ACM* 40, no. 1 (January 1997).

Johnson, Deborah G., and **John M. Mulvey.** "Accountability and Computer Decision Systems." *Communications of the ACM* 38, no. 12 (December 1995).

Keen, Peter and **Mark McDonald**. *The e-Process Edge.* Berkeley, California: Osborne/McGraw-Hill (2000).

King, Julia. "It's CYA Time." *Computerworld* (March 30, 1992).

Kling, Rob. "When Organizations Are Perpetrators: The Conditions of Computer Abuse and Computer Crime." In *Computerization & Controversy: Value Conflicts & Social Choices,* edited by Charles Dunlop and Rob Kling. New York: Academic Press (1991).

Kreie, Jennifer, and **Timothy Paul Cronan**. "Making Ethical Decisions." *Communications of the ACM* 43, no. 12 (December 2000).

Laudon, Kenneth C. "Ethical Concepts and Information Technology." *Communications of the ACM* 38, no. 12 (December 1995).

Martin, David M. Jr., Richard M. Smith, Michael Brittain, Ivan Fetch, and **Hailin Wu**. "The Privacy Practices of Web Browser Extensions." *Communications of the ACM* 44, no. 2 (February 2001).

Mason, Richard O. "Applying Ethics to Information Technology Issues." *Communications of the ACM* 38, no. 12 (December 1995).

Mason, Richard O. "Four Ethical Issues in the Information Age." *MIS Quarterly* 10, no. 1 (March 1986).

Memon, Nasir, and **Ping Wah Wong.** "Protecting Digital Media Content." *Communications of the ACM* 41, no. 7 (July 1998).

Milberg, Sandra J., Sandra J. Burke, H. Jeff Smith, and **Ernest A. Kallman.** "Values, Personal Information Privacy, and Regulatory Approaches." *Communications of the ACM* 38, no. 12 (December 1995).

Moores, Trevor, and **Gurpreet Dhillon.** "Software Piracy: A View from Hong Kong." *Communications of the ACM* 43, no. 12, (December 2000).

Mykytyn, Kathleen, Peter P. Mykytyn, Jr., and **Craig W. Slinkman.** "Expert Systems: A Question of Liability." *MIS Quarterly* 14, no. 1 (March 1990).

National Telecommunications & Information Administration. U.S. Department of Commerce. "Falling Through the Net: Defining the Digital Divide." July 8, 1999.

Nissenbaum, Helen. "Computing and Accountability." *Communications of the ACM* 37, no. 1 (January 1994).

Okerson, Ann. "Who Owns Digital Works?" *Scientific American* (July 1996).

O'Rourke, Maureen A. "Is Virtual Trespass an Apt Analogy?" *Communications of the ACM* 44, no. 2 (February 2001).

Oz, Effy. "Ethical Standards for Information Systems Professionals." *MIS Quarterly* 16, no. 4 (December 1992).

———. *Ethics for the Information Age.* Dubuque, Iowa: W. C. Brown (1994).

Rainie, Lee, and **Dan Packel.** "More Online, Doing More." The Pew Internet and American Life Project (Febuary 18, 2001).

Reagle, Joseph, and **Lorrie Faith Cranor.** "The Platform for Privacy Preferences." *Communications of the ACM* 42, no. 2 (February 1999).

Redman, Thomas C. "The Impact of Poor Data Quality on the Typical Enterprise." *Communications of the ACM* 41, no. 2 (February 1998).

Rifkin, Jeremy. "Watch Out for Trickle-Down Technology." *The New York Times* (March 16, 1993).

Rigdon, Joan E. "Frequent Glitches in New Software Bug Users." *The Wall Street Journal* (January 18, 1995).

Rotenberg, Marc. "Communications Privacy: Implications for Network Design." *Communications of the ACM* 36, no. 8 (August 1993).

Samuelson, Pamela. "Computer Programs and Copyright's Fair Use Doctrine." *Communications of the ACM* 36, no. 9 (September 1993).

———. "Copyright's Fair Use Doctrine and Digital Data." *Communications of the ACM* 37, no. 1 (January 1994).

———. "Liability for Defective Electronic Information." *Communications of the ACM* 36, no. 1 (January 1993).

———. "Self Plagiarism or Fair Use?" *Communications of the ACM* 37, no. 8 (August 1994).

———. "The Ups and Downs of Look and Feel." *Communications of the ACM* 36, no. 4 (April 1993).

Sewell, Graham, and **James R. Barker.** "Neither Good, nor Bad, but Dangerous: Surveillance as an Ethical Paradox." *Ethics and Information Technology* 3, no. 3 (2001).

Sipior, Janice C., and **Burke T. Ward.** "The Dark Side of Employee Email." *Communications of the ACM* 42, no.7 (July 1999).

———. "The Ethical and Legal Quandary of E-mail Privacy." *Communications of the ACM* 38, no. 12 (December 1995).

Smith, H. Jeff. "Privacy Policies and Practices: Inside the Organizational Maze." *Communications of the ACM* 36, no. 12, (December 1993).

Smith, H. Jeff, and John Hasnas. "Ethics and Information Systems: The Corporate Domain." *MIS Quarterly* 23, no. 1 (March 1999).

Smith, H. Jeff, Sandra J. Milberg, and Sandra J. Burke. "Information Privacy: Measuring Individuals' Concerns about Organizational Practices." *MIS Quarterly* 20, no. 2 (June 1996).

Straub, Detmar W., Jr., and Rosann Webb Collins. "Key Information Liability Issues Facing Managers: Software Piracy, Proprietary Databases, and Individual Rights to Privacy." *MIS Quarterly* 14, no. 2 (June 1990).

Straub, Detmar W., Jr., and William D. Nance. "Discovering and Disciplining Computer Abuse in Organizations: A Field Study." *MIS Quarterly* 14, no. 1 (March 1990).

Sullivan, Brian. "IT Worker Pleads Guilty to Sabotaging Computers." *Computerworld* (March 26, 2001).

The Telecommunications Policy Roundtable. "Renewing the Commitment to a Public Interest Telecommunications Policy." *Communications of the ACM* 37, no. 1 (January 1994).

Thong, James Y. L., and Chee-Sing Yap. "Testing an Ethical Decision-Making Theory." *Journal of Management Information Systems* 15, no. 1 (Summer 1998).

Tuttle, Brad, Adrian Harrell, and Paul Harrison. "Moral Hazard, Ethical Considerations, and the Decision to Implement an Information System." *Journal of Management Information Systems* 13, no. 4 (Spring 1997).

United States Department of Health, Education, and Welfare. *Records, Computers, and the Rights of Citizens.* Cambridge: MIT Press (1973).

Urbaczewski, Andrew, and Leonard M. Jessup. "Does Electronic Monitoring of Employee Internet Usage Work?" *Communications of the ACM* 45, no. 1 (January 2002).

Vijayan, Jaikumar. "Caught in the Middle." *Computerworld* (July 24, 2000).

Volokh, Eugene. "Personalization and Privacy." *Communications of the ACM* 43, no. 8 (August 2000).

Wang, Huaiqing, Matthew K. O. Lee, and Chen Wang. "Consumer Privacy Concerns about Internet Marketing." *Communications of the ACM* 41, no. 3 (March 1998).

Zviran, Moshe, and William J. Haga. "Password Security: An Empirical Study." *Journal of Management Information Systems* 15, no. 4 (Spring 1999).

CHAPTER 6

Alison, Diana. "IT Takes on Handheld Management." *Information Week* (May 29, 2000).

Backus, John, "Funding the Computing Revolution's Third Wave." *Communications of the ACM* 44, no. 11 (November 2001).

Bell, Gordon, and Jim Gray. "What's Next in High-Performance Computing?" *Communications of the ACM* 45, no. 1 (January 2002).

Benamati, John, and Albert L. Lederer. "Coping with Rapid Changes in IT." *Communications of the ACM* 44, no. 8 (August 2001).

Bosak, Jon, and Tim Bray. "XML and the Second-Generation Web." *Scientific American* (May 1999).

Clark, Don. "The End of Software." *The Wall Street Journal Technology Report* (November 15, 1999).

David, Julie Smith, David Schuff, and Robert St. Louis. "Managing Your IT Total Cost of Ownership." *Communications of the ACM* 45, no. 1 (January 2002).

Dempsey, Bert J., Debra Weiss, Paul Jones, and Jane Greenberg. "What Is an Open Source Software Developer?" *Communications of the ACM* 45, no. 1 (January 2001).

Fayad, Mohamed, and Marshall P. Cline. "Aspects of Software Adaptability." *Communications of the ACM* 39, no. 10 (October 1996).

Fitzmaurice, George W., Rvain Balakrishnan, and Gordon Kurtenbach. "Sampling, Synthesis, and Input Devices." *Communications of the ACM* 42, no. 8 (August 1999).

Fulton, Susan M. "Speak Softly, Carry a Big Chip." *The New York Times Circuits* (March 30, 2000).

Gibson, Garth A., and Rodney Van Meter. "Network Attached Storage Architecture." *Communications of the ACM* 43, no. 11 (November 2000).

Gomes, Lee. "Somebody Else's Problem." *The Wall Street Journal Technology Report* (November 15, 1999).

Hardaway, Don, and Richard P. Will. "Digital Multimedia Offers Key to Educational Reform." *Communications of the ACM* 40, no. 4 (April 1997).

Jacobs, April. "The Network Computer: Where It's Going." *Computerworld* (December 23, 1997/January 2, 1998).

Kim, Yongbeom, and Edward A. Stohr. "Software Reuse." *Journal of Management Information Systems* 14, no. 4 (Spring 1998).

Korson, Tim, and John D. McGregor. "Understanding Object-Oriented: A Unifying Paradigm." *Communications of the ACM* 33, no. 9 (September 1990).

Linthicum, David S. "EAI Application Integration Exposed." *Software Magazine* (February/March 2000).

Mandelkern, David. "Graphical User Interfaces: The Next Generation." *Communications of the ACM* 36, no. 4 (April 1993).

Messina, Paul, David Culler, Wayne Pfeiffer, William Martin, J. Tinsley Oden, and Gary Smith. "Architecture." *Communications of the ACM* 41, no. 11 (November 1998).

Noffsinger, W. B., Robert Niedbalski, Michael Blanks, and Niall Emmart. "Legacy Object Modeling Speeds Software Integration." *Communications of the ACM* 41, no. 12 (December 1998).

Pancake, Cherri M., and Christian Lengauer. "High-Performance Java." *Communications of the ACM* 44, no. 10 (October 2001).

Paul, Lauren Gibbons. "What Price Ownership?" *Datamation* (December/January 1998).

Post, Gerald V. "How Often Should a Firm Buy New PCs?" *Communications of the ACM* 42, no. 5 (May 1999).

Poulin, Jeffrey S. "Reuse: Been There, Done That." *Communications of the ACM* 42, no. 5 (May 1999).

Robinson, Teri. "NASDAQ Is Bullish on Technology." *Information Week* (May 22, 2000).

Schuff, David, and Robert St. Louis. "Centralization vs. Decentralization of Application Software." *Communications of the ACM* 44, no. 6 (June 2001).

Selker, Ted. "New Paradigms for Using Computers." *Communications of the ACM* 39, no. 8 (August 1996).

Sheetz, Steven D., Gretchen Irwin, David P. Tegarden, H. James Nelson, and David E. Monarchi. "Exploring the Difficulties of Learning Object-Oriented Techniques." *Journal of Management Information Systems* 14, no. 2 (Fall 1997).

Tennenhouse, David. "Proactive Computing." *Communications of the ACM* 43, no. 5 (May 2000).

Vassiliou, Yannis. "On the Interactive Use of Databases: Query Languages." *Journal of Management Information Systems* 1 (Winter 1984–1985).

Von Hippel, Eric. "Learning from Open-Source Software." *Sloan Management Review* 42, no. 4 (Summer 2001).

CHAPTER 7

Belkin, Nicholas J., and **W. Bruce Croft.** "Information Filtering and Information Retrieval: Two Sides of the Same Coin?" *Communications of the ACM* 35, no. 12 (November 1992).

Chang, Shih-Fu, John R. Amith, Mandis Beigi, and **Ana Benitez.** "Visual Information Retrieval from Large Distributed On-line Repositories." *Communications of the ACM* 40, no. 12 (December 1997).

Clifford, James, Albert Croker, and **Alex Tuzhilin.** "On Data Representation and Use in a Temporal Relational DBMS." *Information Systems Research* 7, no. 3 (September 1996).

Cooper, Brian L., Hugh J. Watson, Barbara H. Wixom, and **Dale L. Goodhue.** "Data Warehousing Supports Corporate Strategy at First American Corporation." *MIS Quarterly* (December 2000).

Fiori, Rich. "The Information Warehouse." *Relational Database Journal* (January–February 1995).

Gardner, Stephen R. "Building the Data Warehouse." *Communications of the ACM* 41, no. 9 (September 1998).

Goldstein, R. C., and **J. B. McCririck.** "What Do Data Administrators Really Do?" *Datamation* 26 (August 1980).

Goodhue, Dale L., Judith A. Quillard, and **John F. Rockart.** "Managing the Data Resource: A Contingency Perspective." *MIS Quarterly* (September 1988).

Goodhue, Dale L., Laurie J. Kirsch, Judith A. Quillard, and **Michael D. Wybo.** "Strategic Data Planning: Lessons from the Field." *MIS Quarterly* 16, no. 1 (March 1992).

Goodhue, Dale L., Michael D. Wybo, and **Laurie J. Kirsch.** "The Impact of Data Integration on the Costs and Benefits of Information Systems." *MIS Quarterly* 16, no. 3 (September 1992).

Grosky, William I. "Managing Multimedia Information in Database Systems." *Communications of the ACM* 40, no. 12 (December 1997).

Grover, Varun, and **James Teng.** "How Effective Is Data Resource Management?" *Journal of Information Systems Management* (Summer 1991).

Gupta, Amarnath, and **Ranesh Jain.** "Visual Information Retrieval." *Communications of the ACM* 40, no. 5 (May 1997).

Hirji, Karim K. "Exploring Data Mining Implementation." *Communications of the ACM* 44, no. 7 (July 2001).

Inman, W. H. "The Data Warehouse and Data Mining." *Communications of the ACM* 39, no. 11 (November 1996).

Kahn, Beverly K. "Some Realities of Data Administration." *Communications of the ACM* 26 (October 1983).

King, John L., and **Kenneth Kraemer.** "Information Resource Management Cannot Work." *Information and Management* (1988).

Kroenke, David. *Database Processing: Fundamentals, Design, and Implementation,* 8th ed. Upper Saddle River, NJ: Prentice Hall (2002).

Lange, Danny B. "An Object-Oriented Design Approach for Developing Hypermedia Information Systems." *Journal of Organizational Computing and Electronic Commerce* 6, no. 2 (1996).

March, Salvatore T., and **Young-Gul Kim.** "Information Resource Management: A Metadata Perspective." *Journal of Management Information Systems* 5, no. 3 (Winter 1988–1989).

McCarthy, John. "Phenomenal Data Mining." *Communications of the ACM* 43, no. 8 (August 2000).

McFadden, Fred R., Jeffrey A. Hoffer, and **Mary B. Prescott.** *Modern Database Management,* Sixth Edition. Upper Saddle River, NJ: Prentice-Hall (2002).

Rundensteiner, Elke A, Andreas Koeller, and **Xin Zhang.** "Maintaining Data Warehouses over Changing Information Sources." *Communications of the ACM* 43, no. 6 (June 2000).

Silberschatz, Avi, Michael Stonebraker, and **Jeff Ullman,** eds. "Database Systems: Achievements and Opportunities." *Communications of the ACM* 34, no. 10 (October 1991).

Smith, John B., and **Stephen F. Weiss.** "Hypertext." *Communications of the ACM* 31, no. 7 (July 1988).

Truman, Gregory E. "Integration in Electronic Exchange Environments." *Journal of Management Information Systems* 17, no. 1 (Summer 2000).

Watson, Hugh J., and **Barbara J. Haley.** "Managerial Considerations." *Communications of the ACM* 41, no. 9 (September 1998).

Woods, Tony, and **Kate O'Rourke.** "Keeping Track of Customers." *E-Doc* (May/June 2000).

CHAPTER 8

Boston Consulting Group. "Mobile Commerce: Winning the On-Air Consumer" (November 2000).

Brunner, Marcus, Bernhard Plattner, and **Rolf Stadler.** "Service Creation and Management in Active Telecom Networks." *Communications of the ACM* 44, no. 4 (April 2001).

Carr, Jim. "The Forgotten Networks." *mBusiness* (June 2001).

Chatfield, Akemi Takeoka, and **Philip Yetton.** "Strategic Payoff from EDI as a Function of EDI Embeddedness." *Journal of Management Information Systems* 16, no. 4 (Spring 2000).

Chatterjee, Samir. "Requirements for Success in Gigabit Networking." *Communications of the ACM* 40, no. 7 (July 1997).

Chatterjee, Samir, and **Suzanne Pawlowski.** "All-Optical Networks." *Communications of the ACM* 42, no. 6 (June 1999).

Concours Group. "Managing and Exploiting Corporate Intranets" (1999).

Damsgaard Jan, and **Kalle Lyytinen.** "Building Electronic Trading Infrastructues: A Public or Private Responsibility?" *Journal of Organizational Computing and Electronic Commerce* 11, no. 2 (2001).

Duchessi, Peter, and **InduShobha Chengalur-Smith.** "Client/Server Benefits, Problems, Best Practices." *Communications of the ACM* 41, no. 5 (May 1998).

Dutta, Amitava. "Telecommunications and Economic Activity: An Analysis of Granger Causality." *Journal of Management Information Systems* 17, no. 4 (Spring 2001).

Gefen, David, and **Detmar W. Straub.** "Gender Differences in the Perception and Use of E-Mail: An Extension to the Technology Acceptance Model." *MIS Quarterly* 21, no. 4 (December 1997).

Grover, Varun, and **Martin D. Goslar.** "Initiation, Adoption, and Implementation of Telecommunications Technologies in U.S. Organizations." *Journal of Management Information Systems* 10, no. 1 (Summer 1993).

Hart, Paul J., and **Carol Stoak Saunders.** "Emerging Electronic Partnerships: Antecedents and Dimensions of EDI Use from the Supplier's Perspective." *Journal of Management Information Systems* 14, no. 4 (Spring 1998).

Heywood, Peter. "Charge of the Light Brigade." *Red Herring* (February 2000).

Hill, G. Christian. "First Voice, Now Data." *The Wall Street Journal* (September 20, 1999).

Housel, Tom, and **Eric Skopec.** *Global Telecommunication Revolution: The Business Perspective.* New York: McGraw-Hill (2001).

Imielinski, Tomasz, and **B. R. Badrinath.** "Mobile Wireless Computing: Challenges in Data Management." *Communications of the ACM* 37, no. 10 (October 1994).

Karahanna, Elena, and **Moez Limayem.** "E-Mail and V-Mail Usage: Generalizing Across Technologies." *Journal of Organizational Computing and Electronic Commerce* 10, no. 1 (2000).

Keen, Peter G. W. *Competing in Time: Using Telecommunications for Competitive Advantage.* Cambridge, MA: Ballinger Publishing Company (1986).

Kim, B. G., and **P. Wang.** "ATM Network: Goals and Challenges." *Communications of the ACM* 38, no. 2 (February 1995).

Lee, Ho Geun, Theodore Clark, and **Kar Yan Tam.** "Research Report: Can EDI Benefit Adopters?" *Information Systems Research* 10, no. 2 (June 1999).

Massetti, Brenda, and **Robert W. Zmud.** "Measuring the Extent of EDI Usage in Complex Organizations. Strategies and Illustrative Examples." *MIS Quarterly* 20, no. 3 (September 1996).

Mears, Rena, and **Jason Salzetti.** "The New Wireless Enterprise." *Information Week* (September 18, 2000).

Meister, Frank, Jeetu Patel, and **Joe Fenner.** "E-Commerce Platforms Mature." *Information Week* (Ocrober 23, 2000).

Mueller, Milton. "Universal Service and the Telecommunications Act: Myth Made Law." *Communications of the ACM* 40, no. 3 (March 1997).

Nakamura, Kiyoh, Toshihiro Ide, and **Yukio Kiyokane.** "Roles of Multimedia Technology in Telework." *Journal of Organizational Computing and Electronic Commerce* 6, no. 4 (1996).

Ngwenyama, Ojelanki, and **Allen S. Lee.** "Communication Richness in Electronic Mail: Critical Social Theory and the Contextuality of Meaning." *MIS Quarterly* 21, no. 2 (June 1997).

Panko, Raymond R. *Business Data Networks and Telecommunications.* Upper Saddle River, NJ: Prentice-Hall (2002).

Passmore, David. "Scaling Large E-Commerce Infrastructures." *Packet Magazine* (Third Quarter 1999).

Pottie, G. J., and **W. J. Kaiser.** "Wireless Integrated Network Sensors." *Communications of the ACM* 43, no. 5 (May 2000).

Premkumar, G., K. Ramamurthy, and **Sree Nilakanta.** "Implementation of Electronic Data Interchange: An Innovation Diffusion Perspective." *Journal of Management Information Systems* 11, no. 2 (Fall 1994).

Raymond, Louis, and **Francois Bergeron.** "EDI Success in Small- and Medium-sized Enterprises: A Field Study." *Journal of Organizational Computing and Electronic Commerce* 6, no. 2 (1996).

Sharda, Nalin. "Multimedia Networks: Fundamentals and Future Directions." *Communications of the Association for Information Systems* (February 1999).

Sinha, Alok. "Client-Server Computing." *Communications of the ACM* 35, no. 7 (July 1992).

Teo, Hock-Hai, Bernard C. Y. Tan, and **Kwok-Kee Wei.** "Organizational Transformation Using Electronic Data Interchange: The Case of TradeNet in Singapore." *Journal of Management Information Systems* 13, no. 4 (Spring 1997).

Thompson, Marjorie Sarbough, and **Martha S. Feldman.** "Electronic Mail and Organizational Communication." *Organization Science* 9, no. 6 (November–December 1998).

Torkzadeh, Gholamreza, and **Weidong Xia.** "Managing Telecommunications Strategy by Steering Committee." *MIS Quarterly* 16, no. 2 (June 1992).

Varshney, Upkar. "Networking Support for Mobile Computing." *Communications of the Association for Information Systems* 1 (January 1999).

——— and Ron Vetter. "Emerging Mobile and Wireless Networks." *Communications of the ACM* 42, no. 6 (June 2000).

Vetter, Ronald J. "ATM Concepts, Architectures, and Protocols." *Communications of the ACM* 38, no. 2 (February 1995).

Waldo, Jim. "The Jini Architecture for Network-centric Computing." *Communications of the ACM* 42, no. 7 (July 1999).

Whitman, Michael E., Anthony M. Townsend, and **Robert J. Aalberts.** "Considerations for Effective Telecommunications-Use Policy." *Communications of the ACM* 42, no. 6 (June 1999).

CHAPTER 9

Amor, Daniel. *The E-Business Revolution,* 2nd edition. Upper Saddle River, NJ: Prentice-Hall (2002).

Berners-Lee, Tim, Robert Cailliau, Ari Luotonen, Henrik Frystyk Nielsen, and **Arthur Secret.** "The World-Wide Web." *Communications of the ACM* 37, no. 8 (August 1994).

Bikson, Tora K., Cathleen Stasz, and **Donald A. Monkin.** "Computer-Mediated Work: Individual and Organizational Impact on One Corporate Headquarters." Rand Corporation (1985).

Borriello, Gaetano, and **Roy Want.** "Embedded Computation Meets the World Wide Web." *Communications of the ACM* 43, no. 5 (May 2000).

Byrd, Terry Anthony. "Measuring the Flexibility of Information Technology Infrastructure: Exploratory Analysis of a Construct." *Journal of Management Information Systems* 17, no. 1 (Summer 2000).

Cheyne, Tanya L., and **Frank E. Ritter.** "Targeting Audiences on the Internet." *Communications of the ACM* 44, no. 4 (April 2001).

Farhoomand, Ali, Pauline S. P. Ng, and **Justin K. H. Yue.** "The Building of a New Business Ecosystem: Sustaining National Competitive Advantage through Electronic Commerce." *Journal of Organizational Computing and Electronic Commerce* 11, no. 4 (2001).

Garner, Rochelle. "Internet2..and Counting," *CIO Magazine* (September 1, 1999).

George, Tischelle, and **Sandra Swanson.** "Not Just Kid Stuff." *Information Week* (September 3, 2001).

Glezer, Chanan, and **Surya B. Yadav.** "A Conceptual Model of an Intelligent Catalog Search System." *Journal of Organizational Computing and Electronic Commerce* 11, no. 1 (2001).

Glover, Eric J., Steve Lawrence, Michael D. Gordon, William P. Birmingham, and **C. Lee Giles.** "Web Search-Your Way." *Communications of the ACM* 44, no. 12 (December 2001).

Goodman, S. E., L. I. Press, S. R. Ruth, and **A. M. Rutkowski.** "The Global Diffusion of the Internet: Patterns and Problems." *Communications of the ACM* 37, no. 8 (August 1994).

Greengard, Samuel. "All for One." *Internet World* (March 1, 2001).

Huff, Sid, Malcolm C. Munro, and **Barbara H. Martin.** "Growth Stages of End User Computing." *Communications of the ACM* (May 1988).

Hardman, Vicky, Martina Angela Sasse, and **Isidor Kouvelas.** "Successful Multiparty Audio Communication over the Internet." *Communications of the ACM* 41, no. 5 (May 1998).

Isakowitz, Tomas, Michael Bieber, and **Fabio Vitali.** "Web Information Systems." *Communications of the ACM* 41, no. 7 (July 1998).

Kanter, Rosabeth Moss. "The Ten Deadly Mistakes of Wanna-Dots." *Harvard Business Review* (January 2001).

Kautz, Henry, Bart Selman, and **Mehul Shah.** "ReferralWeb: Combining Social Networks and Collaborative Filtering." *Communications of the ACM* 40, no. 3 (March 1997).

Keen, Peter. "Ready for the 'New' B2B?" *Computerworld* (September 11, 2000).

Kendall, Kenneth E., and **Julie E. Kendall.** "Information Delivery Systems: An Exploration of Web Push and Pull Technologies." *Communications of the Association for Information Systems* 1 (April 1999).

Kuo, Geng-Sheng, and **Jing-Pei Lin.** "New Design Concepts for an Intelligent Internet." *Communications of the ACM* 41, no. 11 (November 1998).

Lieberman, Henry, Christopher Fry, and **Louis Weitzman.** "Exploring the Web with Reconnaissance Agents." *Communications of the ACM* 44, no. 8 (August 2001).

Lohse, Gerald L., and **Peter Spiller.** "Electronic Shopping." *Communications of the ACM* 41, no. 7 (July 1998).

Papazoglou, Mike P. "Agent-Oriented Technology in Support of E-Business." *Communications of the ACM* 44, no. 4 (April 2001).

Sweeney, Terry. "Voice Over IP Builds Momentum." *Information Week* (November 20, 2000).

Valera, Francisco, Jorge E. López de Vergara, José I. Moreno, Víctor A. Villagrá, and **Julio Berrocal.** "Communication Management Experiences in E-commerce." *Communications of the ACM* 44, no. 4 (April 2001).

Varshney, Upkar, Andy Snow, Matt McGivern, and **Christi Howard.** "Voice Over IP." *Communications of the ACM* 45, no. 1 (January 2002).

Vetter, Ron. "The Wireless Web." *Communications of the ACM* 44, no. 3 (March 2001).

Weiser, Mark. "What Ever Happened to the Next-Generation Internet?" *Communications of the ACM* 44, no. 9 (September 2001).

Westin, Alan F., Heather A. Schweder, Michael A. Baker, and **Sheila Lehman.** *The Changing Workplace.* New York: Knowledge Industries (1995).

CHAPTER 10

Ackerman, Mark S., and **Christine A. Halverson.** "Reexamining Organizational Memory." *Communications of the ACM* 43, no. 1 (January 2000).

Alavi, Maryam, and **Dorothy Leidner.** "Knowledge Management Systems: Issues, Challenges, and Benefits." *Communications of the Association for Information Systems* 1 (February 1999).

Maryam Alavi, and **Dorothy E. Leidner.** "Knowledge Management and Knowledge Management Systems." *MIS Quarterly* 25, no. 1 (March 2001).

Allen, Bradley P. "CASE-Based Reasoning: Business Applications." *Communications of the ACM* 37, no. 3 (March 1994).

Asakawa, Kazuo, and **Hideyuki Takagi.** "Neural Networks in Japan." *Communications of the ACM* 37, no. 3 (March 1994).

Badler, Norman I., Martha S. Palmer, and **Rama Bindiganavale.** "Animation Control for Real-time Virtual Humans." *Communications of the ACM* 42, no. 8 (August 1999).

Balasubramanian, V., and **Alf Bashian.** "Document Management and Web Technologies: Alice Marries the Mad Hatter." *Communications of the ACM* 41, no. 7 (July 1998).

Barker, Virginia E., and **Dennis E. O'Connor.** "Expert Systems for Configuration at Digital: XCON and Beyond." *Communications of the ACM* (March 1989).

Becerra-Fernandez, Irma, and **Rajiv Sabherwal.** "Organizational Knowledge Management: A Contingency Perspective." *Journal of Management Information Systems* 18, no. 1 (Summer 2001).

Beer, Randall D., Roger D. Quinn, Hillel J. Chiel, and **Roy E. Ritzman.** "Biologically Inspired Approaches to Robots." *Communications of the ACM* 40, no. 3 (March 1997).

Blanning, Robert W., David R. King, James R. Marsden, and **Ann C. Seror.** "Intelligent Models of Human Organizations: The State of the Art." *Journal of Organizational Computing* 2, no. 2 (1992).

Brutzman, Don. "The Virtual Reality Modeling Language and Java." *Communications of the ACM* 41, no. 6 (June 1998).

Burtka, Michael. "Generic Algorithms." *The Stern Information Systems Review* 1, no. 1 (Spring 1993).

Busch, Elizabeth, Matti Hamalainen, Clyde W. Holsapple, Yongmoo Suh, and **Andrew B. Whinston.** "Issues and Obstacles in the Development of Team Support Systems." *Journal of Organizational Computing* 1, no. 2 (April–June 1991).

Cho, Sungzoon, Chigeun Han, Dae Hee Han, and **Hyung-Il Kim.** "Web-Based Keystroke Dynamics Identity Verification Using Neural Network." *Journal of Organizational Computing and Electronic Commerce* 10, no. 4 (2000).

Churchland, Paul M., and **Patricia Smith Churchland.** "Could a Machine Think?" *Scientific American* (January 1990).

Cole, Kevin, Olivier Fischer, and **Phyllis Saltzman.** "Just-in-Time Knowledge Delivery." *Communications of the ACM* 40, no. 7 (July 1997).

Cole-Gomolski, Barbara. "Customer Service with a :-)" *Computerworld* (March 30, 1998).

Cross, Rob, and **Lloyd Baird.** "Technology is Not Enough: Improving Performance by Building Organizational Memory." *Sloan Management Review* 41, no. 3 (Spring 2000).

Davenport, Thomas H., David W. DeLong, and **Michael C. Beers.** "Successful Knowledge Management Projects." *Sloan Management Review* 39, no. 2 (Winter 1998).

Davenport, Thomas H., and **Lawrence Prusak.** *Working Knowledge: How Organizations Manage What They Know.* Boston, MA: Harvard Business School Press (1997).

Dhar, Vasant. "Plausibility and Scope of Expert Systems in Management." *Journal of Management Information Systems* (Summer 1987).

Dhar, Vasant, and **Roger Stein.** *Intelligent Decision Support Methods: The Science of Knowledge Work.* Upper Saddle River, NJ: Prentice Hall (1997).

Earl, Michael. "Knowledge Management Strategies: Toward a Taxonomy." *Journal of Management Information Systems* 18, no. 1 (Summer 2001).

Earl, Michael J., and **Ian A. Scott.** "What Is a Chief Knowledge Officer?" *Sloan Management Review* 40, no. 2 (Winter 1999).

El Najdawi, M. K., and **Anthony C. Stylianou.** "Expert Support Systems: Integrating AI Technologies." *Communications of the ACM* 36, no. 12 (December 1993).

Favela, Jesus. "Capture and Dissemination of Specialized Knowledge in Network Organizations." *Journal of Organizational Computing and Electronic Commerce* 7, nos. 2 and 3 (1997).

Fazlollahi, Bijan, and **Rustam Vahidov.** "A Method for Generation of Alternatives by Decision Support Systems." *Journal of Management Information Systems* 18, no. 2 (Fall 2001).

Feigenbaum, Edward A. "The Art of Artificial Intelligence: Themes and Case Studies in Knowledge Engineering." *Proceedings of the IJCAI* (1977).

Flash, Cynthia. "Who is the CKO?" *Knowledge Management* (May 2001).

Gelernter, David. "The Metamorphosis of Information Management." *Scientific American* (August 1989).

Giuliao, Vincent E. "The Mechanization of Office Work." *Scientific American* (September 1982).

Glushko, Robert J., Jay M. Tenenbaum, and **Bart Meltzer.** "An XML Framework for Agent-Based E-Commerce." *Communications of the ACM* 42, no. 3 (March 1999).

Gold, Andrew H., Arvind Malhotra, and **Albert H. Segars.** "Knowledge Management: An Organizational Capabilities Perspective." *Journal of Management Information Systems* 18, no. 1 (Summer 2001).

Goldberg, David E. "Genetic and Evolutionary Algorithms Come of Age." *Communications of the ACM* 37, no. 3 (March 1994).

Grant, Robert M. "Prospering in Dynamically-Competitive Environments: Organizational Capability as Knowledge Integration." *Organization Science* 7, no. 4 (July–August 1996).

Gregor, Shirley, and **Izak Benbasat.** "Explanations from Intelligent Systems: Theoretical Foundations and Implications for Practice." *MIS Quarterly* 23, no. 4 (December 1999).

Grover, Varun, and **Thomas H. Davenport.** "General Perspectives on Knowledge Management: Fostering a Research Agenda." *Journal of Management Information Systems* 18, no. 1 (Summer 2001).

Guerra, Anthony. "Goldman Sachs Embraces Rules-Based Solution." *Wall Street and Technology* (May 2001).

Hansen, Morton, and **Bolko von Oetinger.** "Introducing T-Shaped Managers: Knowledge Management's Next Generation." *Harvard Business Review* (March 2001).

Hansen, Morton T., Nitin Nohria, and **Thomas Tierney.** "What's Your Strategy for Knowledge Management?" *Harvard Business Review* (March–April 1999).

Hayes-Roth, Frederick. "Knowledge-Based Expert Systems." *Spectrum IEEE* (October 1987).

Hayes-Roth, Frederick, and **Neil Jacobstein.** "The State of Knowledge-Based Systems." *Communications of the ACM* 37, no. 3 (March 1994).

Hinton, Gregory. "How Neural Networks Learn from Experience." *Scientific American* (September 1992).

Holland, John H. "Genetic Algorithms." *Scientific American* (July 1992).

Housel Tom, and **Arthur A. Bell.** *Measuring and Managing Knowledge.* New York: McGraw-Hill (2001).

Jarvenpaa, Sirkka L., and **D. Sandy Staples.** "Exploring Perceptions of Organizational Ownership of Information and Expertise."*Journal of Management Information Systems* 18, no. 1 (Summer 2001).

Johansen, Robert. "Groupware: Future Directions and Wild Cards." *Journal of Organizational Computing* 1, no. 2 (April–June 1991).

Kim, Steven H. "An Architecture for Advanced Services in Cyberspace through Data Mining: A Framework with Case Studies in Finance and Engineering." *Journal of Organizational Computing and Electronic Commerce* 10, no. 4 (2000).

Kock, Ned, and **Robert J. McQueen.** "An Action Research Study of Effects of Asynchronous Groupware Support on Productivity and Outcome Quality in Process Redesign Groups." *Journal of Organizational Computing and Electronic Commerce* 8, no. 2 (1998).

Lee, Soonchul. "The Impact of Office Information Systems on Power and Influence." *Journal of Management Information Systems* 8, no. 2 (Fall 1991).

Leonard-Barton, Dorothy, and **John J. Sviokla.** "Putting Expert Systems to Work." *Harvard Business Review* (March–April 1988).

Liu, Ziming, and **David G. Stork.** "Is Paperless Really More?" *Communications of the ACM* 43, no. 11 (November 2000).

Lou, Hao, and **Richard W. Scannell.** "Acceptance of Groupware: The Relationships Among Use, Satisfaction, and Outcomes." *Journal of Organizational Computing and Electronic Commerce* 6, no. 2 (1996).

Maes, Patti. "Agents that Reduce Work and Information Overload." *Communications of the ACM* 38, no. 7 (July 1994).

Maes, Patti, Robert H. Guttman, and **Alexandros G. Moukas.** "Agents that Buy and Sell." *Communications of the ACM* 42, no. 3 (March 1999).

Malhotra, Arvind, Ann Majchrzak, Robert Carman, and **Vern Lott.** "Radical Innovation without Collocation: A Case Study at Boeing Rocketdyne." *MIS Quarterly* 25, no. 2 (June 2001).

Malhotra, Yogesh. "Toward a Knowledge Ecology for Organizational White-Waters." Keynote Presentations for the Knowledge Ecology Fair '98 (1998).

Markus, M. Lynne. "Toward a Theory of Knowledge Reuse: Types of Knowledge Reuse Situations and Factors in Reuse Success." *Journal of Management Information Systems* 18, no. 1 (Summer 2001).

McCarthy, John. "Generality in Artificial Intelligence." *Communications of the ACM* (December 1987).

Munakata, Toshinori, and **Yashvant Jani.** "Fuzzy Systems: An Overview." *Communications of the ACM* 37, no. 3 (March 1994).

Nidumolu, Sarma R., Mani Subramani, and **Alan Aldrich**. "Situated Learning and the Situated Knowledge Web: Exploring the Ground Beneath Knowledge Management." *Journal of Management Information Systems* 18, no. 1 (Summer 2001).

O'Leary, Daniel, and **Peter Selfridge.** "Knowledge Management for Best Practices." *Communications of the ACM* 43, no. 11, (November 2000).

O'Leary, Daniel, Daniel Kuokka, and **Robert Plant.** "Artificial Intelligence and Virtual Organizations." *Communications of the ACM* 40, no. 1 (January 1997).

Orlikowski, Wanda J. "Learning from Notes: Organizational Issues in Groupware Implementation." Sloan Working Paper, no. 3428. Cambridge, MA: Sloan School of Management, Massachusetts Institute of Technology.

Pan, Shan L., Ming-Huei Hsieh, and **Helen Chen.** "Knowledge Sharing through Intranet-Based Learning." *Journal of Organizational Computing and Electronic Commerce* 11, no. 3 (2001).

Piccoli, Gabriele, Rami Ahmad, and **Blake Ives.** "Web-Based Virtual Learning Environments: A Research Framework and a Preliminary Assessment of Effectiveness in Basic IT Skills Training." *MIS Quarterly* 25, no. 4 (December 2001).

Porat, Marc. "The Information Economy: Definition and Measurement." Washington, DC: U.S. Department of Commerce, Office of Telecommunications (May 1977).

Press, Lawrence. "Lotus Notes (Groupware) in Context." *Journal of Organizational Computing* 2, nos. 3 and 4 (1992b).

Ruhleder, Karen, and **John Leslie King.** "Computer Support for Work Across Space, Time, and Social Worlds." *Journal of Organizational Computing* 1, no. 4 (1991).

Rumelhart, David E., Bernard Widrow, and **Michael A. Lehr.** "The Basic Ideas in Neural Networks." *Communications of the ACM* 37, no. 3 (March 1994).

Salisbury, J. Kenneth, Jr. "Making Graphics Physically Tangible." *Communications of the ACM* 42, no. 8 (August 1999).

Schultze, Ulrike, and **Betty Vandenbosch.** "Information Overload in a Groupware Environment: Now You See It, Now You Don't." *Journal of Organizational Computing and Electronic Commerce* 8, no. 2 (1998).

Selker, Ted. "Coach: A Teaching Agent that Learns." *Communications of the ACM* 37, no. 7 (July 1994).

Sibigtroth, James M. "Implementing Fuzzy Expert Rules in Hardware." *AI Expert* (April 1992).

Sproull, Lee, and **Sara Kiesler.** *Connections: New Ways of Working in the Networked Organization.* Cambridge, MA: MIT Press (1992).

Starbuck, William H. "Learning by Knowledge-Intensive Firms." *Journal of Management Studies* 29, no. 6 (November 1992).

Storey, Veda C., and **Robert C. Goldstein.** "Knowledge-Based Approaches to Database Design," *MIS Quarterly* 17, no. 1 (March 1993).

Stylianou, Anthony C., Gregory R. Madey, and **Robert D. Smith.** "Selection Criteria for Expert System Shells: A Socio-Technical

Framework." *Communications of the ACM* 35, no. 10 (October 1992).

Sukhatme, Gaurav S., and **Maja J. Mataric.** "Embedding Robots into the Internet." *Communications of the ACM* 43, no. 5 (May 2000).

Sviokla, John J. "An Examination of the Impact of Expert Systems on the Firm: The Case of XCON." *MIS Quarterly* 14, no. 5 (June 1990).

———. "Expert Systems And Their Impact On The Firm: The Effects of Planpower Use On The Information Processing Capacity Of The Financial Collaborative." *Journal Of Management Information Systems* 6, No. 3 (Winter 1989–1990).

Trippi, Robert, and **Efraim Turban.** "The Impact of Parallel and Neural Computing on Managerial Decision Making." *Journal of Management Information Systems* 6, no. 3 (Winter 1989–1990).

Vandenbosch, Betty, and **Michael J. Ginzberg.** "Lotus Notes and Collaboration: Plus ca change . . ." *Journal of Management Information Systems* 13, no. 3 (Winter 1997).

Wakefield, Julie. "Complexity's Business Model." *Scientific American* (January 2001).

Walczak, Stephen. "An Emprical Analysis of Data Requirements for Financial Forecasting with Neural Networks." *Journal of Management Information Systems* 17, no. 4 (Spring 2001).

Walczak, Steven. "Gaining Competitive Advantage for Trading in Emerging Capital Markets with Neural Networks. " *Journal of Management Information Systems* 16, no. 2 (Fall 1999).

Weitzel, John R., and **Larry Kerschberg.** "Developing Knowledge Based Systems: Reorganizing the System Development Life Cycle." *Communications of the ACM* (April 1989).

Wijnhoven, Fons. "Designing Organizational Memories: Concept and Method." *Journal of Organizational Computing and Electronic Commerce* 8, no. 1 (1998).

Widrow, Bernard, David E. Rumelhart, and **Michael A. Lehr.** "Neural Networks: Applications in Industry, Business, and Science." *Communications of the ACM* 37, no. 3 (March 1994).

Wong, David, Noemi Paciorek, and **Dana Moore.** "Java-Based Mobile Agents." *Communications of the ACM* 42, no. 3 (March 1999).

Zadeh, Lotfi A. "The Calculus of Fuzzy If/Then Rules." *AI Expert* (March 1992).

Zadeh, Lotfi A. "Fuzzy Logic, Neural Networks, and Soft Computing." *Communications of the ACM* 37, no. 3 (March 1994).

Zhao, J. Leon, Akhil Kumar, and **Edward W. Stohr.** "Workflow-Centric Information Distribution through E-Mail." *Journal of Management Information Systems* 17, no. 3 (Winter 2000-2001).

Zhao, J. Leon, and **Vincent H. Resh.** "Internet Publishing and Transformation of Knowledge Processes." *Communications of the ACM* 44, no. 12 (December 2001).

CHAPTER 11

Alavi, Maryam, and **Erich A. Joachimsthaler.** "Revisiting DSS Implementation Research: A Meta-Analysis of the Literature and Suggestions for Researchers." *MIS Quarterly* 16, no. 1 (March 1992).

Baldwin, Howard. "Pioneer Natural Resources' Simulation Technology." *CIO Magazine* (June 15, 1998).

Barkhi, Reza. "The Effects of Decision Guidance and Problem Modeling on Group Decision-Making." *Journal of Management Information Systems* 18, no. 3 (Winter 2001-2002).

Brachman, Ronald J., Tom Khabaza, Willi Kloesgen, Gregory Piatetsky-Shapiro, and **Evangelos Simoudis.** "Mining Business Databases." *Communications of the ACM* 39, no. 11 (November 1996).

Caouette, Margarette J., and **Bridget N. O'Connor.** "The Impact of Group Support Systems on Corporate Teams' Stages of

Development." *Journal of Organizational Computing and Electronic Commerce* 8, no. 1 (1998).

Chidambaram, Laku. "Relational Development in Computer-Supported Groups." *MIS Quarterly* 20, no. 2 (June 1996).

De, Prabudda and **Thomas W. Ferrat.** "An Information System Involving Competing Organizations." *Communications of the ACM* 41, no. 12 (December 1998).

Del Rosario, Elise. "Logistical Nightmare." *OR/MS Today,* (April 1999).

Dennis, Alan R. "Information Exchange and Use in Group Decision Making: You Can Lead a Group to Information, but You Can't Make It Think." *MIS Quarterly* 20, no. 4 (December 1996).

Dennis, Alan R., Craig K. Tyran, Douglas R. Vogel, and **Jay Nunamaker, Jr.** "Group Support Systems for Strategic Planning." *Journal of Management Information Systems* 14, no. 1 (Summer 1997).

Dennis, Alan R., Jay E. Aronson, William G. Henriger, and **Edward D. Walker III.** "Structuring Time and Task in Electronic Brainstorming." *MIS Quarterly* 23, no. 1 (March 1999).

Dennis, Alan R., Jay F. Nunamaker, Jr., and **Douglas R. Vogel.** "A Comparison of Laboratory and Field Research in the Study of Electronic Meeting Systems." *Journal of Management Information Systems* 7, no. 3 (Winter 1990–1991).

Dennis, Alan R., Joey F. George, Len M. Jessup, Jay F. Nunamaker, and **Douglas R. Vogel.** "Information Technology to Support Electronic Meetings." *MIS Quarterly* 12, no. 4 (December 1988).

Dennis, Alan R., Sridar K. Pootheri, and **Vijaya L. Natarajan.** "Lessons from Early Adopters of Web Groupware." *Journal of Management Information Systems* 14, no. 4 (Spring 1998).

Dennis, Alan R., and **Barbara H. Wixom,** "Investigating the Moderators of Group Support Systems Use with Meta-Analysis." *Journal of Management Information Systems* 18, no. 3 (Winter 2001-2002).

Dennis, Alan R., Barbara H. Wixom, and **Robert J. Vandenberg.** "Understanding Fit and Appropriation Effects in Group Support Systems Via Meta-Analysis." *MIS Quarterly* 25, no. 2 (June 2001).

DeSanctis, Geraldine, and **R. Brent Gallupe.** "A Foundation for the Study of Group Decision Support Systems." *Management Science* 33, no. 5 (May 1987).

Dietrich, Brenda, Nick Donofrio, Grace Lin, and **Jane Snowdon.** "Big Benefits for Big Blue." *OR/MS Today* (June 2000).

Dutta, Soumitra, Berend Wierenga, and **Arco Dalebout.** "Designing Management Support Systems Using an Integrative Perspective." *Communications of the ACM* 40, no. 6 (June 1997).

Edelstein, Herb. "Technology How To: Mining Data Warehouses." *Information Week* (January 8, 1996).

El Sawy, Omar. "Personal Information Systems for Strategic Scanning in Turbulent Environments." *MIS Quarterly* 9, no. 1 (March 1985).

El Sherif, Hisham, and **Omar A. El Sawy.** "Issue-Based Decision Support Systems for the Egyptian Cabinet." *MIS Quarterly* 12, no. 4 (December 1988).

Fjermestad, Jerry. "An Integrated Framework for Group Support Systems." *Journal of Organizational Computing and Electronic Commerce* 8, no. 2 (1998).

Fjermestad, Jerry, and **Starr Roxanne Hiltz.** "An Assessment of Group Support Systems Experimental Research: Methodology, and Results." *Journal of Management Information Systems* 15, no. 3 (Winter, 1998–1999).

———. "Group Support Systems: A Descriptive Evaluation of Case and Field Studies." *Journal of Management Information Systems* 17, no. 3 (Winter 2000-2001).

Forgionne, Guiseppe. "Management Support System Effectiveness: Further Empirical Evidence." *Journal of the Association for Information Systems* 1 (May 2000).

Gallupe, R. Brent, Geraldine DeSanctis, and **Gary W. Dickson.** "Computer-Based Support for Group Problem-Finding: An Experimental Investigation." *MIS Quarterly* 12, no. 2 (June 1988).

George, Joey. "Organizational Decision Support Systems." *Journal of Management Information Systems* 8, no. 3 (Winter 1991–1992).

Ginzberg, Michael J., W. R. Reitman, and **E. A. Stohr,** eds. *Decision Support Systems.* New York: North Holland Publishing Co. (1982).

Grobowski, Ron, Chris McGoff, Doug Vogel, Ben Martz, and **Jay Nunamaker.** "Implementing Electronic Meeting Systems at IBM: Lessons Learned and Success Factors." *MIS Quarterly* 14, no. 4 (December 1990).

Henderson, John C., and **David A. Schilling.** "Design and Implementation of Decision Support Systems in the Public Sector." *MIS Quarterly* (June 1985).

Hilmer, Kelly M., and **Alan R. Dennis.** "Stimulating Thinking: Cultivating Better Decisions with Groupware through Categorization." *Journal of Management Information Systems* 17, no. 3 (Winter 2000-2001).

Ho, T. H., and **K. S. Raman.** "The Effect of GDSS on Small Group Meetings." *Journal of Management Information Systems* 8, no. 2 (Fall 1991).

Hogue, Jack T. "Decision Support Systems and the Traditional Computer Information System Function: An Examination of Relationships During DSS Application Development." *Journal of Management Information Systems* (Summer 1985).

Hogue, Jack T. "A Framework for the Examination of Management Involvement in Decision Support Systems." *Journal of Management Information Systems* 4, no. 1 (Summer 1987).

Houdeshel, George, and **Hugh J. Watson.** "The Management Information and Decision Support (MIDS) System at Lockheed, Georgia." *MIS Quarterly* 11, no. 2 (March 1987).

Jessup, Leonard M., Terry Connolly, and **Jolene Galegher.** "The Effects of Anonymity on GDSS Group Process with an Idea-Generating Task." *MIS Quarterly* 14, no. 3 (September 1990).

Jones, Jack William, Carol Saunders, and **Raymond McLeod, Jr.,** "Media Usage and Velocity in Executive Information Acquisition: An Exploratory Study." *European Journal of Information Systems* 2 (1993).

Kalakota, Ravi, Jan Stallaert, and **Andrew B. Whinston.** "Worldwide Real-Time Decision Support Systems for Electronic Commerce Applications." *Journal of Organizational Computing and Electronic Commerce* 6, no. 1 (1996).

Keen, Peter G. W., and **M. S. Scott Morton.** *Decision Support Systems: An Organizational Perspective.* Reading, MA: Addison-Wesley (1982).

King, John. "Successful Implementation of Large Scale Decision Support Systems: Computerized Models in U.S. Economic Policy Making." *Systems Objectives Solutions* (November 1983).

Kraemer, Kenneth L., and **John Leslie King.** "Computer-Based Systems for Cooperative Work and Group Decision Making." *ACM Computing Surveys* 20, no. 2 (June 1988).

Leidner, Dorothy E., and **Joyce Elam.** "Executive Information Systems: Their Impact on Executive Decision Making." *Journal of Management Information Systems* (Winter 1993–1994).

Leidner, Dorothy E., and **Joyce Elam.** "The Impact of Executive Information Systems on Organizational Design, Intelligence, and Decision Making." *Organization Science* 6, no. 6 (November–December 1995).

Lewe, Henrik, and **Helmut Krcmar.** "A Computer-Supported Cooperative Work Research Laboratory." *Journal of Management Information Systems* 8, no. 3 (Winter 1991–1992).

McCune, Jenny C. "Measuring Value." *Beyond Computing* (July/August 2000).

Miranda, Shaila M., and **Robert P. Bostrum.** "The Impact of Group Support Systems on Group Conflict and Conflict Management." *Journal of Management Information Systems* 10, no. 3 (Winter 1993–1994).

———. "Meeting Facilitation: Process versus Content Interventions." *Journal of Management Information Systems* 15, no. 4 (Spring 1999).

Nidumolu, Sarma R., Seymour E. Goodman, Douglas R. Vogel, and **Ann K. Danowitz.** "Information Technology for Local Administration Support: The Governorates Project in Egypt." *MIS Quarterly* 20, no. 2 (June 1996).

Niederman, Fred, Catherine M. Beise, and **Peggy M. Beranek.** "Issues and Concerns about Computer-Supported Meetings: The Facilitator's Perspective." *MIS Quarterly* 20, no. 1 (March 1996).

Nunamaker, J. F., Alan R. Dennis, Joseph S. Valacich, Douglas R. Vogel, and **Joey F. George.** "Electronic Meeting Systems to Support Group Work." *Communications of the ACM* 34, no. 7 (July 1991).

Nunamaker, Jay, Robert O. Briggs, Daniel D. Mittleman, Douglas R. Vogel, and **Pierre A. Balthazard.** "Lessons from a Dozen Years of Group Support Systems Research: A Discussion of Lab and Field Findings." *Journal of Management Information Systems* 13, no. 3 (Winter 1997).

O'Keefe, Robert M., and **Tim McEachern.** "Web-based Customer Decision Support Systems." *Communications of the ACM* 41, no. 3 (March 1998).

Pinsonneault, Alain, Henri Barki, R. Brent Gallupe, and **Norberto Hoppen.** "Electronic Brainstorming: The Illusion of Productivity." *Information Systems Research* 10, no. 2 (July 1999).

Radding, Alan. "Analyze Your Customers." *Datamation* (September 25, 2000).

Rockart, John F., and **David W. DeLong.** *Executive Support Systems: The Emergence of Top Management Computer Use.* Homewood, IL: Dow-Jones Irwin (1988).

Schwabe, Gerhard. "Providing for Organizational Memory in Computer-Supported Meetings." *Journal of Organizational Computing and Electronic Commerce* 9, no. 2 and 3 (1999).

Shand, Dawne. "Making It Up as You Go." *Knowledge Management* (April 2000).

Sharda, Ramesh, and **David M. Steiger.** "Inductive Model Analysis Systems: Enhancing Model Analysis in Decision Support Systems." *Information Systems Research* 7, no. 3 (September 1996).

Silver, Mark S. "Decision Support Systems: Directed and Nondirected Change." *Information Systems Research* 1, no. 1 (March 1990).

Sprague, R. H., and **E. D. Carlson.** *Building Effective Decision Support Systems.* Englewood Cliffs, NJ: Prentice Hall (1982).

Todd, Peter, and **Izak Benbasat.** "Evaluating the Impact of DSS, Cognitive Effort, and Incentives on Strategy Selection. *Information Systems Research* 10, no. 4 (December 1999).

"The New Role for 'Executive Information Systems.' " *I/S Analyzer* (January 1992).

Turban, Efraim, and **Jay E. Aronson.** *Decision Support Systems and Intelligent Systems: Management Support Systems,* 6th ed. Upper Saddle River, NJ: Prentice Hall (2001).

Tyran, Craig K., Alan R. Dennis, Douglas R. Vogel, and J. F. Nunamaker, Jr. "The Application of Electronic Meeting Technology to Support Senior Management." *MIS Quarterly* 16, no. 3 (September 1992).

Van der Zee, J.T.M., and Berend de Jong. "Alignment Is Not Enough: Integrating Business and Information Technology Management." *Journal of Management Information Systems* 16, no. 2 (Fall 1999).

Vedder, Richard G., Michael T. Vanacek, C. Stephen Guynes, and James J. Cappel. "CEO and CIO Perspectives on Competitive Intelligence." *Communications of the ACM 42,* no. 8 (August 1999).

Vogel, Douglas R., Jay F. Nunamaker, William Benjamin Martz, Jr., Ronald Grobowski, and Christopher McGoff. "Electronic Meeting System Experience at IBM." *Journal of Management Information Systems* 6, no. 3 (Winter 1989–1990).

Volonino, Linda, and Hugh J. Watson. "The Strategic Business Objectives Method For Eis Development." *Journal of Management Information Systems* 7, No. 3 (Winter 1990–1991).

Walls, Joseph G., George R. Widmeyer, and Omar A. El Sawy. "Building an Information System Design Theory for Vigilant EIS." *Information Systems Research* 3, no. 1 (March 1992).

Watson, Hugh J., Astrid Lipp, Pamela Z. Jackson, Abdelhafid Dahmani, and William B. Fredenberger. "Organizational Support for Decision Support Systems." *Journal of Management Information Systems* 5, no. 4 (Spring 1989).

Watson, Hugh J., R. Kelly Rainer, Jr., and Chang E. Koh. "Executive Information Systems: A Framework for Development and a Survey of Current Practices." *MIS Quarterly* 15, no. 1 (March 1991).

Watson, Richard T., Teck-Hua Ho, and K. S. Raman. "Culture: A Fourth Dimension of Group Support Systems." *Communications of the ACM* 37, no. 10 (October 1994).

Yoo, Youngjin, and Maryam Alavi. "Media and Group Cohesion: Relative Influences on Social Presence, Task Participation, and Group Consensus." *MIS Quarterly* 25, no. 3 (September 2001).

CHAPTER 12

Agarwal, Ritu, Prabudda De, Atish P. Sinha, and Mohan Tanniru. "On the Usability of OO Representations." *Comunications of the ACM* 43, no. 10 (October 2000).

Agarwal, Ritu, Jayesh Prasad, Mohan Tanniru, and John Lynch. "Risks of Rapid Application Development." *Communications of the ACM* 43, no. 11es (November 2000).

Ahituv, Niv, and Seev Neumann. "A Flexible Approach to Information System Development." *MIS Quarterly* (June 1984).

Alavi, Maryam, R. Ryan Nelson, and Ira R. Weiss. "Strategies for End-User Computing: An Integrative Framework." *Journal of Management Information Systems* 4, no. 3 (Winter 1987–1988).

Alavi, Maryam. "An Assessment of the Prototyping Approach to Information System Development." *Communications of the ACM* 27 (June 1984).

Anderson, Evan A. "Choice Models for the Evaluation and Selection of Software Packages." *Journal of Management Information Systems* 6, no. 4 (Spring 1990).

Barua, Anitesh, Sophie C. H. Lee, and Andrew B. Whinston. "The Calculus of Reengineering." *Information Systems Research* 7, no. 4 (December 1996).

Baskerville, Richard L., and Jan Stage. "Controlling Prototype Development through Risk Analysis." *MIS Quarterly* 20, no. 4 (December 1996).

Brier, Tom, Jerry Luftman, and Raymond Papp. "Enablers and Inhibitors of Business—IT Alignment." *Communications of the Association for Information Systems* 1 (March 1999).

Broadbent, Marianne, Peter Weill, and Don St. Clair. "The Implications of Information Technology Infrastructure for Business Process Redesign." *MIS Quarterly* 23, no. 2 (June 1999).

Bullen, Christine, and John F. Rockart. "A Primer on Critical Success Factors." Cambridge, MA: Center for Information Systems Research, Sloan School of Management (1981).

Cline, Marshall, and Mike Girou. "Enduring Business Themes." *Communications of the ACM* 43, no. 5 (May 2000).

Davenport, Thomas H., and James E. Short. "The New Industrial Engineering: Information Technology and Business Process Redesign." *Sloan Management Review* 31, no. 4 (Summer 1990).

Davidson, W. H. "Beyond Engineering: The Three Phases of Business Transformation." *IBM Systems Journal* 32, No. 1 (1993).

Davis, Gordon B. "Determining Management Information Needs: A Comparison of Methods." *MIS Quarterly* 1 (June 1977).

———. "Information Analysis for Information System Development." In *Systems Analysis and Design: A Foundation for the 1980's,* edited by W. W. Cotterman, J. D. Cougar, N. L. Enger, and F. Harold. New York: Wiley (1981).

———. "Strategies for Information Requirements Determination." *IBM Systems Journal* 1 (1982).

Earl, Michael, and Bushra Khan. "E-Commerce Is Changing the Face of IT." *Sloan Management Review,* (Fall 2001).

Ein Dor Philip, and Eli Segev. "Strategic Planning for Management Information Systems." *Management Science* 24, no. 15 (1978).

Fingar, Peter. "Component-Based Frameworks for E-Commerce." *Communications of the ACM* 43, no. 10 (October 2000).

Fuller, Mary K. and E. Burton Swanson. "Information Centers as Organizational Innovation." *Journal of Management Information Systems* 9, no. 1 (Summer 1992).

Gill, Philip. "Flower Power." *Oracle Profit Magazine* (August 1998).

Hagel, John III, and John Seeley Brown. "Your Next IT Strategy." *Harvard Business Review* (October, 2001).

Hammer, Michael, and James Champy. *Reengineering the Corporation.* New York: HarperCollins Publishers (1993).

Hammer, Michael, and Steven A. Stanton. *The Reengineering Revolution.* New York: HarperCollins (1995).

Hammer, Michael. "Reengineering Work: Don't Automate, Obliterate." *Harvard Business Review* (July–August 1990).

Heeseok Lee, and Woojong Suh. "A Workflow-Based Methodology for Developing Hypermedia Information Systems." *Journal of Organizational Computing and Electronic Commerce* 11, no. 2 (2001).

Hirscheim, Rudy, and Mary Lacity. "The Myths and Realities of Information Technology Insourcing." *Communications of the ACM* 43, no. 2 (February 2000).

Hoffer, Jeffrey, Joey George, and Joseph Valacich. *Modern Systems Analysis and Design,* 3rd ed. Upper Saddle River, NJ: Prentice-Hall (2002).

Hopkins, Jon. "Component Primer." *Communications of the ACM* 43, no. 10 (October 2000).

Huizing, Ard, Esther Koster, and Wim Bouman. "Balance in Business Process Reengineering: An Empirical Study of Fit and Performance." *Journal of Management Information Systems* 14, no. 1 (Summer 1997).

Ivari, Juhani, Rudy Hirscheim, and Heinz K. Klein. "A Dynamic Framework for Classifying Information Systems Development Methodologies and Approaches." *Journal of Management Information Systems* 17, no. 3 (Winter 2000-2001).

Jesser, Ryan, Rodney Smith, Mark Stupeck, and William F. Wright. "Information Technology Process Reengineering and Performance Measurement." *Communications of the Association for Information Systems* 1 (February 1999).

Johnson, Richard A. "The Ups and Downs of Object-Oriented Systems Development." *Communications of the ACM* 43, no.10 (October 2000).

Keen, Peter G. W. *Shaping the Future: Business Design Through Information Technology.* Cambridge, MA: Harvard Business School Press (1991).

Kendall, Kenneth E., and Julie E. Kendall. *Systems Analysis and Design,* 5th ed. Upper Saddle River, NJ: Prentice Hall (2002).

Lee, Jae Nam, and Young-Gul Kim. "Effect of Partnership Quality on IS Outsourcing Success." *Journal of Management Information Systems* 15, no. 4 (Spring 1999).

McDougall, Paul et al. "Decoding Web Services." *Information Week* (October 1, 2001).

Martin, J., and C. McClure. "Buying Software Off the Rack." *Harvard Business Review* (November–December 1983).

Martin, James. *Application Development without Programmers.* Englewood Cliffs, NJ: Prentice Hall (1982).

Matos, Victor M., and Paul J. Jalics. "An Experimental Analysis of the Performance of Fourth-Generation Tools on PCs." *Communications of the ACM* 32, no. 11 (November 1989).

Nerson, Jean-Marc. "Applying Object-Oriented Analysis and Design." *Communications of the ACM* 35, no. 9 (September 1992).

Nissen, Mark E. "Redesigning Reengineering through Measurement-Driven Inference," *MIS Quarterly* 22, no. 4 (December 1998).

Pancake, Cherri M. "The Promise and the Cost of Object Technology: A Five-Year Forecast." *Communications of the ACM* 38, no. 10 (October 1995).

Parker, M. M. "Enterprise Information Analysis: Cost-Benefit Analysis and the Data-Managed System." *IBM Systems Journal* 21 (1982).

Prahalad, C. K., and M.S. Krishnan. "The New Meaning of Quality in the Information Age." *Harvard Business Review* (September–October 1999).

Rivard, Suzanne, and Sid L. Huff. "Factors of Success for End-User Computing." *Communications of the ACM* 31, no. 5 (May 1988).

Rockart, John F. "Chief Executives Define Their Own Data Needs." *Harvard Business Review* (March–April 1979).

Rockart, John F., and Lauren S. Flannery. "The Management of End-User Computing." *Communications of the ACM* 26, no. 10 (October 1983).

Rockart, John F., and Michael E. Treacy. "The CEO Goes On-Line." *Harvard Business Review* (January–February 1982).

Sabherwahl, Rajiv. "The Role of Trust in IS Outsourcing Development Projects." *Communications of the ACM* 42, no. 2 (February 1999).

Schmidt, Douglas C., and Mohamed E. Fayad. "Lessons Learned Building Reusable OO Frameworks for Distributed Software." *Communications of the ACM* 40, no. 10 (October 1997).

Segars, Albert H., and Varun Grover. "Profiles of Strategic Information Systems Planning." *Information Systems Research* 10, no. 3 (September 1999).

Shank, Michael E., Andrew C. Boynton, and Robert W. Zmud. "Critical Success Factor Analysis as a Methodology for MIS Planning." *MIS Quarterly* (June 1985).

Sircar, Sumit, Sridhar P. Nerur, and Radhakanta Mahapatra. "Revolution or Evolution? A Comparison of Object-Oriented and Structured Systems Development Methods." *MIS Quarterly* 25, no. 4 (December 2001).

Swanson, E. Burton, and Enrique Dans. "System Life Expectancy and the Maintenance Effort: Exploring their Equilibration." *MIS Quarterly* 24, no. 2 (June 2000).

Sprott, David. "Componentizing the Enterprise Application Packages." *Communications of the ACM* 43, no. 3 (April 2000).

Tam, Kar Yan, and Kai Lung Hui. "A Choice Model for the Selection of Computer Vendors and Its Empirical Estimation." *Journal of Management Information Systems* 17, no. 4 (Spring 2001).

Thong, James Y. L., Chee-Sing Yap, and Kin-Lee Seah. "Business Process Reengineering in the Public Sector: The Case of the Housing Development Board in Singapore." *Journal of Management Information Systems* 17, no. 1 (Summer 2000).

Venkatraman, N. "Beyond Outsourcing: Managing IT Resources as a Value Center." *Sloan Management Review* (Spring 1997).

Vessey, Iris, and Sue A. Conger. "Requirements Specification: Learning Object, Process, and Data Methodologies." *Communications of the ACM* 37, no. 5 (May 1994).

Vessey, Iris, and Sue Conger. "Learning to Specify Information Requirements: The Relationship between Application and Methodology." *Journal of Management Information Systems* 10, no. 2 (Fall 1993).

Watad, Mahmoud M., and Frank J. DiSanzo. "Case Study: The Synergism of Telecommuting and Office Automation." *Sloan Management Review* 41, no. 2 (Winter 2000).

Willis, T. Hillman, and Debbie B. Tesch. "An Assessment of Systems Development Methodologies." *Journal of Information Technology Management* 2, no. 2 (1991).

Zachman, J. A. "Business Systems Planning and Business Information Control Study: A Comparison." *IBM Systems Journal* 21 (1982).

CHAPTER 13

Alter, Steven, and Michael Ginzberg. "Managing Uncertainty in MIS Implementation." *Sloan Management Review* 20 (Fall 1978).

Andres, Howard P., and Robert W. Zmud. "A Contingency Approach to Software Project Coordination." *Journal of Management Information Systems* 18, no. 3 (Winter 2001-2002).

Armstrong, Curtis P., and V. Sambamurthy. "Information Technology Assimilation in Firms: The Influence of Senior Leadership and IT Infrastructures." *Information Systems Research* 10, no. 4 (December 1999).

Attewell, Paul. "Technology Diffusion and Organizational Learning: The Case of Business Computing." *Organization Science,* no. 3 (1992).

Banker, Rajiv. "Value Implications of Relative Investments in Information Technology." Department of Information Systems and Center for Digital Economy Research, University of Texas at Dallas, January 23, 2001.

Barki, Henri, and Jon Hartwick. "Interpersonal Conflict and Its Management in Information Systems Development." *MIS Quarterly* 25, no.2 (June 2001).

Barki, Henri, Suzanne Rivard, and Jean Talbot. "An Integrative Contingency Model of Software Project Risk Management." *Journal of Management Information Systems* 17, no. 4 (Spring 2001).

Beath, Cynthia Mathis, and Wanda J. Orlikowski. "The Contradictory Structure of Systems Development Methodologies: Deconstructing the IS-User Relationship in Information Engineering." *Information Systems Research* 5, no. 4 (December 1994).

Benaroch, Michel, and Robert J. Kauffman. "Justifying Electronic Banking Network Expansion Using Real Options Analysis." *MIS Quarterly* 24, no. 2 (June 2000).

Berinato, Scott. "The Secret to Software Success." *CIO Magazine* (July 1, 2001).

Bharadwaj, Anandhi. "A Resource-Based Perspective on Information Technology Capability and Firm Performance." *MIS Quarterly* 24, no. 1 (March 2000).

Bhattacherjee, Anoi. "Understanding Information Systems Continuance: An Expectation-Confirmation Model." *MIS Quarterly* 25, no.3 (September 2001).

Bhattacharjee, Sudip, and **R. Ramesh.** "Enterprise Computing Environments and Cost Assessment." *Communications of the ACM* 43, no. 10 (October 2000).

Bostrom, R. P., and **J. S. Heinen.** "MIS Problems and Failures: A Socio-Technical Perspective. Part I: The Causes." *MIS Quarterly* 1 (September 1977); "Part II: The Application of Socio-Technical Theory." *MIS Quarterly* 1 (December 1977).

Brooks, Frederick P. "The Mythical Man-Month." *Datamation* (December 1974).

Brynjolfsson, Erik. "The Contribution of Information Technology to Consumer Welfare." *Information Systems Research* 7, no. 3 (September 1996).

———. "The Productivity Paradox of Information Technology." *Communications of the ACM* 36, no. 12 (December 1993).

Brynjolfsson, Erik, and **Lorin M. Hitt.** "Information Technology and Organizational Design: Evidence from Micro Data." (January 1998).

Brynjolfsson, Erik, and **Lorin M. Hitt.** "Beyond the Productivity Paradox." *Communications of the ACM* 41, no. 8 (August 1998).

———. "New Evidence on the Returns to Information Systems." MIT Sloan School of Management (October 1993).

Brynjolfsson, Erik, and **S. Yang.** "Intangible Assets: How the Interaction of Computers and Organizational Structure Affects Stock Markets." MIT Sloan School of Management (2000).

Burkhardt, Grey E., Seymour E. Goodman, Arun Mehta, and **Larry Press.** "The Internet in India: Better Times Ahead?" *Communications of the ACM* 41, no. 11 (November 1998).

Buss, Martin D. J. "How to Rank Computer Projects." *Harvard Business Review* (January 1983).

Clement, Andrew, and **Peter Van den Besselaar.** "A Retrospective Look at PD Projects." *Communications of the ACM* 36, no. 4 (June 1993).

Concours Group. "Delivering Large-Scale System Projects." (2000).

Cooper, Randolph B. "Information Technology Development Creativity: A Case Study of Attempted Radical Change." *MIS Quarterly* 24, no. 2 (June 2000).

Davenport, Thomas H. *Mission Critical: Realizing the Promise of Enterprise Systems.* Boston, MA: Harvard Business School Press (2000).

Davern, Michael J., and **Robert J. Kauffman.** "Discovering Potential and Realizing Value from Information Technology Investments." *Journal of Management Information Systems* 16, no. 4 (Spring 2000).

Davis, Fred R. "Perceived Usefulness, Ease of Use, and User Acceptance of Information Technology." *MIS Quarterly* 13, no. 3 (September 1989).

De Berranger, Pascal, David Tucker, and **Laurie Jones.** "Internet Diffusion in Creative Micro-Businesses: Identifying Change Agent Characteristics as Critical Success Factors." *Journal of Organizational Computing and Electronic Commerce* 11, no. 3 (2001).

Desmarais, Michel C., Richard Leclair, Jean-Yves Fiset, and **Hichem Talbi.** "Cost-Justifying Electronic Performance Support Systems." *Communications of the ACM* 40, no. 7 (July 1997).

Doll, William J. "Avenues for Top Management Involvement in Successful MIS Development." *MIS Quarterly* (March 1985).

Dos Santos, Brian. "Justifying Investments in New Information Technologies." *Journal of Management Information Systems* 7, no. 4 (Spring 1991).

Ein-Dor, Philip, and **Eli Segev.** "Organizational Context and the Success of Management Information Systems." *Management Science* 24 (June 1978).

El Sawy, Omar, and **Burt Nanus.** "Toward the Design of Robust Information Systems." *Journal of Management Information Systems* 5, no. 4 (Spring 1989).

Emery, James C. "Cost/Benefit Analysis of Information Systems." Chicago: Society for Management Information Systems Workshop Report No. 1 (1971).

Farhoomand, Ali, Virpi Kristiina Tuunainen, and **Lester W. Yee.** "Barrier to Global Electronic Commerce: A Cross-Country Study of Hong Kong and Finland." *Journal of Organizational Computing and Electronic Commerce* 10, no. 1 (2000).

Fichman, Robert G. "The Role of Aggregation in the Measurement of IT-Related Organizational Innovation." *MIS Quarterly* 25, no. 4 (December 2001).

Fichman, Robert G., and **Scott A. Moses.** "An Incremental Process for Software Implementation." *Sloan Management Review* 40, no. 2 (Winter 1999).

Franz, Charles, and **Daniel Robey.** "An Investigation of User-Led System Design: Rational and Political Perspectives." *Communications of the ACM* 27 (December 1984).

Gardner, Julia. "Strengthening the Focus on Users' Working Practices." *Communications of the ACM* 42, no. 5 (May 1999)

Giaglis, George. "Focus Issue on Legacy Information Systems and Business Process Change: On the Integrated Design and Evaluation of Business Processes and Information Systems." *Communications of the AIS* 2, (July 1999).

Ginzberg, Michael J. "Early Diagnosis of MIS Implementation Failure: Promising Results and Unanswered Questions." *Management Science* 27 (April 1981).

Gogan, Janis L., Jane Fedorowicz, and **Ashok Rao.** "Assessing Risks in Two Projects: A Strategic Opportunity and a Necessary Evil." *Communications of the Association for Information Systems* 1 (May 1999).

Grover, Varun. "IS Investment Priorities in Contemporary Organizations." *Communications of the ACM* 41, no. 2 (February 1998).

Helms, Glenn L., and **Ira R. Weiss.** "The Cost of Internally Developed Applications: Analysis of Problems and Cost Control Methods." *Journal of Management Information Systems* (Fall 1986).

Housel, Thomas J., Omar El Sawy, Jianfang J. Zhong, and **Waymond Rodgers.** "Measuring the Return on e-Business Initiatives at the Process Level: The Knowledge Value-Added Approach." ICIS (2001).

Hunton, James E., and **Beeler, Jesse D.** "Effects of User Participation in Systems Development: A Longitudinal Field Study." *MIS Quarterly* 21, no. 4 (December 1997).

Irani, Zahir, and **Peter E.D. Love.** "The Propagation of Technology Management Taxonomies for Evaluating Investments in Information Systems." *Journal of Management Information Systems* 17, no.3 (Winter 2000-2001).

Joshi, Kailash. "A Model of Users' Perspective on Change: The Case of Information Systems Technology Implementation." *MIS Quarterly* 15, no. 2 (June 1991).

Karat, John. "Evolving the Scope of User-Centered Design." *Communications of the ACM* 40, no. 7 (July 1997).

Keen, Peter W. "Information Systems and Organizational Change." *Communications of the ACM* 24 (January 1981).

Keil, Mark, Bernard C.Y. Tan, Kwok-Kee Wei, Timo Saarinen, Virpi Tuunainen, and Arjen Waassenaar. "A Cross-Cultural Study on Escalation of Commitment Behavior in Software Projects." *MIS Quarterly* 24, no. 2 (June 2000).

Keil, Mark, Paul E. Cule, Kalle Lyytinen, and Roy C. Schmidt. "A Framework for Identifying Software Project Risks." *Communications of the ACM* 41, 11 (November 1998).

Keil, Mark, and Daniel Robey. "Blowing the Whistle on Troubled Software Projects." *Communications of the ACM* 44, no. 4 (April 2001).

Keil, Mark, and Ramiro Montealegre. "Cutting Your Losses: Extricating Your Organization When a Big Project Goes Awry." *Sloan Management Review* 41, no. 3 (Spring 2000).

Keil, Mark, Richard Mixon, Timo Saarinen, and Virpi Tuunairen. "Understanding Runaway IT Projects." *Journal of Management Information Systems* 11, no. 3 (Winter 1994–95).

Keil, Mark, Joan Mann, and Arun Rai. "Why Software Projects Escalate: An Empirical Analysis and Test of Four Theoretical Models." *MIS Quarterly* 24, no. 4 (December 2000).

Kelly, Sue, Nicola Gibson, Christopher P. Holland, and Ben Light. "Focus Issue on Legacy Information Systems and Business Process Change: A Business Perspective of Legacy Information Systems." *Communications of the AIS* 2 (July 1999).

Kien, Sia Siew, and Boon Siong Neo. "Reengineering Effectiveness and the Redesign of Organizational Control: A Case Study of the Inland Revenue Authority in Singapore." *Journal of Management Information Systems* 14, no. 1 (Summer 1997).

King, Julia. "Reengineering Slammed." *Computerworld* (June 13, 1994).

Kolb, D. A., and A. L. Frohman. "An Organization Development Approach to Consulting." *Sloan Management Review* 12 (Fall 1970).

Lassila, Kathy S., and James C. Brancheau. "Adoption and Utilization of Commercial Software Packages: Exploring Utilization Equilibria, Transitions, Triggers, and Tracks." *Journal of Management Information Systems* 16, no. 2 (Fall 1999).

Laudon, Kenneth C. "CIOs Beware: Very Large Scale Systems." Center for Research on Information Systems, New York University Stern School of Business, working paper (1989).

Lederer, Albert, and Jayesh Prasad. "Nine Management Guidelines for Better Cost Estimating." *Communications of the ACM* 35, no. 2 (February 1992).

Lientz, Bennett P., and E. Burton Swanson. *Software Maintenance Management.* Reading, MA: Addison-Wesley (1980).

Lipin, Steven, and Nikhil Deogun. "Big Mergers of 90s Prove Disappointing to Shareholders." *The Wall Street Journal* (October 30, 2000).

Lohse, Gerald L., and Peter Spiller. "Internet Retail Store Design: How the User Interface Influences Traffic and Sales." *Journal of Computer-Mediated Communication* 5, no. 2 (December 1999).

Lucas, Henry C., Jr. *Implementation: The Key to Successful Information Systems.* New York: Columbia University Press (1981).

Mahmood, Mo Adam, Laura Hall, and Daniel Leonard Swanberg, "Factors Affecting Information Technology Usage: A Meta-Analysis of the Empirical Literature." *Journal of Organizational Computing and Electronic Commerce* 11, no. 2 (November 2, 2001)

Markus, M. Lynne, Conelis Tanis, and Paul C. van Fenema. "Multisite ERP Implementations." *Communications of the ACM* 43, no. 3 (April 2000).

Markus, M. Lynne, and Mark Keil. "If We Build It, They Will Come: Designing Information Systems That People Want to Use." *Sloan Management Review* (Summer 1994).

Markus, M. Lynne, and Robert I. Benjamin. "Change Agentry—The Next IS Frontier." *MIS Quarterly* 20, no. 4 (December 1996).

Markus, M. Lynne, and Robert I. Benjamin. "The Magic Bullet Theory of IT-Enabled Transformation." *Sloan Management Review* (Winter 1997).

Matlin, Gerald. "What Is the Value of Investment in Information Systems?" *MIS Quarterly* 13, no. 3 (September 1989).

McCormack, Alan. "Product-Development Practices that Work: How Internet Companies Build Software." *Sloan Management Review* 42, no. 2 (Winter 2001).

McDonnell, Sharon. "Putting CRM To Work." *Computerworld* (March 12, 2001).

McFarlan, F. Warren. "Portfolio Approach to Information Systems." *Harvard Business Review* (September–October 1981).

McGrath, Rita Gunther and Ian C. McMillan. "Assessing Technology Projects Using Real Options Reasoning." *Industrial Research Institute* (2000).

McKeen, James D., and Tor Guimaraes. "Successful Strategies for User Participation in Systems Development." *Journal of Management Information Systems* 14, no. 2 (Fall 1997).

Mumford, Enid, and Mary Weir. *Computer Systems in Work Design: The ETHICS Method.* New York: John Wiley (1979).

Nambisan, Satish, and Yu-Ming Wang. "Web Technology Adoption and Knowledge Barriers." *Journal of Organizational Computing and Electronic Commerce* 10, no. 2 (2000).

Nolan, Richard. "Managing Information Systems by Committee." *Harvard Business Review* (July–August 1982).

Orlikowski, Wanda J., and J. Debra Hofman. "An Improvisational Change Model for Change Management: The Case of Groupware Technologies." *Sloan Management Review* (Winter 1997).

Panko, Raymond R. "Is Office Productivity Stagnant?" *MIS Quarterly* 15, no. 2 (June 1991).

Petrazzini, Ben, and Mugo Kibati. "The Internet in Developing Countries." *Communications of the ACM* 42, no. 6 (June 1999).

Rai, Arun, Ravi Patnayakuni, and Nainika Patnayakuni. "Technology Investment and Business Performance." *Communications of the ACM* 40, no. 7 (July 1997).

Randall, Dave, John Hughes, Jon O'Brien, Tom Rodden, Mark Rouncefield, Ian Sommerville, and Peter Tolmie. "Focus Issue on Legacy Information Systems and Business Process Change: Banking on the Old Technology: Understanding the Organisational Context of 'Legacy' Issues." *Communications of the AIS* 2, (July 1999).

Robey, Daniel, and M. Lynne Markus. "Rituals in Information System Design." *MIS Quarterly* (March 1984).

Roach, Stephen S. "Industrialization of the Information Economy." New York: Morgan Stanley and Co. (1984).

———. "Making Technology Work." New York: Morgan Stanley and Co. (1993).

———. "Services Under Siege—The Restructuring Imperative." *Harvard Business Review* (September–October 1991).

———. "Technology and the Service Sector." *Technological Forecasting and Social Change* 34, no. 4 (December 1988).

———. "The Hollow Ring of the Productivity Revival." *Harvard Business Review* (November–December 1996).

Ryan, Sherry D., and David A. Harrison. "Considering Social Subsystem Costs and Benefits in Information Technology Investment Decisions: A View from the Field on Anticipated Payoffs." *Journal of Management Information Systems* 16, no. 4 (Spring 2000).

Scheer, August–Wilhelm, and **Frank Habermann.** "Making ERP a Success." *Communications of the ACM* 43, no. 3 (April 2000).

Schmidt, Roy, Kalle Lyytinen, Mark Keil, and **Paul Cule.** "Identifying Software Project Risks: An International Delphi Study." *Journal of Management Information Systems* 17, no. 4 (Spring 2001).

Schneiderman, Ben. "Universal Usability." *Communications of the ACM* 43, no. 5 (May 2000).

Sircar, Sumit, Joe L. Turnbow, and **Bijoy Bordoloi.** "A Framework for Assessing the Relationship between Information Technology Investments and Firm Performance." *Journal of Management Information Systems* 16, no. 4 (Spring 2000).

Smith, H. Jeff, Mark Keil, and **Gordon Depledge.** "Keeping Mum as the Project Goes Under." *Journal of Management Information Systems* 18, no. 2 (Fall 2001).

Soh, Christina, Sia Siew Kien, and **Joanne Tay-Yap.** "Cultural Fits and Misfits: Is ERP a Universal Solution? "*Communications of the ACM* 43, no. 3 (April 2000).

Steinbart, Paul John, and **Ravinder Nath.** "Problems and Issues in the Management of International Data Networks." *MIS Quarterly* 16, no. 1 (March 1992).

Straub, Detmar W. "The Effect of Culture on IT Diffusion: E-Mail and FAX in Japan and the U.S." *Information Systems Research* 5, no. 1 (March 1994).

Swanson, E. Burton. *Information System Implementation.* Homewood, IL: Richard D. Irwin (1988).

Tallon, Paul P, Kenneth L. Kraemer, and **Vijay Gurbaxani.** "Executives' Perceptions of the Business Value of Information Technology: A Process-Oriented Approach." *Journal of Management Information Systems* 16, no. 4 (Spring 2000).

Tan, Zixiang, William Foster, and **Seymour Goodman.** "China's State-Coordinated Internet Infrastructure." *Communications of the ACM* 42, no. 6 (June 1999).

Taudes, Alfred, Markus Feurstein, and **Andreas Mild.** "Options Analysis of Software Platform Decisions: A Case Study." *MIS Quarterly* 24, no. 2 (June 2000).

Teng, James T. C., Seung Ryul Jeong, and **Varun Grover.** "Profiling Successful Reengineering Projects." *Communications of the ACM* 41, no. 6 (June 1998).

Thatcher, Matt E., and **Jim R. Oliver.** "The Impact of Technology Invesments on a Firm's Production Efficiency, Product Quality, and Productivity." *Journal of Management Information Systems* 18, no. 2 (Fall 2001).

Tornatsky, Louis G., J. D. Eveland, M. G. Boylan, W. A. Hetzner, E. C. Johnson, D. Roitman, and **J. Schneider.** *The Process of Technological Innovation: Reviewing the Literature.* Washington, DC: National Science Foundation (1983).

Truex, Duane P., Richard Baskerville, and **Heinz Klein.** "Growing Systems in Emergent Organizations." *Communications of the ACM* 42, no. 8 (August 1999).

Turner, Jon A. "Computer Mediated Work: The Interplay Between Technology and Structured Jobs." *Communications of the ACM* 27 (December 1984).

Wastell, David G. "Learning Dysfunctions in Information Systems Development: Overcoming the Social Defenses with Transitional Objects." *MIS Quarterly* 23, no. 1 (December 1999).

Yin, Robert K. "Life Histories of Innovations: How New Practices Become Routinized." *Public Administration Review* (January–February 1981).

Yu, Larry. "Successful Customer Relationship Management." *Sloan Management Review* 42, no. 4 (Summer 2001).

CHAPTER 14

Abdel-Hamid, Tarek K. Kishore Sengupta, and **Clint Swett**. "The Impact of Goals on Software Project Management: An Experimental Investigation." *MIS Quarterly* 23, no. 4 (December 1999).

Alberts, David S. "The Economics of Software Quality Assurance." Washington, DC: National Computer Conference, 1976 Proceedings.

Banker, Rajiv D., and **Chris F. Kemerer.** "Performance Evaluation Metrics in Information Systems Development: A Principal-Agent Model." *Information Systems Research* 3, no. 4 (December 1992).

Banker, Rajiv D., Robert J. Kaufmann, and **Rachna Kumar.** "An Empirical Test of Object-Based Output Measurement Metrics in a Computer-Aided Software Engineering (CASE) Environment." *Journal of Management Information Systems* 8, no. 3 (Winter 1991–1992).

Banker, Rajiv D., Srikant M. Datar, Chris F. Kemerer, and **Dani Zweig.** "Software Complexity and Maintenance Costs." *Communications of the ACM* 36, no. 11 (November 1993).

Barthelemy, Jerome. "The Hidden Costs of IT Outsourcing." *Sloan Management Review* 42, no. 3 (Spring 2001).

Bertin, Michael. "The New Security Threats." *Smart Business Magazine* (February 2001).

Bertino, Elisa, Elena Pagani, Gian Paolo Rossi, and **Pierangela Samarat**i. "Protecting Information on the Web." *Communications of the ACM* 43, no.11 (Novemer 2000).

Blackburn, Joseph, Gary Scudder, and **Luk N. Van Wassenhove.** "Concurrent Software Development." *Communications of the ACM* 43, no. 11es (November 2000).

Boehm, Barry W. "Understanding and Controlling Software Costs." *IEEE Transactions on Software Engineering* 14, no. 10 (October 1988).

Chin, Shu-Kai. "High-Confidence Design for Security." *Communications of the ACM* 42, no. 7 (July 1999).

Choy, Manhoi, Hong Va Leong, and **Man Hon Wong.** "Disaster Recovery Techniques for Database Systems." *Communications of the ACM* 43, no. 11 (November 2000).

Corbato, Fernando J. "On Building Systems that Will Fail." *Communications of the ACM* 34, no. 9 (September 1991).

Dekleva, Sasa M. "The Influence of Information Systems Development Approach on Maintenance." *MIS Quarterly* 16, no. 3 (September 1992).

DeMarco, Tom. *Structured Analysis and System Specification.* New York: Yourdon Press (1978).

Dijkstra, E. "Structured Programming." In *Classics in Software Engineering,* edited by Edward Nash Yourdon. New York: Yourdon Press (1979).

Domges, Rolf, and **Klaus Pohl.** "Adapting Traceability Environments to Project-Specific Needs." *Communications of the ACM* 41, no. 12 (December 1998).

Durst, Robert, Terrence Champion, Brian Witten, Eric Miller, and **Luigi Spagnuolo.** "Testing and Evaluating Computer Intrusion Detection Systems." *Communications of the ACM* 42, no. 7 (July 1999).

Dutta, Soumitra, Luk N. Van Wassenhove, and **Selvan Kulandaiswamy.** "Benchmarking European Software Management Practices." *Communications of the ACM* 41, no. 6 (June 1998).

Forrest, Stephanie, Steven A. Hofmeyr, and **Anil Somayaji.** "Computer Immunology." *Communications of the ACM* 40, no. 10 (October 1997).

Fraser, Martin D., and Vijay K. Vaishnavi. "A Formal Specifications Maturity Model." *Communications of the ACM* 40, no. 12 (December 1997).

Gane, Chris, and Trish Sarson. *Structured Systems Analysis: Tools and Techniques.* Englewood Cliffs, NJ: Prentice Hall (1979).

Ghosh, Anup K., and Jeffrey M. Voas. "Inoculating Software for Survivability." *Communications of the ACM* 42, no. 7, (July 1999).

Ghosh, Anup K., and Tara M. Swaminatha. "Software Security and Privacy Risks in Mobile E-Commerce." *Communications of the ACM* 44, no. 2 (February 2001).

Goan, Terrance. "A Cop on the Beat: Collecting and Appraising Intrusion Evidence." *Communications of the ACM* 42, no. 7 (July 1999).

Goslar, Martin. "The New E-Security Frontier." *Information Week* (July 10, 2000).

Jajoda, Sushil, Catherine D. McCollum, and Paul Ammann. "Trusted Recovery." *Communications of the ACM* 42, no. 7 (July 1999).

Jarzabek, Stan, and Riri Huang. "The Case for User-Centered CASE Tools." *Communications of the ACM* 41, no. 8 (August 1998).

Joshi, James B.D., Walid G. Aref, Arif Ghafoor, and Eugene H. Spafford." Security Models for Web-Based Applications." *Communications of the ACM* 44, no. 2 (February 2001).

Johnson, Philip M. "Reengineering Inspection." *Communications of the ACM* 41, no. 2 (February 1998).

Kaplan, David, Ramayya Krishnan, Rema Padman, and James Peters. "Assessing Data Quality in Accounting Information Systems." *Communications of the ACM* 41, no. 2 (February 1998).

Kemerer, Chris F. "Progress, Obstacles, and Opportunities in Software Engineering Economics." *Communications of the ACM* 41, no. 8 (August 1998).

Klein, Barbara D., Dale L. Goodhue, and Gordon B. Davis. "Can Humans Detect Errors in Data?" *MIS Quarterly* 21, no. 2 (June 1997).

Laudon, Kenneth C. "Data Quality and Due Process in Large Interorganizational Record Systems." *Communications of the ACM* 29 (January 1986a).

———. *Dossier Society: Value Choices in the Design of National Information Systems.* New York: Columbia University Press (1986b).

Lientz, Bennett P., and E. Burton Swanson. *Software Maintenance Management.* Reading, MA: Addison-Wesley (1980).

Littlewood, Bev, and Lorenzo Strigini. "The Risks of Software." *Scientific American* 267, no. 5 (November 1992).

———. "Validation of Ultra-high Dependability for Software-based Systems." *Communications of the ACM* 36, no. 11 (November 1993).

Loch, Karen D., Houston H. Carr, and Merrill E. Warkentin. "Threats to Information Systems: Today's Reality, Yesterday's Understanding." *MIS Quarterly* 16, no. 2 (June 1992).

Marer, Eva and Patrick Thibodeau. "Companies Confront Rising Network Threats." *Datamation* (July 2, 2001).

Martin, James, and Carma McClure. *Structured Techniques: The Basis of CASE.* Englewood Cliffs, NJ: Prentice Hall (1988).

Mazzucchelli, Louis. "Structured Analysis Can Streamline Software Design." *Computerworld* (December 9, 1985).

Needham, Roger M. "Denial of Service: An Example." *Communications of the ACM* 37, no. 11 (November 1994).

Nerson, Jean-Marc. "Applying Object-Oriented Analysis and Design." *Communications of the ACM* 35, no. 9 (September 1992).

Neumann, Peter G. "Risks Considered Global(ly)." *Communications of the ACM* 35, no. 1 (January 1993).

Oppliger, Rolf. "Internet Security, Firewalls, and Beyond." *Communications of the ACM* 40, no. 7 (May 1997).

Orr, Kenneth. "Data Quality and Systems Theory." *Communications of the ACM* 41, no. 2 (February 1998).

Parsons, Jeffrey, and Yair Wand. "Using Objects for Systems Analysis." *Communications of the ACM* 40, no. 12 (December 1997).

Rainer, Rex Kelley, Jr., Charles A. Snyder, and Houston H. Carr. "Risk Analysis for Information Technology." *Journal of Management Information Systems* 8, no. 1 (Summer 1991).

Ravichandran, T., and Arun Rai. "Total Quality Management in Information Systems Development." *Journal of Management Information Systems* 16, no. 3 (Winter 1999-2000).

Redman, Thomas. "The Impact of Poor Data Quality on the Typical Enterprise." *Communications of the ACM* 41, no. 2 (February 1998).

Scott, Louise, Levente Horvath, and Donald Day. "Characterizing CASE Constraints." *Communications of the ACM* 43, no. 11 (November 2000).

Segev, Arie, Janna Porra, and Malu Roldan. "Internet Security and the Case of Bank of America." *Communications of the ACM* 41, no. 10 (October 1998).

Sharma, Srinarayan, and Arun Rai. "CASE Deployment in IS Organizations." *Communications of the ACM* 43, no. 1 (January 2000).

Slaughter, Sandra A., Donald E. Harter, and Mayuram S. Krishnan. "Evaluating the Cost of Software Quality." *Communications of the ACM* 41, no. 8 (August 1998).

Stillerman, Matthew, Carla Marceau, and Maureen Stillman. "Intrusion Detection for Distributed Applications." *Communications of the ACM* 42, no. 7 (July 1999).

Straub, Detmar W., and Richard J. Welke. "Coping with Systems Risk: Security Planning Models for Management Decision Making." *MIS Quarterly* 22, no. 4 (December 1998).

Strong, Diane M., Yang W. Lee, and Richard Y. Wang. "Data Quality in Context." *Communications of the ACM* 40, no. 5 (May 1997).

Swanson, Kent, Dave McComb, Jill Smith, and Don McCubbrey. "The Application Software Factory: Applying Total Quality Techniques to Systems Development." *MIS Quarterly* 15, no. 4 (December 1991).

Tayi, Giri Kumar, and Donald P. Ballou. "Examining Data Quality." *Communications of the ACM* 41, no. 2 (February 1998).

Viega, John, Tadayoshi Koho, and Bruce Potter. "Trust (and Mistrust) in Secure Applications." *Communications of the ACM* 44, no. 2 (February 2001).

Wand, Yair, and Richard Y. Wang. "Anchoring Data Quality Dimensions in Ontological Foundations." *Communications of the ACM* 39, no. 11 (November 1996).

Wang, Richard Y., Yang W. Lee, Leo L. Pipino, and Diane M. Strong. "Manage Your Information as a Product." *Sloan Management Review* 39, no. 4 (Summer 1998).

Wang, Richard. "A Product Perspective on Total Data Quality Management." *Communications of the ACM* 41, no. 2 (February 1998).

Weber, Ron. *Information Systems Control and Audit.* New York: McGraw-Hill (1999).

Wessel, David. "NASA Explores Future of Software." *The Wall Street Journal* (April 26, 2001).

Ye, Nong, Joseph Giordano, and John Feldman. "A Process Control Approach to Cyber Attack Detection." *Communications of the ACM* 44, no. 8 (August 2001).

Yourdon, Edward, and L. L. Constantine. *Structured Design.* New York: Yourdon Press (1978).

Zhou, Jianying. "Achieving Fair Nonrepudiation in Electronic Transactions." *Journal of Organizational Computing and Electronic Commerce* 11, no. 4 (2001)

INDEXES

Organizations Index

INTERNATIONAL ORGANIZATIONS INDEX

SUBJECT INDEX

PHOTO AND SCREEN SHOT CREDITS

Contributors

 **CANADA**
Len Fertuck, University of Toronto

GERMANY
Helmut Krcmar, University of Hohenheim
Gerhard Schwabe, University of University of Koblenz-Landau
Stephen Wilczek, University of Hohenheim

 **HONG KONG**
Ali Farhoomand, University of Hong Kong
Amir Hoosain, University of Hong Kong
Shamza Khan, University of Hong Kong
Dennis Kira, University of Hong Kong

SWITZERLAND
Donald A. Marchand, International Institute for Management Development
Katarina Paddack, International Institute for Management Development

Consultants

AUSTRALIA
Robert MacGregor, University of Wollongong
Alan Underwood, Queensland University of Technology

CANADA
Wynne W. Chin, University of Calgary
Len Fertuck, University of Toronto
Robert C. Goldstein, University of British Columbia
Rebecca Grant, University of Victoria
Kevin Leonard, Wilfrid Laurier University
Anne B. Pidduck, University of Waterloo

GREECE
Anastasios V. Katos, University of Macedonia

HONG KONG
Enoch Tse, Hong Kong Baptist University

INDIA
Sanjiv D. Vaidya, Indian Institute of Management, Calcutta

ISRAEL
Phillip Ein-Dor, Tel-Aviv University
Peretz Shoval, Ben Gurion University

MEXICO
Noe Urzua Bustamante, Universidad Tecnológica de México

NETHERLANDS
E.O. de Brock, University of Groningen
Theo Thiadens, University of Twente
Charles Van Der Mast, Delft University of Technology

PUERTO RICO, Commonwealth of the United States
Brunilda Marrero, University of Puerto Rico

SWEDEN
Mats Daniels, Uppsala University

SWITZERLAND
Andrew C. Boynton, International Institute for Management Development

UNITED KINGDOM

ENGLAND
G.R. Hidderley, University of Central England, Birmingham
Christopher Kimble, University of York
Jonathan Liebenau, London School of Economics and Political Science
Kecheng Liu, Staffordshire University

SCOTLAND
William N. Dyer, Falkirk College of Technology